A *Complete* Commentary on

PROVERBS

God's Guide for Successful Living

A *Complete* Commentary on

PROVERBS

God's Guide for Successful Living

Darwin and Meige Easter

EastBron Publishing

Alexander City, AL 35010

A *Complete* Commentary on
PROVERBS
God's Guide for Successful Living

Copyright © 2022 by Darwin Easter and Meige Easter

All Rights Reserved

Conditions of Use: Permission is granted to make up to 300 copies of individual pages from the book for classroom use only. The pages may not be modified in any manner. Credit must be given to the authors. Any other use of these pages must be approved by the authors.

deasterinalabama@gmail.com
meigeeaster@gmail.com

ISBN: 979-8-218-03388-0

Cover design by Mary Wright

Website: www.marywrightdesign.com
Thank you for your tremendous help and encouragement on this project.

All Scripture references are from the King James Translation of the Bible.

TABLE OF CONTENTS

SECTION I	1
CHAPTER ONE	3
CHAPTER TWO	21
CHAPTER THREE	31
CHAPTER FOUR	51
CHAPTER FIVE	63
CHAPTER SIX	73
CHAPTER SEVEN	83
CHAPTER EIGHT	91
CHAPTER NINE	105
SECTION II	115
CHAPTER TEN	117
CHAPTER ELEVEN	137
CHAPTER TWELVE	161
CHAPTER THIRTEEN	185
CHAPTER FOURTEEN	207
CHAPTER FIFTEEN	237
CHAPTER SIXTEEN	263
CHAPTER SEVENTEEN	289
CHAPTER EIGHTEEN	311
CHAPTER NINETEEN	333

CHAPTER TWENTY	357
CHAPTER TWENTY-ONE	383
CHAPTER TWENTY-TWO	411
CHAPTER TWENTY-THREE	433
CHAPTER TWENTY-FOUR	449
SECTION III	467
CHAPTER TWENTY-FIVE	469
CHAPTER TWENTY-SIX	487
CHAPTER TWENTY-SEVEN	503
CHAPTER TWENTY-EIGHT	519
CHAPTER TWENTY-NINE	543
SECTION IV	565
CHAPTER THIRTY	567
CHAPTER THIRTY-ONE	583
END NOTES	601
APPENDIX	607
KINGS OF THE OF THE NATION OF ISRAEL	609
PERSONIFIED WISDOM IS NOT CHRIST	610
POETICAL DEVICES IN THE BOOK OF PROVERBS	612
PROVERBS REFERRED TO IN NEW TESTAMENT	614
TIME LINE OF KING SOLOMON'S LIFE	615
BIBLIOGRAPHY	619
INDEX	625

INTRODUCTION

"Surely I *am* more brutish than *any* man and have not the understanding of a man. I neither learned wisdom, nor have the knowledge of the holy" – so said wise, humble Agur of himself (Proverbs 30:1-2). And from the "Virtuous Woman" of chapter 31 (the paradigm of female wisdom) – not one of her words is recorded, yet she is praised to the sky for her exemplary life of wisdom.

Those like Agur and the "Virtuous Woman" who actually become wise are diligent, determined, relentless seekers. They yearn to know how to navigate through this life, not just more effectively but rather in *the most effective* manner. They desire to minimize evil influences and to maximize the good. They are not lazy, arrogant, evil, or ignorant. Neither are they manipulators. They learn first from God, then good people, and good books.

Proverbs 3:5-6 reinforces the truth found throughout the Book of Proverbs that wisdom is built on two main girders: an awesome respect for God and personal humility. "Trust in the LORD with all thine heart; and lean not unto thine own understanding. In all thy ways acknowledge him, and he shall direct thy paths." The humble wise person is guided through this life by God's instructions and by the Holy Spirit.

Inspired by the Spirit of God, King Solomon wrote the Book of Proverbs to teach wisdom to eager, humble disciples of God. *This commentary is an aid* to a better understanding of the Book of Proverbs by providing explanations of its dark sayings, defining its difficult terms and phrases, detailing original intent, and connecting each proverb with other Scriptures throughout the Bible. The enlightened path of wisdom gleaned from the word of God is one with "Christ the power of God, and the wisdom of God" (1 Corinthians 1:24)

My wife, Meige, and I have worked together in various phases of ministry for 48 years as a pastor, evangelist, mission agency director, school teacher, and principal. Writing a commentary on the Book of Proverbs has been a six-and-a-half-year labor of love done in these latter years of our lives.

Enriching the understanding of each verse of Proverbs is the goal of this writing and it is our desire that the reader become aware of God's wise way of living. A sagacious person understands the difference between good and evil. He knows right from wrong. He knows how to: effectively interact with other people, avoid dangerous people and situations, properly evaluate and handle wealth, live honestly, and establish godly goals. Learning and following God's instructions will produce wisdom.

"When wisdom entereth into thine heart, and knowledge is pleasant unto thy soul; discretion shall preserve thee, understanding shall keep thee:" (Proverbs 2:10-11) As a result of studying this commentary, the reader can gain a good understanding of each verse of Proverbs that leads to a grasp of God's wisdom.

Scripture references under each proverb are of paramount importance for two reasons: First, they give an unparalleled understanding to the proverb. Second, the proverb broadens the understanding of the reference. This commentary would have been shorter without these Scripture references, but it would be of little value.

SECTION I
(Chapters 1-9)

Section I contains nine chapters and is written in dialogue form. It does not have many of the well-known pithy sayings like those concentrated in chapter 10-29. These first nine chapters utilize characters (as do chapters 30 and 31) to exemplify, define and teach about wisdom and foolishness. The reader is given insight into the way God thinks (with wisdom, knowledge, and understanding) and acts (with justice, judgment, and equity) so that he can learn the wisdom of being like Him.

Wisdom is personified in this first section as a lady who appeals to some and is opposed by others. She speaks fluently and boldly when describing her personal, eternal, and intimate relationship with God. She also declares her strengths, character, reactions to opposition, and rewards to those attracted to her, and she specifies her rejection and condemnation of those who resist.

Another speaking and acting identity is the wicked adulteress, the antithesis of the personified wisdom. She openly reveals her evil methods of appeal, the depth of her wicked heart, and the consequences for those she victimizes.

The ruthless gang is introduced to teach the reader about the remorseless depth of aggregate wickedness and the severe consequences of evil associations.

Solomon proceeds in Section II to introduce the short, pithy, dark sayings that are concise, memorable, and rich in meaning. Those proverbs are for the student seeking godly wisdom but are useless to the reader who chooses the way of evil and refuses the wise way of righteousness and wisdom. The seeker of wisdom is admonished to read the entire book carefully, meditate upon the words and choose the right path. Proverbs is designed to make the reader aware of the consequences of both good and evil choices and provide the believer with instructions to successfully live his earthly life according to God's wisdom.

CHAPTER ONE

> **Outline of Chapter 1**
>
> I. Credit Is Given to the Author/Owner of the Proverbs. - Solomon, Son of David, King of Israel (verse 1)
>
> II. Goals for Solomon's proverbs are given: (verses 2-6)
>   A. To know wisdom and instruction. (Goal 1) (verse 2)
>   B. To perceive the words of understanding. (Goal 2) (verse 2)
>   C. To receive instruction of wisdom, justice, judgment, and equity. (Goal 3) (verse 3)
>   D. To give subtilty to the simple. (Goal 4) (verse 4a)
>   E. To give knowledge and discretion to the young man. (Goal 5) (verse 4b)
>   F. To understand a proverb, the interpretation and the words of the wise–dark sayings. (Goal 6) (verse 6)
>
> III. The foundation for learning is established. – "*The Fear of the Lord* is the beginning of knowledge." (verse 7a)
>
> IV. Delineation between the wise and the fool is made.
>   A. A wise man will hear, and will increase learning; and a man of understanding will attain unto wise counsels. (verse 5)
>   B. Fools despise wisdom and instruction. (verse 7b)
>
> V. Process for becoming obviously wise is declared.
>   A. Hear and retain parents' instruction. (verse 8)
>   B. Wear the rewards of a wise son. (verse 9)
>
> VI. Warning is made against camaraderie with sinners. (verses 10-14)
>
> VII. Reasons to walk away from sinners are given. (verses 15-19)
>
> VIII. Glorious call of wisdom is described. (verses 20-33)
>   A. Wisdom is refused. (verses 24-25)
>   B. Wisdom rebuffs the fool. (verses 26-32)
>   C. Wisdom reminds the wise of safety and peace. (verse 33)

Proverbs 1:1 The proverbs of Solomon the son of David, king of Israel.

"**The Proverbs of Solomon the Son of David, king of Israel**" (verse 1) is a phrase that establishes both the Hebrew title of the Book of Proverbs and the identification of Solomon as author/owner. Although there are very few proverbs in Chapters 1-9, figurative speech abounds.

Proverbs 1:2-6 To know wisdom and instruction; to perceive the words of understanding;
3. To receive the instruction of wisdom, justice, and judgment, and equity;
4. To give subtilty to the simple, to the young man knowledge and discretion.
5. A wise *man* will hear, and will increase learning; and a man of understanding shall attain unto wise counsels:
6. To understand a proverb, and the interpretation; the words of the wise, and their dark sayings.

Verses 1 - 4 and verse 6 constitute clearly established goals for Solomon's proverbs and likely served as filters used to determine which of his 3,000 proverbs would be allowed in the compilation. Verse 5 is a parenthesis providing clarity to the fact that it is *the wise* to whom these goals will receive fulfillment, for they are the ones who **"will hear and will increase learning"** and not *the foolish,* as identified in the second part of verse 7 who **"despise wisdom and instruction."**

1 Kings 4:32 And he spake three thousand proverbs: and his songs were a thousand and five.

ESTABLISHMENT OF GOALS is essential to success enabling wise men to know what they intend to accomplish before starting their journey or project. EXCEPT, there indeed are those rare times when God will simply instruct a leader to move without telling him where or why, like He did with Abraham.

> Hebrews 11:8 By faith Abraham, when he was called to go out into a place which he should after receive for an inheritance, obeyed; and he went out, not knowing whither he went.

OBTAINING WISDOM and **AVOIDING WICKED PEOPLE** are the main topics of Chapter One, and various proverbs make it clear that the exertion of effort will be necessary for the student to be successful. He cannot be lazy. He must put forth effort **"to know," "to perceive," "to receive,"** and **"to understand"** the profound wisdom that only comes from God.

FIRST GOAL: "To know wisdom and instruction" (verse 2) is substantially different from *being familiar* with the same. "Instruction" includes discipline, rebuke, reproof, chastening, and correction. "Wisdom" in Proverbs focuses on living in a godly manner that pleases God and follows His line of thinking and reasoning rather than that of the world. It teaches the highest level of moral and ethical principles that lead along a Scripturally-lighted pathway to produce a skillful, safe life intentionally separated from evil.

Wisdom isn't attained through a lackadaisical attitude, and the learning process begins with the believer having a **"fear of God"** (verse 7). Such a fear *[awesome respect for God, reverence]* drives a person to be instructed in *God's principles of living*. In fact, Bridges writes that the great purpose of this book is to teach *"not secular or political wisdom . . . but that knowledge of God . . . which, while it 'maketh wise unto salvation, perfects and furnishes the man of God unto all good works.'"*[1]

A wise person becomes "a man of understanding." (verse 5) Wisdom is the godly way of thinking that enables a person to make the best possible decisions when facing life's never-ending challenges.

> "A disposition to 'receive instruction,' is the first and most important lesson for all, and especially for youth; – a humble, docile, self-diffident temper, -a mind open to the admission of sound advice, and desirous to apply it to practice. This disposition is the opposite of self-conceit, and self-will, which are amongst the greatest obstacles to improvement."[2]

The pursuit of a knowledge of wisdom and instruction begins with prayer and a conscientious study of Proverbs, plus a careful review of supporting Scripture. Such study will provide knowledge of what God has revealed about: (1) Himself as related to wisdom, (2) men as they react *(positively or negatively)* to the instruction of wisdom, and (3) the consequential effects *(immediate and eternal)* of both wisdom and foolishness. The Book of Proverbs supports other Scriptures that declare that God has a personal relationship with those seeking wisdom; but that He resists the proud, arrogant ones who oppose Him and His wisdom.

> **The person with wisdom** has the ability,
> because of a proper relationship with God,
> to be able to navigate through the challenges and opportunities of life
> in the most effective manner
> thereby minimizing evil influences and maximizing godly outcomes.

Second Goal: "To perceive the words of understanding." (verse 2b) Solomon's second goal is for the student to **"perceive** *[become aware of by the senses, discern,* **and** *understand]"* the teacher's words *(words of understanding)*. **"Understanding"** means wise discernment, to which Barnes adds, **"understanding"** is the power of distinguishing right from wrong and truth from falsehood.[3]

The student learns right from wrong, good from bad, true from counterfeit based on the explanations and instruction received from the Bible. Such Scriptural instruction often comes through godly people such as parents, teachers, and advisors. When the prudent listener *perceives* and acts on these **"words of understanding,"** the implication from these verses is that the listener will then be able to think and consequently to live in a wise manner minimizing evil influences and maximizing godly outcomes. An astute student will be still and have his learning enhanced through personal observations of his surroundings, people's actions, attitudes, and words.

Worldly wisdom opposes and rejects **"words of understanding"** taught through the Bible. To the fool, the words of the Bible are nonsense rather than **"words of understanding,"** and he will *not* receive them. Consequently, because of the fool's predetermined mindset, he has little hope of perceiving those words.

> Proverbs 10:8 The wise in heart will receive commandments: but a prating fool shall fall.
> Proverbs 15:5 A fool despiseth his father's instruction: but he that regardeth reproof is prudent.

Third Goal: "To receive the instruction of wisdom, justice, judgment and equity." (verse 3) **"Justice, judgment, and equity"** as a grouping of words is found again in Proverbs 2:9; only the English word **"righteousness"** is substituted for **"justice"**; however, the Hebrew word *tsedeq* is the same in both verses. Obviously, **"justice"** and **"righteousness"** are inseparable. The student of wisdom will receive this *God-given trio of godly correctness* as he grows in wisdom. These traits should become evident in his walk as he matures.

"Justice, judgment, and equity" are character traits that constitute GOD'S ABSOLUTE CORRECTNESS. They are Bible terms describing His innate perfect character and His composite wisdom, which He shares with those who seek wisdom. When a person **receives** *[takes, lays hold of, accepts]* the instruction of wisdom, he takes it into his heart. It becomes part of his being, the way he thinks, who he is. It directs his ways and his thoughts. When he receives wisdom from God, a wise person will develop godly character that exemplifies "judgment, justice, and equity." When a person fulfills Solomon's goal of *receiving the instruction* of "justice, and judgment, and equity," he will become a person who has "all the attributes of one upright in all his relations to God and man."[4]

"Justice," as a developed character trait of man and as received from God, "specifies what is right, not only as measured by a code of law, but also by what makes for right relationships as well as harmony and peace."[5] "Justice consists in giving to every one what is his due; practical conformity to the laws and principles of rightness in the dealings of men with each other; honesty; integrity in commerce and life; impartiality."[6] Justice is what is righteous in business, law, and life.

"Judgment" is the ability to make a righteous determination between right and wrong, not only in court; but also in daily life. It is the result of discerning between good and evil to determine what is in agreement with God's idea of right.

"Equity" refers to even, fair, and impartial judgment and justice. Also, "equity" adds the additional connotation of fairness and impartiality in reaching life's decisions and in the treatment of others.

When the student of wisdom receives God's instruction, he consequently learns: (1) to be just (righteous) in every aspect of his life, (2) to make righteous judgments from his knowledge of God's ideas of right and wrong, and (3) to be fair (to practice **equity**) in all his dealings. Then, because He has learned wisdom from God, he will have learned to think and reason and live in a manner that is favorable and pleasing to God. Additionally, he has opened the door for good relationships with other wise people.

Wisdom teaches people to evaluate situations and the actions of people impartially and fairly as God does. These three words of right thinking and acting **("judgment" "justice" and "equity")** are used together in a very negative sense in Isaiah 59:14, showing the believer what happens when God's wisdom is *not* respected, protected, and practiced.

> Isaiah 59:14 And judgment is turned away backward, and justice standeth afar off: for truth is fallen in the street, and equity cannot enter.

The Pulpit Commentary explains **"Judgment is turned away backward."**

> "... the crying sin of perversion of justice is admitted with much amplification.
> (1) RIGHT JUDGMENT is exactly inverted, the innocent are condemned, the guilty acquitted.
> (2) JUSTICE standeth afar off, too far off to be able to hear those who make appeal to it.
> (3) TRUTH is fallen in the street; *i.e., a* false witness prevails over true in the courts of justice.
> (4) EQUITY cannot enter, is not admitted inside the courts, but waits without."[7]

"The teaching of Proverbs is to lead us to pass a right *sentence* upon human actions, whether our own or anothers."[8] This *sentence* is not to prove ourselves more righteous than others but to adjust our own behavior. RECEIVING THE INSTRUCTION OF JUSTICE, JUDGMENT, AND EQUITY IS TO RECEIVE GOD'S INSTRUCTION WHICH TEACHES MEN "THEIR WHOLE DUTY TO GOD, THEIR NEIGHBOR, AND THEMSELVES."[9] If a man possesses these attributes, he will be upright in ALL his relations to God and man.

> For the LORD giveth wisdom:
> out of his mouth cometh knowledge and understanding.
> He layeth up sound wisdom for the righteous: he is a buckler to them that walk uprightly.
> He keepeth the paths of judgment, and preserveth the way of his saints.
> **Then shalt thou understand righteousness** *[tsedeq]*, **and judgment, and equity;**
> yea, every good path. (Proverbs 2:6-9)

When a person obtains wisdom from God, he will have ***God's understanding*** of the matters at hand which is the proper standard of correctness. The three Hebrew words for **"justice, judgment, and equity"** have very slight differences in meaning, but they all point to ***some aspect of "right"*** *[righteous, just, and fair]* which only comes from God. Verse 3 (reinforced by Proverbs 2:6-9) states that God's instruction is right–is right–is right! There is NO error in God's teaching! It is always right! And to **"receive the instruction"** is to absorb the instruction, take it to heart, take ownership of it, knowing that it is the right way of thinking and reasoning that agrees with the way God thinks and reasons about a given matter.

> Psalm 119:137-138; 142 TZADDI. Righteous *art* thou, O LORD, and upright *are* thy judgments. Thy testimonies *that* thou hast commanded *are* righteous and very faithful . . . Thy righteousness *is* an everlasting righteousness, and thy law *is* the truth.
> Zephaniah 3:5 The just LORD *is* in the midst thereof; he will not do iniquity: every morning doth he bring his judgment to light, he faileth not; but the unjust knoweth no shame.
> John 16:8-11 And when he is come, he will reprove the world of sin, and of righteousness, and of judgment: Of sin, because they believe not on me; Of righteousness, because I go to my Father, and ye see me no more; Of judgment, because the prince of this world is judged.
> *[See also Deuteronomy 32:4; Psalm 71:19, 97:2, 98:9, 111:7; Jeremiah 9:23-24]*

Sad to say that the depraved, foolish human mind creates his own flawed standard of correctness because his thinking is corrupt. As noted above in John 16:8-11, the Holy Spirit reproves man of his error.

Fourth Goal: "To give subtilty to the simple." (verse 4a) **"Simple"** *[seducible, easily-deceived]* people are undecided in their views and are easily influenced – *like a child*. A simple person is naive and untaught. However, he is NOT one who cannot comprehend OR a fool who despises wisdom. Instead, he is one whose exposure to life and wisdom has been limited. Because of inexperience, he is gullible and easily influenced. Simple persons are people of weak capacities and shallow understandings. They are incautious and easily imposed upon.[10] "Literally, *(the simple are)* those who are open to good impressions and influences, but who also can be easily led astray."[11]

In the Book of Proverbs, **"subtilty"** is used to mean having "prudence or discretion" rather than its often-used opposite meaning, which is "trickery or guile." Discretion gives the wise the ability to govern themselves and proceed cautiously to guard against being misled. A simple person *(if he advances in wisdom)* must learn to evaluate people and situations so that he can take the godly path of wisdom rather than the path of a fool. In so doing he will gain "subtilty," and thus discretion, a product of wisdom. Webster's *Dictionary* defines "prudent" as "cautious; circumspect; practically wise; careful of the consequences of enterprises, measures or actions; cautious not to act when the end is of doubtful utility, or probably impracticable."[12]

Verses 4 and 5 identify three categories of people – the SIMPLE, the YOUNG, and the WISE. Later the Book of Proverbs will discuss the FOOLISH, the SCORNER, the SLOTHFUL, the EVIL, the STRANGE, and the FROWARD. Wisdom teaches the believer to recognize these various categories of people so that he can identify their traits, behaviors, successes, and failures in order to acquire those characteristics that reflect God and shun those traits that are evil. IDENTIFYING PEOPLE ACCORDING TO THEIR TRAITS, BEHAVIORS, SUCCESSES, AND FAILURES IS NOT THE SAME AS CONDEMNING OR JUDGING THEM. Wise people learn to be *observant* without being hateful, demeaning, or arrogant. Notice how the observer was taught from observation and proper evaluation about a desperate situation in the following verses.

> Proverbs 24:30-34 I went by the field of the slothful, and by the vineyard of the man void of understanding; And, lo, it was all grown over with thorns, and nettles had covered the face thereof, and the stone wall thereof was broken down. Then I saw, and considered it well: I looked upon it, and received instruction. Yet a little sleep, a little slumber, a little folding of the hands to sleep: So shall thy poverty come as one that travelleth; and thy want as an armed man.

Fifth Goal: "To the young man knowledge and discretion." (verse 4b) In the Book of Proverbs and in the Bible at large, **"knowledge"** often refers to knowing important facts; but, more importantly, to *knowing God's view*. Directly and through life illustrations, the word of God explains how He wants His children to act and think; and it reveals sinful behavior and sinful people to avoid. Thus the Bible teaches the Christian to have the same view of right and wrong as God has and, consequently, to become wise. Acceptance of such divine knowledge changes the way a person thinks and reasons, thus giving the believer ability to live a successful life in the world that was specifically created and designed by God for man. The word "knowledge" is used in forty-one verses in Proverbs.

> Proverbs 2:3-6 Yea, if thou criest after knowledge, *and* liftest up thy voice for understanding; If thou seekest her as silver, and searchest for her as *for* hid treasures; Then shalt thou understand the fear of the LORD, and find the knowledge of God. For the LORD giveth wisdom: out of his mouth *cometh* knowledge and understanding.

In the Garden of Eden, God gave Adam and Eve a perfect place to live, and at first, their minds were pure having **"knowledge"** of only good. They were "clothed" in righteousness, no evil having entered their minds. At first their thinking was in total harmony with God. When Satan introduced evil, they foolishly believed that there was a better way than God's way.

God *did not* want Adam and Eve to know evil. In the model prayer in Matthew 6:13, Jesus taught His disciples to pray asking God to ". . . deliver us from evil . . ." To "keep me from evil that it may not grieve me," was Jabez' request in 1 Chronicles 4:10. Every godly person recognizes that as he draws closer to evil, he separates from godly wisdom and he distances himself from God. Although He did not want man to know evil, God gave him a free will to make his own choice. One of the critical goals of the Book of Proverbs is to provide instruction that enables a person to recognize the difference between good and evil – between God's way and any other way. Such knowledge gives the student of wisdom the ability to become discreet; and discretion is *the believer's first line of defense*, keeping him from evil, harmful associations, and dangerous situations. It is a guide to quality living. "Discretion" will cause a person:

(1) To survey the result of his own and other people's actions or words.
(2) To change his actions or speech to be in alignment with God's word.
(3) To seek the best personal outcome.

"Discretion" is that drink of good sense drawn out of the well of wisdom that will cause the wise person to make sober, sane, and safe decisions such as staying away from a harlot of Proverbs Chapters 5-7.

> Proverbs 2:11-12 Discretion shall preserve thee, understanding shall keep thee: to deliver thee from the way of the evil man, from the man that speaketh froward things.
> Proverbs 3:21-22 My son, let not them depart from thine eyes: keep sound wisdom and discretion: so shall they be life unto thy soul, and grace to thy neck.

Proverbs 1:5-6 A wise *man* will hear, and will increase learning; and a man of understanding shall attain unto wise counsels: 6. To understand a proverb, and the interpretation; the words of the wise, and their dark sayings.

"A wise man will hear, and will increase learning." (verse 5a) The student of wisdom cannot allow any hindrances to learning. He incrementally gains knowledge and begins to have understanding. His desire must be to successfully *hear and increase learning* and to succeed in *attaining to wise counsels.* Such dedication defines the **"wise man"** who is a **"man of understanding."** Foolish people believe they know and understand innately, ***without God***, and such flawed thinking is in part what defines them as fools.

> Proverbs 9:9 Give *instruction* to a wise *man,* and he will be yet wiser: teach a just *man,* and he will increase in learning.
> Proverbs 18:15 The heart of the prudent getteth knowledge; and the ear of the wise seeketh knowledge.

"And a man of understanding shall attain unto wise counsels" (verse 5b) which is that good advice drawn from those persons who advise and steer in ways that are righteous – in other words, from those men who are following the leadership of God, who believe God, and who obey His word. A man who associates with wise men shall himself become wise because every person's speech, actions, and ways of thinking are all influenced to some degree by others. It is vital to **"attain** *[possess or acquire]* **unto wise counsels"** who can *positively affect* the seeker while avoiding the foolish ones who can *infect* with sin and wrong thinking. The wise **"shall attain unto wise counsels"** meaning that he seeks out (makes positive effort to acquire) proper associations with the intent of grasping wisdom. The consequence is clear for such an eager learner; he **"will hear and will increase learning."** He can not succeed at becoming **"a man of understanding"** without insisting on having "wise counsels." He can recognize potentially **"wise counsels"** because their advice lines up with Scripture, and he will strive to gain a close relationship with them in order to be taught their way of thinking. He will be identified as **"a man of understanding"** for the very reason that he seeks wisdom where and from whom it can be found. And, of course, the Holy Spirit, the Comforter, will quietly still his heart and soul when He agrees with a good source of righteous instruction.

> Job 28:28 And unto man he said, Behold, the fear of the Lord, that *is* wisdom; and to depart from evil *is* understanding.
>
> Psalm 1: 1-2 Blessed is the man that walketh not in the counsel of the ungodly, nor standeth in the way of sinners, nor sitteth in the seat of the scornful. But his delight is in the law of the LORD; and in his law doth he meditate day and night

Goal Six: "To understand a proverb, and the interpretation; the words of the wise, and their dark sayings." (verse 6) It is through the *hearing* and *attaining unto wise counsels* (verse 5) that *understanding* (verse 6) *of a proverb* is gained. The student of wisdom will *come to an understanding* from having learned **"the interpretation"** from **"wise counsels."** Every *proverb and dark saying* [a riddle or dark obscure utterance, a difficult or perplexing question] has an intended single meaning. In fact, EVERY SCRIPTURE HAS ONLY ONE INTERPRETATION THOUGH THERE MAY BE MANY APPLICATIONS. And to reiterate from verse 2, just *being familiar* with instruction is a great distance from actually *having an understanding*. To hear, to memorize, and to quote the **"words of the wise"** yields very little *without* understanding. Wise counselors will be sought by curious seekers to help them understand "proverbs" and "dark sayings."

> Proverbs 22:17 Bow down thine ear, and hear the words of the wise, and apply thine heart unto my knowledge.
>
> Ecclesiastes 12:11 The words of the wise *are* as goads, and as nails fastened *by* the masters of assemblies, *which* are given from one shepherd.
>
> 1 Corinthians 2:12-16 Now we have received, not the spirit of the world, but the spirit which is of God; that we might know the things that are freely given to us of God. Which things also we speak, not in the words which man's wisdom teacheth, but which the Holy Ghost teacheth; comparing spiritual things with spiritual. But the natural man receiveth not the things of the Spirit of God: for they are foolishness unto him: neither can he know *them,* because they are spiritually discerned. But he that is spiritual judgeth all things, yet he himself is judged of no man. For who hath known the mind of the Lord, that he may instruct him? But we have the mind of Christ.

Proverbs 1:7 The fear of the LORD is the beginning of knowledge: but fools despise wisdom and instruction.

Verse 7 provides a sudden change in narrative from previous verses. The first part of this verse specifies that the beginning action needed to reach the goals established in verses 1-6 is to FIRST *have a* **"fear of the LORD,"** *which is an awesome respect for God*. If the student of wisdom does not regard God as the all-knowing Creator and the complete fulfillment of all knowledge, he will not be able to learn.

"The fear of the LORD is the beginning of knowledge." (verse 7a) This passage *does **not** mean* that the **"fear of the Lord"** ceases when **"knowledge"** begins. Quite the contrary, the "fear of the Lord" is foundational to the believer's learning about God and His instructions. It allows for a mutual relationship of respect and trust and, consequently, a line of communication between God and the believer is made, whereby the Christian can properly receive God's word.

> Deuteronomy 17:18-20 And it shall be, when he sitteth upon the throne of his kingdom, that he shall write him a copy of this law in a book out of *that which is* before the priests the Levites: And it shall be with him, and he shall read therein all the days of his life: that he may learn to fear the LORD his God, to keep all the words of this law and these statutes, to do them: That his heart be not lifted up above his brethren, and that he turn not aside from the commandment, *to* the right hand, or *to* the left: to the end that he may prolong *his* days in his kingdom, he, and his children, in the midst of Israel.

Righteous men have a desire to hear God's word and to listen to the wisdom of godly men. They learn to walk with the LORD daily. The fool does NOT choose the fear of the LORD. (Proverbs 1:29)

One cannot gain knowledge of the spiritual if he begins with a wrong premise about God. He must fear the Lord by recognizing God's character and responding by revering, trusting, worshiping, obeying, and serving Him.[13] Because the fool hates knowledge and does not choose the "fear of the LORD" (verse 29) he travels steadily down a road of ignorance and destruction.

The second part of this verse teaches that fools will never learn those teachings from God because "fools despise wisdom and instruction." They have an improper view of themselves and of God.

"But fools despise wisdom and instruction." (verse 7b) *Because the foundational assumption of a fool is that God doesn't exist* – "There is no God" – the fool does NOT have an awesome respect for Him. Therefore he cannot even take the first step toward wisdom and instruction. He hates the idea of being taught anything about God and about living in a manner that reflects God's plan for man. He is arrogant. The mind and the heart of a fool are so evil and depraved that he despises *[holds in contempt]* God's precious gifts of wisdom and instruction. Thinking himself wiser and more knowledgeable, he rejects the instruction of the Bible and godly men. Because of his attitude, he is doomed.

> Psalm 14:1 . . . The fool hath said in his heart, *There is* no God. They are corrupt, they have done abominable works, *there is* none that doeth good.
>
> Revelation 21:8 But the fearful, and unbelieving, and the abominable, and murderers, and whoremongers, and sorcerers, and idolaters, and all liars, shall have their part in the lake which burneth with fire and brimstone: which is the second death.

Below is a summary chart of all the advantages to be gained from having an awesome respect for God.

In summary, according to the Scriptures below, the **"fear of the LORD"**

(1) Is the beginning of knowledge
(2) Is strong confidence
(3) Is the beginning of wisdom
(4) Is the instruction of wisdom
(5) Tends to life
(6) Prolongs days
(7) Is a fountain of life
(8) Is to hate pride, arrogancy, and the evil way
(9) Causes men to depart from evil
(10) Is better to have it with little than to have the trouble that comes with great riches
(11) Produces riches, and honour, and life

(12) In addition, he that has the **"fear of the Lord"** shall abide satisfied; he shall not be visited with evil.

Supporting passages for the above chart include:

> 2Chronicles 19:9 And he charged them, saying, Thus shall ye do in the fear of the LORD, faithfully, and with a perfect heart.
>
> Job 28:28 And unto man he said, Behold, the fear of the Lord, that is wisdom; and to depart from evil *is* understanding.
>
> Psalm 19:9 The fear of the LORD is clean, enduring for ever: the judgments of the LORD are true and righteous altogether.
>
> Psalm 111:10 The fear of the LORD *is* the beginning of wisdom: a good understanding have all they that do *his commandments:* his praise endureth for ever.
>
> Proverbs 1:7 The fear of the LORD is the beginning of knowledge: but fools despise wisdom and instruction.
>
> Proverbs 1:28-30 Then shall they call upon me, but I will not answer; they shall seek me early, but they shall not find me: For that they hated knowledge, and did not choose the fear of the LORD: They would none of my counsel: they despised all my reproof.
>
> Proverbs 2:3-5 Yea, if thou criest after knowledge, *and* liftest up thy voice for understanding; if thou seekest her as silver, and searchest for her as for hid treasures; then shalt thou understand the fear of the Lord, and find the knowledge of God.
>
> Proverbs 8:13 The fear of the LORD is to hate evil: pride, and arrogancy, and the evil way, and the froward mouth, do I hate.
> *[Repeated verbatim Proverbs 23:17]*
>
> Proverbs 9:10 The fear of the LORD is the beginning of wisdom: and the knowledge of the holy is understanding.
>
> Proverbs 10:27 The fear of the LORD prolongeth days: but the years of the wicked shall be shortened.
>
> Proverbs 14:26 In the fear of the LORD is strong confidence: and his children shall have a place of refuge.
>
> Proverbs 14:27 The fear of the LORD is a fountain of life, to depart from the snares of death.
>
> Proverbs 15:16 Better is little with the fear of the LORD than great treasure and trouble therewith.
>
> Proverbs 15:33 The fear of the LORD is the instruction of wisdom; and before honour is humility.
>
> Proverbs 16:6 By mercy and truth iniquity is purged: and by the fear of the LORD men depart from evil.
>
> Proverbs 19:23 The fear of the LORD tendeth to life: and he that hath it shall abide satisfied; he shall not be visited with evil.
>
> Proverbs 22:4 By humility and the fear of the LORD are riches, and honour, and life.

In His humanity, Jesus demonstrated this awesome respect for God known as FEAR OF THE LORD. He provided the perfect example for believers with His being submissive, obedient, and totally reflective of HIS Father's thoughts and will.

> Isaiah 11:2-5 And the spirit of the LORD shall rest upon him, the spirit of wisdom and understanding, the spirit of counsel and might, the spirit of knowledge and of the fear of the LORD; And shall make him of quick understanding in the fear of the LORD: and he shall not judge after the sight of his eyes, neither reprove after the hearing of his ears: But with righteousness shall he judge the poor, and reprove with equity for the meek of the earth: and he shall smite the earth with the rod of his mouth, and with the breath of his lips shall he slay the wicked. And righteousness shall be the girdle of his loins, and faithfulness the girdle of his reins.

Isaiah 33:6 And wisdom and knowledge shall be the stability of thy times, and strength of salvation: the fear of the LORD is his treasure.

> **NOTE:** The phrase **"fear of the Lord"** *can have a totally different meaning* depending on the Hebrew word used for "fear" and the "fear of the Lord" in the context in which the Hebrew word is used. Rather than meaning an awesome respect for God as in Proverbs, "fear" can have a frightening meaning.
>
> This **"fear"** is translated from the Hebrew word *pachad* (phonetically pronounced *pakh'-ad*), which, according to *Strong's Concordance*, means dread or great terror.
>
> *Pachad* is a fear which God struck upon men to such a degree that they had no heart to withstand. This fear fell upon the nations whom Israel was to conquer or came upon lost men whom God was about to judge.
>
> 1 Samuel 11:7 And he took a yoke of oxen, and hewed them in pieces, and sent them throughout all the coasts of Israel by the hands of messengers, saying, Whosoever cometh not forth after Saul and after Samuel, so shall it be done unto his oxen. And the fear of the LORD fell on the people, and they came out with one consent.
>
> 2 Chronicles 14:14 And they smote all the cities round about Gerar; for the fear of the LORD came upon them: and they spoiled all the cities; for there was exceeding much spoil in them.
>
> Isaiah 2:19 And they shall go into the holes of the rocks, and into the caves of the earth, for fear of the LORD, and for the glory of his majesty, when he ariseth to shake terribly the earth.
>
> [Also see the following: 2 Chronicles 17:10, 2 Chronicles 19:7, Isaiah 2:10, Isaiah 2:21.]

Proverbs 1:8-9 My son, hear the instruction of thy father, and forsake not the law of thy mother:
9. For they *shall be* an ornament of grace unto thy head, and chains about thy neck.

"My son," is used as an affectionate term for a child, a student, a follower, or a disciple and it can be applied to a believer in God. The Hebrew word translated here as "my son," *ben* appears 4,923 times in the Bible; and has been translated as "son" and also as "ye children" in Proverbs 4:1; 5:7; 7:24; and 8:32. *Ben* means *"the house continues,"* and is a description of the one who continues the house (*family line*) into the next generation.[14] The "house" that has been continued by believers studying the Book of Proverbs is the **"house" of *faith in God.*** Those being addressed as "my son" or "ye children" are those offspring and students who believe in God, keep His word, and trust His promises. The seed being carried forward in our current Christian world includes the seed of faith. Believers are all the children of God.

John 1:12 But as many as received him, to them gave he power to become the sons of God, *even* to them that believe on his name.

Romans 8:14-17 For as many as are led by the Spirit of God, they are the sons of God. For ye have not received the spirit of bondage again to fear; but ye have received the Spirit of adoption, whereby we cry, Abba, Father. The Spirit itself beareth witness with our spirit, that we are the children of God: And if children, then heirs; heirs of God, and joint-heirs with Christ; if so be that we suffer with *him,* that we may be also glorified together.

Romans 8:29 For whom he did foreknow, he also did predestinate *to be* conformed to the image of his Son, that he might be the firstborn among many brethren.

2 Corinthians 6:18 And will be a Father unto you, and ye shall be my sons and daughters, saith the Lord Almighty.

Galatians 3:26 For ye are all the children of God by faith in Christ Jesus.

"Hear the instruction of thy father, and forsake not the law of thy mother." (verse 8) **"Hear"** in this context does not just mean to perceive sounds through the ears. The son was not just to hear his father and mother's words, but he was actually to apply the instruction as guides to his life.

In the life of the Hebrew, the main instructors and disciplinarians were fathers and mothers (Proverbs 1:8 and 6:20). The passing on of wisdom teaching for Israel lay firmly in the parents' hands, and included the Torah *[the Pentateuch or first five books of the Bible]*. Scripture was their guide to knowledge of God and to godly living.

Deuteronomy 11:18-19 Therefore shall ye lay up these my words in your heart and in your soul, and bind them for a sign upon your hand, that they may be as frontlets between your eyes. And ye shall teach them your children, speaking of them when thou sittest in thine house, and when thou walkest by the way, when thou liest down, and when thou risest up.

Deuteronomy 32:7 Remember the days of old, consider the years of many generations: ask thy father, and he will shew thee; thy elders, and they will tell thee.

In chapter 3 where the 'law' and 'commandments' are expressed in terms of Solomon's wisdom teaching, Solomon sees himself as re-presenting the Scriptures. He can thus speak of 'my law' and 'my commandments'. The teaching of the word of God had become internalized, personalized, and then presented to their children.[15]

> Exodus 19:5-6 Now therefore, if ye will obey my voice indeed, and keep my covenant, then ye shall be a peculiar treasure unto me above all people: for all the earth *is* mine: And ye shall be unto me a kingdom of priests, and an holy nation. These *are* the words which thou shalt speak unto the children of Israel.

"For they *shall be* an ornament of grace unto thy head, and chains about thy neck." (verse 9) To retain the *instruction of one's godly father and the law of one's godly mother* meant for their teachings to be obvious in the communication and conduct of the child. When one conducts his life so that it reflects the biblical instruction of godly parents, those mannerisms are recognized, honored, and praised as though they were golden medals of honor. Obedient godly behavior gives the child dignity, honor and respect. His life reflects his parents' righteous teachings which are as obvious as an ***ornament of grace around his head and chains about his neck.***

Proverbs 1:10 My son, if sinners entice thee, consent thou not.

This verse assumes that the student of wisdom – **"my son"** – is mature and savvy enough to be able to identify the bad characteristics of evil persons (**"sinners"**) and to make a judgment concerning personal response to their enticements. Though not explicitly stated in the following verses, it is implied, and certainly true, that in order to join these sinners who are both thieves and murderers, the son must abandon the loving companionship and excellent teaching of his parents. *This situation is a test of his wisdom*, and his response will reveal his personal ability to resist evil. Because peer pressure is often the first major test of any young person's character, it is imperative that all young people learn to identify persons who lack spiritual and moral values that can potentially threaten their well being. Their companions should be persons who agree with their spiritual and moral values; otherwise, the ornament around the head (verse 9) will be disgrace rather than grace, and the chain around the neck will be as worthless plastic rather than gold or silver.

"The first great danger which besets the simple and the young is that of evil companionship."[16]

Life is filled with judgments to be made, and they must be made with a proper humble view of self and a respect for others as taught by Scripture. There are many admonitions in Scripture to carefully choose friends and associates based on their speech and conduct. People of all ages should be able to identify enticements to do evil and to know the ramifications of being lured into doing wrong. Hate for others is always wrong but every young person should be taught to identify people who are bent on ungodly behavior and avoid them. In order to follow the admonition of **"My son, if sinners entice thee, consent thou not,"** judgment and discernment must occur! *The first step to succumbing to the devastation caused by sin is **"consent."***

Proverbs 1:11 If they say, Come with us, let us lay wait for blood, let us lurk privily for the innocent without cause:

"If they say, Come with us," these ungodly youths are telling the son to abandon godly parents and mentors and take up company or walk with evildoers. When such evil individuals get together in numbers to do evil things, then the bad is enhanced and multiplied. Furthermore, it is childishly illogical to assume that because *"all these people"* are doing any particular activity, then *"it must be right"*; however, a child or a simple person may have precisely that misunderstanding. But if young people are taught to *live by biblical principles rather than to try to justify every situation according to the circumstances*, then individual enticements are more easily resisted. As an example, if a child is taught, from this proverb, that he is never to become friends with people belonging to gangs, then by abiding by the principle, he will walk away and avoid involvement. The gang member's words, **"Come with us,"** will be completely disregarded.

"Let us lay wait for blood" is a clause that is obviously intended to mean to lurk (hide secretly) with the idea of shedding blood or taking a life in order to take possession of whatever money or goods the victim has. **"Let us lurk privily for the innocent without cause"** signals that the gang has nothing but evil reasons to set up an ambush (**"lurk privily"**). Because their victims are innocent of wrongdoing and the gang has no cause to attack them, the evil men's criminal behavior seems even worse and their wicked heart even darker. This wicked gang will make a surprise attack on anyone they view as a good prospect without any justifiable reason.

Believers should keep in mind: innocent people are a condemnation to evil people. Just the mere presence of persons of good moral values, and especially those of Christian values, incites rage in the ungodly. The believer who walks away from such an evil invitation will cause the criminals to mock at him.

> Proverbs 29:27 An unjust man *is* an abomination to the just: and *he that is* upright in the way *is* abomination to the wicked.

Proverbs 1:12   Let us swallow them up alive as the grave; and whole, as those that go down into the pit.

People can't **"swallow"** other people **"whole"** or "alive;" therefore, it is obvious that the clause utilizes figurative language *(hyperbole* and *simile)* to make the lesson to be learned more stunning, graphic, and easy to remember. Furthermore, the vile hostile acts of this wicked gang are made even more graphic with the use of such descriptive terms as **"grave"** where maggots and other insects continue their work and **"pit"** being a hole or a well into which an unwary traveler falls and is never heard from again. Gang members thus identify themselves as being covetous, heartless, vile, and cruel.

> "The appeal of the wicked, so attractive initially, is presented in its full scope. A foolish person is dazzled by the prospects of acquiring wealth easily and being gratified quickly by the immediate, but a wise person views the consequence of such sin and folly.
>
> The pressure of peers can be strong, especially on young people. Therefore they need to avoid the invitations by the wrong kind of people (sinners) who invite them to take part in murder and theft. To give in to such influence is a downward step. Let's lie in wait for someone's blood (Proverbs 12:6) clearly spells out their murderous intentions. These sinners are ready to take people's lives in order to take their money."[17]

Proverbs 1:13   We shall find all precious substance, we shall fill our houses with spoil.

This gang has the stated purpose of taking valuable items from their victims, who are those *swallowed up alive as the grave*, as noted from the previous verse. *After* they have disabled or destroyed their innocent prey, they **"find all precious substance."** And they believe that the reward of their evil acts will result in enough **"spoil"** (monetary or property gain) to fill their houses.

> "'**We shall find all precious substance**,'... gold and silver and precious stones, everything that is valuable; not considering that hereby they were in danger of losing the more precious substance, their immortal souls; and the most precious substance of all, the enjoyment of God, and happiness with him to all eternity, which is the 'more enduring substance:' the things of this world, properly speaking, are not substance, though wicked men so judge them; they are things that are not; nor are they 'precious', in comparison of spiritual and heavenly things; but they are what carnal men set a high price and value upon, and risk the loss of their name, lives, and souls for.
>
> '**We shall fill our houses with spoil**'... their money, commodities, and goods they were traveling with, which in time would be so large as to fill every one of their houses; covetousness lies at the bottom of all this wickedness; the love of money is the root of all evil (1 Timothy 6:10)."[18]

Proverbs 1:14   Cast in thy lot among us; let us all have one purse.

Though the youth being enticed is a novice, it is implied that he will be given immediate status as an equal and is promised an equal share of the spoil; thus, there is to be only **"one purse"** belonging to each member without partiality as indicated by **"lot."** By joining the gang (**"cast in thy lot among us"**) the newly-duped member would be freeing himself from the godly, loving, caring grasp of his parents and entangling himself in a web of destruction stretched out in his pathway by this vile, future-destroying, character-killing, ungodly monster called a "gang." This poor, misguided young man is being enticed into believing that the feeling of belonging to a group is somehow better than belonging to his godly family.

Proverbs 1:15   My son, walk not thou in the way with them; refrain thy foot from their path.

With this statement, the father begins telling the son to say "NO;" the specific instruction here is to stay out of the very **"path"** of wicked people. Don't even walk where they walk! Psalm One gives an equal admonition "Blessed is the man that walketh not in the counsel of the ungodly, nor standeth in the way of sinners, nor sitteth in the seat of the scornful." Avoiding the first step of walking with evil people (or of becoming their companion) necessarily means that additional steps will be avoided; so the evil situation will be dodged completely.

"Walk not thou in the way with them; refrain thy foot from their path." (verse 15b) The teacher warned the simple young man in Proverbs 1:10 – "My son, if sinners entice thee, consent thou not." Knowing the strong temptation of a peer's invitation to easy wealth, the father now reminds the youth again to not get involved with such people. To set foot on the **"way** *[a course of life or mode of action]***"** with them will lead to actions that entangles him in sin and bloodshed. Habits formed by just walking with evil men cannot be easily and quickly broken except by surrendering to God. Solomon's father David had warned his son of the danger of walking with evil, and now Solomon warns his son. Repeatedly Scripture gives the same warning.

> Exodus 23:2 Thou shalt not follow a multitude to *do* evil . . .
>
> Psalm 1:1 Blessed *is* the man that walketh not in the counsel of the ungodly, nor standeth in the way of sinners, nor sitteth in the seat of the scornful.
>
> Proverbs 4:14-15 Enter not into the path of the wicked, and go not in the way of evil *men.* Avoid it, pass not by it, turn from it, and pass away.
>
> Proverbs 13:20 He that walketh with wise men shall be wise: but a companion of fools shall be destroyed.
>
> Proverbs 14:12 There is a way which seemeth right unto a man, but the end thereof are the ways of death. *[Proverbs 16:25 is almost verbatim to 14:12.]*
>
> 2 Corinthians 6:17-18 Wherefore come out from among them, and be ye separate, saith the Lord, and touch not the unclean thing; and I will receive you, And will be a Father unto you, and ye shall be my sons and daughters, saith the Lord Almighty.

"Refrain thy foot from their path" is another way of saying, "Stay away from evil men. Don't even walk where they walk." The command has to be repeated often enough for the young man to remember!

Proverbs 1:16   For their feet run to evil, and make haste to shed blood.

Wisdom teaches the father to give reasons for making such a demand as the previous verse states, and the reason that he gives is that these wicked people run toward evil and toward shedding blood. Their minds are given over to evil, so they do wrong and do it as fast as their feet will carry them. They don't care to consider their wrong anymore, they just want to do it and do it rapidly. In verse eleven, the wicked gang implied that they would proceed slowly – "let us lay wait for blood." Now greed has overwhelmed them and they race to fulfill their wicked thoughts. They can't commit evil quickly enough; they **"make haste to shed blood."** All the while, these doers of evil find themselves an abomination to God.

> Proverbs 6:16-17 These six things doth the LORD hate: yea, seven are an abomination unto him: A proud look, a lying tongue, and hands that shed innocent blood.
>
> Proverbs 19:2 Also, that the soul be without knowledge, it is not good; and he that hasteth with his feet sinneth.

Proverbs 1:17   Surely in vain the net is spread in the sight of any bird.

This verse provides the father's second reason for warning his son to get away from evil men, for not walking with them, and for keeping his feet off their path. Even when a bird that certainly does not have the understanding of a man sees a danger that threatens its well-being, it will fly away to safety rather than continue after the baited trap; but fools are running so hard after evil and are so blinded by their greed for riches that they fail to see the cleverly-set trap. All they can see is riches and wealth before them. They do not visualize themselves standing before an earthly judge or behind bars or laying in a casket; and they certainly don't see themselves before the Great White Throne where God will pronounce their eternal damnation in the Lake of Fire. Not only does greed act to blind good reasoning ability, thus making danger invisible; but intelligence, as a guide, is replaced by the thoughtless, devious emotion of being accepted into a gang.

> **Proverbs 1:18** And they lay wait for their *own* blood; they lurk privily for their *own* lives.

These criminal gang members (including any simple youth who has yoked up with them) are both the hunted and the hunter. They actively hunt for an easy prey; and while doing so, they establish themselves as outlaws who are hunted by legal authorities and possibly loved ones of their victims. These evil people may be caught up with in this life by officers of the law and certainly in eternity by a just God. Unknown to themselves, they **"lay wait for their own blood: they lurk privily for their own lives."**

> Proverbs 26:27 Whoso diggeth a pit shall fall therein: and he that rolleth a stone, it will return upon him.
>
> Proverbs 28:10 Whoso causeth the righteous to go astray in an evil way, he shall fall himself into his own pit: but the upright shall have good things in possession.

> **Proverbs 1:19** So *are* the ways of everyone that is greedy of gain; *which* taketh away the life of the owners thereof.

This verse is a concluding, summarizing statement to the previous eleven verses. Because of greed and thirst for blood, these criminals' minds are muddled, their path laden with snares and pits, and their light of conscience is dark. Their ideas of freedom through wealth are illusionary and constitute a trap that will eventually capture its owners. Their evil ways lead them to an evil reward. Unjust gain takes away the life of those that are under its powers.

Students of wisdom should read these verses and be alert to both the *sources of evil* and the *people of wicked devices*. Good judgment is mandatory to evaluate men and their actions. Gang members have rapacious **"ways"** *[manners of life, habits]* that establish them in the same category as **"everyone that is greedy of gain."** Greed blinds a person's mind to the trap he is setting for himself. The person consumed with greed doesn't realize that his ability to think properly has been restricted so much that he barely thinks of anything other than getting something for himself. His mind is filled with his own selfish desires and he has no thought of God's plan or his victim's life. Covetousness is always destructive to true, contented life, and ill-gotten gain cannot be enjoyed.

> Proverbs 10:2 Treasures of wickedness profit nothing: but righteousness delivereth from death.
>
> Proverbs 21:7 The robbery of the wicked shall destroy them; because they refuse to do judgment.
>
> Luke 12:15 And he said unto them, Take heed, and beware of covetousness: for a man's life consisteth not in the abundance of the things which he possesseth.
>
> 1 Timothy 6:10 For the love of money is the root of all evil: which while some coveted after, they have erred from the faith, and pierced themselves through with many sorrows.

> **Proverbs 1:20** Wisdom crieth without; she uttereth her voice in the streets:

Now that Solomon has given his introductory set of instructions to "My Son," he introduces another speaker of truth, the lady "Wisdom." She is a PERSONIFICATION, so named Wisdom because she is used to vocalize the thinking and reasoning of God. She is not God, but she is an illustration to show the way God thinks.

All Scripture was given by inspiration of the Holy Spirit directly through different men who each expressed themselves with different words and with various methods of writing. These inspired men employed diverse writing techniques and multiple figures of speech to present the truth. Solomon was obviously free to utilize *several personalities or identities* to speak throughout the Book of Proverbs including Solomon himself, Wisdom, a father, Agur and king Lemuel. Each of these identities was given a "voice" and was used by Solomon to teach aspects of godly wisdom, later in the book called "sound wisdom."

In this chapter, beginning with verse 20, "Wisdom" as a personality is introduced. *Pulpit Helps* refers to this personification of wisdom (Hebrew *chokmoth*) as "all the varieties under which wisdom *par excellence* may be regarded and is comprehended."[19] This Hebrew word for "wisdom," is found in *only* the four verses below: twice as the personified Wisdom (Proverbs 1:20; 9:1), once as describing a woman who epitomized this wisdom (Proverbs 14:1) and once to specify that which a fool can't reach. (Proverbs 24:7)

NOTE: Very interesting is the fact that the only other use of *chokmoth* in the Old Testament is found in Psalm 49:3, also quoted below. Because David loved God and served Him with his whole heart, he is able to speak wisdom. Note that the use of *chokmoth* is confined to these two books of the Bible – Psalms and Proverbs. There are six other Hebrew words translated into the English word "wisdom" in the book of Proverbs.

> Psalm 49:3 My mouth shall speak of wisdom; and the meditation of my heart *shall be* of understanding.
>
> Proverbs 1:20 Wisdom crieth without; she uttereth her voice in the streets . . .
>
> Proverbs 9:1 Wisdom hath builded her house, she hath hewn out her seven pillars . . .
>
> Proverbs 14:1 Every wise woman buildeth her house: but the foolish plucketh it down with her hands.
>
> Proverbs 24:7 Wisdom *is* too high for a fool: he openeth not his mouth in the gate.

Wisdom is that particular and perfect line of reasoning and thinking that originates from God. Any other idea *(worldly wisdom)* that identifies itself as wisdom is innately flawed. Wise men, who learn from God to think in a manner that is approved by Him, submit themselves, as much as is possible, to God's will and to His word. They learn to distinguish between right and wrong and good and evil because they keep His wisdom in their minds. They can now speak wisdom to others because such wisdom from God is what fills their hearts.

> Proverbs 2:7 He layeth up sound wisdom for the righteous: he is a buckler to them that walk uprightly.
>
> Proverbs 3:21 My son, let not them depart from thine eyes: keep sound wisdom and discretion. . .
>
> Proverbs 8:14 Counsel is mine, and sound wisdom: I am understanding; I have strength.
>
> II Timothy 3:16-17 All scripture is given by inspiration of God, and is profitable for doctrine, for reproof, for correction, for instruction in righteousness: That the man of God may be perfect, throughly furnished unto all good works.

THE RELATIONSHIP BETWEEN JESUS AND PERSONIFIED WISDOM EXPLAINED

Because Jesus is Scripturally identified as "Wisdom," and because many of the characteristics that are said of wisdom are also said of Jesus, and because of the eternal presence of both wisdom and Jesus, many believe that these verses in Proverbs are actually spoken by Jesus and not the personified Wisdom.

First Corinthians 1:24 identifies Christ as "the wisdom of God" and Colossians 2:2-3 gives more detail and clarity, saying ". . . and of Christ: In whom are hid all the treasures of wisdom and knowledge." Unquestionably, these verses verify that within Christ Jesus – wisdom is fully manifested. Because of these and other verses of Scripture, there is no doubt that WISDOM IS THE *WAY* JESUS THINKS, REASONS, SPEAKS, AND ACTS. His every action reveals "wisdom" beginning with creation and proceeding to His being the living Word of God.

> 1Corinthians 1:24 But unto them which are called, both Jews and Greeks, Christ the power of God, and the wisdom of God.
>
> Colossians 2:2-3 That their hearts might be comforted, being knit together in love, and unto all riches of the full assurance of understanding, to the acknowledgment of the mystery of God, and of the Father, and of Christ; In whom are hid all the treasures of wisdom and knowledge.

A comparison of Luke 11:49 and Matthew 23:34 *[see below]* reveals that Jesus and "the wisdom of God" are the one source from which prophets, apostles, wise men, and scribes originated. Jesus is the speaker in both verses; however, He identifies Himself as "the wisdom of God" in Luke 11:49. It is by "the wisdom of God" that Jesus speaks for Jesus is God and He fully speaks and thinks and reasons with the same perfect wisdom that His Father speaks. Furthermore, those apostles, prophets, wise men and scribes were told what to say by the Holy Spirit; therefore those Spirit-produced utterances were utterances of wisdom.

> Luke 11:49 Therefore also said the wisdom of God, I will send them prophets and apostles, and some of them they shall slay and persecute . . .
>
> Matthew 23:34 Wherefore, behold, I send unto you prophets, and wise men, and scribes: and some of them ye shall kill and crucify; and some of them shall ye scourge in your synagogues, and persecute them from city to city. . . *[Jesus is speaking]*

Proverbs 3:19 plus Proverbs 8:22-31 tell of Wisdom *as being used* in the creation process and also *possessed by* the LORD; thus, it is obvious that wisdom is said to be something other than the entire being of God, though it is used of God. WISDOM IS THE PERFECT *WAY* HE THINKS AND REASONS; HENCE, JESUS IS SAID TO BE WISDOM because wisdom is the expression of His mind, and that of His Father, and unquestionably that of the Holy Spirit.

> Proverbs 3:19 The LORD by wisdom hath founded the earth; by understanding hath he established the heavens.

Proverbs 8:22-31 *[Personified wisdom speaks in these verses.]* The LORD possessed me in the beginning of his way, before his works of old. I was set up from everlasting, from the beginning, or ever the earth was. When there were no depths, I was brought forth; when there were no fountains abounding with water. Before the mountains were settled, before the hills was I brought forth: While as yet he had not made the earth, nor the fields, nor the highest part of the dust of the world. When he prepared the heavens, I was there: when he set a compass upon the face of the depth: When he established the clouds above: when he strengthened the fountains of the deep: When he gave to the sea his decree, that the waters should not pass his commandment: when he appointed the foundations of the earth: Then I was by him, as one brought up with him: and I was daily his delight, rejoicing always before him; Rejoicing in the habitable part of his earth; and my delights were with the sons of men.

All of the following verses describe Jesus as the Creator. Wisdom is the perfect way of thinking whereby the Creator created all things. Jesus is much more than the single aspect of wisdom.

John 1:1-4 In the beginning was the Word, and the Word was with God, and the Word was God. The same was in the beginning with God. All things were made by him; and without him was not any thing made that was made. In him was life; and the life was the light of men.

John 17:5 And now, O Father, glorify thou me with thine own self with the glory which I had with thee before the world was.

Ephesians 3:9 And to make all men see what is the fellowship of the mystery, which from the beginning of the world hath been hid in God, who created all things by Jesus Christ:

Colossians 1:15-17 Who is the image of the invisible God, the firstborn of every creature: For by him were all things created, that are in heaven, and that are in earth, visible and invisible, whether they be thrones, or dominions, or principalities, or powers: all things were created by him, and for him: And he is before all things, and by him all things consist.

Hebrews 1:2 Hath in these last days spoken unto us by his Son, whom he hath appointed heir of all things, by whom also he made the worlds...

Hebrews 1:10 And, Thou, Lord, in the beginning hast laid the foundation of the earth; and the heavens are the works of thine hands...

Hebrews 3:3-4 For this man was counted worthy of more glory than Moses, inasmuch as he who hath builded the house hath more honour than the house. For every house is builded by some man; but he that built all things is God.

"... The Word was made flesh and dwelt among us" (John 1:14); simultaneously, wisdom was also made obvious through Jesus. The word of God provides knowledge for the believer to know how to yield himself to his Creator and thereby live wisely – in a most effective manner.

Multi-faceted wisdom is a gift *from God* to individuals who desire the same. As this chapter begins to point out, wisdom is taught primarily through the entire body of Scripture, but identities are occasionally given voice to express the same truths given in Biblical directives. As Chapters 2 through 9 progress, the reader will be introduced to some other voices of wisdom, but now the voice of personified Wisdom *(capitalized by the author to differentiate her from the word "wisdom")* will be heard.

NOTE: In the Appendix, there is a lengthy *(but well worth the read)* dissertation that declares the distinction between the personified Wisdom and Jesus. Please see.

ಉಲಉಲಉಲಉಲಉಲಉಲಉಲಉಲಉಲ

"Wisdom crieth without; she uttereth her voice in the streets." (verse 20) Wisdom cries out from all of God's creation–from **"without"**– from **"the streets."**

> **Proverbs 1:21-32** She crieth in the chief place of concourse, in the openings of the gates: in the city she uttereth her words, *saying*,
> 22. How long, ye simple ones, will ye love simplicity? and the scorners delight in their scorning, and fools hate knowledge?
> 23. Turn you at my reproof: behold, I will pour out my spirit unto you, I will make known my words unto you.
> 24. Because I have called, and ye refused; I have stretched out my hand, and no man regarded;
> 25. But ye have set at nought all my counsel, and would none of my reproof:
> 26. I also will laugh at your calamity; I will mock when your fear cometh;
> 27. When your fear cometh as desolation, and your destruction cometh as a whirlwind; when distress and anguish cometh upon you.
> 28. Then shall they call upon me, but I will not answer; they shall seek me early, but they shall not find me:
> 29. For that they hated knowledge, and did not choose the fear of the LORD:
> 30. They would none of my counsel: they despised all my reproof.
> 31. Therefore shall they eat of the fruit of their own way, and be filled with their own devices.
> 32. For the turning away of the simple shall slay them, and the prosperity of fools shall destroy them.

"She crieth in the chief place of concourse, in the openings of the gates: in the city she uttereth her words." (verse 21) The **"chief place of concourse"** describes a place where a crowd of people have gathered together to talk, and **"concourse"** describes the noise that people make when they merge together in a group. It is a public place like the **"openings of the gates." She cried out** (proclaimed) where the most people were gathered, and where the leaders of the city would meet in the gates.

Wisdom is certainly not ashamed of the message she bears, and it is worthy of being proclaimed in every place. JESUS IS THE EMBODIMENT AND THE FULFILLMENT OF ALL THE WORD OF GOD AND OF GODLY WISDOM; consequently, when He speaks, He does so with perfect wisdom. Like the personified wisdom in Proverbs, He cried out or preached **"in the chief place of concourse."** Three great passages that illustrate the crying out publicly of the Lord Jesus Christ are:

> John 7:28 Then cried Jesus in the temple as he taught, saying, ye both know me and ye know whence I am: and I am not come of myself, but he that sent me is true, whom ye know not.
>
> John 7:37-39 In the last day, that great day of the feast, Jesus stood and cried, saying, If any man thirst, let him come unto me, and drink. He that believeth on me, as the scripture hath said, out of his belly shall flow rivers of living water. (But this spake he of the Spirit, which they that believe on him should receive: for the Holy Ghost was not yet given; because that Jesus was not yet glorified.)
>
> Matthew 23:1 and 37 Then spake Jesus to the multitude and to his disciples . . . O Jerusalem, Jerusalem, thou that killest the prophets, and stonest them which are sent unto thee, how often would I have gathered thy children together, even as a hen gathereth her chickens under her wings, and ye would not!

"How long, ye simple ones, will ye love simplicity? and the scorners delight in their scorning, and fools hate knowledge?" (verse 22) Wisdom doesn't mince words as she calls out to the sinners in the chief places where people gather. In this passage she identifies three categories of rejecters of godly wisdom as **"simple ones," "scorners,"** and **"fools."**

The **"simple ones" "love simplicity."** They love being easily led astray because they don't want to think for themselves for various reasons including having to face opposition, being unpopular, and submitting to God. Blinded by their love of sin, they live as if there were no God and no eternity.

"Scorners" mock wisdom, the truths of the Bible, and anyone who believes the same; and they **"delight** *[take pleasure]* **in their scorning."** They encourage the simple, but *not* to do good. They take pleasure in deriding the truth of Scripture and the people of God and righteous living. The scorner and the fool **"hate knowledge"** (especially the knowledge of God) because if they listen to wisdom they would have to acknowledge their sins and recognize the existence of God and the validity of His laws and precepts. Psalm 53:1 states, "The fool has said in his heart, *There is* no God." The question of Wisdom is, **"How long, ye simple ones, will ye love simplicity? and the scorners delight in their scorning, and fools hate knowledge?"**

How long? – until they turn away from their hatred of God and look unto Him for salvation.

"Turn you at my reproof: behold, I will pour out my spirit unto you, I will make known my words unto you." (verse 23) Here, Wisdom speaks the word of God in partnership with the Spirit of God. The Spirit of God uses the word of God to reprove and convict the sinner that he is wrong. To **"turn you at my reproof** *[chastisement, correction]*" means to repent. Upon repentance the Spirit of God is *poured out* or floods the repentant one with His indescribable presence. When a person receives correction by God and receives the Spirit of God, he is in a position to receive Scriptural instruction.

> Psalm 19:7 The law of the LORD is perfect, converting the soul: the testimony of the LORD is sure, making wise the simple.
> Psalm 119:130 The entrance of thy words giveth light; it giveth understanding unto the simple.
> Hebrews 4:12 For the word of God *is* quick, and powerful, and sharper than any twoedged sword, piercing even to the dividing asunder of soul and spirit, and of the joints and marrow, and *is* a discerner of the thoughts and intents of the heart.

"I will pour out my spirit unto you, I will make known my words unto you" (verse 23b) indicates the fact that the word of God is sent from God, is spiritual and has to be spiritually understood with the help of the Holy Spirit. The Spirit works abundantly – He is **"poured out** *[gushes forth]*" – to those who repent – who **"turn you at my reproof;"** thus, by repentance, they manifest a genuine desire to know God, including everything He has to say – His wisdom.

> Psalm 25:14 The secret of the LORD *is* with them that fear him; and he will shew them his covenant.
> John 7:17 If any man will do his will, he shall know of the doctrine, whether it be of God, or *whether* I speak of myself.
> 1Corinthians 2:9-14 But as it is written, Eye hath not seen, nor ear heard, neither have entered into the heart of man, the things which God hath prepared for them that love him. But God hath revealed *them* unto us by his Spirit: for the Spirit searcheth all things, yea, the deep things of God. For what man knoweth the things of a man, save the spirit of man which is in him? even so the things of God knoweth no man, but the Spirit of God. Now we have received, not the spirit of the world, but the spirit which is of God; that we might know the things that are freely given to us of God. Which things also we speak, not in the words which man's wisdom teacheth, but which the Holy Ghost teacheth; comparing spiritual things with spiritual. But the natural man receiveth not the things of the Spirit of God: for they are foolishness unto him: neither can he know *them,* because they are spiritually discerned.

Ever since God formed man out of the dirt, breathed in him the breath of life, and then placed him in the Garden of Eden, God has continually reached out to man. God desires that man trust His great wisdom and believe that He knows what is best for him in every regard. Adam refused and failed miserably. But God has continually reached out to persuade man that He knows best for His creation. God has spoken directly to man as He did first in the Garden, then through dreams and visions, then through prophets, then through His word, and finally through His only begotten Son. Even all the elements of creation demand that man acknowledge the magnificent wisdom of God. Believing that he is wise within himself, man, for the most part, refuses the wisdom of God in every form. God fully expressed His wisdom and His great desire for man to come to his senses by the direct communication from Jesus, Who was and is the hope of mankind. Jesus has reached out to all men and He wants all men saved, but all do not accept such divine wisdom.

> John 3:17 For God sent not his Son into the world to condemn the world; but that the world through him might be saved.
> John 10:9 I am the door: by me if any man enter in, he shall be saved, and shall go in and out, and find pasture.
> Romans 10:13 For whosoever shall call upon the name of the Lord shall be saved.
> Romans 10:17 So then faith cometh by hearing, and hearing by the word of God.
> I Timothy 2:4 Who will have all men to be saved, and to come unto the knowledge of the truth.

"Because I have called, and ye refused; I have stretched out my hand, and no man regarded." (verse 24) This is not the first call of Wisdom, but rather the last.

> Isaiah 65:2 I have spread out my hands all the day unto a rebellious people, which walketh in a way *that was* not good, after their own thoughts;
> Romans 10:21 But to Israel he saith, All day long I have stretched forth my hands unto a disobedient and gainsaying people.

God gets man's attention by His word, His providence, His ministers, and man's conscience; but the invitation eventually changes from mercy to judgment. This sad passage of rejection parallels the reaching out of Jesus to the Jews and their refusal to hear–as illustrated in the following passages:

> Matthew 23:37-38 O Jerusalem, Jerusalem, thou that killest the prophets, and stonest them which are sent unto thee, how often would I have gathered thy children together, even as a hen gathereth her chickens under her wings, and ye would not! Behold, your house is left unto you desolate.
> Luke 14:17-18 And sent his servant at supper time to say to them that were bidden, Come; for all things are now ready. And they all with one consent began to make excuse. The first said unto him, I have bought a piece of ground, and I must needs go and see it: I pray thee have me excused.
> John 1:11-13 He came unto his own, and his own received him not.

"But ye have set at nought all my counsel, and would none of my reproof." (verse 25) Wisdom is said to cry out here to the "simple ones," the "scorners," and the "fools" (of verse 22) and ask them to "turn." To reject and ignore wisdom has serious consequences. This was their choice; they refused to hear. Now they will face judgment. In the Book of Revelation, the church of Laodicia is a picture of rejection:

> Revelation 3:18-19 I counsel thee to buy of me gold tried in the fire, that thou mayest be rich; and white raiment, that thou mayest be clothed, and that the shame of thy nakedness do not appear; and anoint thine eyes with eyesalve, that thou mayest see. As many as I love, I rebuke and chasten: be zealous therefore, and repent.

"I also will laugh at your calamity; I will mock when your fear cometh." (verse 26) Wisdom continues to address the "simple ones," "scorners," and "fools" of verse 22, giving here her response to them when their rejection turns finally into great **"fear"** because of destruction. They have rejected wisdom and have spurned wisdom's teachers and preachers, the wooing of the Spirit, and their own consciences. This verse is very similar to other passages in the Bible that reflect the calm, unshaken resolve of God who will judge all men according to wisdom's admonition for each one, individually, to believe, trust and have a personal relationship with Him.

> Luke 14:24 For I say unto you, That none of those men which were bidden shall taste of my supper.

"When your fear cometh as desolation, and your destruction cometh as a whirlwind; when distress and anguish cometh upon you." (verse 27) This verse and the previous one speak of an extreme fear like one would have of a suddenly approaching category five tornado. There is no defense, no time to run, and no place of security. This verse refers to the severity of distress and anguish that will eventually come upon those who reject godly wisdom. All of these terms (**"calamity," "fear," "desolation," "destruction," "distress,"** and **"anguish"**) remind the reader of Hell and the Lake of Fire. " The whirlwind is often symbolic of God's wrath and destructive fury visited upon the wicked."[20] The words of this verse speak for themselves as far as misery is concerned and the verses below give a broader understanding of the completeness of the judgment. A dismal picture is drawn with the compilation of fear, desolation, destruction, distress, and anguish.

> Proverbs 6:12-15 A naughty person, a wicked man, walketh with a froward mouth. He winketh with his eyes, he speaketh with his feet, he teacheth with his fingers; Frowardness *is* in his heart, he deviseth mischief continually; he soweth discord. Therefore shall his calamity come suddenly; suddenly shall he be broken without remedy.
>
> Jeremiah 23:19 Behold, a whirlwind of the LORD is gone forth in fury, even a grievous whirlwind: it shall fall grievously upon the head of the wicked.
>
> Nahum 1:3 The LORD *is* slow to anger, and great in power, and will not at all acquit *the wicked:* the LORD hath his way in the whirlwind and in the storm, and the clouds *are* the dust of his feet.

"Then shall they call upon me, but I will not answer; they shall seek me early, but they shall not find me." (verse 28) **"Then shall they call upon me"** refers to the time when those who refused the call of Wisdom understand the foolishness of their choice. When trouble comes, they will wake up **"early"** to diligently seek wisdom (the teachings of God), but their decisions during their lifetime had already proved that they **"hated knowledge,"** the knowledge of God. They refused to have **"the fear of the LORD."** They didn't want to hear anything that Wisdom had to say or as the verse states **"my counsel."**

Verses 24-33 are specific in stating that there is an opportunity to call on God in true repentance, and that there will come a time when the invitation will expire. Men establish themselves against God by hating to know about Him, by refusing to have a respect for Him, by refusing to be counseled by Him, and by hating His chastisement. The opportunity for calling on God will expire.

> Genesis 6:3 And the LORD said, My spirit shall not always strive with man, for that he also is flesh: yet his days shall be an hundred and twenty years.
>
> Romans 1:32 Who knowing the judgment of God, that they which commit such things are worthy of death, not only do the same, but have pleasure in them that do them.
>
> 2Thessalanians 2:8-12 And then shall that Wicked be revealed, whom the Lord shall consume with the spirit of his mouth, and shall destroy with the brightness of his coming: *Even him,* whose coming is after the working of Satan with all power and signs and lying wonders, And with all deceivableness of unrighteousness in them that perish; because they received not the love of the truth, that they might be saved. And for this cause God shall send them strong delusion, that they should believe a lie: That they all might be damned who believed not the truth, but had pleasure in unrighteousness.
>
> Revelation 20:11-15 And I saw a great white throne, and him that sat on it, from whose face the earth and the heaven fled away; and there was found no place for them. And I saw the dead, small and great, stand before God; and the books were opened: and another book was opened, which is *the book* of life: and the dead were judged out of those things which were written in the books, according to their works. And the sea gave up the dead which were in it; and death and hell delivered up the dead which were in them: and they were judged every man according to their works. And death and hell were cast into the lake of fire. This is the second death. And whosoever was not found written in the book of life was cast into the lake of fire.

"For that they hated knowledge, and did not choose the fear of the LORD: They would none of my counsel: they despised all my reproof." (verses 29-30) These verses restate the charges presented in verses 22 and 25. Wisdom disregards the sinners because they disregard her call to them. When they did not **"choose"** the **"fear of the LORD"** they showed their lack of love and respect for God. They "despised" wisdom's reproof with scorn.

> Job 21:14 Therefore they say unto God, Depart from us; for we desire not the knowledge of thy ways.
> Proverbs 1:7 The fear of the LORD *is* the beginning of knowledge: *but* fools despise wisdom and instruction.
> Proverbs 1:22 How long, ye simple ones, will ye love simplicity? and the scorners delight in their scorning, and fools hate knowledge?
> Proverbs 5:12-13 And say, How have I hated instruction, and my heart despised reproof; And have not obeyed the voice of my teachers, nor inclined mine ear to them that instructed me!
> Proverbs 6:23 For the commandment *is* a lamp; and the law *is* light; and reproofs of instruction *are* the way of life.
> Isaiah 65:12 Therefore will I number you to the sword, and ye shall all bow down to the slaughter: because when I called, ye did not answer; when I spake, ye did not hear; but did evil before mine eyes, and did choose *that* wherein I delighted not.
> Isaiah 66:4 I also will choose their delusions, and will bring their fears upon them; because when I called, none did answer; when I spake, they did not hear: but they did evil before mine eyes, and chose *that* in which I delighted not.

"Therefore shall they eat of the fruit of their own way, and be filled with their own devices." (verse 31) To **"eat the fruit of their own way"** is to receive punishments equal to their sins. "What was sweet in their mouths shall be bitter in their bellies and that destruction which they have plotted against others shall fall upon themselves."[21]

> Jeremiah 6:19 Hear, O earth: behold, I will bring evil upon this people, *even* the fruit of their thoughts, because they have not hearkened unto my words, nor to my law, but rejected it.
> Galatians 6:7-8 Be not deceived; God is not mocked: for whatsoever a man soweth, that shall he also reap. For he that soweth to his flesh shall of the flesh reap corruption; but he that soweth to the Spirit shall of the Spirit reap life everlasting.

They have chosen their own miserable end and are filled with their own devices. This end was not God' choice for them but was their own choice. God wanted their fruit to be holiness and their destiny to be the joy of everlasting life.

> "Let me impress upon the mind and conscience of every one the reason, and the only reason, of the issue so fearfully described. There is not a word here of inability; it is all unwillingness. And point me out one passage of the Bible, where it is otherwise; where sinners are represented as condemned for inability, – for not doing what they could not do. The blessed God is no such tantalizer. It is never, 'Ye could not' – but 'ye would not:'– and when, at any time, inability is spoken of, it is inability all of a moral nature, and resolves itself into unwillingness. And this alone leaves the blameworthiness where it ought to lie – not with God, but with the sinner."[22]

"For the turning away of the simple shall slay them." (verse 32) Wisdom had called on the simple to turn and turn they did – but *not* toward Wisdom – but rather away from her invitation. This **"turning away"** will destroy them. To turn away from the word of God will be followed by a rejection of Jesus. If a person will not receive the teachings of God, neither will he receive the Son of God.

"The prosperity of fools shall destroy them." (verse 32) The fool can prosper financially in this life; however, the outward appearance of being secure through prosperity without God can lead the simple to turn away from God. Prosperity may lead to a false sense of security, causing the wealthy to trust themselves and their money. Better to trust in God and let Him provide as He deems right.

"But whoso hearkeneth unto me *[Wisdom]* **shall dwell safely, and shall be quiet from fear of evil."** (verse 33) Notice the promises given to those who **"hearkeneth to me"** (those who hear and obey Wisdom). They shall **"dwell safely"** *[without care]*, **"be quiet"** *[be at peace]* without a **"fear of evil."** When people turn away from the teachings of God, they turn away from their our own best interests and from the safest place in all of eternity. There will be no **"fear of evil"** for the redeemed because evil has no claim on them and it is impossible for evil to approach them because they are under His wings.

> Isaiah 48:18 O that thou hadst hearkened to my commandments! then had thy peace been as a river, and thy righteousness as the waves of the sea . . .
> John 10:27-28 My sheep hear my voice, and I know them, and they follow me: And I give unto them eternal life; and they shall never perish, neither shall any man pluck them out of my hand.
> Romans 8:35-39 Who shall separate us from the love of Christ? *shall* tribulation, or distress, or persecution, or famine, or nakedness, or peril, or sword? As it is written, For thy sake we are killed all the day long; we are accounted as sheep for the slaughter. Nay, in all these things we are more than conquerors through him that loved us. For I am persuaded, that neither death, nor life, nor angels, nor principalities, nor powers, nor things present, nor things to come, Nor height, nor depth, nor any other creature, shall be able to separate us from the love of God, which is in Christ Jesus our Lord.

CHAPTER TWO

> **The Protected Life That Comes from Obtaining Wisdom**
> (Outline of Chapter 2)
>
> I. The starting point
>   A. Receive Wisdom's words and hide her commandments in your heart. (verse 1)
>   B. Incline your ear unto wisdom. (verse 2a)
>   C. Apply your heart to understanding. (verse 2b)
>   D. Cry after, seek and search for wisdom, knowledge and understanding as one would a valuable treasure. (verses 3-4)
> II. Step 1
>   A. Obtain an understanding of "the fear of the LORD" and find "the knowledge of God." (verse 5)
>   B. Obtain an understanding of "righteousness, and judgment, and equity; yea, every good path." (verse 9)
> III. Step 2
>   A. Wisdom must enter your heart. (verse 10a)
>   B. Knowledge must be pleasant to your soul. (verse 10b)
> IV. The successful protected life
>   A. Discretion shall preserve/understanding shall keep (guard) you (verse 11)
>   1. From evil men. (verse 12)
>   2. From strange women. (verse 16)
>   B. Successfully walk in the way of good men and keep the paths of the righteous. (verse 20)

Proverbs 2:1-5 My son, if thou wilt receive my words, and hide my commandments with thee;
2. So that thou incline thine ear unto wisdom, *and* apply thine heart to understanding;
3. Yea, if thou criest after knowledge, *and* liftest up thy voice for understanding;
4. If thou seekest her as silver, and searchest for her as *for* hid treasures;
5. Then shalt thou understand the fear of the LORD, and find the knowledge of God.

Affectionately, Solomon begins Chapter Two with **"My son,"** which is an endearing term often used for a son or disciple. Such an affectionate salutation indicates that the person he is addressing has a relationship that is personal. Because the **"son"** is *not* a casual observer or a careless student but is rather an astute and serious learner, his teacher lays out the *serious and demanding* requirements for success. Any mediocre attempt will be met with failure. He must:

(1) **Receive** *[take hold of]* wisdom's words and **hide** *[hoard, protect]* her commandments. (verse 1)
(2) **Incline** his ear unto wisdom, and **apply** his heart to understanding. (verse 2)
(3) **Cry** after knowledge of God and His wisdom, **lift up** his voice (ask God) for understanding. (verse 3)
(4) **Seek and search** for wisdom, knowledge, and understanding like one would look for valuable treasure. (verse 4)

*These 4 requirements represent **significant effort**,* and most people are just not willing to exert themselves or give themselves to God to such a high degree; however, for those who *are* willing, the result is that the student will obtain an understanding that few people have and will develop a strong personal relationship with God that has unparalleled rewards.

A person with understanding has an awesome respect for God and a proper perspective of self. He respects God as Creator and humbly views himself as created by God. He understands that God is ALL POWERFUL and that he has very limited power. He also understands that God has complete knowledge while he has little knowledge. As a result of his respectful attitude, he will minimize himself and fully trust God and His word. Also, this type of fear (as distinguished from a frightful, shaking, alarming fear) directs a person to act in a trusting manner that is pleasing to God. A person who learns to fear and serve God will enjoy God's favor and a good relationship with Him.

"Fear of the Lord" restrains a person from attaching himself to anything or any position ***not*** led by and approved of God. It requires BOTH belief in the ever-present God and an intentional and positive action by the believer to submit himself to God. Like John the Baptist, the believer must determine in his heart that "He must increase, but I must decrease." Obtaining this "FEAR OF THE LORD" has numerous benefits:

> "**The fear of the Lord** [*yir'athyehovah*] . . . is the beginning . . . [*and*] the highest form of knowledge and the greatest good. Elsewhere it is represented as a fountain of life. All true wisdom is summed up in 'the fear of the Lord.' It here means the reverence due to him, and so comprises the whole range of the religious affections and feelings, which respond to various attributes of the Divine character as they are revealed, and which find their expression in holy worship. **The knowledge of God** [*da'ath Elohim*], literally, *the knowledge of Elohim [is]* not merely cognition, but knowledge in its wider sense. The two ideas of '**the fear of the Lord**' and '**the knowledge of God**' act reciprocally on each other. Just as without reverence of God there can be no knowledge of him in its true sense, so the knowledge of God will increase and deepen the feeling of reverence. But it is noticeable that the teacher here, as in Proverbs 9:10, where, however, it is 'the knowledge of the holy' [*daathk'doshim*], gives the chief place to reverence, and thus indicates that it is the basis of knowledge, which is its fruit and result. The relation here suggested is analogous to that which subsists between faith and knowledge, and recalls the celebrated dictum of Anselm: 'Neque enim quaero intelligere ut credam; sed credo, ut intelligam.'"[23] [*Latin for "I believe so that I may understand."*][24]

When one has the fear of the LORD, he is enabled to begin to receive wisdom, knowledge and understanding. Obtaining this ***"fear of the LORD"*** is the foundation, the beginning, the initial stage for the Spirit of God to work in the heart of His disciple. "Fear of the LORD" is the correct frame of mind concerning God that enables the disciple to begin to learn and gain a **"knowledge of God."** Success comes through studying His word, experiencing prayers answered, and seeing His word fulfilled. Studying Scripture reveals illustrations of God's character and His interactions with human beings. Thus, studying purposefully to improve one's **"knowledge of God"** involves a life-long pursuit of discovering His expectations and of learning what pleases Him.

BENEFITS OF HAVING the "Fear of the LORD"

(1) **It is the beginning of wisdom.**
Psalm 111:10 The fear of the LORD *is* the beginning of wisdom: a good understanding have all they that do *his commandments:* his praise endureth for ever.
Proverbs 9:10 The fear of the LORD *is* the beginning of wisdom: and the knowledge of the holy *is* understanding.

(2) **It initiates finding the knowledge of God.**
Proverbs 2:5 Then shalt thou understand the fear of the LORD, and find the knowledge of God.

(3) **It prolongs days.**
Proverbs 10:27 The fear of the LORD prolongeth days: but the years of the wicked shall be shortened.

(3) **It is strong confidence.**
Proverbs 14:26 In the fear of the LORD *is* strong confidence: and his children shall have a place of refuge.

(4) **It is a fountain of life.**
Proverbs 14:27 The fear of the LORD *is* a fountain of life, to depart from the snares of death.

(5) **It is better to have it with little than great treasure and trouble therewith.**
Proverbs 15:16 Better *is* little with the fear of the LORD than great treasure and trouble therewith.

(6) **It is the instruction of wisdom.**
Proverbs 15:33 The fear of the LORD *is* the instruction of wisdom; and before honour *is* humility.

(7) **It causes men to depart from evil.**
Proverbs 16:6 By mercy and truth iniquity is purged: and by the fear of the LORD *men* depart from evil.

(8) **It tendeth to life.**
Proverbs 19:23 The fear of the LORD *tendeth* to life: and *he that hath it* shall abide satisfied; he shall not be visited with evil.

(9) **It causes those that have it to abide satisfied and not be visited with evil.**
Proverbs 19:23 The fear of the LORD *tendeth* to life: and *he that hath it* shall abide satisfied; he shall not be visited with evil.

(10) **It produces riches, and honour, and life in conjunction with humility.**
Proverbs 22:4 By humility *and* the fear of the LORD *are* riches, and honour, and life.

(11) **It is wisdom.**
Job 28:28 And unto man he said, Behold, the fear of the Lord, that *is* wisdom; and to depart from evil *is* understanding.

"It is important to note the final goals [*of the Book of Proverbs*] . . . Paradoxically the aim is to understand God's awesomeness and hiddenness and holiness (the fear of JEHOVAH), whilst at the same time coming to know Him as He is (the knowledge of God), not theoretically through theology, but practically through experience of God. Whilst He is far off, He is to be seen as ever near. As Solomon would say elsewhere, 'behold, the heaven and heaven of heavens cannot contain thee' (1Kings 8:27). And yet now he confirms that He reveals Himself to those who seek Him. This is the wonder of our God."[25]

> **Proverbs 2:6-8** For the LORD giveth wisdom: out of his mouth *cometh* knowledge and understanding.
> 7. He layeth up sound wisdom for the righteous: *he is* a buckler to them that walk uprightly.
> 8. He keepeth the paths of judgment, and preserveth the way of his saints.

God is actively involved with those who genuinely seek His wisdom. (verses 6-8)
- He BESTOWS wisdom, knowledge and understanding. (verses 6-7a)
- He BECOMES a buckler to the righteous. (verse 7b)
- He BARRICADES to keep the believer on the paths of judgment and to preserve the way of his saints. (verse 8)

"For the LORD giveth wisdom: out of his mouth *cometh* knowledge and understanding" (verse 6); and ONLY FROM HIM do these come. There is no other source. He gives these gifts mainly through His word because it is **"out of his mouth"** that wisdom, knowledge, and understanding come. Also, when Jesus spoke, His words were no less than the Father's. Likewise, His prophets also spoke for Him as do the eternal, inerrant Scriptures.

"Wisdom" is accessible but *is beyond human reach without a right relationship with God* **and** *without a great deal of effort.* As described earlier in verse five, the process begins with the believer having a "fear of God" and then gaining a "knowledge of God" through study, prayer, and obedience to His word. In addition, the Apostle Paul, in I Corinthians 2 describes how important it is for Christians desiring to know God intimately to be sensitive to Holy Spirit leadership.

> 1 Corinthians 2:11-16 For what man knoweth the things of a man, save the spirit of man which is in him? even so the things of God knoweth no man, but the Spirit of God. Now we have received, not the spirit of the world, but the spirit which is of God; that we might know the things that are freely given to us of God. Which things also we speak, not in the words which man's wisdom teacheth, but which the Holy Ghost teacheth; comparing spiritual things with spiritual. But the natural man receiveth not the things of the Spirit of God: for they are foolishness unto him: neither can he know them, because they are spiritually discerned. But he that is spiritual judgeth all things, yet he himself is judged of no man. For who hath known the mind of the Lord, that he may instruct him? But we have the mind of Christ.

After Jesus' Ascension, the Holy Spirit, the third Person of the Trinity began to teach the disciples of Jesus, and now He also the teaches the children of God (*the "my son's"*) who are seeking wisdom.

> John 14:26 But the Comforter, *which is* the Holy Ghost, whom the Father will send in my name, he shall teach you all things, and bring all things to your remembrance, whatsoever I have said unto you.

Proverbs deals with both practical living and spiritual living. In a proper relationship, man interacts with God through His word and His Spirit to gain wisdom from God. The learning process involves mentally digging through His word as described earlier in this chapter and subsequently applying learned biblical truths to be able to properly evaluate actions of people and situations encountered in life. A wise person has knowledge of God's word from which he increases his knowledge of God. When the believer gains an understanding heart through having the mind of Christ, that individual knows much that God has revealed about Himself, this world that He created, and the interactions of wise and foolish men. The resulting wisdom allows man the opportunity to make the best possible decisions.

> *WISDOM produces the ability, because of a proper relationship with God, to navigate through the challenges and opportunities of life in the most effective manner thereby minimizing evil influences and maximizing godly outcomes.*

"He layeth up sound wisdom for the righteous: he is a buckler to them that walk uprightly." (verse 7) **"Sound wisdom"** is said to be **"sound"** because it comes from God and is eternal – it is right, stable, and unchanging. It is **"sound"** because it is a way of thinking and reasoning that is instructed by God that is initiated by a proper relationship with Him; hence, it is efficient having abiding success. Wisdom from God is everlasting and unchanging, in contrast with worldly wisdom which is unstable and perishes. Matthew Henry describes "sound wisdom" as "its foundations firm, its principles solid, and its products of lasting advantage."[26] The only ones who receive "sound wisdom" are those who **"walk uprightly"** *[in integrity, innocence, simplicity]* thus having a walk with God. He walks with those whom He considers righteous.

> "Wisdom . . . is the foundation of security and safety . . . God is not only the Source of wisdom; he is also the Ensurer of safety, the Source of salvation to those who act uprightly."[27]
>
> Proverbs 3:21 My son, let not them depart from thine eyes: keep sound wisdom and discretion. . .
>
> Proverbs 8:14 Counsel *is* mine, and sound wisdom: I am understanding; I have strength.

> **NOTE**: in the New Testament, "sound" is translated from the Greek *hugiano* which metaphorically means free from any error, uncorrupted. It also means to be in health or whole. It is used to describe "doctrine" (1 Timothy 1:10; 2 Timothy 4:3; Titus 1:9, 13; Titus 2:1), "words" (1 Timothy 6:3; 2 Timothy 1:13), "faith" (Titus 2:2), and "health" (3 John 1:2). The understanding is that if a believer walks with God, he will be spiritually healthy because he has the wisdom that comes from God.

In addition to a tremendous love of God toward **"the righteous,"** verse 7 describes a powerful and precious relationship that He has with a serious Christian who is seeking to walk with Him to the fullest extent of his or her ability. This is not a casual relationship. When one seeks wisdom, he seeks God. Those who seek God are known as "the righteous," and God puts in reserve for them **("lays up")** **"sound wisdom"** which facilitates quality of life.

In studying wisdom, one has to consider that the wise person has double protection. That first layer of protection or line of defense is wisdom itself which keeps the believer safely away from dangerous situations and dangerous people *(evil men and strange women)*. Then the second layer or line of defense is God, Who has declared here and in other Scriptures *that He is the believer's buckler*, which is symbolic for protector. Specifically God is **"a buckler to them that walk uprightly."** Of the eleven verses containing the word "buckler" in the King James Bible, six references to "buckler" are used to describe a characteristic of God as shield or protector.

"He keepeth the paths of judgment." (verse 8a) **"Paths of judgment"** are the pathways of proper, godly reasoning that lead to righteous opinions or conclusions. **"Judgment"** is the ability to make a righteous determination between right and wrong, not only in court but in daily life. It is the result of discerning between good and evil to determine what agrees with God's idea of right. Such opinions or conclusions are right judgments because they agree with God and are gleaned from His instructive word. (*The world's system has a different path* or way of reasoning and draws different conclusions than do God and His people.) *God guards or keeps the path* (godly way of thinking and living) of those who eagerly seek, receive, cherish, apply, and consequently live by His words. *Wisdom taught by the word of God becomes a way of thinking (path of judgment); therefore, the godly person develops **a path of thinking kept by God**.* Wise persons study the Scriptures to know this wisdom – the mind of God.

> Philippians 1:27 Only let your conversation be as it becometh the gospel of Christ: that whether I come and see you, or else be absent, I may hear of your affairs, that ye stand fast in one spirit, with one mind striving together for the faith of the gospel . . .
> Philippians 2:5 Let this mind be in you, which was also in Christ Jesus . . .

He **"preserveth the way of his saints."** (verse 8b) God *preserves* [hedges in, guards, protects] **the way** [course of life] of **His saints** [the devout, God-fearing holy ones]. Wisdom *makes a person aware* of the mannerisms of evil people, of evil situations, and of evil ways of thinking; consequently, the wise person knows how to avoid these evil people and bad situations. *NOT getting into a situation is better than having to figure a way out.* When situations are unavoidable, God will preserve His child, if need be, by supernatural means. Satan can only inflect damage that God allows.

> 1 Samuel 2:9 He will keep the feet of his saints, and the wicked shall be silent in darkness; for by strength shall no man prevail.
> Job 1:10 Hast not thou made an hedge about him, and about his house, and about all that he hath on every side? thou hast blessed the work of his hands, and his substance is increased in the land.
> Psalm 37:23 The steps of a *good* man are ordered by the LORD: and he delighteth in his way. Though he fall, he shall not be utterly cast down: for the LORD upholdeth *him with* his hand.
> Psalm 121:5-8 The LORD *is* thy keeper: the LORD *is* thy shade upon thy right hand. The sun shall not smite thee by day, nor the moon by night. The LORD shall preserve thee from all evil: he shall preserve thy soul. The LORD shall preserve thy going out and thy coming in from this time forth, and even for evermore.
> Proverbs 3:21-24 My son, let not them depart from thine eyes: keep sound wisdom and discretion: So shall they be life unto thy soul, and grace to thy neck. Then shalt thou walk in thy way safely, and thy foot shall not stumble. When thou liest down, thou shalt not be afraid: yea, thou shalt lie down, and thy sleep shall be sweet.
> Acts 18:10 For I am with thee, and no man shall set on thee to hurt thee: for I have much people in this city.
> 1 Peter 1:5 Who are kept by the power of God through faith unto salvation ready to be revealed in the last time.
> Jude 1:24 Now unto him that is able to keep you from falling, and to present *you* faultless before the presence of his glory with exceeding joy.

Proverbs 2:9 Then shalt thou understand righteousness, and judgment, and equity; yea, every good path.

"Justice, judgment and equity" is that grouping of three words used in Proverbs 1:3 to explain the *comprehensiveness of the rightness (correctness) of God's wisdom.* It also describes the wise way of acting which man is to learn from God. The same grouping of Hebrew words appears here in Proverbs 2:9 except the English word **"righteousness"** is substituted for the English word **"justice;"** however, the Hebrew word *tsedeq* is the same in both verses. *(See page 5 for a detailed discussion of these terms.)*

In this passage **"then"** is a very important word indicating that there is a proper order for becoming wise and thereby *understanding what is right.* One *can't* comprehend **"righteousness, and judgment and equity: yea, every good path"** without first having a great desire for it while diligently studying the Scriptures. *(See verse 1.)* **"If"** a person will *receive God's words and hide his commandments in his heart* and hunger for wisdom (verses 1-4), **"then"** comes an understanding of **"the fear of the LORD"** and **"knowledge of God"** (verse 5). With these God-given tools, a person can **"then"** **"understand righteousness, and judgment, and equity." "Yea,"** a person can *understand* **"every good path"** that identifies with God, that walks with Him (as Enoch did), and that follows His leadership. Because they want to follow His leadership to be able to interact with every person discreetly and handle every situation wisely, wise people seek to know God's understanding and view of matters. THE RIGHT WAY IS ALWAYS GOD'S WAY, AND IT CAN BE KNOWN; however, it takes desire and effort.

The promise is that the student will *understand the right paths of life,* which are the **"good" paths**, because he is following God's lead. He is learning wisdom from God; thus, he is learning to live his life with "righteousness, judgment and equity" as taught by God. It is through righteousness, judgment, and equity that God established and continues to govern His universe. His governing is right; but it is opposed by the world's system, the flesh, and the devil. Abraham is an example of a person who understood that the right way was always God's way.

> Genesis 18:19 For I *[the LORD]* know him *[Abraham]* that he will command his children and his household after him, and they shall keep the way of the LORD, to do justice and judgment; that the LORD may bring upon Abraham that which he hath spoken of him.

"Understand" is another key word in verse 9. It comes from personal effort and interaction with God; hence, Abraham understood thinking and acting that was right with God and he commanded his children and household to "keep the way of the LORD, to do justice and judgment." Eve no doubt understood but *did not believe* that the ways of the LORD would always be right. Somehow she believed that there could be *another right way*, although it opposed God's instructions. King Saul also understood but decided that there was *another* right way other than God's way and lost his reign and his life. King David understood and believed that God knew right but allowed lust to control his actions and decided to take a wrong and sinful path with Bathsheba; consequently, he had to go through the agony of watching his son die besides enduring terrible memories of his conduct concerning Bathsheba and her husband. To **"understand the Fear of the LORD"** and to **"understand righteousness, and judgment, and equity; yea every good path"** is paramount to enjoying all the benefits of wise living.

Proverbs 2:10-11 When wisdom entereth into thine heart, and knowledge is pleasant unto thy soul;
11. Discretion shall preserve thee, understanding shall keep thee:

Here in verses 10-11 appears again that splendid trio of words – wisdom, knowledge, and understanding – so often found in Scripture within the same paragraph and often in the same verse. The trio is intermixed within the two verses and introduced with the *word* **"when"** indicating that conditions are going to have to be met first before **"discretion"** and **"understanding"** become effective within the believer.

The first prerequisite given in verse ten is that *wisdom must enter the heart* – meaning that wisdom must have found a home in the heart *[mind, emotions, will]* and consequently must become a defining part of who the disciple is. When wisdom has entered his heart, the disciple has a view of life that agrees with God's view.

The second prerequisite is that *knowledge has become pleasant to the soul,* meaning that gaining knowledge of God is a treat, delight, a pleasant, lovely, beautiful thing. Acquiring knowledge will be an ongoing process as additional knowledge is intentionally gained daily by the wise disciple eagerly searching out God's word to learn more about Him.

When these two prerequisites are met, the special protection promised is that the disciple will be *preserved* or kept by using wise thinking, which manifests itself with godly "**discretion**" and "**understanding.**" In the Book of Proverbs, "**discretion**" is usually the outward manifestation of wisdom; it tests what is uncertain and avoids danger.[28]

"**When**" the believer gets to the spiritual place where *wisdom enters into his heart, and knowledge is pleasant unto his soul,* then the "**discretion**" and "**understanding**" of verse eleven will be effective. At this point the child of God is fully listening to the instructions of the Father and is obedient to God's continued daily instruction.

"**Understanding**" and "**discretion**" are two parts that make up the whole. "**Understanding**" begins in the brain, and through effort, permeates one's thought process to govern all actions. For wisdom to be fully understood and heartfelt means that wisdom has settled within the heart and thus *keeps the wise person* by being the basis of all reasoning. Understanding enables a person to make godly judgments because it gives a proper godly perspective to discern right from wrong. It causes the wise to establish boundaries for his own speaking and acting. "**Discretion**" is thus a product of "**understanding.**" Without "**understanding**" there would be no "**discretion**" to govern all actions by developing a plan of action to avoid evil results. Discretion is the *first line of defense* for the believer. It produces that ounce of prevention that is worth a pound of cure. Discretion keeps, hedges in, guards the child of God against "evil men" and "strange women" who would do severe damage where possible.

> Proverbs 1:4 To give subtilty to the simple, to the young man knowledge and discretion.
> Proverbs 2:11-12 Discretion shall preserve thee, understanding shall keep thee: to deliver thee from the way of the evil man, from the man that speaketh froward things.
> Proverbs 3:21-22 My son, let not them depart from thine eyes: keep sound wisdom and discretion: so shall they be life unto thy soul, and grace to thy neck.

In the Book of Proverbs, **discretion** will cause a person (1) to look at the result of his own and other people's personal actions or words, (2) to change his personal actions or speech to be in alignment with God's word, (3) and to seek a better personal outcome. "**Discretion**" is that drink of good sense drawn out of the well of wisdom and that will cause the wise person to make sober, sane and safe decisions such as to stay away from a harlot. DISCRETION INVOLVES HAVING A PLAN to avoid certain people and places and ideas. God will guide the reasoning and judging process so that the disciple can avoid the "evil men" of verses twelve through fifteen, and the "strange woman" of verses sixteen through nineteen.

Proverbs 2:12-15 To deliver thee from the way of the evil *man,* from the man that speaketh froward things;
13. Who leave the paths of uprightness, to walk in the ways of darkness;
14. Who rejoice to do evil, *and* delight in the frowardness of the wicked;
15. Whose ways *are* crooked, and *they* froward in their paths:

Discretion will help the believer to develop a plan "**. . . to deliver thee from the way of the evil *man,* from the man that speaketh froward things.**" (verse 12) The "**evil man**" of this verse is the one known to *speak froward things.* His rebellious, offensive, and hateful words reveal the wickedness that is in his heart.

> Proverbs 15:28 The heart of the righteous studieth to answer: but the mouth of the wicked poureth out evil things.
> Matthew 12:34 O generation of vipers, how can ye, being evil, speak good things? for out of the abundance of the heart the mouth speaketh.
> Luke 6:45 A good man out of the good treasure of his heart bringeth forth that which is good; and an evil man out of the evil treasure of his heart bringeth forth that which is evil: for of the abundance of the heart his mouth speaketh.

"**Froward**" (NOT *forward*) means habitually disposed to disobedience and opposition – in other words, perverse. The evil man who is froward in his speaking is opposed to what is right – to justice, judgment, and equity. He is likely to call what is good "evil" and what is evil "good." He is diametrically opposed to the word of God and the God of the word. Notice what God says about the froward:

> Deuteronomy 32:20 And he said, I will hide my face from them, I will see what their end shall be: for they are a very froward generation, children in whom is no faith.

"**Who leave the paths of uprightness, to walk in the ways of darkness; Who rejoice to do evil,** *and* **delight in the frowardness of the wicked; Whose ways** *are* **crooked, and** *they* **froward in their paths.**" (verses 13-15). These verses describe the conduct and emotions of the evil man. He intentionally makes his course of life crooked so as to deviate from righteousness. His chosen path is that of darkness, away from God and in willful ignorance of Him. He enjoys being in opposition to God and in harmony with perverseness. Whatever God is for, the evil man is against – he is **"froward."** He delights when other people are froward. Getting wisdom, knowledge, and understanding from God gives a wise man understanding and discretion to avoid such evil people who **"rejoice to do evil,"** and delight in being froward. The evil man's **"ways are crooked"** in that he swerves away from the way that is righteous, the way that follows the word of God. He is intentionally **"froward"** in his path, that is, he intentionally opposes God.

The depths to which the evil man has fallen appear in the verbs **"rejoice"** and **"delight in."** His wickedness is heartfelt and ingrained in his mental and emotional composition, just as wisdom is heartfelt for the wise person. He avoids the bright, sunlit straight path of uprightness. He is full of "crooked ways, perverse counsels, and deeds of darkness,"[29] and he has sunk to the point of *rejoicing* when he can commit an evil act, and he *delights* in the frowardness and wickedness of others.

When wisdom has entered into the heart of the godly young man, it will be through *understanding and discretion* that he is delivered from this evil, froward man. The following verses identify the second category of evil that the youth will be delivered from as the **strange woman**.

> **Proverbs 2:16-19** To deliver thee from the strange woman, even from the stranger which flattereth with her words;
> 17. Which forsaketh the guide of her youth, and forgetteth the covenant of her God.
> 18. For her house inclineth unto death, and her paths unto the dead.
> 19. None that go unto her return again, neither take they hold of the paths of life.

Not only will "understanding" and "discretion" deliver thee from the way of **"evil men"** (verses 11 and 12), but they will also **"deliver thee from the strange woman."** (verse 16) "Discretion" will **"deliver"** *[snatch away]* the wise man from the adulteress because he will refuse to even go near her house which he "understands" to be filled with wickedness. The **"strange woman"** in this text is one who has "turned aside" or away from her honorable place as her husband's loyal wife, friend, and companion to become evil. She is an adulteress and has become a harlot who entices her victims to the ultimate destruction of body and soul as described in Proverbs Chapters Five, Six, and Seven.

Wisdom hidden within a wise man's heart will keep him away from the snare of the **"strange woman."** Scripture, through testimonies of both Job and Jesus, gives wise counsel concerning this temptation that destroys many men. "Discretion" is that part of wisdom that shows man to make a plan to avoid evil.

> Job 31:1 I made a covenant with mine eyes; why then should I think upon a maid?
>
> Matthew 5:27-29 Ye have heard that it was said by them of old time, Thou shalt not commit adultery: But I say unto you, That whosoever looketh on a woman to lust after her hath committed adultery with her already in his heart. And if thy right eye offend thee, pluck it out, and cast it from thee: for it is profitable for thee that one of thy members should perish, and not that thy whole body should be cast into hell.

The strange woman **"flattereth with her words"** (verse 16). "Flattereth" is a verb translated from a Hebrew word that means figuratively to be smooth. It is a form of lying.

> "Whereas wicked men use perverse words or speak froward things (Proverbs 2:12), the adulteress uses seductive or flattering words (Proverbs 5:3; 6:24; 7:5; 7:21). The **"guide of her youth"** refers to her husband (Proverbs 5:18), and the **"covenant"** which she ignored is her marriage vows. Forgetting her commitment to her husband, she became promiscuous. To be involved with such a person (in her house) leads to **"death"**; adultery puts a person on an irretrievable path that eventually results in physical death (Proverbs 5:5; 7:27). It is fatal."[30]

The adulteress, *with her flattering words,* intends to make the foolish youth think that he is special, that she has selected him, and that no other man has all the tremendous characteristics of manliness that he has. She would like for him to believe that all her preparations leading up to their meeting have been done especially for him; when, in fact, she probably doesn't even know him. Notice the flattering words of the adulteress from Proverbs 7:14-20:

> "*I have* peace offerings with me; this day have I payed my vows. Therefore came I forth to meet thee, diligently to seek thy face, and I have found thee. I have decked my bed with coverings of tapestry, with carved *works,* with fine linen of Egypt. I have perfumed my bed with myrrh, aloes, and cinnamon. Come, let us take our fill of love until the morning: let us solace ourselves with loves. For the goodman *is* not at home, he is gone a long journey: He hath taken a bag of money with him, *and* will come home at the day appointed."

Her hypocrisy is especially obvious in her serving the meat that she had left over from her peace offering (sacrificed in thanksgiving for God's blessings) to entice the youth to a meal. He listens to her words and believes that she kept it especially for him *because he wants her more than he wants the truth.* She then describes how she beautified her bedroom, insinuating that it was "just for him." She then suggestively tells him that her husband is out of town.

"Which forsaketh the guide of her youth, and forgetteth the covenant of her God." (verse 17) The Bible points out that this evil woman had made two extremely bad choices in her forsaking and forgetting. **"Forsaketh"** means to desert or leave, but the word itself exudes the thoughts of darkness and loneliness. **"Guide"** means friend or intimate, but when the phrase "of her youth" is added the reader realizes the phrase is talking about her husband. God is also spoken of as the "guide of my youth" in Jeremiah 3:4. There is no doubt that she has forsaken the greatest Guide of her life in the next phrase **"forgetteth the covenant of her God."** "The sin of the adulteress is not against man only but against the law of God, against His covenant. The words point to a religious formula of espousals."[31] Notice Malachi 2:13-14 which describes God's view of marriage infidelity:

> Malachi 2:13-14 And this have ye done again, covering the altar of the LORD with tears, with weeping, and with crying out, insomuch that he regardeth not the offering any more, or receiveth *it* with good will at your hand. Yet ye say, Wherefore? Because the LORD hath been witness between thee and the wife of thy youth, against whom thou hast dealt treacherously: yet *is* she thy companion, and the wife of thy covenant.

"For her house inclineth unto death, and her paths unto the dead." (verse 18) Wisdom and discretion remind the youth not to go down that path because **"her house inclineth unto death"** (verse 18a). *Her house is symbolic of pure evil.* It reminds one of what she stands for because it is the place of her sins. To go through her door is to make a definite choice to enter the pathway to death – to separate from God.

"And her paths unto the dead." (verse 18b) She leads her victims to spiritual death and possibly to physical death. Because of her indiscriminate involvement with multiple victims, she is likely to transmit disease that also threatens to bring physical death. She is wicked and continually moves away from God and she inclines *[sinks]* toward death and the place of the dead.

"None that go unto her return again, neither take they hold of the paths of life." (verse 19) Certainly there is no sin that cannot be forgiven other than blasphemy against the Holy Spirit, but returning to the clear conscience that preceded this sin is impossible for a man.

> 1 Corinthians 6:9-11 Know ye not that the unrighteous shall not inherit the kingdom of God? Be not deceived: neither fornicators, nor idolaters, nor adulterers, nor effeminate, nor abusers of themselves with mankind, Nor thieves, nor covetous, nor drunkards, nor revilers, nor extortioners, shall inherit the kingdom of God. And such were some of you: but ye are washed, but ye are sanctified, but ye are justified in the name of the Lord Jesus, and by the Spirit of our God.
>
> Hebrews 13:4 Marriage is honourable in all, and the bed undefiled: but whoremongers and adulterers God will judge.

God has promised that He will forgive the sinner, if he will repent and ask in faith.

> John 10:10 The thief cometh not, but for to steal, and to kill, and to destroy: I am come that they might have life, and that they might have *it* more abundantly.
>
> 1 John 1:9 If we confess our sins, he is faithful and just to forgive us our sins, and to cleanse us from all unrighteousness.

Ultimately, some sins, more than others, follow a person. Getting forgiveness is one thing, but putting some sins out of one's mind is yet another. After being with the harlot, there will be no returning to the purity that existed before such an encounter. The harlot robs a man of being able to walk **"the paths of life"** that produce peace and purity of heart and conscience. He may have to avoid particular conversations and some people all the days of his life to keep from revealing the secrets of his heart. However, some adulterers may become so hardened by the power and deceitfulness of their sin that they cannot bring themselves to return to God.

> Ecclesiastes 7:26 And I find more bitter than death the woman, whose heart is snares and nets, and her hands as bands: whoso pleaseth God shall escape from her; but the sinner shall be taken by her.

Understanding and discretion will keep a man from making this horrible mistake. The next verse says that by avoiding the adulteress the young man can stay on the "paths of the righteous."

> **Proverbs 2:20-22** That thou mayest walk in the way of good men, and keep the paths of the righteous.
> 21. For the upright shall dwell in the land, and the perfect shall remain in it.
> 22. But the wicked shall be cut off from the earth, and the transgressors shall be rooted out of it.

"That thou mayest walk in the way of good *men,* and keep the paths of the righteous." (verse 20) ***Discretion*** will protect the wise person from evil ones who hate the people and works of God. The wise person will have the choice and the privilege of being a friend to other wise people and not a companion to fools. He will seek to live around people who have their hearts set on pleasing God and living a profitable life of integrity, which this verse describes with the following two phrases: **"the way of good men"** and **"the paths of the righteous."** Both phrases have the same meaning and are obviously repeated to give emphasis.

"For the upright shall dwell in the land, and the perfect shall remain in it." (verse 21) Along with this wonderful promise, God has a marvelous future for His children who have trusted in Christ. There will be a "new heaven and a new earth" where *no* wicked person will enter and God's people will remain forever because they cannot be moved once He establishes them.

> Psalm 37:29 The righteous shall inherit the land, and dwell therein for ever.
>
> Proverbs 10:30 The righteous shall never be removed: but the wicked shall not inhabit the earth.
>
> 2 Corinthians 5:8 We are confident, I say, and willing rather to be absent from the body, and to be present with the Lord.
>
> Hebrews 11:16 But now they desire a better country, that is, an heavenly: wherefore God is not ashamed to be called their God: for he hath prepared for them a city.
>
> 2 Peter 3:13 Nevertheless we, according to his promise, look for new heavens and a new earth, wherein dwelleth righteousness.
>
> Revelation 21:1-7 And I saw a new heaven and a new earth: for the first heaven and the first earth were passed away; and there was no more sea. And I John saw the holy city, new Jerusalem, coming down from God out of heaven, prepared as a bride adorned for her husband. And I heard a great voice out of heaven saying, Behold, the tabernacle of God is with men, and he will dwell with them, and they shall be his people, and God himself shall be with them, and be their God.

"But the wicked shall be cut off from the earth, and the transgressors shall be rooted out of it." (verse 22) Those who reject the wisdom of God are incompatible with Him and His Son Jesus Christ and thus unworthy of His reward and eternal fellowship. They will be **"cut off"** from the earth and **"rooted out"** of eternal life with God and all believers.

> Psalm 1:6 For the LORD knoweth the way of the righteous: but the way of the ungodly shall perish.
>
> Proverbs 10:24-25 The fear of the wicked, it shall come upon him: but the desire of the righteous shall be granted. As the whirlwind passeth, so is the wicked no more: but the righteous is an everlasting foundation.
>
> Malachi 4:1-2 For, behold, the day cometh, that shall burn as an oven; and all the proud, yea, and all that do wickedly, shall be stubble: and the day that cometh shall burn them up, saith the LORD of hosts, that it shall leave them neither root nor branch. But unto you that fear my name shall the Sun of righteousness arise with healing in his wings; and ye shall go forth, and grow up as calves of the stall.
>
> Revelation 20:15 And whosoever was not found written in the book of life was cast into the lake of fire.

CHAPTER THREE

> **Chapter Three Identifies the Following:**
>
> **GOD'S RELATIONSHIPS:**
> (1) Loving relationships with those who seek God – like a father and son.
> (2) Bad relationships with those who oppose God – like an enemy.
>
> **GOD'S RESPONSES to the wise and to the unwise:**
> (1) God's *resistance* is toward the froward.
> (2) God's *secret* is with the righteous.
> (3) God's *curse* is in the house of the wicked.
> (4) God's *blessing* is in the habitation of those who are faithful and trusting.
> (5) God's *scorning* is toward the scorners.
> (6) God's *favor* is toward the righteous who love Him and His word.
>
> **GOD'S REWARDS to the righteous and to the ungodly:**
> (1) Wise shall inherit glory.
> (2) Fools shall inherit shame.

Proverbs 3:1-2 My son, forget not my law; but let thine heart keep my commandments:
2. For length of days, and long life, and peace, shall they add to thee.

"My son" is an affectionate term for a student, a follower, or a disciple; and in this verse "My son" refers to a believer in God, a student of wisdom. The Hebrew word *ben* is used four thousand, nine hundred two times in the Bible and most often translated as "son" and secondly as "children." *Ben* means "the house continues" and speaks of the one who continues the house into the next generation.[32] The "house" or family name to be continued in the Book of Proverbs is the house of faith in God. Those being spoken to and often identified as "my son" or "ye children" are those who will carry forward a belief in God, keep His word, and trust in His promises. The seed being carried forward is the seed of faith not the seed of humanity.

> Hebrews 3:5-6 And Moses verily *was* faithful in all his house, as a servant, for a testimony of those things which were to be spoken after; But Christ as a son over his own house; whose house are we, if we hold fast the confidence and the rejoicing of the hope firm unto the end.

"Forget not my law" (verse 1) "Forgetting here is not so much oblivion arising from defective memory, as a wilful disregard and/or neglect of the admonitions of the teacher."[33] Verse 1 is a beckoning from God to the wise in heart to retain God's word, with effort, in the conscious thinking – NOT the secondary subconscious.

> **NOTE:** Placed at the end of verse one and in the middle of verse seven, the colon, a simple mark of punctuation, indicates that the following words are the interpretation, or a list, or an explanation – in these cases an explanation. Also note that the Hebrew does not use punctuation as does English.

"But let thine heart *[mind, emotions, will]* **keep my commandments."** (verse 1) The teacher advises the student to engage himself beyond merely learning the words of God's commandments. In other words, he is to have affection for the word of God, to love it. These three actions concerning the word of God are requested by the teacher: (1) remembrance, (2) affection, and (3) obedience.[34] Chapter Three begins by teaching the student's necessity of having a heart for the word of God. The son's having an obedient heart is primary to the father/son relationship that God obviously intends to be developed between Himself and those with sound wisdom. Service to the LORD should always be from the heart.

Isaiah 29:13-14 Wherefore the Lord said, Forasmuch as this people draw near *me* with their mouth, and with their lips do honour me, but have removed their heart far from me, and their fear toward me is taught by the precept of men: Therefore, behold, I will proceed to do a marvellous work among this people, even a marvellous work and a wonder: for the wisdom of their wise men shall perish, and the understanding of their prudent men shall be hid.

I Samuel 16:7 ... for *the LORD seeth* not as man seeth; for man looketh on the outward appearance, but the LORD looketh on the heart.

Psalm 119:11 Thy word have I hid in my heart, that I might not sin against thee.

John 14:15 If ye love me, keep my commandments.

John 14:21 He that hath my commandments, and keepeth them, he it is that loveth me ...

Judas Iscariot, who betrayed Jesus, most likely *had the intellect* to remember the laws and commandments of Jesus though he *never had the heart* for serving; and obviously had no affection for Him.

Verse two contains a promise given to believers who keep God's commandments. (Verses one and two are actually two parts of one sentence.) **"For length of days, and long life, and peace, shall they add to thee."** (verse 2) According to Noah Webster's *Dictionary of American English (1828)*, the word **"for"** is the word by which a reason is introduced. It means "because, on this account, that."[35] Obviously remembering the law and keeping the commandments bring the promise of adding **"length of days, and long life, and peace."** These are tremendous gifts for those who want a relationship with God and obey His word. The expression **"length of days"** literally means "extension of days" and signifies the prolongation of life. It occurs again in the following passages:

Job 12:12 With the ancient *is* wisdom; and in length of days understanding.

Proverbs 3:16 Length of days *is* in her right hand; *and* in her left hand riches and honour.

Psalm 21:4 He asked life of thee, *and* thou gavest *it* him, *even* length of days for ever and ever.

"Length of days" is represented as a blessing in the Old Testament, *but the blessing is conditional on the fulfilment of certain actions*. In the fifth commandment it is dependent on the honoring of parents.

Exodus 20:12 Honour thy father and thy mother: that thy days may be long upon the land which the LORD thy God giveth thee.

Length of days was promised to Solomon at Gibeon, if he walked in God's way, and kept the statutes, and commandments of God.

1 Kings 3:14 And if thou wilt walk in my ways, to keep my statutes and my commandments, as thy father David did walk, then I will lengthen thy days.

"Long life" implies a long earthly life of fellowship with God followed by eternal life hereafter with Him. The law of Moses promised a long life to those who kept the law, and the Gospel of Christ promises all believers in Him that they shall not perish, but shall have everlasting life.

John 3:16 For God so loved the world, that he gave his only begotten Son, that whosoever believeth in him should not perish, but have everlasting life.

1 Timothy 4:7 ... but godliness is profitable unto all things, having promise of the life that now is, and of that which is to come.

"Length of days" and **"Long life"** have fundamentally the same meaning in that life will be extended to those who love God's law. By repeating **"length of days"** with different words, there is a poetic implication that God will be present during that extended lifetime.

The specific advantage of being in God's presence noted in this verse is **"peace"** like only God can provide. (There are other advantages and privileges to wisely walking with God.) It is the mercy of God to His people to shorten the days of trouble when life becomes a burden or when the judgment of God is being pronounced, but this shortening of days also becomes a curse to the wicked.

Psalm 89:45 The days of his youth hast thou shortened: thou hast covered him with shame. Selah.

Psalm 102:23 He weakened my strength in the way; he shortened my days.

Proverbs 10:27 The fear of the LORD prolongeth days: but the years of the wicked shall be shortened.

Matthew 24:22 And except those days should be shortened, there should no flesh be saved: but for the elect's sake those days shall be shortened.

Mark 13:20 And except that the Lord had shortened those days, no flesh should be saved: but for the elect's sake, whom he hath chosen, he hath shortened the days.

The blessing of **"peace"** is a benefit from having a personal, loving, obedient relationship with God and receiving His written promises. His personal presence brings a peace of body, soul, and spirit that can't be self-produced. Like the other eight elements of the fruit of the spirit, peace is a natural by-product, a consequence of trusting and walking with God.

The psalmist represents God's peace as belonging to those who love God's law and are never offended by His law or His word. Peace is denied the wicked.

> Psalm 119:165 Great peace have they which love thy law: and nothing shall offend them.
>
> Isaiah 48:22 *There is* no peace, saith the LORD, unto the wicked. *[Repeated in Isaiah 57:21.]*
>
> Galatians 5:22-23 But the fruit of the Spirit is love, joy, peace, longsuffering, gentleness, goodness, faith, meekness, temperance: against such there is no law.

Proverbs 3:3-4 Let not mercy and truth forsake thee: bind them about thy neck; write them upon the table of thine heart: 4. So shalt thou find favour and good understanding in the sight of God and man.

"Let not mercy and truth forsake thee." (verse 3a) **"Mercy and truth"** of God are often presented together in the Bible, especially in the Book of Psalms (11 times). They identify two aspects of the character of God, and of a morally upright, wise person. To be like Him, the believer must strive to weave these two qualities of character into the fabric of his being so that they govern the way he thinks and acts.

> Psalm 25:10 All the paths of the LORD *are* mercy and truth unto such as keep his covenant and his testimonies.

> **NOTE: Defining of "Paths of the LORD" from Psalm 25:10.** "Paths *[orchoth]* signify the tracks or ruts made by the wheels of wagons by often passing over the same ground. **"Mercy and truth"** are the paths in which God constantly walks in reference to the children of men; and so frequently does he show them mercy, and so frequently does he fulfill his truth that his paths are easily discerned. How frequent, how deeply indented, and how multiplied are those tracks to every family and individual! Wherever we go, we see that God's mercy and truth have been there by the deep tracks they have left behind them. But he is more abundantly merciful to those who keep his covenant and his testimonies; i.e. those who are conformed, not only to the letter, but to the spirit of his pure religion." (Adam Clarke, *Commentary on the Bible*, (1715-1832), e-Sword 12.0.1)

"Mercy" is the aspect of God's love that causes Him to help the miserable who may be so either because of breaking God's law *or* because of circumstances beyond their control, like blindness or leprosy. Because God is merciful, He expects His children to be merciful.[36] **"Truth"** means truth as spoken, truth of testimony and judgment, truth of divine instruction, truth as a body of ethical or religious knowledge, true doctrine. Truth is faithful, sure, reliable, and stable. The greatest act of **"mercy"** that God ever performed was to graciously send His Son (Truth) to pay the sin debt for depraved mankind and thus provide a way to Himself.

> John 14:6 Jesus saith unto him, I am the way, the truth and the life; no man cometh to the Father, but by me.

Hosea tells of God's discontentment when the character traits of **"mercy and truth"** (plus knowledge of God) are missing in His people. Failure to apply "mercy and truth" in one's life reveals an ignorance of a basic knowledge and understanding of God and a walk with Him.

> Hosea 4:1 Hear the word of the LORD, ye children of Israel: for the LORD hath a controversy with the inhabitants of the land, because there is no truth, nor mercy, nor knowledge of God in the land.

In his commentary on Hosea 4:1, Albert Barnes wrote the following concerning the absence of **"truth"** and **"mercy."** There is:

> "No regard for known truth; no conscience, no sincerity, no uprightness; no truth of words; no truth of promises; no truth in witnessing; no making good in deeds what was said in words . . . '**Mercy**' . . . includes all love of one to another . . . loving-kindness, piety to parents, natural affection, forgiveness, tenderness, beneficence, goodness."[37]

"Bind them about thy neck." (verse 3b) Because they are an intrinsic part of a wise person's personality, **"mercy and truth"** are pictured as tied together around a person's neck like a necklace. These two are to be so characteristic of the way that the believer conducts his life and business that they "catch the eye" of the beholder just as would a glistening golden necklace. They are the descriptive terms by which other people ought to identify the godly person. Mercy and truth should be what those familiar with a Christian think of when they see him approaching.

"Write them upon the table of thine heart." (verse 3c) Mercy and truth are to become part of the fabric of the godly, wise person's character. They are not just some good habits that are learned but are rather a means of resembling and pleasing God. Hence, a wise person stirs these character traits into his soul until they become totally blended into the way he thinks.

Ezekiel 36:26-27 A new heart also will I give you, and a new spirit will I put within you: and I will take away the stony heart out of your flesh, and I will give you an heart of flesh. And I will put my spirit within you, and cause you to walk in my statutes, and ye shall keep my judgments, and do *them*.

Mercy and truth are to be written upon the heart so that they filter every thought, flavor every word, and forbid every wrong. **"Table"** in this verse has reference to *(calls to mind)* a writing tablet, and **"heart"** refers to his complete being whereby he responds to God and man. Mercy and truth are foundational to good understanding, clear conscience, and strength of character.

"So shalt thou find favour and good understanding in the sight of God and man." (verse 4) To be obedient to His word, and consequently to incorporate these two main qualities of God's character **("mercy and truth")** into the heart and life is a definite inward step of obedience. Doing so proves a strong desire to be like God and to be favored by Him. In addition to being favored, there will be **"good understanding"** between God's obedient servant and God. It is not to be taken lightly that godly men who respect and honor God, also find **"favor and good understanding"** with each other. They are on the common ground of godly reasoning and thinking, so the natural outcome is **"favor and good understanding."** *Scripture teaches the believer to think and reason in a manner led by God.*

> Romans 12:2 And be not conformed to this world: but be ye transformed by the renewing of your mind, that ye may prove what is that good, and acceptable, and perfect, will of God.
> 1 Corinthians 2:16 For who hath known the mind of the Lord, that he may instruct him? But we have the mind of Christ.
> *[See also Philippians 2:5-8 and 2 Timothy 3:16-17.]*

The Hebrew word for **"favour"** is often translated as "grace" and means the same. Both Samuel and Jesus were said to have lived in favor with God and man.

> 1 Samuel 2:26 And the child Samuel grew on, and was in favour both with the LORD, and also with men.
> Luke 2:52 And Jesus increased in wisdom and stature, and in favour with God and man.

Noah found grace in the eyes of the Lord (Genesis 6:8 and Exodus 33:12), as did Israel in Jeremiah 31:2 and certainly Mary in Luke 1:30.[38] Joseph found favor with the keeper of the prison in Genesis 39:4. Absolutely, God does favor some people over others because those favored ones have proven to be in pursuit of Him.

> Psalm 42:1 As the hart panteth after the water brooks, so panteth my soul after thee, O God.
> Psalm 145:18 The LORD *is* nigh unto all them that call upon him, to all that call upon him in truth.
> Zechariah 1:3 Therefore say thou unto them, Thus saith the LORD of hosts; Turn ye unto me, saith the LORD of hosts, and I will turn unto you, saith the LORD of hosts.
> *[See also 1 Chronicles 28:9; 2 Chronicles 15:2; Malachi 3:7; and James 4:8.]*

God has given man His word as a guide so that he can know how to conduct himself in a manner acceptable to *both* God and man. Such living exemplifies wisdom. After having become personal character traits, **"mercy and truth"** will tenderly serve to create good relationships with others; and thus disarm the divisive, competitive spirit of aggression that so often causes contention between men. Because truth spoken without mercy can be abrasive and damaging, *it takes mercy and truth working together to be effective in creating favor.* Speaking of truth *without mercy* creates hostility and pierces the heart like a sword, but mercy and truth together exemplify love and a reaching out to help rather than to compete.

"Favour" is an important and a major biblical topic that should be given serious study. There are sixteen references to "favor" in Proverbs (utilizing four different Hebrew words) and seventy references in the Bible that mention favor of God or man.

Proverbs 3:5-6 Trust in the LORD with all thine heart; and lean not unto thine own understanding.
6. In all thy ways acknowledge him, and he shall direct thy paths.

To **"trust in the LORD"** (verse 5a) is to have confidence in Him, in His unlimited understanding, and in His unhindered abilities. There can be no godly wisdom without a firm foundation of trust in God.

> Isaiah 55:8-9 For my thoughts *are* not your thoughts, neither *are* your ways my ways, saith the LORD. For *as* the heavens are higher than the earth, so are my ways higher than your ways, and my thoughts than your thoughts.
> Romans 11:33-34 O the depth of the riches both of the wisdom and knowledge of God! how unsearchable *are* his judgments, and his ways past finding out! For who hath known the mind of the Lord? or who hath been his counsellor?

There are seventy-five verses with the Hebrew word *leb* translated **"heart"** in the Book of Proverbs. **"Heart"** is a comprehensive term that includes the mind, emotions, and will of a person. The **"heart"** is also that third portion of man also known as the soul. The other two parts of a man consist of body and spirit. Within the "heart" of man, thinking and reasoning blend facts with emotion to activate his will. Because of this blending, in the "heart," a person becomes thoroughly convinced of something. To **"trust in the LORD with all thine heart"** is to have no reservations about trusting God; no holdouts; no hesitation in the mind, emotions, or will.

"Lean not unto thine own understanding." (verse 5b) At the very best, man has a limited understanding with which he can interpret words, actions, and other available information. Because only God has perfect understanding, a godly wise person learns to pray asking God to give insight, to bring thoughts to his mind, and to lead him. Also, he knows the great value of counsel from other wise people, which God often directs or makes available.

> Proverbs 12:15 The way of a fool *is* right in his own eyes: but he that hearkeneth unto counsel *is* wise.
> Proverbs 26:12 Seest thou a man wise in his own conceit? *there is* more hope of a fool than of him.

"In all thy ways acknowledge him." (verse 6) **"Acknowledge"** means to recognize God's part and presence in everything – "not in acts of solemn worship or great crises only, but 'in all thy ways.'"[39] **"Ways"** refers to one's behavior as reflects character, manner, and habits – the way a person acts as well as what he speaks. Acknowledge Him in thinking, and watching, and responding to other people, and in interacting in various situations. Acknowledge Him in work, in worship, and in recreation. Seek God for guidance in everything to ensure that no activity is out of harmony with His teachings.

> "'Acknowledge' . . . signifies 'to know, recognize.' To acknowledge God is, therefore, to recognize, in all our dealings and undertakings, God's overruling providence, which 'shapes our ends, rough hew them as we will.' It is not a mere theoretical acknowledgment, but one that engages the whole energies of the soul (Delitzsch), and sees in God power, wisdom, providence, goodness, and justice."[40]

> "There are two ways in which people pass through life. They pass through it remembering God, or they pass through it forgetting Him. They go through it with Him in their minds, though they cannot see Him; or they go through it as if they had nothing to do with Him. They live as if this world were all they had to think about, or they remember that another life is coming, though they know they have to die in this world. And, of course, in what they do, this great difference shows itself. Either they 'lean upon their own understanding'; they are satisfied with what they see and have learnt about the ways and wisdom and good things of this present world, and will not listen even to God, when He tells them a different story about what men think so much of here; or they trust in the Lord with all their heart, knowing that 'it is not in man that walketh to direct his steps,' and that it would profit a man nothing if he were to 'gain the whole world, and lose his own soul.'"[41]

> Jeremiah 9:23-24 Thus saith the LORD, Let not the wise man glory in his wisdom, neither let the mighty man glory in his might, let not the rich man glory in his riches: But let him that glorieth glory in this, that he understandeth and knoweth me, that I am the LORD which exercise lovingkindness, judgment, and righteousness, in the earth: for in these things I delight, saith the LORD.
> Jeremiah 10:23 O LORD, I know that the way of man *is* not in himself: *it is* not in man that walketh to direct his steps.

> "(1) **In order to acknowledge God truly there must be a real conviction that God rules the world. – An atheist**, who believes that no God exists, or **a theist,** who believes in His existence but not in His active government of earthly things, or **a fatalist,** who dreams that all things proceed by an iron necessity which nothing can change – **not one of these men can really acknowledge God as the text requires**. It is presupposed that we believe in the existence of an almighty, free, intelligent Spirit, from whom all things have sprung, and on whom all things depend; that He fills the whole universe with His presence, or illumines it with His smile; that He is guiding, controlling, and disposing all its affairs for the consummation of holy and glorious purposes; that He cares for the well-being of all His creatures, from the highest seraph who flames before His throne down to the little sparrow which cannot fall to the ground until He permits it; that He has special care for the dignity and well-being of men, and most of all for those who fear Him or who hope in His mercy. A settled conviction of all this is essential to a right acknowledgment of God. **If there be no God, it is unreasonable to acknowledge any.** If God be not a free or almighty intelligence, but a blind or necessary force, we may as well do homage to the storm that lays waste our fields, or to the earthquake that converts our home into ruins. If God has no care for the concerns of this lower world, to acknowledge Him is useless; if He acts in all things quite independently of our conduct, acknowledging Him is an impertinence. If He is not graciously disposed to accept our prayer and our trust, we may as well give them to the winds. In a word, in order to yield any acknowledgment of God which is worthy of the name, there must be that state of mind described by the Apostle as the condition of all acceptable coming to God—the belief "that he is, and that he is the rewarder of them that diligently seek him. (Hebrews 11:6)
> (2) **It follows that we must have communion with Him**. It is impossible that any one can really be acknowledging God – can be thinking of anything but worldly things – who does not pray by himself in secret, and pray every day regularly . . .
> (3) **Then, to acknowledge God in all our ways is honestly to *admit to Him in each particular case that the matter is in His hands*, and that it is to be ordered as He may see fit**. We are presumed to feel that God is actively present in all the concerns of this world, from the least to the greatest. Our own concerns, therefore, are neither too vast nor too trifling to engage His attention. Small as things may be in themselves, they are still parts of the great whole, links in the chain which girds the world and reaches up into the hand of God . . .

(4) Along with all this there is to be *a sincere dependence upon God for direction and help.* – This is the practical bearing of our conscious reference to God. In the absence of this it is useless to believe in His supreme rule, or to advert to His universal presence... But such a devout regard implies humble reliance upon His guidance..."[42]

"And he shall direct thy paths." (verse 6b) God directs the believer's paths primarily through the teachings of the Bible and godly counsel. The believer is to take a path that avoids evil situations, evil places, and evil people; but more than avoiding certain people, places, and things, Scripture will teach the believer how to think and reason wisely. When Jesus left to go back to heaven, He sent the Holy Spirit to occupy every Christian. The Holy Spirit speaks often through the conscience or by providing a mental "roadblock" or "wall" to keep the believer from going to certain places or being involved with certain people or certain situations; and occasionally He speaks directly into the believer's mind to **"direct thy paths."**

Psalm 32:8 I will instruct thee and teach thee in the way which thou shalt go: I will guide thee with mine eye.
Psalm 48:14 For this God *is* our God for ever and ever: he will be our guide *even* unto death.
Psalm 73:24 Thou shalt guide me with thy counsel, and afterward receive me *to* glory.
Proverbs 8:20 I lead in the way of righteousness, in the midst of the paths of judgment . . .
Proverbs 15:19 The way of the slothful *man is* as an hedge of thorns: but the way of the righteous *is* made plain.
Proverbs 16:9 A man's heart deviseth his way: but the LORD directeth his steps.
Jeremiah 10:23 O LORD, I know that the way of man *is* not in himself: *it is* not in man that walketh to direct his steps.
Isaiah 30:21 And thine ears shall hear a word behind thee, saying, This *is* the way, walk ye in it, when ye turn to the right hand, and when ye turn to the left.
Isaiah 48:17 Thus saith the LORD, thy Redeemer, the Holy One of Israel; I *am* the LORD thy God which teacheth thee to profit, which leadeth thee by the way *that* thou shouldest go.
2 Timothy 2:15 Study to shew thyself approved unto God, a workman that needeth not to be ashamed, rightly dividing the word of truth.

"We should take God for the guide of our life. None of us can take care of ourselves. A young man said boastfully, 'I am my own master.'
'Do you know what a grave responsibility you have assumed?' asked a friend.
No man is wise enough to undertake the direction of his own or any other person's life. Young people need much advice – they should have an older friend, who knows life and can give them good counsel. Bad advice has wrecked many a destiny. Here we are told that we may have the Lord for our confidential friend, acknowledging Him in all our ways, and then receiving His direction at every point. We may trust His counsel, for He never advises any one wrongly."[43]

Proverbs 3:7-8 Be not wise in thine own eyes: fear the LORD, and depart from evil.
8. It shall be health to thy navel, and marrow to thy bones.

"Be not wise in thine own eyes." (verse 7) To loftily think of oneself as wise, to be full of pride in believing that one has superior innate ability is being **"wise in thine own eyes."** Pride is a sin that causes a person to be resisted by God (1 Peter 5:5). A much better way of thinking is to **"fear the LORD, and depart from evil,"** – beginning with the evil of pride.

"'**Be not wise in thine own eyes.**' (verse 7)"So as to act independently of God; not to trust in him, nor acknowledge him, nor seek to him for help and direction; nor ask nor take the advice of others; but, being conceited and self-sufficient, lean to thine own understanding, as being wise enough to conduct all affairs in life by thy own discretion; and in matters of religion wiser than thy teachers, and even than the Scriptures."[44]

A person who believes that he is wise in and of himself, is proud and arrogant, has a swelled head, and is the opposite of humble. Just as humility is a crowning virtue, self-conceit is the finishing touch put to sin. A person who thinks humbly of himself is more likely to have a regard for the LORD; but a person who is *wise in his own eyes* is more likely to believe that since he already has the answers, he does not need to look to God.[45]

Job 11:12 For vain man would be wise, though man be born *like* a wild ass's colt.
Proverbs 26:12 Seest thou a man wise in his own conceit? *there is* more hope of a fool than of him.
Proverbs 26:16 The sluggard *is* wiser in his own conceit than seven men that can render a reason.
Isaiah 5:21 Woe unto *them that are* wise in their own eyes, and prudent in their own sight!
John 9:41 Jesus said unto them, If ye were blind, ye should have no sin: but now ye say, We see; therefore your sin remaineth.
Romans 11:25 For I would not, brethren, that ye should be ignorant of this mystery, lest ye should be wise in your own conceits; that blindness in part is happened to Israel, until the fulness of the Gentiles be come in.
Romans 12:16 Be of the same mind one toward another. Mind not high things, but condescend to men of low estate. Be not wise in your own conceits. *["In your own conceits" corresponds to "in your own eyes."]*

1 Corinthians 3:18-20 Let no man deceive himself. If any man among you seemeth to be wise in this world, let him become a fool, that he may be wise. For the wisdom of this world is foolishness with God. For it is written, He taketh the wise in their own craftiness. And again, The Lord knoweth the thoughts of the wise, that they are vain.

"Fear the LORD, and depart from evil" (verse 7b) answers the first clause of this verse and addresses, primarily, the departing from evil *induced by self-conceit*. **"Fear the LORD"** means to have an awesome respect for God, resulting in reverence for God, faith in Him, dependence on Him, acknowledgment of Him, seeking to Him for direction, and carefulness not to offend Him[46] – all of which is the opposite of self-conceit warned against in the first part of this verse.

Genesis 39:9-10 *There is* none greater in this house than I; neither hath he kept back any thing from me but thee, because thou *art* his wife: how then can I do this great wickedness, and sin against God? And it came to pass, as she spake to Joseph day by day, that he hearkened not unto her, to lie by her, *or* to be with her.

Nehemiah 5:15 But the former governors that *had been* before me were chargeable unto the people, and had taken of them bread and wine, beside forty shekels of silver; yea, even their servants bare rule over the people: but so did not I, because of the fear of God.

Job 28:28 And unto man he said, Behold, the fear of the Lord, that *is* wisdom; and to depart from evil *is* understanding.

Proverbs 14:27 The fear of the LORD *is* a fountain of life, to depart from the snares of death.

Proverbs 16:6 By mercy and truth iniquity is purged: and by the fear of the LORD *men* depart from evil.

"It shall be health to thy navel, and marrow to thy bones." (verse 8) **"It"** refers to verse 7 which states, "fear the LORD, and depart from evil." Doing so is healthy for the entire person. It keeps his conscience clear, brings peace, keeps his body safely away from dangerous places, keeps his mind calm and free of fear, and keeps his spirit sensitive and in communion with God. Used here as a figure of speech, **"navel"** represents the whole body because the umbilical cord that joins to it is the source of all nutrients from the mother. "The umbilical cord has three functions for the developing fetus: it supplies oxygen, it delivers nutrients, and it helps to withdraw blood rich in carbon dioxide and depleted in nutrients."[47] It is the lifeline between mother and child while the child is in the womb. Likewise, God is the lifeline between Himself and His children who have a fear of the LORD causing them to depart from evil.

"Marrow to thy bones." (verse 8b) Used here symbolically of good health, **"marrow"** produces moisture in that it generates red and white blood cells and platelets. Red blood cells transport oxygen to the cells. White blood cells fight infection and disease. Platelets help with blood clotting.[48] When the bone marrow becomes unhealthy, the whole body is in danger of returning to dust.

Leviticus 17:11 For the life of the flesh is in the blood: and I have given it to you upon the altar to make an atonement for your souls: for it is the blood that maketh an atonement for the soul.

Fear of the LORD *leads one to* salvation and wisdom, but it can also *keep one away from* contracting diseases that are often associated with evil encounters involving sinful lust and passion. Being right with God is like having music throughout one's body that synchronizes all the flowing of healthy fluids and connects all the electrical aspects in beautiful harmony. It calms and cures. ***Fear of the LORD and departure from evil*** eliminate excess stress and lead to good health. The following verses indicate how various conditions of life affect one's health.

Proverbs 12:4 A virtuous woman is a crown to her husband: but she that maketh ashamed is as rottenness in his bones.

Proverbs 14:30 A sound heart is the life of the flesh: but envy the rottenness of the bones.

Proverbs 15:30 The light of the eyes rejoiceth the heart: and a good report maketh the bones fat.

Proverbs 16:24 Pleasant words are as an honeycomb, sweet to the soul, and health to the bones.

Proverbs 17:22 A merry heart doeth good like a medicine: but a broken spirit drieth the bones.

Proverbs 3:9-10   Honour the LORD with thy substance, and with the firstfruits of all thine increase:
10.   So shall thy barns be filled with plenty, and thy presses shall burst out with new wine.

"Honour the LORD with thy substance" deals with giving respect and gratitude to God through gifts taken from an individual's own personal wealth.

Deuteronomy 8:18 But thou shalt remember the LORD thy God: for it is he that giveth thee power to get wealth, that he may establish his covenant which he sware unto thy fathers, as it is this day. *[See tithing instructions in Deuteronomy 26:1-4 … 9-14.]*

Verses nine and ten demonstrate the fact that God appreciates being respected and thanked for His gifts and that He promises to give back much more than was given in honor to Him. "The Israelites ***honored Jehovah with their substance*** when they contributed toward the erection of the tabernacle in the wilderness, and later they assisted in the preparations for the building of the temple, and in the payment of tithes. All of the above came from their substance.'"[49]

"With the firstfruits." (verse 9) The law of the first fruits is found in Exodus 22:29, Exodus 23:19, Exodus 34:20, Numbers 18:12, Deuteronomy 18:4, and Deuteronomy 26:1-3. Presented by every Israelite to the priests in token of gratitude and humble thankfulness to Jehovah, the first fruits consisted of the produce of the land in its natural state or prepared for human food. The **"first fruits"** also carried the idea of being the best. It is well known that the priests "lived of the sacrifice" and were "partakers of the altar," and as their support by these means tended to the maintenance of Divine worship, so those who supported them were in the highest degree 'honoring God.'"[50] Notice that the priests were recipients of the firstfruits.

> Deuteronomy 18:3-5 And this shall be the priest's due from the people, from them that offer a sacrifice, whether it be ox or sheep; and they shall give unto the priest the shoulder, and the two cheeks, and the maw. The firstfruit also of thy corn, of thy wine, and of thine oil, and the first of the fleece of thy sheep, shalt thou give him. For the LORD thy God hath chosen him out of all thy tribes, to stand to minister in the name of the LORD, him and his sons for ever.

These injunctions also show that the honoring of God does not consist simply of lip service, or of showing humility and confidence in him; but also of external worship, and in giving of corporeal things. These injunctions oppose all *selfish* use of God's temporal gifts and lead to the thought that, in obeying God's word we are only giving back to God what is already His own.[51]

> Haggai 2:8 The silver *is* mine and the gold *is* mine, saith the Lord of hosts.

"So shall thy barns be filled with plenty, and thy presses shall burst out with new wine." (verse 10)
The word picture is one of a storehouse filled with food and grapes so abundant that there is difficulty finding enough containers to hold that precious juice as it is pressed out. Bible students will be reminded of Jesus' promise to Christians concerning giving.

> Luke 6:38 Give, and it shall be given unto you; good measure, pressed down, and shaken together, and running over, shall men give into your bosom. For with the same measure that ye mete withal it shall be measured to you again.

So far in Chapter 3, God has promised the following *with contingencies*: (1) length of days, long life, peace (verse 2); (2) favor, good understanding (verse 5); (3) direction (verse 6); (4) health (verse 8); and now (5) prosperity (verse 10). Remember, the contingencies are: (1) keeping His commandments; (2) maintaining mercy and truth; (3) avoiding self-dependency and always departing from evil; (4) acknowledging (by praise and thanksgiving) what God has done and what He has given.

Proverbs 3:11-12 My son, despise not the chastening of the LORD; neither be weary of his correction:
12. For whom the LORD loveth he correcteth; even as a father the son in whom he delighteth.

"My son" is a phrase showing endearment. Because the phrase is singular, it can be concluded: that God chastises people as individuals, that he distinguishes between them in chastisement, that He knows the particular type and amount of discipline needed for each person. God's chastening of His beloved child will add to the individual's character *if* he accepts it in submission, patiently, and with appreciation. Such chastening means that God has taken each individual in hand, that He is Himself presiding over each individual's education, and that He loves every one of His children and desires for them to have spiritual growth.

The one being chastened or corrected should be alert to make sure his attitude is one of humility, knowing that God always knows best and that He will not fail to chasten His children when necessary. He should not grow **"weary"** and run away from being disciplined. The believer should submit to God's correction and thus honor Him. His human nature is prone to do wrong, and he needs God's correction *even* if he gets corrected often. There will be times when the individual finds himself in the middle of discipline before he can escape to a quiet place to allow God to bring to his mind the cause for his failure.

> Job 5:17-18 Behold, happy is the man whom God correcteth: therefore despise not thou the chastening of the Almighty: For he maketh sore, and bindeth up: he woundeth, and his hands make whole.
> Proverbs 1:23 Turn you at my reproof: behold, I will pour out my spirit unto you, I will make known my words unto you.

"For whom the LORD loveth, he correcteth; even as a father the son in whom he delighteth." (verse 12) Knowing that correction comes from the loving heavenly Father who is *always* on the side of His children is sufficient to give confidence and peace that the correction will be beneficial and never harmful. Notice how the New Testament refers to verses 11-12:

Hebrews 12:5-8 And ye have forgotten the exhortation which speaketh unto you as unto children, My son, despise not thou the chastening of the Lord, nor faint when thou art rebuked of him: For whom the Lord loveth he chasteneth, and scourgeth every son whom he receiveth. If ye endure chastening, God dealeth with you as with sons; for what son is he whom the father chasteneth not? But if ye be without chastisement, whereof all are partakers, then are ye bastards, and not sons.

Proverbs 3:13-18 Happy *is* the man *that* findeth wisdom, and the man *that* getteth understanding.
14. For the merchandise of it *is* better than the merchandise of silver, and the gain thereof than fine gold.
15. She *is* more precious than rubies: and all the things thou canst desire are not to be compared unto her.
16. Length of days *is* in her right hand; *and* in her left hand riches and honour.
17. Her ways *are* ways of pleasantness, and all her paths *are* peace.
18. She *is* a tree of life to them that lay hold upon her: and happy *is every one* that retaineth her.

"Happy is the man the findeth wisdom . . . that getteth understanding"

Because Wisdom is:
  (1) **Profitable** beyond earth's valuables (gold and silver) (verse 14)
  (2) **Precious** beyond comparison. (verse 15)

Because Wisdom Provides:
  (1) **Prolonged Life** (verse 16a)   (4) **Peaceful** Pathway (verse 17b)
  (2) **Prosperity** (verse 16b)   (5) **Permanent Tree of Life** (verse 18a)
  (3) **Pleasant Pathway** (verse 17a)   (6) **Perpetual Happiness** (verse 18b)

"Happy *is* the man *that* findeth wisdom, and the man *that* getteth understanding." (verse 13) *Happiness* that comes from an association with God and from being blessed with God's personal directions for living (**"wisdom"**) is beyond any carnal happiness. It is spiritually induced from the Spirit of God and is perceived through the spirit of man. It is jubilant happiness derived from being blessed of God.

Romans 8:16 The Spirit itself beareth witness with our spirit, that we are the children of God.

Even *if* there were no other benefits *(but there are many)*, the very act of communicating with God brings happiness. Add to that communication an awareness that God is personally gifting wisdom, and one experiences abounding happiness.

Because they are very similar in meaning, the two verbs **"findeth"** and **"getteth** *[to draw out or bring forth]*" are important to the understanding of this verse. Also, because there are only nuances of differences between the meanings of the words **"wisdom"** and **"understanding,"** the second phrase repeats the intent of the first, but using different words. This repetition is purposefully used *to intensify the thoughts and feelings of happiness* gained from having wisdom and understanding.

Finding **wisdom** as taught by the Bible requires a search that begins with having an *awesome respect for God* as described in Proverbs Chapter One followed by an exercise of *diligent effort* as described in Proverbs Chapter Two. "Finding" and "getting" "wisdom" and "understanding" involves desire and effort.

Proverbs 8:35 For whoso findeth me findeth life, and shall obtain favour of the LORD.

Proverbs 9:10 The fear of the LORD *is* the beginning of wisdom: and the knowledge of the holy *is* understanding.

Getting heart-felt understanding requires that **"wisdom"** must be established in the heart *[mind, emotions, and will]* to keep the wise person by becoming the basis of *all* his reasoning. **"Understanding"** enables a person to make godly judgments by using a proper godly perspective to discern right from wrong. It causes the wise to establish boundaries for his own speaking and acting. *Getting understanding* involves changing the way one reasons to a way that is different from that of the world. It is the godly way, the wise way. This understanding comes from first knowing God and then from receiving instructional wisdom from Him and then feeling about everything the way God does because the believer has been taught by Him. Wisdom produces understanding that begins with a knowledge of God. "Let this mind be in you, which was also in Christ Jesus . . . " (Philippians 2:5)

Proverbs 4:5 Get wisdom, get understanding: forget *it* not; neither decline from the words of my mouth.

Proverbs 4:7 Wisdom *is* the principal thing; *therefore* get wisdom: and with all thy getting get understanding.

Proverbs 16:16 How much better *is it* to get wisdom than gold! and to get understanding rather to be chosen than silver!

"For the merchandise of it *is* better than the merchandise of silver, and the gain thereof than fine gold." (verse 14) *Merchandising* is the buying and selling of a product with the specific idea of making a profit. The *profit from obtaining wisdom and understanding* is identified in the following verses as length of days, riches and honor, pleasantness, peace, tree of life, and happiness. Today, **"fine gold"** refers to gold that is almost pure,[52] and likely meant the same in Biblical times. Neither gold or silver brings the profit or advantages to a person's life that wisdom gives. The benefits of gold and silver are many and valuable to a person, albeit temporary and certainly negligible compared to the temporal, as well as eternal blessings of wisdom and understanding.

> "We must trade for it. We read here of the merchandise of wisdom, which intimates, (1) That we must make it our business, and not a by-business, as the merchant bestows the main of his thoughts and time upon his merchandise. (2) That we must venture all in it, as a stock in trade, and be willing to part with all for it. This is that pearl of great price which, when we have found it, we must willingly sell all for the purchase of. ***Buy the truth***; he does not say at what rate, because we must buy it at any rate rather than miss it."[53]

> Job 28:12-19 But where shall wisdom be found? and where *is* the place of understanding? Man knoweth not the price thereof; neither is it found in the land of the living. The depth saith, It *is* not in me: and the sea saith, *It is* not with me. It cannot be gotten for gold, neither shall silver be weighed *for* the price thereof. It cannot be valued with the gold of Ophir, with the precious onyx, or the sapphire. The gold and the crystal cannot equal it: and the exchange of it *shall not be for* jewels of fine gold. No mention shall be made of coral, or of pearls: for the price of wisdom *is* above rubies. The topaz of Ethiopia shall not equal it, neither shall it be valued with pure gold.

> Proverbs 2:1-5 My son, if thou wilt receive my words, and hide my commandments with thee; So that thou incline thine ear unto wisdom, *and* apply thine heart to understanding; Yea, if thou criest after knowledge, *and* liftest up thy voice for understanding; If thou seekest her as silver, and searchest for her as *for* hid treasures; Then shalt thou understand the fear of the LORD, and find the knowledge of God.

> Proverbs 8:10-11 Receive my instruction, and not silver; and knowledge rather than choice gold. For wisdom *is* better than rubies; and all the things that may be desired are not to be compared to it.

> Proverbs 8:19 My fruit *is* better than gold, yea, than fine gold; and my revenue than choice silver.

> Ecclesiastes 5:10-11 He that loveth silver shall not be satisfied with silver; nor he that loveth abundance with increase: this *is* also vanity. When goods increase, they are increased that eat them: and what good *is there* to the owners thereof, saving the beholding *of them* with their eyes?

"She *is* more precious than rubies: and all the things thou canst desire are not to be compared unto her." (verse 15) In verses 15-18, Wisdom is again personified as a lady who reaches out to those seeking this great gift that comes only and directly from God. Verse 15 is simply declaring that wisdom is of more value than all the wealth that a person can accumulate. *[See verses above.]* Wealth can purchase many things of great earthly value; but wisdom teaches a man to think, reason, and act in a manner that is pleasing to his Creator; and it establishes a relationship that is unknown to those seeking wealth and *not* God and His Son Jesus Christ. Verses 16-18 provide details as to why wisdom is so valuable.

"Length of days *is* in her right hand; *and* in her left hand riches and honour." (verse 16) The Bible now explains one reason WHY wisdom is so valuable. The believer realizes that among wisdom's gifts are long life, riches and honor, pleasantness, and peace. She is pictured as holding valuables in both hands, ready to share the same. In one hand is **long life**, even eternal life, and in the other is **riches and honor**. The promise is that of a long and prosperous temporary life here on earth in addition to eternal life in heaven.[54] Length of days is eternity itself.

> Matthew 6:31-33 Therefore take no thought, saying, What shall we eat? or, What shall we drink? or, Wherewithal shall we be clothed? (For after all these things do the Gentiles seek:) for your heavenly Father knoweth that ye have need of all these things. But seek ye first the kingdom of God, and his righteousness; and all these things shall be added unto you.

> 1 Timothy 4:8 For bodily exercise profiteth little: but godliness is profitable unto all things, having promise of the life that now is, and of that which is to come.

"Riches and honour" are pictured in this verse as being conferred by the personified Wisdom to a person whose life is demonstrative of wisdom and understanding. **"Riches and honour"** enhance quality of life and give dignity to the favored child of God. Other Scriptures, listed below, provide amplification to this gift of **"riches and honor."**

> 1 Chronicles 29:11-12 Thine, O LORD, is the greatness, and the power, and the glory, and the victory, and the majesty: for all that is in the heaven and in the earth is thine; thine is the kingdom, O LORD, and thou art exalted as head above all. Both riches and honour come of thee, and thou reignest over all; and in thine hand is power and might; and in thine hand it is to make great, and to give strength unto all.

> Proverbs 8:18 Riches and honour are with me; yea, durable riches, and righteousness.

> Proverbs 21:20-21 *There is* treasure to be desired and oil in the dwelling of the wise; but a foolish man spendeth it up. He that followeth after righteousness and mercy findeth life, righteousness, and honour.

> Proverbs 22:4 By humility *and* the fear of the LORD *are* riches, and honour, and life.

Having **"honour"** in wisdom's left hand reminds of other passages:

> I Samuel 2:30 Them that honour me I will honour, and they that despise me shall be lightly esteemed.
>
> John 5:44 How can ye believe, which receive honour one of another, and seek not the honour that cometh from God only?
>
> John 12:26 If any man serve me, let him follow me; and where I am, there shall also my servant be: if any man serve me, him will my Father honour.

"Her ways are ways of pleasantness and all her paths are peace." (verse 17) Wisdom teaches her students to recognize the many characteristics of foolish behavior that oppose the peaceful and pleasant ways of God, so that through discernment, contact with evil people and wicked situations are minimized. Whenever those evil situations are unavoidable, the wise person relies on wisdom to handle them discretely, to maintain a spirit of peace, and to diminish involvement. *Pleasantness* [*delightfulness, favor, and agreeableness*] and peace are some of the benefits of walking under the direction of the Prince of Peace. Those who are *on* His side remain *by* His side and *"under His wings."* Peace is a calmness within the soul that comes from trusting in God.

> Psalm 91:4 He shall cover thee with his feathers, and under his wings shalt thou trust: his truth shall be thy shield and buckler.
>
> Jeremiah 29:11 For I know the thoughts that I think toward you, saith the LORD, thoughts of peace, and not of evil, to give you an expected end.
>
> John 14:27 Peace I leave with you, my peace I give unto you: not as the world giveth, give I unto you. Let not your heart be troubled, neither let it be afraid.
>
> Romans 8:6 For to be carnally minded *is* death; but to be spiritually minded *is* life and peace.
>
> Romans 14:17 For the kingdom of God is not meat and drink; but righteousness, and peace, and joy in the Holy Ghost.
>
> Galatians 5:22-23 But the fruit of the Spirit is love, joy, peace, longsuffering, gentleness, goodness, faith, Meekness, temperance: against such there is no law.
>
> Philippians 4:6-7 Be careful for nothing; but in every thing by prayer and supplication with thanksgiving let your requests be made known unto God. And the peace of God, which passeth all understanding, shall keep your hearts and minds through Christ Jesus.
>
> James 3:17-18 But the wisdom that is from above is first pure, then peaceable, gentle, *and* easy to be intreated, full of mercy and good fruits, without partiality, and without hypocrisy. And the fruit of righteousness is sown in peace of them that make peace.

"She *is* a tree of life to them that lay hold upon her: and happy *is every one* that retaineth her." (verse 18) Wisdom is spoken of as a **"tree of life"** because "she" (wisdom) directs the student of wisdom to abundant life with God on earth and eternal life with Him in heaven. To **"lay hold on her"** is to lay hold upon God's instructions. To *retain her* is to absorb wisdom's instructions into the heart so as to convert one's thinking away from the world's way of foolish reasoning to God's way of wise reasoning. The consequence of taking hold of His word produces abundant living beyond anything that the world's system can offer or even know. To *lay hold of wisdom* and to *retain wisdom* is equivalent to (figuratively speaking) eating from a tree of life. Proverbs 4:13 states, "Take fast hold of instruction; let her not go: keep her; for she is thy life."

Happy is every one who retains wisdom because godly wisdom maintains man in the spiritual life of God's grace, and the communion of His Spirit.[55] Wisdom is a tree of life, eternal life, open to all who embrace God's instructions. One can only imagine the sorrow that filled the hearts of Adam and Eve after they rejected God's wisdom and the way to the tree of life was blocked (Genesis 3:22-24). People who know the value of this great gift of wisdom, this "tree of life," "... **lay hold upon her.**" "The tenacious grasp with which the shipwrecked sinking sailor lays hold on any spar or plank floating near will illustrate the kind of grasp with which Wisdom is to be held. *(Muffet)*"[56]

> Hebrews 2:1 Therefore we ought to give the more earnest heed to the things which we have heard, lest at any time we should let them *slip.*

Additional verses concerning the tree of life in Proverbs are as follows, and these will be discussed later in this commentary:

> Proverbs 11:30 "The fruit of the righteous is a tree of life . . . "
>
> Proverbs 13:12 "Hope deferred maketh the heart sick: but *when* the desire cometh, *it is* a tree of life."
>
> Proverbs 15:4 "A wholesome tongue is a tree of life . . . "

"Happy is everyone that retaineth her." (verse 18) One day a distraught alcoholic friend said, "I'd just like to be happy!" He isn't alone, many people would like to be happy, but they continue looking in the wrong places. There is no happiness in the little gods of this world such as alcohol, riches, sex, or in any transgression against God. Wisdom, and consequently happiness, are available to the person who **"retains"** [*lays hold of, grasps*] the instructions of God so that his ways embody the teachings of God. When he learns to think and act according to the word of God, he will behave as God intended and find happiness.

Proverbs 3:13 Happy is the man that findeth wisdom, and the man that getteth understanding.

Proverbs 16:20 He that handleth a matter wisely shall find good: and whoso trusteth in the LORD, happy is he.

Proverbs 28:14 Happy is the man that feareth alway: but he that hardeneth his heart shall fall into mischief.

Proverbs 29:18 Where there is no vision, the people perish: but he that keepeth the law, happy is he.

The unbeliever may gain riches and short-lived honor, but he will not attain the happiness and peace of the believer. The unbeliever will even receive a "long life" (an eternal life), but it will be spent in hell. As R. G. Lee preached in the famous message "Payday Someday," ". . . Satan always pays in counterfeit money . . . all his pearls are paste pearls . . . the nectar he offers is poisoned through and through. Oh, that men would learn the truth and be warned by the truth that if they eat the Devil's corn, he will choke them with the cob."

> **Proverbs 3:19-20**   The LORD by wisdom hath founded the earth; by understanding hath he established the heavens.
> 20.   By his knowledge the depths are broken up, and the clouds drop down the dew.

Again, in these two verses appear the marvelous trio of words – **wisdom, knowledge** and **understanding** – by which God created the world. Wise people who seek after the same learn to think, reason, and effectively commune with the Creator. Such communication facilitates a happy, blessed and productive life in this world created by God and designed to operate according to His plan. Much like the trinity of words – *justice, judgment*, and *equity* – gives an enhanced and emphasized understanding to the *"rightness"* of God, the threesome of *wisdom, knowledge*, and *understanding* gives an enhanced and emphasized meaning to the totality of God's *reasoning*. It is by His great comprehension of all things (wisdom, knowledge, and understanding) that He created the worlds; and it is by His great righteousness (justice, judgment, equity) that He governs.

Verse 20 gives an example of His wisdom by bringing to mind how water cycles on earth. It explains the greatness of God's wisdom – **"the depths are broken up, and the clouds drop down the dew."** *["Depths" refers to the subterranean water supply.]* Only God could have created such a cycle whereby the earth's water breaks down small enough to rise into the atmosphere and then collect again to return as the dew. What a refreshing gift to man! His glorious works declare His majesty, His love, and His marvelous creative mind.

Psalm 104:24 O LORD, how manifold are thy works! in wisdom hast thou made them all: the earth is full of thy riches.

Psalm 136:5 To him that by wisdom made the heavens: for his mercy *endureth* for ever.

Proverbs 8:22-31 The LORD possessed me in the beginning of his way, before his works of old. I was set up from everlasting, from the beginning, or ever the earth was. When *there were* no depths, I was brought forth; when *there were* no fountains abounding with water. Before the mountains were settled, before the hills was I brought forth: While as yet he had not made the earth, nor the fields, nor the highest part of the dust of the world. When he prepared the heavens, I *was* there: when he set a compass upon the face of the depth: When he established the clouds above: when he strengthened the fountains of the deep: When he gave to the sea his decree, that the waters should not pass his commandment: when he appointed the foundations of the earth: Then I was by him, *as* one brought up *with him:* and I was daily *his* delight, rejoicing always before him; Rejoicing in the habitable part of his earth; and my delights *were* with the sons of men.

Jeremiah 10:12 He hath made the earth by his power, he hath established the world by his wisdom, and hath stretched out the heavens by his discretion.

Jeremiah 51:15 He hath made the earth by his power, he hath established the world by his wisdom, and hath stretched out the heaven by his understanding.

> **Proverbs 3:21-26**   My son, let not them depart from thine eyes: keep sound wisdom and discretion:
> 22.   So shall they be life unto thy soul, and grace to thy neck.
> 23.   Then shalt thou walk in thy way safely, and thy foot shall not stumble.
> 24.   When thou liest down, thou shalt not be afraid: yea, thou shalt lie down, and thy sleep shall be sweet.
> 25.   Be not afraid of sudden fear, neither of the desolation of the wicked, when it cometh.
> 26.   For the LORD shall be thy confidence, and shall keep thy foot from being taken.

My son, let not them depart from thine eyes: keep sound wisdom and discretion: So shall they be life unto thy soul and grace to thy neck. (verses 21-22)

> **Embracing Sound Wisdom and Discretion** (verses 21-26) **Provides:**
> 1. Sustenance (life) to the soul. (verse 22a)
> 2. Style (grace) to the neck. (verse 22b)
> 3. Safety to the pathway. (verse 23a)
> 4. Sureness to the faithful who walk with God. (verse 23b)
> 5. Sweetness of safety and sleep. (verse 24)
> 6. Safety from sudden desolation of the wicked. (verse 25)
> 7. Secure walk with the LORD. (verse 26)

"My son" appears again as it does in 23 places in the book of Proverbs. In most of these places, it is the affectionate term for a positive relationship between wisdom and those children and students eager to learn.

> Isaiah 28:9 Whom shall he teach knowledge? and whom shall he make to understand doctrine? *them that are* weaned from the milk, *and* drawn from the breasts. For precept *must be* upon precept, precept upon precept; line upon line, line upon line; here a little, *and* there a little . . .

"Let them *[sound wisdom and discretion]* **not depart from thine eyes."** (verse 21) With the powerful and persuasive information just given (verses 19 and 20) that by wisdom, knowledge, and understanding, God performed His creative acts, Solomon tenderly addresses again his student, whom he obviously believes to have the will to keep such information constantly in his thoughts. The student is instructed to keep a protective watch on **"sound wisdom and discretion,"** ensuring that they are guarded continuously because they are of more value than words can express.

> Deuteronomy 11:18-20 Therefore shall ye lay up these my words in your heart and in your soul, and bind them for a sign upon your hand, that they may be as frontlets between your eyes. And ye shall teach them your children, speaking of them when thou sittest in thine house, and when thou walkest by the way, when thou liest down, and when thou risest up. And thou shalt write them upon the door posts of thine house, and upon thy gates.
>
> 2 Peter 1:12 Wherefore I will not be negligent to put you always in remembrance of these things, though ye know *them,* and be established in the present truth.

"Keep sound wisdom and discretion." Wisdom is "sound" *[successful, efficient]* because it comes straight from God. Sound wisdom reflects the mind of Christ – the same mind as His Father's and that of the Holy Spirit. As expressed throughout Proverbs, in its totality, sound wisdom consists of wisdom, knowledge, and understanding. God's wisdom is beautifully complete, His understanding unmeasurable, and His knowledge comprehensive. With these attributes, He created and sustains the world. So, yes, this wisdom from God is sound. It is unshakable. It can't be improved upon. The expression **"sound wisdom"** occurs three times in the Bible and all three times in Proverbs.

> Proverbs 2:7 He layeth up sound wisdom for the righteous: *he is* a buckler to them that walk uprightly.
>
> Proverbs 3:21 My son, let not them depart from thine eyes: keep sound wisdom and discretion . . .
>
> Proverbs 8:14 Counsel *is* mine, and sound wisdom: I *am* understanding; I have strength.

The word **"discretion,"** as defined by Noah Webster, means "prudence, or knowledge and prudence; that discernment which enables a person to judge critically of what is correct and proper, united with caution . . . directed by circumspection, and primarily regarding one's own conduct."[57] In the Book of Proverbs, discretion will cause a person (1) to look at the result of his own and other people's personal actions or words, (2) to change his actions or speech to be in alignment with God's word, and (3) to seek a better personal outcome. Regarding Proverbs 1:4, *Pulpit Commentary* states that "Discretion is . . . that which sets a man on his guard and prevents him from being duped by others."[58] It is that *drink of good sense* drawn *out of the well of wisdom* and will cause the wise person to make sober, sane, and safe decisions such as staying away from a harlot. (The English word "discretion" is translated from three different Hebrew words, each slightly different in meaning. Discretion is referred to six times in the Book of Proverbs.)

"So shall they *[sound wisdom and discretion]* **be life unto thy soul, and grace to thy neck."** (verse 22) There shouldn't be any reasonable question that **"life"** comes from God as does **"sound wisdom and discretion."** Strange, though, is the fact that many prefer plastic, artificial, worldly wisdom, (which reveals blatant rebellion and willful ignorance) due to the fact that "the god of this world hath blinded the minds of them which believe not . . ." (2 Corinthians 4:4) Life, sound wisdom, and discretion all flow from God, the fountain of life. To make "sound wisdom and discretion" a way of thinking and acting is to live in a manner pleasing to God; hence, they become like an ornament about the neck, bringing honor to the one so submitted to Him. Below are biblical examples of applied "sound wisdom and discretion" that brought honor.

1 Samuel 25:32-33 And David said to Abigail, Blessed be the LORD God of Israel, which sent thee this day to meet me: And blessed be thy advice, and blessed be thou, which hast kept me this day from coming to shed blood, and from avenging myself with mine own hand.

1 Kings 3:28 And all Israel heard of the judgment which the king *[Solomon]* had judged; and they feared the king: for they saw that the wisdom of God was in him, to do judgment.

John 8:4-9 They say unto him, Master, this woman was taken in adultery, in the very act. Now Moses in the law commanded us, that such should be stoned: but what sayest thou? This they said, tempting him, that they might have to accuse him. But Jesus stooped down, and with his finger wrote on the ground, as though he heard them not. So when they continued asking him, he lifted up himself, and said unto them, He that is without sin among you, let him first cast a stone at her. And again he stooped down, and wrote on the ground. And they which heard it, being convicted by their own conscience, went out one by one, beginning at the eldest, even unto the last: and Jesus was left alone, and the woman standing in the midst.

Proverbs 3:23   Then shalt thou walk in thy way safely, and thy foot shall not stumble.

"Sound wisdom and discretion" will keep the young man from traveling on that wrong path and from being allied with evil people with whom sin prevails and danger lurks. The **"way"** is well lighted by the precise instructions of the Father (word of God). With this guidance, the believer can **"walk in thy way safely, and thy foot shall not stumble."**

Psalm 37:2-24 The steps of a *good* man are ordered by the LORD: and he delighteth in his way. Though he fall, he shall not be utterly cast down: for the LORD upholdeth *him with* his hand.

Proverbs 1:33 But whoso hearkeneth unto me shall dwell safely, and shall be quiet from fear of evil.

Proverbs 2:8 He keepeth the paths of judgment, and preserveth the way of his saints.

Proverbs 2:11-12 Discretion shall preserve thee, understanding shall keep thee: To deliver thee from the way of the evil *man,* from the man that speaketh froward things;

Proverbs 2:16-17 To deliver thee from the strange woman, *even* from the stranger *which* flattereth with her words. Which forsaketh the guide of her youth, and forgetteth the covenant of her God.

Proverbs 2:20 That thou mayest walk in the way of good *men,* and keep the paths of the righteous.

In the Book of Proverbs, the person who has successfully obtained godly, sound wisdom has the ability, because of a proper relationship with God, to be able to navigate through the challenges and opportunities of life in the most effective manner, thereby minimizing evil influences and maximizing godly outcomes.

Proverbs 3:24   When thou liest down, thou shalt not be afraid: yea, thou shalt lie down, and thy sleep shall be sweet.

Persons with wisdom and discretion are free from constant worrisome, distracting troubles that overwhelm with fear and disturb the sleep of the ungodly. The wise have peace in knowing that God favors them because they are obedient, submissive, and teachable. God providentially cares for His faithful children; hence, fear is suppressed, and sleep is sweet.

Psalm 4:8 I will both lay me down in peace, and sleep: for thou, LORD, only makest me dwell in safety.

Proverbs 6:22 When thou goest, it *[the law and commandments]* shall lead thee; when thou sleepest, it shall keep thee; and *when* thou awakest, it shall talk with thee.

Having chosen to fully trust in the Lord and thereby having taken "sound wisdom and discretion" (verse 21) close to his bosom, the believer has learned that all of God's promises are true and that he and God are partners in this journey through life. Therefore the obedient believer is led to the safe place to rest, realizing that "He will not suffer thy foot to be moved: he that keepeth thee will not slumber. Behold, he that keepeth Israel shall neither slumber nor sleep." (Psalm 121:3-4)

> **Proverbs 3:25-26** Be not afraid of sudden fear, neither of the desolation of the wicked, when it cometh.
> 26. For the LORD shall be thy confidence, and shall keep thy foot from being taken.

"Be not afraid of sudden fear." Don't fill the mind with worry about something bad that *might* come up from nowhere, that *might* blind side and cause a catastrophe (**"sudden fear"**). Living in fear of potential, unsubstantiated, conjectured catastrophes only makes life miserable. Shakespeare spoke of such unwarranted fear when he said "A coward dies a thousand times before his death, but the valiant taste of death but once. " (William Shakespeare, *Julius Caesar*)

- Psalm 91:1 He that dwelleth in the secret place of the most High shall abide under the shadow of the Almighty.
- Psalm 118:8-9 It is better to trust in the LORD than to put confidence in man. It is better to trust in the LORD than to put confidence in princes.
- Psalm 121:3-8 He will not suffer thy foot to be moved: he that keepeth thee will not slumber.   Behold, he that keepeth Israel shall neither slumber nor sleep. The LORD is thy keeper: the LORD is thy shade upon thy right hand. The sun shall not smite thee by day, nor the moon by night. The LORD shall preserve thee from all evil: he shall preserve thy soul. The LORD shall preserve thy going out and thy coming in from this time forth, and even for evermore.
- Matthew 6:34 Take therefore no thought for the morrow: for the morrow shall take thought for the things of itself. Sufficient unto the day *is* the evil thereof.
- 2 Timothy 1:7 For God hath not given us the spirit of fear; but of power, and of love, and of a sound mind.

Verse 25b adds, don't be afraid of **"the desolation of the wicked, when it cometh."** Wicked men will be brought into desolation *[devastation, ruin]* in a moment. When the wicked's punishment comes, timorous saints may be apprehensive that they will be caught up in the calamity. Saints should remember that even though judgments may be close enough to be felt, God knows those who are His; He knows how to separate between the precious and the vile. "For the LORD shall be thy confidence, and shall keep thy foot from being taken."

"Therefore be not afraid of that which appears most formidable *[desolation of the wicked]*, for *"the Lord shall be* not only thy protector to keep thee safe, but *thy confidence* to keep thee secure, so that thy foot *shall not be taken* by thy enemies nor ensnared by thy own fears." God has engaged to keep the feet of his saints."[59]

"Though the paths of life are dangerous and difficult, yet we shall stand fast, for Jehovah will not permit our feet to slide; and if he will not suffer it we shall not suffer it. If our foot will be thus kept we may be sure that our head and heart will be preserved also . . . Promised preservation should be the subject of perpetual prayer; and we may pray believing; for those who have God for their keeper shall be safe from all the perils of the way. Among the hills and ravines of Palestine the literal keeping of the feet is a great mercy; but in the slippery ways of a tried and afflicted life, the boon of upholding is of priceless value, for a single false step might cause us a fall fraught with awful danger. To stand erect and pursue the even tenor of our way is a blessing which only God can give, which is worthy of the divine hand, and worthy also of perennial gratitude. Our feet shall move in progress, but they shall not be moved to their overthrow."[60]

- Deuteronomy 33:27 The eternal God is thy refuge, and underneath are the everlasting arms: and he shall thrust out the enemy from before thee; and shall say, Destroy them.
- Psalm 37:23-4 The steps of a good man are ordered by the LORD: and he delighteth in his way. Though he fall, he shall not be utterly cast down: for the LORD upholdeth him with his hand.
- Proverbs 1:33 But whoso hearkeneth unto me shall dwell safely, and shall be quiet from fear of evil.
- Isaiah 26:20-21   Come, my people, enter thou into thy chambers, and shut thy doors about thee: hide thyself as it were for a little moment, until the indignation be overpast. For, behold, the LORD cometh out of his place to punish the inhabitants of the earth for their iniquity: the earth also shall disclose her blood, and shall no more cover her slain.
- 2 Timothy 2:19 Nevertheless the foundation of God standeth sure, having this seal, The Lord knoweth them that are his. And, Let every one that nameth the name of Christ depart from iniquity.

> **Proverbs 3: 27-35** Withhold not good from them to whom it is due, when it is in the power of thine hand to do *it.*
> 28. Say not unto thy neighbour, Go, and come again, and to morrow I will give; when thou hast it by thee.
> 29. Devise not evil against thy neighbour, seeing he dwelleth securely by thee.
> 30. Strive not with a man without cause, if he have done thee no harm.
> 31. Envy thou not the oppressor, and choose none of his ways.
> 32. For the froward is abomination to the LORD: but his secret is with the righteous.
> 33. The curse of the LORD is in the house of the wicked: but he blesseth the habitation of the just.
> 34. Surely he scorneth the scorners: but he giveth grace unto the lowly.
> 35. The wise shall inherit glory: but shame shall be the promotion of fools.

> **Relationships with Others** (Outline of Proverbs 3:27-35)
>
> I. **God's Prescribed *Benevolence*** to one's neighbor.
>   A. Don't **deny** available help to others from your wealth. (verse 27)
>   B. Don't **delay** available help to others from your wealth. (verse 28)
>   C. Don't **devise** evil to others. (verse 29)
>   D. Don't **disturb** the peace by striving with others without a cause. (verse 30)
>
> II. **God's Prescribed *Bewares*** against emulating and/or associating with oppressors.
>   A. Don't **envy** the oppressor. (verse 31a)
>   B. Don't **emulate** any ways of the oppressor. (verse 31b)
>
> III. **God's Prescribed *Blasting*** of fools AND ***Blessings*** to the righteous.
>   A. **Froward are disgusting** (an abomination) to Him. (verse 32) BUT **Righteous are delightful** – *God will share secrets* with Him
>   B. **Wicked receive a curse** to their dwelling. (verse 33a) BUT **Just receive continued blessings** to theirs. (verse 33b)
>   C. **Scorners receive scorning.** (verse 34a) BUT **Lowly receive special favor** (grace). (verse 34b)
>   D. **Fools are promoted to shame.** (verse 35b) BUT **Wise are promoted to splendor** (inherit glory). (verse 35a)

"Withhold not good from them to whom it is due, When it is in the power of thine hand to do it." (verse 27) The wise servant is to do **"good"** **"to them to whom it is due,"** meaning to those who are the *owner of a need*. *["Due" is translated from the Hebrew ba'al meaning owner.]* The "good" that the righteous may have available to help with could be in several forms: counsel, correction, a physical item such as food or tools, money, labor, demonstration of love, *or* simply a word of encouragement. The second part of this verse identifies those who are capable of doing "good" as those who have ***the power in their hand to do good***. No one is responsible "to do good" with that which he doesn't have; however, sharing with others is a common theme throughout the word of God. A failure to help where possible is a breach of trust that God has placed in the holder, the steward, whom He has entrusted with such assets as substance or ability.

> Psalm 37:21 The wicked borroweth, and payeth not again: but the righteous sheweth mercy, and giveth.
>
> Jeremiah 22:13-16 Woe unto him that buildeth his house by unrighteousness, and his chambers by wrong; that useth his neighbour's service without wages, and giveth him not for his work; That saith, I will build me a wide house and large chambers, and cutteth him out windows; and it is cieled with cedar, and painted with vermilion. Shalt thou reign, because thou closest thyself in cedar? did not thy father eat and drink, and do judgment and justice, and then it was well with him? He judged the cause of the poor and needy; then it was well with him: was not this to know me? saith the LORD.

"Say not unto thy neighbour, Go, and come again, and to morrow I will give; when thou hast it by thee." (verse 28) Emphasizing and amplifying verse twenty-seven, this verse states the necessity of not putting off helping others, but rather giving immediately with urgency because the need is urgent. *DELAY* IN MERCY is the subject of verse 28, while the previous verse refers to the *DENIAL* OF MERCY. The *admonition is against greed and selfishness* since *a failure to act likely stems from a failure to trust God for replenishment*. Verse 33 addresses the fact that God blesses "the habitation of the just," therefore, the just shouldn't be fearful of doing good where it is needed.

> Galatians 6:10 While we have therefore opportunity, let us do good unto all men, especially unto them who are of the household of faith.
>
> Titus 2:13-14 Looking for that blessed hope, and the glorious appearing of the great God and our Saviour Jesus Christ; Who gave himself for us, that he might redeem us from all iniquity, and purify unto himself a peculiar people, zealous of good works.
>
> James 2:15-16 If a brother or sister be naked, and destitute of daily food, And one of you say unto them, Depart in peace, be *ye* warmed and filled; notwithstanding ye give them not those things which are needful to the body; what *doth it* profit?
>
> James 5:4 Behold, the hire of the labourers who have reaped down your fields, which is of you kept back by fraud, crieth: and the cries of them which have reaped are entered into the ears of the Lord of sabaoth.

"Devise not evil against thy neighbour, seeing he dwelleth securely by thee." (verse 29) The word **"devise"** implies *secretly contriving to do something evil*. **"He dwelleth securely by thee"** means that the person lives close by and has been led to believe that he lives and converses **"securely"** (in safety) with his neighbor, who is relying upon the integrity of his friend. The reader has to wonder if perhaps one of them has shared private matters that he was sure would be safe and secure with his neighbor, his friend. Surely their conversations would forever be kept confidential – or would they? It seems a shame to have to instruct not to contrive evil against anyone, especially a close neighbor, but no doubt the instruction is necessary. Such instruction will strike the heart and conscience of a righteous person who has been loose with his tongue in some manner unworthy of friendship.

> Proverbs 6:12-14 A naughty person, a wicked man, walketh with a froward mouth. He winketh with his eyes, he speaketh with his feet, he teacheth with his fingers; Frowardness is in his heart, he deviseth mischief continually; he soweth discord.

Micah 2:1-2 Woe to them that devise iniquity, and work evil upon their beds! when the morning is light, they practise it, because it is in the power of their hand. And they covet fields, and take them by violence; and houses, and take them away: so they oppress a man and his house, even a man and his heritage.

Zechariah 7:9-10 Thus speaketh the LORD of hosts, saying, Execute true judgment, and shew mercy and compassions every man to his brother: And oppress not the widow, nor the fatherless, the stranger, nor the poor; and let none of you imagine evil against his brother in your heart.

"Strive not with a man without cause, if he have done thee no harm." (verse 30) Part of being wise is being able to discern the difference between the important and the trivial or between an issue that has merit and that which is unimportant – especially when there has been no harm done. The wise person will avoid strife whenever possible, and there are situations where doing so requires him to sustain losses. Then there are also situations, as in this proverb where *strife presents itself*; but there is no justification whatever for such strife to exist. There is no reason for it. Sometimes avoiding strife means just pleasantly excusing oneself.

2 Timothy 2:24 And the servant of the Lord must not strive, but be gentle unto all *men*, apt to teach, patient.

"Envy thou not the oppressor, and choose none of his ways." (verse 31) The **"oppressor"** is one who gets his wealth by violating others in one manner or another. Perhaps he cheats, steals, or uses his powerful position or family name to take from others. The warning is to *not* set your mind upon the things that the oppressor possesses with any idea of envy. This verse instructs the wise person to avoid lusting after the oppressor's things and the command is to **"choose none of his ways"** which are ways of oppression to get unjust wealth or position or fame.

Psalm 37:1-2 Fret not thyself because of evildoers, neither be thou envious against the workers of iniquity. For they shall soon be cut down like the grass, and wither as the green herb.

"For the froward [turned aside, devious, perverse] **is abomination to the Lord: But his secret *is* with the righteous."** (verse 32) This verse amplifies the previous one to describe the "oppressor" as **"froward."** The froward man is one who lives his life contrary to the teachings of God and the godly. He always opposes what is good and right; consequently, he is disgusting to the Lord – an "abomination."

In contrast to **"the froward"** are **"the righteous"** who are considered so because they are right with God. They have learned to think and act in a manner that is pleasing to the LORD. The **"righteous"** are favored of God as indicated by His sharing with them such things as His presence, His peace, His plans, and His instructions. His communication is considered **"secret"** because only the righteous will hear Him. "His close, intimate communion as of 'friend with friend,' is with the righteous."[61]

Job 15:8 Hast thou heard the secret of God? and dost thou restrain wisdom to thyself?

Psalm 25:14 The secret of the LORD is with them that fear him; and he will shew them his covenant.

Proverbs 1:7 The fear of the LORD is the beginning of knowledge: but fools despise wisdom and instruction.

Albert Barnes has the following to say about "secret" in relation to the Lord.

"The word rendered 'secret' *[sod]* means properly a 'couch' or 'cushion,' on which one reclines – whether for sleep or at a table, or as a divan. Hence, it means a divan, or circle of persons sitting together for familiar conversation... or of judges, counselors, or advisers for consultation, as the word 'divan' is now used in Oriental countries. Then it means any consultation, counsel, familiar conversation, or intimacy.

Here God is represented in Oriental language as seated in a 'divan,' or council of state: there is deliberation about the concerns of his government; important questions are agitated and decided; and *[in Job 15:8]* Eliphaz asks of Job whether he had been admitted to that council, and had heard those deliberations; and whether, if he had not, he was qualified to pronounce as he had done, on the plans and purposes of the Almighty."[62]

When Jesus began to speak to the Jews in parables, making the interpretation known only to His disciples, the disciples asked Him, "Why speakest thou unto them in parables?" (Matthew 13:10) His answer is a strong reminder of this verse's statement, **"his secret is with the righteous."**

Matthew 13:11-13 He answered and said unto them, Because it is given unto you to know the mysteries of the kingdom of heaven, but to them it is not given. For whosoever hath, to him shall be given, and he shall have more abundance: but whosoever hath not, from him shall be taken away even that he hath. Therefore speak I to them in parables: because they seeing see not; and hearing they hear not, neither do they understand.

The born-again disciples (in Matthew 13 above) were being groomed to testify of the Gospel, which at this point had been revealed. The masses that followed Jesus were earthly and sensual, and followed Him for His healing or free food. They did not believe that He was the Savior; in fact, the religious leaders among those crowds sought to find fault with Him and to kill Him out of jealousy and hatred. Accusing Him of blasphemy, they scorned Jesus and refused to believe the truth.

Christ's disciples could not get enough of the truth. They longed to learn more about Him, and left all to follow Him. Therefore, He would tell His righteous followers the truths, ***the secrets*** of the Kingdom of Heaven. When Jesus decided to share details about unknown future events with His disciples, He made this statement in John 15:15 – "Henceforth I call you not servants; for the servant knoweth not what his lord doeth: but I have called you friends; for all things that

I have heard of my Father I have made known unto you." He was admitting His disciples to that circle of intimate friends. What an honor and a blessing! **"His secret is with the righteous."** Judas Iscariot, of course, eventually separated himself from righteousness and the Righteous One.

"The curse of the Lord is in the house of the wicked: But he blesseth the habitation the just." (verse 33) From the verses below, it can be observed in various situations that **"the curse of the Lord"** is an act of judgment by the Lord upon a recipient whereby consequences of that judgment are unfavorable. The opposite is true where God blesses, for where He blesses, as in **"the habitation of the just,"** consequences are purposefully favorable.

> Genesis 3:14 -19 And the LORD God said unto the serpent, Because thou hast done this, thou *art* cursed above all cattle, and above every beast of the field; upon thy belly shalt thou go, and dust shalt thou eat all the days of thy life: And I will put enmity between thee and the woman, and between thy seed and her seed; it shall bruise thy head, and thou shalt bruise his heel. Unto the woman he said, I will greatly multiply thy sorrow and thy conception; in sorrow thou shalt bring forth children; and thy desire *shall be* to thy husband, and he shall rule over thee. And unto Adam he said, Because thou hast hearkened unto the voice of thy wife, and hast eaten of the tree, of which I commanded thee, saying, Thou shalt not eat of it: cursed *is* the ground for thy sake; in sorrow shalt thou eat *of* it all the days of thy life; Thorns also and thistles shall it bring forth to thee; and thou shalt eat the herb of the field; In the sweat of thy face shalt thou eat bread, till thou return unto the ground; for out of it wast thou taken: for dust thou *art,* and unto dust shalt thou return.
>
> Genesis 5:29 And he called his name Noah, saying, This *same* shall comfort us concerning our work and toil of our hands, because of the ground which the LORD hath cursed.
>
> Genesis 8:21 And the LORD smelled a sweet savour; and the LORD said in his heart, I will not again curse the ground any more for man's sake; for the imagination of man's heart *is* evil from his youth; neither will I again smite any more every thing living, as I have done.
>
> Genesis 12:3 And I will bless them that bless thee *[Abram]*, and curse him that curseth thee: and in thee shall all families of the earth be blessed.
>
> Deuteronomy 28:15-19 But it shall come to pass, if thou wilt not hearken unto the voice of the LORD thy God, to observe to do all his commandments and his statutes which I command thee this day; that all these curses shall come upon thee, and overtake thee: Cursed *shalt* thou *be* in the city, and cursed *shalt* thou *be* in the field. Cursed *shall be* thy basket and thy store. Cursed *shall be* the fruit of thy body, and the fruit of thy land, the increase of thy kine, and the flocks of thy sheep. Cursed *shalt* thou *be* when thou comest in, and cursed *shalt* thou *be* when thou goest out.
>
> Isaiah 24:6 Therefore hath the curse devoured the earth, and they that dwell therein are desolate: therefore the inhabitants of the earth are burned, and few men left.
>
> Lamentations 3:65 Give them sorrow of heart, thy curse unto them.
>
> Malachi 1:14 But cursed *be* the deceiver, which hath in his flock a male, and voweth, and sacrificeth unto the Lord a corrupt thing: for I *am* a great King, saith the LORD of hosts, and my name *is* dreadful among the heathen.
>
> Malachi 2:2 If ye *[priests]* will not hear, and if ye will not lay *it* to heart, to give glory unto my name, saith the LORD of hosts, I will even send a curse upon you, and I will curse your blessings: yea, I have cursed them already, because ye do not lay *it* to heart.
>
> Malachi 4:5-6 Behold, I will send you Elijah the prophet before the coming of the great and dreadful day of the LORD: And he shall turn the heart of the fathers to the children, and the heart of the children to their fathers, lest I come and smite the earth with a curse.
>
> Matthew 25:41 Then shall he say also unto them on the left hand, Depart from me, ye cursed, into everlasting fire, prepared for the devil and his angels . . .
>
> Hebrews 6:7 For the earth which drinketh in the rain that cometh oft upon it, and bringeth forth herbs meet for them by whom it is dressed, receiveth blessing from God: But that which beareth thorns and briers *is* rejected, and *is* nigh unto cursing; whose end *is* to be burned.

Wicked people despise the presence or even the influence of God. Anywhere that God is disinvited is an invitation for trouble, even without a specific **"curse of the Lord."** Any calamities that befall a wicked head of the house will be felt by the family and household associates; hence, the wise are encouraged to distance themselves from "the wicked."

> Joshua 6:17-18 And the city *[Jericho]*   shall be accursed, *even* it, and all that *are* therein, to the LORD: only Rahab the harlot shall live, she and all that *are* with her in the house, because she hid the messengers that we sent. And ye, in any wise keep *yourselves* from the accursed thing, lest ye make *yourselves* accursed, when ye take of the accursed thing, and make the camp of Israel a curse, and trouble it.
>
> 2 Kings 10:11 So Jehu slew all that remained of the house of Ahab in Jezreel, and all his great men, and his kinsfolks, and his priests, until he left him none remaining.
>
> Zechariah 5:3-4 Then said he unto me, This *is* the curse that goeth forth over the face of the whole earth: for every one that stealeth shall be cut off *as* on this side according to it; and every one that sweareth shall be cut off *as* on that side according to it. I will bring it forth, saith the LORD of hosts, and it shall enter into the house of the thief, and into the house of him that sweareth falsely by my name: and it shall remain in the midst of his house, and shall consume it with the timber thereof and the stones thereof.

In contrast, a blessing or a pronouncement for good or for well-being will be upon a place where God is welcome and makes Himself known. The **"habitation"** may be in the field, under the stars with the sheep, or in a stable. Any **"habitation"** where the **"just"** live and where God takes up abode is better than any **"house"** or palace or mansion where He is not welcome.

Psalm 37:22-24 For *such as be* blessed of him shall inherit the earth; and *they that be* cursed of him shall be cut off. The steps of a *good* man are ordered by the LORD: and he delighteth in his way. Though he fall, he shall not be utterly cast down: for the LORD upholdeth *him with* his hand.

2 Corinthians 6:14-18 Be ye not unequally yoked together with unbelievers: for what fellowship hath righteousness with unrighteousness? and what communion hath light with darkness? And what concord hath Christ with Belial? or what part hath he that believeth with an infidel? And what agreement hath the temple of God with idols? for ye are the temple of the living God; as God hath said, I will dwell in them, and walk in *them;* and I will be their God, and they shall be my people. Wherefore come out from among them, and be ye separate, saith the Lord, and touch not the unclean *thing;* and I will receive you, And will be a Father unto you, and ye shall be my sons and daughters, saith the Lord Almighty.

"Surely he scorneth the scorners: But he giveth grace unto the lowly." (verse 34) *["Scorneth" and "scorners" are translated from the Hebrew luts which means to make mouths at, to mock, to deride.]* Although God would have all men come to Him and receive His blessings, it is obvious that the scorners, who are of the froward category of wicked men, prefer not to serve Him. Consequently, the scorners suffer, both here on earth and in eternity. All mankind have a free will to serve God or not. All those who scorn His word, His grace, His holiness, or His love, will eventually discover that He will find their whole being to be just as repugnant as they thought Him to be.

Psalm 2:1-4 Why do the heathen rage, and the people imagine a vain thing? The kings of the earth set themselves, and the rulers take counsel together, against the LORD, and against his anointed, *saying,* Let us break their bands asunder, and cast away their cords from us. He that sitteth in the heavens shall laugh: the Lord shall have them in derision.

Psalm 18:25-26 With the merciful thou wilt shew thyself merciful; with an upright man thou wilt shew thyself upright; With the pure thou wilt shew thyself pure; and with the froward thou wilt shew thyself froward.

Psalm 81:11-12 But my people would not hearken to my voice; and Israel would none of me. So I gave them up unto their own hearts' lust: *and* they walked in their own counsels.

James 4:6 But he giveth more grace. Wherefore he saith, God resisteth the proud, but giveth grace unto the humble.

1 Peter 5:5 Likewise, ye younger, submit yourselves unto the elder. Yea, all of you be subject one to another, and be clothed with humility: for God resisteth the proud, and giveth grace to the humble.

[Also see Romans 1:18-32 where scorning is not mentioned, but attitude and conduct involves scorning.]

"The wise shall inherit glory: but shame shall be the promotion of fools." (verse 35) This verse serves as a statement of conclusion to this section of Scripture (verses 27-35). **"Glory"** *[splendor, honor, dignity]* brings to mind all the marvelous teachings in the word of God concerning the exceeding beauty and radiance of heaven's assets. The "glory of God" in heaven is resplendent with thrones, untold number of saints, angels, the light of God, a street of gold, great and beautiful high walls, twelve glorious foundations, gates of pearl, and all with such splendor that the human mind cannot conceive. All of this **"glory"** is the inheritance of the wise. It will surround them and they will possess it in eternity. *(See Revelation 21-22.)*

On the other hand, **"Shame"** *[dishonor, personal disgrace]* is the **"promotion of fools."** Shame encircles them, constitutes their awful reward, and is like an ominous cloud of stink that follows them into hell. Instead of being raised up into heavenly places, they shall fall into the eternal miseries of hell.

Daniel 12:2-3 And many of them that sleep in the dust of the earth shall awake, some to everlasting life, and some to shame *and* everlasting contempt. And they that be wise shall shine as the brightness of the firmament; and they that turn many to righteousness as the stars for ever and ever.

Matthew 13:41-43 The Son of man shall send forth his angels, and they shall gather out of his kingdom all things that offend, and them which do iniquity; And shall cast them into a furnace of fire: there shall be wailing and gnashing of teeth. Then shall the righteous shine forth as the sun in the kingdom of their Father. Who hath ears to hear, let him hear.

In summary, Chapter Three has presented: (1) God's relationship with those who seek God, (2) God's relationship with those who oppose God, (3) God's responses to the wise and to the unwise; (4) God's rewards to the wise and the unwise, and (5) believers' relationships with others.

GOD'S PRECIOUS PROMISES to the believer who seeks Him with all his heart (Proverbs 3)

IF the believer will do this	God will provide this	Scripture
Keep the word of God (Law and Commandments)	Length of days, long life and peace	Proverbs 3:1-2
Make mercy and truth part of one's personal being	Good understanding and favor with God and man	Proverbs 3:3-4
Trust in the LORD with all one's heart rather than in personal understanding. Acknowledge the LORD in all ways.	Direction for one's path	Proverbs 3:5-6
Refuse to be proud with personal wisdom. Fear God. Depart from evil	Physical strength from God	Proverbs 3:7-8
Honor God with substance and with first fruits	Filling of one's storehouse with goods plus new wine (joy)	Proverbs 3:9-10
Accept God's correction	Personal Relationship with God like a father to his son	Proverbs 3:11-12
Get wisdom, knowledge and understanding	Length of days, riches, honor, life to thy soul, grace to thy neck, safety, solid walking, and peace	Proverbs 3:13-26
Don't: withhold help **or** devise evil **or** strive unnecessarily **or** envy the oppressor **or** choose any of the oppressor's ways	Grace and glory to the righteous	Proverbs 3:27-35

CHAPTER FOUR

> **Proverbs 4: 1-4** Hear, ye children, the instruction of a father, and attend to know understanding.
> 2. For I give you good doctrine, forsake ye not my law.
> 3. For I was my father's son, tender and only *beloved* in the sight of my mother.
> 4. He taught me also, and said unto me, Let thine heart retain my words: keep my commandments, and live.

"Hear *[listen to, obey]*, **ye children, the instruction of a father, and attend to know understanding."**(verse 1) Chapter Four introduces a change in the noun of direct address from the previously used **"my son"** to **"ye children."** Both are translated from the same Hebrew word, *ben*. These disciples being instructed are the next generation of believers seeking wisdom from God, and wisdom continues to be taught by Solomon through an anonymous identity known as **"a father."** (The words "hear," "ye children, " and "attend" indicate the writer is starting a new section of instruction.)

"Hear" and **"attend"** are synonyms emphasizing that the **"children"** are to pay close attention so that the instruction of wisdom can be both heard and internalized. Once this wonderful instruction is acquired, they can advance to **"understanding,"** as is indicated in verse seven – "Wisdom is the principal thing; therefore get wisdom: and with all thy getting get understanding." Children *[simple ones]* can be taught *wise directives* without fully understanding; however, as a person matures, he should develop an understanding of why he is required to act in a given manner. Biblical truths are often understood through the advantage of remembering Scripture and then applying the verses to an experience. It is then, with the application of experience to wise instruction, that "the light comes on" and understanding has been added to wisdom. In seeking to understand the challenging situations of life, wise people have a huge advantage over the unwise because of internalized wisdom that has been learned from the Scriptures and godly wise mentors.

> **The person with wisdom** has the ability,
> because of a proper relationship with God,
> to be able to navigate through the challenges and opportunities of life
> in the most effective manner
> thereby minimizing evil influences and maximizing godly outcomes.

The appeal to **"attend"** or to **"hear"** *[to pay close attention and to obey]* is also found in the following places in Proverbs:
> Proverbs 2:1-5 My son, if thou wilt receive my words, and hide my commandments with thee; So that thou incline thine ear unto wisdom, and apply thine heart to understanding; Yea, if thou criest after knowledge, and liftest up thy voice for understanding; If thou seekest her as silver, and searchest for her as for hid treasures; Then shalt thou understand the fear of the LORD, and find the knowledge of God.
> Proverbs 5:1-2 My son, attend unto my wisdom, and bow thine ear to my understanding: That thou mayest regard discretion, and that thy lips may keep knowledge.
> Proverbs 8:32-36 Now therefore hearken unto me, O ye children: for blessed are they that keep my ways. Hear instruction, and be wise, and refuse it not. Blessed is the man that heareth me, watching daily at my gates, waiting at the posts of my doors. For whoso findeth me findeth life, and shall obtain favour of the LORD. But he that sinneth against me wrongeth his own soul: all they that hate me love death.
> Proverbs 19:20 Hear counsel, and receive instruction, that thou mayest be wise in thy latter end.
> Proverbs 22:17-18 Bow down thine ear, and hear the words of the wise, and apply thine heart unto my knowledge. For it is a pleasant thing if thou keep them within thee; they shall withal be fitted in thy lips.

None of the word of God was ever intended to be read *without close attention and obedience* because it is only with intent and diligence that a person can know the mind of Christ. It is disrespectful to fail to pay close attention when being taught by a parent or elder and even more disrespectful when God gives instruction. To fail to pay close attention, *without* proper reason, is to prove that one does not have a **"fear of God,"** which is *the qualifying starting place for getting wisdom, knowledge and understanding.* In this passage the words uttered to **"ye children"** are the instructions of **"a father."** The earthly believing father serves as a mouthpiece for the heavenly Father. It is incumbent upon a child to learn to respect other people (especially elders) and, even more important, his parents. Failure to teach a child to respect others has the terrible consequence of disrespect for God, which, if not corrected, will have eternal consequences. (What a tremendous blessing and advantage to have godly parents who teach wisdom!)

"For [because] **I give you good doctrine, forsake ye not my law."** (verse 2) The tremendously valuable *gift* offered here, "good doctrine," is "not vain, or foolish, or false, or pernicious counsels; but such as are true and profitable."[63] The fact that the instruction originated from God's word (godly parents get their instruction from God) necessitates that it is **"good."** No better or greater gift can parents give their children than God's word, especially when it is *taught by example* and *with understanding*. This "good doctrine" is to be taken to heart, to be learned, and to be lived by and never forsaken.

"Forsake ye not my law *[instructions, or directions]***."** (verse 2b) Here the text presents the word **"law"** from the Hebrew word *torah* as found in the first five books of the Bible. These instructions or directions of wisdom obtained from the Scriptures are being given by **"a father."** The directive is similar to Proverbs 1:8 which states: "My son, hear the instruction of thy father, and forsake not the law of thy mother." The father has paternal authority over his children, and he loves them. He teaches God's commandments to guide them as they tread the treacherous paths of this life, and he wants only good for his children. Therefore they receive the eternal and totally accurate word of God. Not so with fools who will turn their back on the law of God in favor of this world's opposing view of what is right. To forsake this invaluable gift is indeed the epitome of foolishness that takes the fool onto an earthly pathway of life replete with disgusting, terrible, unnecessary struggles and into eternal separation from God in hell.

"For I was my father's son, tender and only *beloved* **in the sight of my mother. He taught me also, and said unto me, Let thine heart retain my words: keep my commandments, and live."** (verses 3-4) These two verses tell the reader that the parents' instruction or doctrine was not only **"good"** (verse 2), but it was given with affection and favor (**"tender and only beloved"**). These two verses provide insight into Solomon's personal life when they state that he was favored by his parents. From an early age he must have demonstrated the fact that he had great potential and that he was teachable.

> 1 Chronicles 28:5-7 And of all my sons, (for the LORD hath given me many sons), he hath chosen Solomon my son to sit upon the throne of the kingdom of the LORD over Israel. And he said unto me, Solomon thy son, he shall build my house and my courts: for I have chosen him *to be* my son, and I will be his father. Moreover I will establish his kingdom for ever, if he be constant to do my commandments and my judgments, as at this day.

"I was my father's son" (verse 3a) is a statement showing personal intimacy, relationship, two-way responsibility, and interactive love. It also illustrates the authority of the father and high expectations that he has for this one bearing the family name. This son is expected to respect his father's name and thereby have a high regard for "who he is" and "who his father is." Solomon was his most beloved son and the one chosen to succeed him on the throne.

"Tender and only *beloved* **in the sight of my mother"** (verse 3b) emphasizes the tenderness and affection given by his mother who was with him during his formative years. She teaches and admonishes him to be wise in every aspect of life. Both parents knew the importance of the early years of teaching and would not neglect to give their royal son what he needed to be successful.

> "'Only beloved.' The word *yâchîd* originally signified an "only" (son), as in Zechariah 12:10. Then it came to mean 'beloved as an only son,' and that appears to be the sense of it in Genesis 22:2, as applied to Isaac (for Ishmael was then living), and to Solomon here (for Bath-sheba had other children by David, 1Chronicles 3:5). In New Testament Greek translations it is rendered 'only-begotten' and 'well-beloved,' epithets applied in their highest sense to Christ (John 1:14; Matthew 3:17)."[64]
>
> Genesis 22:2 And he said, Take now thy son, thine only *son* Isaac, whom thou lovest, and get thee into the land of Moriah; and offer him there for a burnt offering upon one of the mountains which I will tell thee of.
>
> Matthew 3:17 And lo a voice from heaven, saying, This is my beloved Son, in whom I am well pleased.
>
> John 1:14 And the Word was made flesh, and dwelt among us, (and we beheld his glory, the glory as of the only begotten of the Father,) full of grace and truth.

In the following three verses, Solomon recalls the instruction of his father David, the king. **"He taught me also, and said unto me"** (verse 4a) emphasizes more than mere speaking. There is teaching going on here! There is eye to eye contact with all distractions being removed! The father is drawing on the fact that this is his son, not a servant or a stranger or even a friend, and because of that relationship, the child will be taught the right way. He will at least hear the words! He will pay attention to the instruction!

"Let thine heart retain my words" (verse 4b) presses home that the wise son is not to *just* retain the words as head knowledge or in passing. Because the words are given from the heart and because those words have been proven to be of extreme value, the words must be taken to heart. Proverbs 3:1 expresses the same thought: "My son, forget not my law; but let thine heart keep my commandments." Every child should be taught from the standpoint that he will mature and be on his own one day; consequently, the child must retain the teaching in order to make wise decisions from his own heart and mind. The parents won't always be there for him.

Deuteronomy 6:6 And these words, which I command thee this day, shall be in thine heart . . .

"Keep *[guard, heed]* **my commandments, and live."** (verse 4c) Wisdom expressed through the **"words"** and **"commandments"** of the parent is to be *kept* because wisdom is more valuable than anything this world offers. Wisdom offers a child (student) the possibility to **"live"** with quality and longevity. Realizing the value of Scripture, godly parents teach from the deep well of God's word. It gives instruction for a *life* of quality. Children learn, among many other things, to respect and honor God and to avoid foolish people and threatening situations. The child can truly **"live"** with quality and enjoy the great blessings of God and His wonderful creation made especially for those who adore Him and His instructions. The obedient child can also expect a longer life for the same reasons. Learning to avoid the pitfalls of life keeps stress and danger to a minimum.

Proverbs 4:5-13 Get wisdom, get understanding: forget it not; neither decline from the words of my mouth.
6. Forsake her not, and she shall preserve thee: love her, and she shall keep thee.
7. Wisdom is the principal thing; therefore get wisdom: and with all thy getting get understanding.
8. Exalt her, and she shall promote thee: she shall bring thee to honour, when thou dost embrace her.
9. She shall give to thine head an ornament of grace: a crown of glory shall she deliver to thee.
10. Hear, O my son, and receive my sayings; and the years of thy life shall be many.
11. I have taught thee in the way of wisdom; I have led thee in right paths.
12. When thou goest, thy steps shall not be straitened; and when thou runnest, thou shalt not stumble.
13. Take fast hold of instruction; let her not go: keep her; for she is thy life.

I HAVE LED THEE IN RIGHT PATHS
Outline of Proverbs 4:5-13

I. STRONG ADMONITION
    A. Get Wisdom. (verses 5 and 7)
    B. Get Understanding. (verses 5 and 7)
    C. Don't Forget it. (verse 7)
    D. Don't Decline from my Words. (verse 5)
    E. Take fast hold of instruction: Let her not go: keep her. (verse 13)

II. SURE ADVICE
    A. Wisdom is the principal thing; therefore get wisdom: and with all thy getting get understanding. (verse 7)
    B. Hear, O my son, and receive my sayings. (verse 10)
    C. I have taught thee in the way of wisdom; I have led thee in right paths. (verse 11)

III. SPECIAL ARRANGEMENTS
    A. Don't forsake her *and she will preserve thee.* (verse 6)
    B. Love her *and she shall keep thee.* (verse 6)
    C. Exalt her *and she shall promote thee.* (verse 8)
    D. Embrace her and *she shall bring thee to honor.* (verse 8)
        She shall give to thine head an ornament of grace. (verse 9)
        She shall deliver a crown of glory to thee. (verse 9)

CONCLUSION
    When thou goest, thy steps shall not be straitened. (verse 12)
    When thou runnest, thou shalt not stumble. (verse 12)
    She (WISDOM) is thy life. (verse 13)

"**Get wisdom, get** *[acquire, possess]* **understanding"**(verse 5a) is the *parental mandate*; however, whether the child actually *gets* wisdom and understanding will be up to him. Although a child can't be forced to obtain wisdom, when there is a proper bond between parents and children, as described in verse three, the child naturally desires to please them. As explained in Chapter Two, taking ownership of wisdom and understanding is to be accomplished with great personal obligation and effort. Wisdom, knowledge, and understanding will NOT come through flippancy. The wise son must and will *(because he is wise)* consider the three guides of life – **wisdom, knowledge,** and **understanding** – to have great value and realize he must seek diligently for them. It is a foolish son who rebels against such teachings.

The student/son is instructed authoritatively to acquire wisdom, knowledge, and understanding. *No mention is made of refusal or failure to obtain.* Cost is not a factor, particularly the cost of effort. Nothing is to interfere with the obtaining because wisdom's value is beyond gold, silver, or any other commodity. The emphatic instruction is to "get wisdom … get understanding!"

> Proverbs 23:23 Buy the truth, and sell it not; also wisdom, and instruction, and understanding.

"Forget it not; neither decline from the words of my mouth." (verse 5b) The father completes his teaching cycle by not only instructing *what must be done* (**"get wisdom, get understanding"**) but also by teaching what *not* to do – *don't forget and don't turn away from my instruction.* Giving this negative instruction intensifies the previously given positive aspect of procuring wisdom and understanding. The instruction on wisdom must not be forgotten.

"Forsake her not, and she shall preserve thee: love her, and she shall keep thee." (verse 6) When a child is young, parents can watch and protect him and guard him to keep evil away; but when he grows older, his own wisdom, knowledge, and understanding must protect and guide him. In verse 2, the son was told not to forsake his father's law – that is, he was not to leave or depart from it, to neglect or desert it. Now he is told not to forsake **"her,"** referring to the "wisdom" and "understanding" of verse 5. The father declares that forsaking wisdom and understanding would mean that the child would be leaving his guard, his protector. Wisdom and understanding hedge a person in to protect against dangerous people and insidious situations of life.

"Love her, and she shall keep thee." (verse 6b) Again, **"she"** refers to wisdom and understanding. To love something is to have affection for it, thereby showing priority, tenderness, and care. Wisdom and understanding are personified in this verse as though "she" has personal feelings and thereby can reciprocate by giving protection to the one who loves her – the promise of verse 6.

"Wisdom is the principal thing; therefore get wisdom: and with all thy getting get understanding." (verse 7) Getting godly wisdom is **"the principal thing"** because wisdom causes the owner to view the world the same way that God does. Additionally, it puts the recipient in agreement with God and causes him to function in the effective manner that God intended. Wisdom makes one Christlike and worthy of being called Christian.

> "Amidst all thy other acquisitions acquire this, without which all others will be useless and even hurtful. (Menochius)"[65]
> "The world's maxim . . . is – 'Money is the principal thing; therefore get money; and with all thy getting, get more.' – Fausset."[66]
> "Venture all for wisdom rather than miss it.
>   1. What we lose is transitory, what we get is durable.
>   2. What we lose is hollow and empty, what we get is full and substantial.
>   3. What We lose is vain, what we get is profitable.
>   4. What we lose is often matter of danger, what we get is matter of safety and security." – Francis Taylor[67]

"And with all thy getting, get understanding." (verse 7b) The only way to acquire wisdom and understanding is to get it from God. The word of God is the instruction book for life. In it lies wisdom and understanding. As stated in verse one, when understanding is added to wisdom, the individual: (1) has the proper reasoning from God that comprehends life's situations and understands people's actions as well as root causes for their actions, and (2) can anticipate future developments of a given situation as to whether it will turn out good or bad.

A person can act wisely because of having been taught to avoid certain people and situations and can choose to speak or avoid speaking at certain times. Children can be taught these wise directives without fully understanding. *As a person matures, he should develop an understanding of why he is acting in a given manner as directed by wisdom.*

Wisdom and understanding come from God. The **"getting"** or obtaining is up to the individual, and the "getting" comes with effort.

Proverbs 2:4-6 If thou seekest her as silver, and searchest for her as *for* hid treasures; Then shalt thou understand the fear of the LORD, and find the knowledge of God. For the LORD giveth wisdom: out of his mouth *cometh* knowledge and understanding.

"Exalt her, and she shall promote thee: she shall bring thee to honour, when thou dost embrace her." (verse 8) Lift up – exalt – make much of wisdom and wisdom will lift you up – raise you up – promote you "to honor, both with God and men; which Solomon knew by experience."[68] Some rewards gained by *exalting wisdom* are respect and confidence of others and elevation to offices of trust. When a person makes wisdom his way of thinking and acting, he becomes pleasing to God and is respected by others.

> Genesis 41:41-43 And Pharaoh said unto Joseph, See, I have set thee over all the land of Egypt. And Pharaoh took off his ring from his hand, and put it upon Joseph's hand, and arrayed him in vestures of fine linen, and put a gold chain about his neck; And he made him to ride in the second chariot which he had; and they cried before him, Bow the knee: and he made him ruler over all the land of Egypt.
>
> 1 Samuel 25:32-33 And David said to Abigail, Blessed be the LORD God of Israel, which sent thee this day to meet me: And blessed be thy advice, and blessed be thou, which hast kept me this day from coming to shed blood, and from avenging myself with mine own hand.
>
> 1 Kings 3:28 And all Israel heard of the judgment which the king had judged; and they feared the king: for they saw that the wisdom of God was in him, to do judgment.
>
> Daniel 2:47-49 The king answered unto Daniel, and said, Of a truth it is, that your God is a God of gods, and a Lord of kings, and a revealer of secrets, seeing thou couldest reveal this secret. Then the king made Daniel a great man, and gave him many great gifts, and made him ruler over the whole province of Babylon, and chief of the governors over all the wise men of Babylon. Then Daniel requested of the king, and he set Shadrach, Meshach, and Abednego, over the affairs of the province of Babylon: but Daniel sat in the gate of the king.

"She shall bring thee to honour, when thou dost embrace her." (verse 8b) **"Embrace her"** in a loving and affectionate manner, as a husband does his wife, or a son his mother."[69] In other words, draw her close; do not have her at a distance, but treat her with affection. She is precious. Through her wise direction she **"brings"** the one who *embraces her* to places where he could not go by himself, to places and positions of **"honor."**

"She shall give to thine head an ornament of grace: a crown of glory shall she deliver to thee." (verse 9) The **"ornament of grace"** and **"crown of glory"** are both *symbolic* and represent *favor* and *honor* whereby the wise person is looked on with respect and honor and dignity and is the opposite of a foolish person who is viewed with disdain, reproach, and dishonor having "egg on his face."

"Hear, O my son, and receive my sayings." (verse 10) This verse is a call very similar to verse one in that the son is to give undivided attention to the wonderful instruction. He is to do more than hear; he is to **"receive my sayings."** When one hears and receives, the teaching process is complete. Simply hearing does not constitute being taught and failing to receive the instruction can indicate anything from not having enough sleep to rebellion.

"And the years of thy life shall be many." When the instruction *has been received* and has become part of his thought process, the resulting proper actions tend to have a longer life for several reasons, including the following. *First*, when one is seeking wisdom, he will be at peace, and consequently, his "sleep will be sweet." Sleep is necessary for the body to heal and for the mind to function properly. Quick thinking and proper reasoning are huge factors in avoiding danger. *Second*, he will employ discretion to avoid "evil men" and "strange women" who have a way of degrading life physically, emotionally, and spiritually. *Third*, and most important, he will have the protection and favor of God.

> Proverbs 3:24 When thou liest down, thou shalt not be afraid: yea, thou shalt lie down, and thy sleep shall be sweet.
>
> Proverbs 2:10-12; 16 When wisdom entereth into thine heart, and knowledge is pleasant unto thy soul; Discretion shall preserve thee, understanding shall keep thee: To deliver thee from the way of the evil *man,* from the man that speaketh froward things . . . To deliver thee from the strange woman, *even* from the stranger *which* flattereth with her words . . .

"I have taught thee in the way of wisdom; I have led thee in right paths. When thou goest, thy steps shall not be straightened; and when thou runnest, thou shalt not stumble." (verses 11-12) The **"way of wisdom"** in the first clause is identified in the second as **"the right path."** It is "right" because it is the way approved by God, and it is the way taught and led by the loving, godly father who always has his children's best interest in mind. The wicked way is a dark path where many dangers lurk, and the end is eternal damnation. (The horror of being taught the wicked way by a wicked father is an awful thought!)

Teaching and **leading** are not the same, though they are supportive of each other. Giving instruction is easier than demonstrating it with one's life. Some fathers concentrate on teaching their children specific areas of development like morals or social interaction. Other fathers teach by godly wisdom from God's word and LEAD their children along the right path. If the teacher is also the demonstrative leader, as in this passage, then the student will more likely become an imitator. Sometimes fathers teach one thing with their mouths and lead another way by their actions.

>Psalm 23:3 He restoreth my soul: He leadeth me in the paths of righteousness for his name's sake.
>
>Proverbs 14:12 There is a way that seemeth right unto a man, but the end thereof are the ways of death.

"When thou goest, thy steps shall not be straitened" (verse 12 a) means that the wise son *shall not be bound* or *be constricted* while walking life's course. He will have freedom from unnecessary pressures that result in traveling the wrong roads and walking with the wrong people. He knows what is right because he is being directed by the wisdom of God rather than the mandates of the world's system. He has great freedom and liberty. Christianity does not **"straiten"** *[narrow or confine]* a person by forbidding quality of life and adventures; rather, it gives the opportunity for life at its fullest. The wise person's conscience is clean, his rest peaceful, and his mind clear; so that he sees, takes note, and avoids people and situations that would constrict his path.

>Proverbs 10:9 He that walketh uprightly walketh surely: but he that perverteth his ways shall be known.
>
>Isaiah 48:17-18 Thus saith the LORD, thy Redeemer, the Holy One of Israel; I am the LORD thy God which teacheth thee to profit, which leadeth thee by the way that thou shouldest go. O that thou hadst hearkened to my commandments! then had thy peace been as a river, and thy righteousness as the waves of the sea . . .

"And when thou runnest, thou shalt not stumble." (verse 12 b) Running provides a faster pace than taking steps and walking (**"when thou goest"**) noted in the first part of this verse. At times life requires quick responses to situations, thereby causing stumbling over objects in the pathway, like fallen limbs, holes, or large rocks. These items represent evil people or dangerous situations that have to be recognized in advance so that the runner can avoid tripping. In this verse, the figurative language tells us that a wise person will be observant concerning obstacles that will cause him problems.

>Proverbs 3:21-23 My son, let not them depart from thine eyes: keep sound wisdom and discretion: So shall they be life unto thy soul, and grace to thy neck. Then shalt thou walk in thy way safely, and thy foot shall not stumble.

"Take fast hold of instruction; let her not go: keep her; for she is thy life." (verse 13) How tightly should instruction be grasped? Imagine a young son's grasp of his father's arm as the child dangles over a cliff.

>Hebrews 2:1. Therefore we ought to give the more earnest heed to the things which we have heard, lest at any time we should let them *slip*.

"Keep her; for she is thy life." (verse 13b) Because wisdom is reasoning derived from God, the wise person's ways, thoughts, and words become that which is learned from the heavenly Father. Such instruction provides a "life" abundant, full of light, and guided by God.

A story is told of a huge wounded whale that swam close to the ship, then it swam out a great distance, and then suddenly turned to violently charge the ship. When the ship received the great force of the sudden impact, it came loose at the seams. Because it was quickly taking on water, the men began to jump ship. All seemed safe when two men suddenly returned to the sinking ship. It looked as though they were going down in the vortex of the sinking ship, but they were soon seen to surface. What was the treasure worth risking their lives for? It was the ship's compass, without which they would never have found their way home. It amounted to their life.

Similarly, wisdom, that way of thinking and reasoning that pleases God, shows the righteous traveler in this life the way to the Father and the Son. Wisdom is also a guide around the many obstacles and unnecessary problems of this earthly life. Furthermore, it teaches the pleasantness of living a contented life that is pleasing to God and good men.

>Proverbs 3:1-2 My son, forget not my law; but let thine heart keep my commandments: For length of days, and long life, and peace, shall they add to thee.
>
>Proverbs 3:16 Length of days *is* in her right hand; *and* in her left hand riches and honour.
>
>Proverbs 3:18 She *[wisdom] is* a tree of life to them that lay hold upon her; and happy *is everyone* that retaineth her.

Ultimately, all of God's wisdom points to His Son, the Lord Jesus Christ. He is the One to cling to, the manifested Word of God, the full expression of wisdom, the only way to the Father.

>John 1:4 In him was life; and the life was the light of men.
>
>John 3:36 He that believeth on the Son hath everlasting life: and he that believeth not the Son shall not see life; but the wrath of God abideth on him.
>
>John 5:24 Verily, verily, I say unto you, He that heareth my word, and believeth on him that sent me, hath everlasting life, and shall not come into condemnation; but is passed from death unto life.

John 14:6 Jesus saith unto him, I am the way, the truth, and the life: no man cometh to the Father but by me.

John 17:3 And this is life eternal, that they might know thee the only true God, and Jesus Christ, whom thou hast sent.

Galatians 2:20 I am crucified with Christ: nevertheless I live; yet not I, but Christ liveth in me: and the life which I now live in the flesh I live by the faith of the Son of God, who loved me, and gave himself for me.

1 John 5:12 He that hath the Son hath life; *and* he that hath not the Son of God hath not life.

Proverbs 4:14-19 Enter not into the path of the wicked, and go not in the way of evil *men*.
15. Avoid it, pass not by it, turn from it, and pass away.
16. For they sleep not, except they have done mischief; and their sleep is taken away, unless they cause *some* to fall.
17. For they eat the bread of wickedness, and drink the wine of violence.
18. But the path of the just *is* as the shining light, that shineth more and more unto the perfect day.
19. The way of the wicked *is* as darkness: they know not at what they stumble.

"Enter not into the path of the wicked, and go not in the way of evil *men*. Avoid it, pass not by it, turn from it, and pass away." (verses 14-15) In the Book of Proverbs, **"two paths"** is a common theme that accentuates the difference between the **"path of the wicked"** and the **"path of the just."** God gives wisdom whereby the godly person knows good from bad, right from wrong, godly from ungodly, safe from unsafe. Since he knows the difference, it is the believer's duty to avoid the wrong, evil path. It is much easier to **"avoid"** going near wickedness than it is to wash out the stain and stink from body and soul – a stink that can and often does linger for a lifetime. (What a blessing is a pure and clean conscience!)

Because sin appeals to the flesh like a magnet to iron, it can draw a person into dark places where God will not accompany him. The "son" is mandated to totally **"avoid"** the **"path of the wicked"** to **"pass not by it"** to **"turn from it and pass away."** The same instruction is given in Chapter Five concerning the adulteress.

Proverbs 5:8 Remove thy way far from her, and come not nigh the door of her house.

Ephesians 5:11 And have no fellowship with the unfruitful works of darkness, but rather reprove *them*. For it is a shame even to speak of those things which are done of them in secret.

"For they sleep not, except they have done mischief; and their sleep is taken away, unless they cause *some* to fall. For they eat the bread of wickedness, and drink the wine of violence." (verses 16-17) Notice that the word **"they"** in verse sixteen refers to the **"evil men"** of verse fourteen who are so labeled because they not only have a separate path from God but also oppose Him. They hate God, His doctrine, His ways, and His thoughts. In this passage the reader is told that these "evil men" have such a twisted mind that they are *comforted by evil*: they cannot sleep unless they have done evil. Evil provides them a sense of accomplishment and success because when **"they cause *some* to fall"** into their trap *(which was set in the darkness of sin without mercy or pity)*, they easily rob others of their valuables or their very life. Such wicked accomplishment is a sleeping pill to their wicked minds nourished *(symbolically, of course)* by **"bread of wickedness"** and **"wine of violence."**

Isaiah 5:20 Woe unto them that call evil good, and good evil; that put darkness for light, and light for darkness; that put bitter for sweet, and sweet for bitter!

"But the path of the just *is* as the shining light, that shineth more and more unto the perfect day." (verse 18) This verse continues to use figurative speech, comparing wisdom of the wise with the increasing brightness of a new day. Daybreak's light grows brighter every second until the full light of noonday is reached. Wise men begin their pathway with God in a twilight of knowledge; and continue to learn until later, in eternity, they have full understanding of God and total light of Christ.

Psalm 119:105 Thy word *is* a lamp unto my feet, and a light unto my path.

John 1:9 That is the true light, which lighteth every man that cometh into the world.

Revelation 22:5 And there shall be no night there; and they need no candle, neither light of the sun; for the Lord God giveth them light: and they shall reign for ever and ever.

"The way of the wicked *is* as darkness: they know not at what they stumble." (verse 19) *Spiritual darkness is ignorance of God.* It is the lost soul's supreme mistake. Deciding to disbelieve and reject God and His word puts one on a road (**"way"**) distanced from where the tracks of God are common. Such a way deepens the darkness over the soul of the sinner himself, blinding his eyes, distorting his vision, and confusing his perceptions. Then, sin leads to the ruin that attends darkness and ends in making the sinner blind to the true character of his own transgressions so that **"they

know not at what they stumble." Blind they are, also, to God.[70] **"The way of the wicked is as darkness"** because his mind is full of darkness. He has rejected the light proceeding from God and His Son. It is a dark path of his own choosing as he refuses to know God and lives by none of God's principles. "Wickedness puts out the eyes of the soul, and, like a blind Samson, it sits in darkness and the shadow of death . . ."[71]

"They know not at what they stumble" because they refuse the light. They had rather fall into the dangers of the damned than be lifted up into the safety of the Savior. *(Review verse 12b, page 56.)*

> Job 5:14 They meet with darkness in the daytime, and grope in the noonday as in the night.
> Job 18:5-6 Yea, the light of the wicked shall be put out, and the spark of his fire shall not shine. The light shall be dark in his tabernacle, and his candle shall be put out with him.
> Job 18:18 He shall be driven from light into darkness, and chased out of the world.
> Jeremiah 13:16 Give glory to the LORD your God, before he cause darkness, and before your feet stumble upon the dark mountains, and, while ye look for light, he turn it into the shadow of death, *and* make *it* gross darkness.
> John 12:35 Then Jesus said unto them, Yet a little while is the light with you. Walk while ye have the light, lest darkness come upon you: for he that walketh in darkness knoweth not whither he goeth.

Proverbs 4:20-22. My son, attend to my words; incline thine ear unto my sayings.
21. Let them not depart from thine eyes; keep them in the midst of thine heart.
22. For they *are* life unto those that find them, and health to all their flesh.

"My son, attend to my words; incline thine ear unto my sayings." (verse 20) Again the son is exhorted to pay close attention to these most important teachings by his loving and protective father, who is totally interested in every aspect of his life. He is the one who cares for him more than anyone else ever will, and his advice reflects the same. In Proverbs 3:1; 4:1; 5:1; 6:20-21, similar words emphasize that the student must pay very close attention to the instruction. The words of verses twenty through twenty-two are certainly more than mere suggestions, especially in view of the previous serious instructions concerning staying away from the path of wicked people.

> "The motives that call for our attention are exceedingly powerful. It is a father that speaks. The things which are spoken are of quickening and invigorating virtue. They are life to such as find them, and health not only to the soul, but to the body; not to a particular part of it, but to all flesh. A medicine effectual to the cure of a single member might soon enrich the inventor of it. Here is a medicine for all the flesh, and yet the physician that prescribes it without reward finds so few willing to make use of it that he must proclaim its virtues again and again. Here is a physician of infinite value; attend to the directions which he gives for the management of our whole life. (G. Lawson.)"[72]

"Let them not depart from thine eyes" (verse 21) reminds the believer about keeping words of wisdom constantly in view as the *guide for living*. One is to set his eyes upon them as one would a point of reference on the seashore amidst a great storm. He keeps his eyes focused there so as not to lose his way. Looking away can mean a loss of direction and potential death.

> Proverbs 3:21 My son, let not them depart from thine eyes: keep sound wisdom and discretion.
> Proverbs 2:1 My son, if thou will receive my words and hide my commandments with thee . . .

"Keep them in the midst of thine heart." (verse 21) Words of wisdom are to be kept within the innermost recesses of the heart where they can be guarded like a treasure and cherished with affection. The spirit of this instruction is found in the following two verses:[73]

> Deuteronomy 6:6 And these words which I command thee this day shall be in thine heart . . .
> Deuteronomy 6:8 And thou shalt bind them for a sign upon thine hand, and they shall be as frontlets between thine eyes.

> "These repeated injunctions are an admirable pattern to the Christian parent or minister. The desire of wisdom, the first step in the path, is encouraged. The means of obtaining, and the privilege when obtained, are pointed out. Eye, then, the treasure of wisdom habitually. A neglected Bible is the melancholy proof of a heart 'alienated from God.' For how can we have a spark of love to him, if that Book, which is the full manifestation of his glory, be despised? And yet a superficial acquaintance with it is of no avail. If our ears were bored to the doors of the sanctuary; if the words never departed from our eyes; yet, except they were *kept in the heart*, our religion would be a notion, not a principle; speculative, not practical; conviction, not love. Nor even here must they possess the mere threshold. Let the word *be kept in the midst of the heart*. Here only can it be operative; 'for out of the heart are the issues of life' (Proverbs 4:23). Here it becomes lively and substantial truth. Here, then, let a home be made for it, a consecrated sanctuary in the most honored chambers *of the heart*. This inhabitation of the word is a covenant promise – the test of our interest in the Lord."[74]

Jeremiah 31:33 But this *shall be* the covenant that I will make with the house of Israel; After those days, saith the LORD, I will put my law in their inward parts, and write it in their hearts; and will be their God, and they shall be my people. And they shall teach no more every man his neighbour, and every man his brother, saying, Know the LORD: for they shall all know me, from the least of them unto the greatest of them, saith the LORD: for I will forgive their iniquity, and I will remember their sin no more.

"For they *(words from God's wisdom)* **are life unto those that find them, and health to all their flesh."** (verse 22) There is an aspect of quality, holy living that causes one to avoid certain diseases that come from improper sexual relationships or from excessive drinking of alcohol that damages internal organs. There is also an aspect of health enriched because of peaceful, adequate sleep; and there is a greater, yea tremendous, peace of mind that comes from a close relationship with God.

Internalizing wisdom keeps the words of wisdom as frontlets before one's eyes and hidden deep within one's heart; furthermore, it creates a personal relationship with God whereby the believer's life can be said to be like Enoch as he walked with God. Being close to God brings benefits such as protection, provisions, and a personal relationship. Jesus said:

> John 10:10 "The thief cometh not, but for to steal, and to kill, and to destroy: I am come that they might have life, and that they might have *it* more abundantly."

A greater quality of life is promised to those who take to heart God's instruction.

> Proverbs 4:4 He taught me also, and said unto me, Let thine heart retain my words: keep my commandments, and live.

The word **"health"** is translated from the Hebrew *marpe,* which carries an understanding of a *cure* or *deliverance* from illness. When taken to heart, the words of God provide a **"life"** that is enhanced by the presence of God and **"health"** that responds to the healing power of God.

Proverbs 4:23-27   Keep thy heart with all diligence; for out of it *are* the issues of life.
24.   Put away from thee a froward mouth, and perverse lips put far from thee.
25.   Let thine eyes look right on, and let thine eyelids look straight before thee.
26.   Ponder the path of thy feet, and let all thy ways be established.
27.   Turn not to the right hand nor to the left: remove thy foot from evil.

Three Hearts of Proverbs 4

I.   The *Wise Heart* of righteous people that internalizes the doctrines of wisdom. (verses 1-13)
II. The *Wicked Heart* of evil people that rejects the doctrines of wisdom and walks a dark path. (verses 14-19)
III. The *Watched Heart* of righteous people that securely guards the doctrines of wisdom and controls the mouth, eyes, and feet. (verses 20-27)

The wise person is to guard his whole person, beginning with his vulnerable heart, thereby ensuring good character that reflects a person that is pleasing to God and worthy of His companionship.

"Keep thy heart with all diligence; for out of it *are* the issues of life." (verse 23) Body, soul, and spirit comprise the three parts of man, and commonly the word **"heart"** is used to represent his soul. The soul or heart also has three parts (*mind, emotions,* and *will*) whereby all the **"issues"** *(actions and communication of a person's life)* originate. With his *mind* he thinks about his actions. With his *emotions* he feels and pressures his thinking to adjust one way or another. With his *will* he determines to put his thoughts into action. The instruction is to **"keep"** the heart *[mind* (thinking)*, emotions* (feelings)*,* and *will* (determination)*]* **"with all diligence."**

> "'Thy heart.' The heart here, and in other parts of Holy Scripture, is that part of a man for whom the Bible exists, that in man to whom the revelation of God appeals, that which places a great gulf between him and all other creatures in the world, that which links him to the angels of God, that which entails upon him responsibilities and endows him with capabilities which will last throughout all the ages to come. It is that spiritual nature which our Lord calls a man's 'own soul' (Matthew 16:26), which Paul speaks of as the 'inner man' (Ephesians 3:16) . . . Keeping of the heart includes a guarding of every inlet of temptation, a watchfulness over the senses, and any organ of the outward man which might lead us into temptation. Hence Solomon exhorts his son to guard his *'eyes'* and his *'feet'* . . . There is much in the heart, both of good and evil, which entered by those gates. There are thoughts there which have been kindled by what we have seen, as Achan's covetous desires were created by the sight of the goodly spoils of Jericho. The eye of David was the entrance-gate of the thought which ended in adultery and murder. And the feet may lead us in forbidden paths – into the way of temptation – into the society of those whose words, finding entrance by the ear, may sow seeds of impurity within."[75]

The heart gives birth to those attitudes and dispositions, words, and actions that may be evil or good. All evil proceeds from the heart, therefore, the believer must guard what issues from the heart.

> Deuteronomy 4:9 Only take heed to thyself, and keep thy soul diligently, lest thou forget the things which thine eyes have seen, and lest they depart from thy heart all the days of thy life: but teach them thy sons, and thy sons' sons . . .
>
> Luke 6:44 -45 For every tree is known by his own fruit. For of thorns men do not gather figs, nor of a bramble bush gather they grapes. A good man out of the good treasure of his heart bringeth forth that which is good; and an evil man out of the evil treasure of his heart bringeth forth that which is evil: for of the abundance of the heart his mouth speaketh.

The last verses contain a command to guard one's heart, including what issues out of it through the mouth. He is to also guard what he feeds his soul with through his eyes, and he is to guard his heart by preventing his feet from carrying himself to wicked places that will pollute his heart with sin.

"Put away from thee a froward mouth, and perverse lips put far from thee." (verse 24) **"A froward mouth"** and **"perverse lips"** are synonyms: both mean *perverseness of mouth and waywardness of lips*. These are figures of speech that tell the reader about the hateful, lying, and vulgar words that come out of the fool's mouth because of the evil in his heart and remind the believer not to use such words.

> **"Perversity of mouth"** is fraudulent, deceitful speech; that which twists, distorts, perverts, or misrepresents what is true, and hence falsehood. The Book of James declares that the tongue is a most difficult member to control. (James 3:1-12) Speech is an indication of the spiritual condition of the mind. Vigilance over the heart is vigilance over the mouth, inasmuch as "out of the abundance of the heart the mouth speaketh" (Matthew 12:34).[76]
>
> Proverbs 6:12 A naughty person, a wicked man, walketh with a froward mouth.
>
> Proverbs 19:1 Better *is* the poor that walketh in his integrity, than he that is perverse in his lips, and is a fool.

Jesus stated, "I am the way, the truth, and the life: no man cometh unto the Father, but by me." Being ***truthful*** and putting away **"perverse lips"** is in this manner being like Jesus, for He is "the truth." The believer should reject froward and perverse speech: **"Put away from thee."**

> Ephesians 4:29 Let no corrupt communication proceed out of your mouth, but that which is good to the use of edifying, that it may minister grace unto the hearers.

The believer's prayer should be:

> Psalm 19:14 Let the words of my mouth, and the meditation of my heart, be acceptable in thy sight, O LORD, my strength, and my redeemer.
>
> Psalm 141:3-4 Set a watch, O LORD, before my mouth; keep the door of my lips. Incline not my heart to *any* evil thing, to practise wicked works with men that work iniquity: and let me not eat of their dainties.

"Let thine eyes look right on, and let thine eyelids look straight before thee." (verse 25) If one wishes to *keep his heart*, as directed in verse twenty-three, he must be guided by *simplicity of sight* meaning that he is not looking everywhere out of lust and greed. Seductions and temptations surround people and endanger the onward and upward progress of the soul. Evil is everywhere available, but the godly person is instructed to **"look straight before thee"** to avoid evil. The believer's goal is to love and serve God with his whole heart, and he should resist looking curiously looking around to see the evil in the world.

This passage brings to mind the **"single eye"** that is *intent on heaven and on God*. When the person is *intent on serving God* and controls his behavior accordingly, he is single-minded and has a "single eye." Thus, his heart is pure before God, and he is walking in the path God has chosen for him. He is not led away by temptations because he has his eyes on God's word and will. He is sensitive to the leadership of the Holy Spirit.

> Matthew 6:22-23 The light of the body is the eye: if therefore thine eye be single, thy whole body shall be full of light. But if thine eye be evil, thy whole body shall be full of darkness. If therefore the light that is in thee be darkness, how great is that darkness.

"Ponder the path of thy feet, and let all thy ways be established." (verse 26) The wise person will **"ponder"** (examine or prepare) the path of his feet so that he determines *if* the path he is traveling meets God's approval, *if* he is walking circumspectly (watchfully and discreetly with caution), and *if* his steps are going in the right direction based on what he knows to be right. **"Let all thy ways be established"** means to be wise and consequently pleasing to God so as to obtain His blessings and good success.[77]

> Ephesians 5:15 See then that ye walk circumspectly, not as fools, but as wise.

"Turn not to the right hand nor to the left: remove thy foot from evil." (verse 27) A recurring theme of the Book of Proverbs, this verse further explains previous instructions. Keep God's instructions in the heart and avoid the dark path of evil. If the right pathway is taken by keeping a straight and guarded walk with God, the foot will be removed from evil *before* getting to that wicked place – not afterward. Prevention is much easier than repair and less expensive in every way.

> Deuteronomy 28:14 And thou shalt not go aside from any of the words which I command thee this day, *to* the right hand, or *to* the left, to go after other gods to serve them.
>
> Joshua 23:6 Be ye therefore very courageous to keep and to do all that is written in the book of the law of Moses, that ye turn not aside therefrom *to* the right hand or *to* the left . . .
>
> Psalm 40:2-3 He brought me up also out of an horrible pit, out of the miry clay, and set my feet upon a rock, and established my goings. And he hath put a new song in my mouth, even praise unto our God: many shall see it, and fear, and shall trust in the LORD.

CHAPTER FIVE

Introduction:

As in Chapter Four, "a father" continues to give affectionate, wise counsel to his son. In this chapter, he deals with the discomforting topic – the "strange woman" – who is an adulteress. Most people and even "a father" are likely to find discussing this topic challenging, uncomfortable, and stressful, to say the least; however, the word of God tackles the most difficult subjects with boldness. Instructions in this chapter include:

(1) Avoidance of the evil adulterous woman (including a description of self-induced tragedies brought on by participating in her sins). (verses 1-14)
(2) Enjoyment of a personal, intimate relationship in marriage. (verses 15-20)
(3) Recognition of the all-seeing eye of God. (verse 21)
(4) Avoidance of the catastrophic binding penalties for the wicked who refuse instruction from wisdom. (verses 22-23)

Chapters Five through Seven issue serious warnings for failing or refusing to **"attend unto"** wisdom's instructions.

The Father Warns the Son about the Wicked Adulteress
(Outline of Chapter 5:1-14)

I. Attention of the Son is Mandatory:
   A. Bow Thine Ear to Understanding and Wisdom (verse 1)
   B. Bind This Knowledge in your heart (verses 2, 7)
   C. Bend Thy Path Away from Her (verse 8)

II. Attributes of the Adulteress are Masked by Her:
   A. Slick and Sweet Talk (verse 3)
   B. Sharp and Bitter End (verse 4)
   C. Slide to hell (verse 5)
   D. Staggering unstable ways (verse 6)

III. Admonitions of the Father against Massive Potential Loss Of:
   A. Honor (verse 9)
   B. Youthful Years (verse 9)
   C. Wealth (verse 10)
   D. Labor (verse 10)
   E. Joy (verse 11)
   F. Health (verse 11)
   G. Peace of Mind (verses 12-14)

> **Proverbs 5:1-14** My son, attend unto my wisdom, *and* bow thine ear to my understanding:
> 2. That thou mayest regard discretion, and *that* thy lips may keep knowledge.
> 3. For the lips of a strange woman drop *as* an honeycomb, and her mouth *is* smoother than oil:
> 4. But her end is bitter as wormwood, sharp as a twoedged sword.
> 5. Her feet go down to death; her steps take hold on hell.
> 6. Lest thou shouldest ponder the path of life, her ways are moveable, *that* thou canst not know *them.*
> 7. Hear me now therefore, O ye children, and depart not from the words of my mouth.
> 8. Remove thy way far from her, and come not nigh the door of her house:
> 9. Lest thou give thine honour unto others, and thy years unto the cruel:
> 10. Lest strangers be filled with thy wealth; and thy labours *be* in the house of a stranger;
> 11. And thou mourn at the last, when thy flesh and thy body are consumed,
> 12. And say, How have I hated instruction, and my heart despised reproof;
> 13. And have not obeyed the voice of my teachers, nor inclined mine ear to them that instructed me!
> 14. I was almost in all evil in the midst of the congregation and assembly.

Solomon utilizes several *identities* in the Book of Proverbs to instruct, including himself, the personified Wisdom, a father, Agur, and the mother of king Lemuel. **"My son"** is the noun of direct address used by all of the following identities: Solomon, the personified Wisdom, a father, mother of king Lemuel. (In Chapter 30, Agur does not address his students as "My son," but he is a distinct identity who provides words of wisdom.)

"My son, attend unto my wisdom." (verse 1a) This chapter begins with **"My son,"** the noun of direct address used in twenty-three verses of the Book of Proverbs. Throughout Scripture, **"my son"** often identifies a cherished relationship between a pupil and instructor. The instructor does not necessarily have to be a parent, and the "son" may not actually be an offspring, but every situation pictures a tender relationship as if a father were teaching his son. In this chapter, Solomon is teaching the student wisdom under the identity of "a father."

"Attend unto my wisdom." (verse 1b) This **"wisdom"** that the son is being urged to **"attend unto"** is *NOT* earthly wisdom but is godly. Psalm 119:9 states –"Wherewithal shall a young man cleanse his way? by taking heed thereto according to thy word." The New Testament states: "Howbeit we speak wisdom among them that are perfect: yet not the wisdom of this world, nor of the princes of this world, that come to nought: But we speak the wisdom of God in a mystery, *even* the hidden *wisdom,* which God ordained before the world unto our glory: Which none of the princes of this world knew: for had they known *it,* they would not have crucified the Lord of glory." (1 Corinthians 2:6-8)

> **Godly wisdom** gives one the ability,
> because of a proper relationship with God,
> to be able to navigate through the challenges and opportunities of life
> in the most effective manner
> thereby minimizing evil influences and maximizing godly outcomes.

"And bow thine ear" (verse 1b) is the suggested physical, or at least a symbolic mental posture, to take that will assure the father that the son is focused and attentive to his most important words of wisdom. In four other passages of the Bible, either the Lord or certain people are requested to "bow down thine ear," indicating that such symbolic posture was well understood as body language displaying focused and attentive listening. Solomon uses the phrase again when he asks the student to hear the words of the wise (Proverbs 22:17). *Notice the urgency* portrayed in the following verses, an urgency that is equally displayed in this verse.

> 2 Kings 19:16 LORD, bow down thine ear, and hear: open, LORD, thine eyes, and see: and hear the words of Sennacherib, which hath sent him to reproach the living God.
>
> Psalm 31:2 Bow down thine ear to me; deliver me speedily: be thou my strong rock, for an house of defence to save me.
>
> Psalm 86:1 A Prayer of David. Bow down thine ear, O LORD, hear me: for I am poor and needy.
>
> Proverbs 22:17 Bow down thine ear, and hear the words of the wise, and apply thine heart unto my knowledge.

"**To my understanding**" is stated by the teacher to make the student aware that his teacher of wisdom comprehensively knows what he is teaching. The wise student will consequently make sure he attends to every word. As previously quoted by Albert Barnes, "understanding" includes the power of distinguishing right from wrong and truth from falsehood.[78] Failure to receive this instruction, this understanding, from wisdom can result in physical, financial, and family disasters, as well as loss of honor as described in verses eight through eleven.

>Proverbs 1:5 A wise *man* will hear, and increase learning; and a man of understanding shall attain unto wise counsels.
>
>Proverbs 1:22 . . . and fools hate knowledge.
>
>Proverbs 1:28-30 Then shall they call upon me, but I will not answer; they shall seek me early, but they shall not find me; For that they hated knowledge, and did not choose the fear of the LORD: They would none of my counsel: they despised all my reproof.

"**That thou mayest regard discretion.**" (verse 2a) Solomon's FIRST REASON for his exhortation to "attend unto my wisdom, and bow thine ear to my understanding" is to develop a capacity to "**regard** *[heed]* **discretion.**" Discretion gives a wise individual the ability to proceed cautiously to guard against being misled. A person must learn to evaluate the words and actions of people and situations so that he can take the godly path of wisdom rather than the path of a fool. In so doing, he will gain discretion, a product of wisdom. *The wise youth who **regards discretion** will develop a plan to AVOID the evil man and the adulterous woman.* He *will PLAN NOT TO LISTEN to their ploys and LOOK FOR AN AVENUE OF ESCAPE from their presence.* Chapter Two taught the reader that "discretion" is the wise person's first line of defense to protect himself against "evil men" and "strange women." *[See Chapters Two and Four for a detailed discussion.]*

In the Book of Proverbs, "discretion" will cause a wise person to evaluate the circumstance that he is encountering and formulate a plan for how to best act. "Discretion" cannot be had until one first has wisdom; hence, the reader has been instructed in verse one to **attend unto wisdom and bow down thine ear to my understanding**. The wise person will "regard discretion," meaning that he is obliged *to pay close attention to and guard* that arsenal of excellent thinking that is developed from wisdom. Because he has wisdom, knowledge, and understanding, the wise person has the potential to not only act properly but also speak appropriately. "Discretion" is that drink of good sense drawn out of the well of wisdom, and it will cause the wise person to make sober, sane, and safe decisions – such as to stay away from a harlot or an evil man.

"**And that thy lips may keep knowledge.**" (verse 2b) "**Lips**" in this sentence is used as a synecdoche *(a figure of speech in which a part of the body represents the entire person)*. Without direction from the brain, a lip doesn't have the ability to form words in and of itself. Speech reveals the quality and kind of knowledge (including attitudes) that have been placed in the mind of a person. The "lips" of the wise son in verse two are contrasted with the "lips" of the "strange" ungodly woman in verse three. Her way of thinking and acting is evil, and she likes being evil. *In contrast,* the lips of a wise person reveal that he or she has studied to learn from God and that such knowledge has been cultivated and developed into a way of thinking that reveals godliness through speech. In this SECOND REASON to listen carefully, the student of wisdom is urged to "**regard discretion**" and to "**keep knowledge**" meaning that *he is to hedge in, to protect, to guard that knowledge of righteousness that produces wise speech and godly actions*. Retained righteous information is more precious than gold, and it contributes to speech that is highly favored by God.

>Proverbs 15:2 The tongue of the wise useth knowledge aright: but the mouth of fools poureth out foolishness.
>
>Proverbs 15:7 The lips of the wise disperse knowledge: but the heart of the foolish *doeth* not so.
>
>Proverbs 16:23 The heart of the wise teacheth his mouth, and addeth learning to his lips.
>
>Proverbs 20:15 There is gold, and a multitude of rubies: but the lips of knowledge *are* a precious jewel.

"**For the lips of a strange woman drop *as* an honeycomb.**" (verse 3a) The phrase "strange woman" appeared first in Chapter 2:16 – " To deliver thee from the strange woman, even from the stranger which flattereth with her words."

> **NOTE:** The "lips" of the father *speak* wisdom and understanding, the "lips" of the son *keep* godly knowledge, and the "lips" of the strange woman are *steeped in* flattery and hypocrisy. Forty-two verses in the Book of Proverbs alone describe the type of speech the wise student should listen for in order to separate and discern the difference between the wise and the foolish. And many of these verses tell what the lips of the wise person are supposed to speak. Thus, the wise believer is warned to listen to the words of others and discreetly evaluate them.

The **"strange woman"** *[translated from the Hebrew word zur]* in this text is one who has "turned aside" or away from her honorable place as a loyal wife and friend and companion to become dishonorable, disloyal, and an enemy of righteousness. She is "One that is not thy own, whether Jewess or heathen."[79] She is an adulteress who entices her victims to their ultimate destruction of body and soul as described in Proverbs Chapters Five, Six, and Seven.

Her **"lips ... drop as an honeycomb"** and **"her mouth is smoother than oil"** (verse 3) are two descriptive clauses that describe the sweetest and smoothest substances in ancient Israel[80] (honeycomb and oil) and thus illustrate the extremely deceptive conversation of the "strange woman." She allures her victim with flattering and enticing, sweet, slick speech. Proverbs 7:5 states that she "flattereth with her words," and an example of those words are as follows.

> Proverbs 7:14-20 *I have* peace offerings with me; this day have I payed my vows. Therefore came I forth to meet thee, diligently to seek thy face, and I have found thee. I have decked my bed with coverings of tapestry, with carved *works,* with fine linen of Egypt. I have perfumed my bed with myrrh, aloes, and cinnamon. Come, let us take our fill of love until the morning: let us solace ourselves with loves. For the goodman *is* not at home, he is gone a long journey: He hath taken a bag of money with him, *and* will come home at the day appointed.

Her lying hypocrisy is appalling but typical of "strange women." In Chapter 7:14, the reader also learns she had been to the temple and had hypocritically given a sacrifice to God in gratitude for His blessings. Portions of such sacrifices were taken home by the offerer. Since they had no refrigerator, the offerer had to consume the leftovers quickly – a situation that usually mandated a feast. The strange woman *says* she is looking for just the right person to share the dinner. Notice how she covers her lewd sexual sin and behavior with a mask of righteousness and devotion to God. The simple youth believes her smooth, sweet words and is convinced that he is special. He is deceived because he wants her more than he wants the truth.

As honey is sweet and attractive to the taste, so in a higher degree are her words pleasant to the senses.[81] Song of Solomon uses the same words in a proper and good sense in the context of marriage.

> Song of Solomon 4:11 Thy lips, O my spouse, drop as a honeycomb

"But her end is bitter as wormwood, sharp as a two edged sword." (verse 4) Because illicit love is full of potential bitterness, wormwood is a fitting emblem for the final dose of poison (figuratively speaking) that she so artfully administers. Wormwood is "something as excessive in its bitterness as honey is in its sweetness."[82] "The pleasures of fleshly lust are very tempting (like the wine that *gives its colour in the cup* and *moves itself aright*); its mouth, the kisses of its mouth, the words of its mouth, are *smoother than oil,* that the poisonous pill may go down glibly and there may be no suspicion of harm in it."[83] The opening descriptive figures of speech **"drop as a honeycomb,"** and **"smoother than oil"** (verse 3) are a shocking contrast to verse four's *bitter end is like "wormwood sharp as a "two-edged sword."* The contrast between her enticements and her **"end"** should be enough to startle the mind of a youth dazzled by a beautiful adulteress.

Her seduction leads him along a path to death where the end is more bitter than the beginning was sweet. After a short pleasure follows extended pain whereby the victim's health, strength, estate, and credibility are left as wreckage. His conscience is no longer clear, his spirit no longer free. Like a double-edged sword that cuts both going and coming, the "strange woman" has wounded body, soul, and spirit. "The physical and moral suffering of the deluded profligate are notoriously terrible."[84]

It should be apparent that honey-dripping speech is a common method of entrapment, and the wise person should be alert and avoid people and situations that flatter. Flattery is a lie that uses untruthful, insincere compliments or praise. David described the deceptive, flattering words of his friend as "drawn swords" *(ready to kill)*.

> Psalm 55:21 *The words* of his mouth were smoother than butter, but war *was* in his heart: his words were softer than oil, yet *were* they drawn swords.

"Her feet go down to death; her steps take hold on hell." (verse 5) God's grave warning is this: To become involved with this woman, whether casually or otherwise, is like entering a ramp that leads onto the road of destruction. There can be no doubt of this fact. "First, the death of the body; and then the damnation of the soul. These are the tendencies of connections with such women."[85]

> Ecclesiastes 7:26 And I find more bitter than death the woman, whose heart *is* snares and nets, *and* her hands *as* bands: whoso pleaseth God shall escape from her; but the sinner shall be taken by her.

"Lest thou shouldest ponder the path of life, her ways are moveable, *that* thou canst not know *them.*" (verse 6) **"Lest"** *["for fear that"⁸⁶]* one should **"ponder"** *[weigh in his mind]* the danger he can reap from the adulterer's **"path of life,"** she tricks him by staying on the move, by constantly changing her **"path,"** thus, preventing him from fully seeing the awful danger of association with her. Wisdom would have him know that "**her ways are movable** *[staggering or unstable]* **that thou canst not know them."** *Her actions are unpredictable and are anything but constant and faithful.* Her ways are subject to change because she lives a crooked, vile life of deception. Dishonesty drives her. There is no stability with her. It is no surprise to the wise person that ultimately her shifty tracks will find their way to death and hell. She keeps on the move, always hiding her true wicked self *lest she become known* for all her wicked, malicious trickery. She hides her bitter end and the hell that she is headed toward.

"Hear me now therefore, O ye children, and depart not from the words of my mouth." (verse 7) Wisdom repeatedly (Chapters 1, 4,5,8,19,22, and 23) gives instructions *to listen*, *to attend*, and to **"hear"** what is being said. It is easily observed that only those who want wisdom will **"bow thine ear"** so as not only to hear the words but take them to heart. The instruction given in conjunction with **"hear me now"** is to **"depart not from"** the teacher's words of wisdom. The noun of direct address changes in this verse from "my son" to "ye children," giving the implication that the student(s) (no matter his/their age) should just simply receive the words of wisdom, as would a child with childlike faith.

"Remove thy way far from her, and come not nigh the door of her house." (verse 8) Without a doubt, the young man is told to stay far away from the adulteress and not to even go *near the door* of her house because of the danger of giving in to her lying flattery, devious lifestyle, and obvious temptations. A young drug addict once told his preacher, "Whenever I get close to people doing cocaine, the association is like a whirlpool and just sucks me under." The same is true with the adulterous woman. Getting too close will suck many under her sway and power.

> 1Corinthians 6:18 Flee fornication. Every sin that a man doeth is without the body; but he that committeth fornication sinneth against his own body.

"Lest thou give thine honour unto others, and thy years unto the cruel." (verse 9) When a young man associates himself with an adulterous woman, he loses that imposing appearance, that grandeur of respect that attends right doing. He loses his **"honour."** He gives up respectability in favor of this immoral association. He is viewed as a man who lacks wisdom and who has no control of himself; thus, his youthful strength is bartered for weakness.

Involvement with the wicked adulteress places an individual on that meandering path where **"the cruel"** *[the merciless one, destitute of pity]* ambushes the young man who is "void of understanding." Although the adulteress pretends love, she has no concern for her victims. She will enjoy her sexual fling until she tires of him and casts him off for another. She is "cruel" and will gleefully receive "thy years" (meaning those beautiful, youthful years of great strength) to her greedy advantage. For example, Delilah had no conscience about taking money from Israel's enemies to take advantage of her lover (Samson) and to turn him over to be cruelly blinded, humiliated, and abused by the Philistines.

> Judges 16:19-21 And she made him sleep upon her knees; and she called for a man, and she caused him to shave off the seven locks of his head; and she began to afflict him, and his strength went from him. And she said, The Philistines *be* upon thee, Samson. And he awoke out of his sleep, and said, I will go out as at other times before, and shake myself. And he wist not that the LORD was departed from him. But the Philistines took him, and put out his eyes, and brought him down to Gaza, and bound him with fetters of brass; and he did grind in the prison house.
>
> Proverbs 6:26 For by means of a whorish woman *a man is brought* to a piece of bread: and the adulteress will hunt for the precious life.
>
> Proverbs 29:3 Whoso loveth wisdom rejoiceth his father: but he that keepeth company with harlots spendeth *his* substance.
>
> "Failure to keep away from the adulteress can result in many losses: loss of strength (which may mean losing one's health, self-respect, or both), loss of a long life (Proverbs 5:9), loss of money (Proverbs 6:26; 29:3) - by paying the adulteress, paying her husband, or paying child support - and loss of health (Proverbs 5:11).⁸⁷

"Lest strangers be filled with thy wealth; and thy labours *be* in the house of a stranger." (verse 10) God gives a person power to get "wealth," but an adulterous woman can snatch it away. She can rob a young man of his honor so that he won't be suitable for any work that requires honor (such as a judge) – or her husband can require more than the foolish young man can pay – or she can require hush money. The "strange woman" selfishly uses up her victims, but wisdom provides for those who seek her.

> Deuteronomy 8:18 But thou shalt remembers the LORD thy God: for it is he that giveth thee power to get wealth . . .
>
> Proverbs 3:16 Length of days is in her *[wisdom's]* right hand; and in her left hand riches and honour.
>
> Proverbs 8:18 Riches and honour are with me *[wisdom]*; yea, durable riches and righteousness.

"And thou mourn at the last, when thy flesh and thy body are consumed." (verse 11) After the flower of youth has passed, when age takes its toll and the man taken in by the **"strange woman"** meditates on his spent life, he will **"mourn"** (growl or moan) within his unwise self. He will realize that he spent his best years – when his flesh was unwrinkled, and his muscles, bones, and heart were strong – playing the part of a fool. For those who contracted a sexually transmitted disease from their foolish actions, their flesh and body will have suffered from the infection.

> "The mourning here spoken of is of the most excessive kind: the word *naham* is often applied to the growling of a lion, and the hoarse incessant murmuring of the sea. In the line of my duty, I have been often called to attend the death-bed of such persons, where groans and shrieks were incessant through the jaculating pains in their bones and flesh. Whoever has witnessed a closing scene like this will at once perceive with what force and propriety the wise man speaks."[88]
>
> **And thou mourn at the last** . . . "expressing great distress of mind, horror of conscience, and vehement lamentations; and yet not having and exercising true repentance, but declaring a worldly sorrow, which worketh death. This mourning is too late, and not so much on account of the evil of sin as the evil that comes by it; it is when the man could have no pleasure from it and in it; when he has not only lost his substance by it, but his health also, the loss of both which must be very distressing: it is at the end of life, in his last days; in his old age . . . when he can no longer pursue his unclean practices."[89]

"At the last" is a thought-provoking phrase used in the Book of Proverbs to emphasize the end results of two very attractive sins. Drunkenness and wild partying with friends, like the encounter with the adulterous, seems so enjoyable and happy at the time. However, Proverbs 23:32 describes the end of the partying – "At the last it biteth like the serpent and stingeth like the adder." The participant in either of these sins thinks he is living a wonderful life, but the end results are bitterness and suffering.

"And say, How have I hated instruction, and my heart despised reproof *[chastisement, figuratively by words]*; **And have not obeyed the voice of my teachers, nor inclined mine ear to them that instructed me!"** (verses 12-13) Thirteen times in the Book of Proverbs Solomon mentions **"reproof."** Reproof comes from the Scripture and from godly counselors and instructors. Wise people are glad to receive reproof so that they can improve, but fools hate to be corrected and will not receive such.

> Proverbs 1:23 Turn you at my reproof: behold, I will pour out my spirit unto you, I will make known my words unto you.
>
> Proverbs 1:25-27 But ye have set at nought all my counsel, and would none of my reproof: I *[personified Wisdom]* also will laugh at your calamity; I will mock when your fear cometh; When your fear cometh as desolation, and your destruction cometh as a whirlwind; when distress and anguish cometh upon you. *[See also verses 29-30.]*
>
> Proverbs 10:17 He is in the way of life that keepeth instruction: but he that refuseth reproof erreth.
>
> Proverbs 12:1 Whoso loveth instruction loveth knowledge: but he that hateth reproof is brutish.
>
> Proverbs 13:18 Poverty and shame shall be to him that refuseth instruction: but he that regardeth reproof shall be honoured.
>
> Proverbs 15:5 A fool despiseth his father's instruction: but he that regardeth reproof is prudent.
>
> Proverbs 15:10 Correction is grievous unto him that forsaketh the way: and he that hateth reproof shall die.
>
> Proverbs 15:31-32 The ear that heareth the reproof of life abideth among the wise. He that refuseth instruction despiseth his own soul: but he that heareth reproof getteth understanding.
>
> Proverbs 17:10 A reproof entereth more into a wise man than an hundred stripes into a fool.
>
> Proverbs 29:15 The rod and reproof give wisdom: but a child left to himself bringeth his mother to shame.
>
> 2 Timothy 3:16-17 All scripture is given by inspiration of God, and is profitable for doctrine, for reproof, for correction, for instruction in righteousness: That the man of God may be perfect, throughly furnished unto all good works.

"Falling prey to lust also brings remorse when a person recognizes too late that he did not heed his parents' (here called **"teachers"**) instructions which inevitably leads to ruin and disgrace before others."[90] Verses 12-14 reflect hypothetical words of a conscience-stricken young man who fell prey to the adulteress because he *hated instruction* and *refused to obey the voice of his teachers.* He deeply regrets that *he would not so much as pay attention (incline his ear)* when they were trying to help him and prevent grievous sorrow from overwhelming him.

"I was almost in all evil in the midst of the congregation and assembly." (verse 14) **"Almost in all evil"** indicates that the lust had such a grip on him that he would have done almost any kind of wickedness and not been restrained *even* **"in the midst of the congregation and assembly"** or among the worshipers of Jehovah. Evil had begun in his heart through his lusting after the adulteress. It progressed to the level that his soul had been taken captive by evil – to the point of unconcern for penalties of the Law as given in Leviticus and Deuteronomy.

> Leviticus 20:10 And the man that committeth adultery with *another* man's wife, *even he* that committeth adultery with his neighbour's wife, the adulterer and the adulteress shall surely be put to death.
>
> Deuteronomy 22:22 If a man be found lying with a woman married to an husband, then they shall both of them die, *both* the man that lay with the woman, and the woman: so shalt thou put away evil from Israel.

If he had progressed beyond the point of **"almost"** being given over to *every form of evil,* he would have been subject to death under Mosaic law. The public scandal of his sin would be the final step of the young man's progression down the dark path to destruction.

> **Chapter 5:15-19**   Drink waters out of thine own cistern, and running waters out of thine own well.
> 16.   Let thy fountains be dispersed abroad, *and* rivers of waters in the streets.
> 17.   Let them be only thine own, and not strangers' with thee.
> 18.   Let thy fountain be blessed: and rejoice with the wife of thy youth.
> 19.   *Let her be as* the loving hind and pleasant roe; let her breasts satisfy thee at all times; and be thou ravished always with her love.

"Drink waters out of thine own cistern, and running waters out of thine own well." (verse 15) Individual households were responsible for maintaining a pure source of water for the family by digging their **"own well"** and maintaining their **"own cistern."** Verses fifteen through eighteen form an allegory whereby the purity of water and the sources of pure water are symbolic of a virtuous and dedicated wife.

> 2Kings 18:31 Hearken not to Hezekiah: for thus saith the king of Assyria, Make *an agreement* with me by a present, and come out to me, and *then* eat ye every man of his own vine, and every one of his fig tree, and drink ye every one the waters of his cistern ...

In verse 15, the **"cistern"** and **"well"** symbolize the wife who is to be valued in the same vitally important way that the source of water would be valued for its life-giving qualities. She is the one who gives birth to, feeds, clothes, and cares for the family – the one who teaches the children, who helps her husband at every turn, and who lives her life for the Lord and teaches the children to do the same. The faithful and pure wife is *presented as a contrast to* **the adulterous woman**, who represents a corrupted stream and muddy cistern, potentially bringing poor health and even death.

> Proverbs 23:27-28 For a whore *is* a deep ditch; and a strange woman *is* a narrow pit. She also lieth in wait as for a prey, and increaseth the transgressors among men.
> Proverbs 9:16-18 Whoso *is* simple, let him turn in hither: and *as for* him that wanteth understanding, she saith to him, Stolen waters are sweet, and bread *eaten* in secret is pleasant. But he knoweth not that the dead *are* there; *and that* her guests *are* in the depths of hell.

As every man formerly had his own cistern to collect water for his own use, so every man should have his own wife.[91] The instruction to the husband is to be faithful to his pure and true wife.

> Ecclesiastes 9:9 Live joyfully with the wife whom thou lovest all the days of the life of thy vanity, which he hath given thee under the sun, all the days of thy vanity: for that *is* thy portion in *this* life, and in thy labour which thou takest under the sun.

> **Other Scriptural Relationships associated with Pure Water**
>
> *Concerning spiritual adultery* observe the following passage.
>
> > Jeremiah 2:13 For my people have committed two evils; they have forsaken me the fountain of living waters, and hewed them out cisterns, broken cisterns, that can hold no water.
>
> *Concerning the purity of the relationship with Jesus* observe the following conversation that took place between Jesus and the adulteress in John Chapter Four.
>
> > John 4:10-14   Jesus answered and said unto her, If thou knewest the gift of God, and who it is that saith to thee, Give me to drink; thou wouldest have asked of him, and he would have given thee living water. The woman saith unto him, Sir, thou hast nothing to draw with, and the well is deep: from whence then hast thou that living water? Art thou greater than our father Jacob, which gave us the well, and drank thereof himself, and his children, and his cattle? Jesus answered and said unto her, Whosoever drinketh of this water shall thirst again: But whosoever drinketh of the water that I shall give him shall never thirst; but the water that I shall give him shall be in him a well of water springing up into everlasting life.

"Let thy fountains be dispersed abroad, *and* rivers of waters in the streets." (verse 16) "The figurative language is continued; and under the terms **'fountains'** and **'rivers of waters'** are to be understood children, the legitimate issue of lawful marriage."[92] *(See passages below.)* The children of a pure marriage grow up to engage in honorable chaste marriages. In this manner, they are "dispersed abroad" to become fountains to others and public blessings like "rivers of waters in the street."

> Deuteronomy 33:28 Israel then shall dwell in safety alone: the fountain of Jacob *shall be* upon a land of corn and wine; also his heavens shall drop down dew.
> Psalm 68:26 Bless ye God in the congregations, *even* the Lord, from the fountain of Israel. There *is* little Benjamin *with* their ruler, the princes of Judah *and* their council, the princes of Zebulun, *and* the princes of Naphtali.

"Let them be only thine own, and not strangers' with thee." (verse 17) **"Them"** refers to the children of verse sixteen. This verse means that the children should be only the father's, and they certainly would be his in a pure marriage where the husband and wife are faithful to each other. **"And not strangers"** would refer to the uncertainty of not knowing who is the father of an adulterous woman's offspring.[93]

"Let thy fountain be blessed: and rejoice with the wife of thy youth." (verse 18) **"Fountain"** in this verse is the source of water and thereby refers to the wife. The wife is **"blessed"** when God allows her to become a mother. Having children was considered a blessing in Israel, but being barren indicated God was withholding His blessings.

"Rejoice with thy wife." The gleeful, cheerful, making merry, and joy of this verse is explained in detail with the acts of lovemaking described in verses nineteen and twenty. His delight should be in her and her alone throughout all their years together.

"Let her be as* the loving hind** *[female deer]* **and pleasant roe** *[female mountain goat]."** (verse 19a) Let the wife be "as amiable and delightful as the hinds are to princes and great men, who used to make them tame and familiar, and to take great delight in them, as has been observed by many writers *[other than Scripture]*."[94] The faithful wife is to *delight* the faithful husband.

> Psalm 18:33 He maketh my feet like hinds' *feet,* and setteth me upon my high places.
> Song of Solomon 2:9 My beloved is like a roe or a young hart: behold, he standeth behind our wall, he looketh forth at the windows, shewing himself through the lattice.
> Song of Solomon 2:17 Until the day break, and the shadows flee away, turn, my beloved, and be thou like a roe or a young hart upon the mountains of Bether.
> Song of Solomon 7:3 Thy two breasts *are* like two young roes *that are* twins.
> Song of Solomon 8:14 Make haste, my beloved, and be thou like to a roe or to a young hart upon the mountains of spices.

"Let her breasts satisfy thee at all times" (verse 19b) refers to "her loves and embraces, expressed by lying between the breasts."[95]

> Song of Solomon 1:13 A bundle of myrrh *is* my wellbeloved unto me; he shall lie all night betwixt my breasts.
> Ezekiel 23:3 And they committed whoredoms in Egypt; they committed whoredoms in their youth: there were their breasts pressed, and there they bruised the teats of their virginity.
> Ezekiel 23:8 Neither left she her whoredoms *brought* from Egypt: for in her youth they lay with her, and they bruised the breasts of her virginity, and poured their whoredom upon her.

"And be thou ravished always with her love." (verse 19c) "That is let it intoxicate thee. The teacher, by a bold figure, describes the entire fascination which the husband is to allow the wife to exercise over him."[96] "Love her fervently."[97]

> **Chapter 5:20-23**   And why wilt thou, my son, be ravished with a strange woman, and embrace the bosom of a stranger?
> 21.   For the ways of man *are* before the eyes of the LORD, and he pondereth all his goings.
> 22.   His own iniquities shall take the wicked himself, and he shall be holden with the cords of his sins
> 23.   He shall die without instruction; and in the greatness of his folly he shall go astray.

"And why wilt thou, my son, be ravished with a strange woman, and embrace the bosom of a stranger? For the ways of man *are* before the eyes of the LORD, and he pondereth all his goings." (verses 20-21)   With a well-placed rhetorical question, Solomon calls for wisdom to prevail. The son must remember that God sees and considers every action. (verse 21) Nothing escapes Him.

2Chronicles 16:9 For the eyes of the LORD run to and fro throughout the whole earth, to shew himself strong in the behalf of *them* whose heart *is* perfect toward him. Herein thou hast done foolishly: therefore from henceforth thou shalt have wars.

Job 34:21 For his eyes *are* upon the ways of man, and he seeth all his goings.

Proverbs 15:3 The eyes of the LORD *are* in every place, beholding the evil and the good.

Jeremiah 16:17 For mine eyes *are* upon all their ways: they are not hid from my face, neither is their iniquity hid from mine eyes.

Hebrews 4:13 Neither is there any creature that is not manifest in his sight: but all things *are* naked and opened unto the eyes of him with whom we have to do. *[See also Psalm 139:1-12.]*

When a person is adequately informed *and then deliberately* ignores the danger, he puts his foolishness on display. Wise men listen to God's warnings and act accordingly. The wise man is blessed to know that God is observing his words, thoughts, and deeds.

"His own iniquities shall take the wicked himself, and he shall be holden with the cords of his sins." (verse 22) Using the metaphor **"cords of his sins,"** this proverb speaks figuratively to describe the awful impact of sin on the sinner. Though the sins are not actually physical cords, the spiritual result is the same. Sin ensnares the sinner and binds him, and leads him to death. God sees even the act of adultery committed in secret and judges the hidden sin.

> "Most people who follow unlawful pleasures, think they can give them up whenever they please; but sin repeated becomes customary; custom soon engenders habit; and habit in the end assumes the form of necessity; the man becomes bound with his own cords, and so is led captive by the devil at his will."[98]

Proverbs 11:5-6 The righteousness of the perfect shall direct his way: but the wicked shall fall by his own wickedness. The righteousness of the upright shall deliver them: but transgressors shall be taken in *their own* naughtiness.

Proverbs 29:6 In the transgression of an evil man *there is* a snare: but the righteous doth sing and rejoice.

Ecclesiastes 12:14 For God shall bring every work into judgment, with every secret thing, whether *it be* good, or whether *it be* evil.

In verses nine through twelve, five miserable conditions are attached to the unrepentant adulterer and are like **"cords of his sins:"**

(1) Shame (verse 9) – for he has surrendered his honor;
(2) Loss of wealth (verse 10) – for strangers now possess his wealth and the fruit of his labors;
(3) Illness (verse 11) – as his flesh and body are consumed;
(4) Mental disturbance (verses 12-14, 21) – for everyone knows of his sins, especially God; and
(5) Remorse (though not specifically named in these verses) follows sooner in this life or later when he stands before God. He has lost peace of mind.

"He shall die without instruction" (verse 23) – not because instruction was not given, but because it was not received. He would not "attend unto" instruction when it is given. He has sold himself to sensual desire, which has blocked his gate of reasoning. In a figurative manner of speaking, wisdom stands outside, rejected and despised. Having preferred and chosen unrighteousness over wisdom, "the wicked" will consequently die without instruction in the company of fools. He exposed himself to endless torments for indulging in fleeting pleasures of sinful lusts.

Psalm 14:1 The fool hath said in his heart, *There is* no God. They are corrupt, they have done abominable works, *there is* none that doeth good.

Proverbs 1:7 The fear of the LORD *is* the beginning of knowledge: *but* fools despise wisdom and instruction.

Proverbs 1:22 How long, ye simple ones, will ye love simplicity? and the scorners delight in their scorning, and fools hate knowledge?

Proverbs 1:29-31 For that they hated knowledge, and did not choose the fear of the LORD: They would none of my counsel: they despised all my reproof. Therefore shall they eat of the fruit of their own way, and be filled with their own devices.

"And in the greatness of his folly he shall go astray." (verse 23b) *The Ancient Hebrew Lexicon of the Bible* states that "folly" means to be without wisdom.[99] Although yielding to sexual lust is sinful "folly," there are other foolish acts, all of which are laden with sin. They start small and swell to become ***greatness of folly.*** Foolish conduct never ends well, always taking its owner "astray" to a path separate from God and His goodness and where sin, like a roaring lion, pounces upon him.

> "A climax is reached in the manner in which the end of the adulterer is portrayed. His end is without a gleam of hope or satisfaction. With an understanding darkened and rendered callous by unrestrained indulgence in lust, and by folly which has reached its utmost limits and cannot, as it were, be surpassed, in that it has persistently and willfully set aside and scorned wisdom and true happiness, the adulterer, like the drunkard, who is oblivious of the danger before him, shall stagger to ruin."[100]

CHAPTER SIX

INTRODUCTION:

Instructions concerning *different types of bindings* join Chapters Five, Six, and Seven. In Chapter Five, the reader is instructed that sins are like cords that bind – especially the sin of adultery (5:22). Chapter Six takes up the thought of being bound or snared with unwise decisions like being surety (6:2). In verses twenty and twenty-one, the reader is instructed about a helpful binding, not with cords, but with the commandments of his father and laws of his mother that were learned from God and passed to him. This binding about the neck is not a confinement but more like a golden necklace representing the principles of wisdom. Wisdom will keep the wise man from being ensnared by bad decisions, evil men, and strange women. Chapter Seven continues with teachings stating that protection from the adulteress comes from binding the commandments about the fingers and writing them upon the heart (7:3). To be obedient to God's commandments and to thus dwell under His protection is the safest and most secure place on earth.

> Proverbs 5:22 His own iniquities shall take the wicked himself, and he shall be holden with the cords of his sins.
> Proverbs 6:2 Thou art snared with the words of thy mouth, thou art taken with the words of thy mouth.
> Proverbs 6:20-21 My son, keep thy father's commandment, and forsake not the law of thy mother. Bind them continually upon thine heart, *and* tie them about thy neck.
> Proverbs 7:2-3 Keep my commandments, and live; and my law as the apple of thine eye. Bind them upon thy fingers, write them upon the table of thine heart.

Proverbs 6:1-5 My son, if thou be surety for thy friend, *if* thou hast stricken thy hand with a stranger,
2. Thou art snared with the words of thy mouth, thou art taken with the words of thy mouth.
3. Do this now, my son, and deliver thyself, when thou art come into the hand of thy friend; go, humble thyself, and make sure thy friend.
4. Give not sleep to thine eyes, nor slumber to thine eyelids.
5. Deliver thyself as a roe from the hand *of the hunter,* and as a bird from the hand of the fowler.

NOTE: "**My son**" is translated from the Hebrew word *ben* and is used as an affectionate term for a child, a student, a follower, or a disciple, and it can refer to a believer in God. *Ben* is used four thousand, nine hundred two times in the Bible; and has been translated as "son" and also as "children." (It is translated "ye children" in Proverbs 4:1; 5:7; 7:24; and 8:32.) *Ben* means "the house continues" and is a description of the one who continues the house (family line) into the next generation. The house to be continued in the Book of Proverbs is the house of *faith in God*. Those being addressed as "my son" or "ye children" are those who will believe in God, keep His word, and trust in His promises. The seed being carried forward is the seed of faith, not the seed of humanity.

"**My son, if thou be surety for thy friend,**" *(verse 1a)* To be surety for another person (**"friend"**) is to declare that **"if"** the friend can't repay the money, then the one being *cosigner* or **"surety"** will pay. **"Surety"** is translated from the Hebrew word *'arab,* meaning *intermix.* When a person cosigns for another, he mingles his finances with the finances of another person who does not have the financial strength to obtain credit or stand good for a loan. The cosigner mingles his financial ability with the financial inability of the person making the loan – think of diluting a milkshake with water.

"***If*** **thou hast stricken thy hand with a stranger.**" *(verse 1b)* This ***striking hands*** is the physical act of committing to becoming a cosigner. We would call it "shaking hands." Here in the second part of the verse, the reader is provided with the additional information that the person loaning the money is a **"stranger."** "Stranger" as used in this context means that he is not a Jew. "The usurers in Israel, who lent money to others for their necessary occasions, upon condition of paying use for it, were either heathens, or were reputed as bad as heathens, because this practice was forbidden by God's law."[101]

Deuteronomy 23:19-20 Thou shalt not lend upon usury to thy brother; usury of money, usury of victuals, usury of any thing that is lent upon usury: Unto a stranger *[nokiry - meaning foreign]* thou mayest lend upon usury; but unto thy brother thou shalt not lend upon usury: that the LORD thy God may bless thee in all that thou settest thine hand to in the land whither thou goest to possess it. *["Usury" is figuratively oppressing someone with the charging of interest.]*

"Thou art snared with the words of thy mouth, thou art taken with the words of thy mouth." (verse 2) **"Thou art snared"** and **"thou art taken"** give shocking understanding to the cosigner that he is trapped into and bound by an agreement that has the potential to be financially disastrous should the **"friend"** not be able to pay. When he lays down to sleep, the cosigner will probably bolt up in the middle of the night, saying to himself, "What have I done?" His thoughts may become consumed with the possible disaster that looms over his head, and he can not reason properly about other important matters. His peace of mind is threatened, and his financial strength is weakened. He has positioned himself outside God's guidelines by participating in a financial arrangement that is threatening to his personal finances and his walk with God. For a Hebrew to borrow from anyone charging interest, was outside the scope of God's intended blessings for His people.

"Do this now, my son, and deliver thyself, when thou art come into the hand of thy friend; go, humble thyself, and make sure thy friend. Give not sleep to thine eyes, nor slumber to thine eyelids. Deliver thyself as a roe from the hand *of the hunter,* and as a bird from the hand of the fowler." (verses 3-5) The urgency expressed to the cosigner (surety) is to **"deliver thyself"** from the trap. The entrapment is compared with the capture of a mountain goat or a bird that is securely in **"the hand of the hunter"** or the **"fowler."** The cosigner is warned not to waste time sleeping, but to **"deliver thyself"** as soon as possible. In going to the **"friend"** quickly and humbly, the cosigner may be able to keep his friend and convince him that he should immediately return the money to the money lender (the usurer, the investor who made the loan), or possibly give something in collateral so as to release him from the obligation and return his freedom of mind and money. **"Make sure"** indicates that he needs to beg, plead, or use boisterous persuasion to disentangle himself from the unwise arrangement.

> **Proverbs 6:6-11** Go to the ant, thou sluggard; consider her ways, and be wise:
> 7. Which having no guide, overseer, or ruler,
> 8. Provideth her meat in the summer, *and* gathereth her food in the harvest.
> 9. How long wilt thou sleep, O sluggard? when wilt thou arise out of thy sleep?
> 10. Yet a little sleep, a little slumber, a little folding of the hands to sleep:
> 11. So shall thy poverty come as one that travelleth, and thy want as an armed man.

"Go to the ant, thou sluggard; consider her ways, and be wise: Which having no guide, overseer, or ruler, provideth her meat in the summer, and gathereth her food in the harvest." The ant has no overseer, yet she diligently searches for her food in the summer and during the harvest. The ant is fully prepared for winter, having energetically placed food in storage. *The sluggard is admonished to consider the ways of the ant* **"and be wise."** In other words watch the work ethic of the ant and learn from her.

> "What evidence of the degradation of the fall, that 'man, created in the image of God' and made wiser than the creation (Genesis 1:26, Job 35:11), should be sent, as here, to this insignificant school for instruction! The ant, having no guide to direct her work, no overseer to inspect her, or ruler to call her to account; yet gathers with diligent foresight the summer and harvest store for her winter need. Let the sluggard consider her ways, and be wise. He sleeps over his work, and, if for a moment half-startled by some rousing call, still pleads for a little more sleep, and folds his hands to sleep. Present ease is all he calculates on, all he provides for. The future he carefully keeps out of sight, to be provided for, like the present, when it comes. Thus life runs to waste. Poverty comes step by step as one that travels, and like an armed man, with irresistible violence."[102]
>
> Job 35:10-11 But none saith, Where *is* God my maker, who giveth songs in the night; Who teacheth us more than the beasts of the earth, and maketh us wiser than the fowls of heaven?

In the verses below, *the sluggard is contrasted with the upright, he*: will go hungry, irritates everyone that has any dealings with him, covets but won't work *(a complaining victim mentality),* is too lazy to eat, will be reduced to begging, will lose even the field or equipment that could make money for him because he won't work, thinks he is right (wise in his own conceit) in not working and makes up stories to avoid work. He has no understanding of the physical or spiritual consequences that his laziness is producing. What an unsavory character!

Proverbs 10:26 As vinegar to the teeth, and as smoke to the eyes, so is the sluggard to them that send him.

Proverbs 13:4 The soul of the sluggard desireth, and hath nothing: but the soul of the diligent shall be made fat.

Proverbs 15:19 The way of the slothful man is as an hedge of thorns: but the way of the righteous is made plain.

Proverbs 19:15 Slothfulness casteth into a deep sleep; and an idle soul shall suffer hunger.

Proverbs 19:24 A slothful man hideth his hand in his bosom, and will not so much as bring it to his mouth again.

Proverbs 20:4 The sluggard will not plow by reason of the cold; therefore shall he beg in harvest, and have nothing.

Proverbs 21:25-6 The desire of the slothful killeth him; for his hands refuse to labour. He coveteth greedily all the day long: but the righteous giveth and spareth not.

Proverbs 24:30-34 I went by the field of the slothful, and by the vineyard of the man void of understanding; And, lo, it was all grown over with thorns, and nettles had covered the face thereof, and the stone wall thereof was broken down. Then I saw, and considered it well: I looked upon it, and received instruction. Yet a little sleep, a little slumber, a little folding of the hands to sleep: So shall thy poverty come as one that travelleth; and thy want as an armed man.

Proverbs 26:13 The slothful man saith, There is a lion in the way; a lion is in the streets.

Proverbs 26:14-16 As the door turneth upon his hinges, so doth the slothful upon his bed. The slothful hideth his hand in his bosom; it grieveth him to bring it again to his mouth. The sluggard is wiser in his own conceit than seven men that can render a reason.

The spiritual sluggard is just as bad. He sleeps away opportunities of grace, takes his salvation for granted, hopes to harvest the rich blessings of God from fields where he has not worked, and disregards his guides (conscience, Scripture, ministers). Faith without work is a slumbering delusion. Slothfulness is not an infirmity but rather a sin that spreads its power over the entire person. It should be resisted in all forms.[103]

"How long wilt thou sleep, O sluggard? when wilt thou arise out of thy sleep?" Totally unlike the ant who works day and night, as described above, to store provisions, the sluggard is obviously a person who would rather stay in bed than diligently earn a living.

"How long then wilt thou sleep, O Sluggard?" – is God's solemn declaration of disapproval and plea for change. The sluggard's sleep is not the refreshing kind enjoyed after a hard day's work; but is rather like the X-ray technician's lead vest that seems to get heavier and heavier. It is the slumber of death–physically and spiritually. 'Awake, thou that sleepest, and Christ shall give thee light' (Ephesians 5:14). The call is ignored and the spell grows stronger, as resistance is delayed. Every day's slumber makes it more improbable, and leaves doubt that the sluggard will ever awaken. The intended struggle of tomorrow is a delusion. A thousand such tomorrows there may be; and yet the sluggard is found at last perishing in *poverty*, and the King of terror *will come as an armed man* to summon him to judgment.

But how one is made to feel that from this deep slumber no voice but Omnipotence can rouse! Enter *the sluggard's* chamber; put aside his curtain; hang over his bed; sound a solemn cry in his ears – *How long?* endeavour even to open his eyelids to the light of day; and yet the spell is too strong for man. He shifts his posture, murmurs his cry – a little more sleep – and slumbers again."[104]

"Yet a little sleep, a little slumber, a little folding of the hands to sleep." (verse 10) Sleep and even drowsiness will cause poverty to sneak up on a foolish man. At first he enjoys a little sleep, and then a little more, and a little more. Lying flat on the back with hands clasped across his belly is a common posture for him. The ant works hard to get in its supplies, but the sluggard begs for more sleep.

"So shall thy poverty come as one that travelleth, and thy want *[poverty, need]* **as an armed man."** (verse 11) This verse presents a word picture to best describe the sluggard's threatening situation. **"Poverty"** is personified as being like a potential predator who threatens the sluggard's wealth and well-being. Poverty is depicted as: (1) the *traveler,* who is "the thief in the night," appearing suddenly to steal and destroy, and (2) the **'armed man'** (man carrying a weapon) appearing with the added threat of a weapon to do the same. Slothfulness is a sure way to **"poverty"** and **"want,"** which convey the idea of utter destitution that is both certain and irresistible. *Poverty,* the personified traveler, will come to the sluggard with determination, swiftness, and precision, making every step count to reach his destination at the appropriate time. Because the sluggard is impoverished, he succumbs to his unfulfilled wants as irresistibly and helplessly as if such want were an armed man pouncing unexpectedly on him. On such an occasion, there is no defense against poverty, no remedy, no other alternative.[105]

Note: **"Want"** and **"poverty"** are synonyms, as are **"one that travelleth"** and **"an armed man."** Using these two pair of synonyms heightens the strength of the verse.

In verses 12-15, the wise instructor introduces another area of concern that the wise student must recognize and avoid: the *froward deceitful person* who is continually thinking up evil and stirring up strife. Notice the similarity of this wicked man's characteristics to those traits that are an abomination to God in verses 16-19.

> **Proverbs 6:12-15** A naughty person, a wicked man, walketh with a froward mouth.
> 13. He winketh with his eyes, he speaketh with his feet, he teacheth with his fingers;
> 14. Frowardness *is* in his heart, he deviseth mischief continually; he soweth discord.
> 15. Therefore shall his calamity come suddenly; suddenly shall he be broken without remedy.

In the 21st century, **"naughty"** has evolved to mean a child who misbehaves in a silly way; however, the original Hebrew meaning as used in this verse, referred to an evil, ungodly person, a man of Belial, a man who was not to be trusted. Because of his look, his gestures, and his speech, the "naughty" person is discoverable; and the wise are warned to identify him. Solomon begins his warning about this person by giving general terms of his nature and character. The first and foremost identifying feature is that he ***walks*** or lives through willful and intentional lies. He has a ***froward mouth.*** "His whole life and conduct are marked by craftiness, deceit, perversion, misrepresentation, and an utter want of truth. *Walking* is here, as elsewhere in Scripture, used of some particular course of conduct."[106] His *froward mouth* is within itself "a world of iniquity."

> James 3:6 And the tongue *is* a fire, a world of iniquity: so is the tongue among our members, that it defileth the whole body, and setteth on fire the course of nature; and it is set on fire of hell.

His *heart* is a "laboratory of evil."[107]

> Matthew 15:18-19 But those things which proceed out of the mouth come forth from the heart; and they defile the man. For out of the heart proceed evil thoughts, murders, adulteries, fornications, thefts, false witness, blasphemies . . .

"He winketh with his eyes, he speaketh with his feet, he teacheth with his fingers." (verse 13) At least sixty percent of all communication is nonverbal. Body language overpowers spoken language so that a person may say "yes" verbally, but his body language says "no." In other words, the "yes" was a lie clarified (often unintentionally) with gestures. The wicked man's *eyes, feet, and fingers* are all "instruments of unrighteousness unto sin." People speak with their entire body in various ways, and the wicked man is no exception. The wise man learns to pay attention to "everything" that is being "said" (verbally and nonverbally). Then he (the wise man) must become established on the right path by predetermining to avoid wicked people.

> Romans 6:13-14 Neither yield ye your members *as* instruments of unrighteousness unto sin: but yield yourselves unto God, as those that are alive from the dead, and your members *as* instruments of righteousness unto God. For sin shall not have dominion over you: for ye are not under the law, but under grace.

"Frowardness *is* in his heart *[mind, emotions, and will]*, **he deviseth mischief continually; he soweth discord."** (verse 14) Here ("in his heart") is the restless *devising of mischief, sowing of discord*, instead of righteousness, and love. Such a wicked person brings on himself his own ruin, *suddenly and without remedy.*[108]

> "Devising mischief is a step beyond the doing of it as opportunities may present themselves. It implies the setting of the wits to work in inventing and studying plans of evil and the means of carrying them into effect. Of similar characters it is said by the Psalmist, 'He deviseth mischief upon his bed' – devises by night, and executes by day."[109]

> "He deviseth mischief continually; against his neighbours, and especially against good men; he is continually planning schemes, contriving methods, ways, and means, how to disturb, distress, and ruin men; being a true child of Belial, or of the devil, his heart is the forge where he is continually framing wickedness in one shape or another; and the ground which he is always ploughing up and labouring at to bring forth sin and wickedness, and with which it is fruitful."[110]

A froward person causes discord in the family, in the community, in the country, and even in the assembly of believers. Later in this chapter (verse 19), there is a declaration that God hates and finds abominable "he that soweth discord among the brethren."

"Therefore shall his calamity come suddenly; suddenly shall he be broken without remedy." (verse 15) This catastrophic retribution to the "wicked man" is pictured as being totally destructive like the shattered fragments of a potter's vessel, which are impossible to reunite – **"broken without remedy."** *[Notice Isaiah's poetic description of such calamity in the Scriptures below.]* So, for the froward man whose life has been one of fraud, deceit, and malice, there is coming a sudden and unrecoverable end. The language is graphic and specific causing the wise to understand and avoid not only his walk but also his wreck.

> Proverbs 29:1 He, that being often reproved hardeneth *his* neck, shall suddenly be destroyed, and that without remedy.

> Isaiah 30:12-14 Wherefore thus saith the Holy One of Israel, Because ye despise this word, and trust in oppression and perverseness, and stay thereon: Therefore this iniquity shall be to you as a breach ready to fall, swelling out in a high wall, whose breaking cometh suddenly at an instant. And he shall break it as the breaking of the potters' vessel that is broken in pieces; he shall not spare: so that there shall not be found in the bursting of it a sherd to take fire from the hearth, or to take water *withal* out of the pit.

> **Proverbs 6:16-19** These six *things* doth the LORD hate: yea, seven *are* an abomination unto him:
> 17. A proud look, a lying tongue, and hands that shed innocent blood,
> 18. An heart that deviseth wicked imaginations, feet that be swift in running to mischief,
> 19. A false witness *that* speaketh lies, and he that soweth discord among brethren.

> **"Abomination"** is translated from the Hebrew word *to'ebah*, which means something morally disgusting. In some passages, "abomination" is connected with idolatry. But it is never used in this sense in the Proverbs. Note that 12 of the 20 verses below state something that is "abomination to the LORD."
>
> Proverbs 3:32   For the froward *is* abomination to the LORD . . .
> Proverbs 6:16   These six *things* doth the LORD hate: yea, seven *are* an abomination unto him . . .
> Proverbs 8:7   . . . wickedness *is* an abomination to my lips.
> Proverbs 11:1   A false balance *is* abomination to the LORD . . .
> Proverbs 11:20   They that are of a froward heart *are* abomination to the LORD . . .
> Proverbs 12:22   Lying lips *are* abomination to the LORD . . .
> Proverbs 13:19   . . . *it is* abomination to fools to depart from evil.
> Proverbs 15:8   The sacrifice of the wicked *is* an abomination to the LORD . . .
> Proverbs 15:9   The way of the wicked *is* an abomination unto the LORD . . .
> Proverbs 15:26   The thoughts of the wicked *are* an abomination to the LORD . . .
> Proverbs 16:5   Every one *that is* proud in heart *is* an abomination to the LORD . . .
> Proverbs 16:12   *It is* an abomination to kings to commit wickedness . . .
> Proverbs 17:15   He that justifieth the wicked, and he that condemneth the just, even they both *are* abomination to the LORD.
> Proverbs 20:10   Divers weights, *and* divers measures, both of them *are* alike abomination to the LORD.
> Proverbs 20:23   Divers weights *are* an abomination unto the LORD . . .
> Proverbs 21:27   The sacrifice of the wicked *is* abomination: how much more, *when* he bringeth it with a wicked mind?
> Proverbs 24:9   . . . the scorner *is* an abomination to men.
> Proverbs 26:25   When he speaketh fair, believe him not: for *there are* seven abominations in his heart.
> Proverbs 28:9   He that turneth away his ear from hearing the law, even his prayer *shall be* abomination.
> Proverbs 29:27   An unjust man *is* an abomination to the just: and *he that is* upright in the way *is* abomination to the wicked.

The strong descriptive language of verse 16 identifying God's attitude toward specific wicked behavior should encourage any spiritually sensitive person to: (1) ensure that *none* of these character traits belong to him and (2) avoid any association with a person exhibiting these characteristics. Verse 19 specifically names two categories of people that are abominable to God: the "false witness" and "he that soweth discord."

From head to foot, the evil man utilizes members of his body to disrupt the peace and comfort of other people. Each of his hateful aspects toward other persons is abominable to God. The wicked person has no respect or regard for God or other men.

> 1 John 4:20   If a man say, I love God, and hateth his brother, he is a liar: for he that loveth not his brother whom he hath seen, how can he love God whom he hath not seen?

Besides the wink in his **"eyes"** that speaks of deception (verse 13), he exhibits a **"proud look."** His **"froward mouth"** houses a **"lying tongue"** as he is **"a false witness that speaketh lies."** He has **"hands that shed innocent blood"** with **"fingers that teach"** his treachery. All of his actions reveal that **"frowardness is in his heart,"** which **"deviseth wicked imaginations."** He has **"feet that be swift in running to mischief,"** and all the while, **"he soweth discord."** Should a single person exhibit all these characteristics, he would indeed be evil from head to foot.

> Romans 6:19-20   I speak after the manner of men because of the infirmity of your flesh: for as ye have yielded your members servants to uncleanness and to iniquity unto iniquity; even so now yield your members servants to righteousness unto holiness. For when ye were the servants of sin, ye were free from righteousness. *[See also examples in Genesis 6:5; Psalm 10:7-9; 35:19-21; 36:1-4; Proverbs 10:10 and Isaiah 3:16.]*

> "The whole structure and arrangement of the thoughts which occur in verses 16-19 clearly show that this is not an independent section, but one closely allied to that which has just preceded. The object is to show that those evil qualities of deceit and malice which are disastrous to man are equally odious in the sight of Jehovah, and consequently within the scope of the Divine displeasure."[111]

> NOTE: A Hebrew literary mode of writing identified as *graded numerical sequence* (such as "these six things doeth the LORD hate: yea, seven . . .") is used effectively in verses 16-19 to express the summary of God's disgust with the wicked person.

Known for charity and for a loving, forgiving spirit, the Christian is instructed "to think on" (reckon, take inventory of) "whatsoever things are lovely, of good report" (Philippians 4:8); but, at the same time, he must be able to recognize evil characteristics of a wicked individual. Sin is disgusting in the sight of God and should be disgusting in the sight of every Christian. Notice the believer's attitude toward sin in the following verses.

> Psalm 119:113 SAMECH. I hate *vain* thoughts: but thy law do I love.
>
> Psalm 119:163 I hate and abhor lying: *but* thy law do I love.
>
> Proverbs 8:13 The fear of the LORD *is* to hate evil: pride, and arrogancy, and the evil way, and the froward mouth, do I hate.

Seven specific sins regarding abuse and hatred of others are mentioned in verses 16-19, but these certainly do not comprise every sinful action of man that God despises. The hatefulness of these and other sins to God should be its greatest condemnation, not only because God will punish it, but because it separates the individual from the love of God.[112]

> **Proverbs 6:20-35** My son, keep thy father's commandment, and forsake not the law of thy mother:
> 21. Bind them continually upon thine heart, *and* tie them about thy neck.
> 22. When thou goest, it shall lead thee; when thou sleepest, it shall keep thee; and *when* thou awakest, it shall talk with thee.
> 23. For the commandment *is* a lamp; and the law *is* light; and reproofs of instruction *are* the way of life:
> 24. To keep thee from the evil woman, from the flattery of the tongue of a strange woman.
> 25. Lust not after her beauty in thine heart; neither let her take thee with her eyelids.
> 26. For by means of a whorish woman *a man is brought* to a piece of bread: and the adulteress will hunt for the precious life.
> 27. Can a man take fire in his bosom, and his clothes not be burned?
> 28. Can one go upon hot coals, and his feet not be burned?
> 29. So he that goeth in to his neighbour's wife; whosoever toucheth her shall not be innocent.
> 30. *Men* do not despise a thief, if he steal to satisfy his soul when he is hungry;
> 31. But *if* he be found, he shall restore sevenfold; he shall give all the substance of his house.
> 32. *But* whoso committeth adultery with a woman lacketh understanding: he *that* doeth it destroyeth his own soul.
> 33. A wound and dishonour shall he get; and his reproach shall not be wiped away.
> 34. For jealousy *is* the rage of a man: therefore he will not spare in the day of vengeance.
> 35. He will not regard any ransom; neither will he rest content, though thou givest many gifts.

Outline of Verses 20-35

I. **Instruction (commandments and law) provides quality life:**
   A. Tenaciously hold to it. (verse 20)
   B. Own it. (verse 21)
   C. Outwardly express it. (verse 21)
   D. Walk with it. (verse 22)
   E. Sleep with it. (verse 22)
   F. Listen to it. (verse 22)
   G. See and be led by it. (verse 23)
   H. Make life corrections by it. (verse 23)
   I. Restrict relationships by it. (verse 24)

II. **The adulteress hunts for her prey, so beware that:**
   A. Her beauty is betraying. (verse 25)
   B. She batters one's wealth. (verse 26)
   C. She baits for one's life. (verse 26)

III. **The adulterer faces certain destruction that is as sure as:**
   A. Taking fire into one's bosom will burn one's clothes. (verse 27)
   B. Walking on hot coals will burn one's feet. (verse 28)

IV. **The adulterer lacks understanding because adultery will:**
   A. Wound him. (verse 33)
   B. Bring dishonor. (verse 33)
   C. Bring permanent reproach. (verse 33)

V. **The husband of the adulteress will not be appeased.**
   A. He will rage with jealousy. (verse 34)
   B. He will not spare in the day of vengeance. (verse 34)
   C. He will not regard ransom. (verse 35)
   D. He will not be bought off with gifts. (verse 35)

"My son, keep thy father's commandment, and forsake not the law of thy mother." (verse 20) Notice the similarity between verse 20 and Proverbs 1:8-9: "My son, hear the instruction of thy father, and forsake not the law of thy mother: For they *shall be* an ornament of grace unto thy head, and chains about thy neck."

> "The authority of parental instruction is again enforced. God never intended young people to be independent of their parents. Instruction from every quarter is valuable. But from parents – always supposing them to be godly parents – it is the ordinance of God. They will bring you God's word, not their own."[113]

To retain the ***commandment of one's father*** and the ***law of one's mother*** meant for their teachings to be internalized, not just given a courtesy listening. The "son" is not to allow any other teaching to uproot or dislodge or replace those wise instructions of his father and mother. The understanding is that the father and mother are teaching the words given by God and that they are godly parents.

"Bind them continually upon thine heart." (verse 21a) The picture given here is that the "son" receives the words and secures them to his "heart," which represents that part of thinking that couples the intellect with the emotion and will. The instruction will then be not only known but also felt. When this happens, parental instruction will have become part of the "son's" active thinking and reasoning. The truths imparted by the godly parents will accompany him day and night.

"*And* tie them about thy neck." (verse 21b) When these Biblical teachings can be observed in the life of an individual, in his every decision, and in the principles that guide his life, the person is visibly obeying what he has learned. In other words, when the "father's commandment" and "law of thy mother" are internalized, the result will be evident in the communication and conduct of the child. Obedient behavior brings the child dignity, honor, and respect from family, friends, and acquaintances. His life reflects the godly teachings of his parents, and their teachings are as apparent as an ornament of grace around his head and decorative chains about his neck. Proverbs 1:9 repeats this illustration – "For they *shall* be an ornament of grace unto thy head, and chains about thy neck."

"When thou goest, it *[commandment; law]* shall lead thee; when thou sleepest, it shall keep thee; and *when* thou awakest, it shall talk with thee. For the commandment *is* a lamp; and the law *is* light; and reproofs of instruction *are* the way of life." (verses 22-23) Teachings of the word of God which are passed on to the "son" by his parents lead his life, give him peaceful sleep, and speak through his conscience to cause him to make right decisions. These teachings always show the right way to please God and avoid evil. Should he deviate into a evil, dark path, the doctrine will instruct him and draw him back to the way of life. A light or lamp shows the individual where to go and how to walk safely in the dark. Deuteronomy 6:6-9 contains the commandment behind these verses.

> Deuteronomy 6:6-9 And these words, which I command thee this day, shall be in thine heart: And thou shalt teach them diligently unto thy children, and shalt talk of them when thou sittest in thine house, and when thou walkest by the way, and when thou liest down, and when thou risest up. And thou shalt bind them for a sign upon thine hand, and they shall be as frontlets between thine eyes. And thou shalt write them upon the posts of thy house, and on thy gates.

> "Therefore *bind it continually about thine heart*, as thy rule; *about thy neck*, as thine adorning. Let the law be thy friend for all times and circumstances – a guide by day; a solace by night, yea – a friend for thy *waking* moments. Take care that nothing hinders thy early converse with this faithful counselor before the world comes in; as the best means of keeping the world out. 'Happy is the mind to which the word is an undivided companion.' A *lamp*, so full of *light*, in this dark world is an inestimable gift. Its reproofs of instruction, the discipline of our wayward will, are to us as *the way of life*."[114]

> 1 Timothy 3:16-17 All scripture *is* given by inspiration of God, and *is* profitable for doctrine, for reproof, for correction, for instruction in righteousness: That the man of God may be perfect, throughly furnished unto all good works. *[See also Deuteronomy 11:18-19 ; Psalm 119:11, 115-116; 139: 17-18; Proverbs 3:3-4, 21-26, 4:12 and 7:2-3.]*

"To keep thee from the evil woman, from the flattery of the tongue of a strange woman." (verse 24) Having been instructed in the Scriptures by his father and mother, the "son" will know the truth about the evil adulteress. He will recognize the way of righteousness; so that he is aware of the dangers associated with such a person. He knows to stay away from "the evil woman," knowing that she is devious in every respect. Even her words of praise are lies.

"Lust not after her beauty in thine heart." (verse 25a) The admonition is a warning to repress the very first inclinations to unchaste desires. Sin originates in the heart of man. This coveting another man's wife "may be unobserved and undetected by others, but they are known to ourselves, and the first duty of repressing them calls for an act of determination and will on our part."[115] Jesus taught the following:

> Matthew 5:28 But I say unto you, That whosoever looketh on a woman to lust after her hath committed adultery with her already in his heart.

According to Proverbs 31:30, "beauty is vain." It will not last past the ravages of sickness, turmoil, or time. Better to find a wife who fears the Lord and stay with her.

"Neither let her take thee with her eyelids." (verse 25b) History records that it was a custom to seductively paint the eyelids,[116] which was likely to draw attention to her amorous, seductive glances toward her victim. The adulteress **"takes"** (captures) the foolish youth with her flattering tongue and her eyes that let him know she is wanton and willing.

> Genesis 39:7 And it came to pass after these things, that his master's wife cast her eyes upon Joseph; and she said, Lie with me.
> Isaiah 3:16 Moreover the LORD saith, Because the daughters of Zion are haughty, and walk with stretched forth necks and wanton eyes, walking and mincing as they go, and making a tinkling with their feet . . .
> 2 Peter 2:13-14 And shall receive the reward of unrighteousness, as they that count it pleasure to riot in the day time. Spots *they are* and blemishes, sporting themselves with their own deceivings while they feast with you; Having eyes full of adultery, and that cannot cease from sin; beguiling unstable souls: an heart they have exercised with covetous practices; cursed children . . .

"For by means of a whorish woman *a man is brought* to a piece of bread: and the adulteress will hunt for the precious life." (verse 26) Used to express that the value of something is nearly worthless, "a piece of bread" is properly "a circle of bread, a small round piece of bread, such as is still baked in Italy and in the East, here an expression for the smallest piece (Fleischer)."[117] *(See the use of this figure of speech in these additional verses below.)*

> 1 Samuel 2:36 And it shall come to pass, *that* every one that is left in thine house shall come *and* crouch to him for a piece of silver and a morsel of bread, and shall say, Put me, I pray thee, into one of the priests' offices, that I may eat a piece of bread.
> Proverbs 28:21 To have respect of persons *is* not good: for for a piece of bread *that* man will transgress.

To be **"*brought* to a piece of bread"** is expressive of extreme poverty and want to which the harlot reduces a man as she heartlessly strips him of all his substance and then sends him to get his bread as best he can. Thus, having spent his substance in riotous living with harlots, the prodigal was so reduced as to desire the husks which swine ate (Luke 15:13-16). Similarly, spiritual fornication or idolatry, leaves men without bread for their souls, brings them into spiritual poverty, and some even to desperation and death.

"The adulteress will hunt for the precious life" (verse 26b) because she is, by Webster's definition, a **predator**– "one that preys, destroys, or devours."[118] She is secretive and lurks hidden when she is on the hunt. Using flattery, she seduces the unwary youth. When she catches her prey, she will destroy his **"precious** *[valuable and honorable]* **life,"** bringing him down to dishonor and near worthlessness as Delilah did to Samson, and as Potiphar's wife would have done to Joseph, except for his strength of character and the providence of God.

> Genesis 39:18-20 And it came to pass, as I lifted up my voice and cried, that he left his garment with me, and fled out. And it came to pass, when his master heard the words of his wife, which she spake unto him, saying, After this manner did thy servant to me; that his wrath was kindled. And Joseph's master took him, and put him into the prison, a place where the king's prisoners were bound: and he was there in the prison.
> Judges 16:18 And when Delilah saw that he had told her all his heart, she sent and called for the lords of the Philistines, saying, Come up this once, for he hath shewed me all his heart. Then the lords of the Philistines came up unto her, and brought money in their hand.

Scripture is very frank in calling the adulteress a **"whorish woman,"** which means that she has all the character of a prostitute or a low-moral woman. She may be from an impoverished neighborhood, the street, or even a wealthy and high place; but her character is a warning to the youth to stay away from her.

"Can a man take fire in his bosom, and his clothes not be burned? Can one go upon hot coals, and his feet not be burned? So he that goeth in to his neighbour's wife; whosoever toucheth her shall not be innocent." (verses 27-29) Using two rhetorical questions ("Can a man take fire in his bosom, and his clothes not be burned? Can one go upon hot coals, and his feet not be burned?"), the Bible makes the point of these two verses very plain. It is foolish to think that a person's clothes will not be burned if he puts fire on them or that his feet will not be burned if he walks on hot coals. Therefore, it is not only absurd but also inconceivable that a person could conclude that he will be unharmed by committing adultery.

"Men do not despise a thief, if he steal to satisfy his soul when he is hungry; But *if* he be found, he shall restore sevenfold; he shall give all the substance of his house. But whoso committeth adultery with a woman lacketh understanding: he *that* doeth it destroyeth his own soul. A wound and dishonour shall he get; and his reproach shall not be wiped away." (verses 30-33) Honest people typically have little use for a thief and treat him with contempt, but they generally will not have the same disdain for the robber if the theft was carried out **"to satisfy his soul when he is hungry."** Although stealing because one is hungry lessens the resentment, the thief, under Mosaic law, would still have been forced to **"restore sevenfold"** and **"give all the substance of his house."** Statutes concerning thieves are found in Exodus 22:1-4.

Compared to a hungry thief who steals food to *preserve* his soul *[life, person]*, the adulterer steals the sacredness of a marriage. He *lacks understanding* of his own depth of wickedness, of God's judgment of his actions, and the extent of the damage he inflicts, as well as personal damage that he has invited to himself. The adulterer receives **"a wound and dishonor,"** and **"his reproach shall not be wiped away."** When yielding to the desire for pleasure supersedes the desire to be a man or woman of integrity, there is a high price to pay. His family and the community will no longer respect the man, and he may even lose his family in the process. He wears a shame that will not be removed by the passing years.

"For jealousy *is* the rage of a man: therefore he will not spare in the day of vengeance. He will not regard any ransom; neither will he rest content, though thou givest many gifts." (verses 34-35) These two verses express the intense emotions and possible lethal reactions of a husband wronged by adultery. By no means are the words intended to express approval for vengeance, but they do state a common human response. The adulterer should be made aware that his life is in danger by going down that sorrowful road that robs a husband of his wife, family, and peace of mind. Jealousy fuels anger in a man, especially when he has been robbed of that which belongs to him. "Day of vengeance" is simply that day when the husband explodes and decides to take action.

> Romans 12:19 Dearly beloved, avenge not yourselves, but *rather* give place unto wrath: for it is written, Vengeance *is* mine; I will repay, saith the Lord.

CHAPTER SEVEN

Adultery – The Route to Ruin   (Outline of Chapter 7)

Introduction: Wisdom and understanding offer a protection plan against the adulteress. (verses 1-5)
   A. Closely guard and bind wisdom with her laws and commandments to body and heart. (verses 1-4)
   B. Claim wisdom to the special, protective place of close kin. (verse 4)

I. **The pitiful plight of a foolish young man who meets an evil, seductive adulteress.** (verses 6-23)
   A. The young man is described as:
      1. Simple (verse 7)
      2. Void of understanding (verse 7)
      3. Moving in darkness toward her house (verses 8-9)
   B. The Adulteress Is Described As:
      1. Dressing like a harlot (verse 10)
      2. Disguising of her heart (verse 10)
      3. Distasteful with a loud voice (verse 11)
      4. Demandingly stubborn (verse 11)
      5. Displaying restlessness and aggression in seeking her victim (verses 11-12)
      6. Decisively aggressive, uninhibited, bold, brazen. (verse 13)
      7. Defiantly hypocritical (verse 14)
      8. Deviously luring her victim with flattery (verses 15-16)
   C. The Adulteress' Description of Delight:
      1. Special arrangements and elegance of her bed (verse 16)
      2. Sweet perfume (verse 17)
      3. Salacious night (verse 18)
      4. Safety from worry about her husband's return (verses 19-20)
   D. Wisdom's Description of the Young Man's Disaster: (verse 21)
      1. Like an ox going to the slaughter (verse 22)
      2. Like a fool to the stocks (verse 22)
      3. Like a bird to the snare (verse 23)

II. **The Preferred Pathway To Deliverance:** (verses 24-25)
   A. Do listen to the words of Wisdom (verse 25)
   B. Don't let thine heart decline to the adulteress' ways (verse 25)
   C. Don't go astray in her paths (verse 25)

III. **The powerful pull of the adulteress:** (verses 26-27)
   A. She has cast down many wounded men. (verse 26)
   B. She has slain many strong men. (verse 26)
   C. She has made her house the way to hell–going down to the chambers of death. (verse 27)

Proverbs 7:1-5 My son, keep my words, and lay up my commandments with thee.
2. Keep my commandments, and live; and my law as the apple of thine eye.
3. Bind them upon thy fingers, write them upon the table of thine heart.
4. Say unto wisdom, Thou *art* my sister; and call understanding *thy* kinswoman:
5. That they may keep thee from the strange woman, from the stranger *which* flattereth with her words.

"My son, keep my words, and lay up my commandments with thee." (verse 1) Using the now-familiar salutation **"My son,"** the reoccurring plea is given by the father to his son to hear, listen, and obey his parent's words. The commandments of the godly father are equal to the commandments of God because the father's heart has been fully given over to the LORD. As instructed by the word of God, he has assimilated the same into the fabric of his soul. Now he teaches them to his son.

Because the words are indeed the wisdom of God, the son is instructed to *keep the words* of his father and mother and store them within his heart like a precious treasure. The phrase **"keep my words"** means to guard the precious instruction of wisdom protectively as one would pay attention to, guard, and watch over his small child in a dangerous environment. These words being given by the father are the priceless commandments of God. **"Lay up my commandments"** means to hide in reserve the commandments of wisdom in the heart as one would hide and protect precious, costly jewels.

"Keep my commandments, and live." (verse 2a) This wisdom being taught concerns how to have a relationship with God and how to live life to its fullest according to God's great plan for man. Following God's commandments teaches man how to be productive in all that he does, to have the best relationships with other people, and to be blessed of God (enjoying His protection, presence, and provisions), all of which amount to quality life.

> "We must lay up God's commandments safely. Not only, Keep them, and you shall live; but, Keep them as those that cannot live without them. Those that blame strict and careful walking as needless and too precise, consider not that the law is to be kept as the apple of the eye; indeed the law in the heart is the eye of the soul. Let the word of God dwell in us, and so be written where it will be always at hand to be read. Thus we shall be kept from the fatal effects of our own passions, and the snares of Satan. Let God's word confirm our dread of sin, and resolutions against it."[119]

"And my law as the apple of thine eye." (verse 2b) The **"apple of thine eye"** is the center or the pupil. **"Keep my law as the apple of thine eye"** means to protect and guard the commandments in a similar manner as a man guards his eyesight. The natural reaction to a threat to the eye's being injured is to *shield it* with a body part of lesser value, such as the hand or forearm, or to turn the face and receive the injury to another part of the head. **Any bodily injury** is spontaneously and instinctively preferred to one that threatens priceless, precious, light-giving, life-guiding eyesight. Likewise, the **"commandments"** of wisdom are of inestimable value providing *insight, light, and guidance to quality of life*. Therefore, they should be given the highest level of priority and protection possible.

The command of verses 1 and 2 starts with keeping God's "words," proceeds to keeping God's "commandments," and then goes to keeping His "law" (Torah). The whole of the word of God is to be the godly person's precious treasure as he is ready to listen and obey every instruction.

"Bind them upon thy fingers, write them upon the table of thine heart." (verse 3) The commands of wisdom are to be received down deeper than the intellect. They are to be written **"upon the table of thine heart."** It is in the **"heart"** wherein lies the totality of the way a man thinks and feels and wills. When the commandments are willfully, obediently, intentionally, and purposefully written on the heart, the person will be spiritually, emotionally, and intellectually attached to them. With a determined will, the believer lives by this deep-seated internal guidance instead of a superficial, flippant, on-again, off-again, insincere lifestyle that takes instruction now from the world and then from God. It is in the heart where daily decisions are made that determine quality of life. If the commandments of wisdom are written (inscribed) there, they will give light to every step, guidance to every thought, and a guard for every word.

> Psalm 119:11 Thy word have I hid in mine heart, that I might not sin against thee.
>
> Psalm 119:105 NUN. Thy word *is* a lamp unto my feet, and a light unto my path.
>
> Proverbs 2:1, 11-12, 16 My son, if thou wilt receive my words, and hide my commandments with thee ... Discretion shall preserve thee, understanding shall keep thee: to deliver thee from the way of the evil *man,* from the man that speaketh froward things: ... to deliver thee from the strange woman, *even* from the stranger *which* flattereth with her words.
>
> Jeremiah 31:33 But this *shall be* the covenant that I will make with the house of Israel; After those days, saith the LORD, I will put my law in their inward parts, and write it in their hearts; and will be their God, and they shall be my people.
>
> 2 Corinthians 3:3 *Forasmuch as ye are* manifestly declared to be the epistle of Christ ministered by us, written not with ink, but with the Spirit of the living God; not in tables of stone, but in fleshy tables of the heart.

Not only are the commands to be so regarded in the heart, but they are to be kept before the eyes of a wise man as though he did **"bind them upon thy fingers."** Fingers often host beautiful rings, especially wedding rings; and they are worn there because it is on a finger that they are easily seen and serve as a reminder of vows made. This Scripture does not mean that anyone is to physically write the commands of wisdom on the heart (which would be impossible), nor does it intend for the commands to be physically bound upon the fingers; rather, it *uses figurative language* to teach the grave importance of both *internalizing and being in constant observation of God's instruction.*

"Say unto wisdom, Thou *art* my sister; and call understanding *thy* kinswoman: That they may keep thee from the strange woman, from the stranger *which* flattereth with her words." (verses 4-5) The understanding behind saying to wisdom **"thou *art* my sister"** and calling **"understanding *thy* kinswoman"** is to express the close, personal, loving relationship with wisdom and understanding; thus, the Song of Solomon refers to his wife as "sister."

Song of Solomon 4:9-10 Thou hast ravished my heart, my sister, my spouse; thou hast ravished my heart with one of thine eyes, with one chain of thy neck. How fair is thy love, my sister, my spouse! how much better is thy love than wine! and the smell of thine ointments than all spices!

Song of Solomon 4:12 A garden inclosed is my sister, my spouse; a spring shut up, a fountain sealed.

These verses express God's desire for His people to be as familiar and as close to wisdom and understanding as to a sister or wife who are understood to be godly, chaste women, as exemplified in Proverbs 31. When a wise person treats **"wisdom"** with the respect and love of a **"sister"** and **"understanding"** with the respect and love of a **"kinswoman,"** then there will be a close bond, a precious fellowship, and delightful, hearty counsel *received and adhered to.* It would be impossible to hearken to the words of wisdom and to those of the adulteress at the same time. Staying close to one naturally creates a great distance from the other. The words "sister" and "kinswoman" are used to give a sharp contrast to the "strange woman" and the "stranger."

"Strange" is a term used to identify the adulteress – "one that is *not thy own*, whether Jewess or heathen."[120] Everything about the **"strange woman"** is foreign to the things of God and His teachings of wisdom.

An affectionate relationship with "wisdom" and "understanding" specifically means that the wise person will be taking to heart the instructions of "wisdom" and seeking to gain "understanding." A proper relationship with a **"sister"** or **"kinswoman"** is precious and tender and involves much respectful affection and is therefore protected with one's life, if necessary.

Proverbs 7:6-27 For at the window of my house I looked through my casement,
7. And beheld among the simple ones, I discerned among the youths, a young man void of understanding,
8. Passing through the street near her corner; and he went the way to her house,
9. In the twilight, in the evening, in the black and dark night:
10. And, behold, there met him a woman *with* the attire of an harlot, and subtil of heart.
11. (She *is* loud and stubborn; her feet abide not in her house:
12. Now *is she* without, now in the streets, and lieth in wait at every corner.)
13. So she caught him, and kissed him, *and* with an impudent face said unto him,
14. I have peace offerings with me; this day have I payed my vows.
15. Therefore came I forth to meet thee, diligently to seek thy face, and I have found thee.
16. I have decked my bed with coverings of tapestry, with carved *works,* with fine linen of Egypt.
17. I have perfumed my bed with myrrh, aloes, and cinnamon.
18. Come, let us take our fill of love until the morning: let us solace ourselves with loves.
19. For the goodman *is* not at home, he is gone a long journey:
20. He hath taken a bag of money with him, *and* will come home at the day appointed.
21. With her much fair speech she caused him to yield, with the flattering of her lips she forced him.
22. He goeth after her straightway, as an ox goeth to the slaughter, or as a fool to the correction of the stocks;
23. Till a dart strike through his liver; as a bird hasteth to the snare, and knoweth not that it *is* for his life.
24. Hearken unto me now therefore, O ye children, and attend to the words of my mouth.
25. Let not thine heart decline to her ways, go not astray in her paths.
26. For she hath cast down many wounded: yea, many strong *men* have been slain by her.
27. Her house *is* the way to hell, going down to the chambers of death.

"For at the window of my house I looked through my casement." (verse 6) After explaining the value of wisdom in protecting a young man from the clever, wicked adulteress, he uses the word **"for"** (because) to introduce a real-life example of her slick, well-rehearsed, professional entrapment of a foolish young man who is too stubborn to accept the teachings of wisdom, too simple to recognize that he has been duped, and too shallow in his understanding to imagine the danger that lies ahead. These verses read like the narrator's eyewitness account of a pitiful event viewed from the window of his home. Clarke explains the meaning of casement.

> "The **casement** is a small aperture in a large window, or a window opening on hinges. Here it means the lattice, for they had no glass windows in the East. And the latticed windows produced a double advantage (1) Making the apartments sufficiently private; and (2) Admitting fresh air to keep them cool."[121]

"And beheld among the simple ones, I discerned among the youths, a young man void of understanding." (verse 7) The Bible describes a casual meeting of youths below the narrator's window. People like to congregate and enjoy each other's fellowship, and typically, they separate by age group. These youths are all somebody's sons. Growing up in Israel, they should have been taught by their parents what God expected of them; however, the narrator describes the youths as "simple."

> **NOTE: Simple** people are undecided in their views and are easily influenced – like a child. A simple person is naive and untaught. However, he is NOT one who cannot comprehend OR a fool who despises wisdom. Instead, he is one whose exposure to life and wisdom has been limited. Because of inexperience, he is gullible and easily influenced. Simple persons are people of weak capacities and shallow understandings. They are incautious and easily imposed upon. *Quoted from Proverbs 1:3 of this commentary.*

Then the narrator proceeds to provide informative and shocking detail about what he is observing. Verse seven declares that the narrator discerned (observed and wisely gained insight) that one "among the youths" was **"void of understanding,"** a condition that manifested itself due to the young man's careless, intentional path that placed him dangerously close to the harlot. His attitude or cocky speech probably further gave him away, as well as his failure to watch and discern the danger he is about to face. Obviously, he does not understand where his involvement with the adulteress will take him, and he has no heart for wisdom. Instead, he has thrown his hat into the ring with fools and is becoming one of them. Other verses that identify a person as **"void of understanding"** are listed below.

> Proverbs 10:13 In the lips of him that hath understanding wisdom is found: but a rod *is* for the back of him that is void of understanding.
> Proverbs 11:12 He that is void of wisdom despiseth his neighbour: but a man of understanding holdeth his peace.
> Proverbs 12:11 He that tilleth his land shall be satisfied with bread: but he that followeth vain *persons is* void of understanding.
> Proverbs 24:30-31 I went by the field of the slothful, and by the vineyard of the man void of understanding; And, lo, it was all grown over with thorns, *and* nettles had covered the face thereof, and the stone wall thereof was broken down.

> **One bad decision can lead a person to disaster.**

"Passing through the street near her corner; and he went the way to her house, In the twilight, in the evening, in the black and dark night." (verses 8-9) Having been informed that the young man is **"simple," "void of understanding,"** the reader mentally watches as the indiscreet youth leaves the other youths; and by himself **"went"** *[with a determined walk, like a march]* on **"the way to her house"** where she lurks as an evil predator. His lack of understanding has set him on a course to make bad decisions and placed him in harm's way.

"Twilight," "evening," and **"black and dark night"** are terms used to denote a steady symbolic descending from light to dark, both physically and spiritually. **"In the black and dark night"** is similar to the expression used in Proverbs 20:20 to denote the middle of the night. Darkness will provide temporary cover for his sin, but not from the all-seeing God and not from his own conscience; nor will it provide an escape from future fears that will spring up in his heart induced by an angry, vengeful husband or the disrespect from those godly people who learn of his encounter. The following verses gives insight concerning those who wander in darkness and whose works are darkness.

> Job 24:13-17 They are of those that rebel against the light; they know not the ways thereof, nor abide in the paths thereof. The murderer rising with the light killeth the poor and needy, and in the night is as a thief. The eye also of the adulterer waiteth for the twilight, saying, No eye shall see me: and disguiseth *his* face. In the dark they dig through houses, *which* they had marked for themselves in the daytime: they know not the light. For the morning *is* to them even as the shadow of death: if *one* know *them, they are in* the terrors of the shadow of death.
> John 3:18-21 He that believeth on him is not condemned: but he that believeth not is condemned already, because he hath not believed in the name of the only begotten Son of God. And this is the condemnation, that light is come into the world, and men loved darkness rather than light, because their deeds were evil. For every one that doeth evil hateth the light, neither cometh to the light, lest his deeds should be reproved. But he that doeth truth cometh to the light, that his deeds may be made manifest, that they are wrought in God.
> Romans 13:12-13 The night is far spent, the day is at hand: let us therefore cast off the works of darkness, and let us put on the armour of light. Let us walk honestly, as in the day; not in rioting and drunkenness, not in chambering and wantonness, not in strife and envying.
> *[See also Job 12:24-25; Proverbs 2:11-13; 20:20; Isaiah 29:15; Luke 22:52-53.]*

"And, behold, there met him a woman *with* the attire of an harlot, and subtil of heart." (verse 10) The **"attire of an harlot"** is not always the same in all places nor in all periods. Still the general population of every society and culture would be able to identify a harlot by her attire. For example, the Genesis 38 passage describes the fully-covered attire of the idolatrous temple prostitute. Judah apparently was unaware that the harlot was his own daughter-in-law.

> Genesis 38:14-15, 19 And she put her widow's garments off from her, and covered her with a vail, and wrapped herself, and sat in an open place, which *is* by the way to Timnath; for she saw that Shelah was grown, and she was not given unto him to wife. When Judah saw her, he thought her *to be* an harlot; because she had covered her face. And she arose, and went away, and laid by her vail from her, and put on the garments of her widowhood.

The adulteress of verse 10 *may have been clothed*

> "with showy, gaudy garments, such as the Athenian whores wore, or short ones, as the Romans; the word signifies one fitted to her body, neat and well shaped, to recommend her: so the woman, the whore of Rome, is said to be arrayed in purple and scarlet colour, and decked with gold, and precious stones, and pearls; signifying the outward pomp and splendour of the Romish religion, designed to captivate weak and unwary minds."[122]

> Revelation 17:4-5 And the woman was arrayed in purple and scarlet colour, and decked with gold and precious stones and pearls, having a golden cup in her hand full of abominations and filthiness of her fornication: And upon her forehead *was* a name written, MYSTERY, BABYLON THE GREAT, THE MOTHER OF HARLOTS AND ABOMINATIONS OF THE EARTH.

Because she was skillfully setting a salacious trap, the **"subtil of heart"** (verse 10b) adulteress had to hide her intent. Consequently, she revealed only carefully selected personal information that she thought the young man might find of interest, and that would not frighten him off. If he could have looked into her heart, he might have seen and heard the many, terrible horrors of hell.

"(She *is* loud and stubborn; her feet abide not in her house: Now *is she* without, now in the streets, and lieth in wait at every corner.)" (verses 11-12) **"She is loud"** or said another way, she is boisterous or noisy, full of clamorous talk, especially with the foolish young man beside her, when she pours out deceptive, enticing words to lure him. Her *loudness* indicates a lack of refinement.

> Proverbs 9:13 A foolish woman *is* clamorous: *she is* simple, and knoweth nothing.

"Stubborn" is a descriptive term that is normally applied to an ungovernable brute beast, like a bellowing animal that will not bear the yoke. The word **"stubborn"** encompasses her attitude of rebellion, self-will, disobedience to her husband, rebelliousness against God, and incorrigibleness obvious to the wise observer. Notice the Bible's condemnation of stubbornness:

> 1 Samuel 15:23 For rebellion *is as* the sin of witchcraft, and stubbornness *is as* iniquity and idolatry. Because thou hast rejected the word of the LORD, he hath also rejected thee from *being* king.

Peter describes the character trait that God values in a godly woman, and it is the opposite of the adulterous woman.

> Peter 3:3-4 Whose adorning let it not be that outward adorning of plaiting the hair, and of wearing of gold, or of putting on of apparel; But let it be the hidden man of the heart, in that which is not corruptible, even the ornament of a meek and quiet spirit, which is in the sight of God of great price.

"Her feet abide not in her house." She is obviously *discontented* and *bored* with being a faithful and honorable wife. Also, she is *restless* because her window of opportunity to trap a simple man who will be willing to come to her house for a salacious event is limited. Her devious and evil work has to be conducted quickly and under the cover of darkness. Time is of the essence. She has given a great deal of thought and effort into making both herself and her bed appealing, and now she talks and moves with energy.

> *The talebearing widows of 1 Timothy had a problem common with the adulteress of abiding not in their house and thus wandering about, revealing their discontentment and disregard for righteousness.*
>
> > 1 Timothy 5:13 And withal they learn *to be* idle, wandering about from house to house; and not only idle, but tattlers also and busybodies, speaking things which they ought not.

God declares the "sin of Sodom" to be "pride, fulness of bread, and abundance of idleness" (Ezekiel 16:49). The adulteress and the young man both act like they have time on their hands and are responsible to no one.

> "She minds not her business, which lies in her own house, but gives herself wholly up to idleness and pleasure, which she seeks in gadding abroad, and in changing her place and company. Now she is without – Standing, or waiting nigh the door of her house; now in the streets – In places of resort; 'and lieth in wait at every corner' – To pick up such as she can make a prey of."[123]

"Lieth in wait at every corner" indicates that she would take the first easy prey she could find. Pity the unwise man who flatters himself into thinking he's special.

"So she caught him, and kissed him." (verse 13a) She recognized something about him indicating he was an easy prey. In addition to his steady walk on "the way to her house," perhaps the simple young man carried himself in a particular way, or had a look of defiance in his eye, or wore his clothes in a suggestive manner, or spoke with loudness and off-color speech, or there was a cocky swagger in his step. No doubt, he exhibited an "attitude that assured her he would be an easy prey. So, she laid hold on him and then immediately kissed him "in order to stir up wanton affections and impure desires in him."[124]

"And **with an impudent face said unto him."** (verse 13b) Her **"impudent face"** indicates that she is strong and hardened in her desire and has predetermined to follow through with her wicked and dangerous scheme. She is defiant and determined to do evil. Proverbs 6:12-14 shows how body language reveals a person's character and path of life. Her facial expressions reveal the character of her malignant heart.

> Proverbs 6:12-14 A naughty person, a wicked man, walketh with a froward mouth. He winketh with his eyes, he speaketh with his feet, he teacheth with his fingers; Frowardness is in his heart, he deviseth mischief continually; he soweth discord.

"I have **peace offerings with me; this day have I payed my vows. Therefore came I forth to meet thee, diligently to seek thy face, and I have found thee."** (verses 14-15) These two verses reveal two pretenses *(lies)* by the adulteress: (1) She pretends, with the act of offering a peace offering, to be a worshiper of God with a genuine heart of submission to Him. (2) She also pretends that she made the sacrifice while having this particular young man in mind and thereby intended to share the feast with him.

"I have **peace offerings with me"** (verse 14) shows that she was still in possession of the sacrifice which she would consume with her household, as part of the act of thanksgiving to God for His provisions, either past or future. Peace offerings were designed to make peace between the worshiper and God by making up for the breach that sin had caused. When the blood was poured out at the altar of sacrifice, and the fat burned there, the breast and the right shoulder were given to the priests. Part of the animal was burned up as a sacrifice to God, and the rest belonged to the worshiper, who was free to carry it home to enjoy in a feast with friends. Sacrifices were made of the best sheep, goat, or bullock that the worshiper had.[125]

Leviticus 7:11-18   THE LAW GOVERNING PEACE OFFERINGS
(See also Leviticus 3:1-11)

And this *is* the law of the sacrifice of peace offerings, which he shall offer unto the LORD. If he offer it for a thanksgiving, then he shall offer with the sacrifice of thanksgiving unleavened cakes mingled with oil, and unleavened wafers anointed with oil, and cakes mingled with oil, of fine flour, fried. Besides the cakes, he shall offer *for* his offering leavened bread with the sacrifice of thanksgiving of his peace offerings. And of it he shall offer one out of the whole oblation *for* an heave offering unto the LORD, *and* it shall be the priest's that sprinkleth the blood of the peace offerings. And the flesh of the sacrifice of his peace offerings for thanksgiving shall be eaten the same day that it is offered; he shall not leave any of it until the morning. But if the sacrifice of his offering *be* a vow, or a voluntary offering, it shall be eaten the same day that he offereth his sacrifice: and on the morrow also the remainder of it shall be eaten: But the remainder of the flesh of the sacrifice on the third day shall be burnt with fire. And if *any* of the flesh of the sacrifice of his peace offerings be eaten at all on the third day, it shall not be accepted, neither shall it be imputed unto him that offereth it: it shall be an abomination, and the soul that eateth of it shall bear his iniquity.

"This day have I payed my vows. Therefore came I forth to meet thee, diligently to seek thy face, and I have found thee." (verse 14b-15) The implication is that the adulteress then came out specifically to meet with him for the purpose of completing the worship process that involved eating the feast at home. As seen in the following verses, her own words tell that she intended on doing evil rather than righteousness.

"I have decked my bed with coverings of tapestry, with carved *works,* with fine linen of Egypt. I have perfumed my bed with myrrh, aloes, and cinnamon." (verses 16-17) The first piece of bait that the adulteress threw out to the foolish young man was the invitation to a sumptuous, delicious feast with her under the guise of religion. She then immediately tosses him another piece of bait by describing her living arrangements as one of high culture; so, he will think of himself as being elevated to a finer life rather than being taken down to the level of sin and destruction.

"**Come, let us take our fill of love until the morning: let us solace ourselves with loves. For the goodman *is* not at home, he is gone a long journey: He hath taken a bag of money with him, *and* will come home at the day appointed.**"(verses 18-20) These verses describe the third incentive to come and partake of adultery with her. Though she had immediately kissed the young man upon seeing him, an action which was suggestive enough in itself, now she moves rapidly to verbalize her desire for a night of lascivious behavior. To make the bait more palatable, she assures him that her husband will not return anytime soon. She is openly seducing the simple youth. He should run like Joseph did when Potiphar's wife said "Lie with me." (Genesis 39:7). But the simple youth is missing the "fear of the LORD" that Joseph so obviously possessed; thus, he is "void of understanding." He lacks wisdom.

"**With her much fair speech she caused him to yield, with the flattering of her lips she forced him.**" (verse 21) The text (verses 13-21) implies that her kisses alone were not persuasive enough, and he might have observed something about her that alarmed him and then showed signs of turning away; but because of her continuing speech concerning the feast, then his visualizing the richness of her lifestyle, then imagining the sweet smells, and finally receiving a specific offer of adultery, he yielded. "His body followed the lead of his blinded mind."[126]

The Hebrew word for "**fair speech**" is translated as "learning" or "doctrine" in earlier passages in Proverbs. Here the expression is used as irony to show there is nothing fair or educational in a positive way about her speech or actions. As previously stated, her lying, flattering words caused him to yield where her kisses did not. "No provocation to sin is a sufficient excuse for it."[127] It was the lying words of the serpent that caused Adam and Eve to fall.

> *Deception is always the consequence of a lack of discernment.*

"**He goeth after her straightway, as an ox goeth to the slaughter, or as a fool to the correction of the stocks; Till a dart strike through his liver; as a bird hasteth to the snare, and knoweth not that it *is* for his life.**" (verses 22-23) He "**goeth after her straightway**" or without hesitancy because he has been duped – deceived. She has convinced him to follow her and he "**knoweth not that it is for his life.**" Wisdom, in these two verses, compares his stupidity with that of "**an ox**" going to the slaughterhouse with no idea of where he is being led, "**a fool**" going to the stocks, and "**a bird**" being lured into a snare or trap. Shamefully, the young man is compared to *animals or beasts* that are not able to understand and to a *fool* who has refused the good path of wisdom. Instead, he has chosen the path that leads to hell. He is "void of understanding." "**Till a dart strike through his liver**" compares the foolish youth with an unintelligent animal that is to be slaughtered, which meets its doom by being stabbed in a vital organ. The adulteress has stripped the unwary youth of the life that God intended him to have by leading him on the route through "her house" on his "**way to hell, going down to the chambers of death.**" (verse 27)

"**Hearken unto me now therefore, O ye children, and attend to the words of my mouth.**" (verse 24) Wisdom again pleads for attention to the words being spoken. The reasons are most obvious from previous verses and from the last three of this chapter. The Hebrew word for "my son" *ben* is translated as "children" in this verse. "**O ye children**" refers to the next generation, including Solomon's own children and anyone of future generations interested in learning the truths of wisdom.

"**Let not thine heart decline to her ways, go not astray in her paths. For she hath cast down many wounded: yea, many strong *men* have been slain by her. Her house *is* the way to hell, going down to the chambers of death.**" (verses 25-27) In verse three, the son was instructed to write the commandments of wisdom upon the table of his heart so as to internalize them; and in verse five, the reader learned that wisdom would "keep thee from the strange woman." To "**decline to her ways**" (verse 25) would be to deviate from wisdom's path and the way to God and thereby enter the path of an adulteress, which is the way to destruction and death. By saying in verse two, "Keep my commandments and live," Wisdom declares that life rather than death is available to the wise.

This young man is not the first to have been seduced. The house of the adulteress is compared with a battlefield strewn with the bodies of many men who have been drawn into such a killing field. "**For she hath cast down many wounded: yea, many strong *men* have been slain by her.**" (verse 26) Such words provide the reason for Wisdom's exhortation in verse twenty-four: "Hearken unto me now therefore, O ye children, and attend to the words of my mouth." The adulteress had victimized many others ("**cast down many wounded**") with her temptations.

"Wounded in their name, character, and reputation; in their bodies by diseases; and in their souls by guilt, shame, and horror, through a compliance with her sinful lusts: these she 'cast down' from the honors they were possessed of, from the health they enjoyed, and from the peace and tranquillity of mind they formerly felt within them. And not a single person, as the young man instanced in, or a few only, but 'many'; great multitudes, hundreds and thousands, and those not weak, and foolish, and inconstant, as he might be thought to be; but such as were 'great' and mighty, as the word also signifies; men of great riches, and wisdom, and courage; as soldiers, mighty men of war, such as wound and kill others; which seems the true sense of the word here used: and therefore none ought to trust in themselves, nor trust themselves in her company, nor in the least decline to her ways; and especially such as are weak and unskillful, and ignorant of her devices . . ."[128]

"Her house *is* the way to hell, going down to the chambers of death." (verse 27) "In short, to follow her unto her house is the direct way to hell: every step taken to her bed is, in truth, a *going down to the* dismal *chambers of death,* and to the most horrid miseries."[129] "To hell, *sheol*, the pit, the grave, the place of the dead, the eternal and infernal world. And they who, through such, fall into the grave, descend lower, into the chambers of death; the place where pleasure is at an end, and illusion mocks no more."[130]

- Colossians 3:1-7 If ye then be risen with Christ, seek those things which are above, where Christ sitteth on the right hand of God. Set your affection on things above, not on things on the earth. For ye are dead, and your life is hid with Christ in God. When Christ, who is our life, shall appear, then shall ye also appear with him in glory. Mortify therefore your members which are upon the earth; fornication, uncleanness, inordinate affection, evil concupiscence, and covetousness, which is idolatry: For which things' sake the wrath of God cometh on the children of disobedience: In the which ye also walked some time, when ye lived in them.
- 1 Thessalonians 4:3-7 For this is the will of God, even your sanctification, that ye should abstain from fornication: That every one of you should know how to possess his vessel in sanctification and honour; Not in the lust of concupiscence, even as the Gentiles which know not God: That no man go beyond and defraud his brother in any matter: because that the Lord is the avenger of all such, as we also have forewarned you and testified. For God hath not called us unto uncleanness, but unto holiness.
- 2 Timothy 2:22 Flee also youthful lusts: but follow righteousness, faith, charity, peace, with them that call on the Lord out of a pure heart.

CHAPTER EIGHT

Outline Chapter Eight

I. **The Proclamations of Wisdom to Mankind** (verses 1-21)
   A. Wisdom's Words Proclaimed in Many Places (verses 1-3)
      1. In the top of the high places (verse 2)
      2. In the paths (verse 2)
      3. In the gates of the city (verse 3)
      4. In the doorways (verse 3)
   B. Wisdom's Words Proclaimed to All People (verses 4-5)
      1. To all of mankind (verse 4)
      2. To the simple (verse 5)
      3. To fools (verse 5)
   C. Wisdom's Words Perfect for Mankind (verses 6-9)
      1. Wisdom speaks excellent things (verse 6)
      2. Wisdom speaks right things (verse 6)
      3. Wisdom speaks truthful things (verse 7)
      4. Wisdom speaks righteous things (verse 8)
      5. Wisdom speaks plain, right things (verse 9)
   D. Wisdom's Words Priceless for Mankind (verse 10-11)
      1. Wisdom's words greater value than silver (verse 10)
      2. Wisdom's words greater value than choice gold (verse 10)
      3. Wisdom's words greater value than rubies (verse 11)
      4. Wisdom's words greater value than everything (verse 11)
   E. Wisdom's Words Powerful for Mankind (verses 12-16)
      1. Powerful to Common Men (verses 12-13)
         a. Because of prudence and persistence (verse 12)
         b. Because of partiality to and fear of God (verse 13)
      2. Powerful to Crowned Men (verses 14-16)
         a. Because wisdom is the source of counsel, soundness, understanding and strength (verse 14)
         b. Because wisdom is the prescription for justice (verse 15)
         c. Because wisdom is the rule of princes, nobles and judges (verse 16)
   F. Wisdom's Words a Pathway for Mankind (verses 17-21)
      1. Wisdom directs men to God's love (verse 17)
      2. Wisdom directs men to riches and honor of righteousness (verse 18-19)
      3. Wisdom directs men to righteous judgment (verse 20)
      4. Wisdom directs men to godly substance and valuables (verse 21)

II. **The Preexistence of Wisdom** (verses 22-30)
   A. Wisdom Existed in the Beginning of Creation (verse 22)
   B. Wisdom Existed from Eternity past (verse 23)
   C. Wisdom Existed Before Depths and Fountains (verse 24)
   D. Wisdom Existed Before the Mountains Settled (verse 25)
   E. Wisdom Existed Before the Earth Was Made (verse 26)
   F. Wisdom Existed When God Prepared the Heavens (verse 27)
   G. Wisdom Was Present When God Made World a Circle (verse 27)
   H. Wisdom Was Present When God Established the Clouds (verse 28)
   I. Wisdom Was Present When God Strengthened the Fountains of the Deep (verse 28)
   J. Wisdom Was Present When God Set the Boundaries of the Seas (verse 29)

III. **The Pleasure of Wisdom** (verse 30-31)
   A. Wisdom Rejoiced always in the Presence of God (verse 30)
   B. Wisdom Rejoiced in the Habitable Part of the Earth with Mankind (verse 30-31)

IV. **The Pleas of Wisdom** (verses 32-36)
   A. Listen to me (verse 32)
   B. Keep My Ways and Be Blessed (verse 32)
   C. Hear Instruction and Be Wise (verse 33)
   D. Hear, Watch and Wait for Wisdom and Be Blessed (verse 34)
   E. Find Wisdom and Find Life and Favor of God (verse 35)

V. **The Persons Who Reject Wisdom** (verses 35-36)
   A. Mistreat Themselves (verse 35)
   B. Love Death (verse 36)

> **Proverbs 8:1-21** Doth not wisdom cry? and understanding put forth her voice?
> 2. She standeth in the top of high places, by the way in the places of the paths.
> 3. She crieth at the gates, at the entry of the city, at the coming in at the doors.
> 4. Unto you, O men, I call; and my voice *is* to the sons of man.
> 5. O ye simple, understand wisdom: and, ye fools, be ye of an understanding heart.
> 6. Hear; for I will speak of excellent things; and the opening of my lips *shall be* right things.
> 7. For my mouth shall speak truth; and wickedness *is* an abomination to my lips.
> 8. All the words of my mouth *are* in righteousness; *there is* nothing froward or perverse in them.
> 9. They *are* all plain to him that understandeth, and right to them that find knowledge.
> 10. Receive my instruction, and not silver; and knowledge rather than choice gold.
> 11. For wisdom *is* better than rubies; and all the things that may be desired are not to be compared to it.
> 12. I wisdom dwell with prudence, and find out knowledge of witty inventions.
> 13. The fear of the LORD *is* to hate evil: pride, and arrogancy, and the evil way, and the froward mouth, do I hate.
> 14. Counsel *is* mine, and sound wisdom: I *am* understanding; I have strength.
> 15. By me kings reign, and princes decree justice.
> 16. By me princes rule, and nobles, *even* all the judges of the earth.
> 17. I love them that love me; and those that seek me early shall find me.
> 18. Riches and honour *are* with me; *yea,* durable riches and righteousness.
> 19. My fruit *is* better than gold, yea, than fine gold; and my revenue than choice silver.
> 20. I lead in the way of righteousness, in the midst of the paths of judgment:
> 21. That I may cause those that love me to inherit substance; and I will fill their treasures.

"Doth not wisdom cry? and understanding put forth her voice? She standeth in the top of high places, by the way in the places of the paths. She crieth at the gates, at the entry of the city, at the coming in at the doors." (verses 1-3) The righteous **personified Wisdom** of Chapter Eight is set in sharp contrast to the **evil adulteress** of Chapter Seven, who pictures fleshly lust, pride, arrogance, and hateful rebellion against God. The adulteress is nervously **secretive**, working under cover of darkness so as to disguise her pathway to hell and the final doom of her duped victims. Wisdom, on the other hand, **"standeth in the top of high places, by the way in the places of the paths."** (verse 2) Publicly and from the most frequented places, she lifts her voice unashamedly in the **"gates,"** **"at the entry of the city,"** and the **"coming in at the doors."** Unashamedly, she establishes herself along well-trodden paths where she cries out her invitation to come into agreement with God. Broadcast in open daylight, her message is holy, life-saving, and life-giving. It is for any of the "sons of man" who have an ear to hear to come "forsake the foolish and live."

> Isaiah 30:21 And thine ears shall hear a word behind thee, saying, This *is* the way, walk ye in it, when ye turn to the right hand, and when ye turn to the left.

> **NOTE: Wisdom** taught by the Bible is accessible but *is beyond human reach without a right relationship with God* and without substantial effort applied as described in Proverbs Two. The process begins with the believer having a "fear of God" (Proverbs 1:7) and then gaining a knowledge of God through intense study, prayer, and obedience to His word. In addition, the Apostle Paul, in I Corinthians Two describes how important it is for Christians to be sensitive to Holy Spirit leadership. Proverbs deals with both practical living **and** spiritual living. In a proper relationship, man interacts with God, through His word and His Spirit, to gain wisdom from God. The learning process involves mentally digging through His word as described in Proverbs Two and subsequently applying learned biblical truths so as to be able to properly evaluate the actions of people and situations. A wise person has knowledge of God's word and consequently increases his knowledge of God. *By studying the Book of Proverbs, one can develop an understanding of human nature and an appreciation of the justice, judgment, and equity that is revealed in God's interaction with man.* An understanding heart comes through having the mind of Christ so that the individual knows much that God has revealed about Himself, this world that He created, and the interactions of wise and foolish men. The resulting wisdom allows man the opportunity to make the best possible decisions.
>
> *In the Book of Proverbs, the person with wisdom has the ability,*
> *because of a proper relationship with God,*
> *to be able to navigate through the challenges and opportunities of life in the most effective manner*
> *thereby minimizing evil influences and maximizing godly outcomes.*

> "Wisdom, unlike the vicious woman (Chapter 7) who lurks in the twilight at the corner of the street which contains her lair, stands in the open places; she makes herself as manifest as may be by occupying some elevated position, from which her ringing voice may be heard down the streets and up the cross-ways, and may attract the attention of those who are entering the city gates or the doors of the houses. As her voice is strong and clear, so her words are full and rounded; there is no whispering, no muttering, no dark hint, no subtle incitement to secret pleasures; her tone is breezy and stirring as the dawn; there is something about it which makes one involuntarily think of the open air, and the wide sky, and the great works of God. (verses 1-6) There is the beauty of goodness in all that she says; there are the charming directness and openness of truth; she abhors tortuous and obscure ways; and if some of her sayings seem paradoxes or enigmas, a little difficult to understand, that is the fault of the hearer; to a tortuous mind straight things appear crooked; to the ignorant and uninstructed mind the eternal laws of God appear foolishness; but all that she says is plain to one who understands, and right to those who find knowledge. (verses 7-9) She walks always in a certain and undeviating course–it is the way of righteousness and judgment–and only those who tread the same path can expect to perceive the meaning of what she says, or to appreciate the soundness of all her counsels. (verse 20) And now she proclaims the grounds on which she demands the attention of men, in a noble appeal, which rises to a passionate eloquence and deepens in spiritual significance as it advances."[131]

Throughout Proverbs Chapter Eight, the reader can readily identify the parallel preaching characteristics of Jesus with those of the personified Wisdom. Chapter Eight (verses 1-3) begins with a description of Wisdom *publically proclaiming her truth to all*; and every student who is familiar with the preaching of Jesus would have to declare that their preaching is amazingly similar. Like wisdom, He preached in the high places, on the streets, and in the gates. However, **Jesus is much more than wisdom**. He is the Creator. He is "Wonderful, Counsellor, The mighty God, The everlasting Father, The Prince of Peace." (Isaiah 9:6) He is the Saviour, full of all love, and all power. Wisdom is the way Christ Jesus thinks and how He spoke.

> Matthew 5:1-2 And seeing the multitudes, he went up into a mountain: and when he was set, his disciples came unto him: And he opened his mouth, and taught them, saying . . .
> Mark 6:34 And Jesus, when he came out, saw much people, and was moved with compassion toward them, because they were as sheep not having a shepherd: and he began to teach them many things.
> Luke 4:15-16 And he taught in their synagogues, being glorified of all. And he came to Nazareth, where he had been brought up: and, as his custom was, he went into the synagogue on the Sabbath day, and stood up for to read.
> John 7:14 Now about the midst of the feast Jesus went up into the temple, and taught.
> John 7:26 But, lo, he speaketh boldly, and they say nothing unto him. Do the rulers know indeed that this is the very Christ?
> John 18:20 Jesus answered him, I spake openly to the world; I ever taught in the synagogue, and in the temple, whither the Jews always resort; and in secret have I said nothing.

Since they could not observe the life and ministry of Jesus, none of the Old Testament prophets could have comprehended the full prophetic understanding of their writings; and it is not conceivable that Solomon, who was not a prophet per se, knew that the personified wisdom he wrote about would preview the eternal Person and various aspects of the earthly ministry of Jesus. Twenty-first century believers can see that the life of Jesus and the descriptions of wisdom are remarkably similar. Before the Incarnation of Jesus, *God revealed His wisdom*, first through speaking directly with Adam, then through dreams, then through chosen prophets, statesmen and kings; and finally, He preserved His wisdom in the written Old Testament. When Jesus came to earth, He revealed additional thoughts (wisdom) of His Father through His personal conversations, preaching, words, and miraculous actions. To hear Him speak was to hear His Father speak, and every utterance is a proclamation of wisdom. *His words were totally and authentically the words of wisdom.* After the resurrection of Jesus, the wisdom of God was preserved through the Spirit-breathed New Testament Scriptures. As marvelous as is His Wisdom, the believer must never forget His great love and sacrifice!

Throughout this chapter and continuing through verse six of Chapter Nine, wisdom again can be observed as a personification. She reasons and expresses her values and instructions in a manner that is common to the mind of God and to the mind of godly men. Those who turn away from wisdom's cry also reject God. Wisdom dwells within the souls of those men who desire to communicate with God. She shows a diligent student right from wrong and brings instruction from God, whose word is pure, untarnished, and perfectly right, having no wrong with it. In like manner with pure wisdom, Jesus spoke publicly and privately; and when He went back to His Father, the Holy Spirit was sent to guide men into all truth. He guides men with wisdom to a place of acceptance, comfort, light, and also to a successful life filled with goodness and love. Men with wisdom hate the things that God hates and love the things that He loves. God has always possessed and delighted in wisdom – that attribute (inherent characteristic) whereby God knows all things. He shares part of that vast ability with willing men so that they can, in a human measure, know and understand His mind and will. Although wisdom cries out to all the sons of men, most will refuse even to hear.

Today wisdom cries out in every available place (illustrations in nature and life, high places, paths, gates, entry of the city, and so on) and is available to every person. Still, only those who hunger after God receive the same. She is speaking through the mouth of godly men and women and godly parents. The word of God speaks wisdom to those who listen. Also, God has sent the following witnesses who testify of His truth: prophets, preachers, apostles, and believers. Furthermore, He has given witness in nature, and in observance of other men, both good and evil.

> Psalm 19:1-3 The heavens declare the glory of God; and the firmament sheweth his handywork. Day unto day uttereth speech, and night unto night sheweth knowledge. *There is* no speech nor language, *where* their voice is not heard.
>
> Proverbs 2:4-7 If thou seekest her as silver, and searchest for her as *for* hid treasures; Then shalt thou understand the fear of the LORD, and find the knowledge of God. For the LORD giveth wisdom: out of his mouth *cometh* knowledge and understanding. He layeth up sound wisdom for the righteous: *he is* a buckler to them that walk uprightly.
>
> Proverbs 24:30-32 I went by the field of the slothful, and by the vineyard of the man void of understanding; And, lo, it was all grown over with thorns, *and* nettles had covered the face thereof, and the stone wall thereof was broken down. Then I saw, *and* considered *it* well: I looked upon *it,* and received instruction.
>
> 1 Corinthians 1:23-24 But we preach Christ crucified, unto the Jews a stumblingblock, and unto the Greeks foolishness; But unto them which are called, both Jews and Greeks, Christ the power of God, and the wisdom of God.
>
> 2 Timothy 3:15 And that from a child thou hast known the holy scriptures, which are able to make thee wise unto salvation through faith which is in Christ Jesus.

"Unto you, O men, I call; and my voice *is* to the sons of man. O ye simple, understand wisdom: and, ye fools, be ye of an understanding heart."(verses 4-5) Wisdom is instructive and honest, calling out to *every person* to hear the truth – **"men," "sons of man," "simple,"** and even **"fools"** are included. She gives her message to anyone who will listen. She calls both "low and high, rich and poor." (Psalm 49: 1-3) She calls to everyone because the Lord is "not willing that any should perish, but that all should come to repentance." (2 Peter 3:9)

"O ye simple, understand wisdom: and, ye fools, be ye of an understanding heart." (verse 5) An individual cannot become a person **"of an understanding heart,"** nor can he **"understand wisdom"** unless *he first listens and obeys the message, the "call," "the voice."* Hence, words such as "hear" or "incline thine ear," or "attend to my words" are repeated numerous times in the Book of Proverbs, as well as in Psalms and other books of the Bible. Understanding is a part of being wise.

> Psalm 49:1-3 Hear this, all *ye* people; give ear, all *ye* inhabitants of the world: Both low and high, rich and poor, together. My mouth shall speak of wisdom; and the meditation of my heart *shall be* of understanding.
>
> Matthew 11:15 He that hath ears to hear, let him hear.
>
> John 3:16 For God so loved the world, that he gave his only begotten Son, that whosoever believeth in him should not perish, but have everlasting life.
>
> Colossians 1:23; 28 If ye continue in the faith grounded and settled, and *be* not moved away from the hope of the gospel, which ye have heard, *and* which was preached to every creature which is under heaven; whereof I Paul am made a minister ... Whom we preach, warning every man, and teaching every man in all wisdom; that we may present every man perfect in Christ Jesus . . .
>
> Titus 2:11 For the grace of God that bringeth salvation hath appeared to all men . . .
>
> Revelation 22:17 And the Spirit and the bride say, Come. And let him that heareth say, Come. And let him that is athirst come. And whosoever will, let him take the water of life freely.

"Hear; for I will speak of excellent things; and the opening of my lips *shall be* right things. For my mouth shall speak truth; and wickedness *is* an abomination to my lips. All the words of my mouth *are* in righteousness; *there is* nothing froward or perverse in them. They *are* all plain to him that understandeth, and right to them that find knowledge."(verses 6-9)   The adulteress of Chapter Seven woos her unsuspecting, "void of understanding," pleasure-seeker "with the flattering of her lips"; and he follows her vain evil lies "as an ox goeth to the slaughter" and "as a fool to the correction of the stocks." Personified Wisdom is exactly the opposite of the adulteress, being straightforward, full of integrity, and faultless. Words of wisdom are described as **"excellent," "right," "truth," "plain,"** and **"wickedness is an abomination to my lips"** – terms which describe the extremely high quality, correctness, accuracy, ease of understanding, and purity of wisdom. To those who depart from evil, a heart condition that involves understanding, her words are plain and agreeable. Yet to those who choose to be in opposition to God, they are difficult and complicated. They don't have ears to hear. Ordinary people, even the simple ones, gladly hear and understand wisdom's great truths. Wisdom leads to life while the adulteress leads to death.

> *"All God's precepts concerning all things are right. They are of unquestionable truth. Wisdom's doctrines, upon which her laws are founded, are such as we may venture our immortal souls upon: My mouth shall speak truth (Proverbs 8:7), the whole truth, and nothing but the truth, for it is a testimony to the world. Every word of God is true; there are not so much as pious frauds in it, nor are we imposed upon in that which is told us for our good."*[132]
>
> Psalm 19:7-11 The law of the LORD *is* perfect, converting the soul: the testimony of the LORD *is* sure, making wise the simple. The statutes of the LORD *are* right, rejoicing the heart: the commandment of the LORD *is* pure, enlightening the eyes. The fear of the LORD *is* clean, enduring for ever: the judgments of the LORD *are* true *and* righteous altogether. More to be desired *are they*

than gold, yea, than much fine gold: sweeter also than honey and the honeycomb. Moreover by them is thy servant warned: *and* in keeping of them *there is* great reward.

Proverbs 4:2 For I give you good doctrine, forsake ye not my law.

Proverbs 4:20-22 My son, attend to my words; incline thine ear unto my sayings. Let them not depart from thine eyes; keep them in the midst of thine heart. For they *are* life unto those that find them, and health to all their flesh.

Proverbs 22:20-21 Have not I written to thee excellent things in counsels and knowledge, That I might make thee know the certainty of the words of truth; that thou mightest answer the words of truth to them that send unto thee?

1Corinthians 2:6-7 Howbeit we speak wisdom among them that are perfect: yet not the wisdom of this world, nor of the princes of this world, that come to nought: But we speak the wisdom of God in a mystery, *even* the hidden *wisdom,* which God ordained before the world unto our glory . . .

"Receive my instruction, and not silver; and knowledge rather than choice gold. For wisdom is better than rubies; and all the things that may be desired are not to be compared to it." (verses 10-11) The adulteress of Chapter Seven used the following shallow *symbols of wealth* (which were also sexually suggestive) to entice her victim: "I have decked my bed with coverings of tapestry, with carved *works,* with fine linen of Egypt. I have perfumed my bed with myrrh, aloes, and cinnamon."

In contrast, Wisdom is not driven by lust but rather by love for God. To the person who *chooses to receive wisdom's instruction over silver and knowledge over gold*, wisdom proves, through issues of life, to be far *better than rubies, and yea, of greater value than anything in this world*. Part of wisdom's great value is guiding a person around many potential disasters of life. She warns of impending dangers, teaches a right view of sin, guides to righteousness, and shows those who love her how and where to position themselves so that God will bless every aspect of their lives.

Psalm 1:1-6 Blessed *is* the man that walketh not in the counsel of the ungodly, nor standeth in the way of sinners, nor sitteth in the seat of the scornful. But his delight *is* in the law of the LORD; and in his law doth he meditate day and night. And he shall be like a tree planted by the rivers of water, that bringeth forth his fruit in his season; his leaf also shall not wither; and whatsoever he doeth shall prosper. The ungodly *are* not so: but *are* like the chaff which the wind driveth away. Therefore the ungodly shall not stand in the judgment, nor sinners in the congregation of the righteous. For the LORD knoweth the way of the righteous: but the way of the ungodly shall perish.

Psalm 119:72 The law of thy mouth *is* better unto me than thousands of gold and silver.

Psalm 119:127 Therefore I love thy commandments above gold; yea, above fine gold.

Psalm 119:162 I rejoice at thy word, as one that findeth great spoil.

Proverbs 3:13-14 Happy *is* the man *that* findeth wisdom, and the man *that* getteth understanding. For the merchandise of it *is* better than the merchandise of silver, and the gain thereof than fine gold.

Proverbs 16:16 How much better *is it* to get wisdom than gold! and to get understanding rather to be chosen than silver!

Proverbs 23:23 Buy the truth, and sell *it* not; *also* wisdom, and instruction, and understanding.

"I wisdom dwell with prudence, and find out knowledge of witty inventions." (verse 12) **"Wisdom"** and **"prudence"** are both personified and pictured as dwelling together to emphasize the fact that when a wise person acts, he will do so in a "prudent" *[discreet]* manner. Wisdom always leads a wise person to act with prudence at exactly the right time, in the best place, and in the proper manner. Wisdom is not to be fooled by **"witty inventions"** or shrewdness, schemes, or such like that have the intent of damage or destruction – for she will always *find them out* before they can do her damage. Chapter Two details how discretion from wisdom acts as a line of defense to protect against "evil men" and "strange women." Wisdom identifies such persons by their words and conduct and consequently takes the necessary, prudent action to minimize any damage they might intend to cause.

"The fear of the LORD *is* to hate evil: pride, and arrogancy, and the evil way, and the froward mouth, do I hate." (verse 13) By saying the "fear of the LORD" is to hate the specific things that God, through His wisdom, hates, this verse creates an identity between wisdom, God, and the wise person. The **"fear of the LORD"** is having AN AWESOME RESPECT FOR GOD, and such respect is the foundation that wisdom builds upon within the heart of the believer. Wisdom hates these products of evil described in this verse, and so does the wise person. To hate the things wisdom hates and to love the things wisdom loves is to identify with God–to have His understanding, His way of thinking. On the other hand, to sympathize with evil that God hates produces a separation between God and man, not only in this life but in eternity. Evil destabilizes the well-being, peace of mind, and safety of its victims. Evil is never satisfied with the extent of damage and is never to be pitied or endorsed in any manner. *To allow any emotion to produce sympathy for evil threatens this wonderful relationship with God.* The adulterous woman represents everything that the person having the "fear of the LORD" hates. She mocks God with her fake sacrifices and her loud froward mouth, and she masterfully uses lust of the flesh to lure men away from a love for God. She arrogantly leads men down a clear evil pathway to hell.

"The passion of hatred is natural; it has a useful, though a low place in the array of spiritual forces. It is abused when it is spent upon persons, but it is rightly indulged against evil principles and practices. We are morally defective unless we can feel 'the hate of hate, and scorn of scorn.' One of the means by which we are helped to resist sin is found in this hatred of it. It is not enough that we disapprove of it. We must loathe and abhor it from the very bottom of our hearts."[133]

Job 28:28 And unto man he said, Behold, the fear of the Lord, that *is* wisdom; and to depart from evil *is* understanding.
Psalm 97:10 Ye that love the LORD, hate evil: he preserveth the souls of his saints; he delivereth them out of the hand of the wicked.
Psalm 101:3 I will set no wicked thing before mine eyes: I hate the work of them that turn aside; *it* shall not cleave to me.
Psalm 119:104 Through thy precepts I get understanding: therefore I hate every false way.
Psalm 119:163 I hate and abhor lying: *but* thy law do I love.
Proverbs 3:7 Be not wise in thine own eyes: fear the LORD, and depart from evil.
Proverbs 14:16 A wise man feareth, and departeth from evil: but the fool rageth, and is confident.
Proverbs 16:6 By mercy and truth iniquity is purged: and by the fear of the LORD men depart from evil.

Poole states that ***hating evil*** "consists in a careful abstinence from all sin, and that not from carnal or prudential motives, but from a true dislike and hatred of it."[134] God hates evil, and believers must hate it also. "If evil is not hated, God is not feared."[135] *Hatred for people is never acceptable regardless of their sin.*

Matthew 6:24 No man can serve two masters: for either he will hate the one, and love the other; or else he will hold to the one, and despise the other. Ye cannot serve God and mammon.

One of the descriptive of Jesus' virtues, humility, is the opposite of **"pride,"** which God hates (Proverbs 6:16-19) and which is also here specified as being hated by wisdom. In verse 12, wisdom was said to "dwell with prudence" and here, the conclusion has to be drawn that wisdom could *never* dwell with pride.[136]

"Pride" produces three polluted streams described as **"arrogancy,"** **"the evil way,"** and **"the froward mouth"** – each declared to be hated by wisdom. All are evil. It is by these three actions that pride manifests its wicked self. In addition to being characteristic of the adulteress described in Chapter Seven *and* the chief characteristic of Satan, pride represents opposition to wisdom and to God. **"Pride"** causes a person to think more highly of himself than he should, and consequently, he doesn't realize a need for wisdom. **"Arrogancy** (arrogance)**,"** the acting out of superior thoughts in an offensive manner, can be observed in the eye as well as in the walk.

"The evil way" is seen in the actions of evil people. It is the way they live; it is their life. **"The evil way"** is a path chosen to oppose God as well as His teachings, and the **"froward mouth"** speaks in opposition and disobedience to wisdom.

1 Samuel 2:3 Talk no more so exceeding proudly; let not arrogancy come out of your mouth: for the LORD is a God of knowledge, and by him actions are weighed.
Psalm 45:7 Thou lovest righteousness, and hatest wickedness: therefore God, thy God, hath anointed thee with the oil of gladness above thy fellows.
Proverbs 4:24 Put away from thee a froward mouth, and perverse lips put far from thee.
Proverbs 6:12-14 A naughty person, a wicked man, walketh with a froward mouth. He winketh with his eyes, he speaketh with his feet, he teacheth with his fingers; Frowardness is in his heart, he deviseth mischief continually; he soweth discord.
Proverbs 6:16-19 These six things doth the LORD hate: yea, seven are an abomination unto him: A proud look, a lying tongue, and hands that shed innocent blood, An heart that deviseth wicked imaginations, feet that be swift in running to mischief, A false witness that speaketh lies, and he that soweth discord among brethren.
Proverbs 16:5 Every one that is proud in heart is an abomination to the LORD: though hand join in hand, he shall not be unpunished.

"Counsel *is* mine, and sound wisdom: I *am* understanding; I have strength." (verse 14) Wisdom here speaks of her **"counsel,"** which is that advice mined out of her heart of pure truth, unparalleled understanding, and knowledge. Any counsel that originates from any other source than godly wisdom is inferior. By wisdom, all of Creation was fashioned and set in motion. To get advice from the Creator of all things is to get counsel from the very deepest well of **"understanding."** This wisdom is **"sound"** because there is nothing about it that is uncertain. Any other wisdom is superficial, without understanding: it is only speculation and perhaps the best guess that can be assumed with limited knowledge and understanding. Godly wisdom has **"strength"** because it originates with God, who is all-powerful, all-knowing and everywhere present. "Counsel" and "sound wisdom" and "understanding" are not flowing from Jesus Christ, they are part of His essence.[137] He is "Counselor" (Isaiah 9:6). Everything that can be said of wisdom can also be said of Jesus, for He is the "express image" of His Father (Hebrews 1:3). He is the "Word of God." (Revelation 19:13)

Job 12:12 With the ancient is wisdom; and in length of days understanding. With him is wisdom and strength, he hath counsel and understanding.

Psalm 147:5 Great is our Lord, and of great power: his understanding is infinite.

Proverbs 2:6-7 For the LORD giveth wisdom: out of his mouth *cometh* knowledge and understanding. He layeth up sound wisdom for the righteous: *he is* a buckler to them that walk uprightly.

Proverbs 21:30 There is no wisdom nor understanding nor counsel against the LORD.

Isaiah 9:6 For unto us a child is born, unto us a son is given: and the government shall be upon his shoulder: and his name shall be called Wonderful, Counsellor, The mighty God, The everlasting Father, The Prince of Peace.

Isaiah 11:1-2 And there shall come forth a rod out of the stem of Jesse, and a Branch shall grow out of his roots: And the spirit of the LORD shall rest upon him, the spirit of wisdom and understanding, the spirit of counsel and might, the spirit of knowledge and of the fear of the LORD.

Isaiah 26:4 Trust ye in the LORD for ever: for in the LORD JEHOVAH is everlasting strength . . .

Isaiah 40:13-14 Who hath directed the Spirit of the LORD, or being his counsellor hath taught him? With whom took he counsel, and who instructed him, and taught him in the path of judgment, and taught him knowledge, and shewed to him the way of understanding?

Isaiah 40:28 Hast thou not known? hast thou not heard, that the everlasting God, the LORD, the Creator of the ends of the earth, fainteth not, neither is weary? there is no searching of his understanding.

Romans 11:33-36 O the depth of the riches both of the wisdom and knowledge of God! how unsearchable *are* his judgments, and his ways past finding out! For who hath known the mind of the Lord? or who hath been his counsellor? Or who hath first given to him, and it shall be recompensed unto him again? For of him, and through him, and to him, *are* all things: to whom *be* glory for ever. Amen.

1 Corinthians 1:24 But unto them which are called, both Jews and Greeks, Christ the power of God, and the wisdom of God.

"By me kings reign, and princes decree justice. By me princes rule, and nobles, *even* all the judges of the earth." (verses 15-16) "By possession of wisdom kings are enabled to discharge their functions duly and righteously. So Solomon prayed for wisdom to enable him to rule his subjects properly (I Kings 3:9)."[138] For leadership to be effective, the leader (king, prince, noble, judge) must comprehend what it means to trust God for wisdom, knowledge, and understanding. In doing so, a wise leader will treat all people, at every level, fairly and gain their respect; thus, he will have the ability to interact with them, and with God, in a productive manner. *(Remember the three traits of God that believers must apply in their lives: justice or righteousness, judgment, and equity See pages 5- 6.)* Of course, not all leaders are godly. Many don't want to know God's way of thinking and reasoning because they are filled with pride. Such men never submit to God's leadership. But *for a king to reign effectively,* for a prince to decree justice, and for princes, nobles, and judges of the earth to rule in truth and with peace, they must have God's help. They must become wise.

1 Kings 3:9 Give therefore thy servant an understanding heart to judge thy people, that I may discern between good and bad: for who is able to judge this thy so great a people?

Isaiah 9:6 For unto us a child is born, unto us a son is given: and the government shall be upon his shoulder: and his name shall be called Wonderful, Counsellor, The mighty God, The everlasting Father, The Prince of Peace.

Daniel 2:21 And he changeth the times and the seasons: he removeth kings, and setteth up kings: he giveth wisdom unto the wise, and knowledge to them that know understanding . . .

Daniel 4:32 And they shall drive thee from men, and thy dwelling *shall be* with the beasts of the field: they shall make thee to eat grass as oxen, and seven times shall pass over thee, until thou know that the most High ruleth in the kingdom of men, and giveth it to whomsoever he will.

Daniel 5:24-28 Then was the part of the hand sent from him; and this writing was written. And this *is* the writing that was written, MENE, MENE, TEKEL, UPHARSIN. This *is* the interpretation of the thing: MENE; God hath numbered thy kingdom, and finished it. TEKEL; Thou art weighed in the balances, and art found wanting. PERES; Thy kingdom is divided, and given to the Medes and Persians.

"I love them that love me." (verse 17a) Wisdom is available for everyone, but only those who love her will acquire her. The sluggard is too lazy to expend the effort, the proud too full of self, the wicked too full of hate, and the average person too comfortable in his ignorance. But for those who love wisdom, she advances to embrace them.

"Wisdom shows itself; teaches man the knowledge of himself; shows him also the will of God concerning him; manifests the snares and dangers of life, the allurements and unsatisfactory nature of all sensual and sinful pleasures, the blessedness of true religion, and the solid happiness which an upright soul derives from the peace and approbation of its Maker. If, then, the heart embraces this wisdom, follows this Divine teaching, and gives itself to God, his love will be shed abroad in it by the influence of the Holy Spirit. Thus we love God because he hath first loved us and the more we love him, the more we shall feel of his love, which will enable us to love him yet more and more; and thus we may go on increasing to eternity. Blessed be God!"[139]

Because wisdom comes from God and Jesus was the manifestation of wisdom, no person can love wisdom without respecting, honoring, and loving God.

Psalm 9:14-16 Because he hath set his love upon me, therefore will I deliver him: I will set him on high, because he hath known my name. He shall call upon me, and I will answer him: I *will be* with him in trouble; I will deliver him, and honour him. With long life will I satisfy him, and shew him my salvation.

John 14:21 He that hath my commandments, and keepeth them, he it is that loveth me: and he that loveth me shall be loved of my Father, and I will love him, and will manifest myself to him.

John 14:23 Jesus answered and said unto him, If a man love me, he will keep my words: and my Father will love him, and we will come unto him, and make our abode with him.

John 16:27 For the Father himself loveth you, because ye have loved me, and have believed that I came out from God.

1 John 4:19 We love him, because he first loved us.

"And those that seek me early shall find me." (verse 17b) **"Seek me early"** implies an urgency that alerts a person to the great need and value of wisdom, focuses his thinking on getting this wisdom, and energizes him to remove all obstacles and pursue wisdom relentlessly.

James 1:5 If any of you lack wisdom, let him ask of God, that giveth to all *men* liberally, and upbraideth not; and it shall be given him.

Proverbs 1:24-31 expresses the *personified Wisdom's* frustration toward those who refuse to love and to seek her.

Proverbs 1:24-31 Because I have called, and ye refused; I have stretched out my hand, and no man regarded; But ye have set at nought all my counsel, and would none of my reproof: I also will laugh at your calamity; I will mock when your fear cometh; When your fear cometh as desolation, and your destruction cometh as a whirlwind; when distress and anguish cometh upon you. Then shall they call upon me, but I will not answer; they shall seek me early, but they shall not find me: For that they hated knowledge, and did not choose the fear of the LORD: They would none of my counsel: they despised all my reproof. Therefore shall they eat of the fruit of their own way, and be filled with their own devices.

Proverbs 8:18-21 Riches and honour are with me; yea, durable riches and righteousness.
19. My fruit is better than gold, yea, than fine gold; and my revenue than choice silver.
20. I lead in the way of righteousness, in the midst of the paths of judgment:
21. That I may cause those that love me to inherit substance; and I will fill their treasures.

"Riches and honour are with me." (verse 18a) **"Riches"** is coupled in this verse with **"honour"** indicating that the type of **"riches"** attained will also bring **"honour"** because wisdom would only lead a person to increase wealth in a righteous manner that pleases God. Honorable gain by wisdom is without dishonesty, fraud, oppression, or any ungodly practice. When wisdom produces "riches and honor," there will be: quality of living, a clear conscience, peace of mind, a good name, a loving family, and certainly wisdom itself.

Proverbs 3:16 Length of days *is* in her right hand; *and* in her left hand riches and honour.

"Yea, durable riches and righteousness" (verse 18b) amplifies the first part of this verse and describes the category of wealth gained through wise living as being **"durable** *[valued and enduring]* **and righteous** *[just, right]*.**"** It is "durable" in that it is valuable, enduring, lasts throughout a lifetime and throughout eternity especially when used in the work of God to bring others into the family of God. It is "righteous" in that it is gained in a manner approved of God and it bears His blessings. Verse nineteen continues to amplify and give understanding to assets attained through wisdom.

"My fruit *[income, produce, gain]* ***is*** **better than gold, yea, than fine gold; and my revenue than choice silver."** (verse 19) "In Wisdom's promises believers have goods laid up, not for days and years, but for eternity; her fruit therefore is *better than gold*."[140]

Proverbs 3:13-15 Happy *is* the man *that* findeth wisdom, and the man *that* getteth understanding. For the merchandise of it *is* better than the merchandise of silver, and the gain thereof than fine gold. She *is* more precious than rubies: and all the things thou canst desire are not to be compared unto her.

Proverbs 8:10-11 Receive my instruction, and not silver; and knowledge rather than choice gold. For wisdom *is* better than rubies; and all the things that may be desired are not to be compared to it.

Ecclesiastes 7:11-12 Wisdom *is* good with an inheritance: and *by it there is* profit to them that see the sun. For wisdom *is* a defence, *and* money *is* a defence: but the excellency of knowledge *is, that* wisdom giveth life to them that have it.

Matthew 25:34 Then shall the King say unto them on his right hand, Come, ye blessed of my Father, inherit the kingdom prepared for you from the foundation of the world:

Luke 10:41-42 And Jesus answered and said unto her, Martha, Martha, thou art careful and troubled about many things: But one thing is needful: and Mary hath chosen that good part, which shall not be taken away from her.

Hebrews 10:34 For ye had compassion of me in my bonds, and took joyfully the spoiling of your goods, knowing in yourselves that ye have in heaven a better and an enduring substance.

Revelation 3:17-18 Because thou sayest, I am rich, and increased with goods, and have need of nothing; and knowest not that thou art wretched, and miserable, and poor, and blind, and naked: I counsel thee to buy of me gold tried in the fire, that thou mayest be rich; and white raiment, that thou mayest be clothed, and t h a t the shame of thy nakedness do not appear; and anoint thine eyes with eyesalve, that thou mayest see.

"I lead in the way of righteousness, in the midst of the paths of judgment." (verse 20) Wisdom says, **"I lead"** to explain that she is always up front showing the way. Thus, for a person to say that they are in the *"permissive will of God"* and *living a life without* righteousness is unfounded. Godly wisdom does not lead in any way other than in righteousness – "in the way of truth, justice, and mercy, of holiness and happiness; the way in which God would have men to walk, and which will certainly bring them to the desired end."[141] The **"way of righteousness"** is the way that is right. **"Paths of judgment"** is another way of saying in the right path. **"In the midst"** means nowhere near the edge (too close to unrighteousness) where a believer's actions might be seen by an observer as *not right*.

> Proverbs 3:6 In all thy ways acknowledge him, and he shall direct thy paths.
>
> Proverbs 4:11-12 I have taught thee in the way of wisdom; I have led thee in right paths. When thou goest, thy steps shall not be straitened; and when thou runnest, thou shalt not stumble.
>
> Proverbs 6:20-22 My son, keep thy father's commandment, and forsake not the law of thy mother: Bind them continually upon thine heart, *and* tie them about thy neck. When thou goest, it shall lead thee; when thou sleepest, it shall keep thee; and *when* thou awakest, it shall talk with thee.
>
> Isaiah 48:17 Thus saith the LORD, thy Redeemer, the Holy One of Israel; I *am* the LORD thy God which teacheth thee to profit, which leadeth thee by the way *that* thou shouldest go.
>
> Isaiah 49:10 They shall not hunger nor thirst; neither shall the heat nor sun smite them: for he that hath mercy on them shall lead them, even by the springs of water shall he guide them.
>
> 1 Thessalonians 5:22 Abstain from all appearance of evil.

"That I may cause those that love me to inherit substance; and I will fill their treasures." (verse 21) This verse declares earthly rewards to be given by wisdom. Such gifts are her acts of love and appreciation in response to those that love her and follow her instructions. Wisdom makes marvelous things happen by always leading in the way of understanding. Because Wisdom thinks and reasons in the same manner as God, she will **"cause"** *the inheriting of substance* and *filling of treasures*, thus always showing the one who loves her how to live, in every regard, in the most effective manner. **"Substance"** is a term that may include anything that exists, and *Pulpit Helps* defines it as "real, valuable possessions."[142] This verse describes substance as that which *fills their treasures* [storehouses]. *It should be noted that the inheritance of substance on earth is only a token of the eternal inheritance of heaven that comes from loving God and His wisdom.*

Wisdom instructs man, first of all, on how to honor God and worship Him in truth and spirit. It also teaches man how to most effectively interact with other people, including how to effectively conduct one's financial life and responsibilities. People, who don't have a personal relationship with God, do not have His direct guidance in their lives, do not have a proper motive in their relationship with others, do not have a proper concept of wealth, and cannot expect God to directly affect their *inheritance of substance* or *to fill their treasures*. This statement is not given to support the modern-day concept of a "prosperity gospel," but it is stated to emphasize that *wisdom will direct every aspect of a Christian's life*, including his wise handling of life that results in personal gain and reveals an obvious blessing of God. Ignorance of God's word leads to poverty both physically and spiritually.

> Psalm 112:1-3 Praise ye the LORD. Blessed *is* the man *that* feareth the LORD, *that* delighteth greatly in his commandments. His seed shall be mighty upon earth: the generation of the upright shall be blessed. Wealth and riches *shall be* in his house: and his righteousness endureth for ever.
>
> Proverbs 3:13-16 Happy *is* the man *that* findeth wisdom, and the man *that* getteth understanding. For the merchandise of it *is* better than the merchandise of silver, and the gain thereof than fine gold. She *is* more precious than rubies: and all the things thou canst desire are not to be compared unto her. Length of days *is* in her right hand; *and* in her left hand riches and honour.
>
> Proverbs 14:24 The crown of the wise *is* their riches: *but* the foolishness of fools *is* folly.
>
> Proverbs 15:6 In the house of the righteous *is* much treasure: but in the revenues of the wicked is trouble.
>
> Proverbs 22:4 By humility *and* the fear of the LORD *are* riches, and honour, and life.
>
> Matthew 6:19-21 Lay not up for yourselves treasures upon earth, where moth and rust doth corrupt, and where thieves break through and steal: But lay up for yourselves treasures in heaven, where neither moth nor rust doth corrupt, and where thieves do not break through nor steal: For where your treasure is, there will your heart be also.
>
> Matthew 6:33 But seek ye first the kingdom of God, and his righteousness; and all these things shall be added unto you.
>
> Luke 12:33-34 Sell that ye have, and give alms; provide yourselves bags which wax not old, a treasure in the heavens that faileth not, where no thief approacheth, neither moth corrupteth. For where your treasure is, there will your heart be also.
>
> Hebrews 10:34 For ye had compassion of me in my bonds, and took joyfully the spoiling of your goods, knowing in yourselves that ye have in heaven a better and an enduring substance.
>
> 1Peter 1:3-5 Blessed *be* the God and Father of our Lord Jesus Christ, which according to his abundant mercy hath begotten us again unto a lively hope by the resurrection of Jesus Christ from the dead, To an inheritance incorruptible, and undefiled, and that fadeth not away, reserved in heaven for you, who are kept by the power of God through faith unto salvation ready to be revealed in the last time.

Sections I, II, and III of the outline below (verses 22-31) portray *the reasons why* **Wisdom's** claims as given in Proverbs 8:6-21 are creditable. After she validates her claims, she makes a final plea for the people of the world to acquire wisdom (verses 32-36).

> **Wisdom is Eternal – Therefore Listen to Wisdom** (Outline of Chapter 8:22-36)
>
> I. **Wisdom Preexisted:** (verses 22-26)
>   A. In the beginning of Creation (verse 22)
>   B. From eternity past (verse 23)
>   C. Before the depths and fountains (verse 24)
>   D. Before the mountains were settled (verse 25)
>   E. Before the earth was made (verse 26)
> II. **Wisdom Was Present:** (verses 27-29)
>   A. When God prepared the heavens (verse 27)
>   B. When God made the world a circle (verse 27)
>   C. When God established the clouds (verse 28)
>   D. When God strengthened the fountains of the deep (verse 28)
>   E. When God set the boundaries of the seas (verse 29)
> III. **Wisdom Pleasantly Rejoiced:** (verses 30-31)
>   A. In the presence of God (verse 30)
>   B. In the habitable part of the earth with mankind (verses 30 31)
> IV. **Wisdom Pleads:** (verses 32-36)
>   A. Listen to me (verse 32)
>   B. Keep my ways and be blessed (verse 32)
>   C. Hear instruction and be wise (verse 33)
>   D. Hear, watch and wait for wisdom and be blessed (verse 34)
>   E. Find wisdom, life, and favor of God (verse 35)
> **Conclusion:** (verse 36)
>   A. "But he that sinneth against me wrongeth his own soul:..."
>   B. "All they that hate me love death."

"The LORD possessed me in the beginning of his way, before his works of old." (verse 22) The personified Wisdom here declares that **"The LORD possessed me"** (verse 22a) means "acquired" and "owned" and that from eternity. Charles Bridges in his *Commentary on Proverbs* said that this subject "is much safer to adore than to expound." Nonetheless, *wisdom is obviously inherently and eternally the way each member of the Trinity thinks and reasons; and such wisdom can be observed in the life of Jesus.*

> Matthew 13:54 And when he was come into his own country, he taught them in their synagogue, insomuch that they were astonished, and said, Whence hath this *man* this wisdom, and *these* mighty works?
> Luke 2:40 And the child grew, and waxed strong in spirit, filled with wisdom: and the grace of God was upon him.
> Luke 2:52 And Jesus increased in wisdom and stature, and in favour with God and man.
> 1Corinthians 1:24 But unto them which are called, both Jews and Greeks, Christ the power of God, and the wisdom of God.
> 1Corinthians 1:30 But of him are ye in Christ Jesus, who of God is made unto us wisdom, and righteousness, and sanctification, and redemption:
> John 1:1 In the beginning was the Word, and the Word was with God, and the Word was God.

"In the beginning of his way, before his works of old" (verse 22b) refers to the beginning of creation as detailed in subsequent verses. This Scripture appears to be in place to substantiate the fact that God was *never without wisdom*. All of God's attributes are part of Himself and just as eternal as Himself.[143] The creation of the heavens and the earth was His work along with His Son's, who was there creating with Him; and like the Father, Jesus also possessed wisdom. In His incarnation, Jesus exemplified this marvelous eternal wisdom to the world.

> Psalm 136:5 To him that by wisdom made the heavens: for his mercy endureth for ever.
> Proverbs 3:19 The LORD by wisdom hath founded the earth; by understanding hath he established the heavens.
> Jeremiah 10:12 He hath made the earth by his power, he hath established the world by his wisdom, and hath stretched out the heavens by his discretion.
> Jeremiah 51:15 He hath made the earth by his power, he hath established the world by his wisdom, and hath stretched out the heaven by his understanding.

"I was set up from everlasting, from the beginning, or ever the earth was." (verse 23) Wisdom reiterates the fact that she was with God before creation and is part of the "fabric" of Who God is. This verse states that wisdom was **"set up from everlasting,"** indicating that along with the eternal God was also eternal wisdom. How Wisdom was "set up" will remain a mystery until God chooses to explain the same in heaven. She was there with God **"from the beginning, or ever the earth was,"** leaving no doubt that Wisdom was always with God.

"When *there were* no depths, I was brought forth; when *there were* no fountains abounding with water. Before the mountains were settled, before the hills was I brought forth." (verses 24-25) Wisdom was **"brought forth,"** meaning that she was *made apparent* as *the thought process* whereby God created the world. Wardlow gives the following explanation:

> "...infinite wisdom directed all the divine counsels, – all the prospective plans of the Godhead being devised by it from everlasting, with unerring, with infinite skill. We are accustomed to speak of a man consulting his understanding, his judgment, his good sense and discretion. Divine wisdom, belonging essentially to the nature of God, was from eternity. But as a person she here speaks of herself as 'brought forth' previously

to the commencement of creation and providence, with obvious reference to the application of her counsels in the purposes and plans of the Godhead. The language of figure is not, of course, to be interpreted literally and strictly."[144]

"While as yet he had not made the earth, nor the fields, nor the highest part of the dust of the world." (verse 26) Wisdom was there before day three of Creation.

> Genesis 1:9-13 And God said, Let the waters under the heaven be gathered together unto one place, and let the dry land appear: and it was so. And God called the dry land Earth; and the gathering together of the waters called he Seas: and God saw that it was good. And God said, Let the earth bring forth grass, the herb yielding seed, and the fruit tree yielding fruit after his kind, whose seed is in itself, upon the earth: and it was so. And the earth brought forth grass, and herb yielding seed after his kind, and the tree yielding fruit, whose seed was in itself, after his kind: and God saw that it was good. And the evening and the morning were the third day.

From the beginning of the Bible, God demonstrated the meaning of *"decently and in order"* (1 Corinthians 14:40). Waters had to be gathered together before the earth could appear. Since the **"highest part of the dust of the world"** refers to the topsoil that has nutrients suitable for growing crops instead of dirt that has no nutrients, the nutrients had to be in place so that the plants could appear.

"When he prepared the heavens, I *was* there: when he set a compass upon the face of the depth." (verse 27) Wisdom was there when God spoke the heavens into place.

> Psalm 33:6 By the word of the LORD were the heavens made; and all the host of them by the breath of his mouth.
> Psalm 102:25 Of old hast thou laid the foundation of the earth: and the heavens *are* the work of thy hands.
> Psalm 136:5 To him that by wisdom made the heavens: for his mercy *endureth* for ever.
> Jeremiah 10:12 He hath made the earth by his power, he hath established the world by his wisdom, and hath stretched out the heavens by his discretion.
> Colossians 1:16-17 For by him were all things created, that are in heaven, and that are in earth, visible and invisible, whether *they be* thrones, or dominions, or principalities, or powers: all things were created by him, and for him: And he is before all things, and by him all things consist.
> Hebrews 1:10 And, Thou, Lord, in the beginning hast laid the foundation of the earth; and the heavens are the works of thine hands . . .

"I *was* there: when he set a compass upon the face of the depth." God's setting **"a compass upon the face of the depth"** meant that He made the earth in the shape of a **"compass"** (a globe or a circle), and Wisdom was present. When he established the heavens, Wisdom was there.

> Isaiah 40:22 *It is* he that sitteth upon the circle of the earth . . .

"When he established the clouds above: when he strengthened the fountains of the deep." (verse 28) God placed the clouds and waters of the earth where He wanted them and commanded them to be "at home" there. He made the clouds with substance so that one could see them in the heavens, but He also prepared them so that they could let loose drops of water (raindrops). By the strength of God's command, the clouds and fountains are properly placed and restrained. When that happened, Wisdom was there.

> Genesis 1:6-8 And God said, Let there be a firmament in the midst of the waters, and let it divide the waters from the waters. And God made the firmament, and divided the waters which *were* under the firmament from the waters which *were* above the firmament: and it was so. And God called the firmament Heaven. And the evening and the morning were the second day.

"When he gave to the sea his decree, that the waters should not pass his commandment: when he appointed the foundations of the earth." (verse 29) The authority seen in the previous verse is observed again when God ordered the sea and the foundations of the earth to remain in place. When God did this, Wisdom was present.

> Psalm 104:5-10 Who laid the foundations of the earth, that it should not be removed for ever. Thou coveredst it with the deep as with a garment: the waters stood above the mountains. At thy rebuke they fled; at the voice of thy thunder they hasted away. They go up by the mountains; they go down by the valleys unto the place which thou hast founded for them. Thou hast set a bound that they may not pass over; that they turn not again to cover the earth. He sendeth the springs into the valleys, which run among the hills.
> Jeremiah 5:21-22 Hear now this, O foolish people, and without understanding; which have eyes, and see not; which have ears, and hear not: Fear ye not me? saith the LORD: will ye not tremble at my presence, which have placed the sand for the bound of the sea by a perpetual decree, that it cannot pass it: and though the waves thereof toss themselves, yet can they not prevail; though they roar, yet can they not pass over it? *[See also Job 38:4-11.]*

"Then I was by him, *as* one brought up *with him*: and I was daily *his* delight, rejoicing always before him; Rejoicing in the habitable part of his earth; and my delights *were* with the sons of men." (verses 30-31) **"Then I was**

by him" describes the closeness that the *personified Wisdom* maintained to God, especially during the Creation. Wisdom is as much an attribute of God as is the attribute of love.

"As one brought up with him and I was daily his delight rejoicing always before him" (verse 30b) indicates the closeness and gladness that attended the constant victories that the Creator brought about through wisdom. God called the light He created "good," the separation of the Earth and the seas "good," the creation of the vegetation "good," the creation of the sun and moon "good," and the creation of the fish and the fowl "good." On the sixth day (Genesis 1:31) "God saw everything that he had made, and, behold, it was *very good*." Wisdom rejoiced with God in each day of Creation. Wisdom rejoiced in everything God created.

"Rejoicing in the habitable part of his earth" (verse 31a) speaks of personified Wisdom's rejoicing in that part of the earth where wise men abide and interact with God. God rejoices with those who thirst after Him and His wisdom and His Son.

"And my delights were with the sons of men." (verse 31b) Because God has always desired to commune with man daily, He created mankind. It is God's delight to reveal Himself to the sons of men, and it was the delight of wisdom in the incarnate Son to take on human flesh and live among men. As C.S. Lewis wrote in his well-known book *Mere Christianity*, "The Son of God became a man to enable men to become sons of God."

> Philippians 2:6-8 Who, being in the form of God, thought it not robbery to be equal with God: But made himself of no reputation, and took upon him the form of a servant, and was made in the likeness of men: And being found in fashion as a man, he humbled himself, and became obedient unto death, even the death of the cross.

Proverbs 8:32-36 Now therefore hearken unto me, O ye children: for blessed *are they that* keep my ways.
33. Hear instruction, and be wise, and refuse it not.
34. Blessed *is* the man that heareth me, watching daily at my gates, waiting at the posts of my doors.
35. For whoso findeth me findeth life, and shall obtain favour of the LORD.
36. But he that sinneth against me wrongeth his own soul: all they that hate me love death.

After Wisdom demonstrated to the reader that she existed before the creation of the world and shared Jehovah's joy at His accomplishments in the Creation, she makes a final plea for the people of the world to acquire wisdom in verses 32-36.

Personified Wisdom continues to speak in verses 32-36. She tells her audience to **"hear instruction"** and addresses them as **"ye children"** as "the father" did. *Ben* is translated as "ye children" in Proverbs 4:1, 5:7, and 7:24. In each of those verses, the word "hear" or "hearken" is stressed.

"Now therefore hearken unto me, O ye children: for blessed *are they that* keep my ways." (verse 32) **"Now therefore"** refers to the words wisdom has already stated about her fruits and about her being so close to God in Creation. Because of her superior qualifications, plus the promised rewards of being "blessed" (verse 32), becoming "wise" (verse 33), having "life," and obtaining "favor of the LORD" (verse 35), she encourages close attention. Notice also the call to obedience in **"blessed are they that keep my ways."** It is for their own benefit that the children listen to her and obey the word of God. Being blessed comes through obedience and submission to God's will.

> Proverbs 8:12; 14–19 I wisdom dwell with prudence, and find out knowledge of witty inventions . . . Counsel is mine, and sound wisdom: I am understanding; I have strength. By me kings reign, and princes decree justice. By me princes rule, and nobles, even all the judges of the earth. I love them that love me; and those that seek me early shall find me. Riches and honour are with me; yea, durable riches and righteousness. My fruit is better than gold, yea, than fine gold; and my revenue than choice silver.

"Hear instruction, and be wise, and refuse it not." (verse 33) Notice how the words "hear" or "hearken" are closely identified with the word "blessed" in verses 32-34. This linked repetition emphasizes the conditional rewards of listening attentively. **"Hear"** *[to perceive by the ear with the implication of attention and obedience]* with great concentration the words that wisdom has to say because the **"instruction"** is the exact thoughts and views of God; and the **"instruction,"** *if heard and followed*, will make the recipient **"wise."** **"Refuse it not"** or else become a victim of "evil men" and "strange women" because of a lack of discretion. *(See Proverbs 2.)*

"Blessed *is* the man that heareth me, watching daily at my gates, waiting at the posts of my doors. For whoso findeth me findeth life, and shall obtain favour of the LORD." (verses 34-35) The mental image given in the statement **"blessed *is* the man that heareth me, watching daily at my gates, waiting at the posts of my doors"** is that of an enthusiastic person eager to learn wise living from this unparalleled instructor. The hungry-to-learn student arrives early and eagerly waits by the schoolhouse door so as not to miss even one word that will bring him to living a wise **"life"** and **"favor of the LORD."** Men always have a choice of *how they live their lives*. And the pathway they choose to walk can either be wise and bring fullness of joy because the walk is according to God's design, or it can be full of heartaches and disaster when lived in opposition to the Creator. Wisdom will instruct on the better way; and such a wonderful, rewarding walk with God begins with paying close attention.

"Favour of the LORD" is a phrase used three times in the Book of Proverbs:
> Proverbs 8:35 For whoso findeth me findeth life, and shall obtain favour of the LORD.
> Proverbs 12:2 A good *man* obtaineth favour of the LORD: but a man of wicked devices will he condemn.
> Proverbs 18:22 *Whoso* findeth a wife findeth a good *thing,* and obtaineth favour of the LORD.

When God favors a person like He did David, Solomon, Daniel, Ruth, and many others, He makes His presence known to them in special ways by dropping "handfuls of purpose" all along the way. Also He provides protection, peace, power, and provisions that the average person never knows. God hears their prayers and communes with them spiritually. To have a desire for wisdom is to have a desire to think like God, to view the world as He does, to love everything He loves, and to hate the sin He hates – thus, having much in common.

"But he that sinneth against me wrongeth his own soul: all they that hate me love death." (verse 36) In the first clause of verse 36, the *sin that wrongs a person's soul* is defined in the second as *those who hate wisdom.* When a person despises wisdom, he hates the way God thinks and reasons and acts. He is against God. Such a person is full of pride, resisted by God, and unable to understand that his thinking causes him to **"love death."** Death is his sentence, his judgment from the Judge. Such a one has separated himself from quality of life on earth and damned himself to hell. Jesus is the expression and communication of the word of God. He is both the incarnate and the inspired Word, and He is the final and ultimate expression of God's love for man. He is also the manifestation of such wisdom from the mind of God that provides man with a way of forgiveness for his sins and a path back to the Father. "Greater love hath no man than this, that a man lay down his life for his friends." (John 15:13)

> Deuteronomy 30:16-20 In that I command thee this day to love the LORD thy God, to walk in his ways, and to keep his commandments and his statutes and his judgments, that thou mayest live and multiply: and the LORD thy God shall bless thee in the land whither thou goest to possess it. But if thine heart turn away, so that thou wilt not hear, but shalt be drawn away, and worship other gods, and serve them; I denounce unto you this day, that ye shall surely perish, *and that* ye shall not prolong *your* days upon the land, whither thou passest over Jordan to go to possess it. I call heaven and earth to record this day against you, *that* I have set before you life and death, blessing and cursing: therefore choose life, that both thou and thy seed may live: That thou mayest love the LORD thy God, *and* that thou mayest obey his voice, and that thou mayest cleave unto him: for he *is* thy life, and the length of thy days: that thou mayest dwell in the land which the LORD sware unto thy fathers, to Abraham, to Isaac, and to Jacob, to give them.
> Proverbs 1:29-31 For that they hated knowledge, and did not choose the fear of the LORD: They would none of my counsel: they despised all my reproof. Therefore shall they eat of the fruit of their own way, and be filled with their own devices.
> Proverbs 11:19 As righteousness *tendeth* to life: so he that pursueth evil *pursueth it* to his own death.
> John 3:19-20 And this is the condemnation, that light is come into the world, and men loved darkness rather than light, because their deeds were evil. For every one that doeth evil hateth the light, neither cometh to the light, lest his deeds should be reproved.
> Hebrews 10:26-29 For if we sin wilfully after that we have received the knowledge of the truth, there remaineth no more sacrifice for sins, But a certain fearful looking for of judgment and fiery indignation, which shall devour the adversaries. He that despised Moses' law died without mercy under two or three witnesses: Of how much sorer punishment, suppose ye, shall he be thought worthy, who hath trodden under foot the Son of God, and hath counted the blood of the covenant, wherewith he was sanctified, an unholy thing, and hath done despite unto the Spirit of grace?

Two choices have been presented to the readers of the Book of Proverbs: the way of wisdom or the way of foolishness. These choices will continue to be presented in the next chapter.

CHAPTER NINE

> **Choose You This Day** (Outline of Proverbs 9)
> I. **Follow Wisdom and Live**
>   A. Wisdom's Mansion (verses 1-6)
>   B. Wisdom's Message to her Missionaries (verses 7-9)
>   C. Wisdom's Method to get to God (verse 10)
>   D. Wisdom's Multiplication in Life (verse 11)
>   E. Wisdom's Meat of the matter–Individual Accountability (verse 12)
> II. **Favor Folly and Die**
>   A. Folly's Emptiness (verse 13)
>   B. Folly's Elevation of Self (verse 14)
>   C. Folly's Invitation (verse 15-16)
>   D. Folly's Enticement (verse 17)
>   E. Folly's Evil End (verse 18)

> **Proverbs 9:1-6** Wisdom hath builded her house, she hath hewn out her seven pillars:
> 2. She hath killed her beasts; she hath mingled her wine; she hath also furnished her table.
> 3. She hath sent forth her maidens: she crieth upon the highest places of the city,
> 4. Whoso *is* simple, let him turn in hither: *as for* him that wanteth understanding, she saith to him,
> 5. Come, eat of my bread, and drink of the wine *which* I have mingled.
> 6. Forsake the foolish, and live; and go in the way of understanding.

These first six verses of Chapter 9 continue to provide information and understanding concerning Wisdom's mansion spoken of in Chapter 8. The narrative contained in chapters 7, 8, and 9 contrasts personified *Wisdom's* depth of godly beauty, strength, and permanent honor with the temporary, shallow, wicked, ugliness of the *adulteress*. To choose the righteous way expressed by Wisdom's words and character is to choose abundant and eternal life. To choose the way of folly represented by the harlot and adulteress is to choose a miserable physical life and an eternity in hell.

Described in these first six verses, personified Wisdom's mansion and meal picture symbolically the wise person's relationship with God that produces eternal life, joy, peace, abundance, and blessings of life.

> "The Palace of Wisdom is very attractive; well built and well furnished, it rings with the sounds of hospitality; and, with its open colonnades, it seems of itself to invite all passers-by to enter in as guests. It is reared upon seven well-hewn marble pillars, in a quadrangular form, With the entrance side left wide open. This is no shifting tent or tottering hut, but an eternal mansion, that lacks nothing of stability, or completeness, or beauty. Through the spacious doorways may be seen the great courtyard, in which appear the preparations for a perpetual feast. The beasts are killed and dressed: the wine stands in tall flagons ready mixed for drinking: the tables are spread and decked. All is open, generous, large, a contrast to that unhallowed private supper to which the unwary youth was invited by his seducer. (Proverbs 7:14) There are no secret chambers, no twilight suggestions and insinuations: the broad light shines over all; there is a promise of social joy; it seems that they will be blessed who sit down together at this board. And now the beautiful owner of the palace has sent forth her maidens into the public ways of the city: theirs is a gracious errand; they are not to chide with sour and censorious rebukes, but they are to invite with winning friendliness; they are to offer this rare repast, which is now ready, to all those who are willing to acknowledge their need of it. 'Come, eat ye of my bread, and drink of the wine which I have mingled.'" (Proverbs 9:5)[145]

In addition to her other great values, Wisdom has been described as eternally excellent and true, righteous, and plain-spoken, with words of promise that are of greater value than all the gold and silver on earth *because they lead to God and His Son*. Her appeal comes symbolically through the depth, strength, and beauty of her stately house, the delicacy of her special meal, the delivery of the invitation by her maidens, and the distinct, beautiful, compelling appeal for mankind to come to their senses and follow after the teachings of God.

"Wisdom hath builded her house, she hath hewn out her seven pillars." (verse 1) Notice the symbolism in this verse. Scripture relates the building of a house to the building of the family of God; and the quality of the house built by God represents the quality of the Builder.

> Hebrews 3:3-4 For this *man* was counted worthy of more glory than Moses, inasmuch as he who hath builded the house hath more honour than the house. For every house is builded by some *man;* but he that built all things *is* God.

Personified Wisdom built this mansion to symbolically express her love for and delight to be with the believing sons of men. Later, the same love and delight are expressed with Jesus' preparations of a beautiful place and a feast for the sons of men who believe in Him.

> Proverbs 8:32 ". . . and my delights *were* with the sons of men."
>
> John 14:2 In my Father's house are many mansions: if it were not so, I would have told you. I go to prepare a place for you.
>
> Revelation 19:7-9 Let us be glad and rejoice, and give honour to him: for the marriage of the Lamb is come, and his wife hath made herself ready. And to her was granted that she should be arrayed in fine linen, clean and white: for the fine linen is the righteousness of saints. And he saith unto me, Write, Blessed *are* they which are called unto the marriage supper of the Lamb. And he saith unto me, These are the true sayings of God.

This imagery of Wisdom's **"house"** gives the reader a picture of the builder's great character; and the magnificent home represents the beauty, stability, strength, and completeness that reflect the owner's eternal spirit of excellence. Her splendid, perfect, and careful preparations are done for the benefit of those honored guests who have *chosen to become wise; and her very special meticulous preparations are symbolic of God's great love and care for those who choose God's wisdom.* Every person who chooses to forsake folly and to enter the beautiful estate of Wisdom will be given instruction directly from God, the source of wisdom.

The **"seven pillars"** hewn out of stone reveal the rock-solidness of all that Wisdom represents and teaches. Her doctrines are permanently established. The structure will not be moved by the winds of time or the settling of earth. Standing in solid contrast to the ever-shifting feet of the adulteress, Wisdom's deep and wide foundations remain ETERNALLY strong and straight without cracks or bowing. Seven is a number found frequently in Scripture to indicate completeness, and the fact that **"she hath hewn out her seven pillars"** represents her undeterred spirit of excellence and persistent labor in completing what she starts. The vast, substantial structure will provide adequately for all guests who seek to know wisdom to the fullest. Listening to the wisdom of God produces a heart that harmonizes with God's heart and a body that shuns sin and enjoys abundant living that begins here on earth and extends throughout eternity in the presence of God.

"She hath killed her beasts; she hath mingled her wine; she hath also furnished her table" (verse 2) Wisdom is fully prepared for those "sons of man" who have chosen to come into her stately mansion and partake of a perfectly-prepared, life-sustaining meal, including the best meats and joyous wine set at her table in a most memorable fashion. All Wisdom's food, drink, and furnishings symbolize *interaction with God through CHOOSING to respect, obey, submit and depend upon God and His wisdom.* Everything that Wisdom does is designed to sustain life, and **"her beasts"** are the finest of meat that symbolizes perfect doctrine. Her gifts are designed to align the mind and manners of her guests with that of God. In contrast is the adulteress who lures to evil, weakness, sickness, and death. The adulteress consistently paves a pathway to hell and misery.

> "Flesh and wine are figures of the nourishment for the mind and the heart which is found with wisdom, and, without asking what the flesh and the wine specially mean, are figures of the manifold enjoyment which makes at once strong and happy."[146]

"She hath mingled her wine." (verse 2) In the box below is a survey of how wine was viewed and used throughout Scripture. From that survey, it should be evident that *wine was a vital symbolic part of Wisdom's total preparations.* She summoned the "simple" and "him that wanteth understanding" to "come, eat of my bread, and drink of the wine which I have mingled." (verse 4)

*Coming to dine with Wisdom indicates a **FORSAKING of the foolish** and a **PARTAKING in life** (righteousness with God).* (verse 6) It is to "go in the way of understanding" – the way of God, of righteousness, of holiness, of wise living (verse 6). Isaiah expressed the great opportunity to walk with God in this way: "Ho, every one that thirsteth, come ye to the waters, and he that hath no money; come ye, buy, and eat; yea, come, buy wine and milk without money and without price." (Isaiah 55:1)

Wine is a product of the fruit of the vine grown out of the ground. As such, it was reflective of the fact that Israel was an agricultural society and that she was directly dependent on God. He gave them (or withheld from them when Israel disobeyed) all the right weather conditions for a good harvest. As a crop, this fruit of the vine symbolized a spiritual connection, interaction, and blessings from God when they were obedient. But, without OBEDIENCE, blessings (symbolized by wine) were withheld.

NOTE: It is beyond the scope of this chapter to discuss all the aspects of wine, especially fermentation. The following chart is provided to reveal the importance of wine in Israel's earlier days and why it was an important factor in Wisdom's preparation.

A Survey of How Wine Was Viewed and Used in Biblical Times

I. Throughout the Old Testament, wine is regarded as a necessity of life and in no way as a mere luxury. It was a necessary part of even the simplest meal.

Genesis 14:18 And Melchizedek king of Salem brought forth bread and wine: and he *was* the priest of the most high God.

Judges 19:19 Yet there is both straw and provender for our asses; and there is bread and wine also for me, and for thy handmaid, and for the young man *which is* with thy servants: *there is* no want of any thing.

1 Samuel 16:20 And Jesse took an ass *laden* with bread, and a bottle of wine, and a kid, and sent *them* by David his son unto Saul.

Isaiah 55:1 Ho, every one that thirsteth, come ye to the waters, and he that hath no money; come ye, buy, and eat; yea, come, buy wine and milk without money and without price.

II. *Wine* was an indispensable provision for a fortress.

2 Chronicles 11:11 And he fortified the strong holds, and put captains in them, and store of victual, and of oil and wine.

III. *Wine* was drunk by all classes.

Lamentations 2:12 They say to their mothers, Where *is* corn and wine? when they swooned as the wounded in the streets of the city, when their soul was poured out into their mothers' bosom.

Zechariah 9:17 For how great *is* his goodness, and how great *is* his beauty! corn shall make the young men cheerful, and new wine the maids.

IV. "Wine" is bracketed with "grain" as a basic staple.

Genesis 27:28 Therefore God give thee of the dew of heaven, and the fatness of the earth, and plenty of corn and wine . . .

V. Failure of the wine crop or its destruction by foreigners was a terrible calamity.

Deuteronomy 28:30 Thou shalt betroth a wife, and another man shall lie with her: thou shalt build an house, and thou shalt not dwell therein: thou shalt plant a vineyard, and shalt not gather the grapes thereof.

Deuteronomy 28:39 Thou shalt plant vineyards, and dress *them,* but shalt neither drink *of* the wine, nor gather *the grapes;* for the worms shall eat them.

Isaiah 62:8 The LORD hath sworn by his right hand, and by the arm of his strength, Surely I will no more give thy corn *to be* meat for thine enemies; and the sons of the stranger shall not drink thy wine, for the which thou hast laboured . . .

Isaiah 65:21 And they shall build houses, and inhabit *them;* and they shall plant vineyards, and eat the fruit of them.

Micah 6:15 Thou shalt sow, but thou shalt not reap; thou shalt tread the olives, but thou shalt not anoint thee with oil; and sweet wine, but shalt not drink wine.

Zephaniah 1:13 Therefore their goods shall become a booty, and their houses a desolation: they shall also build houses, but not inhabit *them;* and they shall plant vineyards, but not drink the wine thereof.

VI. On the other hand, abundance of wine was a special token of God's blessing.

Genesis 27:28 Therefore God give thee of the dew of heaven, and the fatness of the earth, and plenty of corn and wine . . .

Deuteronomy 7:13 And he will love thee, and bless thee, and multiply thee: he will also bless the fruit of thy womb, and the fruit of thy land, thy corn, and thy wine, and thine oil, the increase of thy kine, and the flocks of thy sheep, in the land which he sware unto thy fathers to give thee.

Amos 9:14 And I will bring again the captivity of my people of Israel, and they shall build the waste cities, and inhabit *them;* and they shall plant vineyards, and drink the wine thereof; they shall also make gardens, and eat the fruit of them

VII. Wine in extraordinary abundance will be a token of the Messianic age.

Amos 9:13 Behold, the days come, saith the LORD, that the plowman shall overtake the reaper, and the treader of grapes him that soweth seed; and the mountains shall drop sweet wine, and all the hills shall melt.

Joel 3:18 And it shall come to pass in that day, *that* the mountains shall drop down new wine, and the hills shall flow with milk, and all the rivers of Judah shall flow with waters, and a fountain shall come forth of the house of the LORD, and shall water the valley of Shittim.

Zechariah 9:17 For how great *is* his goodness, and how great *is* his beauty! corn shall make the young men cheerful, and new wine the maids.

Continued on next page.

> **A Survey of How Wine Was Viewed and Used in Biblical Times** – Continued
>
> VIII. **A **moderate "gladdening of the heart" through wine was mentioned in several places.**
>
> Psalm 104:15 And wine *that* maketh glad the heart of man, *and* oil to make *his* face to shine, and bread *which* strengtheneth man's heart.
>
> Ecclesiastes 9:7 Go thy way, eat thy bread with joy, and drink thy wine with a merry heart; for God now accepteth thy works.
>
> Ecclesiastes 10:19 A feast is made for laughter, and wine maketh merry: but money answereth all *things*.
>
> Zechariah 10:7 And *they of* Ephraim shall be like a mighty *man,* and their heart shall rejoice as through wine: yea, their children shall see *it,* and be glad; their heart shall rejoice in the LORD.
>
> Judges 9:13 And the vine said unto them, Should I leave my wine, which cheereth God and man, and go to be promoted over the trees?
>
> ****The excessive use of wine and strong drink is condemned in the Scriptures.****
>
> IX. **"Drink offerings," were of course a part of the prescribed ritual.**
>
> Leviticus 23:13 And the meat offering thereof *shall be* two tenth deals of fine flour mingled with oil, an offering made by fire unto the LORD *for* a sweet savour: and the drink offering thereof *shall be* of wine, the fourth *part* of an hin.
>
> X. **A store of wine was kept in the temple (tabernacle) to ensure the part in the ritual.**
>
> 1 Chronicles 9:29 *Some* of them also *were* appointed to oversee the vessels, and all the instruments of the sanctuary, and the fine flour, and the wine, and the oil, and the frankincense, and the spices.
>
> XI. **Christ adapted Himself to Jewish customs.**
>
> Matthew 11:19 The Son of man came eating and drinking, and they say, Behold a man gluttonous, and a winebibber, a friend of publicans and sinners. But wisdom is justified of her children. (Luke 7:34; 22:18)
>
> (Outline summarized from James Orr, *International Standard Bible Encyclopedia*, 1915, 1939, e-Sword 12.0.1.)

"Undiluted wine was considered distasteful by the Jews, and the wine for the Passover consisted of three parts water and one part wine."[147] Also, if desired, to enhance its flavor, they had a custom of mixing spices with the wine.

Both symbolic gestures of eating of Wisdom's beasts and drinking of her mingled wine indicated a full partaking of a life-sustaining walk with God.

The personified Wisdom invites all men to come to God. Many Old Testament saints came through faith in Jehovah and by obedience to the Mosaic law, and they symbolized their faith with the giving of sacrifices. However, after Jesus, the Lamb of God, was sacrificed, no more sacrifices were necessary or accepted. Jesus came "In the fullness of time" and, through His sacrifice, gives a full pardon to those who seek Him through faith in Him.

Galatians 3:23-26 But before faith came, we were kept under the law, shut up unto the faith which should afterwards be revealed. Wherefore the law was our schoolmaster *to bring us* unto Christ, that we might be justified by faith. But after that faith is come, we are no longer under a schoolmaster. For ye are all the children of God by faith in Christ Jesus.

Galatians 4:4-7 But when the fulness of the time was come, God sent forth his Son, made of a woman, made under the law, To redeem them that were under the law, that we might receive the adoption of sons. And because ye are sons, God hath sent forth the Spirit of his Son into your hearts, crying, Abba, Father. Wherefore thou art no more a servant, but a son; and if a son, then an heir of God through Christ.

Hebrews 1:1-3 God, who at sundry times and in divers manners spake in time past unto the fathers by the prophets, Hath in these last days spoken unto us by *his* Son, whom he hath appointed heir of all things, by whom also he made the worlds; Who being the brightness of *his* glory, and the express image of his person, and upholding all things by the word of his power, when he had by himself purged our sins, sat down on the right hand of the Majesty on high . . .

Today there is no greater example of the wisdom of God than that exemplified in the life and words of Jesus, and there is no offer of eternal life today except through Jesus. He utilized the symbolism of the bread and the wine during His last meal with His apostles. The bread and the wine symbolized His body and His blood. His command was "do this in remembrance of me," and the Holy Spirit had this command repeated four times.

Matthew 26:26-29 And as they were eating, Jesus took bread, and blessed it, and brake it, and gave it to the disciples, and said, Take, eat; this is my body. And he took the cup, and gave thanks, and gave it to them, saying, Drink ye all of it; For this is my blood of the new testament, which is shed for many for the remission of sins. But I say unto you, I will not drink henceforth of this fruit of the vine, until that day when I drink it new with you in my Father's kingdom. *[Also see Mark 14:22-25; Luke 22:15-20.]*

1 Corinthians 11:23-26 For I have received of the Lord that which also I delivered unto you, That the Lord Jesus the same night in which he was betrayed took bread: And when he had given thanks, he brake it, and said, Take, eat: this is my body, which is broken for you: this do in remembrance of me. After the same manner also he took the cup, when he had supped, saying, This

cup is the new testament in my blood: this do ye, as oft as ye drink it, in remembrance of me. For as often as ye eat this bread, and drink this cup, ye do shew the Lord's death till he come.

"She hath sent forth her maidens: she crieth upon the highest places of the city." (verse 3) Wisdom cries aloud through the persons of her missionary maidens in the highest places of the city, which are the high hills and rooftops. (The foolish woman of Proverbs 9:13 invites men to her evil house.)

Both Wisdom and the adulteress cry out to the same people to come. Wisdom beckons to come to life at its fullest through the Truth. The adulteress beckons, but purposefully fails to inform her hearers that her victims end in hell. Both offer a feast, one to nurture spiritual life, the other to poison with spiritual death. The adulteress cries using similar words to Wisdom:

> Proverbs 9:16-18 Whoso is simple, let him turn in hither: and as for him that wanteth understanding, she saith to him, Stolen waters are sweet, and bread eaten in secret is pleasant. But he knoweth not that the dead are there; and that her guests are in the depths of hell.

"Whoso *is* simple, let him turn in hither: *as for* him that wanteth understanding, she saith to him . . ." (verse 4) The **"simple"** are those who are "ignorant, weak, liable to be deceived, but *willing* to learn."[148] The simple and anyone else who lacks understanding can come and learn about God, and also about life and people. The call continues to be made today from Wisdom to come to God through His Son, the Lamb of God – rather than through the Mosaic law regarding faith and animal sacrifice.

> Luke 14:16-22 Then said he unto him, A certain man made a great supper, and bade many And sent his servant at supper time to say to them that were bidden, Come; for all things are now ready. And they all with one *consent* began to make excuse. The first said unto him, I have bought a piece of ground, and I must needs go and see it I pray thee have me excused. And another said, I have bought five yoke of oxen, and I go to prove them I pray thee have me excused. And another said, I have married a wife, and therefore I cannot come. So that servant came, and shewed his lord these things. Then the master of the house being angry said to his servant, Go out quickly into the streets and lanes of the city, and bring in hither the poor, and the maimed, and the halt, and the blind. And the servant said, Lord, it is done as thou hast commanded, and yet there is room. And the lord said unto the servant, Go out into the highways and hedges, and compel *them* to come in, that my house may be filled. For I say unto you, That none of those men which were bidden shall taste of my supper.

> "Yes, our Lord, the Wisdom Incarnate, has glorious ideas of hospitality; He keeps open house; His purpose is to call mankind to a great feast; the 'bread and the wine' are prepared; the sacrifice which furnishes the meat is slain. His messengers are commissioned . . . with good tidings which they are to publish in the high places. His word is always, Come. His desire is that men should live, and therefore He calls them into the way of understanding. (Proverbs 9:6) If a man lacks wisdom, if he recognizes his ignorance, his frailty, his folly, if he is at any rate wise enough to know that he is foolish, well enough to know that he is sick, righteous enough to know that he is sinful, let him approach this noble mansion with its lordly feast. Here is bread which is meat indeed; here is wine which is life-giving, the fruit of the Vine which God has planted."[149]

The response to Wisdom's plea to **"turn in hither,"** requires leaving the masses to come to this spiritual meal where Wisdom is the hostess with her most wonderful companions – God and prudence. (Proverbs 8:12 states: "I wisdom dwell with prudence ...") Everyone is asked to come to Wisdom as everyone is asked to come to Jesus.

> Matthew 7:13-14 Enter ye in at the strait gate: for wide *is* the gate, and broad *is* the way, that leadeth to destruction, and many there be which go in thereat: Because strait *is* the gate, and narrow *is* the way, which leadeth unto life, and few there be that find it.
> Matthew 11:28-29 Come unto me, all *ye* that labour and are heavy laden, and I will give you rest. Take my yoke upon you, and learn of me; for I am meek and lowly in heart: and ye shall find rest unto your souls.
> Matthew 19:14 But Jesus said, Suffer little children, and forbid them not, to come unto me: for of such is the kingdom of heaven. *[See also Mark 10:14; Luke 18:16.]*
> John 7:37 In the last day, that great *day* of the feast, Jesus stood and cried, saying, If any man thirst, let him come unto me, and drink.

"Come, eat of my bread, and drink of the wine *which* I have mingled." (verse 5) Wisdom's invitation is simple and straightforward, "come" and partake of nourishment from God that produces eternal life with God.

> Isaiah 55:1-3 Ho, every one that thirsteth, come ye to the waters, and he that hath no money; come ye, buy, and eat; yea, come, buy wine and milk without money and without price. Wherefore do ye spend money for *that which is* not bread? and your labour for *that which* satisfieth not? hearken diligently unto me, and eat ye *that which is* good, and let your soul delight itself in fatness. Incline your ear, and come unto me: hear, and your soul shall live; and I will make an everlasting covenant with you, *even* the sure mercies of David.
> Matthew 11:28-29 and John 7:37 *[See above.]*
> Revelation 22:17 And the Spirit and the bride say, Come. And let him that heareth say, Come. And let him that is athirst come. And whosoever will, let him take the water of life freely.

"Forsake the foolish, and live; and go in the way of understanding." (verse 6) The plea is to **"forsake the foolish,"** to break from the influence of foolish people, represented by the lustful adulteress, who stand in opposition to God. As in verse four, this decision offers a definite choice and a positive move in the direction toward God and toward understanding.

> Proverbs 21:16 The man that wandereth out of the way of understanding shall remain in the congregation of the dead.
>
> James 4:8 Draw nigh to God, and he will draw nigh to you. Cleanse *your* hands, *ye* sinners; and purify *your* hearts, *ye* double minded.

The **"way of understanding"** is the pathway of the wise, those who love God and are loved by God. The foolish go away from wisdom, from God, from prudence, and from understanding. Those who love the adulteress love foolishness. They love death.

Proverbs 9:7-12 He that reproveth a scorner getteth to himself shame: and he that rebuketh a wicked *man getteth* himself a blot.
8. Reprove not a scorner, lest he hate thee: rebuke a wise man, and he will love thee.
9. Give *instruction* to a wise *man,* and he will be yet wiser: teach a just *man,* and he will increase in learning.
10. The fear of the LORD *is* the beginning of wisdom: and the knowledge of the holy *is* understanding.
11. For by me thy days shall be multiplied, and the years of thy life shall be increased.
12. If thou be wise, thou shalt be wise for thyself: but *if* thou scornest, thou alone shalt bear *it*.

Verses 7-12 form a single-purpose block of parenthetical instruction to the "maidens" who are "sent forth." Presenting a shocking deviation from the dialog (verses 1-6 and verses 13-18), these six verses contrast the significant differences between the righteous invitation of Wisdom and the wicked one of the adulteress.

Specifically, this parenthesis breaks in on the dialog with instruction to the messengers that there are certain people who will never respect or regard their holy invitation from Wisdom. Although the call to come to God is broadcast to everyone "upon the highest places of the city, **the "scorner"** and the **"wicked"** will not only refuse but will create a shameful situation for the faithful messengers. Ignoring an invitation to come to God is within itself a condemnation of the person's ungodliness.

"He that reproveth a scorner getteth to himself shame: and he that rebuketh a wicked *man getteth* himself a blot." "Reprove not a scorner, lest he hate thee: rebuke a wise man, and he will love thee." (verses 7-8) The **"scorner"** is one who mocks God and the teachings of wisdom. Because he hates God, he is likely to focus his hate on individuals who follow God. He adheres to a standard of behavior set by his spiritual father, Satan, and is convinced that wisdom lies within himself – not with God. The reward one receives for correcting such a prideful scorner is **"shame."**

> "But now we are to note that the invitation of Wisdom is addressed only to the simple, not to the scorner. (Proverbs 9:7) She lets the scorner pass by, because a word to him would recoil only in shame on herself, bringing a blush to her queenly face, and would add to the scorner's wickedness by increasing his hatred of her. Her reproof would not benefit him, but it would bring a blot upon herself, it would exhibit her as ineffectual and helpless. The bitter words of a scorner can make wisdom appear foolish, and cover virtue with a confusion which should belong only to vice. 'Speak not in the hearing of a fool; for he will despise the wisdom of thy words.' (Proverbs 23:9) Indeed, there is no character so hopeless as that of the scorner; there proceeds from him, as it were, a fierce blast, which blows away all the approaches which goodness makes to him. Reproof cannot come near him; (Proverbs 13:1) he cannot find wisdom, though he seek it; (Proverbs 14:6) and as a matter of fact, he never seeks it.(Proverbs 15:12) If one attempts to punish him it can only be with the hope that others may benefit by the example; it will have no effect upon him. (Proverbs 19:25) To be rid of him must be the desire of every wise man, for he is an abomination to all, (Proverbs 24:9) and with his departure contention disappears. (Proverbs 22:10) They that scoff at things holy, and scorn the Divine Power, must be left to themselves until the beginnings of wisdom appear in them-the first sense of fear that there is a God who may not be mocked, the first recognition that there is a sanctity which they would do well at all events to reverence. There must be a little wisdom in the heart before a man can enter the Palace of Wisdom; there must be a humbling, a self-mistrust, a diffident misgiving before the scorner will give heed to her invitation."[150]
>
> 2 Chronicles 36:14-16 Moreover all the chief of the priests, and the people, transgressed very much after all the abominations of the heathen; and polluted the house of the LORD which he had hallowed in Jerusalem. And the LORD God of their fathers sent to them by his messengers, rising up betimes, and sending; because he had compassion on his people, and on his dwelling place: But they mocked the messengers of God, and despised his words, and misused his prophets, until the wrath of the LORD arose against his people, till *there was* no remedy.
>
> Proverbs 15:12 A scorner loveth not one that reproveth him: neither will he go unto the wise.

"**He that reproveth a scorner getteth to himself shame.**" (verse 7a) Shame in the form of being made to appear ridiculous comes to the one reproving a scorner who has a habit of mocking with large mouth motions and other exaggerated body gestures.

"**And he that rebuketh a wicked** *man getteth* **himself a blot.**" (verse 7b) This **"blot"** *("stain on character"[151])* comes in the form of getting a bad name, a scandal concerning himself, a rumor of misconduct, or perhaps a lawsuit, all originating from lies told by the **"wicked man"** and carried forth by his friends who are talebearers.

"**Reprove not a scorner, lest he hate thee.**"(verse 8a) Because the **"scorner"** believes himself to be wiser than the godly, he mocks at righteousness, which he considers to be foolishness and beneath him. To correct him only incites rage and exposes one to becoming a recipient of his hate, which may be acted out in various forms, including verbal (and possibly physical) assault. Today, faithful ministers often find themselves becoming targets of scorners by simply fulfilling their duty in preaching the Scriptures, which are ". . . profitable for doctrine, for reproof, for correction, for instruction in righteousness." (2 Timothy 3:16)

"**Rebuke a wise man, and he will love thee.**" (verse 8b) "**Give** *instruction* **to a wise** *man,* **and he will be yet wiser: teach a just** *man,* **and he will increase in learning.**"(verse 9) In every case (verses 7-9), *the effect produced by instruction is dependent on the attitude of those who hear.* Because a wise man is one who has learned to live by God's principles, the one characteristic that stands out about him is that he is alert and eager to make the best of every situation that confronts him; and he *will* receive instruction. He learns from the good situations as well as the bad – always getting wiser.

> "Truth is practically infinite. But our knowledge of it varies according as we are able to attain to a large and yet a discriminating receptivity. To the nut its shell is its universe. The man who locks himself up in the dungeon of prejudice will never see anything but his own prison walls."[152]

"**The fear of the LORD** *is* **the beginning of wisdom: and the knowledge of the holy** *is* **understanding.**"(verse 10) The **"fear of the LORD"** is the same in this verse as in previous chapters of the Book of Proverbs – having an awesome respect for God as opposed to a **"fear"** that believes God rules with an iron fist and will punish anyone severely for the least problem. Having respect for the awesomeness of God establishes the proper frame of mind for interacting with and consequently learning about God. *The more a person knows about God's reasoning and actions, the more he has* **"understanding."** But please note *that simply being familiar with* anything is different from *knowing*.

In the parable of the pounds, Jesus gave the example of the man who feared God because he thought God ruled with an iron fist. This man was fearful of being punished rather than having an awesome respect for God, and such fear squeezed out his ability to trust the Lord and to have a meaningful relationship.

> Luke 19:20-24 And another came, saying, Lord, behold, here is thy pound, which I have kept laid up in a napkin: For me feared thee, because thou art and austere man: thou takest up that thou layedst not down, and reapest that thou didst not sow. And he saith unto him, Out of thine own mouth will I judge thee, thou wicked servant. Thou knewest that I was an austere man, taking up that I laid not down, and reaping that I did not sow: Wherefore then gavest not thou my money into the bank, that at my coming I might have required mine own with usury? And he said unto them that stood by, Take from him the pound, and give it to him that hath ten pounds.

> **NOTE:** Here again, the person delivering the message about the "fear of the LORD" must be sensitive about the person to whom he is speaking. Is he a "simple" person because he has not heard about Jehovah and the wisdom He offers? Or, is he wilfully ignorant? Or, is he intentionally a "scorner" or a "wicked" man, or is he simply ignorant? According to 1 Timothy 1:13, Paul sinned ignorantly and described himself: "Who was before a blasphemer, and a persecutor, and injurious: but I obtained mercy, because I did *it* ignorantly in unbelief." Jesus also spoke of those who *wilfully* disregarded God in Matthew 10:14-15–"And whosoever shall not receive you, nor hear your words, when ye depart out of that house or city, shake off the dust of your feet. Verily I say unto you, It shall be more tolerable for the land of Sodom and Gomorrha in the day of judgment, than for that city."

Because there is a direct correlation between *wisdom, knowledge,* and *understanding*, it takes all three to produce a meaningful relationship of interactive wisdom with God. Wisdom, understanding, and knowledge together provide a person, as much as is humanly possible, with the ability to view life and situations as God does.

> Job 28:28 And unto man he said, Behold, the fear of the Lord, that *is* wisdom; and to depart from evil *is* understanding.

Psalm 111:10 The fear of the LORD *is* the beginning of wisdom: a good understanding have all they that do *his commandments:* his praise endureth for ever.

Proverbs 2:6 For the LORD giveth wisdom: out of his mouth *cometh* knowledge and understanding.

Proverbs 9:10 The fear of the LORD *is* the beginning of wisdom: and the knowledge of the holy *is* understanding.

"For by me thy days shall be multiplied, and the years of thy life shall be increased. If thou be wise, thou shalt be wise for thyself: but *if* thou scornest, thou alone shalt bear *it*." (verses 11-12) Having wisdom and understanding teaches a person to position himself under the umbrella of God's protection, to avoid unnecessary pitfalls, confrontations, evil people, and diseases. Thereby, it can be said, **"for by me thy days shall be multiplied, and the years of thy life shall be increased."** Life can be lived to its fullest with favor from God, including increased health to body, soul, and spirit.

Furthermore, if a person is wise, it is to his personal advantage; or as the text says, **"thou shalt be wise for thyself."** The **"scorner,"** while mocking God, **condemns himself** to a life of suffering physically, emotionally, and mentally. Ultimately he will suffer eternal separation from God in hell.

Deuteronomy 6:24 And the LORD commanded us to do all these statutes, to fear the LORD our God, for our good always, that he might preserve us alive, as *it is* at this day.

Deuteronomy 10:13 To keep the commandments of the LORD, and his statutes, which I command thee this day for thy good?

Ezekiel 18:20 The soul that sinneth, it shall die. The son shall not bear the iniquity of the father, neither shall the father bear the iniquity of the son: the righteousness of the righteous shall be upon him, and the wickedness of the wicked shall be upon him.

Proverbs 9:13-18. A foolish woman *is* clamorous: *she is* simple, and knoweth nothing.
14. For she sitteth at the door of her house, on a seat in the high places of the city,
15. To call passengers who go right on their ways:
16. Whoso *is* simple, let him turn in hither: and *as for* him that wanteth understanding, she saith to him,
17. Stolen waters are sweet, and bread *eaten* in secret is pleasant.
18. But he knoweth not that the dead *are* there; *and that* her guests *are* in the depths of hell.

For the remainder of this chapter, the subject of the dialogue returns to the foolish woman who also calls the simple to a feast at her house, as does Wisdom. Her allurement comes from a different quarter of the city than the call to righteousness given by the wealthy and wise lady Wisdom. Fleshly lusts are here presented in opposition to divine wisdom.[153] The simple youth is open-minded to all forms of evil; and without a "fear of the Lord" and leadership of the Holy Spirit and the Scriptures, he foolishly, willfully, and recklessly follows the adulteress to the "depths of hell." Without spiritual guidance, he is deceived by the adulterous woman who represents evil.

"A foolish woman *is* clamorous: *she is* simple, and knoweth nothing." (verse 13) Because she is the opposite of a wise woman, the **"foolish woman"** is **"clamorous,"** meaning that she makes a commotion with her personal communications or interactions with others so as to draw attention to herself.

Proverbs 7:9-12 In the twilight, in the evening, in the black and dark night: And, behold, there met him a woman *with* the attire of an harlot, and subtil of heart. (She *is* loud and stubborn; her feet abide not in her house: Now *is she* without, now in the streets, and lieth in wait at every corner.)

She lacks discretion and has chosen to be ignorant of wisdom. Showing no respect for God or man, she loudly and proudly flaunts herself.

"And knoweth nothing" doesn't mean that she doesn't know who her mother is or how to count to ten. It just means that she has the overwhelming appearance of being ignorant, not understanding righteousness, and thereby disrespecting both God and man. She knows nothing about wisdom *or* about godliness, as proved by the facts surrounding her lifestyle given in the last five verses of this chapter. Part of her being ignorant to God's teachings and consequently to discretion is being **"simple."** According to Barnes, she is "simple in the worse sense, as open to all forms of evil."[154] Her simplicity is emphasized by the fact that her resistance to righteousness and intensified sensual appetite rule her conduct. She has no direction from God, and she doesn't even act according to human reasoning. So, she seeks out **"whoso is simple"** and **"wanteth understanding"** with the obvious intent of entangling him in sensual pleasure, which tends to keep him on a pathway that opposes God.

"For she sitteth at the door of her house, on a seat in the high places of the city, To call passengers who go right on their ways." (verses 14-15) With a desire to effectively set her evil trap, she, without shame or fear of reprisal, advertises herself **"at the door of her house"** and **"on a seat in the high places of the city."** Her selected participants are the **"passengers,"** meaning those traveling from one place to another. These itinerant "passengers" are less likely to be discovered for having been with a harlot.

"Whoso *is* simple, let him turn in hither: and *as for* him that wanteth understanding, she saith to him, Stolen waters are sweet, and bread *eaten* in secret is pleasant." (verses 16-17) *The harlot's person of interest* is one of the "simple" ones who has not yet made his "final choice, can still be swayed by lower considerations, and may be led astray easily. Such persons find it hard to distinguish between the good and the evil, the false and the true, especially when their sensual appetite is aroused and sides with the temptress."[155] In addition, this wicked woman is seeking **"him that wanteth understanding."** ("Wanteth" means lacking or without.) "This is the other class addressed by Wisdom, and which Folly now solicits, urging them to follow her on the path of pleasure, promising sensual enjoyment and security."[156]

Wisdom's invitation in Proverbs 8:5 and 9:4 also calls out to the simple: "O ye simple, understand wisdom: and, ye fools, be ye of an understanding heart." "Whoso is simple, let him turn in hither;" however, Wisdom's character and motives are opposite those of the harlot. When we read the rest of Wisdom's invitation, the contrast between her and the adulterous woman is pronounced:

> Proverbs 9:5-6 Come, eat of my bread, and drink of the wine which I have mingled. Forsake the foolish, and live; and go in the way of understanding.

Wisdom's guests are invited to come and eat and drink with the choice of leaving their simple ways. They are introduced to "the fear of the LORD" with a plea for them to seek God and His ways, and they are given opportunity for having eternal life. All of her hospitality is for their blessing and their benefit.

BUT, notice the difference in the invitation of "a foolish woman" when she says the following, **"Stolen waters are sweet, and bread *eaten* in secret is pleasant."** (verse 17) Her words intentionally make her appeal for participation in the sinful act seem to be **"sweet"** and **"pleasant"** without any element of harm. **"Stolen waters"** is a euphemism (or a much softer, less direct term) for having an adulterous relationship. "Stolen waters" is also a term that is contrasted to the "waters" (mentioned in Proverbs 5:15), which signify the chaste relationship in a lawful marriage. Notice also the words of Scripture from Hebrews whereby God distinctly clarifies that He has a different attitude toward honorable sexual relationship within marriage than He has for sexual relationship outside of marriage.

> Proverbs 5:15 Drink waters out of thine own cistern, and running waters out of thine own well.
>
> Hebrews 13:4 Marriage *is* honourable in all, and the bed undefiled: but whoremongers and adulterers God will judge.

What the adulteress fails to tell her victim is that being with her may be temporarily enjoyable to the flesh but will eternally have a consequence that will be *anything but* **"pleasant."** Proverbs previously stated (Proverbs 6:2) that a man lured by an evil woman will be brought down to a piece of bread (something of little value). Not only does he ruin his life here on earth, but he establishes himself on a pathway to hell.

"But he knoweth not that the dead *are* there; *and that* her guests *are* in the depths of hell." (verse 18) To be with her is to transition away from God and to place oneself under the umbrella of Satan. Her wicked home is a staging area for the hell bound. Since she has separated herself from God, "death" with her is primarily spiritual and secondarily physical (should a sexually transmitted disease appear). To enter her abode is to leave the paths of righteousness and walk in the paths leading to the destruction of body and soul.

> Proverbs 21:16 The man that wandereth out of the way of understanding shall remain in the congregation of the dead.
>
> Proverbs 22:3 A prudent *man* foreseeth the evil, and hideth himself: but the simple pass on, and are punished.

SECTION II
(Chapters 10-24)

This section is introduced with the phrase "The proverbs of Solomon," giving it a distinct formal separation from Sections I and III. The short, sharp, intense statements, ripe with figurative language contrast wisdom with foolishness. These statements are often, though not always, the concise, two-line proverbs for which the book is famous and by which it is frequently identified.

Proverbs are traditionally referred to as "dark sayings" because understanding is not always immediately discoverable. These sayings are a small portion of the inspired word of God that reveals the mind of Christ, which is wisdom. Without these proverbs, the volume of Scripture would be incomplete.

The meanings of these verses are discoverable by anyone seeking to know how God views the difference between wise and foolish actions of men. However, the fool will immediately reject these words of wisdom because they sharply condemn his ways of thinking and acting. But for the student of wisdom who wants to know how to live successfully in a world of continuous decision making, he will find these proverbs to be a goldmine–in multiple ways.

To unfold the truths of these verses, the student must first have an awesome respect for God and a humble spirit. He must be teachable. Understanding takes time, study, and, more importantly, great desire.

Students must realize the value of understanding the meaning of each word and how it is used within the context. It is also of great importance to know that supportive and related Scriptures are routinely THE light that shines on dark sayings.

Focus statements are provided for each proverb in Sections II and III to give the reader a quick view of the central idea. These are best read in conjunction with the specific verse or verses under consideration. Focus statements are NOT interpretations.

CHAPTER TEN

> **Proverbs 10:1** The proverbs of Solomon. A wise son maketh a glad father: but a foolish son *is* the heaviness of his mother.

Focus: This proverb emphasizes that a child's wisdom (or lack thereof) affects his parents' happiness.

A **"wise son"** is one who is behaving in such a manner that he pleases both God and his parents; thus, his choice of words, actions, and relationships reflect obedience to the godly instructions of his parents who are teaching him about God. Conversely, a **"foolish son"** is driven to be disobedient because of selfishness, rebellion, and pride. These attributes cause him to disregard the teachings and feelings of his parents. When he rejects their instructions concerning God's word, his parents bear excessive burdens and unnecessary grief or "heaviness."

"It is impossible to estimate the tremendous influence which children have on the happiness of their parents. The unfortunate thing about it is that the children are the last to realize it. It may be that a misplaced modesty inclines them to imagine that their course in life cannot be of much consequence to any one. In many cases, unhappily, gross selfishness engenders sheer indifference to the feelings of those who have most claim upon them, so that they never give a thought to the pain they are inflicting. But behind these special points there is the universal fact that no one can understand the depth and overpowering intensity of a parent's love until he becomes a parent himself. Then, in the yearning anxiety he experiences for his own children, a man may have a revelation of the love which he had received all the days of his life without ever dreaming of its wonderful power. But surely, up to their capacity for understanding it, children should realize the great trust that is given to them. They are entrusted with the happiness of their parents. After receiving from them life, food, shelter, innumerable good things and a watchful, tender love throughout, they have it in their power to make bright the evening of their father's and mother's life, or to cloud it with a deep, dark gloom of hopeless misery."[157]

Genesis 5:28-29 And Lamech lived an hundred eighty and two years, and begat a son: And he called his name Noah, saying, This *same* shall comfort us concerning our work and toil of our hands, because of the ground which the LORD hath cursed.

Genesis 33:5 And he lifted up his eyes, and saw the women and the children; and said, Who *are* those with thee? And he said, The children which God hath graciously given thy servant.

Genesis 45:28 And Israel said, *It is* enough; Joseph my son *is* yet alive: I will go and see him before I die.

Genesis 46:30 And Israel said unto Joseph, Now let me die, since I have seen thy face, because thou *art* yet alive.

Psalm 127:3 Lo, children *are* an heritage of the LORD: *and* the fruit of the womb *is his* reward.

Proverbs 23:15-16 My son, if thine heart be wise, my heart shall rejoice, even mine. Yea, my reins shall rejoice, when thy lips speak right things.

Proverbs 23:24-25 The father of the righteous shall greatly rejoice: and he that begetteth a wise *child* shall have joy of him. Thy father and thy mother shall be glad, and she that bare thee shall rejoice.

Proverbs 27:11 My son, be wise, and make my heart glad, that I may answer him that reproacheth me.

Proverbs 29:3 Whoso loveth wisdom rejoiceth his father: but he that keepeth company with harlots spendeth *his* substance.

> **Proverbs 10:2** Treasures of wickedness profit nothing: but righteousness delivereth from death.

Focus: This proverb contrasts the unprofitableness of wickedness with the effective deliverance that comes from having righteousness.

"Treasures of wickedness" describes *ill-gotten gain* that comes into the possession of a person through wicked acts such as theft, fraud, oppression, or extortion. In his twisted thinking, a foolish person who performs such evil may believe that he has a *treasure* in his stolen merchandise, but his gain ***will not profit*** in the end. All that he has taken is as void of profit as he is of understanding. *Wickedness separates a person from God, from society, and from peace of mind.* Both the treasure and the thief are not only void of God's blessings but are also under a curse.

> "They do the possessor no good, but, which is implied from the opposite member, much hurt; they do not only *not* deliver him from death, but oft expose him to it; either from men, who take away his life that they may enjoy his wealth; or from God, who shortens his days, and makes his death more terrible, as being attended with guilt, and with the second death."[158]
>
> Proverbs 3:33 The curse of the LORD is in the house of the wicked: but he blesseth the habitation of the just.
>
> Proverbs 13:11 Wealth gotten by vanity shall be diminished: but he that gathereth by labour shall increase
>
> Proverbs 16:8 Better is a little with righteousness than great revenues without right.
>
> Proverbs 21:6 The getting of treasures by a lying tongue is a vanity tossed to and fro of them that seek death.
>
> Proverbs 21:7 The robbery of the wicked shall destroy them; because they refuse to do judgment.
>
> Isaiah 10:2-3 To turn aside the needy from judgment, and to take away the right from the poor of my people, that widows may be their prey, and *that* they may rob the fatherless! And what will ye do in the day of visitation, and in the desolation *which* shall come from far? to whom will ye flee for help? and where will ye leave your glory?
>
> Zephaniah 1:18 Neither their silver nor their gold shall be able to deliver them in the day of the LORD'S wrath; but the whole land shall be devoured by the fire of his jealousy: for he shall make even a speedy riddance of all them that dwell in the land.

Verse two's second clause, **"but righteousness delivereth from death,"** shines a clear and bright light on the wonderful, advantageous reward of ***righteousness,*** which (in its simplest form) means being right with God. Establishing that honorable posture with the Lord has the potential of preventing a person from premature death, such as can be brought about from being in the company of hunted and hated thieves. Righteous men place themselves under the umbrella of God's protection; thus, they are supernaturally led away from wicked places of activity where impending death and disaster loom. Also, life may be extended through good persons who render aid to such righteous persons where there is danger. Furthermore, they are under God's covenant of protection from eternal death – the second death.[159]

> Proverbs 11:4 Riches profit not in the day of wrath: but righteousness delivereth from death.
>
> Proverbs 12:28 In the way of righteousness *is* life; and *in* the pathway *thereof there is* no death.
>
> Proverbs 14:27 The fear of the LORD is a fountain of life, to depart from the snares of death.
>
> Romans 5:21 That as sin hath reigned unto death, even so might grace reign through righteousness unto eternal life by Jesus Christ our Lord.
>
> Revelation 21:6-8 And he said unto me, It is done. I am Alpha and Omega, the beginning and the end. I will give unto him that is athirst of the fountain of the water of life freely. He that overcometh shall inherit all things; and I will be his God, and he shall be my son. But the fearful, and unbelieving, and the abominable, and murderers, and whoremongers, and sorcerers, and idolaters, and all liars, shall have their part in the lake which burneth with fire and brimstone: which is the second death.

Proverbs 10:3 The LORD will not suffer the soul of the righteous to famish: but he casteth away the substance of the wicked.

Focus: This proverb contrasts God's protection of the righteous with His disregard of even the substance of the wicked.

"Substance of the wicked" in this verse includes their ill-gotten treasure (verse 2), which represents the desire of their hearts; and, ill-gotten or not, it is that which they place confidence in rather than in God. They have a great desire for their wickedness and ill-gotten gain; and, they value their substance as protection against catastrophe and are not aware that God can ***cast it away.*** It is contaminated and infected with the wickedness of its owner.

"Righteous" people desire to please God and are determined to be content with whatever He provides. But the desire of the wicked is for "substance," of which no amount is satisfying; consequently, they are not particular as to what means they have to use or how much damage they inflict to obtain their "stuff." Because God's personal protective relationship with the righteous shields them from hunger, they won't **"famish,"** and He provides their necessities; but the wicked should be aware that whatever they have is in danger of being **"cast away"** by God. Because evil people make themselves obnoxious to God, He exercises no protection for their personal well-being or for their substance.

> Job 20:12-15 Though wickedness be sweet in his mouth, *though* he hide it under his tongue; *Though* he spare it, and forsake it not; but keep it still within his mouth: *Yet* his meat in his bowels is turned, *it is* the gall of asps within him. He hath swallowed down riches, and he shall vomit them up again: God shall cast them out of his belly.
>
> Psalm 33:18-19 Behold, the eye of the LORD *is* upon them that fear him, upon them that hope in his mercy; To deliver their soul from death, and to keep them alive in famine.

Proverbs 13:25 The righteous eateth to the satisfying of his soul: but the belly of the wicked shall want.

Proverbs 14:32 The wicked is driven away in his wickedness: but the righteous hath hope in his death.

Matthew 6:30-33 Wherefore, if God so clothe the grass of the field, which to day is, and to morrow is cast into the oven, *shall he* not much more *clothe* you, O ye of little faith? Therefore take no thought, saying, What shall we eat? or, What shall we drink? or, Wherewithal shall we be clothed? (For after all these things do the Gentiles seek:) for your heavenly Father knoweth that ye have need of all these things. But seek ye first the kingdom of God, and his righteousness; and all these things shall be added unto you. Take therefore no thought for the morrow: for the morrow shall take thought for the things of itself. Sufficient unto the day *is* the evil thereof.

Proverbs 10:4   He becometh poor that dealeth *with* a slack hand: but the hand of the diligent maketh rich.

Focus: This proverb declares that laziness produces want, while diligence produces wealth.

A wise man will understand from Scripture that it is God who gives a person "power to get wealth," and consequently, he will labor with God's leadership and under God's enablement to grow his wealth. A **"slack hand"** is one that is idle or not working. In this verse, the first "hand" mentioned is the **"slack hand"** which is translated from the Hebrew word *kaph*. It means the open, ineffective hand or palm. The second **"hand"** mentioned is the **"hand of the diligent."** It is translated from the Hebrew term *yad,* and means the hand ready and eager for work. Even though he realizes at all times that God is the provider, a believer knows that God puts the opportunity to get wealth in his path and gives him ability to secure it. *God has His part to do, and man has his.* A diligent man will be astute to God's provision and follow through with effort, but a sluggard will ruin opportunities with laziness.

Deuteronomy 8:17-18 And thou say in thine heart, My power and the might of *mine* hand hath gotten me this wealth. But thou shalt remember the LORD thy God: for *it is* he that giveth thee power to get wealth, that he may establish his covenant which he sware unto thy fathers, as *it is* this day.

Proverbs 6:9-11 How long wilt thou sleep, O sluggard? when wilt thou arise out of thy sleep? *Yet* a little sleep, a little slumber, a little folding of the hands to sleep: So shall thy poverty come as one that travelleth, and thy want as an armed man.

Proverbs 19:15 Slothfulness casteth into a deep sleep; and an idle soul shall suffer hunger.

Proverbs 12:24 The hand of the diligent shall bear rule: but the slothful shall be under tribute.

> **NOTE:** Many Scriptures condemn the *attitude and character* of "the rich," and at the same time, there are Scriptures that praise the *attitude and character* of "rich men" like Abram and Boaz. This differentiation is a consequence of who and what they worshiped.
>
> Abram's priority in life was his relationship with God; consequently, God praised him and made him rich. When conflict arose between Abram's laborers and those of his nephew Lot, Abram offered Lot the first choice of the land, knowing that God would give him whatever wealth and other substance He wanted him to have. Another example is Job, who had all his riches taken away, yet he did not lose his integrity with God because his riches were not his priority. Wicked rich men ("the rich") are a category of men who live for their wealth and crave more, make biased decisions based on their money, and are generally driven to be rich for themselves rather than rich toward God.

During the ages that Scripture was written, Hebrew families earned their living through farming; consequently, everyone knew firsthand the importance of working hard during particular seasons, such as planting and harvest time. These were timely windows of opportunity when work was mandatory. The sluggard or slothful man who **"dealeth *with* a slack hand"** would use any excuse to avoid putting his hands to the work. Scripture shows that he will manufacture an excuse for his behavior.

Proverbs 20:4 The sluggard will not plow by reason of the cold; therefore shall he beg in harvest, and have nothing.

Proverbs 26:16 The sluggard is wiser in his own conceit than seven men that can render a reason.

Proverbs 22:13 The slothful man saith, There is a lion without, I shall be slain in the streets.

Wisdom involves ***knowing*** the right things to do at the right time (wise, effective work) but also actually ***doing*** the right things at the right time (energetic, diligent work). Every phase of life opens windows of opportunity, and a wise person will recognize those times and try to capitalize on them. There are windows of opportunity to save money for retirement when a person is young and physically able to work, but the window will close with time. There are often windows of opportunity for education when a person is young, but learning capacity diminishes with age, and people who don't learn as a child will struggle later with a poor foundation. There are opportunities to develop valuable youthful friendships that can last a lifetime, but that time will also pass away. Wise people diligently gain wealth (of various kinds) when the opportunity avails itself, *but he becomes poor (in various ways) who deals with a slack hand.*

Proverbs 10:5 He that gathereth in summer *is* a wise son: *but* he that sleepeth in harvest *is* a son that causeth shame.

Focus: This proverb provides an illustration of the truth taught in verse 4 where indolence (dealing with a "slack hand") was contrasted with diligence.

A diligent person shows evidence that he is "wise" when he properly **gathers during the harvest season**, thus, bringing **honor** rather than **"shame"** to himself and to his family. Each kind of farm work has its own suitable season wherein such work is effective and profitable. In times when the ground is frozen solid, or when mud is boot high are certainly not the right times to plow the fields; and when the crops are ripe for picking is not the time for sleeping.

> "The wise son will thus *gather* his blessing at the fittest time. *The freshness of youth is a summer harvest.* It is as much the will of God, that the young should gather knowledge, as that the farmer should gather his harvest. The *wise gathering in this summer* gives substance, vigour, high tone and power of usefulness in after-life! How often may we trace poverty of mind, enervation of character, unprofitable habits, to *sleeping in* this fruitful *harvest!* 'He who idles away the time of his youth will bear the shame of it when he is old.'"[160]

Ecclesiastes 3:1 To every *thing there is* a season, and a time to every purpose under the heaven . . .

Ecclesiastes 8:5 Whoso keepeth the commandment shall feel no evil thing: and a wise man's heart discerneth both time and judgment.

Proverbs 10:6 Blessings *are* upon the head of the just: but violence covereth the mouth of the wicked.

Focus: This proverb *contrasts* the good, peaceful *blessings* from God that rest upon the righteous *with* the bad, violent disasters that fly in the face of the wicked.

"Blessings *are* upon the head of the just." "Blessings" are benefits, presents, or rewards given by God to those who love and obey Him. He gives His children things they need daily, guards their path, and honors their prayerful requests.

> Psalm 1:1-3 BLESSED is the man that walketh not in the counsel of the ungodly, nor standeth in the way of sinners, nor sitteth in the seat of the scornful. But his delight is in the law of the LORD ; and in his law doth he meditate day and night. And he shall be like a tree planted by the rivers of water, that bringeth forth his fruit in his season; his leaf also shall not wither; and whatsoever he doeth shall prosper.
>
> Psalm 68:1 Blessed *be* the Lord, *who* daily loadeth us *with benefits, even* the God of our salvation. Selah.
>
> Isaiah 41:10 Fear thou not; for I am with thee: be not dismayed; for I am thy God: I will strengthen thee; yea, I will help thee; yea, I will uphold thee with the right hand of my righteousness.
>
> Proverbs 16:7 When a mans ways please the LORD, he maketh even his enemies to be at peace with him.
>
> Jeremiah 17:7-8 Blessed is the man that trusteth in the LORD , and whose hope the LORD is. For he shall be as a tree planted by the waters, and that spreadeth out her roots by the river, and shall not see when heat cometh, but her leaf shall be green; and shall not be careful in the year of drought, neither shall cease from yielding fruit.
>
> Malachi 3:10 Bring ye all the tithes into the storehouse, that there may be meat in mine house, and prove me now herewith, saith the LORD of hosts, if I will not open you the windows of heaven, and pour you out a blessing, that there shall not be room enough to receive it.

"Upon the head of the just" is a phrase used to express that blessings are poured onto the entire person. The just wear the blessings of God and enjoy a life of peace, protection, and provision. In being right with God their wise decisions turn to prosperity. They live and work in harmony with God, then God blesses them, and the blessings are obvious to everyone. Being in a position to receive God's blessings is like "*being under the spout where the glory pours out.*"

"But violence covereth the mouth of the wicked." **"Covereth the mouth"** is a phrase that expresses the fact that the **"wicked"** "blow" out unrighteousness, evil speaking, and violence that is in their heart as they oppose God and good people; and *it rebounds in their faces.* The wicked live in an atmosphere of violence because they are always opposed to God, and they can not help but spew rebellion out of their mouth with hostile words. They are constantly fighting and struggling with themselves, others, and God.

> Isaiah 57:20 But the wicked *are* like the troubled sea, when it cannot rest, whose waters cast up mire and dirt.

Proverbs 12:6 The words of the wicked are to lie in wait for blood: but the mouth of the upright shall deliver them.
Proverbs 15:28 The heart of the righteous studieth to answer: but the mouth of the wicked poureth out evil things.
Proverbs 19:28 An ungodly witness scorneth judgment: and the mouth of the wicked devoureth iniquity.
Matthew 12:34 O generation of vipers, how can ye, being evil, speak good things? for out of the abundance of the heart the mouth speaketh.

Proverbs 10:7 The memory of the just is blessed: but the name of the wicked shall rot.

Focus: This proverb contrasts the blessed way that the righteous are remembered with the accursed way the wicked are remembered.

"Memory of the just" and **"name of the wicked"** both refer to the memory that one person has of another. The **"just"** are those right with God who live a life that is pleasing to God and beneficial to those who know them. The **"wicked"** are those who oppose God and everything that is good. They set themselves to be enemies of godly persons and their beliefs.

"The memory of the just is blessed." A righteous (just) person will be remembered for his love for God, uplifting words, godly counsel, and loving, encouraging example. A believer will be blessed as he remembers how a certain righteous person touched his life. "The memory of the just is blessed" because he gave an example of how to live a godly productive life. He provided help to those in need and was the source of strength to many people. There was no evil in his ways nor hate in his heart.

Psalm 72:17 His name shall endure for ever: his name shall be continued as long as the sun: and *men* shall be blessed in him: all nations shall call him blessed.
Psalm 112:1; 6; 9 Praise ye the LORD. Blessed *is* the man *that* feareth the LORD, *that* delighteth greatly in his commandments. His seed shall be mighty upon earth: the generation of the upright shall be blessed. Wealth and riches *shall be* in his house: and his righteousness endureth for ever....Surely he shall not be moved for ever: the righteous shall be in everlasting remembrance....He hath dispersed, he hath given to the poor; his righteousness endureth for ever; his horn shall be exalted with honour.
Ecclesiastes 7:1 A good name *is* better than precious ointment; and the day of death than the day of one's birth.
Hebrews 11:1-2 Now faith is the substance of things hoped for, the evidence of things not seen. For by it the elders obtained a good report.

"But the name of the wicked shall rot." The very name of the wicked brings offensive memories to those he mistreated directly or had an ill effect upon. Evil men, especially those who hated, murdered, stole, or otherwise disturbed peace and civility, will be remembered as the smell of something putrefied and abhorrent. "Like their character, even their names are corrupt, rotting like a corpse."[161]

Job 18:17 His remembrance shall perish from the earth, and he shall have no name in the street.
Psalm 49:11-12 Their inward thought *is, that* their houses *shall continue* for ever, *and* their dwelling places to all generations; they call *their* lands after their own names. Nevertheless man *being* in honour abideth not: he is like the beasts *that* perish
Psalm 109:13 Let his posterity be cut off; *and* in the generation following let their name be blotted out.
Ecclesiastes 8:10 And so I saw the wicked buried, who had come and gone from the place of the holy, and they were forgotten in the city where they had so done: this *is* also vanity.
Isaiah 65:15 And ye shall leave your name for a curse unto my chosen: for the Lord GOD shall slay thee, and call his servants by another name:
Jeremiah 22:18-19 Therefore thus saith the LORD concerning Jehoiakim the son of Josiah king of Judah; They shall not lament for him, *saying,* Ah my brother! or, Ah sister! they shall not lament for him, *saying,* Ah lord! or, Ah his glory! He shall be buried with the burial of an ass, drawn and cast forth beyond the gates of Jerusalem.

Proverbs 10:8 The wise in heart will receive commandments: but a prating fool shall fall.

Focus: This proverb contrasts the stability of a wise in heart listener with the instability of a foolish hearted, incessantly speaking fool.

"The wise in heart will receive commandments." To avoid dangerous situations and evil people that would cause him to fall spiritually or physically, the wise person has learned to listen quietly and receive instruction, especially from

Scripture. Someone has said, *"God gave us two ears and one mouth so that we could listen twice as much as we talk."* The wise man will train himself to stop talking and listen to God, Scripture, and wise counsel so that he can **"receive"** *[take, seize]* into his heart the best information that directs his behavior to produce the most favorable outcome. He has learned to flee from counterproductive conversations, such as gossip, flattery, and endless petty talk. He is strong and stable because he has received into his heart the counsel of God.

> Proverbs 1:5 A wise *man* will hear, and will increase learning; and a man of understanding shall attain unto wise counsels...
> Proverbs 9:9 Give *instruction* to a wise *man,* and he will be yet wiser: teach a just *man,* and he will increase in learning.
> Proverbs 12:1 Whoso loveth instruction loveth knowledge: but he that hateth reproof *is* brutish.

"But a prating fool shall fall" as all fools will, but the **"prating"** one takes a direct, undeterred pathway to destruction since he can't hear others over the roar of his own senseless words. *(Webster's Dictionary states that to prate means to speak excessively and pointlessly or to babble.[162])* He talks almost without hesitation, pouring out foolishness, all the while believing he is giving out wise instruction to others. Pridefully and obstinately, he refuses to hear wise counsel; and tragically, he refuses God's instruction. His life is unstable, and he constantly falls because he is unsupported by wisdom.

> The prating fool stumbles downward "with all his thoughts being outward bound...bold in his own conceit...while his life and temper fearfully contradict his fluent tongue...too blind to respect himself...too proud to listen to counsel."[163]
>
> ...The scorner, ...who refuses to heed those commandments... here described as a 'fool of lips', a loudmouthed fool who mockingly rejects the teaching of his father and mother, and can only bring grief to them. The misuse of the mouth or tongue is a regular way of describing wrongdoers. Indeed, a wayward mouth was the sign of the 'worthless man'. But in the end such a man will 'trip up.' For as he goes on his way with his proud boasting, he will inevitably continually stumble and fall, because he has nothing which guides him in the right way. And one day he will fall, never to rise again.[164]
>
> Proverbs 2:12 To deliver thee from the way of the evil *man,* from the man that speaketh froward things . . .
> Proverbs 4:24 Put away from thee a froward mouth, and perverse lips put far from thee.
> Proverbs 8:13 The fear of the LORD *is* to hate evil: pride, and arrogancy, and the evil way, and the froward mouth, do I hate.
> Proverbs 18:2 A fool hath no delight in understanding, but that his heart may discover itself.
> Proverbs 18:6 A fool's lips enter into contention, and his mouth calleth for strokes. A fool's mouth *is* his destruction, and his lips *are* the snare of his soul.
> Proverbs 29:11 A fool uttereth all his mind: but a wise man keepeth it in till afterwards.
> Ecclesiastes 10:12 The words of a wise man's mouth *are* gracious; but the lips of a fool will swallow up himself.
> Matthew 12:34 O generation of vipers, how can ye, being evil, speak good things? for out of the abundance of the heart the mouth speaketh.
> Luke 6:45 A good man out of the good treasure of his heart bringeth forth that which is good; and an evil man out of the evil treasure of his heart bringeth forth that which is evil: for of the abundance of the heart his mouth speaketh.
> 3John 1:9-10 I wrote unto the church: but Diotrephes, who loveth to have the preeminence among them, receiveth us not. Wherefore, if I come, I will remember his deeds which he doeth, prating against us with malicious words: and not content therewith, neither doth he himself receive the brethren, and forbiddeth them that would, and casteth *them* out of the church.

Proverbs 10:9   He that walketh uprightly walketh surely: but he that perverteth his ways shall be known.

Focus: This proverb contrasts the righteous person's confidently open, steadfast manner of living with the unstable, evasive lifestyle of the evil man.

"He that walketh uprightly walketh surely." **"He that walketh uprightly"** is the one who is just or right with God and consequently with other good persons. He is a person of integrity: walking in the light of Scripture and living by the principles of God's word. His life is on an enlightened path established, protected, and guided by God. Having received his instructions from God, the upright man shall *walk surely* *[safely with a feeling of security]* because he is *sure* that he is doing right and making every effort to prevent ill, evil, or improper conduct that will cause God or himself embarrassment or grief.

> "'Show me an easier path' is nature's cry. 'Show me' cries the child of God, *'the* sure path.' Such is the upright walk under the shield of the Lord's protection, and providence; under the shadow of His promises; in the assurance of his present favor, and in its peaceful end."[165]
>
> Psalm 84:11 For the LORD God is a sun and shield: the LORD will give grace and glory: no good thing will he withhold from them that walk uprightly.

Psalm 119:57-60 CHETH. *Thou art* my portion, O LORD: I have said that I would keep thy words. I intreated thy favour with *my* whole heart: be merciful unto me according to thy word. I thought on my ways, and turned my feet unto thy testimonies. I made haste, and delayed not to keep thy commandments.

Psalm 119:105 Thy word *is* a lamp unto my feet, and a light unto my path.

Proverbs 1:33 But whoso hearkeneth unto me shall dwell safely, and shall be quiet from fear of evil.

"But he that perverteth his ways shall be known." Opposite of the righteous *[upright]* is the person who **"perverteth his ways"** *["ways" are a course of life, moral character, habit]*. For a "way" or "walk" to be perverted means that it is distorted, turned away from the lifestyle that God intended. It is living in a manner that is not pleasing to God and opposed by good men. His life is froward, deceitful, and sinful; and by his evil, he **"shall be known"** publicly, although, certainly he doesn't think so. Though some try to hide their evil way of life, others are brazen about their sinful ways; however, all will eventually be discovered. This perverted man's course of life is regulated by the ever-shifting maxims of worldly demands; thus, he cannot enjoy the sweet confidence of walking with God.

John 6:70-71 Jesus answered them, Have not I chosen you twelve, and one of you is a devil? He spake of Judas Iscariot the son of Simon: for he it was that should betray him, being one of the twelve.

Luke 12:1-3 In the mean time, when there were gathered together an innumerable multitude of people, insomuch that they trode one upon another, he began to say unto his disciples first of all, Beware ye of the leaven of the Pharisees, which is hypocrisy. For there is nothing covered, that shall not be revealed; neither hid, that shall not be known. Therefore whatsoever ye have spoken in darkness shall be heard in the light; and that which ye have spoken in the ear in closets shall be proclaimed upon the housetops.

1 Timothy 5:24 Some men's sins are open beforehand, going before to judgment; and some men they follow after.

Proverbs 10:10 He that winketh with the eye causeth sorrow: but a prating fool shall fall.

Focus: This proverb compares two foolish speakers: The first speaks with his eyes, the other with his tongue; the first is deceptive and produces sorrow to others, while the other is a babbler who trips himself up with his words.

"He that winketh with the eye causeth sorrow." One who **"winketh with the eye"** is sending a non-verbal message that is *intentionally deceitful* (cunning and secretive), while the **"prating fool"** is *blatantly open* with unchecked verbal nonsense. The winker is a source of evil as he intentionally draws his victim into a trap that results in **"sorrow."** "The wink," as used in this proverb, is a message sent privately and deceptively with the intent of nullifying spoken words. In other words, "the winker" is privately saying to one person, with his wink, to disregard what he is saying to another with his words. He is a liar. (Winking with the eye is also a flirtatious action to demonstrate wantonness.)

"But a prating fool shall fall." The **"prating fool"** trips over his own words and **"shall fall"** himself being his own victim. Both the prating fool and the winker are unwise and demonstrate a lack of righteousness. Neither of these two reveals any desire for God's leadership; if they did, they would guard their communication making it pleasing to the Lord and truthful. *(See verse 8 above for more information on the "prating fool.")*

The International Standard Bible Encyclopedia gives the following information about "***the wink***:"

"The act or habit of winking was evidently considered to be evil both in its motives and in its results. The idea of its facetiousness *[joking, often inappropriately]*, prevalent in our day, is nowhere apparent in the Scriptures. It is mentioned frequently, but is always associated with sin, in the Old Testament, especially in the sense of conceit, pride, and rebellion against God: 'Why doth thine heart carry thee away? and what do thy eyes wink at, That thou turnest thy spirit against God, and lettest such words go out of thy mouth?' (Job 15:12-13) So also Psalm 35:19-21: 'Let not them that are mine enemies wrongfully rejoice over me: neither let them wink with the eye that hate me without a cause. For they speak not peace: but they devise deceitful matters against them that are quiet in the land. Yea, they opened their mouth wide against me, and said, Aha, aha, our eye hath seen it.' Also, 'A naughty person, a wicked man, walketh with froward mouth. He winketh with his eyes,' etc. (Proverbs 6:12-13).

In the New Testament the word is used to express the longsuffering patience and forgiveness of God toward erring Israel: 'And the times of this ignorance God winked at; but now commandeth all men every where to repent.' (Acts 17:30)"[166]

Proverbs 6:12-14 A naughty person, a wicked man, walketh with a froward mouth. He winketh with his eyes, he speaketh with his feet, he teacheth with his fingers; Frowardness is in his heart, he deviseth mischief continually; he soweth discord.

Proverbs 18:6-7 A fool's lips enter into contention, and his mouth calleth for strokes. A fool's mouth *is* his destruction, and his lips *are* the snare of his soul.

Proverbs 18:21 Death and life *are* in the power of the tongue: and they that love it shall eat the fruit thereof.

NOTE: From head to foot, the evil man reveals the things about himself that are abominable to God. He has a wink in his "eyes" that speaks of deception and a "proud look." His "froward mouth" houses a "lying tongue" as he is "a false witness that speaketh lies." He has "hands that shed innocent blood" with "fingers that teach" his treachery. His actions reveal that "frowardness is in his heart," and he has a heart that "deviseth wicked imaginations." He has "feet that be swift in running to mischief" while "he soweth discord." *(See also Proverbs 6:13.)*

Proverbs 10:11 The mouth of a righteous *man is* a well of life: but violence covereth the mouth of the wicked.

Focus: This proverb contrasts the godly, edifying conversation of a righteous man with the destructive, evil conversation of a wicked man.

"The mouth of a righteous *man is* a well of life." A **"righteous man"** is one whose heart is right with God, and his words are "continually sending forth waters of life, or such good and wholesome words as are very refreshing and useful, both to themselves and others, for the preserving of their natural life, and for the promoting of their spiritual and eternal life."[167] The life of a righteous man reflects the internal work of the Holy Spirit and teachings received from God's word. His **"mouth"** thus speaks words that flow from a purified heart that has been redeemed and is now **"a well of life."** He speaks truths that flow to others showing them the way to follow God and to have the abundant life described by Jesus.

> Psalm 36:9 For with thee *is* the fountain of life: in thy light shall we see light.
> Proverbs 10:21 The lips of the righteous feed many: but fools die for want of wisdom.
> Proverbs 16:23 The heart of the wise teacheth his mouth, and addeth learning to his lips.
> Proverbs 18:4 The words of a man's mouth *are as* deep waters, *and* the wellspring of wisdom *as* a flowing brook.
> John 7:38-39 He that believeth on me, as the scripture hath said, out of his belly shall flow rivers of living water. (But this spake he of the Spirit, which they that believe on him should receive: for the Holy Ghost was not yet *given;* because that Jesus was not yet glorified.)
> Ephesians 4:29-32 Let no corrupt communication proceed out of your mouth, but that which is good to the use of edifying, that it may minister grace unto the hearers. And grieve not the holy Spirit of God, whereby ye are sealed unto the day of redemption. Let all bitterness, and wrath, and anger, and clamour, and evil speaking, be put away from you, with all malice: And be ye kind one to another, tenderhearted, forgiving one another, even as God for Christ's sake hath forgiven you.

"But violence covereth the mouth of the wicked" illustrates the truth that the wicked are opposite of the righteous in that the wicked spew out violence. Flowing from a heart contaminated by sin and guided by Satan, their words not only injure others; but they, sooner or later, blow back in the face of the wicked who issued them.

> "Like a fountain of living water, continually running and flowing with water, wholesome, reviving, and refreshing; so the righteous man's mouth, out of the abundance of his heart, overflows with good things, which minister grace to the hearers, and are for the use of edifying; things that are pleasant and profitable, grateful and acceptable, comforting, refreshing, and pleasing, and which tend to the good of the life that now is, and that which is to come; but violence covereth the mouth of the wicked; so that nothing comes out of it but what is pernicious *[destructive]* and hurtful; what savours of . . . violence; nothing but lying and deceit, cursing and swearing, and such like filthy and corrupt communication . . ."[168]

Proverbs 10:12 Hatred stirreth up strifes: but love covereth all sins.

Focus: This proverb declares the opposite ways that the emotions of love and hatred drive the way a person responds to wrongs. Hatred encourages a person to look closely and agitate while love encourages a person to look away and appease.

"Hatred stirreth up strifes." **"Hatred"** is a strong, controlling, and dominating emotion initiated within a person's mind because of a perceived threat brought on by envy, contempt, or humiliation. With or without a bona fide threat, hatred can also be taught by family, friends, leaders, mentors, or social groups. It is fueled by allowing hostility to continue within one's mind but is cured by the equal and opposite emotion of love. Both emotions, hate and love, can be nurtured and controlled within the human heart. Hatred renders its victim unreasonable, causing illogical decisions and a striking out at others. When allowed to guide, love will displace hate; and from the opposite perspective, hate, when allowed to control, will drive out love.

Because of envy generated by their father's favoritism for Joseph and because of his dreams, Joseph's brothers "hated him, and could not speak peaceably unto him (Genesis 37:4);" but he loved them and forgave their evil deeds, which included intense hatred, physical, and mental abuse, as well as lying. Because he believed that God was in control of his life, Joseph was able to dismiss the natural human tendency to hate and chose love; and he was convinced that although his brothers meant to do him evil, God meant their wicked deeds for good (Genesis 50:20). Notice some of the Bible's statements about **"hatred."**

> Leviticus 19:17 Thou shalt not hate thy brother in thine heart . . .
>
> Psalm 109:2-3 For the mouth of the wicked and the mouth of the deceitful are opened against me: they have spoken against me with a lying tongue. They compassed me about also with words of hatred; and fought against me without a cause.
>
> Proverbs 15:17-18 Better *is* a dinner of herbs where love is, than a stalled ox and hatred therewith. A wrathful man stirreth up strife: but *he that is* slow to anger appeaseth strife.
>
> Galatians 5:19-21 Now the works of the flesh are manifest, which are these; Adultery, fornication, uncleanness, lasciviousness, Idolatry, witchcraft, hatred, variance, emulations, wrath, strife, seditions, heresies, Envyings, murders, drunkenness, revellings, and such like: of the which I tell you before, as I have also told you in time past, that they which do such things shall not inherit the kingdom of God.
>
> James 4:1 From whence *come* wars and fightings among you? *come they* not hence, *even* of your lusts that war in your members?
>
> 1 John 2:9, 11 He that saith he is in the light, and hateth his brother, is in darkness even until now. But he that hateth his brother is in darkness, and walketh in darkness, and knoweth not whither he goeth, because that darkness hath blinded his eyes.
>
> 1 John 3:15 Whosoever hateth his brother is a murderer: and ye know that no murderer hath eternal life abiding in him.

Hate stirs up strife is a clause that implies that all the elements for strife are already in place, though hidden like mud at the bottom of a peaceful lake. Hatred unnecessarily agitates the waters, causing contention where peace and stillness would otherwise dominate.

"But love covereth all sins." How does love cover sins? Love refuses to stir the waters by simply refusing to agitate the situation. Love *chooses* not to nurture bad thoughts or speak words leading to contention. From a gracious, obedient heart, love consoles and speaks proper words leading to peace and forgiveness; thereby smoothing out waves of contention. Love is the right choice for the believer. As Proverbs 15:1 states, "A soft answer turneth away wrath: but grievous words stir up anger."

> Proverbs 17:9 He that covereth a transgression seeketh love; but he that repeateth a matter separateth *very* friends.
>
> Proverbs 19:11 The discretion of a man deferreth his anger; and *it is* his glory to pass over a transgression.
>
> Matthew 18:15-17 Moreover if thy brother shall trespass against thee, go and tell him his fault between thee and him alone: if he shall hear thee, thou hast gained thy brother. But if he will not hear *thee, then* take with thee one or two more, that in the mouth of two or three witnesses every word may be established. And if he shall neglect to hear them, tell *it* unto the church: but if he neglect to hear the church, let him be unto thee as an heathen man and a publican.
>
> 1 Corinthians 13:4-7 Charity suffereth long, *and* is kind; charity envieth not; charity vaunteth not itself, is not puffed up, Doth not behave itself unseemly, seeketh not her own, is not easily provoked, thinketh no evil; Rejoiceth not in iniquity, but rejoiceth in the truth; Beareth all things, believeth all things, hopeth all things, endureth all things.
>
> Ephesians 4:15-16 But speaking the truth in love, may grow up into him in all things, which is the head, *even* Christ: From whom the whole body fitly joined together and compacted by that which every joint supplieth, according to the effectual working in the measure of every part, maketh increase of the body unto the edifying of itself in love.
>
> James 5:9 Grudge not one against another, brethren, lest ye be condemned: behold, the judge standeth before the door.
>
> 1 Peter 4:8 And above all things have fervent charity among yourselves: for charity shall cover the multitude of sins.

Proverbs 10:13 In the lips of him that hath understanding wisdom is found: but a rod *is* for the back of him that is void of understanding.

Focus: This proverb *contrasts* the way men view the credibility of a man who has understanding *with* the way men view the credibility of a person void of understanding.

"In the lips of him that hath understanding wisdom is found." Persons with understanding are known for discreet words guided by godly wisdom. When the wise and understanding person talks, wisdom-seeking listeners discover that his words are fruitful, favorable, and excellent guidance for godly, profitable living. His responses are always guarded because he withholds talking when he has inadequate knowledge, at improper times, or in inappropriate places. He is careful not to arouse strife, as discussed in the previous verse, and neither does he allow his words to be rash or foolish, thus causing trouble.

> 1 Kings 10:8 Happy *are* thy men, happy *are* these thy servants, which stand continually before thee, *and* that hear thy wisdom.
> Psalm 37:30 The mouth of the righteous speaketh wisdom, and his tongue talketh of judgment.
> Proverbs 10:11 The mouth of a righteous *man is* a well of life: but violence covereth the mouth of the wicked.
> Proverbs 10:21 The lips of the righteous feed many: but fools die for want of wisdom.
> Proverbs 15:7 The lips of the wise disperse knowledge: but the heart of the foolish *doeth* not so.

"But a rod *is* for the back of him that is void of understanding." In contrast to a person of understanding is the person **"void of understanding,"** who is accustomed to speaking rashly with empty words and damaging speech. Consequently, he is chastised and dismissed. A **"rod"** can figuratively represent hardships. The void-of-understanding person's speech brings him well-deserved chastisement, and he gets himself in difficult situations and disfavor with others when he speaks wrong things.

Proverbs 10:14 Wise *men* lay up knowledge: but the mouth of the foolish *is* near destruction.

Focus: This proverb states that wise men speak productively from compiled knowledge and that fools speak destructively from ignorance.

Not only does the foolish man cause a rod (punishment which may be applied to his back, or figuratively trouble and hardships) (verse 13), but his mouth is near destruction. This verse continues to discuss the virtues of wisdom and the catastrophes of foolishness.

"Wise *men* lay up knowledge." A wise man can speak with wisdom because he *lays up knowledge* and has it on hand to be brought out and used at the proper, necessary time as one would valuable treasure. He reserves his knowledge for the right occasion and doesn't speak indiscriminately or brag about what he knows. He listens and learns from observation of life and instruction from God's word and godly people. He intentionally meditates on and remembers what he sees so as to pull out valuable information and apply it when confronted with various life situations.

> Proverbs 18:15 The heart of the prudent getteth knowledge; and the ear of the wise seeketh knowledge.
> Matthew 13:52 Then said he unto them, Therefore every scribe *which is* instructed unto the kingdom of heaven is like unto a man *that is* an householder, which bringeth forth out of his treasure *things* new and old.

"But the mouth of the foolish *is* near destruction." The foolish man reveals that he has neither attempted to learn from observation *or* godly instructors. He hates reproof, and rather than listen, he prefers to talk and reveal his ignorant foolishness, which is sure to come roaring back to his destruction. He speaks unpredictably from a heart of foolishness and falls into one disaster after another until he destroys everything valuable – friends, finances, and future.

> Psalm 12:3-4 The LORD shall cut off all flattering lips, *and* the tongue that speaketh proud things: Who have said, With our tongue will we prevail; our lips *are* our own: who *is* lord over us?
> Psalm 52:1-5 To the chief Musician, Maschil, *A Psalm* of David, when Doeg the Edomite came and told Saul, and said unto him, David is come to the house of Ahimelech. Why boastest thou thyself in mischief, O mighty man? the goodness of God *endureth* continually. Thy tongue deviseth mischiefs; like a sharp razor, working deceitfully. Thou lovest evil more than good; *and* lying rather than to speak righteousness. Selah. Thou lovest all devouring words, O *thou* deceitful tongue. God shall likewise destroy thee for ever, he shall take thee away, and pluck thee out of *thy* dwelling place, and root thee out of the land of the living. Selah.
> 1 Samuel 25:9-11 And when David's young men came, they spake to Nabal according to all those words in the name of David, and ceased. And Nabal answered David's servants, and said, Who *is* David? and who *is* the son of Jesse? there be many servants now a days that break away every man from his master. Shall I then take my bread, and my water, and my flesh that I have killed for my shearers, and give *it* unto men, whom I know not whence they be? ... (1Samuel 25:38) And it came to pass about ten days *after,* that the LORD smote Nabal, that he died.

Proverbs 10:15 The rich man's wealth *is* his strong city: the destruction of the poor *is* their poverty.

Focus: This proverb compares common attitudes toward wealth: both the rich and the poor believe it provides safety.

Both the rich and the poor man believe that their respective financial condition affect their safety and well-being. The wealthy man develops over-confidence in the provisions of his wealth, and the poor man develops hopelessness and defeat. Their attitudes indicate that neither is trusting God.

"The rich man's wealth *is* his strong city." Having no regard for God, a typical **"rich"** person will trust his wealth to provide safety from the calamities of life; and certainly, *to the limit that God allows*, his wealth can purchase a level of safety. He can buy the service of guards, build walls, put back enough money and necessities to survive difficult times, and even hire expensive lawyers to escape prosecution. His **"wealth is his strong city"** means that his wealth is his protection against various kinds of enemies and catastrophes. Seldom does a rich man trust God; however, a rich, wise man, like Job or Abraham, will not allow wealth to circumvent a dependency on God, Who will continue to be his high tower, his strength, and strong city. God provides multiple times better safety than wealth alone.

"The destruction of the poor *is* their poverty." *If* a **"poor"** person can but trust in God and follow His commandments, he can reap the benefits of peace, power, protection, and provisions that God has promised to those who put their trust in Him. Because he feels deprived and helpless, the poor person usually becomes more feeble; thus, he retreats into discouragement and fails to call on the arm of God for help.

BOTH THE RICH AND POOR HAVE THE OPPORTUNITY TO TRUST IN GOD.

Psalm 52:7-8 Lo, *this is* the man *that* made not God his strength; but trusted in the abundance of his riches, *and* strengthened himself in his wickedness. But I *am* like a green olive tree in the house of God: I trust in the mercy of God for ever and ever.

Proverbs 18:10 The name of the LORD *is* a strong tower: the righteous runneth into it, and is safe.

Proverbs 18:11 The rich man's wealth *is* his strong city, and as an high wall in his own conceit.

Mark 10:24-25 And the disciples were astonished at his words. But Jesus answereth again, and saith unto them, Children, how hard is it for them that trust in riches to enter into the kingdom of God! It is easier for a camel to go through the eye of a needle, than for a rich man to enter into the kingdom of God.

1 Timothy 6:17 Charge them that are rich in this world, that they be not highminded, nor trust in uncertain riches, but in the living God, who giveth us richly all things to enjoy;

James 2:5 Hearken, my beloved brethren, Hath not God chosen the poor of this world rich in faith, and heirs of the kingdom which he hath promised to them that love him?

Revelation 3:17-18 Because thou sayest, I am rich, and increased with goods, and have need of nothing; and knowest not that thou art wretched, and miserable, and poor, and blind, and naked: I counsel thee to buy of me gold tried in the fire, that thou mayest be rich; and white raiment, that thou mayest be clothed, and that the shame of thy nakedness do not appear; and anoint thine eyes with eyesalve, that thou mayest see.

Proverbs 10:16 The labour of the righteous *tendeth* to life: the fruit of the wicked to sin.

Focus: This proverb contrasts the fact that a "righteous" person righteously labors to produce life while the "wicked" person labors in wickedness to produce sin and thus death.

"The labour of the righteous *tendeth* to life." Righteous people desire both to please God and to live peaceably with all men so as to have a quality life on earth, plus they look forward to a promised eternal home in heaven. The life of the righteous is a guiding light pointing others toward Jesus, Who is the "Light of the world" and "the Life." Therefore, God works through the righteous person who is "a vessel unto honour, sanctified, and meet for the master's use, and prepared unto every good work (2 Timothy 2:21)." His "labor" is a manifestation of the works for God that **"tendeth to life."**

Proverbs 11:30 The fruit of the righteous *is* a tree of life; and he that winneth souls *is* wise.

Proverbs 12:28 In the way of righteousness *is* life; and *in* the pathway *thereof there is* no death.

Matthew 5:14-16 Ye are the light of the world. A city that is set on an hill cannot be hid. Neither do men light a candle, and put it under a bushel, but on a candlestick; and it giveth light unto all that are in the house. Let your light so shine before men, that they may see your good works, and glorify your Father which is in heaven.

John 6:27 Labour not for the meat which perisheth, but for that meat which endureth unto everlasting life, which the Son of man shall give unto you: for him hath God the Father sealed.

John 8:12 Then spake Jesus again unto them, saying, I am the light of the world: he that followeth me shall not walk in darkness, but shall have the light of life.

John 14:6 Jesus saith unto him, I am the way, the truth, and the life: no man cometh unto the Father, but by me.

2 Timothy 2:21 If a man therefore purge himself from these, he shall be a vessel unto honour, sanctified, and meet for the master's use, *and* prepared unto every good work.

"The fruit of the wicked *[tendeth]* **to sin."** (The "fruit" of a man's life is what he produces.) The wicked man's life is opposed to God. He has no regard for the things of God; consequently, his life produces sin that manifests itself in ungodly behavior, ungodly friends, wicked speech, and a destructive end separated from God in an eternal hell – the second death.

Proverbs 11:19 As righteousness *tendeth* to life: so he that pursueth evil *pursueth it* to his own death.

Isaiah 3:10-11 Say ye to the righteous, that *it shall be* well *with him:* for they shall eat the fruit of their doings. Woe unto the wicked! *it shall be* ill *with him:* for the reward of his hands shall be given him.

Matthew 7:16-18 Ye shall know them by their fruits. Do men gather grapes of thorns, or figs of thistles? Even so every good tree bringeth forth good fruit; but a corrupt tree bringeth forth evil fruit. A good tree cannot bring forth evil fruit, neither *can a* corrupt tree bring forth good fruit.

Matthew 12:33 Either make the tree good, and his fruit good; or else make the tree corrupt, and his fruit corrupt: for the tree is known by *his* fruit.

Galatians 6:7-8 Be not deceived; God is not mocked: for whatsoever a man soweth, that shall he also reap. For he that soweth to his flesh shall of the flesh reap corruption; but he that soweth to the Spirit shall of the Spirit reap life everlasting.

Revelation 21:8 But the fearful, and unbelieving, and the abominable, and murderers, and whoremongers, and sorcerers, and idolaters, and all liars, shall have their part in the lake which burneth with fire and brimstone: which is the second death.

Proverbs 10:17 He *is in* the way of life that keepeth instruction: but he that refuseth reproof erreth.

Focus: This proverb contrasts the person who values and guards instruction from God and godly mentors with the person who refuses the same. One is walking in the way of life while the other has veered off onto the way of death.

The wise, righteous man led by God's instructions follows the **"way of life"** – the way of eternal life that Jesus spoke of. *(See Matthew 19:17 below.)* **"Keepeth instruction"** means to value, to guard, and to protect Scripture's instruction that causes one *to accept the teaching and to change* the course of life accordingly. The wise refuses to allow a scorner, any unbeliever, or a peer to influence him to move away from his faith. He is just as determined to be taught and corrected by the Scriptures as the ungodly person is determined ***not*** to be taught and corrected by Scripture. The believer knows how valuable this instruction is for guiding him to wisdom, to righteousness, and to **"the way of life"** acceptable unto God. In contrast, the one who refuses to be taught and corrected, ***errs*** or goes off onto the *way of death* rather than the *way of life*. How terrible for a person to turn a deaf ear to that which could save him from eternal ruin.

Proverbs 1:23 Turn you at my reproof: behold, I will pour out my spirit unto you, I will make known my words unto you.

Proverbs 4:20-22 My son, attend to my words; incline thine ear unto my sayings. Let them not depart from thine eyes; keep them in the midst of thine heart. For they *are* life unto those that find them, and health to all their flesh.

Proverbs 6:23 For the commandment *is* a lamp; and the law *is* light; and reproofs of instruction *are* the way of life . . .

Proverbs 8:34-35 Blessed *is* the man that heareth me, watching daily at my gates, waiting at the posts of my doors. For whoso findeth me findeth life, and shall obtain favour of the LORD.

Proverbs 12:1 Whoso loveth instruction loveth knowledge: but he that hateth reproof is brutish.

Proverbs 15:5 A fool despiseth his father's instruction: but he that regardeth reproof is prudent.

Proverbs 15:10 Correction is grievous unto him that forsaketh the way: and he that hateth reproof shall die.

Proverbs 15:24 The way of life *is* above to the wise, that he may depart from hell beneath.

Proverbs 15:32 He that refuseth instruction despiseth his own soul: but he that heareth reproof getteth understanding.

Isaiah 35:8 And an highway shall be there, and a way, and it shall be called The way of holiness; the unclean shall not pass over it; but it *shall be* for those: the wayfaring men, though fools, shall not err *therein*.

Jeremiah 21:8 And unto this people thou shalt say, Thus saith the LORD; Behold, I set before you the way of life, and the way of death.

Matthew 19:17 And he said unto him, Why callest thou me good? *there is* none good but one, *that is,* God: but if thou wilt enter into life, keep the commandments.

Proverbs 10:18 He that hideth hatred *with* lying lips, and he that uttereth a slander, *is* a fool.

Focus: This proverb identifies two means by which a fool deals with his personal hatred: lying and slander.

A fool's *corrupt heart of hate is revealed by his speech.* Whether he *lies* about such hatred or else openly expresses his hate with a *slander*, he declares that his foolish heart is controlled by hate. Just as a wise person is known for love, truth, and kindness of speech; so the fool is known for his lying and slanderous speaking. Jesus taught that words make manifest the condition of one's heart. [See Matthew 15:18-19 below.] **"Hatred"** is an evil that infects, corrupts, and then controls the reins of a fool's heart. To the wise observer, "lying" and "slander" are external indicators of internal hate.

> Matthew 12:36-37 But I say unto you, That every idle word that men shall speak, they shall give account thereof in the day of judgment. For by thy words thou shalt be justified, and by thy words thou shalt be condemned.
> Matthew 15:18-19 But those things which proceed out of the mouth come forth from the heart; and they defile the man. For out of the heart proceed evil thoughts, murders, adulteries, fornications, thefts, false witness, blasphemies . . .
> Luke 6:45 A good man out of the good treasure of his heart bringeth forth that which is good; and an evil man out of the evil treasure of his heart bringeth forth that which is evil: for of the abundance of the heart his mouth speaketh.
> John 8:44 Ye are of *your* father the devil, and the lusts of your father ye will do. He was a murderer from the beginning, and abode not in the truth, because there is no truth in him. When he speaketh a lie, he speaketh of his own: for he is a liar, and the father of it.

Proverbs 10:19 In the multitude of words there wanteth not sin: but he that refraineth his lips is wise.

Focus: This proverb observes again that a wise person controls how much he talks, thereby avoiding the sin that develops from excessive talking.

The first clause of this proverb declares that within a **"multitude of words,"** there is sin *(See "prating" in 10:8 and 10:10.)*, and the second clause declares that a wise person avoids this sin by holding back his words. He filters them, making sure that his words are necessary. When speech is unchecked, false statements will eventually be made, and words become injurious to others.

> Proverbs 13:3 He that keepeth his mouth keepeth his life: *but* he that openeth wide his lips shall have destruction.
> Proverbs 17:27 He that hath knowledge spareth his words: *and* a man of understanding is of an excellent spirit.
> Ecclesiastes 5:2-3 Be not rash with thy mouth, and let not thine heart be hasty to utter *any* thing before God: for God *is* in heaven, and thou upon earth: therefore let thy words be few. For a dream cometh through the multitude of business; and a fool's voice *is known* by multitude of words.
> Matthew 12:36-37 But I say unto you, That every idle word that men shall speak, they shall give account thereof in the day of judgment. For by thy words thou shalt be justified, and by thy words thou shalt be condemned.
> James 1:26 If any man among you seem to be religious, and bridleth not his tongue, but deceiveth his own heart, this man's religion *is* vain.
> James 3:2-6 For in many things we offend all. If any man offend not in word, the same *is* a perfect man, *and* able also to bridle the whole body. Behold, we put bits in the horses' mouths, that they may obey us; and we turn about their whole body. Behold also the ships, which though *they be* so great, and *are* driven of fierce winds, yet are they turned about with a very small helm, whithersoever the governor listeth. Even so the tongue is a little member, and boasteth great things. Behold, how great a matter a little fire kindleth! And the tongue *is* a fire, a world of iniquity: so is the tongue among our members, that it defileth the whole body, and setteth on fire the course of nature; and it is set on fire of hell.

Proverbs 10:20 The tongue of the just *is as* choice silver: the heart of the wicked *is* little worth.

Focus: This proverb states that the speech developed from a righteous person's heart is valuable, but speech developed from a wicked person's heart has little value.

At first glance, this proverb seems to compare the value of **"the tongue"** of the **"just"** *[righteous]* with the value of **"the heart"** of the wicked, but a person's tongue has no ability to move without a command from his heart. And the **"heart"** herein referred to is a term representing the deep convictions of a person – *the combination of the way he thinks, feels, and wills himself to talk and act*. This Scripture is therefore using symbolism to say that the tongue of the just (commanded by his godly "heart") is extremely valuable, but the tongue of the wicked (commanded by his ungodly "heart") is not worth much.

"The tongue of the just *is as* choice silver." The **"tongue of the just"** reveals his righteous heart, and his words reflect the teachings of wisdom from God. Consequently, he has a heart of great value – "choice silver"– to God and good people. When he speaks, he speaks out of a treasury of wisdom, knowledge, and understanding put there by wise teachings. His words are **"as choice silver"** because they guide others to abundant living and eternal life. Wise people want to hear wisdom and instruction taught by wise people; consequently, those who have wisdom to speak have valuable information to share.

> Psalm 12:6 The words of the LORD *are* pure words: *as* silver tried in a furnace of earth, purified seven times.

"The heart of the wicked is little worth" because his evil thoughts infect his words and guide his wicked conduct. His speech is highly offensive, objectionable, and unworthy of listening to.

> Genesis 6:5 And GOD saw that the wickedness of man *was* great in the earth, and *that* every imagination of the thoughts of his heart *was* only evil continually.
> Isaiah 32:6 For the vile person will speak villany, and his heart will work iniquity, to practise hypocrisy, and to utter error against the LORD, to make empty the soul of the hungry, and he will cause the drink of the thirsty to fail.
> Jeremiah 17:9-10 The heart *is* deceitful above all *things,* and desperately wicked: who can know it? I the LORD search the heart, *I* try the reins, even to give every man according to his ways, *and* according to the fruit of his doings.
> Matthew 12:34-35 O generation of vipers, how can ye, being evil, speak good things? For out of the abundance of the heart the mouth speaketh. A good man out of the good treasure of the heart bringeth forth good things: and an evil man out of the evil treasure bringeth forth evil things. *[See also Luke 6:45.]*

Proverbs 10:21 The lips of the righteous feed many: but fools die for want of wisdom.

Focus: This proverb contrasts the spiritual value of the righteous one's words with the spiritual worthlessness of the wicked fool's words.

"The lips of the righteous feed many." **"Righteous"** people, whose minds are filled with thoughts of God, **"feed many"** others spiritually with their words because their speech reflects a heart for pleasing God and a mind centered on Him. They strive to learn about God and what He expects of believers, and because they have studied to know what pleases God, they feed other good persons desiring to be wise. They love the things God loves; and because they have the "mind of Christ," when they speak, their words are nourishing and benefit others spiritually with encouragement, comfort, counsel, and guidance.

> Job 4:3 Behold, thou hast instructed many, and thou hast strengthened the weak hands. Thy words have upholden him that was falling, and thou hast strengthened the feeble knees.
> John 6:63 It is the spirit that quickeneth; the flesh profiteth nothing: the words that I speak unto you, *they* are spirit, and *they* are life.
> Acts 5:20 Go, stand and speak in the temple to the people all the words of this life.
> Acts 26:25 But he said, I am not mad, most noble Festus; but speak forth the words of truth and soberness.
> 1 Peter 5:2-3 Feed the flock of God which is among you, taking the oversight *thereof,* not by constraint, but willingly; not for filthy lucre, but of a ready mind; Neither as being lords over *God's* heritage, but being ensamples to the flock.

"But fools die for want of wisdom." They don't have godly wisdom, so they can't effectively maintain their own lives. "Their wrong kind of talking does not even nourish themselves; they are left spiritually undernourished and starved."[169] They refuse to be spiritually fed from God's word or from the **"righteous."** "But if our gospel be hid, it is hid to them that are lost: In whom the god of this world hath blinded the minds of them which believe not, lest the light of the glorious gospel of Christ, who is the image of God, should shine unto them." (2 Corinthians 4:3-4)

> Proverbs 1:29-31 For that they *[simple ones, scorners, fools]* hated knowledge, and did not choose the fear of the LORD: They would none of my counsel: they despised all my reproof. Therefore shall they eat of the fruit of their own way, and be filled with their own devices.
> Proverbs 15:26 The thoughts of the wicked *are* an abomination to the LORD: but *the words* of the pure *are* pleasant words.
> Ecclesiastes 10:12 The words of a wise man's mouth *are* gracious; but the lips of a fool will swallow up himself.
> Matthew 13:19 When any one heareth the word of the kingdom, and understandeth *it* not, then cometh the wicked *one,* and catcheth away that which was sown in his heart. This is he which received seed by the way side.
> Ephesians 5:6 Let no man deceive you with vain words: for because of these things cometh the wrath of God upon the children of disobedience.
> 1 Timothy 6:3-5 If any man teach otherwise, and consent not to wholesome words, *even* the words of our Lord Jesus Christ, and to the doctrine which is according to godliness; He is proud, knowing nothing, but doting about questions and strifes of words,

whereof cometh envy, strife, railings, evil surmisings, Perverse disputings of men of corrupt minds, and destitute of the truth, supposing that gain is godliness: from such withdraw thyself.

Proverbs 10:22 The blessing of the LORD, it maketh rich, and he addeth no sorrow with it.

Focus: This proverb states that riches provided by God *do not* come with the trouble and turmoil of riches that accompany ill-gotten gain.

Wealth given by the Lord will be a blessing and a good thing, and brings with it no added problem. This proverb complements verse 2 of this chapter: "Treasures of wickedness profit nothing: but righteousness delivereth from death."

> 2 Kings 5:25-27 But he went in, and stood before his master. And Elisha said unto him, Whence *comest thou,* Gehazi? And he said, Thy servant went no whither. And he said unto him, Went not mine heart *with thee,* when the man turned again from his chariot to meet thee? *Is it* a time to receive money, and to receive garments, and oliveyards, and vineyards, and sheep, and oxen, and menservants, and maidservants? The leprosy therefore of Naaman shall cleave unto thee, and unto thy seed for ever. And he went out from his presence a leper *as white* as snow.
>
> 1 Chronicles 4:10 And Jabez called on the God of Israel, saying, Oh that thou wouldest bless me indeed, and enlarge my coast, and that thine hand might be with me, and that thou wouldest keep *me* from evil, that it may not grieve me! And God granted him that which he requested.
>
> Proverbs 15:6 In the house of the righteous *is* much treasure: but in the revenues of the wicked is trouble.
>
> Proverbs 15:16 Better *is* little with the fear of the LORD than great treasure and trouble therewith.
>
> Proverbs 28:22 He that hasteth to be rich hath an evil eye, and considereth not that poverty shall come upon him.
>
> Ecclesiastes 5:19 Every man also to whom God hath given riches and wealth, and hath given him power to eat thereof, and to take his portion, and to rejoice in his labour; this *is* the gift of God.

"What comes from the love of God has the grace of God for its companion, to preserve the soul from those turbulent lusts and passions."[170] Lust and passion are the companions of the ungodly who have an insatiable desire to "get all you can and can all you get." Also, ***blessings from the LORD*** bring rich rewards without the dangers and fears that attend wealth acquired improperly. When a thief secures his ill-gotten gain, he still must be continually on guard against retribution from the lawful owner or a law official who might presently barge through his locked door to confiscate his goods and confine him behind bars.

> I Timothy 6:9-10 But they that will be rich fall into temptation and a snare, and *into* many foolish and hurtful lusts, which drown men in destruction and perdition. For the love of money is the root of all evil: which while some coveted after, they have erred from the faith, and pierced themselves through with many sorrows.

Of the blessed man, the Scriptures say: "And he shall be like a tree planted by the rivers of water, that bringeth forth his fruit in his season; his leaf also shall not wither; and whatsoever he doeth shall prosper." (Psalm 1:3)

Proverbs 10:23 *It is* as sport to a fool to do mischief: but a man of understanding hath wisdom.

Focus: This proverb teaches that the fool (because he lacks understanding) prefers and enjoys mischief *(wickedness)*, but the man of understanding prefers wisdom.

It is a light and happy occasion (**"sport to a fool"**) to carry out wickedness (**"mischief"**), **"but a man of understanding hath wisdom"** that prevents him from engaging in such behavior. He comprehends God's expectations of him, and understands how both good and evil work to produce their respective results. The wise and understanding man knows that mischief produces effects that he does not want to be forced to deal with. He prefers the benefits of wisdom.

> While God "is blessing the righteous, fools are laughing at sin. For the mark of 'the fool' is that he considers wickedness (the word contains the thought of evil devices) to be a joke. He laughs at it, and does not take it seriously. Indeed he enjoys it. He plots a negative course. In contrast the man of understanding rejoices in wisdom. He plots a positive course. His way ahead is sure. The fool finds great enjoyment in pleasing himself, the man of understanding in pleasing God."[171]
>
> Proverbs 14:9 Fools make a mock at sin: but among the righteous *there is* favour.
>
> Proverbs 15:21 Folly *is* joy to *him that is* destitute of wisdom: but a man of understanding walketh uprightly.

> **Proverbs 10:24** The fear of the wicked, it shall come upon him: but the desire of the righteous shall be granted.

Focus: Like many Scriptures, this proverb stresses that the wicked will receive their dreaded punishment; but the righteous will receive the desire of their heart.

Eventually, their own fear catches up with the wicked – "**it shall come upon him.**" They have looked for judgment from the time they committed their first evil deed. Notice the dread of Joseph's brothers.

> Genesis 42:21-23 And they said one to another, We are verily guilty concerning our brother, in that we saw the anguish of his soul, when he besought us, and we would not hear; therefore is this distress come upon us. And Reuben answered them, saying, Spake I not unto you, saying, Do not sin against the child; and ye would not hear? therefore, behold, also his blood is required. And they knew not that Joseph understood them; for he spake unto them by an interpreter.
> Proverbs 1:25-27 But ye have set at nought all my *[Wisdom's]* counsel, and would none of my reproof: I also will laugh at your calamity; I will mock when your fear cometh; When your fear cometh as desolation, and your destruction cometh as a whirlwind; when distress and anguish cometh upon you.
> Proverbs 6:14-15 Frowardness is in his heart, he deviseth mischief continually; he soweth discord. Therefore shall his calamity come suddenly; suddenly shall he be broken without remedy.
> Proverbs 10:3 The LORD will not suffer the soul of the righteous to famish: but he casteth away the substance of the wicked.
> Proverbs 11:23 The desire of the righteous *is* only good: *but* the expectation of the wicked *is* wrath.
> Proverbs 11:31 Behold, the righteous shall be recompensed in the earth: much more the wicked and the sinner.
> Proverbs 13:21 Evil pursueth sinners: but to the righteous good shall be repayed.
> Isaiah 66:4 I also will choose their delusions, and will bring their fears upon them; because when I called, none did answer; when I spake, they did not hear: but they did evil before mine eyes, and chose *that* in which I delighted not.
> Hebrews 10:27 But a certain fearful looking for of judgment and fiery indignation, which shall devour the adversaries.

Judgment to the wicked might come in the form of reprisal from a victim, or a verdict through the judicial system, and even if it doesn't come from one of those sources, it will certainly come in the Judgment when God gives a final verdict.

The righteous will get the thing they desire most, and that is the will of God. God gives the godly the desires of their hearts.

> Psalm 37:4 Delight thyself also in the LORD; and he shall give thee the desires of thine heart.
> Psalm 145:19 He will fulfil the desire of them that fear him: he also will hear their cry, and will save them.
> Proverbs 11:27 He that diligently seeketh good procureth favour: but he that seeketh mischief, it shall come unto him.
> Matthew 5:6 Blessed *are* they which do hunger and thirst after righteousness: for they shall be filled.

> **Proverbs 10:25** As the whirlwind passeth, so *is* the wicked no *more*: but the righteous *is* an everlasting foundation.

Focus: This proverb compares the temporary status of the wicked to the permanent status of the righteous.

Whirlwinds come up suddenly and pass through quickly. Likewise, the wicked will be taken away from the presence of God. **"But the righteous is an everlasting foundation"** declares that the righteous will remain with God forever.

Had there been ten righteous persons in Sodom, God would have spared it. As it was, He removed the few righteous before destroying the city. After the Genesis flood, had it not been for Noah and his family, not one person on earth would have been left. The righteous are the "salt" and the "light" of this world, the stay of it, the stable **"foundation"** on which it remains; and when they are taken out at the rapture of the church, God will bring chaos and destruction for seven years such as the world has never seen. The whirlwind of God's wrath will eventually remove the wicked from His sight and presence, but the righteous will dwell with God for eternity.

> Psalm 91:1 He that dwelleth in the secret place of the most High shall abide under the shadow of the Almighty.
> Psalm 125:1-2 A Song of degrees. They that trust in the LORD *shall be* as mount Zion, *which* cannot be removed, *but* abideth for ever. As the mountains *are* round about Jerusalem, so the LORD *is* round about his people from henceforth even for ever.
> Proverbs 1:25-27 But ye have set at nought all my counsel, and would none of my reproof: I also will laugh at your calamity; I will mock when your fear cometh; When your fear cometh as desolation, and your destruction cometh as a whirlwind; when distress and anguish cometh upon you.

Proverbs 6:15 Therefore shall his calamity come suddenly; suddenly shall he be broken without remedy.

Proverbs 10:30 The righteous shall never be removed: but the wicked shall not inhabit the earth.

Proverbs 12:3 A man shall not be established by wickedness: but the root of the righteous shall not be moved.

Proverbs 29:1 He, that being often reproved hardeneth *his* neck, shall suddenly be destroyed, and that without remedy.

Isaiah 28:14-20 Wherefore hear the word of the LORD, ye scornful men, that rule this people which *is* in Jerusalem. Because ye have said, We have made a covenant with death, and with hell are we at agreement; when the overflowing scourge shall pass through, it shall not come unto us: for we have made lies our refuge, and under falsehood have we hid ourselves: Therefore thus saith the Lord GOD, Behold, I lay in Zion for a foundation a stone, a tried stone, a precious corner *stone,* a sure foundation: he that believeth shall not make haste. Judgment also will I lay to the line, and righteousness to the plummet: and the hail shall sweep away the refuge of lies, and the waters shall overflow the hiding place. And your covenant with death shall be disannulled, and your agreement with hell shall not stand; when the overflowing scourge shall pass through, then ye shall be trodden down by it. From the time that it goeth forth it shall take you: for morning by morning shall it pass over, by day and by night: and it shall be a vexation only *to* understand the report. For the bed is shorter than that *a man* can stretch himself *on it:* and the covering narrower than that he can wrap himself *in it.*

Matthew 7:24-27 Therefore whosoever heareth these sayings of mine, and doeth them, I will liken him unto a wise man, which built his house upon a rock: And the rain descended, and the floods came, and the winds blew, and beat upon that house; and it fell not: for it was founded upon a rock. And every one that heareth these sayings of mine, and doeth them not, shall be likened unto a foolish man, which built his house upon the sand: And the rain descended, and the floods came, and the winds blew, and beat upon that house; and it fell: and great was the fall of it.

Proverbs 10:26 As vinegar to the teeth, and as smoke to the eyes, so *is* the sluggard to them that send him.

Focus: This proverb uses two common irritants to illustrate how irritating the sluggard is to those who ask him to do work or run an errand.

The **"sluggard"** is lazy and has no desire to bear responsibility; but if he manages to awake out of his lethargy long enough to gain someone's favor or pity, he will soon become a disappointment and a source of irritation. The sluggard will repeatedly be a source of frustration to his employer.

"Vinegar" sets the teeth on edge and causes one not to want to put anything else in his mouth for a while. **"Smoke"** stings the eyes and causes one not to be able to see momentarily. In both cases, the sufferer is distracted, stunned, aggravated, and totally involved with recovering himself before being able to continue with what he was previously doing – **"so is the sluggard to them that send him."**

Verses 27-30 mention four great blessings that come to the godly believer: the glad hope or expectation of the righteous; added strength; the promise of inheriting the earth; and a long life and eternity with God. The longevity of the righteous as contrasted with the shortened life of the wicked, are recurrent themes in this book of wisdom, as are the eternal blessings of the righteous in contrast to the eternal doom of the ungodly.

Proverbs 10:27 The fear of the LORD prolongeth days: but the years of the wicked shall be shortened.

Focus: This proverb first gives the reason for the godly man's longer life and then contrasts the righteous person's longer life span with the abbreviated one of the wicked.

"The fear of the LORD prolongeth days," because by the "fear of the LORD" wisdom is initiated (See Proverbs 9:10-11 below). The person with wisdom has the ability, because of a proper relationship with God, to be able to navigate through the challenges and opportunities of life in the most effective manner, thereby minimizing evil influences and maximizing godly outcomes – all of which have the potential of adding to the length of one's life.

Psalm 91:15-16 He shall call upon me, and I will answer him: I *will be* with him in trouble; I will deliver him, and honour him. With long life will I satisfy him, and shew him my salvation.

Proverbs 3:1-2 My son, forget not my law; but let thine heart keep my commandments: For length of days, and long life, and peace, shall they add to thee.

Proverbs 4:10 Hear, O my son, and receive my sayings; and the years of thy life shall be many.

Proverbs 9:10-11 The fear of the LORD *is* the beginning of wisdom: and the knowledge of the holy *is* understanding. For by me thy days shall be multiplied, and the years of thy life shall be increased.

Ephesians 6:1-3 Children, obey your parents in the Lord: for this is right. Honour thy father and mother; (which is the first commandment with promise;) That it may be well with thee, and thou mayest live long on the earth.

I Timothy 4:8 For bodily exercise profiteth little: but godliness is profitable unto all things, having promise of the life that now is, and of that which is to come.

1 John 2:16-17 For all that *is* in the world, the lust of the flesh, and the lust of the eyes, and the pride of life, is not of the Father, but is of the world. And the world passeth away, and the lust thereof: but he that doeth the will of God abideth for ever.

"But the years of the wicked shall be shortened." The **"years of the wicked"** are often shortened primarily because the wicked are disassociated with God and therefore unprotected by Him. In addition, because of reprisals, sin-related diseases, and dangerous associations, their life is often cut short. Also, he robs himself of eternal life by refusing the gift of the Son of God.

Proverbs 2:21-22 For the upright shall dwell in the land, and the perfect shall remain in it. But the wicked shall be cut off from the earth, and the transgressors shall be rooted out of it.

Proverbs 10:25 As the whirlwind passeth, so *is* the wicked no *more:* but the righteous *is* an everlasting foundation.

Proverbs 11:7 When a wicked man dieth, *his* expectation shall perish: and the hope of unjust *men* perisheth.

Proverbs 10:28 The hope of the righteous *shall be* gladness: but the expectation of the wicked shall perish.

Focus: This proverb contrasts "the hope" ("expectation") of the righteous with that of the wicked.

The righteous have a hope of a wonderful, enjoyable eternity with Christ that will produce **"gladness."** God has prepared an unimaginably delightful eternal abode for the righteous, and there will be no disappointments.

On the other hand, the wicked will be sadly disappointed in hell. Since they don't believe in God, their trust is misplaced in false teachers who believe that the Bible is false, that there is no hell, no heaven, no Judgment, and no God. Their **"expectation"** is in reincarnation or life that ends with the grave, but their "expectation...shall perish." Having expectation or hope in anything not promised by God can only end poorly.

Psalm 34:15-16 The eyes of the LORD *are* upon the righteous, and his ears *are open* unto their cry. The face of the LORD *is* against them that do evil, to cut off the remembrance of them from the earth.

Psalm 112:10 The wicked shall see *it,* and be grieved; he shall gnash with his teeth, and melt away: the desire of the wicked shall perish.

Proverbs 11:7 When a wicked man dieth, *his* expectation shall perish: and the hope of unjust *men* perisheth.

Proverbs 14:32 The wicked is driven away in his wickedness: but the righteous hath hope in his death.

Job 8:13-14 So *are* the paths of all that forget God; and the hypocrite's hope shall perish: Whose hope shall be cut off, and whose trust *shall be* a spider's web.

Job 11:20 But the eyes of the wicked shall fail, and they shall not escape, and their hope *shall be as* the giving up of the ghost.

Luke 16:23-26 And in hell he lift up his eyes, being in torments, and seeth Abraham afar off, and Lazarus in his bosom. And he cried and said, Father Abraham, have mercy on me, and send Lazarus, that he may dip the tip of his finger in water, and cool my tongue; for I am tormented in this flame. But Abraham said, Son, remember that thou in thy lifetime receivedst thy good things, and likewise Lazarus evil things: but now he is comforted, and thou art tormented. And beside all this, between us and you there is a great gulf fixed: so that they which would pass from hence to you cannot; neither can they pass to us, that *would come* from thence.

Proverbs 10:29 The way of the LORD *is* strength to the upright: but destruction *shall be* to the workers of iniquity.

Focus: This proverb declares that the "way of the LORD" has its two sides: it gives strength to the upright and destruction to the workers of iniquity.

The **"way of the LORD"** is the righteous manner of living prescribed by God. Wisdom always leads her students to submit to this way because it gives **"strength"** *[place or means of safety, protection, refuge, stronghold]* to a person's character, to his reputation, to his mind, and to his body – all because the **"upright"** live in a manner that the Creator declared to be right. It is a manner of living that rejects the lifestyle of the foolish (**"the workers of iniquity"**) and their views of right and wrong.

Because they war against the **"way of the LORD,"** **"the workers of iniquity"** follow their own wicked ***destructive*** way. Instead of being an umbrella of protection, their opposition to God becomes the cause for a landslide of Divine judgment. Instead of viewing God as a loving Father instructing His children through His word, the wicked view God *(if they believe there is a God)* as a stern Judge and will eventually tremble in fear of Him as previous proverbs teach.

> 2Samuel 22:33 God *is* my strength *and* power: and he maketh my way perfect.
>
> Psalm 1:4-6 The ungodly *are* not so: but *are* like the chaff which the wind driveth away. Therefore the ungodly shall not stand in the judgment, nor sinners in the congregation of the righteous. For the LORD knoweth the way of the righteous: but the way of the ungodly shall perish.
>
> Psalm 18:2 The LORD *is* my rock, and my fortress, and my deliverer; my God, my strength, in whom I will trust; my buckler, and the horn of my salvation, *and* my high tower.
>
> Psalm 18:32 *It is* God that girdeth me with strength, and maketh my way perfect.
>
> Psalm 19:14 Let the words of my mouth, and the meditation of my heart, be acceptable in thy sight, O LORD, my strength, and my redeemer.
>
> Psalm 27:1 *A Psalm* of David. The LORD *is* my light and my salvation; whom shall I fear? the LORD *is* the strength of my life; of whom shall I be afraid?
>
> Psalm 37:39 But the salvation of the righteous *is* of the LORD: *he is* their strength in the time of trouble.
>
> Psalm 52:7 Lo, *this is* the man *that* made not God his strength; but trusted in the abundance of his riches, *and* strengthened himself in his wickedness.
>
> Proverbs 2:5-9 Then shalt thou understand the fear of the LORD, and find the knowledge of God. For the LORD giveth wisdom: out of his mouth *cometh* knowledge and understanding. He layeth up sound wisdom for the righteous: *he is* a buckler to them that walk uprightly. He keepeth the paths of judgment, and preserveth the way of his saints. Then shalt thou understand righteousness, and judgment, and equity; *yea,* every good path.
>
> Proverbs 21:15 *It is* joy to the just to do judgment: but destruction *shall be* to the workers of iniquity.
>
> Romans 1:28-32 And even as they did not like to retain God in their knowledge, God gave them over to a reprobate mind, to do those things which are not convenient; Being filled with all unrighteousness, fornication, wickedness, covetousness, maliciousness; full of envy, murder, debate, deceit, malignity; whisperers, Backbiters, haters of God, despiteful, proud, boasters, inventors of evil things, disobedient to parents, Without understanding, covenant breakers, without natural affection, implacable, unmerciful: Who knowing the judgment of God, that they which commit such things are worthy of death, not only do the same, but have pleasure in them that do them.

Proverbs 10:30 The righteous shall never be removed: but the wicked shall not inhabit the earth.

Focus: This proverb declares that the righteous are secure on earth but that the wicked are not: the wicked will be removed.

God had promised Abraham and his offspring the land from the Nile River to the Euphrates River. (Genesis 15:18) They could dwell there safely and securely under one condition–"if thou shalt keep all these commandments." (Deuteronomy 19:8-9) "To dwell in the land was always put forward as the reward of obedience to God's commandments (Exodus 20:12; 25:18; Exodus 26:5), and the phrase conveyed to the Hebrew mind the idea of one of the greatest, if not the greatest, of all temporal blessings. The love of country was a predominant characteristic of the race."[172] In contrast to the faithful and obedient Jews, the disobedient would be rooted out of the land.

Righteous men understand that this earth and everything else that exists belongs to the Creator. He is the Governor and final Judge. He loves those who love righteousness, and He has a unique protective relationship with those who love Him and His Son, Jesus Christ, and these live with tremendous peace and security. However, God allows mankind a free will by permitting him to choose to be wicked and to thus stand in opposition to Him; but there are consequences to this choice because the ground of opposition they stand on is extremely unstable, and they are subject to God's wrath at any time. Their lives are volatile, and God has promised that He will remove them from His presence. With His destruction of Sodom and the worldwide flood of Genesis 6, God has left detailed, vivid examples of His sure judgment for wickedness.

> Genesis 6:5-8 And GOD saw that the wickedness of man *was* great in the earth, and *that* every imagination of the thoughts of his heart *was* only evil continually. And it repented the LORD that he had made man on the earth, and it grieved him at his heart.

And the LORD said, I will destroy man whom I have created from the face of the earth; both man, and beast, and the creeping thing, and the fowls of the air; for it repenteth me that I have made them. But Noah found grace in the eyes of the LORD.

Genesis 18:20-23 And the LORD said, Because the cry of Sodom and Gomorrah is great, and because their sin is very grievous; I will go down now, and see whether they have done altogether according to the cry of it, which is come unto me; and if not, I will know. And the men turned their faces from thence, and went toward Sodom: but Abraham stood yet before the LORD. And Abraham drew near, and said, Wilt thou also destroy the righteous with the wicked?

Psalm 16:8 I have set the LORD always before me: because *he is* at my right hand, I shall not be moved.

Psalm 24:1-4 **A Psalm of David.** The earth *is* the LORD'S, and the fulness thereof; the world, and they that dwell therein. For he hath founded it upon the seas, and established it upon the floods. Who shall ascend into the hill of the LORD? or who shall stand in his holy place? He that hath clean hands, and a pure heart; who hath not lifted up his soul unto vanity, nor sworn deceitfully.

Psalm 37:9-10 For evildoers shall be cut off: but those that wait upon the LORD, they shall inherit the earth. For yet a little while, and the wicked *shall* not *be:* yea, thou shalt diligently consider his place, and it shall not *be*.

Psalm 37:22 For *such as be* blessed of him shall inherit the earth; and *they that be* cursed of him shall be cut off.

Psalm 37:28-29 For the LORD loveth judgment, and forsaketh not his saints; they are preserved for ever: but the seed of the wicked shall be cut off. The righteous shall inherit the land, and dwell therein for ever.

Psalm 52:1-5 **To the chief Musician, Maschil, *A Psalm* of David, when Doeg the Edomite came and told Saul, and said unto him, David is come to the house of Ahimelech.** Why boastest thou thyself in mischief, O mighty man? the goodness of God *endureth* continually. Thy tongue deviseth mischiefs; like a sharp razor, working deceitfully. Thou lovest evil more than good; *and* lying rather than to speak righteousness. Selah. Thou lovest all devouring words, O *thou* deceitful tongue. God shall likewise destroy thee for ever, he shall take thee away, and pluck thee out of *thy* dwelling place, and root thee out of the land of the living. Selah.

Psalm 112:6 Surely he *[good man]* shall not be moved for ever: the righteous shall be in everlasting remembrance.

Psalm 125:1-2 **A Song of degrees.** They that trust in the LORD *shall be* as mount Zion, *which* cannot be removed, *but* abideth for ever. As the mountains *are* round about Jerusalem, so the LORD *is* round about his people from henceforth even for ever.

Revelation 21:8 But the fearful, and unbelieving, and the abominable, and murderers, and whoremongers, and sorcerers, and idolaters, and all liars, shall have their part in the lake which burneth with fire and brimstone: which is the second death.

Proverbs 10:31-32 The mouth of the just bringeth forth wisdom: but the froward tongue shall be cut out.
32. The lips of the righteous know what is acceptable: but the mouth of the wicked *speaketh* frowardness.

Focus: Joined by the subject of talking, these two proverbs contrast godly and ungodly speech as well as their consequences.

Wisdom comes from God, originates with Him, and is placed into the heart of believers so that **"the mouth of the just bringeth forth wisdom"** and **"the lips of the righteous know what is acceptable"** *to God and righteous men.* Every man speaks out of the abundance of the teachings that are hidden in his heart. Those teachings guide his life. With the believer, the word of God is in his heart, forming wise words in his mouth.

The heart of the wicked is obstinate toward God and His wisdom; hence, he is froward and speaks perversely from the wicked ways he has learned. Because the froward are constantly opposed to God and everything He stands for – **"the froward tongue shall be cut out,"** meaning their voice will end. Only those who want the will of God will dwell with Him eternally. There will be no wicked, vile, froward speech in heaven because there will be no froward person there; hence, *froward tongues will be removed or cut out* of that beautiful place.

Psalm 12:3-5 The LORD shall cut off all flattering lips, and the tongue that speaketh proud things: Who have said, With our tongue will we prevail; our lips are our own: who is lord over us? Thy tongue deviseth mischiefs; like a sharp razor, working deceitfully. Thou lovest evil more than good; and lying rather than to speak righteousness. Selah.

Psalm 52:4-5 Thou lovest all devouring words, O thou deceitful tongue. God shall likewise destroy thee for ever, he shall take thee away, and pluck thee out of thy dwelling place, and root thee out of the land of the living. Selah.

Proverbs 18:7 A fool's mouth is his destruction, and his lips are the snare of his soul.

Luke 6:43-5 For a good tree bringeth not forth corrupt fruit; neither doth a corrupt tree bring forth good fruit. For every tree is known by his own fruit. For of thorns men do not gather figs, nor of a bramble bush gather they grapes. A good man out of the good treasure of his heart bringeth forth that which is good; and an evil man out of the evil treasure of his heart bringeth forth that which is evil: for of the abundance of the heart his mouth speaketh.

CHAPTER ELEVEN

Introduction:

This chapter continues to prove that a life of righteousness is much more profitable than one of wickedness. God blesses, guides, protects, and rewards the righteous person; but tribulation and destruction await the transgressor.

> **Proverbs 11:1** A false balance *is* abomination to the LORD: but a just weight *is* his delight.

> Focus: This proverb declares that God considers dishonesty in commerce detestable but honesty in commerce a delight.

For the scale to be constructed or altered in a manner that would give a **"false"** (or fraudulent) indication of weight, one end of the scale's beam would be slightly longer than the other. The **"just weight"** would likely have been a stone of the exact appropriate weight for a counterbalance.[173] God's word specifically commands His people to deal truthfully in every aspect of life, and He is pleased when they do so. God hates or despises corruption in business.

> Leviticus 19:35-37 Ye shall do no unrighteousness in judgment, in meteyard, in weight, or in measure. Just balances, just weights, a just ephah, and a just hin, shall ye have: I *am* the LORD your God, which brought you out of the land of Egypt. Therefore shall ye observe all my statutes, and all my judgments, and do them: I *am* the LORD.
> Deuteronomy 25:13-16 Thou shalt not have in thy bag divers weights, a great and a small. Thou shalt not have in thine house divers measures, a great and a small. *But* thou shalt have a perfect and just weight, a perfect and just measure shalt thou have: that thy days may be lengthened in the land which the LORD thy God giveth thee. For all that do such things, *and* all that do unrighteously, *are* an abomination unto the LORD thy God.
> Proverbs 16:11 A just weight and balance *are* the LORD'S: all the weights of the bag *are* his work.
> Proverbs 20:10 Divers weights, *and* divers measures, both of them *are* alike abomination to the LORD.
> Proverbs 20:23 Divers weights *are* an abomination unto the LORD; and a false balance *is* not good.
> Matthew 7:12 Therefore all things whatsoever ye would that men should do to you, do ye even so to them: for this is the law and the prophets.
> Acts 24:16 And herein do I exercise myself, to have always a conscience void of offence toward God, and *toward* men.
> 1 Corinthians 6:8-10 Nay, ye do wrong, and defraud, and that *your* brethren. Know ye not that the unrighteous shall not inherit the kingdom of God? Be not deceived: neither fornicators, nor idolaters, nor adulterers, nor effeminate, nor abusers of themselves with mankind, Nor thieves, nor covetous, nor drunkards, nor revilers, nor extortioners, shall inherit the kingdom of God.
> Philippians 4:8 Finally, brethren, whatsoever things are true, whatsoever things *are* honest, whatsoever things *are* just, whatsoever things *are* pure, whatsoever things *are* lovely, whatsoever things *are* of good report; if *there be* any virtue, and if *there be* any praise, think on these things.
> 1 Thessalonians 4:6 That no *man* go beyond and defraud his brother in *any* matter: because that the Lord *is* the avenger of all such, as we also have forewarned you and testified.

> **Proverbs 11:2** *When* pride cometh, then cometh shame: but with the lowly *is* wisdom.

> Focus: This proverb states that shame is the product of pride and that wisdom is a companion to lowliness (humility).

"Pride shall have a fall; self-assertion and self-confidence shall meet with mortification and disgrace in the end."[174] Because the humble person knows that there are ramifications for making bad decisions, he asks God for wisdom which is always available upon request; however, the proud person doesn't ask from God because he believes that wisdom exists within himself.

A humble person who seeks the will and mind of God is wise and avoids the painful feelings of humiliation that pride will ultimately produce. Humility avoids the repercussions of pride by asking others for nothing more than justice, by having a proper opinion of self, and by neither expecting nor desiring accolades. When pride causes a person to behave foolishly, shame is lurking in the shadows.

> Psalm 25:9 The meek will he guide in judgment: and the meek will he teach his way.
> Proverbs 3:34-35 Surely he scorneth the scorners: but he giveth grace unto the lowly. The wise shall inherit glory: but shame shall be the promotion of fools.
> Proverbs 15:33 The fear of the LORD *is* the instruction of wisdom; and before honour *is* humility.
> Proverbs 16:18-19 Pride goeth before destruction, and an haughty spirit before a fall. Better it is to be of an humble spirit with the lowly, than to divide the spoil with the proud.
> Proverbs 18:12 Before destruction the heart of man is haughty, and before honour *is* humility.
> Daniel 4:30-32 The king spake, and said, Is not this great Babylon, that I have built for the house of the kingdom by the might of my power, and for the honour of my majesty? While the word *was* in the king's mouth, there fell a voice from heaven, *saying,* O king Nebuchadnezzar, to thee it is spoken; The kingdom is departed from thee. And they shall drive thee from men, and thy dwelling *shall be* with the beasts of the field: they shall make thee to eat grass as oxen, and seven times shall pass over thee, until thou know that the most High ruleth in the kingdom of men, and giveth it to whomsoever he will.
> Micah 6:8 He hath shewed thee, O man, what is good; and what doth the LORD require of thee, but to do justly, and to love mercy, and to walk humbly with thy God?
> Luke 14:11 For whosoever exalteth himself shall be abased; and he that humbleth himself shall be exalted. *[Repeated in Luke 18:14.]*

Proverbs 11:3 The integrity of the upright shall guide them: but the perverseness of transgressors shall destroy them.

Focus: This proverb teaches that the upright are guided by integrity to safety while transgressors are guided by perverseness to destruction.

"The integrity of the upright shall guide them." **"Integrity"** describes the *godly principle of high moral character*. (Webster defines "integrity" as "the entire, unimpaired state of any thing, particularly of the mind; moral soundness or purity; incorruptness; uprightness; honesty. Integrity comprehends the whole moral character, but has a special reference to uprightness in mutual dealings, transfers of property, and agencies for others."[175]) An **"upright"** person is one who is righteous and walks with God. **"Integrity... shall guide..."** the upright by constantly leading him, by his high moral principles, away from destruction and toward God. The integrity of a righteous man leads him away from business practices that are against God's teachings.

"But the perverseness of transgressors shall destroy them." The **"transgressor"** is void of integrity and has the opposite view of a safe life. He willfully opposes the doctrines of God and chooses **"perverseness"** *[crooked, distorted, vicious dealing]* as the guiding rule of his life. He believes that perverseness will guide him to safety, but instead, *he is constantly moving in the direction of destruction.* He has no guidance or help from God. "Such persons shall be caught in their own net; they not only bring punishment on themselves when their evil designs are discovered and frustrated, but they ruin their moral nature, lose all sense of truth and right, and are rejected of God."[176] "The perverse ways, words, and actions of such as transgress the law of God, deal treacherously with God and men, as the word signifies, *and* shall be their ruin."[177]

The prime historical example of a *transgressor* was Judas Iscariot, who demonstrated the epitome of *perverseness* as he betrayed the Son of God. Jesus identified him as the "son of perdition" in John 17:12. There is yet to be another wicked *transgressor* who will also be known as "the son of perdition; Who opposeth and exalteth himself above all that is called God, or that is worshiped; so that he as God sitteth in the temple of God, shewing himself that he is God (2 Thessalonians 2:4)." Albert Barnes wrote this about the "son of perdition," the Antichrist:

> "'The term 'son' was given by the Hebrews to those who possessed the character described by the word or name following. Thus, sons of Belial - those who possessed his character; children of wisdom those who were wise. Thus Judas is called a 'son of perdition' because he had the character of a destroyer. He was a traitor and a murderer. And this shows that he who knew the heart regarded his character as that of a wicked man one whose appropriate name was that of a son of perdition."[178]

It should strike fear in the heart of the "upright" when considering the many who are known as "transgressors" whose "perverseness shall destroy them" – eternally.

> Proverbs 10:9 He that walketh uprightly walketh surely: but he that perverteth his ways shall be known.
>
> Proverbs 10:29 The way of the LORD is strength to the upright: but destruction shall be to the workers of iniquity.
>
> Proverbs 11:6 The righteousness of the upright shall deliver them: but transgressors shall be taken in their own naughtiness.
>
> Proverbs 13:6 Righteousness keepeth him that is upright in the way: but wickedness overthroweth the sinner.
>
> Proverbs 15:4 A wholesome tongue *is* a tree of life: but perverseness therein *is* a breach in the spirit.
>
> Proverbs 19:1 Better is the poor that walketh in his integrity, than he that is perverse in his lips, and is a fool.
>
> John 17:12 While I was with them in the world, I kept them in thy name: those that thou gavest me I have kept, and none of them is lost, but the son of perdition; that the scripture might be fulfilled.
>
> Ephesians 6:14 Stand therefore, having your loins girt about with truth, and having on the breastplate of righteousness.
>
> 2 Thessalonians 2:3-4 Let no man deceive you by any means: for *that day shall not come,* except there come a falling away first, and that man of sin be revealed, the son of perdition; Who opposeth and exalteth himself above all that is called God, or that is worshipped; so that he as God sitteth in the temple of God, shewing himself that he is God.

Proverbs 11:4   Riches profit not in the day of wrath: but righteousness delivereth from death.

Focus: This proverb contrasts the worthlessness of riches with the value of righteousness on the day of wrath.

"Riches profit not in the day of wrath." "The day of wrath" is that day when God brings judgment because of sin and awards appropriate justice. Throughout history, there have been *days of wrath* when God visited men to bring judgment, such as the destruction of Sodom and the flood of Noah's day. The final **"day of wrath"** will come when men are judged according to their sins and Satan is cast into the Lake of Fire. Even *if* a person could take his riches with him to the judgment seat during the "day of wrath," such valuable goods would *not profit him* (not be of any value).

"But righteousness delivereth from death." It is **"righteousness"** that is profitable in any day of God's wrath because being right with God delivers from death. As Proverbs 10:28 expressed, "The hope of the righteous *shall be* gladness: but the expectation of the wicked shall perish."

> Proverbs 10:2 Treasures of wickedness profit nothing: but righteousness delivereth from death.
>
> Proverbs 11:28 He that trusteth in his riches shall fall: but the righteous shall flourish as a branch.
>
> Isaiah 10:3 And what will ye do in the day of visitation, and in the desolation *which* shall come from far? To whom will ye flee for help? And where will ye leave your glory?
>
> Ezekiel 7:19 They shall cast their silver in the streets, and their gold shall be removed: their silver and their gold shall not be able to deliver them in the day of the wrath of the LORD: they shall not satisfy their souls, neither fill their bowels: because it is the stumblingblock of their iniquity.
>
> Zephaniah 1:15-18 That day *is* a day of wrath, a day of trouble and distress, a day of wasteness and desolation, a day of darkness and gloominess, a day of clouds and thick darkness. A day of the trumpet and alarm against the fenced cities, and against the high towers. And I will bring distress upon men, that they shall walk like blind men, because they have sinned against the LORD: and their blood shall be poured out as dust, and their flesh as the dung. Neither their silver nor their gold shall be able to deliver them in the day of the LORD'S wrath; but the whole land shall be devoured by the fire of his jealousy: for he shall make even a speedy riddance of all them that dwell in the land.
>
> Romans 2:4-11 Or despisest thou the riches of his goodness and forbearance and longsuffering; not knowing that the goodness of God leadeth thee to repentance? But after thy hardness and impenitent heart treasurest up unto thyself wrath against the day of wrath and revelation of the righteous judgment of God; Who will render to every man according to his deeds: To them who by patient continuance in well doing seek for glory and honour and immortality, eternal life: But unto them that are contentious, and do not obey the truth, but obey unrighteousness, indignation and wrath, Tribulation and anguish, upon every soul of man that doeth evil, of the Jew first, and also of the Gentile; But glory, honour, and peace, to every man that worketh good, to the Jew first, and also to the Gentile: For there is no respect of persons with God. *[See also Revelation 2:11; 20:6; 20:14 and 21:8.]*

Proverbs 11:5-6 The righteousness of the perfect shall direct his way: but the wicked shall fall by his own wickedness.
   6. The righteousness of the upright shall deliver them: but transgressors shall be taken in *their own* naughtiness.

Focus: These two proverbs state that righteousness directs and delivers, while wickedness takes and destroys.

Even though they utilize slightly different wording, these two proverbs are very similar in meaning. The **"perfect"** and the **"upright"** identify the *godly or righteous.* The **"wicked"** and **"transgressors"** identify the *ungodly.* **"Naughtiness"** and **"wickedness"** are interchangeable words identifying the evil deeds of the ungodly. Proverbs 11:3 is very similar.

> Proverbs 11:3 The integrity of the upright shall guide them: but the perverseness of transgressors shall destroy them.

> NOTE: The contemporary definition of **"naughtiness"** has changed, giving it a more flippant, toned-down meaning. Dictionary.com has the current meaning as "disobedient; mischievous (used especially in speaking to or about children)." However, the seventeenth-century meaning was serious wickedness, perverseness.

"The righteousness of the perfect shall direct his way." ... **"The righteousness of the upright shall deliver them."** Godly people are directed by a principle of living called "righteousness," which is their way of thinking and acting that *focuses on serving and obeying God.* It is that holy way that safely leads the godly to deliver them from both evil people and the penalty of sin. Because of the believer's desire for righteous living, God directs his way and cares for him. It is those who are wise who live righteously.

> Proverbs 3:5-6 Trust in the LORD with all thine heart; and lean not unto thine own understanding. In all thy ways acknowledge him, and he shall direct thy paths.
> Proverbs 11:3 The integrity of the upright shall guide them: but the perverseness of transgressors shall destroy them.
> Proverbs 11:8 The righteous is delivered out of trouble, and the wicked cometh in his stead.
> Proverbs 13:6 Righteousness keepeth *him that is* upright in the way: but wickedness overthroweth the sinner.
> Hosea 14:9 Who *is* wise, and he shall understand these *things?* prudent, and he shall know them? for the ways of the LORD *are* right, and the just shall walk in them: but the transgressors shall fall therein.

"But the wicked shall fall by his own wickedness" ... **"but transgressors shall be taken in *their own* naughtiness."** Because they are *misguided* by their opposition to God and His ways, the wicked walk in spiritual darkness. In doing so, they are perpetually living in a fashion that is contradictory to the way God intended for man. Ultimately their deceitfulness, hate, viciousness, impulsive behavior, and evil comradery blinds their minds to the traps they have set for others and inadvertently, for themselves. Wickedness dooms the transgressor both spiritually and physically.

> 2 Samuel 17:23 And when Ahithophel saw that his counsel was not followed, he saddled *his* ass, and arose, and gat him home to his house, to his city, and put his household in order, and hanged himself, and died, and was buried in the sepulchre of his father.
> Esther 7:9-10 And Harbonah, one of the chamberlains, said before the king, Behold also, the gallows fifty cubits high, which Haman had made for Mordecai, who had spoken good for the king, standeth in the house of Haman. Then the king said, Hang him thereon. So they hanged Haman on the gallows that he had prepared for Mordecai. Then was the king's wrath pacified.
> Psalm 9:15-16 The heathen are sunk down in the pit *that* they made: in the net which they hid is their own foot taken. The LORD is known *by* the judgment *which* he executeth: the wicked is snared in the work of his own hands. Higgaion. Selah.
> Psalm 37:35-38 I have seen the wicked in great power, and spreading himself like a green bay tree. Yet he passed away, and, lo, he *was* not: yea, I sought him, but he could not be found. Mark the perfect *man,* and behold the upright: for the end of *that* man *is* peace. But the transgressors shall be destroyed together: the end of the wicked shall be cut off.
> Proverbs 1:31-32 Therefore shall they eat of the fruit of their own way, and be filled with their own devices. For the turning away of the simple shall slay them, and the prosperity of fools shall destroy them.
> Proverbs 5:22 His own iniquities shall take the wicked himself, and he shall be holden with the cords of his sins.
> Isaiah 1:28 And the destruction of the transgressors and of the sinners *shall be* together, and they that forsake the LORD shall be consumed.
> Matthew 27:4-5 Saying, I have sinned in that I have betrayed the innocent blood. And they said, What *is that* to us? see thou *to that.* And he cast down the pieces of silver in the temple, and departed, and went and hanged himself.

Proverbs 11:7 . When a wicked man dieth, *his* expectation shall perish: and the hope of the unjust *men* perisheth.

Focus: This proverb states the desperate, hopeless end of the wicked.

Both clauses of this proverb make the same statement with different words, thereby doubling the impact of the expressed truth *that there is no eternal hope for the wicked.* (See Luke 16:19-31 for the awful punishment of unjust men.) Notice the parallel elements within the two clauses in this proverb: **"wicked men"** in the first parallels **"unjust men"** in the second; **"hope"** in the first and **"expectation"** in the second are identical in meaning.

Luke 13:28 There shall be weeping and gnashing of teeth, when ye shall see Abraham, and Isaac, and Jacob, and all the prophets, in the kingdom of God, and you *yourselves* thrust out.

Wicked, unjust men set their minds to *believe a variety of conjured theories* about God and eternity, which amount to anything but believing in Him and trusting His word. Some hope that they will be reincarnated as something beautiful, rich, or powerful, while others have hope that there is no God. Some believe that there is no judgment, and others have confidence that the Bible is written by man's imagination and therefore giving its doctrines no value. When a wicked man dies and meets God, his *expectation and hope will evaporate,* for he will meet the God of the Bible.

> "When the wicked dies, everything, except, indeed, the evil influences he has created and circulated, comes to a dreary end. His expectation, his hope, perishes. He can take nothing that he has toiled for into that other world which he is entering. All his laborious exertion, his elaborate contrivances, his selfish schemes, his painful humiliations, come to nothing; they are buried in the grave. He may have a powerful and well stored mind, but he has cherished no desire, has entertained no ambition which reaches beyond the horizon of mortal life, and with the stopping of his heartbeat, every imagination of his spirit perishes; there is an untimely and utter end of all his brightest hopes. A sad and dismal outlook for a human spirit!
>
> How great and how blessed the contrast of a good man! His largest hopes are then on the point of being realized; his purest and brightest expectations are about to be fulfilled. This earth is, more or less, the scene of disappointment; but in the country whose born he is about to cross, he will find himself where 'Trembling Hope shall realize Her full felicity.'"[179]

Job 8:13-15 So *are* the paths of all that forget God; and the hypocrite's hope shall perish: Whose hope shall be cut off, and whose trust *shall be* a spider's web. He shall lean upon his house, but it shall not stand: he shall hold it fast, but it shall not endure.

Psalm 73:17-18 Until I went into the sanctuary of God; *then* understood I their end. Surely thou didst set them in slippery places: thou castedst them down into destruction.

Proverbs 10:28 The hope of the righteous *shall be* gladness: but the expectation of the wicked shall perish.

Proverbs 14:32 The wicked is driven away in his wickedness: but the righteous hath hope in his death.

Job 11:20 But the eyes of the wicked shall fail, and they shall not escape, and their hope *shall be as* the giving up of the ghost.

Proverbs 14:32 The wicked is driven away in his wickedness: but the righteous hath hope in his death.

Luke 12:19-21 And I will say to my soul, Soul, thou hast much goods laid up for many years; take thine ease, eat, drink, *and* be merry. But God said unto him, *Thou* fool, this night thy soul shall be required of thee: then whose shall those things be, which thou hast provided? So *is* he that layeth up treasure for himself, and is not rich toward God.

Proverbs 11:8 The righteous is delivered out of trouble, and the wicked cometh in his stead.

Focus: This proverb is a reminder of God's providential care of the righteous and His judgment of the wicked.

Wicked people often unwittingly travel their life's journey along a pathway that leads to danger; and they don't comprehend, *or don't believe,* the promise of eternal damnation for those who reject Jesus. They don't seem to understand that they need the providential care of God; while, at the same time, pride guides them into self-made traps. Political correctness often blinds their eyes, and Satan steers them into disaster. When this life is over, the righteous will be delivered out of the trouble of eternal damnation through trusting God's perfect guidance, and the wicked will enter the gates of Hell.

> "**The wicked cometh in his stead** - Often God makes this distinction; in public calamities and in sudden accidents he rescues the righteous, and leaves the wicked, who has filled up the measure of his iniquities, to be seized by the hand of death. Justice, then, does its own work; for mercy has been rejected."[180]

> "Thus do these two classes change places in the dispensations of God. The same providence often marks Divine faithfulness and retributive justice. The Israelites *were delivered out of the trouble* of the Red Sea; the Egyptians *came in their stead*. (Exodus 14:21-28) Mordecai was *delivered* from the gallows; Haman was hanged upon it. (Esther 5:14; 7:10) The noble confessors in Babylon were saved from the fire; their executioners were 'slain' by it. (Daniel 3:22-26) Daniel was preserved from the lions; his accusers were devoured by them. (Daniel 6:22-24) Peter was snatched from death; his jailers and persecutors were condemned (Acts 12:6,19, 23)."[181]

Esther 7:9-10 And Harbonah, one of the chamberlains, said before the king, Behold also, the gallows fifty cubits high, which Haman had made for Mordecai, who had spoken good for the king, standeth in the house of Haman. Then the king said, Hang him thereon. So they hanged Haman on the gallows that he had prepared for Mordecai. Then was the king's wrath pacified.

Proverbs 21:18 The wicked *shall be* a ransom for the righteous, and the transgressor for the upright.

Proverbs 12:13 The wicked is snared by the transgression of *his* lips: but the just shall come out of trouble.

Isaiah 43:3-4 For I *am* the LORD thy God, the Holy One of Israel, thy Saviour: I gave Egypt *for* thy ransom, Ethiopia and Seba for thee. Since thou wast precious in my sight, thou hast been honourable, and I have loved thee: therefore will I give men for thee, and people for thy life.

Daniel 6:23-24 Then was the king exceeding glad for him, and commanded that they should take Daniel up out of the den. So Daniel was taken up out of the den, and no manner of hurt was found upon him, because he believed in his God. And the king commanded, and they brought those men which had accused Daniel, and they cast *them* into the den of lions, them, their children, and their wives; and the lions had the mastery of them, and brake all their bones in pieces or ever they came at the bottom of the den.

Proverbs 11:9 An hypocrite with *his* mouth destroyeth his neighbour: but through knowledge shall the just be delivered.

Focus: This proverb shows that a pretender of righteousness will destroy others with his words, but by knowledge, the righteous are delivered from such evil doers.

The **"hypocrite"** described in this verse is one who is evil but pretends to be good. He *uses knowledge about others* to either destroy their reputation, or else lure them into sin. **"Knowledge"** in the second half of this verse includes the believer's Scriptural knowledge plus personal experiential interaction with God. Scripture teaches how to live effectively to please God and how to recognize and avoid deceivers. With this knowledge, the righteous man will recognize evil flattery and deception of a wicked person. It is then wisdom and understanding will guide his pathway and ***deliver*** him from a host of difficulties, dangers, and (most importantly) eternal damnation.

Proverbs 9:10 The fear of the LORD is the beginning of wisdom: and the knowledge of the holy is understanding.

Because they know the leadership of the Holy Spirit and *have knowledge of God's word,* wise people know to stay away from evil people, thus minimizing the opportunity for wickedness against themselves. Therefore, **"just"** (righteous) people are *delivered* from wicked people, including hypocrites.

Psalm 55:21 *The words* of his mouth were smoother than butter, but war *was* in his heart: his words were softer than oil, yet *were* they drawn swords.

Proverbs 10:18 He that hideth hatred with lying lips, and he that uttereth a slander, is a fool.

Proverbs 2:10-16 When wisdom entereth into thine heart, and knowledge is pleasant unto thy soul; Discretion shall preserve thee, understanding shall keep thee: To deliver thee from the way of the evil *man,* from the man that speaketh froward things; Who leave the paths of uprightness, to walk in the ways of darkness; Who rejoice to do evil, *and* delight in the frowardness of the wicked; Whose ways *are* crooked, and *they* froward in their paths: To deliver thee from the strange woman, *even* from the stranger *which* flattereth with her words.

Proverbs 4:5-7 Get wisdom, get understanding: forget *it* not; neither decline from the words of my mouth. Forsake her not, and she shall preserve thee: love her, and she shall keep thee. Wisdom *is* the principal thing; *therefore* get wisdom: and with all thy getting get understanding.

Proverbs 6:23-24 For the commandment *is* a lamp; and the law *is* light; and reproofs of instruction *are* the way of life: To keep thee from the evil woman, from the flattery of the tongue of a strange woman.

Matthew 7:15-16 Beware of false prophets, which come to you in sheep's clothing, but inwardly they are ravening wolves. Ye shall know them by their fruits. Do men gather grapes of thorns, or figs of thistles?

Romans 16:17-19 Now I beseech you, brethren, mark them which cause divisions and offences contrary to the doctrine which ye have learned; and avoid them. For they that are such serve not our Lord Jesus Christ, but their own belly; and by good words and fair speeches deceive the hearts of the simple. For your obedience is come abroad unto all *men.* I am glad therefore on your behalf: but yet I would have you wise unto that which is good, and simple concerning evil.

2 Peter 3:16-18 As also in all *his* epistles, speaking in them of these things; in which are some things hard to be understood, which they that are unlearned and unstable wrest, as *they do* also the other scriptures, unto their own destruction. Ye therefore, beloved, seeing ye know *these things* before, beware lest ye also, being led away with the error of the wicked, fall from your own stedfastness. But grow in grace, and *in* the knowledge of our Lord and Saviour Jesus Christ. To him *be* glory both now and for ever. Amen.

I Kings 13:18-26 tells of a godly prophet who was lied to by a hypocritical prophet; and, falling into his trap, lost his life through the judgment of God. The godly prophet had the **"knowledge"** of God's orders that would have guided him to avoid the lying, hypocritical prophet, but he failed to be obedient to God's instructions.

Proverbs 11:10 When it goeth well with the righteous, the city rejoiceth: and when the wicked perish, *there is* shouting.

Focus: This proverb declares two reasons for joy and joyous shouting: when the righteous are in leadership and when the wicked are no longer in leadership.

"When it goeth well with the righteous" (when righteous men rise to authoritative positions of honor), then people of the city have reason to rejoice knowing that godly leadership will bring about a better, more equitable, safer life within the city. **"When the wicked perish,"** the same people shout for gratitude, knowing that the wicked influence is over, allowing justice and freedom to return.

> Esther 8:15-16 And Mordecai went out from the presence of the king in royal apparel of blue and white, and with a great crown of gold, and with a garment of fine linen and purple: and the city of Shushan rejoiced and was glad. The Jews had light, and gladness, and joy, and honour.
> Psalm 58:10-11 The righteous shall rejoice when he seeth the vengeance: he shall wash his feet in the blood of the wicked. So that a man shall say, Verily *there is* a reward for the righteous: verily he is a God that judgeth in the earth.
> Proverbs 28:12 When righteous *men* do rejoice, *there is* great glory: but when the wicked rise, a man is hidden.
> Proverbs 28:28 When the wicked rise, men hide themselves: but when they perish, the righteous increase.
> Proverbs 29:2 When the righteous are in authority, the people rejoice: but when the wicked beareth rule, the people mourn.
> Revelation 19:6-7 And I heard as it were the voice of a great multitude, and as the voice of many waters, and as the voice of mighty thunderings, saying, Alleluia: for the Lord God omnipotent reigneth. Let us be glad and rejoice, and give honour to him: for the marriage of the Lamb is come, and his wife hath made herself ready. *[See also 2 Kings 11:19-21, 1 Chronicles 12:38-40, and 2 Chronicles 23:21.]*

Proverbs 11:11 By the blessing of the upright the city is exalted: but it is overthrown by the mouth of the wicked.

Focus: This proverb states that the *blessing* of the upright (righteous) uplifts a city whereas the verbal *blasting* of the wicked tears it down.

"By the blessing of the upright the city is exalted." **"Blessing of the upright"** can be *both* that which comes *to* them as a gift from God and that which goes *from* them through such verbal communications as prayers, counsel, praise, and otherwise sagacious speech. Thus, the upright have the potential to both receive blessings and give blessings. Such blessings come, in part, simply because the righteous are very close, personal friends with God; and He is near them to give ear to their earnest prayers; whereas He is far from the wicked and turns away from their hypocritical pleas. Since God gives special attention and blessings to His own people, the wicked may inadvertently benefit simply by association. A godly person may choose to buy from the ungodly, who would thus make a profit; or, in a court of law, a falsely charged person, even though he is an ungodly person, can have the blessing of being found not guilty through the honest testimony of a righteous person. The city is also ***blessed by the upright*** because of their peaceful lifestyle, their prayers, and the high standards, high integrity, and the highly-efficient principles of the word of God by which they live. Therefore, the city is **"exalted"** *[raised up]* to a greater degree of order, peace, and honesty at every level; and the city is blessed economically, as well as morally.

> Genesis 18:23-24, 32 And Abraham drew near, and said, Wilt thou also destroy the righteous with the wicked? Peradventure there be fifty righteous within the city: wilt thou also destroy and not spare the place for the fifty righteous that *are* therein?...And he said, Oh let not the Lord be angry, and I will speak yet but this once: Peradventure ten shall be found there. And he said, I will not destroy *it* for ten's sake.
> Genesis 30:27-30 And Laban said unto him, I pray thee, if I have found favour in thine eyes, *tarry: for* I have learned by experience that the LORD hath blessed me for thy sake. And he said, Appoint me thy wages, and I will give *it.* And he said unto him, Thou knowest how I have served thee, and how thy cattle was with me. For *it was* little which thou hadst before I *came,* and it is *now* increased unto a multitude; and the LORD hath blessed thee since my coming: and now when shall I provide for mine own house also?
> Esther 8:15 And Mordecai went out from the presence of the king in royal apparel of blue and white, and with a great crown of gold, and with a garment of fine linen and purple: and the city of Shushan rejoiced and was glad.
> Job 22:30 He shall deliver the island of the innocent: and it is delivered by the pureness of thine hands.
> Psalm 112:1-3 Praise ye the LORD. Blessed *is* the man *that* feareth the LORD, *that* delighteth greatly in his commandments. His seed shall be mighty upon earth: the generation of the upright shall be blessed. Wealth and riches *shall be* in his house: and his righteousness endureth for ever.
> Proverbs 14:34 Righteousness exalteth a nation: but sin *is* a reproach to any people.
> Proverbs 16:7 When a man's ways please the LORD, he maketh even his enemies to be at peace with him.

"**But it is overthrown by the mouth of the wicked.**" *Wicked people are known for their ungodly mouths* by which they flatter, slander, deceive, and plan crimes such as murder and robbery – all of which contribute to the ***overthrowing*** of a city's moral and economic stability, peace, and overall desirability as a place to live. *In addition to the destructive overthrowing done by wicked citizens*, the **"mouth"** *of wicked rulers* may gender strife that leads to retaliation by the city's enemies or to conflicts among the citizens. Several verses in Proverbs refer to the wicked stirring up strife:

> Proverbs 15:18 A wrathful man stirreth up strife: but *he that is* slow to anger appeaseth strife.
> Proverbs 16:28 A froward man soweth strife: and a whisperer separateth chief friends.
> Proverbs 17:19 He loveth transgression that loveth strife: and he that exalteth his gate seeketh destruction.
> Proverbs 20:3 Proverbs 22:10 Cast out the scorner, and contention shall go out; yea, strife and reproach shall cease.
> Proverbs 26:21 As coals *are* to burning coals, and wood to fire; so *is* a contentious man to kindle strife.
> Proverbs 28:12 When righteous *men* do rejoice, *there is* great glory: but when the wicked rise, a man is hidden.
> Proverbs 28:25 He that is of a proud heart stirreth up strife: but he that putteth his trust in the LORD shall be made fat.
> Proverbs 28:28 When the wicked rise, men hide themselves: but when they perish, the righteous increase.
> Proverbs 29:22 An angry man stirreth up strife, and a furious man aboundeth in transgression.

Proverbs 11:12 He that is void of wisdom despiseth his neighbour: but a man of understanding holdeth his peace.

Focus: This proverb contrasts a hating, tongue-wagging man without wisdom with a wise man of understanding who controls his speech.

"**He that is void of wisdom despiseth his neighbour.**" Mr. **"void of wisdom"** may speak contemptibly of **"his neighbor"** for a variety of prideful reasons including: a belief that he is wiser, a belief that his wealth has placed him into a category that is better than his poorer neighbor, or a belief that he is more righteous. When a person despises others, he is giving proof that he lacks wisdom.

> 1 Samuel 10:26-27 And Saul also went home to Gibeah; and there went with him a band of men, whose hearts God had touched. But the children of Belial said, How shall this man save us? And they despised him, and brought him no presents. But he held his peace.
> Proverbs 6:2 Thou art snared with the words of thy mouth, thou art taken with the words of thy mouth.
> Proverbs 10:19 In the multitude of words there wanteth not sin: but he that refraineth his lips *is* wise.
> Proverbs 14:21 He that despiseth his neighbour sinneth: but he that hath mercy on the poor, happy is he.
> Ecclesiastes 5:3 For a dream cometh through the multitude of business; and a fool's voice *is* known by multitude of words.
> Matthew 18:15 Moreover if thy brother shall trespass against thee, go and tell him his fault between thee and him alone: if he shall hear thee, thou hast gained thy brother.
> Luke 10:16 He that heareth you heareth me; and he that despiseth you despiseth me; and he that despiseth me despiseth him that sent me.
> 1 Thessalonians 4:8 He therefore that despiseth, despiseth not man, but God, who hath also given unto us his holy Spirit.

"**But a man of understanding holdeth his peace.**" A **"man of understanding"** will usually see much in **"his neighbour"** to excite his pity and stir up his prayers, but nothing to *despise*. He may be called openly to condemn the neighbor, but his general course will be loving forbearance, *holding his peace*.[182] "**Holdeth his peace**" has the simple meaning of being silent and keeping quiet. Because of a loving heart, the wise man, overlooks many of his neighbor's faults and does not speak of them. Because he is wise, and if he cannot admire or praise, he at least knows how to be silent. He has nothing ill to say.

Keeping quiet will also give the wise man an opportunity for self-evaluation, which is an effective tool that reveals personal faults. It will cause the wise person to fasten down any and all loose words lest they come back to haunt him. Such personal evaluation also factors into a person's thinking to form a person of love rather than one of hate. Also, a desire to be pleasing to the Lord and to live wisely mandates that he overlook much of what others say and do. Words can reveal *a heart that despises* others, just as words can reveal an understanding, discreet heart that loves others. A wise person doesn't despise others and proves it by being very careful with his words.

> Proverbs 10:13 In the lips of him that hath understanding wisdom is found: but a rod *is* for the back of him that is void of understanding.
> Proverbs 17:27 He that hath knowledge spareth his words: *and* a man of understanding is of an excellent spirit.

Ecclesiastes 10:12 The words of a wise man's mouth *are* gracious; but the lips of a fool will swallow up himself.
1 Corinthians 13:4-7 Charity suffereth long, *and* is kind; charity envieth not; charity vaunteth not itself, is not puffed up, Doth not behave itself unseemly, seeketh not her own, is not easily provoked, thinketh no evil; Rejoiceth not in iniquity, but rejoiceth in the truth; Beareth all things, believeth all things, hopeth all things, endureth all things.
1 Peter 2:23 Who, when he was reviled, reviled not again; when he suffered, he threatened not; but committed *himself* to him that judgeth righteously . . .

Proverbs 11:13 A talebearer revealeth secrets: but he that is of a faithful spirit concealeth the matter.

Focus: This proverb contrasts two opposite characters: the talebearer who *cannot* be trusted to keep a secret and the faithful man who *can* be trusted with the same secret.

"A talebearer revealeth secrets." The gossiper, slanderer, or informer, identified in this proverb as a **"talebearer,"** *has an unfaithful spirit* meaning that he is not faithful to keep private, personal, or governmental strategy that was told to him in confidence. The talebearer could either be a supposed friend, or he could be a government official in a private conversation with the king or head of state. In either case, the talebearer carefully picks up private information from one person, and speaks it in the ear of another, then travels with the secret to another; so a talebearer goes from house to house, king's palace, or courthouse to the newspaper, or to the enemy picking up tales at one place and telling them in another. Such a person "forfeits all the privileges of friendship and conversation."[183] He may even be a traitor to his country. He should be identified as untrustworthy.

"But he that is of a faithful spirit concealeth the matter." The believer cannot be a talebearer and be right with God. **"A faithful**(supportive, trusted, reliable) **spirit"** is one that is faithful to the person who shared a private matter with the intent that it would not be told. The faithful man supports the person with whom he has spoken by keeping words spoken in confidence, – confidential. He can be trusted to *NOT* broadcast any information told in secret. A faithful spirit can be entrusted with matters of state or secrets of the heart shared from one friend to another.

Usually, a desire to please the Lord Jesus Christ and a love for others are the two factors that create **"a faithful spirit"** and thereby encourage the Christian to refuse to reveal information that would stir up strife or have an ill effect. *Love covers a multitude of sins* (1Peter 4:8); and, on the flip side, it is perhaps hate or contempt (as in verse 12), that publishes information that would otherwise be best left unsaid. This principle doesn't teach that a person should be quiet when he witnesses a crime, or that he should agree to keep silent when another reveals that he is about to commit an illegal or immoral act. Such an attitude would be ***un*faithfulness**.

Leviticus 19:16 Thou shalt not go up and down *as* a talebearer among thy people: neither shalt thou stand against the blood of thy neighbour: I *am* the LORD.
Nehemiah 6:17-19 Moreover in those days the nobles of Judah sent many letters unto Tobiah, and *the letters* of Tobiah came unto them. For *there were* many in Judah sworn unto him, because he *was* the son in law of Shechaniah the son of Arah; and his son Johanan had taken the daughter of Meshullam the son of Berechiah. Also they reported his good deeds before me, and uttered my words to him. *And* Tobiah sent letters to put me in fear.
Proverbs 16:28 A froward man soweth strife: and a whisperer separateth chief friends.
Proverbs 20:19 He that goeth about as a talebearer revealeth secrets: therefore meddle not with him that flattereth with his lips.
Proverbs 25:9-10 Debate thy cause with thy neighbour *himself;* and discover not a secret to another: Lest he that heareth *it* put thee to shame, and thine infamy turn not away.
Proverbs 26:20-22 Where no wood is, *there* the fire goeth out: so where *there is* no talebearer, the strife ceaseth. As coals *are* to burning coals, and wood to fire; so *is* a contentious man to kindle strife. The words of a talebearer *are* as wounds, and they go down into the innermost parts of the belly.
2 Thessalonians 3:10-12 For even when we were with you, this we commanded you, that if any would not work, neither should he eat. For we hear that there are some which walk among you disorderly, working not at all, but are busybodies. Now them that are such we command and exhort by our Lord Jesus Christ, that with quietness they work, and eat their own bread.
1 Timothy 5:13 And withal they learn to be idle, wandering about from house to house; and not only idle, but tattlers also and busybodies, speaking things which they ought not.
1 Peter 4:8 And above all things have fervent charity among yourselves: for charity shall cover the multitude of sins.
1 Peter 4:15 But let none of you suffer as a murderer, or *as* a thief, or *as* an evildoer, or as a busybody in other men's matters.

> **Proverbs 11:14** Where no counsel *is,* the people fall: but in the multitude of counsellors *there is* safety.

Focus: This proverb declares a very important reason for seeking counsel.

Without proper counsel to the leader, the people, who are dependent upon that leader for wise decisions and ultimately safety, will **"fall."** They will be defeated *physically* through war or *economically* through bad policies or *legally* through corrupt judges.

The primary meaning as to *who* will "fall" in this verse is obviously intended to mean countries that are under the leadership of a king. Without proper counsel to their king, the people will become victims to his inadequate leadership and will likely fall prostrate before their enemies.

Application can be made to businesses, families, churches, and any other group where people depend upon the leader for wise decisions. Because the phrase **"the people"** is plural, the reader understands that this proverb is speaking about the safety of a group of people (family, tribe, city, nation, church) rather than an individual, although the application is undoubtedly appropriate for individuals.

A leader is foolish to think (1) that he has the same broad view and, ultimately comprehension, as does a group of wise counselors, *or* (2) that he can be given all aspects of a given situation with input from "yes-men" who will not disagree with him. Different people have different perceptions of the same situation or conversation or circumstance. A wise leader wants to have an understanding of every aspect of a situation before endangering others. *Without* this counsel, the nation can be destroyed, but *with* wise counsel, the people can remain safe. They will not crumble into factions or fall prey to their enemies due to their leader's failure to understand all aspects of the threat.

> 1Kings 12:6-8 And King Rehoboam consulted with the old men, that stood before Solomon his father while he yet lived, and said, How do ye advise that I may answer this people? And they spake unto him, saying, If thou wilt be a servant unto this people this day, and wilt serve them, and answer them, and speak good words to them, then they will be thy servants for ever. But he forsook the counsel of the old men, which they had given him, and consulted with the young men that were grown up with him, *and* which stood before him:
> Proverbs 1:5 A wise *man* will hear, and will increase learning; and a man of understanding shall attain unto wise counsels:
> Proverbs 15:22 Without counsel purposes are disappointed: but in the multitude of counsellors they are established.
> Proverbs 20:18 *Every* purpose is established by counsel: and with good advice make war.
> Proverbs 24:6 For by wise counsel thou shalt make thy war: and in multitude of counsellors *there is* safety.

The result of having a **"multitude of counselors"** is **"safety"** *[deliverance, victory]*. The greatest counsel available to every person, family, tribe, city, or nation is found in the Scriptures that teach wise living *that includes* getting counsel from good, godly people.

> Isaiah 9:6 For unto us a child is born, unto us a son is given: and the government shall be upon his shoulder: and his name shall be called Wonderful, Counsellor, The mighty God, The everlasting Father, The Prince of Peace.

> **Proverbs 11:15** He that is surety for a stranger shall smart *for it:* and he that hateth suretiship is sure.

Focus: This proverb states the danger of cosigning for someone and the security found in being adamantly against cosigning.

> NOTE from Chapter 6: To be **"surety"** for another is to declare that **"if"** the **"friend"** (person making the debt) cannot repay the debt, the one being *cosigner* or **"surety"** will pay. According to the definition of **"surety,"** which is the Hebrew word '*arab*, one mingles his finances with the finances of another person who does not have the financial strength to obtain credit or stand good for a loan. In doing so, the cosigner mingles his financial ability with the financial inability of the person making the loan – think of diluting a milkshake with water.

Becoming a **"surety"** or cosigning means becoming responsible for another person's debt if that person fails to pay. To be surety for a **"stranger"** is especially unwise since very little, if anything is known about the stranger's financial dealings or his character, and the fact that he needs someone to cosign indicates that he is not and *perhaps cannot* be fully trusted. It is wise to hate **"suretyship"** since engaging in the practice has the potential of causing harm both financially and emotionally between the parties involved. They will **"smart for it."** According to the King James translators, **"smart"** means "to be sore broken."[184] To engage in any practice forbidden by the Bible is dangerous. **"Sure"** means to feel safe or secure, and certainly, the person who does *not* become a surety will not be threatened by the same.

> Proverbs 6:1-5 My son, if thou be surety for thy friend, *if* thou hast stricken thy hand with a stranger, Thou art snared with the words of thy mouth, thou art taken with the words of thy mouth. Do this now, my son, and deliver thyself, when thou art come into the hand of thy friend; go, humble thyself, and make sure thy friend. Give not sleep to thine eyes, nor slumber to thine eyelids. Deliver thyself as a roe from the hand *of the hunter,* and as a bird from the hand of the fowler.
>
> Proverbs 17:18 A man void of understanding striketh hands, and becometh surety in the presence of his friend.
>
> Proverbs 22:26-27 Be not thou *one* of them that strike hands, *or* of them that are sureties for debts. If thou hast nothing to pay, why should he take away thy bed from under thee?
>
> Proverbs 27:13 Take his garment that is surety for a stranger, and take a pledge of him for a strange woman.

NOTE: "Stranger" in Proverbs 6 is a non-Hebrew usurer. Here in Chapter 11, "stranger" is an unknown person. In Chapter 27, the first "stranger" is an unknown person, and second is an adulteress.

NOTE: To classify Jesus as Surety for the sinner is a stretch of the interpretation. Atonement, expiation, and propitiation are synonyms that describe the sacrificial work of Jesus and are unlike surety which is a legal and contractual act of securing a business transaction.

Proverbs 11:16 A gracious woman retaineth honour: and strong *men* retain riches.

Focus: This proverb declares that strength is necessary to retain valuable assets.

The purpose of this proverb is to emphasize the rewards for having *strength* to maintain righteous living. Both the "gracious woman" and "strong *men*" retain their gains through strength, but by different motives and methods.

The **"gracious woman"** is given respect and honor because of her kind, gracious behavior. Webster defines "gracious" as "that in manner, deportment or language which renders it appropriate and agreeable; suitableness; elegance with appropriate dignity."[185] This godly woman needs diligence, desire, determination, will power, and certainly Divine help to **"retain"** the godly character whereby the Scriptures would identify her as "honorable" (deserving of respect of others). She has the *strength of character* pictured in the Proverbs 31 lady who was determined and persistent in her goals and behavior.

"Strong *men*" *[mighty oppressor, terror-striking]* strike terror in others to keep their riches. "One who strikes terror because of his wickedness" cannot enjoy "honor, respect or even peace of mind."[186] His raw, oppressive strength used to retain wealth is set in contrast to the gracious woman's strength of righteousness used to retain honor in the sight of God.

A **"gracious woman"** is one who is kind and hospitable, who carries herself respectfully and properly before God and man. She will recognize situations whereby someone (especially a man) could threaten her reputation, and she is astute to avoid those situations. Also, she will not dress or carry herself in a manner that suggests that she is anything but honorable. By not allowing herself to be lured into any situation that would threaten her honor, this woman of grace is a bearer of the "excellency of godliness;" that "outward garment" of quality and craftsmanship that reflects inward righteous strength. When her body finally mingles with dust, still her graciousness, her inner ornaments of godliness *remain.* Though she is "the weaker vessel," still, just as surely as a strong man retains riches, she retains honor. She preserves an unblemished character showing her children, extended family and friends the way to holiness.[187] Her family praise her and "call her blessed."

> Proverbs 22:1 A *good* name *is* rather to be chosen than great riches, and loving favour rather than silver and gold.
>
> Proverbs 31:30-31 Favour is deceitful, and beauty is vain: but a woman that feareth the LORD, she shall be praised. Give her of the fruit of her hands; and let her own works praise her in the gates.
>
> Luke 11:21 When a strong man armed keepeth his palace, his goods are in peace: But when a stronger than he shall come upon him, and overcome him, he taketh from him all his armour wherein he trusted, and divideth his spoils.
>
> 1 Timothy 2:9-10 In like manner also, that women adorn themselves in modest apparel, with shamefacedness and sobriety; not with broided hair, or gold, or pearls, or costly array; But (which becometh women professing godliness) with good works.
>
> 1 Peter 3:7 Likewise, ye husbands, dwell with *them* according to knowledge, giving honour unto the wife, as unto the weaker vessel, and as being heirs together of the grace of life; that your prayers be not hindered.

> **Proverbs 11:17** The merciful man doeth good to his own soul: but *he that is* cruel troubleth his own flesh.

Focus: This proverb contrasts the good that a merciful man brings to himself with the trouble that a cruel man brings to himself.

"The merciful man doeth good to his own soul." He is kind and good to others, and he pities others that are not as blessed as himself, perhaps because of their own weaknesses. Mercy originates from sympathy and compassion in the believer's heart. He does good to himself or "to his own soul" because his good deeds return in blessings, as Matthew 5:7 states – "Blessed are the merciful: for they shall obtain mercy." Since the Scriptures declare instructions and examples of being merciful, God obviously intends for His people to know how He views mercy.[188] Other examples are given below.

Mercy is a reflection of the Christian's likeness to the Father.
> Luke 6:36 Be ye therefore merciful, as your Father also is merciful

Mercy is a response from the Christian's soul where godly love and kindness are in reserve, waiting for an opportunity to be activated.
> Luke 10:33-35 But a certain Samaritan, as he journeyed, came where he was: and when he saw him, he had compassion *on him, And went to him,* and bound up his wounds, pouring in oil and wine, and set him on his own beast, and brought him to an inn, and took care of him. And on the morrow when he departed, he took out two pence, and gave *them* to the host, and said unto him, Take care of him; and whatsoever thou spendest more, when I come again, I will repay thee.

Mercy is reciprocated to the Christian, in kind, by God.
> Psalm 41:1-3 Blessed *is* he that considereth the poor: the LORD will deliver him in time of trouble. The LORD will preserve him, and keep him alive; *and* he shall be blessed upon the earth: and thou wilt not deliver him unto the will of his enemies. The LORD will strengthen him upon the bed of languishing: thou wilt make all his bed in his sickness.
> Proverbs 21:21 He that followeth after righteousness and mercy findeth life, righteousness, and honour
> Matthew 5:7 Blessed are the merciful: for they shall obtain mercy.

Mercy is a recognizable trait of Christianity.
> Matthew 5:44 But I say unto you, Love your enemies, bless them that curse you, do good to them that hate you, and pray for them which despitefully use you, and persecute you;

"The merciful man" is one who extends compassion, help, forgiveness, or favor to someone in need, such as the poor, or to those who have been offensive or damaging or threatening in some manner. The merciful man ***does good to himself** because he is at peace with God and others*. He will *receive mercy* since he has been merciful.

> Isaiah 58:7-11 *Is* it not to deal thy bread to the hungry, and that thou bring the poor that are cast out to thy house? when thou seest the naked, that thou cover him; and that thou hide not thyself from thine own flesh? Then shall thy light break forth as the morning, and thine health shall spring forth speedily: and thy righteousness shall go before thee; the glory of the LORD shall be thy rereward. Then shalt thou call, and the LORD shall answer; thou shalt cry, and he shall say, Here I *am*. If thou take away from the midst of thee the yoke, the putting forth of the finger, and speaking vanity; And *if* thou draw out thy soul to the hungry, and satisfy the afflicted soul; then shall thy light rise in obscurity, and thy darkness *be* as the noonday: And the LORD shall guide thee continually, and satisfy thy soul in drought, and make fat thy bones: and thou shalt be like a watered garden, and like a spring of water, whose waters fail not.
> Matthew 6:14-15 For if ye forgive men their trespasses, your heavenly Father will also forgive you: But if ye forgive not men their trespasses, neither will your Father forgive your trespasses.
> Matthew 25:34-40 Then shall the King say unto them on his right hand, Come, ye blessed of my Father, inherit the kingdom prepared for you from the foundation of the world: For I was an hungred, and ye gave me meat: I was thirsty, and ye gave me drink: I was a stranger, and ye took me in: Naked, and ye clothed me: I was sick, and ye visited me: I was in prison, and ye came unto me. Then shall the righteous answer him, saying, Lord, when saw we thee an hungred, and fed *thee?* or thirsty, and gave *thee* drink? When saw we thee a stranger, and took *thee* in? or naked, and clothed *thee?* Or when saw we thee sick, or in prison, and came unto thee? And the King shall answer and say unto them, Verily I say unto you, Inasmuch as ye have done *it* unto one of the least of these my brethren, ye have done *it* unto me.

The opposite of being merciful is to be **"cruel"** *by refusing to show compassion or give help or extend forgiveness or favor*. The definition of "cruel" is "destitute of pity, compassion, or kindness."

"But *he that is* cruel troubleth his own flesh." Because the "cruel" person has no peace with God or man, he makes himself unhealthy mentally and often physically. Additionally, whatever attitude a person extends to others, he often receives in return. Such a man places himself in a dangerous position because of being cruel to others and facing condemnation from both God and man.

> Genesis 42:21 And they said one to another, We *are* verily guilty concerning our brother, in that we saw the anguish of his soul, when he besought us, and we would not hear; therefore is this distress come upon us.
> Proverbs 12:10 A righteous man regardeth the life of his beast: but the tender mercies of the wicked are cruel.
> Proverbs 14:21-22 He that despiseth his neighbour sinneth: but he that hath mercy on the poor, happy *is* he. Do they not err that devise evil? but mercy and truth *shall be* to them that devise good.
> Proverbs 21:13 Whoso stoppeth his ears at the cry of the poor, he also shall cry himself, but shall not be heard.
> Matthew 23:23 Woe unto you, scribes and Pharisees, hypocrites! for ye pay tithe of mint and anise and cummin, and have omitted the weightier *matters* of the law, judgment, mercy, and faith: these ought ye to have done, and not to leave the other undone.
> James 2:13 For he shall have judgment without mercy, that hath shewed no mercy; and mercy rejoiceth against judgment. *[See also Judges 1:6-7; 1 Kings 22:38; 2 Kings 9:35-37; Job 20:19-23; James 5:1-6.]*

Proverbs 11:18 The wicked worketh a deceitful work: but to him that soweth righteousness *shall be* a sure reward.

Focus: This proverb declares that rewards are given in response to works.

"The wicked worketh a deceitful work" carrying out their evil schemes. The consequence of their evil lives and labor *is not* any better than their wicked works. Their evil works will produce evil rewards. R. G. Lee, in his sermon "Payday, Someday" said, "The devil always pays off, but he always pays in counterfeit money." In contrast, the person whose life and labor *sows* or scatters the seeds of **"righteousness"** will anticipate a **"sure reward."** Having worked according to God's instruction, the righteous man will receive a reward through God's blessings.

Queen Jezebel, the evil wife of King Ahab, employed deceitfulness and lying wicked accomplices to murder righteous Naboth and steal his vineyard. No doubt the wicked couple believed that they would be able to enjoy the ill-gotten gain, but God sent Elijah to tell Ahab "...Thus saith the LORD, Hast thou killed, and also taken possession? ...Thus saith the LORD, In the place where dogs licked the blood of Naboth shall dogs lick thy blood, even thine. And Ahab said to Elijah, Hast thou found me, O mine enemy? And he answered, I have found *thee:* because thou hast sold thyself to work evil in the sight of the LORD." (1 Kings 21:19-20)

> "Pharaoh's attempt to decrease Israel resulted in their increase and his own destruction. Caiaphas seeking by murderous expediency to save the nation of Israel brought about its ruin. The persecution of the Church at Jerusalem led to the greater diffusion of the gospel."[189]
> Job 4:8 Even as I have seen, they that plow iniquity, and sow wickedness, reap the same.
> Proverbs 5:22-23 His own iniquities shall take the wicked himself, and he shall be holden with the cords of his sins. He shall die without instruction; and in the greatness of his folly he shall go astray.
> Proverbs 10:2-3 Treasures of wickedness profit nothing: but righteousness delivereth from death. The LORD will not suffer the soul of the righteous to famish: but he casteth away the substance of the wicked.

When a man who fears the LORD *sows righteousness* by leading a righteous, godly life, he reaps rewards that are beneficial and lasting. Just as the Bible recorded the wicked works that evil men sowed, it recorded the works of the people who sowed righteousness. Noah believed God, did all that was commanded by God and was rewarded accordingly.

> Hebrews 11:7 By faith Noah, being warned of God of things not seen as yet, moved with fear, prepared an ark to the saving of his house; by the which he condemned the world, and became heir of the righteousness which is by faith.

Abraham believed God, and his life revealed works of righteousness. God rewarded Abraham accordingly.

> Hebrews 6:13-15 For when God made promise to Abraham, because he could swear by no greater, he sware by himself, Saying, Surely blessing I will bless thee, and multiplying I will multiply thee. And so, after he had patiently endured, he obtained the promise.

Christians believe God and labor in righteousness, sowing good seed, knowing for sure that God will reward each one as He said He would.

> 1 Corinthians 15:58 Therefore, my beloved brethren, be ye stedfast, unmoveable, always abounding in the work of the Lord, forasmuch as ye know that your labour is not in vain in the Lord.

Galatians 6:8-9 For he that soweth to his flesh shall of the flesh reap corruption; but he that soweth to the Spirit shall of the Spirit reap life everlasting. And let us not be weary in well doing: for in due season we shall reap, if we faint not.

2 Timothy 4:7-8 I have fought a good fight, I have finished *my* course, I have kept the faith: Henceforth there is laid up for me a crown of righteousness, which the Lord, the righteous judge, shall give me at that day: and not to me only, but unto all them also that love his appearing.

Proverbs 11:19 As righteousness *tendeth* to life: so he that pursueth evil *pursueth it* to his own death.

Focus: This proverb makes the point that the pursuit of righteousness is a pursuit unto life, while the pursuit of evil is a pursuit unto death.

"As righteousness *tendeth* to life." **"Righteousness"** (holy and upright living) is seen in attitudes, actions, and words of a person in pursuit of pleasing God. His chosen pathway **tends** or inclines toward **"life"** because walking according to God's instructions is characteristic of wisdom and is the safest and most productive path that leads to living abundantly on earth and eternally in heaven. Such wise, righteous living avoids evil people, who, by their very nature tend toward dangerous situations where reside many of the perils and pitfalls that either bring personal harm or physical death. God is the source of life and through Jesus comes abundant living and eternal life.

Proverbs 10:16 The labour of the righteous *tendeth* to life: the fruit of the wicked to sin.

Proverbs 11:3-4 The integrity of the upright shall guide them: but the perverseness of transgressors shall destroy them. Riches profit not in the day of wrath: but righteousness delivereth from death.

Proverbs 12:28 In the way of righteousness *is* life; and *in* the pathway *thereof there is* no death.

Proverbs 19:23 The fear of the LORD *tendeth* to life: and *he that hath it* shall abide satisfied; he shall not be visited with evil.

John 10:10 The thief cometh not, but for to steal, and to kill, and to destroy: I am come that they might have life, and that they might have *it* more abundantly.

1 Timothy 4:8 For bodily exercise profiteth little: but godliness is profitable unto all things, having promise of the life that now is, and of that which is to come.

1 John 3:7,10 Little children, let no man deceive you: he that doeth righteousness is righteous, even as he is righteous... In this the children of God are manifest, and the children of the devil: whosoever doeth not righteousness is not of God, neither he that loveth not his brother.

"So he that pursueth evil *pursueth it* to his own death." *Pursuing evil [running after evil]* begins with a frame of mind, a predisposition that is intent on living in a manner that is counter to righteousness. There is nothing safe or rewarding, in a positive manner, for the person following hard after evil which always manifest itself in people and situations that oppose God and His instructions. His path is full of danger and trouble, rewarding him negatively with **"his own death."** And the more vigorously he pursues evil, the closer he comes to his own destruction. Such a mindset that opposes God believes that he can prove God a liar. He doesn't believe the truth of God's word when He said in Genesis, "In the day that thou eatest thereof thou shalt surely die." He is convinced of Satan's lie that "Ye shall not surely die." Adam's spiritual death on the day of his disobedience of God's instruction was the seed of, and guarantee of, his physical death that came later. Men who don't believe God is good for His word die to a number of things: peace of mind, presence of God, privilege of God's protection, His provision and His power. And all such loss in this life is compounded with eternal separation from God ("second death") whereby hell will be their permanent dwelling. "The man who builds himself a house upon the side of a volcano may promise himself, or may be promised by others, safety and peace, but unless he can quench the internal fires, that promise cannot be kept. The elements of destruction are ever at work under his very feet, the day will come when the devouring flame will burst forth and consume the work and the worker together."[190]

Proverbs 1:16-18 For their feet run to evil, and make haste to shed blood. Surely in vain the net is spread in the sight of any bird. And they lay wait for their *own* blood; they lurk privily for their *own* lives.

Proverbs 13:21 Evil pursueth sinners: but to the righteous good shall be repayed.

Romans 2:8-11 But unto them that are contentious, and do not obey the truth, but obey unrighteousness, indignation and wrath, Tribulation and anguish, upon every soul of man that doeth evil, of the Jew first, and also of the Gentile; But glory, honour, and peace, to every man that worketh good, to the Jew first, and also to the Gentile: For there is no respect of persons with God.

Romans 6:23 For the wages of sin *is* death; but the gift of God *is* eternal life through Jesus Christ our Lord.

Galatians 6:7-8 Be not deceived; God is not mocked: for whatsoever a man soweth, that shall he also reap. For he that soweth to his flesh shall of the flesh reap corruption; but he that soweth to the Spirit shall of the Spirit reap life everlasting.

Revelation 21:8 But the fearful, and unbelieving, and the abominable, and murderers, and whoremongers, and sorcerers, and idolaters, and all liars, shall have their part in the lake which burneth with fire and brimstone: which is the second death.

Proverbs 11:20 They that are of a froward heart are abomination to the LORD: but such as are upright in their way are his delight.

Focus: This proverb teaches that God abhors the froward, but He delights in the upright.

The evil man is **"froward** *[distorted, false; twisted, crooked, perverted]*" in his life because he is opposed to God's way of operating. He is likely to call that which is good, "evil," and to call that which is evil, "good." He is diametrically opposed to the word of God and the God of the word, willfully refusing to comply with God's instructions. The froward person doesn't simply have *a thought* of opposition; instead, opposition is deeply implanted in his heart to the extent that the LORD considers him an **"abomination"** *[morally disgusting]*.

The opposite of being froward is being upright. The **"upright in their way"** are those who have a heart for pleasing God, walking by faith in Him, and traveling the paths of truth and holiness. With intent and purpose, they please God; consequently, they are God's **"delight."** Being God's delight, the upright have a personal relationship with God, as is described in Job 1:8. "Hast thou *[Satan]* considered my servant Job, that *there is* none like him in the earth, a perfect and an upright man that feareth God, and escheweth evil?" Scripture adds in Job 2:3 – "and still he *[Job]* holdeth fast his integrity, although thou movedst me against him, to destroy him without cause."

    1 Samuel 15:22 And Samuel said, Hath the LORD *as great* delight in burnt offerings and sacrifices, as in obeying the voice of the LORD? Behold, to obey *is* better than sacrifice, *and* to hearken than the fat of rams.

    Psalm 11:5-7 The LORD trieth the righteous: but the wicked and him that loveth violence his soul hateth. Upon the wicked he shall rain snares, fire and brimstone, and an horrible tempest: *this shall be* the portion of their cup. For the righteous LORD loveth righteousness; his countenance doth behold the upright.

    Psalm 119:1 ALEPH. Blessed *are* the undefiled in the way, who walk in the law of the LORD.

    Proverbs 3:32 For the froward *is* abomination to the LORD: but his secret *is* with the righteous.

    Proverbs 6:12-15 A naughty person, a wicked man, walketh with a froward mouth. He winketh with his eyes, he speaketh with his feet, he teacheth with his fingers; Frowardness *is* in his heart, he deviseth mischief continually; he soweth discord. Therefore shall his calamity come suddenly; suddenly shall he be broken without remedy.

    Proverbs 12:22 Lying lips *are* abomination to the LORD: but they that deal truly *are* his delight.

    Proverbs 29:27 An unjust man *is* an abomination to the just: and *he that is* upright in the way *is* abomination to the wicked.

Proverbs 11:21 Though hand *join* in hand, the wicked shall not be unpunished: but the seed of the righteous shall be delivered.

Focus: This proverb declares that God's punishment of the wicked is specific to the individual (regardless of the size of his anti-God confederation), but His deliverance from punishment is to the righteous and to their offspring.

When *the wicked join hand in hand in agreement*, their children will typically follow in their footsteps and likewise their ungodly friends. Though they feel a false sense of confidence *because of their aggregate numbers*, they will certainly be individually *punished by the all-powerful God*. In Revelation 19:19, the kings of the earth and their armies will band together to make war against Jesus. Being froward, they are too devoted to Satan, too confident of their confederacy, and too blinded by hate and rebellion to realize that they are on a collision course with the Son of God.

    "'Hand in hand' is the emblem of union; of united power; of pledged combination:-and the sentiment seems to be, as expressed in our authorized version, that sinners, combining their counsel and their power,-encouraging one another in evil,-braving the 'terrors of the Lord,'-jointly laughing away their fears, and perpetrating evil with a high and determined hand, shall not be the more secure from the penal consequences of their sins. 'There is no wisdom, nor understanding, nor counsel,' no, nor might, whether personal or combined, 'against the Lord.' They may combine successfully against human authority and vigilance, and may successfully resist the power of an earthly government; but if God be against them, escape they cannot."[191]

    Exodus 23:2 Thou shalt not follow a multitude to do evil; neither shalt thou speak in a cause to decline after many to wrest judgment...

    Proverbs 16:5 Every one *that is* proud in heart *is* an abomination to the LORD: *though* hand *join* in hand, he shall not be unpunished.

    Proverbs 21:30 *There is* no wisdom nor understanding nor counsel against the LORD.

Revelation 19:19-21 And I saw the beast, and the kings of the earth, and their armies, gathered together to make war against him that sat on the horse, and against his army. And the beast was taken, and with him the false prophet that wrought miracles before him, with which he deceived them that had received the mark of the beast, and them that worshiped his image. These both were cast alive into a lake of fire burning with brimstone. And the remnant were slain with the sword of him that sat upon the horse, which *sword* proceeded out of his mouth: and all the fowls were filled with their flesh.

The wicked, though they are many, will ultimately be punished individually. But the upright, though he stands alone, **"shall be delivered**[*released, escape*]**,"** and such deliverance potentially extends even to ***his righteous seed*** because they have been taught to also be righteous. ("Seed" means first of all children, but figuratively extends to everyone under the upright's influential instruction.) Being in a family of godly parents has many benefits, with the most important being God's personal interest in the righteous household who together serve God. Children from a godly home have the benefit of being taught wisdom, thereby knowing how to navigate through life delivered from many unnecessary heartaches, dangerous relationships, and damaging repercussions from evil-driven, bad decisions. They are more importantly delivered from the judgment of the damned because they believe God, His written word, and His Son.

Genesis 18:19 For I know him, that he will command his children and his household after him, and they shall keep the way of the LORD, to do justice and judgment; that the LORD may bring upon Abraham that which he hath spoken of him.
Psalm 112:1-2 Praise ye the LORD. Blessed *is* the man *that* feareth the LORD, *that* delighteth greatly in his commandments. His seed shall be mighty upon earth: the generation of the upright shall be blessed.
Jeremiah 32:39 And I will give them one heart, and one way, that they may fear me for ever, for the good of them, and of their children after them:
Acts 2:39 For the promise is unto you, and to your children, and to all that are afar off, *even* as many as the Lord our God shall call.

Proverbs 11:22 *As* a jewel of gold in a swine's snout, *so is* a fair woman which is without discretion.

Focus: This proverb vividly describes the level of disgust felt when an onlooker is surprised to see a beautiful lady conducting herself "without discretion."

"A fair woman which is without discretion" means "literally, 'without taste,' void of the subtle tact and grace, without which mere outward beauty is as ill-bestowed as the nose-ring in the snout of the unclean beast."[192] The use of vulgar, profane language is enough to dull the light of her beauty, but should she exhibit immoral, dissolute behavior, she would be repugnant no matter how attractive she is physically. She would be morally ugly. Her behavior would be as shockingly out of place as would be the sight of a ***golden jewel*** dangling from a filthy ***"pig's snout,"*** which is used to root around mud and manure looking for anything that could be considered food. Conversely, a "jewel of gold" is thought of as something beautiful, delicately placed on a part of the body or clothing to represent beauty, wealth, and the finer things of life.

Proverbs 9:13 A foolish woman *is* clamorous: *she is* simple, and knoweth nothing.
Proverbs 31:30 Favour *is* deceitful, and beauty *is* vain: *but* a woman *that* feareth the LORD, she shall be praised.
1Peter 3:1-5 Likewise, ye wives, *be* in subjection to your own husbands; that, if any obey not the word, they also may without the word be won by the conversation of the wives; While they behold your chaste conversation *coupled* with fear. Whose adorning let it not be that outward *adorning* of plaiting the hair, and of wearing of gold, or of putting on of apparel; But *let it be* the hidden man of the heart, in that which is not corruptible, *even the ornament* of a meek and quiet spirit, which is in the sight of God of great price. For after this manner in the old time the holy women also, who trusted in God, adorned themselves, being in subjection unto their own husbands . . .

Proverbs 11:23 The desire of the righteous *is* only good: *but* the expectation of the wicked *is* wrath.

Focus: This proverb specifies that the longings of the righteous are opposite the longings of the wicked.

When a person is **"righteous,"** he *desires [longs, wishes] to please God as well as others*, and his actions and words reflect the same. He desires that situations work out to be **"good"** *[agreeable, at ease, in favour, gracious, most pleasant]* so that God is glorified, and he is residing under God's good favor and protection.

On the other hand, ***the wicked person*** desires (and expects) to execute **"wrath"** *[outbursts of passion, rage, anger]* on every person he chooses to victimize. He fully expects to live to inflict such hostilities, and he may be able to fulfill his wrathful desires; however, in the end, he will receive the wrath of God.

> Psalm 10:17 LORD, thou hast heard the desire of the humble: thou wilt prepare their heart, thou wilt cause thine ear to hear.
>
> Psalm 27:4 One thing have I desired of the LORD, that will I seek after; that I may dwell in the house of the LORD all the days of my life, to behold the beauty of the LORD, and to enquire in his temple.
>
> Proverbs 10:24 The fear of the wicked, it shall come upon him: but the desire of the righteous shall be granted.
>
> Proverbs 10:28 The hope of the righteous *shall be* gladness: but the expectation of the wicked shall perish.
>
> Proverbs 11:7 When a wicked man dieth, *his* expectation shall perish: and the hope of unjust *men* perisheth.
>
> Proverbs 21:24 Proud *and* haughty scorner *is* his name, who dealeth in proud wrath.
>
> Romans 2:8-11 But unto them that are contentious, and do not obey the truth, but obey unrighteousness, indignation and wrath, Tribulation and anguish, upon every soul of man that doeth evil, of the Jew first, and also of the Gentile; But glory, honour, and peace, to every man that worketh good, to the Jew first, and also to the Gentile: For there is no respect of persons with God.

Verse 23 reveals the fact that the hearts of believers desire to do good. Amplifying that righteous desire, verses 24-26 encourage believers to be generous with their finances. God intends for His people to help those less fortunate than themselves. Verse 24 gives a paradox explaining that being generous to those in need prospers the giver, whereas stingy giving leads to poverty. Verse 25 indicates that if the believer blesses others, he will receive blessings in return. Verse 26 talks about generously selling grain in time of famine.

Proverbs 11:24 There is that scattereth, and yet increaseth; and *there is* that withholdeth more than is meet, but *it tendeth* to poverty.

Focus: This proverb presents the paradox that Scriptural giving produces an increase while selfish withholding produces a decrease.

There are situations (especially those directed by God) whereby a person can **"scatter"** *[disperse]* wealth by giving in numerous places, and yet his wealth paradoxically increases rather than decreases. The disbursements may be to those in need or to those who are indebted to the giver.

On the other hand, there are situations where a person who is stingy, selfish, and disobedient to the Scriptures withholds **"more than is meet"** by refusing to pay the full amount properly owed a worker or simply refusing to help those in need. Perhaps he heartlessly refuses to sell his grain in time of famine because he is storing it up for personal gain (verse 26). Maybe he refuses to share water in time of drought when he owns the lake (verse 25). Rather than showing an increase in his wealth, his finances decrease. All of his devious efforts to gain wealth turn against him, and he becomes the worse for it. Most of all, he misses God's blessings to the obedient, as He "daily loadeth us *with benefits*" (Psalm 68:19).

> Leviticus 23:22 And when ye reap the harvest of your land, thou shalt not make clean riddance of the corners of thy field when thou reapest, neither shalt thou gather any gleaning of thy harvest: thou shalt leave them unto the poor, and to the stranger: I *am* the LORD your God.
>
> Deuteronomy 24:19 When thou cuttest down thine harvest in thy field, and hast forgot a sheaf in the field, thou shalt not go again to fetch it: it shall be for the stranger, for the fatherless, and for the widow: that the LORD thy God may bless thee in all the work of thine hands.
>
> Psalm 112:9 He hath dispersed, he hath given to the poor; his righteousness endureth for ever; his horn shall be exalted with honour.
>
> Proverbs 3:27-28 Withhold not good from them to whom it is due, when it is in the power of thine hand to do *it*. Say not unto thy neighbour, Go, and come again, and to morrow I will give; when thou hast it by thee.
>
> Proverbs 28:27 He that giveth unto the poor shall not lack: but he that hideth his eyes shall have many a curse.
>
> Galatians 6:10 As we have therefore opportunity, let us do good unto all men, especially unto them who are of the household of faith.
>
> Hebrews 13:16 But to do good and to communicate forget not: for with such sacrifices God is well pleased.
>
> James 5:4 Behold, the hire of the labourers who have reaped down your fields, which is of you kept back by fraud, crieth: and the cries of them which have reaped are entered into the ears of the Lord of sabaoth.

> **Proverbs 11:25** The liberal soul shall be made fat: and he that watereth shall be watered also himself.

Focus: This proverb states that the one who gives to others or waters others shall have blessings come back to himself.

"The liberal soul shall be made fat" or shall be blessed. He is one who concerns himself with others around him and consequently shares his blessings in the form of money or items. Literally, "the liberal soul" means the soul that blesses, that gives freely and fully. He is not stingy, but he gives generously. When one person blesses another, God blesses that generous person spiritually and financially. Because the liberal or generous soul helps by giving to others, God sees to it that he receives even more in return to work with – **"he that watereth shall be watered also himself."** Water is one of the essentials of life, and to water others signifies giving to sustain the life or well-being of that person. Kindly acts to others come back to the giver like the refreshing dew and soft rain falls from heaven upon a thirsty land. Other verses in the Old Testament echo this same sentiment.

> Deuteronomy 15:9-11 Beware that there be not a thought in thy wicked heart, saying, The seventh year, the year of release, is at hand; and thine eye be evil against thy poor brother, and thou givest him nought; and he cry unto the LORD against thee, and it be sin unto thee. Thou shalt surely give him, and thine heart shall not be grieved when thou givest unto him: because that for this thing the LORD thy God shall bless thee in all thy works, and in all that thou puttest thine hand unto. For the poor shall never cease out of the land: therefore I command thee, saying, Thou shalt open thine hand wide unto thy brother, to thy poor, and to thy needy, in thy land.
>
> Deuteronomy 24:19 When thou cuttest down thine harvest in thy field, and hast forgot a sheaf in the field, thou shalt not go again to fetch it: it shall be for the stranger, for the fatherless, and for the widow: that the LORD thy God may bless thee in all the work of thine hands.
>
> Proverbs 11:17 The merciful man doeth good to his own soul: but *he that is* cruel troubleth his own flesh.
>
> Proverbs 19:17 He that hath pity upon the poor lendeth unto the LORD; and that which he hath given will he pay him again.
>
> Proverbs 28:27 He that giveth unto the poor shall not lack: but he that hideth his eyes shall have many a curse.
>
> Ecclesiastes 11:1-2 Cast thy bread upon the waters: for thou shalt find it after many days. Give a portion to seven, and also to eight; for thou knowest not what evil shall be upon the earth.
>
> Isaiah 58:10-11 And *if* thou draw out thy soul to the hungry, and satisfy the afflicted soul; then shall thy light rise in obscurity, and thy darkness *be* as the noonday: And the LORD shall guide thee continually, and satisfy thy soul in drought, and make fat thy bones: and thou shalt be like a watered garden, and like a spring of water, whose waters fail not.
>
> Malachi 3:10 Bring ye all the tithes into the storehouse, that there may be meat in mine house, and prove me now herewith, saith the LORD of hosts, if I will not open you the windows of heaven, and pour you out a blessing, that *there shall* not be room enough *to receive it.*

In Ecclesiastes 11:1-2 (quoted above), Solomon himself spoke of the sowing and reaping principle of Proverbs 11:25.

> "Solomon here probably alludes to the manner of planting rice in the eastern countries; for, as Sir John Chardin observes in his note on Isaiah 32:20, 'They sow it upon the water; and, before sowing, while the earth is covered with water, they cause the ground to be trodden by oxen, horses, and asses, which go mid-leg deep; and this is the way of preparing the ground for sowing. And, as they sow the rice in the water, they transplant it in the water.'
>
> 'But, though Solomon alludes to this, it is evident he means in these words to inculcate liberality to the poor. As if he had said, *Cast* That is, freely and liberally bestow; *thy bread* — That is, thy money, or provisions, or the necessaries of life, of whatever kind; *upon the waters* – Upon the poor, on whom thy bounty may at first, and for a time, appear to be lost. (as the seed does, which a man casts upon the waters,) through their unthankfulness or inability to make thee any returns: yet, *thou shalt find it* – It shall be restored to thee, either by God or men, more certainly than the rice or other seed corn, cast upon the marshy or watery ground, produces fruit in due season: *after many days* – The return may be slow, but it is sure, and will be so much the more plentiful the longer it is delayed."[193]

Jesus echoed this principle in Luke.

> Luke 6:38 Give, and it shall be given unto you; good measure, pressed down, and shaken together, and running over, shall men give into your bosom. For with the same measure that ye mete withal it shall be measured to you again.

Jesus also taught the importance of not only loving God with all your heart and with all your soul and with all your mind but also loving your neighbor as yourself. Proverbs 11:24 and 25 express that there is a reward for putting such love into action.

> Matthew 22:36-40 Master, which *is* the great commandment in the law? Jesus said unto him, Thou shalt love the Lord thy God with all thy heart, and with all thy soul, and with all thy mind. This is the first and great commandment. And the second *is* like unto it, Thou shalt love thy neighbour as thyself. On these two commandments hang all the law and the prophets.

> **Proverbs 11:26** He that withholdeth corn, the people shall curse him: but blessing *shall be* upon the head of him that selleth *it*.

Focus: This proverb describes how the people react to business practices that are inhumane.

Knowledge of Israel's farming society lends itself to an easy understanding of this proverb. The *initial implication* is that the corn is greatly needed because the people are desperate to get food; otherwise, there would be no particular concern about it being sold immediately. *The second implication* is that the corn is being withheld for the personal gain of the owner. Perhaps he is holding out, planning to sell later at a higher price; perhaps there is a famine, and he is hoarding it while people die of starvation. *In either case, the implication* is that the person having possession of the corn is conspicuously self-serving. His greater concern is self-preservation and profit, *not* that the people are starving.

Scripture repeatedly teaches that the desire for personal gain is not to have precedent over treating people with respect, dignity, and compassion. In a farming society like Israel, a farmer who sold his grain instead of hoarding it was a blessing, especially when food was scarce. Having a respectful relationship with other people reflects a proper relationship with God.

> Genesis 47:23-25 Then Joseph said unto the people, Behold, I have bought you this day and your land for Pharaoh: lo, *here is* seed for you, and ye shall sow the land. And it shall come to pass in the increase, that ye shall give the fifth *part* unto Pharaoh, and four parts shall be your own, for seed of the field, and for your food, and for them of your households, and for food for your little ones. And they said, Thou hast saved our lives: let us find grace in the sight of my lord, and we will be Pharaoh's servants.
>
> Amos 8:4-7 Hear this, O ye that swallow up the needy, even to make the poor of the land to fail, Saying, When will the new moon be gone, that we may sell corn? and the sabbath, that we may set forth wheat, making the ephah small, and the shekel great, and falsifying the balances by deceit? That we may buy the poor for silver, and the needy for a pair of shoes; *yea,* and sell the refuse of the wheat? The LORD hath sworn by the excellency of Jacob, Surely I will never forget any of their works.

The ones from whom grain is being withheld will "**curse**" *[to malign or execrate, that is, stab with words]* or use very sharp words in speaking about the profiteer, causing him to dread coming into their presence. The farmer who withholds will not receive any blessings for his actions, as does the one who has compassion and sells his grain.

"**Blessing** *[benediction and by implication prosperity;gift, present]* **shall be upon the head of him that selleth it.**" Not only will the man who sells the grain at a fair rate receive the goodwill and the pleasant conversation of the people, but he will be blessed by God for adhering to the truth of His word. Blessings from God will come upon the man's head who sacrifices his own interests for other people's good. As Proverbs 10:6 states – "Blessings *are* upon the head of the just."

> Deuteronomy 28:1-6 And it shall come to pass, if thou shalt hearken diligently unto the voice of the LORD thy God, to observe *and* to do all his commandments which I command thee this day, that the LORD thy God will set thee on high above all nations of the earth: And all these blessings shall come on thee, and overtake thee, if thou shalt hearken unto the voice of the LORD thy God. Blessed *shalt* thou *be* in the city, and blessed *shalt* thou *be* in the field. Blessed *shall be* the fruit of thy body, and the fruit of thy ground, and the fruit of thy cattle, the increase of thy kine, and the flocks of thy sheep. Blessed *shall be* thy basket and thy store. Blessed *shalt* thou *be* when thou comest in, and blessed *shalt* thou *be* when thou goest out.
>
> Job 29:11-13 When the ear heard *me,* then it blessed me; and when the eye saw *me,* it gave witness to me: Because I delivered the poor that cried, and the fatherless, and *him that had* none to help him. The blessing of him that was ready to perish came upon me: and I caused the widow's heart to sing for joy.
>
> Proverbs 28:20 A faithful man shall abound with blessings: but he that maketh haste to be rich shall not be innocent.

> **NOTE**: *Berakah* (the Hebrew word used for "blessing" in this verse) means "to do or give something of value to another. God 'blesses' us by providing for our needs, and we in turn 'bless' God by giving Him of ourselves as His servants." [Jeff Benner, *Ancient Hebrew Word Meanings,* as quoted on https://nuggets4u.files.wordpress.com/2013/04/ancient-hebrew-word-meanings.doc.]

> **Proverbs 11:27** He that diligently seeketh good procureth favour: but he that seeketh mischief, it shall come unto him.

Focus: This proverb declares that men receive according to their seeking.

"**He that diligently seeketh good procureth favour.**" A person demonstrates that he wants to please God when he *diligently seeks good*. Obviously, seeking "**good**" *[welfare, benefit, good things]* is the opposite of seeking "**mischief**" *[evil,* *misery, distress, harm]*; therefore, the effects are opposite. When a person seeks good, he obtains favor from both God and good men.

He that diligently seeks good arises from his bed early with the goal of seeking earnestly and painstakingly to do **good** for himself, his family, and others during the day. He ***procures favor*** because he is seeking to please his Maker. Most likely, his first seeking of the day is to Jehovah, and he has learned to pray earnestly.

"But he that seeketh mischief, it shall come unto him." The characteristic of this second seeker is that he *seeks mischief [evil]*, and the mischief he sought after for himself and others **"shall come to him."** Psalm 36 describes the wicked man who seeks after evil.

> Psalm 36:1-4 To the chief Musician, *A Psalm* of David the servant of the LORD. The transgression of the wicked saith within my heart, *that there is* no fear of God before his eyes. For he flattereth himself in his own eyes, until his iniquity be found to be hateful. The words of his mouth *are* iniquity and deceit: he hath left off to be wise, *and* to do good. He deviseth mischief upon his bed; he setteth himself in a way *that is* not good; he abhorreth not evil.

When evil is sought, evil will be found, but not to the seeker's advantage for he loses favor with both God and men. The verses below give ample proof of which of the two characteristics God blesses.

> Psalm 1:3-5 And he shall be like a tree planted by the rivers of water, that bringeth forth his fruit in his season; his leaf also shall not wither; and whatsoever he doeth shall prosper. The ungodly are not so: but are like the chaff which the wind driveth away. Therefore the ungodly shall not stand in the judgment, nor sinners in the congregation of the righteous.
>
> Psalm 9:15 The heathen are sunk down in the pit *that* they made: in the net which they hid is their own foot taken.
>
> Psalm 37:1-3 *A Psalm* of David. Fret not thyself because of evildoers, neither be thou envious against the workers of iniquity. For they shall soon be cut down like the grass, and wither as the green herb. Trust in the LORD, and do good; *so* shalt thou dwell in the land, and verily thou shalt be fed.
>
> Proverbs 8:34-36 Blessed is the man that heareth me, watching daily at my gates, waiting at the posts of my doors. For whoso findeth me findeth life, and shall obtain favour of the LORD. But he that sinneth against me wrongeth his own soul: all they that hate me love death.
>
> Proverbs 11:17 The merciful man doeth good to his own soul: but he that is cruel troubleth his own flesh.
>
> Proverbs 12:21 There shall no evil happen to the just: but the wicked shall be filled with mischief.
>
> Galatians 6:7 Be not deceived; God is not mocked: for whatsoever a man soweth, that shall he also reap.
>
> Revelation 13:10 He that leadeth into captivity shall go into captivity: he that killeth with the sword must be killed with the sword. Here is the patience and the faith of the saints.

Proverbs 11:28 He that trusteth in his riches shall fall: but the righteous shall flourish as a branch.

Focus: This proverb contrasts the consequences to a person who trusts in riches with the consequences to a person who trusts in God.

"He that trusteth in his riches shall fall" like a dead autumn leaf descending from a tree shaken by the wind, **"but the righteous shall flourish as a branch"** firmly attached to the life-sustaining vine and able to weather severe storms.

God has given abundant reasons why man is not to trust in his riches. Riches are not a source or a provider of life, but are instead a provision by God, the Giver of Life. Also, a man was not made to serve riches, but rather riches were made to serve man – to provide for his necessities and enjoyments; but never to be worshiped or to be the recipient of confidence, adoration, or dependence that should properly be placed in God. When man inverts God's order, he becomes weak and succumbs to the luring, controlling power of the enemy that will guide him to destruction.

> "A golden key will not open the gate of heaven. Therefore 'Charge them that are rich in this world, that they be not high-minded, nor trust in uncertain riches, but in the living God (1Timothy 6:17).'"[194]
>
> "There are things that earthly riches cannot do. They can never satisfy Divine justice, nor pacify Divine wrath, nor quiet a guilty conscience. And till these things are done, the man is undone."[195]
>
> Deuteronomy 8:17-20 And thou say in thine heart, My power and the might of *mine* hand hath gotten me this wealth. But thou shalt remember the LORD thy God: for *it is* he that giveth thee power to get wealth, that he may establish his covenant which he sware unto thy fathers, as *it is* this day. And it shall be, if thou do at all forget the LORD thy God, and walk after other gods, and serve them, and worship them, I testify against you this day that ye shall surely perish. As the nations which the LORD destroyeth before your face, so shall ye perish; because ye would not be obedient unto the voice of the LORD your God.

Mark 10:23-25 And Jesus looked round about, and saith unto his disciples, How hardly shall they that have riches enter into the kingdom of God! And the disciples were astonished at his words. But Jesus answereth again, and saith unto them, Children, how hard is it for them that trust in riches to enter into the kingdom of God! It is easier for a camel to go through the eye of a needle, than for a rich man to enter into the kingdom of God.

Luke 12:16-21 And he spake a parable unto them, saying, The ground of a certain rich man brought forth plentifully: And he thought within himself, saying, What shall I do, because I have no room where to bestow my fruits? And he said, This will I do: I will pull down my barns, and build greater; and there will I bestow all my fruits and my goods. And I will say to my soul, Soul, thou hast much goods laid up for many years; take thine ease, eat, drink, *and* be merry. But God said unto him, *Thou* fool, this night thy soul shall be required of thee: then whose shall those things be, which thou hast provided? So *is* he that layeth up treasure for himself, and is not rich toward God.

1Timothy 6:17 Charge them that are rich in this world, that they be not highminded, nor trust in uncertain riches, but in the living God, who giveth us richly all things to enjoy.

James 1:10-11 But the rich, in that he is made low: because as the flower of the grass he shall pass away. For the sun is no sooner risen with a burning heat, but it withereth the grass, and the flower thereof falleth, and the grace of the fashion of it perisheth: so also shall the rich man fade away in his ways.

"But the righteous shall flourish *[grow, spread abroad abundantly]* **as a branch"** because their trust is in God – not in riches, and they live their lives in a manner that reflects the same. **"Riches"** can buy merchandise to create comfort or purchase the service of the best lawyer, but riches cannot obtain the favor of God – Who alone determines man's fate.

"The righteous shall flourish as a branch" because the branch is attached to and dependent upon the vine, and has the following promise from Jesus – "Abide in me, and I in you. As the branch cannot bear fruit of itself, except it abide in the vine; no more can ye, except ye abide in me. I am the vine, ye *are* the branches: He that abideth in me, and I in him, the same bringeth forth much fruit: for without me ye can do nothing. (John 15:4-5)

Psalm 1:3 And he shall be like a tree planted by the rivers of water, that bringeth forth his fruit in his season; his leaf also shall not wither; and whatsoever he doeth shall prosper.

Psalm 72:7 In his days shall the righteous flourish; and abundance of peace so long as the moon endureth. *[David's Psalm for Solomon]*

Psalm 92:12-15 The righteous shall flourish like the palm tree: he shall grow like a cedar in Lebanon. Those that be planted in the house of the LORD shall flourish in the courts of our God. They shall still bring forth fruit in old age; they shall be fat and flourishing; To shew that the LORD *is* upright: *he is* my rock, and *there is* no unrighteousness in him.

Proverbs 10:2 Treasures of wickedness profit nothing: but righteousness delivereth from death.

Proverbs 18:10-11 The name of the LORD *is* a strong tower: the righteous runneth into it, and is safe. The rich man's wealth *is* his strong city, and as an high wall in his own conceit.

Proverbs 14:11 The house of the wicked shall be overthrown: but the tabernacle of the upright shall flourish.

Jeremiah 9:23-24 Thus saith the LORD, Let not the wise *man* glory in his wisdom, neither let the mighty *man* glory in his might, let not the rich *man* glory in his riches: But let him that glorieth glory in this, that he understandeth and knoweth me, that I *am* the LORD which exercise lovingkindness, judgment, and righteousness, in the earth: for in these *things* I delight, saith the LORD.

Jeremiah 17:7-8 Blessed *is* the man that trusteth in the LORD, and whose hope the LORD is. For he shall be as a tree planted by the waters, and *that* spreadeth out her roots by the river, and shall not see when heat cometh, but her leaf shall be green; and shall not be careful in the year of drought, neither shall cease from yielding fruit.

Proverbs 11:29   He that troubleth his own house shall inherit the wind: and the fool *shall be* servant to the wise of heart.

Focus: This proverb compares the demeaning and destitute consequences of a foolish trouble-making family member with the fool who is destined to servanthood.

"He that troubleth *[disturb, afflict, stir]* **his own house"** is one who keeps the family from having peace. Such disruption can come through selfishness, slothfulness, greed, quick violent temper, arrogance, wastefulness, addictions, stealing, or other foolish destructive, disruptive behavior whereby everyone around the person becomes miserable. The family loses respect for the wayward one, who destroys not only peace, but also potentially the family's standing in the community, and often their financial stability.

He **"shall inherit the wind"** indicates that he "shall be as unable to keep and enjoy what he gets as a man is to hold the wind in his fist, or to feed and satisfy himself with it; he shall be brought to poverty."[196] He is unable to retain relationships or riches. The patriarch of the family may leave his riches and lands to another relative who does not destroy the peace of the household. If the self-indulgent father is the problem, and he wastes the family fortunes through greed, addiction, laziness, or other sinful behavior, the family may lose respect for him and leave him alone in poverty.

"And the fool *shall be* servant to the wise of heart." Just as the trouble maker destroys peace and his own prosperity, the fool destroys any ability to rise above the level of a servant. He will always be a servant to the wise. The trouble maker and the fool are alike in that they have both lost credibility. After the prodigal son played the fool by asking for his inheritance and wasting it on riotous living, he came to his senses and wanted to ask his father to make him like one of the hired servants – a level of acceptance that he obviously felt that he had reduced himself to. (Luke 15:19)

> Psalm 133:1-3   Behold, how good and how pleasant it is for brethren to dwell together in unity! It is like the precious ointment upon the head, that ran down upon the beard, even Aaron's beard: that went down to the skirts of his garments; As the dew of Hermon, and as the dew that descended upon the mountains of Zion: for there the LORD commanded the blessing, even life for evermore.
> Proverbs 14:1 Every wise woman buildeth her house: but the foolish plucketh it down with her hands.
> Proverbs 15:27 He that is greedy of gain troubleth his own house; but he that hateth gifts shall live.
> Proverbs 17:2 A wise servant shall have rule over a son that causeth shame, and shall have part of the inheritance among the brethren.
> Habakkuk 2:9 Woe to him that coveteth an evil covetousness to his house, that he may set his nest on high, that he may be delivered from the power of evil!

Proverbs 11:30   The fruit of the righteous *is* a tree of life; and he that winneth souls *is* wise.

Focus: This proverb declares (1) that the actions of the righteous person's life ("fruit") has life enabling qualities, and (2) that the wise are those righteous ones who persuade others.

"The fruit of the righteous" describes a person's influence, lifestyle, instruction, and his example. The fruit is a combination of the qualities that others notice about the believer in his daily life. The Hebrew word for **"fruit"** can mean the produce of the ground, reward, or offspring, but in this case, the fruit is defined *figuratively* as the person's actions. **"The righteous"** are those who are lawful, correct, and right with God.

> **"The fruit of the righteous"** describes the *spiritual nourishment* that is gained from being associated with the righteous. This fruit that is gleaned from the godly is specifically the wise way he handles his affairs, deals with problems and challenges of everyday life, manages his family and finances, and generally, the way that he serves God in every aspect of his life. It also includes his charity, his exhortations and prayers, his spiritual reproofs and instructions, his interest in heaven, and his spiritual influence on earth. Like the fruit of a tree, this fruit is "precious and useful, contributing to the support and increase of the spiritual life in many, and nourishing them up to eternal life."[197]

The context further declares that the **"fruit of righteousness is a tree of life"** because such wise, godly living shows others how to live in a way that pleases God, the giver of life. The person who is a "tree of life" to others lives a godly life, and speaks kindly words of comfort, support, good counsel, love, respect, joy, and righteousness. This person will also speak words from the Scriptures and share his wealth, time and labor with those in need.
(See Genesis 2:9; 3:22; 3:24; Proverbs 3:18; 11:30;13:12; 15:4; Revelation 2:7; 22:2; 22:14 for "tree of life" in Scripture.)

"And he that winneth souls *is* wise." Since he knows the great value of being righteous, he naturally wants others to have all the rich rewards and blessings given to him by God, so *he extends himself to others in order to win them over to the same walk with God.* Winning souls over to serve God is a sign of wisdom in the righteous. Only Jesus can save a man's soul, but believers can certainly exhibit Christ in their life and words. They can be the salt that makes a man thirsty for Christ, and they can be a light to the paths of those struggling in sin. The wise man **wins souls** by attracting them to himself, and inducing them to follow his example of righteousness.

> Proverbs 3:13-18 Happy *is* the man *that* findeth wisdom, and the man *that* getteth understanding. For the merchandise of it *is* better than the merchandise of silver, and the gain thereof than fine gold. She *is* more precious than rubies: and all the things thou canst desire are not to be compared unto her. Length of days *is* in her right hand; *and* in her left hand riches and honour. Her ways *are* ways of pleasantness, and all her paths *are* peace. She is a tree of life to them that lay hold upon her: and happy *is every one* that retaineth her.
> Proverbs 4:13 Take fast hold of instruction; let her not go: keep her; for she is thy life.
> Proverbs 10:11 The mouth of a righteous *man is* a well of life: but violence covereth the mouth of the wicked.

Proverbs 10:21 The lips of the righteous feed many: but fools die for want of wisdom.
   [See also Proverbs 12:14; 13:2; 15:28; and 18:4.]

"Souls can only be won . . . The soul can only be won *to* God by the same kind of power as it was won *from* God, viz., by that of **persuasion**. If the tempter had tried **force** he would have failed with our first parents. He knew human nature too well to attempt the use of such means. Force is of no avail to bring about a *friendship*, and the winning of a soul is bringing about a *friendship* between man and God. Therefore the Apostle 'beseeches' and 'prays' men to be reconciled to God.

Souls are won by fruit . . . Human nature will not be influenced by words without actions. The actions which make up a holy life are here called *fruit*. When two men are at variance and hatred is deeply rooted, he who would be a peace-maker must *be* something as well as *say* something. Words alone will not kill enmity—there must be correspondent deeds.

This constituted our Lord Jesus Christ the great Reconciler—that He brought forth the fruits of holiness and self-sacrifice, and so gave weight to His words of persuasion. So many souls have been won by him because so much fruit was brought forth by him. And all who would win souls must in their measure do likewise. In this sense they must obey His injunction and be made partakers of His promise: Matthew 4:18-20 And Jesus, walking by the sea of Galilee, saw two brethren, Simon called Peter, and Andrew his brother, casting a net into the sea: for they were fishers. And he saith unto them, Follow me, and I will make you fishers of men. And they straightway left *their* nets, and followed him.

. . . When he who seeks to win souls brings one to taste the sweets of godliness for himself, there is joy for both. The righteous man is a "tree of righteousness," hence he is himself a "tree of life." Others partake of his fruit and live unto holiness, and become fruit-bearing trees in their turn. And in this sense "he that reapeth and he who soweth rejoice together," and the precious harvest is a "tree of life"—an undying source of soul-satisfaction to both."[198]

"Those that would win souls have need of wisdom to know how to deal with them; and those that do win souls show that they are wise."[199]

In 2013, Peter Pett made the following comments:

"The crowning blessing of the righteous is that they become a blessing to others. Their fruit is a tree of life, a lifegiving tree. By their lives, the 'natural' product of their walking in wisdom with God, they are a source of life and well being to others. Through their wisely lived lives they win the hearts of men … It does not strictly mean 'winning souls' in an evangelistic sense, although that is undoubtedly one of its outcomes. If we would 'win men's souls' we must first win men's hearts … The reference to the tree of life indicates that God's purpose for the spiritually wise, who follow God's wisdom, is that they will play their part in restoring what has been lost by the fall. And they do it by attracting others to God's way of wisdom. It is part of the process of restoration. We too are to be a tree of life to men and women as we attract men to Christ by the beauty of our lives, and of course by proclaiming His wisdom."[200]

Matthew 5:13-16 "You are the salt of the earth. But if the salt loses its saltiness, how can it be made salty again? It is no longer good for anything, except to be thrown out and trampled underfoot. You are the light of the world. A town built on a hill cannot be hidden. Neither do people light a lamp and put it under a bowl. Instead they put it on its stand, and it gives light to everyone in the house. Let your light shine before men, that they may see your good works, and glorify your Father which is in heaven.

A well-known quote attributed to St. Francis of Assisi:
" PREACH THE GOSPEL ALL THE TIME AND, IF NECESSARY, USE WORDS."

Proverbs 11:31 Behold, the righteous shall be recompensed in the earth: much more the wicked and the sinner.

Focus: This proverb declares that the righteous will be punished in the earth for their wrongs, and since they will be punished, much more will the wicked (who is without any favor of God) be punished.

"Behold" *is an expression of surprise* used here to grab the attention of some who may have forgotten (if they ever knew) the truth that is about to be expounded, and that is that the **"recompense"** (on the earth) to the ungodly for their wrongs is greater than the recompense (on the earth) to the godly for their wrongs. This truth that the wicked are punished on this earth is not always observable; nonetheless, it is a declared truth of Scripture. *(See Proverbs 11:19 and "the way of the sinner is hard," Proverbs 13:15.)*

"The wicked and the sinner" stand in opposition to God and hate Him, and their sins are intentional. The "righteous" will sin against God, but not because they are opposed to Him or hate Him. Still, the sins of the righteous are ***"recompensed"*** but ***"much more the wicked and the sinner."*** Scripture specifies that God favors His children, but it also specifies that He will recompense them for wrong that they do. Since He will recompense His children, He will certainly recompense the wicked and the sinner who have no favor with Him and are not His children.

- Deuteronomy 7:9-10 Know therefore that the LORD thy God, he *is* God, the faithful God, which keepeth covenant and mercy with them that love him and keep his commandments to a thousand generations; And repayeth them that hate him to their face, to destroy them: he will not be slack to him that hateth him, he will repay him to his face.
- Psalm 21:8-9 Thine hand shall find out all thine enemies: thy right hand shall find out those that hate thee. Thou shalt make them as a fiery oven in the time of thine anger: the LORD shall swallow them up in his wrath, and the fire shall devour them.
- Psalm 89:30-32 If his children forsake my law, and walk not in my judgments; If they break my statutes, and keep not my commandments; Then will I visit their transgression with the rod, and their iniquity with stripes.
- Proverbs 11:21 Though hand join in hand, the wicked shall not be unpunished: but the seed of the righteous shall be delivered.
- Amos 3:1-2 Hear this word that the LORD hath spoken against you, O children of Israel, against the whole family which I brought up from the land of Egypt, saying, You only have I known of all the families of the earth: therefore I will punish you for all your iniquities.
- 1Peter 4:17-18 For the time *is come* that judgment must begin at the house of God: and if *it* first *begin* at us, what shall the end *be* of them that obey not the gospel of God? And if the righteous scarcely be saved, where shall the ungodly and the sinner appear?
- Hebrews 12:5-11 And ye have forgotten the exhortation which speaketh unto you as unto children, My son, despise not thou the chastening of the Lord, nor faint when thou art rebuked of him: For whom the Lord loveth he chasteneth, and scourgeth every son whom he receiveth. If ye endure chastening, God dealeth with you as with sons; for what son is he whom the father chasteneth not? But if ye be without chastisement, whereof all are partakers, then are ye bastards, and not sons. Furthermore we have had fathers of our flesh which corrected *us,* and we gave *them* reverence: shall we not much rather be in subjection unto the Father of spirits, and live? For they verily for a few days chastened *us* after their own pleasure; but he for *our* profit, that *we* might be partakers of his holiness. Now no chastening for the present seemeth to be joyous, but grievous: nevertheless afterward it yieldeth the peaceable fruit of righteousness unto them which are exercised thereby.

CHAPTER TWELVE

> **Proverbs 12:1**   Whoso loveth instruction loveth knowledge: but he that hateth reproof *is* brutish.

Focus: This proverb declares a difference between someone who loves to be taught and someone who hates to be corrected with instruction.

"Instruction" *[chastisement, warning, discipline, doctrine]* teaches the learner information that is right; consequently, it *reproves* *[corrects, chastises]* where there is wrong. No instruction is complete or effective until the student receives it and determines to incorporate it into his reasoning. *When a person loves the type of instruction that identifies where he is wrong and gives him correction, he is in a position to improve his life. When he loves to gain knowledge so that it can change his life*, he will enjoy being successful and wise, especially in the pursuit of God. A person who hates the kind of instruction that gives reproof is indeed **"brutish"** *[stupid]* and is compared in this verse to an animal that can't rise any higher in its understanding. In refusing to be corrected, such a person has become "an enemy to himself and to his own happiness."[201] To learn from Scripture is to learn from and about God, how He interacts with man, and what He thinks and expects of man; consequently, a man who wants to be corrected can and will make changes according to those instructions. **"Brutish,"** which means to be brutish or dull-minded like an animal, [202] is used in only two places in Proverbs: 12:1 and 30:2.

> 'The love of instruction. It is by instruction that knowledge comes. He who fancies he has all in himself will never learn. -Again, in proportion to the love of instruction will be the acquisition of knowledge... The love of instruction implies humility. It argues a sense of ignorance and need of information. It is a common thing for men to allow pride to cheat them of much valuable knowledge. ...That the knowledge of duty as well as of truth is here to be included may be inferred from the latter part of the verse – **'but he that refuseth reproof is brutish.'** Such conduct is 'brutish' as irrational, senseless, unworthy of a creature endowed with intellect; distinguished by reason from the beasts of the field, and distinguished from them too by his immorality"[203]
>
> Psalm 32:9 Be ye not as the horse, or as the mule, which have no understanding: whose mouth must be held in with bit and bridle, lest they come near unto thee.
>
> Psalm 50:17-20 Seeing thou hatest instruction, and castest my words behind thee. When thou sawest a thief, then thou consentedst with him, and hast been partaker with adulterers. Thou givest thy mouth to evil, and thy tongue frameth deceit. Thou sittest *and* speakest against thy brother; thou slanderest thine own mother's son.
>
> Psalm 92:5-6 O LORD, how great are thy works! and thy thoughts are very deep. A brutish man knoweth not; neither doth a fool understand this.
>
> Psalm 119:26-27 I have declared my ways, and thou heardest me: teach me thy statutes. Make me to understand the way of thy precepts: so shall I talk of thy wondrous works.
>
> Psalm 119:97-100 MEM. O how love I thy law! it is my meditation all the day. Thou through thy commandments hast made me wiser than mine enemies: for they are ever with me. I have more understanding than all my teachers: for thy testimonies are my meditation. I understand more than the ancients, because I keep thy precepts.
>
> Proverbs 1:5 A wise *man* will hear, and will increase learning; and a man of understanding shall attain unto wise counsels. . .
>
> Proverbs 1:25-29 But ye have set at nought all my counsel, and would none of my reproof: I also will laugh at your calamity; I will mock when your fear cometh; When your fear cometh as desolation, and your destruction cometh as a whirlwind; when distress and anguish cometh upon you. Then shall they call upon me, but I will not answer; they shall seek me early, but they shall not find me: For that they hated knowledge, and did not choose the fear of the LORD:
>
> Proverbs 2:10-11 When wisdom entereth into thine heart, and knowledge is pleasant unto thy soul; Discretion shall preserve thee, understanding shall keep thee:
>
> Proverbs 4:13 Take fast hold of instruction; let *her* not go: keep her; for she *is* thy life.
>
> Proverbs 9:7-9 He that reproveth a scorner getteth to himself shame: and he that rebuketh a wicked man getteth himself a blot. Reprove not a scorner, lest he hate thee: rebuke a wise man, and he will love thee. Give instruction to a wise man, and he will be yet wiser: teach a just man, and he will increase in learning.
>
> Proverbs 10:17 He *is in* the way of life that keepeth instruction: but he that refuseth reproof erreth.
>
> Proverbs 15:10 Correction *is* grievous unto him that forsaketh the way: *and* he that hateth reproof shall die.

Proverbs 30:2-3 Surely I am more brutish than any man, and have not the understanding of a man. I neither learned wisdom, nor have the knowledge of the holy.

Isaiah 1:2-4 Hear, O heavens, and give ear, O earth: for the LORD hath spoken, I have nourished and brought up children, and they have rebelled against me. The ox knoweth his owner, and the ass his master's crib: but Israel doth not know, my people doth not consider. Ah sinful nation, a people laden with iniquity, a seed of evildoers, children that are corrupters: they have forsaken the LORD, they have provoked the Holy One of Israel unto anger, they are gone away backward.

John 3:19-21 And this is the condemnation, that light is come into the world, and men loved darkness rather than light, because their deeds were evil. For every one that doeth evil hateth the light, neither cometh to the light, lest his deeds should be reproved. But he that doeth truth cometh to the light, that his deeds may be made manifest, that they are wrought in God.

2Thessalonians 2:10-12 And with all deceivableness of unrighteousness in them that perish; because they received not the love of the truth, that they might be saved. And for this cause God shall send them strong delusion, that they should believe a lie: That they all might be damned who believed not the truth, but had pleasure in unrighteousness.

2 Timothy 3:16-17 All scripture *is* given by inspiration of God, and *is* profitable for doctrine, for reproof, for correction, for instruction in righteousness: That the man of God may be perfect, throughly furnished unto all good works.

Proverbs 12:2 A good *man* obtaineth favour of the LORD: but a man of wicked devices will he condemn.

Focus: This proverb teaches that God interacts and responds to men individually, according to the condition of their heart.

"A good man obtaineth favour of the LORD." The Book of Proverbs uses the following descriptive terms for righteous and wise persons: upright, blameless, man of understanding, trustworthy, kind, generous, prudent, and truthful.[204] The term **"good"** is a general term that describes all these characteristics and more. No man is good naturally but is made so through the indwelling of God. A ***good man obtains favor*** from the LORD because he seeks to be righteous and opposes evil. He controls his flesh and forces himself to think and behave in a manner that pleases the LORD. ***Goodness*** is also a fruit of the Spirit, and being thus filled with the Spirit of God, the good person is led by Him; consequently, he has no need or desire or likeness for scheming. Manipulation of others is foreign to his thinking. He ***obtains favor from God*** through answered prayer and through his footsteps being guided by God. In addition, he enjoys a peace that passes all understanding, and God makes His presence known to him and protects him against evil by giving him godly wisdom, knowledge, and understanding. He is guided by God through this life and into eternity, where only those who love God and are loved by Him will abide forever.

Psalm 37:23-24 The steps of a *good* man are ordered by the LORD: and he delighteth in his way. Though he fall, he shall not be utterly cast down: for the LORD upholdeth *him with* his hand.

Psalm 112:1-9 Praise ye the LORD. Blessed *is* the man *that* feareth the LORD, *that* delighteth greatly in his commandments. His seed shall be mighty upon earth: the generation of the upright shall be blessed. Wealth and riches *shall be* in his house: and his righteousness endureth for ever. Unto the upright there ariseth light in the darkness: *he is* gracious, and full of compassion, and righteous. A good man sheweth favour, and lendeth: he will guide his affairs with discretion. Surely he shall not be moved for ever: the righteous shall be in everlasting remembrance. He shall not be afraid of evil tidings: his heart is fixed, trusting in the LORD. His heart *is* established, he shall not be afraid, until he see *his desire* upon his enemies. He hath dispersed, he hath given to the poor; his righteousness endureth for ever; his horn shall be exalted with honour.

Proverbs 8:35-36 For whoso findeth me *[Wisdom]* findeth life, and shall obtain favour of the LORD. But he that sinneth against me wrongeth his own soul: all they that hate me love death.

Proverbs 14:9 Fools make a mock at sin: but among the righteous *there is* favour.

Proverbs 14:22 Do they not err that devise evil? but mercy and truth *shall be* to them that devise good.

1 Peter 3:12 For the eyes of the Lord *are* over the righteous, and his ears *are open* unto their prayers: but the face of the Lord *is* against them that do evil.

"But a man of wicked devices will he condemn." A man of wicked devices schemes to do wrong and displeases God by living in an ungodly manner. If he were only a man in whom wicked devices were found, he would certainly find disapproval among good men and God, *but* to be **"a man of wicked devices"** implies that he has the stink of such evil scheming all over himself. He is as much a part of such wickedness as it is of him. His mind is geared the opposite of the "good man," and he has no identity with the Holy Spirit. He will be ***condemned by God*** because he fully opposes God and His teachings.

Proverbs 6:16-19 These six *things* doth the LORD hate: yea, seven *are* an abomination unto him: A proud look, a lying tongue, and hands that shed innocent blood, An heart that deviseth wicked imaginations, feet that be swift in running to mischief, A false witness *that* speaketh lies, and he that soweth discord among brethren.

Isaiah 32:6-7 For the vile person will speak villany, and his heart will work iniquity, to practise hypocrisy, and to utter error against the LORD, to make empty the soul of the hungry, and he will cause the drink of the thirsty to fail. The instruments also of the churl *are* evil: he deviseth wicked devices to destroy the poor with lying words, even when the needy speaketh right.

John 3:17-21 For God sent not his Son into the world to condemn the world; but that the world through him might be saved. He that believeth on him is not condemned: but he that believeth not is condemned already, because he hath not believed in the name of the only begotten Son of God. And this is the condemnation, that light is come into the world, and men loved darkness rather than light, because their deeds were evil. For every one that doeth evil hateth the light, neither cometh to the light, lest his deeds should be reproved. But he that doeth truth cometh to the light, that his deeds may be made manifest, that they are wrought in God.

Proverbs 12:3   A man shall not be established by wickedness: but the root of the righteous shall not be moved.

Focus: This proverb declares that wickedness causes instability while righteousness causes stability.

"A man shall not be established by wickedness." Among other evil practices, **"wickedness"** manifests itself with a disregard for righteousness, justice, honor, truth, integrity, godliness, and most importantly – God. For one to believe that he can **"be established by wickedness"** would necessitate him having an evil mind that believes his ill-gotten gain is secure, that his pleasure and prosperity are permanent, and that his wicked beliefs about God, life, death, and eternity have a solid soil for its roots to anchor into. But he is mistaken; he **"shall not be established by wickedness,"** for God is opposed to him.

The roots of the wicked are anchored in the wickedness of the lies of Satan. All the wickedness that he teaches is false, temporary, and condemned by God, and all who put their roots down into that soil are known as **"the wicked."** Along with Satan and his angels, they will face the judgment of God and be cast into the Lake of Fire.

"But the root of the righteous shall not be moved." **"Righteous"** people are often compared to trees in Scripture, as is true in this verse. And *their root shall not be moved* is true because it steadfastly grows and anchors deep into the good, rich, godly soil comprised of the doctrines given and inspired by God Himself. His word is eternal and fixed, and there is nothing more steadfast. Roots growing in Scriptural soil will never budge. The righteous life is a stable, permanent life because the upright believe and live out the doctrines of God. This earthly life, as well as life in eternity, are both rooted and grounded on these doctrines and steadfastly, unquestionably depend on its permanency.

Job 20:5-9 That the triumphing of the wicked is short, and the joy of the hypocrite but for a moment? Though his excellency mount up to the heavens, and his head reach unto the clouds; Yet he shall perish for ever like his own dung: they which have seen him shall say, Where is he? He shall fly away as a dream, and shall not be found: yea, he shall be chased away as a vision of the night. The eye also which saw him shall see him no more; neither shall his place any more behold him.

Job 27:16-18 Though he heap up silver as the dust, and prepare raiment as the clay; He may prepare it, but the just shall put it on, and the innocent shall divide the silver. He buildeth his house as a moth, and as a booth that the keeper maketh.

Psalm 1:1-6 Blessed is the man that walketh not in the counsel of the ungodly, nor standeth in the way of sinners, nor sitteth in the seat of the scornful. But his delight is in the law of the LORD; and in his law doth he meditate day and night. And he shall be like a tree planted by the rivers of water, that bringeth forth his fruit in his season; his leaf also shall not wither; and whatsoever he doeth shall prosper. The ungodly are not so: but are like the chaff which the wind driveth away. Therefore the ungodly shall not stand in the judgment, nor sinners in the congregation of the righteous. For the LORD knoweth the way of the righteous: but the way of the ungodly shall perish.

Psalm 125:1-2 A Song of degrees. They that trust in the LORD shall be as mount Zion, which cannot be removed, but abideth for ever. As the mountains are round about Jerusalem, so the LORD is round about his people from henceforth even for ever.

Proverbs 10:25 As the whirlwind passeth, so is the wicked no more: but the righteous is an everlasting foundation.

Proverbs 12:7 The wicked are overthrown, and are not: but the house of the righteous shall stand.

Matthew 7:24-27 Therefore whosoever heareth these sayings of mine, and doeth them, I will liken him unto a wise man, which built his house upon a rock: And the rain descended, and the floods came, and the winds blew, and beat upon that house; and it fell not: for it was founded upon a rock. And every one that heareth these sayings of mine, and doeth them not, shall be likened unto a foolish man, which built his house upon the sand: And the rain descended, and the floods came, and the winds blew, and beat upon that house; and it fell: and great was the fall of it.

Matthew 13:20-21 But he that received the seed into stony places, the same is he that heareth the word, and anon with joy receiveth it; Yet hath he not root in himself, but dureth for a while: for when tribulation or persecution ariseth because of the word, by and by he is offended.

Luke 8:13 They on the rock *are they*, which, when they hear, receive the word with joy; and these have no root, which for a while believe, and in time of temptation fall away.

Matthew 24:35 Heaven and earth shall pass away, but my words shall not pass away.

Colossians 2:7 Rooted and built up in him, and stablished in the faith, as ye have been taught, abounding therein with thanksgiving.

Proverbs 12:4   A virtuous woman is a crown to her husband: but she that maketh ashamed is as rottenness in his bones.

Focus: This proverb contrasts the glorious effect that the virtuous wife has on her husband with the disgraceful, degenerative effect the vile wife has on her husband.

The **"virtuous woman"** combines the ideas of moral goodness and bodily vigor and activity.[205] The woman "that maketh ashamed" lacks these traits and drains her husband's strength and dignity to the point she figuratively decays his bones. *["Virtuous" comes from the Hebrew chayil or [hayhil] which means probably a force, whether of men, means or other resources; an army, wealth, virtue, valor, strength, ability, activity, goods, might, power, riches, and/or worthy, efficiency.]*

Virtue is a by-product of wisdom, which initiates from "fear of the LORD." A **"virtuous woman"** is, in general, a *woman of strength.* She is a powerful person because she is wise. In this verse, the virtuous woman's strength of wisdom enables her to be a **"crown to her husband,"** a mark of dignity, respectability, and reputation to the man she married. Wisdom gives the ability to live one's life to its fullest and has a positive effect on every association, especially the spouse.

Proverbs 31:23 Her husband is known in the gates, when he sitteth among the elders of the land.

1 Corinthians 11:7 For a man indeed ought not to cover his head, forasmuch as he is the image and glory of God: but the woman is the glory of the man.

The life of a virtuous woman is detailed in Proverbs 31, which describes her *strength of wisdom* in her ability to properly handle the matters of life, and especially that of her house, with credibility, dignity, and honor. She is wise, industrious, and energetic; there is no evil about her. The virtuous woman is successful because she follows the blueprint of God's law, which has made her wise and consequently strong (virtuous) in all the ways taught by wisdom. Thus, she is full of kindness and loves the laws of God.

"Virtuous" is used to describe Ruth – "And now, my daughter, fear not; I will do to thee all that thou requirest: for all the city of my people doth know that thou art a virtuous *[chayil]* woman." (Ruth 3:11) The same Hebrew word is used to describe Boaz, but it is translated "wealth." "And Naomi had a kinsman of her husband's, a mighty man of wealth *[chayil]*, of the family of Elimelech; and his name was Boaz." (Ruth 2:1) *Chayil* is also used to describe the virtuous woman of Proverbs 31.

"The worthy (strong, capable) woman has been revealed as the one who instructs her children in the Torah (Proverbs 1:8), and who tenderly loves and trains them (Proverbs 4:3). She grieves over their folly (Proverbs 10:1). She ensures that their thoughts are righteous (Proverbs12:5). She builds up her household (Proverbs 14:1). Thus she makes a full contribution in the rearing of the children in wisdom and knowledge and adds to her husband's status. She is a crown to him, just as his worthy children are a floral wreath of flowers on his head (Proverbs 1:9). She makes him look and feel like a king. The community admire him for his worthy family."[206]

"A crown was not only the sign of the power of a king, but it was also a sign of joy and gladness."[207] On the day when the groom appeared at the bride's father's house to escort her to their new home, he would wear a crown of gold or silver or flowers[208] to symbolize what she meant to him. Because of this custom, the Hebrews of Solomon's day would immediately understand the significance of this verse.

If the term **"virtuous woman"** embodies all that is good in the fairer sex, then certainly **"she that maketh ashamed"** manifests the opposite, and the total opposite of the virtuous woman is the adulteress who is also a fool. Proverbs mentions several behaviors that **"maketh ashamed."** Two particular behaviors that seem to be the most often mentioned: folly in taking care of business and sexual wickedness.

The **"rottenness in his bones"** is brought about by the foolish woman's being a constant grief and worry to her husband. When he can't trust her because she is not faithful, or she won't support his desire to serve God, or she doesn't care for the children or other responsibilities of the home, or she nags and complains continually, or she runs her husband down publicly and privately, or she spends more money than is contained in the family coffers, his health is broken down and his joy is taken away. The joyful **"crown"** of the wedding day is tarnished, if not broken. **"Rottenness in his bones"** pictures a man whose legs have become so structurally weak they cannot hold up his body.

> "Such a wife poisons her husband's life, deprives him of strength and vigour; though she is made 'bone of his bones, and flesh of his flesh (Genesis 2:23), far from being a helpmate for him, she saps his very existence." [209]
>
> Proverbs 14:1 Every wise woman buildeth her house: but the foolish plucketh it down with her hands.
>
> Proverbs 19:13-14 A foolish son is the calamity of his father: and the contentions of a wife are a continual dropping. House and riches are the inheritance of fathers: and a prudent wife is from the LORD.
>
> Proverbs 21:9 It is better to dwell in a corner of the housetop, than with a brawling woman in a wide house.
>
> Proverbs 21:19 It is better to dwell in the wilderness, than with a contentious and an angry woman.
>
> Proverbs 27:15-16 A continual dropping in a very rainy day and a contentious woman are alike. Whosoever hideth her hideth the wind, and the ointment of his right hand, which bewrayeth itself.

Verses five through eight contrast the righteous with the wicked in regard to their thoughts, words, final judgment, and wisdom or lack thereof.

Proverbs 12:5 The thoughts of the righteous are right: but the counsels of the wicked are deceit.

Focus: This proverb contrasts the right thoughts of the righteous with the deceitful counsels of the wicked.

"The thoughts of the righteous are right." A righteous man is one who is **"right"** with God, therefore he will corral any evil thoughts and refuse for them to be a part of his reasoning. Thus, any counsel or steering he gives will originate from thoughts that are pleasing to God.

"But the counsels of the wicked are deceit *[fraudulent]***"** because their counsel originates from wicked thoughts. Because they have no regard for righteousness, their advice is the fruit of unrestrained, improper thoughts which imagine whatever evil their wicked heart desires to pursue.

> "'**The thoughts of the righteous are right** . . .' The thoughts of men's hearts are naturally evil, nor can any think a good thought of themselves; but the thoughts of the righteous are directed and influenced by the grace of God, and are formed according to that word which is a discerner of the thoughts and intents of the heart; their thoughts concerning God and religion, concerning Christ and his Gospel, his ways and worship, his truths and ordinances, they are judiciously framed according to the rule of God's word, the revelation he has made, and so are right; and such are their resolutions and designs to serve the Lord their God, and him only, and to cleave to him with full purpose of heart **but the counsels of the wicked are deceit**; the designs, schemes, and contrivances of wicked men, are to trick, and overreach, and defraud their neighbours in civil affairs; and of false teachers, to deceive the hearts of the simple in religious ones. The coming of the man of sin was with all deceivableness; and all the gaudy show and pageantry he makes, and pretended miracles he works, are to deceive the inhabitants of the earth; and by his sorceries all nations are deceived." (2Thessalonians 2:10)[210]
>
> 2 Chronicles 22:2-4 Forty and two years old *was* Ahaziah when he began to reign, and he reigned one year in Jerusalem. His mother's name also *was* Athaliah the daughter of Omri. He also walked in the ways of the house of Ahab: for his mother was his counsellor to do wickedly. Wherefore he did evil in the sight of the LORD like the house of Ahab: for they were his counsellors after the death of his father to his destruction.
>
> Psalm 36:1-4 The transgression of the wicked saith within my heart, *that there is* no fear of God before his eyes. For he flattereth himself in his own eyes, until his iniquity be found to be hateful. The words of his mouth *are* iniquity and deceit: he hath left off to be wise, *and* to do good. He deviseth mischief upon his bed; he setteth himself in a way *that is* not good; he abhorreth not evil.
>
> Psalm 139:23-24 Search me, O God, and know my heart: try me, and know my thoughts: And see if there be any wicked way in me, and lead me in the way everlasting.
>
> Proverbs 26:24 He that hateth dissembleth with his lips, and layeth up deceit within him; When he speaketh fair, believe him not: for *there are* seven abominations in his heart. *Whose* hatred is covered by deceit, his wickedness shall be shewed before the *whole* congregation.
>
> Romans 8:6 For to be carnally minded is death; but to be spiritually minded is life and peace.

> **Proverbs 12:6** The words of the wicked are to lie in wait for blood: but the mouth of the upright shall deliver them.

Focus: This proverb contrasts the ungodly purpose of the wicked person's talk with the godly purpose of the righteous person's talk.

"The words of the wicked are to lie in wait for blood." Words are products of thoughts as discussed in the previous verse. Figuratively speaking, words form the foundation on which actions are constructed. After his wicked mind develops evil ideas and plots, the wicked speak deceitful, shrewd words with the desire to destroy lives.

The following verses are examples of **"wicked"** words that plotted destruction.

> 2 Samuel 17:1-2 Moreover Ahithophel said unto Absalom, Let me now choose out twelve thousand men, and I will arise and pursue after David this night: And I will come upon him while he is weary and weak handed, and will make him afraid: and all the people that are with him shall flee; and I will smite the king only:
> 1 Kings 21:13 And there came in two men, children of Belial, and sat before him: and the men of Belial witnessed against him, even against Naboth, in the presence of the people, saying, Naboth did blaspheme God and the king. Then they carried him forth out of the city, and stoned him with stones, that he died.
> Esther 3:8-9 And Haman said unto king Ahasuerus, There is a certain people scattered abroad and dispersed among the people in all the provinces of thy kingdom; and their laws are diverse from all people; neither keep they the king's laws: therefore it is not for the king's profit to suffer them. If it please the king, let it be written that they may be destroyed: and I will pay ten thousand talents of silver to the hands of those that have the charge of the business, to bring it into the king's treasuries.
> Revelation 13:15 And he *[Antichrist]* had power to give life unto the image of the beast, that the image of the beast should both speak, and cause that as many as would not worship the image of the beast should be killed.

"But the mouth of the upright shall deliver them." "The mouth of the upright" refers to the speech of righteous persons whose mouth can sometimes do great good with a single well-spoken, timely, and proper word. Because those with a heart for God speak of peace, preservation of life, and equitable treatment for the downtrodden, this proverb says that the upright's speech **"delivers"** *[snatches away, rescues, recovers]*. There is a commanding power associated with spoken truth that demands a response. History reveals that many innocent people have been released from the grip of wicked men of authority by the truth being spoken. Jesus foretold of wars and persecution to the Christian but also stated that when brought before civil authorities, they would have a testimony and that they were not to meditate on how to answer because ". . . I will give you a mouth and wisdom, which all your adversaries shall not be able to gainsay nor resist." (Luke 21:15)

> Proverbs 15:26 The thoughts of the wicked *are* an abomination to the LORD: but *the words* of the pure *are* pleasant words.
> Proverbs 16:23-24 The heart of the wise teacheth his mouth, and addeth learning to his lips. Pleasant words *are as* an honeycomb, sweet to the soul, and health to the bones.
> Proverbs 21:23 Whoso keepeth his mouth and his tongue keepeth his soul from troubles.
> Proverbs 22:20-21 Have not I written to thee excellent things in counsels and knowledge, That I might make thee know the certainty of the words of truth; that thou mightest answer the words of truth to them that send unto thee?
> Proverbs 31:8-9 Open thy mouth for the dumb in the cause of all such as are appointed to destruction. Open thy mouth, judge righteously, and plead the cause of the poor and needy.

> **Proverbs 12:7** The wicked are overthrown, and are not: but the house of the righteous shall stand.

Focus: This proverb contrasts the instability and removal of the wicked with the steadfastness of the righteous.

"The wicked are overthrown, and are not." The ungodly have already crossed the line with God; and, in His mind, according to this Scripture, are already judged – only they await future sentencing at the Great White Throne Judgment. A preview of God's judgment against sin is seen in Genesis 7, when the world was destroyed with a flood, and in Genesis 19, when He destroyed Sodom and Gomorrah with brimstone and fire. Evil people spread their ideas of opposing God to the minds of their family, friends, and associates, but that will end at the Great White Throne Judgment when all those in opposition to God will be eternally separated in the Lake of Fire. Also, concerning the "house" or family of the ungodly, "the wicked seldom have many generations in a direct line. This is God's mercy, that the entail of iniquity may be in some sort cut off, so that the same vices may not be strengthened by successive generations. For generally, the bad root produces not only a bad plant, but one worse than itself."[211]

"But, the house of the righteous shall stand." This **"house of the righteous"** is a family that individually and collectively serve God so that the "house" or family is known to be "righteous." They are right with God and thus undergirded and strengthened by Him. Though they will face adversity, their roots drive deep into the soil of God's doctrines; and they are and will be forever secure and steadfast with God. The righteous have chosen to follow God's way and to refuse everything that opposes Him and His commandments; therefore, God is their stronghold both now and forever.

> Genesis 6:5-8 And GOD saw that the wickedness of man *was* great in the earth, and *that* every imagination of the thoughts of his heart *was* only evil continually. And it repented the LORD that he had made man on the earth, and it grieved him at his heart. And the LORD said, I will destroy man whom I have created from the face of the earth; both man, and beast, and the creeping thing, and the fowls of the air; for it repenteth me that I have made them. But Noah found grace in the eyes of the LORD.
> Genesis 19:29 And it came to pass, when God destroyed the cities of the plain, that God remembered Abraham, and sent Lot out of the midst of the overthrow, when he overthrew the cities in the which Lot dwelt.
> Job 18:15-21 It shall dwell in his tabernacle, because *it is* none of his: brimstone shall be scattered upon his habitation. His roots shall be dried up beneath, and above shall his branch be cut off. His remembrance shall perish from the earth, and he shall have no name in the street. He shall be driven from light into darkness, and chased out of the world. He shall neither have son nor nephew among his people, nor any remaining in his dwellings. They that come after *him* shall be astonied at his day, as they that went before were affrighted. Surely such *are* the dwellings of the wicked, and this *is* the place *of him that* knoweth not God.
> Psalm 37:35-40 I have seen the wicked in great power, and spreading himself like a green bay tree. Yet he passed away, and, lo, he was not: yea, I sought him, but he could not be found. Mark the perfect man, and behold the upright: for the end of that man is peace. But the transgressors shall be destroyed together: the end of the wicked shall be cut off. But the salvation of the righteous is of the LORD: he is their strength in the time of trouble. And the LORD shall help them, and deliver them: he shall deliver them from the wicked, and save them, because they trust in him.
> Psalm 125:1-2 A Song of degrees. They that trust in the LORD shall be as mount Zion, which cannot be removed, but abideth for ever. As the mountains are round about Jerusalem, so the LORD is round about his people from henceforth even for ever.
> Proverbs 1:17-18 Surely in vain the net is spread in the sight of any bird. And they lay wait for their own blood; they lurk privily for their own lives.
> Proverbs 10:25 As the whirlwind passeth, so is the wicked no more: but the righteous is an everlasting foundation.
> Proverbs 12:3 A man shall not be established by wickedness: but the root of the righteous shall not be moved.
> Proverbs 14:11 The house of the wicked shall be overthrown: but the tabernacle of the upright shall flourish.
> Isaiah 26:4-5 Trust ye in the LORD for ever: for in the LORD JEHOVAH is everlasting strength: For he bringeth down them that dwell on high; the lofty city, he layeth it low; he layeth it low, even to the ground; he bringeth it even to the dust.
> Matthew 7:24-27 Therefore whosoever heareth these sayings of mine, and doeth them, I will liken him unto a wise man, which built his house upon a rock: And the rain descended, and the floods came, and the winds blew, and beat upon that house; and it fell not: for it was founded upon a rock. And every one that heareth these sayings of mine, and doeth them not, shall be likened unto a foolish man, which built his house upon the sand: And the rain descended, and the floods came, and the winds blew, and beat upon that house; and it fell: and great was the fall of it.

Proverbs 12:8 A man shall be commended according to his wisdom: but he that is of a perverse heart shall be despised.

Focus: This proverb contrasts people's different reactive attitudes toward the wise and toward the "perverse" (wicked).

If a man is truly wise, people often commend him because his wise handling of affairs usually has a bearing on their personal lives, either directly or indirectly. Relatives, friends, and associates all have the potential of being affected by the actions and decisions of a wise person.

Opposite of wisdom is ***perverseness,*** whereby the perverse heart continually produces words and actions that are contrary to those desired by God and man. The **"perverse"** person speaks against God and against good people. His actions oppose the teachings of Scripture. He is obstinate and has a habit of pursuing wrong. The perverse person has a warped and crooked mind; his thinking is distorted. ***He is despised*** and consequently shunned because his life adversely affects his family, friends, and associates.

> Genesis 41:39 And Pharaoh said unto Joseph, Forasmuch as God hath shewed thee all this, there is none so discreet and wise as thou art . . .
> 1 Samuel 18:5 And David went out whithersoever Saul sent him, and behaved himself wisely: and Saul set him over the men of war, and he was accepted in the sight of all the people, and also in the sight of Saul's servants.

1 Samuel 18:30 Then the princes of the Philistines went forth: and it came to pass, after they went forth, that David behaved himself more wisely than all the servants of Saul; so that his name was much set by.

Proverbs 3:35 The wise shall inherit glory: but shame shall be the promotion of fools.

Proverbs 18:3 When the wicked cometh, then cometh also contempt, and with ignominy reproach.

Malachi 2:8-9 But ye are departed out of the way; ye have caused many to stumble at the law; ye have corrupted the covenant of Levi, saith the LORD of hosts. Therefore have I also made you contemptible and base before all the people, according as ye have not kept my ways, but have been partial in the law.

Matthew 27:3-5 Then Judas, which had betrayed him, when he saw that he was condemned, repented himself, and brought again the thirty pieces of silver to the chief priests and elders, Saying, I have sinned in that I have betrayed the innocent blood. And they said, What is that to us? see thou to that. And he cast down the pieces of silver in the temple, and departed, and went and hanged himself.

Luke 16:8 And the lord commended the unjust steward, because he had done wisely: for the children of this world are in their generation wiser than the children of light.

Verses nine through eleven continue to compare the righteous and the wicked, but the setting is now in the home and on the farm. In verse 9, when the contrasting "better than" is used in place of the conjunction "but," it illustrates that the first item is superior to the second.

> **Proverbs 12:9** *He that is* despised, and hath a servant, *is* better than he that honoureth himself, and lacketh bread.

Focus: This proverb answers the unspoken question: what good does it do to act important when there is not enough money to put food on the table?

"*He that is* **despised**" describes one who is *held in contempt* by those who think they are superior because of his poverty and their plenty. Such despising of "the poor" was a common attitude of "the rich" in biblical times and is so even now. For a person to **honor himself** by exceeding his financial capacity in order to give the impression of belonging to a higher class is foolishness. He can create greater problems for himself by such outlandish acts, especially if such pretensions force him into deeper poverty. If the one despised privately has ample provision and even **"a servant"** to help with his struggling life, he is better off than someone publicly faking that he lives in a higher class but actually lacks adequate food to maintain good health. "Respectable mediocrity is better than boastful poverty."[212]

1 Samuel 18:23 And Saul's servants spake those words in the ears of David. And David said, Seemeth it to you a light thing to be a king's son in law, seeing that I am a poor man, and lightly esteemed?

Proverbs 13:7 There is that maketh himself rich, yet hath nothing: there is that maketh himself poor, yet hath great riches.

Proverbs 19:1 Better is the poor that walketh in his integrity, than he that is perverse in his lips, and is a fool.

Proverbs 30:8-9 Remove far from me vanity and lies: give me neither poverty nor riches; feed me with food convenient for me: Lest I be full, and deny thee, and say, Who is the LORD? or lest I be poor, and steal, and take the name of my God in vain.

Luke 14:11 For whosoever exalteth himself shall be abased; and he that humbleth himself shall be exalted.

> **Proverbs 12:10** A righteous *man* regardeth the life of his beast: but the tender mercies of the wicked *are* cruel.

Focus: This proverb contrasts a righteous person's demonstrative compassion with the disguised cruelty of a wicked person.

A righteous man's tenderheartedness toward his animal reflects his true righteousness, whereas a wicked person's demonstration of compassion is actually a disguise of his cruelty.

"**A righteous *man* regardeth** *[knows, including observation, care, and instruction]* **the life of his beast.**" The context of this verse amplifies the meaning of **"regardeth."** It includes the understanding that the righteous man, because of being very familiar with his animals coupled with his tender mercy, takes special care of them. Because they are precious gifts from God, he makes it his business to be aware of their needs. A man who is right with God has feelings of mercy for other people, and that same tenderness can be observed throughout all aspects of his life, not just in how he treats people. He will not intentionally push his working animals to perform beyond their strength nor cause them cruel, unnecessary pain.

In addition, he will teach his children to respect every animal and to never mistreat them for amusement because such cruelty will "... demoralize their whole character and harden them against all the sympathies of social life. For, it can be observed that, 'they who delight in the sufferings and destruction of inferior creatures, will not be apt to be very compassionate and benign to those of their own kind.'"[213]

Although God gave man dominion over the animals (Genesis 1:28; 9:2-3), Scripture teaches that the godly person is to help the over-burdened beast, even those of his enemy (Exodus 23:4-5). He gives them proper rest as directed by God (Exodus 20:10). Because he understands and regards their abilities, he wisely places them for labor, not unequally yoking the ox with the donkey (Deuteronomy 22:10). He feeds them well as is evident by the Scripture forbidding the muzzling of the ox when treading out corn (Deuteronomy 25:4). His tender mercy is extended to the little birds so that he will not even take a sitting bird from her little brood (Deuteronomy 22:6). Nor will he cook a goat in its mother's milk (Exodus 23:19), thereby showing tenderness for "relation between parent and child, mother and suckling.[214]

"But the tender mercies of the wicked *are* cruel." "Cruel" means "disposed to give pain in body or mind, destitute of pity, compassion or kindness; applied to persons and their dispositions."[215] "What should be mercy and love are in an evil man only hard-heartedness and cruelty."[216]

The highest level of hypocritical evidence that a truly wicked person might try to muster (to make others believe that he possesses kindness or has regard for life) would actually manifest itself only in cruelty. A truly wicked, godless person has no feelings of mercy because he has *no* regard for God, *no* belief in eternity, and little or no respect for life. He is cruel in his heart, afraid only of getting caught for the evil he does. His conscience is seared, and he refuses the counsel of Scripture. He has no feelings for the life, property, or dignity due to other human beings *or* his animals.

> Genesis 24:31-32 And he said, Come in, thou blessed of the LORD; wherefore standest thou without? for I have prepared the house, and room for the camels. And the man came into the house: and he ungirded his camels, and gave straw and provender for the camels, and water to wash his feet, and the men's feet that *were* with him.
> Genesis 33:13-14 And he said unto him, My lord knoweth that the children *are* tender, and the flocks and herds with young *are* with me: and if men should overdrive them one day, all the flock will die. Let my lord, I pray thee, pass over before his servant: and I will lead on softly, according as the cattle that goeth before me and the children be able to endure, until I come unto my lord unto Seir.
> Exodus 20:10 But the seventh day *is* the sabbath of the LORD thy God: *in it* thou shalt not do any work, thou, nor thy son, nor thy daughter, thy manservant, nor thy maidservant, nor thy cattle, nor thy stranger that *is* within thy gates:
> Exodus 23:4-5 If thou meet thine enemy's ox or his ass going astray, thou shalt surely bring it back to him again. If thou see the ass of him that hateth thee lying under his burden, and wouldest forbear to help him, thou shalt surely help with him.
> Numbers 22:27-33 And when the ass saw the angel of the LORD, she fell down under Balaam: and Balaam's anger was kindled, and he smote the ass with a staff. And the LORD opened the mouth of the ass, and she said unto Balaam, What have I done unto thee, that thou hast smitten me these three times? And Balaam said unto the ass, Because thou hast mocked me: I would there were a sword in mine hand, for now would I kill thee. And the ass said unto Balaam, *Am* not I thine ass, upon which thou hast ridden ever since *I was* thine unto this day? was I ever wont to do so unto thee? And he said, Nay. Then the LORD opened the eyes of Balaam, and he saw the angel of the LORD standing in the way, and his sword drawn in his hand: and he bowed down his head, and fell flat on his face. And the angel of the LORD said unto him, Wherefore hast thou smitten thine ass these three times? behold, I went out to withstand thee, because *thy* way is perverse before me: And the ass saw me, and turned from me these three times: unless she had turned from me, surely now also I had slain thee, and saved her alive.
> Deuteronomy 22:6-7, 10 If a bird's nest chance to be before thee in the way in any tree, or on the ground, whether they be young ones, or eggs, and the dam sitting upon the young, or upon the eggs, thou shalt not take the dam with the young: But thou shalt in any wise let the dam go, and take the young to thee; that it may be well with thee, and that thou mayest prolong thy days...Thou shalt not plow with an ox and an ass together.
> Deuteronomy 25:4 Thou shalt not muzzle the ox when he treadeth out the corn. *[Also see 1 Timothy 5:18; 1 Corinthians 9:9.]*
> Psalm 36:6 Thy righteousness is like the great mountains; thy judgments are a great deep: O LORD, thou preservest man and beast.
> Psalm 145:9 The LORD is good to all: and his tender mercies are over all his works.
> Proverbs 27:23 Be thou diligent to know the state of thy flocks, and look well to thy herds.
> Jonah 4:11 And should not I spare Nineveh, that great city, wherein are more than sixscore thousand persons that cannot discern between their right hand and their left hand; and *also* much cattle?

Proverbs 12:11 He that tilleth his land shall be satisfied with bread: but he that followeth vain *persons is* void of understanding.

Focus: This proverb contrasts the wise, responsible person who labors to be productive with the foolish, irresponsible renegade.

"He that tilleth his land shall be satisfied with bread." **"Tilleth his land"** is a figurative expression that uses *tilling* to describe the entire work process involved in producing a crop. The work extends from tilling the ground to harvesting the crop (not just plowing land). If a person has knowledge of farming and works the land properly, he should enjoy a good harvest that will feed his family. When God's blessings are added, his satisfaction will be even greater.

"But he that followeth vain *persons* is void of understanding." If a person *follows after vain* [empty, worthless] *persons*, rather than taking care of his business, he will receive poverty rather than provision because the land will lay idle, producing nothing. And even worse than a failed crop, his *following after vain people* places him in the company of perpetual trouble. Being with other **"vain *persons*"** encourages foolishness and foolish thinking. It drives a person farther away from God and onto a pathway of perverseness. Notice also the following:

> Psalm 128:2 For thou shalt eat the labour of thine hands: *happy* shalt thou *be*, and *it shall be* well with thee.
> Proverbs 13:20 He that walketh with wise men shall be wise: but a companion of fools shall be destroyed.
> Proverbs 13:23 Much food *is* in the tillage of the poor: but there is *that is* destroyed for want of judgment.
> Proverbs 28:19 He that tilleth his land shall have plenty of bread: but he that followeth after vain persons shall have poverty enough.
> Proverbs 14:23 In all labour there is profit: but the talk of the lips *tendeth* only to penury.
> Ephesians 4:28 Let him that stole steal no more: but rather let him labour, working with *his* hands the thing which is good, that he may have to give to him that needeth.

In the well-known parable of the prodigal son given by Jesus, the foolish son decided to follow after **"vain persons;"** and except for his repentance followed by the forgiveness of his father, he would have spent the remainder of his life in misery and poverty. *[See Luke 15:11-24.]*

The Book of Proverbs identifies five individuals who are **"void of understanding"** as follows:
    (1) those foolish young men lacking wisdom who go to the adulteress' house (7:7);
    (2) those who lack wisdom (10:13);
    (3) those who speak ill of their neighbor (11:12);
    (4) those who are slothful and who sleep rather than care for their vineyard (24:30-31); and
    (5) those foolish ones who follow after vain persons rather than work in the fields. (12:11)

Clearly, persons who are "void of understanding" take self-destructive actions. In each case, the person is not wise enough to understand the consequences of his actions. *(See Proverbs 13:20 above.)*

Proverbs 12:12 The wicked desireth the net of evil *men*: but the root of the righteous yieldeth *fruit*.

Focus: This proverb contrasts the *evil desire of the wicked* with the righteous productivity of the upright.

"The wicked desireth the net of evil *men*." *Nets* are typically used to catch prey, such as fish or animals. Here "net" is used as a figure of speech to symbolize that taken into possession by robbery and depicting that such gain was taken by subtle, insidious means. *"The wicked* emulate each other in wickedness; and if they see *other evil men* more successful than themselves, they *desire their net*; to discover their plans, in order to imitate them. Not satisfied with the honest 'gain of godliness,' they *desire a net*, in which they may grasp richer treasures of this world's vanity."[217] Their "net" is filled with ill-gotten gain obtained through dishonesty and if necessary, with force, employing such criminal methods as lying, stealing, cheating, embezzlement, and perhaps murder.

> "When 'the wicked' see the devices of 'evil men' succeed, they desire to try the same arts. Instead of any moral detestation of the means, they look only at the end. They see that attained. They are envious. They are tempted to imitate; and, there being little or no principle to offer resistance, the desire is at once put into practice. The violation of right sits but lightly on their consciences. The barrier of what men call duty and conscience, is easily thrown down. The sole question is, whether the plan be feasible,-whether it holds out a fair prospect of success."[218]

Psalm 10:8-10 He sitteth in the lurking places of the villages: in the secret places doth he murder the innocent: his eyes are privily set against the poor. He lieth in wait secretly as a lion in his den: he lieth in wait to catch the poor: he doth catch the poor, when he draweth him into his net. He croucheth, *and* humbleth himself, that the poor may fall by his strong ones.

Proverbs 4:16 For they sleep not, except they have done mischief; and their sleep is taken away, unless they cause some to fall.

Proverbs 21:10 The soul of the wicked desireth evil: his neighbour findeth no favour in his eyes.

Proverbs 29:5 A man that flattereth his neighbour spreadeth a net for his feet.

Jeremiah 5:25-28 Your iniquities have turned away these *things,* and your sins have withholden good *things* from you. For among my people are found wicked *men:* they lay wait, as he that setteth snares; they set a trap, they catch men. As a cage is full of birds, so *are* their houses full of deceit: therefore they are become great, and waxen rich. They are waxen fat, they shine: yea, they overpass the deeds of the wicked: they judge not the cause, the cause of the fatherless, yet they prosper; and the right of the needy do they not judge.

Opposite to the desire of the wicked is desire of the righteous for good. The righteous have a relationship with God and consequently prosper because they are *rooted in the doctrines of their God.* They prosper and have plenty, not needing or wanting the "net of evil men." The ***root of the righteous yields fruit*** because the principles they live by are guarded and guided by God; consequently, they are established, stable, blessed, and fruitful without the need or desire for anything belonging to others–especially using any illegal or ungodly means to accomplish their desire.

Psalm 1:3-4 And he shall be like a tree planted by the rivers of water, that bringeth forth his fruit in his season; his leaf also shall not wither; and whatsoever he doeth shall prosper. The ungodly are not so: but are like the chaff which the wind driveth away. *[See also Jeremiah 17:8.]*

Proverbs 10:3 The LORD will not suffer the soul of the righteous to famish: but he casteth away the substance of the wicked.

Proverbs 11:23 The desire of the righteous *is* only good: *but* the expectation of the wicked *is* wrath.

Proverbs 11:27-28 He that diligently seeketh good procureth favour: but he that seeketh mischief, it shall come unto him. He that trusteth in his riches shall fall: but the righteous shall flourish as a branch.

Proverbs 13:21 Evil pursueth sinners: but to the righteous good shall be repayed.

John 15:5 I am the vine, ye are the branches: He that abideth in me, and I in him, the same bringeth forth much fruit: for without me ye can do nothing.

Proverbs 12:13 The wicked is snared by the transgression of his lips: but the just shall come out of trouble.

Focus: This proverb contrasts the wicked's entrapment because of their sinful speech with the liberation that the righteous (just) enjoy because of their godly speech.

"The wicked is snared by the transgression of his lips." Wicked people eventually get caught or snared by the sin revealed through their words. They lie to cover up a previous lie, spew out poisonous words in an attempt to destroy the reputation of others, or plot in a confederate manner to do some evil.

Psalm 64:8 So they shall make their own tongue to fall upon themselves: all that see them shall flee away.

Proverbs 18:6-7 A fool's lips enter into contention, and his mouth calleth for strokes. A fool's mouth *is* his destruction, and his lips *are* the snare of his soul.

Proverbs 21:23 Whoso keepeth his mouth and his tongue keepeth his soul from troubles.

Daniel 6:24 And the king commanded, and they brought those men which had accused Daniel, and they cast *them* into the den of lions, them, their children, and their wives; and the lions had the mastery of them, and brake all their bones in pieces or ever they came at the bottom of the den.

Matthew 27:25 Then answered all the people, and said, His blood *be* on us, and on our children.

"But the just shall come out of trouble." In contrast to the wicked words of the ungodly, truthful words revealing honesty are spoken by righteous people. Because God commands him to love his brother as himself, the **"just"** one is restrained in his speech and avoids being trapped through evil speaking. Even if telling the truth puts the righteous person into a time of tribulation, he will stand before God at the judgment with a clean heart. Also, the upright person is taught by God's word to humble himself and apologize when necessary. He is to live peaceably with all men and to secure honorable relationships.

Proverbs 10:11-14 The mouth of a righteous man is a well of life: but violence covereth the mouth of the wicked. Hatred stirreth up strifes: but love covereth all sins. In the lips of him that hath understanding wisdom is found: but a rod is for the back of him that is void of understanding. Wise men lay up knowledge: but the mouth of the foolish is near destruction.

Proverbs 10:18-21 He that hideth hatred with lying lips, and he that uttereth a slander, is a fool. In the multitude of words there wanteth not sin: but he that refraineth his lips is wise. The tongue of the just is as choice silver: the heart of the wicked is little worth. The lips of the righteous feed many: but fools die for want of wisdom.

Proverbs 11:9 An hypocrite with his mouth destroyeth his neighbour: but through knowledge shall the just be delivered.

Proverbs 11:11 By the blessing of the upright the city is exalted: but it is overthrown by the mouth of the wicked.

Proverbs 11:12 He that is void of wisdom despiseth his neighbour: but a man of understanding holdeth his peace.

Proverbs 11:13 A talebearer revealeth secrets: but he that is of a faithful spirit concealeth the matter.

Proverbs 11:8 The righteous is delivered out of trouble, and the wicked cometh in his stead.

Matthew 12:33-37 Either make the tree good, and his fruit good; or else make the tree corrupt, and his fruit corrupt: for the tree is known by his fruit. O generation of vipers, how can ye, being evil, speak good things? for out of the abundance of the heart the mouth speaketh. A good man out of the good treasure of the heart bringeth forth good things: and an evil man out of the evil treasure bringeth forth evil things. But I say unto you, That every idle word that men shall speak, they shall give account thereof in the day of judgment. For by thy words thou shalt be justified, and by thy words thou shalt be condemned.

Proverbs 12:14 A man shall be satisfied with good by the fruit of *his* mouth: and the recompence of a man's hands shall be rendered unto him.

Focus: This proverb declares that satisfying results (fruit) are produced by good words as well as by good work.

"A man shall be satisfied with good by the fruit of *his* mouth." The godly man has a heart trained by the laws of God; so he knows when to speak and when to remain quiet, and he chooses his words carefully from thoughts that arise from a desire to always stay close to the center of God's will. His wisdom extends to friends and others who seek his counsel, and *he is satisfied because his words prove to be wise.* **"Satisfied"** means to have enough. **"Fruit"** means reward, fruit that results from actions.

"And the recompence of a man's hands shall be rendered unto him." As the verse moves from *fruit of mouth* to **"recompense of a man's hands** *[reward of a person's labor]*,**"** Solomon teaches that *excellent rewards are the product of a righteous man's work.* "Hands" in this verse are symbolic of labor. Just as the righteous man speaks from an upright heart, he also works from an upright heart. He will be known for fairness, quality, work completion, and all the good qualities that a man who desires to please God can produce. He is a man of godly character that is reflected in both his words and his work, and he will be recompensed by God and man.

Job 1:9-10 Then Satan answered the LORD, and said, Doth Job fear God for nought? Hast not thou made an hedge about him, and about his house, and about all that he hath on every side? thou hast blessed the work of his hands, and his substance is increased in the land.

Proverbs 12:18 There is that speaketh like the piercings of a sword: but the tongue of the wise is health.

Proverbs 13:2 A man shall eat good by the fruit of his mouth: but the soul of the transgressors shall eat violence.

Proverbs 14:14 The backslider in heart shall be filled with his own ways: and a good man shall be satisfied from himself.

Proverbs 18:20-21 A man's belly shall be satisfied with the fruit of his mouth; and with the increase of his lips shall he be filled. Death and life are in the power of the tongue: and they that love it shall eat the fruit thereof.

Isaiah 3:10-11 Say ye to the righteous, that *it shall be* well *with him:* for they shall eat the fruit of their doings. Woe unto the wicked! *it shall be* ill *with him:* for the reward of his hands shall be given him.

Matthew 12:37 For by thy words thou shalt be justified, and by thy words thou shalt be condemned.

Proverbs 12:15 The way of a fool *is* right in his own eyes: but he that hearkeneth unto counsel *is* wise.

Focus: This proverb contrasts the self-approved way of a fool with the well-counseled way of a wise person.

A fool doesn't want counsel because he is convinced he is right no matter what anyone else has to say – including the words of Christ and all of Scripture, but a wise man might be heard praying something like "O my God! Save me from myself – from my own self-deceitfulness."[219] The fool's overwhelming danger is his sense of false security which leads him to destruction. It would behoove him to awaken to an acknowledgment of God and an awareness of his own limitations.

Because a wise person has the perception to know that it is impossible for him to independently understand every situation, he not only seeks counsel, but he also hearkens to the same. Scripture verses such as this present one urge the wise person to seek counsel from other sagacious people.

> Proverbs 1:5 A wise man will hear, and will increase learning; and a man of understanding shall attain unto wise counsels . . .
> Proverbs 1:7 The fear of the LORD is the beginning of knowledge: but fools despise wisdom and instruction.
> Proverbs 9:9 Give instruction to a wise man, and he will be yet wiser: teach a just man, and he will increase in learning.
> Proverbs 10:17 He is in the way of life that keepeth instruction: but he that refuseth reproof erreth.
> Proverbs 11:14 Where no counsel is, the people fall: but in the multitude of counsellors there is safety.
> Proverbs 14:12 There is a way which seemeth right unto a man, but the end thereof are the ways of death. *[Also, see 16:25.]*
> Proverbs 14:16 A wise man feareth, and departeth from evil: but the fool rageth, and is confident.
> Proverbs 19:20 Hear counsel, and receive instruction, that thou mayest be wise in thy latter end.
> Proverbs 26:16 The sluggard is wiser in his own conceit than seven men that can render a reason.
> Matthew 7:24-27 Therefore whosoever heareth these sayings of mine, and doeth them, I will liken him unto a wise man, which built his house upon a rock: and the rain descended, and the floods came, and the winds blew, and beat upon that house; and it fell not: for it was founded upon the rock. And every one that heareth these words of mine, and doeth them not, shall be likened unto a foolish man, who built his house upon the sand: and the rain descended, and the floods came, and the winds blew, and smote upon that house; and it fell: and great was the fall thereof.

Proverbs 12:16 A fool's wrath is presently known: but a prudent *man* covereth shame.

Focus: This proverb contrasts the unguarded, demonstrative, wrathful emotions of a fool with the guarded, reticent expressions of the prudent.

"A fool's wrath is presently known" meaning that it is immediate and obvious. "It is to be seen in the fire of his eyes, in the frowns of his face, in the gnashing of his teeth, and in the stamping of his feet, as well as in the bitter expressions of his mouth."[220] Also, his anger stirs up contention. He has no filter on his words or actions and is not restrained by counsel from the Scriptures or from his parents or from wise people. He chooses instead to get support for his irrational behavior from like-minded unwise people.

"But a prudent *man* covereth shame." Regarding his words and conduct, **"a prudent man"** filters and measures his words and actions. He doesn't want to embarrass his Lord or others who love and respect him; consequently, he is concerned about his behavior. In addition, he is a peacemaker, choosing to hide wrath in order to diffuse situations with calmness rather than ignite them with anger. He knows that it is much better to defuse situations than to inflame them. The shame he covers is sometimes his own; and other times, it could be mistakes, shame, reproach, or injurious remarks others have made that he would choose to not expose. He has learned to wait until he has seen every aspect, heard every detail, and received leadership from God before responding. In this proverb, **"covers"** means that he *controls his response* to insults, not that he ignores them.

> Judges 8:1-3 And the men of Ephraim said unto him, Why hast thou served us thus, that thou calledst us not, when thou wentest to fight with the Midianites? And they did chide with him sharply. And he said unto them, What have I done now in comparison of you? *Is* not the gleaning of the grapes of Ephraim better than the vintage of Abiezer? God hath delivered into your hands the princes of Midian, Oreb and Zeeb: and what was I able to do in comparison of you? Then their anger was abated toward him, when he had said that.
> 1 Samuel 10:27 But the children of Belial said, How shall this man save us? And they despised him, and brought him no presents. But he held his peace.
> Esther 3:5 And when Haman saw that Mordecai bowed not, nor did him reverence, then was Haman full of wrath.
> Proverbs 10:12 Hatred stirreth up strifes: but love covereth all sins.
> Proverbs 14:17 *He that is* soon angry dealeth foolishly: and a man of wicked devices is hated.
> Proverbs 14:29 *He that is* slow to wrath *is* of great understanding: but *he that is* hasty of spirit exalteth folly.
> Proverbs 16:32 *He that is* slow to anger *is* better than the mighty; and he that ruleth his spirit than he that taketh a city.
> Proverbs 17:9 He that covereth a transgression seeketh love; but he that repeateth a matter separateth very friends.

Proverbs 19:11 The discretion of a man deferreth his anger; and *it is* his glory to pass over a transgression.

Proverbs 20:3 *It is* an honour for a man to cease from strife: but every fool will be meddling.

Proverbs 25:28 He that hath no rule over his own spirit is like a city that is broken down, and without walls.

Proverbs 29:11 A fool uttereth all his mind: but a wise man keepeth it in till afterwards.

Ecclesiastes 7:9 Be not hasty in thy spirit to be angry: for anger resteth in the bosom of fools.

Daniel 3:19 Then was Nebuchadnezzar full of fury, and the form of his visage was changed against Shadrach, Meshach, and Abednego: *therefore* he spake, and commanded that they should heat the furnace one seven times more than it was wont to be heated.

Matthew 5:9 Blessed are the peacemakers: for they shall be called the children of God.

Matthew 18:15 Moreover if thy brother shall trespass against thee, go and tell him his fault between thee and him alone: if he shall hear thee, thou hast gained thy brother.

Romans 12:18-21 If it be possible, as much as lieth in you, live peaceably with all men. Dearly beloved, avenge not yourselves, but *rather* give place unto wrath: for it is written, Vengeance *is* mine; I will repay, saith the Lord. Therefore if thine enemy hunger, feed him; if he thirst, give him drink: for in so doing thou shalt heap coals of fire on his head. Be not overcome of evil, but overcome evil with good.

2 Timothy 2:23-25 But foolish and unlearned questions avoid, knowing that they do gender strifes. And the servant of the Lord must not strive; but be gentle unto all men, apt to teach, patient, In meekness instructing those that oppose themselves; if God peradventure will give them repentance to the acknowledging of the truth;

James 1:19-20 Wherefore, my beloved brethren, let every man be swift to hear, slow to speak, slow to wrath: For the wrath of man worketh not the righteousness of God.

1 Peter 2:23 Who, when he was reviled, reviled not again; when he suffered, he threatened not; but committed *himself* to him that judgeth righteously:

1 Peter 4:8 And above all things have fervent charity among yourselves: for charity shall cover the multitude of sins.

NOTE: Although the Hebrew word for **"prudent"** (*'arum*) in the Bible may be used in a negative sense, the Book of Proverbs only uses it to describe a positive trait. Notice how the word is used in Proverbs.

Proverbs 12:16 A fool's wrath is presently known: but a prudent *man* covereth shame.

Proverbs 12:23 A prudent man concealeth knowledge: but the heart of fools proclaimeth foolishness.

Proverbs 13:16 Every prudent *man* dealeth with knowledge: but a fool layeth open *his* folly.

Proverbs 14:8 The wisdom of the prudent *is* to understand his way: but the folly of fools *is* deceit.
Proverbs 14:15 The simple believeth every word: but the prudent *man* looketh well to his going.
Proverbs 14:18 The simple inherit folly: but the prudent are crowned with knowledge.

Proverbs 22:3 & 27:12 A prudent *man* foreseeth the evil, and hideth himself: but the simple pass on, and are punished.

In his *Dictionary of American English (1828)*, Noah Webster defines **prudent** as "Cautious; circumspect; practically wise; careful of the consequences of enterprises, measures or actions; cautious not to act when the end is of doubtful utility, or probably impracticable."

Proverbs 12:17 *He that* speaketh truth sheweth forth righteousness: but a false witness deceit.

Focus: This proverb declares that a truthful tongue reflects a righteous heart, and a lying tongue reflects a deceitful heart.

"Witness" in this proverb indicates that a legal matter is likely at hand, and people are being called upon to testify about what they have seen or heard. *["**False witness**" – lying or deceitful testimony-- is presented in Proverbs 6:19, 12:17, 14:5, 19:5, 19:9, and 25:18.]* If the inner man *[heart, mind]* of the witness is righteous, he will speak truthfully, revealing righteousness. He does not have to be under oath to tell the truth because *righteousness* and *truthfulness* are character traits of a godly person, but neither one is a character trait of a fool. If the inner man is a deceiver, he *will* speak false words. A righteous person is compelled to tell the truth, while a deceiver is compelled to speak lies. A righteous person tells the truth because his overwhelming concern is to be pleasing to God; while the deceiver tells lies because his father, the devil, is a deceiver. He speaks whatever he believes will protect his personal interest or give him gain. The heart of a person is revealed by his tongue, which potentially has the power to enable justice with truth or else subvert it with a lie.

Proverbs 6:16-19 These six things doth the LORD hate: yea, seven are an abomination unto him: A proud look, a lying tongue, and hands that shed innocent blood, An heart that deviseth wicked imaginations, feet that be swift in running to mischief, A false witness that speaketh lies, and he that soweth discord among brethren.

Proverbs 13:5 A righteous man hateth lying: but a wicked man is loathsome, and cometh to shame.

Proverbs 14:5 A faithful witness will not lie: but a false witness will utter lies.

Proverbs 14:25 A true witness delivereth souls: but a deceitful witness speaketh lies.

Proverbs 19:5 A false witness shall not be unpunished, and he that speaketh lies shall not escape.

Proverbs 21:28 A false witness shall perish: but the man that heareth speaketh constantly.

Matthew 26:60-61 But found none: yea, though many false witnesses came, yet found they none. At the last came two false witnesses, And said, This fellow said, I am able to destroy the temple of God, and to build it in three days.

Luke 6:45 A good man out of the good treasure of his heart bringeth forth that which is good; and an evil man out of the evil treasure of his heart bringeth forth that which is evil: for of the abundance of the heart his mouth speaketh.

Ephesians 4:22-25 That ye put off concerning the former conversation the old man, which is corrupt according to the deceitful lusts; And be renewed in the spirit of your mind; And that ye put on the new man, which after God is created in righteousness and true holiness. Wherefore putting away lying, speak every man truth with his neighbour: for we are members one of another.

Proverbs 12:18 There is that speaketh like the piercings of a sword: but the tongue of the wise *is* health.

Focus: This proverb compares the wound that can be caused by wicked speaking with the healing that can be accomplished by wise (righteous) speaking.

Words of a false witness, a slanderer, or a backbiter can pierce like a sword, wounding the heart or relationships, dividing families and friends, and even causing death by inciting revenge or suicide. Piercing words can destroy reputations, good names, credibility, and friendships. On the other hand, a wise person can use his speech to heal broken hearts, relationships, divided families, and hurting friends. And because he is known to be a person of strong character, the wise man can have credibility enough, that through wise speech, he can overturn damage done by others–especially in a legal situation involving sworn witnesses. Words of evil men cut and injure others; but the words of wise men heal wounds and bring health, reconciliation, comfort, and encouragement.

> "...words may inflict a more deadly wound than a sword. If spoken *to a man* they may break his heart, if spoken *of him* they may kill his reputation, which no sword of steel can touch, and which to the best men is much more precious than bodily life. A lying or even a *babbling* tongue can pierce a much more vital organ than flesh and blood – it can enter the human spirit, and hurt it in its most sensitive part; or by slander it can destroy all the joy of a man's earthly life. And as a sword can in a moment sever the spirit and the body of a man, and work such ruin and misery as can never be done away with, so a lying tongue may by one word, or one conversation, do mischief that can never be undone. The sword of steel can divide human friends locally; but it cannot sever their love; it tends rather to increase and brighten the flame; but a word of slander may do all this, and estrange those who were bound in the tenderest ties, until the God of Truth shall bring the truth to light. Though the lying tongue is comparatively 'but for a moment,' yet in a moment it can deal a thrust that will last as long as life. It can open a wound whence will flow out all the joy of life, as the heart's blood flows from a mortally wounded man."[221]

Psalm 52:2 Thy tongue deviseth mischiefs; like a sharp razor, working deceitfully.

Psalm 57:4 My soul is among lions: and I lie even among them that are set on fire, even the sons of men, whose teeth are spears and arrows, and their tongue a sharp sword.

Psalm 64:3 Who whet their tongue like a sword, and bend their bows to shoot their arrows, even bitter words:

Proverbs 10:20 The tongue of the just is as choice silver: the heart of the wicked is little worth.

Proverbs 15:4 A wholesome tongue is a tree of life: but perverseness therein is a breach in the spirit.

Proverbs 16:24 Pleasant words are as an honeycomb, sweet to the soul, and health to the bones.

Proverbs 25:18 A man that beareth false witness against his neighbour is a maul, and a sword, and a sharp arrow.

Proverbs 12:25 Heaviness in the heart of man maketh it stoop: but a good word maketh it glad.

Proverbs 15:4 A wholesome tongue is a tree of life: but perverseness therein is a breach in the spirit.

Proverbs 12:19 The lip of truth shall be established for ever: but a lying tongue is but for a moment.

Focus: This proverb contrasts the long endurance of the words of the truth-teller *against* the short life of a lie told by a liar.

"The lip of truth shall be established for ever." The **"lip of truth"** is a figure of speech for *spoken truth*. Truthful words proceed from an honest, truthful heart and mind. Truth spoken by an honest person may be challenged, temporarily disputed, and improperly deemed a lie; but eventually, truth will prevail, thus establishing not only the truth but the honorable person who told the truth. And it should be remembered that God's words are everlasting truth regardless of how often they are disputed.

"But a lying tongue is but for a moment." A **"lying tongue"** is a phrase that is expressive of a spoken lie. Lying words come from a deceitful heart and mind. The lie may prevail momentarily, but the truth will eventually manifest itself, and both the lie and the liar will be disestablished and identified properly.

> "**A lying tongue is but for a moment** – Truth stands for ever; because its foundation is indestructible: but falsehood may soon be detected; and, though it gain credit for a while, it had that credit because it was supposed to be truth."[222]

> Joshua 9:16 And it came to pass at the end of three days after they had made a league with them, that they heard that they *were* their neighbours, and *that* they dwelt among them. *[See Joshua 9:1-27.]*

> Job 20:4-5 Knowest thou not this of old, since man was placed upon earth, That the triumphing of the wicked is short, and the joy of the hypocrite but for a moment?

> Proverbs 12:22 Lying lips are abomination to the LORD: but they that deal truly are his delight.

> Proverbs 19:9 A false witness shall not be unpunished, and *he that* speaketh lies shall perish.

> Matthew 24:35 Heaven and earth shall pass away, but my words shall not pass away.

> Acts 5:3-5 But Peter said, Ananias, why hath Satan filled thine heart to lie to the Holy Ghost, and to keep back *part* of the price of the land? Whiles it remained, was it not thine own? and after it was sold, was it not in thine own power? why hast thou conceived this thing in thine heart? thou hast not lied unto men, but unto God. And Ananias hearing these words fell down, and gave up the ghost: and great fear came on all them that heard these things. *[See Acts 5: 6-10.]*

Proverbs 12:20 Deceit *is* in the heart of them that imagine evil: but to the counsellors of peace *is* joy.

Focus: This proverb *contrasts* the deceit-filled heart of a person known to promote evil *with* the joyous heart of a person known to promote peace.

"Deceit is in the heart of them that imagine evil." They have been deceived by the Deceiver (Satan) and by the deceitfulness of sin into believing that their evil doings will bring joy and victory. Within their **"heart"** *[mind]*, they create a harbor for evil, dreaming up wicked plots against others, thinking to deceive them in some manner and to do them wrong. But evil has a way of boomeranging and becomes like a poison dart to the evil dreamer's heart. Thus, he is forever being deceived himself and hosting sorrow where there should be joy. To say that a person *imagines evil in his heart* is a very clear way of saying that he is *evil in his innermost being* and that he intends to pursue a life of evil. He skillfully carves deceitful, evil imaginations in his mind, just as a talented sculptor would carve an image from stone. Such wickedness produces a miserable lifestyle and a heart where joy is missing. The deceitfulness of those **"that imagine evil"** eventually manifests itself, and such people become known as unhappy deceivers.

"But to the counsellors of peace *is* joy." In contrast to "them that imagine evil," are "counsellors of peace," who have a heart that yearns for and skillfully nurtures peace through truthfulness; and these wonderful people are known for their **"joy."** Psalm 16:11 gives the reason for this "joy" – "Thou wilt shew me the path of life: in thy presence *is* fulness of joy; at thy right hand *there are* pleasures for evermore."

> Proverbs 3:29 Devise not evil against thy neighbour, seeing he dwelleth securely by thee.

> Proverbs 6:14 Frowardness is in his heart, he deviseth mischief continually; he soweth discord.

> Proverbs 12:5 The thoughts of the righteous are right: but the counsels of the wicked are deceit.

> Proverbs 14:8 The wisdom of the prudent is to understand his way: but the folly of fools is deceit.

> Proverbs 14:22 Do they not err that devise evil? but mercy and truth *shall be* to them that devise good.

> Proverbs 15:21 Folly *is* joy to *him that is* destitute of wisdom: but a man of understanding walketh uprightly.

> Jeremiah 17:9-10 The heart is deceitful above all things, and desperately wicked: who can know it? I the LORD search the heart, I try the reins, even to give every man according to his ways, and according to the fruit of his doings.

Micah 2:1 Woe to them that devise iniquity, and work evil upon their beds! when the morning is light, they practise it, because it is in the power of their hand.

Matthew 5:9 Blessed are the peacemakers: for they shall be called the children of God.

Romans 12:18 If it be possible, as much as lieth in you, live peaceably with all men.

Galatians 5:22-23 But the fruit of the Spirit is love, joy, peace, longsuffering, gentleness, goodness, faith, Meekness, temperance: against such there is no law.

1 Peter 3:8-12 Finally, be ye all of one mind, having compassion one of another, love as brethren, be pitiful, be courteous: Not rendering evil for evil, or railing for railing: but contrariwise blessing; knowing that ye are thereunto called, that ye should inherit a blessing. For he that will love life, and see good days, let him refrain his tongue from evil, and his lips that they speak no guile: Let him eschew evil, and do good; let him seek peace, and ensue it. For the eyes of the Lord are over the righteous, and his ears are open unto their prayers: but the face of the Lord is against them that do evil.

Proverbs 12:21   There shall no evil happen to the just: but the wicked shall be filled with mischief.

Focus: This proverb contrasts the *close association with mischief* (evil) that the ungodly have with the *avoidance of mischief* experienced by the godly.

"There shall no evil happen to the just." **"Evil"** *[trouble, wickedness]* in the first half of this verse and **"mischief"** *[evil]* in the second are synonyms and is that which fills the minds of ungodly people. *No evil shall ever **just happen** to the righteous person because* "The steps of a *good* man are ordered by the LORD: and he delighteth in his way." (Psalm 37:23) If evil comes, it is because God chooses to allow it as He did with Job. God provides a hedge for the righteous.

"But the wicked shall be filled with mischief *[evil, (naturally or morally), misery, distress]*.**"**   The wicked do not have God's protection, because the devil is their spiritual father. *Satan does not protect his children; rather he uses them to produce more evil.* Evil befalls the wicked because they live a lifestyle that associates with other ungodly people, their minds are continually on evil, their feet walk with dedication in the direction of mischief, and their bodies are ultimately caught in the entrapments that they set for others. **"The just,"** who are the ones right with God, are spared from this **"mischief"** because they walk a totally different pathway that avoids known evil and is guarded by God. *Mischief fills the wicked* because *inwardly,* they produce and harbor wicked thoughts; *outwardly*, they resist righteous relationships and nurture evil ones; and *upwardly,* they resist God.

Genesis 15:1 After these things the word of the LORD came unto Abram in a vision, saying, Fear not, Abram: I am thy shield, and thy exceeding great reward.

Job 1:9-12 Then Satan answered the LORD, and said, Doth Job fear God for nought? Hast not thou made an hedge about him, and about his house, and about all that he hath on every side? thou hast blessed the work of his hands, and his substance is increased in the land. But put forth thine hand now, and touch all that he hath, and he will curse thee to thy face. And the LORD said unto Satan, Behold, all that he hath is in thy power; only upon himself put not forth thine hand. So Satan went forth from the presence of the LORD.

Psalm 1:3-4 And he shall be like a tree planted by the rivers of water, that bringeth forth his fruit in his season; his leaf also shall not wither; and whatsoever he doeth shall prosper. The ungodly are not so: but are like the chaff which the wind driveth away.

Psalm 5:12 For thou, LORD, wilt bless the righteous; with favour wilt thou compass him as with a shield.

Psalm 18:2 The LORD is my rock, and my fortress, and my deliverer; my God, my strength, in whom I will trust; my buckler, and the horn of my salvation, and my high tower.

Psalm 32:10 Many sorrows *shall be* to the wicked: but he that trusteth in the LORD, mercy shall compass him about.

Psalm 34:7 The angel of the LORD encampeth round about them that fear him, and delivereth them.

Psalm 91:9-10 Because thou hast made the LORD, *which is* my refuge, *even* the most High, thy habitation; There shall no evil befall thee, neither shall any plague come nigh thy dwelling.

Proverbs 1:31 Therefore shall they eat of the fruit of their own way, and be filled with their own devices.

Proverbs 11:8 The righteous is delivered out of trouble, and the wicked cometh in his stead.

Proverbs 11:21 *Though* hand *join* in hand, the wicked shall not be unpunished: but the seed of the righteous shall be delivered.

Proverbs 19:23 The fear of the LORD *tendeth* to life: and *he that hath it* shall abide satisfied; he shall not be visited with evil.

Proverbs 21:10 The soul of the wicked desireth evil: his neighbour findeth no favour in his eyes.

Romans 8:28 And we know that all things work together for good to them that love God, to them who are the called according to *his* purpose

> **Proverbs 12:22** Lying lips are abomination to the LORD: but they that deal truly are his delight.

Focus: This proverb contrasts God's attitude toward those who lie with His attitude toward those who are truthful.

"Lying lips are abomination to the LORD." **"Lying lips"** is a figure of speech representing the entire person who lies. Foundationally, he is ***disgusting*** to God because lying originates from an evil heart that refuses to trust in God. Lying is as much a part of wickedness as truthfulness is a part of righteousness. Truthfulness respects God and others, while lying is self-seeking, disrespectful, and harmful. All relationships are built on trust; and since the liar can't be trusted, he destroys meaningful relationships with God and men.

"But they that deal truly are his delight." **"They that deal truly"** are those who *both* speak and act with honesty to produce truth. God finds these to be **"his delight."** Such a godly person will be upright in every aspect of his business, personal, social, and spiritual life. Righteous people choose to tell the truth because they follow God's instruction, and they believe that God will control the outcome. In this verse, the believer is taught:

> "1. To hate lying, and to keep at the utmost distance from it, because it is an abomination to the Lord, and renders those abominable in his sight that allow themselves in it, not only because it is a breach of his law, but because it is destructive to human society. 2. To make conscience of truth, not only in our words, but in all our actions, because those that *deal truly* and sincerely in all their dealings are *his delight,* and he is well pleased with them. We delight to converse with, and make use of, those that are honest and that we may put a confidence in; such therefore let us be, that we may recommend ourselves to the favour both of God and man."[223]
>
> Psalm 5:6 Thou shalt destroy them that speak leasing *[lying, falsehood]*: the LORD will abhor the bloody and deceitful man.
>
> Proverbs 6:16-19 These six things doth the LORD hate: yea, seven are an abomination unto him: A proud look, a lying tongue, and hands that shed innocent blood, An heart that deviseth wicked imaginations, feet that be swift in running to mischief, A false witness that speaketh lies, and he that soweth discord among brethren.
>
> Proverbs 12:17 He that speaketh truth sheweth forth righteousness: but a false witness deceit.
>
> Proverbs 12:19 The lip of truth shall be established for ever: but a lying tongue is but for a moment.
>
> Proverbs 14:25 A true witness delivereth souls: but a deceitful witness speaketh lies.
>
> Isaiah 9:15 The ancient and honourable, he is the head; and the prophet that teacheth lies, he is the tail.
>
> Ezekiel 13:19 And will ye pollute me among my people for handfuls of barley and for pieces of bread, to slay the souls that should not die, and to save the souls alive that should not live, by your lying to my people that hear your lies?
>
> Ezekiel 13:22 Because with lies ye have made the heart of the righteous sad, whom I have not made sad; and strengthened the hands of the wicked, that he should not return from his wicked way, by promising him life …
>
> Revelation 21:8 But the fearful, and unbelieving, and the abominable, and murderers, and whoremongers, and sorcerers, and idolaters, and all liars, shall have their part in the lake which burneth with fire and brimstone: which is the second death.
>
> Revelation 22:15 For without are dogs, and sorcerers, and whoremongers, and murderers, and idolaters, and whosoever loveth and maketh a lie.

> **Proverbs 12:23** A prudent man concealeth knowledge: but the heart of fools proclaimeth foolishness.

Focus: This proverb contrasts the discreet way that a prudent person shares information with the unrestrained way of a fool's speaking.

"A prudent man concealeth knowledge." A prudent man is able to properly evaluate all the important circumstances concerning his present situation and then speak or act accordingly. His goal will be to minimize, if not totally avoid, any damage to himself or others by his words (or non-verbal responses). He will humble himself, avoiding all glory-seeking and all conversation that has the potential of harming others. He knows that all non-public information doesn't need to be shared and that all personal information needs to be kept secure. It is not a matter of whether or not the prudent man has proper and valuable information to share, but rather whether or not the circumstances are right for him to reveal such. A prudent man is a wise man. *(See verse 16 of this chapter for more information on prudence.)*

> Genesis 42:6-8 And Joseph was the governor over the land, and he it was that sold to all the people of the land: and Joseph's brethren came, and bowed down themselves before him with their faces to the earth. And Joseph saw his brethren, and he knew them, but made himself strange unto them, and spake roughly unto them; and he said unto them, Whence come ye? And they said, From the land of Canaan to buy food. And Joseph knew his brethren, but they knew not him.

Esther 2:10 Esther had not shewed her people nor her kindred: for Mordecai had charged her that she should not shew it.

Ecclesiastes 3:1,7 To every thing there is a season, and a time to every purpose under the heaven . . . A time to rend, and a time to sew; a time to keep silence, and a time to speak;

Matthew 7:6 Give not that which is holy unto the dogs, neither cast ye your pearls before swine, lest they trample them under their feet, and turn again and rend you.

Matthew 17:9 And as they came down from the mountain, Jesus charged them, saying, Tell the vision to no man, until the Son of man be risen again from the dead.

John 16:12-13 I have yet many things to say unto you, but ye cannot bear them now. Howbeit when he, the Spirit of truth, is come, he will guide you into all truth: for he shall not speak of himself; but whatsoever he shall hear, that shall he speak: and he will shew you things to come. *[See also verses below.]*

"But the heart of fools proclaimeth foolishness." A fool doesn't control his speech but blurts out the foolishness that fills his heart. Being driven by pride (and thus resisted by God), he believes that he has all the answers and that everyone needs to hear all he has to say. His concern is for himself, not for the well-being of others, and he doesn't know that he doesn't understand; therefore, his speech reveals a lack of wisdom.

Judges 16:17 That he *[Samson]* told her all his heart, and said unto her, There hath not come a razor upon mine head; for I have been a Nazarite unto God from my mother's womb: if I be shaven, then my strength will go from me, and I shall become weak, and be like any other man.

Ecclesiastes 10:3, 12-14 Yea also, when he that is a fool walketh by the way, his wisdom faileth him, and he saith to every one that he is a fool . . .The words of a wise man's mouth are gracious; but the lips of a fool will swallow up himself. The beginning of the words of his mouth is foolishness: and the end of his talk is mischievous madness. A fool also is full of words: a man cannot tell what shall be; and what shall be after him, who can tell him?

The following verses deal with both wise and foolish speaking.

Proverbs 10:14 Wise *men* lay up knowledge: but the mouth of the foolish *is* near destruction.

Proverbs 10:19 In the multitude of words there wanteth not sin: but he that refraineth his lips is wise.

Proverbs 11:13 A talebearer revealeth secrets: but he that is of a faithful spirit concealeth the matter.

Proverbs 13:16 Every prudent man dealeth with knowledge: but a fool layeth open his folly.

Proverbs 14:33 Wisdom resteth in the heart of him that hath understanding: but *that which is* in the midst of fools is made known.

Proverbs 15:2 The tongue of the wise useth knowledge aright: but the mouth of fools poureth out foolishness.

Proverbs 29:11 A fool uttereth all his mind: but a wise *man* keepeth it in till afterwards.

Proverbs 12:24 The hand of the diligent shall bear rule: but the slothful shall be under tribute.

Focus: This proverb stresses that a "diligent" person will eventually have victory or "bear rule" over the designated task; and using a play on words, the proverb states that the lazy person will be bound to the task.

"Diligent" *[determined, eager]* is further explained by Noah Webster as "steady in application to business, constant in effort or exertion to accomplish what is undertaken, industrious, not idle or negligent."[224] Diligent persons are the ones who typically rise to positions of leadership because they eagerly see a task through to the end; but the opposite is true for the **"slothful"** who have their minds set on stopping all work rather than completing the job, thus causing such lazy persons to **"be under tribute"** or under the control of the task, project, or chore which rules them rather than their ruling it. The task beats them or conquers them.

"Slothful" *[remissness, laxness, deceit, treachery, idleness]* is further explained by Webster as "remiss; backward; not using due diligence; not earnest or eager; as slack in duty or service; slack in business."[225] A slothful person has an element of deceitfulness about him (as is implied by the definition); and when left without supervision, he won't work enough to provide food and will eventually have to beg. For such a slothful person to be improperly placed in a position of leadership brings defeat and discouragement to everyone involved.

A country under tribute means that the conquered country is subject to the victor and forced to pay the demanded tax or tribute. When an individual is put **"under tribute,"** he has been defeated, made subject to another, and forced to do labor.

1 Kings 11:28 And the man Jeroboam was a mighty man of valour: and Solomon seeing the young man that he was industrious, he made him ruler over all the charge of the house of Joseph.

Proverbs 10:4 He becometh poor that dealeth with a slack hand: but the hand of the diligent maketh rich.

Proverbs 13:4 The soul of the sluggard desireth, and *hath* nothing: but the soul of the diligent shall be made fat.

Proverbs 22:29 Seest thou a man diligent in his business? he shall stand before kings; he shall not stand before mean men.

Ecclesiastes 9:10 Whatsoever thy hand findeth to do, do it with thy might; for there is no work, nor device, nor knowledge, nor wisdom, in the grave, whither thou goest.

Matthew 25:21 His lord said unto him, Well done, thou good and faithful servant: thou hast been faithful over a few things, I will make thee ruler over many things: enter thou into the joy of thy lord.

Romans 12:11 Not slothful in business; fervent in spirit; serving the Lord . . .

Colossians 3:23-24 And whatsoever ye do, do it heartily, as to the Lord, and not unto men; Knowing that of the Lord ye shall receive the reward of the inheritance: for ye serve the Lord Christ.

Proverbs 12:25. Heaviness in the heart of man maketh it stoop: but a good word maketh it glad.

Focus: This proverb declares the good effect that proper words can have on a depressed individual.

"Heaviness in the heart of man maketh it stoop." "Heaviness" *[anxiety, fear, or sorrow]* can be triggered by a several sources, including guilt from sin, ill health, bad finances, poor relationships, improper communications, despairing news, failures of various kinds, and so on. Anxiety causes a man to stoop because he is weighed down and depressed over a situation. He is unhappy and his body shows it by stooping *[bowing down]*.

"In the heart" is synonymous with *in the mind,* but the *heart* is typically referenced when emotions are a significant factor. Emotion can, on various levels, either have a negative impact and overpower good rationale or have a positive effect and enhance one's ability to reason. A person's happiness will be directly affected depending on how the "heart" processes news of any kind.

"**'A good word maketh it glad.'** Such words sometimes take the form of a promise of help. A man bowed down by disease is made glad by the word of the physician, which assures him that his malady can be cured. The debtor who feels himself hopelessly involved is made glad by the promise of one who engages to meet his debts. The man who is bowed down under a sense of guilt is lifted out of his heaviness by the promises of a forgiving God. In all these cases the worth of the word depends upon the character of him who utters them. It is a 'good word' if it is not only a *cheering* word, but a *reliable* word – if the promise is uttered by one whom we know would not promise what he was unable to perform. It is this certainty which makes every promise of God so *good* a *word* to the soul. And when a man's heaviness of heart arises from a source which is beyond the power of human help, there is no greater service that a friend can do him than to remind him of some 'good word' of the Heavenly Father which is suitable to his case."[226]

It is the good word of God that has a profound effect on the heart of a believer, especially when given from the mouth of a trusted preacher or simply from the heart of a friend. Such words are powerful and uplifting. Notice how words can comfort in the following verses.

2 Chronicles 32:8 With him *is* an arm of flesh; but with us *is* the LORD our God to help us, and to fight our battles. And the people rested themselves upon the words of Hezekiah king of Judah.

Psalm 42:10-11 As with a sword in my bones, mine enemies reproach me; while they say daily unto me, Where is thy God? Why art thou cast down, O my soul? and why art thou disquieted within me? hope thou in God: for I shall yet praise him, who is the health of my countenance, and my God.\

Proverbs 12:18 There is that speaketh like the piercings of a sword: but the tongue of the wise is health.

Proverbs 15:23 A man hath joy by the answer of his mouth: and a word spoken in due season, how good is it!

Proverbs 16:24 Pleasant words are as an honeycomb, sweet to the soul, and health to the bones.

Proverbs 25:11 A word fitly spoken is like apples of gold in pictures of silver.

Proverbs 27:9 Ointment and perfume rejoice the heart: so doth the sweetness of a man's friend by hearty counsel.

Isaiah 50:4 The Lord GOD hath given me the tongue of the learned, that I should know how to speak a word in season to him that is weary: he wakeneth morning by morning, he wakeneth mine ear to hear as the learned.

Matthew 11:28-29 Come unto me, all *ye* that labour and are heavy laden, and I will give you rest. Take my yoke upon you, and learn of me; for I am meek and lowly in heart: and ye shall find rest unto your souls.

Matthew 14:26-27 And when the disciples saw him walking on the sea, they were troubled, saying, It is a spirit; and they cried out for fear. But straightway Jesus spake unto them, saying, Be of good cheer; it is I; be not afraid.

2 Corinthians 1:3-4 Blessed *be* God, even the Father of our Lord Jesus Christ, the Father of mercies, and the God of all comfort; Who comforteth us in all our tribulation, that we may be able to comfort them which are in any trouble, by the comfort wherewith we ourselves are comforted of God.

Proverbs 12:26 The righteous is more excellent than his neighbour: but the way of the wicked seduceth them.

Focus: This proverb declares that the righteous have a way about them that helps their neighbor while the wicked have a way about them that causes harm.

Examining the second clause of this proverb helps in understanding the first. The **"way"** *[course of action, moral character, habit]* of the **"wicked"** person is to seduce or *[lead another person astray,]* as their own wicked, unstable mind leads themselves farther astray. The wicked constantly plan to be unjust, to steal, to wound another's spirit or body, and to hate both neighbor and God. They have no intention of doing good, but **"the righteous is more excellent than his neighbor."** Neighbor in this context is general, meaning simply other people (who are implied to be either *not* righteous or immature believers). The righteous **"is more excellent"** because he is capable of leading others to an abundant life where there is peace, prosperity, and quality of living and where men honor and respect each other and worship God. The significant difference between the righteous and the wicked is that the godly person leads his neighbor in a **"more excellent"** path toward God, while "the wicked" seduces his neighbor to err from the godly path and turn to the wicked's way.

> *"More excellent* is he in character, *more abundant* in privilege, *than his neighbour*, be his external advantage and endowments ever so great. Look at his birth, a child of God; his dignity, a king; his connections, a member of the family of heaven; his inheritance, a title to both worlds; his food, the bread of everlasting life; his clothing, the righteousness of the Savior; his prospects, infinite and everlasting joy.
>
> *Mark the honour which his God puts upon him.* He is the fullness of Christ; 'the temple of the Holy Ghost,' throwing the splendor of Solomon's temple into the shade. Angels, while 'beholding the face of their Father which is in heaven,' count it an honour to 'minister to him as an heir of salvation.'
>
> And then – passing to the last contemplation – see him in the full enjoyment of his present prospects, 'carried by the angels into Abraham's bosom;' 'entering into the joy of his Lord;' welcome before the assembled world; then fixed on the throne of his Lord, to be with him, near him, like him, for ever – what are *his neighbour's* prospects, but as hell compared with heaven? Can we doubt this testimony – *The righteous is more excellent than his neighbour?*'"[227]

Psalm 28:3 Draw me not away with the wicked, and with the workers of iniquity, which speak peace to their neighbours, but mischief *is* in their hearts.

Psalm 122:8-9 For my brethren and companions' sakes, I will now say, Peace *be* within thee. Because of the house of the LORD our God I will seek thy good.

Proverb 3:29 Devise not evil against thy neighbour, seeing he dwelleth securely by thee.

Proverbs 14:12 There is a way which seemeth right unto a man, but the end thereof are the ways of death.

Proverbs 15:9 The way of the wicked is an abomination unto the LORD: but he loveth him that followeth after righteousness.

Proverbs 16:29 A violent man enticeth his neighbour, and leadeth him into the way *that is* not good.

Proverbs 21:10 The soul of the wicked desireth evil: his neighbour findeth no favour in his eyes.

Proverbs 12:27 The slothful *man* roasteth not that which he took in hunting: but the substance of a diligent man *is* precious.

Focus: This proverb contrasts the *value* that diligent people place on important things with the *disregard* that the slothful have for the same.

"The slothful *man* roasteth not that which he took in hunting." A **"slothful man"** doesn't want to expend energy, so he devalues anything that might require work to obtain or retain. In this proverb, he had enough energy to go hunting. However, the effort was probably a deceitful attempt to give others a false impression that he had some level of conscientiousness. Whatever may have inspired him to make the minimal effort wasn't sufficient to encourage him to complete the process of converting the carcass into a meal. He had neither respect for the carcass as a source of food nor energy for the task. Slothful people have an overwhelming characteristic of quitting before a project is finished, but a dominant characteristic of a diligent person is to stay with a project until it is complete.

Proverbs 13:4 The soul of the sluggard desireth, and hath nothing: but the soul of the diligent shall be made fat.

Proverbs 21:25 The desire of the slothful killeth him; for his hands refuse to labour.

Proverbs 26:15 The slothful hideth his hand in his bosom; it grieveth him to bring it again to his mouth.

Ecclesiastes 9:10 Whatsoever thy hand findeth to do, do it with thy might; for there is no work, nor device, nor knowledge, nor wisdom, in the grave, whither thou goest.

Colossians 3:23-24 And whatsoever ye do, do it heartily, as to the Lord, and not unto men; Knowing that of the Lord ye shall receive the reward of the inheritance: for ye serve the Lord Christ.

2 Thessalonians 3:10 For even when we were with you, this we commanded you, that if any would not work, neither should he eat.

"But the substance of a diligent man *is* precious." "The substance *[riches or sufficiency]* **of a diligent man is precious** *[highly-valued],***"** meaning whatever thing of value a "diligent man" has is respected by him, considered important, and given value. Webster's definition of **"diligent"** is worthy of repeating here. He states that "diligent" means "steady in application to business, constant in effort or exertion to accomplish what is undertaken, industrious, not idle or negligent."[228] A diligent person eagerly puts forth whatever energy and determination are necessary. He stays with the project to the end, and gives proper care and protection for his property. He is diligent *because* he understands value and considers his efforts worthwhile. It is important to remember that diligence is an attribute of God; hence it is an attribute sought after by the righteous who do everything possible to both mimic and to obey Him.

Isaiah 40:28 Hast thou not known? hast thou not heard, *that* the everlasting God, the LORD, the Creator of the ends of the earth, fainteth not, neither is weary? *there is* no searching of his understanding.

Unquestionably, Jesus was diligent in every matter seeing every task to completion.

Luke 9:51 And it came to pass, when the time was come that he should be received up, he stedfastly set his face to go to Jerusalem

John 5:17 But Jesus answered them, My Father worketh hitherto, and I work.

Proverbs 12:28 In the way of righteousness *is* life; and in the pathway *thereof there is* no death.

Focus: This proverb promises that the earthly pathway of the righteous is one of abundant life followed by immortality for eternity.

"In the way of righteousness *is* life." The **"way of righteousness"** is the "highway," the "way of holiness" on which the ones who are right with God travel with Him. This proverb is similar to Proverbs 12:21, "There shall no evil happen to the just: but the wicked shall be filled with mischief." In both these proverbs, the righteous walk a supernaturally protected and preserved pathway. Righteous conduct is righteous because it agrees with the instructions of God taken from Scripture. It is conduct that believes and trusts in God and avoids evil and evil people.

"And in the pathway *thereof there is* no death." The wicked walk a way of impending death, both temporally and eternally. They have rejected God, His word, and His Son. And their deeds, as well as their associations, are, by choice, evil. **"There is no death"** *in the way of the righteous* because the way is designed by God, who dedicated it for His children, and He will deliver them to Heaven. Death has no claim on them because His Son has paid the price of sin with His own perfect, sinless life. They will put off this flesh only as a means to acquire a new body that will last for eternity. God, the Author of life, takes up abode with them. The "second death" has absolutely no power over them.

"The way of righteousness is the way of God's salvation in which his children come to him; the way of his commandments, in which they love to walk with him. (Isaiah 35:8) *In this way is* present life (Proverbs 8:35; 10:16), a passage from death unto life eternal. (John 5:24) Enjoying the sense of God's love; confiding in his unspeakable, satisfying friendship; consecrating ourselves in spiritual devotedness to his service; anticipating the fullness of his eternal joy – this is *life* indeed for – eternity. For where the life of grace is possessed, the life of glory is secured. It is 'hid with Christ in God' (Colossians 3:3); so that – ' because I live, ye shall live also.' (John 14:19)"

"In this pathway there is no death. (John 8:51; 11:25) The curse of the first death hath passed away. The power of the second death cannot hurt. (Revelation 2:11; 20:6) 'The body is dead because of sin.' (Romans 8:10; 5:12) Yet it 'sleeps,' rather than dies, under the care of Jesus. (Acts 7:60; 1Thessalonians 4:14) Surely the bitterness of death is passed. Now, 'O death! where is thy sting?' (1Corinthians 15:55) Sheathed in the body of Jesus."[229]

Deuteronomy 30:15-20 See, I have set before thee this day life and good, and death and evil; In that I command thee this day to love the LORD thy God, to walk in his ways, and to keep his commandments and his statutes and his judgments, that thou mayest live and multiply: and the LORD thy God shall bless thee in the land whither thou goest to possess it. But if thine heart turn away, so that thou wilt not hear, but shalt be drawn away, and worship other gods, and serve them; I denounce unto you this day, that ye shall surely perish, *and that* ye shall not prolong *your* days upon the land, whither thou passest over Jordan to go to possess it. I call heaven and earth to record this day against you, *that* I have set before you life and death, blessing and cursing: therefore choose life, that both thou and thy seed may live: That thou mayest love the LORD thy God, *and* that thou mayest obey his voice, and that thou mayest cleave unto him: for he *is* thy life, and the length of thy days: that thou mayest dwell in the land which the LORD sware unto thy fathers, to Abraham, to Isaac, and to Jacob, to give them.

Psalm 5:8 Lead me, O LORD, in thy righteousness because of mine enemies; make thy way straight before my face.

Proverbs 8:20 I lead in the way of righteousness, in the midst of the paths of judgment . . .

Proverbs 8:35-36 For whoso findeth me findeth life, and shall obtain favour of the LORD. But he that sinneth against me wrongeth his own soul: all they that hate me love death.

Proverbs 9:10-11 The fear of the LORD is the beginning of wisdom: and the knowledge of the holy is understanding. For by me thy days shall be multiplied, and the years of thy life shall be increased.

Proverbs 10:2 Treasures of wickedness profit nothing: but righteousness delivereth from death.

Proverbs 10:16 The labour of the righteous tendeth to life: the fruit of the wicked to sin.

Proverbs 11:5-6 The righteousness of the perfect shall direct his way: but the wicked shall fall by his own wickedness. The righteousness of the upright shall deliver them: but transgressors shall be taken in *their own* naughtiness.

Proverbs 11:19 As righteousness tendeth to life: so he that pursueth evil pursueth it to his own death.

Proverbs 15:9 The way of the wicked *is* an abomination unto the LORD: but he loveth him that followeth after righteousness.

Proverbs 16:17 The highway of the upright *is* to depart from evil: he that keepeth his way preserveth his soul.

Proverbs 16:25 There is a way that seemeth right unto a man, but the end thereof *are* the ways of death.

Isaiah 35:8 And an highway shall be there, and a way, and it shall be called The way of holiness; the unclean shall not pass over it; but it *shall be* for those: the wayfaring men, though fools, shall not err *therein*.

Ezekiel 18:9 Hath walked in my statutes, and hath kept my judgments, to deal truly; he is just, he shall surely live, saith the Lord GOD.

John 8:51 Verily, verily, I say unto you, If a man keep my saying, he shall never see death.

John 11:25 Jesus said unto her, I am the resurrection, and the life: he that believeth in me, though he were dead, yet shall he live:

Romans 5:21 That as sin hath reigned unto death, even so might grace reign through righteousness unto eternal life by Jesus Christ our Lord.

Romans 6:21-23 What fruit had ye then in those things whereof ye are now ashamed? for the end of those things is death. But now being made free from sin, and become servants to God, ye have your fruit unto holiness, and the end everlasting life. For the wages of sin is death; but the gift of God is eternal life through Jesus Christ our Lord.

Romans 8:6 For to be carnally minded *is* death; but to be spiritually minded *is* life and peace.

CHAPTER THIRTEEN

> **Proverbs 13:1** A wise son *heareth* his father's instruction: but a scorner heareth not rebuke.

Focus: This proverb contrasts the willingness of a wise son to hear instruction ("rebuke") with the refusal of the scorner to hear.

"A wise son" is *eager to listen and be taught*. He will follow through with obedience – as is implied by the meaning of the word **hear**. The father's instruction is from Scripture which reproves, rebukes and exhorts. (2 Timothy 4:2)

Contrariwise, a **"scorner"** blocks out all **"rebuke"** *[chiding, reproof]*. Webster defines a **"scorner"** as "in Scripture, one who scoffs at religion, its ordinances and teachers, and who makes a mock of sin and the judgments and threatenings of God against sinners."[230] The godly parent gives God's instructions to the child, but at some point this child rejects that instruction and begins to think he is wiser than his parents or God. He begins to delight in making fun of his godly parents and deriding the truths of Scripture. At this point he has gone past the stage of quietly resisting to openly mocking his father's instruction – he has become a "scorner." It becomes apparent that he has neither fear of God or respect for others. Scripture states that he is an abomination to men, that reproof of the scorner only gains shame for the reprover, that he will hate anyone who reproves him, and that wherever he is there is contention. (Some righteous parents lose their boldness in his presence, and others sadly realize that he will face many hardships in this life, and live in eternity without God.)

> Proverbs 3:34 Surely he scorneth the scorners: but he giveth grace unto the lowly.
> Proverbs 9:7-9 He that reproveth a scorner getteth to himself shame: and he that rebuketh a wicked man getteth himself a blot. Reprove not a scorner, lest he hate thee: rebuke a wise man, and he will love thee. Give instruction to a wise man, and he will be yet wiser: teach a just man, and he will increase in learning.
> Proverbs 10:17 He is in the way of life that keepeth instruction: but he that refuseth reproof erreth.
> Proverbs 12:1 Whoso loveth instruction loveth knowledge: but he that hateth reproof is brutish.
> Proverbs 14:6-7 A scorner seeketh wisdom, and findeth it not: but knowledge is easy unto him that understandeth. Go from the presence of a foolish man, when thou perceivest not *in him* the lips of knowledge.
> Proverbs 15:5 A fool despiseth his father's instruction: but he that regardeth reproof is prudent.
> Proverbs 15:12 A scorner loveth not one that reproveth him: neither will he go unto the wise.
> Proverbs 17:10 A reproof entereth more into a wise man than an hundred stripes into a fool.
> Proverbs 19:29 Judgments are prepared for scorners, and stripes for the back of fools.
> Proverbs 21:11 When the scorner is punished, the simple is made wise: and when the wise is instructed, he receiveth knowledge.
> Proverbs 22:10, 12 Cast out the scorner, and contention shall go out; yea, strife and reproach shall cease...The eyes of the LORD preserve knowledge, and he overthroweth the words of the transgressor.
> Proverbs 24:9 The thought of foolishness is sin: and the scorner is an abomination to men.

> **Proverbs 13:2** A man shall eat good by the fruit of *his* mouth: but the soul of the transgressors *shall eat* violence.

Focus: This proverb contrasts the peaceful, beneficial results that redound to a righteous man because of his words with the violent, cursed results that redound to a transgressor because of his words.

"A man shall eat good by the fruit of *his* mouth." **"Fruit of *his* mouth"** is a phrase used three times in Proverbs to mean the good *or* bad produced by a person's words. A person's words come out of the heart and indicate his deep-seated beliefs and feelings. Proverbs 11:23 states, "The desire of the righteous *is* only good: *but* the expectation of the wicked *is* wrath." The righteous person speaks words from a heart that desires only good; consequently, his words bring good to himself and others. He ministers good to himself when he speaks or instructs others, and others reap good to themselves from his words. The phrase **"eat good"** is used metaphorically to describe the good that comes back to him.

> "The sense is, that a good man brings forth good things out of the good treasure of his heart by his mouth; which not only minister grace to the hearers, and are for the use of edifying to others, but also to himself; while he gives wholesome counsel and advice to others, it is of service to himself; while he comforts others, he comforts himself; and while he teaches and instructs others, he teaches and instructs himself: so a good minister of Jesus Christ, while he feeds others with knowledge and understanding, he himself is nourished up with the words of faith and good doctrine."[231]

> "The man who is charitable in his judgments, and disposed to speak well of others, will be himself the subject of charitable judgment and of cordial commendation. All will love, and honour, and bless the man 'in whose tongue is the law of kindness.' Thus he 'shall eat good by the fruit of his mouth.'"[232]

" But the soul of the transgressors *shall eat* violence." "Transgressors" *[deceitful, treacherous, faithless, wicked people]* bring retribution on themselves because of hateful communication. Their wicked desire for evil and injury to others is reflected in their speech, and it comes back on themselves. They consume (eat) violence that they intended for others. According to Vines' *Dictionary of Old Testament Words*, **"violence"** means wrong or maliciousness and violent wrongdoing; and it "connotes the disruption of the divinely established order of things."[233]

The words of a transgressor, whether they are deceitful, violent, hateful, derogatory, or in some other way improper, cause an unpleasant reaction in the person who hears them. When the listener receives words, he evaluates them and then determines the extent he is willing to interact verbally, emotionally, and spiritually with the one talking. Wise people learn to walk away from the volatile words of wicked people, but others may react "in kind" or in the way that they are spoken to. Often, communication has as much to do with how the words are spoken as it does with actual words. *Angry, hateful, mean-spirited tones reflect the transgressor's wicked heart.*

Proverbs 10:14 Wise men lay up knowledge: but the mouth of the foolish is near destruction.
Proverbs 10:20 The tongue of the just is as choice silver: the heart of the wicked is little worth.
Proverbs 12:14 A man shall be satisfied with good by the fruit of his mouth: and the recompence of a man's hands shall be rendered unto him.
Proverbs 12:18 There is that speaketh like the piercings of a sword: but the tongue of the wise is health.
Proverbs 14:3 In the mouth of the foolish is a rod of pride: but the lips of the wise shall preserve them.
Proverbs 15:23 A man hath joy by the answer of his mouth: and a word spoken in due season, how good is it!
Proverbs 18:6-7 A fool's lips enter into contention, and his mouth calleth for strokes. A fool's mouth is his destruction, and his lips are the snare of his soul.
Proverbs 18:20-21 A man's belly shall be satisfied with the fruit of his mouth; and with the increase of his lips shall he be filled. Death and life are in the power of the tongue: and they that love it shall eat the fruit thereof.
Matthew 12:37 For by thy words thou shalt be justified, and by thy words thou shalt be condemned.
Luke 6:45 A good man out of the good treasure of his heart bringeth forth that which is good; and an evil man out of the evil treasure of his heart bringeth forth that which is evil: for of the abundance of the heart his mouth speaketh.

A believer who is walking with God will always strive to have godly communication. **"A man shall eat good by the fruit of his mouth"** shows that *good reactions* will come to those who choose words with discretion and speak them in a proper manner. Bad reactions are the consequence of the ***transgressor's*** *words*. A wise person is a godly person who speaks with tones of love and kindness; consequently, he receives in kind.

Proverbs 13:3 He that keepeth his mouth keepeth his life: *but* he that openeth wide his lips shall have destruction.

Focus: This proverb emphasizes a proven fact that a wise man who considers and chooses his words carefully will avoid trouble, whereas a man who speaks hastily and rashly brings on trouble.

If a person can keep or guard his speech, he can, in many cases, keep his life from unnecessary damage. The person who opens wide his lips, saying whatever comes to mind without discretion, is racing toward **"destruction."** Every wise person desires to **keep** *[to hedge about, guard, protect]* **his life,** thereby giving quality to his time on earth. A person with a run-away, unfiltered mouth is not trusted to be discreet, to develop good relationships, *or* to be wise in everyday dealings.

An unfiltered tongue reveals a heart that lacks understanding and the ability to avoid the pitfalls of life that are disruptive and destructive to peace, comfort, stability, and civility.

> "A guard upon the lips is a guard to the soul. He that is cautious, that thinks twice before he speaks once, that, if he have *thought evil, lays his hand upon his mouth* to suppress it, that keeps a strong bridle on his tongue and a strict hand on that bridle, he *keeps his soul* from a great deal both of guilt and grief and saves himself the trouble of many bitter reflections on himself and reflections of others upon him.
>
> There is many a one ruined by an ungoverned tongue. *He that opens widely his lips,* to let his *quod in buccam venerit - whatever comes uppermost;* that loves to bawl, and bluster, and make a noise, and affects such a liberty of speech as bids defiance both to God and man, he *shall have destruction.* It will be the destruction of his reputation, his interest, his comfort, and his soul for ever."[234]

> "Two things are clear. (1) But for the blood of Christ, the mass of guilt from the sins of the tongue would have condemned us for ever; and (2) in proportion as the 'little member' is bridled, 'the peace of God rules in the heart.'"[235]

Psalm 34:11-13 Come, ye children, hearken unto me: I will teach you the fear of the LORD. What man *is he that* desireth life, *and* loveth *many* days, that he may see good? Keep thy tongue from evil, and thy lips from speaking guile. Depart from evil, and do good; seek peace, and pursue it.

Psalm 39:1 To the chief Musician, even to Jeduthun, A Psalm of David. I said, I will take heed to my ways, that I sin not with my tongue: I will keep my mouth with a bridle, while the wicked is before me.

Psalm 141:3 Set a watch, O LORD, before my mouth; keep the door of my lips.

Proverbs 10:6 Blessings *are* upon the head of the just: but violence covereth the mouth of the wicked.

Proverbs 12:13 The wicked is snared by the transgression of his lips: but the just shall come out of trouble.

Proverbs 14:3 In the mouth of the foolish *is* a rod of pride: but the lips of the wise shall preserve them.

Proverbs 21:23 Whoso keepeth his mouth and his tongue keepeth his soul from troubles.

Matthew 12:37 For by thy words thou shalt be justified, and by thy words thou shalt be condemned.

James 1:26 If any man among you seem to be religious, and bridleth not his tongue, but deceiveth his own heart, this man's religion is vain.

James 3:6 And the tongue *is* a fire, a world of iniquity: so is the tongue among our members, that it defileth the whole body, and setteth on fire the course of nature; and it is set on fire of hell.

Proverbs 13:4 The soul of the sluggard desireth, and *hath* nothing: but the soul of the diligent shall be made fat.

> Focus: This proverb states that both the sluggard and the diligent have desires but the sluggard has nothing, and the diligent is satisfied.

Used in verses two, three, and four, *nephesh* – translated as **"the soul"** or **"life"** – refers to a man's being, especially that part of him which can understand and have desire. The soul is composed of the mind, the emotions, and the will. In his mind, he observes and consequently desires – all of which require no exertion of energy or effort – he is simply thinking. Both the sluggard and the diligent are alike in having desire.

However, **"The soul of the sluggard desireth, and *hath* nothing." "Sluggard"** *[indolent, slothful, sluggish, lazy]* is used 14 times in the Book of Proverbs and in no other book of the Old Testament. If the man is a **"sluggard,"** he sees something and would like to possess it, but he will not exert himself because he has only wish-power but no will-power. He desires the gains but avoids the pains that the diligent employ to obtain what is wanted. He will not expend the energy necessary to get possession. The thing desired could be physical or spiritual. He might crave a new table, but obtaining it would require work. He might wish to be a Christian, but he can never bring himself to read the Bible or go hear a sermon; and if he did manage to read God's word once or twice or listen to a sermon, he wouldn't have the energy to follow through. The issue is not that the sluggard cannot comprehend the good things of life, including a personal relationship with God and men; it is because he doesn't care to expend the energy. Consequently, he has **"nothing."** He has no good relationship with God or men and lacks the comfort given a man who honors God with his work ethic.

> "He wastes his strength and life in unsatisfied longings for something which he has not energy to gain. The wish to do great or good things may sometimes be taken for the deed, but if the hindrance is from a man's own sloth, it does but add to his condemnation."[236]

Ecclesiastes 9:10 Whatsoever thy hand findeth to do, do it with thy might; for there is no work, nor device, nor knowledge, nor wisdom, in the grave, whither thou goest.

Proverbs 10:4 He becometh poor that dealeth *with* a slack hand: but the hand of the diligent maketh rich.

Proverbs 20:4 The sluggard will not plow by reason of the cold; *therefore* shall he beg in harvest, and *have* nothing.

Proverbs 21:25 The desire of the slothful killeth him; for his hands refuse to labour.

Matthew 25:24-29 Then he which had received the one talent came and said, Lord, I knew thee that thou art an hard man, reaping where thou hast not sown, and gathering where thou hast not strawed: And I was afraid, and went and hid thy talent in the earth: lo, there thou hast that is thine. His lord answered and said unto him, Thou wicked and slothful servant, thou knewest that I reap where I sowed not, and gather where I have not strawed: Thou oughtest therefore to have put my money to the exchangers, and then at my coming I should have received mine own with usury. Take therefore the talent from him, and give it unto him which hath ten talents. For unto every one that hath shall be given, and he shall have abundance: but from him that hath not shall be taken away even that which he hath.

2 Thessalonians 3:10-12 For even when we were with you, this we commanded you, that if any would not work, neither should he eat. For we hear that there are some which walk among you disorderly, working not at all, but are busybodies. Now them that are such we command and exhort by our Lord Jesus Christ, that with quietness they work, and eat their own bread.

A **"diligent"** person *("steady in application to business, constant in effort or exertion to accomplish what is undertaken, industrious, not idle or negligent"[237])* has both *desire* and *determination* to meet the need. The diligent is *steady* in his business application, constant in effort and exertion to accomplish his task, attentive to his work, and industrious and not idle. He is careful to do things right. No wonder the Scriptures state in Proverbs 22:9 – "Seest thou a man diligent in his business? he shall stand before kings; he shall not stand before mean *men*."

"But the soul of the diligent shall be made fat." His soul is **"made fat"** or is satisfied because he has made a steady and consistent effort to get the thing desired. "Fatness, the sleek, well-filled look of health, becomes the figure of prosperity, as leanness of misfortune."[238] **"Diligent"** people are rewarded with the sense of being satisfied with the accomplishments of their labor, and then with the ability to get other things because of their labor.

Proverbs 12:24 The hand of the diligent shall bear rule: but the slothful shall be under tribute.

Romans 12:11 Not slothful in business; fervent in spirit; serving the Lord;

Galatians 6:9 And let us not be weary in well doing: for in due season we shall reap, if we faint not.

Colossians 3:23 And whatsoever ye do, do *it* heartily, as to the Lord, and not unto men; Knowing that of the Lord ye shall receive the reward of the inheritance: for ye serve the Lord Christ.

2 Peter 1:5-11 And beside this, giving all diligence, add to your faith virtue; and to virtue knowledge; And to knowledge temperance; and to temperance patience; and to patience godliness; And to godliness brotherly kindness; and to brotherly kindness charity. For if these things be in you, and abound, they make you that ye shall neither be barren nor unfruitful in the knowledge of our Lord Jesus Christ. But he that lacketh these things is blind, and cannot see afar off, and hath forgotten that he was purged from his old sins. Wherefore the rather, brethren, give diligence to make your calling and election sure: for if ye do these things, ye shall never fall: For so an entrance shall be ministered unto you abundantly into the everlasting kingdom of our Lord and Saviour Jesus Christ.

"There is a general principle here that lazy people want things in their 'inner man, appetite' *nephesh*, but often don't get them because of their laziness. They lie in bed and let the years slip away. In contrast diligent people set about things, and get what they want and more. Thus their 'inner men' will be 'made fat', that is, will prosper and enjoy prosperity.

But in the context of guiding and listening, and of solid teaching there is here special reference to the gathering of wisdom and truth. The lazy person wants to have wisdom and understanding, and every now and then he wants to know God and His word, but he never gets round to seeking them. Thus he ends up spiritually poor. Indeed he ends up with nothing that is worthwhile. But the one who from his heart (his inner person) diligently seeks, and makes an effort to understand, will not only find, but will grow and enjoy fullness of blessing. What such people receive they will 'roast', in other words, will take time and effort over it in order to enjoy it to the full. They will enjoy what is most precious in the earth."[239]

Proverbs 6:6-11 Go to the ant, thou sluggard; consider her ways, and be wise: Which having no guide, overseer, or ruler, Provideth her meat in the summer, *and* gathereth her food in the harvest. How long wilt thou sleep, O sluggard? when wilt thou arise out of thy sleep? *Yet* a little sleep, a little slumber, a little folding of the hands to sleep: So shall thy poverty come as one that travelleth, and thy want as an armed man.

Proverbs 12:27 The slothful *man* roasteth not that which he took in hunting: but the substance of a diligent man *is* precious.

Proverbs 13:5   A righteous *man* hateth lying: but a wicked *man* is loathsome, and cometh to shame.

Focus: This proverb specifies that a *hate for lying* shields the righteous person from the offensiveness and shame that shrouds a wicked liar.

"A righteous man hateth lying" in himself and in others for several reasons, including the following: (1) Because God commands him not to lie. (2) Because lying would identify him with Satan and condemn him as ungodly. (3) Because lying is wicked, he despises the shame that covers a **"wicked man"** like a cloak. (4) Because one lie has to be supported by an additional lie creating an unstable, shameful life. (5) Because lying is evidence of mistrusting God.

"**But a wicked *man* is loathsome**" meaning that he "'causes' or 'spreads a stink.'"[240] Furthermore, he stinks in the nostrils of those desiring to be truthful and honorable in the sight of God. He is morally offensive **"and cometh to shame"** for the following reasons: (1) He can never be trusted. Once he is labeled as a liar, men expect a lie every time he talks. (2) His lies materialize with damage to lives causing ill will to reflect on the liar. (3) His lies breach relationships causing any person who trusted him to become cynical and to have mistrust in other potentially good relationships that rely on truth for good, effective communication.

When the wicked person's lies are discovered on earth, he is put to shame for only as long as he lives; but when he faces God, he will be put to shame eternally in Hell. "And yet how often, even in the Church, is this feature of godliness obscured! Is not strict truth often sacrificed to courtesy? Is not *lying* sometimes acted, insinuated, or implied, where we should be ashamed of plainly speaking it? Is not the simple truth often colored with exaggeration? "Abstain from all appearance of evil" (1Thessalonians 5:22) is the rule for the man of God. Commit the tongue to the only safe ordering, the restraint and guidance of the God of Truth. (Psalm 19:14; 141:3)"[241]

> Psalm 19:14 Let the words of my mouth, and the meditation of my heart, be acceptable in thy sight, O LORD, my strength, and my redeemer.
> Psalm 119:163 I hate and abhor lying: but thy law do I love.
> Psalm 141:3 Set a watch, O LORD, before my mouth; keep the door of my lips.
> Proverbs 3:35 The wise shall inherit glory: but shame shall be the promotion of fools.
> Proverbs 6:16-17 These six things doth the LORD hate: yea, seven are an abomination unto him: A proud look, a lying tongue, and hands that shed innocent blood . . .
> Proverbs 12:22 Lying lips *are* abomination to the LORD: but they that deal truly *are* his delight.
> Proverbs 30:8 Remove far from me vanity and lies: give me neither poverty nor riches; feed me with food convenient for me . . .
> Daniel 3:16-18 Shadrach, Meshach, and Abednego, answered and said to the king, O Nebuchadnezzar, we *are* not careful to answer thee in this matter. If it be *so,* our God whom we serve is able to deliver us from the burning fiery furnace, and he will deliver *us* out of thine hand, O king. But if not, be it known unto thee, O king, that we will not serve thy gods, nor worship the golden image which thou hast set up.
> Ephesians 4:25 Wherefore putting away lying, speak every man truth with his neighbour: for we are members one of another.
> Colossians 3:9 Lie not one to another, seeing that ye have put off the old man with his deeds . . .
> Revelation 21:8 But the fearful, and unbelieving, and the abominable, and murderers, and whoremongers, and sorcerers, and idolaters, and all liars, shall have their part in the lake which burneth with fire and brimstone: which is the second death.

Proverbs 13:6   Righteousness keepeth *him that is* upright in the way: but wickedness overthroweth the sinner.

Focus: This proverb declares that righteousness serves to guard the way of an upright individual, whereas wickedness serves to endanger and ruin the sinner.

"Righteousness keepeth *him that is* upright in the way." "Righteousness" *[Holy and upright living in accordance with God's standard]* is rightness with God. A person who is right with God listens to His instructions and abides by those wise commands; consequently, he is given discretion to keep him from the evil man and the strange woman, as is taught in Chapter Two. Discretion is his first line of defense. Righteous, wise living is a consequence of an obedient right relationship with God and it ***keeps*** (guards) the **"upright"** *[righteous]* by *preventing him* from being at evil places where violence is a potential, by *positioning him* in proper places where God can bless with peace and safety, and by *procuring him* a personal communication link with God so that he can always be sensitive to His leadership. As Ephesians 6:14 states, righteousness is like a breastplate keeping the godly protected from the many arrows of sin.

> Genesis 7:1 And the LORD said unto Noah, Come thou and all thy house into the ark; for thee have I seen righteous before me in this generation.
> Psalm 25:21 Let integrity and uprightness preserve me; for I wait on thee.
> Psalm 26:1 A Psalm of David. Judge me, O LORD; for I have walked in mine integrity: I have trusted also in the LORD; therefore I shall not slide.
> Psalm 119:105 NUN. Thy word is a lamp unto my feet, and a light unto my path.
> Proverbs 2:11 Discretion shall preserve thee, understanding shall keep thee . . .

Proverbs 4:4-6 He taught me also, and said unto me, Let thine heart retain my words: keep my commandments, and live. Get wisdom, get understanding: forget *it* not; neither decline from the words of my mouth. Forsake her not, and she shall preserve thee: love her, and she shall keep thee.

Proverbs 11:3-6 The integrity of the upright shall guide them: but the perverseness of transgressors shall destroy them. Riches profit not in the day of wrath: but righteousness delivereth from death. The righteousness of the perfect shall direct his way: but the wicked shall fall by his own wickedness. The righteousness of the upright shall deliver them: but transgressors shall be taken in their own naughtiness.

Proverbs 12:21 There shall no evil happen to the just: but the wicked shall be filled with mischief.

Ephesians 6:14 Stand therefore, having your loins girt about with truth, and having on the breastplate of righteousness . . .

2 Peter 2:7-9 And delivered just Lot, vexed with the filthy conversation of the wicked: (For that righteous man dwelling among them, in seeing and hearing, vexed *his* righteous soul from day to day with *their* unlawful deeds;) The Lord knoweth how to deliver the godly out of temptations, and to reserve the unjust unto the day of judgment to be punished:

"But wickedness overthroweth *[ruins]* **the sinner."** Because the sinner is guided by wickedness, he goes to dangerous, evil places where other sinners go; and he learns from them how to be even more wicked. His wickedness is self-perpetuating because he refuses instruction and any communication with God. The wickedness he loves separates him from God and godly people both here on earth and eternally.

The Bible describes King Ahaz's overthrow – "For he sacrificed unto the gods of Damascus, which smote him: and he said, Because the gods of the kings of Syria help them, *therefore* will I sacrifice to them, that they may help me. But they were the ruin of him, and of all Israel." (2 Chronicles 28:23)

"**Wickedness Is the Sinner's Ruin.**
1. It exhausts his property. Sin is a very expensive thing. The passions are clamorous, exorbitant, and reckless, till gratified.
2. It blasts his reputation. Sin can never be deemed honorable, on correct principles.
3. It destroys his health. Intemperance has a natural tendency to undermine the best constitution.
4. It hastens the approach of death.
5. It effects the damnation of the soul. Coming to sin beyond remedy, he goes to his own place."[242]

Psalm 140:11 Let not an evil speaker be established in the earth: evil shall hunt the violent man to overthrow him.

Proverbs 5:21-23 For the ways of man are before the eyes of the LORD, and he pondereth all his goings. His own iniquities shall take the wicked himself, and he shall be holden with the cords of his sins. He shall die without instruction; and in the greatness of his folly he shall go astray.

Proverbs 21:12 The righteous man wisely considereth the house of the wicked: but God overthroweth the wicked for their wickedness.

Proverbs 13:7 There is that maketh himself rich, yet *hath* nothing: *there is* that maketh himself poor, yet *hath* great riches.

Focus: This proverb contrasts two individuals whose **apparent** physical wealth is inconsistent with their **actual** spiritual well-being.

"There is that maketh himself rich, yet *hath* nothing." *Being wise and living wisely* is the fundamental theme that permeates all of the Book of Proverbs. The wise person is often contrasted with the fool, the godly with the wicked, the sluggard with the industrious. Here, in this verse, the *rich toward God (wise) is contrasted with those who are rich toward the world (the foolish)*.

The person in the first clause *makes himself rich* with the goods of this life, yet he has **"nothing"** with God, **"nothing"** of eternal value. His life is empty; his riches do not satisfy. He does not enjoy the comfort he has worked to obtain because he has no relationship with his Creator. Obviously God is not helping him, and his wealth is coming through earthly wisdom.

"*There is* that maketh himself poor, yet *hath* great riches." The person of the second clause has *made himself poor*. Outwardly he seems to be just another poor man, yet he has wealth sufficient for his every need. He decreases his wealth by helping others, yet he has **"great riches."** Because he is righteous, he has determined that he will have nothing that God doesn't want him to have. He follows God's directives for wisdom and waits on Him to provide; thus, he has **"great riches"** in his spiritual relationship with God. He is content and satisfied with whatever material things that God provides. A person satisfied with God and thus with himself is wealthy indeed.

Genesis 14:22-15:1 And Abram said to the king of Sodom, I have lift up mine hand unto the LORD, the most high God, the possessor of heaven and earth, That I will not *take* from a thread even to a shoelatchet, and that I will not take any thing that *is* thine, lest thou shouldest say, I have made Abram rich: Save only that which the young men have eaten, and the portion of the men which went with me, Aner, Eshcol, and Mamre; let them take their portion. After these things the word of the LORD came unto Abram in a vision, saying, Fear not, Abram: I *am* thy shield, *and* thy exceeding great reward.

Genesis 39:3 And his master saw that the LORD *was* with him, and that the LORD made all that he did to prosper in his hand.

Deuteronomy 29:9 Keep therefore the words of this covenant, and do them, that ye may prosper in all that ye do.

1 Kings 2:1 Now the days of David drew nigh that he should die; and he charged Solomon his son, saying, I go the way of all the earth: be thou strong therefore, and shew thyself a man; And keep the charge of the LORD thy God, to walk in his ways, to keep his statutes, and his commandments, and his judgments, and his testimonies, as it is written in the law of Moses, that thou mayest prosper in all that thou doest, and whithersoever thou turnest thyself . . .

Psalm 112:1-3 Praise ye the LORD. Blessed is the man that feareth the LORD, that delighteth greatly in his commandments. His seed shall be mighty upon earth: the generation of the upright shall be blessed. Wealth and riches shall be in his house: and his righteousness endureth for ever.

Proverbs 8:20-21 I lead in the way of righteousness, in the midst of the paths of judgment: That I may cause those that love me to inherit substance; and I will fill their treasures.

Proverbs 11:24 There is that scattereth, and yet increaseth; and *there is* that withholdeth more than is meet, but *it tendeth* to poverty.

Proverbs 15:6 In the house of the righteous is much treasure: but in the revenues of the wicked is trouble.

Proverbs 21:20 There is treasure to be desired and oil in the dwelling of the wise; but a foolish man spendeth it up.

Ecclesiastes 5:13-14 There is a sore evil which I have seen under the sun, namely, riches kept for the owners thereof to their hurt. But those riches perish by evil travail: and he begetteth a son, and there is nothing in his hand.

2 Corinthians 6:10 As sorrowful, yet alway rejoicing; as poor, yet making many rich; as having nothing, and yet possessing all things.

Revelation 3:17-18 Because thou sayest, I am rich, and increased with goods, and have need of nothing; and knowest not that thou art wretched, and miserable, and poor, and blind, and naked: I counsel thee to buy of me gold tried in the fire, that thou mayest be rich; and white raiment, that thou mayest be clothed, and *that* the shame of thy nakedness do not appear; and anoint thine eyes with eyesalve, that thou mayest see.

Proverbs 13:8   The ransom of a man's life *are* his riches: but the poor heareth not rebuke.

Focus: This proverb contrasts the reaction of a rich man to a major threat against his life with the reaction of a poor man to a "threat" as minor as a rebuke.

"The ransom of a man's life *are* his riches."   A rich person relies on his wealth (not on God) for every aspect of his life: such as safety, health, comfort, luxury, friends, and needs. If his life is threatened, he might be able to pay a ransom *[price of a life, bribe]* and thus get himself out of trouble. Not only does he have the threat of some envious person wanting to take his riches in court, or his family fears someone will kidnap him for ransom, but he also has a daily fear that someone will break in and steal some of his valuables. He hires bodyguards and puts up locks and walls and gates to protect himself. He is often arrogant because of having a large amount of wealth, an attitude which also encourages others to attack him in one way or another. He always has an element of fear that keeps him from total peace and is always on guard anticipating a predator. The rich man responds to his threats and fears by trusting in his riches.

However, some rich people, such as Abraham, are not vulnerable to such threats. He was wealthy and at the same time totally dependent on God, even though he had a trained army. Such a wealthy person is at peace knowing that God is his provider and protector.

"But the poor heareth not rebuke." The poor person is not fearfully protective of his wealth because he doesn't have any. Obviously poor people don't get threatened for ransom; thus, they avoid the threats faced by the rich person. Additionally, they will typically exhibit a humble spirit so as not to provoke others, and such a spirit of humility invokes pity rather than hostility.   Unless a man were insane as well as wicked, he wouldn't envy, or prosecute, or defraud, or demand a ransom from a man who has nothing.   But if someone did manage to issue a **"rebuke"** (threat) to the poor person, he would ***not so much as hear*** the same.

> **"The ransom of a man's life are his riches.** A rich man can save himself from many difficulties and dangers by the sacrifice of a portion of his wealth, *e.g.* when his money or his life is demanded by a robber; when men in authority make extortionate demands on pain of death; or when he has incurred extreme penalty by infringement of law. . . **The poor heareth not rebuke;** has not to listen to threats from the covetous or abuse from the envious. He has nothing to lose, and no one can gain anything by interfering with him. So the poor man is at peace. 'A hundred men cannot rob one pauper.'"[243]

> Psalm 49:6-10 They that trust in their wealth, and boast themselves in the multitude of their riches; None of them can by any means redeem his brother, nor give to God a ransom for him: (For the redemption of their soul is precious, and it ceaseth for ever:) That he should still live for ever, and not see corruption. For he seeth that wise men die, likewise the fool and the brutish person perish, and leave their wealth to others.

In an interesting historical note related to this verse, when Babylon conquered Israel, the king carried away 832 persons (Jeremiah 52:29). The rest were either killed or died by famine or deserted to the Babylonians so that only the poor of the land were left behind to till the ground and take care of the vineyards. Jeremiah 39:10 states, "But Nebuzaradan the captain of the guard left of the poor of the people, which had nothing, in the land of Judah, and gave them vineyards and fields at the same time." Matthew Henry comments:

> "Sometimes poverty is a protection; for those that have nothing have nothing to lose. When the rich Jews, who had been oppressive to the poor, were made strangers, nay, prisoners, in an enemy's country, the poor whom they had despised and oppressed had liberty and peace in their own country. Thus Providence sometimes remarkably humbles the proud and favours those of low degree."[244]
>
> 2 Kings 25:11-12 Now the rest of the people *that were* left in the city, and the fugitives that fell away to the king of Babylon, with the remnant of the multitude, did Nebuzaradan the captain of the guard carry away. But the captain of the guard left of the poor of the land *to be* vinedressers and husbandmen.

An application for this proverb involves the payment for the sin debt. No man has enough riches to pay his way out of hell. On this ground, the rich and the poor are equal. They both must obtain salvation on the same basis. Proverbs 22:2 states, "The rich and poor meet together: the LORD *is* the maker of them all." He provided Himself the salvation for all men who would believe.

> 1 Peter 1:18-21 Forasmuch as ye know that ye were not redeemed with corruptible things, *as* silver and gold, from your vain conversation *received* by tradition from your fathers; But with the precious blood of Christ, as of a lamb without blemish and without spot: Who verily was foreordained before the foundation of the world, but was manifest in these last times for you, Who by him do believe in God, that raised him up from the dead, and gave him glory; that your faith and hope might be in God.

Proverbs 13:9   The light of the righteous rejoiceth: but the lamp of the wicked shall be put out.

Focus: This proverb contrasts the rejoicing growing light of the righteous with the sad diminishing lamp of the wicked.

"The light of the righteous rejoiceth." **"Light"** primarily means illumination, and symbolically, it denotes comprehension. **"The light of the righteous"** is the radiance of God that surrounds them. It is initiated by an indwelling of God whereby the believer's entire life is modified so that he radiates the presence of God joyfully from himself. Such illumination ***"rejoiceth** [grows or brightens, gleesome]"* the more the righteous person studies and lives to serve God. His life shines in this dark world to become a guide whereby individuals can come to know God and His Son.

> "Who can estimate the worth of a Christian's bright shining *light?* (Matthew 5:14-16; Philippians 2:15; Proverbs 4:18) Happy in his own soul, like his counterpart in the heavens, he sheds a *joyous* light around him. But how glowing, then, is the light of the Church in the combined shining of all her members! Many of them have no remarkable individual splendour; yet, like the lesser stars forming the milky way, they present a bright path of holiness in the spiritual firmament. This happy heavenly *light* 'shineth into perfect day,' and that day will never set. (Isaiah 60:19-20) Sometimes it may be obscured, but only that it may break out more gloriously (Micah 7:8); and soon will it be a day without a cloud. (Revelation 21:23-24)"[245]
>
> Psalm 112:4 Unto the upright there ariseth light in the darkness: he is gracious, and full of compassion, and righteous.
>
> Psalm 119:105 NUN. Thy word is a lamp unto my feet, and a light unto my path.
>
> Psalm 119:130 The entrance of thy words giveth light; it giveth understanding unto the simple.
>
> Proverbs 4:18 But the path of the just is as the shining light, that shineth more and more unto the perfect day.
>
> Proverbs 6:23 For the commandment is a lamp; and the law is light; and reproofs of instruction are the way of life . . .
>
> Matthew 5:14-16 Ye are the light of the world. A city that is set on an hill cannot be hid. Neither do men light a candle, and put it under a bushel, but on a candlestick; and it giveth light unto all that are in the house. Let your light so shine before men, that they may see your good works, and glorify your Father which is in heaven.
>
> Ephesians 5:8 For ye were sometimes darkness, but now *are ye* light in the Lord: walk as children of light:
>
> Philippians 2:15 That ye may be blameless and harmless, the sons of God, without rebuke, in the midst of a crooked and perverse nation, among whom ye shine as lights in the world . . .
>
> 1 Peter 2:9 But ye *are* a chosen generation, a royal priesthood, an holy nation, a peculiar people; that ye should shew forth the praises of him who hath called you out of darkness into his marvellous light:

Revelation 21:23 And the city had no need of the sun, neither of the moon, to shine in it: for the glory of God did lighten it, and the Lamb is the light thereof.

"But the lamp of the wicked shall be put out." God makes Himself known to the wicked when he views creation, associates with the righteous, and perhaps even hears Scripture; still, he considers the concept of God as being ridiculous. Since he has refused any understanding of God and His word, he must depend on his own foolish thoughts to guide his steps; consequently, he stumbles in spiritual darkness. What illumination he has been exposed to only grows dimmer through rejection and will be **"put out"** at his death, and he will meet with the total darkness of hell. His **"lamp"** is dim, at best, and short-lived.

"The wicked have their *lamp,* a cold profession of the name of religion. But being without oil, it will soon *be put out* (Job 18:5-6; Matthew 25:8). Even while it lasts, it *rejoiceth not.* It sheds no light upon the soul. It guides no fellow-pilgrim with its light. Fearful will be the end. He takes his leave of the light of this world, only to enter into eternal darkness, without even a flickering ray to cheer 'the blackness of darkness for ever.'(Psalm 49:19; Matthew 22:13)"[246]

Job 18:5-6 Yea, the light of the wicked shall be put out, and the spark of his fire shall not shine. The light shall be dark in his tabernacle, and his candle shall be put out with him.

Job 21:17 How oft is the candle of the wicked put out! and how oft cometh their destruction upon them! God distributeth sorrows in his anger.

Psalms 49:19 He shall go to the generation of his fathers; they shall never see light.

Proverbs 4:19 The way of the wicked is as darkness: they know not at what they stumble.

Proverbs 24:20 For there shall be no reward to the evil man; the candle of the wicked shall be put out.

Matthew 22:13 Then said the king to the servants, Bind him hand and foot, and take him away, and cast *him* into outer darkness; there shall be weeping and gnashing of teeth. *[See also Matthew 22:22-13.]*

Matthew 25:8 And the foolish said unto the wise, Give us of your oil; for our lamps are gone out.

Proverbs 13:10 Only by pride cometh contention: but with the well advised is wisdom.

Focus: This proverb declares that pride produces contention but that humility seeks counsel to wisely avoid contention.

"Only by pride cometh contention." Struggles between people often appear to begin over material issues dealing with money, personal possessions, and property or else over moral issues such as lying and stealing; however, as one uncovers the layers of words and committed deeds, he will discover that **"pride"** *[unyielding arrogance]* is the basis. Pride fosters and encourages ungodly character, such as lying, stealing, and grabbing for possessions. It is also the poison that kills relationships. Pride moves an otherwise peaceful situation to one of contention. Ignorance, covetousness, and mistakes can spark contention; but pride is the fuel that makes the situations burn.

"But with the well advised is wisdom." Always an evil to contend with, pride causes a person to believe that he deserves more, that somehow he has been robbed of that which is due him, or that he thinks of himself as superior to others in mind or matter. But the humble spirit of a wise man causes him to prudently consider and seek counsel to find the best solution and avoid contention. For him to be **"well advised,"** he must obtain from other wise people and Scripture a comprehensive evaluation of self and situation so that he is aware of his own strengths and weaknesses, as well as the righteous way of conducting himself. Wisdom persuades a person to act according to prudence rather than passion.

Judges 12:1 And the men of Ephraim gathered themselves together, and went northward, and said unto Jephthah, Wherefore passedst thou over to fight against the children of Ammon, and didst not call us to go with thee? we will burn thine house upon thee with fire.

Proverbs 11:2 When pride cometh, then cometh shame: but with the lowly is wisdom.

Proverbs 12:15 The way of a fool is right in his own eyes: but he that hearkeneth unto counsel is wise.

Proverbs 21:24 Proud and haughty scorner is his name, who dealeth in proud wrath.

Proverbs 28:25 He that is of a proud heart stirreth up strife: but he that putteth his trust in the LORD shall be made fat.

Matthew 20:21, 24 And he said unto her, What wilt thou? She saith unto him, Grant that these my two sons may sit, the one on thy right hand, and the other on the left, in thy kingdom . . . And when the ten heard it, they were moved with indignation against the two brethren.

Luke 22:24 And there was also a strife among them, which of them should be accounted the greatest.

1 Corinthians 3:3-4 For ye are yet carnal: for whereas there is among you envying, and strife, and divisions, are ye not carnal, and walk as men? For while one saith, I am of Paul; and another, I am of Apollos; are ye not carnal?

Philippians 2:3 Let nothing be done through strife or vainglory; but in lowliness of mind let each esteem other better than themselves.

James 4:6-10 But he giveth more grace. Wherefore he saith, God resisteth the proud, but giveth grace unto the humble. Submit yourselves therefore to God. Resist the devil, and he will flee from you. Draw nigh to God, and he will draw nigh to you. Cleanse your hands, ye sinners; and purify your hearts, ye double minded. Be afflicted, and mourn, and weep: let your laughter be turned to mourning, and your joy to heaviness. Humble yourselves in the sight of the Lord, and he shall lift you up.

3 John 1:9-10 I wrote unto the church: but Diotrephes, who loveth to have the preeminence among them, receiveth us not. Wherefore, if I come, I will remember his deeds which he doeth, prating against us with malicious words: and not content therewith, neither doth he himself receive the brethren, and forbiddeth them that would, and casteth *them* out of the church.

Proverbs 13:11 Wealth *gotten* by vanity shall be diminished: but he that gathereth by labour shall increase.

Focus: This proverb compares the end result of wealth acquired by vanity with the end result of wealth gained through labor.

"Wealth *gotten* by vanity shall be diminished." "Wealth gotten by vanity" is gained through *[empty, transitory, and unsatisfactory]* means such as gambling, theft, trickery, exploitation, or fraud. "Wealth gotten by vanity will be bestowed upon vanity."[247] The recipient usually spends his ill-gotten gain lavishly, unnecessarily, and extravagantly. Such gain lacks the blessings of God and will eventually suffer the consequences of His displeasure. Wealth received by some kind of windfall (or even an inheritance) is seldom respected.

"But he that gathereth by labour shall increase." Wealth gotten by **"labor"** is likely to be cared for because the laborer is aware of the effort put into getting it. If the laborer is wise, he recalls his responsibility to God to be a good steward of what God has provided. Also, "The steps of a *good* man are ordered by the LORD;" thus, encouraging him to work with a spirit of excellence, with honesty, and with a promise of God's blessing.

Wisely-handled wealth will naturally **"increase"** when there are no extenuating circumstances, such as a national disaster or bad health. Because he is wise, he will not spend wastefully in a manner that is demonstrative of pride or for the luxury of others. His handling of finances is blessed of God and therefore his wealth increases.

Jeremiah 17:11 As the partridge sitteth on eggs, and hatcheth *them* not; so he that getteth riches, and not by right, shall leave them in the midst of his days, and at his end shall be a fool.

Proverbs 10:2 Treasures of wickedness profit nothing: but righteousness delivereth from death.

Proverbs 13:22 A good *man* leaveth an inheritance to his children's children: and the wealth of the sinner *is* laid up for the just.

Proverbs 20:21 An inheritance *may be* gotten hastily at the beginning; but the end thereof shall not be blessed.

Proverbs 21:6 The getting of treasures by a lying tongue *is* a vanity tossed to and fro of them that seek death.

Proverbs 23:4-5 Labour not to be rich: cease from thine own wisdom. Wilt thou set thine eyes upon that which is not? for *riches* certainly make themselves wings; they fly away as an eagle toward heaven.

Ephesians 4:28 Let him that stole steal no more: but rather let him labour, working with *his* hands the thing which is good, that he may have to give to him that needeth.

Proverbs 13:12 Hope deferred maketh the heart sick: but *when* the desire cometh, *it is* a tree of life.

Focus: This proverb contrasts how deferred hope affects a person with how fulfilled hope affects him.

"Hope deferred maketh the heart sick." If a person believes the instruction of God's word, acts on it, and consequently expects God to honor His word, he does so with **"hope"** *[expectation]*. "The delay of what is anxiously hoped for is very painful to the mind; obtaining it is very pleasant. But spiritual blessings are chiefly intended."[248] When the promised outcome is or seems to be delayed (**"hope deferred"**), the person becomes grieved and disappointed (**"heart sick"**). But, when the expected outcome finally comes and hope has turned into reality, then the person's joy is rejuvenated. To have hope fulfilled is healthy for body, soul, and spirit.

Psalms describes how David felt during his time of "hope deferred."

Psalm 42:1-5 **To the chief Musician, Maschil, for the sons of Korah.** As the hart panteth after the water brooks, so panteth my soul after thee, O God. My soul thirsteth for God, for the living God: when shall I come and appear before God? My tears have been my meat day and night, while they continually say unto me, Where *is* thy God? When I remember these *things*, I pour out my soul in me: for I had gone with the multitude, I went with them to the house of God, with the voice of joy and praise, with a multitude that kept holyday. Why art thou cast down, O my soul? and *why* art thou disquieted in me? hope thou in God: for I shall yet praise him *for* the help of his countenance.

Psalm 69:3 I am weary of my crying: my throat is dried: mine eyes fail while I wait for my God.

Psalm 143:7 Hear me speedily, O LORD: my spirit faileth: hide not thy face from me, lest I be like unto them that go down into the pit.

"But *when* the desire cometh, *it is* a tree of life." Before man sinned in the Garden of Eden, the **"tree of life'** was an actual tree and the means ordained by God for the preservation of lasting life and continual vigor and health. **"The tree of life,"** as referenced in this verse, is symbolic of that which sustains life. When something hoped for is fully realized, the result is that the person's whole being is invigorated. True wisdom maintains man in the spiritual life of God's grace, and the communion of his Spirit.[249] The wise person believes God and waits for the fulfillment of His promises, whereas the fool has no hope. Instead of hope, he scoffs at God's word. To be without hope means to expect no solution or answer or fulfillment. Indeed, without God, there is no hope.

Genesis 21:6-7 And Sarah said, God hath made me to laugh, so that all that hear will laugh with me. And she said, Who would have said unto Abraham, that Sarah should have given children suck? for I have born him a son in his old age.

Genesis 46:30 And Israel said unto Joseph, Now let me die, since I have seen thy face, because thou art yet alive.

1 Samuel 1:26-28 And she said, Oh my lord, as thy soul liveth, my lord, I am the woman that stood by thee here, praying unto the LORD. For this child I prayed; and the LORD hath given me my petition which I asked of him: Therefore also I have lent him to the LORD; as long as he liveth he shall be lent to the LORD. And he worshipped the LORD there.

Psalm 40:2-3 He brought me up also out of an horrible pit, out of the miry clay, and set my feet upon a rock, and established my goings. And he hath put a new song in my mouth, even praise unto our God: many shall see it, and fear, and shall trust in the LORD.

Proverbs 3:5-8 Trust in the LORD with all thine heart; and lean not unto thine own understanding. In all thy ways acknowledge him, and he shall direct thy paths. Be not wise in thine own eyes: fear the LORD, and depart from evil. It shall be health to thy navel, and marrow to thy bones.

Proverbs 3:18 She is a tree of life to them that lay hold upon her: and happy is every one that retaineth her.

Luke 2:29-30 Lord, now lettest thou thy servant depart in peace, according to thy word: For mine eyes have seen thy salvation,

John 16:22 And ye now therefore have sorrow: but I will see you again, and your heart shall rejoice, and your joy no man taketh from you.

Romans 4:18 Who against hope believed in hope, that he might become the father of many nations, according to that which was spoken, So shall thy seed be.

Proverbs 13:13 Whoso despiseth the word shall be destroyed: but he that feareth the commandment shall be rewarded.

Focus: This proverb contrasts the destruction that comes to a person who despises God's word with the rewards that come to one who has reverential fear of His word.

"Whoso despiseth the word shall be destroyed." To hate God's instruction and to despise His word is the epitome of foolishness, arrogance, and pride. If he despises God's word, he is certain to disobey it. When one thinks that he knows more than God concerning anything, he sets himself on a path of destruction both through the making of ruinous, uninformed decisions and through receiving the judgment of God. To hate His word seals a person's doom to foolish behavior and an eternal hell.

"But he that feareth the commandment shall be rewarded." For the believer to fear God is to revere, respect, honor, obey and hold in high regard both God and His instructions. Proof of love of Him and His word is best shown by loving obedience to Scripture. This trusting, obedient, wise behavior is rewarded by the gift of eternal life. *(See John 14:15,21 and 15:10.)* Both earthly and heavenly rewards come to the believer because of obedience to Scriptural instruction and following Holy Spirit leadership. Such obedience leads the believer to make wise decisions and consequently to be directly and personally rewarded by God. The word of God teaches a person how to be pleasing to God and His Son. The "word *is* a lamp unto my feet, and a light unto my path" *(Psalm 119:105)*, ever guiding in the way of holiness, wisdom, and to the cross of Calvary.

Numbers 15:31 Because he hath despised the word of the LORD, and hath broken his commandment, that soul shall utterly be cut off; his iniquity *shall be* upon him.

2Samuel 12:9-10 Wherefore hast thou despised the commandment of the LORD, to do evil in his sight? thou hast killed Uriah the Hittite with the sword, and hast taken his wife *to be* thy wife, and hast slain him with the sword of the children of Ammon. Now therefore the sword shall never depart from thine house; because thou hast despised me, and hast taken the wife of Uriah the Hittite to be thy wife.

2Chronicles 36:16 But they mocked the messengers of God, and despised his words, and misused his prophets, until the wrath of the LORD arose against his people, till *there was* no remedy.

Proverbs 1:25,30-31 But ye have set at nought all my counsel, and would none of my reproof . . . They would none of my counsel: they despised all my reproof. Therefore shall they eat of the fruit of their own way, and be filled with their own devices.

Ezekiel 20:13 But the house of Israel rebelled against me in the wilderness: they walked not in my statutes, and they despised my judgments, which *if* a man do, he shall even live in them; and my sabbaths they greatly polluted: then I said, I would pour out my fury upon them in the wilderness, to consume them.

Luke 16:31 And he said unto him, If they hear not Moses and the prophets, neither will they be persuaded, though one rose from the dead.

John 14:21 He that hath my commandments, and keepeth them, he it is that loveth me: and he that loveth me shall be loved of my Father, and I will love him, and will manifest myself to him. *[See also John 14:15 and 15:10.]*

Hebrews 10:28 He that despised Moses' law died without mercy under two or three witnesses: Of how much sorer punishment, suppose ye, shall he be thought worthy, who hath trodden under foot the Son of God, and hath counted the blood of the covenant, wherewith he was sanctified, an unholy thing, and hath done despite unto the Spirit of grace?

Proverbs 13:14   The law of the wise is a fountain of life, to depart from the snares of death.

Focus: This proverb declares that the "law of the wise," which is God's instruction from His word, is the source of quality life that guides the wise away from Satan's "snares of death."

"The law of the wise is a fountain of life." **"The Law of the wise"** is a composite of the guiding principles gleaned from Scripture. It is by these principles that "the wise" make good decisions to produce the highest quality of life. The believer thus learns to think and act according to the commandments of God; therefore, "in His law doeth he meditate day and night." (Psalm 1:2) Scripture is a **"fountain of life"** provided by the Giver of Life to instruct and guide His people onto a pathway of abundant living and away from the **"snares of death."**

Deuteronomy 6:2 That thou mightest fear the LORD thy God, to keep all his statutes and his commandments, which I command thee, thou, and thy son, and thy son's son, all the days of thy life; and that thy days may be prolonged.

Psalm 17:4 Concerning the works of men, by the word of thy lips I have kept *me from* the paths of the destroyer.

Psalm 36:9 For with thee *is* the fountain of life: in thy light shall we see light.

Proverbs 3:1-2 My son, forget not my law; but let thine heart keep my commandments: For length of days, and long life, and peace, shall they add to thee.

Proverbs 3:16-18 Length of days is in her right hand; and in her left hand riches and honour. Her ways are ways of pleasantness, and all her paths are peace. She is a tree of life to them that lay hold upon her: and happy is every one that retaineth her.

Proverbs 4:20-22 My son, attend to my words; incline thine ear unto my sayings. Let them not depart from thine eyes; keep them in the midst of thine heart. For they *are* life unto those that find them, and health to all their flesh.

Proverbs 8:35-36 For whoso findeth me findeth life, and shall obtain favour of the LORD. But he that sinneth against me wrongeth his own soul: all they that hate me love death.

Proverbs 9:11 For by me thy days shall be multiplied, and the years of thy life shall be increased.

Proverbs 10:11 The mouth of a righteous man is a well of life: but violence covereth the mouth of the wicked.

Proverbs 10:27 The fear of the LORD prolongeth days: but the years of the wicked shall be shortened.

Proverbs 14:27 The fear of the LORD *is* a fountain of life, to depart from the snares of death.

Revelation 21:6 And he said unto me, It is done. I am Alpha and Omega, the beginning and the end. I will give unto him that is athirst of the fountain of the water of life freely.

"To depart from the snares of death." Just as a wise man is *guided* by the commandments of God, the unwise person is *misguided* by the world system and will walk into **"the snares of death."**

2 Corinthians 4:3-4 "But if our gospel be hid, it is hid to them that are lost: In whom the god of this world hath blinded the minds of them which believe not, lest the light of the glorious gospel of Christ, who is the image of God, should shine unto them.

Because unwise men do not heed leadership from God, they walk headlong into traps set by evil people who either attack their victims directly or cause them to be entrapped by improper words and actions. The unwise walk in dangerous places where the wise have been taught not to go. (For example, the Scripture teaches the believer not to conduct business or partner with an unbeliever or not to walk, as Psalm 1 states, "in the counsel of the ungodly or stand in the way with sinners...") Understanding, for the unwise, comes either too late or never. Ultimately, the unwise rejecter of God, the one who has rejected the "fountain of life," is subject to the "second death," which is eternal separation from God in the Lake of Fire.

> Numbers 15:31 Because he hath despised the word of the LORD, and hath broken his commandment, that soul shall utterly be cut off; his iniquity *shall be* upon him.
>
> Proverbs 7:24-27 Hearken unto me now therefore, O ye children, and attend to the words of my mouth. Let not thine heart decline to her ways, go not astray in her paths. For she hath cast down many wounded: yea, many strong *men* have been slain by her. Her house *is* the way to hell, going down to the chambers of death.
>
> Proverbs 16:22 Understanding is a wellspring of life unto him that hath it: but the instruction of fools is folly.
>
> 1 Timothy 6:9-11 But they that will be rich fall into temptation and a snare, and *into* many foolish and hurtful lusts, which drown men in destruction and perdition. For the love of money is the root of all evil: which while some coveted after, they have erred from the faith, and pierced themselves through with many sorrows. But thou, O man of God, flee these things; and follow after righteousness, godliness, faith, love, patience, meekness.
>
> 2 Timothy 2:24-26 And the servant of the Lord must not strive; but be gentle unto all *men,* apt to teach, patient, In meekness instructing those that oppose themselves; if God peradventure will give them repentance to the acknowledging of the truth; And *that* they may recover themselves out of the snare of the devil, who are taken captive by him at his will.

Proverbs 13:15 Good understanding giveth favour: but the way of transgressors *is* hard.

Focus: This proverb *contrasts* the favorable way of life lived by the wise who have "good understanding" *with* the unfavorable, hard, rough way of life lived by sinners.

"Good understanding giveth favour." The phrase **"good understanding"** is used four times in the King James Bible. In two of those verses, "good understanding" is associated with **"favor"** *[grace, acceptance]*.

> 1 Samuel 25:3 Now the name of the man *was* Nabal; and the name of his wife Abigail: and *she was* a woman of good understanding, and of a beautiful countenance: but the man *was* churlish and evil in his doings; and he *was* of the house of Caleb.
>
> Psalm 111:10 The fear of the LORD *is* the beginning of wisdom: a good understanding have all they that do *his* commandments: his praise endureth for ever.
>
> Proverbs 3:4 So shalt thou find favour and good understanding in the sight of God and man. *[See also Luke 2:52 on next page.]*
>
> Proverbs 13:15 Good understanding giveth favour: but the way of transgressors *is* hard.

"Good understanding" *[insight, prudence, good sense]* is that broad mental comprehension of life's matters. It is that mental exercise that puts together all the facts, seen and unseen *(yet often Spiritually-sensed)*, and thereby comprehends how, when, where, and with whom to have proper interaction. A person with "good understanding" is a wise person.

When a person is obedient to God's word, he proves that he strongly desires to please God and be in His favor. God's obedient servant enjoys **"good understanding"** of life's matters because he is being taught by the Creator. Good understanding and obedience to Scripture gives him **"favor"** with God and good men because other persons with "good understanding" are also obedient to God's word.

> 1 Samuel 18:14-16 And David behaved himself wisely in all his ways; and the LORD was with him. Wherefore when Saul saw that he behaved himself very wisely, he was afraid of him. But all Israel and Judah loved David, because he went out and came in before them.
>
> Proverbs 4:7-9 Wisdom is the principal thing; therefore get wisdom: and with all thy getting get understanding. Exalt her, and she shall promote thee: she shall bring thee to honour, when thou dost embrace her. She shall give to thine head an ornament of grace: a crown of glory shall she deliver to thee.

Daniel 1:8 But Daniel purposed in his heart that he would not defile himself with the portion of the king's meat, nor with the wine which he drank: therefore he requested of the prince of the eunuchs that he might not defile himself. Now God had brought Daniel into favour and tender love with the prince of the eunuchs.

Luke 2:52 And Jesus increased in wisdom and stature, and in favour with God and man.

Acts 2:47 Praising God, and having favour with all the people. And the Lord added to the church daily such as should be saved.

Acts 7:9-10 And the patriarchs, moved with envy, sold Joseph into Egypt: but God was with him, And delivered him out of all his afflictions, and gave him favour and wisdom in the sight of Pharaoh king of Egypt; and he made him governor over Egypt and all his house.

Romans 14:17 For the kingdom of God is not meat and drink; but righteousness, and peace, and joy in the Holy Ghost. For he that in these things serveth Christ is acceptable to God, and approved of men.

"But the way of the transgressor is hard" is the antithetical phrase to "good understanding giveth favour." *Transgressors"* [*deceitful, treacherous, faithless, wicked people*] bring retribution on themselves from others because of their evil way of life. Their wicked desire for evil and injury on others is reflected in their speech and it comes back on themselves. *(See Proverbs 13:2.)* The transgressor receives no favor from God because he lives in opposition to the Creator's commandments, laws, and methods. His way is resistive and offensive to both God and good men. **"Transgressors"** face **"hard"** times in this life and later in hell. In this life, he has a constant warfare with his conscience, an absence of peace, and a dread concerning eternal condemnation and suffering.

Job 15:20 The wicked man travaileth with pain all his days, and the number of years is hidden to the oppressor.

Psalm 95:8-11 Harden not your heart, as in the provocation, and as in the day of temptation in the wilderness: When your fathers tempted me, proved me, and saw my work. Forty years long was I grieved with this generation, and said, It is a people that do err in their heart, and they have not known my ways: Unto whom I sware in my wrath that they should not enter into my rest.

Proverbs 15:10 Correction is grievous unto him that forsaketh the way: and he that hateth reproof shall die.

Proverbs 23:29-35 Who hath woe? who hath sorrow? who hath contentions? who hath babbling? who hath wounds without cause? who hath redness of eyes? They that tarry long at the wine; they that go to seek mixed wine. Look not thou upon the wine when it is red, when it giveth his colour in the cup, when it moveth itself aright. At the last it biteth like a serpent, and stingeth like an adder. Thine eyes shall behold strange women, and thine heart shall utter perverse things. Yea, thou shalt be as he that lieth down in the midst of the sea, or as he that lieth upon the top of a mast. They have stricken me, shalt thou say, and I was not sick; they have beaten me, and I felt it not: when shall I awake? I will seek it yet again.

Isaiah 5:18...20-24 Woe unto them that draw iniquity with cords of vanity, and sin as it were with a cart rope . . . Woe unto them that call evil good, and good evil; that put darkness for light, and light for darkness; that put bitter for sweet, and sweet for bitter! Woe unto them that are wise in their own eyes, and prudent in their own sight! Woe unto them that are mighty to drink wine, and men of strength to mingle strong drink: Which justify the wicked for reward, and take away the righteousness of the righteous from him! Therefore as the fire devoureth the stubble, and the flame consumeth the chaff, so their root shall be as rottenness, and their blossom shall go up as dust: because they have cast away the law of the LORD of hosts, and despised the word of the Holy One of Israel.

Isaiah 57:20-21 But the wicked are like the troubled sea, when it cannot rest, whose waters cast up mire and dirt. There is no peace, saith my God, to the wicked.

Isaiah 59:8 The way of peace they know not; and there is no judgment in their goings: they have made them crooked paths: whosoever goeth therein shall not know peace.

Jeremiah 2:19-20 Thine own wickedness shall correct thee, and thy backslidings shall reprove thee: know therefore and see that it is an evil thing and bitter, that thou hast forsaken the LORD thy God, and that my fear is not in thee, saith the Lord GOD of hosts. For of old time I have broken thy yoke, and burst thy bands; and thou saidst, I will not transgress; when upon every high hill and under every green tree thou wanderest, playing the harlot.

Acts 26:14 And when we were all fallen to the earth, I heard a voice speaking unto me, and saying in the Hebrew tongue, Saul, Saul, why persecutest thou me? *it is* hard for thee to kick against the pricks.

Romans 6:20-21 For when ye were the servants of sin, ye were free from righteousness. What fruit had ye then in those things whereof ye are now ashamed? for the end of those things is death.

Proverbs 13:16 Every prudent *man* dealeth with knowledge: but a fool layeth open *his* folly.

Focus: This proverb declares that a prudent person conducts his business ("dealeth") according to knowledge and that a fool jumps ahead without knowledge, thus revealing his foolishness.

"Every prudent *man* dealeth with knowledge." Scriptural knowledge provides him with the guiding principles of wisdom so that he is able to properly evaluate the worth of non-Scriptural knowledge. The **"prudent man"** *("cautious; circumspect; practically wise; careful of the consequences of enterprises, measures or actions; cautious not to act when the end is of doubtful* *utility, or probably impracticable"*[250]*)* cautiously acquires and evaluates knowledge and waits for the proper time, place, and spirit to deal with what he has come to know. He is cautious not to act on inadequate knowledge, or to allow emotions (rather than knowledge) to drive his behavior, or believe every word to be truthful. He only commits himself to others when he has sufficient knowledge of them to do so.

> Proverbs 14:8 The wisdom of the prudent *is* to understand his way: but the folly of fools *is* deceit.
>
> Proverbs 14:15 The simple believeth every word: but the prudent *man* looketh well to his going.
>
> Isaiah 50:4 The Lord GOD hath given me the tongue of the learned, that I should know how to speak a word in season to *him that is* weary: he wakeneth morning by morning, he wakeneth mine ear to hear as the learned.
>
> Isaiah 52:13 Behold, my servant shall deal prudently, he shall be exalted and extolled, and be very high.
>
> Matthew 10:16 Behold, I send you forth as sheep in the midst of wolves: be ye therefore wise as serpents, and harmless as doves.

"But a fool layeth open *his* folly." He places no value on the knowledge of Scripture; consequently, he has no light (guiding principle) whereby he can evaluate the worth of other knowledge. The **"fool"** habitually acts without proper knowledge. His foolishness is *laid open* in public display.

> "A fool by rash and inconsiderate conduct 'layeth open' or 'publishes' his folly. It is implied by contrasting him with the prudent man who "deals with knowledge" that he deals without it, that he leaps before he looks and walks in the dark when he might avail himself of a light to guide him. Such conduct arises from a lack of the sense of responsibility. He does not consider what is involved in his failure, how much misery may thus be entailed on himself and others. Every man who does not weigh results proves himself thereby to be a fool."[251]
>
> 1Samuel 25:10-11 And Nabal answered David's servants, and said, Who *is* David? and who *is* the son of Jesse? there be many servants now a days that break away every man from his master. Shall I then take my bread, and my water, and my flesh that I have killed for my shearers, and give *it* unto men, whom I know not whence they *be?*
>
> Proverbs 4:23-24 Keep thy heart with all diligence; for out of it *are* the issues of life. Put away from thee a froward mouth, and perverse lips put far from thee.
>
> Proverbs 12:16 A fool's wrath is presently known: but a prudent *man* covereth shame.
>
> Proverbs 12:23 A prudent man concealeth knowledge: but the heart of fools proclaimeth foolishness.
>
> Proverbs 18:13 He that answereth a matter before he heareth *it,* it *is* folly and shame unto him.
>
> Proverbs 15:2 The tongue of the wise useth knowledge aright: but the mouth of fools poureth out foolishness.
>
> Proverbs 15:28 The heart of the righteous studieth to answer: but the mouth of the wicked poureth out evil things.
>
> Ecclesiastes 10:3 Yea also, when he that is a fool walketh by the way, his wisdom faileth *him,* and he saith to every one *that* he *is* a fool.
>
> Matthew 14:6-7 But when Herod's birthday was kept, the daughter of Herodias danced before them, and pleased Herod. Whereupon he promised with an oath to give her whatsoever she would ask.

Proverbs 13:17 A wicked messenger falleth into mischief: but a faithful ambassador *is* health.

Focus: This proverb contrasts the evil consequences to a wicked (unfaithful) messenger with the blessings brought by a faithful one.

"A wicked *[criminal, guilty, hostile to God]* **messenger** *[representative, angel]* **falleth into mischief** *[evil, distress, calamity, adversity]***."** In biblical times, when there were no postal services or electronic devices, people often sent important communications by personal messengers. Placing trust in a messenger was (and still is) something to give serious consideration, and the messenger, especially the spiritual one who proclaims God's word, must consider the potential consequences should he be unfaithful. Great **"mischief"** *to the messenger himself*, as well as to the business or friendship, was a threat should he be wicked and distort the intended truth of the message he carried. A **"wicked messenger"** is a betrayer and thus found to be destructive, evil, and repugnant. He will certainly fall into mischief (punishment from God and perhaps those who sent him).

"But a faithful ambassador *[messenger, envoy]* **is health."** "A reliable messenger brings healing, that is, he contributes to the welfare of those for whom he works."[252] He receives safety and benefit for the one sending him and also for himself.[253] As threatening as conditions were in Bible days, the damage caused today by unfaithful messengers of the gospel is far more acute and permanent.[254]

NOTE: Angels are special messengers of God; and their very title, "angel," means *messenger*. Starting with the prophets, God used men as faithful messengers to warn, proclaim, preach and teach His messages.

"**The ill consequences of betraying a trust:** *A **wicked messenger***, who, being sent to negotiate any business, is false to him that employed him, divulges his counsels, and so defeats his designs, cannot expect to prosper, but will certainly ***fall into* some *mischief*** or other, will be discovered and punished, since nothing is more hateful to God and man than the treachery of those that have a confidence reposed in them.

The happy effects of fidelity: An ***ambassador*** who ***faithfully*** discharges his trust, and serves the interests of those who employ him, ***is health***; he is health to those by whom and for whom he is employed, heals differences that are between them, and preserves a good understanding; he is health to himself, for he secures his own interest.

This is applicable to ministers, Christ's messengers and ambassadors; those that are wicked and false to Christ and the souls of men do mischief and *fall into mischief*, but those that are faithful will find sound words to be healing words to others and themselves."[255]

Proverbs 10:26 As vinegar to the teeth, and as smoke to the eyes, so *is* the sluggard to them that send him.

Proverbs 25:13 As the cold of snow in the time of harvest, *so is* a faithful messenger to them that send him: for he refresheth the soul of his masters.

Proverbs 26:6 He that sendeth a message by the hand of a fool cutteth off the feet, *and* drinketh damage.

Jeremiah 23:13-16 And I have seen folly in the prophets of Samaria; they prophesied in Baal, and caused my people Israel to err. I have seen also in the prophets of Jerusalem an horrible thing: they commit adultery, and walk in lies: they strengthen also the hands of evildoers, that none doth return from his wickedness: they are all of them unto me as Sodom, and the inhabitants thereof as Gomorrah. Therefore thus saith the LORD of hosts concerning the prophets; Behold, I will feed them with wormwood, and make them drink the water of gall: for from the prophets of Jerusalem is profaneness gone forth into all the land. Thus saith the LORD of hosts, Hearken not unto the words of the prophets that prophesy unto you: they make you vain: they speak a vision of their own heart, *and* not out of the mouth of the LORD.

Ezekiel 3:18 When I say unto the wicked, Thou shalt surely die; and thou givest him not warning, nor speakest to warn the wicked from his wicked way, to save his life; the same wicked *man* shall die in his iniquity; but his blood will I require at thine hand.

Ezekiel 33:7-8 So thou, O son of man, I have set thee a watchman unto the house of Israel; therefore thou shalt hear the word at my mouth, and warn them from me. When I say unto the wicked, O wicked *man*, thou shalt surely die; if thou dost not speak to warn the wicked from his way, that wicked *man* shall die in his iniquity; but his blood will I require at thine hand.

2 Corinthians 2:17 For we are not as many, which corrupt the word of God: but as of sincerity, but as of God, in the sight of God speak we in Christ.

1 Corinthians 4:1-2 Let a man so account of us, as of the ministers of Christ, and stewards of the mysteries of God. Moreover it is required in stewards, that a man be found faithful.

2 Corinthians 5:20 Now then we are ambassadors for Christ, as though God did beseech *you* by us: we pray *you* in Christ's stead, be ye reconciled to God.

1 Timothy 1:12 And I thank Christ Jesus our Lord, who hath enabled me, for that he counted me faithful, putting me into the ministry;

2 Timothy 2:2 And the things that thou hast heard of me among many witnesses, the same commit thou to faithful men, who shall be able to teach others also.

Proverbs 13:18 Poverty and shame *shall be to* him that refuseth instruction: but he that regardeth reproof shall be honoured.

Focus: This proverb *contrasts the shameful consequences* affecting the person who refuses instruction with the honorable consequences accruing to the person who accepts instruction.

"**Reproof** *[instruction, chastisement, discipline, figuratively reproof]*" in the second clause is a synonym of "**instruction** *[correction, chastisement, reproof]*" in the first. The difference in consequences for refusing "instruction" or "correction" and accepting the same makes it clear that a person who is willing to be instructed to the point of correcting a fault is revealing a contrite soul that is worthy of honor from God and man. He proves that he is teachable and reveals humility, intelligence, and character. On the other hand, the poor soul who refuses to be *instructed in his fault* will be brought to "**poverty and shame**" because he will keep performing the same error though he has been instructed it is wrong. *Refusing to hear corrective instruction* reveals *pride* and identifies a person as "foolish, stubborn and ungovernable."[256]

"One of the **weakest** traits of any person is to be **unwilling** to accept honest criticism and correction. From the foolish child who will never listen to parental authority, on to the foolish man who will never listen to rebuke or reason, pride always goes before a fall. Honest criticism is often a bitter dose to swallow, but most tonics are bitter, and we are the stronger for taking them down bravely.

'If I am censured,' said that godly man, Bishop Griswold, 'then let me correct, but never justify, my faults.' A minister with more zeal than discretion once called on the bishop and belabored him with rather a harsh denunciation. Instead of showing the man out of the door, the bishop calmly replied, 'My dear friend, I don't wonder that they who witness the inconsistencies in my daily conduct should think that I have no religion. I often fear this myself, and I feel very grateful to you for giving me this warning.'

This reply was made in such unaffected meekness and sincerity that the visitor at once begged the bishop's pardon, and always regarded him afterwards as one of the most Christlike Christians he had ever known. He is doubly the fool who not only flings himself into a pit, but resents the friendly hand that tries to help him out of it. (T. G. Cuyler.)"[257]

Job 36:10-12 He openeth also their ear to discipline, and commandeth that they return from iniquity. If they obey and serve him, they shall spend their days in prosperity, and their years in pleasures. But if they obey not, they shall perish by the sword, and they shall die without knowledge.

Proverbs 5:9-14 Lest thou give thine honour unto others, and thy years unto the cruel: Lest strangers be filled with thy wealth; and thy labours be in the house of a stranger; And thou mourn at the last, when thy flesh and thy body are consumed, And say, How have I hated instruction, and my heart despised reproof; And have not obeyed the voice of my teachers, nor inclined mine ear to them that instructed me! I was almost in all evil in the midst of the congregation and assembly.

Proverbs 6:23 For the commandment is a lamp; and the law is light; and reproofs of instruction are the way of life . . .

Proverbs 9:8-10 Reprove not a scorner, lest he hate thee: rebuke a wise man, and he will love thee. Give *instruction* to a wise *man,* and he will be yet wiser: teach a just *man,* and he will increase in learning. The fear of the LORD *is* the beginning of wisdom: and the knowledge of the holy *is* understanding.

Proverbs 12:1 Whoso loveth instruction loveth knowledge: but he that hateth reproof is brutish.

Proverbs 13:13 Whoso despiseth the word shall be destroyed: but he that feareth the commandment shall be rewarded.

Proverbs 15:5 A fool despiseth his father's instruction: but he that regardeth reproof is prudent.

Proverbs 15:31-33 The ear that heareth the reproof of life abideth among the wise. He that refuseth instruction despiseth his own soul: but he that heareth reproof getteth understanding. The fear of the LORD is the instruction of wisdom; and before honour is humility.

Proverbs 25:12 As an earring of gold, and an ornament of fine gold, so is a wise reprover upon an obedient ear.

Proverbs 13:19 The desire accomplished is sweet to the soul: but *it is* abomination to fools to depart from evil.

Focus: This proverb declares that fools will not enjoy the sweet elation gained from righteous accomplishments because their heart desires to do evil.

The second clause specifies that fools love being associated with wickedness so much so that the fool would consider it an **"abomination"** *[a disgusting idea]* **"to depart from evil."** Therefore, he is conflicted since, according to the first clause, he would like to have the *sweetness of accomplishment;* BUT, he would consider it a disgusting thing to leave off his wickedness.

"In spite of the *sweetness of good desires accomplished*, fools will not forsake evil to attain to it. Balaam's desire, 'let me die the death of the righteous' (Numbers 23:10), would have been *"sweet to his soul"* in its accomplishment, but it was abomination to him to depart from 'the wages of unrighteousness.' (2Peter 2:15)"[258]

Numbers 23:10 Who can count the dust of Jacob, and the number of the fourth *part* of Israel? Let me die the death of the righteous, and let my last end be like his!

2 Peter 2:15 Which have forsaken the right way, and are gone astray, following the way of Balaam *the son* of Bosor, who loved the wages of unrighteousness;

It is the deceit of sinful lust that binds the fool to his folly[259] – that keeps him at bay from accomplishing the sweet things of God – that binds his body and blinds his mind to evil so that he will "remain in the congregation of the dead (Proverbs 21:16)" rather than "rejoice evermore" with the living. "For they that are after the flesh do mind the things of the flesh; but they that are after the Spirit the things of the Spirit. For to be carnally minded *is* death; but to be spiritually minded *is* life and peace. Because the carnal mind *is* enmity against God: for it is not subject to the law of God, neither indeed can be. So then they that are in the flesh cannot please God." (Romans 8:5-8)

"May not all enjoy this *sweetness?* All might, but all will not, be happy. The object is so revolting to the 'enmity of the carnal mind.' Perhaps those, who have been early trained in the ways of God, cannot experimentally estimate the bitterness of this enmity. But what can give a more awful view of this principle than the truth, that what is abomination to God to see, *is abomination to the fool to depart from!* (Proverbs 15:21) A striking figure of heaven and hell, in full contrast; with the great gulf that is fixed between them! Holiness makes heaven; sin makes hell. See then for which place the ungodly are fitting. Hatred of holiness is meetness for hell. Oh! what a mighty change must that be, that can slay the enmity, and make it to the soul an abomination to commit *evil*, as it now *is to depart from it!*"[260]

1 Chronicles 4:10 And Jabez called on the God of Israel, saying, Oh that thou wouldest bless me indeed, and enlarge my coast, and that thine hand might be with me, and that thou wouldest keep *me* from evil, that it may not grieve me! And God granted him that which he requested.

Psalm 17:15 As for me, I will behold thy face in righteousness: I shall be satisfied, when I awake, with thy likeness.

Psalm 21:1-2 **To the chief Musician, A Psalm of David.** The king shall joy in thy strength, O LORD; and in thy salvation how greatly shall he rejoice! Thou hast given him his heart's desire, and hast not withholden the request of his lips. Selah.

Proverbs 10:24 The fear of the wicked, it shall come upon him: but the desire of the righteous shall be granted.

Proverbs 11:23 The desire of the righteous *is* only good: *but* the expectation of the wicked *is* wrath.

Proverbs 13:12 Hope deferred maketh the heart sick: but *when* the desire cometh, *it is* a tree of life.

Proverbs 15:21 Folly is joy to him that is destitute of wisdom: but a man of understanding walketh uprightly.

Proverbs 21:16 The man that wandereth out of the way of understanding shall remain in the congregation of the dead.

Proverbs 13:20 He that walketh with wise *men* shall be wise: but a companion of fools shall be destroyed.

Focus: This proverb emphasizes the *power of influence* produced by both wise and foolish companionship.

Wise friends influence a sagacious, constructive lifestyle while foolish ones lead astray to destruction. People will, with time, modify their *values, opinions,* and their *reasoning process* depending upon the people with whom they associate. Because people are peer-pressure-oriented, they like the idea of being accepted by others and of being with groups. Those considered friends produce instruction through both words and actions, sometimes inadvertently, but often intentionally. Consequently, friends learn to have the same values, opinions, and reasoning as the people they **walk with**. If their **companions** are fools, they become fools. If their associations are wise, they become wise. "Friendships are two-edged tools, which may open up for you the way to life or the way to death."[261] "As the health of the body depends upon the kind of food which it assimilates and its power of assimilation, so the health of the mind depends upon the character of the thoughts which it receives and its power of making them its own."[262] *"To walk with a person* implies love and attachment; and it is impossible not to imitate those we love. So we say, 'Show me his company, and I'll tell you the man.' Let me know the company he keeps, and I shall easily guess his moral character.'"[263]

1 Kings 10:8 Happy *are* thy men, happy *are* these thy servants, which stand continually before thee, *and* that hear thy wisdom.

Psalm 1:1-6 Blessed is the man that walketh not in the counsel of the ungodly, nor standeth in the way of sinners, nor sitteth in the seat of the scornful. But his delight is in the law of the LORD; and in his law doth he meditate day and night. And he shall be like a tree planted by the rivers of water, that bringeth forth his fruit in his season; his leaf also shall not wither; and whatsoever he doeth shall prosper. The ungodly are not so: but are like the chaff which the wind driveth away. Therefore the ungodly shall not stand in the judgment, nor sinners in the congregation of the righteous. For the LORD knoweth the way of the righteous: but the way of the ungodly shall perish.

Psalm 119:63 I *am* a companion of all *them* that fear thee, and of them that keep thy precepts.

Proverbs 4:14-16 Enter not into the path of the wicked, and go not in the way of evil men. Avoid it, pass not by it, turn from it, and pass away. For they sleep not, except they have done mischief; and their sleep is taken away, unless they cause some to fall.

Proverbs 22:24-25 Make no friendship with an angry man; and with a furious man thou shalt not go: Lest thou learn his ways, and get a snare to thy soul.

Proverbs 28:7 Whoso keepeth the law is a wise son: but he that is a companion of riotous men shameth his father.

Zechariah 8:23 Thus saith the LORD of hosts; In those days *it shall come to pass,* that ten men shall take hold out of all languages of the nations, even shall take hold of the skirt of him that is a Jew, saying, We will go with you: for we have heard *that* God *is* with you.

Malachi 3:16-18 Then they that feared the LORD spake often one to another: and the LORD hearkened, and heard *it,* and a book of remembrance was written before him for them that feared the LORD, and that thought upon his name. And they shall be mine, saith the LORD of hosts, in that day when I make up my jewels; and I will spare them, as a man spareth his own son that serveth him. Then shall ye return, and discern between the righteous and the wicked, between him that serveth God and him that serveth him not.

2 Corinthians 6:14-18 Be ye not unequally yoked together with unbelievers: for what fellowship hath righteousness with unrighteousness? and what communion hath light with darkness? And what concord hath Christ with Belial? or what part hath he that believeth with an infidel? And what agreement hath the temple of God with idols? for ye are the temple of the living God; as God hath said, I will dwell in them, and walk in *them;* and I will be their God, and they shall be my people. Wherefore come out from among them, and be ye separate, saith the Lord, and touch not the unclean *thing;* and I will receive you, And will be a Father unto you, and ye shall be my sons and daughters, saith the Lord Almighty.

Hebrews 10:24-25 And let us consider one another to provoke unto love and to good works: Not forsaking the assembling of ourselves together, as the manner of some *is;* but exhorting *one another:* and so much the more, as ye see the day approaching.

Revelation 18:4-6 And I heard another voice from heaven, saying, Come out of her, my people, that ye be not partakers of her sins, and that ye receive not of her plagues. For her sins have reached unto heaven, and God hath remembered her iniquities. Reward her even as she rewarded you, and double unto her double according to her works: in the cup which she hath filled fill to her double.

> **Proverbs 13:21** Evil pursueth sinners: but to the righteous good shall be repayed.

Focus: In this proverb, personified evil is identified as a *stalker* who dogs the sinner's steps for bad, whereas good follows and rewards the righteous.

When a person rejects righteousness and favors sin, he essentially places himself into an unprotected, godless environment whereby unrestrained evil follows him.

"**Sinners** suffer not only the natural consequences of crime in external evil, injury to body, estate, reputation, etc. (Psalm 11:6), but also stings of conscience and remorse; even seeming prosperity is often a chastisement, and long impunity is only augmenting the coming retribution. As the shadow attends the substance, so guilt is attached to sin, and brings with it punishment."[264]

Sinners receive evil retribution for their sins, while the righteous receive good because of having produced good. By preference, the righteous person chooses God's companionship and all the benefits and blessings that accompany such a relationship. He seeks and receives God's goodness that is poured out every day.

"As sure as the shadow follows the substance, as *[sure as]* the avenger of blood *pursued* 'the manslayer,' (Numbers 35:19) 'evil shall hunt the violent man to overthrow him.' (Psalm 140:11) Yet often the sinner goes on in his blinded infatuation. 'No one has been witness to his sin. Or no one will make account of it. Or his accusers, being as guilty as himself, will hold their peace; or, should he be discovered, prudence or pleading will secure him from punishment.' And then, though 'the iniquity of his heels compasseth him about' (Psalm 49:5), he thinks only of present gratification, never looks back, and therefore sees not the *evil pursuing him*. His blindness thus makes his ruin more certain. (Deuteronomy 29:19-20; Job 11:20; 1 Thessalonians 5:3) And how dearly are his momentary pleasures purchased at the cost of eternity! (Ecclesiastes 11:9)

Not less sure is *the good, which shall be repaid to the righteous*. (Isaiah 3:10-11; Romans 2:6-10) The evil follows in just retribution. The other is the reward of grace. Not the smallest good – even 'a cup of cold water to a disciple' (Matthew 10:42), or honour showed to his servants (Matthew 10:41; 1 Kings 17:16-23) – shall 'lose its reward.' (Hebrews 6:10) And if a single act is thus remembered, much more 'a course, a fight,' held out to the end. (2 Timothy 4:7-8) How manifestly is this the constitution of grace; that when perfect obedience can claim no recompense (Luke 17:10), such unworthy, such defiled, work should be so honoured with an infinite, overwhelming acceptance!"[265]

Genesis 4:7 If thou doest well, shalt thou not be accepted? and if thou doest not well, sin lieth at the door. And unto thee *shall be* his desire, and thou shalt rule over him.

Numbers 32:23 But if ye will not do so, behold, ye have sinned against the LORD: and be sure your sin will find you out.

Numbers 35:19 The revenger of blood himself shall slay the murderer: when he meeteth him, he shall slay him.

Job 11:18-20 And thou shalt be secure, because there is hope; yea, thou shalt dig *about thee, and* thou shalt take thy rest in safety. Also thou shalt lie down, and none shall make *thee* afraid; yea, many shall make suit unto thee. But the eyes of the wicked shall fail, and they shall not escape, and their hope *shall be as* the giving up of the ghost.

Psalm 11:6 Upon the wicked he shall rain snares, fire and brimstone, and an horrible tempest: *this shall be* the portion of their cup.

Psalm 32:10 Many sorrows *shall be* to the wicked: but he that trusteth in the LORD, mercy shall compass him about.

Psalm 140:11-13 Let not an evil speaker be established in the earth: evil shall hunt the violent man to overthrow *him*. I know that the LORD will maintain the cause of the afflicted, *and* the right of the poor. Surely the righteous shall give thanks unto thy name: the upright shall dwell in thy presence.

Isaiah 3:10-11 Say ye to the righteous, that *it shall be* well *with him:* for they shall eat the fruit of their doings. Woe unto the wicked! *it shall be* ill *with him:* for the reward of his hands shall be given him.

Matthew 10:40-42 He that receiveth you receiveth me, and he that receiveth me receiveth him that sent me. He that receiveth a prophet in the name of a prophet shall receive a prophet's reward; and he that receiveth a righteous man in the name of a righteous man shall receive a righteous man's reward. And whosoever shall give to drink unto one of these little ones a cup of *water* only in the name of a disciple, verily I say unto you, he shall in no wise lose his reward.

Romans 2:7-11 To them who by patient continuance in well doing seek for glory and honour and immortality, eternal life: But unto them that are contentious, and do not obey the truth, but obey unrighteousness, indignation and wrath, Tribulation and anguish, upon every soul of man that doeth evil, of the Jew first, and also of the Gentile; But glory, honour, and peace, to every man that worketh good, to the Jew first, and also to the Gentile: For there is no respect of persons with God.

1 Thessalonians 5:3 For when they shall say, Peace and safety; then sudden destruction cometh upon them, as travail upon a woman with child; and they shall not escape.

2 Timothy 4:7-8 I have fought a good fight, I have finished *my* course, I have kept the faith: Henceforth there is laid up for me a crown of righteousness, which the Lord, the righteous judge, shall give me at that day: and not to me only, but unto all them also that love his appearing.

Hebrews 6:10 For God *is* not unrighteous to forget your work and labour of love, which ye have shewed toward his name, in that ye have ministered to the saints, and do minister. *[See also Deuteronomy 29:18-20; 1 Kings 17:16-23; Psalm 49:5 and Ecclesiastes 11:9.]*

Proverbs 13:22 A good *man* leaveth an inheritance to his children's children: and the wealth of the sinner *is* laid up for the just.

Focus: This proverb declares that the righteous stand to gain from both their righteous earthly parents and from their heavenly Father.

"A good *man* leaveth an inheritance to his children's children." God blesses the godly, and He gives the ability to get wealth. However, there are conditions that can cause good people to lose all wealth, such as war, poor health, critical accidents, thieves, corrupt government, and widespread economic failure; but generally, the longer wise people live, the more wealth they accumulate. Should the **"good"** person lose that wealth or never acquire it for some reason beyond his control, he will certainly leave a storehouse of prayers, his righteous example, and wise instruction. A good man, being blessed of God, leaves an inheritance for his grand-children whom he has taught to be righteous in the sight of God.

"And the wealth of the sinner *is* laid up for the just." Eventually, even that which the evil man has finds its way to the righteous through the providence of God, since the righteous shall "inherit the earth." Ungodly people often accumulate wealth, but they are not in God's favor and are under His wrath. Eventually, their inheritance will find its way to the just, the children of God, who will inherit the wealth of the entire earth when the ungodly are permanently removed.

> Exodus 12:35-36 And the children of Israel did according to the word of Moses; and they borrowed of the Egyptians jewels of silver, and jewels of gold, and raiment: And the LORD gave the people favour in the sight of the Egyptians, so that they lent unto them *such things as they required.* And they spoiled the Egyptians.
> Deuteronomy 8:18 But thou shalt remember the LORD thy God: for *it is* he that giveth thee power to get wealth, that he may establish his covenant which he sware unto thy fathers, as *it is* this day.
> 1 Samuel 2:8 He raiseth up the poor out of the dust, *and* lifteth up the beggar from the dunghill, to set *them* among princes, and to make them inherit the throne of glory: for the pillars of the earth *are* the LORD'S, and he hath set the world upon them.
> Psalm 25:13 His soul shall dwell at ease; and his seed shall inherit the earth.
> Psalm 37:9-11 For evildoers shall be cut off: but those that wait upon the LORD, they shall inherit the earth. For yet a little while, and the wicked shall not *be:* yea, thou shalt diligently consider his place, and it *shall* not *be.* But the meek shall inherit the earth; and shall delight themselves in the abundance of peace.
> Psalm 37:22 For *such as be* blessed of him shall inherit the earth; and *they that be* cursed of him shall be cut off.
> Proverbs 21:20 *There is* treasure to be desired and oil in the dwelling of the wise; but a foolish man spendeth it up.
> Proverbs 28:8 He that by usury and unjust gain increaseth his substance, he shall gather it for him that will pity the poor.
> Job 27:16-17 Though he heap up silver as the dust, and prepare raiment as the clay; He may prepare *it,* but the just shall put *it* on, and the innocent shall divide the silver
> Ecclesiastes 2:26 For *God* giveth to a man that *is* good in his sight wisdom, and knowledge, and joy: but to the sinner he giveth travail, to gather and to heap up, that he may give to *him that is* good before God. This also *is* vanity and vexation of spirit.
> Matthew 5:5 Blessed *are* the meek: for they shall inherit the earth.
> John 3:18 He that believeth on him is not condemned: but he that believeth not is condemned already, because he hath not believed in the name of the only begotten Son of God.
> Revelation 21:7 He that overcometh shall inherit all things; and I will be his God, and he shall be my son.

Proverbs 13:23 Much food *is in* the tillage of the poor: but there is *that is* destroyed for want of judgment.

Focus: This proverb contrasts the potential increase that comes from wise judgment (assessment) with the destruction that comes from poor judgment.

"Much food *is in* the tillage of the poor." A poor person judges his land to be valuable in producing much food and puts his hand to the plow. **"Tillage"** in the context of this proverb is used to represent all the various phases of farming work involved in producing a crop, not just that portion of breaking up new ground. A poor person with good judgment knows that a wise working of his land can bring forth enough food to sustain the life of himself and his family. Proverbs 12:11 also states: "He that tilleth his land shall be satisfied with bread, but he that followeth vain *persons is* void of understanding."

"There are many things in nature in which there exists a latent power to minister to man's needs; but his hand must be put forth to arouse the sleeping power. There is heat in coal to warm him, but he must kindle the coal before it will put it forth. So in the earth, there are stores of life-giving power wrapped up in its bosom, but the hand of man must till it before it will yield him food. And it will yield food to the poor man as well as to the rich; his hard toil will be rewarded by receiving bread for his labour."[266]

"But there is *that is* destroyed for want of judgment." **"Want of judgment"** refers specifically to an *inability to evaluate and understand the potential* of whatever assets are available, large or small, resulting in **"destruction"** *[a sweeping away, ruin, removal]*. A small estate can *go to ruin* simply from a failure to wisely work whatever assets are available, and a large estate can *go to waste* because of a failure to understand and thus manage effectively.

> Proverbs 6:6-11 Go to the ant, thou sluggard; consider her ways, and be wise: Which having no guide, overseer, or ruler, Provideth her meat in the summer, *and* gathereth her food in the harvest. How long wilt thou sleep, O sluggard? when wilt thou arise out of thy sleep? *Yet* a little sleep, a little slumber, a little folding of the hands to sleep: So shall thy poverty come as one that travelleth, and thy want as an armed man.
> Proverbs 24:30-34 I went by the field of the slothful, and by the vineyard of the man void of understanding; And, lo, it was all grown over with thorns, *and* nettles had covered the face thereof, and the stone wall thereof was bSroken down. Then I saw, *and* considered *it* well: I looked upon *it, and* received instruction. *Yet* a little sleep, a little slumber, a little folding of the hands to sleep: So shall thy poverty come *as* one that travelleth; and thy want as an armed man.
> Proverbs 27:23-27 Be thou diligent to know the state of thy flocks, *and* look well to thy herds. For riches *are* not for ever: and doth the crown *endure* to every generation? The hay appeareth, and the tender grass sheweth itself, and herbs of the mountains are gathered. The lambs *are* for thy clothing, and the goats *are* the price of the field. And *thou shalt have* goats' milk enough for thy food, for the food of thy household, and *for* the maintenance for thy maidens.
> Proverbs 28:19 He that tilleth his land shall have plenty of bread: but he that followeth after vain *persons* shall have poverty enough.

Proverbs 13:24 He that spareth his rod hateth his son: but he that loveth him chasteneth him betimes.

Focus: This proverb stresses that the measure of a parent's love is revealed in his willingness (or unwillingness) to properly discipline his children.

Earnest, faithful, and consistent discipline disrupts an otherwise peaceful morning, causes heartache, and is unpleasant for all; but quite necessary. A loving parent will inflict temporary discomfort on his child (and at the same time on himself), so the youngster won't have to face the disasters accompanying an undisciplined life. But the level of a parent's love is questionable when he refuses to discipline.

> Proverbs 19:18 Chasten thy son while there is hope, and let not thy soul spare for his crying.
> Proverbs 22:15 Foolishness *is* bound in the heart of a child; *but* the rod of correction shall drive it far from him.
> Proverbs 23:13 Withhold not correction from the child: for *if* thou beatest him with the rod, he shall not die.
> Proverbs 29:15 The rod and reproof give wisdom: but a child left *to himself* bringeth his mother to shame.
> Proverbs 29:17 Correct thy son, and he shall give thee rest; yea, he shall give delight unto thy soul.
> Hebrews 12:6-8 For whom the Lord loveth he chasteneth, and scourgeth every son whom he receiveth. If ye endure chastening, God dealeth with you as with sons; for what son is he whom the father chasteneth not? But if ye be without chastisement, whereof all are partakers, then are ye bastards, and not sons.

The Rod as an Instrument of Discipline

"Rod" is translated from the Hebrew *shebet* (pronounced *shay'-bet*) from an unused root which means a scion *[small stick or stem]* used for punishing, writing, fighting, ruling, walking. Figuratively it means a clan or tribe.] (From Strong's *Hebrew Dictionary*)

"The word "rod" indicates a thin stick or switch that can be used to give a small amount of physical pain with no lasting physical injury. A child should never be bruised, injured, or cut by a physical correction. The Bible warns that parents should never abuse the power and authority they have over their children while they are young because it provokes the children to righteous anger."

> Ephesians 6:4 And, ye fathers, provoke not your children to wrath: but bring them up in the nurture and admonition of the Lord.
> Colossians 3:21 Fathers, provoke not your children to anger, lest they be discouraged.

"Physical discipline is always done in love, never as a vent to the parent's frustration. It is also just one part of discipline and should be used when the child shows defiance to a clear limit, not in the heat of the moment." From https://www.gotquestions.org/spare-rod-spoil-child.html

---

"The rod without affection is revolting tyranny."[267]

> **Proverbs 13:25** The righteous eateth to the satisfying of his soul: but the belly of the wicked shall want.

Focus: This proverb contrasts the satisfaction of the righteous with the "never satisfaction" of the wicked.

A righteous person is one who lives for God and is satisfied with His provisions. ***Eating*** is here symbolic of consumption of every kind of need and want that a person has. Never satisfied with what they have, the wicked are always wanting, coveting, and willing to take whatever they desire by whatever evil means are necessary. Never satisfied in body, soul or spirit, the wicked are functioning at a hopeless, Christ-less level of dissatisfaction that will forever be uncomfortable and unfulfilling. He lacks the consoling presence of his Creator, Who is Comforter to His own but not to the wicked.

"To the possession of this perfect satisfaction there is but one way. It is the enjoyment of God's Favour. Nothing can satisfy the soul of man but this; and when this is obtained, it will infuse the spirit of satisfaction into every thing. It will enrich every joy; it will alleviate, and sweeten, and sanctify every sorrow. Here lies the secret of true contentment and happiness. God In All Things, And All Things In God, is the sum of the divine lesson."[268]

Genesis 47:12-13 And Joseph nourished his father, and his brethren, and all his father's household, with bread, according to their families. And there was no bread in all the land; for the famine was very sore, so that the land of Egypt and all the land of Canaan fainted by reason of the famine.

Deuteronomy 28:47-48 Because thou servedst not the LORD thy God with joyfulness, and with gladness of heart, for the abundance of all *things;* Therefore shalt thou serve thine enemies which the LORD shall send against thee, in hunger, and in thirst, and in nakedness, and in want of all *things:* and he shall put a yoke of iron upon thy neck, until he have destroyed thee.

Psalm 34:10 The young lions do lack, and suffer hunger: but they that seek the LORD shall not want any good *thing.*

Psalm 37:3 Trust in the LORD, and do good; *so* shalt thou dwell in the land, and verily thou shalt be fed.

Psalm 37:16 A little that a righteous man hath *is* better than the riches of many wicked.

Psalm 37:18-19 The LORD knoweth the days of the upright: and their inheritance shall be for ever. They shall not be ashamed in the evil time: and in the days of famine they shall be satisfied.

Proverbs 10:3 The LORD will not suffer the soul of the righteous to famish: but he casteth away the substance of the wicked.

Isaiah 65:13-14 Therefore thus saith the Lord GOD, Behold, my servants shall eat, but ye shall be hungry: behold, my servants shall drink, but ye shall be thirsty: behold, my servants shall rejoice, but ye shall be ashamed: Behold, my servants shall sing for joy of heart, but ye shall cry for sorrow of heart, and shall howl for vexation of spirit.

Hosea 4:10 For they shall eat, and not have enough: they shall commit whoredom, and shall not increase: because they have left off to take heed to the LORD.

Philippians 4:11-12 Not that I speak in respect of want: for I have learned, in whatsoever state I am, *therewith* to be content. I know both how to be abased, and I know how to abound: every where and in all things I am instructed both to be full and to be hungry, both to abound and to suffer need.

Hebrews 13:5 Let your conversation be without covetousness; and be content with such things as ye have: for he hath said, I will never leave thee, nor forsake thee.

CHAPTER FOURTEEN

> **Proverbs 14:1** Every wise woman buildeth her house: but the foolish plucketh it down with her hands.

Focus: This proverb sharply contrasts the constructive home-building qualities of a wise woman with the destructive qualities of a foolish one.

The wife will typically spend considerably more time with the children than her husband, thus having an enormous effect on their development in every area, including spiritual, mental, emotional, and physical. She has the capacity to ***build her house*** or ***pluck it down***. The *building or plucking down **with her hands*** comes *through actions and words*. **"Hands"** is a term used here symbolically to represent *personal strength*. She has the strength (ability) to destroy or build up every aspect of the family. The verse does not mean that she physically constructs or removes her house's building materials such as brick, wood, or glass. **"House"** in this proverb symbolizes the family, not the physical building itself; and the word "house" is often used in Scripture to symbolize a family line. The overarching term "house" contains numerous aspects of family life such as spiritual commitment, financial soundness, reputation, and peace within the home that the wise woman enhances; and the foolish woman destroys.

The wise woman teaches her children wisdom by educating them in the Scriptures, as well as by demonstrating an example of righteousness. Destruction by the foolish woman comes because of her opposition to God's established biblical principles of living. Her delight in evil things, ways, and relationships results in devastation.

Whether wise or foolish, each woman individually clearly has ownership of the consequences of her words and actions. The wise woman and the foolish one will individually be known in her respective community for her character. The respective families will either be respected or disrespected, accepted or rejected, depending, in large portion, on how she is received. *Wisdom within a person is, by its very nature, constructive, but foolishness is destructive.* A woman with wisdom understands what it takes to guide her family to a proper relationship, first with God, then with others. The foolish woman's actions are rebellious, clamorous, simple, ignorant, and sometimes promiscuous. She is **destructive** to her family – **"she plucketh down her house."**

> 1 Kings 21:25 But there was none like unto Ahab, which did sell himself to work wickedness in the sight of the LORD, whom Jezebel his wife stirred up.
> Ruth 4:11-12 And all the people that were in the gate, and the elders, said, We are witnesses. The LORD make the woman that is come into thine house like Rachel and like Leah, which two did build the house of Israel: and do thou worthily in Ephratah, and be famous in Bethlehem: And let thy house be like the house of Pharez, whom Tamar bare unto Judah, of the seed which the LORD shall give thee of this young woman.
> Psalm 127:1 A Song of degrees for Solomon. Except the LORD build the house, they labour in vain that build it: except the LORD keep the city, the watchman waketh but in vain.
> Proverbs 9:1 Wisdom hath builded her house, she hath hewn out her seven pillars . . .
> Proverbs 9:13 A foolish woman *is* clamorous: *she is* simple, and knoweth nothing.
> Proverbs 12:4 A virtuous woman is a crown to her husband: but she that maketh ashamed is as rottenness in his bones.
> Proverbs 12:7 The wicked are overthrown, and are not: but the house of the righteous shall stand.
> Proverbs 24:3 Through wisdom is an house builded; and by understanding it is established . . .
> Proverbs 31:24-27 She maketh fine linen, and selleth it; and delivereth girdles unto the merchant. Strength and honour are her clothing; and she shall rejoice in time to come. She openeth her mouth with wisdom; and in her tongue is the law of kindness. She looketh well to the ways of her household, and eateth not the bread of idleness.
> 1 Timothy 5:14 I will therefore that the younger women marry, bear children, guide the house, give none occasion to the adversary to speak reproachfully.

> **Proverbs 14:2** He that walketh in his uprightness feareth the LORD: but *he that is* perverse in his ways despiseth him.

Focus: This proverb declares that a person's "walk" or way of living is expressive of his relationship with God.

> ### "Human Conduct"
> "I. **Men differ widely in their daily conduct.**
>   A. **Some men walk uprightly. Walking uprightly implies--**
>   1. **Moral strength.** The man is not bent and crooked by the infirmities of sin or the weight of depravity.
>   2. **Conscious rectitude** *(Righteous or correct in judgment)*. He does not bow down his head, as if ashamed to look his neighbour in the face. He is as open as the day, and as fearless as the sun.
>   B. **Some walk perversely.** They are perverse in their ways. They are crooked in their purposes, policies, and performances. *(They are against God, His word, and His people.)*
> II. **Men reveal their heart towards God in their daily walk.**
>   A. **Right conduct springs from a right feeling towards God.** The man that walks uprightly fears the Lord. There is no true morality without religion. Piety is the first principle of all rectitude. All good living must have respect to God.
>   B. **Wrong conduct springs from wrong feeling towards God.** 'He that is perverse in his ways, despiseth Him'. The wrong doer has no feeling of respect for God. He ignores Him as much as he can. You may know how men feel inwardly toward their Maker by observing how they deal outwardly with each other." D. Thomas, as quoted in Joseph S. Exell, Editor, *The Biblical Illustrator*, 1887-1905, e-Sword 12.0.1.)

Because it aligns with the teachings of Scripture, an upright lifestyle (**"walk"**) gives evidence of love and respect for the LORD. In contrast, an ungodly, **"perverse"** lifestyle expresses dishonor and disdain for the Lord and His word. A person who is "perverse" *[departed, turned aside, gone wrong or crooked]* is the opposite of a person who *fears the LORD.* Proof of believing in the reality of God, in His word, in His Creation of the world, and in His power is shown when an individual is living and walking in the word "all the day long." Conversely, the lost, foolish, perverse man walks in his disbelief and opposition to God all day long.

> Genesis 18:19 For I know him *[Abraham]*, that he will command his children and his household after him, and they shall keep the way of the LORD, to do justice and judgment; that the LORD may bring upon Abraham that which he hath spoken of him.
> 1 Samuel 2:29-30 Wherefore kick ye *[Eli]* at my sacrifice and at mine offering, which I have commanded *in my* habitation; and honourest thy sons *[Hophni and Phinehas]* above me, to make yourselves fat with the chiefest of all the offerings of Israel my people? Wherefore the LORD God of Israel saith, I said indeed *that* thy house, and the house of thy father, should walk before me for ever: but now the LORD saith, Be it far from me; for them that honour me I will honour, and they that despise me shall be lightly esteemed.
> 2 Samuel 12:9-10 Wherefore hast thou *[David]* despised the commandment of the LORD, to do evil in his sight? thou hast killed Uriah the Hittite with the sword, and hast taken his wife *to be* thy wife, and hast slain him with the sword of the children of Ammon. Now therefore the sword shall never depart from thine house; because thou hast despised me, and hast taken the wife of Uriah the Hittite to be thy wife.
> Psalm 111:10 The fear of the LORD *is* the beginning of wisdom: a good understanding have all they that do *his commandments*: his praise endureth for ever.
> Isaiah 30:12-13 Wherefore thus saith the Holy One of Israel, Because ye despise this word, and trust in oppression and perverseness, and stay thereon: Therefore this iniquity shall be to you as a breach ready to fall, swelling out in a high wall, whose breaking cometh suddenly at an instant.
> 2 Timothy 3:1-5 This know also, that in the last days perilous times shall come. For men shall be lovers of their own selves, covetous, boasters, proud, blasphemers, disobedient to parents, unthankful, unholy, Without natural affection, trucebreakers, false accusers, incontinent, fierce, despisers of those that are good, Traitors, heady, highminded, lovers of pleasures more than lovers of God; Having a form of godliness, but denying the power thereof: from such turn away. *[description of perversity]*

> **Proverbs 14:3** In the mouth of the foolish *is* a rod of pride: but the lips of the wise shall preserve them.

Focus: This proverb contrasts the damaging effects of the words of the foolish with the preserving effects of the words of the wise.

"In the mouth of the foolish is a rod of pride." Revealing inward pride, ill-spoken words of the foolish become (figuratively) like **"rods"** or branches with which he beats others and ultimately (though inadvertently) himself. A prideful heart manifests itself with words that are potentially snobbish, imperious, contemptuous, violent, or abusive. Because such words strike at others with a piercing effect, they oftentimes arouse dangerous spiteful responses such as resentment, envy, or hate. Because of their ungoverned tongues, fools bring trouble and correction upon themselves. Rather than submitting themselves to the word of God, fools allow pride to drive their words and actions.

> Exodus 5:2;14:28 And Pharaoh said, Who is the LORD, that I should obey his voice to let Israel go? I know not the LORD, neither will I let Israel go ... Exodus 14:28 And the waters returned, and covered the chariots, and the horsemen, and all the host of Pharaoh that came into the sea after them; there remained not so much as one of them.
>
> 1 Samuel 2:3 Talk no more so exceeding proudly; let not arrogancy come out of your mouth: for the LORD is a God of knowledge, and by him actions are weighed.
>
> Psalm 12:3-4 The LORD shall cut off all flattering lips, and the tongue that speaketh proud things: Who have said, With our tongue will we prevail; our lips are our own: who is lord over us?
>
> Psalm 31:18-20 Let the lying lips be put to silence; which speak grievous things proudly and contemptuously against the righteous. Oh how great is thy goodness, which thou hast laid up for them that fear thee; which thou hast wrought for them that trust in thee before the sons of men! Thou shalt hide them in the secret of thy presence from the pride of man: thou shalt keep them secretly in a pavilion from the strife of tongues.
>
> Psalm 64:2-8 Hide me from the secret counsel of the wicked; from the insurrection of the workers of iniquity: Who whet their tongue like a sword, and bend their bows to shoot their arrows, even bitter words: That they may shoot in secret at the perfect: suddenly do they shoot at him, and fear not. They encourage themselves in an evil matter: they commune of laying snares privily; they say, Who shall see them? They search out iniquities; they accomplish a diligent search: both the inward thought of every one of them, and the heart, is deep. But God shall shoot at them with an arrow; suddenly shall they be wounded. So they shall make their own tongue to fall upon themselves: all that see them shall flee away.
>
> Proverbs 18:6-7 A fool's lips enter into contention, and his mouth calleth for strokes. A fool's mouth is his destruction, and his lips are the snare of his soul.
>
> Jeremiah 18:18 Then said they, Come, and let us devise devices against Jeremiah; for the law shall not perish from the priest, nor counsel from the wise, nor the word from the prophet. Come, and let us smite him with the tongue, and let us not give heed to any of his words.

"But the lips of the wise shall preserve them." In contrast to the words of the foolish, which bring harm, those of the wise bring preservation. Because speech reveals a person's heart, if that person is **"wise,"** he will speak words of humility, meekness, gentleness, kindness, and peace, rather than pride, contempt, violence, and abuse as is spoken by the foolish. **"The wise"** have been taught to carefully choose their words so that their speech represents a humble heart and becomes a ***preserver*** *[guard, protector]* of everything their godly soul represents. The **"lips of the wise"** show forth the fruit of the Spirit, which removes fear and brings peace, deliverance, health, and life.

> Proverbs 10:13 In the lips of him that hath understanding wisdom is found: but a rod is for the back of him that is void of understanding.
>
> Proverbs 12:6 The words of the wicked are to lie in wait for blood: but the mouth of the upright shall deliver them.
>
> Proverbs 12:18 There is that speaketh like the piercings of a sword: but the tongue of the wise is health.
>
> Proverbs 13:3 He that keepeth his mouth keepeth his life: but he that openeth wide his lips shall have destruction.
>
> Proverbs 16:7 When a man's ways please the LORD, he maketh even his enemies to be at peace with him.
>
> Proverbs 28:25 He that is of a proud heart stirreth up strife: but he that putteth his trust in the LORD shall be made fat.
>
> Galatians 5:22-24 But the fruit of the Spirit is love, joy, peace, longsuffering, gentleness, goodness, faith, Meekness, temperance: against such there is no law. And they that are Christ's have crucified the flesh with the affections and lusts.

Proverbs 14:4 Where no oxen are, the crib is clean: but much increase is by the strength of the ox.

Focus: This proverb teaches that profitable endeavors often have their downside.

There is reward to those willing to endure the obnoxious smell, spend time cleaning and caring, feeding and working with the oxen who multiply (through their great strength) the work that a man alone can accomplish. Oxen were the John Deere tractors of Solomon's day and still are in some primitive regions of the world. They have *great strength to pull the plows and wagons* used throughout the entire varied processes of farming; but, along with all that increased food production and potential increase of profit, there was also the cost and effort of filling the crib with food and the unpleasant task of cleaning after the oxen. In one form or another, there is always a price to pay when work is profitable; but after effort and expenditures, a good and effective farmer will have abundant food that is largely attributed to the work of his beasts.

> "A SERIOUS MISTAKE, to prefer nicety or daintiness to fruitfulness or usefulness. This grave mistake is made by the *farmer* who would rather have a clean crib than a quantity of valuable manure; by the *housewife* who cares more for the elegance of the furniture than the comfort of the family; by the *minister* who spends more strength on the wording than on the doctrine of his discourse; by the *teacher* who lays more stress on the composition of classical verses than on the history of his country or than on the strengthening of the mind; by the *poet* who takes infinite pains with his rhymes and gives little thought to his subject or his imagery; by the *statesman* who is particular about the draughting of his bills, and has no objection to introduce retrograde and dishonouring measures; by the *doctor* who insists much on his medicine, and lets his patient go on neglecting all the laws of hygiene; etc."[269]

Proverbs 12:11 He that tilleth his land shall be satisfied with bread: but he that followeth vain persons is void of understanding.

Proverbs 13:23 Much food is in the tillage of the poor: but there is that is destroyed for want of judgment.

Interesting side NOTES: www.wikipedia.com states that male cattle are castrated to make them easier to handle. This bovine is then known as an **"ox"** rather than a bull. Female cattle are called cows. Also, the early definition of a half acre of land was that amount which a yoke of oxen could plow in a half day with a wooden plow. (1 Samuel 14:14)

Proverbs 14:5 A faithful witness will not lie: but a false witness will utter lies.

Focus: This proverb makes clear that the unchanging trait of the false witness is to lie and the established behavior of a faithful witness is to tell the truth.

"A faithful witness will not lie." Lying is not part of the character of a faithful witness, neither is giving a false testimony in a courtroom.

> **"A true witness.** Truth is beautiful, as well as safe and mighty. In the incident related below a boy twelve years old, with only truth as a weapon, conquered a smart and shrewd lawyer, who was fighting for a bad cause. 'Truth is the highest thing that man may keep,' and the noblest child or man is he that keeps the truth ever between his lips. Walter was the important witness in a lawsuit. One of the lawyers, after cross-questioning him severely, said, 'Your father has been talking to you and telling you how to testify, hasn't he? Yes,' said the boy. 'Now,' said the lawyer, 'just tell us how your father told you to testify.' 'Well,' said the boy modestly, 'father told me that the lawyers would try and tangle me in my testimony; but if I would just be careful and tell the truth, I could tell the same thing every time.' The lawyer didn't try to tangle that boy any more. (*The Fireside News*)"[270]

"But a false witness will utter lies." **"False witness"** or lying witness is a common expression used in Proverbs 6:19, 12:17, 14:5, 19:5, 19:9, and 25:18. Because his evil heart desires to speak lies or take a bribe, **"a false witness"** is 100% sure to lie. He is driven to lie because his guiding principles are derived from Satan, the father of lies. *"A false witness has lost all principle of truth."*[271]

> 1 Kings 22:12-14 And all the prophets prophesied so, saying, Go up to Ramothgilead, and prosper: for the LORD shall deliver it into the king's hand. And the messenger that was gone to call Micaiah spake unto him, saying, Behold now, the words of the prophets declare good unto the king with one mouth: let thy word, I pray thee, be like the word of one of them, and speak that which is good. And Micaiah said, As the LORD liveth, what the LORD saith unto me, that will I speak.
>
> Psalm 15:1-2 A Psalm of David. LORD, who shall abide in thy tabernacle? who shall dwell in thy holy hill? He that walketh uprightly, and worketh righteousness, and speaketh the truth in his heart.
>
> Proverbs 6:16-17 These six *things* doth the LORD hate: yea, seven *are* an abomination unto him: A proud look, a lying tongue, and hands that shed innocent blood . . .
>
> Proverbs 12:17 He that speaketh truth sheweth forth righteousness: but a false witness deceit.
>
> Proverbs 13:5 A righteous man hateth lying: but a wicked man is loathsome, and cometh to shame.
>
> Proverbs 14:25 A true witness delivereth souls: but a deceitful witness speaketh lies.
>
> Proverbs 25:19 Confidence in an unfaithful man in time of trouble *is like* a broken tooth, and a foot out of joint.
>
> Isaiah 26:2 Open ye the gates, that the righteous nation which keepeth the truth may enter in.
>
> Jeremiah 9:3 And they bend their tongues like their bow for lies: but they are not valiant for the truth upon the earth; for they proceed from evil to evil, and they know not me, saith the LORD.
>
> John 8:44 Ye are of *your* father the devil, and the lusts of your father ye will do. He was a murderer from the beginning, and abode not in the truth, because there is no truth in him. When he speaketh a lie, he speaketh of his own: for he is a liar, and the father of it.

John 18:37 Pilate therefore said unto him, Art thou a king then? Jesus answered, Thou sayest that I am a king. To this end was I born, and for this cause came I into the world, that I should bear witness unto the truth. Every one that is of the truth heareth my voice.
Revelation 1:5 And from Jesus Christ, who is the faithful witness, and the first begotten of the dead, and the prince of the kings of the earth. Unto him that loved us, and washed us from our sins in his own blood . . .

JESUS CHRIST IS "THE FAITHFUL AND TRUE WITNESS," "the Son of God" sent from Heaven by His Father to testify of the Truth. Every born-again Christian strives to bear the image of Jesus and to be a "faithful witness." He cannot be persuaded to tell a lie by either a threat or a bribe because he hates lying and because he desires to please God and to be acceptable to other good persons.

Proverbs 14:6 A scorner seeketh wisdom, and *findeth it* not: but knowledge *is* easy unto him that understandeth.

Focus: This proverb declares the scorner's utter failure to obtain wisdom while emphasizing the easy success with which the person of understanding obtains it.

"A scorner seeketh wisdom, and *findeth it* not." Every **"scorner"** fails to meet the foundational requirement for obtaining wisdom which is an awesome respect (fear) of God (Proverbs 9:10). Rather than respect God, he hates Him, has a haughty opinion of himself, and displays heinous grandstanding acts of pride and arrogant opposition to God. The scorner blocks his own way to wisdom with hate, resistance, and mocking. The farther the scorner separates himself from God, the farther God separates from him. A scorner would seek to know aspects of wisdom only for more information with which to ridicule God and to feed his own arrogant, prideful self. He could never actually receive wisdom because he hates the same, making it hard for him to even listen once he has forced himself within hearing distance. Wisdom (should he actually hear it) would rebuke his wicked thoughts, bring judgment on his stony heart, and distance him farther from God.

"A contradictory character *[is]* a scorner in quest of wisdom. It would be strange to hear a man ask advice of a physician whose opinion he held in contempt, or to ask guidance of a traveler whose judgment and ability he despised. It would be obvious that the advice given or the rules laid down would not be followed. So a scorner, while he seeks wisdom, scorns the only method of becoming wise. He asks advice of those whom he despises, he inquires the way to wisdom, while he holds the road to it in utter contempt. The antithesis of the verse implies that he does not find wisdom because he lacks understanding – because he finds it above his comprehension. Two children may be equally ignorant of knowledge, but if one has the desire and the will to acquire it, and the other has not, what was hard to both at first will only continue hard to him who despises knowledge. So the scorner fails to find wisdom because he does not value it enough to make an effort to acquire it. The spirit in which he seeks is an effectual barrier against his finding."[272]

Proverbs 9:7-10 He that reproveth a scorner getteth to himself shame: and he that rebuketh a wicked *man getteth* himself a blot. Reprove not a scorner, lest he hate thee: rebuke a wise man, and he will love thee. Give *instruction* to a wise *man,* and he will be yet wiser: teach a just *man,* and he will increase in learning. The fear of the LORD *is* the beginning of wisdom: and the knowledge of the holy *is* understanding.
Proverbs 13:1 A wise son heareth his father's instruction: but a scorner heareth not rebuke.
Proverbs 15:12 A scorner loveth not one that reproveth him: neither will he go unto the wise.
Proverbs 17:16 Wherefore is there a price in the hand of a fool to get wisdom, seeing he hath no heart to it?
Proverbs 18:2 A fool hath no delight in understanding, but that his heart may discover itself.
Proverbs 26:12 Seest thou a man wise in his own conceit? *there is* more hope of a fool than of him.

"But knowledge *is* easy unto him that understandeth." The opposite of a scorner is a person of **understanding** who departs from evil, seeks to do God's commandments, and has knowledge of God and His word. A person of understanding is one who knows the difference between good and evil and right and wrong. As he draws closer to God, then God draws closer to him (James 4:8), and there he finds wisdom, knowledge, and understanding. It is with this closeness that God teaches His chosen vessels. ***Knowledge is easy to him that understands*** because he has the mind of Christ and is a close friend of the Teacher.

Job 28:28 And unto man he said, Behold, the fear of the Lord, that *is* wisdom; and to depart from evil *is* understanding.
Psalm 1:1 Blessed *is* the man that walketh not in the counsel of the ungodly, nor standeth in the way of sinners, nor sitteth in the seat of the scornful.
Psalm 111:10 The fear of the LORD is the beginning of wisdom: a good understanding have all they that do *his commandments: his* praise endureth for ever.
Proverbs 1:7 The fear of the LORD *is* the beginning of knowledge: but fools despise wisdom and instruction.
Proverbs 9:10 The fear of the LORD is the beginning of wisdom: and the knowledge of the holy is understanding.

> **Proverbs 14:7** Go from the presence of a foolish man, when thou perceivest not *in him* the lips of knowledge.

>> Focus: This proverb teaches to depart from the presence of a foolish person once his speech reveals his wicked, foolish heart that lacks the knowledge of God.

The previous proverb indicated that the foolish man cannot receive wisdom; consequently, according to this proverb, when allowed to speak, he will reveal himself for the fool that he is. Although a foolish man might be able to disguise himself for the sake of developing an advantageous relationship, eventually, his **"lips"** (words) will reveal a foolish heart. John Gill advises departure, "when it is observed that his lips pour out foolishness, what is corrupt and unsavory, unchaste and filthy; what does not minister grace to the hearers, nor is for the use of edifying, nor any ways improving in useful knowledge, but all the reverse."[273] Matthew Henry wrote: "*Go from his presence, for thou perceivest* there is no good to be gotten by his company, but danger of getting hurt by it. Sometimes the only way we have of reproving wicked discourse and witnessing against it is by leaving the company and going out of the hearing of it."[274]

Scripture gives several reasons for a departing from the foolish man's presence: (1) lest the person's own heart become contaminated, (2) lest the person become injured from the fallout of God's wrath toward the ungodly, (3) lest the person lose the blessings of God by becoming disobedient to Him, and (4) lest the person find himself too far from the spiritual and perhaps physical place where God intended to meet with him.

> Proverbs 9:6 Forsake the foolish, and live; and go in the way of understanding.
> Proverbs 13:20 He that walketh with wise men shall be wise: but a companion of fools shall be destroyed.
> Proverbs 14:8 The wisdom of the prudent *is* to understand his way: but the folly of fools *is* deceit.
> Proverbs 19:27 Cease, my son, to hear the instruction that causeth to err from the words of knowledge.
> 1 Corinthians 5:11 But now I have written unto you not to keep company, if any man that is called a brother be a fornicator, or covetous, or an idolater, or a railer, or a drunkard, or an extortioner; with such an one no not to eat.
> 1 Timothy 6:3-5 If any man teach otherwise, and consent not to wholesome words, *even* the words of our Lord Jesus Christ, and to the doctrine which is according to godliness; He is proud, knowing nothing, but doting about questions and strifes of words, whereof cometh envy, strife, railings, evil surmisings, Perverse disputings of men of corrupt minds, and destitute of the truth, supposing that gain is godliness: from such withdraw thyself.

Obeying this proverb may seem difficult to the merciful and loving believer, but the Bible illustrates it in 1 Samuel 15:35 "And Samuel came no more to see Saul until the day of his death: nevertheless Samuel mourned for Saul..." "when he saw that remonstrances were unavailing with him, though he continued to 'mourn' for him, remembering from what high estate he had fallen."[275]

> **Proverbs 14:8** The wisdom of the prudent *is* to understand his way: but the folly of fools *is* deceit.

>> Focus: This proverb contrasts the prudent person who has wisdom to understand his way of life with the fool who has foolishness to deceive him about his way of life.

"The wisdom of the prudent is to understand his way." *Prudence* is that part of being wise that causes a person to make good choices; and in the case of this proverb, it is wisdom that causes the prudent person to choose the right path. He **understands his way** because he understands the will of God for his life.

> "'As God hath distributed to every man, as the Lord hath called everyone, so let him walk.' (1Corinthians 7:17) Let the eye do the work of the eye, and the hand of the hand. If Moses prayed on the Mount, and Joshua fought in the valley, it was not because the one was deficient in courage, or the other in prayer; but because each had his appointed work, and understood his own way. Many steps of our way are different from our neighbor's, and may often be difficult to discern; being rather involved in the principles, than expressed in the detail, of Scripture. But the wisdom of the prudent will "understand what the will of the Lord is." (Ephesians 5:17) 'A single eye' (Matthew 6:22) and a 'sound heart' (Psalm 119:80) will make our way plain."[276]
>
> Psalm 119:34-35 Give me understanding, and I shall keep thy law; yea, I shall observe it with my whole heart. Make me to go in the path of thy commandments; for therein do I delight.

Psalm 119:104-105 Through thy precepts I get understanding: therefore I hate every false way. NUN. Thy word *is* a lamp unto my feet, and a light unto my path.

Proverbs 2:7-9 He layeth up sound wisdom for the righteous: he is a buckler to them that walk uprightly. He keepeth the paths of judgment, and preserveth the way of his saints. Then shalt thou understand righteousness, and judgment, and equity; yea, every good path.

Proverbs 14:33 Wisdom resteth in the heart of him that hath understanding: but *that which is* in the midst of fools is made known.

Proverbs 17:24 Wisdom *is* before him that hath understanding; but the eyes of a fool *are* in the ends of the earth.

Colossians 1:9-10 For this cause we also, since the day we heard it, do not cease to pray for you, and to desire that ye might be filled with the knowledge of his will in all wisdom and spiritual understanding; That ye might walk worthy of the Lord unto all pleasing, being fruitful in every good work, and increasing in the knowledge of God . . .

Ephesians 5:17 Wherefore be ye not unwise, but understanding what the will of the Lord *is*.

"But the folly of fools is deceit." The fool's foolishness (which he believes is his wisdom) causes him to misunderstand his way – *to be deceived*, thinking he is right. The fool doesn't comprehend that he doesn't understand, that he has been deceived into believing that his foolishness is wisdom. He thinks too highly of himself and not enough of God, and he is deceived about his earthly pathway and his eternal destiny. His first step to receiving wisdom and prudence is believing and trusting in God and His word, but foolish people will *not* hear the reproof of Scripture, and they will *not* accept the leadership and lordship of Christ. Proof of their deception is publicly visible to all when they reject the word of God and His Son.

The fool does not believe in God, and he has no fear of God – he hates the knowledge of God. He is a liar and a deceiver, and doing evil is such a sport to him that departing from the ***pathway of evil*** is an abomination. Figuratively speaking, he wears a crown of foolishness instead of wearing a crown of wisdom. Furthermore, once a person has chosen the ***path of fools***, he seems drawn into the whirlpool of destruction.

Psalm 36:2-4 For he flattereth himself in his own eyes, until his iniquity be found to be hateful. The words of his mouth *are* iniquity and deceit: he hath left off to be wise, *and* to do good. He deviseth mischief upon his bed; he setteth himself in a way *that is* not good; he abhorreth not evil.

Psalm 53:1-3 To the chief Musician upon Mahalath, Maschil, *A Psalm* of David. The fool hath said in his heart, *There is* no God. Corrupt are they, and have done abominable iniquity: *there is* none that doeth good. God looked down from heaven upon the children of men, to see if there were *any* that did understand, that did seek God. Every one of them is gone back: they are altogether become filthy; *there is* none that doeth good, no, not one.

Proverbs 1:7 The fear of the LORD *is* the beginning of knowledge: *but* fools despise wisdom and instruction.

Proverbs 1:30-32 They would none of my counsel: they despised all my reproof. Therefore shall they eat of the fruit of their own way, and be filled with their own devices. For the turning away of the simple shall slay them, and the prosperity of fools shall destroy them.

Proverbs 10:23 *It is* as sport to a fool to do mischief: but a man of understanding hath wisdom.

Proverbs 12:15 The way of a fool *is* right in his own eyes: but he that hearkeneth unto counsel *is* wise.

Proverbs 18:2 A fool hath no delight in understanding, but that his heart may discover itself.

Proverbs 14:9 Fools make a mock at sin: but among the righteous *there is* favour.

Focus: This proverb states because fools mock at sin, they receive God's disfavor; but the righteous receive favor.

"Fools make a mock at sin." The fool who ***mocks at sin***, finds no favor from God but rather wrath; thus, he victimizes himself. Certainly, the fool (because he is a fool) doesn't understand that it is sin that brought death into the world. Surely, if his mind were not so blinded and his heart so hardened, he would understand that sin is not to be mocked nor the offer of forgiveness from sin taken lightly. Fools mock because they become hardened in their wickedness. To mock at sin is to mock at the sacrifice of Jesus.

"They make a laughing matter of the sins of others, making themselves and their companions merry with that for which they should mourn, and they make a light matter of their own sins, both when they are tempted to sin and when they have committed it; they *call evil good and good evil*, turn it off with a jest, rush into sin (Jeremiah 8:6) and say they shall have peace though they go on. They care not what mischief they do by their sins, and laugh at those that tell them of it. They are advocates for sin, and are ingenious at framing excuses for it."[277]

Proverbs 30:20 Such *is* the way of an adulterous woman; she eateth, and wipeth her mouth, and saith, I have done no wickedness.

Isaiah 5:20 Woe unto them that call evil good, and good evil; that put darkness for light, and light for darkness; that put bitter for sweet, and sweet for bitter!

Jeremiah 8:6 I hearkened and heard, *but* they spake not aright: no man repented him of his wickedness, saying, What have I done? every one turned to his course, as the horse rusheth into the battle.

Romans 1:28, 32 And even as they did not like to retain God in their knowledge, God gave them over to a reprobate mind, to do those things which are not convenient . . . Who knowing the judgment of God, that they which commit such things are worthy of death, not only do the same, but have pleasure in them that do them.

"But among the righteous *there is* favour." Rather than "mock at sin" (as does the fool), the righteous, hate sin, knowing its grave consequences; hence, the righteous are given rewarding **"favor"** from God. He can be found *"under the spout where the glory comes out"* enjoying God's peace, power, provisions, and His marvelous presence.

Psalm 1:3-4 And he shall be like a tree planted by the rivers of water, that bringeth forth his fruit in his season; his leaf also shall not wither; and whatsoever he doeth shall prosper. The ungodly *are* not so: but *are* like the chaff which the wind driveth away.

Proverbs 8:33-35 Hear instruction, and be wise, and refuse it not. Blessed is the man that heareth me, watching daily at my gates, waiting at the posts of my doors. For whoso findeth me findeth life, and shall obtain favour of the LORD.

Proverbs 12:2 A good *man* obtaineth favour of the LORD: but a man of wicked devices will he condemn.

Proverbs 13:15 Good understanding giveth favour: but the way of transgressors is hard.

Hebrews 11:6 But without faith *it is* impossible to please *him*: for he that cometh to God must believe that he is, and *that* he is a rewarder of them that diligently seek him.

Proverbs 14:10 The heart knoweth his own bitterness; and a stranger doth not intermeddle with his joy.

Focus: This proverb emphasizes that no person can fully know and understand the joy or the bitterness of another.

Every individual has a multiplicity of mental inputs from numerous sources that mingle with imperfect memory, erratic emotions, and developing intelligence to potentially produce a great variety of emotional, psychological, intellectual, and spiritual responses within the mind. On one end of the response is extreme bitterness and on the other is extreme joy. Webster defines **"bitterness"** as "keen sorrow, painful affliction; vexation; deep distress of mind."[278] It is impossible for an individual to fully express in words or gestures the depth of his thoughts and feelings. Though no man lives to himself and no man dies to himself, no man ever fully understands exactly how another feels. Consolation and comfort come from the knowledge and communing one has with God, for He alone understands every detail of an individual's every emotion and thought. More likely than not, even an individual doesn't completely understand all of his own feelings of bitterness and joy.

Jeremiah 17:9 The heart *is* deceitful above all *things,* and desperately wicked: who can know it?

God had "shut up Hannah's womb," and she longed to have a child. One year when she made the trip with the family to sacrifice at the altar, which was then at Shiloh, Hannah *"was* in bitterness of soul, and prayed unto the LORD, and wept sore."* (1 Samuel 1:10) The priest, Eli *(who hadn't restrained his own sons' evil ways)* was sitting nearby and thought she was drunk because only her lips moved (1 Samuel 1:13). Clearly Eli did not see into her heart, understand her bitterness, and feel the depth of her prayer; therefore, he misjudged her actions. *Only God can judge the motives of the heart.*

Job's friends couldn't see into the depths of his heart and feel the emotional upheaval of his soul when he said, "Oh that my grief were throughly weighed, and my calamity laid in the balances together! For now it would be heavier than the sand of the sea: therefore my words are swallowed up." (Job 6:2-3) Job's friend Bildad, showed his own lack of understanding when he reproved Job in Chapter 8.

In 2 Kings 4, neither the spiritual prophet Elisha nor his backslidden servant understood the overwhelming sorrow that drove the great Shunammite woman to ride furiously for 33 miles on the back of a donkey to Mt. Carmel. Elisha said, ". . . her soul *is* vexed within her: and the Lord hath hid *it* from me, and hath not told me." (2 Kings 4:27)

In the same way that one person cannot understand and know the inner feelings of another who is enduring a period of tribulation and pain in his life, one person cannot completely understand and partake of the joy felt by another. The Bible doesn't describe the incredible pain that Abraham felt when he heard these words from God: "Take now thy son, thine only *son* Isaac, whom thou lovest, and get thee into the land of Moriah; and offer him there for a burnt offering upon one of the mountains which I will tell thee of." (Genesis 22:2) Neither does it describe the joy that must have flooded Abraham when he heard the words of the angel in Genesis 22:12-13 – "Lay not thine hand upon the lad, neither do thou any thing unto him: for now I know that thou fearest God, seeing thou hast not withheld thy son, thine only *son* from me. And Abraham lifted up his eyes, and looked, and behold behind *him* a ram caught in a thicket by his horns: and Abraham went and took the ram, and offered him up for a burnt offering in the stead of his son." The following quotation from *The Biblical Illustrator* is very telling.

> "Though joy is less self-concealing than sorrow, yet it has depths unknown to any but its possessor and its God. The joy that rushed into Abraham's heart when Isaac descended with him from the altar on Moriah; the joy of the father when he pressed his prodigal son to his bosom *[Luke 15:11-24]*; the joy of the widow of Nain when her only son raised himself from the bier, and returned to gladden her lowly home; the joy of the broken-hearted woman when she heard Christ say, "Thy sins are all forgiven thee" (Luke 7:36-50); such joy has depths that no outward eye could penetrate. The joy of the true Christian is indeed a joy "unspeakable and full of glory."[279]

Unlike Eli, who could not understand the deep bitterness and heartache that moved Hannah to pray so fervently, the believer has a high priest – Jesus Christ, Who made himself a "man of sorrows, and acquainted with grief" that he might save the lost and become the greatest Friend a person could ever have. The Bible declares "he hath borne our griefs, and carried our sorrows." He truly understands our "bitterness" and our "joy" and He is NOT a "**stranger**"to those who walk with Him.

> Isaiah 53:3-5 He is despised and rejected of men; a man of sorrows, and acquainted with grief: and we hid as it were *our* faces from him; he was despised, and we esteemed him not. Surely he hath borne our griefs, and carried our sorrows: yet we did esteem him stricken, smitten of God, and afflicted. But he *was* wounded for our transgressions, *he was* bruised for our iniquities: the chastisement of our peace *was* upon him; and with his stripes we are healed.
> Hebrews 4:13-16 Neither is there any creature that is not manifest in his sight: but all things *are* naked and opened unto the eyes of him with whom we have to do. Seeing then that we have a great high priest, that is passed into the heavens, Jesus the Son of God, let us hold fast *our* profession For we have not an high priest which cannot be touched with the feeling of our infirmities; but was in all points tempted like as *we are, yet* without sin. Let us therefore come boldly unto the throne of grace, that we may obtain mercy, and find grace to help in time of need.

Proverbs 14:11 The house of the wicked shall be overthrown: but the tabernacle of the upright shall flourish.

Focus: This proverb contrasts temporary physical strength and ultimate demise of the wicked with eternal spiritual strength and eternal endurance of the upright.

The **wicked's house** (life), is symbolically constructed of durable building material and appears to be *strong, permanent*, and capable of withstanding storms. His **"house"** is contrasted with the **"tabernacle of the upright"** that appears to be *weak, temporary,* and incapable of withstanding a storm. (A "tabernacle" or tent was usually constructed of fabric or animal hide.) It is fitting that the righteous are depicted as a tabernacle because they spend their lives as "pilgrims and strangers" looking forward to their permanent home with the Father. Their hearts are not to become enamored with the fancies of this world. The righteous are content with whatever God sees fit to give them because they are looking forward to a city with established "foundations whose builder and maker is God."

> Hebrews 11:9-10 By faith he sojourned in the land of promise, as in a strange country, dwelling in tabernacles with Isaac and Jacob, the heirs with him of the same promise: For he looked for a city which hath foundations, whose builder and maker is God.
> Hebrews 11:13-16 These all died in faith, not having received the promises, but having seen them afar off, and were persuaded of them, and embraced them, and confessed that they were strangers and pilgrims on the earth. For they that say such things declare plainly that they seek a country. And truly, if they had been mindful of that country from whence they came out, they might have had opportunity to have returned. But now they desire a better country, that is, an heavenly: wherefore God is not ashamed to be called their God: for he hath prepared for them a city.
> 1 John 2:15-17 Love not the world, neither the things *that are* in the world. If any man love the world, the love of the Father is not in him. For all that *is* in the world, the lust of the flesh, and the lust of the eyes, and the pride of life, is not of the Father, but is of the world. And the world passeth away, and the lust thereof: but he that doeth the will of God abideth for ever.

Taking great pains to increase their material prosperity, wicked people build their lives (houses) through sin. "Their inward thought is, that their houses *shall continue* forever, *and* their dwelling places to all generations; they call *their* lands after *their* own names." (Psalm 49:11)

Upright people build their lives through righteousness and helping others. They have the great strength and stability of a "tree planted by the rivers of water" – because of God's favor. "The ungodly are not so; but are like the chaff which the wind driveth away. Therefore the ungodly shall not stand in the judgment, nor sinners in the congregation of the righteous. For the LORD knoweth the way of the righteous: but the way of the ungodly shall perish." (Psalm 1)

The **"upright"** have the benefit of protection, peace, provision, and partnership with God, thereby giving their "tabernacle" the ability to **"flourish"** throughout eternity. The "wicked" have no such relationship, and their "house" will be overthrown. **"Flourish"** applies metaphorically to the growth, vigor, and increase of a family under the blessing of God.[280]

> Job 8:13-15 So *are* the paths of all that forget God; and the hypocrite's hope shall perish: Whose hope shall be cut off, and whose trust *shall be* a spider's web. He shall lean upon his house, but it shall not stand: he shall hold it fast, but it shall not endure.
>
> Psalm 49:6-13 They that trust in their wealth, and boast themselves in the multitude of their riches; None *of them* can by any means redeem his brother, nor give to God a ransom for him: (For the redemption of their soul *is* precious, and it ceaseth for ever:) That he should still live for ever, *and* not see corruption. For he seeth *that* wise men die, likewise the fool and the brutish person perish, and leave their wealth to others. Their inward thought is, that their houses *shall continue* for ever, *and* their dwelling places to all generations; they call *their* lands after *their* own names. Nevertheless man *being* in honour abideth not: he is like the beasts *that* perish. This their way *is* their folly: yet their posterity approve their sayings. Selah.
>
> Proverbs 3:33 The curse of the LORD *is* in the house of the wicked: but he blesseth the habitation of the just.
>
> Proverbs 12:7 The wicked are overthrown, and *are* not: but the house of the righteous shall stand.
>
> Proverbs 21:12 The righteous man wisely considereth the house of the wicked: but God overthroweth the wicked for their wickedness.
>
> Isaiah 33:20 Look upon Zion, the city of our solemnities: thine eyes shall see Jerusalem a quiet habitation, a tabernacle that shall not be taken down; not one of the stakes thereof shall ever be removed, neither shall any of the cords thereof be broken.
>
> Matthew 7:24-27 Therefore whosoever heareth these sayings of mine, and doeth them, I will liken him unto a wise man, which built his house upon a rock: And the rain descended, and the floods came, and the winds blew, and beat upon that house; and it fell not: for it was founded upon a rock. And every one that heareth these sayings of mine, and doeth them not, shall be likened unto a foolish man, which built his house upon the sand: And the rain descended, and the floods came, and the winds blew, and beat upon that house; and it fell: and great was the fall of it.

Proverbs 14:12 There is a way which seemeth right unto a man, but the end thereof *are* the ways of death.

Focus: This proverb declares that man can have faulty destructive reasoning.

Many men use defective criteria for determining if the **"way"** is right or wrong (judgment). Faulty criteria may include the following: ungodly laws, peer pressure, improper family values, and justified thinking because of distorted personal desires. These and other criteria can lead a person down the wrong way to destruction, but instructions from Scripture will never lead wrong. People are deceived into believing something, or some action is right simply because they want that thing, or they want to perform that act. Coveting has led many into disaster when they believed that acquiring that object or person had to be right because the desire was so strong. Once a person is *comfortably* on a path of error, other pathways for wrong (which seem to be right) present themselves.

> "This verse is a warning against following a perverted or uninstructed conscience. Conscience needs to be informed by God's word and ruled by God's will to make it a safe guide. When properly regulated, it is able to pronounce a verdict upon contemplated action, and its verdict must always he obeyed. But warped by prejudice, weakened by disuse and disobedience, judicially blinded in punishment and in consequence of sin, it loses all power of moral judgment, and becomes inoperative of good; and then, as to the way that seemed at the moment right, **the end thereof are the ways of death.**"[281]

The natural man – the one who doesn't know God – believes strongly that he is right. "The rightness is present only as a phantom, for it arises wholly from a terrible self-deception.[282] He believes others who believe in following the dictates of Scripture are wrong.

> Psalm 1:6 For the LORD knoweth the way of the righteous: but the way of the ungodly shall perish.
>
> Proverbs 3:5-6 Trust in the LORD with all thine heart; and lean not unto thine own understanding. In all thy ways acknowledge him, and he shall direct thy paths.
>
> Proverbs 5:3-5 For the lips of a strange woman drop *as* an honeycomb, and her mouth *is* smoother than oil: But her end is bitter as wormwood, sharp as a twoedged sword. Her feet go down to death; her steps take hold on hell.
>
> Proverbs 12:15 The way of a fool is right in his own eyes: but he that hearkeneth unto counsel is wise.

Proverbs 30:12 *There is* a generation *that are* pure in their own eyes, and *yet* is not washed from their filthiness.

Matthew 7:13-14 Enter ye in at the strait gate: for wide *is* the gate, and broad *is* the way, that leadeth to destruction, and many there be which go in thereat: Because strait *is* the gate, and narrow *is* the way, which leadeth unto life, and few there be that find it.

Romans 1:28, 32 And even as they did not like to retain God in their knowledge, God gave them over to a reprobate mind, to do those things which are not convenient . . . Who knowing the judgment of God, that they which commit such things are worthy of death, not only do the same, but have pleasure in them that do them.

Romans 6:20-21 For when ye were the servants of sin, ye were free from righteousness. What fruit had ye then in those things whereof ye are now ashamed? for the end of those things is death.

James 1:22 But be ye doers of the word, and not hearers only, deceiving your own selves.

The "**way which seemeth right**" may be centered in false views of religion.

"...he may have an imperfect repentance, a false faith, a very false creed; and he may persuade himself that he is in the direct way to heaven. Many of the papists, when they were burning the saints of God in the flames at Smithfield, thought they were doing God service! And in the late Irish massacre, the more of the Protestants they piked to death, shot, or burnt, the more they believed they deserved of God's favor and their Church's gratitude. But cruelty and murder are the short road, the near way, to eternal perdition."[283]

Proverbs 16:25 repeats this proverb except the word "that" is substituted for the word "which."

Proverbs 14:13 Even in laughter the heart is sorrowful; and the end of that mirth *is* heaviness.

Focus: This proverb declares that a person (either wise or foolish) has to contend with mixed emotions – often to the extreme.

Both wicked and righteous persons may experience extreme emotions simultaneously. First, consider the wicked as described by Solomon in Ecclesiastes 7:6. He describes this mirth as "the laughter of fools." It is the forced, boisterous merriment of a fallen man disturbed by the stings of an accusing conscience and oppressed with forebodings of future eternal punishment. It is a hypocritical, put-on merriment for the purpose of drowning out the sorrows and distress of the man's conscience. When left to himself after the boisterous companions have departed, this man is left to contemplate the results of his sinful nature and experiences **"the end of that mirth *is* heaviness"** *[grief, sorrow]*. It can also be seen in the artificial mirth of an unrepentant man about to die.

Ecclesiastes 7:4-6 The heart of the wise *is* in the house of mourning; but the heart of fools *is* in the house of mirth. *It is* better to hear the rebuke of the wise, than for a man to hear the song of fools. For as the crackling of thorns under a pot, so *is* the laughter of the fool: this also *is* vanity.

"**Even in laughter the heart is sorrowful**. . . As Belshazzar's was in the midst of his feast and jollity *[Daniel 5]*, when he saw the writing on the wall; so sin may stare a man in the face, and guilt load his conscience and fill him with sorrow, amidst his merriment; a man may put on a merry countenance, and feign a laugh, when his heart is very sorrowful; and oftentimes this sorrow comes by sinful laughter, by mocking at sin and jesting at religion; **and the end of that mirth** *is* **heaviness**: sometimes in this life a sinner mourns at last, and mourns for his wicked mirth, or that he has made himself so merry with religious persons and things, and oftentimes when it is too late; so the end of that mirth the fool in the Gospel promised himself was heaviness, when his soul was required of him; this was the case of the rich man who had his good things here, and his evil things hereafter."[284] *[See Daniel 5:18-23.]*

There are situations where the righteous person forces laughter and gives the impression that he is joyful; but inwardly, he is sorrowful and hurting. When the laughter stops, the heaviness or sorrow again prevails. J. F. B. Tingling relates the following interview with Opie Read, an American humorist who was in deep heaviness during the time he was writing articles to make others laugh.

"'Sometimes,' says the writer, 'his work is marked by the deepest pathos. He had lost two of his children, to whom he was devotedly attached, and these melancholy events made very marked impressions on the man and his work.'

'When one of my babies died,' said he, in talking of the matter to me, 'I was working for a magazine, and I was required to do just so much work every day. I was compelled to do it – it was my only means of support. During that awful time I would frequently rock the cradle of my dying babe for hours at the time. With one hand I rocked that cradle of death, and with the other I was writing stuff to make people laugh. I sobbed and wept, and watched that angel and wrote that stuff, and I felt every minute as if my heart would burst. And yet some people think this funny business is all sunshine. Sometimes even now I see articles floating around that I wrote while under the shadow of death, and occasionally some editor will preface these very things with some such remark as, 'The genial and sunny-souled Opie Read says so and so,' – yes, about these same things that I penned when my babe was dying and my heart was bursting.'"[285]

Furthermore, wonderful, pleasant memories that emerge after the death of a loved one can create a manifestation of conflicting emotions whereby friends and family experience both laughter and sorrow of heart simultaneously. Also, people often laugh when someone makes a personal derogatory comment about them; but inwardly the comment has pricked their heart, bringing forth feelings of sorrow.

Proverbs 14:14 The backslider in heart shall be filled with his own ways: and a good man *shall be satisfied* from himself.

Focus: This proverb declares that the backslider's heart causes him to act in "his own ways" to satisfy his wicked heart's desire and the good man's heart causes him to act in a manner that satisfies his godly heart's desire.

"The backslider in heart shall be filled with his own ways." The **"backslider in heart"** has surrendered his **"heart"** *[mind, emotions, and will]* to the position and attitude that he endorsed before claiming to be a child of God. Having lost his fervor for God and His word, the backslider has willfully moved away from God. His sin has lured him to partake more and more of evil until he is trapped within its insidious web. At this point, he is **"filled with his own ways,"** meaning that his conduct (or ways) is led by his own sin-distorted and compromised acceptance of right and wrong.

> *"Backsliding* implies a willful step; not always open, but the more dangerous, because hidden. Here was no open apostasy, perhaps no tangible inconsistency. Nay – the man may be looked up to as an eminent saint. But he is *a backslider in heart.* A secret canker of unwatchfulness; worldly conformity (Hosea 7:8), neglect, or indulgence, has insensibly 'devoured his strength.' (Hosea 7:9; Judges 16:20) He was once pressing onward. A langour has now stolen upon him. His heart beats unsteadily. He has become formal and hurried in his prayers; lukewarm in the means of grace: reading his Bible to soothe his conscience, rather than to feed his soul. The first steps, instead of alarming, and bringing him to secret weeping (Matthew 26:75), hurried him onwards from one liberty to another, till he lost all power of resistance. His unsoundness was known to God, long before it was manifested to the Church."[286]

The Bible graphically portrays the backslider's sin. David's backsliding was known to God *before* he took another man's wife and had her husband killed. (2Samuel 11:1-2) After all his accomplishments and trusting God, Hezekiah allowed pride to cause him to backslide and become a warning to later believers to always be watchful. (2 Chronicles 32:31; Philippians 2:12)

> Judges 16:19-20 And she made him sleep upon her knees; and she called for a man, and she caused him to shave off the seven locks of his head; and she began to afflict him, and his strength went from him. And she said, The Philistines be upon thee, Samson. And he awoke out of his sleep, and said, I will go out as at other times before, and shake myself. And he wist not that the LORD was departed from him.
>
> 2 Samuel 11:1-5 And it came to pass, after the year was expired, at the time when kings go forth *to battle,* that David sent Joab, and his servants with him, and all Israel; and they destroyed the children of Ammon, and besieged Rabbah. But David tarried still at Jerusalem. And it came to pass in an eveningtide, that David arose from off his bed, and walked upon the roof of the king's house: and from the roof he saw a woman washing herself; and the woman *was* very beautiful to look upon. And David sent and enquired after the woman. And *one* said, *Is* not this Bathsheba, the daughter of Eliam, the wife of Uriah the Hittite? And David sent messengers, and took her; and she came in unto him, and he lay with her; for she was purified from her uncleanness: and she returned unto her house. And the woman conceived, and sent and told David, and said, I *am* with child.
>
> 2 Chronicles 32:31 Howbeit in *the business of* the ambassadors of the princes of Babylon, who sent unto him to enquire of the wonder that was *done* in the land, God left him *[Hezekiah],* to try him, that he might know all *that was* in his heart.
>
> Hosea 7:8-9 Ephraim, he hath mixed himself among the people; Ephraim is a cake not turned. Strangers have devoured his strength, and he knoweth *it* not: yea, gray hairs are here and there upon him, yet he knoweth not.
>
> Matthew 26:69-75 Now Peter sat without in the palace: and a damsel came unto him, saying, Thou also wast with Jesus of Galilee. But he denied before *them* all, saying, I know not what thou sayest. And when he was gone out into the porch, another *maid* saw him, and said unto them that were there, This *fellow* was also with Jesus of Nazareth. And again he denied with an oath, I do not know the man. And after a while came unto *him* they that stood by, and said to Peter, Surely thou also art *one* of them; for thy speech bewrayeth thee. Then began he to curse and to swear, *saying,* I know not the man. And immediately the cock crew. And Peter remembered the word of Jesus, which said unto him, Before the cock crow, thou shalt deny me thrice. And he went out, and wept bitterly.

When he becomes "filled with his own ways," *the backslider becomes the fountain of his own misery.* He brings problems and tribulations into his own life. When he turns away from God, the backslider will not leave his brutish lusts and passions.

> Proverbs 1:30-31 They would none of my counsel: they despised all my reproof. Therefore shall they eat of the fruit of their own way, and be filled with their own devices.

Proverbs 5:21-22 For the ways of man *are* before the eyes of the LORD, and he pondereth all his goings. His own iniquities shall take the wicked himself, and he shall be holden with the cords of his sins. He shall die without instruction; and in the greatness of his folly he shall go astray.

Jeremiah 2:13 For my people have committed two evils; they have forsaken me the fountain of living waters, *and* hewed them out cisterns, broken cisterns, that can hold no water.

"And a good man *shall be satisfied* from himself." The **"good man"** is good because he walks with God. He is **satisfied** *or filled from within himself* because "from the pious temper of his own heart, which cleaves to the Lord, and from the holy and righteous course of his life, he shall receive unspeakable comfort, both in this world and in the next."[287] His ways are learned from God's word; consequently, his conduct is guided by God and ***satisfying***. Within, he has the witness of the Spirit, Who, among other things, invigorates life, gives joy, and directs his conscience as well as his steps.

Isaiah 3:10-11 Say ye to the righteous, that it shall be well with him: for they shall eat the fruit of their doings. Woe unto the wicked! it shall be ill with him: for the reward of his hands shall be given him.

John 14:16 And I will pray the Father, and he shall give you another Comforter, that he may abide with you for ever; Even the Spirit of truth; whom the world cannot receive, because it seeth him not, neither knoweth him: but ye know him; for he dwelleth with you, and shall be in you.

Romans 8:16 The Spirit itself beareth witness with our spirit, that we are the children of God:

Galatians 5:22-23 But the fruit of the Spirit is love, joy, peace, longsuffering, gentleness, goodness, faith, Meekness, temperance: against such there is no law.

Philippians 2:12-13 Wherefore, my beloved, as ye have always obeyed, not as in my presence only, but now much more in my absence, work out your own salvation with fear and trembling. For it is God which worketh in you both to will and to do of *his* good pleasure.

The next four proverbs discuss the ways of the fool. Verses 15 and 18 contrast the ways of the fool with the prudent's ways.

Proverbs 14:15 The simple believeth every word: but the prudent *man* looketh well to his going.

Focus: This proverb contrasts how information is evaluated by a simple person versus how the same is evaluated by a prudent person.

"The simple believeth every word." "To **believe every word** of God is faith. To believe every word of man is credulity *[gullibility]*."[288] The simple are naive, not having internalized instruction from wisdom; therefore, they fail to challenge the truthfulness of what they have heard. They are easily deceived. Not only do wicked men and women deceive them and cause them to choose the path of the wicked, but false teachers easily dupe them when they peddle false Biblical doctrine or twist the Scriptures to make them more palatable.

Genesis 3:1-6 Now the serpent was more subtil than any beast of the field which the LORD God had made. And he said unto the woman, Yea, hath God said, Ye shall not eat of every tree of the garden? And the woman said unto the serpent, We may eat of the fruit of the trees of the garden: But of the fruit of the tree which is in the midst of the garden, God hath said, Ye shall not eat of it, neither shall ye touch it, lest ye die. And the serpent said unto the woman, Ye shall not surely die: For God doth know that in the day ye eat thereof, then your eyes shall be opened, and ye shall be as gods, knowing good and evil. And when the woman saw that the tree was good for food, and that it was pleasant to the eyes, and a tree to be desired to make one wise, she took of the fruit thereof, and did eat, and gave also unto her husband with her; and he did eat.

Proverbs 7:7-10, 21-24 And beheld among the simple ones, I discerned among the youths, a young man void of understanding, passing through the street near her corner; and he went the way to her house, In the twilight, in the evening, in the black and dark night: And, behold, there met him a woman with the attire of an harlot, and subtil of heart . . . With her much fair speech she caused him to yield, with the flattering of her lips she forced him. He goeth after her straightway, as an ox goeth to the slaughter, or as a fool to the correction of the stocks; Till a dart strike through his liver; as a bird hasteth to the snare, and knoweth not that it is for his life.

"But the prudent *man* looketh well to his going." He is always personally responsible for his own actions; and though there are many times and situations where he must trust others, he is not so simple as to believe everything he is told, especially by untrustworthy or unproven people. *(See pages 198-199 for more explanation of "prudent.")*

"The prudent man looketh well to his going" . . . that is, he judges of men's words and professions by their conduct, which is a good rule. He is cautious, examining before he believes, and trying before he trusts, especially in matters of great moment; and considering things maturely before he does as he is advised. Bochart observes well upon this verse, that 'as prudence without simplicity degenerates into craft, so simplicity without prudence is no better than downright folly. We must follow our Saviour's counsel, and unite the serpent with the dove.'"[289]

Proverbs 14:8 The wisdom of the prudent is to understand his way: but the folly of fools is deceit.

Proverbs 22:3 A prudent man foreseeth the evil, and hideth himself: but the simple pass on, and are punished. *[repeated verbatim in Proverbs 27:12]*

Matthew 10:16 Behold, I send you forth as sheep in the midst of wolves: be ye therefore wise as serpents, and harmless as doves.

John 2:24 But Jesus did not commit himself unto them, because he knew all *men* . . .

Romans 16:17-19 Now I beseech you, brethren, mark them which cause divisions and offences contrary to the doctrine which ye have learned; and avoid them. For they that are such serve not our Lord Jesus Christ, but their own belly; and by good words and fair speeches deceive the hearts of the simple. For your obedience is come abroad unto all men. I am glad therefore on your behalf: but yet I would have you wise unto that which is good, and simple concerning evil.

Ephesians 4:14 That we *henceforth* be no more children, tossed to and fro, and carried about with every wind of doctrine, by the sleight of men, *and* cunning craftiness, whereby they lie in wait to deceive . . .

1 Thessalonians 5:21 Prove all things; hold fast that which is good.

1 John 4:1 Beloved, believe not every spirit, but try the spirits whether they are of God: because many false prophets are gone out into the world.

Proverbs 14:16 A wise *man* feareth, and departeth from evil: but the fool rageth, and is confident.

Focus: This proverb compares the wise person's response to evil with the fool's response to evil.

"A wise *man* feareth, and departeth from evil." The fear of the LORD is the very foundation of a **wise man** (Psalm 111:10; Proverbs 9:10 and 15:33). It is the solid, unmovable ground on which he builds every premise of belief, every principle of action, and every proclamation of truth. He has respect for the awesomeness of God; and it is this "fear," this respect, that causes him to **"depart from evil."** The wise man knows that God is light to him in a dark world and that it is God who provides, protects, and produces all good that he enjoys. Evil threatens the wise person's peace of mind and wonderful relationship with God; therefore, when evil presents itself, he separates from it. As the New Testament states, the wise man will "work out his own salvation with fear and trembling." (Philippians 2:12)

A perfect illustration of a wise man's fearing God and departing from evil is found in Joseph. Potiphar's wife wanted to seduce the handsome young man, but he told her, "how can I do this great wickedness and sin against God." (Genesis 39:9) One day, in an attempt to persuade him, she caught him by his garment, but he fled from her seductive advance. Because she was enraged at his refusal of her, she then charged him falsely to her husband, and Joseph was forced back into prison. God was proving and training the young man for the great leadership task that he would assume later. Consequently, he was blessed and eventually honored for his relentless desire to be true to his God despite frequent devastating personal attacks.

Nehemiah 5:15 But the former governors that had been before me were chargeable unto the people, and had taken of them bread and wine, beside forty shekels of silver; yea, even their servants bare rule over the people: but so did not I, because of the fear of God.

Proverbs 3:7 Be not wise in thine own eyes: fear the LORD, and depart from evil.

Proverbs 16:6 By mercy and truth iniquity is purged: and by the fear of the LORD men depart from evil.

Proverbs 16:17 The highway of the upright is to depart from evil: he that keepeth his way preserveth his soul.

Proverbs 22:3 A prudent *man* foreseeth the evil, and hideth himself: but the simple pass on, and are punished.

"But the fool rageth, and is confident." Not having any regard for God and not fearing God or respecting the warnings of His word, **"the fool"** charges ahead into evil. He is reckless in his pursuit of evil, and he will ***rage*** *(wildly continue in sin)* as he detests and ignores God's word. His arrogance beams from *confidence improperly placed in self* rather than in God. Jezebel was one who charged headlong into evil deeds.

1 Kings 19:2 Then Jezebel sent a messenger unto Elijah, saying, So let the gods do to me, and more also, if I make not thy life as the life of one of them by to morrow about this time.

Rehoboam exemplified himself as a fool, such as is described in this proverb. In his own arrogant self-will and over-confidence, he foolishly ignored the counsel of the older, wise men of the kingdom and listened to his contemporaries who counseled evil. (1 Kings 12:3-17) 1 Kings 12:19 declares the evil circumstances that resulted from Rehoboam's foolish actions – "So Israel rebelled against the house of David unto this day." What should have been a glorious national celebration turned into a chaotic, disorderly, humiliating debacle for Israel's new king as he fled his own coronation to escape assassination by his angry subjects.

Proverbs 14:17 *He that is* soon angry dealeth foolishly: and a man of wicked devices is hated.

Focus: This proverb compares the consequences of being hot-headed with the consequences of one who plans evil.

The out-of-control **"soon angry"** person does much damage because of his quick-temper. He is ruled by his emotions rather than reason and operates from a position of selfish recklessness. The **"man of wicked devices"** schemes and rigorously plans evil in a vindictive and insidious fashion. Both men produce wicked *behavior*; the first man's passions drive him like a madman, and the second is driven by evil inclination. Both men are foolish and both will suffer and cause suffering because of their wrongdoing. The man **"soon angry"** acts foolishly because he consistently and quickly reacts irrationally, whereas the man of **"wicked devices"** carefully plans his evil behavior intending to trap, seduce, or put down another. *He is hated* because people see him as a schemer of evil. The man that is a hothead will be shunned, despicably talked about, and rejected. Those people whose actions produce sorrow, either because of uncontrolled or preplanned behavior, are not welcomed inside an otherwise peaceful environment.

> Esther 9:24-25 Because Haman the son of Hammedatha, the Agagite, the enemy of all the Jews, had devised against the Jews to destroy them, and had cast Pur, that is, the lot, to consume them, and to destroy them; But when Esther came before the king, he commanded by letters that his wicked device, which he devised against the Jews, should return upon his own head, and that he and his sons should be hanged on the gallows.
> Psalm 36:1-4 To the chief Musician, A Psalm of David the servant of the LORD. The transgression of the wicked saith within my heart, that there is no fear of God before his eyes. For he flattereth himself in his own eyes, until his iniquity be found to be hateful. The words of his mouth are iniquity and deceit: he hath left off to be wise, and to do good. He deviseth mischief upon his bed; he setteth himself in a way that is not good; he abhorreth not evil.
> Proverbs 6:16-19 These six *things* doth the LORD hate: yea, seven *are* an abomination unto him: A proud look, a lying tongue, and hands that shed innocent blood, An heart that deviseth wicked imaginations, feet that be swift in running to mischief, A false witness *that* speaketh lies, and he that soweth discord among brethren.
> Proverbs 12:2 A good man obtaineth favour of the LORD: but a man of wicked devices will he condemn.
> Proverbs 14:22 Do they not err that devise evil? but mercy and truth *shall be* to them that devise good.
> Proverbs 14:29 He that is slow to wrath is of great understanding: but he that is hasty of spirit exalteth folly.
> Proverbs 15:18 A wrathful man stirreth up strife: but he that is slow to anger appeaseth strife.
> Proverbs 22:24-25 Make no friendship with an angry man; and with a furious man thou shalt not go: Lest thou learn his ways, and get a snare to thy soul.
> Isaiah 32:6-7 For the vile person will speak villany, and his heart will work iniquity, to practise hypocrisy, and to utter error against the LORD, to make empty the soul of the hungry, and he will cause the drink of the thirsty to fail. The instruments also of the churl *are* evil: he deviseth wicked devices to destroy the poor with lying words, even when the needy speaketh right.
> Colossians 3:8 But now ye also put off all these; anger, wrath, malice, blasphemy, filthy communication out of your mouth.
> James 1:19-20 Wherefore, my beloved brethren, let every man be swift to hear, slow to speak, slow to wrath: For the wrath of man worketh not the righteousness of God.

Proverbs 14:18 The simple inherit folly: but the prudent are crowned with knowledge.

Focus: This proverb compares how the simple acquire foolishness with how the prudent radiate knowledge.

"The simple inherit folly" because they believe every word and fall into whatever trap is set for them. They *gleefully* take ownership of foolishness, *as though it were a valuable inheritance*. They are easily led astray into foolishness that eventually engulfs them like a robe. **"Inherit"** is used figuratively in this verse to specify how easily and freely **"the**

simple" acquire "folly;" however, it is not entirely figurative, for foolishness, being demonstrative of man's fallen nature, is passed from generation to generation and is only overcome through faith in Jesus.

Job declares that the child of Adam *inherits folly* because he is ignorant of the things of God "For vain man would be wise, though man be born *like* a wild ass's colt." (Job 11:12) Peter declares that the Jews *inherited folly* (as a manner of speaking) from the "vain conversation" (foolish, sinful way of life) that they received from their "fathers." He follows by telling of redemption received (not by inheritance, but by faith) in " the precious blood of Christ, as of a lamb without blemish and without spot." (1 Peter 1:18-19)

"But the prudent are crowned with knowledge." Just as the simple have a walk and talk that identifies their habitual relationship with sinful "folly," so the prudent have a walk and talk that identifies their relationship with the ***knowledge of godly wisdom.*** This verse reminds the believer of Proverbs 4:9, which states that wisdom will give one who seeks her a "crown of glory." When a person turns to God, he learns to live in such a way that pleases God and good men; and being known for his lifestyle, he will figuratively *wear such knowledge as a crown*. **"The prudent"**(wise) are the ones who place their honor, joy, and future in knowing and obeying God; and their belief and trust becomes obvious, like a crown on their heads. "Wise heads shall be respected as if they were crowned heads."[290]

> Proverbs 3:35 The wise shall inherit glory: but shame shall be the promotion of fools.
>
> Proverbs 4:7-9 Wisdom *is* the principal thing; *therefore* get wisdom: and with all thy getting get understanding. Exalt her, and she shall promote thee: she shall bring thee to honour, when thou dost embrace her. She shall give to thine head an ornament of grace: a crown of glory shall she deliver to thee.

Wisdom is available to the foolish, simple man if only he would ask.

> James 1:5-8 If any of you lack wisdom, let him ask of God, that giveth to all *men* liberally, and upbraideth not; and it shall be given him. But let him ask in faith, nothing wavering. For he that wavereth is like a wave of the sea driven with the wind and tossed. For let not that man think that he shall receive any thing of the Lord. A double minded man *is* unstable in all his ways.

Proverbs 14:19 The evil bow before the good; and the wicked at the gates of the righteous.

Focus: This proverb declares the eventual submission of the wicked before the righteous.

In this world, evil often triumphs, though its victories are brief; but every student of the Scriptures knows that all of mankind will one day bow before God. Also, in this life, there are times when the wicked will bow before the "righteous" through their actions; and usually, this rare event is brought on when, by a reversal of circumstances, the wicked need the counsel of the righteous whom they have condemned or mocked. There have been times when the *evil bowed before the good* such as when the Egyptians and Joseph's brothers bowed before him (Genesis 41:43, 42:6), Pharaoh and his people before Moses (Exodus 8:8; 9:27-28; 11:8), Saul to David (1 Samuel 24:16-21; 26:21), Jehoram and Naaman before Elisha (2 Kings 3:12; 5:9), Haman before Esther (Esther 7:7), and the magistrates before the apostles (Acts 16:39).

> "More often still is the spirit of this proverb illustrated in the constrained testimony of the wicked to the preeminence of the righteous. (Revelation 3:9) The millennial era will exhibit a more glorious fulfillment. (Isaiah 49:23, 60:14; Revelation 20:4) The grand consummation will set all things right, and shed a Divine splendor over this profound aphorism. 'The upright shall have dominion over the wicked in the morning.' (Psalm 49:14; Malachi 4:1-3) 'The saints shall judge the world.' (1 Corinthians 6:2) They shall there appear in their suitable rank, exalted with their glorious Head over the whole creation. (Revelation 2:26) Oh! let the sunshine of this glory irradiate every clouded morn. If this be not enough to counter-balance the scorn of the ungodly, where is our faith?"[291]
>
> Genesis 42:6 And Joseph was the governor over the land, and he it was that sold to all the people of the land: and Joseph's brethren came, and bowed down themselves before him with their faces to the earth.
>
> Exodus 11:8 And all these thy servants *[Pharaoh's]* shall come down unto me, and bow down themselves unto me, saying, Get thee out, and all the people that follow thee: and after that I will go out. And he went out from Pharaoh in a great anger. *[See also Exodus 12:29-32.]*
>
> 2 Kings 5:8-9 And it was so, when Elisha the man of God had heard that the king of Israel had rent his clothes, that he sent to the king, saying, Wherefore hast thou rent thy clothes? let him come now to me, and he shall know that there is a prophet in Israel. So Naaman came with his horses and with his chariot, and stood at the door of the house of Elisha.
>
> Esther 7:6-8 And Esther said, The adversary and enemy *is* this wicked Haman. Then Haman was afraid before the king and the queen. And the king arising from the banquet of wine in his wrath *went* into the palace garden: and Haman stood up to make request for his life to Esther the queen; for he saw that there was evil determined against him by the king. Then the king returned out of the palace garden

into the place of the banquet of wine; and Haman was fallen upon the bed whereon Esther *was*. Then said the king, Will he force the queen also before me in the house? As the word went out of the king's mouth, they covered Haman's face.

Isaiah 49:23 And kings shall be thy nursing fathers, and their queens thy nursing mothers: they shall bow down to thee with *their* face toward the earth, and lick up the dust of thy feet; and thou shalt know that I *am* the LORD: for they shall not be ashamed that wait for me.

Isaiah 60:14 The sons also of them that afflicted thee shall come bending unto thee; and all they that despised thee shall bow themselves down at the soles of thy feet; and they shall call thee, The city of the LORD, The Zion of the Holy One of Israel.

Micah 7:16-17 The nations shall see and be confounded at all their might: they shall lay their hand upon *their* mouth, their ears shall be deaf. They shall lick the dust like a serpent, they shall move out of their holes like worms of the earth: they shall be afraid of the LORD our God, and shall fear because of thee.

Romans 14:11 For it is written, As I live, saith the Lord, every knee shall bow to me, and every tongue shall confess to God.

1 Corinthians 6:2 Do ye not know that the saints shall judge the world? and if the world shall be judged by you, are ye unworthy to judge the smallest matters?

Revelation 2:26 And he that overcometh, and keepeth my works unto the end, to him will I give power over the nations:

Revelation 3:9 Behold, I will make them of the synagogue of Satan, which say they are Jews, and are not, but do lie; behold, I will make them to come and worship before thy feet, and to know that I have loved thee.

Revelation 20:4 And I saw thrones, and they sat upon them, and judgment was given unto them: and *I saw* the souls of them that were beheaded for the witness of Jesus, and for the word of God, and which had not worshipped the beast, neither his image, neither had received *his* mark upon their foreheads, or in their hands; and they lived and reigned with Christ a thousand years.

[See also 1 Samuel 26:21; 2 Kings 3:11-12; and Malachi 4:1-3]

Proverbs 14:20-21 The poor is hated even of his own neighbour: but the rich *hath* many friends.
21.   He that despiseth his neighbour sinneth: but he that hath mercy on the poor, happy *is* he.

Focus: This proverb: 1) contrasts hatred that the poor experience from others with friendship that the rich experience; 2) identifies such hate for others as sin; and 3) declares a reward for having the opposite and proper attitude of mercy.

"The poor is hated even of his own neighbor*[friend, another person, fellow citizen]*.**"** Verse 20 addresses the disgraceful, worldly attitude of hate for the poor; a condition made more despicable when such hatred comes from those living nearby. Neighbors need each other at various times of their life, but hate divides and eliminates that otherwise good and profitable and respected friendship.

Verse 20b highlights the fact that being poor limits the number of friends one has and acknowledges that ***the rich have many friends.*** Some people obviously think that a friendship with the rich will give them such advantages as prestige, a special place of opportunity, financial gain, enjoyment of a few of the rich's assets, and perhaps even power. Such hypocritically-and-covetously motivated friendships are improper for the Christian. They are deceptive, built on flattery, and likely short lived.

It is a shame for financial status to invalidate a relationship; however, average people, especially the rich, often display an attitude of disdain and contempt for those of lesser circumstances. Evil should be a separating factor–but not financial status! This totally improper attitude is addressed in verse 21 which states that the person who **despises** *[disrespects, holds in contempt, or regards as insignificant]* another person specifically because of poverty is alerted that such ***despising of others is a sin***.

The wise person will heed God's admonition by possessing and demonstrating the attribute of **"mercy"** by realizing that someone has a need and then reaching out to them with assistance. Such an act, especially when done to be pleasing and obedient to God, **brings happiness**. For a Christian to despise anyone grieves the Holy Spirit and consequently, his own spirit. **Mercy** is always in order and puts the Christian's heart in harmony with God and his spirit at peace with the Holy Spirit. Hosea 6:6 states that God desires mercy over observable, but often hypocritical, religion; and Jesus went into lengthy detail to express a proper attitude toward those in need (Matthew 25 below).

Hosea 6:6 For I desired mercy, and not sacrifice; and the knowledge of God more than burnt offerings.

Matthew 9:13 But go ye and learn what *that* meaneth, I will have mercy, and not sacrifice: for I am not come to call the righteous, but sinners to repentance. *[Also see Matthew 12:7]*

Matthew 25:34-46 Then shall the King say unto them on his right hand, Come, ye blessed of my Father, inherit the kingdom prepared for you from the foundation of the world: For I was an hungred, and ye gave me meat: I was thirsty, and ye gave me drink: I was a stranger, and ye took me in: Naked, and ye clothed me: I was sick, and ye visited me: I was in prison, and ye came unto me. Then shall the righteous answer him, saying, Lord, when saw we thee an hungred, and fed *thee?* or thirsty, and gave *thee* drink? When saw we thee a stranger, and took *thee* in? or naked, and clothed *thee?* Or when saw we thee sick, or in prison, and came unto thee? And the King shall answer and say unto them, Verily I say unto you, Inasmuch as ye have done *it* unto one of the least of these my brethren, ye have done *it* unto me. Then shall he say also unto them on the left hand, Depart from me, ye cursed, into everlasting fire, prepared for the devil and his angels: For I was an hungred, and ye gave me no meat: I was thirsty, and ye gave me no drink: I was a stranger, and ye took me not in: naked, and ye clothed me not: sick, and in prison, and ye visited me not. Then shall they also answer him, saying, Lord, when saw we thee an hungred, or athirst, or a stranger, or naked, or sick, or in prison, and did not minister unto thee? Then shall he answer them, saying, Verily I say unto you, Inasmuch as ye did *it* not to one of the least of these, ye did *it* not to me. And these shall go away into everlasting punishment: but the righteous into life eternal.

James 1:27 Pure religion and undefiled before God and the Father is this, To visit the fatherless and widows in their affliction, *and* to keep himself unspotted from the world.

Throughout the Bible, God *demands* that the poor are to be dealt with mercifully. They are to be given help by those blessed by God, and they are to be treated with dignity in the process. **"Happy is he"** that obeys God by having **"mercy on the poor."** Notice among the following verses how often Proverbs calls attention to the treatment of the poor.

Leviticus 25:35 And if thy brother be waxen poor, and fallen in decay with thee; then thou shalt relieve him: yea, though he be a stranger, or a sojourner; that he may live with thee.

Proverbs 14:31 He that oppresseth the poor reproacheth his Maker: but he that honoureth him hath mercy on the poor.

Proverbs 19:4 Wealth maketh many friends; but the poor is separated from his neighbour.

Proverbs 19:6 Many will intreat the favour of the prince: and every man is a friend to him that giveth gifts.

Proverbs 19:7 All the brethren of the poor do hate him: how much more do his friends go far from him? he pursueth them with words, yet they are wanting to him.

Proverbs 19:17 He that hath pity upon the poor lendeth unto the LORD; and that which he hath given will he pay him again.

Proverbs 21:13 Whoso stoppeth his ears at the cry of the poor, he also shall cry himself, but shall not be heard.

Proverbs 22:9 He that hath a bountiful eye shall be blessed; for he giveth of his bread to the poor.

Proverbs 29:7 The righteous considereth the cause of the poor: but the wicked regardeth not to know it.

Ecclesiastes 9:14-16 There was a little city, and few men within it; and there came a great king against it, and besieged it, and built great bulwarks against it: Now there was found in it a poor wise man, and he by his wisdom delivered the city; yet no man remembered that same poor man. Then said I, Wisdom is better than strength: nevertheless the poor man's wisdom is despised, and his words are not heard.

Mark 14:7 For ye have the poor with you always, and whensoever ye will ye may do them good: but me ye have not always.

Luke 15:14-16 And when he *[prodigal son]* had spent all, there arose a mighty famine in that land; and he began to be in want. And he went and joined himself to a citizen of that country; and he sent him into his fields to feed swine. And he would fain have filled his belly with the husks that the swine did eat: and no man gave unto him.

James 2:5-6 Hearken, my beloved brethren, Hath not God chosen the poor of this world rich in faith, and heirs of the kingdom which he hath promised to them that love him? But ye have despised the poor. Do not rich men oppress you, and draw you before the judgment seats?

Proverbs 14:22   Do they not err that devise evil? but mercy and truth *shall be* to them that devise good.

Focus: This proverb declares that those who "devise evil" deviate from the good path where "mercy and truth" exist while those who "devise good" remain on that good path.

"Mercy and truth" are said to be "all the paths of the LORD. . ." (Psalm 25:10), and they are identified as attributes of God in 10 scriptures and are associated with righteous men in 9 scriptures. When one *devises evil*, he uses such tools as lying, manipulation, and hypocrisy. His motivation may have originated from such emotions as hate, greed, resentment, or ambition; and the labor that he expends to fabricate evil is unmistakably pleasing to Satan. He **"errs"** *[goes astray "from the right way, the way of life"[292]]*, thus bringing destruction, tribulation, and a curse upon his victims as well as himself. All his labor, every action, every step, takes him *in the opposite direction from God* and away from **"mercy and truth."** He has chosen to live with, in, and among hatred and lies; ". . . and a man of wicked devices is hated." (Proverbs 14:17)

Mercy" is the aspect of God's love that causes Him to help the miserable who may be so either because of breaking God's law or because of circumstances beyond their control like blindness or leprosy. Finally, because God is merciful, He expects His children to be merciful.[293]

Proverbs 3:27-29 Withhold not good from them to whom it is due, when it is in the power of thine hand to do *it*. Say not unto thy neighbour, Go, and come again, and to morrow I will give; when thou hast it by thee. Devise not evil against thy neighbour, seeing he dwelleth securely by thee.

Proverbs 6:12-15 A naughty person, a wicked man, walketh with a froward mouth. He winketh with his eyes, he speaketh with his feet, he teacheth with his fingers; Frowardness *is* in his heart, he deviseth mischief continually; he soweth discord. Therefore shall his calamity come suddenly; suddenly shall he be broken without remedy.

Proverbs 12:2 A good man obtaineth favour of the LORD: but a man of wicked devices will he condemn.

Proverbs 24:8 He that deviseth to do evil shall be called a mischievous person.

Isaiah 32:6-8 For the vile person will speak villany, and his heart will work iniquity, to practise hypocrisy, and to utter error against the LORD, to make empty the soul of the hungry, and he will cause the drink of the thirsty to fail. The instruments also of the churl are evil: he deviseth wicked devices to destroy the poor with lying words, even when the needy speaketh right. But the liberal deviseth liberal things; and by liberal things shall he stand.

Scripture bears reference to men who devised evil, but they didn't receive honor, praise or their anticipated happiness because their purpose was evil. Look at the shame of the Babel-builders (Genesis 11:9), the unexpected use of Haman's gallows (Esther 7:10), and the disgrace of those who plotted against our beloved Lord. (Psalm 2:1-4)

Genesis 11:6-9 And the LORD said, Behold, the people *is* one, and they have all one language; and this they begin to do: and now nothing will be restrained from them, which they have imagined to do. Go to, let us go down, and there confound their language, that they may not understand one another's speech. So the LORD scattered them abroad from thence upon the face of all the earth: and they left off to build the city. Therefore is the name of it called Babel; because the LORD did there confound the language of all the earth: and from thence did the LORD scatter them abroad upon the face of all the earth.

Esther 7:10 So they hanged Haman on the gallows that he had prepared for Mordecai. Then was the king's wrath pacified.

Psalm 2:1-4 Why do the heathen rage, and the people imagine a vain thing? The kings of the earth set themselves, and the rulers take counsel together, against the LORD, and against his anointed, *saying,* Let us break their bands asunder, and cast away their cords from us. He that sitteth in the heavens shall laugh: the Lord shall have them in derision. Then shall he speak unto them in his wrath, and vex them in his sore displeasure.

Matthew 26:14-16, 27:3-5 Then one of the twelve, called Judas Iscariot, went unto the chief priests, And said *unto them,* What will ye give me, and I will deliver him unto you? And they covenanted with him for thirty pieces of silver. And from that time he sought opportunity to betray him . . . Then Judas, which had betrayed him, when he saw that he was condemned, repented himself, and brought again the thirty pieces of silver to the chief priests and elders, Saying, I have sinned in that I have betrayed the innocent blood. And they said, What *is that* to us? see thou *to that.* And he cast down the pieces of silver in the temple, and departed, and went and hanged himself.

In contrast, those men who **"devise good"** have a fixed mind and a determined will to develop a lifestyle that follows God's directives to know how to live wisely and avoid the many pitfalls and unnecessary sorrows of life. They use such tools as love, mercy, truth, or kindness. They work to benefit others and remain in the pathway where God can provide, protect, and guide them with His **"truth"** because He has **"mercy"** on them. He is merciful even though he knows man's weaknesses and ignorance. Instead of receiving hatred from their neighbors, these men are loved and held in esteem by those who love "good" and hate "evil." **"Mercy"** is given in forgiving them for their sins and **"truth"** is given to guide them in the right way so that they **do not "err."**

Genesis 24:27 And he said, Blessed be the LORD God of my master Abraham, who hath not left destitute my master of his mercy and his truth: I being in the way, the LORD led me to the house of my master's brethren.

Proverbs 3:3-4 Let not mercy and truth forsake thee: bind them about thy neck; write them upon the table of thine heart: So shalt thou find favour and good understanding in the sight of God and man.

Proverbs 16:6 By mercy and truth iniquity is purged: and by the fear of the LORD *men* depart from evil.

Proverbs 20:28 Mercy and truth preserve the king: and his throne is upholden by mercy.

Daniel 9:9 To the Lord our God *belong* mercies and forgivenesses, though we have rebelled against him . . .

Matthew 5:7 Blessed are the merciful: for they shall obtain mercy.

Romans 9:14-16 What shall we say then? *Is there* unrighteousness with God? God forbid. For he saith to Moses, I will have mercy on whom I will have mercy, and I will have compassion on whom I will have compassion. So then *it is* not of him that willeth, nor of him that runneth, but of God that sheweth mercy.

Ephesians 2:4-7 But God, who is rich in mercy, for his great love wherewith he loved us, Even when we were dead in sins, hath quickened us together with Christ, (by grace ye are saved;) And hath raised *us* up together, and made *us* sit together in heavenly *places* in Christ Jesus: That in the ages to come he might shew the exceeding riches of his grace in *his* kindness toward us through Christ Jesus.

1 Timothy 1:13...16 Who was before a blasphemer, and a persecutor, and injurious: but I obtained mercy, because I did *it* ignorantly in unbelief. Howbeit for this cause I obtained mercy, that in me first Jesus Christ might shew forth all longsuffering, for a pattern to them which should hereafter believe on him to life everlasting.

James 1:27 Pure religion and undefiled before God and the Father is this, To visit the fatherless and widows in their affliction, *and* to keep himself unspotted from the world. *[See also Psalms 25:10; 57:3; 61:7; 85:10; 86:15; 89:14; 98:3; and 100:5.]*

"Mercy and truth" are often used together in the Old Testament, and together they are a blessed gift from God. God always acts from a position of **truth** because He is truth. He shows His **mercy** to us even when we fail him. With that being true, this proverb begs the question, **"Do they not err that devise evil?"** and the answer is, "Yes – certainly they do, and they have abandoned God's great rewards of "mercy" and "truth." *(See additional information on "mercy and truth" on page 33)*

Proverbs 14:23 In all labour there is profit: but the talk of the lips *tendeth* only to penury.

Focus: This proverb declares that labor is productive, whereas talking (instead of working) brings poverty.

There is gain or profit to putting forth effort, but useless talking instead of working only brings deficiency or impoverishment (**"penury"**). In this twenty-first century, there are jobs (such as TV and radio personalities, ambassadors) whereby people earn their living by talking (after much preparation); but this proverb speaks of *useless* talk that produces nothing but sore ears, frustration, and perhaps sharp rebuke.

> "'Solomon here,' says Lord Bacon, as quoted by Bishop Patrick, 'separates the fruit of the labour of the tongue, and of the labour of the hands; as if want was the revenue of the one, and wealth the revenue of the other. For it commonly comes to pass that they who talk liberally, boast much, and promise mighty matters, are beggars, and receive no benefit by their brags, or by any thing they discourse of. Nay, rather, for the most part, such men are not industrious and diligent in their employment; but only feed and fill themselves with words as with wind.'"[294]

> Proverbs 10:4 He becometh poor that dealeth *with* a slack hand: but the hand of the diligent maketh rich.
> Ecclesiastes 5:3 For a dream cometh through the multitude of business; and a fool's voice *is known* by multitude of words.
> 2 Thessalonians 3:10-12 For even when we were with you, this we commanded you, that if any would not work, neither should he eat. For we hear that there are some which walk among you disorderly, working not at all, but are busybodies. Now them that are such we command and exhort by our Lord Jesus Christ, that with quietness they work, and eat their own bread.
> 1 Timothy 5:13 And withal they learn *to be* idle, wandering about from house to house; and not only idle, but tattlers also and busybodies, speaking things which they ought not.

Proverbs 14:24 The crown of the wise *is* their riches: *but* the foolishness of fools *is* folly.

Focus: This proverb contrasts the figurative crown or aura of wisdom surrounding a wise person with the fool's aura of foolishness.

A **"wise"** person is one who walks with God by loving Him and being obedient to His commandments. He is not proud or arrogant, and no amount of **"riches"** will take away from his dependence on the LORD. He exalts God with his lifestyle, and he knows that every amount of wealth he owns is there because of the blessings of his heavenly Father. Any riches he possesses only serve to enhance his walk with God and to strengthen his identity as a godly person. He knows how to live effectively, including applying godly methods of handling finances. Outside of adverse circumstances beyond the wise person's control, he will enjoy a good measure of wealth. He is diligent in his work and takes care of everything over which God has given him stewardship; consequently, *an aura of stability and wisdom*, which Proverbs identifies as a **"crown,"** becomes a part of his identity. Those rewards for being wise in the form of riches are themselves like crowns that testify of his wisdom.

> Deuteronomy 8:17-18 And thou say in thine heart, My power and the might of *mine* hand hath gotten me this wealth. But thou shalt remember the LORD thy God: for *it is* he that giveth thee power to get wealth, that he may establish his covenant which he sware unto thy fathers, as *it is* this day.
> 1 Kings 3:12 13 Behold, I have done according to thy words: lo, I have given thee a wise and an understanding heart; so that there was none like thee before thee, neither after thee shall any arise like unto thee. And I have also given thee that which thou hast not asked, both riches, and honour: so that there shall not be any among the kings like unto thee all thy days.
> Psalm 49:6-13 They that trust in their wealth, and boast themselves in the multitude of their riches; None *of them* can by any means redeem his brother, nor give to God a ransom for him: (For the redemption of their soul *is* precious, and it ceaseth for ever:) That he should still live for ever, *and* not see corruption. For he seeth *that* wise men die, likewise the fool and the brutish person perish, and leave their wealth to others. Their inward thought *is, that* their houses *shall continue* for ever, *and* their dwelling places to all generations; they call *their* lands after their own names. Nevertheless man *being* in honour abideth not: he is like the beasts *that* perish. This their way *is* their folly: yet their posterity approve their sayings. Selah.

Psalm 112:1-3 Praise ye the LORD. Blessed is the man that feareth the LORD, that delighteth greatly in his commandments. His seed shall be mighty upon earth: the generation of the upright shall be blessed. Wealth and riches shall be in his house: and his righteousness endureth for ever.

Proverbs 3:16 Length of days is in her *[Wisdom's]* right hand; and in her left hand riches and honour.

Proverbs 14:18 The simple inherit folly: but the prudent are crowned with knowledge.

"The foolishness of fools is folly" is a negative phrase that draws attention to the fact that the fool wears his foolishness like an imitation crown. It has an aura that speaks loudly of his rebellion against God. His wastefulness and folly hang over him like a dark cloud, and he is known by his spirit of foolishness. He either spends up all that comes his way and never sees long-term gain or else uses the riches for mischief and indulgence in more folly.

> The Book of Proverbs points out that foolishness is a major cause of poverty. The characteristics of foolishness that cause poverty include the following:
>
> laziness (10:4, 24:30-34)
> willful ignorance of God's instruction (13:18)
> deceit (14:8)
> too much talk (without toil/labor) (14:23)
> working of iniquity (21:15)
> oppressing the poor (22:16)
>
> love of pleasure (21:17)
> drunkenness and gluttony (23:21)
> following vain (empty) people (28:19)
> hastening to be rich (28:22)
> excessive slumber (6:10-11; 20:13; 23:21; 24:33-34)
>
> While observing how foolishness causes self-inflicted poverty, one must also recognize: "The LORD maketh poor, and maketh rich: he bringeth low, and lifteth up." (1 Samuel 2:7)

Proverbs 14:25 A true witness delivereth souls: but a deceitful *witness* speaketh lies.

Focus: This proverb declares that the true witness provides freedom through truth while the deceitful witness sustains bindings with more lies.

In this verse, the fact that ***souls are delivered by a truthful witness*** is contrasted with the implied fact that ***souls are bound by a lying witness.*** A **"true witness"** will not lie, and his truth *releases the binding* put on others by lies. Contrary to the "true witness" is the **"deceitful witness"** who is sure to lie. He prefers lying to truth, and will continue to lie so that he can bind and destroy innocent lives – not only in the court of law but also in the court of public opinion. He is of his father, the Devil. This proverb repeats the principle of the last part of Proverbs 14:5 – "A faithful witness will not lie: but a false witness will utter lies."

1 Kings 21:9-13 And she wrote in the letters, saying, Proclaim a fast, and set Naboth on high among the people: And set two men, sons of Belial, before him, to bear witness against him, saying, Thou didst blaspheme God and the king. And then carry him out, and stone him, that he may die. And the men of his city, even the elders and the nobles who were the inhabitants in his city, did as Jezebel had sent unto them, and as it was written in the letters which she had sent unto them. They proclaimed a fast, and set Naboth on high among the people. And there came in two men, children of Belial, and sat before him: and the men of Belial witnessed against him, even against Naboth, in the presence of the people, saying, Naboth did blaspheme God and the king. Then they carried him forth out of the city, and stoned him with stones, that he died.

Psalm 24:3-5 Who shall ascend into the hill of the LORD? or who shall stand in his holy place? He that hath clean hands, and a pure heart; who hath not lifted up his soul unto vanity, nor sworn deceitfully. He shall receive the blessing from the LORD, and righteousness from the God of his salvation.

Proverbs 12:6 The words of the wicked *are* to lie in wait for blood: but the mouth of the upright shall deliver them.

Proverbs 12:17 *He that* speaketh truth sheweth forth righteousness: but a false witness deceit.

Proverbs 24:11-12 If thou forbear to deliver them that are drawn unto death, and those that are ready to be slain; If thou sayest, Behold, we knew it not; doth not he that pondereth the heart consider it? and he that keepeth thy soul, doth not he know it? and shall not he render to every man according to his works?

Matthew 26:59-60 Now the chief priests, and elders, and all the council, sought false witness against Jesus, to put him to death; But found none: yea, though many false witnesses came, *yet* found they none. At the last came two false witnesses . . .

Acts 6:11-13 Then they suborned men, which said, We have heard him speak blasphemous words against Moses, and *against* God. And they stirred up the people, and the elders, and the scribes, and came upon *him,* and caught *him,* and brought *him* to the council, And set up false witnesses, which said, This man ceaseth not to speak blasphemous words against this holy place, and the law . . .

> **Proverbs 14:26** In the fear of the LORD *is* strong confidence: and his children shall have a place of refuge.

Focus: This proverb declares that "the fear of the LORD" provides a person with "strong confidence" and his children with a place of safety.

"In the fear of the LORD *is* strong confidence." When a person actually has a **"fear** *[awesome respect, reverence]* **of the LORD,"** he will likely have (at least) a foundational understanding that God is omnipresent, omniscient, and omnipotent. Because he feared God, Abraham would have sacrificed his son: yet was fully confident of his safety, knowing 'that God was able to raise him from the dead (Genesis 22:1; Hebrews 11:17-19). With **"strong confidence"** in their awesome God, the three Hebrew children refused to bow and worship Nebuchadnezzar's image. They were thrown into the fiery furnace (Daniel 3:16-18), which was their **"place of refuge,"** the coolest, most comfortable, safest place in the kingdom.

"His children shall have a place of refuge." When children are verbally taught and also witness their parents' reverence for an interactive walk with God, they will also learn to respect, trust, and walk with God. Parents can give no greater gift to their child than an opportunity to serve the living, protecting, guiding, eternal God. Every wise parent teaches their children to trust God for their safety.

> "...It entails a blessing upon posterity. The children of those that by faith make God their confidence shall be encouraged by the promise that God will be a God to believers and to their seed to flee to him as their refuge, and they shall find shelter in him. The children of religious parents often do the better for their parents' instructions and example and fare the better for their faith and prayers. 'Our fathers trusted in thee, therefore we will.'"[295]

> Proverbs 3:21-26 My son, let not them depart from thine eyes: keep sound wisdom and discretion: So shall they be life unto thy soul, and grace to thy neck. Then shalt thou walk in thy way safely, and thy foot shall not stumble. When thou liest down, thou shalt not be afraid: yea, thou shalt lie down, and thy sleep shall be sweet. Be not afraid of sudden fear, neither of the desolation of the wicked, when it cometh. For the LORD shall be thy confidence, and shall keep thy foot from being taken.
> Hebrews 11:17-19 By faith Abraham, when he was tried, offered up Isaac: and he that had received the promises offered up his only begotten son, Of whom it was said, That in Isaac shall thy seed be called: Accounting that God was able to raise *him* up, even from the dead; from whence also he received him in a figure . . . Genesis 25:11 And it came to pass after the death of Abraham, that God blessed his son Isaac; and Isaac dwelt by the well Lahairoi.
> *[Many verses proclaim safety with God including: Psalm 27:1; 46:1-3; 56:1-4; 91:1-6; 112:1; 143:9; Proverbs 1:33; 18:10; 19:23; 29:25 Isaiah 25:4; Daniel 3:16-18; Romans 8:31.]*

> **Proverbs 14:27** The fear of the LORD *is* a fountain of life, to depart from the snares of death.

Focus: This proverb declares that "The fear of the LORD" is a source of life by leading one away from "the snares of death."

Having an awesome respect for God ("fear of the LORD") enables a trusting relationship with God, the source and sustainer of life *("fountain of life")*. He guides and delivers His own children so that they avoid the many death traps laid by Satan, his demons, and evil people already ensnared by him. The child of God will escape the "second death," which is eternal separation from God pronounced at the Great White Throne Judgment of sinners.

Unwise men (the foolish ones) don't have a respect for God; consequently, they don't heed God's leadership, don't listen to God's word, and walk headlong into traps set by evil people who either attack their victims directly or cause them to be entrapped by improper words and actions. The unwise walk in places where the wise have been taught not to go. They conduct business or partner where danger looms, and understanding comes either too late or never.

> **NOTE**: Proverbs 13:14 "The law of the wise is a fountain of life, to depart from the snares of death" is similar to this verse.

> Deuteronomy 6:2 That thou mightest fear the LORD thy God, to keep all his statutes and his commandments, which I command thee, thou, and thy son, and thy son's son, all the days of thy life; and that thy days may be prolonged.
> Proverbs 2:10-17 When wisdom entereth into thine heart, and knowledge is pleasant unto thy soul; Discretion shall preserve thee, understanding shall keep thee: To deliver thee from the way of the evil *man,* from the man that speaketh froward things; Who leave the paths of uprightness, to walk in the ways of darkness; Who rejoice to do evil, *and* delight in the frowardness of the wicked; Whose ways *are* crooked, and *they* froward in their paths: To deliver thee from the strange woman, *even* from the stranger *which* flattereth with her words; Which forsaketh the guide of her youth, and forgetteth the covenant of her God.

Proverbs 3:1-2 My son, forget not my law; but let thine heart keep my commandments: For length of days, and long life, and peace, shall they add to thee.

Proverbs 3:16-18 Length of days is in her right hand; and in her left hand riches and honour. Her ways are ways of pleasantness, and all her paths are peace. She is a tree of life to them that lay hold upon her: and happy is every one that retaineth her.

Proverbs 3:21-24 My son, let not them depart from thine eyes: keep sound wisdom and discretion: So shall they be life unto thy soul, and grace to thy neck. Then shalt thou walk in thy way safely, and thy foot shall not stumble. When thou liest down, thou shalt not be afraid: yea, thou shalt lie down, and thy sleep shall be sweet.

Proverbs 4:20-22 My son, attend to my words; incline thine ear unto my sayings. Let them not depart from thine eyes; keep them in the midst of thine heart. For they *are* life unto those that find them, and health to all their flesh.

Proverbs 8:35-36 For whoso findeth me findeth life, and shall obtain favour of the LORD. But he that sinneth against me wrongeth his own soul: all they that hate me love death.

Proverbs 9:10-11 The fear of the LORD is the beginning of wisdom: and the knowledge of the holy is understanding. For by me thy days shall be multiplied, and the years of thy life shall be increased.

Proverbs 10:2 Treasures of wickedness profit nothing: but righteousness delivereth from death.

Proverbs 10:11 The mouth of a righteous man is a well of life: but violence covereth the mouth of the wicked.

Proverbs 10:27 The fear of the LORD prolongeth days: but the years of the wicked shall be shortened.

Proverbs 16:6 By mercy and truth iniquity is purged: and by the fear of the LORD *men* depart from evil.

Proverbs 19:23 The fear of the LORD tendeth to life: and he that hath it shall abide satisfied; he shall not be visited with evil.

Proverbs 22:4 By humility and the fear of the LORD are riches, and honour, and life.

Proverbs 14:28 In the multitude of people *is* the king's honour: but in the want of people *is* the destruction of the prince.

Focus: This proverb declares that a vast population size can indicate an honorable and stable leadership by the king, and a small population can indicate a dishonorable and unstable (self-destructive) leadership.

"In the multitude of people *is* the king's honour" indicates that when a king's wise leadership *produces or helps to sustain* a **"multitude of people,"** he is lavished with honor because "it is a sign of a good and wise government, of clemency and righteousness being exercised, of liberty and property being enjoyed, of peace, plenty, and prosperity; which encourage subjects to serve their king cheerfully, and to continue under his reign and government peaceably; and which invites others from different parts to come and settle there also."[296] Kings have various means of control including taxation, declaration of peace or war, and the making of laws. Any of his actions can either enhance or harm the populace.

Solomon unified the nation of Israel through the honor and worship of God and through his God-given wisdom. The nation became strong, secure, and populous. The people had plenty to eat and drink, and they were happily enjoying the comforts of life.

1 Kings 4:20-21, 24-25, 29 Judah and Israel *were* many, as the sand which *is* by the sea in multitude, eating and drinking, and making merry. And Solomon reigned over all kingdoms from the river unto the land of the Philistines, and unto the border of Egypt: they brought presents, and served Solomon all the days of his life ... For he had dominion over all *the region* on this side the river, from Tiphsah even to Azzah, over all the kings on this side the river: and he had peace on all sides round about him. And Judah and Israel dwelt safely, every man under his vine and under his fig tree, from Dan even to Beersheba, all the days of Solomon ... And God gave Solomon wisdom and understanding exceeding much, and largeness of heart, even as the sand that *is* on the sea shore.

"But in the want of people *is* the destruction of the prince." *When leadership is foolish, the people suffer, and the population stands the possibility of decreasing.* War often kills large portions of a nation's people, and military actions can even destroy the ability of the land to produce well enough to sustain the citizens. Enemies have been known to cut down all the trees, trample crops, and poison the streams. All of these actions have the potential of reducing population either because of people fleeing the country or through death. When the population is decreased as a result of a king's foolish acts, such as unnecessary war, failure to take wise counsel, injustice, ungodly laws, and acts contrary to the will of God; all the leadership (princes) suffer the consequences. A severe decrease in the number of citizens can eliminate the possibility of the prince or his offspring inheriting the throne.

"*In the want of people* . . . trade lies dead, the ground lies untilled, the army wants to be recruited, the navy to be manned, and all because there are not hands sufficient. See how much the honour and safety of kings depend upon their people, which is a reason why they should rule by love, and not with rigour. Princes are corrected by those judgments which abate the number of the people, as we find (2Samuel 24)."[297]

2 Samuel 24:10-16 And David's heart smote him after that he had numbered the people. And David said unto the LORD, I have sinned greatly in that I have done: and now, I beseech thee, O LORD, take away the iniquity of thy servant; for I have done very foolishly. For when David was up in the morning, the word of the LORD came unto the prophet Gad, David's seer, saying, Go and say unto David, Thus saith the LORD, I offer thee three *things;* choose thee one of them, that I may *do it* unto thee. So Gad came to David, and told him, and said unto him, Shall seven years of famine come unto thee in thy land? or wilt thou flee three months before thine enemies, while they pursue thee? or that there be three days' pestilence in thy land? now advise, and see what answer I shall return to him that sent me. And David said unto Gad, I am in a great strait: let us fall now into the hand of the LORD; for his mercies *are* great: and let me not fall into the hand of man. So the LORD sent a pestilence upon Israel from the morning even to the time appointed: and there died of the people from Dan even to Beersheba seventy thousand men. And when the angel stretched out his hand upon Jerusalem to destroy it, the LORD repented him of the evil, and said to the angel that destroyed the people, It is enough: stay now thine hand. And the angel of the LORD was by the threshingplace of Araunah the Jebusite. *[See also 1 Chronicles 21.]*

1 Kings 12:16-20 So when all Israel saw that the king hearkened not unto them, the people answered the king, saying, What portion have we in David? neither *have we* inheritance in the son of Jesse: to your tents, O Israel: now see to thine own house, David. So Israel departed unto their tents. But *as for* the children of Israel which dwelt in the cities of Judah, Rehoboam reigned over them. Then king Rehoboam sent Adoram, who *was* over the tribute; and all Israel stoned him with stones, that he died. Therefore king Rehoboam made speed to get him up to his chariot, to flee to Jerusalem. So Israel rebelled against the house of David unto this day. And it came to pass, when all Israel heard that Jeroboam was come again, that they sent and called him unto the congregation, and made him king over all Israel: there was none that followed the house of David, but the tribe of Judah only.

Proverbs 14:29 *He that is* slow to wrath *is* of great understanding: but *he that is* hasty of spirit exalteth folly.

Focus: This proverb declares that the level of a person's self control is either indicative of the level of his understanding or else the level of his foolishness.

Being **"slow to wrath"** is indicative of being under the control of intelligence and reason rather than passion. It pictures the exercise of wisdom, and it demonstrates the wise man's understanding about people in general. A person who is "slow to wrath" understands the potential consequences of his actions. "A man's prudence and wisdom are displayed by his being slow to take offense and being patient under injury."[298] A wise person comprehends that an outburst of anger has the potential to produce adverse, unnecessary, and avoidable ill consequences.

Being **"hasty** *[short-tempered, impatient]* **of spirit exalteth folly"** because it reveals a preference for foolishness and a disregard for acting with wisdom. This character trait is a demonstration of pride that ***lifts folly up high*** (exalts) as though it were a badge of honor. Being **"hasty of spirit"** flaunts its ugliness in the face of others, darkens any light of understanding, and troubles the hearts of innocent people desiring peace.

Proverbs 14:16-17 A wise *man* feareth, and departeth from evil: but the fool rageth, and is confident. *He that is* soon angry dealeth foolishly: and a man of wicked devices is hated.

Proverbs 15:18 A wrathful man stirreth up strife: but *he that is* slow to anger appeaseth strife.

Proverbs 16:32 *He that is* slow to anger *is* better than the mighty; and he that ruleth his spirit than he that taketh a city.

Proverbs 19:11 The discretion of a man deferreth his anger; and *it is* his glory to pass over a transgression.

Proverbs 22:24-25 Make no friendship with an angry man; and with a furious man thou shalt not go: Lest thou learn his ways, and get a snare to thy soul.

Proverbs 25:8 Go not forth hastily to strive, lest *thou know not* what to do in the end thereof, when thy neighbour hath put thee to shame.

Proverbs 25:28 He that *hath* no rule over his own spirit *is like* a city *that is* broken down, *and* without walls.

Ecclesiastes 7:8 Better *is* the end of a thing than the beginning thereof: *and* the patient in spirit *is* better than the proud in spirit. Be not hasty in thy spirit to be angry: for anger resteth in the bosom of fools.

Matthew 11:29 Take my yoke upon you, and learn of me; for I am meek and lowly in heart: and ye shall find rest unto your souls.

1 Corinthians 13:4-5 Charity suffereth long, and is kind; charity envieth not; charity vaunteth not itself, is not puffed up Doth not behave itself unseemly, seeketh not her own, is not easily provoked, thinketh no evil. . .

Galatians 5:22-26 But the fruit of the Spirit is love, joy, peace, longsuffering, gentleness, goodness, faith, Meekness, temperance: against such there is no law. And they that are Christ's have crucified the flesh with the affections and lusts. If we live in the Spirit, let us also walk in the Spirit. Let us not be desirous of vain glory, provoking one another, envying one another.

James 3:17-20 But the wisdom that is from above is first pure, then peaceable, gentle, *and* easy to be intreated, full of mercy and good fruits, without partiality, and without hypocrisy. And the fruit of righteousness is sown in peace of them that make peace.

Wherefore, my beloved brethren, let every man be swift to hear, slow to speak, slow to wrath: For the wrath of man worketh not the righteousness of God.

Proverbs 14:30 A sound heart *is* the life of the flesh: but envy the rottenness of the bones.

Focus: This proverb *contrasts the effects* that "a sound heart" has on a person with the effects of "envy."

"A sound heart *is* the life of the flesh." **"Heart"** is used in a figurative sense referring to that part of man whereby he thinks and feels and has a will – *not* that part of man that pumps blood. **"A sound heart"** means that *the person is at peace* (placid, undisturbed, and calm), or as one writer described it – a "'Heart of health,' . . . in which all emotions and appetites are in a healthy equilibrium."[299] Contrasted with this sound heart is ". . .the **envy** which eats, like a consuming disease, into the very bones and marrow of a man's moral life."[300] A person who is at peace in his **"heart"** is producing harmony and health throughout his **"flesh"** *[body]*.

Knowing God and obeying Him brings a believer this peace as described above. "The Old Testament meaning of peace was completeness, soundness, and well-being of the total person. This peace was considered God-given, obtained by following the Law."[301] Peace is the absence of stress and agitation that produces health problems, such as high blood pressure, heart disease, obesity, and diabetes.[302]

> Proverbs 3:1-2 My son, forget not my law; but let thine heart keep my commandments: For length of days, and long life, and peace, shall they add to thee.
>
> Proverbs 3:13-17 Happy *is* the man *that* findeth wisdom, and the man *that* getteth understanding. For the merchandise of it *is* better than the merchandise of silver, and the gain thereof than fine gold. She *is* more precious than rubies: and all the things thou canst desire are not to be compared unto her. Length of days *is* in her right hand; *and* in her left hand riches and honour. Her ways *are* ways of pleasantness, and all her paths *are* peace.
>
> Isaiah 26:3 Thou wilt keep *him* in perfect peace, *whose* mind *is* stayed *on thee:* because he trusteth in thee.
>
> Isaiah 48:22 *There is* no peace, saith the LORD, unto the wicked.
>
> John 14:26-27 But the Comforter, *which is* the Holy Ghost, whom the Father will send in my name, he shall teach you all things, and bring all things to your remembrance, whatsoever I have said unto you. Peace I leave with you, my peace I give unto you: not as the world giveth, give I unto you. Let not your heart be troubled, neither let it be afraid.

"But envy the rottenness of the bones." Mentioned twice in the Book of Proverbs, **"rottenness** *[decay, used figuratively]* **of the bones"** suggests that physical health is closely associated with spiritual health – a fact well-known today.[303] (See Proverbs 12:4 below.) A spirit of **"envy"** in the soul of man pumps disharmony and destruction to the very foundation of his being. Evidence from this and other Scriptures proves that the over-all health of a person is affected by his emotions. Proper ways of thinking that bring peace within the heart of man produce vitality all the way out to the flesh, while improper thoughts like envy produce enervation all the way into the bones. Other external forces like a sinful relationship, continual bad news, hatred, and guidance from the world system rather than from Scripture can also cause damage to good health.

> Proverbs 3:7-8 Be not wise in thine own eyes: fear the LORD, and depart from evil. It shall be health to thy navel, and marrow to thy bones.
>
> Proverbs 4:20-23 My son, attend to my words; incline thine ear unto my sayings. Let them not depart from thine eyes; keep them in the midst of thine heart. For they are life unto those that find them, and health to all their flesh. Keep thy heart with all diligence; for out of it are the issues of life.
>
> Proverbs 12:4 A virtuous woman *is* a crown to her husband: but she that maketh ashamed *is* as rottenness in his bones.
>
> Proverbs 17:22 A merry heart doeth good *like* a medicine: but a broken spirit drieth the bones.

Proverbs 14:31 He that oppresseth the poor reproacheth his Maker: but he that honoureth him hath mercy on the poor.

Focus: This proverb declares that God considers a person's actions toward the poor as being reflective of his attitude toward God.

"**Oppresseth**" means to defraud, to do violence, or to do wrong to a person. Proverbs 4:21 declares that despising someone is a sin, and Proverbs 22:22-23 testifies that God will take up the cause of the oppressed against the oppressor. Commands against oppression are covered by Zechariah 7:8-10.

> Zechariah 7:8-10 And the word of the LORD came unto Zechariah, saying, Thus speaketh the LORD of hosts, saying, Execute true judgment, and shew mercy and compassions every man to his brother: And oppress not the widow, nor the fatherless, the stranger, nor the poor; and let none of you imagine evil against his brother in your heart.

It is a **reproach**[taunt, blasphemy, defiance] to God to oppress the poor for the simple yet profound reason, that God is the Maker of every man, rich and poor. In extending mercy to the poor, one shows respect for his fellow humans and **"honour"** for God who made them. "Society is a commonwealth of human nature in close connection with God. And so every man becomes his 'brother's keeper.'"[304] Believers should never treat the poor as though they were somehow lesser beings than themselves.

Also, a person dishonors (brings reproach on) and defies God by disobeying His commandments. An early and oft-repeated commandment to pity and take care of the poor was given in Deuteronomy 15:11, which states: "For the poor shall never cease out of the land: therefore I command thee, saying, Thou shalt open thine hand wide unto thy brother, to thy poor, and to thy needy, in thy land."

Furthermore, Jesus, the very Son of God, made Himself poor, and He takes it personally when a poor person is oppressed. Matthew 25:44-45 states – "Then shall they also answer him, saying, Lord, when saw we thee an hungred, or athirst, or a stranger, or naked, or sick, or in prison, and did not minister unto thee? Then shall he answer them, saying, Verily I say unto you, Inasmuch as ye did *it* not to one of the least of these, ye did *it* not to me."

> Psalm 12:5 For the oppression of the poor, for the sighing of the needy, now will I arise, saith the LORD; I will set *him* in safety *from him that* puffeth at him.
> Proverbs 3:27-29 Withhold not good from them to whom it is due, when it is in the power of thine hand to do it. Say not unto thy neighbour, Go, and come again, and tomorrow I will give; when thou hast it by thee. Devise not evil against thy neighbour, seeing he dwelleth securely by thee.
> Proverbs 14:21 He that despiseth his neighbour sinneth: but he that hath mercy on the poor, happy is he.
> Proverbs 17:5 Whoso mocketh the poor reproacheth his Maker: *and* he that is glad at calamities shall not be unpunished.
> Proverbs 19:17 He that hath pity upon the poor lendeth unto the LORD; and that which he hath given will he pay him again.
> Proverbs 22:2 The rich and poor meet together: the LORD *is* the maker of them all.
> Proverbs 22:22-23 Rob not the poor, because he *is* poor: neither oppress the afflicted in the gate: For the LORD will plead their cause, and spoil the soul of those that spoiled them.
> Proverbs 28:27 He that giveth unto the poor shall not lack: but he that hideth his eyes shall have many a curse.
> 2 Corinthians 8:9 For ye know the grace of our Lord Jesus Christ, that, though he was rich, yet for your sakes he became poor, that ye through his poverty might be rich.
> Philippians 2:5-8 Let this mind be in you, which was also in Christ Jesus: Who, being in the form of God, thought it not robbery to be equal with God: But made himself of no reputation, and took upon him the form of a servant, and was made in the likeness of men: And being found in fashion as a man, he humbled himself, and became obedient unto death, even the death of the cross.
> 1 John 3:17-18 But whoso hath this world's good, and seeth his brother have need, and shutteth up his bowels of compassion from him, how dwelleth the love of God in him? My little children, let us not love in word, neither in tongue; but in deed and in truth.

Proverbs 14:32 The wicked is driven away in his wickedness: but the righteous hath hope in his death.

Focus: This proverb compares the final eternal consequences of being wicked with that of being righteous.

"Wickedness" [acts of evil] and **"the wicked"** [an actively bad person, a person hostile to God, guilty of sin. The "lawless ones."[305]] are **"driven away"** [chased away, outcast] from God. When the wicked die, both they and their wickedness depart from God forever, without hope. They will be "driven away from God's favor and presence, and from the society of the just, and from all his hopes of happiness, both in this life and in the next. This expression notes that this is done suddenly, violently, and irresistibly, as the smoke or chaff are driven away by a strong wind." [306]

> Genesis 4:10-14 And he said, What hast thou done? the voice of thy brother's blood crieth unto me from the ground. And now *art* thou cursed from the earth, which hath opened her mouth to receive thy brother's blood from thy hand; When thou tillest the

ground, it shall not henceforth yield unto thee her strength; a fugitive and a vagabond shalt thou be in the earth. And Cain said unto the LORD, My punishment *is* greater than I can bear. Behold, thou hast driven me out this day from the face of the earth; and from thy face shall I be hid; and I shall be a fugitive and a vagabond in the earth; and it shall come to pass, *that* every one that findeth me shall slay me.

Job 18:18 He shall be driven from light into darkness, and chased out of the world.

Psalm 1:4-6 The ungodly *are* not so: but *are* like the chaff which the wind driveth away. Therefore the ungodly shall not stand in the judgment, nor sinners in the congregation of the righteous. For the LORD knoweth the way of the righteous: but the way of the ungodly shall perish.

Psalm 9:17 The wicked shall be turned into hell, and all the nations that forget God.

Proverbs 6:12-15 A naughty person, a wicked man, walketh with a froward mouth. He winketh with his eyes, he speaketh with his feet, he teacheth with his fingers; Frowardness is in his heart, he deviseth mischief continually; he soweth discord. Therefore shall his calamity come suddenly; suddenly shall he be broken without remedy.

Jeremiah 23:12 Wherefore their way shall be unto them as slippery *ways* in the darkness: they shall be driven on, and fall therein: for I will bring evil upon them, *even* the year of their visitation, saith the LORD.

Matthew 7:26-27 And every one that heareth these sayings of mine, and doeth them not, shall be likened unto a foolish man, which built his house upon the sand: And the rain descended, and the floods came, and the winds blew, and beat upon that house; and it fell: and great was the fall of it.

Revelation 20:14-15 And death and hell were cast into the lake of fire. This is the second death. And whosoever was not found written in the book of life was cast into the lake of fire.

"But the righteous hath hope *[have refuge, protection]* **in his death."** At death – the righteous will eternally be with God, surrounded by righteousness; but the wicked will eternally be with Satan, surrounded by wickedness. "Yea, though I walk through the valley of the shadow of death, I will fear no evil: for thou *art* with me; thy rod and thy staff they comfort me." (Psalm 23:4) "He rejoiceth to depart and be with Christ: to him death is gain; he is not reluctant to go – he flies at the call of God."[307] The believer has hope, and he knows the best is yet to come.

Job 19:25-27 For I know *that* my redeemer liveth, and *that* he shall stand at the latter *day* upon the earth: And *though* after my skin *worms* destroy this *body,* yet in my flesh shall I see God: Whom I shall see for myself, and mine eyes shall behold, and not another; *though* my reins be consumed within me.

Proverbs 10:2 Treasures of wickedness profit nothing: but righteousness delivereth from death.

Proverbs 12:28 In the way of righteousness *is* life; and *in* the pathway *thereof there is* no death.

Proverbs 13:21 Evil pursueth sinners: but to the righteous good shall be repayed.

Proverbs 15:24 The way of life *is* above to the wise, that he may depart from hell beneath.

2 Corinthians 5:8 We are confident, *I say,* and willing rather to be absent from the body, and to be present with the Lord.

Philippians 1:21-24 For to me to live is Christ, and to die is gain. But if I live in the flesh, this is the fruit of my labour: yet what I shall choose I wot not. For I am in a strait betwixt two, having a desire to depart, and to be with Christ; which is far better: Nevertheless to abide in the flesh is more needful for you.

Revelation 14:13 And I heard a voice from heaven saying unto me, Write, Blessed are the dead which die in the Lord from henceforth: Yea, saith the Spirit, that they may rest from their labours; and their works do follow them.

Proverbs 14:33 Wisdom resteth in the heart of him that hath understanding: but *that which is* in the midst of fools is made known.

Focus: This proverb states that those with understanding reveal a heart of wisdom, and those who are fools reveal a heart of folly.

A person of understanding knows that there is a right place, right time, and right spirit to handle every situation; so he conceals his thoughts and suppresses his words until the situation can be handled properly. But a fool impetuously, unrestrained, and willingly charges into situations, thereby making it known that he is a fool. He imagines that he possesses great understanding, and his imprudence churns inside him with intense heat and suddenly erupts like lava from a volcano spewing forth volumes of foolishness.

Proverbs 10:20-21 The tongue of the just is as choice silver: the heart of the wicked is little worth. The lips of the righteous feed many: but fools die for want of wisdom.

Proverbs 12:23 A prudent man concealeth knowledge: but the heart of fools proclaimeth foolishness.

Proverbs 13:16 Every prudent man dealeth with knowledge: but a fool layeth open his folly.

Proverbs 15:2 The tongue of the wise useth knowledge aright: but the mouth of fools poureth out foolishness.

Proverbs 15:28 The heart of the righteous studieth to answer: but the mouth of the wicked poureth out evil things.

Proverbs 18:2 A fool hath no delight in understanding, but that his heart may discover itself.

Proverbs 29:11 A fool uttereth all his mind: but a wise *man* keepeth it in till afterwards.

Ecclesiastes 10:2-3 A wise man's heart *is* at his right hand; but a fool's heart at his left. Yea also, when he that is a fool walketh by the way, his wisdom faileth *him,* and he saith to every one *that* he *is* a fool.

Proverbs 14:34 Righteousness exalteth a nation: but sin *is* a reproach to any people.

Focus: This proverb contrasts the effect that righteousness has on a nation with sin's effect on a nation.

"Righteousness exalteth a nation." God gave Israel His word and statutes to live by, declaring, "This is your wisdom and understanding in the sight of the nations." (Deuteronomy 4:5-8) When idolatrous people saw that the Hebrews obeyed the laws given by their God and therefore lived righteously, she was exalted in their sight. Scripture teaches the believer that "a nation's real greatness consists not in its conquests, magnificence, military, or artistic skill, but in its observance of the requirements of justice and religion."[308]

> "What is true of the individual is also true of the nation. When a nation has wisdom resting in it, it behaves righteously. Justice prevails, honesty abounds, taxation is fair and reasonable, the people are as one. It becomes a just and fair society. And as a consequence it is exalted. It is lifted up in the eyes of those round about. It is admired and respected. People see it as an example. It produces a good and wholesome society.
>
> But when sin takes over, and a society becomes unjust and unfair, and full of dissension, and taxation becomes a heavy burden, these things become a reproach and reproof to that society. It is no longer exalted in men's eyes, but looked down on and despised."[309]

> Deuteronomy 4:5-8 Behold, I have taught you statutes and judgments, even as the LORD my God commanded me, that ye should do so in the land whither ye go to possess it. Keep therefore and do them; for this is your wisdom and your understanding in the sight of the nations, which shall hear all these statutes, and say, Surely this great nation is a wise and understanding people. For what nation is there so great, who hath God so nigh unto them, as the LORD our God is in all things that we call upon him for? And what nation is there so great, that hath statutes and judgments so righteous as all this law, which I set before you this day?
>
> Deuteronomy 26:18-19 And the LORD hath avouched thee this day to be his peculiar people, as he hath promised thee, and that thou shouldest keep all his commandments; And to make thee high above all nations which he hath made, in praise, and in name, and in honour; and that thou mayest be an holy people unto the LORD thy God, as he hath spoken.
>
> Proverbs 11:11 By the blessing of the upright the city is exalted: but it is overthrown by the mouth of the wicked.

"But sin is a reproach *[shame]* **to any people"** A nation brings reproach on themselves when reprobate men rule and when the nation's sins take them down and away from God. Righteous people's failure to stand for God, thus, becoming like the world, is a disgrace. Sin in leadership brings contempt and scorn against the nation that has the disgrace of having evil men at the helm.

> Psalm 44:13-14 Thou makest us a reproach to our neighbours, a scorn and a derision to them that are round about us. Thou makest us a byword among the heathen, a shaking of the head among the people.
>
> Jeremiah 44:5-8 But they hearkened not, nor inclined their ear to turn from their wickedness, to burn no incense unto other gods. Wherefore my fury and mine anger was poured forth, and was kindled in the cities of Judah and in the streets of Jerusalem; and they are wasted and desolate, as at this day. Therefore now thus saith the LORD, the God of hosts, the God of Israel; Wherefore commit ye this great evil against your souls, to cut off from you man and woman, child and suckling, out of Judah, to leave you none to remain; In that ye provoke me unto wrath with the works of your hands, burning incense unto other gods in the land of Egypt, whither ye be gone to dwell, that ye might cut yourselves off, and that ye might be a curse and a reproach among all the nations of the earth?

Unfortunately, the nation of Israel was an example of both conditions. When they obeyed God, they were exalted – defeating their enemies and expanding the nation. When their leadership forsook God, the nations about them trampled on them, and they became a reproach.

Proverbs 14:35 The king's favour *is* toward a wise servant: but his wrath is *against* him that causeth shame.

Focus: This proverb compares the king's response to a wise servant with his response to a foolish one who causes shame.

"Wise" *[prudent, wisely understanding, skillful, insightful]* indicates that the servant is wise specifically in regard to the handling of practical matters. The foolish servant causes "shame" because he doesn't know what he is doing, and he makes the king look foolish when his work is not right or when the servant acts like a fool. Notice the wise Joseph and David in the following verses.

> Genesis 41:39-40 And Pharaoh said unto Joseph, Forasmuch as God hath shewed thee all this, *there is* none so discreet and wise as thou *art:* Thou shalt be over my house, and according unto thy word shall all my people be ruled: only in the throne will I be greater than thou.
>
> 1 Samuel 16:18 Then answered one of the servants, and said, Behold, I have seen a son of Jesse the Bethlehemite, that is cunning in playing, and a mighty valiant man, and a man of war, and prudent in matters, and a comely person, and the LORD is with him.

It is indeed foolish to cause shame to a king or to anyone having oversight or authority such as a supervisor on a job. A person has a much better chance of getting promotions, or pay raises, or just good peaceful relationships if he behaves himself wisely in the presence of those having authority.

What would a king's servant do to cause ***shame to the king***? He would act like a fool:

> 1 Kings 2:8-9 And, behold, *thou hast* with thee Shimei the son of Gera, a Benjamite of Bahurim, which cursed me with a grievous curse in the day when I went to Mahanaim: but he came down to meet me at Jordan, and I sware to him by the LORD, saying, I will not put thee to death with the sword. Now therefore hold him not guiltless: for thou *art* a wise man, and knowest what thou oughtest to do unto him; but his hoar head bring thou down to the grave with blood.

```
┌─────────────────────────────────────────────────────┐
│                     A Fool                          │
│                                                     │
│   (1)  lies and utters slanders (Proverbs 10:18)    │
│   (2)  arrogantly won't take counsel (Proverbs 12:15)│
│   (3)  likes to display wrath (Proverbs 12:16)      │
│   (4)  rages with overconfidence (Proverbs 14:16)   │
│   (5)  cannot be reproved or given instructions (Proverbs 15:5)│
│   (6)  can't be corrected (Proverbs 17:10)          │
│   (7)  is contentious (Proverbs 18:6)               │
│   (8)  practices meddling (Proverbs 20:3)           │
│   (9)  causes severe damage to those who trust him (Proverbs 26:6)│
│  (10)  says whatever comes to his mind (Proverbs 29:11)│
└─────────────────────────────────────────────────────┘
```

CHAPTER FIFTEEN

> **Proverbs 15:1** A soft answer turneth away wrath: but grievous words stir up anger.

Focus: This proverb contrasts the effects of a tender response with the effects of a harsh and offensive one.

Verse 1 is the first of seven proverbs in Chapter 15 that reference wise or foolish speaking (verses 1, 2, 4, 7, 14, 23, and 28). In this verse, anger is apparently already present in the situation, and the wise person must quickly and quietly decide his response. He should immediately attempt to turn strife and wrath away with words or actions that are gentle and pleasant. A **"soft answer"** *[a response that is tender, soft]* requires humility from a person who is not interested in seeking his own way but rather in avoiding a conflict that has the potential of damaging everyone involved. Damage can certainly be inflicted emotionally and perhaps spiritually, and maybe physically should the conflict escalate beyond mild words. "A soft answer" may be given *wordlessly* with proper body language, such as with a warm smile. The wise person knows that the tone and loudness of words can inflame or subdue a situation.

"Grievous *[painful or offensive]* **words"** would likely cause an angry person to become more incensed and should be avoided. Also, a wordless response like an angry frown and crossed arms or a sullen silence can generate as much or more wrath than "grievous words." "Being conciliatory in such a situation requires forethought, patience, self-control, and kindness, virtues commonly lauded in Proverbs."[310]

> Judges 8:1-3 And the men of Ephraim said unto him, Why hast thou served us thus, that thou calledst us not, when thou wentest to fight with the Midianites? And they did chide with him sharply. And he said unto them, What have I done now in comparison of you? *Is* not the gleaning of the grapes of Ephraim better than the vintage of Abiezer? God hath delivered into your hands the princes of Midian, Oreb and Zeeb: and what was I able to do in comparison of you? Then their anger was abated toward him, when he had said that.
>
> 1 Samuel 25:10-11, 32-33 And Nabal answered David's servants, and said, Who *is* David? and who *is* the son of Jesse? there be many servants now a days that break away every man from his master. Shall I then take my bread, and my water, and my flesh that I have killed for my shearers, and give *it* unto men, whom I know not whence they be? ... And David said to Abigail, Blessed *be* the LORD God of Israel, which sent thee this day to meet me: And blessed *be* thy advice, and blessed *be* thou, which hast kept me this day from coming to *shed* blood, and from avenging myself with mine own hand.
>
> 1 Kings 12:13 And the king answered the people roughly, and forsook the old men's counsel that they gave him; And spake to them after the counsel of the young men, saying, My father made your yoke heavy, and I will add to your yoke: my father *also* chastised you with whips, but I will chastise you with scorpions.
>
> Proverbs 17:14 The beginning of strife *is as* when one letteth out water: therefore leave off contention, before it be meddled with.
>
> Proverbs 25:15 By long forbearing is a prince persuaded, and a soft tongue breaketh the bone.
>
> Proverbs 29:22 An angry man stirreth up strife, and a furious man aboundeth in transgression.
>
> Hebrews 12:14 Follow peace with all *men,* and holiness, without which no man shall see the Lord ...

> **Proverbs 15:2** The tongue of the wise useth knowledge aright: but the mouth of fools poureth out foolishness.

Focus: This proverb contrasts the gracefully expressed knowledge of a wise person with the foolishly expressed knowledge (or lack thereof) of a fool.

The wise man knows how to use **"knowledge aright"** *[knowledge dealt with in a good fashion, pleasantly, joyfully]*. He carefully considers "knowledge" that he is confident to be true and then decides if he should be part of a conversation or not. His decision will be influenced by consideration of the people present and all influencing circumstances. This careful consideration and making a wise choice is the prudent aspect of wisdom. Showing that he has wisely considered information (**"knowledge"**) before carefully choosing his words, his proper speech will attract men to godly wisdom and consequently, to the Lord.

A carefully chosen response by the wise person is contrasted with the fool who speaks without such consideration and gushes forth foolishness. His conversation is pure folly, revealing not only a lack of knowledge but also his foolish heart. He speaks "plentifully, continually, promiscuously, and vehemently, as a fountain does water."[311] Notice the similarity between this proverb and verse 28.

> Proverbs 15:28 The heart of the righteous studieth to answer: but the mouth of the wicked poureth out evil things.

Waiting for the opportune time and situation, a wise person stores up and reviews knowledge before he speaks. He ensures that the most good and least harm will be accomplished by his carefully chosen words. A wise man once said, "Wait for the right time, the right place, and the right spirit to speak." Contrariwise, the fool blurts out foolishness in the form of misinformation or partial knowledge and likely at an inappropriate time without proper, if any, consideration of collateral damage.

> Proverbs 12:23 A prudent man concealeth knowledge: but the heart of fools proclaimeth foolishness.
> Proverbs 16:23 The heart of the wise teacheth his mouth, and addeth learning to his lips.
> Proverbs 25:11-12 A word fitly spoken *is like* apples of gold in pictures of silver. *As* an earring of gold, and an ornament of fine gold, so is a wise reprover upon an obedient ear.
> Ecclesiastes 10:12-13 The words of a wise man's mouth *are* gracious; but the lips of a fool will swallow up himself. The beginning of the words of his mouth *is* foolishness: and the end of his talk *is* mischievous madness.
> Isaiah 50:4 The Lord GOD hath given me the tongue of the learned, that I should know how to speak a word in season to *him that is* weary: he wakeneth morning by morning, he wakeneth mine ear to hear as the learned.

Proverbs 15:3 The eyes of the LORD *are* in every place, beholding the evil and the good.

Focus: This proverb emphasizes the omniscience and omnipresence of God as He observes every act of every person.

The phrase **"eyes of the LORD"** is the Old Testament's often-used phrase indicating God's omniscience and omnipresence (Genesis 6:8; Deuteronomy 11:12, 13:18; 1 Samuel 26:24; 2 Samuel 15:25; 1 Kings 15:5, 15:11, 16:25, and 22:43; 2 Chronicles 14:2, 16:9, 21:6; 29:6; Psalm 34:15; Proverbs 5:21, 15:3; 22:12; Isaiah 49:5; Jeremiah 52:2; Zechariah 4:10). Nothing done or said by man, good or bad, ever escapes God's observation; and it follows that because God sees every act of man, He is also fully aware of every thought and of every motive. Man will give account for every idle word (Matthew 12:36).

> "The great truths of divinity are of great use to enforce the precepts of morality, and none more than this - That the eye of God is always upon the children of men. An eye to discern all, not only from which nothing can be concealed, but by which every thing is actually inspected, and nothing overlooked or looked slightly upon: *The eyes of the Lord are in every place;* for He not only sees all from on high (Psalm 33:13), but He is every where present. Angels are *full of eyes* (Revelation 4:8), but God is all eye. It denotes not only his omniscience, that he sees all, but his universal providence, that he upholds and governs all. Secret sins, services, and sorrows, are under His eye.
>
> An eye to distinguish both persons and actions. He *beholds the evil and the good,* is displeased with the evil and approves of the good, and will judge men according to the sight of his eyes (Psalm 1:6; 11:4). The wicked shall not go unpunished, nor the righteous unrewarded, for God has his eye upon both and knows their true character; this speaks as much comfort to saints as terror to sinners."[312]

> 2 Chronicles 16:9 For the eyes of the LORD run to and fro throughout the whole earth, to shew himself strong in the behalf of *them* whose heart *is* perfect toward him. Herein thou hast done foolishly: therefore from henceforth thou shalt have wars.
> Job 34:21-22 For his eyes *are* upon the ways of man, and he seeth all his goings. *There is* no darkness, nor shadow of death, where the workers of iniquity may hide themselves.
> Psalm 1:6 For the LORD knoweth the way of the righteous: but the way of the ungodly shall perish.
> Psalm 11:4 The LORD *is* in his holy temple, the LORD'S throne *is* in heaven: his eyes behold, his eyelids try, the children of men.
> Psalm 33:13 The LORD looketh from heaven; he beholdeth all the sons of men.
> Psalm 139:1-4 **To the chief Musician, A Psalm of David.** O LORD, thou hast searched me, and known *me.* Thou knowest my downsitting and mine uprising, thou understandest my thought afar off. Thou compassest my path and my lying down, and art acquainted *with* all my ways. For *there is* not a word in my tongue, *but,* lo, O LORD, thou knowest it altogether.
> Proverbs 5:21 For the ways of man *are* before the eyes of the LORD, and he pondereth all his goings.

Jeremiah 16:17 For mine eyes *are* upon all their ways: they are not hid from my face, neither is their iniquity hid from mine eyes.

Jeremiah 23:24 Can any hide himself in secret places that I shall not see him? saith the LORD. Do not I fill heaven and earth? saith the LORD.

Jeremiah 32:19 Great in counsel, and mighty in work: for thine eyes *are* open upon all the ways of the sons of men: to give every one according to his ways, and according to the fruit of his doings:

Hebrews 4:13 Neither is there any creature that is not manifest in his sight: but all things *are* naked and opened unto the eyes of him with whom we have to do.

Proverbs 15:4 A wholesome tongue *is* a tree of life: but perverseness therein *is* a breach in the spirit.

Focus: This proverb expresses the two extreme opposite capabilities of the tongue whereby it can be a source of joyous living or a source of sorrowful disturbance.

Because context plays a major role in how words are translated, the Hebrew word for **"wholesome***[medicine, cure]***"** was translated "health" in 4:22, 12:18, 13:17, and 16:24; "remedy" in 6:15 and 29:1; "sound" in 14:30; and finally "wholesome" in 15:4. **"Wholesome"** speaking is the ability to use words that have a curing effect, like medicine to the human spirit. It involves words that bring deliverance or healing to wounded consciences, giving comfort. Such words bring peace and love where there are differences and make the home a paradise.[313] They give wholesome advice and good counsel and are labeled a **"tree of life"** because they encourage the heart, strengthen the will, and heal the spirit.

Psalm 45:2 Thou *[The messiah, Jesus Christ]* art fairer than the children of men: grace is poured into thy lips: therefore God hath blessed thee for ever

Proverbs 3:18 She *[wisdom]* is a tree of life to them that lay hold upon her: and happy is every one that retaineth her.

Proverbs 11:30 The fruit of the righteous is a tree of life; and he that winneth souls is wise.

Proverbs 16:24 Pleasant words *are as* an honeycomb, sweet to the soul, and health to the bones.

Perverse words ***breach*** *[fracture, shatter]* ***the spirit*** by disturbing and wounding the spirit of a man that would otherwise be at peace. Such words eat at the listener like a canker, make his soul sad, and bring distress and despair. They can cause depression of one's morale, as exemplified by the perverse words of Job's three "friends."

Psalm 52:1 To the chief Musician, Maschil, A Psalm of David, when Doeg the Edomite came and told Saul, and said unto him, David is come to the house of Ahimelech. Why boastest thou thyself in mischief, O mighty man? the goodness of God *endureth* continually. Thy tongue deviseth mischiefs; like a sharp razor, working deceitfully. Thou lovest evil more than good; *and* lying rather than to speak righteousness. Selah. Thou lovest all devouring words, O *thou* deceitful tongue.

Psalm 69:19-20 Thou hast known my *[David's]* reproach, and my shame, and my dishonour: mine adversaries *are* all before thee. Reproach hath broken my heart; and I am full of heaviness: and I looked *for some* to take pity, but *there was* none; and for comforters, but I found none.

Proverbs 12:18 There is that speaketh like the piercings of a sword: but the tongue of the wise *is* health.

Proverbs 18:14 The spirit of a man will sustain his infirmity; but a wounded spirit who can bear?

Proverbs 18:8 The words of a talebearer *are* as wounds, and they go down into the innermost parts of the belly.

1 Timothy 6:3-5 If any man teach otherwise, and consent not to wholesome words, *even* the words of our Lord Jesus Christ, and to the doctrine which is according to godliness; He is proud, knowing nothing, but doting about questions and strifes of words, whereof cometh envy, strife, railings, evil surmisings, Perverse disputings of men of corrupt minds, and destitute of the truth, supposing that gain is godliness: from such withdraw thyself.

Proverbs 15:5 A fool despiseth his father's instruction: but he that regardeth reproof is prudent.

Focus: This proverb identifies and labels a child according to his willingness to receive instruction from his parent.

The fool doesn't comprehend that he doesn't have the needed knowledge, experience, or skill; therefore, his foolishness is manifest by the fact that he despises reproof, especially from his father. While this verse labels a child who despises and refuses his father's instruction as a fool, Proverbs 12:1 further identifies anyone who hates reproof as *brutish* (dull like an animal). ***Scorners or mockers*** are among those who despise rebuke or reproof (Proverbs 13:1 and 15:12). Such a rebel is ***destroying or killing himself*** (Proverbs 15:10).

A prudent or wise person will not only listen to instruction but will secure it in his heart, giving it special protection and care. Starting by prudently and wisely listening and following his father's instruction, he will continue to grow in wisdom throughout his life.

> 1 Samuel 2:23-25 And he *[Eli the priest]* said unto them, Why do ye such things? for I hear of your evil dealings by all this people. Nay, my sons; for *it is* no good report that I hear: ye make the LORD'S people to transgress. If one man sin against another, the judge shall judge him: but if a man sin against the LORD, who shall intreat for him? Notwithstanding they hearkened not unto the voice of their father, because the LORD would slay them.
>
> 1 Chronicles 28:9 And thou, Solomon my son, know thou the God of thy father, and serve him with a perfect heart and with a willing mind: for the LORD searcheth all hearts, and understandeth all the imaginations of the thoughts: if thou seek him, he will be found of thee; but if thou forsake him, he will cast thee off for ever.
>
> Psalm 141:5 Let the righteous smite me; *it shall be* a kindness: and let him reprove me; *it shall be* an excellent oil, *which* shall not break my head: for yet my prayer also *shall be* in their calamities.
>
> Proverbs 1:7 The fear of the LORD is the beginning of knowledge: but fools despise wisdom and instruction.
>
> Proverbs 12:1 Whoso loveth instruction loveth knowledge: but he that hateth reproof is brutish.
>
> Proverbs 13:1 A wise son *heareth* his father's instruction: but a scorner heareth not rebuke.
>
> Proverbs 15:10 Correction *is* grievous unto him that forsaketh the way: *and* he that hateth reproof shall die.
>
> Proverbs 15:12 A scorner loveth not one that reproveth him: neither will he go unto the wise.
>
> Proverbs 15:32 He that refuseth instruction despiseth his own soul: but he that heareth reproof getteth understanding.
>
> 1 Peter 5:5 Likewise, ye younger, submit yourselves unto the elder. Yea, all *of you* be subject one to another, and be clothed with humility: for God resisteth the proud, and giveth grace to the humble.

Proverbs 15:6 In the house of the righteous *is* much treasure: but in the revenues of the wicked is trouble.

> Focus: This proverb repeats the premise that righteous, wise handling of life and finances generally results in "much treasure," and it reminds the reader that wealth acquired ("revenues") by wickedness results in "trouble" or affliction and problems.

A **"righteous"** person is one who is right with God. Because his priority is to please God in all that he does and with every object that he owns, he is blessed of God and is at peace. He is satisfied and gives great value to everything God has provided either through giving him the ability to get wealth or by sending supernatural provisions. Either way, his home is characterized by peace and appreciation, but the opposite is true of the home and wealth of the **"wicked."** *Trouble is in the wicked's abode* because they get wealth by any means possible, disregarding all instruction from God. Their house is characterized by **"trouble** *[disturbances, calamities]***"** because the extreme heaviness of guilt as well as a curse take away peace. Pride and a lust for more, envy, and contentions rob them of the joy of their revenues and often create hostilities in relationships both within their families and without.[314]

> "The comparison between *the righteous and the wicked*, always turns in favor of *the righteous*. Even in *treasure* (Proverbs 3:33; 15:16-17), the world's idol, he exceeds. For though *his house* may be destitute of money, yet is there *much treasure;* often unseen (2Corinthians 6:10), yet such, that *the revenues of the wicked*, compared with it, sink into nothing. Divine Teaching alone can convey any just apprehension of it. (1Corinthians 2:9) Even eternity cannot fully grasp it; as throughout eternity it will be progressively increasing. 'Drop millions of gold, boundless *revenues*, ample territories, crowns and sceptres; and a poor contemptible worm lays his One God against all of them.' The treasures of the wicked are too much for their good, and too little for their lust. They cannot satisfy their senses, much less their souls. (Ecclesiastes 5:10) They may 'take wings' (Proverbs 23:5) at any moment; and, while they continue, unlike *the treasures of the righteous* (Proverbs 10:22), they are burdened with *trouble*. (Ecclesiastes 4:6) But is it not the crown of the Christian's crown, and the glory of his glory, that his portion is so full, that he cannot desire more? All the excellences of the creation are only dark shadows of its more substantial excellency. What a mercy to be delivered from the idolatrous bait, so ruinous alike to our present peace and eternal welfare! (1Timothy 6:9-10) But a greater mercy still, to be enriched with that *treasure*, beyond the reach of harm, that raises to heaven; a portion in God, his favor, his image, his everlasting joy."[315]
>
> Job 20:19 Because he hath oppressed *and* hath forsaken the poor; *because* he hath violently taken away an house which he builded not; Surely he shall not feel quietness in his belly, he shall not save of that which he desired. There shall none of his meat be left; therefore shall no man look for his goods. In the fulness of his sufficiency he shall be in straits: every hand of the wicked shall come upon him. *When* he is about to fill his belly, *God* shall cast the fury of his wrath upon him, and shall rain *it* upon him while he is eating.
>
> Psalm 112:3 Wealth and riches *shall be* in his house: and his righteousness endureth for ever.
>
> Proverbs 3:33 The curse of the LORD *is* in the house of the wicked: but he blesseth the habitation of the just.

Proverbs 8:18   Riches and honour *are* with me; *yea,* durable riches and righteousness.

Proverbs 8:20-21   I lead in the way of righteousness, in the midst of the paths of judgment: That I may cause those that love me to inherit substance; and I will fill their treasures.

Proverbs 10:22   The blessing of the LORD, it maketh rich, and he addeth no sorrow with it.

Proverbs 15:16-17   Better *is* little with the fear of the LORD than great treasure and trouble therewith. Better *is* a dinner of herbs where love is, than a stalled ox and hatred therewith.

Proverbs 22:4   By humility *and* the fear of the LORD *are* riches, and honour, and life.

Ecclesiastes 4:6   Better *is* an handful *with* quietness, than both the hands full *with* travail and vexation of spirit.

2 Corinthians 6:10   As sorrowful, yet alway rejoicing; as poor, yet making many rich; as having nothing, and *yet* possessing all things.

1 Timothy 6:9-10   But they that will be rich fall into temptation and a snare, and *into* many foolish and hurtful lusts, which drown men in destruction and perdition.   For the love of money is the root of all evil: which while some coveted after, they have erred from the faith, and pierced themselves through with many sorrows.

Proverbs 15:7   The lips of the wise disperse knowledge: but the heart of the foolish *doeth* not so.

Focus: This proverb draws attention to the fact that when wise people speak, they have something worthwhile to say, unlike the fool who is known to blurt out only foolishness.

The wise person assimilates knowledge about God that he learns through studying Scripture, listening to other wise people, and observing God's creation.   Because he has previously *determined* to be wise, the wise person becomes wiser with new knowledge; and when he speaks his beneficial words disperse knowledge which is a joy to hear.   *The true value of knowledge (and also wealth) depends upon its use.*   Since God has put His word in trust with believers, they feel compelled to disperse such knowledge by gladly telling others of truths that affect their temporal and eternal well-being.

The fool can't speak wisely because his heart is wicked; and he hates "to retain God in his knowledge (Romans 1:28)."   He can only produce folly *or* as Proverbs 15:2 states *his mouth pours out foolishness.*

Psalm 37:30   The mouth of the righteous speaketh wisdom, and his tongue talketh of judgment.

Proverbs 4:23-24   Keep thy heart with all diligence; for out of it are the issues of life.   Put away from thee a froward mouth, and perverse lips put far from thee.

Proverbs 5:1-2   My son, attend unto my wisdom, *and* bow thine ear to my understanding: That thou mayest regard discretion, and *that* thy lips may keep knowledge.

Proverbs 10:14   Wise *men* lay up knowledge: but the mouth of the foolish *is* near destruction.

Proverbs 10:20-21   The tongue of the just *is as* choice silver: the heart of the wicked *is* little worth. The lips of the righteous feed many: but fools die for want of wisdom.

Proverbs 10:32   The lips of the righteous know what is acceptable: but the mouth of the wicked *speaketh* frowardness.

Proverbs 15:2   The tongue of the wise useth knowledge aright: but the mouth of fools poureth out foolishness.

Proverbs 15:8   The sacrifice of the wicked *is* an abomination to the LORD: but the prayer of the upright *is* his delight.

Focus: This proverb contrasts God's attitude toward the sacrifice of the wicked with His attitude toward the prayer of the upright.

"The sacrifice of the wicked *is* an abomination to the LORD."   A wicked person thinks and lives *in opposition* to God, *in conflict* with all that He stands for, and *in rejection* of all His laws and commandments.   For him to offer a sacrifice to God would be pure hypocrisy; consequently, God has nothing but disapproval for such action.   He detests such a sacrifice, the ways, and even the thoughts of the wicked (Proverbs 15:26).

1 Samuel 15:22   And Samuel said, Hath the LORD *as great* delight in burnt offerings and sacrifices, as in obeying the voice of the LORD? Behold, to obey *is* better than sacrifice, *and* to hearken than the fat of rams.

Proverbs 7:14   *I have* peace offerings with me; this day have I payed my vows. *[spoken by the hypocritical adulteress]*

Proverbs 15:29   The LORD *is* far from the wicked: but he heareth the prayer of the righteous.

Proverbs 21:27   The sacrifice of the wicked *is* abomination: how much more, *when* he bringeth it with a wicked mind?

Isaiah 1:10-14 Hear the word of the LORD, ye rulers of Sodom; give ear unto the law of our God, ye people of Gomorrah. To what purpose *is* the multitude of your sacrifices unto me? saith the LORD: I am full of the burnt offerings of rams, and the fat of fed beasts; and I delight not in the blood of bullocks, or of lambs, or of he goats. When ye come to appear before me, who hath required this at your hand, to tread my courts? Bring no more vain oblations; incense is an abomination unto me; the new moons and sabbaths, the calling of assemblies, I cannot away with; *it is* iniquity, even the solemn meeting. Your new moons and your appointed feasts my soul hateth: they are a trouble unto me; I am weary to bear *them*.

Jeremiah 6:20 To what purpose cometh there to me incense from Sheba, and the sweet cane from a far country? your burnt offerings *are* not acceptable, nor your sacrifices sweet unto me.

Amos 5:21-22 I hate, I despise your feast days, and I will not smell in your solemn assemblies. Though ye offer me burnt offerings and your meat offerings, I will not accept *them*: neither will I regard the peace offerings of your fat beasts.

In contrast to the wicked who hate God, who have a mind set against Him, and who live in opposition to His laws and commandments are the upright who "follow after righteousness." These are determined to know what thoughts and ways are appropriate toward God and their fellow man, therefore ***when they come to God in prayer*** *(without any expensive sacrifice)*, ***He is delighted*** as stated in verses 11: 20 and 12:22 above. He also hears their prayers (15:29).

Hebrews 13:15 By him therefore let us offer the sacrifice of praise to God continually, that is, the fruit of *our* lips giving thanks to his name.

Proverbs 15:9   The way of the wicked *is* an abomination unto the LORD: but he loveth him that followeth after righteousness.

Focus: This proverb contrasts God's attitude toward the way of the wicked with His attitude toward those who *follow after righteousness*.

"The way *[manner, habits]* **of the wicked *is* an abomination unto the LORD."** The *way* of the wicked is their evil lifestyle – which is representative of *themselves*. Not only does God despise the *sacrifice* of the wicked (verse 8), but He also views his *way* as an abomination and detests his *thoughts* (verse 26). Concerning the wicked, "All of his doings are the corrupt stream from a corrupt fountain. Awful, indeed, is the thought of every step of life as being hateful to God!"[316] The wicked abandon righteousness and pursue wickedness, while the righteous do the opposite – they abandon evil and follow after righteousness. As much as God loves the person in pursuit of righteousness, He despises the person in pursuit of wickedness.

"But he loveth him that followeth after righteousness." Those who *follow after righteousness* in this verse were identified as **"the upright"** in the previous one. The **"way"** of a person is representative of his *entire person (or manner of living)* as can be observed when comparing both sides of this verse and other verses listed below.

Psalm 1:6 For the LORD knoweth the way of the righteous: but the way of the ungodly shall perish.

Psalm 146:8-9 The LORD openeth *the eyes of* the blind: the LORD raiseth them that are bowed down: the LORD loveth the righteous: The LORD preserveth the strangers; he relieveth the fatherless and widow: but the way of the wicked he turneth upside down.

Proverbs 4:19 The way of the wicked *is* as darkness: they know not at what they stumble.

Proverbs 11:19 As righteousness *tendeth* to life: so he that pursueth evil *pursueth it* to his own death.

Proverbs 11:20 They that are of a froward heart *are* abomination to the LORD: but *such as are* upright in their way *are* his delight.

Proverbs 21:21 He that followeth after righteousness and mercy findeth life, righteousness, and honour.

2 Timothy 2:22 Flee also youthful lusts: but follow righteousness, faith, charity, peace, with them that call on the Lord out of a pure heart.

In this chapter, the first nine verses (except verse 3) were antithetical proverbs joined by the negative conjunction "but." In the next three verses, the two parts of the proverb are joined by a colon, and the second part of the proverb expands the thought of the first.

Proverbs 15:10   Correction *is* grievous unto him that forsaketh the way: *and* he that hateth reproof shall die.

Focus: This proverb declares that the one who hates being corrected will forsake the way of righteousness and he will die.

When a person *forsakes the way (God's way)*, he enters the "ways of darkness" (Proverbs 2:13) and "pursueth evil...to his own death." (Proverbs 11:9) Walking with God in *the righteous way* is nonsense to the fool; furthermore, he is **grieved over being corrected.** Consequently, he refuses and *will die to the things of God,* eventually suffering the "second death," which is eternal separation from God. "He that hates reproof shall perish in his sins, since he would not be parted from them."³¹⁷

"There is no surer step to ruin than this **hatred of reproof** ... But *[if]* correction turns back him, who had forsaken the way. ...Then it is *grievous* no more . . . For surely so long as the physician administers the medicine, there is no ground for despondency."³¹⁸

Psalm 119:1 ALEPH. Blessed *are* the undefiled in the way, who walk in the law of the LORD.

Proverbs 5:11-12 And thou mourn at the last, when thy flesh and thy body are consumed, And say, How have I hated instruction, and my heart despised reproof;

Proverbs 5:22 His own iniquities shall take the wicked himself, and he shall be holden with the cords of his sins. He shall die without instruction; and in the greatness of his folly he shall go astray.

Proverbs 10:17 He *is in* the way of life that keepeth instruction: but he that refuseth reproof erreth.

Proverbs 12:1 Whoso loveth instruction loveth knowledge: but he that hateth reproof *is* brutish.

Proverbs 13:1 A wise son *heareth* his father's instruction: but a scorner heareth not rebuke.

Proverbs 14:32 The wicked is driven away in his wickedness: but the righteous hath hope in his death.

John 3:20 For every one that doeth evil hateth the light, neither cometh to the light, lest his deeds should be reproved.

Proverbs 15:11 Hell and destruction *are* before the LORD: how much more then the hearts of the children of men?

Focus: This proverb declares that there is nothing hidden from God – not the depths of Hell nor the hearts of men – nothing is hidden from God.

"Hell and destruction *are* before the LORD" refers to all the condemned world on the other side of this life, including the place of decaying bodies and that of departed spirits. **"Hell"** is translated from the Hebrew word *sheol*, which is ". . . used generally as the place to which the souls of the dead are consigned – the receptacle of all departed spirits, whether good or bad."³¹⁹ **"Destruction"** is translated from the Hebrew *'abaddon* which means place of destruction, ruin. It is "the place and state of the damned, of which men know nothing but by Divine revelation."³²⁰ "*Abaddon* is the lowest depth of hell, the 'abyss' *[Greek abussos]* of Luke 8:31; Revelation 9:2, 20:1."³²¹

"This confirms what was said (Proverbs 15:3) concerning God's omnipresence, in order to his judging of evil and good. God knows all things, even those things that are hidden from the eyes of all living: *Hell and destruction are before the Lord,* not only the center of the earth, and its subterraneous caverns, but the grave, and all the dead bodies which are there buried out of our sight; they are all *before the Lord,* all under his eye, so that none of them can be lost or be *sought for* when they are to be raised again. He knows where every man lies buried, even Moses, even those that are buried in the greatest obscurity; nor needs he any monument with a *Hic jacet - Here he lies,* to direct him. The place of the damned in particular, and all their torments, which are inexpressible, the state of separate souls in general, and all their circumstances, are under God's eye. The word here used for *destruction* is *Abaddon*, which is one of the devil's names (Revelation 9:11). That destroyer, though he deceives us, cannot evade or elude the divine cognizance."³²²

Job 26:6 Hell *is* naked before him, and destruction hath no covering.

Proverbs 15:3 The eyes of the LORD *are* in every place, beholding the evil and the good.

Hebrews 4:13 Neither is there any creature that is not manifest in his sight: but all things *are* naked and opened unto the eyes of him with whom we have to do.

Revelation 9:1 And the fifth angel sounded, and I saw a star fall from heaven unto the earth: and to him was given the key of the bottomless pit.

Revelation 9:11 And they had a king over them, *which is* the angel of the bottomless pit, whose name in the Hebrew tongue *is* Abaddon, but in the Greek tongue hath *his* name Apollyon.

"How much more then the hearts of the children of men?" The depth of the heart of man is shallow compared to the depth of "hell and destruction." It is *not* challenging for God to know every aspect, every thought, every word or scheme. Man doesn't need to speak words for God to know his heart for "The LORD knoweth the thoughts of man" (Psalm 94:11). To Him the attitudes of every man are as bright and clear as the noonday sun. How vain is sinful man to think otherwise.

2 Chronicles 6:30-31 Then hear thou from heaven thy dwelling place, and forgive, and render unto every man according unto all his ways, whose heart thou knowest; (for thou only knowest the hearts of the children of men:) That they may fear thee, to walk in thy ways, so long as they live in the land which thou gavest unto our fathers.

Psalm 139:7-13 Whither shall I go from thy spirit? or whither shall I flee from thy presence? If I ascend up into heaven, thou *art* there: if I make my bed in hell, behold, thou *art there. If* I take the wings of the morning, *and* dwell in the uttermost parts of the sea; Even there shall thy hand lead me, and thy right hand shall hold me. If I say, Surely the darkness shall cover me; even the night shall be light about me. Yea, the darkness hideth not from thee; but the night shineth as the day: the darkness and the light *are* both alike *to thee*. For thou hast possessed my reins: thou hast covered me in my mother's womb.

Isaiah 29:15 Woe unto them that seek deep to hide their counsel from the LORD, and their works are in the dark, and they say, Who seeth us? and who knoweth us?

Jeremiah 17:9-10 The heart is deceitful above all things, and desperately wicked: who can know it? I the LORD search the heart, I try the reins, even to give every man according to his ways, and according to the fruit of his doings.

John 2:24-25 But Jesus did not commit himself unto them, because he knew all men, and needed not that any should testify of man: for he knew what was in man.

1 John 3:20 For if our heart condemn us, God is greater than our heart, and knoweth all things.

Proverbs 15:12 A scorner loveth not one that reproveth him: neither will he go unto the wise.

Focus: This proverb expresses two profound characteristics of a scorner.

Because of the scorner's attitude of hate for God's instruction, he is in a doomed, disastrous condition. He harms himself by thinking that he is a master teacher and by hating anyone attempting to correct his folly. **"A scorner loveth not one that reproveth him"** because scorners "are conceited, arrogant persons, freethinkers, indifferent to or skeptical of religion, and too self-opinionated to be open to advice or reproof. **Neither will he go unto the wise,** who would correct and teach him."[323]

"The words of the wise and the lives of the wise reprove the scorner by increasing his light, and thus adding to his guilt. He therefore 'cometh not to the light lest his deeds should be reproved' (John 3:20). He is like a man who is conscious that he is suffering from a dangerous disease, but who will not submit to the examination of the physician because he knows he would prescribe treatment which, though it would cure, would be painful. No men love reproof any more than they love the surgeon's knife; but wise men submit to the one and the other for the sake of the health to soul and to body which will follow. But the scorner hates the keen-edged weapon of reproof because he does not value the good that would result from patiently bearing the incision . . . Ignorance is a crime only when the means of enlightenment are within reach. He who scorns to avail himself of those means, he who will not submit to reproof, he who rejects the invitation and despises the threatening of Divine Wisdom commits moral suicide."[324]

Proverbs 9:7-8 He that reproveth a scorner getteth to himself shame: and he that rebuketh a wicked *man getteth* himself a blot. Reprove not a scorner, lest he hate thee: rebuke a wise man, and he will love thee.

Proverbs 12:1 Whoso loveth instruction loveth knowledge: but he that hateth reproof *is* brutish.

Proverbs 15:10 Correction *is* grievous unto him that forsaketh the way: *and* he that hateth reproof shall die.

Amos 5:10 They hate him that rebuketh in the gate, and they abhor him that speaketh uprightly.

John 3:18-21 He that believeth on him is not condemned: but he that believeth not is condemned already, because he hath not believed in the name of the only begotten Son of God. And this is the condemnation, that light is come into the world, and men loved darkness rather than light, because their deeds were evil. For every one that doeth evil hateth the light, neither cometh to the light, lest his deeds should be reproved. But he that doeth truth cometh to the light, that his deeds may be made manifest, that they are wrought in God.

Proverbs 15:13 A merry heart maketh a cheerful countenance: but by sorrow of the heart the spirit is broken.

Focus: This proverb specifies that the emotional condition of a person's heart is reflected in his countenance and in his spirit.

"Countenance" is the facial display of a person's emotions, whether merry, sorrowful, or otherwise; and a ***spirit broken*** because of a sorrowful heart is visible in a person's face, shoulders, words, and walk. "How close is the sympathy between the body and soul, though framed of such opposite elements. A man's countenance is the index of his spirit."[325]

"A merry heart" is not referring to the boisterous, false, temporary merriment that accompanies excessive drinking of alcohol. It is rather, *in its most pure form*, the inward peace and joy imparted by God to a person who seeks to fulfill His will. For example, when Hannah realized that God had answered her prayer, "her countenance was no more sad."

1 Samuel 1:14-18 And Eli said unto her, How long wilt thou be drunken? put away thy wine from thee. And Hannah answered and said, No, my lord, I am a woman of a sorrowful spirit: I have drunk neither wine nor strong drink, but have poured out my soul before the LORD. Count not thine handmaid for a daughter of Belial: for out of the abundance of my complaint and grief have I spoken hitherto.

Then Eli answered and said, Go in peace: and the God of Israel grant thee thy petition that thou hast asked of him. And she said, Let thine handmaid find grace in thy sight. So the woman went her way, and did eat, and her countenance was no more sad.

Nehemiah, a captive Jew and foreigner in the Medo-Persian Empire, had the important, life-threatening, high- ranking, and trusted position of serving as King Artaxerxes' cupbearer. When the king read Nehemiah's countenance as being sad, he was naturally and wisely alarmed. He quickly wanted to know what was wrong. (His first thought must have been that Nehemiah's heart was troubled because of a quarrel with the king or his kingdom – a sorrowful heart for this reason was punishable by death.) King Artaxerxes knew that a person's countenance reflected his heart condition, but when Nehemiah revealed that his heart was troubled about the condition of the gates and walls around Jerusalem, the king was relieved and offered Nehemiah a massive amount of help to rectify the problem.

> Nehemiah 2:2 Wherefore the king said unto me, Why *is* thy countenance sad, seeing thou *art* not sick? this *is* nothing *else* but sorrow of heart. Then I was very sore afraid,
> Proverbs 12:25 Heaviness in the heart of man maketh it stoop: but a good word maketh it glad.
> Proverbs 17:22 A merry heart doeth good *like* a medicine: but a broken spirit drieth the bones.
> Proverbs 18:14 The spirit of a man will sustain his infirmity; but a wounded spirit who can bear?
> 2 Corinthians 7:10 For godly sorrow worketh repentance to salvation not to be repented of: but the sorrow of the world worketh death.

Everyone experiences **"sorrow of heart"** on occasions, such as the death of a loved one, severe disappointments from defeat of a hopeful situation, or when a friend violates trust. All such situations have the potential of being reflected in a person's countenance, and these sorrows when extended and accumulated over a long period break the spirit, deprive it of its vigor, and make a person unfit for active life.[326] But the Christian must take refuge in the promises of Scripture and not permit a defeated life else he lose his testimony and joy. "Sorrow of heart" that breaks the spirit and ultimately reveals itself in the countenance should not be an ongoing condition of a believer. *(See also Proverbs 15:15.)* God's word and godly counsel should help the downcast believer choose a better way.

> **"The effect of sorrow upon the human spirit**: it 'breaks' it. When a vessel's timbers are shivered by the fury of the storm she may not go to pieces altogether. But she is no longer able to hold her own against the elements, which she could once use as forces to convey her from land to land. If she were now to put to sea, instead of riding over the waves and making them her servants, she would be a passive thing in their hands, a mere helpless bundle of timbers to be tossed whithersoever they pleased, instead of 'walking the waters like a thing of life.' So it is with the human spirit when the cross seas and angry winds of adverse circumstances have quenched the hope and paralyzed the energy that once governed and inspired the man, he is no longer able to face the storms of life, and outride them, or even make them advance his interests. He is passive amid the changes and chances of mortal life, and they drift him on wheresoever they will. But this can never be the case unless a man has lost faith in the character of God and his own high and immortal destiny. Then, indeed, the elements which he was built to rule will rule him, and he will fail to fulfil the end for which God launched him on the sea of life."[327]
> Psalm 13:1-6 To the chief Musician, A Psalm of David. How long wilt thou forget me, O LORD? for ever? how long wilt thou hide thy face from me? How long shall I take counsel in my soul, *having* sorrow in my heart daily? how long shall mine enemy be exalted over me? Consider *and* hear me, O LORD my God: lighten mine eyes, lest I sleep the *sleep of* death; Lest mine enemy say, I have prevailed against him; *and* those that trouble me rejoice when I am moved. But I have trusted in thy mercy; my heart shall rejoice in thy salvation. I will sing unto the LORD, because he hath dealt bountifully with me.
> Ecclesiastes 9:7 Go thy way, eat thy bread with joy, and drink thy wine with a merry heart; for God now accepteth thy works.
> John 14:1 Let not your heart be troubled: ye believe in God, believe also in me.
> 2 Corinthians 2:7 So that contrariwise ye *ought* rather to forgive *him,* and comfort *him,* lest perhaps such a one should be swallowed up with overmuch sorrow.
> 2 Corinthians 7:9-10 Now I rejoice, not that ye were made sorry, but that ye sorrowed to repentance: for ye were made sorry after a godly manner, that ye might receive damage by us in nothing. For godly sorrow worketh repentance to salvation not to be repented of: but the sorrow of the world worketh death.

Paul and Silas could have been thrown into deep depression and suffered a **broken spirit** when they were beaten and cast into prison because they loved the lost people of Philippi enough to tell them the truth about Christ. However, notice how they reacted.

> Acts 16:22-26 And the multitude rose up together against them: and the magistrates rent off their clothes, and commanded to beat *them.* And when they had laid many stripes upon them, they cast them into prison, charging the jailor to keep them safely: Who, having received such a charge, thrust them into the inner prison, and made their feet fast in the stocks. And at midnight Paul and Silas prayed, and sang praises unto God: and the prisoners heard them. And suddenly there was a great earthquake, so that the foundations of the prison were shaken: and immediately all the doors were opened, and every one's bands were loosed.

Proverbs 15:14 The heart of him that hath understanding seeketh knowledge: but the mouth of fools feedeth on foolishness.

Focus: This proverb contrasts the eagerness for gathering knowledge by a person of understanding with the eagerness for gathering foolishness by the fool.

"The heart of him that hath understanding seeketh knowledge." The **"heart,"** sometimes called "the inner man" or the "soul," is his *mind* that he thinks with, his *emotions* that he feels with, and his *will* that he is determined with. Thus, a person's "heart" is representative of the way he carries on his life; and when he has **"understanding** *[the power to distinguish right from wrong and truth from falsehood[328]],"* he will desire a greater **knowledge** of God so that he can walk closer to Him and live as wisely as possible.

> Proverbs 1:5 A wise *man* will hear, and will increase learning; and a man of understanding shall attain unto wise counsels . . .
>
> Proverbs 2:2-5 So that thou incline thine ear unto wisdom, *and* apply thine heart to understanding; Yea, if thou criest after knowledge, *and* liftest up thy voice for understanding; If thou seekest her as silver, and searchest for her as *for* hid treasures; Then shalt thou understand the fear of the LORD, and find the knowledge of God.
>
> Proverbs 9:9-10 Give *instruction* to a wise *man,* and he will be yet wiser: teach a just *man,* and he will increase in learning. The fear of the LORD *is* the beginning of wisdom: and the knowledge of the holy *is* understanding.
>
> Proverbs 18:15 The heart of the prudent getteth knowledge; and the ear of the wise seeketh knowledge.
>
> 2 Peter 3:18 But grow in grace, and in the knowledge of our Lord and Saviour Jesus Christ. To him be glory both now and for ever. Amen.

"The mouth of fools feedeth on foolishness" means that he is hungry for reinforcement from foolish people or foolish misunderstandings to support and sustain his own foolishness which he considers wisdom. "His brutish taste *feeds upon foolishness,* as his meat and his drink."[329] Figuratively speaking, the fool is constantly gulping down every silly, slanderous, evil word that he hears; and then he will blab it to anyone who will listen.

> Proverbs 15:2 The tongue of the wise useth knowledge aright: but the mouth of fools poureth out foolishness.
>
> Proverbs 15:21 Folly *is* joy to *him that is* destitute of wisdom: but a man of understanding walketh uprightly.
>
> Proverbs 17:24 Wisdom *is* before him that hath understanding; but the eyes of a fool *are* in the ends of the earth.
>
> Proverbs 18:2 A fool hath no delight in understanding, but that his heart may discover itself.

Proverbs 15:15 All the days of the afflicted *are* evil: but he that is of a merry heart *hath* a continual feast.

Focus: This proverb contrasts the consequences of having an afflicted heart with the consequences of having a merry heart.

The **"afflicted** *[wretched, depressed]"* here is translated from the Hebrew '*aniy* which means the opposite of **"merry** *[good, pleasant, happy]."* In other words the "afflicted" goes around under a cloud of misery because he sees **"evil"** (bad) in everything. He is bogged down with a bad attitude.

All people have both good and bad to come their way, and everyone has to deal with his own particular and individual circumstances of life. To choose to dwell on the bad and thus minimize or ignore the good is to set one's path down misery lane. To decide to have a **"merry heart"** and to find that ray of sunshine (though circumstances may be challenging), and to thus minimize the bad, is a choice that sets one down a path of happiness.

"A merry heart" is *in its most pure form,* the inward peace and joy imparted by God to a person who seeks to fulfill His will. For example, a believer might have a flat tire; but he rejoices because a lost man came by to help, and he had the opportunity to witness about Jesus. Or perhaps he just enjoyed the sights and sounds of a beautiful day while he was changing the tire *(all the while remembering that God had given him the job and the money to buy the car).* So, a man with this attitude of finding good will enjoy a **"continual feast"** of enjoying life despite difficult circumstances.

> **"But he that is of a merry heart *hath* a continual feast"** is one that has "a heart that has 'the kingdom of God' in it, which lies 'not *in* meat and drink, but *in* righteousness, peace, and joy in the Holy Ghost,' (Romans 14:17) which has the love of God shed abroad in it by the Spirit, where Christ dwells by faith; and that lives by faith in him, and on the provisions of his grace; all this is a constant continual feast to a gracious soul, made joyful hereby."[330]
>
> Nehemiah 8:10 Then he said unto them, Go your way, eat the fat, and drink the sweet, and send portions unto them for whom nothing is prepared: for *this* day *is* holy unto our Lord: neither be ye sorry; for the joy of the LORD is your strength.
>
> Proverbs 15:13 A merry heart maketh a cheerful countenance: but by sorrow of the heart the spirit is broken.
>
> Proverbs 17:22 A merry heart doeth good like a medicine: but a broken spirit drieth the bones.

Habakkuk 3:17-19 Although the fig tree shall not blossom, neither shall fruit be in the vines; the labour of the olive shall fail, and the fields shall yield no meat; the flock shall be cut off from the fold, and there shall be no herd in the stalls: Yet I will rejoice in the LORD, I will joy in the God of my salvation. The LORD God is my strength, and he will make my feet like hinds' feet, and he will make me to walk upon mine high places. To the chief singer on my stringed instruments.

Romans 5:1-5 Therefore being justified by faith, we have peace with God through our Lord Jesus Christ: By whom also we have access by faith into this grace wherein we stand, and rejoice in hope of the glory of God. And not only *so,* but we glory in tribulations also: knowing that tribulation worketh patience. And patience, experience; and experience, hope: And hope maketh not ashamed; because the love of God is shed abroad in our hearts by the Holy Ghost which is given unto us.

Philippians 4:4 Rejoice in the Lord alway: *and* again I say, Rejoice.

Philippians 4:6-8 Be careful for nothing; but in every thing by prayer and supplication with thanksgiving let your requests be made known unto God. And the peace of God, which passeth all understanding, shall keep your hearts and minds through Christ Jesus. Finally, brethren, whatsoever things are true, whatsoever things *are* honest, whatsoever things are just, whatsoever things *are* pure, whatsoever things are lovely, whatsoever things *are* of good report; if *there be* any virtue, and if *there be* any praise, think on these things.

James 1:2 My brethren, count it all joy when ye fall into divers temptations...

James 1:9-10 Let the brother of low degree rejoice in that he is exalted: But the rich, in that he is made low: because as the flower of the grass he shall pass away.

1 Peter 1:8 Whom having not seen, ye love; in whom, though now ye see *him* not, yet believing, ye rejoice with joy unspeakable and full of glory...

1 Peter 4:12-13 Beloved, think it not strange concerning the fiery trial which is to try you, as though some strange thing happened unto you: But rejoice, inasmuch as ye are partakers of Christ's sufferings; that, when his glory shall be revealed, ye may be glad also with exceeding joy.

NOTE: Verse 16 and the following verse are two of twenty verses in the Book of Proverbs that use the "better...than" method of contrasting two ideas rather than using the conjunction "but."

Proverbs 15:16 Better *is* little with the fear of the LORD than great treasure and trouble therewith.

Focus: This proverb declares a great value of having the "fear of the LORD" (even though meager in lifestyle) as opposed to having wealth where there is trouble.

A person who has the **"fear of the LORD"** *[an awesome respect for God]* views Him as the all-knowing, all-powerful, and all-present One. When the relationship is right between man and God, the man can have *peace and enjoyment* even though he has very little wealth. And if the peace and joy of God are all he has, he is much better off than the wealthy man whose life is full of misery because his soul is out of sorts with God.

"Great treasure" in and of itself doesn't bring trouble. It has no ability within itself as an inanimate object to produce anything. However, if the person who owns "great treasure" disregards God (as implied in the verse) and lives a life in violation of God's directions, he can expect trouble both here on earth and in eternity.

Psalm 37:16 A little that a righteous man hath *is* better than the riches of many wicked.

Proverbs 10:22 The blessing of the LORD, it maketh rich, and he addeth no sorrow with it.

Proverbs 15:6 In the house of the righteous is much treasure: but in the revenues of the wicked is trouble.

Proverbs 16:8 Better is a little with righteousness than great revenues without right.

Proverbs 17:1 Better is a dry morsel, and quietness therewith, than an house full of sacrifices with strife.

Proverbs 28:6 Better is the poor that walketh in his uprightness, than he that is perverse in his ways, though he be rich.

Ecclesiastes 4:6 Better is an handful with quietness, than both the hands full with travail and vexation of spirit.

Ecclesiastes 5:12 The sleep of a labouring man is sweet, whether he eat little or much: but the abundance of the rich will not suffer him to sleep.

Isaiah 33:6 And wisdom and knowledge shall be the stability of thy times, and strength of salvation: the fear of the LORD is his treasure.

Matthew 6:33 But seek ye first the kingdom of God, and his righteousness; and all these things shall be added unto you.

Luke 12:15 And he said unto them, Take heed, and beware of covetousness: for a man's life consisteth not in the abundance of the things which he possesseth.

1 Timothy 6:6-9 But godliness with contentment is great gain. For we brought nothing into this world, and it is certain we can carry nothing out. And having food and raiment let us be therewith content. But they that will be rich fall into temptation and a snare, and into many foolish and hurtful lusts, which drown men in destruction and perdition.

> **Proverbs 15:17** Better *is* a dinner of herbs where love is, than a stalled ox and hatred therewith.

Focus: This proverb declares the overarching great value of love over hatred.

Love sets the tone for good relationships and makes the least expensive of meals taste better than the most valuable dinners. Hatred destroys the value of finery, separates family and friends, and alienates God. In other words, enjoy a supper of beans and peas (**"herbs"**) rather than steak – if hatred is involved. "Love makes one's difficult circumstances endurable, whereas hatred undoes all the enjoyments that good food might otherwise bring."[331] All the joyful benefits of having sufficient working animals, and to occasionally butcher one for a feast, loses value when the home is a place of hatred rather than love. Dinner is better with love and only the bare minimum of food because love is the perfect "seasoning" while hate is the perfect "poison."

"A stalled ox" is one that is kept up in a pen and fattened up for the table. Malachi 4:2 refers to the stalled ox when it states, "But unto you that fear my name shall the Sun of righteousness arise with healing in his wings; and ye shall go forth, and grow up as calves of the stall." When the prodigal came home, the father brought out the "fatted calf" for the celebration. (Luke 15:23)

>> Psalm 37:16 A little that a righteous man hath *is* better than the riches of many wicked.
>> Psalm 133:1 A Song of degrees of David. Behold, how good and how pleasant *it is* for brethren to dwell together in unity!
>> Proverbs 16:8 Better *is* a little with righteousness than great revenues without right.
>> Proverbs 17:1 Better *is* a dry morsel, and quietness therewith, than an house full of sacrifices *with* strife.
>> Ecclesiastes 4:6 Better *is* an handful *with* quietness, than both the hands full *with* travail and vexation of spirit.

> **Proverbs 15:18** A wrathful man stirreth up strife: but *he that is* slow to anger appeaseth strife.

Focus: This proverb declares that strife is inflamed by an angry man and tamped down by a man slow to anger.

A godly person trains and controls himself according to the principles of God's word, but a wrathful man has surrendered self-control to passion. Wardlaw describes the wrathful man as "hasty, hot, resentful spirit, which startles touchily at every word or look; finds meanings in them that have no existence but in a perverted fancy; catches fire in a moment; breathes vengeance; and by high words stirs up the spirits of others, and kindles the flames of discord."[332] The righteous person, like his heavenly Father, is slow to become angry. He speaks softly to turn away wrath, and he walks in love. "The LORD *is* merciful and gracious, slow to anger, and plenteous in mercy."(Psalm 103:8)

Three other Proverbs (listed below) cover this same topic: Proverbs 29:22, 26:21, and 28:25. The first two Scriptures and the Acts 6 reference below exemplify how strife is appeased by a man who follows the principles of God's word.

>> "... A man of a wrathful disposition, of a furious spirit, of an angry temper; that is under the power and dominion of such a passion, and indulges it, and takes all opportunities to gratify it; he stirs up strife and contention where there was none, or where it was laid; as a man stirs up coals of fire and raises a flame, (See Proverbs 26:21.) He stirs up strife in families, sets one relation against another, and the house in an uproar; he stirs up contentions in neighborhoods, and sets one friend and neighbor against another, whence proceed quarrels and lawsuits: he stirs up strife in churches, breaks brotherly love, and causes animosities and divisions; he stirs up strife in kingdoms and states, whence come wars and fightings, confusion, and every evil work; but *he that is* slow to anger appeaseth strife: a man of a quiet and peaceable disposition, possessed of the true grace of charity; who is not easily provoked, longsuffering, bears and endures all things; he allays the heat of anger; he quenches the coals of contention; he calms the storm and makes it quiet … he 'mitigates strifes raised …' He composes differences, reconciles the parties at variance, and makes all hush and still; and so prevents the ill consequences of contention and strife."[333]
>> Genesis 13:8-9 And Abram said unto Lot, Let there be no strife, I pray thee, between me and thee, and between my herdmen and thy herdmen; for we *be* brethren. *Is* not the whole land before thee? separate thyself, I pray thee, from me: if *thou wilt take* the left hand, then I will go to the right; or if *thou depart* to the right hand, then I will go to the left.
>> Genesis 32:19-20 And so commanded he the second, and the third, and all that followed the droves, saying, On this manner shall ye speak unto Esau, when ye find him. And say ye moreover, Behold, thy servant Jacob *is* behind us. For he said, I will appease him with the present that goeth before me, and afterward I will see his face; peradventure he will accept of me.
>> Proverbs 10:12 Hatred stirreth up strifes: but love covereth all sins.

Proverbs 14:16-17 A wise man feareth, and departeth from evil: but the fool rageth, and is confident. He that is soon angry dealeth foolishly: and a man of wicked devices is hated.

Proverbs 14:29 *He that is* slow to wrath *is* of great understanding: but *he that is* hasty of spirit exaltata folly.

Proverbs 15:1 A soft answer turneth away wrath: but grievous words stir up anger.

Proverbs 16:32 He that is slow to anger is better than the mighty; and he that ruleth his spirit than he that taketh a city.

Proverbs 19:11 The discretion of a man deferreth his anger; and it is his glory to pass over a transgression.

Proverbs 22:24-25 Make no friendship with an angry man; and with a furious man thou shalt not go: Lest thou learn his ways, and get a snare to thy soul.

Proverbs 26:21 As coals are to burning coals, and wood to fire; so is a contentious man to kindle strife.

Proverbs 28:25 He that is of a proud heart stirreth up strife: but he that putteth his trust in the LORD shall be made fat.

Proverbs 29:22 An angry man stirreth up strife, and a furious man aboundeth in transgression.

Matthew 5:9 Blessed *are* the peacemakers: for they shall be called the children of God.

James 1:19-20 Wherefore, my beloved brethren, let every man be swift to hear, slow to speak, slow to wrath: For the wrath of man worketh not the righteousness of God.

Proverbs 15:19 The way of the slothful *man is* as an hedge of thorns: but the way of the righteous *is* made plain.

Focus: This proverb contrasts the attitude toward life that a slothful man has with the attitude toward life that a righteous person has.

The previous three proverbs have revealed that hatred, greed, and anger produce problems; and in verse 19 it is slothfulness that hinders. By contrasting laziness with righteousness, *Scripture brings attention to the fact that slothfulness is also a spiritual issue.*

In this Proverb, two different attitudes toward life are presented through the phrases **"the way** *[derek]* **of the slothful"** and **"the way** *[orach]* **of the righteous."** *(Notice the wordplay in the words.)* Both ways refer to a path or a road and also figuratively to a manner of living. A lazy person envisions his pathway as blockaded by **"a hedge of thorns"** (dangerous obstacles) – only one of the reasons a **"slothful"** person dreams up to explain why he can't accomplish necessary tasks of the day. The pathway to success is too difficult for him to travel because he imagines it filled with obstacles or difficulties symbolized in this verse by **"thorns."** In his mind he is trying to force himself through this hedge of thorns, which *might* tear his flesh. He sees hindrances and problems everywhere. After a feeble, half-hearted struggle he convinces himself he cannot go on and gives up the effort. He approaches both the physical and the spiritual in the same manner.

Completely opposite in attitude from **"the slothful,"** the righteous person envisions himself rising above any obstacles so that his pathway is **"made plain,"** and he is free to proceed with life. He prays and seeks God's help to accomplish the safest and most productive walk through life. Obtaining counsel from Scripture and from godly men, he can work diligently with confidence and peace. Difficulties *are faced;* if they can't be removed from the path, they are handled wisely. The believer's attitude is to overcome with God's help. He approaches both the physical and the spiritual with the same level of valuable worth.

The concept of **"the way of the righteous"** being **"made plain"** is mentioned several times in the Bible. **"Made plain"** in the Hebrew refers to the creation of the king's highway which is made smooth.

> "The idea is taken from the practice of Eastern monarchs, who whenever they entered on a journey or an expedition, especially through a barren and unfrequented or inhospitable country, sent harbingers or heralds before them to prepare the way. To do this, it was necessary for them to provide supplies, and make bridges, or find fording places over the streams; to level hills, and construct causeways over valleys, or fill them up; and to make a way through the forest which might lie in their intended line of march."[334]

> "Observe God's estimate of him *[slothful person]*. He contrasts with him, not the diligent, but *the righteous;* marking him as a 'wicked, because a *slothful* servant.' (Matthew 25:26). The difficulties are far more in the mind than in the path. For while *the slothful* sits down by his *hedge-side* in despair, *the way of the righteous*, in itself not more easy, *is made plain*. He does not expect God to work for him in an indolent habit. But he finds that God helps those that help themselves. Working with diligence, he finds that he can work in comfort. Following his commands, feeding upon his promises, continuing in prayer, in waiting and watching for an answer to prayer – *his way is raised up*, before him. He believes what is written, and acts upon it without disputing, without delay. As soon as ever the light comes into his mind – at the very first dawn – this determines the direction of his steps, and the order of his proceedings. Thus his stumbling-blocks are removed (Numbers 13:30; 14:6-9; Isaiah 57:14). Industrious wisdom performs what lazy foolishness deemed impossible. *Thorns* there are doubtless in the way, but not an impassable *hedge of thorns;* only such, as while they pierce his flesh, are overruled as a blessing to his soul. (2 Corinthians 12:7-8)"[335]

Proverbs 3:5-6 Trust in the LORD with all thine heart; and lean not unto thine own understanding. In all thy ways acknowledge him, and he shall direct thy paths.

Proverbs 26:13 The slothful *man* saith, *There is* a lion in the way; a lion is in the streets.

Isaiah 42:16 And I will bring the blind by a way that they knew not; I will lead them in paths that they have not known: I will make darkness light before them, and crooked things straight. These things will I do unto them, and not forsake them.

Proverbs 15:20 A wise son maketh a glad father: but a foolish man despiseth his mother.

Focus: This proverb *contrasts the glad effect* that a wise son has on his father *with the grieving effect* that a foolish son has on his mother.

An attitude of love and respect from children to parents is mandatory for a contented, well-functioning family. Because he has good relationships with his teachers and especially with his father and mother *(his first and most important teachers)*, a wise child can be taught. On the other hand, a fool despises his parents, especially his mother, because she is usually more dogmatic about details of learning and spends more time trying to make him conform to what is right, especially in regard to God. Because a fool despises such teaching and consequently the teacher, his mother is made sad. Concerning a grown child Matthew Henry wrote, "A foolish son despises his mother, that had most sorrow with him and perhaps had too much indulged him, which makes his sin in despising her the more sinful and her sorrow the more sorrowful."[336]

Proverbs 10:1 The proverbs of Solomon. A wise son maketh a glad father: but a foolish son is the heaviness of his mother.
Proverbs 13:1 A wise son heareth his father's instruction: but a scorner heareth not rebuke.
Proverbs 17:21 He that begetteth a fool doeth it to his sorrow: and the father of a fool hath no joy.
Proverbs 17:25 A foolish son is a grief to his father, and bitterness to her that bare him.
Proverbs 19:13 A foolish son is the calamity of his father: and the contentions of a wife are a continual dropping.
Proverbs 23:15-16 My son, if thine heart be wise, my heart shall rejoice, even mine. Yea, my reins shall rejoice, when thy lips speak right things.
Proverbs 23:22 Hearken unto thy father that begat thee, and despise not thy mother when she is old.
Proverbs 23:24 The father of the righteous shall greatly rejoice: and he that begetteth a wise child shall have joy of him.
Proverbs 27:11 My son, be wise, and make my heart glad, that I may answer him that reproacheth me.
Proverbs 28:7 Whoso keepeth the law is a wise son: but he that is a companion of riotous men shameth his father.
Proverbs 29:3 Whoso loveth wisdom rejoiceth his father: but he that keepeth company with harlots spendeth his substance.
Proverbs 30:17 The eye that mocketh at his father, and despiseth to obey his mother, the ravens of the valley shall pick it out, and the young eagles shall eat it.

Proverbs 15:21 Folly *is* joy to *him that is* destitute of wisdom: but a man of understanding walketh uprightly.

Focus: This proverb contrasts the fool (destitute of wisdom) who joyously walks in foolishness with the wise person (man of understanding) who joyously walks in righteousness.

The fool enjoys living a life of foolishness, whereas the upright enjoys a life of wise living for God. When **"wisdom"** is **"destitute"** *[lacking]* in a person, that individual's actions are being driven by a foolish heart, which makes him joyful about doing wickedness. Wisdom would prick his perverted conscience and drive him in a different direction toward pleasing God, but he has no understanding of or desire for such righteousness. "It is as sport to a fool to do mischief: but a man of understanding hath wisdom." (Proverbs 10:23)

The person who **walks uprightly** is a wise person who understands the payback for sinful living, and intentionally lives his life in a manner that is right with God. He has observed that foolishness brings hardships and heartaches and avoids wicked behavior. His joy is walking with God, and he avoids the foolishness of sin. "The empty-hearted, rejoicing in folly, goes the wrong way; the man of understanding, rejoicing in wisdom, goes the right way."[337]

"A fool lives at large, walks at all adventures, by no rule, acts with no sincerity or steadiness; but a man of understanding, the eyes of whose understanding are enlightened by the Spirit (and those that have not a good understanding have no understanding), walks uprightly, lives a sober, orderly, regular life, and studies in every thing to conform himself to the will of God; and this is a constant pleasure and joy to him. But what foolishness remains in him, or proceeds from him at any time, is a grief to him, and he is ashamed of it. By these characters we may try ourselves."[338]

Job 28:28 And unto man he said, Behold, the fear of the Lord, that is wisdom; and to depart from evil is understanding.

Psalm 111:10 The fear of the LORD is the beginning of wisdom: a good understanding have all they that do his commandments: his praise endureth for ever.

Proverbs 1:7 The fear of the LORD is the beginning of knowledge: but fools despise wisdom and instruction.

Proverbs 14:6-9 A scorner seeketh wisdom, and findeth it not: but knowledge is easy unto him that understandeth. Go from the presence of a foolish man, when thou perceivest not in him the lips of knowledge. The wisdom of the prudent is to understand his way: but the folly of fools is deceit. Fools make a mock at sin: but among the righteous there is favour.

Proverbs 14:16-17 A wise man feareth, and departeth from evil: but the fool rageth, and is confident. For they eat the bread of wickedness, and drink the wine of violence.

Proverbs 19:1-3 Better is the poor that walketh in his integrity, than he that is perverse in his lips, and is a fool. Also, that the soul be without knowledge, it is not good; and he that hasteth with his feet sinneth. The foolishness of man perverteth his way: and his heart fretteth against the LORD.

Proverbs 28:26 He that trusteth in his own heart is a fool: but whoso walketh wisely, he shall be delivered.

Ephesians 5:15 See then that ye walk circumspectly, not as fools, but as wise,

James 3:13 Who is a wise man and endued with knowledge among you? let him shew out of a good conversation his works with meekness of wisdom.

Proverbs 15:22 Without counsel purposes are disappointed: but in the multitude of counsellors they are established.

Focus: This proverb contrasts the success of purposes empowered through counsel with the defeat of those lacking counsel.

The old saying is true – "*Plus vident oculi quam oculus* – Many eyes see more than one."[339] Four times in the Book of Proverbs, this importance of seeking counsel is stressed.

Proverbs 11:14 Where no counsel is, the people fall: but in the multitude of counsellors there is safety.

Proverbs 15:22 Without counsel purposes are disappointed: but in the multitude of counsellors they are established.

Proverbs 20:18 *Every* purpose is established by counsel: and with good advice make war.

Proverbs 24:6 For by wise counsel thou shalt make thy war: and in multitude of counsellors there is safety.

Court counselors, like Jonathan, David's uncle (1Chronicles 27:32), served to give the king advice. With the counsel of godly, mature men, the purposes of countries are made sure; and obviously, a wise, proper choice of counselors is mandatory. Foolish counselors can only produce foolishness.

In 1Kings 12, the story of Rehoboam, Solomon's son, illustrates what happens when the leadership of a country doesn't listen to wise counsel. Jeroboam, with "all the congregation of Israel," came and said that they would follow Rehoboam as king if he would reduce the burden of taxes and the people's workload. Rehoboam called in two groups of counselors – the older, wise men who had served as Solomon's advisors and some of the young men who had grown up with him. He chose the counsel of the younger, inexperienced, foolish men, who advised Rehoboam to deal harshly with the people. As a result, Israel rebelled and followed Jeroboam with ten of the tribes to form the Northern kingdom of Israel. The country was divided because Rehoboam listened to terrible, unworthy counselors who were young, inexperienced, and foolish yes-men.

Plans are best carried out when well-advised. Because a fool is full of pride and believes that he knows more than others (even others collectively), he doesn't seek counsel or else seeks it from those in agreement with his folly. Every wise person will first seek the advice from God's word as a foundational way of thinking in conjunction with asking counsel from honorable, wise persons. One of Jesus' titles is "Counselor" – "For unto us a child is born, unto us a son is given: and the government shall be upon his shoulder: and his name shall be called Wonderful, Counsellor, The mighty God, The everlasting Father, The Prince of Peace." (Isaiah 9:6)

1 Chronicles 27:32 Also Jonathan David's uncle was a counsellor, a wise man, and a scribe …

Psalm 119:24 Thy testimonies also are my delight and my counsellors.

Proverbs 1:24-27 Because I *[wisdom]* have called, and ye refused; I have stretched out my hand, and no man regarded; But ye have set at nought all my counsel, and would none of my reproof: I also will laugh at your calamity; I will mock when your fear cometh; When your fear cometh as desolation, and your destruction cometh as a whirlwind; when distress and anguish cometh upon you.

Proverbs 3:5-6 Trust in the LORD with all thine heart; and lean not unto thine own understanding. In all thy ways acknowledge him, and he shall direct thy paths.

Proverbs 12:15 The way of a fool is right in his own eyes: but he that hearkeneth unto counsel is wise.

Proverbs 19:20 Hear counsel, and receive instruction, that thou mayest be wise in thy latter end.

Proverbs 19:21 There are many devices in a man's heart; nevertheless the counsel of the LORD, that shall stand.

Proverbs 20:5 Counsel in the heart of man is like deep water; but a man of understanding will draw it out.

Proverbs 27:9 Ointment and perfume rejoice the heart: so doth the sweetness of a man's friend by hearty counsel.

Whenever the teaching of this proverb has been applied to a local church assembly, disaster has been avoided. In Acts 15:2, there arose a disagreement about circumcision; consequently, the apostles and elders wisely came together to discuss the matter. After studying the Scriptures and being led by the Holy Spirit, they sent a letter of resolve to the Gentile brethren.

Proverbs 15:23 A man hath joy by the answer of his mouth: and a word *spoken* in due season, how good *is it!*

Focus: This proverb declares that joy and good come from speaking wisely.

When a person becomes wise enough to consistently produce positive results with his personal verbal communication, he will certainly avoid much sorrow and increase his joy of living. The damage that is caused by improper speech can be, and often is, beyond description. The believer should pray for the "tongue of the learned" as in Isaiah 50:4 – "The Lord GOD hath given me the tongue of the learned, that I should know how to speak a word in season to him that is weary: he wakeneth morning by morning, he wakeneth mine ear to hear as the learned."

Ecclesiastes 3:1, 7 To every thing there is a season, and a time to every purpose under the heaven ... A time to rend, and a time to sew; a time to keep silence, and a time to speak...

Knowing the right place and time to speak along with having the right spirit are conditions that every wise person learns because of his desire to properly and effectively communicate. Good communication has a direct effect on personal joy as does poor communication.

1 Samuel 25:32-33 And David said to Abigail, Blessed be the LORD God of Israel, which sent thee this day to meet me: And blessed be thy advice, and blessed be thou, which hast kept me this day from coming to shed blood, and from avenging myself with mine own hand.

Proverbs 12:14 A man shall be satisfied with good by the fruit of his mouth: and the recompence of a man's hands shall be rendered unto him.

Proverbs 12:25 Heaviness in the heart of man maketh it stoop: but a good word maketh it glad.

Proverbs 13:2 A man shall eat good by the fruit of his mouth: but the soul of the transgressors shall eat violence.

Proverbs 16:13 Righteous lips are the delight of kings; and they love him that speaketh right.

Proverbs 24:26 Every man shall kiss his lips that giveth a right answer.

Proverbs 25:11-12 A word fitly spoken is like apples of gold in pictures of silver. As an earring of gold, and an ornament of fine gold, so is a wise reprover upon an obedient ear.

Ephesians 4:29 Let no corrupt communication proceed out of your mouth, but that which is good to the use of edifying, that it may minister grace unto the hearers.

Proverbs 15:24 The way of life *is* above to the wise, that he may depart from hell beneath.

Focus: This proverb specifies that the way of life takes a wise person both toward God and away from hell.

The wise person's desire is to please God, leading him upward toward heaven and away from **"hell beneath."** Though both the fool and the wise face physical death, the wise escape the damnation of hell because they choose God's way, **"the way of life."** Beginning with their response to the Holy Spirit to trust in and to follow Jesus, wise people additionally learn from God to be discreet with their words, selective about associations, and cautious concerning every type of action and decision of life. By choosing the right path, the wise avoid many problems on earth and have the promise of living with Christ for eternity.

> "The way of life is above to the wise – The way which a wise man takes to preserve and obtain spiritual and eternal life, is to place his heart, treasure, and conversation in things above; and to manage all his affairs in this world with due respect and subserviency to the happiness of another world; that he may depart from hell beneath – Or, *from the lowest hell;* not *from the grave,* as this word is sometimes used, for no wisdom can preserve from that, but from *hell,* properly so called, as this word elsewhere signifies . . ."[340]

> "The further we walk in this way above, the further we depart from hell beneath. Heaven and Hell are here before us. Soon will our state be fixed for eternity . . . Those who walk in the way above — 'their conversation is in heaven;' their hope is fixed on the Lord's coming from thence; their everlasting joy will be the complete transformation into his own image. There is no downward tendency. It is still upwards. It is all rising ground. Mount ever so high, the ascent is ever before us; an immense distance still appears, ere we gain the summit. Yet the moment we desire this heavenly state, we have begun to know it, and we shall rise higher and higher heavenward, till we take our place before the throne of God. Thus 'he that is truly wise, in this holy way of obedience, walketh to eternal life.'"[341]

Psalm 16:11 Thou wilt shew me the path of life: in thy presence is fulness of joy; at thy right hand there are pleasures for evermore.

Psalm 139:23-24 Search me, O God, and know my heart: try me, and know my thoughts: And see if there be any wicked way in me, and lead me in the way everlasting.

Proverbs 2:18-19 For her house inclineth unto death, and her paths unto the dead. None that go unto her return again, neither take they hold of the paths of life.

Proverbs 5:3-5 For the lips of a strange woman drop as an honeycomb, and her mouth is smoother than oil: But her end is bitter as wormwood, sharp as a twoedged sword. Her feet go down to death; her steps take hold on hell.

Proverbs 6:23 For the commandment is a lamp; and the law is light; and reproofs of instruction are the way of life . . .

Proverbs 7:25-27 Let not thine heart decline to her ways, go not astray in her paths. For she hath cast down many wounded: yea, many strong men have been slain by her. Her house is the way to hell, going down to the chambers of death.

Jeremiah 21:8 And unto this people thou shalt say, Thus saith the LORD; Behold, I set before you the way of life, and the way of death.

Matthew 7:14 Because strait *is* the gate, and narrow *is* the way, which leadeth unto life, and few there be that find it.

John 14:6 Jesus saith unto him, I am the way, the truth, and the life: no man cometh unto the Father, but by me.

Philippians 3:17-20 Brethren, be followers together of me, and mark them which walk so as ye have us for an ensample. (For many walk, of whom I have told you often, and now tell you even weeping, that they are the enemies of the cross of Christ: Whose end is destruction, whose God is their belly, and whose glory is in their shame, who mind earthly things.) For our conversation is in heaven; from whence also we look for the Saviour, the Lord Jesus Christ . . .

Colossians 3:1-2 If ye then be risen with Christ, seek those things which are above, where Christ sitteth on the right hand of God. Set your affection on things above, not on things on the earth.

> TWO WAYS AND TWO CHOICES are presented in the Book of Proverbs. One way leads upward to God; the other leads away from God to hell.

THE WAY TOWARD GOD IS:		THE WAY AWAY FROM GOD IS:	
Proverbs 2:8	the way of his saints	Proverbs 2:12	the way of the evil *man*
Proverbs 2:20	the way of good *men*	Proverbs 4:14	the way of evil *men*
Proverbs 4:11	the way of wisdom	Proverbs 4:19, 12:26, 15:19, 16:25	the way of the wicked the way that is not good
Proverbs 6:23, 10:17 15:24	the way of life	Proverbs 12:15 19:3	the way of a fool
Proverbs 8:20, 12:28, 16:31	the way of righteousness	Proverbs 13:15	the way of transgressors
Proverbs 9:6, 21:16	the way of understanding	Proverbs 14:12 16:25	the way that seemeth right
Proverbs 10:29	the way of the LORD	Proverbs 15:19	the way of the slothful
Proverbs 11:20, 16:11	the way of the upright	Proverbs 21:2, 21:8	the way of a man, way of man
Proverbs 16:31	the way of the righteous	Proverbs 22:5	the way of the froward
		Proverbs 7:27, 30:20	the way of an adulterous woman

Proverbs 15:25 The LORD will destroy the house of the proud: but he will establish the border of the widow.

Focus: This proverb declares that God acts *both* punitively to destroy the house of the proud and protectively to establish the border of the widow.

Pride is a trademark of wicked men, and God will destroy their houses (wicked families or family lines), which they believe will continue forever. While magnifying themselves and defying God, they trample on the poor.

Esther 7:10 So they hanged Haman on the gallows that he had prepared for Mordecai. Then was the king's wrath pacified.

Psalm 12:3-5 The LORD shall cut off all flattering lips, *and* the tongue that speaketh proud things: Who have said, With our tongue will we prevail; our lips *are* our own: who *is* lord over us? For the oppression of the poor, for the sighing of the needy, now will I arise, saith the LORD; I will set *him* in safety *from him that* puffeth at him.

Proverbs 14:11 The house of the wicked shall be overthrown: but the tabernacle of the upright shall flourish.

Proverbs 16:5 Every one *that is* proud in heart *is* an abomination to the LORD: *though* hand *join* in hand, he shall not be unpunished.

Proverbs 16:18-19 Pride goeth before destruction, and an haughty spirit before a fall. Better it is to be of an humble spirit with the lowly, than to divide the spoil with the proud.

Isaiah 2:11-12 The lofty looks of man shall be humbled, and the haughtiness of men shall be bowed down, and the LORD alone shall be exalted in that day. For the day of the LORD of hosts shall be upon every one that is proud and lofty, and upon every one that is lifted up; and he shall be brought low:

Luke 1:51-52 He hath shewed strength with his arm; he hath scattered the proud in the imagination of their hearts. He hath put down the mighty from their seats, and exalted them of low degree.

James 4:6 But he giveth more grace. Wherefore he saith, God resisteth the proud, but giveth grace unto the humble.

God has ordered the believer to look after the widow. Not only that, He will avenge any mistreatment of the helpless.

Exodus 22:22-24 Ye shall not afflict any widow, or fatherless child. If thou afflict them in any wise, and they cry at all unto me, I will surely hear their cry; And my wrath shall wax hot, and I will kill you with the sword; and your wives shall be widows, and your children fatherless.

Deuteronomy 10:17-18 For the LORD your God is God of gods, and Lord of lords, a great God, a mighty, and a terrible, which regardeth not persons, nor taketh reward: He doth execute the judgment of the fatherless and widow, and loveth the stranger, in giving him food and raiment.

Deuteronomy 26:12-13 When thou hast made an end of tithing all the tithes of thine increase the third year, which is the year of tithing, and hast given it unto the Levite, the stranger, the fatherless, and the widow, that they may eat within thy gates, and be filled; Then thou shalt say before the LORD thy God, I have brought away the hallowed things out of mine house, and also have given them unto the Levite, and unto the stranger, to the fatherless, and to the widow, according to all thy commandments which thou hast commanded me: I have not transgressed thy commandments, neither have I forgotten them . . .

Proverbs 22:22-23 Rob not the poor, because he is poor: neither oppress the afflicted in the gate: For the LORD will plead their cause, and spoil the soul of those that spoiled them.

Property borders were marked by objects such as large stones, which could be moved by a wicked person who would then be in danger of God ***destroying his house.*** A widow had no husband to protect her when a powerful neighbor moved the landmarks and took part of her land – but God promised to **"establish the border of the widow"** – that is, make her secure in her home. Notice again the contrast of God's promised actions in this verse between *establishing* the **"border of the widow"** and *destroying* the **"house of the proud."**

Deuteronomy 27:17 Cursed be he that removeth his neighbour's landmark. And all the people shall say, Amen.

Psalm 10:14 Thou hast seen it; for thou beholdest mischief and spite, to requite it with thy hand: the poor committeth himself unto thee; thou art the helper of the fatherless.

Psalm 68:5 A father of the fatherless, and a judge of the widows, is God in his holy habitation.

Psalm 138:6 Though the LORD be high, yet hath he respect unto the lowly: but the proud he knoweth afar off.

Psalm 146:9 The LORD preserveth the strangers; he relieveth the fatherless and widow: but the way of the wicked he turneth upside down.

Proverbs 12:7 The wicked are overthrown, and are not: but the house of the righteous shall stand.

Proverbs 14:11 The house of the wicked shall be overthrown: but the tabernacle of the upright shall flourish.

Proverbs 15:26 The thoughts of the wicked *are* an abomination to the LORD: but *the words* of the pure *are* pleasant words.

Focus: This proverb contrasts God's attitude toward the thoughts of the wicked with His attitude toward the words of the righteous.

Before the wicked can produce hateful words from their evil mind, God knows their wicked thoughts; and they ***"are an abomination"*** to Him. Righteous people have a mind in harmony with God and thus produce ***words that are pleasant to Him***. Those who follow God, identified here as **"the pure"** are also known as "the righteous," "the godly," the "born-again," and "the saints." These are not pure within or of themselves but are so because they have submitted themselves to God and are counseled by His word; consequently, their words reflect the mind of God. They learn to think like God, to reason as He reasons, to love as He loves, and to live in a godly manner because they desire to please Him. They hide His words in their hearts, thereby producing thoughts and speaking words that are agreeable to God.

". . .But thoughts are the seminal principles of sin. And as the cause virtually includes its effects; so do they contain, like the seed in its little body, all the after fruit. They are also the index of character. Watch their infinite variety; not so much those that are under the control of circumstances, or thrown up by the occasion, as the voluntary flow, following the habitual train of our associations. 'For as he thinketh in his heart, so is he.' (Proverbs 23:7) Let the Christian yield himself up to the clear radiance of 'the word, as a discerner of the thoughts and intents of the heart:' and what a mass of vanity does only one day, one hour, bring to account! As to the wicked? 'Evil thoughts' are the first bubbling of the corrupt fountain. (Matthew 15:19) The tide of evil rolls on unceasingly in 'thoughts of iniquity' (Isaiah 59:7), in order to give effect to the malevolent temper; dwelling on wickedness with complacency; pursuing it with determined purpose. What can such thoughts be, but an abomination to the LORD?"[342]

Genesis 6:5-7 And GOD saw that the wickedness of man was great in the earth, and that every imagination of the thoughts of his heart was only evil continually. And it repented the LORD that he had made man on the earth, and it grieved him at his heart. And the LORD said, I will destroy man whom I have created from the face of the earth; both man, and beast, and the creeping thing, and the fowls of the air; for it repenteth me that I have made them.

Psalm 19:14 Let the words of my mouth, and the meditation of my heart, be acceptable in thy sight, O LORD, my strength, and my redeemer.

Psalm 37:30-31 The mouth of the righteous speaketh wisdom, and his tongue talketh of judgment. The law of his God is in his heart; none of his steps shall slide.

Psalm 139:1-4 **To the chief Musician, A Psalm of David.** O LORD, thou hast searched me, and known me. Thou knowest my downsitting and mine uprising, thou understandest my thought afar off. Thou compassest my path and my lying down, and art acquainted with all my ways. For there is not a word in my tongue, but, lo, O LORD, thou knowest it altogether.

Proverbs 6:16-19 These six things doth the LORD hate: yea, seven are an abomination unto him: A proud look, a lying tongue, and hands that shed innocent blood, An heart that deviseth wicked imaginations, feet that be swift in running to mischief, A false witness that speaketh lies, and he that soweth discord among brethren.

Proverbs 23:6-7 Eat thou not the bread of him that hath an evil eye, neither desire thou his dainty meats: For as he thinketh in his heart, so is he: Eat and drink, saith he to thee; but his heart is not with thee.

Proverbs 24:9 The thought of foolishness is sin: and the scorner is an abomination to men.

Isaiah 59:1-7 Behold, the LORD'S hand is not shortened, that it cannot save; neither his ear heavy, that it cannot hear: But your iniquities have separated between you and your God, and your sins have hid his face from you, that he will not hear. For your hands are defiled with blood, and your fingers with iniquity; your lips have spoken lies, your tongue hath muttered perverseness. None calleth for justice, nor any pleadeth for truth: they trust in vanity, and speak lies; they conceive mischief, and bring forth iniquity. They hatch cockatrice' eggs, and weave the spider's web: he that eateth of their eggs dieth, and that which is crushed breaketh out into a viper. Their webs shall not become garments, neither shall they cover themselves with their works: their works are works of iniquity, and the act of violence is in their hands. Their feet run to evil, and they make haste to shed innocent blood: their thoughts are thoughts of iniquity; wasting and destruction are in their paths.

Malachi 3:16-17 Then they that feared the LORD spake often one to another: and the LORD hearkened, and heard it, and a book of remembrance was written before him for them that feared the LORD, and that thought upon his name. And they shall be mine, saith the LORD of hosts, in that day when I make up my jewels; and I will spare them, as a man spareth his own son that serveth him.

Matthew 12:34-37 O generation of vipers, how can ye, being evil, speak good things? for out of the abundance of the heart the mouth speaketh. A good man out of the good treasure of the heart bringeth forth good things: and an evil man out of the evil treasure bringeth forth evil things. But I say unto you, That every idle word that men shall speak, they shall give account thereof in the day of judgment. For by thy words thou shalt be justified, and by thy words thou shalt be condemned.

Matthew 15:18-19 But those things which proceed out of the mouth come forth from the heart; and they defile the man. For out of the heart proceed evil thoughts, murders, adulteries, fornications, thefts, false witness, blasphemies:

Hebrews 4:12-13 For the word of God is quick, and powerful, and sharper than any twoedged sword, piercing even to the dividing asunder of soul and spirit, and of the joints and marrow, and is a discerner of the thoughts and intents of the heart. Neither is there any creature that is not manifest in his sight: but all things are naked and opened unto the eyes of him with whom we have to do.

Proverbs 15:27 He that is greedy of gain troubleth his own house; but he that hateth gifts shall live.

Focus: This proverb contrasts the troubled life that greed causes with the pleasurable life that hatred for greed gives. *(Receiving a bribe is evidence of greed.)*

Demanding excessive gain, **greed** blinds its host to reality, distorts his judgment, twists his tongue, and ruins his name. It drives his desire to enrich himself at the sacrifice of peaceful satisfaction, safety, and service to God. *The covetous person is driven to obtain unjust gain.*

Those in certain leadership positions attempt to satisfy their greed by accepting bribes which are referred to in this proverb as **"gifts."** Since no one lives or dies to himself, covetousness often brings unnecessary problems to those nearest him, especially his family. His family or **"house"** suffers because of their personal association with him *and* community repercussions. The person who chooses to enrich himself by taking bribes (gifts for unjust favors) ***brings trouble into his own house*** – trouble that binds a person and keeps him from living freely in peace and with a clear conscience. It robs the home of sanctuary status.

Because gifts are purposefully given to these persons to pervert justice, the evil condemned by this proverb is especially true for those who are in a position to make crucial decisions, such as a judge, a king, or even today's supervisor.

Exodus 23:8 And thou shalt take no gift: for the gift blindeth the wise, and perverteth the words of the righteous.

Exodus 18:21 Moreover thou shalt provide out of all the people able men, such as fear God, men of truth, hating covetousness; and place such over them, to be rulers of thousands, and rulers of hundreds, rulers of fifties, and rulers of tens . . .

Deuteronomy 16:18-19 Judges and officers shalt thou make thee in all thy gates, which the LORD thy God giveth thee, throughout thy tribes: and they shall judge the people with just judgment. Thou shalt not wrest judgment; thou shalt not respect persons, neither take a gift: for a gift doth blind the eyes of the wise, and pervert the words of the righteous.

Proverbs 1:18-19 And they lay wait for their own blood; they lurk privily for their own lives. So are the ways of every one that is greedy of gain; which taketh away the life of the owners thereof.

Ecclesiastes 7:7 Surely oppression maketh a wise man mad; and a gift destroyeth the heart.

Isaiah 1:23 Thy princes are rebellious, and companions of thieves: every one loveth gifts, and followeth after rewards: they judge not the fatherless, neither doth the cause of the widow come unto them.

Habakkuk 2:9-10 Woe to him that coveteth an evil covetousness to his house, that he may set his nest on high, that he may be delivered from the power of evil! Thou hast consulted shame to thy house by cutting off many people, and hast sinned against thy soul.

He that hates gifts shall live has a primary reference to judges but certainly applies to everyone in a position to receive a bribe. The righteous leader who hates gifts will save his family from ruin – from the curse of greediness, from the inheritance of a bad name, from dishonor, hatred of others, and the displeasure of God. He **"shall live"** having the blessings of God, a good name, peace of mind, worthy friends, and a general enjoyment of an honest life. *[See also verses 8-9, 25 above.]* Jeremiah 22:13-19 below describes God's attitude toward covetousness.

Proverbs 10:2-3 Treasures of wickedness profit nothing: but righteousness delivereth from death. The LORD will not suffer the soul of the righteous to famish: but he casteth away the substance of the wicked.

Proverbs 28:16 The prince that wanteth understanding is also a great oppressor: but he that hateth covetousness shall prolong his days.

Jeremiah 22:13-19 Woe unto him that buildeth his house by unrighteousness, and his chambers by wrong; that useth his neighbour's service without wages, and giveth him not for his work; That saith, I will build me a wide house and large chambers, and cutteth him out windows; and it is cieled with cedar, and painted with vermilion. Shalt thou reign, because thou closest thyself in cedar? did not thy father eat and drink, and do judgment and justice, and then it was well with him? He judged the cause of the poor and needy; then it was well with him: was not this to know me? saith the LORD. But thine eyes and thine heart are not but for thy covetousness, and for to shed innocent blood, and for oppression, and for violence, to do it. Therefore thus saith the LORD concerning Jehoiakim the son of Josiah king of Judah; They shall not lament for him, saying, Ah my brother! or, Ah sister! they shall not lament for him, saying, Ah lord! or, Ah his glory! He shall be buried with the burial of an ass, drawn and cast forth beyond the gates of Jerusalem.

1 Timothy 6:9-10 But they that will be rich fall into temptation and a snare, and into many foolish and hurtful lusts, which drown men in destruction and perdition. For the love of money is the root of all evil: which while some coveted after, they have erred from the faith, and pierced themselves through with many sorrows.

Proverbs 15:28 The heart of the righteous studieth to answer: but the mouth of the wicked poureth out evil things.

Focus: This proverb contrasts the cautious speaking of the righteous with the careless, abundant, evil-speaking of the wicked.

The righteous person ***studies to answer*** (meditates and considers every aspect) before speaking, making sure that what he says has no evil content. The Hebrew definition of **"studieth to answer"** presents a word picture of a man talking to himself *[murmuring, moaning, growling, muttering]* as he meditates on the proper course of action or the right words to say. He wants to ensure that his words are truthful, accurate and not harmful to anyone. Indeed, he must decide whether or not he should speak at all. "Think twice before speaking once" is excellent advice for the cautious believer. The wicked are not burdened about truthfulness, accuracy, or harm that their words may cause. Their loose flowing words pour out of hearts poisoned with evil.

"Many stumblings have been made by speaking from the impulse of the moment, from warm feelings, rather than from a well-balanced and considerate judgment. In this haste, Joshua was beguiled by the Gibeonites; David indulged a burst of murderous revenge; Peter would fain have dissuaded his Master from the work, which he came down from heaven to do, and without which we should have been a world eternally lost. Cultivate a pondering mind. If ever asked to open an important subject, throw it not off hastily, nor give an answer, till we have obtained it from God. For the heart's study to answer necessarily implies prayer, the only medium of receiving the 'wisdom that is profitable to direct.' Nehemiah darted up his prayer; and how graciously was the answer for the moment vouchsafed!"[343]

Proverbs 8:13 The fear of the LORD is to hate evil: pride, and arrogancy, and the evil way, and the froward mouth, do I hate.

Proverbs 10:19 In the multitude of words there wanteth not sin: but he that refraineth his lips is wise.

Proverbs 10:32 The lips of the righteous know what is acceptable: but the mouth of the wicked speaketh frowardness.

Proverbs 13:16 Every prudent man dealeth with knowledge: but a fool layeth open his folly.

Proverbs 15:2 The tongue of the wise useth knowledge aright: but the mouth of fools poureth out foolishness.

Proverbs 16:23 The heart of the wise teacheth his mouth, and addeth learning to his lips.

Proverbs 29:11 A fool uttereth all his mind: but a wise man keepeth it in till afterwards.

Ecclesiastes 5:2 Be not rash with thy mouth, and let not thine heart be hasty to utter any thing before God: for God is in heaven, and thou upon earth: therefore let thy words be few.

Ecclesiastes 5:6 Suffer not thy mouth to cause thy flesh to sin; neither say thou before the angel, that it was an error: wherefore should God be angry at thy voice, and destroy the work of thine hands?

Ecclesiastes 10:10-14 If the iron be blunt, and he do not whet the edge, then must he put to more strength: but wisdom is profitable to direct. Surely the serpent will bite without enchantment; and a babbler is no better. The words of a wise man's mouth are gracious; but the lips of a fool will swallow up himself. The beginning of the words of his mouth is foolishness: and the end of his talk is mischievous madness. A fool also is full of words: a man cannot tell what shall be; and what shall be after him, who can tell him?

Matthew 12:34 O generation of vipers, how can ye, being evil, speak good things? for out of the abundance of the heart the mouth speaketh.

Matthew 16:23 But he turned, and said unto Peter, Get thee behind me, Satan: thou art an offence unto me: for thou savourest not the things that be of God, but those that be of men. *[See also Mark 8:33 and Luke 4:8.]*

1 Timothy 6:3-5 If any man teach otherwise, and consent not to wholesome words, even the words of our Lord Jesus Christ, and to the doctrine which is according to godliness; He is proud, knowing nothing, but doting about questions and strifes of words, whereof cometh envy, strife, railings, evil surmisings, Perverse disputings of men of corrupt minds, and destitute of the truth, supposing that gain is godliness: from such withdraw thyself.

Titus 1:10-11 For there are many unruly and vain talkers and deceivers, specially they of the circumcision: Whose mouths must be stopped, who subvert whole houses, teaching things which they ought not, for filthy lucre's sake.

Proverbs 15:29 The LORD *is* far from the wicked: but he heareth the prayer of the righteous.

Focus: This proverb contrasts the distance that God puts between Himself and the wicked with the closeness that He maintains with the righteous.

"The LORD is far from the wicked" because they prefer to be far from Him. They hate Him, His law, and His commandments. Consequently, God is not near them to hear their cries or near them to extend His peace or provisions or power. His presence is unknown to them. Many are God's invitations, but they choose rather to disregard them. An example is, "Let the wicked forsake his way, and the unrighteous man his thoughts: and let him return unto the LORD, and he will have mercy upon him; and to our God, for he will abundantly pardon" (Isaiah 55:7) God would have all men come to Him. "For whosoever shall call upon the name of the Lord shall be saved." (Romans 10:13) Eternally, they will be far from Him when they shall be cast into the Lake of Fire. Judgment is the consequence of rejected mercy, and all men have a free will to receive or reject God's Son, through Whom comes mercy and forgiveness.

"'**The Lord *is* far from the wicked**' . . . Not as to his essence or powerful presence, which is everywhere, for he is God omnipresent; but with respect to his favour and good will, he is far from helping in distress, and from hearing their cries when they apply unto him in desperate circumstances; nor does he admit them to nearness and communion with him now, as he does the righteous; nor will he receive them to himself at the last day, but bid them depart from him; they are far from him and from his law, and from all righteousness; and he is far from them, and keeps them at a distance from him; '**but he heareth the prayer of the righteous**'; they draw nigh to him, and he draws nigh to them; he is nigh to all that call upon him in truth; and there is none like them that has God so nigh them as they have; his eyes are upon them, and his ears are open to their cries; he is a God hearing and answering their prayers, and bestows upon them the favours they ask for, and stand in need of."[344]

"God sets himself at a distance from those that set him at defiance: The wicked say to the Almighty, Depart from us, and he is, accordingly, far from them; he does not manifest himself to them, has no communion with them, will not hear them, will not help them, no, not in the time of their need. They shall be for ever banished from his presence and he will behold them afar off. Depart from me, you cursed. He will draw nigh to those in a way of mercy who draw nigh to him in a way of duty: He hears the prayer of the righteous, accepts it, is well pleased with it, and will grant an answer of peace to it. It is the prayer of a righteous man that avails much (James 5:16.) He is nigh to them, a present help, in all that they call upon him for."[345]

"But he heareth the prayer of the righteous." This is only one of many Scriptures that teach of God's distancing Himself from **"the wicked"** and of His drawing nigh to **"the righteous."** Prayers of "the righteous" are the delight of God because they reveal a desire to communicate with Him in a humble manner. In addition to that, prayers are acts of obedience and the righteous person's desire to pray is but the beginning of eternal personal communication with God.

Psalm 34:15-17 The eyes of the LORD are upon the righteous, and his ears are open unto their cry. The face of the LORD is against them that do evil, to cut off the remembrance of them from the earth. The righteous cry, and the LORD heareth, and delivereth them out of all their troubles.

Psalm 66:18-19 If I regard iniquity in my heart, the Lord will not hear me: But verily God hath heard me; he hath attended to the voice of my prayer.

Psalm 73:27 For, lo, they that are far from thee shall perish: thou hast destroyed all them that go a whoring from thee.

Psalm 138:6 Though the LORD be high, yet hath he respect unto the lowly: but the proud he knoweth afar off.

Psalm 145:18-19 The LORD is nigh unto all them that call upon him, to all that call upon him in truth. He will fulfil the desire of them that fear him: he also will hear their cry, and will save them.

Proverbs 15:8 The sacrifice of the wicked is an abomination to the LORD: but the prayer of the upright is his delight.

Isaiah 59:1-2 Behold, the LORD'S hand is not shortened, that it cannot save; neither his ear heavy, that it cannot hear: But your iniquities have separated between you and your God, and your sins have hid his face from you, that he will not hear.

John 9:31 Now we know that God heareth not sinners: but if any man be a worshipper of God, and doeth his will, him he heareth.
Ephesians 2:12-13 That at that time ye were without Christ, being aliens from the commonwealth of Israel, and strangers from the covenants of promise, having no hope, and without God in the world: But now in Christ Jesus ye who sometimes were far off are made nigh by the blood of Christ.
James 5:16 Confess your faults one to another, and pray one for another, that ye may be healed. The effectual fervent prayer of a righteous man availeth much.
1 Peter 3:12 For the eyes of the Lord are over the righteous, and his ears are open unto their prayers: but the face of the Lord is against them that do evil.
1 John 3:22 And whatsoever we ask, we receive of him, because we keep his commandments, and do those things that are pleasing in his sight.

Proverbs 15:30. The light of the eyes rejoiceth the heart: *and* a good report maketh the bones fat.

Focus: This proverb declares that cheerfulness seen in another person's eyes has a joyful effect on the beholder's heart and that hearing a "good report" has a positive overall effect.

"The light of the eyes rejoiceth the heart." "The light of the eyes" is understood to be the twinkle or beam in a person's eyes as he looks upon someone he loves or perhaps someone that he is sharing a humorous event with. Both the **"light of the eyes"** and a **"good report"** are uplifting and bring physical, spiritual, and emotional encouragement. Good thoughts stir up emotions deep within one's heart, which are then involuntary manifested as a sparkle to the eye.   Notice the following verses which illustrate the truth that the thoughts of the heart are mirrored in the eyes of the countenance.

Ezra 9:8 And now for a little space grace hath been *shewed* from the LORD our God, to leave us a remnant to escape, and to give us a nail in his holy place, that our God may lighten our eyes, and give us a little reviving in our bondage.
Proverbs 15:13 A merry heart maketh a cheerful countenance: but by sorrow of the heart the spirit is broken.

"It is good for the man himself. If sunlight gives strength to the body this sunlight of the soul is strengthening to the whole man. Cheerfulness gives courage to face the difficulties of life – that gladness of heart which springs from 'doing justly, loving mercy, and walking with God' is a power which no man for his own sake can afford to throw away. But it is also a duty which we owe to others: In this sense 'the light of the eyes rejoices the heart,' the incoming of a cheerful man into a house where the inhabitants are depressed and sad is like the entrance of sunlight into a darkened room – it changes the entire aspect of things. The influence of such a man is like a shower upon the parched earth – everything seems to spring into new life after it. If it has so reviving and cheering an effect in a world where there is so much to sadden and to weaken men's energies, every man is bound to cultivate a habit of cheerfulness as a matter of duty. It is part of the duty which men owe to God. It is a manifestation of confidence in His righteous character and merciful purposes towards His creatures. It reveals contentment with the lot in life which He has assigned to us – a spirit of submission to His will. Therefore it is an apostolic command, 'Rejoice in the Lord alway: and again I say, rejoice (Philippians 4:4).'" [346]

"*And* a good report maketh the bones fat." "A good report" gives relaxing comfort by setting the mind at ease and allowing all the body to function properly and healthily, as the phrase **"maketh the bones fat"** means. "Maketh the bones fat" is closely associated with the words "marrow to the bones" as used in Proverbs 3:7-8. "...fear the LORD, and depart from evil. It shall be health to thy navel, and marrow to thy bones." Marrow produces moisture in that it generates red and white blood cells and platelets. Red blood cells transport oxygen to the cells. White blood cells fight infection and disease. Platelets help with blood clotting.[347] When the bone marrow becomes unhealthy, the whole body is in danger of returning to dust.

Psalm 63:5 My soul shall be satisfied as with marrow and fatness; and my mouth shall praise thee with joyful lips . . .
Proverbs 4:20 My son, attend to my words; incline thine ear unto my sayings. Let them not depart from thine eyes; keep them in the midst of thine heart. For they are life unto those that find them, and health to all their flesh.
Isaiah 55:2 Wherefore do ye spend money for that which is not bread? and your labour for that which satisfieth not? hearken diligently unto me, and eat ye that which is good, and let your soul delight itself in fatness.
Isaiah 58:11 And the LORD shall guide thee continually, and satisfy thy soul in drought, and make fat thy bones: and thou shalt be like a watered garden, and like a spring of water, whose waters fail not.

"A good report" is a positive, hopeful, encouraging message concerning any number of areas, such as good personal health, well-being of family or friends, or a potential blessing with a job. All such good reports edify a person's emotions, bring comfort to his heart, and strengthen the person who receives them. When the wagons came to take Jacob's family to Egypt, he rejoiced because his son whom he thought was dead was alive and sending for him. Scripture describes Jacob's reaction as "the spirit of Jacob their father revived." (Genesis 45:27) Similarly, a loving look, or the cheerful beaming of a friendly eye make the recipient happy and bring encouragement. Such was the "cheerful countenance" spoken of in verse 13, which has such an inspirational effect on those who see it that it **"rejoiceth the heart."**

> Ezra 9:8 And now for a little space grace hath been shewed from the LORD our God, to leave us a remnant to escape, and to give us a nail in his holy place, that our God may lighten our eyes, and give us a little reviving in our bondage.
> Psalm 34:4 I sought the LORD, and he heard me, and delivered me from all my fears. They looked unto him, and were lightened: and their faces were not ashamed.
> Proverbs 13:9 The light of the righteous rejoiceth: but the lamp of the wicked shall be put out.
> Proverbs 15:13 A merry heart maketh a cheerful countenance: but by sorrow of the heart the spirit is broken.
> Proverbs 16:15 In the light of the king's countenance is life; and his favour is as a cloud of the latter rain.
> Proverbs 17:22 A merry heart doeth good like a medicine: but a broken spirit drieth the bones.
> Proverbs 15:23 A man hath joy by the answer of his mouth: and a word spoken in due season, how good is it!
> Proverbs 16:24 Pleasant words are as an honeycomb, sweet to the soul, and health to the bones.
> Proverbs 25:25 As cold waters to a thirsty soul, so is good news from a far country.
> Isaiah 52:7 How beautiful upon the mountains are the feet of him that bringeth good tidings, that publisheth peace; that bringeth good tidings of good, that publisheth salvation; that saith unto Zion, Thy God reigneth!
> Luke 2:10-11 And the angel said unto them, Fear not: for, behold, I bring you good tidings of great joy, which shall be to all people. For unto you is born this day in the city of David a Saviour, which is Christ the Lord.

Proverbs 15:31 The ear that heareth the reproof of life abideth among the wise.

Focus: This proverb declares that the receiving of righteous correction (reproof of life) positions a person among others who receive righteous correction (the wise).

Wise people are such because they have subjected themselves to evaluation and correction, especially from the word of God and from righteous wise men of whom they determine to abide *[to stay with permanently]*. They appreciate positive criticism that helps rid themselves of ideas, thoughts, behaviors, or anything else that diminishes their ability to walk with God and good men. *Refusing reproof* is the foundational action that causes a person to remain a fool rather than to become wise. **"The ear"** is a figure of speech that represents the entire person, and the **"reproof of life"** is God's instruction that shows the way to a righteous life and salvation. The **"reproof of life"** may come directly from God's word or from the Holy Spirit speaking through a righteous person. *["Heareth" means to perceive by the ear and it implies attention and obedience.]* By refusing to hear, the fool throws a protective cover over all his faults, thus shielding his most dangerous enemies; it is in this state of mind of refusing instruction that he fixes his position among the enemies of God.[348] In contrast, wise persons hear corrective instruction and enjoy life on the path approved and attended by God.

> Psalm 141:5 Let the righteous smite me; it shall be a kindness: and let him reprove me; it shall be an excellent oil, which shall not break my head: for yet my prayer also shall be in their calamities.
> Proverbs 1:23 Turn you at my reproof: behold, I will pour out my spirit unto you, I will make known my words unto you.
> Proverbs 6:23 For the commandment is a lamp; and the law is light; and reproofs of instruction are the way of life . . .
> Proverbs 10:17 He is in the way of life that keepeth instruction: but he that refuseth reproof erreth.
> Proverbs 13:20 He that walketh with wise men shall be wise: but a companion of fools shall be destroyed.
> Proverbs 15:10 Correction is grievous unto him that forsaketh the way: and he that hateth reproof shall die.
> Isaiah 55:3 Incline your ear, and come unto me: hear, and your soul shall live; and I will make an everlasting covenant with you, even the sure mercies of David.
> 2 Timothy 3:16-17 All scripture is given by inspiration of God, and is profitable for doctrine, for reproof, for correction, for instruction in righteousness: That the man of God may be perfect, throughly furnished unto all good works.

Proverbs 15:32 He that refuseth instruction despiseth his own soul: but he that heareth reproof getteth understanding.

Focus: This proverb emphasizes that refusing instruction is destructive and receiving instruction is constructive.

Refusing instruction is the foundational reason why a person becomes a fool. To refuse instruction, especially God's, is to rebel against authority, thus establishing a person solidly on the road to destruction. He therefore will fail to sufficiently learn the truths about God and God's designed wisdom for man. Since he has established himself on this road to destruction, his actions give the appearance that he ***despises his own soul***. His act of rejection may very well cut his life short and will eventually lead him to hell with all others who reject the Son of God. "Sinners undervalue their own souls; therefore they prefer the body before the soul, and wrong the soul to please the body."[349] The most crucial **"instruction"** or **"reproof"** that a person can obtain is that about Jesus Christ; and such truth is instructed in the Scriptures, by godly parents in the sanctity of a Christian home, through a special friend, or under the ministry of a church.

Through corrective instruction (reproof) a person learns the wisdom of God, which gives him a proper perspective of God, himself, and others. When he gains such wise perspectives, he will ***get understanding*** and be able to navigate through the challenges and opportunities of life in the most effective manner, minimize evil influences and maximize godly outcomes, especially the final outcome whereby men face God's judgment..

> "'**Despiseth his own soul**' … shows that he makes no account of it *[his soul]*, has no regard for it or care about it, when it is so precious a jewel, and the loss of it irreparable; not that a man can strictly and properly despise his soul, but comparatively, having a greater regard for his body, and especially for his carnal lusts and pleasures, than for that; or as a man diseased and refuses proper medicines may be said to despise his health; '**But he that heareth reproof getteth understanding**' … by listening to reproof, and behaving according to it; he better understands himself and his case, what he should shun and avoid, what he should receive, embrace, and do; instead of losing his soul, as the man that refuses correction does, he finds the life of it, and possesses it, and with it a large share of experience and spiritual wisdom."[350]

> Proverbs 1:24-26 Because I *[wisdom]* have called, and ye refused; I have stretched out my hand, and no man regarded; But ye have set at nought all my counsel, and would none of my reproof: I also will laugh at your calamity; I will mock when your fear cometh...
>
> Proverbs 5:11-13 And thou mourn at the last, when thy flesh and thy body are consumed, And say, How have I hated instruction, and my heart despised reproof; And have not obeyed the voice of my teachers, nor inclined mine ear to them that instructed me!
>
> Proverbs 6:23 For the commandment is a lamp; and the law is light; and reproofs of instruction are the way of life …
>
> Proverbs 8:33-36 Hear instruction, and be wise, and refuse it not. Blessed is the man that heareth me, watching daily at my gates, waiting at the posts of my doors. For whoso findeth me findeth life, and shall obtain favour of the LORD. But he that sinneth against me wrongeth his own soul: all they that hate me love death.
>
> Proverbs 15:10 Correction is grievous unto him that forsaketh the way: and he that hateth reproof shall die.
>
> Proverbs 19:8 He that getteth wisdom loveth his own soul: he that keepeth understanding shall find good.
>
> Proverbs 29:1 He, that being often reproved hardeneth his neck, shall suddenly be destroyed, and that without remedy.
>
> John 3:16-21 For God so loved the world, that he gave his only begotten Son, that whosoever believeth in him should not perish, but have everlasting life. For God sent not his Son into the world to condemn the world; but that the world through him might be saved. He that believeth on him is not condemned: but he that believeth not is condemned already, because he hath not believed in the name of the only begotten Son of God. And this is the condemnation, that light is come into the world, and men loved darkness rather than light, because their deeds were evil. For every one that doeth evil hateth the light, neither cometh to the light, lest his deeds should be reproved. But he that doeth truth cometh to the light, that his deeds may be made manifest, that they are wrought in God.
>
> Romans 10:17 So then faith *cometh* by hearing, and hearing by the word of God.
>
> Revelation 3:19 As many as I love, I rebuke and chasten: be zealous therefore, and repent.

Proverbs 15:33 The fear of the LORD *is* the instruction of wisdom; and before honour *is* humility.

Focus: This proverb declares that before a person can receive honor (from being wise) he must be humble so as to have a proper "fear of the LORD."

A person is honored by God when he has wisdom, but such honor comes through a proper order. **"Humility"** lays the groundwork for having a **"fear of the LORD** *[a healthy fear directed toward God and encompassing feelings of reverence, awe, and respect]*,**" which lays the groundwork for obtaining **"wisdom,"** which lays the groundwork for receiving **"honor."** The very first requirement for ultimately being honored by God is to be humble. Humility has a direct relationship with a "fear of the LORD."

> "The fear of God and humility go together, where the one is the other is; and as the one is the way to wisdom, the other is the way to glory; Christ's humiliation was before his exaltation; men are first humbled and laid low in their own eyes, and then they are raised out of their low estate, and are set among princes; and shall inherit the throne of glory, being made kings and priests unto God; it is a frequent saying of Christ's, 'he that humbleth himself shall be exalted.'" (Luke 14:11)[351]

"'I am not worthy,' is the voice of the saints. They know God, and God knows them. **Moses** was the meekest man upon earth, and therefore God is said to know him by name (Exodus 33:17). 'I am not worthy of the least of all thy mercies,' saith **Jacob** (Genesis 32:10). Lo, he was honored to be father of the twelve tribes, and heir of the blessing. 'Who am I, O Lord?' says **David**. He was advanced from that lowly conceit to be king of Israel. 'I am not worthy to loose the latchet of Christ's shoe,' saith **John Baptist** (Matthew 3:11). Lo, he was esteemed worthy to lay his hand on Christ's head. 'I am not worthy that thou shouldest come under my roof,' says the **centurion**, therefore Christ commended him. 'I have not found so great faith; no, not in Israel' (Matthew 8:8). 'I am the least of the apostles,' saith **Paul**; 'not worthy to be called an apostle' (1Corinthins 15:9). Therefore he is honored with the title of the apostle. 'Behold the handmaid of the Lord,' saith the **holy virgin**; therefore she was honored to be the mother of the Lord, and to have all generations call her blessed. This . . . humble annihilation of themselves, hath gotten them the honor of saints. In spiritual graces let us study to be great, and not to know it, as the fixed stars are everyone bigger than the earth, yet appear to us less than torches. Not to be high-minded in high deserts is the way to blessed preferment. Humility is not only a virtue itself, but a vessel to contain other virtues; like embers, which keep the fire alive that is hidden under it. It emptieth itself by a modest estimation of its own worth, that Christ may fill it."[352]

Job 28:28 And unto man he said, Behold, the fear of the Lord, that *is* wisdom; and to depart from evil *is* understanding.

Psalm 111:10 The fear of the LORD *is* the beginning of wisdom: a good understanding have all they that do *his commandments:* his praise endureth for ever.

Proverbs 1:7 The fear of the LORD *is* the beginning of knowledge: *but* fools despise wisdom and instruction.

Proverbs 3:16 Length of days *is* in her right hand; *and* in her left hand riches and honour.

Proverbs 8:13 The fear of the LORD *is* to hate evil: pride, and arrogancy, and the evil way, and the froward mouth, do I hate.

Proverbs 18:12 Before destruction the heart of man is haughty, and before honour *is* humility.

Proverbs 22:4 By humility *and* the fear of the LORD *are* riches, and honour, and life.

Proverbs 29:23 A man's pride shall bring him low: but honour shall uphold the humble in spirit.

Luke 14:11 For whosoever exalteth himself shall be abased; and he that humbleth himself shall be exalted.

James 4:10 Humble yourselves in the sight of the Lord, and he shall lift you up.

1 Peter 5:5 Likewise, ye younger, submit yourselves unto the elder. Yea, all *of you* be subject one to another, and be clothed with humility: for God resisteth the proud, and giveth grace to the humble.

CHAPTER SIXTEEN

> **Proverbs 16:1** The preparations of the heart in man, and the answer of the tongue, *is* from the LORD.

Focus: This proverb expresses God's *steering effect on a person's* thinking and speaking.

Proverbs 16:1 is one of many verses in the Book of Proverbs that indirectly teach the importance of giving a carefully chosen right answer. The righteous person believes that his mind belongs to God; consequently, he studies His word, learns His laws, and yields himself to His leadership. Not so with the ungodly, but the man who will be pleasing to God ***prepares his heart*** with Scripture that becomes the groundwork for the way he thinks and chooses his words. He either learns to speak words that are pleasing to God or suffers a shared internal grief with the Holy Spirit. Ephesians 4:29-31 states – "Let no corrupt communication proceed out of your mouth, but that which is good to the use of edifying, that it may minister grace unto the hearers. And grieve not the holy Spirit of God, whereby ye are sealed unto the day of redemption. Let all bitterness, and wrath, and anger, and clamour, and evil speaking, be put away from you, with all malice."

> Proverbs 15:26 The thoughts of the wicked *are* an abomination to the LORD: but *the words* of the pure *are* pleasant words.
>
> Proverbs 15:28 The heart of the righteous studieth to answer: but the mouth of the wicked poureth out evil things.

God ***prepares*** the believer's heart with His word and *guides his speech* with His Spirit. The believer's mind (**"heart"**) may have various plans, words, and ideas come in; but when he fully submits his life to God, he will be marvelously blessed by having the LORD guide every aspect of his life.

Philippians 2:13 is a complimentary New Testament verse stating – "For it is God which worketh in you both to will and to do of *his* good pleasure." It is God Who created such a mysterious and marvelously complicated human brain; along with that creation, He gave man a free will to think, speak, and act without (and even against) his Creator, if he so foolishly chooses. It is God, the Creator, who has given mankind the ability to make preparations in his heart and the ability to speak with his tongue. While it is true that wicked, foolish men contrive wickedness in their heart and pour out profane words; it is also true that godly, wise men meditate on instructions from God and try to imitate Him in both holiness of words and deeds. God is sovereign over the believer's plans. In the wise man, God guides what comes from his heart and pours from his mouth. On the other hand, the fool disregards the teachings from God and consequently allows evil scheming to fill his mind and profane words to pour from his mouth.

> Exodus 4:11-12 And the LORD said unto him, Who hath made man's mouth? or who maketh the dumb, or deaf, or the seeing, or the blind? have not I the LORD? Now therefore go, and I will be with thy mouth, and teach thee what thou shalt say.
>
> Exodus 4:15 And thou shalt speak unto him, and put words in his mouth: and I will be with thy mouth, and with his mouth, and will teach you what ye shall do.
>
> Proverbs 16:9 A man's heart deviseth his way: but the LORD directeth his steps.
>
> Proverbs 21:1 The king's heart *is* in the hand of the LORD, *as* the rivers of water: he turneth it whithersoever he will.
>
> Jeremiah 1:7-9 But the LORD said unto me, Say not, I *am* a child: for thou shalt go to all that I shall send thee, and whatsoever I command thee thou shalt speak. Be not afraid of their faces: for I *am* with thee to deliver thee, saith the LORD. Then the LORD put forth his hand, and touched my mouth. And the LORD said unto me, Behold, I have put my words in thy mouth.
>
> Micah 3:7 Then shall the seers be ashamed, and the diviners confounded: yea, they shall all cover their lips; for *there is* no answer of God. But truly I am full of power by the spirit of the LORD, and of judgment, and of might, to declare unto Jacob his transgression, and to Israel his sin.
>
> Matthew 10:19-20 But when they deliver you up, take no thought how or what ye shall speak: for it shall be given you in that same hour what ye shall speak. For it is not ye that speak, but the Spirit of your Father which speaketh in you.
>
> 2 Corinthians 3:5 Not that we are sufficient of ourselves to think any thing as of ourselves; but our sufficiency *is* of God

One example of a false prophet being unable to speak what he wanted, and being forced to speak God's words is found in the Old Testament.

> "Whatever thoughts and purposes are in a man's mind, – whatever sentiments it may be his intention to utter; if they are such as are likely to have any influence, or to produce effects of any consequence, – they are all under supreme control. We have an exemplification of the fact in the case of Balaam. The preparation of his mind and heart was his own. He left his country on the invitation of Balak, with a certain purpose; designing to utter what was in harmony with his 'love of the wages of unrighteousness.' But 'the Lord God turned the curse into a blessing.' He made the infatuated false prophet to feel his dependence; so that, bent as his heart was to utter one thing, his tongue was constrained to utter another. (Numbers 22:18, 38; 23: 26; 24:12-13) Thus it often is – in ways for which the speakers and agents themselves cannot at the time account. One of these ways is, that, by imperative, unanticipated circumstances, men are brought to say the very contrary of what they intended. They have previously made up their minds. But either their memory fails them, in a manner they are at a loss to understand, and that which they had with pains prepared forsakes them in the time of need; or something different occurs suddenly to the mind just at the necessary juncture, which all their previous study had not suggested; or some incident-something it may be said or done by another, changes, in a moment, the current of their thoughts and the tenor of their words."[353]

Proverbs 16:2   All the ways of a man *are* clean in his own eyes; but the LORD weigheth the spirits.

Focus: This proverb contrasts the biased view that man has of himself with God's unbiased omniscient view.

As used in this verse, a person's ***spirit*** refers to those deep ideas of right and wrong that motivate and determine intentions. When God ***weighs the spirit*** of a man, He balances the words and actions of that person against His knowledge of that person's actual heart-felt intentions, his real motives that perhaps only he and God know. Sometimes a person tries to mask his ***spirit;*** however, God knows every secret thought, feeling, and motive. In other words, God evaluates a person's **"ways,"** not according to the person's idea of self-righteousness, but according to His knowledge of man's heart. That person can convince himself that his own personal behavior (**"ways"**) are **"clean"** *[figuratively righteous]*; but God knows when a lying spirit, a hateful one, or a spirit of covetousness is driving his hypocritical behavior. A person may convince himself that his actions are honest and pure or even righteous when compared to others, but God knows his "spirit." God alone can see the motives of the heart of man. He alone can judge man for his sin.

> "We are all apt to be partial in judging of ourselves: *All the ways of a man,* all his designs, all his doings, *are clean in his own eyes,* and he sees nothing amiss in them, nothing for which to condemn himself, or which should make his projects prove otherwise than well; and therefore he is confident of success, and that the answer of the tongue shall be according to the expectations of the heart; but there is a great deal of pollution cleaving to our ways, which we are not aware of, or do not think so ill of as we ought. The judgment of God concerning us, we are sure, is according to truth: He *weighs the spirits* in a just and unerring balance, knows what is in us, and passes a judgment upon us accordingly, writing *Tekel* upon that which passed our scale with approbation – *weighed in the balance and found wanting;* and by his judgment we must stand or fall. He not only sees men's ways but tries their spirits, and we are as our spirits are."[354]

> "Sometimes we see this delusion under the most shadowy cover: Pilate washed his hands, and was *clean in his own eyes*, from the blood of his condemned victim. (Matthew 27:24) The murderers of Christ were clean, by refraining from the defilement of the judgment-hall, and by eating the passover. (John 18:28) The persecutors of the Church blinded their consciences in the sincerity of unbelief. (Acts 26:9) Often has the self-deceiver passed into eternity under a creditable profession. But how does he stand before God? He never acted from principle. He had the form and the shape of a Christian, so drawn to life as to pass for a living man. But the eyes that are as a flame of fire, bare witness – 'Thou hast a name that thou livest, and art dead.'" (Revelation 3:1)[355]

Proverbs 17:3 The fining pot is for silver, and the furnace for gold: but the LORD trieth the hearts.

Proverbs 20:27 The spirit of man is the candle of the LORD, searching all the inward parts of the belly.

Proverbs 21:2 Every way of a man is right in his own eyes: but the LORD pondereth the hearts.

Proverbs 24:12 If thou sayest, Behold, we knew it not; doth not he that pondereth the heart consider *it?* and he that keepeth thy soul, doth *not* he know *it?* and shall *not* he render to *every* man according to his works?

Jeremiah 17:9-10 The heart *is* deceitful above all *things*, and desperately wicked: who can know it. I the LORD search the heart, I try the reins, even to give every man according to his ways, and according to the fruit of his doings.

John 2:23-25 Now when he was in Jerusalem at the passover, in the feast *day*, many believed in his name, when they saw the miracles which he did. But Jesus did not commit himself unto them, because he knew all men, And needed not that any should testify of man: for he knew what was in man.

John 18:28 Then led they Jesus from Caiaphas unto the hall of judgment: and it was early; and they themselves went not into the judgment hall, lest they should be defiled; but that they might eat the passover.

Hebrews 4:12 For the word of God *is* quick, and powerful, and sharper than any twoedged sword, piercing even to the dividing asunder of soul and spirit, and of the joints and marrow, and is a discerner of the thoughts and intents of the heart.

Revelation 2:23 And I will kill her children with death; and all the churches shall know that I am he which searcheth the reins and hearts: and I will give unto every one of you according to your works.

[Scriptures that testify to the omniscience of God are too numerous to mention here, but a sampling includes the following: Genesis 6:5; 1 Samuel 16:7; Matthew 12:25; Luke 18:11-14; Luke 16:15.]

Proverbs 16:3   Commit thy works unto the LORD, and thy thoughts shall be established.

Focus: This proverb instructs about how to have a settled mind.

For a person to ***commit his works unto the Lord***, he must believe that God is directing his thoughts and labor and that God will be the controlling agent of outcomes. Literally, the word **"commit"** means "to roll," and the context instructs the rolling of works off one's back and onto God. "Roll" describes a man transferring a burden from his own back to the back of a stronger person who is better able to bear the burden.[356] When a person "has, by faith and in prayer, committed himself, his case, his ways, and works to the Lord,"[357] his ***thoughts become established*** *[made firm, stable, fixed]*, and a person's mind is free from anxiety, from sleeplessness, from peace-disrupting thoughts, from grief. Only when a person truly believes that he is pleasing to God and that God is pleased to totally interact in his life can his thoughts be established.

The wise man believes that God will produce the proper results from his righteous labor. He has learned not to second guess himself because he has done his best, and God will do the rest. He has learned to labor with the idea of pleasing God with a spirit of excellence and at the same time he knows that the results are God's business, not his; consequently, his mind is at ease, his thoughts established.

1 Samuel 17:45 Then said David to the Philistine, Thou comest to me with a sword, and with a spear, and with a shield: but I come to thee in the name of the LORD of hosts, the God of the armies of Israel, whom thou hast defied. This day will the LORD deliver thee into mine hand; and I will smite thee, and take thine head from thee; and I will give the carcases of the host of the Philistines this day unto the fowls of the air, and to the wild beasts of the earth; that all the earth may know that there is a God in Israel.

1 Samuel 30:8 And David enquired at the LORD, saying, Shall I pursue after this troop? shall I overtake them? And he answered him, Pursue: for thou shalt surely overtake them, and without fail recover all.

Ruth 2:11-12 And Boaz answered and said unto her, It hath fully been shewed me, all that thou hast done unto thy mother in law since the death of thine husband: and how thou hast left thy father and thy mother, and the land of thy nativity, and art come unto a people which thou knewest not heretofore. The LORD recompense thy work, and a full reward be given thee of the LORD God of Israel, under whose wings thou art come to trust.

Psalm 37:4-5 Delight thyself also in the LORD; and he shall give thee the desires of thine heart. Commit thy way unto the LORD; trust also in him; and he shall bring *it* to pass.

Psalm 55:22 Cast thy burden upon the LORD, and he shall sustain thee: he shall never suffer the righteous to be moved.

Psalm 112:5-8 A good man sheweth favour, and lendeth: he will guide his affairs with discretion. Surely he shall not be moved for ever: the righteous shall be in everlasting remembrance. He shall not be afraid of evil tidings: his heart is fixed, trusting in the LORD. His heart is established, he shall not be afraid, until he see his desire upon his enemies.

Psalm 127:2 *It is* vain for you to rise up early, to sit up late, to eat the bread of sorrows: *for* so he giveth his beloved sleep.

Proverbs 3:5-6 Trust in the LORD with all thine heart; and lean not unto thine own understanding. In all thy ways acknowledge him, and he shall direct thy paths.

Isaiah 26:3-4 Thou wilt keep him in perfect peace, whose mind is stayed on thee: because he trusteth in thee. Trust ye in the LORD for ever: for in the LORD JEHOVAH is everlasting strength:

Isaiah 50:7-9 For the Lord GOD will help me; therefore shall I not be confounded: therefore have I set my face like a flint, and I know that I shall not be ashamed. He is near that justifieth me; who will contend with me? let us stand together: who is mine adversary? let him come near to me. Behold, the Lord GOD will help me; who is he that shall condemn me? lo, they all shall wax old as a garment; the moth shall eat them up.

Philippians 4:6-7 Be careful for nothing; but in every thing by prayer and supplication with thanksgiving let your requests be made known unto God. And the peace of God, which passeth all understanding, shall keep your hearts and minds through Christ Jesus.

2 Timothy 1:12 For the which cause I also suffer these things: nevertheless I am not ashamed: for I know whom I have believed, and am persuaded that he is able to keep that which I have committed unto him against that day.

Hebrews 4:3 For we which have believed do enter into rest, as he said, As I have sworn in my wrath, if they shall enter into my rest: although the works were finished from the foundation of the world.

1 Peter 5:6-7 Humble yourselves therefore under the mighty hand of God, that he may exalt you in due time: Casting all your care upon him; for he careth for you.

> **Proverbs 16:4**   The LORD hath made all *things* for himself: yea, even the wicked for the day of evil.

Focus: This proverb declares that everything in the world was created by God and for God, even the wicked who emerged from God's creation.

"The LORD hath made all *things* for himself." Before God began the process of creating, there was nothing and no one other than Himself; consequently, God did not confer with anyone. With this in mind, it is certainly understandable that God made everything **"for Himself"** (Father, Son, and Holy Spirit), for His holy self, Who allows no wickedness near Himself, including Lucifer or any wicked person. God is righteous, and there is no evil about Him; therefore, His creation was made in holiness as a means of pleasing Him. It is impossible for anything wicked to please God, for "He is holy" (Psalm 99), His Spirit is identified as the Holy Spirit (Luke 11:13), and Jesus the Son of God is holy (Luke 1:35). At the Great White Throne Judgment, every wicked person will be far removed from God and His children.

> Genesis 1:26 And God said, Let us make man in our image, after our likeness: and let them have dominion over the fish of the sea, and over the fowl of the air, and over the cattle, and over all the earth, and over every creeping thing that creepeth upon the earth.
> Revelation 4:11 Thou art worthy, O Lord, to receive glory and honour and power: for thou hast created all things, and for thy pleasure they are and were created.

"Yea, even the wicked *[actively bad people, hostile to God, guilty of sin. The "lawless ones"[358]]* **for the day of evil."** God created man with the ability to choose to be wicked or to be righteous; and because of this free will, *indirectly*, it can be said that God made the wicked. Men often choose to do horrible things and consequentially face God with their evil deeds, and the most wicked thing that a person can do is reject the Son of God. Of course, God knew that men would often choose to be wicked, and He planned **"for the day of evil"** (Judgment Day) whereby **"the wicked"** would be removed for eternity, and no sin (opposition to God) would ever exist again in His creation. It should be noted that ". . . no man can be brought to a **"day of evil"** except by his own consent."[359]

God created man *(not mindless robots)* in His image with a mind capable of knowing God, a heart and emotions capable of loving God, and a will capable of choosing to obey God. With this free will, man could either choose or refuse God; and God being omniscient, knew who would refuse Him. His plan before "the foundation of the world" was that He would send His Son to be the perfect sacrifice for the sins of man. God, in his foreknowledge, knew each person who would turn to Him in repentance and faith. He also knew beforehand every man who would choose to reject him.

> "It is not the sense of this text, nor of any other passage of Scripture, that God made man to damn him; nor is this to be inferred from the doctrine of predestination: God made man, neither to damn him, nor to save him, but for his own glory; and that is secured, whether in his salvation or damnation; nor did or does God make men wicked; he made man upright, and he *[evil mankind]* has made himself wicked; and, being so, God may justly appoint him to damnation for his wickedness, in doing which he glorifies his justice. 'The day of evil', or 'evil day', is the day of wrath and ruin, unto which wicked men are reserved by the appointment of God . . . "[360]
>
> Isaiah 43:7 *Even* every one that is called by my name: for I have created him for my glory, I have formed him; yea, I have made him.
> Isaiah 43:21 This people have I formed for myself; they shall shew forth my praise.
> Romans 2:5-11 But after thy hardness and impenitent heart treasurest up unto thyself wrath against the day of wrath and revelation of the righteous judgment of God; Who will render to every man according to his deeds: To them who by patient continuance in well doing seek for glory and honour and immortality, eternal life: But unto them that are contentious, and do not obey the truth, but obey unrighteousness, indignation and wrath, Tribulation and anguish, upon every soul of man that doeth evil, of the Jew first, and also of the Gentile; But glory, honour, and peace, to every man that worketh good, to the Jew first, and also to the Gentile: For there is no respect of persons with God.
> Romans 8:29-30 For whom he did foreknow, he also did predestinate to be conformed to the image of his Son, that he might be the firstborn among many brethren. Moreover whom he did predestinate, them he also called: and whom he called, them he also justified: and whom he justified, them he also glorified.
> Ephesians 1:3-6 Blessed be the God and Father of our Lord Jesus Christ, who hath blessed us with all spiritual blessings in heavenly places in Christ: According as he hath chosen us in him before the foundation of the world, that we should be holy and without blame before him in love: Having predestinated us unto the adoption of children by Jesus Christ to himself, according to the good pleasure of his will, To the praise of the glory of his grace, wherein he hath made us accepted in the beloved.
> 1 Peter 1:18-21 Forasmuch as ye know that ye were not redeemed with corruptible things, as silver and gold, from your vain conversation received by tradition from your fathers; But with the precious blood of Christ, as of a lamb without blemish and without spot: Who verily was foreordained before the foundation of the world, but was manifest in these last times for you, Who by him do believe in God, that raised him up from the dead, and gave him glory; that your faith and hope might be in God.
> Revelation 13:4-8 And they worshipped the dragon which gave power unto the beast: and they worshipped the beast, saying, Who is like unto the beast? who is able to make war with him? And there was given unto him a mouth speaking great things and blasphemies; and power was given unto him to continue forty and two months. And he opened his mouth in blasphemy against

God, to blaspheme his name, and his tabernacle, and them that dwell in heaven. And it was given unto him to make war with the saints, and to overcome them: and power was given him over all kindreds, and tongues, and nations. And all that dwell upon the earth shall worship him, whose names are not written in the book of life of the Lamb slain from the foundation of the world.

"Because His creatures were not robots, there was the risk of *[their making]* a negative choice. But God, by His sovereign will, purpose, and foreknowledge, determined to allow this, indeed, He ordained it by His own eternal wisdom without Himself being the cause. Many struggle with this, but in the process of all that has occurred, God's glory is supremely revealed in all His Holy attributes – His holiness, righteousness, justice, mercy, grace, and love, veracity, truth, etc. God did not cause the creature to sin. If the creature was to really have the freedom to know, love, and choose for God and respond in worship and obedience as a free and independent agent, he had to have true freedom of choice. Thus, compare the temptation of Eve by the devil. He attacked her knowledge and understanding of God to get her to doubt God's love, etc. The race fell because of Adam and Eve's negative response to the grace of God. But in the process, God's character and glory is revealed in a more total or complete way. So, through the cross, man's sin, like diamonds reflecting the light against the backdrop of black velvet, reflects God's love, mercy, grace, holiness and justice in infinite ways."[361]

God made a perfect and righteous man (Adam) with a free will to continue a perfect relationship or to mar it with disobedience. Then Satan, the chief of angelic disobedience to God, introduced Adam and Eve to his line of rebellious thinking. Though Adam and Eve had previously known only righteousness, through disobeying God, they came to know evil.

God created mankind "for his own glory and service; for the discovery and illustration of his own wisdom, power, goodness, truth, justice, and his other most glorious perfections."[362] He gave every man a mind, emotions, and will; and evil men use these gifts from God to choose to be wicked.

> Ecclesiastes 7:29 Lo, this only have I found, that God hath made man upright; but they have sought out many inventions.
> Romans 9:22-24 What if God, willing to shew his wrath, and to make his power known, endured with much longsuffering the vessels of wrath fitted to destruction: And that he might make known the riches of his glory on the vessels of mercy, which he had afore prepared unto glory, Even us, whom he hath called, not of the Jews only, but also of the Gentiles?
> Hebrews 4:2-3 For unto us was the gospel preached, as well as unto them: but the word preached did not profit them, not being mixed with faith in them that heard it. For we which have believed do enter into rest, as he said, As I have sworn in my wrath, if they shall enter into my rest: although the works were finished from the foundation of the world.
> 2 Peter 3:9 The Lord is not slack concerning his promise, as some men count slackness; but is longsuffering to us-ward, not willing that any should perish, but that all should come to repentance.
> 1 John 3:4-5 Whosoever committeth sin transgresseth also the law: for sin is the transgression of the law. And ye know that he was manifested to take away our sins; and in him is no sin.

Proverbs 16:5 Every one *that is* proud in heart is an abomination to the LORD: *though* hand *join* in hand, he shall not be unpunished.

Focus: This proverb declares God's attitude toward the proud and toward their collective efforts against Him.

"Though hand join in hand" from the second clause implies a confederacy of opposition by a group of prideful people who oppose God. Obviously, the group believes that because they are large in number and multiplied in strength, their opposition must be right, and ultimately, victory belongs to them. In this verse, God declares that such reasoning is faulty and that they will all receive just punishment regardless of their numbers. Ungodly agreement, especially against God, only brings multiplied grief, sorrow, and ultimate punishment from Him. In this life, as at the Tower of Babel *(an example of "hand join to hand")*, punishment is temporal; but punishment will be eternal in the absence of salvation.

> Genesis 11:1-9 And the whole earth was of one language, and of one speech. And it came to pass, as they journeyed from the east, that they found a plain in the land of Shinar; and they dwelt there. And they said one to another, Go to, let us make brick, and burn them throughly. And they had brick for stone, and slime had they for morter. And they said, Go to, let us build us a city and a tower, whose top may reach unto heaven; and let us make us a name, lest we be scattered abroad upon the face of the whole earth. And the LORD came down to see the city and the tower, which the children of men builded. And the LORD said, Behold, the people is one, and they have all one language; and this they begin to do: and now nothing will be restrained from them, which they have imagined to do. Go to, let us go down, and there confound their language, that they may not understand one another's speech. So the LORD scattered them abroad from thence upon the face of all the earth: and they left off to build the city. Therefore is the name of it called Babel; because the LORD did there confound the language of all the earth: and from thence did the LORD scatter them abroad upon the face of all the earth.
> Proverbs 6:16-17 These six things doth the LORD hate: yea, seven are an abomination unto him: A proud look, a lying tongue, and hands that shed innocent blood…
> Proverbs 8:13 The fear of the LORD is to hate evil: pride, and arrogancy, and the evil way, and the froward mouth, do I hate.

Proverbs 11:21 Though hand join in hand, the wicked shall not be unpunished: but the seed of the righteous shall be delivered.

Isaiah 14:12-15 How art thou fallen from heaven, O Lucifer, son of the morning! how art thou cut down to the ground, which didst weaken the nations! For thou hast said in thine heart, I will ascend into heaven, I will exalt my throne above the stars of God: I will sit also upon the mount of the congregation, in the sides of the north: I will ascend above the heights of the clouds; I will be like the most High. Yet thou shalt be brought down to hell, to the sides of the pit.

Isaiah 45:9 Woe unto him that striveth with his Maker! Let the potsherd *strive* with the potsherds of the earth. Shall the clay say to him that fashioneth it, What makest thou? or thy work, He hath no hands?

Ezekiel 28:2 Son of man, say unto the prince of Tyrus, Thus saith the Lord GOD; Because thine heart is lifted up, and thou hast said, I am a God, I sit in the seat of God, in the midst of the seas; yet thou art a man, and not God, though thou set thine heart as the heart of God:

James 4:6 But he giveth more grace. Wherefore he saith, God resisteth the proud, but giveth grace unto the humble.

1 Peter 5:5-6 Likewise, ye younger, submit yourselves unto the elder. Yea, all of you be subject one to another, and be clothed with humility: for God resisteth the proud, and giveth grace to the humble. Humble yourselves therefore under the mighty hand of God, that he may exalt you in due time...

Proverbs 16:6 By mercy and truth iniquity is purged: and by the fear of the LORD *men* depart from evil.

Focus: This proverb declares the qualities of God whereby iniquity is purged and the attitude man has to have toward God so that he can separate from evil.

"By mercy and truth iniquity is purged." Often presented together in the Bible, the " mercy and truth" of God identifies two aspects of His character. In order to be like Him, one must strive to weave these two qualities of character into the fabric of his being so that they govern the way he thinks and acts. **"Mercy"** is a gesture of love that is extended to those in need. It is especially noted when the one in need is as helpless as is every sinner in need of salvation. **"Truth** *[faithful, sure, reliable, stable]* **"** is the absence of anything false and is perfectly illustrated in Jesus, Who is Truth in every respect. When "mercy and truth" are extended by God's love, through Jesus, and with the wooing of the Holy Spirit, sin (when repented of) is purged.

NOTE: **"Mercy"** translated from the Hebrew *chesed* which means goodness, loving kindness, pity. In the Old Testament *chesed* is translated "lovingkindness (es)" in 29 verses and "mercy" in 139 verses; but **is NOT** translated "lovingkindness" in Proverbs. **"Mercy"** is the aspect of God's love that causes Him to help the miserable who may be so either because of breaking God's law or because of circumstances beyond their control like blindness or leprosy. Finally, because God is merciful, He expects His children to be merciful.[363]

Hosea 6:6 For I desired mercy, and not sacrifice; and the knowledge of God more than burnt offerings.

Matthew 9:13 But go ye and learn what *that* meaneth, I will have mercy, and not sacrifice: for I am not come to call the righteous, but sinners to repentance.

"By the fear of the LORD *men* depart from evil. The **"fear of the Lord,"** is that awesome respect for God that keeps people from abusing God's mercy and turning to evil. When men have such an awesome respect for God, they will learn "to hate evil: pride, and arrogancy, and the evil way, and the froward mouth." (Proverbs 8:13)

Psalm 25:12 What man *is* he that feareth the LORD? him shall he teach in the way *that* he shall choose.

Proverbs 3:5-7 Trust in the LORD with all thine heart; and lean not unto thine own understanding. In all thy ways acknowledge him, and he shall direct thy paths. Be not wise in thine own eyes: fear the LORD, and depart from evil.

Proverbs 14:16 A wise man feareth, and departeth from evil: but the fool rageth, and is confident.

Proverbs 14:27 The fear of the LORD is a fountain of life, to depart from the snares of death.

2 Corinthians 7:1 Having therefore these promises, dearly beloved, let us cleanse ourselves from all filthiness of the flesh and spirit, perfecting holiness in the fear of God.

Proverbs 16:7 When a man's ways please the LORD, he maketh even his enemies to be at peace with him.

Focus: This proverb specifies the manner of life that obtains God's favor and, in turn, peace with enemies.

This verse certainly does *not* mean that *all* man's enemies will be at peace with him, as can be exemplified by the life of Jesus. He had a perfect godly character and lifestyle, yet had many enemies. Likewise, the apostles and martyrs throughout the years had enemies who declared war on them – not peace. Men that hate God will hate the child of God. However, there have been and will continue to be, enemies of the child of God who change and become peaceful because God changes their hearts.

Led by Scripture and the Holy Spirit, wise people know when, where, and how to speak properly. They know how to treat other people with respect, how to be honest and sincere, and how to genuinely love people (especially those who oppose themselves – 2 Timothy 2:5). They also know how to distance themselves from certain people, and how to observe all other ways that please the Lord as taught in the Scriptures. God, Who created the human mind, knows how His children should best interact with the world; and He also has the power to persuade and change the hearts of enemies.

> "**When a man's ways please the Lord** – The best way to have our enemies reconciled unto us, is for us first to be reconciled unto God; for such is the love which the Lord hath to pious and virtuous persons, that when all their designs and actions are such as he approves, he often inclines even those that were their foes to become their friends, disposing their hearts to kindness toward them."[364]

> "God can turn foes into friends when he pleases. He that has all hearts in his hand has access to men's spirits and power over them, working insensibly, but irresistibly upon them, can make *a man;s enemies to be at peace with him,* can change their minds, or force them into a feigned submission. He can slay all enemies, and bring those together that were at the greatest distance from each other.

> He will do it for us when we please him. If we make it our care to be reconciled to God, and to keep ourselves in his love, he will incline those that have been envious towards us, and vexatious to us, to entertain a good opinion of us and to become our friends. God made Esau to be at peace with Jacob, Abimelech with Isaac, and David's enemies to court his favour and desire a league with Israel."[365]

> Genesis 26:26-28 Then Abimelech went to him from Gerar, and Ahuzzath one of his friends, and Phichol the chief captain of his army. And Isaac said unto them, Wherefore come ye to me, seeing ye hate me, and have sent me away from you? And they said, We saw certainly that the LORD was with thee: and we said, Let there be now an oath betwixt us, *even* betwixt us and thee, and let us make a covenant with thee;
> Joshua 3:7 And the LORD said unto Joshua, This day will I begin to magnify thee in the sight of all Israel, that they may know that, as I was with Moses, so I will be with thee.
> Joshua 4:14 On that day the LORD magnified Joshua in the sight of all Israel; and they feared him, as they feared Moses, all the days of his life.
> 1 Chronicles 29:24-25 And all the princes, and the mighty men, and all the sons likewise of king David, submitted themselves unto Solomon the king. And the LORD magnified Solomon exceedingly in the sight of all Israel, and bestowed upon him such royal majesty as had not been on any king before him in Israel.
> 2 Chronicles 1:1 And Solomon the son of David was strengthened in his kingdom, and the LORD his God was with him, and magnified him exceedingly.
> 2 Chronicles 17:10-11 And the fear of the LORD fell upon all the kingdoms of the lands that were round about Judah, so that they made no war against Jehoshaphat. Also some of the Philistines brought Jehoshaphat presents, and tribute silver; and the Arabians brought him flocks, seven thousand and seven hundred rams, and seven thousand and seven hundred he goats.

Proverbs 16:8   Better is a little with righteousness than great revenues without right.

Focus: This proverb specifies the preferred balance between wealth and righteousness.

This proverb can be visualized as God's set of balance scales. On the left side is *righteousness with a little wealth*, and on the right side is *no righteousness but much ill-gotten wealth*. The scales are totally depressed on the left side indicating that righteousness has exceedingly greater value than wealth.

While God puts great value on living righteously, men most often put great value on obtaining wealth by any means possible; but this verse clearly states that a little wealth with righteousness is better than much wealth without righteousness. Righteousness is better because of the friendship and favor of our all-providing God and for peace of mind. Righteousness is better because it lays the foundation for answered prayer, for honest dealings man to man, and for fertile soil with which to receive the promises of God. Moreover, the peace that it brings is far better than the trouble that accompanies wickedly-gotten wealth.

> Psalm 37:16-17 A little that a righteous man hath is better than the riches of many wicked. For the arms of the wicked shall be broken: but the LORD upholdeth the righteous.
> Proverbs 15:6 In the house of the righteous *is* much treasure: but in the revenues of the wicked is trouble.
> Proverbs 15:16 Better *is* little with the fear of the LORD than great treasure and trouble therewith.

Proverbs 15:29 The LORD is far from the wicked: but he heareth the prayer of the righteous.

Proverbs 21:6-7 The getting of treasures by a lying tongue is a vanity tossed to and fro of them that seek death. The robbery of the wicked shall destroy them; because they refuse to do judgment.

Proverbs 28:6 Better is the poor that walketh in his uprightness, than he that is perverse in his ways, though he be rich.

Ecclesiastes 4:6 Better *is* an handful *with* quietness, than both the hands full *with* travail and vexation of spirit.

Jeremiah 17:11 As the partridge sitteth on eggs, and hatcheth them not; so he that getteth riches, and not by right, shall leave them in the midst of his days, and at his end shall be a fool.

Jeremiah 22:13 Woe unto him that buildeth his house by unrighteousness, and his chambers by wrong; that useth his neighbour's service without wages, and giveth him not for his work . . .

Luke 12:15 And he said unto them, Take heed, and beware of covetousness: for a man's life consisteth not in the abundance of the things which he possesseth.

1 Timothy 6:6-9 But godliness with contentment is great gain. For we brought nothing into this world, and it is certain we can carry nothing out. And having food and raiment let us be therewith content. But they that will be rich fall into temptation and a snare, and into many foolish and hurtful lusts, which drown men in destruction and perdition.

Proverbs 16:9   A man's heart deviseth his way: but the LORD directeth his steps.

Focus: This proverb declares that a man makes plans, but the Lord determines what, if anything, he will actually do.

A man can form a plan as to what he wants to accomplish in a day or week or even as far out as the end of his working days (or even his life), but it is God who determines if the plan will be allowed and will come to fruition. Certainly men should make short-term and long-term plans; but they should always keep in mind that God may alter their course without conferring with them because **God directs a man's steps.** This proverb is "a fine description of the Sovereign government of God."[366]

Men often contrive plans (both evil and good) that are allowed by God. He certainly does *not* direct a man's steps to do evil but often allows a wicked man to proceed to his own destruction. As evidenced by the Psalms and his early life, David knew to have his steps directed by the Holy Spirit; but he sometimes allowed his fleshly desire to overrule and caused himself and others much grief. Christian men today would do well to grasp the following Scriptural admonition "*This* I say then, Walk in the Spirit, and ye shall not fulfil the lust of the flesh." (Galatians 5:16)

"Man without his free will is a machine. God without his unchangeable purpose ceases to be God. As rational agents we think, consult, act freely. As dependent agents, the LORD exercises his own power in permitting, overruling, or furthering our acts. Thus man proposes; God disposes. Man devises; the LORD directs. He orders our will, without infringing our liberty, or disturbing our responsibility. For while we act as we please, we must be answerable. . . How little did Joseph's brethren contemplate the overruling *direction* to their evil *devisings!* When Saul's *heart was devising* 'slaughter against the disciples of the Lord;' when the renegade slave was running in his own path, little did they think of that gracious *direction of their steps,* to the salvation of their souls. When David simply went at his father's bidding, little did he know the grand crisis, to which *the LORD was directing his steps.* As little did the captive girl calculate upon the weighty results from her banishment from her country. Often also hath the path of the Lord's people been encouraged by the counteracting of their enemies' *devising,* and the backward *direction of their steps,* at the moment when they were ready to grasp their prey!"[367]

Genesis 50:18-20 And his brethren also went and fell down before his face; and they said, Behold, we *be* thy servants. And Joseph said unto them, Fear not: for *am* I in the place of God? But as for you, ye thought evil against me; *but* God meant it unto good, to bring to pass, as *it is* this day, to save much people alive.

Job 23:8-12 Behold, I go forward, but he *is* not *there;* and backward, but I cannot perceive him: On the left hand, where he doth work, but I cannot behold *him:* he hideth himself on the right hand, that I cannot see him: But he knoweth the way that I take: *when* he hath tried me, I shall come forth as gold. My foot hath held his steps, his way have I kept, and not declined. Neither have I gone back from the commandment of his lips; I have esteemed the words of his mouth more than my necessary *food.*

Psalm 37:23 The steps of a good man are ordered by the LORD: and he delighteth in his way.

Psalm 40:1-2 To the chief Musician, A Psalm of David. I waited patiently for the LORD; and he inclined unto me, and heard my cry. He brought me up also out of an horrible pit, out of the miry clay, and set my feet upon a rock, *and* established my goings.

Psalm 119:133 Order my steps in thy word: and let not any iniquity have dominion over me.

Psalm 121:8 The LORD shall preserve thy going out and thy coming in from this time forth, and even for evermore.

Proverbs 20:24 Man's goings are of the LORD; how can a man then understand his own way?

Proverbs 21:30 *There is* no wisdom nor understanding nor counsel against the LORD.

Jeremiah 10:23 O LORD, I know that the way of man is not in himself: it is not in man that walketh to direct his steps.

> **Proverbs 16:10** A divine sentence is in the lips of the king: his mouth transgresseth not in judgment.

Focus: This proverb establishes the righteous level of judgment that is expected of kings when they speak as a representative of God.

Starting with verse 10 and proceeding through verse 15, a manual for kings is laid out – not showing what they are but what they should be if they want the blessings of God on their kingdom.

If a king submits himself to God for instruction and leadership and after that follows such guidance, he will give a **"divine sentence"** (proper discernment between right and wrong, guilt and innocence), and *his mouth **will not transgress in judgment** [a verdict–favorable or unfavorable]*. Kings are not born wiser than average persons, and they do not have an innate ability to give *divine sentences*. Therefore, it is the expectation that the king will get direct intervention from God and that God will give him proper reasoning, wisdom, and spiritual judgments. Evidenced by their unquestionably bad judgment in trying to destroy the work of God and the prophets of God, the wicked, ungodly kings of the northern Kingdom of Israel had no such God-given ability to discern properly.

The first criteria for the king is to have a **"divine sentence in the lips"** meaning that he is to speak what God would have him to speak because he is walking in the righteousness he has learned from God. In order to be successful and have God's blessing on himself and the kingdom, the king must seek the wisdom of God. He should have no interest of his own except glorifying God and seeking the good of the kingdom.

> "We wish this were always true as a proposition, and we ought to make it our prayer for kings, and all in authority, that a *divine sentence* may be in their lips, both in giving orders, that they may do that in wisdom, and in giving sentence, that they may do that in equity, both which are included in *judgment,* and that in neither their mouth may transgress."[368]
>
> 2 Samuel 14:17 Then thine handmaid said, The word of my lord the king shall now be comfortable: for as an angel of God, so is my lord the king to discern good and bad: therefore the LORD thy God will be with thee.
> 2 Samuel 23:3 The God of Israel said, the Rock of Israel spake to me, He that ruleth over men must be just, ruling in the fear of God.
> 1 Kings 3:9 Give therefore thy servant an understanding heart to judge thy people, that I may discern between good and bad: for who is able to judge this thy so great a people?
> 1 Kings 3:27-28 Then the king answered and said, Give her the living child, and in no wise slay it: she is the mother thereof. And all Israel heard of the judgment which the king had judged; and they feared the king: for they saw that the wisdom of God was in him, to do judgment.
> Proverbs 8:15 By me *[wisdom]* kings reign, and princes decree justice.
> Proverbs 16:12-13 It is an abomination to kings to commit wickedness: for the throne is established by righteousness. Righteous lips are the delight of kings; and they love him that speaketh right.
> Isaiah 32:1 Behold, a king shall reign in righteousness, and princes shall rule in judgment.
> Jeremiah 23:5 Behold, the days come, saith the LORD, that I will raise unto David a righteous Branch, and a King shall reign and prosper, and shall execute judgment and justice in the earth.
> 1 Timothy 2:1-2 I exhort therefore, that, first of all, supplications, prayers, intercessions, *and* giving of thanks, be made for all men; For kings, and *for* all that are in authority; that we may lead a quiet and peaceable life in all godliness and honesty.

> **Proverbs 16:11** A just weight and balance *are* the LORD'S: all the weights of the bag *are* his work.

Focus: This proverb utilizes balance scales to symbolize God's demand for honesty.

Even though this Proverb has application to unjust practices of businessmen, as shown below, ultimately, it is part of the instruction about the righteousness of kings (and certainly applies to spiritual leaders). God stated that there must be just weights and balances in Leviticus 19 and Deuteronomy 25. (When Absalom's hair was weighed in 2 Samuel 14:26, it was weighed "after the king's weight" showing that this was under the oversight of the king.) When a king allowed businessmen to change the fixed establishment of the weights and balances, he was not honoring God; and this wickedness God would judge.

> "A most "important part of their *[the king's]* official duty *[was]* to promote among their subjects, to the utmost extent of their power, **the principles and the practice of equity between man and man**. The prevalence, indeed, of mutual confidence is indispensable to the comfort and prosperity of society . . . that depends on trade and commerce."[369]

Leviticus 19:35-36 Ye shall do no unrighteousness in judgment, in meteyard, in weight, or in measure. Just balances, just weights, a just ephah, and a just hin, shall ye have: I am the LORD your God, which brought you out of the land of Egypt.

Ezekiel 45:9-12 Thus saith the Lord GOD; Let it suffice you, O princes of Israel: remove violence and spoil, and execute judgment and justice, take away your exactions from my people, saith the Lord GOD. Ye shall have just balances, and a just ephah, and a just bath. The ephah and the bath shall be of one measure, that the bath may contain the tenth part of an homer, and the ephah the tenth part of an homer: the measure thereof shall be after the homer. And the shekel *shall be* twenty gerahs: twenty shekels, five and twenty shekels, fifteen shekels, shall be your maneh.

"A just weight and balance are the LORD'S." The LORD has ordered that the "weight and balance" must be "just" (accurate, right, truthful). *"People are not to think that trade lies outside the divine law. God has commanded there also all that belongs to truth and right."*[370] God insists on honesty, truthfulness, and integrity from His people. Such just dealings are not the way of those wicked, evil people who are defined by their cheating and lying.

Job 31:6 Let me be weighed in an even balance, that God may know mine integrity.

Psalm 62:9 Surely men of low degree *are* vanity, *and* men of high degree *are* a lie: to be laid in the balance, they *are* altogether *lighter* than vanity.

"All the weights of the bag are his work" is an inculcation (teaching or impressing upon the mind by frequent instruction or repetition) of the first clause emphasizing that HONESTY IS DEMANDED BY GOD and reflects to Him. Weights used as a counterbalance for measuring must be true because they represent: (1) the truthfulness of God and (2) dependence on His provision rather than on any necessity for cheating by the ungodly.

"In the Bible, 'balances' are often used in a figurative way. The Lord told the Israelites, 'You shall have just balances, just weights' (Leviticus 19:36; Ezekiel 45:10). The "just balances" symbolize honesty, righteousness, justice, and fair dealing (Job 31:6; Psalm 62:9; Proverbs 16:11). 'False balances' symbolize evil and bring the displeasure and judgment of God (Proverbs 11:1; Micah 6:11)."[371]

Truth is one of the primary identifying characteristics of God, so it should be no surprise that He expects *truthfulness* and *honesty* from His people. *Any interaction that a godly individual has with others must be reflective of the teachings and expectations of his heavenly Father.* Specifically illustrated in this verse are truthfulness and honesty in financial dealings. Truthful, accurate weights used to measure silver or gold for trading must be accurate simply because God expects honesty from His children. People who do business with the righteous know that righteous people honor God in all their dealings; consequently, even dishonest businessmen trust those who are believers.

"Whether used by kings or businessmen, the accurate balance and scales which ensure fair dealings are the only ones that have YHWH's approval. They alone are His, and acknowledged by Him. Indeed, the very weights which the businessman keeps in a bag are His work if they are accurate and reliable. And if they are not then He repudiates them. They come under His disapproval . . . God is with a king or businessman in his endeavours when he deals honestly, but rejects him when he does not. It is also an important indication of the emphasis that God puts on honest dealings."[372]

Deuteronomy 25:13-16 Thou shalt not have in thy bag divers weights, a great and a small. Thou shalt not have in thine house divers measures, a great and a small. But thou shalt have a perfect and just weight, a perfect and just measure shalt thou have: that thy days may be lengthened in the land which the LORD thy God giveth thee. For all that do such things, *and* all that do unrighteously, *are* an abomination unto the LORD thy God.

Proverbs 11:1 A false balance is abomination to the LORD: but a just weight is his delight.

Proverbs 20:10 Divers weights, and divers measures, both of them are alike abomination to the LORD.

Proverbs 20:23 Divers weights are an abomination unto the LORD; and a false balance is not good.

Ezekiel 45:10 Ye shall have just balances, and a just ephah, and a just bath.

Micah 6:11 Shall I count them pure with the wicked balances, and with the bag of deceitful weights?

1 Thessalonians 4:6-7 That no *man* go beyond and defraud his brother in *any* matter: because that the Lord *is* the avenger of all such, as we also have forewarned you and testified. For God hath not called us unto uncleanness, but unto holiness.

Proverbs 16:12 *It is* an abomination to kings to commit wickedness: for the throne is established by righteousness.

Focus: This proverb establishes the proper attitude that kings should have toward wickedness.

This proverb teaches that good kings hate wickedness in anyone (including themselves). They know that righteousness establishes and stabilizes a kingdom while wickedness undermines, destabilizes, and otherwise weakens. A godly, upright king will strive to maintain righteous behavior before God, and he will require righteousness in his servants and subjects. The Lord puts up kings and establishes them by righteousness for a long, peaceful reign, but kings are overthrown by wickedness.

2 Samuel 23:3 The God of Israel said, the Rock of Israel spake to me, He that ruleth over men *must be* just, ruling in the fear of God.

Proverbs 20:8 A king that sitteth in the throne of judgment scattereth away all evil with his eyes.

Proverbs 20:26 A wise king scattereth the wicked, and bringeth the wheel over them.

Proverbs 20:28 Mercy and truth preserve the king: and his throne is upholden by mercy.

Proverbs 22:11 He that loveth pureness of heart, for the grace of his lips the king shall be his friend.

Proverbs 25:5 Take away the wicked from before the king, and his throne shall be established in righteousness.

Proverbs 29:4 The king by judgment establisheth the land: but he that receiveth gifts overthroweth it.

Proverbs 29:14 The king that faithfully judgeth the poor, his throne shall be established for ever.

Although God provided the Scriptures as a guide to godly living as well as to righteous leadership, the only One perfectly meeting the criteria of a righteous king will be Jesus Christ, the Son of God. The righteousness of our Lord and King Jesus Christ will be visible to all. His holy leadership will establish the Kingdom of God forever.

Isaiah 9:6-7 For unto us a child is born, unto us a son is given: and the government shall be upon his shoulder: and his name shall be called Wonderful, Counsellor, The mighty God, The everlasting Father, The Prince of Peace. Of the increase of his government and peace there shall be no end, upon the throne of David, and upon his kingdom, to order it, and to establish it with judgment and with justice from henceforth even for ever. The zeal of the LORD of hosts will perform this.

Jeremiah 23:5 Behold, the days come, saith the LORD, that I will raise unto David a righteous Branch, and a King shall reign and prosper, and shall execute judgment and justice in the earth.

> **Proverbs 16:13** Righteous lips *are* the delight of kings; and they love him that speaketh right.

Focus: This proverb specifies the kind of people whom the king enjoys and loves.

Carrying further the idea presented in verse 12, this proverb declares that good kings delight in and love those who speak righteously. **"Righteous lips"** is a figure of speech representing a person who is right with God and who speaks accordingly. Wise leadership welcomes such and does not want to be flattered or lied to because the truth is necessary to make wise decisions. **"Right" speaking** is straight, upright, just, fitting, and proper.

Also, proper communication between godly people promotes not only a feeling of safety, but also the joy of righteous fellowship. Not only does the king love righteous people in his court as his counselors and friends, but righteous subjects love and respect the king who speaks and lives according to God's standard. Notice carefully what the righteous king wrote in Psalm 101.

Psalm 101:3-8 I will set no wicked thing before mine eyes: I hate the work of them that turn aside; *it* shall not cleave to me. A froward heart shall depart from me: I will not know a wicked *person.* Whoso privily slandereth his neighbour, him will I cut off: him that hath an high look and a proud heart will not I suffer. Mine eyes *shall be* upon the faithful of the land, that they may dwell with me: he that walketh in a perfect way, he shall serve me. He that worketh deceit shall not dwell within my house: he that telleth lies shall not tarry in my sight. I will early destroy all the wicked of the land; that I may cut off all wicked doers from the city of the LORD.

Proverbs 10:20 The tongue of the just *is as* choice silver: the heart of the wicked *is* little worth.

Proverbs 14:35 The king's favour *is* toward a wise servant: but his wrath is *against* him that causeth shame.

Proverbs 22:11 He that loveth pureness of heart, *for* the grace of his lips the king *shall be* his friend.

Proverbs 29:12 If a ruler hearken to lies, all his servants *are* wicked.

Ungodly kings would certainly rather have those around them who flatter and otherwise say what is pleasing to them, but wise righteous kings delight in knowing the truth from trusted individuals. Foolish people do not receive instruction, and wicked persons do not give righteous instruction. An unrighteous king encourages distortions of the truth in order to obtain a temporary measure of delight from such nonsense. This truth is illustrated with Ahab, king of Israel, who hated the prophet Micaiah because he told him only the truth as he received it from God (2 Chronicles 18:7).

2 Chronicles 18:7 And the king of Israel said unto Jehoshaphat, There is yet one man, by whom we may enquire of the LORD: but I hate him; for he never prophesied good unto me, but always evil: the same is Micaiah the son of Imla. And Jehoshaphat said, Let not the king say so.

"Happy is it for the prince who feels and acts as this verse describes; who desires honest and faithful counsel; who prefers unpalatable truth to palatable falsehood; who rejects with dignity and scorn the advisers whom he detects putting a bandage over his eyes, and who places those proportionally near to him and in the light of his favour, who assist him to see clearly things as they actually are, and suggest, with the fidelity of conscientious conviction, the measures that will make things as they ought to be!"[373]

> **Proverbs 16:14** The wrath of a king *is as* messengers of death: but a wise man will pacify it.

Focus: This proverb describes the awfulness of a king's wrath and the category of man who can appease the same.

A man of **"wrath"** is controlled and driven by anger. He has little or no self-control but allows his emotions to dictate his actions. Consequently, he fails to apply wisdom to situations that are displeasing to him and repeatedly causes himself serious repercussions and unnecessary problems.

When the **"wrath"** *[rage, hot displeasure, venom]* of a king is aroused, great terror comes over his target because the sentence of death may come upon the recipient of his great anger. **"Messengers of death"** may soon be sent to execute the sentence of death pronounced by the angry, all-powerful monarch.

There are situations where having wisdom to know how to give a proper response (smooth over hostilities) at the right time can quell an otherwise lethal situation and abort an order of disaster. A wise man will **"pacify"** the king's anger by knowing when to speak, having the right spirit, and being respectful to him.

> "Wrath soon finds executioners. Under the despotic governments of the East there are frequently no forms of trial. A man may not know that he is condemned, or even accused, until the executioner, the **'messenger of death,'** comes to take his head off; perhaps in his own house, in the midst of his family, or wherever he meets him."[374]
>
> Genesis 32:20 And say ye moreover, Behold, thy servant Jacob is behind us. For he said, I will appease him with the present that goeth before me, and afterward I will see his face; peradventure he will accept of me.
>
> 1 Samuel 19:4-6 And Jonathan spake good of David unto Saul his father, and said unto him, Let not the king sin against his servant, against David; because he hath not sinned against thee, and because his works have been to thee-ward very good: For he did put his life in his hand, and slew the Philistine, and the LORD wrought a great salvation for all Israel: thou sawest it, and didst rejoice: wherefore then wilt thou sin against innocent blood, to slay David without a cause? And Saul hearkened unto the voice of Jonathan: and Saul sware, As the LORD liveth, he shall not be slain.
>
> 1 Samuel 25:23-26 And when Abigail saw David, she hasted, and lighted off the ass, and fell before David on her face, and bowed herself to the ground, And fell at his feet, and said, Upon me, my lord, *upon* me *let this* iniquity *be:* and let thine handmaid, I pray thee, speak in thine audience, and hear the words of thine handmaid. Let not my lord, I pray thee, regard this man of Belial, *even* Nabal: for as his name *is,* so *is* he; Nabal *is* his name, and folly *is* with him: but I thine handmaid saw not the young men of my lord, whom thou didst send. Now therefore, my lord, *as* the LORD liveth, and *as* thy soul liveth, seeing the LORD hath withholden thee from coming to *shed* blood, and from avenging thyself with thine own hand, now let thine enemies, and they that seek evil to my lord, be as Nabal.
>
> Esther 7:7-10 And the king arising from the banquet of wine in his wrath went into the palace garden: and Haman stood up to make request for his life to Esther the queen; for he saw that there was evil determined against him by the king. Then the king returned out of the palace garden into the place of the banquet of wine; and Haman was fallen upon the bed whereon Esther was. Then said the king, Will he force the queen also before me in the house? As the word went out of the king's mouth, they covered Haman's face. And Harbonah, one of the chamberlains, said before the king, Behold also, the gallows fifty cubits high, which Haman had made for Mordecai, who had spoken good for the king, standeth in the house of Haman. Then the king said, Hang him thereon. So they hanged Haman on the gallows that he had prepared for Mordecai. Then was the king's wrath pacified.
>
> Proverbs 15:12 A soft answer turneth away wrath: but grievous words stir up anger. The tongue of the wise useth knowledge aright: but the mouth of fools poureth out foolishness.
>
> Proverbs 19:12 The king's wrath is as the roaring of a lion; but his favour is as dew upon the grass.
>
> Proverbs 20:2 The fear of a king is as the roaring of a lion: whoso provoketh him to anger sinneth against his own soul.
>
> Proverbs 25:15 By long forbearing is a prince persuaded, and a soft tongue breaketh the bone.
>
> Ecclesiastes 8:2-5 I counsel thee to keep the king's commandment, and that in regard of the oath of God. Be not hasty to go out of his sight: stand not in an evil thing; for he doeth whatsoever pleaseth him. Where the word of a king is, there is power: and who may say unto him, What doest thou? Whoso keepeth the commandment shall feel no evil thing: and a wise man's heart discerneth both time and judgment.

> **Proverbs 16:15** In the light of the king's countenance is life; and his favour is as a cloud of the latter rain.

Focus: This proverb describes the benefit of a king's delight and, consequently, his favor.

"The light of the king's countenance" speaks of his shining face of approval. The king has the power to kill or to allow to live; and when his countenance reflects pleasure instead of wrath, it is as refreshing as **"a cloud of the latter rain."** The life-giving latter rain comes in March or April just before harvest, and leading these wonderful refreshing showers are clouds that give delightful and welcome shade from the scorching sun to the field laborers. *(See Deuteronomy 11:13-15 for God's promise of first and latter rains to Israel.)*

One way to brighten up the king's face was given in Proverbs 16:13 – "Righteous lips are the delight of kings; and they love him that speaketh right." Like other righteous people, a godly king is delighted when those around him, especially his counselors and members of the court, speak of righteousness and judgment. He will surely grant them favor.

> Psalm 4:6 There be many that say, Who will shew us any good? LORD, lift thou up the light of thy countenance upon us.
>
> Psalm 21:6 For thou hast made him most blessed for ever: thou hast made him exceeding glad with thy countenance.
>
> Proverbs 19:12 The king's wrath is as the roaring of a lion; but his favour is as dew upon the grass.
>
> Acts 2:28 Thou hast made known to me the ways of life; thou shalt make me full of joy with thy countenance.

Proverbs 16:16 How much better is it to get wisdom than gold! and to get understanding rather to be chosen than silver!

Focus: This proverb names something better to have than wealth.

It is of inestimably more value to obtain **"wisdom"** than wealth as represented in this verse by **"silver"** and **"gold."** Precious metals are valuable, tangible items that can be used to purchase necessities and niceties of life. At the same time, **"wisdom"** is an attribute that can enhance every aspect of life, *including* the ability to accumulate wealth. Wisdom is like a great river, while gold might be considered a tributary. **"Understanding"** *["the power of distinguishing right from wrong and truth from falsehood* [375]*]* is closely related to and part of wisdom. Wisdom, knowledge, and understanding are often found together in Scripture and are used together to *embody a whole godly way of reasoning.* One term is often substituted for the other. All three provide a person with the *unlimited ability to enjoy God and every aspect of His creation.* Precious metals, on the other hand, have limited value.

> Proverbs 2:3-5 Yea, if thou criest after knowledge, and liftest up thy voice for understanding; If thou seekest her as silver, and searchest for her as for hid treasures; Then shalt thou understand the fear of the LORD, and find the knowledge of God.
>
> Proverbs 3:13-15 Happy *is* the man that findeth wisdom, and the man that getteth understanding. For the merchandise of it is better than the merchandise of silver, and the gain thereof than fine gold. She *is* more precious than rubies: and all the things thou canst desire are not to be compared unto her.
>
> Proverbs 4:5-8 Get wisdom, get understanding: forget it not; neither decline from the words of my mouth. Forsake her not, and she shall preserve thee: love her, and she shall keep thee. Wisdom is the principal thing; therefore get wisdom: and with all thy getting get understanding. Exalt her, and she shall promote thee: she shall bring thee to honour, when thou dost embrace her.
>
> Proverbs 8:10-11 Receive my instruction, and not silver; and knowledge rather than choice gold. For wisdom is better than rubies; and all the things that may be desired are not to be compared to it.
>
> Proverbs 8:19 My fruit is better than gold, yea, than fine gold; and my revenue than choice silver.
>
> Proverbs 23:23 Buy the truth, and sell it not; also wisdom, and instruction, and understanding.
>
> 1 Corinthians 1:24 But unto them which are called, both Jews and Greeks, Christ the power of God, and the wisdom of God.
>
> Philippians 3:7-8 But what things were gain to me, those I counted loss for Christ. Yea doubtless, and I count all things but loss for the excellency of the knowledge of Christ Jesus my Lord: for whom I have suffered the loss of all things, and do count them but dung, that I may win Christ…

Proverbs 16:17 The highway of the upright *is* to depart from evil: he that keepeth his way preserveth his soul.

Focus: This proverb declares that the way of the righteous is a separate way from evil and that the guarding of that way has a great reward.

The **"highway of the upright"** *[the righteous, just]* is a figure of speech for the way in which the righteous live by God's precepts. A person will enjoy a walk with God when he ***departs from evil***, follows God's commandments, loves the things He loves, and hates the things He hates. To maintain this privileged pathway, one has to protect, guard, and preserve his godly lifestyle and consequently himself against evil. Staying on the **"highway"** with God is staying on "the way of holiness" (Isaiah 35:8) and is the way of spiritual safety and preservation. Today, embarking on that highway requires salvation through belief in Jesus.

To **"depart from evil"** is "an abomination to fools" (Proverbs 13:19), but it is the beloved way of the wise. When he departs from evil by choosing the narrow way and walking in the "fear of the LORD" (Proverbs 3:7, 16:6) ; God ***preserves his soul*** from unnecessary trouble, evil people, and His displeasure.

> Psalm 119:1-3   ALEPH. Blessed are the undefiled in the way, who walk in the law of the LORD. Blessed are they that keep his testimonies, and that seek him with the whole heart. They also do no iniquity: they walk in his ways.
>
> Job 28:28   And unto man he said, Behold, the fear of the Lord, that is wisdom; and to depart from evil is understanding.
>
> Proverbs 2:11-20   Discretion shall preserve thee, understanding shall keep thee: To deliver thee from the way of the evil *man,* from the man that speaketh froward things; Who leave the paths of uprightness, to walk in the ways of darkness; Who rejoice to do evil, *and* delight in the frowardness of the wicked; Whose ways *are* crooked, and *they* froward in their paths: To deliver thee from the strange woman, *even* from the stranger *which* flattereth with her words; Which forsaketh the guide of her youth, and forgetteth the covenant of her God. For her house inclineth unto death, and her paths unto the dead. None that go unto her return again, neither take they hold of the paths of life. That thou mayest walk in the way of good *men,* and keep the paths of the righteous.
>
> Proverbs 3:6-7   In all thy ways acknowledge him, and he shall direct thy paths. Be not wise in thine own eyes: fear the LORD, and depart from evil.
>
> Proverbs 4:14-16   Enter not into the path of the wicked, and go not in the way of evil *men.* Avoid it, pass not by it, turn from it, and pass away. For they sleep not, except they have done mischief; and their sleep is taken away, unless they cause *some* to fall.
>
> Proverbs 4:18   But the path of the just *is* as the shining light, that shineth more and more unto the perfect day.
>
> Proverbs 4:23-27   Keep thy heart with all diligence; for out of it are the issues of life. Put away from thee a froward mouth, and perverse lips put far from thee. Let thine eyes look right on, and let thine eyelids look straight before thee. Ponder the path of thy feet, and let all thy ways be established. Turn not to the right hand nor to the left: remove thy foot from evil.
>
> Proverbs 8:13   The fear of the LORD is to hate evil: pride, and arrogancy, and the evil way, and the froward mouth, do I hate.
>
> Proverbs 11:20   They that are of a froward heart are abomination to the LORD: but such as are upright in their way are his delight.
>
> Proverbs 14:2   He that walketh in his uprightness feareth the LORD: but he that is perverse in his ways despiseth him.
>
> Proverbs 14:16   A wise man feareth, and departeth from evil: but the fool rageth, and is confident.
>
> Proverbs 15:19   The way of the slothful man is as an hedge of thorns: but the way of the righteous is made plain.
>
> Proverbs 16:6   By mercy and truth iniquity is purged: and by the fear of the LORD *men* depart from evil.
>
> Proverbs 19:16   He that keepeth the commandment keepeth his own soul; but he that despiseth his ways shall die.
>
> Proverbs 22:5   Thorns and snares are in the way of the froward: he that doth keep his soul shall be far from them.
>
> Isaiah 35:8   And an highway shall be there, and a way, and it shall be called The way of holiness; the unclean shall not pass over it; but it shall be for those: the wayfaring men, though fools, shall not err therein.
>
> Matthew 7:13-14   Enter ye in at the strait gate: for wide *is* the gate, and broad *is* the way, that leadeth to destruction, and many there be which go in thereat: Because strait *is* the gate, and narrow *is* the way, which leadeth unto life, and few there be that find it.
>
> 1 John 2:15-17   Love not the world, neither the things *that are* in the world. If any man love the world, the love of the Father is not in him. For all that *is* in the world, the lust of the flesh, and the lust of the eyes, and the pride of life, is not of the Father, but is of the world. And the world passeth away, and the lust thereof: but he that doeth the will of God abideth for ever.
>
> 1 John 5:18   We know that whosoever is born of God sinneth not; but he that is begotten of God keepeth himself, and that wicked one toucheth him not.

Proverbs 16:18   Pride *goeth* before destruction, and an haughty spirit before a fall.

Focus: This proverb declares pride as a personal characteristic that brings destruction and failure.

The disastrous consequences of pride is the subject of this verse located in the very center of the Book of Proverbs.[376] It is immediately followed by Proverbs 16:19 extolling humility.

"Pride *goeth* before destruction." Pride *[arrogancy, self-exaltation]* tarnishes the way a person thinks and skews his reasoning ability, causing the self-centered one to fall into destructive traps that he might otherwise observe and avoid. Eve is the first and most significant example of destruction by pride. She opposed God for the purpose of elevating herself, thus dragging Adam and mankind into a whirlpool of human disaster. Not being satisfied by living in a beautiful garden and knowing only good, Eve wanted to be as gods (Genesis 3:5), knowing good and evil. Destruction came upon them and their offspring. Pride causes people to eventually ruin themselves, their environment, and their valuable relationships. *(**NOTE**: Eve's prideful words are similar to Satan's words in Isaiah 14:14,* "I will ascend above the heights of the clouds; I will be like the most High."*)*

"And an haughty *[arrogant]* spirit before a fall" repeats the first clause in different words so as to strengthen and support it. Pride produces a spirit of haughtiness that can be seen in a person's walk, word choice, and eyes. This ungodly trait is hated by God as well as by other people, even others full of the same evil. It is insidiously taught constantly on television, radio, in schools, and even in many churches. Pride is the exact opposite of humility taught by the Scriptures.

> "According to Christian teachers, the essential vice, the utmost evil, is Pride. Unchastity, anger, greed, drunkenness, and all that, are mere flea bites in comparison: it was through Pride that the devil became the devil: Pride leads to every other vice: it is the complete anti-God state of mind . . . it is Pride which has been the chief cause of misery in every nation and every family since the world began."[377]

> Esther 6:6 and 7:10 So Haman came in. And the king said unto him, What shall be done unto the man whom the king delighteth to honour? Now Haman thought in his heart, To whom would the king delight to do honour more than to myself? . . . . So they hanged Haman on the gallows that he had prepared for Mordecai. Then was the king's wrath pacified.
> Psalm 12:3 The LORD shall cut off all flattering lips, and the tongue that speaketh proud things . . .
> Psalm 101:5 Whoso privily slandereth his neighbour, him will I cut off: him that hath an high look and a proud heart will not I suffer.
> Proverbs 8:13 The fear of the LORD is to hate evil: pride, and arrogancy, and the evil way, and the froward mouth, do I hate.
> Proverbs 11:2 When pride cometh, then cometh shame: but with the lowly is wisdom.
> Proverbs 17:19 He loveth transgression that loveth strife: *and* he that exalteth his gate seeketh destruction.
> Proverbs 18:12 Before destruction the heart of man is haughty, and before honour is humility.
> Proverbs 29:23 A man's pride shall bring him low: but honour shall uphold the humble in spirit.
> Isaiah 2:11-12 The lofty looks of man shall be humbled, and the haughtiness of men shall be bowed down, and the LORD alone shall be exalted in that day. For the day of the LORD of hosts *shall be* upon every *one that is* proud and lofty, and upon every *one that is* lifted up; and he shall be brought low . . .
> 1 Timothy 3:6 Not a novice, lest being lifted up with pride he fall into the condemnation of the devil.
> James 4:6 But he giveth more grace. Wherefore he saith, God resisteth the proud, but giveth grace unto the humble.
> *[See also Proverbs 15:33, 21:4; Daniel 4:30-31, 5:18-23; Mark 7:20-23; Luke 11:43, 18:10-14; Acts 12:21-23; 1 Corinthians 4:6-7; 2 Timothy 3:1-2; Revelation 18:7]*

Proverbs 16:19 Better *it is to be* of an humble spirit with the lowly, than to divide the spoil with the proud.

Focus: This proverb declares what is better than being proud and having much.

"Better *it is to be* of an humble spirit with the lowly." **"Humble spirit"** refers to a person's attitude that is opposite of being proud. This person is not ashamed to humble himself, nor is he ashamed of association with others of the same spirit. The proud travel on a road of destruction while the humble are protected by God and enjoy His presence. On a practical, observable level, when comparing the humble with the proud, one can observe the following: Humble people are usually contented, cheerful, submissive, joyful, and loving while the proud are self-seeking, discontented, and constantly generating a competitive spirit rather than a compassionate agreeable one. When a person chooses to humble himself before God, he becomes a companion to other humble people; however, the opposite is true of the proud person who resists God and becomes a companion to other arrogant persons.

The last part of the verse, **"to divide the spoil with the proud,"** is given in a condemnatory fashion. **"Spoil"** refers to any booty, illegal gain, or wealth acquired through violence (such as war) or dishonest means (such as robbery). Such dishonesty will not go unpunished. To do without gain obtained through some form of violence and to follow God's commandments will secure the favor of God.

> Exodus 15:9-10 The enemy said, I will pursue, I will overtake, I will divide the spoil; my lust shall be satisfied upon them; I will draw my sword, my hand shall destroy them. Thou didst blow with thy wind, the sea covered them: they sank as lead in the mighty waters.
> Proverbs 18:12 Before destruction the heart of man is haughty, and before honour *is* humility.
> Psalm 34:18 The LORD is nigh unto them that are of a broken heart; and saveth such as be of a contrite spirit.
> Psalm 84:10 For a day in thy courts is better than a thousand. I had rather be a doorkeeper in the house of my God, than to dwell in the tents of wickedness.
> Psalm 138:6 Though the LORD be high, yet hath he respect unto the lowly: but the proud he knoweth afar off.

Proverbs 1:10-19 My son, if sinners entice thee, consent thou not. If they say, Come with us, let us lay wait for blood, let us lurk privily for the innocent without cause: Let us swallow them up alive as the grave; and whole, as those that go down into the pit: We shall find all precious substance, we shall fill our houses with spoil: Cast in thy lot among us; let us all have one purse: My son, walk not thou in the way with them; refrain thy foot from their path: For their feet run to evil, and make haste to shed blood. Surely in vain the net is spread in the sight of any bird. And they lay wait for their own blood; they lurk privily for their own lives. So are the ways of every one that is greedy of gain; which taketh away the life of the owners thereof.

Proverbs 15:25 The LORD will destroy the house of the proud: but he will establish the border of the widow.

Proverbs 16:5 Every one that is proud in heart is an abomination to the LORD: though hand join in hand, he shall not be unpunished.

Proverbs 16:8 Better is a little with righteousness than great revenues without right.

Isaiah 57:15 For thus saith the high and lofty One that inhabiteth eternity, whose name is Holy; I dwell in the high and holy place, with him also that is of a contrite and humble spirit, to revive the spirit of the humble, and to revive the heart of the contrite ones.

James 4:6 But he giveth more grace. Wherefore he saith, God resisteth the proud, but giveth grace unto the humble.

1 Peter 5:5 Likewise, ye younger, submit yourselves unto the elder. Yea, all of you be subject one to another, and be clothed with humility: for God resisteth the proud, and giveth grace to the humble.

Proverbs 16:20 He that handleth a matter wisely shall find good: and whoso trusteth in the LORD, happy *is* he.

Focus: This proverb declares the results of wisely handling matters and trusting in the LORD.

Wisdom teaches how to best deal with the issues of life so that problems handled wisely turn out to the **"good,"** and **trusting God** teaches us to be **"happy"** waiting on Him. Exemplifying full trust in God, the wise person seeks to know everything that God can teach him so that he becomes wise. Consequently, he will be led to places and people who are good and will learn how to use words properly, to treat people right, to conduct business in an honorable manner, and to avoid certain people while making friends with others. The wise person has insight, intuitiveness, and specific instructions from God about matters that the foolish person never understands or accepts.

Being wise and trusting in God brings good as well as happiness. "Two things are needed for the success of a matter – wisdom and faith. One teaches us what to do for ourselves, the other what to expect from God."[378]

> *"...He that handles a matter wisely (that is master of his trade and makes it to appear he understands what he undertakes, that is considerate in his affairs, and, when he speaks or writes on any subject, does it pertinently) shall find good,* shall come into good repute, and perhaps may make a good hand of it. But it is piety only that will secure men's true happiness: Those that *handle a matter wisely,* if they are proud and lean to their own understanding, though they may find some good, yet they will have no great satisfaction in it; but he that *trusts in the Lord,* and not in his own wisdom, *happy is he,* and shall speed better at last."[379]

Genesis 41:38-40 And Pharaoh said unto his servants, Can we find such a one as this is, a man in whom the Spirit of God is? And Pharaoh said unto Joseph, Forasmuch as God hath shewed thee all this, there is none so discreet and wise as thou art: Thou shalt be over my house, and according unto thy word shall all my people be ruled: only in the throne will I be greater than thou.

Psalm 2:12 Kiss the Son, lest he be angry, and ye perish from the way, when his wrath is kindled but a little. Blessed are all they that put their trust in him.

Proverbs 3:5-6 Trust in the LORD with all thine heart; and lean not unto thine own understanding. In all thy ways acknowledge him, and he shall direct thy paths.

Proverbs 19:8 He that getteth wisdom loveth his own soul: he that keepeth understanding shall find good.

Jeremiah 17:7-8 Blessed is the man that trusteth in the LORD, and whose hope the LORD is. For he shall be as a tree planted by the waters, and that spreadeth out her roots by the river, and shall not see when heat cometh, but her leaf shall be green; and shall not be careful in the year of drought, neither shall cease from yielding fruit.

Daniel 1:19-21 And the king communed with them; and among them all was found none like Daniel, Hananiah, Mishael, and Azariah: therefore stood they before the king. And in all matters of wisdom and understanding, that the king enquired of them, he found them ten times better than all the magicians and astrologers that were in all his realm. And Daniel continued even unto the first year of king Cyrus.

Acts 6:1-7 And in those days, when the number of the disciples was multiplied, there arose a murmuring of the Grecians against the Hebrews, because their widows were neglected in the daily ministration. Then the twelve called the multitude of the disciples unto them, and said, It is not reason that we should leave the word of God, and serve tables. Wherefore, brethren, look ye out among you seven men of honest report, full of the Holy Ghost and wisdom, whom we may appoint over this business. But we will give ourselves continually to prayer, and to the ministry of the word. And the saying pleased the whole multitude: and they chose Stephen, a man full of faith and of the Holy Ghost, and Philip, and Prochorus, and Nicanor, and Timon, and Parmenas, and Nicolas a proselyte of Antioch: Whom they set before the apostles: and when they had prayed, they laid their hands on them. And the word of God increased; and the number of the disciples multiplied in Jerusalem greatly; and a great company of the priests were obedient to the faith.

> **Proverbs 16:21** The wise in heart shall be called prudent: and the sweetness of the lips increaseth learning.

Focus: This proverb labels the person who is wise in heart and declares the result of his pleasant, proper speech in teaching others.

"The wise in heart" results from a changed heart rather than just advanced knowledge. These are under the influence of sound principles and know how to "order their affairs with discretion."[380] They have learned to listen and receive instruction and have trained themselves to be sensitive to the Holy Spirit, Scriptures, and wise counselors. They are astute to flee from gossip, flattery, evil speaking, and verbose, senseless-speaking people.

> NOTE: "Wise in heart" appears three times in Proverbs and is translated in seven Old Testament verses as "wise-hearted." These people conduct their lives with wisdom and help others learn more. In Proverbs 10:8, the "wise in heart" are said to "receive commandments." In Proverbs 11:29, "The fool shall be servant to the wise of heart." In 16:23, "the heart of the wise teaches his mouth."

"The wise in heart" are identified as **"prudent"** because they wisely choose their words, associations and actions so as to avoid repercussions from evil. *[Prudent means discerning, understanding, discreet.]* They have understanding of the challenges of life being able to perceive the difference between right and wrong and also between that which is true and that which is false. They have been trained according to God's standards so that they can make good choices.

"The sweetness of the lips" is a figure of speech for speaking in a pleasant manner. People recognize one who is **"wise in heart"** because he has learned to speak in a manner that edifies and is interesting and challenging. His listeners will desire to learn from him, and he will learn more as he studies to answer properly. The wise person thinks about what he is going to say as well as about his tone of voice. This type of controlled wise speech promotes and **"increases learning"** through proper communications whereas harsh words break down communications impeding the learning process. The **"sweetness of lips"** is described as:

> "... a flowing easy style; can clothe their thoughts with proper words, and convey their ideas in clear expressions, in a very edifying and instructive manner: these communicate knowledge to others, and increase it in themselves: for, while they are improving others, they improve themselves and learning also, whether it be divine or human; these are such who are 'apt to teach' (1 Timothy 3:2); and if they have proper hearers to attend them, they will 'increase in learning' (Proverbs 9:9) as a just man does."[381]

> Psalm 45:2 Thou art fairer than the children of men: grace is poured into thy lips: therefore God hath blessed thee for ever.
>
> Proverbs 9:9 Give instruction to a wise man, and he will be yet wiser: teach a just man, and he will increase in learning.
>
> Proverbs 15:1-2 A soft answer turneth away wrath: but grievous words stir up anger. The tongue of the wise useth knowledge aright: but the mouth of fools poureth out foolishness.
>
> Proverbs 15:7 The lips of the wise disperse knowledge: but the heart of the foolish doeth not so.
>
> Proverbs 16:23-24 The heart of the wise teacheth his mouth, and addeth learning to his lips. Pleasant words are as an honeycomb, sweet to the soul, and health to the bones.
>
> Ecclesiastes 12:10-11 The preacher sought to find out acceptable words: and that which was written was upright, even words of truth. The words of the wise are as goads, and as nails fastened by the masters of assemblies, which are given from one shepherd.
>
> Isaiah 50:4 The Lord GOD hath given me the tongue of the learned, that I should know how to speak a word in season to him that is weary: he wakeneth morning by morning, he wakeneth mine ear to hear as the learned.
>
> Hosea 14:9 Who is wise, and he shall understand these things? prudent, and he shall know them? for the ways of the LORD are right, and the just shall walk in them: but the transgressors shall fall therein.
>
> Matthew 12:34 O generation of vipers, how can ye, being evil, speak good things? for out of the abundance of the heart the mouth speaketh.
>
> Luke 4:22 And all bare him witness, and wondered at the gracious words which proceeded out of his mouth. And they said, Is not this Joseph's son?
>
> John 7:46 The officers answered, Never man spake like this man.
>
> 1 Corinthians 2:1-5 And I, brethren, when I came to you, came not with excellency of speech or of wisdom, declaring unto you the testimony of God. For I determined not to know any thing among you, save Jesus Christ, and him crucified. And I was with you in weakness, and in fear, and in much trembling. And my speech and my preaching was not with enticing words of man's wisdom, but in demonstration of the Spirit and of power: That your faith should not stand in the wisdom of men, but in the power of God.
>
> James 3:17 But the wisdom that is from above is first pure, then peaceable, gentle, and easy to be intreated, full of mercy and good fruits, without partiality, and without hypocrisy.

> **Proverbs 16:22** Understanding is a wellspring of life unto him that hath it: but the instruction of fools is folly.

Focus: This proverb contrasts the value that a wise person's understanding has to himself with the worthlessness that a fool's folly has to himself.

A wise person (a person of **"understanding"**) produces a **"wellspring** *[figuratively, a source]* **of life"** for himself. In the Book of Proverbs, **"understanding,"** alongwith knowledge and wisdom, is that which comes from God causing a person to be able to discern between right and wrong, good and bad, proper and improper. The person with understanding helps himself by making good judgments based on a deep desire to please God. When he shares his understanding *(of God and His wisdom)* with others, he becomes a source of life for God to them.

Conversely, the fool can only draw foolishness out of his heart because that is what he has insisted on putting there. He just keeps on instructing himself and others (should they listen) with folly because he has poisoned his thought process. "His own folly is the scourge which punishes him; refusing the teaching of wisdom, he makes misery for himself, deprives himself of the happiness which virtue gives, and pierces himself through with many sorrows."[382]

> Job 11:12 For vain man would be wise, though man be born like a wild ass's colt.
> Proverbs 1:7 The fear of the LORD is the beginning of knowledge: but fools despise wisdom and instruction.
> Proverbs 10:11 The mouth of a righteous man is a well of life: but violence covereth the mouth of the wicked.
> Proverbs 13:13-15 Whoso despiseth the word shall be destroyed: but he that feareth the commandment shall be rewarded. The law of the wise is a fountain of life, to depart from the snares of death. Good understanding giveth favour: but the way of transgressors is hard.
> Proverbs 14:27 The fear of the LORD is a fountain of life, to depart from the snares of death.
> Proverbs 15:2 The tongue of the wise useth knowledge aright: but the mouth of fools poureth out foolishness.
> Proverbs 15:14 The heart of him that hath understanding seeketh knowledge: but the mouth of fools feedeth on foolishness.
> Proverbs 15:28 The heart of the righteous studieth to answer: but the mouth of the wicked poureth out evil things.
> Proverbs 18:4 The words of a man's mouth are as deep waters, and the wellspring of wisdom as a flowing brook.
> Matthew 15:14 Let them alone: they be blind leaders of the blind. And if the blind lead the blind, both shall fall into the ditch.
> John 4:14 But whosoever drinketh of the water that I shall give him shall never thirst; but the water that I shall give him shall be in him a well of water springing up into everlasting life.
> John 6:68 Then Simon Peter answered him, Lord, to whom shall we go? thou hast the words of eternal life.

> **Proverbs 16:23** The heart of the wise teacheth his mouth, and addeth learning to his lips.

Focus: This proverb declares that wisdom within a person's heart generates wise verbal communication.

"Teacheth his mouth" is an interesting figurative way of saying that the wise person patiently and painstakingly trains himself to carefully choose his words. Discipline and patience are his common characteristics. **"Addeth learning to his lips"** means that because the wise person studies to answer every situation properly, he is constantly learning from the process and is teaching himself, as well as those who observe and listen. "His wisdom and learning do not remain hidden in his heart, but continually rise to his lips, like the waters of an ever flowing fountain, for the instruction of others."[383]

> Psalm 37:30-31 The mouth of the righteous speaketh wisdom, and his tongue talketh of judgment. The law of his God is in his heart; none of his steps shall slide.
> Proverbs 15:2 The tongue of the wise useth knowledge aright: but the mouth of fools poureth out foolishness.
> Proverbs 15:28 The heart of the righteous studieth to answer: but the mouth of the wicked poureth out evil things.
> Proverbs 22:17-18 Bow down thine ear, and hear the words of the wise, and apply thine heart unto my knowledge. For it is a pleasant thing if thou keep them within thee; they shall withal be fitted in thy lips.
> Matthew 12:34-37 O generation of vipers, how can ye, being evil, speak good things? for out of the abundance of the heart the mouth speaketh. A good man out of the good treasure of the heart bringeth forth good things: and an evil man out of the evil treasure bringeth forth evil things. But I say unto you, That every idle word that men shall speak, they shall give account thereof in the day of judgment. For by thy words thou shalt be justified, and by thy words thou shalt be condemned.

> **Proverbs 16:24** Pleasant words *are as* an honeycomb, sweet to the soul, and health to the bones.

Focus: This proverb compares the delightful and healthy qualities of a honeycomb to pleasant words.

Words that are **"pleasant"** *[delightful, kind, agreeable]* are words that encourage, calm, counsel, praise, and otherwise uplift the hearer. These **"sweet"** words potentially cause the listener to feel better emotionally and physically by causing his heart and soul to become peaceful. In turn, peace drives away the fear, anxiety, and anguish that are damaging to good health and a hindrance to making good decisions. When David was running from Saul, Jonathan strengthened David's "hand in God" with his pleasant words.

> 1 Samuel 23:15-17 And David saw that Saul was come out to seek his life: and David was in the wilderness of Ziph in a wood. And Jonathan Saul's son arose, and went to David into the wood, and strengthened his hand in God. And he said unto him, Fear not: for the hand of Saul my father shall not find thee; and thou shalt be king over Israel, and I shall be next unto thee; and that also Saul my father knoweth.

The ancient Israelites who prized honey as a luxurious sweetener also used it on account of its medicinal qualities. Science has proven its worth as a wound dressing and as a cough suppressant. Notice how the honey revived Jonathan.

> 1 Samuel 14:24-27 And the men of Israel were distressed that day: for Saul had adjured the people, saying, Cursed be the man that eateth any food until evening, that I may be avenged on mine enemies. So none of the people tasted any food. And all they of the land came to a wood; and there was honey upon the ground. And when the people were come into the wood, behold, the honey dropped; but no man put his hand to his mouth: for the people feared the oath. But Jonathan heard not when his father charged the people with the oath: wherefore he put forth the end of the rod that was in his hand, and dipped it in an honeycomb, and put his hand to his mouth; and his eyes were enlightened.

"Honey took its place not only among the luxuries, but among the medicines of the Israelites. This two-fold use made it all the more suitable to be an emblem both of the true Wisdom which is also true obedience, and of the "pleasant words" in which that Wisdom speaks."[384]

Pleasant words enable counseling during both perilous and good times. Like Solomon, the wise person today studies to know God's word. It directs Him in every aspect of life, especially with verbal communication.

"They (words of God) are wholesome. Many things are pleasant that are not profitable, but these pleasant words are health to the bones, to the inward man, as well as sweet to the soul. They make the bones, which sin has broken and put out of joint, to rejoice. The bones are the strength of the body; and the good word of God is a means of spiritual strength, curing the diseases that weaken us."[385]

> Psalm 19:9-11 The fear of the LORD is clean, enduring for ever: the judgments of the LORD are true and righteous altogether. More to be desired are they than gold, yea, than much fine gold: sweeter also than honey and the honeycomb. Moreover by them is thy servant warned: and in keeping of them there is great reward.
>
> Psalm 119:102-104 I have not departed from thy judgments: for thou hast taught me. How sweet are thy words unto my taste! yea, sweeter than honey to my mouth! Through thy precepts I get understanding: therefore I hate every false way.
>
> Proverbs 3:7-8 Be not wise in thine own eyes: fear the LORD, and depart from evil. It shall be health to thy navel, and marrow to thy bones.
>
> Proverbs 4:20-22 My son, attend to my words; incline thine ear unto my sayings. Let them not depart from thine eyes; keep them in the midst of thine heart. For they are life unto those that find them, and health to all their flesh.
>
> Proverbs 12:18 There is that speaketh like the piercings of a sword: but the tongue of the wise is health.
>
> Proverbs 15:23 A man hath joy by the answer of his mouth: and a word spoken in due season, how good is it!
>
> Proverbs 15:26 The thoughts of the wicked are an abomination to the LORD: but the words of the pure are pleasant words.
>
> Proverbs 24:13-14 My son, eat thou honey, because it is good; and the honeycomb, which is sweet to thy taste: So shall the knowledge of wisdom be unto thy soul: when thou hast found it, then there shall be a reward, and thy expectation shall not be cut off.
>
> Proverbs 27:9 Ointment and perfume rejoice the heart: so doth the sweetness of a man's friend by hearty counsel.

> **Proverbs 16:25**. There is a way that seemeth right unto a man, but the end thereof are the ways of death.

Focus: This proverb declares that the man's human reasoning can misguide him.

"There is a way that seemeth right unto a man." People have different criteria for determining right and wrong, such as laws of the land, peer pressure, family values, or simply their own personal desires. They can be deceived into thinking something or some action is right simply because they want that thing or action, more than they want the truth. Coveting has led many into disaster because they believed that acquiring that object (or person) had to be *right* just because the *desire* was so strong. All of the various criteria for right and wrong mentioned above may be contrary to the ultimate authority which is God's word; and if so, the end result is likely to be disaster. (See Scriptures below.)

Once a person becomes comfortable on a path of error, other pathways for doing wrong (which seem to be right) present themselves. The natural man, the one who doesn't know God, believes strongly that he is right, and others who believe in following the dictates of Scripture are wrong. (Proverbs 14:12 is the same as this proverb except the word "that" is substituted for the word "which.")

> "The rightness is present only as a phantom, for it arises wholly from a terrible self-deception; the man judges falsely and goes astray when, without regard to God and His word, he follows only his own opinions."[386]

> "This verse is a warning against following a perverted or uninstructed conscience. Conscience needs to be informed by God's Word and ruled by God's will to make it a safe guide. When properly regulated, it is able to pronounce a verdict upon contemplated action, and its verdict must always he obeyed. But warped by prejudice, weakened by disuse and disobedience, judicially blinded in punishment and in consequence of sin, it loses all power of moral judgment, and becomes inoperative of good; and then, as to the way that seemed at the moment right, the end thereof are the ways of death."[387]

> Psalm 1:6 For the LORD knoweth the way of the righteous: but the way of the ungodly shall perish.

> Proverbs 3:5-6 Trust in the LORD with all thine heart; and lean not unto thine own understanding. In all thy ways acknowledge him, and he shall direct thy paths.

> Proverbs 5:3-5 For the lips of a strange woman drop as an honeycomb, and her mouth is smoother than oil: But her end is bitter as wormwood, sharp as a twoedged sword. Her feet go down to death; her steps take hold on hell.

> Proverbs 12:15 The way of a fool is right in his own eyes: but he that hearkeneth unto counsel is wise.

> Proverbs 30:12 There is a generation that are pure in their own eyes, and yet is not washed from their filthiness.

> Matthew 7:13-14 Enter ye in at the strait gate: for wide is the gate, and broad is the way, that leadeth to destruction, and many there be which go in thereat: Because strait is the gate, and narrow *is* the way, which leadeth unto life, and few there be that find it.

> Romans 1:28, 32 And even as they did not like to retain God in their knowledge, God gave them over to a reprobate mind, to do those things which are not convenient . . . Who knowing the judgment of God, that they which commit such things are worthy of death, not only do the same, but have pleasure in them that do them.

> 1 Corinthians 2:14 But the natural man receiveth not the things of the Spirit of God: for they are foolishness unto him: neither can he know *them,* because they are spiritually discerned.

The **"way which seemeth right"** may be centered in false views of religion:

> "...he may have an imperfect repentance, a false faith, a very false creed; and he may persuade himself that he is in the direct way to heaven. Many of the papists, when they were burning the saints of God in the flames at Smithfield, thought they were doing God service! And in the late Irish massacre, the more of the Protestants they piked to death, shot, or burnt, the more they believed they deserved of God's favor and their Church's gratitude. But cruelty and murder are the short road, the near way, to eternal perdition."[388]

Proverbs 16:26 He that laboureth laboureth for himself; for his mouth craveth it of him.

Focus: This proverb identifies the beneficiary of and the motivation for personal labor.

Even though a man is working for another person and drawing a wage, he is actually laboring for himself in order to buy food to satisfy that ***craving of his mouth***. Without hunger, a lazy man would sit down and not work another day. Hunger is an alarm that triggers the brain to either provide nourishment for the body or suffer starvation. "**Hunger** can motivate people, sometimes even lazy people, to work so that they can buy food with their wages. This verse has an interesting wordplay: though a person works as a laborer for someone else, his **appetite** is "working" for himself."[389]

> Ecclesiastes 6:7 All the labour of man is for his mouth, and yet the appetite is not filled.

> 2 Thessalonians 3:8-12 Neither did we eat any man's bread for nought; but wrought with labour and travail night and day, that we might not be chargeable to any of you: Not because we have not power, but to make ourselves an ensample unto you to follow us. For even when we were with you, this we commanded you, that if any would not work, neither should he eat. For we hear that there are some which walk among you disorderly, working not at all, but are busybodies. Now them that are such we command and exhort by our Lord Jesus Christ, that with quietness they work, and eat their own bread.

Scriptures speak of both physical and spiritual hunger. Although one is eternal while the other is only temporal, the absence of spiritual food is just as lethal to the well-being of the believer as is the lack of the physical. "Hunger of some kind is the spring of all hearty labour. Without that a man would sit down and take his ease. So also, unless there is hunger in the soul, craving to be fed, there can be no labor after righteousness and wisdom."[390]

> Matthew 5:6 Blessed are they which do hunger and thirst after righteousness: for they shall be filled.
>
> John 6:58 This is that bread which came down from heaven: not as your fathers did eat manna, and are dead: he that eateth of this bread shall live for ever.

Proverbs 16:27-30 An ungodly man diggeth up evil: and in his lips *there is* as a burning fire.
28. A froward man soweth strife: and a whisperer separateth chief friends.
29. A violent man enticeth his neighbour, and leadeth him into the way *that is* not good.
30. He shutteth his eyes to devise froward things: moving his lips he bringeth evil to pass.

In these four verses is a brief, sharp description of an **"ungodly man"** (a man of Belial). Scripture presents this wicked man as froward, a whisperer, and violent. He is a person who digs up evil so he can broadcast it in a damaging manner, who meditates on how to do wickedness, and one who uses his lips to further his damage.

"An ungodly man diggeth up evil: and in his lips there is as a burning fire." (verse 27)

> Focus: This proverb describes the wicked determined effort and the destructive effects of an ungodly man.

"An ungodly man" *[a worthless, wicked, lawless, base fellow]* draws shameful comments from people by asking questions, listening to private conversations, and sneaking into places uninvited. He is trying to discover something evil that can be spread with his wicked lips that are set on fire of hell. In other words, he ***digs up evil.***

Using another metaphor, the second part of verse 27 compares the words the ungodly person speaks to a conflagration that burns and injures another – **"in his lips there is a burning fire."** He sows discord, starts arguments, betrays trust, and lures weaker men into his traps. Perhaps most of all, he delights in seeing the righteous fall. James 3:5-6 and Proverbs 26:18-25 *(See below.)* describe the fire that can be lit from the words of an ungodly man.

> Psalm 52:1-4 To the chief Musician, Maschil, A Psalm of David, when Doeg the Edomite came and told Saul, and said unto him, David is come to the house of Ahimelech. Why boastest thou thyself in mischief, O mighty man? the goodness of God endureth continually. Thy tongue deviseth mischiefs; like a sharp razor, working deceitfully. Thou lovest evil more than good; and lying rather than to speak righteousness. Selah. Thou lovest all devouring words, O thou deceitful tongue.
>
> Psalm 57:4 My soul is among lions: and I lie even among them that are set on fire, even the sons of men, whose teeth are spears and arrows, and their tongue a sharp sword.
>
> Proverbs 4:14-17 Enter not into the path of the wicked, and go not in the way of evil men. Avoid it, pass not by it, turn from it, and pass away. For they sleep not, except they have done mischief; and their sleep is taken away, unless they cause some to fall. For they eat the bread of wickedness, and drink the wine of violence.
>
> Proverbs 6:12-14 A naughty person, a wicked man, walketh with a froward mouth. He winketh with his eyes, he speaketh with his feet, he teacheth with his fingers; Frowardness is in his heart, he deviseth mischief continually; he soweth discord.
>
> Proverbs 26:18-25 As a mad man who casteth firebrands, arrows, and death, So is the man that deceiveth his neighbour, and saith, Am not I in sport? Where no wood is, there the fire goeth out: so where there is no talebearer, the strife ceaseth. As coals are to burning coals, and wood to fire; so is a contentious man to kindle strife. The words of a talebearer are as wounds, and they go down into the innermost parts of the belly. Burning lips and a wicked heart are like a potsherd covered with silver dross. He that hateth dissembleth with his lips, and layeth up deceit within him; When he speaketh fair, believe him not: for there are seven abominations in his heart.
>
> Isaiah 32:6-7 For the vile person will speak villany, and his heart will work iniquity, to practise hypocrisy, and to utter error against the LORD, to make empty the soul of the hungry, and he will cause the drink of the thirsty to fail. The instruments also of the churl are evil: he deviseth wicked devices to destroy the poor with lying words, even when the needy speaketh right.
>
> Romans 3:10-18 As it is written, There is none righteous, no, not one: There is none that understandeth, there is none that seeketh after God. They are all gone out of the way, they are together become unprofitable; there is none that doeth good, no, not one. Their throat is an open sepulchre; with their tongues they have used deceit; the poison of asps is under their lips: Whose mouth is full of cursing and bitterness: Their feet are swift to shed blood: Destruction and misery are in their ways: And the way of peace have they not known: There is no fear of God before their eyes.

James 3:5-6 Even so the tongue is a little member, and boasteth great things. Behold, how great a matter a little fire kindleth! And the tongue is a fire, a world of iniquity: so is the tongue among our members, that it defileth the whole body, and setteth on fire the course of nature; and it is set on fire of hell.

"A froward man soweth strife: and a whisperer separateth chief friends." (verse 28)

Focus: This proverb names two wicked works of the evil, ungodly person's tongue.

"A froward man soweth strife." "Froward" *[NOT forward]* means habitually disposed to disobedience and opposition. The evil man who is froward in his speaking is opposed to what is right – to justice, judgment, and equity. He is likely to call what is good "evil" and what is evil "good." He is diametrically opposed to the word of God and the God of the word. Notice what God says about the froward:

Deuteronomy 32:20 And he said, I will hide my face from them, I will see what their end shall be: for they are a very froward generation, children in whom is no faith.

"And a whisperer *[backbiter, slanderer, talebearer]* **separateth chief friends."** Being froward to his core, he is habitually disposed to opposing God and godliness. He is driven to cause a much damage and ill will between people as possible. He is evil. Through infiltration, he goes about dividing families, work associates, and church members. Because he is a sneaky whisperer, a slanderer, and a talebearer, he causes strife by telling things that he should not, thereby pitting one person against another and causing close friendships to cease. He **pretends** to be a friend by telling secrets, but he is actually an enemy.

Leviticus 19:16 Thou shalt not go up and down as a talebearer among thy people: neither shalt thou stand against the blood of thy neighbour: I am the LORD.
Psalm 52:2-4 Thy tongue deviseth mischiefs; like a sharp razor, working deceitfully. Thou lovest evil more than good; and lying rather than to speak righteousness. Selah. Thou lovest all devouring words, O thou deceitful tongue.
Proverbs 6:12-14 A naughty person, a wicked man, walketh with a froward mouth. He winketh with his eyes, he speaketh with his feet, he teacheth with his fingers; Frowardness is in his heart, he deviseth mischief continually; he soweth discord.
Proverbs 8:13 The fear of the LORD is to hate evil: pride, and arrogancy, and the evil way, and the froward mouth, do I hate.
Proverbs 10:18 He that hideth hatred with lying lips, and he that uttereth a slander, is a fool.
Proverbs 10:32 The lips of the righteous know what is acceptable: but the mouth of the wicked speaketh frowardness.
Proverbs 17:9 He that covereth a transgression seeketh love; but he that repeateth a matter separateth very friends.
Proverbs 18:8 The words of a talebearer are as wounds, and they go down into the innermost parts of the belly.
Proverbs 26:20 Where no wood is, there the fire goeth out: so where there is no talebearer, the strife ceaseth.
Romans 1:28-32 And even as they did not like to retain God in their knowledge, God gave them over to a reprobate mind, to do those things which are not convenient; Being filled with all unrighteousness, fornication, wickedness, covetousness, maliciousness; full of envy, murder, debate, deceit, malignity; whisperers, Backbiters, haters of God, despiteful, proud, boasters, inventors of evil things, disobedient to parents, Without understanding, covenantbreakers, without natural affection, implacable, unmerciful: Who knowing the judgment of God, that they which commit such things are worthy of death, not only do the same, but have pleasure in them that do them.
James 3:14-16 But if ye have bitter envying and strife in your hearts, glory not, and lie not against the truth. This wisdom descendeth not from above, but is earthly, sensual, devilish. For where envying and strife is, there is confusion and every evil work.

"A violent man enticeth his neighbour, and leadeth him into the way that is not good." (verse 29)

Focus: This proverb describes two uncanny, evil persuasive abilities that a violent man practices with others.

This **"violent man"** is evil, luring, deceptive, froward, conniving, and bent on causing damage to his victim of choice. He has the ability to lead his victims into an evil path as well as the ability to command other wicked persons to fulfill his diabolical plans. He is evil. The character of the violent man is well drawn in Proverbs 1:10-16. *(See below.)*

"Such as (like Satan) do all the mischief they can by force and violence, as roaring lions, and not only by fraud and insinuation, as subtle serpents: They are violent men, that d*o all by rapine [forcible seizure of another's property]* and oppression, that shut their eyes, meditating with the closest intention and application of mind to devise froward things, to contrive how they may do the greatest mischief to their neighbour, to do it effectually and yet securely to themselves; and then moving their lips, giving the word of command to their agents, they bring the evil to pass, and accomplish the wicked device . . . When the wicked plots against the just he gnasheth upon him with his teeth (Psalm 37:12).

Such as (like Satan) do all they can to *entice* and draw in others to join with them in doing mischief, *leading them in a way that is not good,* that is not honest, nor honourable, nor safe, but offensive to God, and which will be in the end pernicious to the sinner. Thus he aims to ruin some in this world by bringing them into trouble, and others in the other world by bringing them into sin."[391]

Job 16:9 He teareth *me* in his wrath, who hateth me: he gnasheth upon me with his teeth; mine enemy sharpeneth his eyes upon me.

Psalm 37:12 The wicked plotteth against the just, and gnasheth upon him with his teeth.

Proverbs 1:10-16 My son, if sinners entice thee, consent thou not. If they say, Come with us, let us lay wait for blood, let us lurk privily for the innocent without cause: Let us swallow them up alive as the grave; and whole, as those that go down into the pit: We shall find all precious substance, we shall fill our houses with spoil: Cast in thy lot among us; let us all have one purse: My son, walk not thou in the way with them; refrain thy foot from their path: For their feet run to evil, and make haste to shed blood.

Proverbs 2:10-15 When wisdom entereth into thine heart, and knowledge is pleasant unto thy soul; Discretion shall preserve thee, understanding shall keep thee: To deliver thee from the way of the evil man, from the man that speaketh froward things; Who leave the paths of uprightness, to walk in the ways of darkness; Who rejoice to do evil, and delight in the frowardness of the wicked; Whose ways are crooked, and they froward in their paths . . .

Acts 20:30 Also of your own selves shall men arise, speaking perverse things, to draw away disciples after them.

"He shutteth his eyes to devise froward things: moving his lips he bringeth evil to pass." (verse 30)

Focus: This proverb pictures the dedication of the *violent man's* evil scheming and delivery.

He *shuts his eyes* so he will not be distracted from making his evil schemes. Even in his bed while other men sleep, he contrives **"froward things"** (ideas and acts in opposition to right). Then he *moves his lips,* engaging conversation or orders to underlings in order to accomplish his ungodliness.

Psalm 36:1-4 To the chief Musician, A Psalm of David the servant of the LORD. The transgression of the wicked saith within my heart, that there is no fear of God before his eyes. For he flattereth himself in his own eyes, until his iniquity be found to be hateful. The words of his mouth are iniquity and deceit: he hath left off to be wise, and to do good. He deviseth mischief upon his bed; he setteth himself in a way that is not good; he abhorreth not evil.

Proverbs 4:14-17 Enter not into the path of the wicked, and go not in the way of evil men. Avoid it, pass not by it, turn from it, and pass away. For they sleep not, except they have done mischief; and their sleep is taken away, unless they cause some to fall.

Proverbs 4:17 For they eat the bread of wickedness, and drink the wine of violence.

Isaiah 32:6-7 For the vile person will speak villany, and his heart will work iniquity, to practise hypocrisy, and to utter error against the LORD, to make empty the soul of the hungry, and he will cause the drink of the thirsty to fail. The instruments also of the churl are evil: he deviseth wicked devices to destroy the poor with lying words, even when the needy speaketh right.

Proverbs 16:31 The hoary head *is* a crown of glory, *if* it be found in the way of righteousness.

Focus: This Proverb describes the condition under which an aged person's gray hair is to be regarded as a crown of glory.

"Hoary [gray hairs of old age] **head "** was, to the Hebrew, ornamental and beautiful because it spoke of gravity, wisdom, and prudence; and the possessor was due reverence and respect *if* he lived his life for God.

Crown of Glory

NOTE: In its first use in Proverbs 4:9, the "Crown of Glory" symbolizes the gift of wisdom given to the believer who chooses to live his life for God.

Proverbs 4:9 She shall give to thine head an ornament of grace: a crown of glory shall she deliver to thee.

A godly woman who lives her life for the Lord is such a blessing that she is considered a **"crown"** to her husband.

Proverbs 12:4 A virtuous woman *is* a crown to her husband: but she that maketh ashamed *is* as rottenness in his bones.

Riches obtained wisely by a believer who has given his life to the service of the Lord is considered a crown and an ornament. To the fool, riches only enhance his foolishness.

Proverbs 14:24 The crown of the wise *is* their riches: *but* the foolishness of fools *is* folly.

It is an honor and crown for grandparents to have grandchildren who are following the Lord. Godly grandchildren advance the reputation of their families.

Proverbs 17:6 Children's children *are* the crown of old men; and the glory of children *are* their fathers.

So, the phrase "crown of glory" represents the honor placed upon those who live their life for God. There is an aura that accompanies them as they represent the Father through their walk in this life.

"The text points out what we must all recognize for an aesthetic truth, that it is the association of age with goodness which makes it (gray or white hair) truly respectable, venerable, beautiful."[392] Sitting on one of older age, with soon-coming feebleness nearing the end of life's journey, the "hoary head," along with a life of righteousness, reflects meaningful beauty to God and other righteous people. However, not all older folks have lived righteously. Neither here nor in eternity will there be a crown or glory or approval from God for a wicked person. Nor is any good to come for him.

> Leviticus 19:32 Thou shalt rise up before the hoary head, and honour the face of the old man, and fear thy God: I am the LORD.
>
> Psalm 71:17-18 O God, thou hast taught me from my youth: and hitherto have I declared thy wondrous works. Now also when I am old and grayheaded, O God, forsake me not; until I have shewed thy strength unto this generation, and thy power to every one that is to come.
>
> Proverbs 4:7-9 Wisdom *is* the principal thing; *therefore* get wisdom: and with all thy getting get understanding. Exalt her, and she shall promote thee: she shall bring thee to honour, when thou dost embrace her. She shall give to thine head an ornament of grace: a crown of glory shall she deliver to thee.
>
> Proverbs 9:10-11 The fear of the LORD is the beginning of wisdom: and the knowledge of the holy is understanding. For by me thy days shall be multiplied, and the years of thy life shall be increased.
>
> Proverbs 10:27 The fear of the LORD prolongeth days: but the years of the wicked shall be shortened.
>
> Proverbs 20:29 The glory of young men is their strength: and the beauty of old men is the gray head.

Proverbs 16:32 *He that is* slow to anger *is* better than the mighty; and he that ruleth his spirit than he that taketh a city.

Focus: This proverb declares that having control of one's spirit is preferred to being a mighty warrior.

Gaining self-control begins with sincere desire. The process is private and humbling, takes relentless effort, seldom receives praise, but has great personal rewards. This conquering of self is better than being a powerful person with great military skills because a person who cannot control his anger will sooner or later have his mind blinded with rage and do very foolish things, thereby undoing all his positive accomplishments. To be slow to anger, as was Jesus, is a desire of the righteous. Controlling one's temperament and submitting to Holy Spirit leadership produces a life that is wisely guarded in word and deed.

> "The careless soul slumbers over a mine of dynamite in the region of its own passions. It needs a supreme effort to quell and curb and rule such a foe."[393]
>
> "A man who loses the balance of a good temper will certainly 'deal foolishly.' We are never at our best when we are angry. Our judgment is disturbed; our mental faculties are disordered; they lose their true proportion. We do not speak as wisely, we do not act as judiciously, as we otherwise should. In all probability, we speak and act with positive folly, in a way which brings regret on our own part and reproach from our neighbour. Very possibly we say and do that which cannot easily, if ever, be undone. We take the bloom off a fair friendship; we plant a root of bitterness which we are not able to pluck up; we start a train of consequences which will run we know not whither."[394]
>
> "To take a city is, in part, to triumph over physical obstacles, over walls and moats and bullets; but he that ruleth his spirit is doing battle with evil tempers and unholy inclinations and unworthy impulses. He is striving 'not against flesh and blood,' but against the mightier enemies that couch and spring on the human soul; he is fighting with far nobler weapons than sword or bayonet or cannon with thought, with spiritual energy, with deep resolve, with strenuous will, with conscience, with prayer. The victory is fought and won on the highest ground, the arena of a human spirit."[395]
>
> "It is much easier to subdue an enemy without than one within. There have been many kings who had conquered nations, and yet were slaves to their own passions. Alexander, who conquered the world, was a slave to intemperate anger, and in a fit of it slew Clytus, the best and most intimate of all his friends, and one whom he loved beyond all others."[396]
>
> Psalm 103:8 The LORD *is* merciful and gracious, slow to anger, and plenteous in mercy.
>
> Proverbs 14:17 He that is soon angry dealeth foolishly: and a man of wicked devices is hated.
>
> Proverbs 14:29 He that is slow to wrath is of great understanding: but he that is hasty of spirit exalteth folly.
>
> Proverbs 15:18 A wrathful man stirreth up strife: but *he that is* slow to anger appeaseth strife.
>
> Proverbs 19:11 The discretion of a man deferreth his anger; and *it is* his glory to pass over a transgression.
>
> Proverbs 25:28 He that hath no rule over his own spirit is like a city that is broken down, and without walls.
>
> Ecclesiastes 7:8-9 Better *is* the end of a thing than the beginning thereof: *and* the patient in spirit *is* better than the proud in spirit. Be not hasty in thy spirit to be angry: for anger resteth in the bosom of fools.

Romans 12:18-21 If it be possible, as much as lieth in you, live peaceably with all men. Dearly beloved, avenge not yourselves, but *rather* give place unto wrath: for it is written, Vengeance *is* mine; I will repay, saith the Lord. Therefore if thine enemy hunger, feed him; if he thirst, give him drink: for in so doing thou shalt heap coals of fire on his head. Be not overcome of evil, but overcome evil with good.

1 Corinthians 9:25-27 And every man that striveth for the mastery is temperate in all things. Now they do it to obtain a corruptible crown; but we an incorruptible. I therefore so run, not as uncertainly; so fight I, not as one that beateth the air: But I keep under my body, and bring it into subjection: lest that by any means, when I have preached to others, I myself should be a castaway.

James 1:19-20 Wherefore, my beloved brethren, let every man be swift to hear, slow to speak, slow to wrath: For the wrath of man worketh not the righteousness of God.

Proverbs 16:33 The lot is cast into the lap; but the whole disposing thereof *is* of the LORD.

Focus: This proverb speaks to the sovereign providence of the Lord.

Scripture specifies instances whereby God made His will known by the casting of lots. Although the practice seems strange to the modern mind, it is clear from this proverb and other Scripture that God has, on occasion, directed the results of cast lots.

"The practice of casting lots occurs most often in connection with the division of the land under Joshua (Joshua 14-21), a procedure that God instructed the Israelites on several times in the book of Numbers (Numbers 26:55, 33:54, 34:13, 36:2). God allowed the Israelites to cast lots in order to determine His will for a given situation (Joshua 18:6-10; 1 Chronicles 24:5,31). Various offices and functions in the temple were also determined by lot (1 Chronicles 24:5, 31; 25:8-9; 26:13-14). The sailors on Jonah's ship (Jonah 1:7) also cast lots to determine who had brought God's wrath upon their ship."[397]

In these specific situations where God directly controlled the process as well as the outcome, the person doing the casting of the lot had no part other than the actual casting of the lot. God determined the outcome. "The whole disposing thereof *is* of the LORD."

"The word "lots" occurs seventy times in the Old Testament and seven in the New Testament. Most of the occurrences were in the early period when little of the Bible was available and when God approved of this means for determining His will." The completion of the written word of God and the ministry of the Holy Spirit caused the use of casting "lots" to cease by Acts 1:26.[398]

Joshua 7:18 And he brought his household man by man; and Achan, the son of Carmi, the son of Zabdi, the son of Zerah, of the tribe of Judah, was taken.

1 Samuel 14:41-42 Therefore Saul said unto the LORD God of Israel, Give a perfect *lot.* And Saul and Jonathan were taken: but the people escaped. And Saul said, Cast *lots* between me and Jonathan my son. And Jonathan was taken.

Proverbs 18:18 The lot causeth contentions to cease, and parteth between the mighty.

Jonah 1:7 And they said every one to his fellow, Come, and let us cast lots, that we may know for whose cause this evil *is* upon us. So they cast lots, and the lot fell upon Jonah.

Christians are to determine the will of God by praying, following directives from Scripture, and being sensitive to leadership from the Holy Spirit; therefore, Christians today have a perpetual and personal interactive leadership from God.

"'We have' at least 'a more sure word of prophecy, whereunto we do well that we take heed, as unto a light that shineth in a dark place.' (2Peter 1:19) The book of God is given us expressly as 'a lamp to our feet, and a light to our path.' (Psalm 119:105) The rule is more clear in itself, and linked with a most encouraging promise – 'In all thy ways acknowledge him, and he shall direct thy paths.' (Proverbs 3:6) It is far better to exercise faith, than indolently to tamper with personal responsibility."[399]

Galatians 5:16-18 *This* I say then, Walk in the Spirit, and ye shall not fulfil the lust of the flesh. For the flesh lusteth against the Spirit, and the Spirit against the flesh: and these are contrary the one to the other: so that ye cannot do the things that ye would. But if ye be led of the Spirit, ye are not under the law.

CHAPTER SEVENTEEN

> **Proverbs 17:1** Better *is* a dry morsel, and quietness therewith, than an house full of sacrifices *with* strife.

Focus: This proverb declares the great value of living in peace without strife.

It is better to have only **"a dry morsel"** *(an insignificant amount of food)* with **"quietness"** than to have **"a house full of sacrifices"** *(an excessive amount of savory meat)* *"with* strife" *(quarreling, contention)*. **"Quietness"** *[peace, security]* pictures the absence of strife and quarreling. Quietness cannot coexist with **"strife,"** which is that ugly manifestation of pride (Proverbs 13:10) that creates upsetting vibrations of unwanted, unnecessary and unpleasant competition. The absence of strife in a home is of more value than an overabundance of the best meat available ("house full of sacrifices"). This text declares that it would be better to have a "dry morsel," a small dry bit of food like a soda cracker or parched corn which is difficult to swallow, than a seemingly unlimited feast, if the home can just be peaceful.

"Sacrifices" refer to the portion of sacrificial meat that was authorized to be taken home and consumed by the worshiper, his family, and friends. Part of the required sacrifice that the worshiper offered to God was burned on the altar at the temple, and a part was given to the priest. The worshiper had a feast on what was left. There was no better meat than that given in sacrifices because it was hand-picked and inspected, thus ensuring that it was flawless and healthy. Ironically this particular offering was called a "peace offering" *(because it promoted peaceful relations with God)*. There can be no peace with God when the offerer is hateful to others.

When reading this proverb, the Hebrew reader would probably have been reminded of the "worthy portion" of the sacrifice given to Hannah by her husband Elkanah in 1 Samuel 1. Scripture states that the worthy portion was specifically provided to Hannah because Elkanah loved her; however, that double portion lost its preciousness because of the "strife" that existed within her house with Elkanah's other wife, Peninnah, who provoked Hannah and made her fret.

> 1 Samuel 1:3-7 And this man *[Elkanah]* went up out of his city yearly to worship and to sacrifice unto the LORD of hosts in Shiloh. And the two sons of Eli, Hophni and Phinehas, the priests of the LORD, were there. And when the time was that Elkanah offered, he gave to Peninnah his wife, and to all her sons and her daughters, portions *[See note below.]*: But unto Hannah he gave a worthy portion; for he loved Hannah: but the LORD had shut up her womb. And her adversary also provoked her sore, for to make her fret, because the LORD had shut up her womb. And *as* he did so year by year, when she went up to the house of the LORD, so she provoked her; therefore she wept, and did not eat.

> *(Note concerning sacrificed portions in 1 Samuel 1:4)* "Portions – Of those parts of the peace-offerings which belonged to the offerer. These were the whole, except the fat, which belonged to the Lord, and the breast and right shoulder, which were due to the priest, Leviticus 7:34; with the rest the sacrificer made a feast for himself, his family, and friends, giving to every one a portion of the sacrifice, as the master of the feast used to do to the guests. And they ate all before the Lord, and hereby were supposed to have communion with him, by partaking with him of his sacrifices, which had been offered to him at his altar."[400]

> Leviticus 7:14-17 And of it he shall offer one out of the whole oblation for an heave offering unto the LORD, and it shall be the priest's that sprinkleth the blood of the peace offerings. And the flesh of the sacrifice of his peace offerings for thanksgiving shall be eaten the same day that it is offered; he shall not leave any of it until the morning. But if the sacrifice of his offering be a vow, or a voluntary offering, it shall be eaten the same day that he offereth his sacrifice: and on the morrow also the remainder of it shall be eaten: But the remainder of the flesh of the sacrifice on the third day shall be burnt with fire.

In the New Testament the love feasts of the early church sometimes was served with strife. *Pulpit Commentary* described the unhappy occurrences. "The joyous family festival often degenerated into excess, which naturally led to quarrels and strife. So the *agapae* of the early Church were desecrated by license and selfishness."[401]

> 1 Corinthians 11:20-22 When ye come together therefore into one place, *this* is not to eat the Lord's supper. For in eating every one taketh before *other* his own supper: and one is hungry, and another is drunken. What? have ye not houses to eat and to drink in? or despise ye the church of God, and shame them that have not? What shall I say to you? shall I praise you in this? I praise *you* not.

"Those that live in contention, that are always jarring and brawling, and reflecting upon one another, though they have plenty of dainties, *a house full of sacrifices,* live uncomfortably; they cannot expect the blessing of God upon them and what they have, nor can they have any true relish of their enjoyments, much less any peace in their own consciences. Love will sweeten a *dry morsel,* but strife will sour and embitter *a house full of sacrifices.* A little of the leaven of malice will leaven all the enjoyments."[402]

Proverbs 17:2   A wise servant shall have rule over a son that causeth shame, and shall have part of the inheritance among the brethren.

Focus: This proverb designates one of the potential, yet unusual, benefits of living wisely regardless of station in life.

In this proverb, **"a wise servant"** is given authority over the shameful, foolish son, and then given priority to the wayward youth's inheritance. **"A son,"** who is called such because of having been born into a family, only has to properly conduct himself before his parents and God to keep his rightful place of inheritance. Unfortunately, *foolishness threatens* such a wonderful opportunity. If the son gives himself to folly, he will proceed through a life of disastrous happenings and, if not born-again, into a Christ-less eternity. In addition, a wise servant may be assigned the unpleasant task of helping to control the foolish son, whose shameful behavior may cause him to be disinherited.

"Wise" refers to the servant's aspect of wisdom involving prudence, circumspection, and understanding. *A son that causes shame* would indicate that he is a disgrace to the family. Some of the ways mentioned in Proverbs that a son can cause shame include: (1) being a scorner (9:7), (2) being lazy especially in harvest (10:5), (3) being proud and haughty (11:2), (4) being full of wrath (12:16) and strife (25:8), (5) being a liar and wicked (13:5), (6) refusing reproof or instruction (13:18), (7) dealing violently with his father and mother (19:26), (8) keeping company with harlots (29:3) or (9) engaging in riotous living (23:20, 28:7). A wise servant, or any wise person, will avoid these behaviors.

One of the advantages of being wise, though only a servant, is that a "wise servant" has the possibility of obtaining a son's part of the inheritance. He also has the potential of bearing a leadership position if the son causes shame by playing the part of a fool. For example, Jeroboam, the son of a servant (1Kings 11:26-28), rose over Solomon's son Rehoboam, who disgraced himself by not listening to the counsel of his late father's older, wiser advisors. Because Rehoboam listened to his foolish peers and followed their hateful advice, Jeroboam became leader of ten of the twelve tribes of Israel. (1 Kings 12 and 2Chronicles 10) Only two tribes remained with Rehoboam.

> 2 Chronicles 10:6-8 And king Rehoboam took counsel with the old men that had stood before Solomon his father while he yet lived, saying, What counsel give ye *me* to return answer to this people? And they spake unto him, saying, If thou be kind to this people, and please them, and speak good words to them, they will be thy servants for ever. But he forsook the counsel which the old men gave him, and took counsel with the young men that were brought up with him, that stood before him.

Eliezer of Damascus, the steward of Abraham's house, diligently and faithfully conducted himself as a servant; and Abraham, impatiently lacking the promised son, stressed to God that the wise servant must be his replacement heir. Afterward, God, Who is always good for His word and always works on His own schedule, gave Abraham a son.

> Genesis 15:2-3 And Abram said, Lord GOD, what wilt thou give me, seeing I go childless, and the steward of my house *is* this Eliezer of Damascus? And Abram said, Behold, to me thou hast given no seed: and, lo, one born in my house is mine heir.
>
> Proverbs 10:5 He that gathereth in summer is a wise son: but he that sleepeth in harvest is a son that causeth shame.
>
> Proverbs 11:29 He that troubleth his own house shall inherit the wind: and the fool shall be servant to the wise of heart.
>
> Proverbs 12:24 The hand of the diligent shall bear rule: but the slothful shall be under tribute.
>
> Proverbs 14:35 The king's favour is toward a wise servant: but his wrath is against him that causeth shame.
>
> Proverbs 19:26 He that wasteth his father, and chaseth away his mother, is a son that causeth shame, and bringeth reproach.
>
> Proverbs 27:18 Whoso keepeth the fig tree shall eat the fruit thereof: so he that waiteth on his master shall be honoured.
>
> Proverbs 29:21 He that delicately bringeth up his servant from a child shall have him become *his* son at the length.

Proverbs 17:3.   The fining pot *is* for silver, and the furnace for gold: but the LORD trieth the hearts.

Focus: This proverb compares purifying of metals with God's proving of the human heart.

"The fining pot *is* for silver, and the furnace for gold" introduces a comparison of separating expensive metals from ores with God's process of purifying a man and making him fit for heaven. High temperatures in the furnace and refining pot or crucible will separate dross from pure metal, such as silver and gold, making obvious which is to be kept and which is to be discarded.

"But the LORD trieth *[to test, especially metals, to prove, to examine]* **the hearts."** God allows trials, pressures, or troubles into the lives of those He loves to cause them to either separate from their sins or else to prove themselves free from specific sins (as He did with Job). Likewise, God's furnace of affliction purges away the contaminants of sin and corruption that have hindered those persons from achieving God's purpose and God's will for their lives. Silver mixed with dross is of little value. Likewise, until the individual's sinful habits and desires are brought to his mind so that he can recognize the evil and deal with it, the person remains in a low or no state of spiritual usefulness. Men may refine the gold and silver, but only God can refine the heart.

> "The gold and the silver ores are thrown into the crucible and placed over the fire, in order that it may be made manifest how much there is of real worth in them, and the human soul is subjected to trials of various kinds by the Great Searcher of hearts, in order that both the good and the evil that is therein may be seen, and the one separated from the other. The proverb seems rather to refer to the *testing*, than to the purifying process."[403]

> "God's process is the application of sorrow, sickness, temptation, that, duly meeting these, the soul may emerge from the trial as pure gold, fit for the Master's use."[404]

Deuteronomy 8:2 And thou shalt remember all the way which the LORD thy God led thee these forty years in the wilderness, to humble thee, and to prove thee, to know what was in thine heart, whether thou wouldest keep his commandments, or no.

Psalm 66:10 For thou, O God, hast proved us: thou hast tried us, as silver is tried.

Proverbs 27:21 As the fining pot for silver, and the furnace for gold; so is a man to his praise.

Isaiah 1:25-26 And I will turn my hand upon thee, and purely purge away thy dross, and take away all thy tin: And I will restore thy judges as at the first, and thy counsellors as at the beginning: afterward thou shalt be called, The city of righteousness, the faithful city.

Jeremiah 17:10 I the LORD search the heart, I try the reins, even to give every man according to his ways, and according to the fruit of his doings.

Zechariah 13:9 And I will bring the third part through the fire, and will refine them as silver is refined, and will try them as gold is tried: they shall call on my name, and I will hear them: I will say, It is my people: and they shall say, The LORD is my God.

1 Corinthians 3:11-15 For other foundation can no man lay than that is laid, which is Jesus Christ. Now if any man build upon this foundation gold, silver, precious stones, wood, hay, stubble; Every man's work shall be made manifest: for the day shall declare it, because it shall be revealed by fire; and the fire shall try every man's work of what sort it is. If any man's work abide which he hath built thereupon, he shall receive a reward. If any man's work shall be burned, he shall suffer loss: but he himself shall be saved; yet so as by fire.

James 1:2-4 My brethren, count it all joy when ye fall into divers temptations; Knowing this, that the trying of your faith worketh patience. But let patience have *her* perfect work, that ye may be perfect and entire, wanting nothing.

Revelation 2:23 And I will kill her children with death; and all the churches shall know that I am he which searcheth the reins and hearts: and I will give unto every one of you according to your works.

> "Wonderful as is the separation of the pure metal from the dross with which it has mingled, there is something yet more wonderful in the divine discipline which purifies the good that lies hid, like a grain of gold, even in rough and common natures, and frees it from all admixture of evil."[405]

Malachi 3:2-3 But who may abide the day of his coming? and who shall stand when he appeareth? for he is like a refiner's fire, and like fullers' soap: And he shall sit as a refiner and purifier of silver: and he shall purify the sons of Levi, and purge them as gold and silver, that they may offer unto the LORD an offering in righteousness.

1 Peter 1:7-9 That the trial of your faith, being much more precious than of gold that perisheth, though it be tried with fire, might be found unto praise and honour and glory at the appearing of Jesus Christ: Whom having not seen, ye love; in whom, though now ye see *him* not, yet believing, ye rejoice with joy unspeakable and full of glory: Receiving the end of your faith, *even* the salvation of *your* souls.

Proverbs 17:4 A wicked doer giveth heed to false lips; *and* a liar giveth ear to a naughty tongue.

Focus: This proverb teaches that wicked people fuel each other's wickedness with their lies.

Nourishing their unholy lives through people like themselves who are also liars, the **"wicked doer"** and the *wicked speaker* desire conversation that will be destructive to others. They are prone to **give heed** or **give ear** to listen and delight in gossip and evil talk that plots wickedness, falsehoods, and slander. *Both the wicked doer and the liar seek the stimulation and encouragement of the other to increase their unholy activities.* Notice how eagerly Ahab listened to the counsels of his wicked wife Jezebel to secure his vineyard.

- 1 Kings 21:3-7 And Naboth said to Ahab, The LORD forbid it me, that I should give the inheritance of my fathers unto thee. And Ahab came into his house heavy and displeased because of the word which Naboth the Jezreelite had spoken to him: for he had said, I will not give thee the inheritance of my fathers. And he laid him down upon his bed, and turned away his face, and would eat no bread. But Jezebel his wife came to him, and said unto him, Why is thy spirit so sad, that thou eatest no bread? And he said unto her, Because I spake unto Naboth the Jezreelite, and said unto him, Give me thy vineyard for money; or else, if it please thee, I will give thee another vineyard for it: and he answered, I will not give thee my vineyard. And Jezebel his wife said unto him, Dost thou now govern the kingdom of Israel? arise, and eat bread, and let thine heart be merry: I will give thee the vineyard of Naboth the Jezreelite.
- Psalm 5:9 For *there is* no faithfulness in their mouth; their inward part *is* very wickedness; their throat *is* an open sepulchre; they flatter with their tongue.
- Psalm 38:12 They also that seek after my life lay snares *for me:* and they that seek my hurt speak mischievous things, and imagine deceits all the day long.
- Psalm 52:2-4 Thy tongue deviseth mischiefs; like a sharp razor, working deceitfully. Thou lovest evil more than good; *and* lying rather than to speak righteousness. Selah. Thou lovest all devouring words, O *thou* deceitful tongue.
- Proverbs 6:12 A naughty person, a wicked man, walketh with a froward mouth.
- Proverbs 28:4 They that forsake the law praise the wicked: but such as keep the law contend with them.
- 2 Timothy 4:3-4 For the time will come when they will not endure sound doctrine; but after their own lusts shall they heap to themselves teachers, having itching ears; And they shall turn away their ears from the truth, and shall be turned unto fables.

Proverbs 17:5 Whoso mocketh the poor reproacheth his Maker: *and* he that is glad at calamities shall not be unpunished.

Focus: This proverb reveals God's attitude toward those who demonstrate foolish arrogance.

Being disrespectful to others is an act of foolish arrogance, whether in the form of **mocking the poor** or *being "glad at calamities."* Only a person who is full of pride and who believes he is better than others would engage in such mistreatment. Neither the mocker of the poor or the one rejoicing at someone else's calamities will go unpunished.

"Whoso mocketh the poor reproacheth his Maker." Mocking the poor reproaches *[taunts, upbraids, defies]* God because it is against His commandments. In addition, all men have the common denominator of being made in the image of God and by God; consequently mocking another because he is poor is equal to discrediting or **reproaching his Maker**.

Being **"glad"** *[rejoicing, making merry]* at **"calamities"** *[misfortunes, distress, disaster]* of others brings judgment from God. A proper response to mankind is to count humanity as a brother or sister and to have compassion on them regardless of their inabilities, difficulties in handling matters of life, or misfortunes. This Scripture specifically states that it is unacceptable with God to be *glad or rejoice when others have calamities.*

"In Proverbs 16:32 we learned of the one who was slow to anger and who ruled his spirit, *[and was]* controlled and thoughtful in all that he did. Now we have described those who reveal the opposite traits. They do not control themselves. They hear and react unwisely. They listen to unrighteous lips and do evil, because they are evildoers. (The righteous man would not have done it). They listen to mischievous gossip and slander, and, with some relish, pass on the lies, thereby revealing themselves as themselves liars. They see a man's poverty and deride him, not realizing that thereby they are reproaching the One Who made him. They see calamity coming on men and are even glad at it, revealing themselves as callous and uncaring. But none of them will be unpunished, for in each case what they are doing is reproaching the One Who made their victims, and the One Who tries the hearts (Proverbs 17:3) will see and will repay."[406]

- Job 31:29-30 If I rejoiced at the destruction of him that hated me, or lifted up myself when evil found him: Neither have I suffered my mouth to sin by wishing a curse to his soul.
- Proverbs 14:31 He that oppresseth the poor reproacheth his Maker: but he that honoureth him hath mercy on the poor.
- Proverbs 24:17-18 Rejoice not when thine enemy falleth, and let not thine heart be glad when he stumbleth: Lest the LORD see it, and it displease him, and he turn away his wrath from him.
- Matthew 25:44-46 Then shall they also answer him, saying, Lord, when saw we thee an hungred, or athirst, or a stranger, or naked, or sick, or in prison, and did not minister unto thee? Then shall he answer them, saying, Verily I say unto you, Inasmuch as ye did it not to one of the least of these, ye did it not to me. And these shall go away into everlasting punishment: but the righteous into life eternal.
- Romans 12:14-21 Bless them which persecute you: bless, and curse not. Rejoice with them that do rejoice, and weep with them that weep. Be of the same mind one toward another. Mind not high things, but condescend to men of low estate. Be not wise in your own conceits. Recompense to no man evil for evil. Provide things honest in the sight of all men. If it be possible, as much as lieth in you, live

peaceably with all men. Dearly beloved, avenge not yourselves, but *rather* give place unto wrath: for it is written, Vengeance *is* mine; I will repay, saith the Lord. Therefore if thine enemy hunger, feed him; if he thirst, give him drink: for in so doing thou shalt heap coals of fire on his head. Be not overcome of evil, but overcome evil with good.

1 Peter 2:17 Honour all men. Love the brotherhood. Fear God. Honour the king.

Proverbs 17:6 Children's children *are* the crown of old men; and the glory of children *are* their fathers.

Focus: This proverb states that children and ancestors are equally proud of each other.

"Children's children *are* the crown of old men." A **"crown"** is an ornament worn to designate honor. The Philippians and the Thessalonians were the Apostle Paul's "joy and crown" because their godly lives were representative of the Christian truths and values that he diligently worked and suffered severely to teach (Philippians 4:1, 1 Thessalonians 2:19). They became sources of energy, encouragement, and reward for his labor. Had their lives been ungodly, they would have been a 'crown of thorns' rather than a crown of honor. In like manner, a person's children and grandchildren have the potential of being a "crown" to him.

"And the glory of children *are* their fathers." **"Glory"** means *[ornament, beauty, splendor]*. During the time of Christ, the Jews were prone to say, "we have Abraham for our father," thus expressing their pride and dignity in having such a godly, ancestor.

> "Children are a blessing from God (Psalm 127 and 128); thus, a family circle consisting of children and grandchildren (including great-grandchildren) is as a crown of glory surrounding the grey-haired patriarch; and again, children have glory and honour in their parents, for to have a man of an honoured name, or of a blessed memory, as a father, is the most effective commendation, and has for the son, even though he is unlike his father, always important and beneficial consequences."[407]

> "Those are unnatural children who reckon their aged parents a burden to them, and think they live too long; whereas, if the children be wise and good, it is as much their honour as can be that thereby they are comforts to their parents in the unpleasant days of their old age."[408]

> Genesis 48:9-11 And Joseph said unto his father, They are my sons, whom God hath given me in this place. And he said, Bring them, I pray thee, unto me, and I will bless them. Now the eyes of Israel were dim for age, so that he could not see. And he brought them near unto him; and he kissed them, and embraced them. And Israel said unto Joseph, I had not thought to see thy face: and, lo, God hath shewed me also thy seed.

> Genesis 50:22-23 And Joseph dwelt in Egypt, he, and his father's house: and Joseph lived an hundred and ten years. And Joseph saw Ephraim's children of the third generation: the children also of Machir the son of Manasseh were brought up upon Joseph's knees.

> Psalm 127:3-5 Lo, children are an heritage of the LORD: and the fruit of the womb is his reward. As arrows are in the hand of a mighty man; so are children of the youth. Happy is the man that hath his quiver full of them: they shall not be ashamed, but they shall speak with the enemies in the gate.

> Psalm 128:4-6 Behold, that thus shall the man be blessed that feareth the LORD. The LORD shall bless thee out of Zion: and thou shalt see the good of Jerusalem all the days of thy life. Yea, thou shalt see thy children's children, and peace upon Israel.

> Matthew 3:7-9 But when he saw many of the Pharisees and Sadducees come to his baptism, he said unto them, O generation of vipers, who hath warned you to flee from the wrath to come? Bring forth therefore fruits meet for repentance: And think not to say within yourselves, We have Abraham to *our* father: for I say unto you, that God is able of these stones to raise up children unto Abraham. *[Also see Luke 3:7-8.]*

> Philippians 4:1 Therefore, my brethren dearly beloved and longed for, my joy and crown, so stand fast in the Lord, *my* dearly beloved.

> 1 Thessalonians 2:19-20 For what *is* our hope, or joy, or crown of rejoicing? *Are* not even ye in the presence of our Lord Jesus Christ at his coming? For ye are our glory and joy.

In verses 7-9, appear a trilogy of various forms of wicked speech and injustice: lying, bribing with a gift, and slandering by not overlooking a transgression to spread it to others.

Proverbs 17:7 Excellent speech becometh not a fool: much less do lying lips a prince.

Focus: This proverb declares that some speech is uncharacteristic of a person's character or position.

"Excellent speech becometh not a fool." "Excellent speech" is that which pleases God and good men. It reveals wisdom as learned from Scripture and from others known to have spiritual insight. "Fool" in this verse is translated from the Hebrew *nabal* and refers to a person who lacks spiritual insight; he is wicked and vile. He resents and resists the things of God and even the idea of being a student of righteousness. Excellent speech in him is as out of place as a "jewel of gold in a swine's snout." No matter how efficient his arguments, how vivid and clear his illustrations, however powerful and convincing his appeals, his foolish character is known to be inconsistent what he is saying. Should a wicked man speak of the excellent things of Christ, his words would seem as mockery.

> "'Excellent speech' probably refers to wise and sensible words. The idea is that fools, and wise and sensible words, do not go together. Nor do lying words and a prince (someone in authority). Indeed, the opposite should be the case. We would expect wise and sensible words from one in authority, and lying lips from a fool."[409]

> Psalm 14:1 To the chief Musician, *A Psalm* of David. The fool *[nabal]* hath said in his heart, There is no God. They are corrupt, they have done abominable works, *there is* none that doeth good.

> Psalm 50:16-17 But unto the wicked God saith, What hast thou to do to declare my statutes, or *that* thou shouldest take my covenant in thy mouth? Seeing thou hatest instruction, and castest my words behind thee.

> Psalm 74:22 Arise, O God, plead thine own cause: remember how the foolish *[nabal]* man reproacheth thee daily.

> Proverbs 26:7-9 The legs of the lame are not equal: so *is* a parable in the mouth of fools. As he that bindeth a stone in a sling, so *is* he that giveth honour to a fool. *As* a thorn goeth up into the hand of a drunkard, so *is* a parable in the mouth of fools.

> Isaiah 32:6 For the vile person will speak villany, and his heart will work iniquity, to practise hypocrisy, and to utter error against the LORD, to make empty the soul of the hungry, and he will cause the drink of the thirsty to fail.

"Much less do lying lips a prince." By definition, a **"prince,"** is one who is noble of mind and character. He is expected to be a man of integrity, honesty, and trustworthiness. If such a leader were to lie, everyone would be shocked. His speech would be even more unbecoming than a fool with excellent speech. Such speech would be disconcerting and incongruent with that expected.

> 2 Samuel 23:1-3 Now these *be* the last words of David. David the son of Jesse said, and the man *who was* raised up on high, the anointed of the God of Jacob, and the sweet psalmist of Israel, said, The Spirit of the LORD spake by me, and his word *was* in my tongue. The God of Israel said, the Rock of Israel spake to me, He that ruleth over men *must be* just, ruling in the fear of God.

> Proverbs 16:12-13 *It is* an abomination to kings to commit wickedness: for the throne is established by righteousness. Righteous lips are the delight of kings; and they love him that speaketh right.

> Ephesians 4:29 Let no corrupt communication proceed out of your mouth, but that which is good to the use of edifying, that it may minister grace unto the hearers.

> Colossians 4:6 Let your speech *be* alway with grace, seasoned with salt, that ye may know how ye ought to answer every man.

Proverbs 17:8 A gift *is as* a precious stone in the eyes of him that hath it: whithersoever it turneth, it prospereth.

Focus: This proverb describes a wicked person's view of the power of a bribe.

The wording of verse 8 indicates that the **"gift"** is used to obtain something desired without any consideration of pleasing the Lord. It is a bribe. "From the giver's perspective; a bribe 'works like a charm.'"[410] **"In the eyes of him that hath it,"** the gift is an item that is considered to have substantial value, as does a **"precious stone."** The owner admires the gift because, as the supportive phrase indicates, it is a prosperous thing wherever and to whomever it is presented – **"withersoever it turneth."** Just as the precious stone glistens from turning it against the light, so the giver sees the bribe as having an ungodly but productive glow wherever presented. The gift could be any item of great value.

This is the second consecutive proverb describing something a believer or righteous leader should not involve himself with. Bribery is condemned in Scripture.

> Exodus 23:8 And thou shalt take no gift: for the gift blindeth the wise, and perverteth the words of the righteous.

> Deuteronomy 16:19 Thou shalt not wrest judgment; thou shalt not respect persons, neither take a gift: for a gift doth blind the eyes of the wise, and pervert the words of the righteous.

> 1 Samuel 12:3 Behold, here I am: witness against me before the LORD, and before his anointed: whose ox have I taken? or whose ass have I taken? or whom have I defrauded? whom have I oppressed? or of whose hand have I received any bribe to blind mine eyes therewith? and I will restore it you.

> Proverbs 15:27 He that is greedy of gain troubleth his own house; but he that hateth gifts shall live.

> Proverbs 17:23 A wicked man taketh a gift out of the bosom to pervert the ways of judgment.

> Proverbs 19:6 Many will intreat the favour of the prince: and every man is a friend to him that giveth gifts.

Isaiah 1:23 Thy princes *are* rebellious, and companions of thieves: every one loveth gifts, and followeth after rewards: they judge not the fatherless, neither doth the cause of the widow come unto them.

Micah 7:2-3 The good *man* is perished out of the earth: and *there is* none upright among men: they all lie in wait for blood; they hunt every man his brother with a net. That they may do evil with both hands earnestly, the prince asketh, and the judge *asketh* for a reward; and the great *man,* he uttereth his mischievous desire: so they wrap it up.

NOTE: Other uses of the word "gift" such as the use of "present" in Genesis 33:9-11 below may be considered wise. That "present" was evidence of Jacob's good will. The context and the Hebrew word used will determine the meaning.

Genesis 33:9-11 And Esau said, I have enough, my brother; keep that thou hast unto thyself. And Jacob said, Nay, I pray thee, if now I have found grace in thy sight, then receive my present at my hand: for therefore I have seen thy face, as though I had seen the face of God, and thou wast pleased with me. Take, I pray thee, my blessing that is brought to thee; because God hath dealt graciously with me, and because I have enough. And he urged him, and he took *it.*

Proverbs 17:9 He that covereth a transgression seeketh love; but he that repeateth a matter separateth *very* friends.

Focus: This proverb contrasts the motive of suppressing damaging information with the consequence of repeating it.

If a person **covers a transgression** *(refuses to talk about a sin of another)*, his desire is to **seek love** *(foster love among friends)*. Conversely, if a person **repeats a matter** *[gossips about another's sins[411]]*, his actions frequently **separate very friends**. The actions and words of people reflect their motives. When a person's motive is to create an environment of **love**, he will be known for his actions of kindness and peace that result in a loving environment. **"To cover a transgression"** helps to maintain good relationships. Actions, such as repeating a transgression, reveal that the motive is something less noble than love; and the atmosphere is likely to become contentious. The potential consequence of such misconduct is that friends are separated. Vindictive tale-bearing persuades others to turn against and condemn friends.

Leviticus 19:18 Thou shalt not avenge, nor bear any grudge against the children of thy people, but thou shalt love thy neighbour as thyself: I am the LORD.

Proverbs 10:12 Hatred stirreth up strifes: but love covereth all sins.

Proverbs 12:16 A fool's wrath is presently known: but a prudent *man* covereth shame.

Proverbs 16:28 A froward man soweth strife: and a whisperer separateth chief friends.

1 Corinthians 13:4-7 Charity suffereth long, and is kind; charity envieth not; charity vaunteth not itself, is not puffed up, Doth not behave itself unseemly, seeketh not her own, is not easily provoked, thinketh no evil; Rejoiceth not in iniquity, but rejoiceth in the truth; Beareth all things, believeth all things, hopeth all things, endureth all things.

Ephesians 5:1-2 Be ye therefore followers of God, as dear children; And walk in love, as Christ also hath loved us, and hath given himself for us an offering and a sacrifice to God for a sweet smelling savour.

1 Peter 4:8 And above all things have fervent charity among yourselves: for charity shall cover the multitude of sins.

1 John 4:16 And we have known and believed the love that God hath to us. God is love; and he that dwelleth in love dwelleth in God, and God in him.

Some form of evil or foolish action is described in verses ten to sixteen. These actions include refusing to accept instruction or reproof, punishing a rebel, dealing with a fool, rewarding evil for good, avoiding contention, and justifying the wicked.

Proverbs 17:10 A reproof entereth more into a wise man than an hundred stripes into a fool.

Focus: This proverb contrasts the sensitivity that a wise person has to correction with that of a fool.

A wise man is readily corrected by simply being spoken to. Tell such a wise man something that needs to be corrected in his life (**"reproof"**), and he will mentally absorb every word and respond accordingly. **"Entering"** of a reproof means that it *enters the heart* of a wise person. The fool stops the flow of corrective or instructive words at his ear. The wise person has sufficient good character to use the reproof to better his life. He lives and thinks in a godly manner because of his desire to please the Lord regardless of the pain or effort to make proper corrections. He desires to be in agreement with God. The **"fool"** is a rebel; consequently, even a beating will not cause his heart to welcome such correction. He stops up his ears. The more he is reprimanded and even beaten with stripes, the more he opposes.

> Psalm 141:5 Let the righteous smite me; *it shall be* a kindness: and let him reprove me; *it shall be* an excellent oil, *which* shall not break my head: for yet my prayer also *shall be* in their calamities.
>
> Proverbs 1:7 The fear of the LORD is the beginning of knowledge: but fools despise wisdom and instruction.
>
> Proverbs 6:23 For the commandment *is* a lamp; and the law *is* light; and reproofs of instruction *are* the way of life:
>
> Proverbs 9:8-9 Reprove not a scorner, lest he hate thee: rebuke a wise man, and he will love thee. Give instruction to a wise man, and he will be yet wiser: teach a just man, and he will increase in learning.
>
> Proverbs 13:1 A wise son heareth his father's instruction: but a scorner heareth not rebuke.
>
> Proverbs 13:18 Poverty and shame *shall be to* him that refuseth instruction: but he that regardeth reproof shall be honoured.
>
> Proverbs 15:5 A fool despiseth his father's instruction: but he that regardeth reproof is prudent.
>
> Proverbs 15:31 The ear that heareth the reproof of life abideth among the wise.
>
> Proverbs 15:32 He that refuseth instruction despiseth his own soul: but he that heareth reproof getteth understanding.
>
> Proverbs 17:11 An evil *man* seeketh only rebellion: therefore a cruel messenger shall be sent against him.
>
> Proverbs 19:25 Smite a scorner, and the simple will beware: and reprove one that hath understanding, and he will understand knowledge.
>
> Proverbs 27:22 Though thou shouldest bray a fool in a mortar among wheat with a pestle, yet will not his foolishness depart from him.
>
> 2 Timothy 3:16 All scripture *is* given by inspiration of God, and *is* profitable for doctrine, for reproof, for correction, for instruction in righteousness

Notice the reaction of different men to God's reproof in the verses below. Sometimes a reproof from God comes in the form of tribulation.

> Exodus 9:33-35 And Moses went out of the city from Pharaoh, and spread abroad his hands unto the LORD: and the thunders and hail ceased, and the rain was not poured upon the earth. And when Pharaoh saw that the rain and the hail and the thunders were ceased, he sinned yet more, and hardened his heart, he and his servants. And the heart of Pharaoh was hardened, neither would he let the children of Israel go; as the LORD had spoken by Moses.
>
> 2 Samuel 12:13 And David said unto Nathan *[after being chastised by the prophet]*, I have sinned against the LORD. And Nathan said unto David, The LORD also hath put away thy sin; thou shalt not die.
>
> 2 Samuel 24:13, 14 So Gad came to David, and told him, and said unto him, Shall seven years of famine come unto thee in thy land? or wilt thou flee three months before thine enemies, while they pursue thee? or that there be three days' pestilence in thy land? now advise, and see what answer I shall return to him that sent me . . . And David said unto Gad, I am in a great strait: let us fall now into the hand of the LORD; for his mercies *are* great: and let me not fall into the hand of man.
>
> 2 Chronicles 28:20 And Tilgathpilneser king of Assyria came unto him, and distressed him, but strengthened him not. For Ahaz took away a portion *out* of the house of the LORD, and *out* of the house of the king, and of the princes, and gave *it* unto the king of Assyria: but he helped him not. And in the time of his distress did he trespass yet more against the LORD: this *is that* king Ahaz.
>
> Luke 22:61-62 And the Lord turned, and looked upon Peter. And Peter remembered the word of the Lord, how he had said unto him, Before the cock crow, thou shalt deny me thrice. And Peter went out, and wept bitterly.
>
> "What then makes the difference as to the effect of *reproof?* ... A needle pierces deeper into flesh, than a sword into stone. A wakeful ear, a tender conscience, a softened heart, a teachable spirit – these are the practical exercises, by which a wise and loving father disciplines his children for his service, for his cross, and for his crown."[412]

Proverbs 17:11 An evil *man* seeketh only rebellion: therefore a cruel messenger shall be sent against him.

Focus: This proverb declares rebellion is the motivation behind *an evil man's* actions and he should expect a dire consequence.

The **"evil *man*"** is the same as the fool in the previous proverb. Since he can't be corrected by word or beating, a **"cruel messenger"** is dispatched, bringing a dreadful judgment, such as a **"messenger"** of death, an officer of the law to arrest him, or an executioner to destroy him. A "cruel messenger" is "one that will not be turned from his work."[413]

The chief characteristic of an evil person is rebellion against God. ***An evil man seeks only rebellion*** is a clause indicating that rebellion is in all of his thoughts and is the foundation for other sins. Wickedness is the fountain that burst forth from him to reveal his stubborn rebellious will, violent acts, and words of hate. It may be disguised under a cloak of eerie, quiet verbiage; but the sense is that the rebellion lies deep within like a crouched animal ready to pounce.

1 Samuel 15:23 For rebellion is as the sin of witchcraft, and stubbornness is as iniquity and idolatry. Because thou hast rejected the word of the LORD, he hath also rejected thee from being king.

2 Samuel 18:14-15 Then said Joab, I may not tarry thus with thee. And he took three darts in his hand, and thrust them through the heart of Absalom, while he *was* yet alive in the midst of the oak. And ten young men that bare Joab's armour compassed about and smote Absalom, and slew him.

1 Kings 2:24-25 Now therefore, *as* the LORD liveth, which hath established me, and set me on the throne of David my father, and who hath made me an house, as he promised, Adonijah shall be put to death this day. And king Solomon sent by the hand of Benaiah the son of Jehoiada; and he fell upon him that he died.

Romans 2:8-9 But unto them that are contentious, and do not obey the truth, but obey unrighteousness, indignation and wrath, Tribulation and anguish, upon every soul of man that doeth evil, of the Jew first, and also of the Gentile … *[See also Deuteronomy 21:18-21 for how harshly the Mosaic law dealt with rebellion.]*

Proverbs 17:12 Let a bear robbed of her whelps meet a man, rather than a fool in his folly.

Focus: This proverb describes the potential inestimable amount of ungoverned violence that resides within a fool.

A she-bear that has been robbed of her cubs may enter into a blind rage attacking every creature within reach. Several biblical examples show the aptness of comparing the uncontrollable anger of a fool to the anger of a savage bear. (1) Jacob's cruel and uncontrolled sons killed every man in a city because of the actions of a single foolish man who lived there. (Genesis 34:25) (2) Wicked Saul ordered the murder of 85 priests because they supported David. (1 Samuel 22:18) (3) Deranged and Satan-controlled Herod ordered the ruthless killing of all children under two years old in Ramah. (Matthew 2:16)

"Fool in his folly" does not refer to the teasing talk of a loquacious, conceited fool; but it relates to the danger of the murderous rage of a *wicked* foolish man. Unlike a she-bear that only has animal intelligence, the fool does have human intelligence; consequently, he is capable of relentlessly and cruelly contriving evil. There is a chance that a she-bear **"robbed of her whelps"** *(cubs)* can be frightened away, but the foolishness of a dangerously evil fool inspires him to fulfill his wicked intentions.

"…a fool acting in his folly is more dangerous than a bear robbed of her cubs, which is outside of itself in grief and desire for revenge. This is the fool of Proverbs 17:11. He is uncontrolled and violent. He plans only evil. He has refused to let the folly be driven out of him by the lash. He is without restraint."[414]

"The strength and accuracy of the figure can scarcely be surpassed. The savage beast under the strongest excitement – a bear robbed of her whelps – is less dangerous to meet *[than a man in his folly]*… was not all this the rage of a beast, not the reason of a man? Humbling, indeed, is this picture of man, once "created in the image of God." (Genesis 1:27)[415]

Genesis 34:25 And it came to pass on the third day, when they were sore, that two of the sons of Jacob, Simeon and Levi, Dinah's brethren, took each man his sword, and came upon the city boldly, and slew all the males.

1 Samuel 22:18-19 And the king said to Doeg, Turn thou, and fall upon the priests. And Doeg the Edomite turned, and he fell upon the priests, and slew on that day fourscore and five persons that did wear a linen ephod. And Nob, the city of the priests, smote he with the edge of the sword, both men and women, children and sucklings, and oxen, and asses, and sheep, with the edge of the sword.

Proverbs 27:3 A stone *is* heavy, and the sand weighty; but a fool's wrath *is* heavier than them both.

Proverbs 28:15 *As* a roaring lion, and a ranging bear; *so is* a wicked ruler over the poor people.

Matthew 2:16 Then Herod, when he saw that he was mocked of the wise men, was exceeding wroth, and sent forth, and slew all the children that were in Bethlehem, and in all the coasts thereof, from two years old and under, according to the time which he had diligently enquired of the wise men.

Proverbs 17:13 Whoso rewardeth evil for good, evil shall not depart from his house.

Focus: This proverb declares just retribution for the person who rewards evil for good.

"Whoso rewardeth evil for good" is conduct that is the *very opposite of that taught by God* through Scripture. For a person to refuse to show gratitude for good done to him is disrespectful and shows a lack of understanding, but to repay **"evil for good"** is demonstrative of a human heart controlled by Satan. Nabal was such a person who demonstrated hate for David after he had protected Nabal's estate (1 Samuel 25). A Satan-controlled mob mandated the crucifixion of Jesus after He had bestowed the love of God on them for three and a half years. (Matthew 27) David rewarded evil to his good soldier and loyal follower Uriah and received the specific punishment of this verse – *evil did not depart from his house.* David and his family faced God's judgment with unusual calamities and deaths. (2 Samuel 12:10-14)

> "To render good for evil is Divine, good for good is human, evil for evil is brutish, evil for good is devilish. – *Trapp.*"[416]

> 1 Samuel 24:17 And he said to David, Thou art more righteous than I: for thou hast rewarded me good, whereas I have rewarded thee evil.
> 1 Samuel 25:21 Now David had said, Surely in vain have I kept all that this *fellow* hath in the wilderness, so that nothing was missed of all that *pertained* unto him: and he hath requited me evil for good.
> Psalm 35:12 They rewarded me evil for good to the spoiling of my soul.
> Psalm 38:20 They also that render evil for good are mine adversaries; because I follow *the thing that* good *is.*
> Psalm 109:5 And they have rewarded me evil for good, and hatred for my love.
> Proverbs 13:21 Evil pursueth sinners: but to the righteous good shall be repayed.
> Jeremiah 18:20-21 Shall evil be recompensed for good? for they have digged a pit for my soul. Remember that I stood before thee to speak good for them, *and* to turn away thy wrath from them. Therefore deliver up their children to the famine, and pour out their *blood* by the force of the sword; and let their wives be bereaved of their children, and *be* widows; and let their men be put to death; *let* their young men *be* slain by the sword in battle.
> Matthew 27:23-25 And the governor said, Why, what evil hath he done? But they cried out the more, saying, Let him be crucified. When Pilate saw that he could prevail nothing, but that rather a tumult was made, he took water, and washed his hands before the multitude, saying, I am innocent of the blood of this just person: see ye to it. Then answered all the people, and said, His blood be on us, and on our children.
> Luke 22:48 But Jesus said unto him, Judas, betrayest thou the Son of man with a kiss?

Proverbs 17:14 The beginning of strife *is as* when one letteth out water: therefore leave off contention, before it be meddled with.

Focus: This proverb teaches the wise way to handle contention before it explodes.

"The beginning of strife *is as* when one letteth out water." Strife often starts small and grows. In Genesis 3:8, if Abram had not acted to eliminate the strife, it could have led to violence between Lot and Abram's herdsmen and thus potentially degenerated into bad relations between family members. Not only should the wise person watch his words, but he should recognize when the angry, spiteful words begin to bubble up in another. He should remember that "A soft answer turneth away wrath: but grievous words stir up anger" (Proverbs 15:1). If he cannot calm the situation (or calm himself, if he is at fault), the wise person is to seek an exit from the situation **"before it be meddled with"** *[breaks out]* like a flood of waters.

> "The figure is taken from the great tank or reservoir upon which Eastern cities often depended for their supply of water. The beginning of strife is compared to the first crack in the mound of such a reservoir. At first a few drops ooze out, but after a time the whole mass of waters pour themselves forth with fury, and it is hard to set limits to the destruction which they cause."[417]

Pride will cause a person to stand his ground when doing so is a foolish alternative. The whole of this proverb's instruction is to refuse to be contentious and avoid being part of strife.

> Genesis 13:8-9 And Abram said unto Lot, Let there be no strife, I pray thee, between me and thee, and between my herdmen and thy herdmen; for we be brethren. *Is* not the whole land before thee? separate thyself, I pray thee, from me: if *thou wilt take* the left hand, then I will go to the right; or if thou depart to the right hand, then I will go to the left.
> Proverbs 13:10 Only by pride cometh contention: but with the well advised *is* wisdom.
> Proverbs 17:19 He loveth transgression that loveth strife: *and* he that exalteth his gate seeketh destruction.
> Proverbs 19:11 The discretion of a man deferreth his anger; and *it is* his glory to pass over a transgression.
> Proverbs 20:3 *It is* an honour for a man to cease from strife: but every fool will be meddling.
> Proverbs 25:8 Go not forth hastily to strive, lest *thou know not* what to do in the end thereof, when thy neighbour hath put thee to shame.
> Proverbs 26:21 *As* coals *are* to burning coals, and wood to fire; so *is* a contentious man to kindle strife.
> Ecclesiastes 7:8 Better is the end of a thing than the beginning thereof: and the patient in spirit is better than the proud in spirit.
> Matthew 5:39-41 But I say unto you, That ye resist not evil: but whosoever shall smite thee on thy right cheek, turn to him the other also. And if any man will sue thee at the law, and take away thy coat, let him have *thy* cloke also. And whosoever shall compel thee to go a mile, go with him twain.
> Romans 12:18 If it be possible, as much as lieth in you, live peaceably with all men.

James 3:14-18 But if ye have bitter envying and strife in your hearts, glory not, and lie not against the truth. This wisdom descendeth not from above, but *is* earthly, sensual, devilish. For where envying and strife is, there is confusion and every evil work. But the wisdom that is from above is first pure, then peaceable, gentle, *and* easy to be intreated, full of mercy and good fruits, without partiality, and without hypocrisy. And the fruit of righteousness is sown in peace of them that make peace.

Proverbs 17:15 He that justifieth the wicked, and he that condemneth the just, even they both *are* abomination to the LORD.

Focus: This proverb identifies two wicked acts that are despicable to the LORD.

In this verse, ***justifying the wicked*** means to make the wicked appear to be in the right. By nature of who they are, evil people ***justify the wicked*** and ***condemn the just***. Such actions define them as wicked. This evil category of people could represent a judge in a courtroom or a citizen on the street. They are fully engaged in opposing righteousness in every form; consequently, they are an abomination to other men, which can cause them severe problems; but to be an abhorrence to God is to guarantee disaster and eternal damnation. In the courtroom, they defeat the purpose of government, which is to protect the good and punish the bad; therefore, they are an abomination to God.

"People need to be warned against an unjust acquittal, no less than against unjust condemnation. The word 'justifieth' has its forensic sense, 'to declare righteous,' to acquit."[418]

"It was a saying of Solon, the Athenian lawgiver, that a republic walks upon two feet; one being just punishment for the unworthy, the other due reward for the worthy. If it fail in either of these, it necessarily goes lame. How if it fail in both?"[419]

Exodus 23:7 Keep thee far from a false matter; and the innocent and righteous slay thou not: for I will not justify the wicked.

Deuteronomy 25:1 If there be a controversy between men, and they come unto judgment, that *the judges* may judge them; then they shall justify the righteous, and condemn the wicked.

1 Kings 21:13-19 And there came in two men, children of Belial, and sat before him: and the men of Belial witnessed against him, even against Naboth, in the presence of the people, saying, Naboth did blaspheme God and the king. Then they carried him forth out of the city, and stoned him with stones, that he died. Then they sent to Jezebel, saying, Naboth is stoned, and is dead. And it came to pass, when Jezebel heard that Naboth was stoned, and was dead, that Jezebel said to Ahab, Arise, take possession of the vineyard of Naboth the Jezreelite, which he refused to give thee for money: for Naboth is not alive, but dead. And it came to pass, when Ahab heard that Naboth was dead, that Ahab rose up to go down to the vineyard of Naboth the Jezreelite, to take possession of it. And the word of the LORD came to Elijah the Tishbite, saying, Arise, go down to meet Ahab king of Israel, which is in Samaria: behold, he is in the vineyard of Naboth, whither he is gone down to possess it. And thou shalt speak unto him, saying, Thus saith the LORD, Hast thou killed, and also taken possession? And thou shalt speak unto him, saying, Thus saith the LORD, In the place where dogs licked the blood of Naboth shall dogs lick thy blood, even thine.

Proverbs 24:23-25 These *things* also *belong* to the wise. *It is* not good to have respect of persons in judgment. He that saith unto the wicked, Thou *art* righteous; him shall the people curse, nations shall abhor him: But to them that rebuke *him* shall be delight, and a good blessing shall come upon them.

Isaiah 5:22-24 Woe unto *them that are* mighty to drink wine, and men of strength to mingle strong drink: Which justify the wicked for reward, and take away the righteousness of the righteous from him! Therefore as the fire devoureth the stubble, and the flame consumeth the chaff, *so* their root shall be as rottenness, and their blossom shall go up as dust: because they have cast away the law of the LORD of hosts, and despised the word of the Holy One of Israel.

Luke 23:24-25 And Pilate gave sentence that it should be as they required. And he released unto them him that for sedition and murder was cast into prison, whom they had desired; but he delivered Jesus to their will.

Romans 13:3-5 For rulers are not a terror to good works, but to the evil. Wilt thou then not be afraid of the power? do that which is good, and thou shalt have praise of the same: For he is the minister of God to thee for good. But if thou do that which is evil, be afraid; for he beareth not the sword in vain: for he is the minister of God, a revenger to *execute* wrath upon him that doeth evil. Wherefore *ye* must needs be subject, not only for wrath, but also for conscience sake.

Proverbs 17:16 Wherefore *is there* a price in the hand of a fool to get wisdom, seeing *he hath* no heart *to it?*

Focus: This proverb specifies that a lack of desire for wisdom keeps the fool a fool.

Wisdom comes directly from God, and the *fool has no thirst for God or the things of God*. If such a thirst were possible for a fool, wisdom could not be purchased with his money any more than God can be purchased with money.

Fools neither fear God nor favor wisdom. They have **"no heart to it"** *[no inclination, no mental desire, no will for it]*. "The fear of the LORD is the beginning of knowledge: but fools despise wisdom and instruction." (Proverbs 1:7) In Nazareth of Galilee, where Jesus grew up and performed many miracles, the townsmen turned themselves away from Jesus and His wisdom. The Gadarenes bid Him leave, dismissing their only hope. Herod looked at Him with curiosity, but power, sex, and evil consumed his mind. Pilate saw His innocence but not His deity and succumbed to evil disorder and the power of a mob. The rich young ruler preferred his personal wealth to God.

More than one Hebrew word is translated "fool" in Proverbs. In this verse, the Hebrew *kesiyl* indicates a person so simple he thinks he can buy wisdom but fails to understand he has no desire for it.[420] His other characteristics also preclude his ability to receive wisdom. He is characterized by a dull, closed mind, and he is thickheaded and stubborn. Because he is lazy and shortsighted, this kind of fool rejects information from others.

> "That which 'is more precious than rubies' (Proverbs 3:15) is to him more worthless than a pebble. That which 'is more sweet than honey,' is tasteless as the 'white of an egg.' He lives for himself, as if there was no God in the world. His heart is given to the world, as if it could *be a God* to him, or could fill up God's vacant place in his heart! Yet thus the realities of eternity – the mighty things of the Gospel – things that should drink up our spirits, are like 'a tale that is told.' Enough that they should have a place in our creed, though never in our hearts. The world is preferred to heaven, time to eternity; and the immortal soul, for which such a cost has been paid, and such prospects prepared, perishes in folly."[421]

> Deuteronomy 5:29 O that there were such an heart in them, that they would fear me, and keep all my commandments always, that it might be well with them, and with their children for ever!
>
> Psalm 81:11-13 But my people would not hearken to my voice; and Israel would none of me. So I gave them up unto their own hearts' lust: *and* they walked in their own counsels. Oh that my people had hearkened unto me, *and* Israel had walked in my ways!
>
> Proverbs 1:22 How long, ye simple ones, will ye love simplicity? and the scorners delight in their scorning, and fools hate knowledge?
>
> Proverbs 14:6 A scorner seeketh wisdom, and *findeth it* not: but knowledge is easy unto him that understandeth.
>
> Hosea 4:6-11 My people are destroyed for lack of knowledge: because thou hast rejected knowledge, I will also reject thee, that thou shalt be no priest to me: seeing thou hast forgotten the law of thy God, I will also forget thy children. As they were increased, so they sinned against me: therefore will I change their glory into shame. They eat up the sin of my people, and they set their heart on their iniquity. And there shall be, like people, like priest: and I will punish them for their ways, and reward them their doings. For they shall eat, and not have enough: they shall commit whoredom, and shall not increase: because they have left off to take heed to the LORD. Whoredom and wine and new wine take away the heart.
>
> John 3:20 For every one that doeth evil hateth the light, neither cometh to the light, lest his deeds should be reproved.
>
> Acts 28:26-27 Saying, Go unto this people, and say, Hearing ye shall hear, and shall not understand; and seeing ye shall see, and not perceive: For the heart of this people is waxed gross, and their ears are dull of hearing, and their eyes have they closed; lest they should see with their eyes, and hear with *their* ears, and understand with *their* heart, and should be converted, and I should heal them.

Proverbs 17:17 A friend loveth at all times, and a brother is born for adversity.

Focus: This proverb declares the constant love of a friend and his transformation to the status of a "brother" during "adversity."

The consistent loyalty of a true friend is noted as one who is there during every positive and negative phase of life. When serious trouble comes so that difficulty turns to distress, the true friend remains faithful and becomes even closer, like a "brother." False friends forsake when there is adversity – when the relationship no longer works for their selfish advantage.

> "...the true *friend loveth at all times*, through 'evil as well as good report.' He does not change, when circumstances change. He is the same, whether we are in wealth or need. He proves himself in *adversity*, by rising in warmth, and exerting every nerve, in proportion as his aid is needed. He is not ashamed of poverty or of a prison. In any jarrings of the flesh, *adversity* cements love. The *loving friend* becomes now *a brother born for adversity*."[422]

Naomi needed a true friend and "sister" in her time of adversity.

> Ruth 1:14-17 And they lifted up their voice, and wept again: and Orpah kissed her mother in law; but Ruth clave unto her. And she said, Behold, thy sister in law is gone back unto her people, and unto her gods: return thou after thy sister in law. And Ruth said, Intreat me not to leave thee, *or* to return from following after thee: for whither thou goest, I will go; and where thou lodgest, I will lodge: thy people *shall be* my people, and thy God my God: Where thou diest, will I die, and there will I be buried: the LORD do so to me, and more also, *if ought* but death part thee and me.

There is no question to the Christian that God brings friends into his life who will be there during special times of need. Such a **"friend"** deserves the additional title of **"brother."**

> "Adversity is the time when affection is put to the proof. It is hardly at all tried among relatives, when all is going-well, and there is no call in providence for sacrifices on the part of any members of the domestic circle, in behalf of the others. But when, through unforeseen circumstances, privation and distress become the lot of any of them, then is the test of the sincerity and strength of natural affection. Brethren are born to help each other in need. This is the will and purpose of God in placing them in their near relationship. It is sad when this fails; and beautiful when it is displayed. It is not when Naomi 'goes out full,' but when 'the Lord brings her home again empty,' that the fond attachment of Ruth draws to the eye the tear of approving and delighted sympathy. It is in the reverses and fallen fortunes of his kinswoman-widowed, desolate, and dependent-that the fidelity and generosity of Boaz are brought out into conspicuous manifestation.-We shudder at the unnatural conduct of Joseph's brethren; while in Joseph himself-whether viewed in the providential arrangements of his history, or in his amiably pious and forgiving disposition, – we see 'a brother born for adversity.'"[423]

> "But – Ah! it is to *Jesus* that we must look as the perfect exemplar. To see the Son of God in our nature, that he might be our *friend and brother* (Hebrews 2:14); to hear him 'not ashamed to call us brethren' (Hebrews 2:11-13) – this is a mystery of *friendship* – unsearchable. Truly is this Friend – he alone, worthy of our unlimited confidence. Such is the constancy of his *love — at all times* (John 13:1) – even unto death – unaltered by the most undutiful returns – 'turning and looking upon' the disciple (a look so full of tenderness and power!) (Luke 22:61) whom we should have excommunicated. Such the sympathy of his love – *born for adversity;* so united to us – the friend and the brother we need; never nearer to us than when in our lowest depths of trouble; and, though now our glorified *Brother* in heaven, yet still 'touched with the feeling of our infirmities' (Hebrews 4:15); still 'afflicted in all our afflictions' (Isaiah 63:9); presenting us to his Father, as his own elect, the purchase of his blood, 'the members of his body, of his flesh, and of his bones.' (Ephesians 5:30) Here is sympathy in all its fullness, and all its helpfulness. Here is indeed *'a Brother born for adversity.'* 'Trust him,' O ye trembling believers, 'at all times,' and in all places. You will then be possessed of the happy art of living beyond the reach of all disappointment.'"[424]

1 Samuel 18:3 Then Jonathan and David made a covenant, because he loved him as his own soul.

1 Samuel 19:1-2 And Saul spake to Jonathan his son, and to all his servants, that they should kill David. But Jonathan Saul's son delighted much in David: and Jonathan told David, saying, Saul my father seeketh to kill thee: now therefore, I pray thee, take heed to thyself until the morning, and abide in a secret *place.* and hide thyself:

Esther 4:14 For if thou altogether holdest thy peace at this time, then shall there enlargement and deliverance arise to the Jews from another place; but thou and thy father's house shall be destroyed: and who knoweth whether thou art come to the kingdom for such a time as this?

Proverbs 18:24 A man that hath friends must shew himself friendly: and there is a friend that sticketh closer than a brother.

Isaiah 63:9 In all their affliction he was afflicted, and the angel of his presence saved them: in his love and in his pity he redeemed them; and he bare them, and carried them all the days of old.

Luke 22:61 And the Lord turned, and looked upon Peter. And Peter remembered the word of the Lord, how he had said unto him, Before the cock crow, thou shalt deny me thrice.

John 13:1 Now before the feast of the passover, when Jesus knew that his hour was come that he should depart out of this world unto the Father, having loved his own which were in the world, he loved them unto the end.

Ephesians 5:30 For we are members of his body, of his flesh, and of his bones.

Hebrews 2:11-15 For both he that sanctifieth and they who are sanctified *are* all of one: for which cause he is not ashamed to call them brethren, Saying, I will declare thy name unto my brethren, in the midst of the church will I sing praise unto thee. And again, I will put my trust in him. And again, Behold I and the children which God hath given me. Forasmuch then as the children are partakers of flesh and blood, he also himself likewise took part of the same; that through death he might destroy him that had the power of death, that is, the devil; And deliver them who through fear of death were all their lifetime subject to bondage.

Proverbs 17:18 A man void of understanding striketh hands, *and* becometh surety in the presence of his friend.

Focus: This proverb declares the lack of understanding involved in cosigning for a friend.

To be **"surety"** for another is to declare that "if" the "friend" (poor person making the debt) cannot repay, then the one being cosigner or **"surety"** will be responsible. The cosigner, in effect, mingles his financial ability with the financial inability of the person making the loan. Becoming surety for anyone and namely, a friend, as in this verse, shows a void *[lack]* of understanding.

The surety (cosigner who guarantees the loan) **"striketh hands"** (with the person who has money to loan), thereby securing the debt. *Striking hands* is similar to shaking hands to show honorable intent to fulfill the agreement. This action assures the lender that the surety will repay his friend's loan if necessary. The **"friend"** in this verse is *present* and watching the agreement.

Like an addendum to the previous proverb, this one specifies a *point of limitation* to friendship as a place where the financial security of one's personal family is threatened. To become surety for a friend at the risk of one's own family being deprived of the necessities of life is beyond reason, and to do so would prove that the potential surety is **"void of understanding."** No true friend would ask his friend to cosign for him under such conditions. In addition, experience shows that friendships most often dissolve when a surety agreement is made because of failed expectations, embarrassment, and the changes in relation status (cosigner is no longer an equal friend but has leverage – a higher status). People usually need cosigners because of poor credit or reputation, or sometimes because of youth and thus having no credit rating, or because of not being old enough to have established credibility.

A foolish man, ***void of understanding***, will walk into problems without thinking, or just as bad, allow emotions rather than intellect to drive his decisions. A wise man will avoid becoming a surety, he will choose godly friends, and he will rely on God at all times. If the person becoming surety or cosigner has ample finances and willingly (and best secretly) considers the act a gift rather than a potential debt, the outcome is more likely to be successful.

> Proverbs 6:1-5 My son, if thou be surety for thy friend, if thou hast stricken thy hand with a stranger, Thou art snared with the words of thy mouth, thou art taken with the words of thy mouth. Do this now, my son, and deliver thyself, when thou art come into the hand of thy friend; go, humble thyself, and make sure thy friend. Give not sleep to thine eyes, nor slumber to thine eyelids. Deliver thyself as a roe from the hand *of the hunter*, and as a bird from the hand of the fowler.
> Proverbs 11:15 He that is surety for a stranger shall smart *for it*: and he that hateth suretiship is sure.
> Proverbs 22:26-27 Be not thou one of them that strike hands, *or* of them that are sureties for debts. If thou hast nothing to pay, why should he take away thy bed from under thee?

Proverbs 17:19 He loveth transgression that loveth strife: *and* he that exalteth his gate seeketh destruction.

Focus: This proverb declares that strife is natural to a person who loves transgression, and destruction is the natural consequence of arrogance.

According to 1John 3:4, "sin is the transgression of the law." **"Transgression"** means a revolt, nationally, morally, or religiously (a sin against God). Because they are full of pride, rebels are, by nature, quarrelsome. They are *lovers of strife,* and they will be noted for their arrogance because their foolish conduct is driven by pride. The transgressor's foolishness places him into a loop of conduct, bringing never-ending strife and destruction.

To ***exalt one's gate*** is an idiom meaning to lift oneself in pride above his rank as an individual would by building a high gate or showy entrance into his home purely to be ostentatious. The immediate potential problem is that the high gate provides easy access for enemies who may come inside to destroy him and take his possessions. In the same manner, pride thus lifts one high and exposes him to enemies. Also, to insist upon a title such as "Rabbi" or *any other term like "Doctor" for the purpose of elevating one above his peers* is to ***exalt one's gate***.

> "In different parts of Palestine they are obliged to have the doors of their courts and houses very low, not more than three feet high, to prevent the Arabs, who scarcely ever leave the backs of their horses, from riding into the courts and houses, and spoiling their goods. He, then, who, through pride and ostentation, made a high gate, exposed himself to destruction; and is said here to seek it, because he must know that this would be a necessary consequence of exalting his gate."[425]
> Proverbs 16:18 Pride *goeth* before destruction, and an haughty spirit before a fall.
> Proverbs 16:28 A froward man soweth strife: and a whisperer separateth chief friends.
> Proverbs 18:12 Before destruction the heart of man is haughty, and before honour is humility.
> Proverbs 29:22-23 An angry man stirreth up strife, and a furious man aboundeth in transgression. A man's pride shall bring him low: but honour shall uphold the humble in spirit.
> Matthew 23:5-12 But all their works they do for to be seen of men: they make broad their phylacteries, and enlarge the borders of their garments, And love the uppermost rooms at feasts, and the chief seats in the synagogues, And greetings in the markets, and to be called of men, Rabbi, Rabbi. But be not ye called Rabbi: for one is your Master, *even* Christ; and all ye are brethren. And call no *man* your father upon the earth: for one is your Father, which is in heaven. Neither be ye called masters: for one is your Master, *even* Christ. But he that is greatest among you shall be your servant. And whosoever shall exalt himself shall be abased; and he that shall humble himself shall be exalted.
> James 4:6-7 But he giveth more grace. Wherefore he saith, God resisteth the proud, but giveth grace unto the humble. Submit yourselves therefore to God. Resist the devil, and he will flee from you.
> James 3:14-16 But if ye have bitter envying and strife in your hearts, glory not, and lie not against the truth. This wisdom descendeth not from above, but is earthly, sensual, devilish. For where envying and strife is, there is confusion and every evil work.

1 Peter 5:5-6 Likewise, ye younger, submit yourselves unto the elder. Yea, all of you be subject one to another, and be clothed with humility: for God resisteth the proud, and giveth grace to the humble. Humble yourselves therefore under the mighty hand of God, that he may exalt you in due time.

Proverbs 17:20 He that hath a froward heart findeth no good: and he that hath a perverse tongue falleth into mischief.

Focus: This proverb declares the bad consequence of a froward heart that reveals itself with a perverse tongue.

"He that hath a froward heart findeth no good." The consequence of having a **"froward heart"** *[a mind habitually disposed to disobedience and opposition]* is that the person **"findeth no good"** *(faces evil or bad circumstances continually)*. **"A froward heart"** is **"perverse,"** or "willfully determined or disposed to go counter to what is expected or desired: contrary."[426] This person is constantly faced with the bad that this world has to offer since he does not solicit the help of God but instead opposes Him. He avoids the good blessings of life because his heart loves the bad, the wicked, the things that God condemns for the benefit of men. His froward heart has a proclivity toward evil, and like a vulture circling over a dead body, he focuses his life on mischief, and his evil tongue reveals the darkness of his soul.

"And he that hath a perverse tongue falleth into mischief." "A perverse tongue" (wicked speech) in this second clause is a product of the **"froward heart"** named in the first. In other words, a "froward heart" produces a "perverse tongue." If he could control his tongue, this foolish, wicked person could avoid many self-induced problems; but his doing right is not likely. This ungodly, perverse tongue continuously leads him into **"mischief,"** which, as the Hebrew definition shows, could include any or all of the following: bad, evil, adversity, affliction, calamity, displeasure, distress, or wretchedness. With his evil words, he provokes his enemies, perturbs his friends, and perpetually places himself in the exact location of trouble.

The opposite of this proverb is found in Proverbs 16:20, which states–"He that handleth a matter wisely shall find good: and whoso trusteth in the LORD, happy *is* he." Wise people who trust God and handle actions and words wisely "find good," which indicates happiness in life because they follow God's laws and seek His mind before they conduct business and life's many matters. Wise people intentionally follow God and avoid trouble.

Proverbs 2:12-15 To deliver thee from the way of the evil *man*, from the man that speaketh froward things; Who leave the paths of uprightness, to walk in the ways of darkness; Who rejoice to do evil, and delight in the frowardness of the wicked; Whose ways are crooked, and they froward in their paths . . .

Proverbs 8:13 The fear of the LORD is to hate evil: pride, and arrogancy, and the evil way, and the froward mouth, do I hate.

Proverbs 10:14 Wise men lay up knowledge: but the mouth of the foolish is near destruction.

Proverbs 10:28 The hope of the righteous shall be gladness: but the expectation of the wicked shall perish.

Proverbs 10:31-32 The mouth of the just bringeth forth wisdom: but the froward tongue shall be cut out. The lips of the righteous know what is acceptable: but the mouth of the wicked *speaketh* frowardness.

Proverbs 11:20 They that are of a froward heart are abomination to the LORD: but such as are upright in their way are his delight.

Proverbs 18:6-7 A fool's lips enter into contention, and his mouth calleth for strokes. A fool's mouth *is* his destruction, and his lips *are* the snare of his soul.

Luke 6:45 A good man out of the good treasure of his heart bringeth forth that which is good; and an evil man out of the evil treasure of his heart bringeth forth that which is evil: for of the abundance of the heart his mouth speaketh.

Acts 13:6-11 And when they had gone through the isle unto Paphos, they found a certain sorcerer, a false prophet, a Jew, whose name was Barjesus: Which was with the deputy of the country, Sergius Paulus, a prudent man; who called for Barnabas and Saul, and desired to hear the word of God. But Elymas the sorcerer (for so is his name by interpretation) withstood them, seeking to turn away the deputy from the faith. Then Saul, (who also is called Paul,) filled with the Holy Ghost, set his eyes on him, And said, O full of all subtilty and all mischief, thou child of the devil, thou enemy of all righteousness, wilt thou not cease to pervert the right ways of the Lord? And now, behold, the hand of the Lord is upon thee, and thou shalt be blind, not seeing the sun for a season. And immediately there fell on him a mist and a darkness; and he went about seeking some to lead him by the hand.

Proverbs 17:21 He that begetteth a fool *doeth it* to his sorrow: and the father of a fool hath no joy.

Focus: This proverb describes the effects of a foolish child on the parents (specifically the father).

Using two different words for **"fool,"** this proverb emphasizes that two kinds of foolish children will bring sadness to a godly father and rob him of his joy, especially parental joy. The first word is *keciyl* and the meaning emphasizes being dull and thickheaded, while the second is *nabal* emphasizing wickedness (lack of spiritual perception and sensitivity).[427] A child that does unwise, foolish things *(keciyl)* is an embarrassment and a worry to his father. An ungodly and vile child (*nabal*) will cause a father to have **"no joy"** most notably in the area of his life that concerns the child. The foolishness of his son will not leave his mind. When either type of foolish child becomes an adult, the parents will have some relief, not being responsible anymore for his actions. But a child's behavior is *never* entirely divorced from parents' minds. Their lives are always mentally and emotionally intertwined.

> "The meaning is more than that he has no joy in that son. The character and conduct of that son serve to infuse 'bitterness' into everything else. There may be many things in his domestic lot fitted to inspire cheerfulness and delight: – but at the happy moments, when his heart, yielding to all the fond impulses of conjugal and parental tenderness, is swelling with the emotions of gladness, the thought of his perverse, rebellious, profligate boy comes over him, sends through that heart the pang of agony, 'turns his harp to mourning, and his organ to the voice of them that weep.'"[428]

1 Samuel 8:3 And his *[Samuel's]* sons walked not in his ways, but turned aside after lucre, and took bribes, and perverted judgment.
2 Samuel 18:33 And the king was much moved, and went up to the chamber over the gate, and wept: and as he went, thus he said,
 O my son Absalom, my son, my son Absalom! would God I had died for thee, O Absalom, my son, my son!
Proverbs 10:1 The proverbs of Solomon. A wise son maketh a glad father: but a foolish son is the heaviness of his mother.
Proverbs 15:20 A wise son maketh a glad father: but a foolish man despiseth his mother.
Proverbs 17:25 A foolish son is a grief to his father, and bitterness to her that bare him.
Proverbs 19:13 A foolish son is the calamity of his father: and the contentions of a wife are a continual dropping.
Proverbs 23:15 My son, if thine heart be wise, my heart shall rejoice, even mine.
Proverbs 23:24 The father of the righteous shall greatly rejoice: and he that begetteth a wise child shall have joy of him.

Proverbs 17:22 A merry heart doeth good *like* a medicine: but a broken spirit drieth the bones.

Focus: This proverb contrasts the effect of a merry heart with the effect of a broken spirit.

A **"merry heart"** and a **"broken spirit"** (being distressed or saddened) are *opposite attitudes toward life* that, in a significant manner, are governed by will power, reliance on God, and associates, including family and friends. A person's frame of mind directly affects his physical well-being, and the instruction in this proverb alerts a person to the importance of keeping a good attitude toward life.

Determining to be happy can have a healing effect on the body. Being continually unhappy can be hurtful. Relationships and fellowship with others, who have a good attitude because of trust in God and belief in His promises, play a significant part in having a good frame of mind. Even the father of a fool, as identified in the previous verse, could be helped by this proverb's advice.

Gained by focusing on God's many blessings, His great love, mercy and grace, and on the positive things of life, a cheerful, contented spirit (**"merry heart"**) promotes a healthy body and the sustaining of life. In contrast, maintaining a continued unhappy **"broken spirit"** by allowing the attacks of Satan to be effective, plus meditating on the bad events of life, contributes to disease and death. *These spiritual truths show a direct link between the way a person thinks and his physical well-being.*

When a person follows God's wisdom, he can *avoid many factors* that cause the fool to be in despair. In Jesus, there is joy and hope, as is evidenced by His words: "These things have I spoken unto you, that my joy might remain in you, and *that* your joy might be full." (John 15:11) "These things I have spoken unto you, that in me ye might have peace. In the world ye shall have tribulation: but be of good cheer; I have overcome the world." (John 16:33). Following the teachings of the Scriptures has a powerful influence on the mind and body. Knowing whom to avoid, when and how to speak properly, where to go and not to go will bring contentment. *To ignore God's instruction can only bring a **broken spirit** and disaster.*

"Dry bones" is a Scriptural expression denoting death or dying. The condition occurs after life has left a person and all moisture has evaporated; however, to a lesser extent, "dry bones" can also occur in advanced age, as the following medical reference specifies.

> "Spinal fluid helps lubricate the discs and vertebrae in the spinal column – making it easy to bend, twist, and otherwise move your back. When this spinal fluid starts to dissipate, the result is often pain, and loss of mobility. But what exactly causes discs to dry out? The most common cause is simple wear and tear over time. As our bodies age, they break down. With time, the discs in the spine can begin to lose fluid, dry out, and shrink."[429]

The "dry bones" of Ezekiel 37 dramatically picture the promise of God that He would bring the "dead" nation of Israel, who had been scattered away from the homeland because of sin, back to her proper place. This vision allowed Israel to have hope. As another prophet wrote in Nehemiah 8:10, "the joy of the LORD is your strength." In like fashion, "A merry heart doeth good like a medicine."

Proverbs 3:7-8 Be not wise in thine own eyes: fear the LORD, and depart from evil. It shall be health to thy navel, and marrow to thy bones.

Proverbs 12:25 Heaviness in the heart of man maketh it stoop: but a good word maketh it glad.

Proverbs 12:4 A virtuous woman is a crown to her husband: but she that maketh ashamed is as rottenness in his bones.

Proverbs 15:13 A merry heart maketh a cheerful countenance: but by sorrow of the heart the spirit is broken.

Proverbs 15:15 All the days of the afflicted are evil: but he that is of a merry heart hath a continual feast.

Proverbs 15:30 The light of the eyes rejoiceth the heart: and a good report maketh the bones fat.

Proverbs 16:24 Pleasant words are as an honeycomb, sweet to the soul, and health to the bones.

Proverbs 18:14 The spirit of a man will sustain his infirmity; but a wounded spirit who can bear?

Ecclesiastes 9:7-9 Go thy way, eat thy bread with joy, and drink thy wine with a merry heart; for God now accepteth thy works. Let thy garments be always white; and let thy head lack no ointment. Live joyfully with the wife whom thou lovest all the days of the life of thy vanity, which he hath given thee under the sun, all the days of thy vanity: for that *is* thy portion in this life, and in thy labour which thou takest under the sun.

2 Corinthians 2:7 So that contrariwise ye *ought* rather to forgive *him*, and comfort *him*, lest perhaps such a one should be swallowed up with overmuch sorrow.

Proverbs 17:23 A wicked *man* taketh a gift out of the bosom to pervert the ways of judgment.

Focus: This proverb specifies the privacy and purpose of a bribe.

Verse eight of this chapter brought attention to the fact that an ungodly man's bribe is precious in his sight in that it provides a tool for him to get what he desires. Here in this verse, the true purpose of a bribe is clearly stated, **"to pervert the ways of judgment."** An accepted bribe makes the recipient *unwilling* to judge between right and wrong. Obviously, those justices and leaders who accept bribes are as wicked as the persons who give them. Because he is driven by greed, a bribe's recipient will put aside a desire for pleasing God or for being just in his dealings with other people. He will eagerly receive it with the intent of aborting righteous judgment.

"Out of the bosom" indicates that the gift is given very privately to the judge or magistrate so as not to be seen or known by others. Little does the wicked man know that God sees every move and hears every word, and He is not pleased with the *perversion of justice*. Temptation tests the principles on which a man bases his life.

Exodus 23:8 And thou shalt take no gift: for the gift blindeth the wise, and perverteth the words of the righteous.

Deuteronomy 16:19 Thou shalt not wrest judgment; thou shalt not respect persons, neither take a gift: for a gift doth blind the eyes of the wise, and pervert the words of the righteous.

1 Samuel 12:3 Behold, here I am: witness against me before the LORD, and before his anointed: whose ox have I taken? or whose ass have I taken? or whom have I defrauded? whom have I oppressed? or of whose hand have I received any bribe to blind mine eyes therewith? and I will restore it you.

Job 34:21-22 For his eyes are upon the ways of man, and he seeth all his goings. There is no darkness, nor shadow of death, where the workers of iniquity may hide themselves.

Psalm 139:7-8 Whither shall I go from thy spirit? or whither shall I flee from thy presence? If I ascend up into heaven, thou art there: if I make my bed in hell, behold, thou art there.

Proverbs 15:27 He that is greedy of gain troubleth his own house; but he that hateth gifts shall live.

Isaiah 1:23-24 Thy princes are rebellious, and companions of thieves: every one loveth gifts, and followeth after rewards: they judge not the fatherless, neither doth the cause of the widow come unto them. Therefore saith the Lord, the LORD of hosts, the mighty One of Israel, Ah, I will ease me of mine adversaries, and avenge me of mine enemies:

Isaiah 33:15-16 He that walketh righteously, and speaketh uprightly; he that despiseth the gain of oppressions, that shaketh his hands from holding of bribes, that stoppeth his ears from hearing of blood, and shutteth his eyes from seeing evil;He shall dwell on high: his place of defence shall be the munitions of rocks: bread shall be given him; his waters shall be sure.

Acts 24:25-26 And as he reasoned of righteousness, temperance, and judgment to come, Felix trembled, and answered, Go thy way for this time; when I have a convenient season, I will call for thee. He hoped also that money should have been given him of Paul, that he might loose him: wherefore he sent for him the oftener, and communed with him.

Proverbs 17:24 Wisdom *is* before him that hath understanding; but the eyes of a fool *are* in the ends of the earth.

Focus: This proverb contrasts the ability (of those with understanding) to acknowledge wisdom with the inability (of the fool) to acknowledge wisdom.

"Wisdom is before him that hath understanding." "Wisdom is before" means that *wisdom is right in front of him–staring him in the face.* God's wisdom is like an ever-present, in-hand compass by which the wise man steers his life. When a man walks with God, wisdom and understanding walk with him.

Having fixed his heart on wisdom, the ***man who has understanding*** is daily learning from God. The fear of the Lord is foundational to the way he thinks, and the word of God is ever in his mind guiding his thoughts. Wisdom is the target at which he aims and the guide by which he directs his path. He searches for wisdom like another would search for buried gold. His wisdom is evident in the way he worships God and interacts with people. The events and developments in his life are further indications of his wisdom and being blessed by God.

"The eyes of a fool *are* in the ends of the earth." A fool is such because in his mind, superstition, magic, his own intellect, or the thoughts of other corrupt minds are more beneficial than God or His wisdom. He looks anywhere and everywhere, except to God, for wisdom. Looking in the **"ends of the earth,"** he will discover the absurd things that satisfy his wickedness and motivate his life. He will look everywhere and wander here and there searching all fleeting earthly vanities. Those things that are of least importance interest him most. These vanities he keeps before himself, determining every decision of his life. Unlike the wise man, he does not have the single objective of pleasing God in view, but he pursues many different ideas and wastes his life without gaining wisdom.

Deuteronomy 30:10-14 If thou shalt hearken unto the voice of the LORD thy God, to keep his commandments and his statutes which are written in this book of the law, *and* if thou turn unto the LORD thy God with all thine heart, and with all thy soul. For this commandment which I command thee this day, it *is* not hidden from thee, neither *is* it far off. It *is* not in heaven, that thou shouldest say, Who shall go up for us to heaven, and bring it unto us, that we may hear it, and do it? Neither *is* it beyond the sea, that thou shouldest say, Who shall go over the sea for us, and bring it unto us, that we may hear it, and do it? But the word *is* very nigh unto thee, in thy mouth, and in thy heart, that thou mayest do it.

Proverbs 2:1-5 My son, if thou wilt receive my words, and hide my commandments with thee; So that thou incline thine ear unto wisdom, and apply thine heart to understanding; Yea, if thou criest after knowledge, and liftest up thy voice for understanding; If thou seekest her as silver, and searchest for her as for hid treasures; Then shalt thou understand the fear of the LORD, and find the knowledge of God.

Proverbs 8:8-9 All the words of my mouth *are* in righteousness; *there is* nothing froward or perverse in them. They *are* all plain to him that understandeth, and right to them that find knowledge.

Proverbs 14:6 A scorner seeketh wisdom, and *findeth it* not: but knowledge *is* easy unto him that understandeth.

Proverbs 14:33 Wisdom resteth in the heart of him that hath understanding: but that which is in the midst of fools is made known.

Proverbs 15:14 The heart of him that hath understanding seeketh knowledge: but the mouth of fools feedeth on foolishness.

Romans 10:8 But what saith it? The word is nigh thee, *even* in thy mouth, and in thy heart: that is, the word of faith, which we preach.

Proverbs 17:25 A foolish son *is* a grief to his father, and bitterness to her that bare him.

Focus: This proverb describes the effect of a foolish son on his parents.

Verse twenty-one above defines the disastrous effect brought on parents by a foolish son as being "sorrow" and lack of "joy," and in this verse, the parents are said to experience **"grief"** and **"bitterness."** All four descriptive terms identify sorrow of heart, making the two proverbs nearly identical. (The Hebrew word for "bitterness" means sorrow.)

Along with all the parents' many heartaches caused by the unwise son is the grief and bitterness of knowing that these sorrows will continue as long as he insists on living a wicked life of rebellion against God. Additionally and tragically, they know that the foolish son faces the eternal penalty of hell. It is of no light matter that when such a son is with his mother and father, there is very little if anything, that they can agree with or be joyous about.

> Genesis 26:34-35 And Esau was forty years old when he took to wife Judith the daughter of Beeri the Hittite, and Bashemath the daughter of Elon the Hittite: Which were a grief of mind unto Isaac and to Rebekah.
> 1 Samuel 2:22 Now Eli was very old, and heard all that his sons did unto all Israel; and how they lay with the women that assembled at the door of the tabernacle of the congregation.
> 1 Samuel 8:3 And his *[Samuel's]* sons walked not in his ways, but turned aside after lucre, and took bribes, and perverted judgment.
> 2 Samuel 18:33 And the king *[David]* was much moved, and went up to the chamber over the gate, and wept: and as he went, thus he said, O my son Absalom, my son, my son Absalom! would God I had died for thee, O Absalom, my son, my son!
> Proverbs 10:1 The proverbs of Solomon. A wise son maketh a glad father: but a foolish son is the heaviness of his mother.
> Proverbs 15:20 A wise son maketh a glad father: but a foolish man despiseth his mother.
> Proverbs 17:21 He that begetteth a fool doeth it to his sorrow: and the father of a fool hath no joy.
> Proverbs 19:13 A foolish son is the calamity of his father: and the contentions of a wife are a continual dropping.
> Proverbs 23:15 My son, if thine heart be wise, my heart shall rejoice, even mine.

Proverbs 17:26 Also to punish the just *is* not good, *nor* to strike princes for equity.

Focus: This proverb identifies two inversions of justice that are bad and opposed by God.

"Also to punish the just *is* not good." Anytime **"the just"** *[righteous]* are punished as though they were evil, justice is perverted. It is **"not good"** in the sight of God or for the abused or for the abuser to punish those who have done no wrong. **"The just"** are those who are right with God and include those who are innocent of doing evil against society or the laws of the land. The righteous are obligated and desire for their actions to please God in every area of society, whether civil or sacred. To punish the just is to summon the wrath of God.

> "**To punish an innocent** person (cf. Proverbs 18:5) **or to flog officials** (only kings or judges could order this to be done) who are serving with **integrity** is, like bribery (Proverbs 17:23), perverting the cause of justice."[430]
>
> Proverbs 17:15 He that justifieth the wicked, and he that condemneth the just, even they both are abomination to the LORD.
> Proverbs 18:5 It is not good to accept the person of the wicked, to overthrow the righteous in judgment.
> John 18:22-23 And when he had thus spoken, one of the officers which stood by struck Jesus with the palm of his hand, saying, Answerest thou the high priest so? Jesus answered him, If I have spoken evil, bear witness of the evil: but if well, why smitest thou me?
> Acts 4:1-3 And as they spake unto the people, the priests, and the captain of the temple, and the Sadducees, came upon them, Being grieved that they taught the people, and preached through Jesus the resurrection from the dead. And they laid hands on them, and put *them* in hold unto the next day: for it was now eventide.
> Romans 13:1-4 Let every soul be subject unto the higher powers. For there is no power but of God: the powers that be are ordained of God. Whosoever therefore resisteth the power, resisteth the ordinance of God: and they that resist shall receive to themselves damnation. For rulers are not a terror to good works, but to the evil. Wilt thou then not be afraid of the power? do that which is good, and thou shalt have praise of the same: For he is the minister of God to thee for good. But if thou do that which is evil, be afraid; for he beareth not the sword in vain: for he is the minister of God, a revenger to *execute* wrath upon him that doeth evil.

"*Nor* to strike princes for equity." The instruction here is that it **"is not good"** to **"strike"** (punish) a **"prince"** *[noble in mind and character, an upright, honest official]* for making an honest and equitable decision. Such maltreatment is blasphemous to God's laws of justice and righteousness and will not go unpunished. When people, including "princes," who are behaving properly are punished as though they were evil doers, the population becomes disturbed, discontented and unstable. Consequently, government leaders, who become corrupt and punish the righteous as though they were evil, "are Ministers of God in authority, but Ministers of Satan in administration."[431] To punish a just or righteous person or to punish a prince or noble leader who serves with integrity is a perversion of justice like the bribery of verse 23.

> Genesis 18:25 That be far from thee to do after this manner, to slay the righteous with the wicked: and that the righteous should be as the wicked, that be far from thee: Shall not the Judge of all the earth do right?
>
> Exodus 22:28 Thou shalt not revile the gods, nor curse the ruler of thy people.

Proverbs 17:27 He that hath knowledge spareth his words: *and* a man of understanding is of an excellent spirit.

Focus: This proverb declares that the man with knowledge (of God and His laws) carefully chooses his words and that a man of understanding reveals to everyone an excellent spirit.

"He that hath knowledge spareth his words." In this proverb, the *wise person* is both the **"he"** who ***has knowledge*** in the first clause and the **"man of understanding"** in the second. Having knowledge from and about God, he knows to cautiously choose his words and ***spare his words.*** "He shows his common sense, not by rash talk or saying all he knows, but by restraining his tongue."[432] He can thus please God and appease men.

> Job 13:5 O that ye would altogether hold your peace! and it should be your wisdom.
>
> Psalm 39:1 To the chief Musician, even to Jeduthun, A Psalm of David. I said, I will take heed to my ways, that I sin not with my tongue: I will keep my mouth with a bridle, while the wicked is before me.
>
> Proverbs 29:11 A fool uttereth all his mind: but a wise man keepeth it in till afterwards.
>
> Matthew 12:36-37 But I say unto you, That every idle word that men shall speak, they shall give account thereof in the day of judgment. For by thy words thou shalt be justified, and by thy words thou shalt be condemned.
>
> James 1:19-20 Wherefore, my beloved brethren, let every man be swift to hear, slow to speak, slow to wrath: For the wrath of man worketh not the righteousness of God.
>
> James 3:2 For in many things we offend all. If any man offend not in word, the same *is* a perfect man, *and* able also to bridle the whole body.

"And a man of understanding is of an excellent spirit." He understands godly wisdom and thus the ways and words of God. From God, he has been taught how to act *in* the world and interact *with* the world according to instructions from the Designer, the Creator. *With a desire to please God, and leadership from the Holy Spirit, he will control his speech and spirit so that it can be said that he has an* **"excellent spirit."** A description of such God-given excellence in both attitude and behavior is found in Galatians 5:22 and identified as the fruit of the Holy Spirit – love, joy, peace, longsuffering, gentleness, goodness, faith, meekness, and temperance. The phrase "excellent spirit" was used to describe Daniel in Daniel 5:12 which states, "as an excellent spirit, and knowledge, and understanding, interpreting of dreams, and shewing of hard sentences, and dissolving of doubts, were found in the same Daniel." (Daniel's "excellent spirit" is also referred to in Daniel 5:14 and 6:3.)

> Proverbs 2:1-6 My son, if thou wilt receive my words, and hide my commandments with thee; So that thou incline thine ear unto wisdom, *and* apply thine heart to understanding; Yea, if thou criest after knowledge, *and* liftest up thy voice for understanding; If thou seekest her as silver, and searchest for her as *for* hid treasures; Then shalt thou understand the fear of the LORD, and find the knowledge of God. For the LORD giveth wisdom: out of his mouth *cometh* knowledge and understanding.
>
> Proverbs 9:10 The fear of the LORD *is* the beginning of wisdom: and the knowledge of the holy *is* understanding.
>
> Proverbs 15:1 The tongue of the wise useth knowledge aright: but the mouth of fools poureth out foolishness.
>
> 1 Peter 3:8-10 Finally, be ye all of one mind, having compassion one of another, love as brethren, be pitiful, be courteous: Not rendering evil for evil, or railing for railing: but contrariwise blessing; knowing that ye are thereunto called, that ye should inherit a blessing. For he that will love life, and see good days, let him refrain his tongue from evil, and his lips that they speak no guile.

Proverbs 17:28 Even a fool, when he holdeth his peace, is counted wise: *and* he that shutteth his lips *is esteemed* a man of understanding.

Focus: This proverb declares how people perceive others who keep quiet.

When a fool remains quiet, he gives the appearance of being wise because of two possible assumptions by observers: First, if the audience doesn't know him, they may suppose that he is being quiet because he is pausing to carefully choose his words before speaking. (Unrestrained, spontaneous speaking is a mark of a fool.) Second, they may surmise that he is a wise person because he is simply exhibiting the wise person's obvious characteristic, which is to be thoughtful and restrained. "He cannot be known for a fool, that says nothing. He is a fool, not who hath unwise thoughts, but who utters them. Even concealed folly is wisdom."[433]

"The fool might get a character for wisdom, had he only wit enough to be quiet; – 'Even a fool, when he holdeth his peace, is counted wise: and he that shutteth his lips is esteemed a man of understanding.' Folly, to be known, must be uttered. If it is kept in, it may pass undiscovered; and the very reserve might contribute to give a stranger the impression of wisdom; since 'he that hath knowledge spareth his words.' But the loss of the fool is, that he 'cannot withhold himself from speaking; and thus he cannot conceal his folly.'"[434]

Psalm 39:1-2 To the chief Musician, *even* to Jeduthun, A Psalm of David. I said, I will take heed to my ways, that I sin not with my tongue: I will keep my mouth with a bridle, while the wicked is before me. I was dumb with silence, I held my peace, *even* from good; and my sorrow was stirred.

Proverbs 15:28 The heart of the righteous studieth to answer: but the mouth of the wicked poureth out evil things.

Matthew 12:36-37 But I say unto you, That every idle word that men shall speak, they shall give account thereof in the day of judgment. For by thy words thou shalt be justified, and by thy words thou shalt be condemned.

James 3:2 For in many things we offend all. If any man offend not in word, the same *is* a perfect man, *and* able also to bridle the whole body.

CHAPTER EIGHTEEN

> **Proverbs 18:1-2** Through desire a man, having separated himself, seeketh *and* intermeddleth with all wisdom.
> 2. A fool hath no delight in understanding, but that his heart may discover itself.

Focus: This proverb (verses 1 and 2) exposes the braggadocious, egotistical heart and motive of a fool who obstinately involves himself with wisdom so that he can demonstrate himself to be the seat of all wisdom (or so he thinks to do).

"Through desire a man, having separated himself, seeketh *and* intermeddleth with all wisdom." This verse speaks of **"a man"** who is further identified as **"a fool"** in verse two. This foolish man is said to take two courses of action: (1) he *separates himself,* (from God and those with godly wisdom) and (2) he *intermeddles with all wisdom.*

When he *intermeddles* [breaks out in contention, is obstinate] with **"all wisdom,"** it is not for the purpose of learning. He does so to prove to himself and others that his superior native wisdom (or so he believes it to be) is greater than the aggregate of all other wisdom. The New Testament church contended with men like him in their ranks.

> 1 Timothy 6:4-5 He is proud, knowing nothing, but doting about questions and strifes of words, whereof cometh envy, strife, railings, evil surmisings, Perverse disputings of men of corrupt minds, and destitute of the truth, supposing that gain is godliness: from such withdraw thyself.
> Titus 1:14 Not giving heed to Jewish fables, and commandments of men, that turn from the truth.

"A fool hath no delight in understanding, but that his heart may discover itself." Verse two gives the fool's motive for the courses of action that he took in verse one– **"that his heart may discover itself."** He wants to hear himself expound, to make a show of what he believes to be his own great native wisdom. He has *no delight in understanding,* he just wants to exhibit himself as he foolishly believes that his demonstration of foolishness is received as wisdom. He believes that he doesn't need any help from anyone else for understanding–especially from God. If the fool would or could actually visualize the emptiness of his wicked heart, he would see "the scantiness of his knowledge and the vanity of his mind."[435]

Wisdom, knowledge, and understanding do not come from within a man; they are gifts of God given through diligent search into the words of God. James also tells the believer that if he lacks wisdom, he should ask God for it (James:1:5).

> Proverbs 2:1-6 My son, if thou wilt receive my words, and hide my commandments with thee; So that thou incline thine ear unto wisdom, *and* apply thine heart to understanding; Yea, if thou criest after knowledge, *and* liftest up thy voice for understanding; If thou seekest her as silver, and searchest for her as *for* hid treasures; Then shalt thou understand the fear of the LORD, and find the knowledge of God. For the LORD giveth wisdom: out of his mouth *cometh* knowledge and understanding.
> Isaiah 26:9 With my soul have I desired thee in the night; yea, with my spirit within me will I seek thee early: for when thy judgments *are* in the earth, the inhabitants of the world will learn righteousness.
> Matthew 13:9-11 Who hath ears to hear, let him hear. And the disciples came, and said unto him, Why speakest thou unto them in parables? He answered and said unto them, Because it is given unto you to know the mysteries of the kingdom of heaven, but to them it is not given.
> 1 Corinthians 2:9-14 But as it is written, Eye hath not seen, nor ear heard, neither have entered into the heart of man, the things which God hath prepared for them that love him. But God hath revealed *them* unto us by his Spirit: for the Spirit searcheth all things, yea, the deep things of God. For what man knoweth the things of a man, save the spirit of man which is in him? even so the things of God knoweth no man, but the Spirit of God. Now we have received, not the spirit of the world, but the spirit which is of God; that we might know the things that are freely given to us of God. Which things also we speak, not in the words which man's wisdom teacheth, but which the Holy Ghost teacheth; comparing spiritual things with spiritual. But the natural man receiveth not the things of the Spirit of God: for they are foolishness unto him: neither can he know *them,* because they are spiritually discerned.

> **Proverbs 18:3** When the wicked cometh, *then* cometh also contempt, and with ignominy reproach.

Focus: This proverb expresses the fact that contempt, ignominy, and reproach accompany the approach of a wicked person.

As part of his being wicked, the evil person brings along (like a bad odor) the misery of **"contempt"** *[degrading disrespect]*, **"ignominy"** *[shame, disgrace]*, and **"reproach"** *[scorn, shame, disgrace]*. It is as though the wicked person dipped himself in the stink of opposition to God and man and the odor follows wherever he goes. The wicked use words of contempt in an attempt to destroy the work of God and to shame the children of God. "When he comes into the house of God, it may be said, 'There comes contempt'; for he comes not to hear the word, in order to receive any profit by it, but to contemn it, and the ministers of it."[436] The **"contempt"** of the wicked bubbles up from deep within his heart and manifests itself through his vile mouth. He uses disgraceful, shameful words whereby he intentionally insults, with the intent to disgrace and to bring reproach upon the righteous.

> Psalm 37:12 The wicked plotteth against the just, and gnasheth upon him with his teeth.
>
> Psalm 58:3 The wicked are estranged from the womb: they go astray as soon as they be born, speaking lies.
>
> Psalm 123:3-4 Have mercy upon us, O LORD, have mercy upon us: for we are exceedingly filled with contempt. Our soul is exceedingly filled with the scorning of those that are at ease, *and* with the contempt of the proud.
>
> Proverbs 11:2 *When* pride cometh, then cometh shame: but with the lowly *is* wisdom.
>
> Proverbs 21:10 The soul of the wicked desireth evil: his neighbour findeth no favour in his eyes.
>
> Proverbs 22:10 Cast out the scorner, and contention shall go out; yea, strife and reproach shall cease.
>
> Isaiah 57:20 But the wicked *are* like the troubled sea, when it cannot rest, whose waters cast up mire and dirt.

The wicked man is full of contempt. He looks down on his neighbors, and his neighbor's poverty or tribulations; and to bring shame he uses his neighbor's calamities as a subject of demeaning conversation.

King Saul's wicked daughter Michal had purposefully been given as a wife to David to "be a snare unto him." (1 Samuel 18:21) She tried to shame David because he loved the Lord; and she is a picture of a wicked wife disrupting an otherwise joyful, God-honoring situation with shame and reproach.

> 2 Samuel 6:16 . . . 20-23 And as the ark of the LORD came into the city of David, Michal Saul's daughter looked through a window, and saw king David leaping and dancing before the LORD; and she despised him in her heart . . . Then David returned to bless his household. And Michal the daughter of Saul came out to meet David, and said, How glorious was the king of Israel to day, who uncovered himself to day in the eyes of the handmaids of his servants, as one of the vain fellows shamelessly uncovereth himself! And David said unto Michal, It was before the LORD, which chose me before thy father, and before all his house, to appoint me ruler over the people of the LORD, over Israel: therefore will I play before the LORD. And I will yet be more vile than thus, and will be base in mine own sight: and of the maidservants which thou hast spoken of, of them shall I be had in honour. Therefore Michal the daughter of Saul had no child unto the day of her death.

Wicked Sanballat and Tobiah approached Nehemiah and the Jewish workers with mockery, shame and contempt while they were trying to rebuilt the wall of Jerusalem.

> Nehemiah 4:1-4 But it came to pass, that when Sanballat heard that we builded the wall, he was wroth, and took great indignation, and mocked the Jews. And he spake before his brethren and the army of Samaria, and said, What do these feeble Jews? will they fortify themselves? will they sacrifice? will they make an end in a day? will they revive the stones out of the heaps of the rubbish which are burned? Now Tobiah the Ammonite was by him, and he said, Even that which they build, if a fox go up, he shall even break down their stone wall. Hear, O our God; for we are despised: and turn their reproach upon their own head, and give them for a prey in the land of captivity:

In addition to His painful death on the Cross, our Lord had to suffer shame and reproach at the hand of the wicked.

> Psalm 69:19-20 Thou hast known my reproach, and my shame, and my dishonour: mine adversaries are all before thee. Reproach hath broken my heart; and I am full of heaviness: and I looked for some to take pity, but there was none; and for comforters, but I found none.
>
> Matthew 10:25 It is enough for the disciple that he be as his master, and the servant as his lord. If they have called the master of the house Beelzebub, how much more shall they call them of his household?
>
> Matthew 27:39-44 And they that passed by reviled him, wagging their heads, And saying, Thou that destroyest the temple, and buildest it in three days, save thyself. If thou be the Son of God, come down from the cross. Likewise also the chief priests mocking him, with the scribes and elders, said, He saved others; himself he cannot save. If he be the King of Israel, let him now

come down from the cross, and we will believe him. He trusted in God; let him deliver him now, if he will have him: for he said, I am the Son of God. The thieves also, which were crucified with him, cast the same in his teeth.

Since the Savior was mocked and shamed by wicked men, Christians will not expect to be respected. Peter describes the mocking and shame that evil people try to bring on new Christians.

> 1 Peter 4:3-4 For the time past of our life may suffice us to have wrought the will of the Gentiles, when we walked in lasciviousness, lusts, excess of wine, revellings, banquetings, and abominable idolatries: Wherein they think it strange that ye run not with them to the same excess of riot, speaking evil of you:
>
> 1 Peter 4:14 If ye be reproached for the name of Christ, happy are ye; for the spirit of glory and of God resteth upon you: on their part he is evil spoken of, but on your part he is glorified.

Evil men will not cease to have contempt for God and good people, and will seek to prove Christians "ignorant and unlearned" as they did the apostles.

> Proverbs 22:10 Cast out the scorner, and contention shall go out; yea, strife and reproach shall cease.
>
> Luke 6:22 Blessed are ye, when men shall hate you, and when they shall separate you from their company, and shall reproach you, and cast out your name as evil, for the Son of man's sake.

Proverbs 18:4 The words of a man's mouth *are as* deep waters, *and* the wellspring of wisdom *as* a flowing brook.

Focus: This proverb describes the intrinsic depth and natural fluency of the words of a wise person.

"The words of a man's mouth *are as* deep waters." The sagacious sayings from a wise man are like "deep waters" (figuratively dark and calm). Because God teaches him wisdom, his foundational reasoning is correct; and he has deep understanding. God has taught the wise person to view the issues of life and the ridiculous arguments of men through the prism of His teachings so that He thinks in a manner instructed by God and consequently speaks with godly wisdom. Like a relic brought up from the dark, calm waters of an ocean, the wise man's words are drawn from the dark sayings of God.

"*And* the wellspring of wisdom *as* a flowing brook" indicating that such a wise person's words have their source and flow from his deep, God-produced pure understanding like a calming, refreshing flow of a mountain stream bubbling over rocks and gentle falls. In order to be a wellspring and source of life, the mouth of the believer must speak the wisdom found in God's word.

> "How shallow is much, if not most, that is spoken in our hearing! It strikes no deeper than 'the hour's event,' than the mere gilding of our life; it only extends to the circumstances or to the conventionalities of life; it deals with tastes and customs, with regulation and proprieties; it goes no further than pecuniary or social expectations; it lies upon the surface and does not touch 'the deep heart and reality of things.' But the wisdom of the wise strikes deep; it goes down into the character; it touches first principles; it has to do with the sources and springs of human action; it concerns itself with the intrinsically true, the really beautiful, the solidly and permanently good."[437]

> "The utterances of men who are not truly wise are lacking in this. They can only repeat what they have learned; they have to consult their 'authorities' in order to know what they should say; they have to labour and strive in order to express themselves. Not so the truly wise. Their words come from them as water from a well spring; their speech is the simple, natural, unconstrained outflow of their soul; they speak from the heart, not from the book. Their spirit is full of Divine wisdom; they 'have understanding' (Proverbs 17:24); they have knowledge, insight, love of the truth; they 'cannot but speak' the truth they have learned of God, the things they have heard and seen. And the spontaneity of their utterance is one real element in their eloquence and their influence . . . They are 'as a flowing brook.' As water that is not pent up like a reservoir, but flows on through the thirsty land, communicating moisture, and thus ministering to life and growth, so the words of the wise are continually flowing; they spread from heart to heart, from land to land, from age to age. And as they flow they minister to the life and the growth of men; they communicate those living truths which enlighten the mind, which soften and change the heart, which transform and ennoble the life. Their career is never closed, for from soul to soul, from lip to lip, from life to life, wisdom passes on in its blessed, unbroken course."[438]

> Proverbs 10:11 The mouth of a righteous *man is* a well of life: but violence covereth the mouth of the wicked.
>
> Proverbs 13:14 The law of the wise *is* a fountain of life, to depart from the snares of death.
>
> Proverbs 16:22 Understanding *is* a wellspring of life unto him that hath it: but the instruction of fools *is* folly.
>
> Proverbs 17:24 Wisdom *is* before him that hath understanding; but the eyes of a fool *are* in the ends of the earth.
>
> Proverbs 20:5 Counsel in the heart of man *is like* deep water; but a man of understanding will draw it out.
>
> Ecclesiastes 7:24 That which is far off, and exceeding deep, who can find it out?
>
> Colossians 3:16 Let the word of Christ dwell in you richly in all wisdom; teaching and admonishing one another in Psalm and hymns and spiritual songs, singing with grace in your hearts to the Lord.

Colossians 4:6 Let your speech *be* alway with grace, seasoned with salt, that ye may know how ye ought to answer every man.

The Importance of Language

Language is one of the principal tests and standards of civilization. The study of language is one of the most naturally interesting and naturally elevating studies with which the human mind can occupy itself.

I. **It is of great intellectual importance.** Only through the instrumentality of language can the thoughts of the mind be revealed and displayed. Nothing bewrays more obviously the rustiness and disorganization of the intellect than inaccuracy and dullness of language.

II. **The moral importance of language is still greater.** As a rule the relations between intellect and conscience are harmonious. When the intellect is illuminated it brightens the conscience; when the conscience is quickened it animates the intellect. Language is often a standard of morals. Exactitude of utterance is seldom compatible with great frequency of utterance. Modern writing and modern speech are impotent because they are slipshod. Language is also a great moral force in the world by reason of its variety. A world of one language would not be a very interesting world.

III. **The great religious importance of language.** The utmost solemnity is attached in the Bible to the use of language. What man can think that words are light and little things when he remembers that it is through the instrumentality of words inspired that God has made known His greatest revelations to mankind?"

(From a sermon by Canon Diggle as quoted in Joseph S. Exell, Editor, *The Biblical Illustrator*, 1887-1905, e-Sword 12.0.1.)

Proverbs 18:5 *It is* not good to accept the person of the wicked, to overthrow the righteous in judgment.

Focus: This proverb specifies the evil of showing partiality to the person (status) of the wicked.

"*It is* not good to accept the person of the wicked." "*It is* not good" is an expression "meaning it is very bad."[439] "To show partiality" to a wicked person because of his political, economic, or social status is wrong. Neither should charisma nor a pleasant persona that does not match true character overwhelm any evidence of wickedness. An evil person should be properly recognized and identified as the wicked person that he is rather than excused because of his possession of power or position. To accept such a person and give him preference over another because of any reason such as the above plus "appearance, manners, fortune, family,"[440] is "an offense to God, an affront to justice, a wrong to mankind, and a real service done to the kingdom of sin and Satan."[441]

"To overthrow the righteous in judgment" is to allow any wicked person's power, position, riches, or other prominence to overthrow proper judgment of the righteous. Wicked men who oppose truthfulness will use their place of power or authority to defeat the righteous in a court of law. Lying is part of their nature, and their opposition to the righteous is a manifestation of their opposition to God.

Leviticus 19:15 Ye shall do no unrighteousness in judgment: thou shalt not respect the person of the poor, nor honour the person of the mighty: *but* in righteousness shalt thou judge thy neighbour.

Deuteronomy 1:17 Ye shall not respect persons in judgment; *but* ye shall hear the small as well as the great; ye shall not be afraid of the face of man; for the judgment *is* God's: and the cause that is too hard for you, bring *it* unto me, and I will hear it.

2 Samuel 23:3 The God of Israel said, the Rock of Israel spake to me, He that ruleth over men *must be* just, ruling in the fear of God.

Psalm 82:2 How long will ye judge unjustly, and accept the persons of the wicked? Selah.

Proverbs 17:15 He that justifieth the wicked, and he that condemneth the just, even they both *are* abomination to the LORD.

Proverbs 17:23 A wicked *man* taketh a gift out of the bosom to pervert the ways of judgment.

Proverbs 17:26 Also to punish the just *is* not good, *nor* to strike princes for equity.

Proverbs 24:23 These *things* also *belong* to the wise. *It is* not good to have respect of persons in judgment.

Proverbs 28:21 To have respect of persons *is* not good: for for a piece of bread *that* man will transgress.

Isaiah 5:22 Woe unto *them that are* mighty to drink wine, and men of strength to mingle strong drink: Which justify the wicked for reward, and take away the righteousness of the righteous from him!

Isaiah 11:4 But with righteousness shall he judge the poor, and reprove with equity for the meek of the earth: and he shall smite the earth with the rod of his mouth, and with the breath of his lips shall he slay the wicked.

Acts 17:30-31 And the times of this ignorance God winked at; but now commandeth all men every where to repent: Because he hath appointed a day, in the which he will judge the world in righteousness by *that* man whom he hath ordained; *whereof* he hath given assurance unto all *men*, in that he hath raised him from the dead.

> **Proverbs 18:6-7** A fool's lips enter into contention, and his mouth calleth for strokes.
> 7. A fool's mouth *is* his destruction, and his lips *are* the snare of his soul.

Focus: This proverb (verses 6 and 7) describes the variety of self-inflicted troubles that are the consequence of a fool's mouth.

"The fool's lips enter into contention, and his mouth calleth for strokes." He walks right into situations, senselessly running his mouth, involving himself when doing so is not only needless but disastrous. "And thus he makes a rod for himself. He puts a weapon into the hands of Satan, with which to beat his own head, and hammers him with fearful *strokes*."[442] An experienced wise person can see strife developing. He watches people like a cook watches a seething pot. As strife begins heating up with the wrong kind of looks and gestures, he sets himself on alert, guards his words, gathers his stuff, and separates himself from a senseless situation. Not so with the fool. If he were to recognize the beginning of strife, he would continue unrestrained. He wouldn't care to heed Paul's admonition, "If it be possible, as much as lieth in you, live peaceably with all men." (Romans 12:18)

"A fool's mouth *is* his destruction, and his lips *are* the snare of his soul." His mouth destroys his own reputation, repose, and relationships. He does this through provocative language that stirs emotions and draws ill responses, through prying into situations where he is obviously out of place and has no business, and through proudly declaring objectives that he can not possibly fulfill. He has a complete disregard for truth. There is no need for others to set a trap for him because his senseless, unfiltered, and uncontrolled talk is a snare of its own.

> Proverbs 10:14 Wise *men* lay up knowledge: but the mouth of the foolish *is* near destruction.
> Proverbs 12:13 The wicked is snared by the transgression of *his* lips: but the just shall come out of trouble.
> Proverbs 13:3 He that keepeth his mouth keepeth his life: *but* he that openeth wide his lips shall have destruction.
> Proverbs 16:27-28 An ungodly man diggeth up evil: and in his lips there is as a burning fire. A froward man soweth strife: and a whisperer separateth chief friends.
> Proverbs 19:29 Judgments are prepared for scorners, and stripes for the back of fools.
> Proverbs 26:3 A whip for the horse, a bridle for the ass, and a rod for the fool's back.
> Romans 3:13-18 Their throat is an open sepulchre; with their tongues they have used deceit; the poison of asps is under their lips: Whose mouth is full of cursing and bitterness: Their feet are swift to shed blood: Destruction and misery are in their ways: And the way of peace have they not known: There is no fear of God before their eyes.
> James 3:6, 8-9 And the tongue is a fire, a world of iniquity: so is the tongue among our members, that it defileth the whole body, and setteth on fire the course of nature; and it is set on fire of hell . . . But the tongue can no man tame; it is an unruly evil, full of deadly poison. Therewith bless we God, even the Father; and therewith curse we men, which are made after the similitude of God.

A fool's words are a continual entanglement to him – the **"snare of his soul."** As Proverbs 5:22 states: "His own iniquities shall take the wicked himself, and he shall be holden with the cords of his sins." Jesus was very specific that a man's words will either condemn or free him on the day of judgment.

> Matthew 12:34-37 O generation of vipers, how can ye, being evil, speak good things? for out of the abundance of the heart the mouth speaketh. A good man out of the good treasure of the heart bringeth forth good things: and an evil man out of the evil treasure bringeth forth evil things. But I say unto you, That every idle word that men shall speak, they shall give account thereof in the day of judgment. For by thy words thou shalt be justified, and by thy words thou shalt be condemned.

Other Scriptures show the immediate punishment that comes upon the wicked because of his evil words.

> 2 Kings 2:23-24 And he went up from thence unto Bethel: and as he was going up by the way, there came forth little children out of the city, and mocked him, and said unto him, Go up, thou bald head; go up, thou bald head. And he turned back, and looked on them, and cursed them in the name of the LORD. And there came forth two she bears out of the wood, and tare forty and two children of them.
> Acts 12:21-23 And upon a set day Herod, arrayed in royal apparel, sat upon his throne, and made an oration unto them. And the people gave a shout, saying, It is the voice of a god, and not of a man. And immediately the angel of the Lord smote him, because he gave not God the glory: and he was eaten of worms, and gave up the ghost.

> **Proverbs 18:8** The words of a talebearer *are* as wounds, and they go down into the innermost parts of the belly.

Focus: This proverb (identical to Proverbs 26:22) expresses the severe damage that talebearing causes.

Like a delicious morsel of food is delightful to eat, the talebearer's lips speak words that are delightful for some people to hear. His words are like sharp knives creating wounds. They are words of discord and strife piercing everyone who "tastes" his concoction. All are harmed – the talebearer, the listener, and the one spoken about. Reputations are ruined, friendships destroyed, feuds initiated, clear consciences made into troubled minds, and peace made into war. God detests the talebearer, and wise people dodge him or show him an angry countenance when he leans to whisper his malicious words.

> Leviticus 19:16 Thou shalt not go up and down *as* a talebearer among thy people: neither shalt thou stand against the blood of thy neighbour: I *am* the LORD.
> Psalm 50:19-20 Thou givest thy mouth to evil, and thy tongue frameth deceit. Thou sittest and speakest against thy brother; thou slanderest thine own mother's son.
> Psalm 52:2 Thy tongue deviseth mischiefs; like a sharp razor, working deceitfully.
> Proverbs 12:18 There is that speaketh like the piercings of a sword: but the tongue of the wise *is* health.
> Proverbs 16:28 A froward man soweth strife: and a whisperer separateth chief friends.
> Proverbs 17:9 He that covereth a transgression seeketh love; but he that repeateth a matter separateth *very* friends.
> 1 Corinthians 13:6 Rejoiceth not in iniquity, but rejoiceth in the truth.

Proverbs 18:9 He also that is slothful in his work is brother to him that is a great waster.

Focus: This proverb specifies that the person slothful in work and the one who is wasteful are equally in the same category of foolishness.

Figuratively speaking, the **"slothful"** and the **"great waster"** come out of the same family. They are **brothers** with the same *family traits* of self-destructiveness, disrespectfulness of God's provisions, and a disregard for God's instructions for living.

> "**Slothfulness and prodigality** *[wastefulness]* **have the same origin**. As brothers are the children of a common parent, so sloth and waste have their root in the common sin of ungodliness; men are spendthrifts or they are lazy, because they have no right sense of their obligations to God and to man – because they do not look upon their life as a stewardship for which they must give an account (Romans 14:12), but as a gift which they are at liberty to spend as they please. The acts of the prodigal and the slothful man differ in themselves, but they all spring from that spirit of self-pleasing which is the essence of ungodliness."[443]

Neither the "slothful" nor the "great waster" is respected by God or godly men. It is difficult to imagine that a genuinely slothful person or a great waster could heed God's instruction for wisdom. The man identified as 'wicked and slothful' in Matthew 25 had a very disrespectful opinion of God and was fearful of interacting with Him; and as a result of such degenerative fear, he hid the Lord's talent rather than interact with Him. On the other hand, the Prodigal who "wasted his goods" eventually repented, respected God, and requested to again be with Him (Luke 16:1).

> "The one folds his arms in sloth. The other opens his hands in wastefulness. The one gets nothing. The other spends what he gets. The one rushes into beggary. The other sits still, and waits its arrival. (Proverbs 6:11) The one dies by a rapid and violent disease. The other by a slow, subtle, but sure, consumption. Thus fearful is the guilt, solemn is the account, certain is the ruin, of both. God gives talents, not only to enrich, but to employ. And whether they be selfishly neglected, or carelessly thrown away – 'Thou wicked servant' will be the condemnation; 'outer darkness' will be the just and eternal doom. (Matthew 25:26-30)"[444]
> Proverbs 6:9-11 How long wilt thou sleep, O sluggard? when wilt thou arise out of thy sleep? *Yet* a little sleep, a little slumber, a little folding of the hands to sleep: So shall thy poverty come as one that travelleth, and thy want as an armed man.
> Proverbs 10:4 He becometh poor that dealeth *with* a slack hand: but the hand of the diligent maketh rich.
> Proverbs 24:30-34 I went by the field of the slothful, and by the vineyard of the man void of understanding; And, lo, it was all grown over with thorns, *and* nettles had covered the face thereof, and the stone wall thereof was broken down. Then I saw, *and* considered *it* well: I looked upon *it, and* received instruction. *Yet* a little sleep, a little slumber, a little folding of the hands to sleep: So shall thy poverty come *as* one that travelleth; and thy want as an armed man.
> Matthew 25:24-30 Then he which had received the one talent came and said, Lord, I knew thee that thou art an hard man, reaping where thou hast not sown, and gathering where thou hast not strawed: And I was afraid, and went and hid thy talent in the earth: lo, *there* thou hast *that is* thine. His lord answered and said unto him, *Thou* wicked and slothful servant, thou knewest that I reap where I sowed not, and gather where I have not strawed: Thou oughtest therefore to have put my money to the exchangers, and *then* at my coming I should have received mine own with usury. Take therefore the talent from him, and give *it* unto him which hath ten talents. For unto every one that hath shall be given, and he shall have abundance: but from him that hath not shall be taken away even that which he hath. And cast ye the unprofitable servant into outer darkness: there shall be weeping and gnashing of teeth.
> Luke 16:1 And he said also unto his disciples, There was a certain rich man, which had a steward; and the same was accused unto him that he had wasted his goods.

Romans 12:11 Not slothful in business; fervent in spirit; serving the Lord ...
Romans 14:12 So then every one of us shall give account of himself to God.
Hebrews 6:12 That ye be not slothful, but followers of them who through faith and patience inherit the promises.

Proverbs 18:10-11 The name of the LORD *is* a strong tower: the righteous runneth into it, and is safe.
11.   The rich man's wealth *is* his strong city, and as an high wall in his own conceit.

Focus: This proverb (verses 10 and 11) contrasts the reality of safety that the righteous have in "the name of the LORD" ("a strong tower") *with* the imagined safety that the wicked have in their "wealth."

The "Name of the Lord" in Scripture

Synonymous with the name of God Himself, the phrase **"the name of the LORD"** is found in 108 verses in the King James Bible. In today's culture, a name is usually a label that sets one person apart from another; but in the Bible, a name is much more than an identifier since personal and place names were formed from words that had their own meanings. Believing there was a vital connection between the name and the person that the name identified, the people of the Bible were very conscious of the meaning of names that represented the person's nature. In Exodus, when God Himself proclaimed the "name of the LORD," He added words that described His character.

> Exodus 34:4-7 And he hewed two tables of stone like unto the first; and Moses rose up early in the morning, and went up unto mount Sinai, as the LORD had commanded him, and took in his hand the two tables of stone. And the LORD descended in the cloud, and stood with him there, and proclaimed the name of the LORD. And the LORD passed by before him, and proclaimed, The LORD, The LORD God, merciful and gracious, longsuffering, and abundant in goodness and truth, Keeping mercy for thousands, forgiving iniquity and transgression and sin, and that will by no means clear *the guilty;* visiting the iniquity of the fathers upon the children, and upon the children's children, unto the third and to the fourth *generation.*

In other places in Scripture, the "name of the LORD" was synonymous with His presence.

> Psalm 75:1 To the chief Musician, Altaschith, A Psalm *or* Song of Asaph. Unto thee, O God, do we give thanks, *unto thee* do we give thanks: for *that* thy name is near thy wondrous works declare.

For a believer to take the "name of the LORD" in vain is to act or speak in a way that is inconsistent with the person's profession that He is God – "Thou shalt not take the name of the LORD thy God in vain; for the LORD will not hold him guiltless that taketh his name in vain" (Exodus 20:7). (When a person uses the "name of the LORD" he is saying he knows God personally.) Furthermore, in the New Testament the "name of the LORD" is synonymous and interchangeable with His Person.

> Acts 4:12 Neither is there salvation in any other: for there is none other name under heaven given among men, whereby we must be saved.
> 2 Timothy 2:19 Nevertheless the foundation of God standeth sure, having this seal, The Lord knoweth them that are his. And, Let every one that nameth the name of Christ depart from iniquity. (From Nelson's *Bible Dictionary*)

God provides a place of refuge and safety for the righteous that can be said to be like a **"strong tower."** He is the place of safety for the righteous, whereas there is no real place of safety for the wicked. Only **"in his own conceit"** (in his mind) is **"the rich man's wealth"** like a **"strong city"** and a **"high wall."**

> 'The Name of the Lord signifies all that God is in himself – his attributes, his love, mercy, power, knowledge; which allow man to regard him as a sure Refuge. 'Thou hast been a Shelter for me,' says the psalmist, 'and a strong Tower from the enemy.' The words bring before us a picture of a capitol, or central fortress, in which, at times of danger, the surrounding population could take refuge."[445]
>
> Deuteronomy 33:27-29 The eternal God *is thy* refuge, and underneath *are* the everlasting arms: and he shall thrust out the enemy from before thee; and shall say, Destroy *them.* Israel then shall dwell in safety alone: the fountain of Jacob *shall be* upon a land of corn and wine; also his heavens shall drop down dew. Happy *art* thou, O Israel: who *is* like unto thee, O people saved by the LORD, the shield of thy help, and who *is* the sword of thy excellency! and thine enemies shall be found liars unto thee; and thou shalt tread upon their high places.
> Exodus 3:13-15 And Moses said unto God, Behold, *when* I come unto the children of Israel, and shall say unto them, The God of your fathers hath sent me unto you; and they shall say to me, What *is* his name? what shall I say unto them? And God said unto Moses, I AM THAT I AM: and he said, Thus shalt thou say unto the children of Israel, I AM hath sent me unto you. And God said moreover unto Moses, Thus shalt thou say unto the children of Israel, The LORD God of your fathers, the God of Abraham, the God of Isaac, and the God of Jacob, hath sent me unto you: this *is* my name for ever, and this *is* my memorial unto all generations.
> Joshua 24:12 And I sent the hornet before you, which drave them out from before you, *even* the two kings of the Amorites; *but* not with thy sword, nor with thy bow.

2 Samuel 22:3 The God of my rock; in him will I trust: *he is* my shield, and the horn of my salvation, my high tower, and my refuge, my saviour; thou savest me from violence.

Psalm 9:10 And they that know thy name will put their trust in thee: for thou, LORD, hast not forsaken them that seek thee.

Psalm 18:2 The LORD *is* my rock, and my fortress, and my deliverer; my God, my strength, in whom I will trust; my buckler, and the horn of my salvation, *and* my high tower.

Psalm 27:1 *A Psalm* of David. The LORD *is* my light and my salvation; whom shall I fear? the LORD *is* the strength of my life; of whom shall I be afraid?

Psalm 61:3 For thou hast been a shelter for me, *and* a strong tower from the enemy.

Psalm 91:1-7 He that dwelleth in the secret place of the most High shall abide under the shadow of the Almighty. I will say of the LORD, *He is* my refuge and my fortress: my God; in him will I trust. Surely he shall deliver thee from the snare of the fowler, *and* from the noisome pestilence. He shall cover thee with his feathers, and under his wings shalt thou trust: his truth *shall be thy* shield and buckler. Thou shalt not be afraid for the terror by night; *nor* for the arrow *that* flieth by day; *Nor* for the pestilence *that* walketh in darkness; *nor* for the destruction *that* wasteth at noonday. A thousand shall fall at thy side, and ten thousand at thy right hand; *but* it shall not come nigh thee.

Proverbs 29:25 The fear of man bringeth a snare: but whoso putteth his trust in the LORD shall be safe.

The **"rich man"** is a term for a category of people who treat their wealth as a god. This verse does *not* refer to individual wealthy people like Abraham who trusted God, but rather to those who fully trust their **"wealth"** to care for them and provide for them in the same way that believers trust in God. A rich man's wealth can purchase things and services and can even purchase a certain "fair-weather" brand of friendship or loyalty from others; however, riches do not have any supernatural powers such as healing or safety. Wealth cannot create illusions in the enemy's mind to make them flee. It cannot supernaturally bring the right person across one's path to provide help or counsel in time of need. Wealth cannot provide "peace like a river," nor can it provide the most important of all things, an eternal home in heaven. Wealth is a **"high wall in his own conceit,"** meaning that in the rich person's imagination his wealth will protect him like the high wall of ancient cities protected the king and the citizens from enemies. The wall of protection provided by the purchasing power of wealth is, in reality, neither high nor strong compared to God, Who is indeed strength and protection. Wealth has no ability to think or reason and is a slave to the desire of its owner; in contrast, God is the loving Companion who communicates with His children while protecting and guiding them through life.

1 Kings 17:2-6 And the word of the LORD came unto him, saying, Get thee hence, and turn thee eastward, and hide thyself by the brook Cherith, that *is* before Jordan. And it shall be, *that* thou shalt drink of the brook; and I have commanded the ravens to feed thee there. So he went and did according unto the word of the LORD: for he went and dwelt by the brook Cherith, that *is* before Jordan. And the ravens brought him bread and flesh in the morning, and bread and flesh in the evening; and he drank of the brook.

2 Kings 7:5-7 And they rose up in the twilight, to go unto the camp of the Syrians: and when they were come to the uttermost part of the camp of Syria, behold, *there was* no man there. For the Lord had made the host of the Syrians to hear a noise of chariots, and a noise of horses, *even* the noise of a great host: and they said one to another, Lo, the king of Israel hath hired against us the kings of the Hittites, and the kings of the Egyptians, to come upon us. Wherefore they arose and fled in the twilight, and left their tents, and their horses, and their asses, even the camp as it *was,* and fled for their life.

Psalm 56:4 In God I will praise his word, in God I have put my trust; I will not fear what flesh can do unto me.

Psalm 91:14 Because he hath set his love upon me, therefore will I deliver him: I will set him on high, because he hath known my name.

Proverbs 10:15 The rich man's wealth *is* his strong city: the destruction of the poor *is* their poverty.

Matthew 7:24-27 Therefore whosoever heareth these sayings of mine, and doeth them, I will liken him unto a wise man, which built his house upon a rock: And the rain descended, and the floods came, and the winds blew, and beat upon that house; and it fell not: for it was founded upon a rock. And every one that heareth these sayings of mine, and doeth them not, shall be likened unto a foolish man, which built his house upon the sand: And the rain descended, and the floods came, and the winds blew, and beat upon that house; and it fell: and great was the fall of it.

Proverbs 18:12 Before destruction the heart of man is haughty, and before honour *is* humility.

Focus: This proverb contrasts the consequence of having a haughty heart with having a humble heart.

"Before destruction the heart of man is haughty *[lifted up in pride]***."** Usually visible in a man's attitude, pride tarnishes the way a person thinks and skews his reasoning ability, thus causing the self-centered one to fall into *destructive traps* that he might otherwise, with clear thinking, observe and avoid. Eve is the first and most significant example of *destruction by pride* as she opposed God to elevate herself, thus dragging Adam into a whirlpool of human disaster. Not being satisfied with living in a beautiful garden and knowing only good, Eve wanted to be as god, knowing good *and* evil. **"Destruction"** came upon them and their offspring. Pride causes people to eventually ruin themselves, their environment, and their relationships. It produces a spirit of haughtiness that can be seen even in a person's walk, word choice, and eyes. It is hated by God as well as by other people, even others full of the same evil. It is insidiously taught constantly on television, radio, in the schools and even in many churches.

> "According to Christian teachers, the essential vice, the utmost evil, is Pride. Unchastity, anger, greed, drunkenness, and all that, are mere flea bites in comparison: it was through Pride that the devil became the devil: Pride leads to every other vice: it is the complete anti-God state of mind ... it is Pride which has been the chief cause of misery in every nation and every family since the world began."[446]

Pride is the predominant sin mentioned throughout Scripture as being hated and judged by God. Because it is the attitude that magnifies self, minimizes God, and musters other sins, No other sin is named or identified so often.

> Psalm 12:3 The LORD shall cut off all flattering lips, and the tongue that speaketh proud things:
>
> Psalm 101:5 Whoso privily slandereth his neighbour, him will I cut off: him that hath an high look and a proud heart will not I suffer
>
> Proverbs 11:2 *When* pride cometh, then cometh shame: but with the lowly *is* wisdom.
>
> Proverbs 16:18 Pride *goeth* before destruction, and an haughty spirit before a fall.
>
> Proverbs 17:19 He loveth transgression that loveth strife: *and* he that exalteth his gate seeketh destruction.
>
> Proverbs 29:23 A man's pride shall bring him low: but honour shall uphold the humble in spirit.
>
> Isaiah 2:11-12 The lofty looks of man shall be humbled, and the haughtiness of men shall be bowed down, and the LORD alone shall be exalted in that day. For the day of the LORD of hosts *shall be* upon every *one that is* proud and lofty, and upon every *one that is* lifted up; and he shall be brought low.
>
> Ezekiel 16:49-50 Behold, this was the iniquity of thy sister Sodom, pride, fulness of bread, and abundance of idleness was in her and in her daughters, neither did she strengthen the hand of the poor and needy. And they were haughty, and committed abomination before me: therefore I took them away as I saw *good.*
>
> Daniel 4:30-31 The king spake, and said, Is not this great Babylon, that I have built for the house of the kingdom by the might of my power, and for the honour of my majesty? While the word was in the king's mouth, there fell a voice from heaven, saying, O king Nebuchadnezzar, to thee it is spoken; The kingdom is departed from thee.
>
> Daniel 5:23-28 But hast lifted up thyself against the Lord of heaven; and they have brought the vessels of his house before thee, and thou, and thy lords, thy wives, and thy concubines, have drunk wine in them; and thou hast praised the gods of silver, and gold, of brass, iron, wood, and stone, which see not, nor hear, nor know: and the God in whose hand thy breath *is,* and whose *are* all thy ways, hast thou not glorified: Then was the part of the hand sent from him; and this writing was written. And this *is* the writing that was written, MENE, MENE, TEKEL, UPHARSIN. This *is* the interpretation of the thing: MENE; God hath numbered thy kingdom, and finished it. TEKEL; Thou art weighed in the balances, and art found wanting. PERES; Thy kingdom is divided, and given to the Medes and Persians.
>
> Luke 14:8-11 When thou art bidden of any *man* to a wedding, sit not down in the highest room; lest a more honourable man than thou be bidden of him; And he that bade thee and him come and say to thee, Give this man place; and thou begin with shame to take the lowest room. But when thou art bidden, go and sit down in the lowest room; that when he that bade thee cometh, he may say unto thee, Friend, go up higher: then shalt thou have worship in the presence of them that sit at meat with thee. For whosoever exalteth himself shall be abased; and he that humbleth himself shall be exalted.
>
> Luke 18:10-14 Two men went up into the temple to pray; the one a Pharisee, and the other a publican. The Pharisee stood and prayed thus with himself, God, I thank thee, that I am not as other men are, extortioners, unjust, adulterers, or even as this publican. I fast twice in the week, I give tithes of all that I possess. And the publican, standing afar off, would not lift up so much as his eyes unto heaven, but smote upon his breast, saying, God be merciful to me a sinner. I tell you, this man went down to his house justified rather than the other: for every one that exalteth himself shall be abased; and he that humbleth himself shall be exalted. *[Also see Matthew 23:12.]*
>
> Acts 12:21-23 And upon a set day Herod, arrayed in royal apparel, sat upon his throne, and made an oration unto them. And the people gave a shout, *saying, It is* the voice of a god, and not of a man. And immediately the angel of the Lord smote him, because he gave not God the glory: and he was eaten of worms, and gave up the ghost.
>
> 1 Corinthians 4:6-7 And these things, brethren, I have in a figure transferred to myself and to Apollos for your sakes; that ye might learn in us not to think of men above that which is written, that no one of you be puffed up for one against another. For who maketh thee to differ from another? and what hast thou that thou didst not receive? now if thou didst receive it, why dost thou glory, as if thou hadst not received it?
>
> 1 Timothy 3:6 Not a novice, lest being lifted up with pride he fall into the condemnation of the devil.
>
> 2 Timothy 3:1-2 This know also, that in the last days perilous times shall come. For men shall be lovers of their own selves, covetous, boasters, proud, blasphemers, disobedient to parents, unthankful, unholy,
>
> James 4:6 But he giveth more grace. Wherefore he saith, God resisteth the proud, but giveth grace unto the humble.
>
> 1 Peter 5:5 Likewise, ye younger, submit yourselves unto the elder. Yea, all *of you* be subject one to another, and be clothed with humility: for God resisteth the proud, and giveth grace to the humble.
>
> Revelation 18:7 How much she hath glorified herself *[false religion - spiritual Babylon]*, and lived deliciously, so much torment and sorrow give her: for she saith in her heart, I sit a queen, and am no widow, and shall see no sorrow. Therefore shall her

plagues come in one day, death, and mourning, and famine; and she shall be utterly burned with fire: for strong is the Lord God who judgeth her.

"And before honour *is* humility." A person must show humility *before God will give honor.* Although men often disregard God's order and erroneously give honor without humility, the hasty action usually results in an exacerbation of arrogance. Then, this accelerated pride results in destruction beginning with rejection from God.

> *"Humility before honour.* Indeed, without *humility, honour* would be our temptation, rather than our glory. Had not the Apostle been kept down by a most humbling trial, his *honour* would have been his ruin. (2Corinthians 12:7-9) The exaltation of the Lord's people in Providence, is therefore often conducted through the valley of *Humiliation.* Joseph was raised from the prison to the throne. Moses and David were taken from the Shepherd's fold to feed the LORD's inheritance. Gideon acknowledged himself to be of 'the least of the families of Israel.' Ruth was humbled by adversity, ere she was raised to the high *honour* of a Mother in Israel, and progenitor of the Savior. Abigail confessed herself unworthy to wash the feet of her lord's servants, before she was honoured to be his wife. And in the daily walk of life, the lowest place is the path-way to *honour* ... And was not this the track of our beloved Lord – Before honour, humility – the cross before the crown? How deep was that descent, by which he, who was infinitely more than man, became 'a worm and no man!' (Psalm 22:6) And yet *the honour*, which rewarded this humility, what tongue can tell! (Philippians 2:9) 'We must not disdain to follow Jesus Christ.' Is it a light privilege to follow in the pathway consecrated by his steps, irradiated by his smile? (Matthew 11:29; 20:28, John 13:14)"[447]

Psalm 22:6 But I *am* a worm, and no man; a reproach of men, and despised of the people.

Proverbs 15:33 The fear of the LORD *is* the instruction of wisdom; and before honour *is* humility

Matthew 11:28-30 Come unto me, all ye that labour and are heavy laden, and I will give you rest. Take my yoke upon you, and learn of me; for I am meek and lowly in heart: and ye shall find rest unto your souls. For my yoke *is* easy, and my burden is light.

Matthew 20:25-28 But Jesus called them *unto him,* and said, Ye know that the princes of the Gentiles exercise dominion over them, and they that are great exercise authority upon them. But it shall not be so among you: but whosoever will be great among you, let him be your minister; And whosoever will be chief among you, let him be your servant: Even as the Son of man came not to be ministered unto, but to minister, and to give his life a ransom for many.

John 13:13-17 Ye call me Master and Lord: and ye say well; for *so* I am. If I then, *your* Lord and Master, have washed your feet; ye also ought to wash one another's feet. For I have given you an example, that ye should do as I have done to you. Verily, verily, I say unto you, The servant is not greater than his lord; neither he that is sent greater than he that sent him. If ye know these things, happy are ye if ye do them.

2 Corinthians 12:7-9 And lest I should be exalted above measure through the abundance of the revelations, there was given to me a thorn in the flesh, the messenger of Satan to buffet me, lest I should be exalted above measure. For this thing I besought the Lord thrice, that it might depart from me. And he said unto me, My grace is sufficient for thee: for my strength is made perfect in weakness. Most gladly therefore will I rather glory in my infirmities, that the power of Christ may rest upon me.

Philippians 2:5-9 Let this mind be in you, which was also in Christ Jesus: Who, being in the form of God, thought it not robbery to be equal with God: But made himself of no reputation, and took upon him the form of a servant, and was made in the likeness of men: And being found in fashion as a man, he humbled himself, and became obedient unto death, even the death of the cross. Wherefore God also hath highly exalted him, and given him a name which is above every name.

Proverbs 18:13 He that answereth a matter before he heareth *it,* it *is* folly and shame unto him.

Focus: This proverb specifies the bad consequences resulting from an impulsive, partially-informed response.

In order to speak wisely and avoid being labeled **"foolish,"** wisdom instructs the believer to gather all information first. The fool thinks he knows the answer before the other finishes speaking. "It is a shameful folly, though he seek the reputation of a wise man by it; as if he could readily and thoroughly understand all that another can say before he has uttered it."[448] **"Shame"** always rides on folly's coattail.

King Darius (Daniel 6) was tricked by the presidents and princes of his kingdom who "sought to find occasion" against Daniel. Their plot was to flatter the king, who (being blinded with a pride-swollen head) would then unwittingly write a law intended to entrap Daniel. Darius did not question their lie, suspect a problem, question their flattering words, or investigate. Instead rushed into signing the decree, and consequently, Daniel was thrown into the den of lions for disobeying the law. Upon realizing his foolish mistake, Darius was "sore displeased with himself, and set *his* heart on delivering Daniel. The king "laboured till the going down of the sun to deliver him," (Daniel 6:14), but to no avail. The immediate outcome revealed the king's **"folly"** which resulted in **"shame;"** however, because of intervention by God, the final outcome was not what the presidents and princes expected. And after realizing the intervention by God and his folly of prideful, premature action, Darius signed another, more thoughtful order to protect the believers in his kingdom.

Daniel 6:24, 26 And the king commanded, and they brought those men which had accused Daniel, and they cast *them* into the den of lions, them, their children, and their wives; and the lions had the mastery of them, and brake all their bones in pieces or ever they came at the bottom of the den . . . I make a decree, That in every dominion of my kingdom men tremble and fear before the God of Daniel: for he *is* the living God, and stedfast for ever, and his kingdom *that* which shall not be destroyed, and his dominion *shall be even* unto the end.

While David was fleeing Saul and not in a state of mind to make important decisions, he was confronted with a situation that appeared to be truthful but, in fact, was a lie with dreadful intent. Without seeking to hear the whole matter, David accepted the circumstantial evidence that seemed to validate Ziba's lie that Mephibosheth wanted to recover his right to the throne. Based on that lie, David gave all of Mephibosheth's property to Ziba. Later, he was confronted with Mephibosheth's side of the story, but substantial damage had already been done.

2 Samuel 16:1-4 And when David was a little past the top *of the hill,* behold, Ziba the servant of Mephibosheth met him, with a couple of asses saddled, and upon them two hundred *loaves* of bread, and an hundred bunches of raisins, and an hundred of summer fruits, and a bottle of wine. And the king said unto Ziba, What meanest thou by these? And Ziba said, The asses *be* for the king's household to ride on; and the bread and summer fruit for the young men to eat; and the wine, that such as be faint in the wilderness may drink. And the king said, And where *is* thy master's son? And Ziba said unto the king, Behold, he abideth at Jerusalem: for he said, To day shall the house of Israel restore me the kingdom of my father. Then said the king to Ziba, Behold, thine *are* all that *pertained* unto Mephibosheth. And Ziba said, I humbly beseech thee *that* I may find grace in thy sight, my lord, O king.

Later, David asked appropriate questions of Mephibosheth, but it was too late.

2 Samuel 19:25-30 And it came to pass, when he was come to Jerusalem to meet the king, that the king said unto him, Wherefore wentest not thou with me, Mephibosheth? And he answered, My lord, O king, my servant deceived me: for thy servant said, I will saddle me an ass, that I may ride thereon, and go to the king; because thy servant *is* lame. And he hath slandered thy servant unto my lord the king; but my lord the king *is* as an angel of God: do therefore *what is* good in thine eyes. For all *of* my father's house were but dead men before my lord the king: yet didst thou set thy servant among them that did eat at thine own table. What right therefore have I yet to cry any more unto the king? And the king said unto him, Why speakest thou any more of thy matters? I have said, Thou and Ziba divide the land. And Mephibosheth said unto the king, Yea, let him take all, forasmuch as my lord the king is come again in peace unto his own house.

"Too often is this Proverb verified in common life. Men will scarcely hear out what is unacceptable to them. They will break in upon a speaker, before they have fully heard him, and therefore *answer a matter*, which they have little weighed, and but imperfectly understood. The eager disputant prides himself on his acute judgment. He interrupts his opponent, and confutes arguments, or contradicts statements, *before he has fairly heard them*. Job's friends seem to have erred here. (Job 20:1-3; 21:1-6) Elihu, on the other hand, considerately restrained' himself, till he had thoroughly heard the matter. (Job 32:4,10-11) Job himself prudently 'searched out the cause that he knew not.'(Job 29:16) This impatient spirit tells little for candor or humility, and only stamps a man's character with folly and shame. It is fraught with injustice in the court of law. (John 7:45-52) Here at least the judge must carefully hear and weigh both sides for a satisfactory verdict. The wise man thoroughly heard his difficult case, before he gave judgment. (1 Kings 3:16-28; Proverbs 25:2) Job was scrupulously exact in thus 'contending with his servant.' (Job 31:13) 'The rich man, when his steward was accused to him, that he had wasted his goods,' did not turn him away upon the mere report, but he examined his accounts. (Luke 16:1-2) On the other hand, Potiphar, from the want of this upright considerateness, was guilty of the most flagrant wrong. (Genesis 39:17-20) The Eastern autocrats seldom cared to sift accusations. Even 'the man after God's heart' grievously sinned in this matter. But their hasty decisions brought *shame* upon them, being either covered over, or virtually retracted. (Esther 3:8-11; 8:5-13, Daniel 6:9; 6:14; 6:24, 2 Samuel 16:1-4; 19:26-30) Our Lord's *matter, was answered before it was heard.* (Luke 26:66-71) The Apostle met with similar treatment, (Acts 22:21-22; 23:2) though at other times he found a more impartial judgment. (Acts 23:30-35; 24:1-22; 25:1-5; 25; 24-27; 26:30-32)

This *folly* was directly forbidden by God's law. (Deuteronomy 13:12-14; John 7:24) It was no less contrary to his own procedure. He examined Adam, before he pronounced judgment. (Genesis 3:9-19) He came down to see Babel and Sodom, previous to their destruction, for the more clear demonstration of his justice. (Genesis 11:5; 18:20-21) While on earth, patient investigation marked his decisions. (Matthew 22:15-22; Isaiah 11:3) 'All his ways are judgment; a God of truth, and without iniquity, just and right is he.'" (Deuteronomy 32:4; 1 Samuel 2:3)[449]

Genesis 11:5; 18:20-21 And the LORD came down to see the city and the tower, which the children of men builded. . . . And the LORD said, Because the cry of Sodom and Gomorrah is great, and because their sin is very grievous; I will go down now, and see whether they have done altogether according to the cry of it, which is come unto me; and if not, I will know.

Genesis 39:17-20 And she spake unto him according to these words, saying, The Hebrew servant, which thou hast brought unto us, came in unto me to mock me: And it came to pass, as I lifted up my voice and cried, that he left his garment with me, and fled out. And it came to pass, when his master heard the words of his wife, which she spake unto him, saying, After this manner did thy servant to me; that his wrath was kindled. And Joseph's master took him, and put him into the prison, a place where the king's prisoners *were* bound: and he was there in the prison.

Deuteronomy 13:12-15 If thou shalt hear *say* in one of thy cities, which the LORD thy God hath given thee to dwell there, saying, *Certain* men, the children of Belial, are gone out from among you, and have withdrawn the inhabitants of their city, saying, Let us go and serve other gods, which ye have not known; Then shalt thou enquire, and make search, and ask diligently; and, behold, *if it be* truth, *and* the thing certain, *that* such abomination is wrought among you; Thou shalt surely smite the inhabitants of that city with the edge of the sword, destroying it utterly, and all that *is* therein, and the cattle thereof, with the edge of the sword.

Job 20:1-3 Then answered Zophar the Naamathite, and said, Therefore do my thoughts cause me to answer, and for *this* I make haste. I have heard the check of my reproach, and the spirit of my understanding causeth me to answer.

Job 21:1-6 But Job answered and said, Hear diligently my speech, and let this be your consolations. Suffer me that I may speak; and after that I have spoken, mock on. As for me, *is* my complaint to man? and if *it were so,* why should not my spirit be troubled? Mark me, and be astonished, and lay *your* hand upon *your* mouth. Even when I remember I am afraid, and trembling taketh hold on my flesh.

Job 31:13 If I did despise the cause of my manservant or of my maidservant, when they contended with me;

Job 32:4; 10-11 Now Elihu had waited till Job had spoken, because they *were* elder than he. . . . Therefore I said, Hearken to me; I also will shew mine opinion. Behold, I waited for your words; I gave ear to your reasons, whilst ye searched out what to say.

Proverbs 25:2 *It is* the glory of God to conceal a thing: but the honour of kings *is* to search out a matter.

Proverbs 26:12 Seest thou a man wise in his own conceit? *there is* more hope of a fool than of him.

Proverbs 29:20 Seest thou a man that is hasty in his words? there is more hope of a fool than of him.

Luke 16:1-2 And he said also unto his disciples, There was a certain rich man, which had a steward; and the same was accused unto him that he had wasted his goods. And he called him, and said unto him, How is it that I hear this of thee? give an account of thy stewardship; for thou mayest be no longer steward.

Luke 22:66-71 And as soon as it was day, the elders of the people and the chief priests and the scribes came together, and led him into their council, saying, Art thou the Christ? tell us. And he said unto them, If I tell you, ye will not believe: And if I also ask *you,* ye will not answer me, nor let *me* go. Hereafter shall the Son of man sit on the right hand of the power of God. Then said they all, Art thou then the Son of God? And he said unto them, Ye say that I am. And they said, What need we any further witness? for we ourselves have heard of his own mouth.

John 7:24 Judge not according to the appearance, but judge righteous judgment.

John 7:51 Doth our law judge *any* man, before it hear him, and know what he doeth?

Proverbs 18:14 The spirit of a man will sustain his infirmity; but a wounded spirit who can bear?

Focus: This proverb contrasts the consequence of a healthy spirit with the consequence of a wounded one.

"The spirit of a man will sustain his infirmity." The **"spirit of a *man*"** *[mind, seat of moral character, will]* includes his *overall attitude* and *his courage.* (This spirit is not the spirit spoken of as the third part of man – body, soul, and spirit. This is rather his way of thinking that reveals itself in a predominate attitude.) Some men are blessed with a greater than normal strength of spirit, a natural courage that will bear them up under the obstacles and tribulations of life. If a person has a strong spirit, he can **"sustain his infirmity"** *(endure an illness or stand up against that which is trying to take him down).* Faith in God often produces an extremely strong courage. Such faith manifests itself as a spirit of strength, and at the same time, a spirit of humility. Notice the following Biblical illustrations:

Job 1:20-21 Then Job arose, and rent his mantle, and shaved his head, and fell down upon the ground, and worshipped, And said, Naked came I out of my mother's womb, and naked shall I return thither: the LORD gave, and the LORD hath taken away; blessed be the name of the LORD.

Job 2:9-10 Then said his wife unto him, Dost thou still retain thine integrity? curse God, and die. But he said unto her, Thou speakest as one of the foolish women speaketh. What? shall we receive good at the hand of God, and shall we not receive evil? In all this did not Job sin with his lips.

Job 19:25-27 For I know that my redeemer liveth, and that he shall stand at the latter day upon the earth: And though after my skin worms destroy this body, yet in my flesh shall I see God: Whom I shall see for myself, and mine eyes shall behold, and not another; though my reins be consumed within me."

2 Corinthians 12:7-10 And lest I should be exalted above measure through the abundance of the revelations, there was given to me a thorn in the flesh, the messenger of Satan to buffet me, lest I should be exalted above measure. For this thing I besought the Lord thrice, that it might depart from me. And he said unto me, My grace is sufficient for thee: for my strength is made perfect in weakness. Most gladly therefore will I rather glory in my infirmities, that the power of Christ may rest upon me. Therefore I take pleasure in infirmities, in reproaches, in necessities, in persecutions, in distresses for Christ's sake: for when I am weak, then am I strong.

"But a wounded spirit who can bear?" The **"wounded spirit"** *(broken spirit)* manifests itself in a person when he is defeated in his mind because of a bad situation, foul words, or a personal sin. Usually, a "wounded spirit" occurs when a person receives a physical or verbal attack from another person causing him to lose his vigor. However, he may have a "wounded spirit" because of physical, personal, or financial setbacks causing turmoil in his life. A person cannot **"bear"** *[endure, lift oneself up]* a desperate situation when he has such a **"wounded spirit."** Depending upon the causes for having a wounded spirit, the believer learns to overcome through repentance of sin, forgiveness of self and others, and faith in God. It is the inner self that gives victory or allows defeat. An individual must humbly trust the Lord to give him necessary strength.

> Isaiah 40:29-31 He giveth power to the faint; and to *them that have* no might he increaseth strength. Even the youths shall faint and be weary, and the young men shall utterly fall: But they that wait upon the LORD shall renew *their* strength; they shall mount up with wings as eagles; they shall run, and not be weary; *and* they shall walk, and not faint.

"It is the office of the spirit, or mind, to govern the body, but not that of the body to govern the mind: therefore, when the body is under 'infirmity,' 'the spirit sustains it: but if the spirit be afflicted, there is nothing which can bear it up' (Proverbs 15:13). 'The spirit of . . . MAN' . . . stands in contrast to 'a broken spirit.' We ought not so to yield to calamity as to suffer the 'spirit' to be 'broken,' but we ought to make 'the name of the LORD' our 'tower of strength.'"[450] (Proverbs 18:10)

The body can, as it were, fall back upon the support of the spirit, when it is distressed and weakened; but when the spirit itself is broken, grieved, wearied, debilitated, it has no resource, no higher faculty to which it can appeal, and it must succumb beneath the pressure. Here is a lesson, too, concerning the treatment of others. We should be more careful not to wound a brother's spirit than we are to refrain from doing a bodily injury; the latter may be healed by medical applications; the former is more severe in its effects, and is often irremediable. In the first clause, 'spirit,' is masculine, in the second it is feminine, intimating by the change of gender that in the former case it is a manly property, virile moral quality, in the latter it has become weakened and depressed through affliction."[451]

> Psalm 147:3 He healeth the broken in heart, and bindeth up their wounds.
>
> Proverbs 15:13 A merry heart maketh a cheerful countenance: but by sorrow of the heart the spirit is broken.
>
> Proverbs 17:22 A merry heart doeth good *like* a medicine: but a broken spirit drieth the bones.
>
> Proverbs 18:10 The name of the LORD *is* a strong tower: the righteous runneth into it, and is safe.
>
> 2 Corinthians 12:9-10 And he said unto me, My grace is sufficient for thee: for my strength is made perfect in weakness. Most gladly therefore will I rather glory in my infirmities, that the power of Christ may rest upon me. Therefore I take pleasure in infirmities, in reproaches, in necessities, in persecutions, in distresses for Christ's sake: for when I am weak, then am I strong.
>
> Hebrews 12:3 For consider him that endured such contradiction of sinners against himself, lest ye be wearied and faint in your minds.

King David faced at least one situation where he could not bear the opposition that came against him. His recourse shows what all believers should do when their own spirit cannot deal with the situation.

> 1 Samuel 30:6 And David was greatly distressed; for the people spake of stoning him, because the soul of all the people was grieved, every man for his sons and for his daughters: but David encouraged himself in the LORD his God.
>
> Psalm 27:13-14 *I had fainted,* unless I had believed to see the goodness of the LORD in the land of the living. Wait on the LORD: be of good courage, and he shall strengthen thine heart: wait, I say, on the LORD.

Proverbs 18:15 The heart of the prudent getteth knowledge; and the ear of the wise seeketh knowledge.

Focus: This proverb specifies the successfulness and sincere eagerness with which the wise pursue knowledge.

"The heart *[man's mind, emotions, and will]*" of the **"prudent** *[a wise, understanding, and discerning person]*" **"getteth"** and **"seeketh knowledge."** He is driven to get knowledge, especially that wonderful knowledge of God; and his heart is fully given to it. Constantly and eagerly, he is listening. Within the **"heart of the prudent"** is a treasury of knowledge of God and consequently of righteousness. Knowledge of God and of His will comprise the very fabric of his life, and by such knowledge, he lives and dies. "Heart" speaks of the whole man, his very soul. "Out of it are the issues of life." (Proverbs 4:23) To say that the knowledge of God is within his heart means that the prudent person has buried it deep within himself–into his core–into the center of himself–from which he forms every thought and produces every action.

To say that **"the ear" "seeketh knowledge"** means that the person is not dull or sluggish or inattentive but is putting forth the effort and energy to not only hear and observe, but also to absorb and retain knowledge. The prudent, wise person is not like the lazy person who thinks about getting knowledge but never makes any effort. The prudent man continually makes the physical effort to listen while positioning himself in the right places with the right people. More importantly, he has learned to be still and listen to instructions from God. He successfully assimilates everything good that he hears into his heart, where such knowledge can direct him to righteous living.

A wise man appreciates knowledge that he can utilize in his life, and he is always seeking to find a practical application for the knowledge he acquires. Spiritually, his heart's desire is that his whole character be an embodiment of the word of God. Psalm 119:11 expresses this concept by stating: "Thy word have I hid in mine heart, that I might not sin against thee."

Proverbs 1:5 A wise *man* will hear, and will increase learning; and a man of understanding shall attain unto wise counsels . . .

Proverbs 2:1-5 My son, if thou wilt receive my words, and hide my commandments with thee; So that thou incline thine ear unto wisdom, and apply thine heart to understanding; Yea, if thou criest after knowledge, and liftest up thy voice for understanding; If thou seekest her as silver, and searchest for her as for hid treasures; Then shalt thou understand the fear of the LORD, and find the knowledge of God.

Proverbs 4:5-7 Get wisdom, get understanding: forget *it* not; neither decline from the words of my mouth . Forsake her not, and she shall preserve thee: love her, and she shall keep thee. Wisdom *is* the principal thing; *therefore* get wisdom: and with all thy getting get understanding.

Proverbs 10:14 Wise *men* lay up knowledge: but the mouth of the foolish *is* near destruction.

Proverbs 15:14 The heart of him that hath understanding seeketh knowledge: but the mouth of fools feedeth on foolishness.

Proverbs 19:20 Hear counsel, and receive instruction, that thou mayest be wise in thy latter end.

Proverbs 23:12 Apply thine heart unto instruction, and thine ears to the words of knowledge.

Luke 8:8-10 And other fell on good ground, and sprang up, and bare fruit an hundredfold. And when he had said these things, he cried, He that hath ears to hear, let him hear. And his disciples asked him, saying, What might this parable be? And he said, Unto you it is given to know the mysteries of the kingdom of God: but to others in parables; that seeing they might not see, and hearing they might not understand.

Luke 10:39 And she had a sister called Mary, which also sat at Jesus' feet, and heard his word.

2 Timothy 3:15-17 And that from a child thou hast known the holy scriptures, which are able to make thee wise unto salvation through faith which is in Christ Jesus. All scripture *is* given by inspiration of God, and *is* profitable for doctrine, for reproof, for correction, for instruction in righteousness: That the man of God may be perfect, throughly furnished unto all good works.

In contrast to the wise, the unwise often seek a kind of knowledge that brings about their spiritual death, as Eve did. In unbelief, she sought after the knowledge of evil that God had forbidden, believing such knowledge "to be good for food, pleasant to the eyes, and a tree to be desired to make one wise." (Genesis 3:6) She obviously believed that she could prove God wrong by gaining knowledge that would make her and Adam "as gods." (Genesis 3:5) Christians are admonished to be humble and to keep from "being lifted up with pride" and from falling "into the condemnation of the devil." (1 Timothy 3:6)

Proverbs 18:16   A man's gift maketh room for him, and bringeth him before great men.

Focus: This proverb declares two benefits of an honorable, legitimate gift.

Depending on the motive, **"A man's gift"** can be given either as a bribe or as a proper representation of respect. This proverb specifically illustrates "the Oriental custom of offering suitable gifts to one in authority when a favor or an audience is desired."[452] In the process of being respectful or honorable, a gift can be a means of assuaging a hostile or angry situation or a method of gaining acceptance and an audience before great men. (In contrast, Proverbs 17:23 describes a gift being given by a wicked man with the desire to pervert justice: "A wicked *man* taketh a gift out of the bosom to pervert the ways of judgment.") In this proverb (18:16), a gift procures the giver access to **"great men,"** meaning men of influence and power. Also, the *gift makes room for him* (enlarges his options) or provides a job or an office so that he may be accepted and have freedom to speak and move about. According to the latter part of this proverb (*and brings him before great men*), the gift is a symbol of respect. It is given to someone of influence with the motive of acting with proper and acceptable protocol.

1 Kings 4:21 And Solomon reigned over all kingdoms from the river unto the land of the Philistines, and unto the border of Egypt: they brought presents, and served Solomon all the days of his life.

1 Kings 10:24-25 And all the earth sought to Solomon, to hear his wisdom, which God had put in his heart. And they brought every man his present, vessels of silver, and vessels of gold, and garments, and armour, and spices, horses, and mules, a rate year by year.

Proverbs 21:14 A gift in secret pacifieth anger: and a reward in the bosom strong wrath.

Abraham sent gifts with his servant so that Laban would listen to the servant's request for a bride for Isaac. Abraham's *gifts made room* for Eliezer, the servant.

Genesis 24:30-31 And it came to pass, when he saw the earring and bracelets upon his sister's hands, and when he heard the words of Rebekah his sister, saying, Thus spake the man unto me; that he came unto the man; and, behold, he stood by the camels at the well. And he said, Come in, thou blessed of the LORD; wherefore standest thou without? for I have prepared the house, and room for the camels.

By sending gifts to his brother Esau, Jacob could calm a very threatening situation. (Genesis 32 - 33:1-11)

> Genesis 32:20 And say ye moreover, Behold, thy servant Jacob *is* behind us. For he said, I will appease him with the present that goeth before me, and afterward I will see his face; peradventure he will accept of me.

Because Joseph had insisted that Benjamin was to be brought to Egypt to prove that the brothers were not spies, Jacob sent a gift to ***make room*** for his sons and have them accepted.

> Genesis 43:7, 11 And they said, The man asked us straitly of our state, and of our kindred, saying, Is your father yet alive? have ye another brother? and we told him according to the tenor of these words: could we certainly know that he would say, Bring your brother down? ... And their father Israel said unto them, If it must be so now, do this; take of the best fruits in the land in your vessels, and carry down the man a present, a little balm, and a little honey, spices, and myrrh, nuts, and almonds ...

When Abigail learned what her wicked husband Nabal had said to David's men, she did not hesitate to take a gift to the future king as an apology designed to save lives.

> 1 Samuel 25:18-19 Then Abigail made haste, and took two hundred loaves, and two bottles of wine, and five sheep ready dressed, and five measures of parched corn, and an hundred clusters of raisins, and two hundred cakes of figs, and laid them on asses. And she said unto her servants, Go on before me; behold, I come after you. But she told not her husband Nabal.

When the "wise men" came to the newborn King, under the direct leadership of God, they brought gifts of "gold, and frankincense, and myrrh." There is no mention from the Scriptures that they gained "room" or any favor; however, there should be no question that God personally favored them for their obedience. Their action of bringing gifts was indicative of proper protocol for a king, and this King of kings was certainly deserving of gifts to recognize His kingship.

> Matthew 2:11 And when they were come into the house, they saw the young child with Mary his mother, and fell down, and worshipped him: and when they had opened their treasures, they presented unto him gifts; gold, and frankincense, and myrrh.

Proverbs 18:17 *He that is* first in his own cause *seemeth* just; but his neighbour cometh and searcheth him.

Focus: This proverb expresses the importance of obtaining every detail from everyone involved (both sides of a story) before reaching conclusions.

The **"first in his own cause"** means the first person to present his cause. **"Seemeth just"** means that he seems to be right in what he has said in that his arguments appear to be sane and honorable. He has been convincing people that his behavior, motives, actions, and speech were proper *until* his **"neighbor cometh and searcheth him** *[examine, investigate]***."** After the neighbor questions him and perhaps presents the actual truth, the "first" is revealed to be untrue in his testimony. Also, along with the testimony of a challenger, the wise adjudicator or judge will know to evaluate each person's history of truthfulness.

As stated in verse 13 of this chapter, it is best to hear the entire matter before making judgment, lest one's immature judgment reveal foolishness and result in shame. The human mind tends to accept the first rendering of a story or even a first explanation of a term, and it is often difficult to be convinced that the first presentation was wrong. However, a wise person will be attentive to this weakness and willing to hear the entire story before being convinced of truth or passing judgment.

> "This shows that one tale is good till another is told. He that speaks first will be sure to tell a straight story, and relate that only which makes for him, and put the best colour he can upon it, so that his cause shall appear good, whether it really be so or no. The plaintiff having done his evidence, it is fit that the defendant should be heard, should have leave to confront the witnesses and cross-examine them, and show the falsehood and fallacy of what has been alleged, which perhaps may make the matter appear quite otherwise than it did. We must therefore remember that we have two ears, to hear both sides before we give judgment."[453]

> 2 Samuel 16:1-4 And when David was a little past the top *of the hill*, behold, Ziba the servant of Mephibosheth met him, with a couple of asses saddled, and upon them two hundred *loaves* of bread, and an hundred bunches of raisins, and an hundred of summer fruits, and a bottle of wine. And the king said unto Ziba, What meanest thou by these? And Ziba said, The asses *be* for the king's household to ride on; and the bread and summer fruit for the young men to eat; and the wine, that such as be faint in the wilderness may drink. And the king said, And where *is* thy master's son? And Ziba said unto the king, Behold, he abideth at Jerusalem: for he said, To day shall the house of Israel restore me the kingdom of my father. Then said the king to Ziba, Behold, thine *are* all that *pertained* unto Mephibosheth. And Ziba said, I humbly beseech thee *that* I may find grace in thy sight, my lord, O king.

> 2 Samuel 19:24-27 And Mephibosheth the son of Saul came down to meet the king, and had neither dressed his feet, nor trimmed his beard, nor washed his clothes, from the day the king departed until the day he came *again* in peace. And it came to pass, when he was come to Jerusalem to meet the king, that the king said unto him, Wherefore wentest not thou with me, Mephibosheth? And he answered, My lord, O king, my servant deceived me: for thy servant said, I will saddle me an ass, that

I may ride thereon, and go to the king; because thy servant *is* lame. And he hath slandered thy servant unto my lord the king; but my lord the king *is* as an angel of God: do therefore *what is* good in thine eyes.

Potiphar's wife was angry when Joseph would not comply with her sorry request, and she told her husband the lie that Joseph had accosted her. Because he failed to determine the truth, Potiphar cast the innocent young man into prison. (Genesis 39)

Proverbs 18:13 He that answereth a matter before he heareth *it,* it *is* folly and shame unto him.

Proverbs 18:18 The lot causeth contentions to cease, and parteth between the mighty.

Focus: This proverb declares the benefits of casting lots.

One way of settling disagreements in Bible times was casting lots. Scripture provides numerous instances whereby God made His will known by the casting of lots; and it is clear from such Scriptures that God was, in fact, supernaturally intervening. The fact must have been obvious and accepted by all present that the person doing the casting of the lot had nothing to do with the outcome; consequently, with such acknowledgments, *contentions ceased.*

Proverbs 16:33 The lot is cast into the lap; but the whole disposing thereof *is* of the LORD.

"**Mighty**" persons (those who powerfully exercised great authority) were more forceful persons than average and would often settle their differences through violence. Apparently, they were unwilling to accept any arguments that they thought not provable; however, when the lot was cast and accepted as being from God, they were humbled and accepted the answer, *thereby separating themselves* from the contending party. Since the Lord was controlling the outcome, there was no disputing the results of the lot and no violence committed.

> "**The lot causeth contentions to cease** – By determining the matters in difference; **and parteth between the mighty** – Maketh a partition, and giveth to each of the contending parties what is right or meet, by the order and disposition of divine providence. It parteth also between mean persons, but he mentions *the mighty,* because they are most prone to contention, and most fierce and obstinate in it, and most capable of doing great mischief to themselves and others by it, and therefore they most need this remedy."[454]

Numbers 26:55-56 Notwithstanding the land shall be divided by lot: according to the names of the tribes of their fathers they shall inherit. According to the lot shall the possession thereof be divided between many and few.

Joshua 14:2 By lot *was* their inheritance, as the LORD commanded by the hand of Moses, for the nine tribes, and *for* the half tribe.

Joshua 18:10 And Joshua cast lots for them in Shiloh before the LORD: and there Joshua divided the land unto the children of Israel according to their divisions.

1 Samuel 10:21 When he had caused the tribe of Benjamin to come near by their families, the family of Matri was taken, and Saul the son of Kish was taken: and when they sought him, he could not be found.

1 Samuel 14:42 And Saul said, Cast *lots* between me and Jonathan my son. And Jonathan was taken.

1 Chronicles 6:63 Unto the sons of Merari *were given* by lot, throughout their families, out of the tribe of Reuben, and out of the tribe of Gad, and out of the tribe of Zebulun, twelve cities.

1 Chronicles 24:31 These likewise cast lots over against their brethren the sons of Aaron in the presence of David the king, and Zadok, and Ahimelech, and the chief of the fathers of the priests and Levites, even the principal fathers over against their younger brethren.

Nehemiah 10:34 And we cast the lots among the priests, the Levites, and the people, for the wood offering, to bring *it* into the house of our God, after the houses of our fathers, at times appointed year by year, to burn upon the altar of the LORD our God, as *it is* written in the law:

Nehemiah 11:1 And the rulers of the people dwelt at Jerusalem: the rest of the people also cast lots, to bring one of ten to dwell in Jerusalem the holy city, and nine parts *to dwell* in *other* cities.

Proverbs 18:19 A brother offended *is harder to be won* than a strong city: and *their* contentions *are* like the bars of a castle.

Focus: This proverb describes the extreme difficulty of reconciliation when bonds of trust have been broken.

When people are close enough *(either blood relatives, fellow Christians, members of the same group like a tribe, union, or military organization)* to be identified as "**brother**" or "brethren," (as Scripture does 542 times), there is by necessity an element of *substantial trust* in the relationship. If that trust is violated so that one of the "**brothers**" is offended *[transgressed* *against]*, then that great trust can turn to great feelings of betrayal, resulting in anger and perhaps violence. Such a betrayal also causes feelings of instability and uncertainty in one's own ability to judge character and to ever again have such a "brother" relationship. To regain the aforementioned trust between brothers is *as difficult as conquering a city that has fortified itself with every means possible*, making it **a "strong city."** The original trusting relationship will be very hard to restore, if not impossible.

When a blood brother causes mistrust in his blood brother through an offense, the great strength that is characterized by an unyielding, never-ending family bond is broken. **"Their contentions are like the bars of a castle,"** indicating that the strife between the brethren is rigid, like bars of steel, so that there is no bending or giving on either side.

There are certain cases in the Bible where such resentment was so aroused between brothers that the situation became violent and resulted in murder, for example – Cain and Abel, and Absalom and Amnon. Other volatile situations received reconciliation, such as Joseph and his brethren, and Esau and Jacob.

> Genesis 27:41 And Esau hated Jacob because of the blessing wherewith his father blessed him: and Esau said in his heart, The days of mourning for my father are at hand; then will I slay my brother Jacob.
>
> Genesis 33:8-12 And he said, What *meanest* thou by all this drove which I met? And he said, *These are* to find grace in the sight of my lord. And Esau said, I have enough, my brother; keep that thou hast unto thyself. And Jacob said, Nay, I pray thee, if now I have found grace in thy sight, then receive my present at my hand: for therefore I have seen thy face, as though I had seen the face of God, and thou wast pleased with me. Take, I pray thee, my blessing that is brought to thee; because God hath dealt graciously with me, and because I have enough. And he urged him, and he took *it*. And he said, Let us take our journey, and let us go, and I will go before thee.
>
> Genesis 37:3-4, 8 Now Israel loved Joseph more than all his children, because he *was* the son of his old age: and he made him a coat of *many* colours. And when his brethren saw that their father loved him more than all his brethren, they hated him, and could not speak peaceably unto him . . . And his brethren said to him, Shalt thou indeed reign over us? or shalt thou indeed have dominion over us? And they hated him yet the more for his dreams, and for his words.
>
> Genesis 50:15-21 And when Joseph's brethren saw that their father was dead, they said, Joseph will peradventure hate us, and will certainly requite us all the evil which we did unto him. And they sent a messenger unto Joseph, saying, Thy father did command before he died, saying, So shall ye say unto Joseph, Forgive, I pray thee now, the trespass of thy brethren, and their sin; for they did unto thee evil: and now, we pray thee, forgive the trespass of the servants of the God of thy father. And Joseph wept when they spake unto him. And his brethren also went and fell down before his face; and they said, Behold, we *be* thy servants. And Joseph said unto them, Fear not: for *am* I in the place of God? But as for you, ye thought evil against me; *but* God meant it unto good, to bring to pass, as *it is* this day, to save much people alive. Now therefore fear ye not: I will nourish you, and your little ones. And he comforted them, and spake kindly unto them.
>
> 2 Samuel 13:22 And Absalom spake unto his brother Amnon neither good nor bad: for Absalom hated Amnon, because he had forced his sister Tamar.
>
> 2 Samuel 13:28-29 Now Absalom had commanded his servants, saying, Mark ye now when Amnon's heart is merry with wine, and when I say unto you, Smite Amnon; then kill him, fear not: have not I commanded you? be courageous, and be valiant. And the servants of Absalom did unto Amnon as Absalom had commanded. Then all the king's sons arose, and every man gat him up upon his mule, and fled.
>
> Psalm 133:1-3 A Song of degrees of David. Behold, how good and how pleasant it is for brethren to dwell together in unity! It is like the precious ointment upon the head, that ran down upon the beard, even Aaron's beard: that went down to the skirts of his garments; As the dew of Hermon, and as the dew that descended upon the mountains of Zion: for there the LORD commanded the blessing, even life for evermore.
>
> Ephesians 4:1-3 I therefore, the prisoner of the Lord, beseech you that ye walk worthy of the vocation wherewith ye are called, With all lowliness and meekness, with longsuffering, forbearing one another in love; Endeavouring to keep the unity of the Spirit in the bond of peace.

Proverbs 18:20 A man's belly shall be satisfied with the fruit of his mouth; *and* with the increase of his lips shall he be filled.

Focus: This proverb teaches that spoken words shape the situations (good or evil) surrounding a man's life.

"A man's belly shall be satisfied with the fruit of his mouth" means that a person's wise or foolish speech has much to do with the level of satisfaction, peace, and happiness in which he lives. The man himself – (figuratively identified as **"a man's belly"**) is directly affected by that which he utters (**"the fruit of his mouth."**)

> "Here an agricultural metaphor is used to describe how a man can benefit himself (or otherwise) by his own words. What he says with his mouth and lips can be to him like fruit which fills his belly (his inner man), or like the produce of his land (his 'increase') which satisfies him, first because of its quantity, and second because it feeds him and his family. In the same way a man can feed himself

with his words, either because they directly affect him as he speaks them, or because they cause a reaction in others which then rebounds on him himself, whether for good or ill."[455]

"With the increase of his lips shall he be filled" is repetitive of the first clause indicating that the more a person speaks (**"increase of his lips"**), the more he *fills his life* with satisfaction *or* defeat. His life will be filled with the consequences of his speech. The words of his mouth will determine his peace and comfort, his enjoyment of life, and his inward satisfaction according to whether the words are good or evil, peaceful or wrathful, honest or dishonest, hateful or loving, to the glory of God, or to the praise of evil. When a wise man realizes he will have to "eat" the results of his words, he will control what he says; however, fools never learn, and the evil in their lives is compounded.

> Proverbs 12:14 A man shall be satisfied with good by the fruit of *his* mouth: and the recompence of a man's hands shall be rendered unto him.
> Proverbs 13:2 A man shall eat good by the fruit of *his* mouth: but the soul of the transgressors *shall eat* violence.
> Proverbs 22:17-18 Bow down thine ear, and hear the words of the wise, and apply thine heart unto my knowledge. For *it is* a pleasant thing if thou keep them within thee; they shall withal be fitted in thy lips.
> Proverbs 25:11 A word fitly spoken *is like* apples of gold in pictures of silver. *[See also the verses below that substantiate verse 21.]*

Proverbs 18:21 Death and life *are* in the power of the tongue: and they that love it shall eat the fruit thereof.

Focus: This proverb tells of the powerful ability and consequences of words.

A continuation of the previous proverb, this one serves to remind that the words of the tongue can destroy or come back to the source, like "chickens coming home to roost." The **"tongue"** is symbolic of speech, and speech is a verbal reflection of the condition of one's heart. *WORDS HAVE POWER* in that they often provoke action. A false witness can cause a jury to find someone guilty when they are actually innocent or *vice versa*. Far too often has an innocent person been declared guilty because of lies, and even more often has an innocent person had his reputation ruined by unfiltered, unbridled, or untruthful words. It is a wise person who knows the seriousness of speaking properly because of **"the power of the tongue."** A foolish person does not know, and more often, doesn't care what harm is caused by his wicked speech.

Words are like seeds that are sown, which eventually produce a crop that will prove to be good or bad, and ***those who love to talk*** shall **"eat the fruit thereof."** A wise person will make his words good so that whatever actions develop from those words and eventually return is good rather than bad. People often want to know who is the source of specific words; consequently, the effects of those words have a way of rebounding to overtake the source. In this manner, **"they that love it shall eat the fruit thereof."** Men may never hold a person responsible for evil speaking or reward them for proper speaking, but eventually, God will.

> **"And they that love it** (the tongue) **shall eat the fruit thereof.** They who use it much must abide the consequences of their words, whether by kind and pure and edifying conversation they contribute health and life to themselves and others, or whether by foul, calumnious, corrupting language they involve themselves and others in mortal sin."[456]
> Job 19:2 How long will ye vex my soul, and break me in pieces with words?
> Psalm 34:12-13 What man is he that desireth life, and loveth many days, that he may see good? Keep thy tongue from evil, and thy lips from speaking guile.
> Psalm 52:2-4 Thy tongue deviseth mischiefs; like a sharp razor, working deceitfully. Thou lovest evil more than good; *and* lying rather than to speak righteousness. Selah. Thou lovest all devouring words, O *thou* deceitful tongue.
> Psalm 141:3 Set a watch, O LORD, before my mouth; keep the door of my lips.
> Proverbs 12:13 The wicked is snared by the transgression of *his* lips: but the just shall come out of trouble.
> Proverbs 12:18 There is that speaketh like the piercings of a sword: but the tongue of the wise *is* health.
> Proverbs 13:2 A man shall eat good by the fruit of his mouth: but the soul of the transgressors shall eat violence.
> Proverbs 18:7 A fool's mouth is his destruction, and his lips are the snare of his soul.
> Proverbs 21:23 Whoso keepeth his mouth and his tongue keepeth his soul from troubles.
> Proverbs 26:28 A lying tongue hateth *those that are* afflicted by it; and a flattering mouth worketh ruin.
> Jeremiah 18:18 Then said they, Come, and let us devise devices against Jeremiah; for the law shall not perish from the priest, nor counsel from the wise, nor the word from the prophet. Come, and let us smite him with the tongue, and let us not give heed to any of his words.

Hosea 10:13 Ye have plowed wickedness, ye have reaped iniquity; ye have eaten the fruit of lies: because thou didst trust in thy way, in the multitude of thy mighty men.

Matthew 12:35-37 A good man out of the good treasure of the heart bringeth forth good things: and an evil man out of the evil treasure bringeth forth evil things. But I say unto you, That every idle word that men shall speak, they shall give account thereof in the day of judgment. For by thy words thou shalt be justified, and by thy words thou shalt be condemned.

Ephesians 4:31 Let all bitterness, and wrath, and anger, and clamour, and evil speaking, be put away from you, with all malice . . .

James 3:6 And the tongue *is* a fire, a world of iniquity: so is the tongue among our members, that it defileth the whole body, and setteth on fire the course of nature; and it is set on fire of hell.

Proverbs 18:22 *Whoso* findeth a wife findeth a good *thing,* and obtaineth favour of the LORD.

Focus: This proverb specifies two advantages for a man who *finds* a wife.

***"Whoso* findeth** *[obtains, gets]* **a wife findeth a good *thing.*"** In the very first few pages of Scripture, God declared that it was not **"a good thing"** for man to be alone (Genesis 2:18), and He desired for the wife to be a *godly wife*. A godly wife is good for her husband *physically* in that she helps with maintaining the household. She is good for him *emotionally* in that her loving spirit keeps him calm and focused. She is good for him *financially* in that she labors to help provide for all the needs of the household. Conversely, an *ungodly* wife brings *grief and sorrow*; consequently, she is definitely not the **"good *thing*"** spoken of in this passage. Additionally, and even more disastrous, due to her wickedness, she brings the *condemnation of God* to herself as part of her family unit.

"And obtaineth *[cause to come out from]* **favour of the LORD."** The second part of the proverb specifies that she is God's gift through God's favor. The good wife is good for the man *spiritually* in that she also seeks the favor of God, thereby helping to keep them both in the right path. She worships and prays with him, and she also teaches their children to love and serve God. *(Notice similar words of praise are said concerning the man in Proverbs 12:2 – "A good man obtaineth favour of the LORD: but a man of wicked devices will he condemn.")*

> "God intended husband and wife to be a spiritual, functional unity, walking in integrity, serving **God,** and keeping His commandments together. When this harmony is operative, society prospers under God's hand . . . Adam was **alone** and that was **not good;** all else in Creation was good (Genesis 1:4, 10, 12, 18, 21). As man began to function as God's representative – naming the animals represented his dominion over them; he became aware of his solitude. **God** therefore put him to **sleep,** and created Eve from his **flesh** and **bone.** God decided to **make a helper suitable** . . . **for** the man."[457]

Proverbs 19:14 House and riches *are* the inheritance of fathers: and a prudent wife *is* from the LORD.

Proverbs 31:10 Who can find a virtuous woman? for her price *is* far above rubies.

Proverbs 18:23 The poor useth intreaties; but the rich answereth roughly.

Focus: This proverb contrasts the way a poor person speaks with the way a rich person speaks to accentuate the attitude differences between the rich and the poor.

"The rich," as mentioned in this verse, is a specific category of wealthy, ungodly people. They often have an egotistical evaluation of themselves and an inflated idea of their personal success and an overestimation of their worth to society. Believing that they don't need anyone else, they are proud, haughty, and self-centered, especially toward a poor person whom they do not envision as ever being needed for their personal advancement. Most importantly, they have no regard for God; consequently, they speak **"roughly"** *[strongly, harshly, fiercely],* not caring how their words are received.

On the other hand, a poor person may feel that he needs as much help as he can get from whoever will give it. Consequently, he speaks with ***entreaties*** *[pleas, requests, supplications],* being careful that his words are received with kindness. He needs help from the rich man, who answers roughly and refuses. Because they want to be pleasing to God, wise rich people know better than trusting riches or treating people *without* the proper consideration.

> Genesis 42:6-7 And Joseph *was* the governor over the land, *and* he *it was* that sold to all the people of the land: and Joseph's brethren came, and bowed down themselves before him *with* their faces to the earth. And Joseph saw his brethren, and he knew them,

but made himself strange unto them, and spake roughly unto them; and he said unto them, Whence come ye? And they said, From the land of Canaan to buy food.

Ruth 2:7 And she said, I pray you, let me glean and gather after the reapers among the sheaves: so she came, and hath continued even from the morning until now, that she tarried a little in the house.

1 Samuel 2:36 And it shall come to pass, *that* every one that is left in thine house shall come *and* crouch to him for a piece of silver and a morsel of bread, and shall say, Put me, I pray thee, into one of the priests' offices, that I may eat a piece of bread.

1 Samuel 25:9-10 And when David's young men came, they spake to Nabal according to all those words in the name of David, and ceased. And Nabal answered David's servants, and said, Who *is* David? and who *is* the son of Jesse? there be many servants now a days that break away every man from his master.

1 Kings 12:13-14 And the king *[Rehoboam]* answered the people roughly, and forsook the old men's counsel that they gave him; And spake to them after the counsel of the young men, saying, My father *[Solomon]* made your yoke heavy, and I will add to your yoke: my father *also* chastised you with whips, but I will chastise you with scorpions.

Proverbs 18:24 A man *that hath* friends must shew himself friendly: and there is a friend *that* sticketh closer than a brother.

Focus: This proverb contrasts having many relationships through improper behavior with having a true friend through proper behavior.

At first glance of this proverb, one would think that ***showing himself friendly*** is a good and honorable thing to do, and it is–if one can be friendly and honest at the same time. However, acting in an unrighteous manner in order to win friends is neither good nor godly. Please read the definitions below.

> **"Friends"** is translated from the Hebrew *rea'* which means an associate (more or less close), brother, companion, fellow, friend, husband, lover, fellow-citizen, another person. In the Book of Proverbs *rea'* is translated "neighbour" in verses: 3:28, 3:29, 6:29, 11:9, 11:12, 12:26, 14:20, 14:21, 16:29, 18:17. 19:4, 21:10, 24:28, 25:8, 25:9, 25:17, 25:18, 26:19, 27:10, and 29:5; "friend (s)" in 6:1, 6:3, 17:17, 17:18, 18:24, 19:6, 22:11, 27:9, 27:10, 27:14, and 27:17.
>
> **"Must shew himself friendly"** is translated from the Hebrew *ra'a'* (pronounced *raw-ah'*), which means properly to be bad or evil, to be injurious, to be wicked. In the Book of Proverbs, not only is *ra'a* translated "they have done mischief" in Proverbs 4:16, it is also translated "smart" in "He that is surety for a stranger shall smart for it" (11:15), "wicked doer" (17:4), "friendly" (18:24), "evil" (24:8 and 24:19), and "displease" (24:18).
>
> **"Friend"** is translated from the Hebrew *ahab* which means to have affection for, to like; human love for another (includes family); act of being a friend, like a friend; human appetite for objects such as food, drink, sleep, wisdom; God's love for man and man's love for God. *Ahab* is translated "friend (s)" twice in Proverbs and "love (s) (eth) twenty-five times.

The use of English words similar in sound but different in meaning (**"friends," "friendly,"** and **"friend"**) punctuates the intended understanding of the proverb. (This contrasting effect is even more obvious in the Hebrew.) In the first clause, **"friends** *[associates, companions]*" is contrasted with **"friend** *[one who loves, has affection for]*."

The person ***that has friends*** or *multiple associates* has to 'go along to get along' *(compromise)* because, if he doesn't agree with these **"friends'"** ideas, ways, *and possibly opposition to God*, the association would be dissolved. On the other hand, there is that particular **"*friend [one who loves]*"** with whom agreement is found in many areas, especially in the love of God. That friend **"sticketh closer than a brother."** That friendship is on good, godly ground and will stand the test of time, and even disagreements.

> "Love begets love; and love requires love as its recompense. If a man do not maintain a friendly carriage, he cannot expect to retain his friends. Friendship is a good plant; but it requires cultivation to make it grow. There is a kind of factitious *[false]* friendship in the world, that, to show one's self friendly in it, is very expensive, and in every way utterly unprofitable: it is maintained by expensive parties. feasts, etc., where the table groans with dainties, and where the conversation is either jejune *[dull]* and insipid *[dull]*, or calumnious *[slanderous]*; backbiting, talebearing, and scandal, being the general topics of the different squads in company."[458]

> "It is not the multitude of so called friends that helps us. They may only embarrass and perplex. What we prize is the one whose love is stronger and purer even than all ties of kindred."[459]

> "The man of many friends, who lays himself out to make friends of bad and good alike, does so to his own ruin. They will feed upon him, and exhaust his resources, but will not stand by him in the day of calamity – nay, rather will give a helping hand to his downfall. It is not the number of so called friends that is really useful and precious. **But there is a friend that sticketh closer than a brother."** (Proverbs 17:17, 27:10)[460]

Deuteronomy 13:6-8 If thy brother, the son of thy mother, or thy son, or thy daughter, or the wife of thy bosom, or thy friend, which *is* as thine own soul, entice thee secretly, saying, Let us go and serve other gods, which thou hast not known, thou, nor thy fathers; *Namely,* of the gods of the people which *are* round about you, nigh unto thee, or far off from thee, from the *one* end of the earth even unto the *other* end of the earth; Thou shalt not consent unto him, nor hearken unto him; neither shall thine eye pity him, neither shalt thou spare, neither shalt thou conceal him:

1 Samuel 18:1 And it came to pass, when he had made an end of speaking unto Saul, that the soul of Jonathan was knit with the soul of David, and Jonathan loved him as his own soul.

1 Samuel 20:42 And Jonathan said to David, Go in peace, forasmuch as we have sworn both of us in the name of the LORD, saying, The LORD be between me and thee, and between my seed and thy seed for ever. And he arose and departed: and Jonathan went into the city.

2 Samuel 21:7 But the king spared Mephibosheth, the son of Jonathan the son of Saul, because of the LORD'S oath that *was* between them, between David and Jonathan the son of Saul.

Ruth 1:17 And Ruth said, Intreat me not to leave thee, or to return from following after thee: for whither thou goest, I will go; and where thou lodgest, I will lodge: thy people shall be my people, and thy God my God . . .

Psalm 41:9 Yea, mine own familiar friend, in whom I trusted, which did eat of my bread, hath lifted up *his* heel against me.

Proverbs 1:10-14 My son, if sinners entice thee, consent thou not. If they say, Come with us, let us lay wait for blood, let us lurk privily for the innocent without cause: Let us swallow them up alive as the grave; and whole, as those that go down into the pit: We shall find all precious substance, we shall fill our houses with spoil: Cast in thy lot among us; let us all have one purse . . .

Proverbs 19:4 Wealth maketh many friends; but the poor is separated from his neighbour.

Proverbs 14:20 The poor is hated even of his own neighbour: but the rich *hath* many friends.

Proverbs 27:9-10 Ointment and perfume rejoice the heart: so *doth* the sweetness of a man's friend by hearty counsel. Thine own friend, and thy father's friend, forsake not; neither go into thy brother's house in the day of thy calamity: *for* better *is* a neighbour *that is* near than a brother far off.

John 6:66-67 From that *time* many of his disciples went back, and walked no more with him. Then said Jesus unto the twelve, Will ye also go away?

John 11:5 Now Jesus loved Martha, and her sister, and Lazarus.

John 15:14-15 Ye are my friends, if ye do whatsoever I command you.   Henceforth I call you not servants; for the servant knoweth not what his lord doeth: but I have called you friends; for all things that I have heard of my Father I have made known unto you.

1 Corinthians 4:17 For this cause have I sent unto you Timotheus, who is my beloved son, and faithful in the Lord, who shall bring you into remembrance of my ways which be in Christ, as I teach every where in every church.

CHAPTER NINETEEN

> **Proverbs 19:1** Better *is* the poor that walketh in his integrity, than *he that is* perverse in his lips, and is a fool.

Focus: This proverb contrasts God's favor for a truthful and wise person (though poor) with His disfavor for a lying fool.

"Better *is* the poor that walketh in his integrity" This poor person with integrity lives in a manner that reflects God's teachings, will, and wisdom; thus, he is better because God loves him, favors him, and remains near to converse with him. He has the light of God's word to guide him, the presence of God Himself to comfort him, and the promises of God to give him hope. This poor person is better because he has good character, a clear conscience, honest and good friends, and because his integrity leads him to quality of life. He doesn't have to fret about the consistency of his word, for he always tells the truth and acts according to godly wisdom. These are they who obey the Scriptures and walk in His ways and of whom "the world was not worthy." (Hebrews 11:38)

> "POVERTY is never a disgrace, except when it is the fruit of ill-conduct. But when adorned with godly *integrity*, it is most honorable. *Better is the poor man, than* he whom riches lift up in his own eyes, and he is given up to his *perverseness and folly*. (Proverbs 28:6) Often man puts under his feet those, whom God lays in his bosom. He honors the *perverse* for their riches, and despises *the poor* for their poverty. 'But what hath the rich, if he hath not God? And what is a poor man, if he hath God? Better be in a wilderness with God, than in Canaan without him.'"[461]

> "It is not, after all, what a man's portion is, but how he uses it, that makes his life a blessing or a curse. A man who walks in integrity makes the righteous law of his God the rule of his life, and this keeping of the Divine commandments brings with it a reward (Psalm 19:11) of which the rebellious fool knows nothing. He knows how to use his more limited opportunities and influence to the best advantage – how to put out his small capital so as to obtain the best interest upon it – how to trade with his five talents so as to make them other five, and so he is daily laying up a treasure which is better than all the fame and wealth that belongs to this world, for it is the riches of a righteous character by which he is raised himself to a higher spiritual level, and by which he is able to make the world better than he found it."[462]

The fool who is known to be **"perverse in his lips"** *[distorts the truth as a way of life]* is worse in God's righteous judgment because he has rebelled against his Maker. He has no favor from God, not even an audience with Him. He has no guidance on earth and no hope for eternity because he has rejected God, and consequently, God has rejected him.

> Proverbs 2:7 He layeth up sound wisdom for the righteous: he is a buckler to them that walk uprightly.
>
> Proverbs 4:24 Put away from thee a froward mouth, and perverse lips put far from thee.
>
> Proverbs 10:9 He that walketh uprightly walketh surely: but he that perverteth his ways shall be known.
>
> Proverbs 11:5 The righteousness of the perfect shall direct his way: but the wicked shall fall by his own wickedness.
>
> Proverbs 15:16 Better *is* little with the fear of the LORD than great treasure and trouble therewith.
>
> Proverbs 16:8 Better *is* a little with righteousness than great revenues without right.
>
> Proverbs 19:22 The desire of a man is his kindness: and a poor man is better than a liar.
>
> Proverbs 28:18 Whoso walketh uprightly shall be saved: but he that is perverse in his ways shall fall at once.
>
> Luke 16:19-23 There was a certain rich man, which was clothed in purple and fine linen, and fared sumptuously every day: And there was a certain beggar named Lazarus, which was laid at his gate, full of sores, And desiring to be fed with the crumbs which fell from the rich man's table: moreover the dogs came and licked his sores. And it came to pass, that the beggar died, and was carried by the angels into Abraham's bosom: the rich man also died, and was buried; And in hell he lift up his eyes, being in torments, and seeth Abraham afar off, and Lazarus in his bosom.
>
> Hebrews 11:37-38 They were stoned, they were sawn asunder, were tempted, were slain with the sword: they wandered about in sheepskins and goatskins; being destitute, afflicted, tormented; (Of whom the world was not worthy:) they wandered in deserts, and *in* mountains, and *in* dens and caves of the earth.
>
> Revelation 2:8-9 And unto the angel of the church in Smyrna write; These things saith the first and the last, which was dead, and is alive; I know thy works, and tribulation, and poverty, (but thou art rich) and *I know* the blasphemy of them which say they are Jews, and are not, but *are* the synagogue of Satan.

> **Proverbs 19:2** Also, *that* the soul *be* without knowledge, *it is* not good; and he that hasteth with *his* feet sinneth.

Focus: This proverb establishes the sinfulness of a lack of knowledge (especially about God) and of making haste without proper knowledge.

"Also, *that* the soul *be* without knowledge, *it is* not good." **"Also"** refers to the perverse fool of the previous proverb and then points to the words of this proverb in order to focus on that which feeds the fool's ***perverseness of lips*** which is his ***lack of*** knowledge, specifically the knowledge of God. "Ignorance gives perpetuity to folly,"[463] meaning that foolishness feeds on ignorance, so that as long as there is ignorance, there is foolishness. Willful ignorance of God is the foundational desire of a fool who will be ***perverse in his lips*** because of his very rebellious nature (coupled with ignorance). *(See Proverbs 2:3-6 below.)*

God convicts, intercedes, teaches, and guides the believer through this life. For a person to be **"without knowledge"** of God is **"not good"** because man without a knowledge of God can only act according to his own desire, his human nature.

Some of mankind refuse to retain any knowledge of God, and the result is a reprobate mind.

> Romans 1: 28-32 And even as they did not like to retain God in *their* knowledge, God gave them over to a reprobate *[unfit, disapproved]* mind, to do those things which are not convenient; Being filled with all unrighteousness, fornication, wickedness, covetousness, maliciousness; full of envy, murder, debate, deceit, malignity; whisperers, Backbiters, haters of God, despiteful, proud, boasters, inventors of evil things, disobedient to parents, Without understanding, covenantbreakers, without natural affection, implacable, unmerciful: Who knowing the judgment of God, that they which commit such things are worthy of death, not only do the same, but have pleasure in them that do them.

To live this life without knowledge, especially knowledge of God, is to walk in darkness; and to hurry into such darkness is absurdly dangerous. Ignorance of God's available word indicates that the ignorant one has purposefully established himself in a position to be ignorant of how to please God. He does not know what it means to have faith in God, how to treat others in a manner that pleases God, or how to resist Satan. Especially he does not know of the work of His Son, Jesus Christ, or how he can get forgiveness for his sins, and he does not know of the promises of God concerning earth or heaven.

"And he that hasteth with his feet sinneth." Swift responses typically do not give the person enough time to gain the knowledge of God's will before acting. For an individual to hasten to a decision implies that he is being drawn into a response and forced to *react* rather than to wait for instructions from God and then *act* accordingly. Under those conditions, the person is certain to blunder, make mistakes, and sin. However, even more significant than simple blunders and mistakes, the person is sure to miss the blessings of eternal life. "And this is life eternal, that they might know thee the only true God, and Jesus Christ, whom thou hast sent." (John 17:3)

> Proverbs 2:3-6 Yea, if thou criest after knowledge, *and* liftest up thy voice for understanding; If thou seekest her as silver, and searchest for her as *for* hid treasures; Then shalt thou understand the fear of the LORD, and find the knowledge of God. For the LORD giveth wisdom: out of his mouth *cometh* knowledge and understanding.
> Proverbs 6:16, 18 These six *things* doth the LORD hate: yea, seven *are* an abomination unto him . . . An heart that deviseth wicked imaginations, feet that be swift in running to mischief,
> Proverbs 9:10 The fear of the LORD *is* the beginning of wisdom: and the knowledge of the holy *is* understanding.
> Proverbs 13:16 Every prudent *man* dealeth with knowledge: but a fool layeth open *his* folly.
> Proverbs 14:18 The simple inherit folly: but the prudent are crowned with knowledge.
> Proverbs 14:29 He that is slow to wrath *is* of great understanding: but *he that is* hasty of spirit exalteth folly.
> Isaiah 1:3-4 The ox knoweth his owner, and the ass his master's crib: *but* Israel doth not know, my people doth not consider. Ah sinful nation, a people laden with iniquity, a seed of evildoers, children that are corrupters: they have forsaken the LORD, they have provoked the Holy One of Israel unto anger, they are gone away backward.
> Isaiah 5:13 Therefore my people are gone into captivity, because *they have* no knowledge: and their honourable men *are* famished, and their multitude dried up with thirst.
> Isaiah 28:16 Therefore thus saith the Lord GOD, Behold, I lay in Zion for a foundation a stone, a tried stone, a precious corner *stone,* a sure foundation: he that believeth shall not make haste.
> Hosea 4:6 My people are destroyed for lack of knowledge: because thou hast rejected knowledge, I will also reject thee, that thou shalt be no priest to me: seeing thou hast forgotten the law of thy God, I will also forget thy children.
> John 12:35-36 Then Jesus said unto them, Yet a little while is the light with you. Walk while ye have the light, lest darkness come upon you: for he that walketh in darkness knoweth not whither he goeth. While ye have light, believe in the light, that ye may be the children of light. These things spake Jesus, and departed, and did hide himself from them.
> John 16:3 And these things will they do unto you, because they have not known the Father, nor me.
> Romans 10:2 For I bear them record that they have a zeal of God, but not according to knowledge.

Philippians 1:9-10 And this I pray, that your love may abound yet more and more in knowledge and *in* all judgment; That ye may approve things that are excellent; that ye may be sincere and without offence till the day of Christ;

2 Thessalonians 1:7-8 And to you who are troubled rest with us, when the Lord Jesus shall be revealed from heaven with his mighty angels, In flaming fire taking vengeance on them that know not God, and that obey not the gospel of our Lord Jesus Christ…

Proverbs 19:3   The foolishness of man perverteth his way: and his heart fretteth against the LORD.

Focus: This proverb declares that foolishness is the root cause of why a foolish person's pathway is overthrown, yet he blames God.

"The foolishness of man perverteth his way." *Foolishness within a man* is a product of his stubbornness and resistance to the leadership of God. His foolishness manifests itself through actions, words, and associations that are improper and unacceptable to God and ultimately bring about his ruin *(pervert his way)*. Until wisdom is personally procured, a man's idea is that he can figure things out on his own and that he does not need any help. However, the truth is that without God's direction, the foolish man discovers himself in situations of self-induced extreme grief and sorrow. He plots his path thinking that he will surely be able to accomplish his plan when suddenly something unexpected overwhelms and overthrows him *(perverts his way)*. Rather than examine to find why he failed, he blames God *(frets against the LORD)*. From the beginning with Adam and Eve, mankind has rebelled in this manner against the instructions of God.

"And his heart fretteth against the LORD." To *fret against the Lord* is to be angry with Him and blame Him in one disingenuous way or another. When Adam foolishly followed Eve to disobey God, he blamed God for giving him Eve in the first place. Man had a perfect life in a perfect environment with a perfect relationship with God when his foolishness undermined and overturned (perverted) his ideal existence. "The non-wisdom which, having brought about disasters by its own perverseness, then turns round and "fretteth," i. e., angrily complains against the Providence of God."[464]

Genesis 3:11-12 And he said, Who told thee that thou *wast* naked? Hast thou eaten of the tree, whereof I commanded thee that thou shouldest not eat? And the man said, The woman whom thou gavest *to be* with me, she gave me of the tree, and I did eat.

Proverbs 13:6 Righteousness keepeth *him that is* upright in the way: but wickedness overthroweth the sinner.

Isaiah 8:21 And they shall pass through it, hardly bestead and hungry: and it shall come to pass, that when they shall be hungry, they shall fret themselves, and curse their king and their God, and look upward

Jeremiah 7:8-10 Behold, ye trust in lying words, that cannot profit. Will ye steal, murder, and commit adultery, and swear falsely, and burn incense unto Baal, and walk after other gods whom ye know not; And come and stand before me in this house, which is called by my name, and say, We are delivered to do all these abominations?

Matthew 23:37-38 O Jerusalem, Jerusalem, thou that killest the prophets, and stonest them which are sent unto thee, how often would I have gathered thy children together, even as a hen gathereth her chickens under her wings, and ye would not! Behold, your house is left unto you desolate.

Romans 9:19-21 Thou wilt say then unto me, Why doth he yet find fault? For who hath resisted his will? Nay but, O man, who art thou that repliest against God? Shall the thing formed say to him that formed it, Why hast thou made me thus? Hath not the potter power over the clay, of the same lump to make one vessel unto honour, and another unto dishonour?

James 1:13-14 Let no man say when he is tempted, I am tempted of God: for God cannot be tempted with evil, neither tempteth he any man: But every man is tempted, when he is drawn away of his own lust, and enticed.

Revelation 16:10-11 And the fifth angel poured out his vial upon the seat of the beast; and his kingdom was full of darkness; and they gnawed their tongues for pain, And blasphemed the God of heaven because of their pains and their sores, and repented not of their deeds.

Revelation 16:21 And there fell upon men a great hail out of heaven, *every stone* about the weight of a talent: and men blasphemed God because of the plague of the hail; for the plague thereof was exceeding great.

Proverbs 19:4   Wealth maketh many friends; but the poor is separated from his neighbour.

Focus: This proverb addresses the typical effect that wealth has on relationships.

In this proverb, **"friends"** and **"neighbor"** are translated from the same Hebrew word, which means *[an associate more or less close]*. These are NOT of the category of people who actually love and have their friends' best interests in mind. Proverbs 18:24 showed the reader that multiple friends were not always true friends.

Proverbs 18:24 A man *that hath* friends must shew himself friendly: and there is a friend *that* sticketh closer than a brother.

"Wealth maketh many friends." People often love others in only a relative manner–relative to their overwhelming love for **"wealth"** in the form of money, status, position, or some other personal gain that can be accomplished through association with a "friend." Such a relationship is often the glue that holds many flighty, fragile relationships together.

"But the poor is separated from his neighbour." There is no pretense of friendship with the poor because there is nothing (no wealth in any form) to gain by being their "friend;" consequently, distance is placed between the rich and the poor. Poor neighbors are not likely to be called and invited to special occasions or visited when they are sick. Wealthy friends, on the other hand, are often special guests at galas and typically receive many invitations.

Even in churches, there is often a substantial difference between the disdainful way the poor are treated, and the affection poured out to the wealthy. This shameful treatment of the poor would not occur if the Scriptures were followed and the Holy Spirit allowed to lead. Far too often, the poor are disowned and neglected by those who should help and befriend them. True Christianity overcomes the selfishness of human nature through obedience to the Scriptures in regard to treating all people equally, regardless of wealth or status, and through demonstrating the fruit of the Spirit: love, joy, peace, longsuffering, gentleness, goodness, faith, meekness and temperance. (Galatians 5:22-23)

> Deuteronomy 15:7 If there be among you a poor man of one of thy brethren within any of thy gates in thy land which the LORD thy God giveth thee, thou shalt not harden thine heart, nor shut thine hand from thy poor brother:
>
> Psalm 40:17 But I am poor and needy; yet the Lord thinketh upon me: thou art my help and my deliverer; make no tarrying, O my God.
>
> Proverbs 14:20 The poor is hated even of his own neighbour: but the rich *hath* many friends.
>
> Proverbs 19:7 All the brethren of the poor do hate him: how much more do his friends go far from him? he pursueth *them with* words, *yet* they *are* wanting *to him.*
>
> Proverbs 19:17 He that hath pity upon the poor lendeth unto the LORD; and that which he hath given will he pay him again.
>
> Luke 14:12-14 Then said he also to him that bade him, When thou makest a dinner or a supper, call not thy friends, nor thy brethren, neither thy kinsmen, nor *thy* rich neighbours; lest they also bid thee again, and a recompence be made thee. But when thou makest a feast, call the poor, the maimed, the lame, the blind: And thou shalt be blessed; for they cannot recompense thee: for thou shalt be recompensed at the resurrection of the just.
>
> James 2:1-4 My brethren, have not the faith of our Lord Jesus Christ, *the Lord* of glory, with respect of persons. For if there come unto your assembly a man with a gold ring, in goodly apparel, and there come in also a poor man in vile raiment; And ye have respect to him that weareth the gay clothing, and say unto him, Sit thou here in a good place; and say to the poor, Stand thou there, or sit here under my footstool: Are ye not then partial in yourselves, and are become judges of evil thoughts?

Proverbs 19:5 A false witness shall not be unpunished, and *he that* speaketh lies shall not escape.

Focus: This proverb declares that lying will receive punishment.

The first clause **("a false witness shall not be unpunished")** implies a court situation in which *a witness lies*, thus causing a wrongful judgment to be imposed on an innocent person. The **"false witness"** will perhaps be punished by others in his lifetime and certainly in eternity by God. The second clause **("and *he that* speaketh lies shall not escape")** reiterates the first truth that *a liar shall not escape,* for God is always the witness to actions, words, and thoughts of men and He will render judgment. The repetition is probably to emphasize the seriousness of lying in court. In America today, the punishment for perjury under oath varies from state to state. Perjury is usually considered a felony carrying a possible prison sentence of at least one year, plus fines and probation, with penalties increasing relative to how much the perjury interfered with the proceeding.

> NOTE: Except for the last verb, this proverb is identical to Proverbs 19:9. "Not escape" in this verse replaces "perish" in 19:9.
>
> Exodus 20:16 Thou shalt not bear false witness against thy neighbour.
>
> Exodus 23:1 Thou shalt not raise a false report: put not thine hand with the wicked to be an unrighteous witness.
>
> Deuteronomy 19:16-19 If a false witness rise up against any man to testify against him *that which is* wrong; Then both the men, between whom the controversy *is,* shall stand before the LORD, before the priests and the judges, which shall be in those days; And the judges shall make diligent inquisition: and, behold, *if* the witness *be* a false witness, *and* hath testified falsely against his brother; Then shall ye do unto him, as he had thought to have done unto his brother: so shalt thou put the evil away from among you.
>
> Proverbs 12:19 The lip of truth shall be established for ever: but a lying tongue *is* but for a moment.
>
> Proverbs 14:5 A faithful witness will not lie: but a false witness will utter lies.
>
> Proverbs 14:25 A true witness delivereth souls: but a deceitful *witness* speaketh lies.

Proverbs 19:9 A false witness shall not be unpunished, and he that speaketh lies shall perish.

Jeremiah 9:3 And they bend their tongues *like* their bow *for* lies: but they are not valiant for the truth upon the earth; for they proceed from evil to evil, and they know not me, saith the LORD.

Revelation 21:8 But the fearful, and unbelieving, and the abominable, and murderers, and whoremongers, and sorcerers, and idolaters, and all liars, shall have their part in the lake which burneth with fire and brimstone: which is the second death.

Proverbs 19:6   Many will intreat the favour of the prince: and every man *is* a friend to him that giveth gifts.

Focus: This proverb describes typical hypocritical behavior that is executed for personal gain.

"Many will intreat *["stroke the face"]* **the favour of the prince."** Many people will do whatever is necessary – including lying, flattery, or giving a bribe – in order to receive some special benefit in return. **"Prince"** is translated from the Hebrew word *nadiyb* which means a liberal (generous) and powerful man.[465]

"And every man *is* **a friend to him that giveth gifts**," though the "friend" spoken of here is not the loving kind but rather an associate more or less close. *(See 14:20, 18:24, and 19:4 above.)* **He that gives gifts** is a person who is generous to others. This giving person may be a prince, a high-ranking official, or someone who simply believes in sharing with others. Whatever the case, people become aware of his free spirit and desire to partake of his generosity. Such friends are only so in outward appearance, but they disguise their covetous hearts with hypocritical, smooth, and favorable words.

Scripture instructs the wisdom of loving everyone while expecting nothing in return, but foolish people "love" the person from whom they expect a benefit. Jude points out this truth: "These are murmurers, complainers, walking after their own lusts; and their mouth speaketh great swelling words, having men's persons in admiration because of advantage." (verse 16)

Proverbs 14:20 The poor is hated even of his own neighbour: but the rich *hath* many friends.

Proverbs 19:4 Wealth maketh many friends; but the poor is separated from his neighbour.

Proverbs 19:7   All the brethren of the poor do hate him: how much more do his friends go far from him? he pursueth *them with* words, *yet* they *are* wanting *to him*.

Focus: This proverb describes the sorry attitude and unmerciful actions that many have for the poor.

"All the brethren of the poor do hate him: how much more do his friends go far from him?" Verses four, six, and seven together provide a description of interpersonal actions based on wealth that many people have with others. Human nature again reveals its innate selfishness and consequential hateful behavior in this verse, showing that ungodly people, even blood relatives, and previous friends, do not want to be bothered by poor people who cannot advantage them in any manner. There is no gain, no personal benefit for the selfish, ungodly person to cause him to desire any measure of relationship or closeness with a poor brother or previous friend who has fallen on hard times.

"He pursueth *them with* **words,** *yet* **they** *are* **wanting** *to him"* is a word picture drawn of an impoverished person walking behind others and pleading with them for help. They arrogantly deny help, stop their ears and walk faster trying to distance themselves. **Wanting** is translated from a Hebrew word which means *nothing*. The result of his pursuing after those who could help is *nothing*. No doubt such behavior is displeasing to God. Every Christian should distance themselves from such unkind, despicable behavior.

Job 19:13-19 He hath put my brethren far from me, and mine acquaintance are verily estranged from me. My kinsfolk have failed, and my familiar friends have forgotten me. They that dwell in mine house, and my maids, count me for a stranger: I am an alien in their sight. I called my servant, and he gave me no answer; I intreated him with my mouth. My breath is strange to my wife, though I intreated for the children's sake of mine own body. Yea, young children despised me; I arose, and they spake against me. All my inward friends abhorred me: and they whom I loved are turned against me.

Proverbs 14:20 The poor is hated even of his own neighbour: but the rich *hath* many friends.

Proverbs 18:23 The poor useth intreaties; but the rich answereth roughly.

Proverbs 19:4 Wealth maketh many friends; but the poor is separated from his neighbour.

Proverbs 21:13 Whoso stoppeth his ears at the cry of the poor, he also shall cry himself, but shall not be heard.

Ecclesiastes 9:14-16 *There was* a little city, and few men within it; and there came a great king against it, and besieged it, and built great bulwarks against it: Now there was found in it a poor wise man, and he by his wisdom delivered the city; yet no man remembered that same poor man. Then said I, Wisdom *is* better than strength: nevertheless the poor man's wisdom *is* despised, and his words are not heard.

1 John 3:17-18 But whoso hath this world's good, and seeth his brother have need, and shutteth up his bowels *of compassion* from him, how dwelleth the love of God in him? My little children, let us not love in word, neither in tongue; but in deed and in truth.

Proverbs 19:8   He that getteth wisdom loveth his own soul: he that keepeth understanding shall find good.

Focus: This proverb declares that a person who wants good things for his life will seek two things.

"He that getteth wisdom loveth his own soul." The Book of Proverbs exhorts the reader to *get wisdom* because it is God's guidebook for navigating this life successfully. Wisdom affects every aspect of a person's life, as well as his relationship with God; therefore, a person who wants the best life will get wisdom.

Proverbs 8:35-36 For whoso findeth me findeth life, and shall obtain favour of the LORD. But he that sinneth against me wrongeth his own soul: all they that hate me love death.

Proverbs 16:20 He that handleth a matter wisely shall find good: and whoso trusteth in the LORD, happy *is* he.

What does having wisdom do for the wise man? Wisdom feeds the soul with proper, godly instruction and protects from much of life's adversity. It prevents the individual from improper damaging relationships, and it proactively teaches how to live according to God's plan for man. It maximizes the effectiveness of interactions with mankind and develops a way of thinking that enhances all the positive benefits of a personal relationship with God.

A disregard for wisdom is the grand act of foolishness that results in self destruction. Refusing God's instruction culminates in refusing Jesus. *Loving his own soul* does not mean that the person is proud and considers himself to be the center of the universe. Every wise person knows that God resists the proud person who arrogantly loves himself and has no heart for God. Wisdom teaches a person to *love his own soul* in a manner that resists pride. At the same time, he strives to be instructed by God in order to be benefitted by a better relationship. Anyone who yearns for these advantages given by wisdom would exhibit the righteous quality of a **love for his own soul.**

"He that keepeth understanding shall find good." Often used in conjunction with and sometimes interchangeably with "wisdom," **"understanding"** shows that a human heart that has become wise has a mind and heart that labor to **"find good"** wherever possible. *Understanding finds good* because understanding knows how to differentiate between good and evil, right and wrong, advantage and disadvantage. *Keeping understanding* takes effort and desire derived from anticipating both short and long-range outcomes. It is best for a healthy, righteous soul. Wisdom, knowledge, and understanding always run counter to the views of evil men; but in the long run, good is habitually produced from the practice of wisdom. Understanding maintains a good relationship with God and with other wise persons. It seeks for good outcomes to potentially harmful situations, peace of mind, provisions from God, and protection from danger, among other good benefits.

Proverbs 2:1-6 My son, if thou wilt receive my words, and hide my commandments with thee; So that thou incline thine ear unto wisdom, and apply thine heart to understanding; Yea, if thou criest after knowledge, and liftest up thy voice for understanding; If thou seekest her as silver, and searchest for her as for hid treasures; Then shalt thou understand the fear of the LORD, and find the knowledge of God. For the LORD giveth wisdom: out of his mouth cometh knowledge and understanding.

Proverbs 4:5-8 Get wisdom, get understanding: forget it not; neither decline from the words of my mouth. Forsake her not, and she shall preserve thee: love her, and she shall keep thee. Wisdom is the principal thing; therefore get wisdom: and with all thy getting get understanding. Exalt her, and she shall promote thee: she shall bring thee to honour, when thou dost embrace her.

John 14:21 He that hath my commandments, and keepeth them, he it is that loveth me: and he that loveth me shall be loved of my Father, and I will love him, and will manifest myself to him.

> **Proverbs 19:9** A false witness shall not be unpunished, and he that speaketh lies shall perish.

Focus: This proverb declares that the liar will not escape punishment.

Except for the last verb, this proverb is identical to Proverbs 19:5. **"Perish"** in this verse replaces "not escape" in verse five. (Please see the notes for verse 5.) This repetition certainly emphasizes God's repugnance for lying (especially lying in court) and the consequences of it. Wise men learn to think like God and they teach themselves to be truthful by yielding themselves to God and obeying His commandments. To be truthful is to be like Christ and to lie is to imitate Satan.

> Jeremiah 28:15-17 Then said the prophet Jeremiah unto Hananiah the prophet, Hear now, Hananiah; The LORD hath not sent thee; but thou makest this people to trust in a lie. Therefore thus saith the LORD; Behold, I will cast thee from off the face of the earth: this year thou shalt die, because thou hast taught rebellion against the LORD. So Hananiah the prophet died the same year in the seventh month.
>
> Malachi 3:5 And I will come near to you to judgment; and I will be a swift witness against the sorcerers, and against the adulterers, and against false swearers, and against those that oppress the hireling in his wages, the widow, and the fatherless, and that turn aside the stranger from his right, and fear not me, saith the LORD of hosts.
>
> John 8:44 Ye are of *your* father the devil, and the lusts of your father ye will do. He was a murderer from the beginning, and abode not in the truth, because there is no truth in him. When he speaketh a lie, he speaketh of his own: for he is a liar, and the father of it.
>
> John 14:6 Jesus saith unto him, I am the way, the truth, and the life: no man cometh unto the Father, but by me.
>
> Revelation 22:15 For without are dogs, and sorcerers, and whoremongers, and murderers, and idolaters, and whosoever loveth and maketh a lie.

> **Proverbs 19:10** Delight is not seemly for a fool; much less for a servant to have rule over princes.

Focus: This proverb declares the awkwardness that exists where privilege and position are improperly given to undeserving recipients.

"Delight is not seemly for a fool." "Delight" *[unrestrained enjoyment[466] for living in luxury, pleasure, plenty, and honor]* is inappropriate for a fool. There is an incongruity between the fool and life as described in this verse. Furthermore, "delight" is not **"seemly"** *[suitable, comely, beautiful]* for a fool because his mind is corrupted by being in opposition to God. He abuses everything that is delicate with his corrupt manners and ill desires. Where there is pleasantness, the fool brings hatefulness. Where there is wealth, the fool brings poverty. Where there is good communication, the fool brings discord.

> "In most cases, the 'fool' cannot bear his good fortune, it renders him vain, insolent, self-sufficient, consequential, and overbearing. He assumes airs, such as only make his imbecility and folly the more apparent, and the unseemliness the greater and the more offensive. And still further, he has not wit enough to use his prosperity rightly. He perverts it to foolish, improper, unbecoming purposes; not only failing to apply it for the glory of God and the true benefit of men, but actually applying it to useless, silly, frivolous, fantastic ends, which expose him to universal ridicule."[467]

"Much less for a servant to have rule over princes." Also, it is even more inappropriate for a servant to rule over those who ought to be ruling. (Placing an ex-servant in a position of ruling over princes is **"much less"** appropriate than placing a man trained to lead in that position.) When a servant is elevated to rule over a prince, he brings ignorance, insolence, and incapable leadership where there should be wisdom, respect, and competence in leadership. "The second clause carries the thought on to what the despotism of Eastern monarchies often presented, the objectionable rule of some favored slave, it might be, of alien birth, over the princes and nobles of the land."[468]

> Proverbs 1:32 For the turning away of the simple shall slay them, and the prosperity of fools shall destroy them.
>
> Proverbs 3:35 The wise shall inherit glory: but shame shall be the promotion of fools.
>
> Proverbs 13:16 Every prudent man dealeth with knowledge: but a fool layeth open his folly.
>
> Proverbs 14:8 The wisdom of the prudent is to understand his way: but the folly of fools is deceit.
>
> Proverbs 17:7 Excellent speech becometh not a fool: much less do lying lips a prince.
>
> Proverbs 18:6 A fool's lips enter into contention, and his mouth calleth for strokes.
>
> Proverbs 21:20 There is treasure to be desired and oil in the dwelling of the wise; but a foolish man spendeth it up.
>
> Proverbs 26:1 As snow in summer, and as rain in harvest, so honour is not seemly for a fool.
>
> Proverbs 26:3 A whip for the horse, a bridle for the ass, and a rod for the fool's back.

Proverbs 30:21-23 For three things the earth is disquieted, and for four which it cannot bear: For a servant when he reigneth; and a fool when he is filled with meat; For an odious woman when she is married; and an handmaid that is heir to her mistress.
Ecclesiastes 10:5-7 There is an evil which I have seen under the sun, as an error which proceedeth from the ruler: Folly is set in great dignity, and the rich sit in low place. I have seen servants upon horses, and princes walking as servants upon the earth.

Proverbs 19:11 The discretion of a man deferreth his anger; and *it is* his glory to pass over a transgression.

Focus: This proverb specifies the particular quality of a wise man that guides him to be in control of his emotions and thus his actions.

"The discretion of a man" is that product of wisdom that leads him to calmly observe and patiently evaluate a personal insult or other transgression and then to thoughtfully determine to be in control of himself. Of utmost importance is the interval between the insult and the response, during which time the wise man measures his words and manages his actions so as to defuse the assault. An open transgression that insults, belittles, or otherwise challenges a wise person becomes a test for him to evaluate whether or not he is a slave to his own emotions.

Discretion is a trait that develops from wisdom. It gives a person the ability to refuse to react or be drawn into an unwanted situation. Instead, the wise person acts decisively and with self-control. A person with discretion does not respond like a fool who allows his emotions to control his behavior; consequently, he is able to defer his anger. When anger is not necessary to produce a given positive outcome, he pushes it away from his thinking and remains fully in control of himself.

"It is his glory to pass over a transgression." "Glory" expresses the wise person's honor as a distinctive but intangible quality surrounding him. It is symbolically worn like an ornament when he shows the wisdom to refuse to allow another person's **"transgression"**(offense) to control his thoughts and actions. Because forgiveness and mercy are godly traits, it is to a person's glory when he passes over an insult. Jesus "openeth not his mouth" (Isaiah 53:7) at insults and afflictions. A wise believer learns to control himself and dismiss a transgression without anger or retribution.

A person who is known to be reactionary has not learned to practice humility and to consider peace to be of greater value than reprisal. Passing over an offense is an indication of God's authority in a man's life, and being humble and gracious like Jesus is the greatest glory of man.

Proverbs 10:12 Hatred stirreth up strifes: but love covereth all sins.
Proverbs 12:16 A fool' wrath is presently known: but a prudent man covereth shame.
Proverbs 14:17 He that is soon angry dealeth foolishly: and a man of wicked devices is hated.
Proverbs 14:29 He that is slow to wrath is of great understanding: but he that is hasty of spirit exalteth folly.
Proverbs 16:32 He that is slow to anger is better than the mighty; and he that ruleth his spirit than he that taketh a city.
Proverbs 17:9 He that covereth a transgression seeketh love; but he that repeateth a matter separateth very friends.
Proverbs 19:19 A man of great wrath shall suffer punishment: for if thou deliver him, yet thou must do it again.
Ecclesiastes 7:9 Be not hasty in thy spirit to be angry: for anger resteth in the bosom of fools.
James 1:19-20 Wherefore, my beloved brethren, let every man be swift to hear, slow to speak, slow to wrath: For the wrath of man worketh not the righteousness of God.

Proverbs 19:12 The king's wrath *is* as the roaring of a lion; but his favour *is* as dew upon the grass.

Focus: This proverb describes the difference between a king's wrath and his favor.

"The king's wrath is as the roaring of a lion." Because it is incredibly loud and menacing, **"the roaring of a lion"** strikes terror in the heart of every nearby creature. The king's wrath and the lion's roar represent a tremendous and terrifying ability to bring death, and there is little defense to abate the attack. No one wants to arouse the king's wrath because it could bring the "messengers of death." (Proverbs 16:14-15) Also, because **"the roaring of a lion"** inspired such terror, rulers often used a statue of a lion to keep that figure in their subject's minds. Solomon was no exception.

1 Kings 10:19-20 The throne *[of King Solomon]* had six steps, and the top of the throne was round behind: and there were stays on either side on the place of the seat, and two lions stood beside the stays. And twelve lions stood there on the one side and on the other upon the six steps: there was not the like made in any kingdom.
Proverbs 16:14-15 The wrath of a king is as messengers of death: but a wise man will pacify it. In the light of the king's countenance is life; and his favour is as a cloud of the latter rain.

The second clause, **"but his favour is as dew upon the grass,"** is this proverb's opposite and more pleasant side. Morning **"dew"** is that cool, life-giving moisture extracted silently from the atmosphere. It is refreshing and promises a renewal of life for vegetation. Likewise, the **favor of a king** brings opportunity for living well because of receiving various rewards that can provide peace and comfort.

"There is no misery like the endurance of the one; there is no blessedness like the enjoyment of the other. The one will sink you to hell; the other will raise you to heaven. Nay, the one is hell; the other is heaven."[469]

Proverbs 20:2 The fear of a king is as the roaring of a lion: whoso provoketh him to anger sinneth against his own soul.
Daniel 2:5-6, 12 The king answered and said to the Chaldeans, The thing is gone from me: if ye will not make known unto me the dream, with the interpretation thereof, ye shall be cut in pieces, and your houses shall be made a dunghill. But if ye shew the dream, and the interpretation thereof, ye shall receive of me gifts and rewards and great honour: therefore shew me the dream, and the interpretation thereof. For this cause the king was angry and very furious, and commanded to destroy all the wise men of Babylon.
Matthew 2:16 Then Herod, when he saw that he was mocked of the wise men, was exceeding wroth, and sent forth, and slew all the children that were in Bethlehem, and in all the coasts thereof, from two years old and under, according to the time which he had diligently enquired of the wise men.

Proverbs 19:13 A foolish son *is* the calamity of his father: and the contentions of a wife *are* a continual dropping.

Focus: This proverb expresses how two family members can render the home miserable by their actions.

It would be difficult to find any conditions that would rob a man of his happiness and make his home life more miserable than a foolish son or a foolish contentious wife. These two people (son and wife) should bring joy from their very presence. Instead, the head of the house might have to leave his home to get away and find peace. A commentator of an earlier time stated, "Many are the miseries of a man's life; but none like that, which cometh from him, who should be the stay of his life."[470] Having a foolish son has been described as "like an overwhelming catastrophe that sucks a person into a deep pit."[471] Making home life intolerable, the contentions of a wife are irritating, uncontrollable, and sometimes visible to the community.

"A foolish son" has a lifestyle and characteristics that are opposite those of a wise son. His behavior may include any of the following: refusal to be instructed, arrogance, prevarication, association with foolish people, laziness, thievery, gang membership, disrespect to God and parents, disobedience, irresponsibility, frowardness, perverseness of speech, fornication, hastiness, or drunkenness. 2 Samuel 13 tells the disastrous and distressing story of David's foolish son Amnon who raped his half-sister and then was killed by Absalom, another of David's sons.

The **"calamity** *[engulfing ruin]*" brought on the father because of a foolish son comes in the form of sleepless nights; disharmony and fighting among family members; financial challenges resulting from riotous living; disrespect from relatives, friends, and neighbors; loss of desire to excel or prepare for the future; agony when considering inheritances going to a fool; and overall loss of enjoyment of life.

Regarding the wife's **"contentions** *[quarreling]*," the **"continual dropping"** is a comparison of the wife's continual quarreling to a leaking roof that constantly reminds the household *(especially the father)* that the problem is ever-present, that the damage is steadily getting worse, and that the expense is growing. "The flat roofs of Eastern houses, formed of planks loosely joined and covered with a coating of clay or plaster, were always subject to leakage in heavy rains."[472] If the leaks were severe and widespread, there would be no place to sit, stand, work or sleep without being dripped on. Such annoyance robs everyone in the house of sleep and sets nerves on edge.

Proverbs 10:1 The proverbs of Solomon. A wise son maketh a glad father: but a foolish son is the heaviness of his mother.
Proverbs 15:20 A wise son maketh a glad father: but a foolish man despiseth his mother.

Proverbs 17:21 He that begetteth a fool doeth it to his sorrow: and the father of a fool hath no joy.

Proverbs 17:25 A foolish son is a grief to his father, and bitterness to her that bare him.

Proverbs 21:9 It is better to dwell in a corner of the housetop, than with a brawling woman in a wide house. *[Repeated nearly verbatim in Proverbs 25:24]*

Proverbs 21:19 It is better to dwell in the wilderness, than with a contentious and an angry woman.

Proverbs 25:24 *It is* better to dwell in the corner of the housetop, than with a brawling woman and in a wide house.

Proverbs 27:15-16 A continual dropping in a very rainy day and a contentious woman are alike. Whosoever hideth her hideth the wind, and the ointment of his right hand, which bewrayeth itself.

Proverbs 19:14 House and riches *are* the inheritance of fathers: and a prudent wife *is* from the LORD.

Focus: This proverb contrasts a parents' gift of substance with God's gift of a prudent wife.

"House and riches are the inheritance of fathers." A man may receive a valuable inheritance of real estate, personal property, and money from parents or others, and all such inheritances can bring a measure of comfort and enjoyment. However, the previous verse demonstrated just how futile it is to have a home without love, discipline, and respect. Hence, a prudent wife has more impact on happiness than a house and riches.

"And a prudent wife is from the Lord." A prudent wife is one who conducts her life wisely. She is a gift *(and a contrast to the quarrelsome wife of verse 13)*. A man is indeed blessed when he admits ignorance as to how to pick the woman who will be the mother of his children, his best friend on earth, the one who runs his household in his absence, the one he trusts with all his possessions, and the one who owns all that he owns and with whom he shares all of his heart. A man can be fooled by sweet talk, size and shape, or beauty. He could be sorry for his choice for the rest of his life. Because only God can see the heart of a woman who might become his wife, every man should pray and trust God to bring him the right wife. In Jewish societies where parents selected the spouse for their children, it would certainly have benefitted the child for his parents to have known and followed the will of God and prayed earnestly for God's choice. Inheritances are wonderful *if* the wife determines to make the home godly. Otherwise, even immense wealth is worthless where there is constant trouble.

Genesis 24:12-14 And he said, O LORD God of my master Abraham, I pray thee, send me good speed this day, and shew kindness unto my master Abraham. Behold, I stand here by the well of water; and the daughters of the men of the city come out to draw water: And let it come to pass, that the damsel to whom I shall say, Let down thy pitcher, I pray thee, that I may drink; and she shall say, Drink, and I will give thy camels drink also: let the same be she that thou hast appointed for thy servant Isaac; and thereby shall I know that thou hast shewed kindness unto my master.

Proverbs 12:4 A virtuous woman is a crown to her husband: but she that maketh ashamed is as rottenness in his bones.

Proverbs 18:22 Whoso findeth a wife findeth a good thing, and obtaineth favour of the LORD.

James 1:17 Every good gift and every perfect gift is from above, and cometh down from the Father of lights, with whom is no variableness, neither shadow of turning.

Proverbs 19:15 Slothfulness casteth into a deep sleep; and an idle soul shall suffer hunger.

Focus: This proverb characterizes the consequences of slothfulness.

"Slothfulness *[sluggishness, laziness, indolence]* **casteth into a deep sleep."** **"Deep sleep** *[lethargy or by implication, trance]*" describes a state of dull mindlessness in which the person is unaware of life. The term was used first in Genesis to describe the supernatural sleep that God placed on Adam when He formed Eve from one of his ribs. *(Genesis 2:21)* It was the condition that came upon Abraham when God made His covenant with him *(Genesis 15:12)*, and it was the condition of Saul and his men produced by God to protect David from them when he walked into their camp. *(1 Samuel 26:12)* "Deep sleep" also describes the dream state of man. *(Job 4:13; 33:15)* Isaiah used the phrase "spirit of deep sleep" to describe an insensibility to danger and spirit of stupidity that God had given the Jews due to their infidelity and impiety.[473] *(Isaiah 29:10)* The sluggard would find this state of unawareness enjoyable. However, eventually, even parents will tire of making provisions for the slothful son or daughter, who will be forced to do some labor to abate hunger. **"An idle soul shall suffer**

hunger." A slothful person does not want to exert energy; consequently, he is indolent, hesitant to move, likes to sleep, has little or no interest in the future, is fearful, and is dependent on others for livelihood. He may even lie to prevent exerting energy. Slothful persons have characteristics and living conditions that are **opposite** that of a wise person.

"...dreaming much, but doing nothing. Slothful people doze away their time, bury their talents, live a useless life, and are the unprofitable burdens of the earth; for any service they do when they are awake they might as well be always asleep. Even their souls are idle and lulled asleep, their rational powers chilled and frozen. It *[slothfulness]* impoverishes men and brings them to want. Those that will not labour cannot expect to eat, but must suffer hunger . . . "[474]

"Slothfulness enervates a man, renders him as useless for labour as if he were actually asleep in his bed; it also enfeebles the mind, corrupts the higher faculties, converts a rational being into a witless animal."[475]

Proverbs 6:9-11 How long wilt thou sleep, O sluggard? when wilt thou arise out of thy sleep? *Yet* a little sleep, a little slumber, a little folding of the hands to sleep: So shall thy poverty come as one that travelleth, and thy want as an armed man.

Proverbs 10:4-5 He becometh poor that dealeth *with* a slack hand: but the hand of the diligent maketh rich. He that gathereth in summer *is* a wise son: *but* he that sleepeth in harvest *is* a son that causeth shame.

Proverbs 12:24 The hand of the diligent shall bear rule: but the slothful shall be under tribute.

Proverbs 12:27 The slothful *man* roasteth not that which he took in hunting: but the substance of a diligent man *is* precious.

Proverbs 15:19 The way of the slothful *man is* as an hedge of thorns: but the way of the righteous *is* made plain.

Proverbs 18:9 He also that is slothful in his work is brother to him that is a great waster.

Proverbs 19:24 A slothful *man* hideth his hand in *his* bosom, and will not so much as bring it to his mouth again.

Proverbs 20:4 The sluggard will not plow by reason of the cold; *therefore* shall he beg in harvest, and *have* nothing.

Proverbs 20:13 Love not sleep, lest thou come to poverty; open thine eyes, and thou shalt be satisfied with bread.

Proverbs 23:21 For the drunkard and the glutton shall come to poverty: and drowsiness shall clothe *a man* with rags.

Proverbs 26:13-14 The slothful *man* saith, *There is* a lion in the way; a lion *is* in the streets. *As* the door turneth upon his hinges, so *doth* the slothful upon his bed.

Matthew 25:25-26 And I was afraid, and went and hid thy talent in the earth: lo, *there* thou hast *that is* thine. His lord answered and said unto him, *Thou* wicked and slothful servant, thou knewest that I reap where I sowed not, and gather where I have not strawed

Colossians 3:23 And whatsoever ye do, do *it* heartily, as to the Lord, and not unto men

2 Thessalonians 3:10 For even when we were with you, this we commanded you, that if any would not work, neither should he eat.

Proverbs 19:16 He that keepeth the commandment keepeth his own soul; *but* he that despiseth his ways shall die.

Focus: This proverb contrasts opposite attitudes toward the commandments of God and gives the consequence of each attitude.

"He that keepeth the commandment keepeth his own soul." From this proverb, one realizes that there is a bond between God and the people who keep His word. God gives peace, power, protection, provision, and a special relationship with the Paraclete to those who love Him and His word. A person proves his love for God when he sets a guard about His word and establishes his life by living out the truths contained in it.

The one major characteristic that separates the wise from the foolish is that the wise keep *(protect, guard, and obey)* the word of God. Building on the word of God as the solid foundation, a wise person learns to live safely and efficiently because of having God and His word as Guide. ***The wise man thus keeps himself (his "soul")*** from evil people, dangerous circumstances, unnecessary heartaches, and the sway of Satan. His relationship with God is personal and unbreakable.

Psalm 103:17-18 But the mercy of the LORD is from everlasting to everlasting upon them that fear him, and his righteousness unto children's children; To such as keep his covenant, and to those that remember his commandments to do them.

Proverbs 1:30-33 They would none of my counsel: they despised all my reproof. Therefore shall they eat of the fruit of their own way, and be filled with their own devices. For the turning away of the simple shall slay them, and the prosperity of fools shall destroy them. But whoso hearkeneth unto me shall dwell safely, and shall be quiet from fear of evil.

Proverbs 6:23 For the commandment *is* a lamp; and the law *is* light; and reproofs of instruction *are* the way of life . . .

Proverbs 13:13 Whoso despiseth the word shall be destroyed: but he that feareth the commandment shall be rewarded.

Proverbs 19:20 Hear counsel, and receive instruction, that thou mayest be wise in thy latter end.

Proverbs 29:18 Where *there is* no vision, the people perish: but he that keepeth the law, happy *is* he.

Ecclesiastes 8:5 Whoso keepeth the commandment shall feel no evil thing: and a wise man's heart discerneth both time and judgment.

Ecclesiastes 12:13 Let us hear the conclusion of the whole matter: Fear God, and keep his commandments: for this *is* the whole *duty* of man.

Jeremiah 7:23 But this thing commanded I them, saying, Obey my voice, and I will be your God, and ye shall be my people: and walk ye in all the ways that I have commanded you, that it may be well unto you.

Luke 11:27-28 And it came to pass, as he spake these things, a certain woman of the company lifted up her voice, and said unto him, Blessed *is* the womb that bare thee, and the paps which thou hast sucked. But he said, Yea rather, blessed *are* they that hear the word of God, and keep it.

John 14:21-23 He that hath my commandments, and keepeth them, he it is that loveth me: and he that loveth me shall be loved of my Father, and I will love him, and will manifest myself to him. Judas saith unto him, not Iscariot, Lord, how is it that thou wilt manifest thyself unto us, and not unto the world? Jesus answered and said unto him, If a man love me, he will keep my words: and my Father will love him, and we will come unto him, and make our abode with him.

1 John 2:3-4 And hereby we do know that we know him, if we keep his commandments. He that saith, I know him, and keepeth not his commandments, is a liar, and the truth is not in him.

1 John 3:22-24 And whatsoever we ask, we receive of him, because we keep his commandments, and do those things that are pleasing in his sight. And this is his commandment, That we should believe on the name of his Son Jesus Christ, and love one another, as he gave us commandment. And he that keepeth his commandments dwelleth in him, and he in him. And hereby we know that he abideth in us, by the Spirit which he hath given us.

Revelation 22:14 Blessed *are* they that do his commandments, that they may have right to the tree of life, and may enter in through the gates into the city.

"*But* **he that despiseth his ways shall die**" is set in opposition to "**he that keepeth the commandment**…" When a person despises something, he has no regard for it; consequently, he does not *keep it* in his ways or lifestyle. He does not protect or guard "**his ways**," thus allowing himself to live outside of biblical guidelines. The commandments of God mean nothing to him; and he considers his life entirely his own to be lived in any manner he chooses, whether he lie, cheat, steal, murder, commit adultery, or whatever situation presents itself to him. Because he has no regard for his own lifestyle, he certainly has none for the commandments of God that would restrict his behavior. His contempt and disdain for God's leadership is exactly why he "**shall die.**" Death is separation from God according to 2 Thessalonians 1:8 and 9 – "… them that know not God, and that obey not the gospel of our Lord Jesus Christ: Who shall be punished with everlasting destruction from the presence of the Lord, and from the glory of his power." In the first death, which is physical, the body is separated from the soul and spirit. In the "second death," which is spiritual, soul and spirit are separated eternally from God in the Lake of Fire.

Numbers 15:31 Because he hath despised the word of the LORD, and hath broken his commandment, that soul shall utterly be cut off; his iniquity *shall be* upon him.

Proverbs 15:10 Correction is grievous unto him that forsaketh the way: and he that hateth reproof shall die.

Ezekiel 33:11 Say unto them, As I live, saith the Lord GOD, I have no pleasure in the death of the wicked; but that the wicked turn from his way and live: turn ye, turn ye from your evil ways; for why will ye die, O house of Israel?

Proverbs 19:17 He that hath pity upon the poor lendeth unto the LORD; and that which he hath given will he pay him again.

Focus: This proverb expresses God's view pitying the poor and His promise to those who give to them.

Having pity *[to have mercy on, to bend or stoop in kindness to an inferior]* **upon the poor** is the first requirement for this special promise from God to be fulfilled. Such giving out of pity comes from a humble heart filled with love for those in need. This kind of *freewill giving* differs from the *command giving* that Israel had during her early years of statehood.

NOTE: Not mentioned in this proverb are at least two other motives behind giving that are *not* considered **loans to God**: (1) Giving with a heart of greed, rather than pity, because one believes that God will repay out of obligation, and (2) Giving because the *right* people are watching.

"**And that which he hath given will he pay him again.**" God *commanded the Hebrews* to feed the poor directly from their farms and from all their surplus. *(See verses below.)* When Jesus walked in Israel, He fed the hungry through personal miracles; and because of the love of Christ within Christians, they are expected to personally feed and care for the poor. When such acts of love and pity are accomplished, it is *as though the believer's gifts were a loan to God, and He promises to repay*. What an astounding promise and opportunity to interact with God!!

"Selfishness would evade the obligation under the cover of prudence. But *what we give* is only a loan, to be paid *again*, and *that* with such security, as can never fail. The Lord of heaven condescends to be the Surety for *the poor*. He takes the debt upon himself, and gives us the bond of his word in promise of payment. Though he has a right to all, and is beholden to none, he becomes a debtor to his own. Many acts of kindness have been buried and forgotten. The witness of our conscience is the only fruit. But here is a safe deposit in the very heart of God. It can never be lost or forgotten. 'If then' – as Bishop Hall writes – 'we will needs lay up, where should we rather repose it, than in the Christian's treasury? The poor man's hand is the treasury of Christ. All my superfluity shall there be hoarded up, where I know it will be safely kept, and surely returned me.'"[476]

"'And that which he hath given will, he pay him again' either in this life, in things temporal and spiritual, increasing his worldly substance, blessing his posterity, granting him larger measures of grace, indulging him with his gracious presence, and giving him peace of mind, which passeth all understanding; or in the world to come; not as a reward of debt, but of grace"[477]

Leviticus 25:35-36 And if thy brother be waxen poor, and fallen in decay with thee; then thou shalt relieve him: *yea, though he be* a stranger, or a sojourner; that he may live with thee. Take thou no usury of him, or increase: but fear thy God; that thy brother may live with thee.

Deuteronomy 15:7-8 If there be among you a poor man of one of thy brethren within any of thy gates in thy land which the LORD thy God giveth thee, thou shalt not harden thine heart, nor shut thine hand from thy poor brother: But thou shalt open thine hand wide unto him, and shalt surely lend him sufficient for his need, *in that* which he wanteth.

Deuteronomy 24:19 When thou cuttest down thine harvest in thy field, and hast forgot a sheaf in the field, thou shalt not go again to fetch it: it shall be for the stranger, for the fatherless, and for the widow: that the LORD thy God may bless thee in all the work of thine hands.

Psalm 41:1-3 To the chief Musician, A Psalm of David. Blessed *is* he that considereth the poor: the LORD will deliver him in time of trouble. The LORD will preserve him, and keep him alive; *and* he shall be blessed upon the earth: and thou wilt not deliver him unto the will of his enemies. The LORD will strengthen him upon the bed of languishing: thou wilt make all his bed in his sickness.

Proverbs 11:24 There is that scattereth, and yet increaseth; and *there is* that withholdeth more than is meet, but *it tendeth* to poverty.

Proverbs 14:21 He that despiseth his neighbour sinneth: but he that hath mercy on the poor, happy *is* he.

Proverbs 14:31 He that oppresseth the poor reproacheth his Maker: but he that honoureth him hath mercy on the poor.

Proverbs 22:9 He that hath a bountiful eye shall be blessed; for he giveth of his bread to the poor.

Proverbs 28:27 He that giveth unto the poor shall not lack: but he that hideth his eyes shall have many a curse.

Proverbs 31:20 She stretcheth out her hand to the poor; yea, she reacheth forth her hands to the needy.

Ecclesiastes 11:1 Cast thy bread upon the waters: for thou shalt find it after many days.

Matthew 5:42 Give to him that asketh thee, and from him that would borrow of thee turn not thou away.

Matthew 25:34-40 Then shall the King say unto them on his right hand, Come, ye blessed of my Father, inherit the kingdom prepared for you from the foundation of the world: For I was an hungred, and ye gave me meat: I was thirsty, and ye gave me drink: I was a stranger, and ye took me in: Naked, and ye clothed me: I was sick, and ye visited me: I was in prison, and ye came unto me. Then shall the righteous answer him, saying, Lord, when saw we thee an hungred, and fed *thee?* or thirsty, and gave *thee* drink? When saw we thee a stranger, and took *thee* in? or naked, and clothed *thee?* Or when saw we thee sick, or in prison, and came unto thee? And the King shall answer and say unto them, Verily I say unto you, Inasmuch as ye have done *it* unto one of the least of these my brethren, ye have done *it* unto me.

Luke 10:35 And on the morrow when he departed, he took out two pence, and gave *them* to the host, and said unto him, Take care of him; and whatsoever thou spendest more, when I come again, I will repay thee.

Luke 14:13-14 But when thou makest a feast, call the poor, the maimed, the lame, the blind: And thou shalt be blessed; for they cannot recompense thee: for thou shalt be recompensed at the resurrection of the just.

Acts 20:35 I have shewed you all things, how that so labouring ye ought to support the weak, and to remember the words of the Lord Jesus, how he said, It is more blessed to give than to receive.

1 Corinthians 13:3 And though I bestow all my goods to feed *the poor,* and though I give my body to be burned, and have not charity, it profiteth me nothing.

James 2:15-16 If a brother or sister be naked, and destitute of daily food, And one of you say unto them, Depart in peace, be *ye* warmed and filled; notwithstanding ye give them not those things which are needful to the body; what *doth it* profit?

1 John 3:17 But whoso hath this world's good, and seeth his brother have need, and shutteth up his bowels *of compassion* from him, how dwelleth the love of God in him?

Proverbs 19:18 Chasten thy son while there is hope, and let not thy soul spare for his crying.

Focus: This proverb establishes two important guidelines for the effective discipline of a child.

"Chasten thy son while there is hope." Chastening *[instructing, correcting, admonishing, teaching]* done by the wise parent is to be given **"while there is hope,"** meaning while he is young enough to be corrected through chastening. The **"hope** *[a cord as an attachment, expectancy, thing longed for]*" is that the child will correct his behavior and adhere to the principles of God's teaching, enjoy a productive life, avoid evil and unnecessary hardships, and anticipate eternity with God.

A loving parent will not have any desire to inflict pain on anyone, especially on his beloved and dear child; however, it is a common fact that adjustments in life usually occur because of some level of discomfort or pain. The infliction of *minimal pain* resulting from parental chastening is an act of mercy because such minimal pain is virtually zero compared to the pain he will suffer if left without correction.

When they are being punished, children are notorious for hypocritically crying so loudly and pitifully that people within earshot think they are surely at the point of death. The warning is for parents to refuse to allow such "crying" to interfere with a proper level of correction being applied in order to keep them from actually dying early in life. **"Let not thy soul spare for his crying"** is an admonition to parents to be resolved to follow through with correction even though his crying is heartbreaking.

> 1 Samuel 3:13 For I have told him that I will judge his house for ever for the iniquity which he knoweth; because his sons made themselves vile, and he restrained them not.
> Proverbs 13:24 He that spareth his rod hateth his son: but he that loveth him chasteneth him betimes.
> Proverbs 19:26 He that wasteth *his* father, *and* chaseth away *his* mother, *is* a son that causeth shame, and bringeth reproach.
> Proverbs 22:15 Foolishness *is* bound in the heart of a child; *but* the rod of correction shall drive it far from him.
> Proverbs 23:13 Withhold not correction from the child: for *if* thou beatest him with the rod, he shall not die.
> Proverbs 23:14 Thou shalt beat him with the rod, and shalt deliver his soul from hell.
> Proverbs 29:15 The rod and reproof give wisdom: but a child left *to himself* bringeth his mother to shame.
> Proverbs 29:17 Correct thy son, and he shall give thee rest; yea, he shall give delight unto thy soul.
> Hebrews 12:11 Now no chastening for the present seemeth to be joyous, but grievous: nevertheless afterward it yieldeth the peaceable fruit of righteousness unto them which are exercised thereby.

Believers need to love their children wisely. Foolish man calls *sparing the rod* "loving the child." That kind of mercy is *false tenderness*. Eli "kindly and tenderly" overlooked his children's sins, only to regret it later when they lay with the women in the temple and took meat out of the offering (1 Samuel 2:22; 3:13). It is far better that a child cries under healthy, loving correction, than that the father and mother should weep at the jail or at the grave.

Special attention, affection, and direction should accompany correction. A child should understand why he is being disciplined, and he should be fully aware of, and sensitive to, his parent's love. "The rod without affection is revolting tyranny."[478] The following is repeated from this commentary's notes on Proverbs 13:24. (See verse above.)

The Rod as an Instrument of Discipline

"**Rod**" is translated from the Hebrew *shebet* (pronounced *shay'-bet*) from an unused root which means a scion *[small stick or stem]* used for punishing, writing, fighting, ruling, walking. Figuratively it means a clan or tribe. (From Strong's *Hebrew Dictionary*)

"The word 'rod' indicates a thin stick or switch that can be used to give a small amount of physical pain with no lasting physical injury. A child should never be bruised, injured, or cut by a physical correction. The Bible warns that parents should never abuse the power and authority they have over their children while they are young because it provokes the children to righteous anger."

> Ephesians 6:4 And, ye fathers, provoke not your children to wrath: but bring them up in the nurture and admonition of the Lord.
> Colossians 3:21 Fathers, provoke not your children to anger, lest they be discouraged.

"Physical discipline is always done in love, never as a vent to the parent's frustration. It is also just one part of discipline and should be used when the child shows defiance to a clear limit, not in the heat of the moment." (From https://www.gotquestions.org/spare-rod-spoil-child.html)

Proverbs 19:19 A man of great wrath shall suffer punishment: for if thou deliver *him*, yet thou must do it again.

Focus: This proverb specifies (1) the consequence to a man of great wrath and (2) the consistency with which he has to be delivered from punishment.

"A man of great wrath shall suffer punishment." **"A man of great wrath"** is controlled by emotions and driven by anger. He has little or no self-control but allows his emotions to dictate his actions. Consequently, he fails to apply wisdom to displeasing situations and repeatedly brings on serious repercussions and unnecessary problems. The anger-controlled man torments himself as well as others because his violent conduct causes disagreements, arguments, loss of friends, and possibly lawsuits. As soon as he gets out of one situation, he faces another.

Scripture mentions several men who were controlled by anger – men such as *Cain,* who slew his brother (Genesis 4); *Baalam,* who wanted to kill his donkey in Numbers 22; *Haman,* who wanted to kill Mordecai and all the Jews in Esther; and *Absalom* who grew angry at his brother Amnon and revenged his sister's rape in 2 Samuel 13. Finally, there is the **"great wrath"** of King Saul, whose violent outbursts led to boiling rage that manifested itself repeatedly over time.

Saul's anger first seemed to erupt when David returned from the slaughter of the Philistines and the women sang this song: "Saul hath slain his thousands, and David his ten thousands . . . And Saul was very wroth... And Saul eyed David from that day and forward." (1 Samuel 18:7-9) Afterward, in his anger and jealousy, Saul twice threw his spear at David, trying to pin him to the wall (1 Samuel 18:10-1; 19:9; 10;12-15). Hoping that he would die while fighting the Philistines, Saul required that David kill one hundred Philistines before he would give him his daughter in marriage (1 Samuel 18:25–29). The wrathful king pursued David continually for more than a decade, forcing him to live in exile and frequently move from hiding place to hiding place (1 Samuel 24: 26). Not only did Saul pursue David without mercy, but he ordered the murder of those who helped him. The king even turned on his own son with murderous intent (1 Samuel 20:30). Saul's anger had no end even though his son, Jonathan, and David tried to reason with him at different times.

"For if thou deliver *him,* yet thou must do it again." Observation of fathers' bailing their children out of situations brought on by anger has affirmed the truth of this proverb. Their children were usually repeat offenders. As the proverb states, it is unwise to **"deliver him"** because he will soon be in another self-induced predicament. Better that he **"suffer punishment"** on his own with the hope that such pain will cause him to correct his ill behavior.

> Genesis 49:5-7 Simeon and Levi *are* brethren; instruments of cruelty *are in* their habitations. O my soul, come not thou into their secret; unto their assembly, mine honour, be not thou united: for in their anger they slew a man, and in their selfwill they digged down a wall. Cursed *be* their anger, for *it was* fierce; and their wrath, for it was cruel: I will divide them in Jacob, and scatter them in Israel.
> Proverbs 15:18 A wrathful man stirreth up strife: but *he that is* slow to anger appeaseth strife.
> Proverbs 18:6 A fool's lips enter into contention, and his mouth calleth for strokes.
> Proverbs 22:24-25 Make no friendship with an angry man; and with a furious man thou shalt not go: Lest thou learn his ways, and get a snare to thy soul.
> Proverbs 25:28 He that *hath* no rule over his own spirit *is like* a city *that is* broken down, *and* without walls.
> Proverbs 27:3-4 A stone *is* heavy, and the sand weighty; but a fool's wrath *is* heavier than them both. Wrath *is* cruel, and anger *is* outrageous; but who *is* able to stand before envy?
> Proverbs 29:22 An angry man stirreth up strife, and a furious man aboundeth in transgression.
> Ecclesiastes 7:9 Be not hasty in thy spirit to be angry: for anger resteth in the bosom of fools.
> Colossians 3:8 But now ye also put off all these; anger, wrath, malice, blasphemy, filthy communication out of your mouth.
> James 1:19-20 Wherefore, my beloved brethren, let every man be swift to hear, slow to speak, slow to wrath: For the wrath of man worketh not the righteousness of God.
> Revelation 12:12 Therefore rejoice, *ye* heavens, and ye that dwell in them. Woe to the inhabiters of the earth and of the sea! for the devil is come down unto you, having great wrath, because he knoweth that he hath but a short time.

Proverbs 19:20 Hear counsel, and receive instruction, that thou mayest be wise in thy latter end.

Focus: This proverb gives the process for becoming wise.

A wise young student of wisdom knows that learning is vital to better living; consequently, he will **"hear counsel,"** especially that of God, and **"receive instruction"** so as to become a person of understanding. Obtaining wisdom is a protracted gradual learning process, and the **"latter end"** is that part when the student has learned the principles of being wise and is actually following them. A gray head is typically respected because of age, and the assumption is that such a bearer has grown wise with experience. However, a failure to "hear counsel" and then actually "receive instruction" from others can only produce foolishness. Every aged person is not wise.

The student of wisdom knows that he can learn from every occasion, every observation, and every person that he meets. He is ever attentive to the *direct* as well as the *indirect* counsel of others. He has trained himself to receive, to mull over, to think deeply about what he has observed, and to ask God to show him where and how to apply it to his life and way of thinking. Furthermore, he knows that the greatest counsel of all, the greatest teacher, is Scripture. These words of God provide excellent counsel and also cause a person to be able to discern good counsel from evil. "The simple believeth every word: but the prudent *man* looketh well to his going." (Proverbs 14:15)

> Deuteronomy 32:28-29 For they *are* a nation void of counsel, neither *is there any* understanding in them. O that they were wise, *that* they understood this, *that* they would consider their latter end!
>
> 1 Kings 12:8 . . . 16 But he forsook the counsel of the old men, which they had given him, and consulted with the young men that were grown up with him, *and* which stood before him . . . So when all Israel saw that the king hearkened not unto them, the people answered the king, saying, What portion have we in David? neither *have we* inheritance in the son of Jesse: to your tents, O Israel: now see to thine own house, David. So Israel departed unto their tents.
>
> Proverbs 5:1-2 My son, attend unto my wisdom, *and* bow thine ear to my understanding: That thou mayest regard discretion, and *that* thy lips may keep knowledge.
>
> Proverbs 8:10 Receive my instruction, and not silver; and knowledge rather than choice gold.
>
> Proverbs 8:33-35 Hear instruction, and be wise, and refuse it not. Blessed *is* the man that heareth me, *[wisdom]* watching daily at my gates, waiting at the posts of my doors. For whoso findeth me findeth life, and shall obtain favour of the LORD.
>
> Proverbs 12:15 The way of a fool *is* right in his own eyes: but he that hearkeneth unto counsel *is* wise.
>
> Proverbs 13:10 Only by pride cometh contention: but with the well advised *is* wisdom.
>
> Proverbs 14:12 There is a way which seemeth right unto a man, but the end thereof *are* the ways of death.
>
> Proverbs 15:31 The ear that heareth the reproof of life abideth among the wise.
>
> Proverbs 15:32 He that refuseth instruction despiseth his own soul: but he that heareth reproof getteth understanding.
>
> Proverbs 24:30-32 I went by the field of the slothful, and by the vineyard of the man void of understanding; And, lo, it was all grown over with thorns, *and* nettles had covered the face thereof, and the stone wall thereof was broken down. Then I saw, *and* considered *it* well: I looked upon *it, and* received instruction.
>
> 1 Corinthians 10:11 Now all these things happened unto them for ensamples: and they are written for our admonition, upon whom the ends of the world are come.
>
> 2 Timothy 3:14-15 But continue thou in the things which thou hast learned and hast been assured of, knowing of whom thou hast learned them; And that from a child thou hast known the holy scriptures, which are able to make thee wise unto salvation through faith which is in Christ Jesus.

Proverbs 19:21 There are many devices in a man's heart; nevertheless the counsel of the LORD, that shall stand.

Focus: This proverb contrasts the many temporary and unstable contrivances that man concocts with the strength and stability of God's counsel.

"There are many devices in a man's heart." Verse 4 reminded the reader that *wealth makes many friends*, and now verse 21 states there are **"many devices in a man's heart."** The **"many friends"** were not *all* good, and neither are the **"many devices"**– "many desires, intentions, and resolutions, – many objects, with the plans and means of their attainment."[479] Though his devices are lodged in his heart and unspoken, they are not hidden from God who knows when man sits and stands and even his thoughts before they come to his mind. (Psalm 139:2) Man's devices are many and dependent upon the will of God for completion, while God's counsel is independent of any outside force or agency. Man's devices have no affect the counsel of God, but His counsel has an absolute effect on man's devices, which He finds humorous. (Psalm 2:1-4)

"Nevertheless the counsel of the LORD, that shall stand." God often allows men plenty of space to move forward with their plans, but eventually, He will cause His will to prevail. It is impossible for a man to ultimately succeed when his contrivances oppose *God's counsel*. A prime example is found in the Book of Esther. Mordecai (a Jew and *one of God's chosen people*) refused to bow to Haman, the wicked prime minister of Persia (Iran). Haman then plotted to destroy not only Mordecai but all the Jews in Persia. He was eventually hanged on the very gallows he had previously built for Mordecai (Esther 3:1-9:25) because God providentially intervened.

Scripture is full of **"the counsel of the LORD"** that is given by implication, through specific life illustrations, and directly through His commandments. Wise men thus study the written *counsel of God* and become sensitive to the leadership of the Spirit of God in order to properly evaluate their own plans, whether they are good or bad, proper or improper, likely to succeed or likely to fail. "Let the word of Christ dwell in you richly in all wisdom; teaching and admonishing one another in psalms and hymns and spiritual songs, singing with grace in your hearts to the Lord." (Colossians 3:16)

> Genesis 37:18-20; 50:20 And when they *[Joseph's brothers]* saw him *[Joseph]* afar off, even before he came near unto them, they conspired against him to slay him. And they said one to another, Behold, this dreamer cometh. Come now therefore, and let us slay him, and cast him into some pit, and we will say, Some evil beast hath devoured him: and we shall see what will become of his dreams . . . But as for you, *[Joseph to his brothers]* ye thought evil against me; *but* God meant it unto good, to bring to pass, as *it is* this day, to save much people alive.
>
> Esther 9:25 But when *Esther* came before the king, he commanded by letters that his wicked device, which he devised against the Jews, should return upon his own head, and that he and his sons should be hanged on the gallows.
>
> Psalm 2:1-6 Why do the heathen rage, and the people imagine a vain thing?   The kings of the earth set themselves, and the rulers take counsel together, against the LORD, and against his anointed, *saying,* Let us break their bands asunder, and cast away their cords from us. He that sitteth in the heavens shall laugh: the Lord shall have them in derision. Then shall he speak unto them in his wrath, and vex them in his sore displeasure. Yet have I set my king upon my holy hill of Zion.
>
> Psalm 33:10-11 The LORD bringeth the counsel of the heathen to nought: he maketh the devices of the people of none effect. The counsel of the LORD standeth for ever, the thoughts of his heart to all generations.
>
> Psalm 81:11-14 But my people would not hearken to my voice; and Israel would none of me. So I gave them up unto their own hearts' lust: and they walked in their own counsels. Oh that my people had hearkened unto me, and Israel had walked in my ways! I should soon have subdued their enemies, and turned my hand against their adversaries.
>
> Psalm 119:89 LAMED. For ever, O LORD, thy word is settled in heaven.
>
> Proverbs 16:9 A man's heart deviseth his way: but the LORD directeth his steps.
>
> Proverbs 21:30 *There is* no wisdom nor understanding nor counsel against the LORD.
>
> Ecclesiastes 7:29 Lo, this only have I found, that God hath made man upright; but they have sought out many inventions.
>
> Isaiah 7:6-7 Let us go up against Judah, and vex it, and let us make a breach therein for us, and set a king in the midst of it, even the son of Tabeal: Thus saith the Lord GOD, It shall not stand, neither shall it come to pass.
>
> Isaiah 46:9-10 Remember the former things of old: for I am God, and there is none else; I am God, and there is none like me, Declaring the end from the beginning, and from ancient times the things that are not yet done, saying, My counsel shall stand, and I will do all my pleasure . . .
>
> Jeremiah 2:13 For my people have committed two evils; they have forsaken me the fountain of living waters, *and* hewed them out cisterns, broken cisterns, that can hold no water.
>
> Acts 5:38-39 And now I say unto you, Refrain from these men, and let them alone: for if this counsel or this work be of men, it will come to nought: But if it be of God, ye cannot overthrow it; lest haply ye be found even to fight against God.
>
> Acts 23:10-11 And when there arose a great dissension, the chief captain, fearing lest Paul should have been pulled in pieces of them, commanded the soldiers to go down, and to take him by force from among them, and to bring him into the castle. And the night following the Lord stood by him, and said, Be of good cheer, Paul: for as thou hast testified of me in Jerusalem, so must thou bear witness also at Rome.
>
> Ephesians 1:11 In whom also we have obtained an inheritance, being predestinated according to the purpose of him who worketh all things after the counsel of his own will:
>
> James 4:13-15 Go to now, ye that say, To day or to morrow we will go into such a city, and continue there a year, and buy and sell, and get gain: Whereas ye know not what shall be on the morrow. For what is your life? It is even a vapour, that appeareth for a little time, and then vanisheth away. For that ye ought to say, If the Lord will, we shall live, and do this, or that.

Proverbs 19:22 The desire of a man *is* his kindness: and a poor man *is* better than a liar.

> Focus: This proverb contrasts a poor person who desires to help others (but with no ability) with a capable hypocritical person who lies about his desire to help others.

"The desire of a man *is* his kindness." This Scripture reveals that a poor man's desire to aid a neighbor in distress is demonstrative of a merciful heart (even if he is unable to carry out his intention). Deep within a person's soul lies the truth of who he is. A person who says that he wants to be merciful and kind, but does not act that way when everything is in place for him to do so, is either untruthful or lacks ability. Only God can judge a man's motives. An act of kindness to others is equal to being a servant to them to meet their needs, but people with large financial capacities often feel powerful and typically prefer to be served rather than to serve. (See Biblical illustration below.)

The second clause, **"And a poor man is better than a liar,"** is a continuation of the first and enhances the overall understanding. In this verse, **"a liar"** *pretends* to have kindness. He has the means to help others, and the situation allows for an act of kindness, but he refuses to do so. Therefore, he is lying about his kindness. He wants people to think that he has a kind heart, but actually he has no desire to be kind to others. "Withhold not good from them to whom it is due, when it is in the power of thine hand to do it. Say not unto thy neighbour, Go, and come again, and to morrow I will give; when thou hast it by thee." (Proverbs 3:27-28) It is better to be poor with a genuine desire to help others than to be a rich liar.

> Exodus 35:5 Take ye from among you an offering unto the LORD: whosoever *is* of a willing heart, let him bring it, an offering of the LORD; gold, and silver, and brass,
>
> Proverbs 11:23 The desire of the righteous *is* only good: *but* the expectation of the wicked *is* wrath.
>
> Proverbs 19:1 Better *is* the poor that walketh in his integrity, than *he that is* perverse in his lips, and is a fool.
>
> Proverbs 23:7 For as he thinketh in his heart, so *is* he: Eat and drink, saith he to thee; but his heart *is* not with thee.
>
> 2 Corinthians 8:12 For if there be first a willing mind, *it is* accepted according to that a man hath, *and* not according to that he hath not.

Rehoboam's Folly

Solomon's son, Rehoboam, assumed his father's throne and was presented with an option to show kindness to those under his reign, but he was both foolish and without kindness. His act of foolish cruelty cost him the loss of 10 of Israel's 12 tribes.

1 Kings 12:7 is a parallel passage to 2 Chronicles 10:7; only the 1 Kings passages states "If thou will be a servant unto this people.." while the 2 Chronicles passage states "If thou be kind to this people..." There is no discrepancy for the meaning is the same in both passages.

To be kind to others means to serve them in some manner; thus agreeing with Webster's definition of the word **"kind"**: "Disposed to do good to others, and to make them happy by granting their requests, supplying their wants, or assisting them in distress." (Noah Webster, *Dictionary of American English (1828)*, e-Sword,12.0.1.)

When Rehoboam "forsook the counsel of the old men", and determined to be more unkind than his father ever dreamed of being (I Kings 12:14,15), "Israel rebelled against the house of David" (I Kings 12:19). This was the beginning of the great division in the twelve tribes of Israel, as Jeroboam led ten of the tribes in revolt away from the house of David, driving a wedge between the ten tribes of Israel and the two tribes of Judah (I Kings 12:20-33).   (From Pastor Ricky Kurth as quoted on https://revivedlife.com/the-biblical-definition-of-kindness)

Proverbs 19:23 The fear of the LORD *tendeth* to life: and *he that hath it* shall abide satisfied; he shall not be visited with evil.

Focus: This proverb declares three personal advantages from having proper respect for God.

"The fear of the LORD *tendeth* to life." "The fear of the LORD" is a type of fear that is an awesome respect for God resulting in love, rather than a type of fear that causes anxiety and mental anguish. Such proper respect leads a person to focus on the awesomeness of God and the minuteness of self. Because of such focus, life is enriched with satisfaction because it is being protected, guided, and favored. According to Scripture, a person who learns to fear and to serve God will enjoy His favor and obtain length of days upon the earth. This "fear of the Lord" restrains a person from attaching himself to anything or anyone who disassociates with God. He **"shall abide satisfied"** because he trusts God, and thus, his conscience is clear and his heart at peace with God, himself and others. He knows that his behavior is proper because he has been instructed by Scripture. He avoids many of the dangers and disasters of life brought on by improper association, actions, and intentions; thus, **"he shall not be visited with evil."** Being close to God puts evil at a distance.

> 1 Samuel 25:39 And when David heard that Nabal was dead, he said, Blessed *be* the LORD, that hath pleaded the cause of my reproach from the hand of Nabal, and hath kept his servant from evil: for the LORD hath returned the wickedness of Nabal upon his own head. And David sent and communed with Abigail, to take her to him to wife.
>
> 1 Chronicles 4:10 And Jabez called on the God of Israel, saying, Oh that thou wouldest bless me indeed, and enlarge my coast, and that thine hand might be with me, and that thou wouldest keep *me* from evil, that it may not grieve me! And God granted him that which he requested.
>
> Psalm 25:12-13 What man *is* he that feareth the LORD? him shall he teach in the way *that* he shall choose.   His soul shall dwell at ease; and his seed shall inherit the earth.
>
> Psalm 33:18-19 Behold, the eye of the LORD *is* upon them that fear him, upon them that hope in his mercy; To deliver their soul from death, and to keep them alive in famine.
>
> Psalm 34:9-10 O fear the LORD, ye his saints: for *there is* no want to them that fear him. The young lions do lack, and suffer hunger: but they that seek the LORD shall not want any good *thing*.
>
> Psalm 91:4 He shall cover thee with his feathers, and under his wings shalt thou trust: his truth shall be thy shield and buckler.
>
> Psalm 121:2-7 My help *cometh* from the LORD, which made heaven and earth. He will not suffer thy foot to be moved: he that keepeth thee will not slumber. Behold, he that keepeth Israel shall neither slumber nor sleep. The LORD *is* thy keeper: the LORD *is* thy shade upon thy right hand. The sun shall not smite thee by day, nor the moon by night. The LORD shall preserve thee from all evil: he shall preserve thy soul.

Proverbs 3:23-26 Then shalt thou walk in thy way safely, and thy foot shall not stumble. When thou liest down, thou shalt not be afraid: yea, thou shalt lie down, and thy sleep shall be sweet. Be not afraid of sudden fear, neither of the desolation of the wicked, when it cometh. For the LORD shall be thy confidence, and shall keep thy foot from being taken.

Proverbs 10:27 The fear of the LORD prolongeth days: but the years of the wicked shall be shortened.

Proverbs 11:19 As righteousness *tendeth* to life: so he that pursueth evil *pursueth it* to his own death.

Proverbs 12:21 There shall no evil happen to the just: but the wicked shall be filled with mischief.

Proverbs 12:28 In the way of righteousness *is* life; and *in* the pathway *thereof there is* no death.

Proverbs 14:26 In the fear of the LORD *is* strong confidence: and his children shall have a place of refuge.

Proverbs 14:27 The fear of the LORD *is* a fountain of life, to depart from the snares of death.

Matthew 6:13 And lead us not into temptation, but deliver us from evil: For thine is the kingdom, and the power, and the glory, for ever. Amen.

John 17:15 I pray not that thou shouldest take them out of the world, but that thou shouldest keep them from the evil.

Romans 8:28 And we know that all things work together for good to them that love God, to them who are the called according to *his* purpose.

2 Thessalonians 3:3 But the Lord is faithful, who shall stablish you, and keep *you* from evil.

2 Timothy 4:18 And the Lord shall deliver me from every evil work, and will preserve *me* unto his heavenly kingdom: to whom *be* glory for ever and ever. Amen.

Proverbs 19:24 A slothful *man* hideth his hand in *his* bosom, and will not so much as bring it to his mouth again.

Focus: This proverb describes the epitome of laziness.

In this comical proverb, the **"slothful man"** is pictured as being so incredibly lazy that when he reaches down to get some food out of his bowl, held dearly close to his bosom, he does not have enough energy and willpower to pick up his hand and bring it to his mouth. Since the inner Hebrew garment had no sleeves, it is possible that the lazy man's hands and arms were covered with the folds of the robe, and he was grieved because it would have taken too much effort to disentangle himself in order to eat. Sarcasm and hyperbole are used here to ridicule the slothful person with the objective that others will not follow the lazy, foolish man's example.

Proverbs 12:27 The slothful man roasteth not that which he took in hunting: but the substance of a diligent man is precious.

Proverbs 19:15 Slothfulness casteth into a deep sleep; and an idle soul shall suffer hunger.

Proverbs 21:25 The desire of the slothful killeth him; for his hands refuse to labour.

Proverbs 24:30-34 I went by the field of the slothful, and by the vineyard of the man void of understanding; And, lo, it was all grown over with thorns, *and* nettles had covered the face thereof, and the stone wall thereof was broken down. Then I saw, *and* considered *it* well: I looked upon *it, and* received instruction. *Yet* a little sleep, a little slumber, a little folding of the hands to sleep: So shall thy poverty come *as* one that travelleth; and thy want as an armed man.

Ecclesiastes 4:5 The fool foldeth his hands together, and eateth his own flesh.

Hebrew Customs Associated with Mealtimes

Hebrew and oriental customs "connected with the eating of a meal, are such a decided contrast to Western habits, that much care should be given to the study of them, if the many references in the Bible to eating, are to be interpreted accurately."

"Old Testament Hebrews did "not use knives, forks, spoons, plates, or napkins which are considered so essential in the West. They say: "What does a man want of a spoon when God has given him so many fingers?" Sheets of bread, about as thick as heavy flannel; take the place of spoons or forks to some extent. A piece from this bread is broken off and shaped so as to put some of the food on it."

"They use this bread to scoop up any partially liquid dish, such as soups, sauces, or gravies. Each torn off piece of bread that thus serves as a spoon is eaten along with the food it contains."

"Meat is usually served in a single large dish and is eaten with the fingers. Broth is served in a separate dish and it is used to moisten the bread. This method of eating is actually not as untidy as might be supposed."

"The invitation Boaz gave to Ruth to eat with his workers, indicates that these same customs must have been in operation in those days: 'And Boaz said unto her, At mealtime come thou hither, and eat of the bread, and dip thy morsel in the vinegar' (Ruth 2:14). And at the last supper JESUS said to His disciples, 'He that dippeth his hand with me in the dish, the same shall betray me' (Matthew 26:23). Furthermore, He spoke of dipping a choice portion of the meat called the sop into the dish (John 13:26)...Most of the Oriental customs of today in regard to eating date back, not only to the days of our Saviour, but also to the Old Testament era." Excerpted from Wight, Fred H, *Manners and Customs of Bible lands*, e-Sword 12.0.1.

> **Proverbs 19:25** Smite a scorner, and the simple will beware: and reprove one that hath understanding, *and* he will understand knowledge.

Focus: In this proverb, the slight effectiveness that correction has with the simple is contrasted with the significant effectiveness that correction has with a person of understanding.

"Smite a scorner *[one who mocks and 'scoffs at religion, its ordinances and teachers, and who makes a mock of sin and the judgments and threatenings of God against sinners[480]]*, **and the simple** *[silly (that is, seducible), naive, foolish, open-minded. "Such as want wisdom, and are easily deceived by others"[481]]* **will beware." "The simple"** are those who are untaught (with limited knowledge and little understanding) and able to be easily persuaded to do wrong. Observing the *smiting of a scorner* creates a lasting, woefully fearful memory for the simple person. The mental image he retains, coupled with the *fear* that he might receive the same pain, will cause him to "beware," meaning that he has his guard up and is paying attention–not that he actually understands. It is doubtful that his comprehension is beyond a raised level of awareness. Because he does not want the pain from a beating, the simple may correct his behavior temporarily; but he may also be seduced by another scorner when his memory fades. "The simple" tend to degenerate and perhaps become a scorner themselves.

> Proverbs 21:11 When the scorner is punished, the simple is made wise: and when the wise is instructed, he receiveth knowledge.
> 1 Timothy 5:20 Them that sin rebuke before all, that others also may fear.

Having rejected the teaching of God, **"a scorner"** becomes hardened and froward, and mocks God and His instructions. He is so hardened that all he has to look forward to is retribution. Proverbs 17:10 states that "a reproof entereth more into a wise man than an hundred stripes into a fool." He is *smitten* because words of instruction to him are ineffective.

> Proverbs 9:12 If thou be wise, thou shalt be wise for thyself: but if thou scornest, thou alone shalt bear it.
> Proverbs 13:1 A wise son heareth his father's instruction: but a scorner heareth not rebuke.
> Proverbs 14:6 A scorner seeketh wisdom, and findeth it not: but knowledge is easy unto him that understandeth.
> Proverbs 19:29 Judgments are prepared for scorners, and stripes for the back of fools.
> Proverbs 21:24 Proud and haughty scorner is his name, who dealeth in proud wrath.
> Proverbs 24:9 The thought of foolishness is sin: and the scorner is an abomination to men.

"One that hath understanding" is a person who is opposite the scorner in his thinking about God and about His teachings. Because he has made up his mind to accept correction in order to please God, he can receive instruction and reproof through simple language. There is certainly no need for physical punishment. **"He will understand knowledge"** means that he will comprehend the correction because he desires to comprehend – and he is NOT in opposition to knowledge about God or mocking those with understanding.

> "The reproof of wise men will be a means of good to themselves. They need not be smitten; a word to the wise is enough. Do but *reprove one that has understanding and he will* so far understand himself and his own interest that he will *understand knowledge* by it, and not miss it again through ignorance and inadvertency when once he has been told of it; so kindly does he take reproof and so wisely improve it."[482]
> Psalm 141:5 Let the righteous smite me; *it shall be* a kindness: and let him reprove me; *it shall be* an excellent oil, *which* shall not break my head: for yet my prayer also *shall be* in their calamities.
> Proverbs 9:6-10 Forsake the foolish, and live; and go in the way of understanding. He that reproveth a scorner getteth to himself shame: and he that rebuketh a wicked *man getteth* himself a blot. Reprove not a scorner, lest he hate thee: rebuke a wise man, and he will love thee. Give *instruction* to a wise *man*, and he will be yet wiser: teach a just *man*, and he will increase in learning. The fear of the LORD *is* the beginning of wisdom: and the knowledge of the holy *is* understanding.
> Proverbs 21:11 When the scorner is punished, the simple is made wise: and when the wise is instructed, he receiveth knowledge.

"Never let us forget the mercy of being kept from sin, or being restored from it, though it be by our Master's sharp and gracious rebuke – 'As many as I love, I rebuke and chasten: be zealous therefore, and repent. (Revelation 3:19)"[483]

> **Proverbs 19:26** He that wasteth *his* father, *and* chaseth away *his* mother, *is* a son that causeth shame, and bringeth reproach.

Focus: This proverb specifies the devastation caused by a parentally abusive and rebellious son.

"Wasteth his father" describes the father's being impoverished by his son. He is diminished in health or wealth because the evil son robs, assaults, or mistreats his father causing losses. A shameful son can use up his father's estate, break down his health, and destroy his comfort through rebellion and extravagant, wild, sinful living. Disregarding the father's godly instruction is bad enough, but to abuse him physically (or in any other manner), steal from him (directly or indirectly), or curse him is disgraceful. The *extreme* point where he **"chaseth away his mother"** represents evil.

> *"He wastes his father,* wastes his estate which he should have to support him in his old age, wastes his spirits, and breaks his heart, and brings his gray head *with sorrow to the grave.* He *chases away his mother,* alienates her affections from him, which cannot be done without a great deal of regret and uneasiness to her; he makes her weary of the house, with his rudeness and insolence, and glad to retire for a little quietness; and, when he has spent all, he turns her out of doors."[484]

Godly parents naturally want to hold their heads up with a proper measure of self-esteem, and they regard the family name as special. However, when a son becomes a rebel, the family name is smeared, and parents are shamed into wondering how the public actually evaluates them as parents. **"Shame"** and **"reproach"** have the same meaning, so the words **"a son that causeth shame, and bringeth reproach,"** provide a double statement of the same meaning; thus, indicating the severity of the shameful situation.

> Proverbs 10:5 He that gathereth in summer *is* a wise son: *but* he that sleepeth in harvest *is* a son that causeth shame.
> Proverbs 13:5 A righteous *man* hateth lying: but a wicked *man* is loathsome, and cometh to shame.
> Proverbs 23:22 Hearken unto thy father that begat thee, and despise not thy mother when she is old.
> Proverbs 28:7 Whoso keepeth the law *is* a wise son: but he that is a companion of riotous *men* shameth his father.
> Proverbs 28:24 Whoso robbeth his father or his mother, and saith, It *is* no transgression; the same *is* the companion of a destroyer.
> Proverbs 30:11 There is a generation that curseth their father, and doth not bless their mother.
> Proverbs 30:17 The eye *that* mocketh at *his* father, and despiseth to obey *his* mother, the ravens of the valley shall pick it out, and the young eagles shall eat it.
> Mark 7:11-13 But ye say, If a man shall say to his father or mother, It is Corban, that is to say, a gift, by whatsoever thou mightest be profited by me; he shall be free. And ye suffer him no more to do ought for his father or his mother; Making the word of God of none effect through your tradition, which ye have delivered: and many such like things do ye.
> Romans 1:30-32 Backbiters, haters of God, despiteful, proud, boasters, inventors of evil things, disobedient to parents, Without understanding, covenantbreakers, without natural affection, implacable, unmerciful: Who knowing the judgment of God, that they which commit such things are worthy of death, not only do the same, but have pleasure in them that do them.
> Ephesians 6:1-3 Children, obey your parents in the Lord: for this is right. Honour thy father and mother; (which is the first commandment with promise;) That it may be well with thee, and thou mayest live long on the earth.

Proverbs 19:27 Cease, my son, to hear the instruction *that causeth* to err from the words of knowledge.

Focus: This proverb is a firm, fatherly admonition to stop listening to false teachers opposed to the word of God.

Any teaching by any person that opposes the truths taught by the word of God should be avoided. Eve would have done well to have ceased hearing Satan's instruction that caused her to transgress the **"words of knowledge"** (word of God) which had been given personally to her husband Adam and relayed to her. The wise are instructed to cherish God's teachings and to stop hearing conflicting false instruction.

Jesus warned of the Pharisees and Sadducees who mixed truth with false doctrine (leaven). (Matthew 6:12) And He also warned of "false prophets." (Matthew 7:15) Notice the following Biblical warnings.

> Deuteronomy 13:1-3 If there arise among you a prophet, or a dreamer of dreams, and giveth thee a sign or a wonder, And the sign or the wonder come to pass, whereof he spake unto thee, saying, Let us go after other gods, which thou hast not known, and let us serve them; Thou shalt not hearken unto the words of that prophet, or that dreamer of dreams: for the LORD your God proveth you, to know whether ye love the LORD your God with all your heart and with all your soul.
> Proverbs 14:7 Go from the presence of a foolish man, when thou perceivest not *in him* the lips of knowledge.
> Matthew 7:15 Beware of false prophets, which come to you in sheep's clothing, but inwardly they are ravening wolves.
> Matthew 16:6, 12 Then Jesus said unto them, Take heed and beware of the leaven of the Pharisees and of the Sadducees. . . . Then understood they how that he bade *them* not beware of the leaven of bread, but of the doctrine of the Pharisees and of the Sadducees.
> Mark 4:24-25 And he said unto them, Take heed what ye hear: with what measure ye mete, it shall be measured to you: and unto you that hear shall more be given. For he that hath, to him shall be given: and he that hath not, from him shall be taken even that which he hath.
> John 10:3-5 To him the porter openeth; and the sheep hear his voice: and he calleth his own sheep by name, and leadeth them out. And when he putteth forth his own sheep, he goeth before them, and the sheep follow him: for they know his voice. And a stranger will they not follow, but will flee from him: for they know not the voice of strangers.

2 Corinthians 11:13-15 For such *are* false apostles, deceitful workers, transforming themselves into the apostles of Christ. And no marvel; for Satan himself is transformed into an angel of light. Therefore *it is* no great thing if his ministers also be transformed as the ministers of righteousness; whose end shall be according to their works.

Ephesians 4:14-15 That we *henceforth* be no more children, tossed to and fro, and carried about with every wind of doctrine, by the sleight of men, *and* cunning craftiness, whereby they lie in wait to deceive; But speaking the truth in love, may grow up into him in all things, which is the head, *even* Christ:

1 Timothy 4:7 But refuse profane and old wives' fables, and exercise thyself *rather* unto godliness.

1 Timothy 6:3-5   If any man teach otherwise, and consent not to wholesome words, *even* the words of our Lord Jesus Christ, and to the doctrine which is according to godliness; He is proud, knowing nothing, but doting about questions and strifes of words, whereof cometh envy, strife, railings, evil surmisings, Perverse disputings of men of corrupt minds, and destitute of the truth, supposing that gain is godliness: from such withdraw thyself.

1 Timothy 6:20-21 O Timothy, keep that which is committed to thy trust, avoiding profane *and* vain babblings, and oppositions of science falsely so called: Which some professing have erred concerning the faith. Grace *be* with thee. Amen.

2 Peter 2:1-2 But there were false prophets also among the people, even as there shall be false teachers among you, who privily shall bring in damnable heresies, even denying the Lord that bought them, and bring upon themselves swift destruction. And many shall follow their pernicious ways; by reason of whom the way of truth shall be evil spoken of.

1 John 4:1 Beloved, believe not every spirit, but try the spirits whether they are of God: because many false prophets are gone out into the world.

2 John 1:9-11 Whosoever transgresseth, and abideth not in the doctrine of Christ, hath not God. He that abideth in the doctrine of Christ, he hath both the Father and the Son. If there come any unto you, and bring not this doctrine, receive him not into *your* house, neither bid him God speed: For he that biddeth him God speed is partaker of his evil deeds.

Revelation 2:2 I know thy works, and thy labour, and thy patience, and how thou canst not bear them which are evil: and thou hast tried them which say they are apostles, and are not, and hast found them liars. . .

Proverbs 19:28   An ungodly witness scorneth judgment: and the mouth of the wicked devoureth iniquity.

Focus: This proverb draws a word picture of how the wicked is an instrument that consumes and breathes out evil.

"An ungodly witness" is an unrighteous fool, a lying testifier, an iniquity-filled person who opposes righteousness and truth, especially the teachings of God. He **"scorneth judgment,"** makes fun of, and casts insulting remarks at the work or process of fulfilling righteous judicial action against wickedness. He is "'a witness of Belial,' according to the Hebrew term."[485] He is so incredibly evil that he **"devoureth iniquity"** as though it were a delicious, wonderful tasting meal for which his hunger is never satisfied. He is evil in all his thoughts and obviously likes his wickedness, so he feeds his ungodly desires to make himself a stronger witness for Satan.

Exodus 23:1 Thou shalt not raise a false report: put not thine hand with the wicked to be an unrighteous witness.

1 Kings 21:9-10 And she *[Jezebel]* wrote in the letters, saying, Proclaim a fast, and set Naboth on high among the people: And set two men, sons of Belial, before him, to bear witness against him, saying, Thou didst blaspheme God and the king. And *then* carry him out, and stone him, that he may die.

Job 15:16 How much more abominable and filthy *is* man, which drinketh iniquity like water?

Job 20:12-13 Though wickedness be sweet in his mouth, *though* he hide it under his tongue; *Though* he spare it, and forsake it not; but keep it still within his mouth:

Psalm 1:1 Blessed *is* the man that walketh not in the counsel of the ungodly, nor standeth in the way of sinners, nor sitteth in the seat of the scornful.

Proverbs 6:12 A naughty person, a wicked man, walketh with a froward mouth.

Proverbs 15:14 The heart of him that hath understanding seeketh knowledge: but the mouth of fools feedeth on foolishness.

Acts 6:11-13 Then they suborned men, which said, We have heard him speak blasphemous words against Moses, and *against* God. And they stirred up the people, and the elders, and the scribes, and came upon *him,* and caught him, and brought *him* to the council, And set up false witnesses, which said, This man ceaseth not to speak blasphemous words against this holy place, and the law…

Proverbs 19:29. Judgments are prepared for scorners, and stripes for the back of fools.

Focus: This proverb declares the consequences for both the scorner and the fool.

"Scorners" are **"fools"** who mock at the works and instructions of God, and they will be sentenced perhaps by earthly judges, but certainly by the Heavenly Judge. They refuse to be instructed but rather mock; consequently, they choose punishment rather than correction. "**'Judgments'** translated from the Hebrew *shephet* is used 16 times in the Old Testament and always used of the punitive judgments of God, even though "they are inflicted by human instrumentality.'"[486] **"Stripes"** are typically given for correction, to get a person's attention so that wrong behavior can be corrected. When the foolish one becomes so saturated with being a fool that he becomes a scorning fool, he is beyond correction and ready for judgment.

> "Another Hebrew parallelism: 'judgments' and 'stripes' go together as do 'scoffers' and 'fools'. The verse is picturing an adult rather than a child, the 'judgments' and 'stripes' being public punishments. A child may be 'foolish' (Proverbs 22:15), but he is not a full-fledged 'fool', but if one grows up, and his foolishness continues, and it is the recognized course of his life, then he is indeed a 'fool'."[487]

> *"Judgments are prepared for scorners* – Either by men, or, at least, by God; although they be deferred for a time, yet they are treasured up for them, and shall infallibly be inflicted upon them: and *stripes for the back of fools* – Nor shall other sinners escape, who sin through want of consideration, but they also shall be punished, though in a less degree."[488]

Exodus 7:4 But Pharaoh shall not hearken unto you, that I may lay my hand upon Egypt, and bring forth mine armies, *and* my people the children of Israel, out of the land of Egypt by great judgments.

Proverbs 1:22 How long, ye simple ones, will ye love simplicity? and the scorners delight in their scorning, and fools hate knowledge?

Proverbs 3:34 Surely he scorneth the scorners: but he giveth grace unto the lowly.

Proverbs 9:12 If thou be wise, thou shalt be wise for thyself: but *if* thou scornest, thou alone shalt bear it.

Proverbs 10:13 In the lips of him that hath understanding wisdom is found: but a rod is for the back of him that is void of understanding.

Proverbs 18:6 A fool's lips enter into contention, and his mouth calleth for strokes.

Proverbs 19:25 Smite a scorner, and the simple will beware: and reprove one that hath understanding, and he will understand knowledge.

Proverbs 26:3 A whip for the horse, a bridle for the ass, and a rod for the fool's back.

Isaiah 28:22 Now therefore be ye not mockers, lest your bands be made strong: for I have heard from the Lord GOD of hosts a consumption, even determined upon the whole earth.

Isaiah 29:20 For the terrible one is brought to nought, and the scorner is consumed, and all that watch for iniquity are cut off. . .

Ezekiel 22:13-14 Behold, therefore I have smitten mine hand at thy dishonest gain which thou hast made, and at thy blood which hath been in the midst of thee. Can thine heart endure, or can thine hands be strong, in the days that I shall deal with thee? I the LORD have spoken it, and will do it.

Hebrews 10:31 It is a fearful thing to fall into the hands of the living God.

2 Peter 3:2-7 That ye may be mindful of the words which were spoken before by the holy prophets, and of the commandment of us the apostles of the Lord and Saviour: Knowing this first, that there shall come in the last days scoffers, walking after their own lusts, And saying, Where is the promise of his coming? for since the fathers fell asleep, all things continue as *they were* from the beginning of the creation. For this they willingly are ignorant of, that by the word of God the heavens were of old, and the earth standing out of the water and in the water: Whereby the world that then was, being overflowed with water, perished: But the heavens and the earth, which are now, by the same word are kept in store, reserved unto fire against the day of judgment and perdition of ungodly men.

CHAPTER TWENTY

Some of the topics discussed in this chapter include wine and strong drink, avoidance of contentions, the sluggard, righteousness and wickedness as exhibited in business affairs, and leadership and daily life. It concludes with the benefit of correction.

> **Proverbs 20:1** Wine *is* a mocker, strong drink *is* raging: and whosoever is deceived thereby is not wise.

> Focus: This proverb declares two characteristics of alcohol and an egregious consequence of being deceived by it.

Verse one begins by personifying alcohol. **"Wine is a mocker** *["to scorn, to make mouths at, deride]***."** Once the **"mocker"** is swallowed and rapidly reaches the brain of its host, it begins to take control, rendering such a one no longer in full control of his thinking and actions. Thus, he is mocked by having his faculties voluntarily numbed. In varying degrees, with each additional swallow, the "mocker" "deprives him of his understanding, and causes him to speak and act like a fool, and thereby renders him ridiculous, and exposes him to shame, contempt, and insult."[489] Lovers of fermented wine, sooner or later, are likely to realize that they are being mocked and grievously deceived by the liquor they love. An enslaved, abuser of wine lives and likely dies with this raging internal scoffer.

"Strong drink is raging." Alcohol mixes with his victim's blood and breath; so that together, this victim and mocker rage with uncontrolled passions and are catapulted down a path destined for suffering and sorrow. Depending on his natural tendencies, the drunk may mock like a fool or rage like a madman. Hypocritically pretending to be a social beverage, whereby friends are made, this raging internal demon is more likely to order its unknowing victim to talk with a stutter, walk with a stagger, and weep like a cry-baby. Furthermore, peace is often robbed from the person who overindulges in wine and from many people who associate with him, especially his children and spouse.

"Whosoever is deceived *[lead astray morally]* **thereby is not wise."** In varying degrees, wine disables the drunkard's cognitive abilities; consequently, he cannot have a proper regard for God, which is the mandatory starting place for obtaining wisdom. Because of the loss of reasoning abilities separating him further from wisdom, he is often unable to adequately meet even moderate challenges and opportunities of life. Since people seldom drink alone, he has placed himself in the company of unwise men and evil influences. He has been deceived into believing that the benefits of alcohol will provide solutions when in fact, it does the opposite – its use creates both immediate and long-term problems, if not disasters.

> 'When wine is in,' says one, 'wit is out' *Whosoever is deceived thereby* –Namely, by wine or strong drink; *is not wise* – Is a fool or a madman, because he deprives himself of the use of his reason. Thus, 'the first precept in this chapter is against drunkenness, as an enemy to *wisdom,* even in common things; much more in those of everlasting consequence: for it commonly expels out of men's minds all reverence, both to God and others, inclining them to take the license to say or do any thing without restraint or discretion.'"[490]

> "The prohibition against *wine or other fermented drink* [*Leviticus 10:8-11 quoted below.*] was probably aimed at keeping their minds clear to fulfill their priestly duty of distinguishing **between the holy and the profane, between the unclean and the clean,** and so being prepared to **teach the Israelites** the rules revealed from God **through Moses** as well as to make decisions about difficult cases."[491]

> Leviticus 10:8-11 And the LORD spake unto Aaron, saying, Do not drink wine nor strong drink, thou, nor thy sons with thee, when ye go into the tabernacle of the congregation, lest ye die: *it shall be* a statute for ever throughout your generations: And that ye may put difference between holy and unholy, and between unclean and clean; And that ye may teach the children of Israel all the statutes which the LORD hath spoken unto them by the hand of Moses.

Deuteronomy 17:9-11 And thou shalt come unto the priests the Levites, and unto the judge that shall be in those days, and enquire; and they shall shew thee the sentence of judgment: And thou shalt do according to the sentence, which they of that place which the LORD shall choose shall shew thee; and thou shalt observe to do according to all that they inform thee: According to the sentence of the law which they shall teach thee, and according to the judgment which they shall tell thee, thou shalt do: thou shalt not decline from the sentence which they shall shew thee, *to* the right hand, nor *to* the left.

Proverbs 23:29-35 Who hath woe? who hath sorrow? who hath contentions? who hath babbling? who hath wounds without cause? who hath redness of eyes? They that tarry long at the wine; they that go to seek mixed wine. Look not thou upon the wine when it is red, when it giveth his colour in the cup, when it moveth itself aright. At the last it biteth like a serpent, and stingeth like an adder. Thine eyes shall behold strange women, and thine heart shall utter perverse things. Yea, thou shalt be as he that lieth down in the midst of the sea, or as he that lieth upon the top of a mast. They have stricken me, shalt thou say, and I was not sick; they have beaten me, and I felt it not: when shall I awake? I will seek it yet again.

Proverbs 31:4-5 It is not for kings, O Lemuel, it is not for kings to drink wine; nor for princes strong drink: Lest they drink, and forget the law, and pervert the judgment of any of the afflicted.

Isaiah 5:11 Woe unto them that rise up early in the morning, that they may follow strong drink; that continue until night, till wine inflame them!

Isaiah 28:7 But they also have erred through wine, and through strong drink are out of the way; the priest and the prophet have erred through strong drink, they are swallowed up of wine, they are out of the way through strong drink; they err in vision, they stumble in judgment.

Hosea 7:75 In the day of our king the princes have made him sick with bottles of wine; he stretched out his hand with scorners.

Habakkuk 2:15 Woe unto him that giveth his neighbour drink, that puttest thy bottle to him, and makest him drunken also, that thou mayest look on their nakedness!

Ephesians 5:17-18 Wherefore be ye not unwise, but understanding what the will of the Lord is. And be not drunk with wine, wherein is excess; but be filled with the Spirit.

Several profound cases of the evil work of alcohol are found in Scripture. The first occurred when *Noah* planted a vineyard and was naked before his sons (Genesis 9:21-23). A few chapters later, *Lot's daughters* used it to seduce their father, so they could have children with him (Genesis 19:31-36). In 2 Samuel 11:13, *David* tried to get Uriah drunk so that he would go home and lie with his wife and thereby not know that David had made her pregnant. *Absalom* commanded his servants to kill an inebriated Amnon in 2 Samuel 13:28. The New Testament clearly states that the unwise man who abuses himself and those around him with his drunken lifestyle will not inherit the kingdom of God.

1 Corinthians 6:9-11 Know ye not that the unrighteous shall not inherit the kingdom of God? Be not deceived: neither fornicators, nor idolaters, nor adulterers, nor effeminate, nor abusers of themselves with mankind, Nor thieves, nor covetous, nor drunkards, nor revilers, nor extortioners, shall inherit the kingdom of God. And such were some of you: but ye are washed, but ye are sanctified, but ye are justified in the name of the Lord Jesus, and by the Spirit of our God.

Galatians 5:19-21 Now the works of the flesh are manifest, which are these; Adultery, fornication, uncleanness, lasciviousness, Idolatry, witchcraft, hatred, variance, emulations, wrath, strife, seditions, heresies, Envyings, murders, drunkenness, revellings, and such like: of the which I tell you before, as I have also told you in time past, that they which do such things shall not inherit the kingdom of God.

Proverbs 20:2 The fear of a king *is* as the roaring of a lion: *whoso* provoketh him to anger sinneth *against* his own soul.

Focus: This proverb declares what the fear of a king is like and the extreme danger of provoking his anger.

Previously, Proverbs compared the wrath of a king to the "roaring of a lion" and the "messengers of death." The king's wrath evokes fear in his subjects. It is dangerous for a subject to go against the king's will by disobeying the laws of the land, leading an insurrection, being angry or, in some cases, disagreeing with the king. In the time of Solomon, it was dangerous to anger a ruler because he had the power to take an offender's life. **"Whoso provoketh him to anger sinneth against** *[condemns]* his own soul." **"Soul"** refers to a living being, the man himself. The Hebrew word for soul is also translated "life."

Proverbs 19:12 The king's wrath is as the roaring of a lion; but his favour is as dew upon the grass.

Proverbs 16:14 The wrath of a king is as messengers of death: but a wise man will pacify it.

Previous to Solomon's inheritance of David's throne, his father's general, Joab, had made the egregious decision to anoint Solomon's older brother, Adonijah, as king rather than Solomon. When Joab heard that the new King Solomon had sent Benaiah to kill him, he justifiably feared "the roaring of the lion" and fled for refuge to the horns of the altar, but to no avail (1 Kings 2:28-34).

Jonathan, even though he was King Saul's son, knowing that he had to appease "the roaring of the lion" in his father, pled for his friend David's life (1 Samuel 19:4-6).

In Romans, Paul gives instructions concerning the authority and terror of a ruler or king.

> Romans 13:3-5 For rulers are not a terror to good works, but to the evil. Wilt thou then not be afraid of the power? do that which is good, and thou shalt have praise of the same: For he is the minister of God to thee for good. But if thou do that which is evil, be afraid; for he beareth not the sword in vain: for he is the minister of God, a revenger to *execute* wrath upon him that doeth evil. Wherefore *ye* must needs be subject, not only for wrath, but also for conscience sake.

Proverbs 20:3   *It is* an honour for a man to cease from strife: but every fool will be meddling.

Focus: This proverb contrasts a wise person's approach to strife to that of a fool.

"It is an honour *[glory or reputation-building]* **for a man to cease from strife."** It is an honor "either to prevent it . . . or put an end to it . . . It is an evidence of their wisdom and power over their passions, and of their respect and obedience to their sovereign Lord, in which their honour and happiness consist."[492] Wisdom teaches the wise person to back away from strife when it first appears as a threat. Because strife disrupts the peace of an individual, every wise man will do his best to eliminate strife by avoiding unnecessary volatile situations and foolish people. If he is trapped in a hostile situation, he will always govern his overall communication and especially his words, making sure that he speaks at the right time, right place, and with the right spirit. The wise person has learned to control himself, thereby never allowing another person *to draw him* into an undesirable *reaction*. He controls himself and always *acts* rather than *reacts* and speaks what he knows is appropriate. Unlike the fool, the wise man does not meddle; consequently, he is flexible except where his core beliefs and faith are threatened. He is willing to yield where possible to avoid strife. When he yields, he obtains the respect and honor of God and reasonable men.

> "Men think, when they are engaged in quarrels, that it would be a shame to them *[not]* to go back and let fall the weapon; whereas really *it is an honour for a man to cease from strife,* an honour to withdraw an action, to drop a controversy, to forgive an injury, and to be friends with those that we have fallen out with. It is the honour of a man, a wise man, a man of spirit, to show the command he has of himself by *ceasing from strife,* yielding, and stooping, and receding from his just demands, for peace-sake, as Abraham, the better man."[493]
>
> Genesis 13:7-9 And there was a strife between the herdmen of Abram's cattle and the herdmen of Lot's cattle: and the Canaanite and the Perizzite dwelled then in the land. And Abram said unto Lot, Let there be no strife, I pray thee, between me and thee, and between my herdmen and thy herdmen; for we *be* brethren. *Is* not the whole land before thee? separate thyself, I pray thee, from me: if *thou wilt take* the left hand, then I will go to the right; or if *thou depart* to the right hand, then I will go to the left.

Ceasing from strife is not the way of a fool since **"every fool will be meddling."** He stirs up strife by injecting his opinion and demanding acceptance of himself and his beliefs without any flexibility. Because of his pride he feels that he has the right to interpose in other men's concerns.

Some proud, foolish people, who lack understanding, find it ***dishonorable*** to **"cease from strife."** Whether they are defending themselves or stirring up an argument over a questionable issue, the resulting strife itself indicates to them that they are wise and powerful. They glory in strife because it enables them to browbeat any criticism or opposition. Their ability to silence others or force them to flee is a vindication of their belief that they are right.

However, to a believer, ceasing from strife is honorable because it shows their wisdom and control over emotions and tongue. Proverbs 19:11 is instructive in this matter: "The discretion of a man deferreth his anger; and **it is his glory to pass over a transgression."** "Ceasing from strife" shows victory over the flesh.

> 2 Samuel 10:3-7 And the princes of the children of Ammon said unto Hanun their lord, Thinkest thou that David doth honour thy father, that he hath sent comforters unto thee? hath not David rather sent his servants unto thee, to search the city, and to spy it out, and to overthrow it? Wherefore Hanun took David's servants, and shaved off the one half of their beards, and cut off their garments in the middle, even to their buttocks, and sent them away. When they told it unto David, he sent to meet them, because the men were greatly ashamed: and the king said, Tarry at Jericho until your beards be grown, and then return. And when the children of Ammon saw that they stank before David, the children of Ammon sent and hired the Syrians of Bethrehob, and the Syrians of Zoba, twenty thousand footmen, and of king Maacah a thousand men, and of Ishtob twelve thousand men. And when David heard of it, he sent Joab, and all the host of the mighty men.
>
> 2 Kings 14:10-12 Thou hast indeed smitten Edom, and thine heart hath lifted thee up: glory *of this,* and tarry at home: for why shouldest thou meddle to *thy* hurt, that thou shouldest fall, *even* thou, and Judah with thee? Amaziah would not hear. Therefore

Jehoash king of Israel went up; and he and Amaziah king of Judah looked one another in the face at Bethshemesh, which *belongeth* to Judah. And Judah was put to the worse before Israel; and they fled every man to their tents.

Proverbs 14:29 He that is slow to wrath is of great understanding: but he that is hasty of spirit exalteth folly.

Proverbs 18:6 A fool's lips enter into contention, and his mouth calleth for strokes.

James 1:19-20 Wherefore, my beloved brethren, let every man be swift to hear, slow to speak, slow to wrath: For the wrath of man worketh not the righteousness of God.

Proverbs 20:4 The sluggard will not plow by reason of the cold; *therefore* shall he beg in harvest, and *have* nothing.

Focus: This proverb is a condemnation of the lazy excuse-maker and specifies the consequence of his indolence.

Israeli farmers prepare their fields for the upcoming planting season after the current harvest, which is in the latter part of autumn toward winter ("November and December when the wind blows commonly from the north"[494]). Because the early wooden plows were fragile, the soil had to be softened by the winter or spring rains.[495] The sluggard makes up excuses to avoid getting out in the cold or the damp or any other weather. Ecclesiastes 11:4 makes the point that there are duties that have to be accomplished regardless of the weather – "He that observeth the wind shall not sow; and he that regardeth the clouds shall not reap." "He that will not submit to the labor of ploughing must submit to the shame of begging."[496]

Man's behavior affects the way others look at him. When men see the sluggard refusing to perform laborious and difficult work, their thoughts become hardened against the indolent one. Even though working men are usually more generous in harvest time, they are rightfully resistant to share what they have diligently acquired by hard work with the sluggard. **"Therefore shall he beg in harvest, and have nothing."**

2 Thessalonians 3:10 For even when we were with you, this we commanded you, that if any would not work, neither should he eat.

2 Thessalonians clearly manifests the fact that God expects man to have a good work ethic, thus earning a living by the sweat of his brow (Genesis 3:19). Moreover, it is neither reasonable nor Scriptural to reward those who won't work by supplying all their needs. Notice below how these verses are applied to the spiritual realm.

"This holds good in spiritual things; such who have been slothful and sluggish about their spiritual affairs, unconcerned for the grace of God, and indolent in the use of means, or performance of duty, will ask when too late, or of wrong persons, and shall not have it; as the foolish virgins ask oil of the wise, when the bridegroom is come; and the rich man for water from Abraham, when in hell (Matthew 25:8, Luke 16:24-25)."[497]

"He hates and avoids all laborious and difficult work, although his own necessity and interest oblige him to do it; *therefore shall he beg, and have nothing* – And not obtain any alms; not even in harvest, that time of plenty and bounty, because men's hearts are justly hardened against that man, who, by his own sloth and wilfulness, hath brought himself to want."[498]

Proverbs 19:15 Slothfulness casteth into a deep sleep; and an idle soul shall suffer hunger.

Proverbs 19:24 A slothful *man* hideth his hand in *his* bosom, and will not so much as bring it to his mouth again.

Proverbs 20:5 Counsel in the heart of man *is like* deep water; but a man of understanding will draw it out.

Focus: This proverb characterizes the depth of counsel within a person and by whom and how it can be fetched.

"Counsel in the heart of man is like deep water" in that both water in a deep well and counsel in the heart of man take effort to remove. His advice is the good counsel of wisdom in Proverbs 18:4 – "The words of a man's mouth are as deep waters, and the wellspring of wisdom as a flowing brook." The inner thoughts of man are easily discerned by God but not nearly so effortlessly discerned by man. However, there are clues an understanding man can observe. Wise men who harbor valuable counsel are often recognized by guarded speech, carefully selected and wise companions, and a successful lifestyle of peace and prosperity provided by God's personal oversight and blessings. The wise person walks in the spiritual light of God's word upon which he studies and meditates. **"A man of understanding will draw it out."** The understanding man can ***draw out the person's counsel***: (1) *By observing* his body language. (2) *By listening* attentively to his words or observing the message of his silence. (3) *By asking* appropriate questions in a timely manner with a proper attitude. (4) By *waiting* patiently for the conversation to develop and information to come forth.

> "It *[this proverb]* sets before us two men, one reticent, and the other skilful in worming out designs which he wishes to penetrate. The former is like a deep draw-well; the latter is like a man who lets down a bucket into it, and winds it up full. 'Still waters are deep.' The faculty of reading men may be abused to bad ends, but is worth cultivating, and may be allied to high aims, and serve to help in accomplishing these. It may aid good men in detecting evil, in knowing how to present God's truth to hearts that need it, in pouring comfort into closely shut spirits."[499]

"A man of understanding" searches out the deep thoughts of another person in order to be yet wiser. He needs good information and advice (**"counsel"**) in order to respond to situations appropriately. The man of understanding is "one who possesses the right criteria for distinguishing between good and bad, true and false, and at the same time has the capacity to look through men and things, draws out… the secret… for he penetrates to the bottom of the deep water. Such an one does not deceive himself with men, he knows how to estimate their conduct according to its last underlying motive and aim."[500]

Depth of wisdom from the Counselor and desire for counsel is made plain in John 4 when Wisdom Himself conversed with the shameful woman of Samaria at Jacob's well. No greater counsel has ever been given, and no greater Counselor has ever lived. Worthy of thought is the observation that "the woman" could have lost the eternal benefit of conversing with Wisdom *should she have failed to be inquisitive.*

> John 4:10-14 Jesus answered and said unto her, If thou knewest the gift of God, and who it is that saith to thee, Give me to drink; thou wouldest have asked of him, and he would have given thee living water. The woman saith unto him, Sir, thou hast nothing to draw with, and the well is deep: from whence then hast thou that living water? Art thou greater than our father Jacob, which gave us the well, and drank thereof himself, and his children, and his cattle? Jesus answered and said unto her, Whosoever drinketh of this water shall thirst again: But whosoever drinketh of the water that I shall give him shall never thirst; but the water that I shall give him shall be in him a well of water springing up into everlasting life.
> Proverbs 13:20 He that walketh with wise *men* shall be wise: but a companion of fools shall be destroyed.

Proverbs 20:6 Most men will proclaim every one his own goodness: but a faithful man who can find?

Focus: This proverb emphasizes the discrepancy between those who claim to have goodness and those who actually have it.

"Most men will proclaim every one his own goodness." There is a great deal said in the Book of Proverbs about both the lips and the hearts of men. It is easy for men to speak about themselves as having **"goodness** *[kindness, faithfulness, mercy, piety]*,**"** but it is a different story for a person to actually faithfully demonstrate such. Not every man who claims to extend pity, to be kind, merciful, and generous, or to seriously love others, actually practices those character traits. The ugly tendency of a man to brag about his **"goodness"** produced special warnings from Jesus:

> Matthew 6:1-6 Take heed that ye do not your alms before men, to be seen of them: otherwise ye have no reward of your Father which is in heaven. Therefore when thou doest *thine* alms, do not sound a trumpet before thee, as the hypocrites do in the synagogues and in the streets, that they may have glory of men. Verily I say unto you, They have their reward. But when thou doest alms, let not thy left hand know what thy right hand doeth: That thine alms may be in secret: and thy Father which seeth in secret himself shall reward thee openly. And when thou prayest, thou shalt not be as the hypocrites *are:* for they love to pray standing in the synagogues and in the corners of the streets, that they may be seen of men. Verily I say unto you, They have their reward. But thou, when thou prayest, enter into thy closet, and when thou hast shut thy door, pray to thy Father which is in secret; and thy Father which seeth in secret shall reward thee openly.
> Luke 18:10-14 Two men went up into the temple to pray; the one a Pharisee, and the other a publican. The Pharisee stood and prayed thus with himself, God, I thank thee, that I am not as other men *are,* extortioners, unjust, adulterers, or even as this publican. I fast twice in the week, I give tithes of all that I possess. And the publican, standing afar off, would not lift up so much as *his* eyes unto heaven, but smote upon his breast, saying, God be merciful to me a sinner. I tell you, this man went down to his house justified *rather* than the other: for every one that exalteth himself shall be abased; and he that humbleth himself shall be exalted.

"But a faithful *[trustworthy]* **man who can find?"** What *faithfulness* means to God and what it means to man may be totally different. "The faithfulness intended is fidelity to promises, the practical execution of the vaunted benevolence; this is rare indeed, so that a psalmist could cry, 'I said in my haste, All men are liars' (Psalm 116:11)."[501]

Yes, there are men who accurately represent the godly character of the faithful man. There are men who are as good as their word, who do not forsake a friend going through hard financial times, who say they will give help and then give it. Though many men talk of their good works and boast of their goodness, it is difficult to find a man in whom God's true love and faithfulness is his character. David speaks of this situation in Psalm 12:1-2 – "Help, LORD; for the godly man ceaseth; for the faithful fail from among the children of men. They speak vanity every one with his neighbour: *with* flattering lips *and* with a double heart do they speak."

Common man easily moves his lip to speak *whatever* his peers want to hear; but when his heart is converted, and his motive is to please God rather than peers, he will prove to be faithful, fulfilling His word. Such faithful men are difficult to find; but they do whatever they say they will do, and they prove to be kind, generous, and loving friends to God and men. To study to *appear* to be good is not the same as to study to *actually be good*.

> "Even the ungodly *proclaims his own goodness*. 'Jehu took no heed to walk in the way of the LORD.' Still – said he – 'Come, see my zeal for the LORD.' Absalom, while treason was at work within, 'stole the hearts' of the people by his loud pretensions to *goodness*. The whole nation, while given up to all manner of iniquity, boasted of its integrity. The Pharisee *proclaimed his goodness* at the corner of the streets; yea – even in the presence of his God. Such is the blindness of a self-deceiving heart! Lord! teach me to remember – 'That which is highly esteemed among men is abomination in the sight of God.'"
>
> 2 Samuel 15:3-4, 10 And Absalom said unto him, See, thy matters *are* good and right; but *there is* no man *deputed* of the king to hear thee. Absalom said moreover, Oh that I were made judge in the land, that every man which hath any suit or cause might come unto me, and I would do him justice!....But Absalom sent spies throughout all the tribes of Israel, saying, As soon as ye hear the sound of the trumpet, then ye shall say, Absalom reigneth in Hebron.
>
> 2 Kings 10:16 and 10:31 And he said, Come with me, and see my zeal for the LORD. So they made him ride in his chariot . . . But Jehu took no heed to walk in the law of the LORD God of Israel with all his heart: for he departed not from the sins of Jeroboam, which made Israel to sin.
>
> Proverbs 16:2 All the ways of a man are clean in his own eyes; but the LORD weigheth the spirits.
>
> Proverbs 21:2 Every way of a man is right in his own eyes: but the LORD pondereth the hearts.
>
> Proverbs 27:2 Let another man praise thee, and not thine own mouth; a stranger, and not thine own lips.
>
> Daniel 6:4-5 Then the presidents and princes sought to find occasion against Daniel concerning the kingdom; but they could find none occasion nor fault; forasmuch as he was faithful, neither was there any error or fault found in him. Then said these men, We shall not find any occasion against this Daniel, except we find it against him concerning the law of his God.
>
> Matthew 23:2-8 Saying, The scribes and the Pharisees sit in Moses' seat: All therefore whatsoever they bid you observe, *that* observe and do; but do not ye after their works: for they say, and do not. For they bind heavy burdens and grievous to be borne, and lay *them* on men's shoulders; but they *themselves* will not move them with one of their fingers. But all their works they do for to be seen of men: they make broad their phylacteries, and enlarge the borders of their garments, And love the uppermost rooms at feasts, and the chief seats in the synagogues, And greetings in the markets, and to be called of men, Rabbi, Rabbi. But be not ye called Rabbi: for one is your Master, *even* Christ; and all ye are brethren.

Proverbs 20:7 The just *man* walketh in his integrity: his children *are* blessed after him.

Focus: This proverb declares how a righteous man lives and how his children are affected by such a walk.

The character of the rare, humble, righteous **"faithful man"** of verse six is the same as the character of the **"just man"** walking **"in his integrity"** here in verse seven. His *walk* or manner of life is upright, innocent, and exemplary so that his children desire to be like him. Children typically mimic their parents in such ways as speech, reasoning, habits, and even the way they walk and wear their clothes. *(The offspring of evil men often suffer from mimicking evil and become evil themselves.)* Children of *a just man walking in his integrity* have the tremendous advantage of observing how to properly live under the protective hand of God. If they are wise, they will realize that the blessings they enjoy are a direct result of their father's walk with God. Such children will learn to follow God in like manner and continue to enjoy being blessed by God throughout their lives. Thus, they will be *blessed after their father.* What a shame when his children are foolish and fail to know the grace of God and the fulfillment of this Scripture.

> Genesis 18:18-19 Seeing that Abraham shall surely become a great and mighty nation, and all the nations of the earth shall be blessed in him? For I know him, that he will command his children and his household after him, and they shall keep the way of the LORD, to do justice and judgment; that the LORD may bring upon Abraham that which he hath spoken of him.
>
> Deuteronomy 4:40 Thou shalt keep therefore his statutes, and his commandments, which I command thee this day, that it may go well with thee, and with thy children after thee, and that thou mayest prolong *thy* days upon the earth, which the LORD thy God giveth thee, for ever.

Psalm 112:1-4 Praise ye the LORD. Blessed *is* the man *that* feareth the LORD, *that* delighteth greatly in his commandments. His seed shall be mighty upon earth: the generation of the upright shall be blessed. Wealth and riches *shall be* in his house: and his righteousness endureth for ever. Unto the upright there ariseth light in the darkness: *he is* gracious, and full of compassion, and righteous.

Isaiah 33:15-16 He that walketh righteously, and speaketh uprightly; he that despiseth the gain of oppressions, that shaketh his hands from holding of bribes, that stoppeth his ears from hearing of blood, and shutteth his eyes from seeing evil; He shall dwell on high: his place of defence shall be the munitions of rocks: bread shall be given him; his waters shall be sure.

2 Timothy 1:3-5 I thank God, whom I serve from *my* forefathers with pure conscience, that without ceasing I have remembrance of thee in my prayers night and day; Greatly desiring to see thee, being mindful of thy tears, that I may be filled with joy; When I call to remembrance the unfeigned faith that is in thee, which dwelt first in thy grandmother Lois, and thy mother Eunice; and I am persuaded that in thee also.

Proverbs 20:8   A king that sitteth in the throne of judgment scattereth away all evil with his eyes.

Focus: This proverb describes the reaction that evil men have to a righteous king sitting in judgment.

As rulers, David and his son Solomon sat in a **"throne of judgment"** and served as chief judges. David described God's requirement for the kings of Israel in 2 Samuel 23:3 – "He that ruleth over men must be just, ruling in the fear of God." Evil kings, like Ahab, *attracted* evil rather than *scattered it away.* Sadly, there were times, such as when he had Uriah killed, that David, rather than scatter away evil, actually concocted evil for disastrous results.

In addition to setting an example of godly behavior, a righteous king will discern the wicked and pronounce justice in order to protect the citizens. **"Scattereth away all evil with his eyes"** is an expression taken from the process of winnowing by which the grain is tossed up into the air allowing the wind to scatter the unwanted chaff. Saying that the king would *scatter away all evil with his eyes* indicated that he would separate evil motives and actions from truth, as chaff is separated from the grain. The dagger-like eyes of a righteous king who hated wickedness would have been piercing and frightful to an evil subject with a guilty conscience. He would have terrified those false witnesses and other evil doers. Solomon used his God-given wisdom to see through wicked devices and pretenses that were a veneer for evil beneath. With such wisdom, he separated the evil mother from the good mother in 1 Kings 3:16-28.

> "... he will easily and quickly discern who is evil, or who is in a bad cause before him, and will pass sentence on him, and drive him away from him with shame and disgrace, and to receive deserved punishment; or he will terrify persons from coming before him with false witness against their neighbour, or with a wrong cause. This may be applied to Christ, the King of kings, and Judge of all; whose eyes are as a flame of fire; who will clearly see into all hearts and actions, when he shall sit on his throne of judgment; and shall pass the righteous and definitive sentence, and shall drive the wicked into hell, into everlasting punishment."[502]

Psalm 11:4 The LORD *is* in his holy temple, the LORD'S throne *is* in heaven: his eyes behold, his eyelids try, the children of men.

Proverbs 20:26 A wise king scattereth the wicked, and bringeth the wheel over them.

Proverbs 16:12-15 It is an abomination to kings to commit wickedness: for the throne is established by righteousness. Righteous lips are the delight of kings; and they love him that speaketh right. The wrath of a king is as messengers of death: but a wise man will pacify it. In the light of the king's countenance is life; and his favour is as a cloud of the latter rain.

Habakkuk 1:13 *Thou art* of purer eyes than to behold evil, and canst not look on iniquity: wherefore lookest thou upon them that deal treacherously, *and* holdest thy tongue when the wicked devoureth *the man that is* more righteous than he?

Matthew 3:12 Whose fan *is* in his hand, and he will throughly purge his floor, and gather his wheat into the garner; but he will burn up the chaff with unquenchable fire.

Romans 13:1-5 Let every soul be subject unto the higher powers. For there is no power but of God: the powers that be are ordained of God. Whosoever therefore resisteth the power, resisteth the ordinance of God: and they that resist shall receive to themselves damnation. For rulers are not a terror to good works, but to the evil. Wilt thou then not be afraid of the power? do that which is good, and thou shalt have praise of the same: For he is the minister of God to thee for good. But if thou do that which is evil, be afraid; for he beareth not the sword in vain: for he is the minister of God, a revenger to *execute* wrath upon him that doeth evil. Wherefore *ye* must needs be subject, not only for wrath, but also for conscience sake.

Proverbs 20:9   Who can say, I have made my heart clean, I am pure from my sin?

Focus: This proverb asks a question that mandates an honest evaluation of one's own human heart and how it can be made clean.

Certainly, the answer to this proverb's question is that *absolutely no person can make his own heart "clean" and pure from sin,* either past ones or present ones or from the ungodly inclinations or from evil desires that arise in his heart. Only through believing in the resurrected Jesus as Lord and Savior can a person have his heart cleansed. "That if thou shalt confess with thy mouth the Lord Jesus, and shalt believe in thine heart that God hath raised him from the dead, thou shalt be saved." (Romans 10:9)

The human mind can only imagine having to stand before the great King of kings sitting in the throne of judgment. On that day, no man will have a place to hide from such scrutiny that has known every thought, seen every deed, heard every word, and discerned every motive of the heart. It will be impossible to say truthfully **"I have made my heart clean."** Also, it must be considered that every person has a *CHOICE* as to whether or not he wants to be cleansed of his sins through repentance and trust in Jesus as Saviour. God sent His only Son, Jesus, the Lamb of God to pay the required price of sin for every willing person and to thereby cleanse his heart, making him fit for heaven. "Who can say, I have made my heart clean. I am pure from my sin?" Nobody!! There is no innocent human being.

> Genesis 8:21 And the LORD smelled a sweet savour; and the LORD said in his heart, I will not again curse the ground any more for man's sake; for the imagination of man's heart *is* evil from his youth; neither will I again smite any more every thing living, as I have done.
>
> 1 Kings 8:46 If they sin against thee, (for *there is* no man that sinneth not,) and thou be angry with them, and deliver them to the enemy, so that they carry them away captives unto the land of the enemy, far or near . . . *[This verse reappears nearly verbatim in 2 Chronicles 6:36.]*
>
> Job 15:14 What *is* man, that he should be clean? and *he which is* born of a woman, that he should be righteous?
>
> Job 25:4 How then can man be justified with God? or how can he be clean that is born of a woman?
>
> Psalm 19:12-14 Who can understand *his* errors? cleanse thou me from secret *faults*. Keep back thy servant also from presumptuous *sins;* let them not have dominion over me: then shall I be upright, and I shall be innocent from the great transgression. Let the words of my mouth, and the meditation of my heart, be acceptable in thy sight, O LORD, my strength, and my redeemer.
>
> Psalm 51:5 Behold, I was shapen in iniquity; and in sin did my mother conceive me.
>
> Ecclesiastes 7:20 For *there is* not a just man upon earth, that doeth good, and sinneth not.
>
> Jeremiah 17:9 The heart *is* deceitful above all *things*, and desperately wicked: who can know it? I the LORD search the heart, *I* try the reins, even to give every man according to his ways, *and* according to the fruit of his doings.
>
> Romans 3:10-12 As it is written, There is none righteous, no, not one: There is none that understandeth, there is none that seeketh after God. They are all gone out of the way, they are together become unprofitable; there is none that doeth good, no, not one.
>
> Romans 3:23 For all have sinned, and come short of the glory of God . . .
>
> Ephesians 5:25-27 . . . Christ also loved the church, and gave himself for it; That he might sanctify and cleanse it with the washing of water by the word, That he might present it to himself a glorious church, not having spot, or wrinkle, or any such thing; but that it should be holy and without blemish.
>
> Hebrews 10:8-12 Above when he said, Sacrifice and offering and burnt offerings and *offering* for sin thou wouldest not, neither hadst pleasure *therein;* which are offered by the law; Then said he, Lo, I come to do thy will, O God. He taketh away the first, that he may establish the second. By the which will we are sanctified through the offering of the body of Jesus Christ once for all. And every priest standeth daily ministering and offering oftentimes the same sacrifices, which can never take away sins: But this man, after he had offered one sacrifice for sins for ever, sat down on the right hand of God.
>
> 1 John 1:8-10 If we say that we have no sin, we deceive ourselves, and the truth is not in us. If we confess our sins, he is faithful and just to forgive us our sins, and to cleanse us from all unrighteousness. If we say that we have not sinned, we make him a liar, and his word is not in us.

Proverbs 20:10 Divers weights, and divers measures, both of them are alike abomination to the LORD.

Focus: This proverb expresses God's disgust for dishonest trading or business practices.

The Hebrew words for **"divers weights"** (*'eben 'eben*) and the two for **"divers measures"** (*'ephah 'ephah*) are doubled in order to indicate two *different* weights and two *different* measures. This repeating is done because "There is no single Hebrew word for 'divers' *[diverse]*"[503] used in the Old Testament. The Hebrew reading for the first phrase is literally, "stone and stone, ephah and ephah." *Ephah* is used as a figure of speech for all kinds of weights and measures.[504]

The *ephah* was used to measure volume. "In delivering out and taking in goods they had *divers measures,* a scanty measure to sell by and a large measure to buy by. This was done wrong with plot and contrivance, and under colour of doing right. Under these is included all manner of fraud and deceit in commerce and trade."[505]

Deuteronomy 25:13-15 gives further clarity to this proverb *[See verses below.]* and God's command against the abominable practice. Weights and measures used for buying and selling were to be the same (equal in weight) – not one large and one small (one the standard, the other less than the standard) that could be swapped around to deceive the buyer or seller into thinking he was getting one weight or measure when he was actually getting less but paying or swapping for more. In the farming society of the early Hebrews, produce was measured and sold on a balance scale and also in a definite measure.

Weights and Measures in the Hebrew Bible

Weights: In ancient times, the balance was used to determine weight. "The balance consisted of a beam supported in the middle with a pan suspended by cords on each end. A known quantity of weight would be placed in the pan on one side of the balance and the object to be weighed on the other side. By adding or removing known weights until each side was equal, the weight of the object could be determined... Most of the weights in the ancient world were made of stone or metal... Since these weights varied from one place to the next, many people carried pouches which contained their own weights (Deuteronomy 25:13; Proverbs 16:11), so they could see if they were receiving just value."

Measures: Measurements recorded in the Bible are of three types: (1) measures of volume (dry or liquid) that could be contained in a vessel; (2) measures of length, height, width, and depth; and (3) measures of total. (Ronald F. Youngblood, General Editor; General Editor of Original Edition: Herbert Lockyer, Sr., *Nelson's New Illustrated Bible Dictionary*, Thomas Nelson Publishers: 1986, 1995, e-Sword 12.0.1.)

Ezekiel 45:10-11 standardized the *bath* (liquid) and the *ephah* (dry), but no exact modern equivalent is known.

The following verses identify the "abominable" in Proverbs.

1. The froward (3:32; 11:20)
2. A proud look, a lying tongue, murderer, wicked thoughts, swiftness in running to evil, a false witness, and he that sows discord among brethren (6:16-19)   Pride (16:5)
3. Wicked speaking (8:7)
4. Crooked business practices (11:1; 20:10; 20:23)
5. Lying (12:22; 26:25)
6. The sacrifice, the lifestyle, and the thoughts of the wicked (15:8,9, 26; 21:27); He that justifies the wicked or condemns the just (17:15); An unjust man (29:27)
7. The scorner (24:9) *and*
8. The prayers of one that rejects the words of Scripture (specifically the law) (28:9)

To put the meaning of **"abomination"** *[morally disgusting]* in perspective, one must notice what practices and who are considered **"abomination"** to God Himself or to righteous men. Any failure to be truthful and thus any act of injustice is an abomination to God. He loathes and detests the actions so much that the "abominable" will be separated from Him in hell.

> Leviticus 19:13 Thou shalt not defraud thy neighbour, neither rob him: the wages of him that is hired shall not abide with thee all night until the morning.
>
> Leviticus 19:35 Ye shall do no unrighteousness in judgment, in meteyard, in weight, or in measure.
>
> Deuteronomy 25:13-15 Thou shalt not have in thy bag divers weights, a great and a small. Thou shalt not have in thine house divers measures, a great and a small. But thou shalt have a perfect and just weight, a perfect and just measure shalt thou have: that thy days may be lengthened in the land which the LORD thy God giveth thee.
>
> Proverbs 11:1 A false balance is abomination to the LORD: but a just weight is his delight.
>
> Proverbs 16:11 A just weight and balance are the LORD'S: all the weights of the bag are his work.
>
> Amos 8:4-7 Hear this, O ye that swallow up the needy, even to make the poor of the land to fail, Saying, When will the new moon be gone, that we may sell corn? and the sabbath, that we may set forth wheat, making the ephah small, and the shekel great, and falsifying the balances by deceit? That we may buy the poor for silver, and the needy for a pair of shoes; yea, and sell the refuse of the wheat? The LORD hath sworn by the excellency of Jacob, Surely I will never forget any of their works.
>
> Revelation 21:8 But the fearful, and unbelieving, and the abominable, and murderers, and whoremongers, and sorcerers, and idolaters, and all liars, shall have their part in the lake which burneth with fire and brimstone: which is the second death.

WHAT GOD FINDS OFFENSIVE, THE RIGHTEOUS SHOULD ALSO FIND OFFENSIVE.

Proverbs 20:11 Even a child is known by his doings, whether his work *be* pure, and whether *it be* right.

Focus: This proverb teaches that the actions of a person (even a child) reveal much about the motives of his heart.

"Doings" and **"work"** are synonyms for whatever acts, deeds, or endeavors a person undertakes. Because human beings routinely observe other people, their conduct is generally known and instinctively evaluated. "Ye shall know them by their fruits *[godly or ungodly works, acts, or deeds]*," said our Lord in Matthew 7:16. The doings of a person reflect his understanding of what he considers acceptable conduct. If his doings are **"pure"** and **"right,"** they will agree with godly standards.

Because children have not yet learned, as most adults have, to discreetly conceal or suppress their feelings and deep thoughts, their life is open, fully observable, and easy to be evaluated. Given the right pressures and circumstances, every person, adult or child, will reveal his heart. The purity, or lack thereof, in the child's behavior, prefigures the potential character qualities he will display in adulthood. In his 1802 poem, "My Heart Leaps Up" William Wordsworth wrote those interesting words "The child is the father of the man."

Daily observation of the **"doings"** of a child gives parents information and insight to serve as a guide to know specifically which area of the child's life needs immediate attention. When godly principles are taught, the child is more likely to become an adult that pleases God and lives a successful life. Notice the favor and personal relationship God gave to Abraham because He was certain that Abraham would give proper parental training to his family. "For I know him, that he will command his children and his household after him, and they shall keep the way of the LORD, to do justice and judgment; that the LORD may bring upon Abraham that which he hath spoken of him." (Genesis 18:19) This verse in Genesis leaves the reader with the understanding that God has a very special relationship with a parent who teaches his family to live godly.

> Proverbs 21:8 The way of man is froward and strange: but as for the pure, his work is right.
> Proverbs 22:6 Train up a child in the way he should go: and when he is old, he will not depart from it.
> Luke 1:15 For he shall be great in the sight of the Lord, and shall drink neither wine nor strong drink; and he shall be filled with the Holy Ghost, even from his mother's womb.
> Luke 6:43-44 For a good tree bringeth not forth corrupt fruit; neither doth a corrupt tree bring forth good fruit. For every tree is known by his own fruit. For of thorns men do not gather figs, nor of a bramble bush gather they grapes.

Proverbs 20:12 The hearing ear, and the seeing eye, the LORD hath made even both of them.

Focus: This proverb declares that God equipped man with the ability to comprehend (both spiritually and physically).

Hearing and seeing are gates whereby information is channeled to the brain for understanding. With such incoming information, man is provided with an enhanced opportunity to explore, interact with, and admire the work of his Creator. Reading the first few pages of our Bible reveals that fellowship between God and man was His motivation for creating such an intelligent being in His image. **"Hearing"** means to perceive by the ear with the implication of attention and obedience. **"Seeing"** can literally mean to see with the eye, or it can mean figuratively to inspect, to consider, or to discern.

> Exodus 4:11 And the LORD said unto him, Who hath made man's mouth? or who maketh the dumb, or deaf, or the seeing, or the blind? have not I the LORD?
> Psalm 139:14 I will praise thee; for I am fearfully *and* wonderfully made: marvellous *are* thy works; and *that* my soul knoweth right well.

Jesus performed various miracles of healing physical disorders, including seeing and hearing, thus helping people see and hear the beauty of God's creation and read and hear His word so that they could know God and more effectively interact with others. "So then faith *cometh* by hearing, and hearing by the word of God." (Romans 10:17)

Biblical references to *"ears that can't hear"* and *"eyes that can't see"* refer to a spiritual condition rather than a physical one. If a man's heart is wicked, then his spiritual senses are diminished, and he can't respond to communications from God. Those who desire the things of God are given a "hearing ear and a seeing eye" so that they can be a participant with God of His great truths.

> "Man is deaf and blind in the things of God – 'Having ears, he hears not; having eyes, he sees not.' (Matthew 13:13-14) The voice of mercy is disregarded. To his need, and to his remedy, he is alike insensible. His ear is open to sound advice, to moral doctrine, to the dictates of external decency. But as to the gospel, he is a mere *statue*, without life. All his senses are blinded, deadened, chained. (2Corintheans 4:3-4) His moral disabilities can only be removed by that Almighty power, which on earth gave ears to the deaf, and sight to the blind... *The hearing ear*, which Solomon intends, is that which believeth and obeyeth what it heareth. The *seeing eye* is that, which

so seeth, as that it followeth the good which it seeth.' But who of us, whose *ears* are wakened, and whose *eyes* are opened, will not rejoice in the adoring acknowledgment – *the LORD hath made both of them?*"⁵⁰⁶

In the following verses, notice God's relationship to "the hearing ear and the seeing eye."

Genesis 21:19 And God opened her eyes, and she saw a well of water; and she went, and filled the bottle with water, and gave the lad drink.

Deuteronomy 29:1-4 These are the words of the covenant, which the LORD commanded Moses to make with the children of Israel in the land of Moab, beside the covenant which he made with them in Horeb. And Moses called unto all Israel, and said unto them, Ye have seen all that the LORD did before your eyes in the land of Egypt unto Pharaoh, and unto all his servants, and unto all his land; The great temptations which thine eyes have seen, the signs, and those great miracles: Yet the LORD hath not given you an heart to perceive, and eyes to see, and ears to hear, unto this day.

1 Samuel 3:9 Therefore Eli said unto Samuel, Go, lie down: and it shall be, if he call thee, that thou shalt say, Speak, LORD; for thy servant heareth. So Samuel went and lay down in his place.

2 Kings 6:17 And Elisha prayed, and said, LORD, I pray thee, open his eyes, that he may see. And the LORD opened the eyes of the young man; and he saw: and, behold, the mountain *was* full of horses and chariots of fire round about Elisha.

Psalm 19:1-3 To the chief Musician, A Psalm of David. The heavens declare the glory of God; and the firmament sheweth his handywork. Day unto day uttereth speech, and night unto night sheweth knowledge. *There is* no speech nor language, *where* their voice is not heard.

Psalm 115:4-8 Their idols *are* silver and gold, the work of men's hands. They have mouths, but they speak not: eyes have they, but they see not: They have ears, but they hear not: noses have they, but they smell not: They have hands, but they handle not: feet have they, but they walk not: neither speak they through their throat. They that make them are like unto them; *so is* every one that trusteth in them.

Psalm 119:18 Open thou mine eyes, that I may behold wondrous things out of thy law.

Matthew 11:15 He that hath ears to hear, let him hear. (Also Mark 4:9; Luke 8:8; Luke 14:35)

Matthew 13:13-16 Therefore speak I to them in parables: because they seeing see not; and hearing they hear not, neither do they understand. And in them is fulfilled the prophecy of Esaias, which saith, By hearing ye shall hear, and shall not understand; and seeing ye shall see, and shall not perceive: For this people's heart is waxed gross, and their ears are dull of hearing, and their eyes they have closed; lest at any time they should see with their eyes, and hear with their ears, and should understand with their heart, and should be converted, and I should heal them. But blessed are your eyes, for they see: and your ears, for they hear.

Acts 16:14 And a certain woman named Lydia, a seller of purple, of the city of Thyatira, which worshipped God, heard *us:* whose heart the Lord opened, that she attended unto the things which were spoken of Paul.

Acts 26:17-18 Delivering thee from the people, and from the Gentiles, unto whom now I send thee, To open their eyes, and to turn them from darkness to light, and from the power of Satan unto God, that they may receive forgiveness of sins, and inheritance among them which are sanctified by faith that is in me.

Ephesians 1:17-18 That the God of our Lord Jesus Christ, the Father of glory, may give unto you the spirit of wisdom and revelation in the knowledge of him: The eyes of your understanding being enlightened; that ye may know what is the hope of his calling, and what the riches of the glory of his inheritance in the saints . . .

2 Corinthians 4:3-4 But if our gospel be hid, it is hid to them that are lost: In whom the god of this world hath blinded the minds of them which believe not, lest the light of the glorious gospel of Christ, who is the image of God, should shine unto them.

Proverbs 20:13 Love not sleep, lest thou come to poverty; open thine eyes, *and* thou shalt be satisfied with bread.

Focus: This proverb relates love of sleep to poverty and effort to success.

"Love not sleep, lest thou come to poverty." Love of sleep is an attitude that indicates a disregard for the activities of life, especially productive work, and it is a characteristic of the ungodly sluggard who had rather sleep than eat or care for his vineyard or be resourceful with that taken in hunting. He loves sleep to the detriment of everything else in his life, including the productive work that keeps him from becoming impoverished.

One should appreciate and enjoy the required times of sleep, knowing that sleep rejuvenates the mind and body, thus preparing for a proper and productive Christian life, for effective work with a spirit of excellence, and for earning the necessities of life. ***To love sleep*** means to have an inordinate affection for sleep, and not simply to view sleep as a necessity to prepare for work and life.

"Open thine eyes, *and* thou shalt be satisfied with bread." Alertness makes a person aware of the needs of life, and work produces the capacity to earn a wage that can be exchanged for other goods, including "bread" or food of various kinds. Scripture is saying, "Shake off the laziness!" Only then will the sluggard have enough to eat for himself and his family.

Proverbs 6:6-11 Go to the ant, thou sluggard; consider her ways, and be wise: Which having no guide, overseer, or ruler, Provideth her meat in the summer, and gathereth her food in the harvest. How long wilt thou sleep, O sluggard? when wilt thou arise out of thy sleep? Yet a little sleep, a little slumber, a little folding of the hands to sleep: So shall thy poverty come as one that travelleth, and thy want as an armed man.

Proverbs 10:4-5 He becometh poor that dealeth with a slack hand: but the hand of the diligent maketh rich. He that gathereth in summer is a wise son: but he that sleepeth in harvest is a son that causeth shame.

Proverbs 19:15 Slothfulness casteth into a deep sleep; and an idle soul shall suffer hunger.

Proverbs 26:12-16 Seest thou a man wise in his own conceit? there is more hope of a fool than of him. The slothful man saith, There is a lion in the way; a lion is in the streets. As the door turneth upon his hinges, so doth the slothful upon his bed. The slothful hideth his hand in his bosom; it grieveth him to bring it again to his mouth. The sluggard is wiser in his own conceit than seven men that can render a reason.

Ecclesiastes 10:18 By much slothfulness the building decayeth; and through idleness of the hands the house droppeth through.

Romans 12:11 Not slothful in business; fervent in spirit; serving the Lord…

2 Thessalonians 3:10-12 For even when we were with you, this we commanded you, that if any would not work, neither should he eat. For we hear that there are some which walk among you disorderly, working not at all, but are busybodies. Now them that are such we command and exhort by our Lord Jesus Christ, that with quietness they work, and eat their own bread.

Proverbs 20:14 *It is* naught, *it is* naught, saith the buyer: but when he is gone his way, then he boasteth.

Focus: This proverb exposes the unacceptable but common business practice of lying about the value of a product to gain a better price.

Verse 10 above warns of the deceitful seller, and here, the warning is about a deceitful buyer. Deceitfulness is wrong, and the one who practices it loses favor with God and man. Though his boasting may obtain a laugh, he will be marked as dishonest. His word will be questioned as to truthfulness from the time he deceives forward.

"*It is* naught, *it is* naught, saith the buyer." When the buyer says, **"*It is* naught**[evil or bad]**, *it is* naught,"** he implies that the merchandise is of inferior quality when it is not, or else he pretends to be uninterested when the opposite is true. The context reveals to the reader is that the buyer is pretending that he is being grossly overcharged for this item. He uses deceitful words to persuade the seller to take less for the item.

"But when he is gone his way, then he boasteth." After convincing the seller of his lie and the buyer has successfully purchased the item for a lower price, he then goes his way and brags to his friends that he was successful with his deception. Like the charlatan using different weights in verse 10, this is another example of deceitful business practices God sees as an abomination. Man may laugh and overlook the sin, but God sees and judges it.

Truth is always the acceptable choice that pleases God. A true believer knows that God can provide more in a second than deception can get in years. "Stand therefore, having your loins girt about with truth, and having on the breastplate of righteousness…" (Ephesians 6:14)

Leviticus 19:11 Ye shall not steal, neither deal falsely, neither lie one to another.

Leviticus 25:14 And if thou sell ought unto thy neighbour, or buyest ought of thy neighbour's hand, ye shall not oppress one another:

Isaiah 5:20 Woe unto them that call evil good, and good evil; that put darkness for light, and light for darkness; that put bitter for sweet, and sweet for bitter!

Matthew 5:37 But let your communication be, Yea, yea; Nay, nay: for whatsoever is more than these cometh of evil.

Matthew 7:12 Therefore all things whatsoever ye would that men should do to you, do ye even so to them: for this is the law and the prophets.

Acts 24:16 And herein do I exercise myself, to have always a conscience void of offence toward God, and *toward* men.

Colossians 3:23-25 And whatsoever ye do, do it heartily, as to the Lord, and not unto men; Knowing that of the Lord ye shall receive the reward of the inheritance: for ye serve the Lord Christ. But he that doeth wrong shall receive for the wrong which he hath done: and there is no respect of persons.

1 Thessalonians 4:6 That no man go beyond and defraud his brother in any matter: because that the Lord is the avenger of all such, as we also have forewarned you and testified.

Proverbs 20:15 There is gold, and a multitude of rubies: but the lips of knowledge *are* a precious jewel.

Focus: This proverb contrasts the superior value of wisdom with the lesser value of wealth.

"Gold" is valuable, **"and a multitude of rubies"** are likely to be even more valuable. Pile all of those rubies and gold on one side of God's scale and **"lips of knowledge"** on the other, and the scale will immediately dive to one side showing that the greatest weight of value, by far, to be "lips of knowledge." "Lips of knowledge" is a phrase used two times in the Book of Proverbs – Proverbs 14:7 and 20:15 – indicating speech given by a wise person who knows God and speaks from a heart full of His wisdom. His words are precious, proving a knowledge of God and His directions for living. He knows how, when, and where to speak effectively, in a pleasing manner, and with purpose. He also knows when to keep quiet.

> "The *lips of knowledge* (a good understanding to guide the lips and a good elocution to diffuse the knowledge) are to be preferred far before gold, and pearl, and rubies; for, 1. They are more rare in themselves, more scarce and hard to be got. *There is gold* in many a man's pocket that has no grace in his heart. In Solomon's time there was plenty of gold (1Kings 10:21) and *abundance of rubies;* everybody wore them; they were to be bought in every town. But wisdom is a rare thing, a precious jewel; few have it so as to do good with it, nor is it to be purchased of the merchants. They are more enriching to us and more adorning. They make us rich toward God, rich in good works, (1Timothy 2:9, 10) Most people are fond of gold, and a ruby or two will not serve, they must have a multitude of them, a cabinet of jewels; but he that has the lips of knowledge despises these, because he knows and possesses better things."[507]

> Proverbs 3:13-15 Happy is the man that findeth wisdom, and the man that getteth understanding. For the merchandise of it is better than the merchandise of silver, and the gain thereof than fine gold. She is more precious than rubies: and all the things thou canst desire are not to be compared unto her.
> Proverbs 14:7 Go from the presence of a foolish man, when thou perceivest not *in him* the lips of knowledge.
> Proverbs 16:16 How much better is it to get wisdom than gold! and to get understanding rather to be chosen than silver!
> Proverbs 25:12 As an earring of gold, and an ornament of fine gold, so is a wise reprover upon an obedient ear.

Nothing is to be compared to wisdom that comes from God, and therefore **"lips of knowledge"** are a precious commodity in man.

> Proverbs 8:10-11 Receive my instruction, and not silver; and knowledge rather than choice gold. For wisdom is better than rubies; and all the things that may be desired are not to be compared to it.
> Proverbs 10:20 The tongue of the just is as choice silver: the heart of the wicked is little worth.
> Proverbs 15:7 The lips of the wise disperse knowledge: but the heart of the foolish doeth not so.

Proverbs 20:16 Take his garment that is surety *for* a stranger: and take a pledge of him for a strange woman.

Focus: This proverb teaches that extra precautionary measures are necessary when dealing with a foolhardy person. *(Identical to Proverbs 27:13)*

A **"surety"** is a person who verifies to a money lender that he will stand good for the debt of someone other than himself (should that someone not be able to pay the specified debt). Today, such a person is called a cosigner. The person who becomes a surety mingles his finances with another person. In this case, the verse describes the *someone else* as a person whom he barely knows (**"stranger"**) and advances in the second clause to identify her as an adulterous woman (**"strange woman"**). The danger of cosigning is stressed in several other passages in Proverbs.

> Proverbs 6:1-5 My son, if thou be surety for thy friend, if thou hast stricken thy hand with a stranger, Thou art snared with the words of thy mouth, thou art taken with the words of thy mouth. Do this now, my son, and deliver thyself, when thou art come into the hand of thy friend; go, humble thyself, and make sure thy friend. Give not sleep to thine eyes, nor slumber to thine eyelids. Deliver thyself as a roe from the hand of the hunter, and as a bird from the hand of the fowler.
> Proverbs 11:15 He that is surety for a stranger shall smart for it: and he that hateth suretiship is sure.
> Proverbs 17:18 A man void of understanding striketh hands, and becometh surety in the presence of his friend.
> Proverbs 22:26-27 Be not thou one of them that strike hands, or of them that are sureties for debts. If thou hast nothing to pay, why should he take away thy bed from under thee?
> Proverbs 27:12-13 A prudent *man* foreseeth the evil, *and* hideth himself; *but* the simple pass on, *and* are punished. Take his garment that is surety for a stranger, and take a pledge of him for a strange woman.

In case the debt is not paid, the item held for collateral, is a **"garment"** in the first clause. In the second clause garment is substituted for the general term **"pledge."** Both sides of the proverb stress that a man who will make himself responsible for the debt of someone only slightly known to himself is foolish and unreliable. So much so that in order for the lender to secure repayment of such a loan, he will be justified in holding the surety's garment *(not the garment of the person receiving the loan)* until the debt is paid. Holding a poor person's garment overnight was forbidden by the Mosaic law, but if the person being responsible ("**surety**") for a stranger's debt is blatantly foolish (not poor), then holding his garment until the debt is paid, appears to be justified. Additionally, a person who would stand good for the debt of a "strange woman" is so foolish that the person making the loan is justified in taking something of substantial value ("pledge"). The implication (by repeating the phrase only with different words) is that the **"pledge"** goes beyond the value of a garment because the risk increases with the introduction of a harlot into the equation.

> "Two sorts of persons are here spoken of that are ruining their own estates, and will be beggars shortly, and therefore are not to be trusted with any good security: 1. Those that will be bound for any body that will ask them, that entangle themselves in rash suretiship to oblige their idle companions; they will break at last, nay, they cannot hold out long; these waste by wholesale. 2. Those that are in league with abandoned women, that treat them, and court them, and keep company with them. They will be beggars in a little time; never give them credit without good pledge. Strange women have strange ways of impoverishing men to enrich themselves."[508]

> **NOTE:** The reason the Law prohibited taking a garment for a pledge was *to protect the poor and unfortunate who were forced to borrow out of necessity*; however, Proverbs 20:16 and 27:13 describe a foolish man, not a poor one, who involves himself with "a strange woman."

> Exodus 22:26-27 If thou at all take thy neighbour's raiment to pledge, thou shalt deliver it unto him by that the sun goeth down: For that is his covering only, it is his raiment for his skin: wherein shall he sleep? and it shall come to pass, when he crieth unto me, that I will hear; for I am gracious.

Proverbs 20:17 Bread of deceit *is* sweet to a man; but afterwards his mouth shall be filled with gravel.

Focus: This proverb graphically depicts that there will be surprisingly unexpected consequences from lying to get gain.

"Bread of deceit" is a phrase used to express anything gained by such unjust means as lying, fraud, theft, or any actions whereby truthfulness is missing. It is gain by evil means. "All the pleasures and profits of sin are 'bread of deceit.'"[509] Wickedness and deceit are part of the daily life of the unregenerate man. His ill-gotten gain is, *at first*, sweet. The proverb is a word picture of a wicked person smacking his lips and holding sweet bread on his tongue to savor the flavor. He finds the **"bread of deceit"** pleasurable for a time, but later **"his mouth shall be filled with gravel."** Afterward the fear of human retribution and the certainty of Divine wrath shakes him to the core.

> "'To eat gravel' was a Hebrew (Lamentations 3:16 – "He hath also broken my teeth with gravel stones, he hath covered me with ashes.), and is an Arabic, phrase for getting into trouble." So "bread," got by deceit, tastes sweet at first, but ends by leaving the hunger of the soul unsatisfied. There is a pleasure in the sense of cleverness felt after a hard bargain or a successful fraud, which must be met by bidding men look on the after consequences."[510]

> Job 20:12-16 Though wickedness be sweet in his mouth, though he hide it under his tongue; Though he spare it, and forsake it not; but keep it still within his mouth: Yet his meat in his bowels is turned, it is the gall of asps within him. He hath swallowed down riches, and he shall vomit them up again: God shall cast them out of his belly. He shall suck the poison of asps: the viper's tongue shall slay him.

> Proverbs 4:17 For they eat the bread of wickedness, and drink the wine of violence.

> Proverbs 9:17-18 Stolen waters are sweet, and bread eaten in secret is pleasant. But he knoweth not that the dead are there; and that her guests are in the depths of hell.

Believers should, like Moses, choose "to suffer affliction with the people of God, rather than enjoy the pleasures of sin for a season." (Hebrews 11:25) Sin always pays off in counterfeit money, but God's blessings and rewards are wonderful beyond words.

> "'*The bread*, which *a man* hath got by fraud and cozenage *[scam]*, seems *sweet* and pleasant at the first taste of it; but by that time he hath chewed it a little, he shall find it to be but harsh gravel, that crasheth between his teeth, galls his jaws, wounds his tongue, and offends his palate.'"[511]

Proverbs 20:18 *Every* purpose is established by counsel: and with good advice make war.

Focus: This proverb stresses the value and necessity of counsel.

"***Every*** **purpose is established by counsel."** Even a wicked leader should know that if his purposes are to succeed, he must listen to the counsel of others. Rarely does a hasty decision, without previous advice, achieve a high level of success. **"Counsel"**(in the first half of the proverb) and **"advice "** (in the second half) are synonyms. By such repetition, it is understood that the defining point for success is that *plans*, especially those that have serious consequences, like declaring war, must be **"established by counsel."**

The second clause is emphatic – **"with good advice make war."** When a king is to declare war, he must anticipate responses at many levels, including that of the people of his own country. He should not embark on a military engagement before meeting with his counsel to discuss the possible outcomes, strategies, and alternatives.

> "'Rashness spoils the best designs, which must be carried on prudently, and with good advice, if we would have them to prove successful. 'And with good advice make war' – Warlike expeditions are not to be undertaken without great deliberation. It should be maturely considered, whether the war ought to be begun or not; whether it be just, whether it be prudent. And, when it is begun, how, and by what arts, it may be successfully prosecuted: for skill is as necessary as *courage*."
>
> Proverbs 1:5 A wise *man* will hear, and will increase learning; and a man of understanding shall attain unto wise counsels . . .
> Proverbs 11:14 Where no counsel is, the people fall: but in the multitude of counsellors there is safety.
>
> Proverbs 15:22 Without counsel purposes are disappointed: but in the multitude of counsellors they are established.
>
> Proverbs 24:6 For by wise counsel thou shalt make thy war: and in multitude of counsellors there is safety.
>
> Luke 14:31-32 Or what king, going to make war against another king, sitteth not down first, and consulteth whether he be able with ten thousand to meet him that cometh against him with twenty thousand? Or else, while the other is yet a great way off, he sendeth an ambassage, and desireth conditions of peace.

David prayed and asked counsel from the Lord before he went to battle.

> 2 Samuel 5:19 And David enquired of the LORD, saying, Shall I go up to the Philistines? wilt thou deliver them into mine hand? And the LORD said unto David, Go up: for I will doubtless deliver the Philistines into thine hand.

Wicked Ahab asked counsel from his 400 false prophets, who unanimously advised him to **"make war."** Those individuals who comprised Ahab's "multitude of counselors" were as ungodly as Ahab himself, and their counsel proved to be disastrous. Four hundred men proved that they were incapable of giving **"good advice,"** as their hearts were opposed to God, and they were all "yes men" to the king.

> 1 Kings 22:6 Then the king of Israel gathered the prophets together, about four hundred men, and said unto them, Shall I go against Ramothgilead to battle, or shall I forbear? And they said, Go up; for the Lord shall deliver it into the hand of the king.

One godly prophet, Micaiah, gave **"good counsel"** that would have saved the life of Ahab, the wicked king of Israel, but the 400 evil counselors led by Zedekiah the son of Chenaahah, prevailed. Consequently, Micaiah was again imprisoned, and Ahab, as prophesied, was killed in battle. Read the entire story of both good and bad counsel recorded in 1 Kings 22.

> 1 Kings 22:26-28 And the king of Israel said, Take Micaiah, and carry him back unto Amon the governor of the city, and to Joash the king's son; And say, Thus saith the king, Put this *fellow* in the prison, and feed him with bread of affliction and with water of affliction, until I come in peace. And Micaiah said, If thou return at all in peace, the LORD hath not spoken by me. And he said, Hearken, O people, every one of you.
> 1 Kings 22:34-35 And a *certain* man drew a bow at a venture, and smote the king of Israel between the joints of the harness: wherefore he said unto the driver of his chariot, Turn thine hand, and carry me out of the host; for I am wounded. And the battle increased that day: and the king was stayed up in his chariot against the Syrians, and died at even: and the blood ran out of the wound into the midst of the chariot.

King Rehoboam asked counsel of the old men with experience and the young men who were his peers. Through lack of God-given discernment, he chose the wrong advice and consequently lost a large part of the kingdom. (1 Kings 12)

> "THE PERMANENT SUCCESS OF AN UNDERTAKING
> IS GENERALLY IN PROPORTION
> TO THE THOUGHT BESTOWED UPON IT BEFOREHAND."
> (Joseph S. Exell, Editor, W. Harris, "Proverbs", in *The Preachers Complete Homiletical Commentary*, 1892, e-Sword 12.0.1.)

The believer must seek God for His wisdom, knowledge and discernment; and he also should look for men who can give godly counsel. The value of counsel is in proportion to the amount of wisdom in the heart. The word of God counsels Christians to avoid individual war or unnecessary conflicts with others.

> Romans 12:18 If it be possible, as much as lieth in you, live peaceably with all men.

2 Timothy 2:24-26 And the servant of the Lord must not strive: but be gentle unto all *men*, apt to teach, patient, In meekness instructing those that oppose themselves; if God peradventure will give them repentance to the acknowledging of the truth; And *that* they may recover themselves out of the snare of the devil, who are taken captive by him at his will.

"God has placed us in society more or less dependent upon each other. And therefore, while it is most important to possess a calm and decided judgment; it is not less so to guard against an obstinate and exclusive adherence to our own opinions."[512]

Proverbs 20:19 He that goeth about *as* a talebearer revealeth secrets: therefore meddle not with him that flattereth with his lips.

Focus: This proverb identifies the devious work of a talebearer and instructs the wise person regarding his relationship with such persons.

A **"talebearer"** goes around the community **revealing secrets**, but *first, he has to go around the community and learn confidential information*. He spends time learning about other people's business and family affairs. He asks many questions and listens with bended ear; and what he learns in a visit at one location, he will carry with him *(he bears it)* and deliver it as a tale *[slander]* at the next.

In Proverbs 11:12-13, the **"talebearer"** is characterized as *having an un-faithful spirit*, meaning that he is not trustworthy to keep secret private, personal, or governmental strategy that was told to him in confidence. The talebearer could be a supposed friend or a government official in a private conversation with the king or head of state. In either case, the talebearer carefully picks up private information from one person and speaks it in the ear of another. He then travels with the secret to another. Such a person "forfeits all the privileges of friendship and conversation."[513] The believer *cannot* be a talebearer and be right with God.

The opposite of one that **"revealeth secrets"** is "a faithful spirit" who is faithful to the person who shared a private matter with the intent that it would not be told. The faithful man supports the person with whom he has listened by keeping his private words confidentially in his heart. He can be trusted *NOT* to broadcast any information told in secret. A faithful spirit can be entrusted with matters of state or secrets of the heart told from one friend to another. Notice how the Bible speaks about the **"talebearer."**

> Proverbs 11:12-13 He that is void of wisdom despiseth his neighbour: but a man of understanding holdeth his peace. A talebearer revealeth secrets: but he that is of a faithful spirit concealeth the matter.
> Proverbs 18:8 The words of a talebearer are as wounds, and they go down into the innermost parts of the belly.
> Proverbs 26:20-22 Where no wood is, there the fire goeth out: so where there is no talebearer, the strife ceaseth. As coals are to burning coals, and wood to fire; so is a contentious man to kindle strife. The words of a talebearer are as wounds, and they go down into the innermost parts of the belly.

If a talebearer overheard a man cursing his wife and children and then repeated what he heard to another, the talebearer would hurt the man in the eyes of his neighbors. Perhaps a man told a talebearer that he intended to find another job but was waiting until a better time. If the talebearer purposefully or maliciously repeated this information to the man's boss, job loss could occur. Certainly the talebearer wounds others with his words, whether they are true or false.

"Therefore meddle *[have fellowship with, share, intermix, be surety for a loan]* **not with him that flattereth with his lips."** "Meddle" is translated from the same Hebrew word translated "surety" in verse 16. As surely as acting as a surety is foolish, associating with a "flatterer" will lead to unnecessary problems. A form of lying, "flattereth" is a verb translated from a Hebrew word that means figuratively to be smooth. "If a man fawn upon you, compliment and commend you, suspect him to have some design upon you, and stand upon your guard."[514] Two other warnings are recognized from Proverbs 20:19.

First, the believer should be wise enough to recognize a talebearer for what he is and then avoid associating or having fellowship with him. His loose and disingenuous talk is designed to enlarge his own position with one person by belittling another. Wise persons will not be drawn into such devious entrapments. This proverbs first warning is to **not** meddle with the flattering talebearer – not to associate with him or fellowship with him. "He that walketh with wise *men* shall be wise: but a companion of fools shall be destroyed." (Proverbs 13:20)

A second warning in the New Testament is that the believer is **not** to be a talebearer personally. Talebearers will have to openly and excessively talk to gain their victim's confidence, and they seem to have too much free time on their hands. Both Paul and Peter identify the talebearer as a "busybody."

> 2 Thessalonians 3:11-12 For we hear that there are some which walk among you disorderly, working not at all, but are busybodies. Now them that are such we command and exhort by our Lord Jesus Christ, that with quietness they work, and eat their own bread.
>
> 1 Timothy 5:13 And withal they learn to be idle, wandering about from house to house; and not only idle, but tattlers also and busybodies, speaking things which they ought not.
>
> 1 Peter 4:15 But let none of you suffer as a murderer, or as a thief, or as an evildoer, or as a busybody in other men's matters.

Wisdom tells a person to refuse to hear gossip, keep private information to himself, and speak discreetly.

> Psalm 12:1-2 Help, LORD; for the godly man ceaseth; for the faithful fail from among the children of men. They speak vanity every one with his neighbour: *with* flattering lips *and* with a double heart do they speak.
>
> Proverbs 13:3 He that keepeth his mouth keepeth his life: but he that openeth wide his lips shall have destruction.
>
> Proverbs 25:9 Debate thy cause with thy neighbour himself; and discover not a secret to another:
>
> Proverbs 25:23 The north wind driveth away rain: so doth an angry countenance a backbiting tongue.
>
> Proverbs 26:20-22 Where no wood is, *there* the fire goeth out: so where *there is* no talebearer, the strife ceaseth. *As* coals *are* to burning coals, and wood to fire; so *is* a contentious man to kindle strife. The words of a talebearer *are* as wounds, and they go down into the innermost parts of the belly.

"Two sorts of people are dangerous to be conversed with:
1. Tale-bearers, though they are commonly flatterers, and by fair speeches insinuate themselves into men's acquaintance. Those are unprincipled people that go about carrying stories, that make mischief among neighbours and relations, that sow in the minds of people jealousies of their governors, of their ministers, and of one another, that reveal secrets which they are entrusted with or which by unfair means they come to the knowledge of, under pretence of guessing at men's thoughts and intentions, tell that of them which is really false. 'Be not familiar with such; do not give them the hearing when they tell their tales and reveal secrets, for you may be sure that they will betray your secrets too and tell tales of you.'
2. Flatterers, for they are commonly tale-bearers. If a man fawn upon you, compliment and commend you, suspect him to have some design upon you, and stand upon your guard; he would pick that out of you which will serve him to make a story of to somebody else to your prejudice; therefore *meddle not with him that flatters with his lips.* Those too dearly love, and too dearly buy, their own praise, that will put confidence in a man and trust him with a secret or business because he flatters them."[515]

Proverbs 20:20 Whoso curseth his father or his mother, his lamp shall be put out in obscure darkness.

Focus: This proverb references the Mosaic law's judgment for a person who curses his father or mother.

As a reminder of the possible enforcement of the fifth commandment, this proverb emphasizes the punishment which the Old Testament community could have legally *(but seldom and not likely)* enforced on an individual who behaved in such a terrible unnatural manner.[516] A wicked person who cursed his parents, treated them with contempt and did not honor them according to the Mosaic law was subject to extremely harsh judgment.

"**Whoso curseth** *[to make light, treat with contempt, bring dishonor, revile]* **his father or his mother**" is disrespectful, hateful, and foolish and the punishment for such maltreatment of parents was potentially severe under the Mosaic law:

> Exodus 20:12 Honour thy father and thy mother: that thy days may be long upon the land which the LORD thy God giveth thee.
>
> Exodus 21:17 And he that curseth his father, or his mother, shall surely be put to death.
>
> Leviticus 20:9 For every one that curseth his father or his mother shall be surely put to death: he hath cursed his father or his mother; his blood shall be upon him.

"**His lamp shall be put out in obscure darkness.**" The following is a quote from *Pulpit Commentary* that reads harshly, but renders the meaning intended by the Hebrew language as it refers to the Mosaic law. Thank God for mercy through repentance and the obtaining of forgiveness through our Lord Jesus Christ. "**Lamp**" is "a metaphor applied to the bodily and the spiritual life, to happiness and prosperity, to a man's fame and reputation, to a man's posterity; and all these senses may be involved in the denunciation of the disobedient and stubborn child. He shall suffer in body and soul, in character, in fortune, in his children. His fate is the exact counterpart of the blessing promised in the Law."[517]

> Proverbs 13:9 The light of the righteous rejoiceth: but the lamp of the wicked shall be put out.

Proverbs 24:20 For there shall be no reward to the evil man; the candle of the wicked shall be put out.

Proverbs 30:11 There is a generation that curseth their father, and doth not bless their mother.

Proverbs 30:17 The eye that mocketh at his father, and despiseth to obey his mother, the ravens of the valley shall pick it out, and the young eagles shall eat it.

Proverbs 23:22 Hearken unto thy father that begat thee, and despise not thy mother when she is old.

Mark 7:10-13 For Moses said, Honour thy father and thy mother; and, Whoso curseth father or mother, let him die the death: But ye say, If a man shall say to his father or mother, It is Corban, that is to say, a gift, by whatsoever thou mightest be profited by me; he shall be free. And ye suffer him no more to do ought for his father or his mother; Making the word of God of none effect through your tradition, which ye have delivered: and many such like things do ye. *[Matthew 15:3-6 is similar.]*

1 Timothy 5:4 But if any widow have children or nephews, let them learn first to shew piety at home, and to requite their parents: for that is good and acceptable before God.

Ephesians 6:2-3 Honour thy father and mother; (which is the first commandment with promise;) That it may be well with thee, and thou mayest live long on the earth.

Verse 21 begins a series of miscellaneous verses on financial dealings, the Lord's knowledge of man's heart, a righteous king, young men and old men, and correction. Some of the later verses share a close relationship with verses discussed at the beginning of the chapter.

> **Proverbs 20:21** An inheritance may be gotten hastily at the beginning; but the end thereof shall not be blessed.

Focus: This proverb is a warning against being an impatient and greedy beneficiary of an inheritance.

"An inheritance may be gotten hastily at the beginning" refers to the greedy, foolish son who gets his inheritance prior to the parents' death. He may get it **"hastily"** either by asking for it early or by using dishonest means, but such wealth will **"not be blessed."** Instead of it being a benefit because it was an inheritance given in love to a righteous son, the inheritance will be "suddenly ruined: it shall wither by God's just judgment, and come to nothing."[518]

The prodigal son in Luke 15 is one example of such greed and foolishness causing a child's inheritance NOT to be blessed. He gets his inheritance early by asking for it, and soon, it is totally gone.

Luke 15:11-14 And he said, A certain man had two sons: And the younger of them said to his father, Father, give me the portion of goods that falleth to me. And he divided unto them his living. And not many days after the younger son gathered all together, and took his journey into a far country, and there wasted his substance with riotous living. And when he had spent all, there arose a mighty famine in that land; and he began to be in want

An inheritance may also be acquired hastily by deceit, dishonesty, or mistreatment of the parents.

Proverbs 28:20 A faithful man shall abound with blessings: but he that maketh haste to be rich shall not be innocent.

Proverbs 28:22 He that hasteth to be rich hath an evil eye, and considereth not that poverty shall come upon him.

Proverbs 28:24 Whoso robbeth his father or his mother, and saith, It is no transgression; the same is the companion of a destroyer.

1 Timothy 6:9-10 But they that will be rich fall into temptation and a snare, and into many foolish and hurtful lusts, which drown men in destruction and perdition. For the love of money is the root of all evil: which while some coveted after, they have erred from the faith, and pierced themselves through with many sorrows.

"The end thereof shall not be blessed" indicates that God will not bless premature and dishonorable gain. Instead of the inheritance growing in amount, which is normal for properly invested wealth, the money decreases rapidly and seems to vaporize. When the absence of God's blessings is added to foolish living and spending, wealth disappears about as fast as it comes.

Wisdom enables men to avoid any love for money, to wait on and depend on God for His personal leadership and provisions, to understand how to properly and effectively interact with men and wealth, and to be content with whatever God gives and when He gives it.

Proverbs 10:2-3 Treasures of wickedness profit nothing: but righteousness delivereth from death. The LORD will not suffer the soul of the righteous to famish: but he casteth away the substance of the wicked.

Proverbs 13:11 Wealth gotten by vanity shall be diminished: but he that gathereth by labour shall increase.

Proverbs 21:5 The thoughts of the diligent tend only to plenteousness; but of every one that is hasty only to want.

Proverbs 28:20 A faithful man shall abound with blessings: but he that maketh haste to be rich shall not be innocent.

> **Proverbs 20:22** Say not thou, I will recompense evil; but wait on the LORD, and he shall save thee.

Focus: This proverb specifies the proper attitude toward vengeance.

God expressly declares that vengeance will be accomplished by Himself; and because of His complete knowledge, He is the only one capable of true equitable justice. He is always righteous and just, whereas we are prejudiced and do not ever possess total information; therefore, we are never fully qualified to **"recompense evil."** The Lord does not allow His people to avenge themselves with their tongues or with a sword, and so – ***don't say, I will recompense evil.***

- Leviticus 19:18 Thou shalt not avenge, nor bear any grudge against the children of thy people, but thou shalt love thy neighbour as thyself: I am the LORD.
- Deuteronomy 32:35 To me belongeth vengeance, and recompence; their foot shall slide in due time: for the day of their calamity is at hand, and the things that shall come upon them make haste.
- Proverbs 24:29 Say not, I will do so to him as he hath done to me: I will render to the man according to his work.
- Luke 18:7-8 And shall not God avenge his own elect, which cry day and night unto him, though he bear long with them? I tell you that he will avenge them speedily. Nevertheless when the Son of man cometh, shall he find faith on the earth?
- Romans 12:14, 17-19 Bless them which persecute you: bless, and curse not . . . Recompense to no man evil for evil. Provide things honest in the sight of all men. If it be possible, as much as lieth in you, live peaceably with all men. Dearly beloved, avenge not yourselves, but rather give place unto wrath: for it is written, Vengeance is mine; I will repay, saith the Lord.
- Hebrews 10:30-31 For we know him that hath said, Vengeance belongeth unto me, I will recompense, saith the Lord. And again, The Lord shall judge his people. It is a fearful thing to fall into the hands of the living God.

"Wait on the LORD, and he shall save thee," not in the hope of seeing vengeance taken on our enemy, but in the certainty that God will help us bear the wrong and deliver us in His own way and in His own timing.[519] Tremendous side benefits to being obedient to this passage and waiting on God include avoiding being consumed with mental anguish, not allowing hatred to drive out love and compassion, and living in peace and enjoying life and God.

- Psalm 27:14 Wait on the LORD: be of good courage, and he shall strengthen thine heart: wait, I say, on the LORD.
- Psalm 37:34 Wait on the LORD, and keep his way, and he shall exalt thee to inherit the land: when the wicked are cut off, thou shalt see it.
- Psalm 37:39-40 But the salvation of the righteous is of the LORD: he is their strength in the time of trouble. And the LORD shall help them, and deliver them: he shall deliver them from the wicked, and save them, because they trust in him.
- 1 Peter 4:19 Wherefore let them that suffer according to the will of God commit the keeping of their souls to him in well doing, as unto a faithful Creator.

Joseph knew what it was like to trust God and wait on Him. Years after surviving intense hate from his brothers, who threw him into the pit and sold him into slavery, he said, "But as for you, ye thought evil against me; but God meant it unto good, to bring to pass, as it is this day, to save much people alive." (Genesis 50:20)

"Those that live in this world must expect to have injuries done them, affronts given them, and trouble wrongfully created them, for we dwell among briers . . . We must not avenge ourselves, no, nor so much as think of revenge, or design it: '*Say not thou,* no, not in thy heart, *I will recompense evil* for evil.' Do not please thyself with the thought that some time or other thou shalt have an opportunity of being quits with him. Do not wish revenge, or hope for it, much less resolve upon it, no, not when the injury is fresh and the resentment of it most deep. Never say that thou wilt do a thing which thou canst not in faith pray to God to assist thee in, and *that* thou canst not do in mediating revenge.

We must refer ourselves to God, and leave it to him to plead our cause, to maintain our right, and reckon with those that do us wrong in such a way and manner as he thinks fit and in his own due time: "*Wait on the Lord,* and attend his pleasure, acquiesce in his will, and he does not say that he will punish him that has injured thee (instead of desiring that thou must forgive him and pray for him), but *he will save thee,* and that is enough. He will protect thee, so that thy passing by one injury shall not (as is commonly feared) expose thee to another; nay, he will recompense good to thee, to balance thy trouble and encourage thy patience," as David hoped, when Shimei cursed him."[520]

2 Samuel 16:12 It may be that the LORD will look on mine affliction, and that the LORD will requite me good for his cursing this day.

1 Peter 2:23-24 Who, when he was reviled, reviled not again; when he suffered, he threatened not; but committed himself to him that judgeth righteously: Who his own self bare our sins in his own body on the tree, that we, being dead to sins, should live unto righteousness: by whose stripes ye were healed.

> **Proverbs 20:23** Divers weights *are* an abomination unto the LORD; and a false balance *is* not good.

> Focus: This proverb describes God's attitude toward men's use of deceptive devices in commerce.

In the farming society of the early Hebrews, produce was measured and priced according to weight as reflected on a balance scale. Some produce was measured in a container and priced according to volume. Weights in the form of stones of precise measurement were selected and placed on one side of the scales; thus, a specific-sized stone on one side of the scales would be counterbalanced on the other side of the scale by the same weight of the selected produce (apples, grapes). A **divers weight** would be different size stones that the owner claimed to be equal but were not and thus used to defraud the buyer or barterer. A substitute stone that weighed less than the designated accurate one would cause the scale to balance at the lesser amount but sold or bartered as though it were the greater amount; thus, the buyer is cheated, and the seller is both a deceiver and a thief.

Three times in this chapter – Proverbs 20:10, 14, and now 23 – dishonesty in trading is severely condemned. *Never* is the believer to deceive another person by any means and specifically through using different "weights" and a "false balance." This verse is reminiscent of one of the purpose statements given by Solomon for the Book of Proverbs in Chapter One: "To receive the instruction of wisdom, justice, and judgment, and equity." (Proverbs 1:3) Every person should be treated fairly, honestly, and righteously. To maintain "diverse weights" and a "false balance" is not only an abomination to God but is **"not good"** meaning that it is wicked. A deceptive person should not fool himself into believing that he is an astute businessman when he is actually a thief.

> Deuteronomy 25:14-16 Thou shalt not have in thine house divers measures, a great and a small. But thou shalt have a perfect and just weight, a perfect and just measure shalt thou have: that thy days may be lengthened in the land which the LORD thy God giveth thee. For all that do such things, and all that do unrighteously, are an abomination unto the LORD thy God.
> 1 Thessalonians 4:6-7 That no man go beyond and defraud his brother in any matter: because that the Lord is the avenger of all such, as we also have forewarned you and testified. For God hath not called us unto uncleanness, but unto holiness.

> **Proverbs 20:24** Man's goings *are* of the LORD; how can a man then understand his own way?

> Focus: This proverb teaches that a man cannot understand his own way because God is secretly steering his life.

"Man's goings are of the Lord." Every action of man is controlled by God's providence, and man's purposes and activities are subject to be frustrated or changed as God sees fit. He can clear the way or block the path through physical and spiritual circumstances, other people, or direct intervention. Regardless of how much control a man thinks he has, he only goes wherever God permits. A believer learns to ask the LORD to control his life, block the path, or open the way according to His will. He knows he cannot see around the corners of life but depends upon the Lord to guide his way.

> "'**Man's goings are of the Lord.**' In the first clause the word for "man" is *geber*, which implies 'a mighty man'; in the second clause the word is *adam*, 'a human creature.'...The proverb says that the steps of a great and powerful man depend, as their final cause, upon the Lord; he conditions and controls results. Man has free will, and is responsible for his actions, but God foreknows them, and holds the thread that connects them together; he gives preventing grace; he gives efficient grace: and man blindly works out the designs of Omnipotence according as he obeys or resists."[521]

A young Christian man had just transferred from one college to another. Before the process of registering at the new college, he came to the conclusion that he would never marry. As he walked on the beautiful hilly grass-covered lawn that sun-filled day to participate in an outdoor registration for classes, he noticed a young lady, a student helping at the English registration table. The Holy Spirit spoke this thought into his mind, "There's your wife." That has been so for over half a century.

> "The man is not moved as a machine, unconscious of its operations and results, but acted upon by intelligent principles. He is not carried along the way, but enabled to walk. He is 'drawn,' not driven, 'with the cords of a man,' not of a beast; and those cords are so wisely applied, that they are felt to be 'bands of love.' (Hosea 11:4) He is enlightened, so that he sees; softened, so that he turns; 'drawn, so that he runs.' (Song of Solomon 1:4; Psalm 119:32) He is moved effectually, but willingly; invincibly, but without constraint. Divine grace acts, not as

in a lifeless machine, but as in a purposing, willing, ever-working creature. Nothing is therefore distorted. There is no unnatural violence. It is 'the day of the LORD's power,' who 'worketh in him to will and to do of his good pleasure.' *His goings are of the LORD*, who at once inspires the effort, and secures the success . . . Little did Israel *understand* the reason of their circuitous *way* to Canaan. Yet did it prove in the end to be 'the right way.' As little did Ahasuerus *understand* the profound reason, why 'on that night could not the king sleep;' a minute incident, seeming scarcely worthy to be recorded, yet a necessary link in the chain of the LORD's everlasting purposes of grace to his Church. (Esther 6:1) Little did Philip *understand his own way*, when he was moved from the wide sphere of preaching the gospel in Samaria, to go into the desert, which ultimately proved a wider extension of the gospel. As little did the great Apostle understand, that his '*prosperous* journey' to see his beloved flock at Rome, would be a narrow escape from shipwreck, and to be conducted a prisoner in chains. Little do we know what we pray for. 'By terrible things wilt thou answer us in righteousness, O God of our salvation.' (Psalm 65:5) We go out in the morning *not understanding our way;* 'not knowing what an hour may bring forth.' (Proverbs 27:1) Some turn, connected with our happiness or misery for life, meets us before night. (John 4:7) Joseph in taking his walk to search for his brethren, never anticipated a more than twenty years' separation from his father. (Genesis 37:14) And what ought those cross ways or dark ways to teach us? Not constant, trembling anxiety, but daily dependence. 'I will bring the blind by a way that they know not: I will lead them in paths that they have not known.' But shall they be left in the dark perplexity? 'I will make darkness light before them, and crooked things straight. These things will I do unto them, and not forsake them.' (Isaiah 42:16) Often do I look back amazed at the strangeness of my course, so different, so contrary to my way. But it is enough for me, that all is in thine hands; that 'my steps are ordered of thee.' (Psalm 37:23; Proverbs 16:9) I dare trust thy wisdom, thy goodness, thy tenderness, thy faithful care. Lead me – uphold me – forsake me not. Thou shalt guide me with thy counsel, and afterwards receive me to glory."[522]

Psalm 25:4 Shew me thy ways, O LORD; teach me thy paths.

Psalm 37:23 The steps of a good man are ordered by the LORD: and he delighteth in his way.

Proverbs 16:9 A man's heart deviseth his way: but the LORD directeth his steps.

Proverbs 21:1 The king's heart is in the hand of the LORD, as the rivers of water: he turneth it whithersoever he will.

Jeremiah 10:23 O LORD, I know that the way of man is not in himself: it is not in man that walketh to direct his steps.

Acts 17:28 For in him we live, and move, and have our being; as certain also of your own poets have said, For we are also his offspring.

After prayer, Abraham's servant came to the well at the exact time to meet Rebekah, the bride he was seeking for Isaac. (Genesis 24:7) After Pharaoh had given the order to kill all the baby boys, his own daughter went out to bathe and found Moses, who had been prayerfully placed in a basket by his parents Amram and Jochebed. (Exodus 2:1-5) She took Moses into the palace and raised him as her own.

Men should do their best to tend to their duties in life and prayerfully and quietly depend on God for the outcome. **"Man's goings are of the LORD; how can a man then understand his own way?"** He cannot.

Proverbs 20:25 *It is* a snare to the man *who* devoureth *that which is* holy, and after vows to make enquiry.

Focus: This proverb specifies what happens when a person misappropriates something that belongs to God or goes back on a vow to God.

"It is a snare to the man who devoureth that which is holy." When a person gives money, *or* brings a sacrifice and gives it to the Lord, *or* promises the Lord that he will serve Him faithfully, that gift or pledge becomes **"holy"** *[a sacred place or thing, set apart, devoted to a particular purpose]* unto the Lord. To *devour that which is holy* is a sin that involves taking anything that belongs to the Lord, *or* to His worship, *or* to His work and using it for one's own private purpose. Ananias and Sapphira *said* they were giving a certain amount of the proceeds received from the sale of land to the Lord's work. However, when they held back part of what they had promised for their own use, they *devoured something set aside for God's work* and set a **"snare"** *[a noose for catching animals, a trap]* for themselves, and God required their life. (Acts 5:1-10) They *devoured that which was holy* since they made personal that which was dedicated to the Lord.

When a church body gives an offering to an evangelist or missionary, and one of the church staff redirects that dedicated money for another purpose in the local church, that local church is *devouring* that holy offering. It is a sin. If the believer has devoted to God a certain time for prayer and study, and then hurries over that sacred time to do something else, he is *devouring that which is holy*.

"Holy" refers to anything that is sanctified or set apart for God's service. Moses was told to take off his shoes because the place he was standing was "holy" ground. (Exodus 3:5) The Sabbath day was set apart for a day of rest, and the Bible states "remember the Sabbath day to keep it holy." (Exodus 20:8) The nation of Israel was a "holy" nation because God chose it and set it apart for Himself. (Exodus 19:6) Notice what the Bible teaches about offerings to the Lord.

> Leviticus 27:9-10 And if it be a beast, whereof men bring an offering unto the LORD, all that any man giveth of such unto the LORD shall be holy. He shall not alter it, nor change it, a good for a bad, or a bad for a good: and if he shall at all change beast for beast, then it and the exchange thereof shall be holy.
>
> Leviticus 27:28-32 Notwithstanding no devoted thing, that a man shall devote unto the LORD of all that he hath, both of man and beast, and of the field of his possession, shall be sold or redeemed: every devoted thing is most holy unto the LORD. None devoted, which shall be devoted of men, shall be redeemed; but shall surely be put to death. And all the tithe of the land, whether of the seed of the land, or of the fruit of the tree, is the LORD'S: it is holy unto the LORD. And if a man will at all redeem ought of his tithes, he shall add thereto the fifth part thereof. And concerning the tithe of the herd, or of the flock, even of whatsoever passeth under the rod, the tenth shall be holy unto the LORD.

"And after vows to make enquiry" describes a situation in which a person has promised or dedicated something to the Lord, then begins to ask himself or others what he can do to get out of fulfilling his vow. A man may be sitting with his sick child and perhaps promises God a large offering if the Great Physician will just heal him. The child recovers, but when the man's fear and worry for his child ceases, his devotion to God ceases. He remembers what he has promised God but begins to look for excuses that can, in his mind, overturn his commitment to God.

> Ecclesiastes 5:4-6 When thou vowest a vow unto God, defer not to pay it; for he hath no pleasure in fools: pay that which thou hast vowed. Better is it that thou shouldest not vow, than that thou shouldest vow and not pay. Suffer not thy mouth to cause thy flesh to sin; neither say thou before the angel, that it was an error: wherefore should God be angry at thy voice, and destroy the work of thine hands?

The scribes and Pharisees often came up with "traditions" that would enable those that needed to get out of a vow or even disobey a commandment. One of the commandments was "honor thy father and mother." A Hebrew was supposed to support his aging parents, but if a selfish and uncaring son wanted to spend his money on himself, he could declare all his possessions "Corban" meaning a gift offered to God. "Corban" was an invention pronounced over money and property donated to the temple and its services. If a son declared that the resources required to support his parents were "Corban," then according to "tradition" he was exempt from God's command to take care of his parents; and his parents had no claim to gain his support (Mark 7:11-12). Timothy was moved to make the following statement:

> 1 Timothy 5:8 But if any provide not for his own, and specially for those of his own house, he hath denied the faith, and is worse than an infidel.

Proverbs 20:26 A wise king scattereth the wicked, and bringeth the wheel over them.

Focus: This proverb declares aggressive actions of justice that a wise king takes against the wicked to protect his kingdom.

Having the responsibility to maintain order and administer justice, a wise, righteous Hebrew king would punish the wicked once their dangerous and destructive plots were discovered. In administering justice, Solomon chose to use two familiar harvesting terms as a comparison to describe such work – ***scattering the wicked*** (winnowing) and ***bringing the wheel over them*** *(threshing)*.

"A wise king scattereth the wicked." *Scattering* refers to the process of winnowing. A king's work in controlling evil by *separating wicked people from the good ones* is compared to separating the good, edible grain from the chaff in the winnowing process. Winnowing occurred when the farmer used a utensil to shovel up the threshed grain mixed with chaff and throw it all up into the breeze. The grain, which was heavier and rounder, would fall straight to the ground, while the larger pieces of stalk would fall off to the side, and the light chaff would be blown even farther away.

Christ is our wise King who will eternally separate the wicked from the righteous.

> Matthew 3:12 Whose fan is in his hand, and he will throughly purge his floor, and gather his wheat into the garner; but he will burn up the chaff with unquenchable fire.
>
> "The pronged winnowing-fork . . . throws up the grain against the wind. The Coming One is to put an end to the present mixture of chaff and corn. He will thoroughly purge the threshing-floor of this world, gathering the good into one safe place, and destroying the evil . . . The present mixture of good and evil shall be brought to an End. All true believers shall finally be brought to perfect unity."[523]
>
> Matthew 13:30 Let both grow together until the harvest: and in the time of harvest I will say to the reapers, Gather ye together first the tares, and bind them in bundles to burn them: but gather the wheat into my barn.

"A wise king . . . bringeth the wheel over them *(the wicked)*.**"** These words describe the *severity of justice administered to the evil* by comparing their punishment to threshing. The harvested stalks were laid out on the threshing floor, and the threshing wheels were rolled over them, thereby cutting up the stalks and separating the heads of grain that were knocked off the stalks – a process illustrated by the term *bringing the wheel over them*.

> "The threshing wheel is meant. *(Isaiah 28:27 Amos 1:3)* This was a wooden frame with three or four rollers under it armed with iron teeth. It was drawn by two oxen, and, aided by the weight of the driver, who had his seat upon it, it crushed out the grain, and cut up the straw into fodder. . .The wise ruler will not only distinguish between the godless and the good, but will show his discrimination by visiting the evil with condign *[fitting]* punishment.[524]

> "What is the business of magistrates. They are to be a terror to evil-doers. They must *scatter the wicked,* who are linked in confederacies to assist and embolden one another in doing mischief; and there is no doing this but by *bringing the wheel over them*, that is, putting the laws in execution against them, crushing their power and quashing their projects. Severity must sometimes be used to rid the country of those that are openly vicious and mischievous, debauched and debauching.

> What is the qualification of magistrates, which is necessary in order to do this. They have need to be both pious and prudent, for it is the wise king, who is both religious and discreet, that is likely to effect the suppression of vice and reformation of manners."[525]

Proverbs 20:27 The spirit of man *is* the candle of the LORD, searching all the inward parts of the belly.

Focus: This proverb declares that the spirit of man is used with and by God as an examiner of man's heart.

In this verse, the **"spirit of man"** is compared to a **"candle"** or a searchlight that illuminates the totally dark heart of a man so that man's conscience "can see" or is alerted to specific sins hidden there. The spirit of man (candle) is comparable to a light in that it alerts and makes his conscience aware of specific sins. The verse strongly implies that *God and man's spirit search together*, looking down into the deep recesses of a man's innermost suppressed thoughts and inventions **("inward parts of the belly")** where he may have hidden secrets previously unknown even to his own conscience. David, in Psalm 139, set the example for believers to plead with God to hold up this candle and bring hidden sin to light so that it can be denounced and forsaken.

> Psalm 139:23-24 Search me, O God, and know my heart: try me, and know my thoughts: And see if there be any wicked way in me, and lead me in the way everlasting.
> John 3:20-21 For every one that doeth evil hateth the light, neither cometh to the light, lest his deeds should be reproved. But he that doeth truth cometh to the light, that his deeds may be made manifest, that they are wrought in God.
> 1 John 1:8-10 If we say that we have no sin, we deceive ourselves, and the truth is not in us. If we confess our sins, he is faithful and just to forgive us our sins, and to cleanse us from all unrighteousness. If we say that we have not sinned, we make him a liar, and his word is not in us.

"Searching all the inward parts of the belly" simply means *searching the whole inner man* for his motives, inward principles, thoughts on his past, and his resolutions for the future. When the lamp is not used, evil remains undetected. Man can become puffed up thinking he is good. Not willing to have a false view of himself, Paul speaks of his desire when he writes in Acts 24:16 – "And herein do I exercise myself, to have always a conscience void of offense toward God, and men."

God *knows every person's* thoughts, desires, motives, loves, and hatreds. Conversely, because man can only hear the outward words and see the actions of another person, his judgments are never totally accurate, as are God's. There will be no rebutting or arguing with God at the final judgment.

> Jeremiah 17:9-10 The heart is deceitful above all things, and desperately wicked: who can know it? I the LORD search the heart, I try the reins, even to give every man according to his ways, and according to the fruit of his doings.
> Hebrews 4:12-13 For the word of God is quick, and powerful, and sharper than any twoedged sword, piercing even to the dividing asunder of soul and spirit, and of the joints and marrow, and is a discerner of the thoughts and intents of the heart. Neither is there any creature that is not manifest in his sight: but all things are naked and opened unto the eyes of him with whom we have to do.

Through the word of God and the Spirit of God interacting with the spirit of man, he can "see" his own heart and know the difference between his right and wrong deeds.

> Job 32:8 But *there is* a spirit in man: and the inspiration of the Almighty giveth them understanding.
> Ecclesiastes 12:7 Then shall the dust return to the earth as it was: and the spirit shall return unto God who gave it.

Matthew 6:23 But if thine eye be evil, thy whole body shall be full of darkness. If therefore the light that is in thee be darkness, how great *is that darkness!*

Hebrews 4:12 For the word of God is quick, and powerful, and sharper than any twoedged sword, piercing even to the dividing asunder of soul and spirit, and of the joints and marrow, and is a discerner of the thoughts and intents of the heart.

"Long ago one could have seen, in not a few churches, upon Christmas Eve, two small lights, symbolizing the Divine and human natures, being gradually brought together until they blended in one brilliant flame. This truth was also typified in the cloven tongues of fire that hovered over the disciples' heads upon the day of Pentecost. So with the restoration of the vital connections between man and God through Jesus Christ, the Holy Spirit shall commingle with our spirit, intensifying the holy flame, so that it shall penetrate to the farthest reaches of life and character. Our moral vision shall be corrected, so that truth and error, right and wrong shall appear to us in sharply-defined contrast. He shall lead us into all truth."[526]

Proverbs 20:28 Mercy and truth preserve the king: and his throne is upholden by mercy.

Focus: This proverb names two attributes of a king's leadership that preserve him and establish his throne.

The king who practices mercy and yearns for truth will discover that God responds with favor. Also, the people will revere him. In this verse, **"Mercy"** for others, as extended by the king, would involve pardon for offenders and help to the poor. Such mercy is recognized and favored by the people, who then in turn strongly support the king. *["**Mercy**" is the aspect of God's love that causes Him to help the miserable who may be so either because of breaking God's law or because of circumstances beyond their control like blindness or leprosy… because God is merciful, He expects His children to be merciful.[527]]* The king's **"truth** *[faithful, sure, reliable, stable.]* **"** is evidenced by keeping his word and his promises. The king's throne is well established when mercy and truth are the two strong pillars of justice holding up his kingdom. Within the population, truth produces reverence – mercy will win the people's hearts. The king's own mercy and truth "are the safeguards of his throne." The righteous king:

"… must be strictly faithful to his word, must be sincere, and abhor all dissimulation, must religiously discharge all the trusts reposed in him, must support and countenance truth. He must likewise rule with clemency, and by all acts of compassion gain the affections of his people. Mercy and truth are the glories of God's throne … These virtues will preserve his person and support his government, will make him easy and safe, beloved by his own people and feared by his enemies, if it be possible that he should have any."[528]

Psalm 21:7 For the king trusteth in the LORD, and through the mercy of the most High he shall not be moved.

Psalm 61:6-7 Thou wilt prolong the king's life: and his years as many generations. He shall abide before God for ever: O prepare mercy and truth, which may preserve him.

Proverbs 3:3-4 Let not mercy and truth forsake thee: bind them about thy neck; write them upon the table of thine heart: So shalt thou find favour and good understanding in the sight of God and man.

Proverbs 14:22 Do they not err that devise evil? but mercy and truth shall be to them that devise good.

Proverbs 16:6 By mercy and truth iniquity is purged: and by the fear of the LORD men depart from evil.

Proverbs 29:14 The king that faithfully judgeth the poor, his throne shall be established for ever.

Isaiah 16:5 And in mercy shall the throne be established: and he shall sit upon it in truth in the tabernacle of David, judging, and seeking judgment, and hasting righteousness.

Proverbs 20:29 The glory of young men *is* their strength: and the beauty of old men *is* the gray head.

Focus: This proverb declares the glory of young men and the beauty of old men.

"The glory *[ornament, renown]* **of young men *is* their strength."** Since they are proud of being both mentally and physically strong, young men typically exercise to make themselves even stronger. God has so designed human development that young men excel in mind and body, and this is a glory to them. It is thus wise and suitable for young men to take on tasks that use such powerful abilities. They can conduct business, go to war and overcome obstacles through endurance and power of fully-functioning faculties. Eventually, age will diminish such great strength, and they will be honored otherwise, such as from being sagacious.

"The beauty of old men is the gray head." The beauty of gray hair adorning a wise old man is so because of being symbolic of the many years of gradually developing wisdom and losing physical strength. What the old men lack in physical strength, they *should* make up for in wisdom appropriate for those who have a gray head. The gray hair is a reminder of an old man's wisdom that comes from walking with God over his lifetime. All the previously mentioned glory and beauty may be turned to shame if youth and old age are lived in opposition to God.

> "Let youth and age however each beware of defacing their glory. Each takes the precedence in some things, and gives place in others. Let them not therefore envy or despise each other's prerogatives. The world – the state – the church needs them both – *the strength of youth* for energy, and the maturity of *age* for wisdom."

Having grown old, the man is honored, not for his strength but for his wisdom and experience. His counsel is as valuable now as his strength once was, only in a different way.

> Psalm 71:17-18   O God, thou hast taught me from my youth: and hitherto have I declared thy wondrous works. Now also when I am old and grayheaded, O God, forsake me not; until I have shewed thy strength unto this generation, and thy power to every one that is to come.
>
> Proverbs 16:31 The hoary head is a crown of glory, if it be found in the way of righteousness.
>
> Ecclesiastes 11:9   Rejoice, O young man, in thy youth; and let thy heart cheer thee in the days of thy youth, and walk in the ways of thine heart, and in the sight of thine eyes: but know thou, that for all these things God will bring thee into judgment.
>
> Jeremiah 9:23-24   Thus saith the LORD, Let not the wise man glory in his wisdom, neither let the mighty man glory in his might, let not the rich man glory in his riches: But let him that glorieth glory in this, that he understandeth and knoweth me, that I am the LORD which exercise lovingkindness, judgment, and righteousness, in the earth: for in these things I delight, saith the LORD.
>
> 1 John 2:14   I have written unto you, fathers, because ye have known him *that is* from the beginning. I have written unto you, young men, because ye are strong, and the word of God abideth in you, and ye have overcome the wicked one.

Proverbs 20:30   The blueness of a wound cleanseth away evil: so *do* stripes the inward parts of the belly.

> Focus: This proverb declares that physical chastisement can leave bruises or stripes on the flesh, and those same external stripes can extend themselves (figuratively) to reach inside to cleanse the heart.

"The blueness of a wound cleanseth away evil." "Blueness of a wound" (bruise) in this first clause is equal to "stripes" in the second. Thus, the effect of a scourging is "stripes" or "blueness of a wound." Bruises caused by severe chastisement on a person effectively correct evil behavior. The KJV marginal notes add that the words "cleanseth away evil" are equivalent to saying that the stripes are a "purging medicine against evil."[529] **"So *do* stripes the inward parts of the belly,"** indicates that while the chastening is being applied externally, it effects "the inward parts of the belly" which is the inner man, his soul or heart.

After his father's death, Manasseh, the son of the godly King Hezekiah, turned to the evil ways of his grandfather Ahaz. He worshiped Molech by sacrificing his son to him, and he killed all that protested his actions. God chastened him and cleansed the evil in his heart. (See 2 Chronicles 33:11-16 below.)

> 2 Chronicles 33:11-16   Wherefore the LORD brought upon them the captains of the host of the king of Assyria, which took Manasseh among the thorns, and bound him with fetters, and carried him to Babylon. And when he was in affliction, he besought the LORD his God, and humbled himself greatly before the God of his fathers, And prayed unto him: and he was intreated of him, and heard his supplication, and brought him again to Jerusalem into his kingdom. Then Manasseh knew that the LORD he was God. Now after this he built a wall without the city of David, on the west side of Gihon, in the valley, even to the entering in at the fish gate, and compassed about Ophel, and raised it up a very great height, and put captains of war in all the fenced cities of Judah. And he took away the strange gods, and the idol out of the house of the LORD, and all the altars that he had built in the mount of the house of the LORD, and in Jerusalem, and cast them out of the city. And he repaired the altar of the LORD, and sacrificed thereon peace offerings and thank offerings, and commanded Judah to serve the LORD God of Israel.

Corinthians reminds the believer that chastisement prevents being condemned with the lost.

> 1 Corinthians 11:31-32   For if we would judge ourselves, we should not be judged. But when we are judged, we are chastened of the Lord, that we should not be condemned with the world.
>
> Hebrews 12:6-11   For whom the Lord loveth he chasteneth, and scourgeth every son whom he receiveth. If ye endure chastening, God dealeth with you as with sons; for what son is he whom the father chasteneth not? But if ye be without chastisement, whereof all are partakers, then are ye bastards, and not sons. Furthermore we have had fathers of our flesh which corrected us, and we gave them reverence: shall we not much rather be in subjection unto the Father of spirits, and live? For they verily for a few days chastened us after their own pleasure; but he for our profit, that we might be partakers of his holiness. Now no chastening for the present seemeth to be joyous, but grievous: nevertheless afterward it yieldeth the peaceable fruit of righteousness unto them which are exercised thereby.

CHAPTER TWENTY-ONE

> **Proverbs 21:1** The king's heart *is* in the hand of the LORD, *as* the rivers of water: he turneth it whithersoever he will.

Focus: This proverb expresses the ease with which God can change the heart of a king.

"The king's heart is in the hand of the LORD." Every human being is subject to his thoughts being guided by God in order to fulfill divine purposes, but the heathen king or any man is most likely to be unaware of such supernatural intervention. The self-willed king's purposes and inclinations seem to himself to be totally private, and he would probably deny that God had anything to do with his personal desires. Each man has a free will to make his own choices in life, but God influences those choices that affect God's purposes in the overall scheme of world events.

> "A ruler is an official and representative person in an eminent degree. What he does affects others directly and indirectly. Providence oft times overrules his thoughts, tastes, passions, purposes, etc., to subserve His own ends, and often works out results altogether foreign to the intention or expectation of the ruler."[530]

The **"rivers of water"** is a wonderful symbol of God's work in specifically *guiding leaders*. **"Rivers"** is a Hebrew term for a flowing channel of personally-released stored water for irrigation purposes. Because of the lack of rain during parts of the year and because the crops often grew in fields too far away to receive any water from a stream or lake, a system of irrigation was devised. Canals or ditches were dug from the reserved water source to the crops. Farmers would collect rain waters in pools or cisterns and then dig ditches designed to carry streams of water from the pools to the fields. They constructed piles of dirt to effectively dam up the flow of water. When he wanted to irrigate a certain field, the farmer would move a portion of the dirt with his foot, and allow the water to escape and flow specifically to the selected field. When necessary, he could close that gap and open another to allow the water to flow to a different field. *(See Psalm 1.)*

> "By hidden influences and providential arrangements God disposes the monarch to order his government so as to carry out his designs, to spread around joy and plenty. The system of irrigation signified in this passage is still to be seen in Eastern lands. 'Flower beds and gardens of herbs are always made at a little lower level than the surrounding ground, and are divided into small squares, a slight edging of earth banking the whole round on each side. Water is then let in, and floods the entire surface till the soil is thoroughly saturated; after which the moisture is turned off to another bed, by simply closing the opening in the one under water, by a turn of the bare foot of the gardener, and making another in the same way with the foot, in the next bed ... Only, in this case, the hand is supposed to make the gap in the clay bank of the streamlet, and divert the current' (Geikie, "Holy Land and Bible," 1:9)."[531]

In the same way that farmers could easily turn rivers of water, God intervenes to carry out His own purposes by causing events to happen, thoughts to occur and words to be spoken or simply forgotten. One Pharaoh's heart was softened to put Joseph in charge of Egypt. Four hundred years later, a selfish and conceited Pharaoh's heart was hardened because it was time for Israel to return to the Promised Land. The Gentile King Cyrus was stirred to do the will of God in sending the Jews back to rebuild the Temple. In the Tribulation, the kings will give their hearts to the Beast. Knowing that our God is truly King of kings, Timothy urged the church to pray for the rulers of this world.

> 1 Timothy 2:1-2 I exhort therefore, that, first of all, supplications, prayers, intercessions, and giving of thanks, be made for all men;
> For kings, and for all that are in authority; that we may lead a quiet and peaceable life in all godliness and honesty.

The Bible gives many illustrations of God's turning the inmost thoughts of kings to do His own will. It is not only the minds of righteous Hebrew kings that God guides, but He also controls the heart of the worldly Gentile rulers. Notice the following Scriptures:

> Genesis 20:2-3 And Abraham said of Sarah his wife, She is my sister: and Abimelech king of Gerar sent, and took Sarah. But God came to Abimelech in a dream by night, and said to him, Behold, thou art but a dead man, for the woman which thou hast taken; for she is a man's wife.

Genesis 41:37-41 And the thing was good in the eyes of Pharaoh, and in the eyes of all his servants. And Pharaoh said unto his servants, Can we find such a one as this is, a man in whom the Spirit of God is? And Pharaoh said unto Joseph, Forasmuch as God hath shewed thee all this, there is none so discreet and wise as thou art: Thou shalt be over my house, and according unto thy word shall all my people be ruled: only in the throne will I be greater than thou. And Pharaoh said unto Joseph, See, I have set thee over all the land of Egypt.

Exodus 7:13 And he hardened Pharaoh's heart, that he hearkened not unto them; as the LORD had said.

Isaiah 44:28 That saith of Cyrus, He is my shepherd, and shall perform all my pleasure: even saying to Jerusalem, Thou shalt be built; and to the temple, Thy foundation shall be laid.

Ezra 1:1-2 Now in the first year of Cyrus king of Persia, that the word of the LORD by the mouth of Jeremiah might be fulfilled, the LORD stirred up the spirit of Cyrus king of Persia, that he made a proclamation throughout all his kingdom, and put it also in writing, saying, Thus saith Cyrus king of Persia, The LORD God of heaven hath given me all the kingdoms of the earth; and he hath charged me to build him an house at Jerusalem, which is in Judah. *[See also 2 Chronicles 36:22-23.]*

Acts 4:25-28 Who by the mouth of thy servant David hast said, Why did the heathen rage, and the people imagine vain things? The kings of the earth stood up, and the rulers were gathered together against the Lord, and against his Christ. For of a truth against thy holy child Jesus, whom thou hast anointed, both Herod, and Pontius Pilate, with the Gentiles, and the people of Israel, were gathered together, For to do whatsoever thy hand and thy counsel determined before to be done.

Revelation 17:16-17 And the ten horns which thou sawest upon the beast, these shall hate the whore, and shall make her desolate and naked, and shall eat her flesh, and burn her with fire. For God hath put in their hearts to fulfil his will, and to agree, and give their kingdom unto the beast, until the words of God shall be fulfilled.

Proverbs 21:2   Every way of a man *is* right in his own eyes: but the LORD pondereth the hearts.

Focus: This proverb contrasts prejudiced self-evaluation with God's unbiased, truthful evaluation.

"Every way of a man is right in his own eyes." A person may think that he talks, thinks, and acts right – *probably because he has compared himself with himself*. Also, it is human nature to minimize and suppress the memory of one's own sins and misdeeds while being quite familiar and unforgiving of others. Believing that he is right in his own reasoning and justified in his own actions, he favors himself, but God has the supernatural ability to scrutinize the motives of our hearts. Thus, He knows not only our words and deeds but also our motives.

"The LORD pondereth the hearts" means that He "weighs them in the balance of righteousness and truth: considers them, having a perfect knowledge of them, and all the springs of action in them; and knows that every way of man is not right, though they may seem so to him."[532] Along with such pondering, God is fully capable of causing a person to smell an odor or feel a particular thing or to see something or hear a sound or word that will bring a suppressed memory rushing to the forefront, and He especially does this with His word in order to bring stinging conviction.

"All the ways of a man are clean in his own eyes; but the LORD weigheth the spirits," Proverbs 16:2 is very similar in words and meaning to this current verse. Obviously, the Holy Spirit wanted this concept repeated in the Book of Proverbs plus other places of Scripture. The wise believer will realize this weakness in self-evaluation and request a candid survey of his heart by God and then wait quietly until God gives His judgment.

Psalm 139:23-24 Search me, O God, and know my heart: try me, and know my thoughts: And see if there be any wicked way in me, and lead me in the way everlasting.

Proverbs 28:6 He that trusteth in his own heart is a fool: but whoso walketh wisely, he shall be delivered.

Many other Scriptures declare the truth of this proverb including the following:

Proverbs 16:25 There is a way that seemeth right unto a man, but the end thereof are the ways of death.

Proverbs 24:12 If thou sayest, Behold, we knew it not; doth not he that pondereth the heart consider it? and he that keepeth thy soul, doth not he know it? and shall not he render to every man according to his works?

Proverbs 30:12 There is a generation that are pure in their own eyes, and yet is not washed from their filthiness.

Jeremiah 17:9-10 The heart is deceitful above all things, and desperately wicked: who can know it? I the LORD search the heart, I try the reins, even to give every man according to his ways, and according to the fruit of his doings.

Luke 16:14-15 And the Pharisees also, who were covetous, heard all these things: and they derided him. And he said unto them, Ye are they which justify yourselves before men; but God knoweth your hearts: for that which is highly esteemed among men is abomination in the sight of God.

Luke 18:9-14 And he spake this parable unto certain which trusted in themselves that they were righteous, and despised others: Two men went up into the temple to pray; the one a Pharisee, and the other a publican. The Pharisee stood and prayed thus with himself, God, I thank thee, that I am not as other men are, extortioners, unjust, adulterers, or even as this publican. I fast twice in the week, I give tithes of all that I possess. And the publican, standing afar off, would not lift up so much as his eyes unto heaven, but smote upon his breast, saying, God be merciful to me a sinner. I tell you, this man went down to his house justified rather than the other: for every one that exalteth himself shall be abased; and he that humbleth himself shall be exalted.

John 2:23-25 Now when he was in Jerusalem at the passover, in the feast day, many believed in his name, when they saw the miracles which he did. But Jesus did not commit himself unto them, because he knew all men, And needed not that any should testify of man: for he knew what was in man.

Galatians 6:3 For if a man think himself to be something, when he is nothing, he deceiveth himself.

Revelation 2:20-23 Notwithstanding I have a few things against thee, because thou sufferest that woman Jezebel, which calleth herself a prophetess, to teach and to seduce my servants to commit fornication, and to eat things sacrificed unto idols. And I gave her space to repent of her fornication; and she repented not. Behold, I will cast her into a bed, and them that commit adultery with her into great tribulation, except they repent of their deeds. And I will kill her children with death; and all the churches shall know that I am he which searcheth the reins and hearts: and I will give unto every one of you according to your works.

Proverbs 21:3 To do justice and judgment *is* more acceptable to the LORD than sacrifice.

Focus: This proverb declares that God prefers righteous living (doing justice and judgment) to religious sacrifices.

Ideally, a line of righteous interaction is supposed to exist between men and also between men and God. This line can be pictured as a triangle whereby God is at the top, the individual man at one of the bottom points, and his "neighbor" at the other. The righteous interaction with God can be hindered or even severed when bad feelings, offenses, or mistreatment occur between people. This interaction can also be severed by sin directly against God. Because the treatment of others reflects the spiritual condition of a person's heart, a significant part of his being right with God is his being right with others.

"To do justice and judgment" means to do *acts of righteousness* involving other people, and both justice and judgment proceed from a foundational love for both God and man – not mere regard to the law.[533]

"To do justice" *is to do what is righteous* in business, law, or life. "Justice consists in giving to every one what is his due; practical conformity to the laws and principles of rightness in the dealings of men with each other; honesty; integrity in commerce and life; impartiality."[534]

"To do ... judgment" *is to make righteous judgments* between right and wrong, not only in court but also in daily life. Exercising judgmental discernment between good and evil *in order to determine righteousness* is necessary to keep the believer in agreement with God's idea of right. *(See also verse 15.)*

When the student of wisdom receives God's instruction so that he has learned "to do justice and judgment," he will have learned to think and reason and live in a manner that is favorable and pleasing to God, for he will have learned from Him.

Isaiah describes how the nation of Israel was highly disapproved of God, even though she made the required sacrifices.

Isaiah 59:14 And judgment is turned away backward, and justice standeth afar off: for truth is fallen in the street, and equity cannot enter.

"Judgment is turned away backward... the crying sin of perversion of justice is admitted with much amplification.
  (1) Right judgment is exactly inverted, the innocent are condemned, the guilty acquitted.
  (2) Justice standeth afar off, too far off to be able to hear those who make appeal to it.
  (3) Truth is fallen in the street; *i.e.,* false witness prevails over true in the courts of justice.
  (4) Equity cannot enter, is not admitted inside the courts, but waits without."[535]

Old Testament **"sacrifices"** were the Mosaic law's acts of obedience toward God. Animal sacrifices given under the law of Moses were instituted by God, were expected to be offered to Him, and were acceptable to Him, *if* done under proper conditions. Sin offerings were expected to be given with a contrite heart and a submission of the person's will to God. *The sin had to be put away with the sacrifice.* No meat offering would be acceptable to God without the offerer's love for his neighbor. Acts of injustice, unmerciful behavior, and arrogance voided any sacrifice regardless of the value or size. (Micah 6:6-8)

Micah 6:6-8 Wherewith shall I come before the LORD, and bow myself before the high God? shall I come before him with burnt offerings, with calves of a year old? Will the LORD be pleased with thousands of rams, or with ten thousands of rivers of oil?

shall I give my firstborn for my transgression, the fruit of my body for the sin of my soul? He hath shewed thee, O man, what is good; and what doth the LORD require of thee, but to do justly, and to love mercy, and to walk humbly with thy God?

Matthew 5:21-24 Ye have heard that it was said by them of old time, Thou shalt not kill; and whosoever shall kill shall be in danger of the judgment: But I say unto you, That whosoever is angry with his brother without a cause shall be in danger of the judgment: and whosoever shall say to his brother, Raca, shall be in danger of the council: but whosoever shall say, Thou fool, shall be in danger of hell fire. Therefore if thou bring thy gift to the altar, and there rememberest that thy brother hath ought against thee; Leave there thy gift before the altar, and go thy way; first be reconciled to thy brother, and then come and offer thy gift.

To desire to do right concerning other people and to follow through with "justice and judgment" is honorable with God; contrariwise, simply going through the motion of making a heartless sacrifice is unacceptable even though done ceremoniously for God. In order **"[to] do justice,"** a person must know how to live among others *in accordance to the expectations of God.*

With no conscience, no regard for God, and no respect for others, unjust men could easily participate ceremoniously in the **"sacrifice"** of animals. Unrighteous Jews simply performed the *formality* of offering expensive personal property (bulls, lambs) as required by the law, but the Lord expressed His detest for this hypocrisy. However, when the sacrifice was performed with a sincere heartfelt desire to please God, it was acceptable and honored. Scriptures make it clear that, to God, participating in the sacrificial system was no substitute for ***doing justice and judgment*** (righteously interacting with others). It is impossible to please God and have improper acts and attitudes toward others.

The superiority of moral obedience over ceremonial worship is often taught in Scripture.[536]

Psalm 51:16-17 For thou desirest not sacrifice; else would I give it: thou delightest not in burnt offering. The sacrifices of God are a broken spirit: a broken and a contrite heart, O God, thou wilt not despise.

Proverbs 15:8 The sacrifice of the wicked is an abomination to the LORD: but the prayer of the upright is his delight.

Hosea 6:6 For I desired mercy, and not sacrifice; and the knowledge of God more than burnt offerings.

Hosea 12:6 Therefore turn thou to thy God: keep mercy and judgment, and wait on thy God continually.

Amos 5:21-24 I hate, I despise your feast days, and I will not smell in your solemn assemblies. Though ye offer me burnt offerings and your meat offerings, I will not accept them: neither will I regard the peace offerings of your fat beasts. Take thou away from me the noise of thy songs; for I will not hear the melody of thy viols. But let judgment run down as waters, and righteousness as a mighty stream.

Micah 6:6-8 *[See above.]*

Matthew 9:13 But go ye and learn what that meaneth, I will have mercy, and not sacrifice: for I am not come to call the righteous, but sinners to repentance.

Matthew 23:23 Woe unto you, scribes and Pharisees, hypocrites! for ye pay tithe of mint and anise and cummin, and have omitted the weightier matters of the law, judgment, mercy, and faith: these ought ye to have done, and not to leave the other undone.

Jesus' conversation with a scribe reveals God's value for daily righteous living and the love of one's neighbor. Verses 32-34 shows that "... a proper understanding of the Old Testament, of its laws and requirements, would prepare the mind for Christianity, and suit a person at once to embrace it when presented."[537]

Mark 12:32-34 And the scribe said unto him, Well, Master, thou hast said the truth: for there is one God; and there is none other but he: And to love him with all the heart, and with all the understanding, and with all the soul, and with all the strength, and to love *his* neighbour as himself, is more than all whole burnt offerings and sacrifices. And when Jesus saw that he answered discreetly, he said unto him, Thou art not far from the kingdom of God. And no man after that durst ask him *any question.*

Proverbs 21:4 An high look, and a proud heart, *and* the plowing of the wicked, *is* sin.

Focus: This proverb declares that everything about a wicked person opposes God.

"An high look" is a snapshot, an instantaneous observation of an arrogant person. It can be seen at a glance and is unmistakable. This look expresses the reprehensible attitude of a **"proud heart"** and informs the observer that this individual believes himself so important that the world revolves around him. Such a look makes a nonverbal yet very loud statement that the person mistakenly concludes that he is fully self-contained, with no need of any other person and with no regard for God. It is a look of superiority setting every individual on alert that to come too close is to encounter hatefulness and self-preservation.

"The proud man by his pride proclaims his moral blindness – his high look is a sure indication that the light within him is darkness – that he has never seen himself as he really is. Hence it follows that he is wrong at the very core and center of his moral being; where pride holds her throne there is no room for God, there is no confession of sin, and no yielding to Divine guidance."[538]

> Psalm 131:1 A Song of degrees of David. LORD, my heart is not haughty, nor mine eyes lofty: neither do I exercise myself in great matters, or in things too high for me.
> Proverbs 6:16-19 These six things doth the LORD hate: yea, seven are an abomination unto him: A proud look, a lying tongue, and hands that shed innocent blood, An heart that deviseth wicked imaginations, feet that be swift in running to mischief, A false witness that speaketh lies, and he that soweth discord among brethren.
> Proverbs 30:13 There is a generation, O how lofty are their eyes! and their eyelids are lifted up.

"The plowing of the wicked" is a phrase that symbolizes *all* of the work of the wicked. At the time of the writing of Proverbs, Israel was primarily an agricultural society. Though there were other trades, husbandry was the primary source of making a living.

> "The man, who plows the soil, acknowledging God in his work, and seeking his strength and blessing – does it acceptably to the glory of God.' It is essentially a religious action. But the wicked, who does the same work without any regard to God – for want of a godly end, his plowing is sin. His idleness is sin against a plain command. (2Thessalonians 3:10) His industry is the sin of ungodliness, putting God out of his own world. The substance of his act is good. But the corrupt principle defiles the very best actions. (Titus 1:15)"[539]

> "While a man's pride keeps him at a moral distance from God, no matter how successful he may be, the taint and curse of unpardoned guilt is upon all his gains and possessions."[540]

> Job 4:8 Even as I have seen, they that plow iniquity, and sow wickedness, reap the same.
> Proverbs 15:8 The sacrifice of the wicked is an abomination to the LORD: but the prayer of the upright is his delight.
> *[See also Isaiah 10:12-13.]*

There is no doubt that everything a wicked person is, and everything he does is sin. He had rather sin than make the sin offering referred to in the previous verse. "Sin is the pride, the ambition, the glory and joy, and the business of wicked men."[541] "In short, the whole husbandry of the godless, or the whole of the field cultivated by them, with all that grows thereon, is sin."[542]

> "Even their civil or natural actions, which in themselves are lawful and good, are made sinful, as they are managed by ungodly men, without any regard to the glory of God, which ought to be the end of all our actions; *is sin* – Is by them turned into sin, and made the occasion of much wickedness."[543]

Proverbs 21:5 The thoughts of the diligent *tend* only to plenteousness; but of every one *that is* hasty only to want.

Focus: This proverb contrasts the different results of the *thoughtfully diligent* with those who are *thoughtlessly hasty*.

"The thoughts of the diligent *tend* only to plenteousness." "The thoughts of the diligent" are driven by a desire to reach a correct solution for whatever situation presents itself. Webster defines **"diligent"** as "steady in application to business, constant in effort or exertion to accomplish what is undertaken, industrious, not idle or negligent."[544] The diligent employ this method of thinking because *the person has trained himself to slow down and get things right and to act on established priorities*. Meditative thinking must come *before* acting in order to be effective. For the believer, thinking a matter through rather than racing to a premature conclusion includes praying, gathering all the facts, considering all the alternatives, receiving opinions and advice from others, and just meditating on the matter for awhile. Thinking a matter through is as important as diligently doing the work. If a matter is properly considered and the person is convinced that he is right in the approach and confident of success, he can diligently work the project all the way to completion. Because a diligent person acts as described above, he is typically successful in obtaining God's help, overcoming obstacles, and operating to completion; thus **"the thoughts of the diligent *tend* only to plenteousness."** Those **"thoughts"** *(that create plans)* lead to gains. A person can either plan his work and work his plan OR aim at nothing and hit nothing.

Even though a **"diligent"** person is *eager and determined* to take on the task at hand, he is not **"hasty."** Hasty persons "are rash and inconsiderate in their affairs, and will not take time to think, ... are greedy of gain, by right or wrong, and make haste to be rich by unjust practices or unwise projects."[545]

"The thoughts... of every one *that is* hasty...[tend] only to want *[poverty, need]*." (The idea written in the first part of this proverb is understood in the second part.) The hasty person is likely to have two prominent and destructive characteristics: he goes into action before getting adequate information and fails to wait for God's peace before advancing. His projects become patchwork and sooner or later have to be redone or left incomplete and poorly done. His actions are but 'beating the air.'"[546]

"**Plenteousness**" versus "**want**" – the implication in this proverb is that the outcome of *thoughtful diligence* produces a surplus of finances while *thoughtless haste* produces loss of wealth. Furthermore, the uses of "diligent" and "diligence" in the Book of Proverbs point to the fact that most diligent men will be prosperous and well-respected leaders.

> Proverbs 10:4 He becometh poor that dealeth with a slack hand: but the hand of the diligent maketh rich.
> Proverbs 12:24 The hand of the diligent shall bear rule: but the slothful shall be under tribute.
> Proverbs 13:4 The soul of the sluggard desireth, and hath nothing: but the soul of the diligent shall be made fat.
> Proverbs 22:29 Seest thou a man diligent in his business? he shall stand before kings; he shall not stand before mean men.

Notice that in Proverbs 10:4 and 13:4 that "diligent" is contrasted with laziness, whereas this verse contrasts **"diligent"** with **"hasty"** adding a new dimension of meaning to the word – **"but of every one that is hasty only to want."** If a person is "diligent," he will not be lazy or hasty.

Proverbs 21:6   The getting of treasures by a lying tongue *is* a vanity tossed to and fro of them that seek death.

Focus: This proverb warns of the emptiness, uncertainty, and danger of lying to obtain wealth.

Driven by an evil mind, **"a lying tongue"** lodges in the mouth of a person who wants riches so much that he is willing to twist the truth in a business agreement, bear false witness in a courtroom, or lie anywhere he has opportunity for gain.

"A vanity *[vapor, breath, figuratively something transitory and unsatisfactory]* **tossed to and fro of them that seek death"** is a profound description of the activities of a person seeking ill-gotten gain through nefarious means. Such ill-gotten gains are as unstable and unpredictable as randomly blown smoke from a chimney. Both the liar and his wealth are likely to be deposited into the hands of destruction and death. "Their own sin is the seed of destruction,"[547] and any riches gained by falsehood will eventually become a trap. 1 Timothy 6:9 warns, "But they that will be rich fall into temptation and a snare, and into many foolish and hurtful lusts, which drown men in destruction and perdition."

> Proverbs 8:10-11 Receive my instruction, and not silver; and knowledge rather than choice gold. For wisdom *is* better than rubies; and all the things that may be desired are not to be compared to it.
> Proverbs 10:2 Treasures of wickedness profit nothing: but righteousness delivereth from death.
> Proverbs 13:11 Wealth *gotten* by vanity shall be diminished: but he that gathereth by labour shall increase.
> Proverbs 20:17 Bread of deceit *is* sweet to a man; but afterwards his mouth shall be filled with gravel.
> Proverbs 23:4 Labour not to be rich: cease from thine own wisdom.
> Proverbs 23:5 Wilt thou set thine eyes upon that which is not? for *riches* certainly make themselves wings; they fly away as an eagle toward heaven.

Proverbs 21:7   The robbery of the wicked shall destroy them; because they refuse to do judgment.

Focus: This proverb declares why wicked robbers have a built-in source of destruction.

The previous verse refers to robbery by deceit; this verse speaks of robbery by violence. **"Robbery"** is a violent act of aggression that includes injustice and oppression enacted against another. When the thief commits robbery, his innocent victims lose money and valuable goods and potentially their physical health, peace of mind, and emotional stability.

Not only does robbery affect the victim, but such action also leads to the destruction of the perpetrator. **"Because they refuse to do judgment,"** *[to do right by discerning right or good from wrong or evil]* they will eventually be destroyed, either through the government's legal system, through a reactive victim, or directly through God's judgment. "*Those that refuse to do justice will choose to do wrong.*"[548] Unbeknown to themselves, they write their own bill of indictment and proceed to *destruction*.

> Psalm 9:15 The heathen are sunk down in the pit *that* they made: in the net which they hid is their own foot taken.
> Proverbs 1:18-19 And they lay wait for their *own* blood; they lurk privily for their *own* lives. So *are* the ways of every one that is greedy of gain; *which* taketh away the life of the owners thereof.

Proverbs 1:24-31 Because I have called, and ye refused; I have stretched out my hand, and no man regarded; But ye have set at nought all my counsel, and would none of my reproof: I also will laugh at your calamity; I will mock when your fear cometh; When your fear cometh as desolation, and your destruction cometh as a whirlwind; when distress and anguish cometh upon you. Then shall they call upon me, but I will not answer; they shall seek me early, but they shall not find me: For that they hated knowledge, and did not choose the fear of the LORD: They would none of my counsel: they despised all my reproof. Therefore shall they eat of the fruit of their own way, and be filled with their own devices.

Proverbs 21:6 The getting of treasures by a lying tongue *is* a vanity tossed to and fro of them that seek death.

Romans 2:6-7 Who will render to every man according to his deeds: To them who by patient continuance in well doing seek for glory and honour and immortality, eternal life:

Galatians 6:7-8 Be not deceived; God is not mocked: for whatsoever a man soweth, that shall he also reap. For he that soweth to his flesh shall of the flesh reap corruption; but he that soweth to the Spirit shall of the Spirit reap life everlasting.

Proverbs 21:8   The way of man *is* froward and strange: but *as for* the pure, his work *is* right.

Focus: This proverb provides God's view of both the sinful man's way of living and the righteous man's way of living.

Adam and Eve were created innocent *of evil*, knowing only good; consequently, they acted in a **"pure"** *[clean, righteous]* manner that was pleasing to God and exhibited love for their Creator. When they yielded to Satan and sinned, their purity and innocence was lost; thus, establishing the **"way of man"** *[moral character, manner, course of life]* that is **"froward and strange"** to God. The Hebrew definition qualifies the **"froward"** as *perverse and crooked,* and the fallen man as **"strange** *[guilty, burdened with guilt, criminal]***."** Since the fall of Adam, the natural or unbelieving man has followed his own way *away from God,* and only when spiritually regenerated will he be **"pure"** and **"right."**

"Evil men have evil ways. If the man be *froward,* his way also is *strange;* and this is the way of most men, such is the general corruption of mankind. *They have all gone aside* (Psalm 14:2,3); all flesh have perverted their way. But the froward man, the man of deceit, that acts by craft and trick in all he does, his way is strange, contrary to all the rules of honour and honesty ... It is strange, for it is alienated from all good and estranges men from God and his favour ...

Men that are pure are proved to be such by their work, for it *is right,* it is just and regular; and they are accepted of God and approved of men. The way of mankind in their apostasy is froward and strange; but as for the pure, those that by the grace of God are recovered out of that *(fallen)* state, of which there is here and there one, *their work is right,* as Noah's was in the old world."[549]

Genesis 7:1 And the LORD said unto Noah, Come thou and all thy house into the ark; for thee have I seen righteous before me in this generation.

Psalm 14:1-3 To the chief Musician, A Psalm of David. The fool hath said in his heart, There is no God. They are corrupt, they have done abominable works, there is none that doeth good. The LORD looked down from heaven upon the children of men, to see if there were any that did understand, *and* seek God. They are all gone aside, they are *all* together become filthy: *there is* none that doeth good, no, not one.

Proverbs 15:26 The thoughts of the wicked are an abomination to the LORD: but the words of the pure are pleasant words.

Proverbs 30:12 *There is* a generation *that are* pure in their own eyes, and *yet* is not washed from their filthiness.

Ecclesiastes 7:29 Lo, this only have I found, that God hath made man upright; but they have sought out many inventions.

Isaiah 53:6 All we like sheep have gone astray; we have turned every one to his own way; and the LORD hath laid on him the iniquity of us all.

Titus 1:15-16 Unto the pure all things are pure: but unto them that are defiled and unbelieving is nothing pure; but even their mind and conscience is defiled. They profess that they know God; but in works they deny him, being abominable, and disobedient, and unto every good work reprobate.

Titus 3:3-7 For we ourselves also were sometimes foolish, disobedient, deceived, serving divers lusts and pleasures, living in malice and envy, hateful, and hating one another. But after that the kindness and love of God our Saviour toward man appeared, Not by works of righteousness which we have done, but according to his mercy he saved us, by the washing of regeneration, and renewing of the Holy Ghost; Which he shed on us abundantly through Jesus Christ our Saviour; That being justified by his grace, we should be made heirs according to the hope of eternal life.

[See also 1 Corinthians 6:9-11; Ephesians 2:1-3; 4:17-18; 24-25.]

In verses nine through nineteen, the Bible continues to contrast the righteous and the wicked. Certain verses indicate that, for the sake of peace in the believer's life, some people should be *marked as ungodly examples*, and some should even be *avoided if possible*.

> **Proverbs 21:9** *It is* better to dwell in a corner of the housetop, than with a brawling woman in a wide house.

Focus: This proverb expresses the misery that a brawling woman can cause.

"*It is* better to dwell in a corner of the housetop." Homes in Israel (and in any other country) have the potential for peace and an enjoyable marriage when both husband and wife are focused on pleasing God. Jewish families were expected to submit to God's doctrine on wise living, but obviously, from this verse, both husband and wife did not always do so.

In Solomon's days, houses were built with a flat roof, and protection from falling off was provided by building a battlement (wall) around the top perimeter. This roof was open to the sun and rain, but people would go up for different reasons, including retirement for the day while taking in the evening beauty, or perhaps to sleep, study, meditate, or pray – but in this case, to escape strife from a hostile spouse. On such a rooftop, against the safety wall the Shunammite woman and her husband provided a room for Elisha on the occasions that he passed that way. "Let us make a little chamber, I pray thee, on the wall; and let us set for him there a bed, and a table, and a stool, and a candlestick: and it shall be, when he cometh to us, that he shall turn in thither." (2 Kings 4:10)

"Than with a brawling woman in a wide house." **"A wide** *[company, society]* **house"** is specifically a house large enough to accommodate more than one family, making the escape to "a corner of the housetop," an even greater sacrifice than such an escape would have been from a normal-sized home. Exchanging comfortable spacious rooms with human fellowship for a small corner of isolation (not mentioning having to deal with the weather elements) speaks of just how dire was the situation. However, such action is certainly a desirable alternative to contending with **"a brawling woman."** **"Brawling"** describes her as being contentious and causing strife by which she relentlessly drives out peace *and her husband*.

> Proverbs 19:13 A foolish son is the calamity of his father: and the contentions of a wife are a continual dropping.
> Proverbs 12:4 A virtuous woman is a crown to her husband: but she that maketh ashamed is as rottenness in his bones.
> Proverbs 25:24 It is better to dwell in the corner of the housetop, than with a brawling woman and in a wide house. *[Same as Proverbs 21:9.]*
> Proverbs 27:15-16 A continual dropping in a very rainy day and a contentious woman are alike. Whosoever hideth her hideth the wind, and the ointment of his right hand, which bewrayeth itself.
> Proverbs 15:16-17 Better is little with the fear of the LORD than great treasure and trouble therewith. Better is a dinner of herbs where love is, than a stalled ox and hatred therewith.
> Proverbs 17:1 Better is a dry morsel, and quietness therewith, than an house full of sacrifices with strife.

> **Proverbs 21:10** The soul of the wicked desireth evil: his neighbour findeth no favour in his eyes.

Focus: This proverb expresses where evil originates within a wicked man and where it reaches.

"The soul of the wicked desireth evil." The Apostle Paul stated that when he did wrong, he hated that he had allowed himself to consent to do so – but this despising of one's evil doings does not happen within the heart of an evil person. Instead, **"the wicked"** *[who are bad, hostile to God, guilty of sin against man and God]* desire deep down in their souls to do evil. They are the *"lawless ones."*[550] Their desire for evil permeates their souls, which produce all their thoughts and feelings and driving desires. Evil motivates them and nothing gives them more delight than to be wicked like their father, the Devil.

> ". . .self to *the wicked* is both his god and his object. Intent upon his own lust, not only his enemy, or a stranger, but even *his neighbor*, who might have a claim upon him, *findeth no favor in his eyes*. His charity does not extend beyond his own door (1 Samuel 25:11). No one is regarded, who stands in the way of his own interest. Friend and brother must give place to selfish gratification."[551]
> 1 Samuel 25: 11 Shall I then take my bread, and my water, and my flesh that I have killed for my shearers, and give *it* unto men, whom I know not whence they *be?*

"**His neighbour** *[associate, more or less close]* **findeth no favour in his eyes.**" The wicked man has no concern or regard for others and especially no love for anyone beyond his personal family – *if* in fact, he has any affection for his own family. He is a hateful character and the extreme opposite of the believer who detests evil, loves his neighbors and his enemies, and prefers the welfare of others before himself. "The wicked" are hostile people and cannot show others **"favour"** *[graciousness, pity, consideration, mercy]*.

> Psalm 36:1-4 To the chief Musician, A Psalm of David the servant of the LORD. The transgression of the wicked saith within my heart, that there is no fear of God before his eyes. For he flattereth himself in his own eyes, until his iniquity be found to be hateful. The words of his mouth are iniquity and deceit: he hath left off to be wise, and to do good. He deviseth mischief upon his bed; he setteth himself in a way that is not good; he abhorreth not evil.
>
> Proverbs 4:16 For they sleep not, except they have done mischief; and their sleep is taken away, unless they cause *some* to fall.
>
> Proverbs 10:23 *It is* as sport to a fool to do mischief: but a man of understanding hath wisdom.
>
> Proverbs 12:10 A righteous *man* regardeth the life of his beast: but the tender mercies of the wicked *are* cruel.
>
> Proverbs 13:19 The desire accomplished is sweet to the soul: but *it is* abomination to fools to depart from evil.
>
> Isaiah 32:6-7 For the vile person will speak villany, and his heart will work iniquity, to practise hypocrisy, and to utter error against the LORD, to make empty the soul of the hungry, and he will cause the drink of the thirsty to fail. The instruments also of the churl are evil: he deviseth wicked devices to destroy the poor with lying words, even when the needy speaketh right.

Proverbs 21:11 When the scorner is punished, the simple is made wise: and when the wise is instructed, he receiveth knowledge.

Focus: This proverb contrasts the difficulty it takes for the simple to learn with the ease with which the wise learn.

"When the scorner is punished, the simple is made wise." The **"scorner"** mocks believers, and he blasphemes God. He verbally belches out hate with derision hoping to attract others, especially simple ones, to his foolish way of thinking. Having rejected the teachings of God, **"a scorner"** becomes increasingly hardened, froward, hateful, and bravely vocal. *When he is punished* indirectly by the actions of God or directly by civil authorities, **"the simple is made wise;"** not because they receive the instruction of words, but because they witness the infliction of pain and do not want the same for themselves. The **"simple"** are untaught, naive, and easily persuaded to believe false doctrine or go with the wrong crowd; but when they see others suffer and realize that they could be punished next, they accept the correction as though it were personal.

The learning process of the wise person is opposite that of the simple. Because he is willing to be taught, the wise man uses every opportunity as a learning experience to increase his understanding. Speak to the wise man, and he will hear. He will take hold of knowledge and become wiser. *"When the wise is instructed"* by other wise persons or directly by the word of God or by overhearing a conversation or even by observation, he **"receiveth knowledge."**

The same thought of this proverb is also given in Proverbs 19:25 – "Smite a scorner, and the simple will beware: and reprove one that hath understanding, and he will understand knowledge."

> Proverbs 9:12 If thou be wise, thou shalt be wise for thyself: but if thou scornest, thou alone shalt bear it.
>
> Proverbs 13:1 A wise son heareth his father's instruction: but a scorner heareth not rebuke.
>
> Proverbs 14:6 A scorner seeketh wisdom, and findeth it not: but knowledge is easy unto him that understandeth.
>
> Proverbs 19:29 Judgments are prepared for scorners, and stripes for the back of fools.
>
> Proverbs 21:24 Proud and haughty scorner is his name, who dealeth in proud wrath.
>
> Proverbs 24:9 The thought of foolishness is sin: and the scorner is an abomination to men.

Proverbs 21:12 The righteous *man* wisely considereth the house of the wicked: *but God* overthroweth the wicked for *their* wickedness.

Focus: This proverb declares that a wise, righteous person cautiously ponders the wicked's house, while knowing that such an evil person is under the judgment of God.

The righteous man wisely considers the house of the wicked. Righteous people know through Scripture, that the wicked are already under God's judgment and that they will eventually face Him for their unjust deeds. Without any desire for his ill-gotten gain, the righteous person peers right through the glow and glistening of the evil man's things and visualizes the throne room of God, where the wicked man stands speechless and condemned for his horrible deeds. Thus, he considers the man's lack of relationship with God and not his riches.

"God overthroweth the wicked for their wickedness." Riches, houses, and anything else gained by wicked actions are always accompanied by trouble; so much so that the first chapter of Proverbs warns the young man to stay away from wicked peers whose acts of evil are a pathway to the judgment of God. Job and John state that the wicked are already condemned.

> Job 27:13-23 This is the portion of a wicked man with God, and the heritage of oppressors, which they shall receive of the Almighty. If his children be multiplied, it is for the sword: and his offspring shall not be satisfied with bread. Those that remain of him shall be buried in death: and his widows shall not weep. Though he heap up silver as the dust, and prepare raiment as the clay; He may prepare it, but the just shall put it on, and the innocent shall divide the silver. He buildeth his house as a moth, and as a booth that the keeper maketh. The rich man shall lie down, but he shall not be gathered: he openeth his eyes, and he is not. Terrors take hold on him as waters, a tempest stealeth him away in the night. The east wind carrieth him away, and he departeth: and as a storm hurleth him out of his place. For God shall cast upon him, and not spare: he would fain flee out of his hand. Men shall clap their hands at him, and shall hiss him out of his place.
>
> John 3:17-19 For God sent not his Son into the world to condemn the world; but that the world through him might be saved. He that believeth on him is not condemned: but he that believeth not is condemned already, because he hath not believed in the name of the only begotten Son of God. And this is the condemnation, that light is come into the world, and men loved darkness rather than light, because their deeds were evil.

Other Scriptures confirm the sinner's doom including the following:

> Job 18:5; 14-18 Yea, the light of the wicked shall be put out, and the spark of his fire shall not shine. His confidence shall be rooted out of his tabernacle, and it shall bring him to the king of terrors. It shall dwell in his tabernacle, because it is none of his: brimstone shall be scattered upon his habitation. His roots shall be dried up beneath, and above shall his branch be cut off. His remembrance shall perish from the earth, and he shall have no name in the street. He shall be driven from light into darkness, and chased out of the world.
>
> Psalm 37:35-36 I have seen the wicked in great power, and spreading himself like a green bay tree. Yet he passed away, and, lo, he was not: yea, I sought him, but he could not be found. *[See also Job 8:13-15; 21:28-30.]*
>
> Proverbs 3:33 The curse of the LORD is in the house of the wicked: but he blesseth the habitation of the just.
>
> Proverbs 1:16-19 For their feet run to evil, and make haste to shed blood. Surely in vain the net is spread in the sight of any bird. And they lay wait for their *own* blood; they lurk privily for their *own* lives. So *are* the ways of every one that is greedy of gain; *which* taketh away the life of the owners thereof.
>
> Proverbs 11:3-7 The integrity of the upright shall guide them: but the perverseness of transgressors shall destroy them. Riches profit not in the day of wrath: but righteousness delivereth from death. The righteousness of the perfect shall direct his way: but the wicked shall fall by his own wickedness. The righteousness of the upright shall deliver them: but transgressors shall be taken in *their own* naughtiness. When a wicked man dieth, *his* expectation shall perish: and the hope of unjust *men* perisheth.
>
> Proverbs 13:6 Righteousness keepeth him that is upright in the way: but wickedness overthroweth the sinner.
>
> Proverbs 14:11 The house of the wicked shall be overthrown: but the tabernacle of the upright shall flourish.
>
> Proverbs 15:27 He that is greedy of gain troubleth his own house; but he that hateth gifts shall live.
>
> Proverbs 21:15 It is joy to the just to do judgment: but destruction shall be to the workers of iniquity.

Proverbs 21:13 Whoso stoppeth his ears at the cry of the poor, he also shall cry himself, but shall not be heard.

Focus: This proverb warns of retribution for those insensitive to the cry of the poor.

"Whoso stoppeth his ears at the cry of the poor." Beginning very early in the Scriptures, God showed His concern for the poor and commanded believers to come to their aid. The **"poor"** person is not just one who lacks money. He may be in the category of the feeble, weak, or helpless, such as, the widow, orphan, stranger in the land, and servant or hired laborer. The **"cry of the poor"** is a cry of distress, and such pleading for help brings to memory the cries of the children of Israel as they were under bondage to Pharaoh.

> Exodus 2:23-24 And it came to pass in process of time, that the king of Egypt died: and the children of Israel sighed by reason of the bondage, and they cried, and their cry came up unto God by reason of the bondage. And God heard their groaning, and God remembered his covenant with Abraham, with Isaac, and with Jacob.

Stopping up one's ears is a phrase that implies not only a lack of sensitivity and compassion for the poor but also strong resistance to obeying the word of God.

> Deuteronomy 15:7-11 If there be among you a poor man of one of thy brethren within any of thy gates in thy land which the LORD thy God giveth thee, thou shalt not harden thine heart, nor shut thine hand from thy poor brother: But thou shalt open thine hand wide unto him, and shalt surely lend him sufficient for his need, in that which he wanteth. Beware that there be not a thought in thy wicked heart, saying, The seventh year, the year of release, is at hand; and thine eye be evil against thy poor brother, and thou givest him nought; and he cry unto the LORD against thee, and it be sin unto thee. Thou shalt surely give him, and thine heart shall not be grieved when thou givest unto him: because that for this thing the LORD thy God shall bless thee in all thy works, and in all that thou puttest thine hand unto. For the poor shall never cease out of the land: therefore I command thee, saying, Thou shalt open thine hand wide unto thy brother, to thy poor, and to thy needy, in thy land.

According to 1 John 3:17, a person's lack of compassion brings into serious question his love for God: "But whoso hath this world's good, and seeth his brother have need, and shutteth up his bowels *of compassion* from him, how dwelleth the love of God in him?" The same measure that the hard-hearted man meted out to the poor will be meted unto him in his time of need. "Give, and it shall be given unto you; good measure, pressed down, and shaken together, and running over, shall men give into your bosom. For with the same measure that ye mete withal it shall be measured to you again." (Luke 6:38)

Notice the blessing God gives to those that are sensitive and help the poor in Proverbs 28:27 – "He that giveth unto the poor shall not lack: but he that hideth his eyes shall have many a curse." In addition, ignoring the need of the poor is wickedness. Proverbs 29:7 states, "The righteous considereth the cause of the poor: *but* the wicked regardeth not to know *it*."

"He also shall cry himself, but shall not be heard." This man who will not listen to the cry of the poor will eventually need God's help only to discover it is not available. *(See Scriptures below.)*

> "And now, as the selfish hardness shows the man has no love to God, he will find no love from God. 'With the same measure that he meted withal, it shall be measured to him again.' Did he *stop his ears at the cry of the poor?* God will stop his ears against his cry. He that would not give a crumb on earth, was denied a drop of water in hell. 'He shall have judgment without mercy, that hath shewed no mercy' (James 2:13)."[552]

> Proverbs 19:17 He that hath pity upon the poor lendeth unto the LORD; and that which he hath given will he pay him again.

> Zechariah 7:9-14 Thus speaketh the LORD of hosts, saying, Execute true judgment, and shew mercy and compassions every man to his brother: And oppress not the widow, nor the fatherless, the stranger, nor the poor; and let none of you imagine evil against his brother in your heart. But they refused to hearken, and pulled away the shoulder, and stopped their ears, that they should not hear. Yea, they made their hearts as an adamant stone, lest they should hear the law, and the words which the LORD of hosts hath sent in his spirit by the former prophets: therefore came a great wrath from the LORD of hosts. Therefore it is come to pass, that as he cried, and they would not hear; so they cried, and I would not hear, saith the LORD of hosts: But I scattered them with a whirlwind among all the nations whom they knew not. Thus the land was desolate after them, that no man passed through nor returned: for they laid the pleasant land desolate.

> Matthew 25:41-46 Then shall he say also unto them on the left hand, Depart from me, ye cursed, into everlasting fire, prepared for the devil and his angels: For I was an hungred, and ye gave me no meat: I was thirsty, and ye gave me no drink: I was a stranger, and ye took me not in: naked, and ye clothed me not: sick, and in prison, and ye visited me not. Then shall they also answer him, saying, Lord, when saw we thee an hungred, or athirst, or a stranger, or naked, or sick, or in prison, and did not minister unto thee? Then shall he answer them, saying, Verily I say unto you, Inasmuch as ye did it not to one of the least of these, ye did it not to me. And these shall go away into everlasting punishment: but the righteous into life eternal.

> James 2:13-17 For he shall have judgment without mercy, that hath shewed no mercy; and mercy rejoiceth against judgment. What doth it profit, my brethren, though a man say he hath faith, and have not works? can faith save him? If a brother or sister be naked, and destitute of daily food, And one of you say unto them, Depart in peace, be ye warmed and filled; notwithstanding ye give them not those things which are needful to the body; what doth it profit? Even so faith, if it hath not works, is dead, being alone.

Proverbs 21:14 A gift in secret pacifieth anger: and a reward in the bosom strong wrath.

Focus: This proverb specifies the calming value of a properly bestowed gift.

The motive of a person's heart and the purpose whereby it is given determines whether the gift is wicked or worthy. Previous Scripture has shown that God condemns a gift or present used as a bribe to gain favor or pervert justice.

> Exodus 23:6-8 Thou shalt not wrest the judgment of thy poor in his cause. Keep thee far from a false matter; and the innocent and righteous slay thou not: for I will not justify the wicked. And thou shalt take no gift: for the gift blindeth the wise, and perverteth the words of the righteous.

Deuteronomy 16:19 Thou shalt not wrest judgment; thou shalt not respect persons, neither take a gift: for a gift doth blind the eyes of the wise, and pervert the words of the righteous.
Proverbs 17:23 A wicked man taketh a gift out of the bosom to pervert the ways of judgment.

"Gift in secret" in the first half of the verse and **"reward in the bosom"** in the second have the same meaning, thus emphasizing through repetition to the idea that this is not a gift given publicly. Many believers have observed that a gift given in secret to someone who is very angry at the giver will often assuage the anger of the offended; especially when the secret gift is given with a spirit of love and concern; and, if needed, a heartfelt apology. Giving the gift in secret makes it more acceptable. Gifts given openly often reek of the giver's ostentation which may unwittingly bring shame or contempt to the receiver.

Jacob's story exemplifies wisely-given gifts to appease anger. Although Jacob and Esau were twins, they competed for their father's blessing, which Jacob finagled away from Esau. Jacob consequently had to flee to Laban (brother of his mother, Rebekah and father of his brides-to-be Rachael and Leah). Later he gave gifts to his brother Esau (though not given in secret), believing that the valuable items would show goodwill and bring peace.

> Genesis 32:13-18 And he lodged there that same night; and took of that which came to his hand a present for Esau his brother; Two hundred she goats, and twenty he goats, two hundred ewes, and twenty rams, Thirty milch camels with their colts, forty kine, and ten bulls, twenty she asses, and ten foals. And he delivered them into the hand of his servants, every drove by themselves; and said unto his servants, Pass over before me, and put a space betwixt drove and drove. And he commanded the foremost, saying, When Esau my brother meeteth thee, and asketh thee, saying, Whose art thou? and whither goest thou? and whose are these before thee? Then thou shalt say, They be thy servant Jacob's; it is a present sent unto my lord Esau: and, behold, also he is behind us.

A second Old Testament example of a gift given to soothe anger is given in 1 Samuel 25. David sent some of his men to a very wealthy man named Nabal *[which means fool, dolt]* to ask for provisions to sustain his men while they were in the wilderness of Maon. Even though David's soldiers protected Nabal's flocks and herdsmen, and the soldier/messengers asked Nabal respectfully, Nabal spurned David's messengers. When the men returned and told David of their treatment, "David said unto his men, Gird ye on every man his sword. And they girded on every man his sword; and David also girded on his sword: and there went up after David about four hundred men; and two hundred abode by the stuff." (1 Samuel 25:13) Meanwhile, Nabal's wife Abigail ("a woman of good understanding, and of a beautiful countenance" –1 Samuel 25:3) heard of the danger her husband caused. She "made haste, and took two hundred loaves, and two bottles of wine, and five sheep ready dressed, and five measures of parched corn, and an hundred clusters of raisins, and two hundred cakes of figs, and laid them on asses. And she said unto her servants, Go on before me; behold, I come after you. But she told not her husband Nabal." (1 Samuel 25:18-19) Abigail gave David the gift of provisions and begged him to spare her and Nabal. So, David spared them and accepted her gift. The following day when Abigail told Nabal what she had done and how David had spared them, he went into shock. Ten days later, God smote Nabal and he died, and the wise Abigail then became David's wife.

Proverbs 21:15 *It is* joy to the just to do judgment: but destruction *shall be* to the workers of iniquity.

Focus: This proverb contrasts the reward of doing righteously with the penalty of doing wickedly.

***It is* joy to the just to do judgment."** Found in several other verses in the Old Testament, **"to do judgment"** means a right and godly opinion or course of action reached after discerning and consideration.[553] After determining what is right, the godly person will then do right. An understanding of "do judgment" can be enhanced by studying the verses below.

> Genesis 18:19 For I know him *[Abram]*, that he will command his children and his household after him, and they shall keep the way of the LORD, to do justice and judgment; that the LORD may bring upon Abraham that which he hath spoken of him.
> 1 Kings 3:28 And all Israel heard of the judgment which the king *[Solomon]* had judged; and they feared the king: for they saw that the wisdom of God *was* in him, to do judgment.
> 1 Kings 10:9 Blessed be the LORD thy God, which delighted in thee *[Solomon]*, to set thee on the throne of Israel: because the LORD loved Israel for ever, therefore made he thee king, to do judgment and justice.
> Proverbs 21:3 To do justice and judgment *is* more acceptable to the LORD than sacrifice.
> Proverbs 21:7 The robbery of the wicked shall destroy them; because they refuse to do judgment.

In Genesis 18 above, righteous Abram judged actions according to whether they were right or wrong in the sight of God. When he knew something was right, he taught his children to do that. His joy was to please God, and he did so by choosing to do right.

Because their conduct and character is to please the Lord, God's people, who are **"the just,"** count it *joy to do judgment.* "The righteous feel real pleasure in doing what is right; they have the answer of a good conscience and the feeling that they are, as far as they can, making God's will their will, and this brings deep comfort and stable joy."[554]

> Psalm 40:8 I delight to do thy will, O my God: yea, thy law is within my heart.
> Psalm 112:1-2 Praise ye the LORD. Blessed is the man that feareth the LORD, that delighteth greatly in his commandments. His seed shall be mighty upon earth: the generation of the upright shall be blessed.
> Psalm 119:16 I will delight myself in thy statutes: I will not forget thy word.
> Proverbs 10:29 The way of the LORD *is* strength to the upright: but destruction *shall be* to the workers of iniquity.
> Proverbs 12:20 Deceit *is* in the heart of them that imagine evil: but to the counsellors of peace *is* joy.
> Proverbs 29:6 In the transgression of an evil man *there is* a snare: but the righteous doth sing and rejoice.
> Ecclesiastes 3:12 I know that there is no good in them, but for a man to rejoice, and to do good in his life.
> Psalm 40:8 I delight to do thy will, O my God: yea, thy law is within my heart.
> Psalm 112:1-2 Praise ye the LORD. Blessed is the man that feareth the LORD, that delighteth greatly in his commandments. His seed shall be mighty upon earth: the generation of the upright shall be blessed.
> Psalm 119:16 I will delight myself in thy statutes: I will not forget thy word.
> Proverbs 10:29 The way of the LORD *is* strength to the upright: but destruction *shall be* to the workers of iniquity.
> Proverbs 12:20 Deceit *is* in the heart of them that imagine evil: but to the counsellors of peace *is* joy.
> Proverbs 29:6 In the transgression of an evil man *there is* a snare: but the righteous doth sing and rejoice.
> Ecclesiastes 3:12 I know that there is no good in them, but for a man to rejoice, and to do good in his life.

To have the wisdom to **"do judgment"** is exactly the meaning of what Solomon asked of God in 1 Kings 3:9 when he said, "Give therefore thy servant an understanding heart to judge thy people, that I may discern between good and bad: for who is able to judge this thy so great a people?"

"But destruction *shall be* to the workers of iniquity." In direct contrast to the attitude of doing right to bring "joy" to the righteous, the **"workers of iniquity"** rejoice to do wickedness. (Proverbs 2:12-15) The wicked choose to do whatever is necessary to satisfy their own greed no matter what wicked thing they have to do. The wicked do not care who they step on for personal advancement and they love themselves, not God. Proverbs 21:10 states – "The soul of the wicked desireth evil..." "They *(workers of iniquity)* cannot trust themselves to do rightly without fear; they cannot commit the result to God, as the righteous do; if ever they do act uprightly, it is against their inclination, and such action will, as they fear, bring them to ruin."[555]

> Proverbs 2:12-15 To deliver thee from the way of the evil *man,* from the man that speaketh froward things; Who leave the paths of uprightness, to walk in the ways of darkness; Who rejoice to do evil, *and* delight in the frowardness of the wicked; Whose ways *are* crooked, and *they* froward in their paths.
> Proverbs 4:16 For they sleep not, except they have done mischief; and their sleep is taken away, unless they cause some to fall.

"... They *(workers of iniquity)* **refuse** to do right and they will eventually be destroyed, either through the government's legal system, through a reactive victim, or directly through the judgment of God. Unbeknown to themselves, they write their own bill of indictment and proceed from there to ***destruction*** ..."[556] The wicked must have a feeling of the impending destruction that God will bring upon them because of their unrighteous acts. Proverbs 11:23 states, "The desire of the righteous *is* only good: *but* the expectation of the wicked *is* wrath." Because of their wickedness, they often face shame and punishment in this life, and their destruction is mentioned often in Scripture:

> Job 31:3 Is not destruction to the wicked? and a strange punishment to the workers of iniquity?
> Proverbs 10:28-29 The hope of the righteous *shall be* gladness: but the expectation of the wicked shall perish. The way of the LORD is strength to the upright: but destruction shall be to the workers of iniquity.
> Matthew 13:41-42 The Son of man shall send forth his angels, and they shall gather out of his kingdom all things that offend, and them which do iniquity; And shall cast them into a furnace of fire: there shall be wailing and gnashing of teeth.
> Luke 13:27-28 But he shall say, I tell you, I know you not whence ye are; depart from me, all ye workers of iniquity. There shall be weeping and gnashing of teeth, when ye shall see Abraham, and Isaac, and Jacob, and all the prophets, in the kingdom of God, and you yourselves thrust out.

Righteous people find satisfaction and joy when the courts administer proper justice, thereby setting the innocent free and properly charging the guilty. In contrast (because of their own evil thoughts and actions), wicked people feel "**destruction**" *[terror, dismay]* when the law is enforced, when wickedness is put down, and when they are forced into hiding because of their evil deeds. As Proverbs 28:1 emphasizes, they are always looking over their shoulder for punishment: "The wicked flee when no man pursueth . . ."

> **Proverbs 21:16** The man that wandereth out of the way of understanding shall remain in the congregation of the dead.

Focus: This proverb specifies the eternal destiny of those who turn away from God.

"Wandereth" means to *vacillate, stray, stagger*. A person who wanders has no attachments, so he goes here or there. The difference between a person who is rooted and attached to the word of God and one who wanders, having no root or attachment, is best described in Psalm 1. The wanderer likes to be with the ungodly, the sinners, and the scornful, having no sincere regard for the word of God. He is likened to the husk of grain, loose grasses, and dust particles that are blown away by the wind during the winnowing process.

> Psalm 1:3-4 And he shall be like a tree planted by the rivers of water, that bringeth forth his fruit in his season; his leaf also shall not wither; and whatsoever he doeth shall prosper. The ungodly *are* not so: but *are* like the chaff which the wind driveth away.

This **wanderer** who goes away from God will not be allowed to stand "in the judgment" with the righteous but will be eternally separated.

> Psalm 1:5-6 Therefore the ungodly shall not stand in the judgment, nor sinners in the congregation of the righteous. For the LORD knoweth the way of the righteous: but the way of the ungodly shall perish.

Because he is being specially cared for by the Master, the person who removes himself from evil influences, delights in the word of God, and meditates on it is said to be like a carefully-planted tree with solid roots, exceptional growth, and perpetual fruit-bearing.

> Psalm 1:3 And he shall be like a tree planted by the rivers of water, that bringeth forth his fruit in his season; his leaf also shall not wither; and whatsoever he doeth shall prosper.

"Way of understanding" is the path taken by the wise man who has the "fear of the LORD" and is trusting his life to God. Earlier in Proverbs appear the following parallel phrases: "the path of the just" (Proverbs 4:18), "the way of righteousness" (Proverbs 12:28), and "the way of life" (Proverbs 15:24), and in Psalm 1:6 "the way of the righteous." Synonyms for "way of understanding, these phrases describe the pathway for people who wisely walk with God. It is God's designated safe pathway where He accompanies, provides and teaches. Those who walk there share an overwhelming and demonstrative love for God, greatly admiring His word, His way, and His will–and He loves them.

However, the person who is the subject of this proverb is described as having wandered OUT OF the "way of understanding" and has thus chosen his own path disassociated with God. "He who forsakes the way of wisdom, the path of virtue, the religious life…thus becomes in proverbial language 'a fool' he shall remain *(rest, dwell)* in the congregation of the dead."[557] A person who becomes familiar with the "way of understanding" and then refuses the same, condemns himself. He is not losing a previous relationship with God, for he only tested and contemplated the same.

Jesus gave the parable of the sower to illustrate that when a crowd of people hear the word of God, there will be two reactions. Some will hear and obey the word, and some will **wander "out of the way of understanding."**

> Matthew 13:18-23 Hear ye therefore the parable of the sower. When any one heareth the word of the kingdom, and understandeth it not, then cometh the wicked one, and catcheth away that which was sown in his heart. This is he which received seed by the way side. But he that received the seed into stony places, the same is he that heareth the word, and anon with joy receiveth it; Yet hath he not root in himself, but dureth for a while: for when tribulation or persecution ariseth because of the word, by and by he is offended. He also that received seed among the thorns is he that heareth the word; and the care of this world, and the deceitfulness of riches, choke the word, and he becometh unfruitful. But he that received seed into the good ground is he that heareth the word, and understandeth it; which also beareth fruit, and bringeth forth, some an hundredfold, some sixty, some thirty.
> *[Also see Luke 8:5-18.]*

"Congregation of the dead" is the large company of the lost who are traveling their chosen path of separation from God. They are spiritually dead.

John 3:19-20 And this is the condemnation, that light is come into the world, and men loved darkness rather than light, because their deeds were evil. For every one that doeth evil hateth the light, neither cometh to the light, lest his deeds should be reproved.

The two paths, one leading to life and one leading to death, are illustrated in the Book of Proverbs through the two women, *Wisdom* and *Folly* (the adulteress). Individually, these women prepare a feast in their separate houses and invite guests. Wisdom offers abundant holy living, while the foolish adulteress offers temptation to evil.

Proverbs 9:1-6; 10-11 Wisdom hath builded her house, she hath hewn out her seven pillars: She hath killed her beasts; she hath mingled her wine; she hath also furnished her table. She hath sent forth her maidens: she crieth upon the highest places of the city, Whoso is simple, let him turn in hither: as for him that wanteth understanding, she saith to him, Come, eat of my bread, and drink of the wine which I have mingled. Forsake the foolish, and live; and go in the way of understanding...The fear of the LORD is the beginning of wisdom: and the knowledge of the holy is understanding. For by me thy days shall be multiplied, and the years of thy life shall be increased. If thou be wise, thou shalt be wise for thyself: but if thou scornest, thou alone shalt bear it.

Proverbs 9:13-18 A foolish woman is clamorous: she is simple, and knoweth nothing. For she sitteth at the door of her house, on a seat in the high places of the city, To call passengers who go right on their ways: Whoso is simple, let him turn in hither: and as for him that wanteth understanding, she saith to him, Stolen waters are sweet, and bread eaten in secret is pleasant. But he knoweth not that the dead are there; and that her guests are in the depths of hell.

God created man a free agent so that he can choose to either follow God or else go away from Him.

Psalm 119:10-12 With my whole heart have I sought thee: O let me not wander from thy commandments. Thy word have I hid in mine heart, that I might not sin against thee. Blessed art thou, O LORD: teach me thy statutes.

Proverbs 2:10-14 When wisdom entereth into thine heart, and knowledge is pleasant unto thy soul; Discretion shall preserve thee, understanding shall keep thee: To deliver thee from the way of the evil man, from the man that speaketh froward things; Who leave the paths of uprightness, to walk in the ways of darkness; Who rejoice to do evil, and delight in the frowardness of the wicked;

Ezekiel 18:23-24 Have I any pleasure at all that the wicked should die? saith the Lord GOD: and not that he should return from his ways, and live? But when the righteous turneth away from his righteousness, and committeth iniquity, and doeth according to all the abominations that the wicked man doeth, shall he live? All his righteousness that he hath done shall not be mentioned: in his trespass that he hath trespassed, and in his sin that he hath sinned, in them shall he die.

Hebrews 6:4-6; 9-10 For it is impossible for those who were once enlightened, and have tasted of the heavenly gift, and were made partakers of the Holy Ghost, And have tasted the good word of God, and the powers of the world to come, If they shall fall away, to renew them again unto repentance; seeing they crucify to themselves the Son of God afresh, and put him to an open shame . . . But, beloved, we are persuaded better things of you, and things that accompany salvation, though we thus speak. For God is not unrighteous to forget your work and labour of love, which ye have shewed toward his name, in that ye have ministered to the saints, and do minister.

Hebrews 10:38-39 Now the just shall live by faith: but if any man draw back, my soul shall have no pleasure in him. But we are not of them who draw back unto perdition; but of them that believe to the saving of the soul.

2 Peter 2:19-22 While they promise them liberty, they themselves are the servants of corruption: for of whom a man is overcome, of the same is he brought in bondage. For if after they have escaped the pollutions of the world through the knowledge of the Lord and Saviour Jesus Christ, they are again entangled therein, and overcome, the latter end is worse with them than the beginning. For it had been better for them not to have known the way of righteousness, than, after they have known it, to turn from the holy commandment delivered unto them. But it is happened unto them according to the true proverb, The dog is turned to his own vomit again; and the sow that was washed to her wallowing in the mire.

1 John 2:18-19 Little children, it is the last time: and as ye have heard that antichrist shall come, even now are there many antichrists; whereby we know that it is the last time. They went out from us, but they were not of us; for if they had been of us, they would no doubt have continued with us: but they went out, that they might be made manifest that they were not all of us.

Proverbs 21:17 He that loveth pleasure *shall be* a poor man: he that loveth wine and oil shall not be rich.

Focus: This proverb declares that love for pleasure and extravagant living robs a person of wealth (both spiritual and financial).

"He that loveth pleasure shall be a poor man." To **"love pleasure"** means to have such a strong and sincere affection for doing pleasurable activities that doing them becomes an obsession, a priority *while neglecting other, more important, proper, and productive responsibilities–especially spiritual ones.* There is certainly no Scriptural condemnation against having pleasure any more than there is to having money. It is the *love of* pleasure just as it is the *love of* money that causes problems. (1 Timothy 6:10)

One who *loves* pleasure **"shall be a poor man"** because the effects of his love for pleasure mimic those of an addiction, in that he becomes controlled by his desire. He would rather enjoy the things he finds pleasurable at the expense of fulfilling his other obligations, primarily those spiritual ones and then secondarily, financial. "He shall become 'a man of want.'"[558] Wise people make decisions based on the guiding principles of Scripture, wise counsel, and leadership from the Holy Spirit. They have an understanding of what is right and proper. Foolish people allow their emotions, such as appetite (or **"love"**) for pleasure, to drive their decisions, and the outcome is ultimately disastrous.

"He that loveth wine and oil shall not be rich." "Wine" and "oil" are representative terms for high, luxurious living since they were those expensive items that carried banquets to a high level of extravagance. As in the first clause of this proverb, the *love of* these pleasures (with an implied neglect of responsibilities) is the problem.

"Shall not be rich" is a phrase that relays the message of a *lack of accumulation*. Lusting after pleasure takes one away from God and is, at the same time, a hole in the pocket. A truly rich person is "rich toward God." *(See Luke 12:16-21 below)*

It can be said of every wise person that he or she lives a life that exemplifies a **love for God.** Having an uncontrolled love for pleasure or high living specifies that these ways of living have taken the place of love for God; and, as such, that addicted person is no longer enjoying the blessings and favor of God – he is not living wisely. The result of forsaking God and living foolishly is spiritual poverty and potentially financial poverty.

>Proverbs 21:20 There is treasure to be desired and oil in the dwelling of the wise; but the foolish man spendeth it up.
>
>Proverbs 23:20-21 Be not among winebibbers; among riotous eaters of flesh: For the drunkard and the glutton shall come to poverty: and drowsiness shall clothe a man with rags.
>
>Proverbs 29:3 Whoso loveth wisdom rejoiceth his father: but he that keepeth company with harlots spendeth *his* substance.
>
>Luke 12:16-21 And he spake a parable unto them, saying, The ground of a certain rich man brought forth plentifully: And he thought within himself, saying, What shall I do, because I have no room where to bestow my fruits? And he said, This will I do: I will pull down my barns, and build greater; and there will I bestow all my fruits and my goods. And I will say to my soul, Soul, thou hast much goods laid up for many years; take thine ease, eat, drink, *and* be merry. But God said unto him, *Thou* fool, this night thy soul shall be required of thee: then whose shall those things be, which thou hast provided? So *is* he that layeth up treasure for himself, and is not rich toward God.
>
>Luke 15:13-16 And not many days after the younger son gathered all together, and took his journey into a far country, and there wasted his substance with riotous living. And when he had spent all, there arose a mighty famine in that land; and he began to be in want. And he went and joined himself to a citizen of that country; and he sent him into his fields to feed swine. And he would fain have filled his belly with the husks that the swine did eat: and no man gave unto him.
>
>1 Timothy 5:5-6 Now she that is a widow indeed, and desolate, trusteth in God, and continueth in supplications and prayers night and day. But she that liveth in pleasure is dead while she liveth.
>
>1 Timothy 6:10 For the love of money is the root of all evil: which while some coveted after, they have erred from the faith, and pierced themselves through with many sorrows.
>
>2 Timothy 3:1-5 This know also, that in the last days perilous times shall come. For men shall be lovers of their own selves, covetous, boasters, proud, blasphemers, disobedient to parents, unthankful, unholy, Without natural affection, trucebreakers, false accusers, incontinent, fierce, despisers of those that are good, Traitors, heady, highminded, lovers of pleasures more than lovers of God; Having a form of godliness, but denying the power thereof: from such turn away.
>
>Hebrews 11:24-26 By faith Moses, when he was come to years, refused to be called the son of Pharaoh's daughter; Choosing rather to suffer affliction with the people of God, than to enjoy the pleasures of sin for a season; Esteeming the reproach of Christ greater riches than the treasures in Egypt: for he had respect unto the recompence of the reward.

Proverbs 21:18 The wicked *shall be* a ransom for the righteous, and the transgressor for the upright.

> Focus: This proverb declares that the wicked transgressor will come in the place of the righteous to receive their intended troubles.

"The wicked" in the first half of this verse and **"the transgressor"** in the second are equivalent. Likewise, **"the righteous"** and **"the upright"** are equivalent on each side of the proverb. Thus, it becomes apparent that the second part of the proverb echos the first for emphasis. "The wicked" and "the transgressor" are opposers of God, holiness, and also godly individuals. "The righteous" and "the upright" are the ones who love God and holiness.

"Ransom" here means to pay the *[price of a life]* by *coming in the place of.* A very similar verse, Proverbs 11:8, states: "The righteous is delivered out of trouble, and the wicked cometh in his stead." The Bible gives several illustrations of evil men taking the place of (or becoming a **"ransom"** for) the righteous in tribulation. One example is given in the Book of Esther, where Haman (Ahasuerus' trusted adviser) took the place of (became a **ransom** for Mordecai) on the gallows that Haman had prepared for Mordecai. An egotistical and ambitious man, Haman demanded that people bow to him as he passed – something that Mordecai, a devout Jew, could not do in good conscience. In a rage, Haman sought revenge by persuading the king to issue an edict that allowed the killing of all the Jews and seizing of their property. Like Proverbs 21:18, God's retributive judgment and overruling providence are remarkably illustrated. His wicked plot backfired on himself; the honors he designed for himself were heaped on the man whom he so scornfully hated. The gallows which he intended to hang Mordecai became that on which he was hanged himself.

> Psalm 7:14-16 Behold, he travaileth with iniquity, and hath conceived mischief, and brought forth falsehood. He made a pit, and digged it, and is fallen into the ditch *which* he made. His mischief shall return upon his own head, and his violent dealing shall come down upon his own pate.

Sometimes punishment of **"the transgressor,"** as in the case of Achan, is the means of averting calamity of the righteous. With God's supernatural help, the Israelites had easily taken the high-walled city of Jericho, but their soldiers were chased, and some killed, at the near-defenseless city of Ai. Joshua knew that the root cause of such a shameful happening was sin in the camp, and he knew God was angry and was punishing Israel because of an unknown transgression. After Joshua earnestly prayed to God to understand why the nation suffered defeat at Ai, God said to him, "Israel hath sinned, and they have also transgressed my covenant which I commanded them: for they have even taken of the accursed thing, and have also stolen, and dissembled also, and they have put it even among their own stuff." (Joshua 7:11)

God had previously commanded, "the city *[Jericho]* shall be accursed, even it, and all that are therein, to the LORD: only Rahab the harlot shall live, she and all that are with her in the house, because she hid the messengers that we sent. And ye, in any wise keep yourselves from the accursed thing, lest ye make yourselves accursed, when ye take of the accursed thing, and make the camp of Israel a curse, and trouble it." (Joshua 6:17-18) When Joshua cast lots among the families to discover the guilty party, Achan's guilt was made known by the lot. He confessed to taking the "accursed thing" in Joshua 7:21 – "a goodly Babylonish garment, and two hundred shekels of silver, and a wedge of gold of fifty shekels weight, then I coveted them, and took them; and, behold, they are hid in the earth in the midst of my tent, and the silver under it." Achan, **"the transgressor,"** and his family served as a **"ransom"** for the nation of Israel – *they died in the place of the nation.*

Isaiah describes how the nation of Israel is so precious in the sight of God that He would destroy wicked nations if need be to preserve Israel. Egypt and Ethiopia thus became a *ransom* for Israel. Isaiah writes:

> Isaiah 43:1-4 But now thus saith the LORD that created thee, O Jacob, and he that formed thee, O Israel, Fear not: for I have redeemed thee, I have called thee by thy name; thou art mine. When thou passest through the waters, I will be with thee; and through the rivers, they shall not overflow thee: when thou walkest through the fire, thou shalt not be burned; neither shall the flame kindle upon thee. For I am the LORD thy God, the Holy One of Israel, thy Saviour: I gave Egypt for thy ransom, Ethiopia and Seba for thee. Since thou wast precious in my sight, thou hast been honourable, and I have loved thee: therefore will I give men for thee, and people for thy life.

Proverbs 21:19 *It is* better to dwell in the wilderness, than with a contentious and an angry woman.

Focus: This proverb depicts the misery of living with a contentious and angry woman.

"It is better to dwell in the wilderness." As does verse 9, this verse pictures the misery of domestic dissension. Living alone in a desolate place is better than living with an aggressive, strife-seeking wife. Escape from such a woman to a wilderness exposes one to the potential misery of severe weather, attack from wild animals, and loneliness; yet, it is a place where the threat of verbal (and perhaps physical) altercation is not imminent. It is a place of peace. This **"contentious and an angry woman"** is ready and waiting for a fight, and she turns every comfort into bitterness. It is most difficult for the wise and the unwise to live under the same roof. By extension of the subject, to own a business together or to have any personal relationship is nearly impossible with a contentious partner.

> 2 Corinthians 6:14 Be ye not unequally yoked together with unbelievers: for what fellowship hath righteousness with unrighteousness? and what communion hath light with darkness?

A domineering, angry, contentious husband can also destroy the peace and comfort of home. Peter added one admonition to the husband.

> 1 Peter 3:7 Likewise, ye husbands, dwell with them according to knowledge, giving honour unto the wife, as unto the weaker vessel, and as being heirs together of the grace of life; that your prayers be not hindered.

As a major subject in the Bible (400 verses), peace is a characteristic of God and those who love God. A man who concludes that it is **better** to dwell in the wilderness (or in the corner of a roof), rather than in a comfortable home is obviously desperate for peace.

> Proverbs 3:17 Her ways *[wisdom] are* ways of pleasantness, and all her paths *are* peace.
> John 16:33 These things I have spoken unto you, that in me ye might have peace. In the world ye shall have tribulation: but be of good cheer; I have overcome the world.
> Romans 8:6 For to be carnally minded *is* death; but to be spiritually minded *is* life and peace.
> Romans 14:19 Let us therefore follow after the things which make for peace, and things wherewith one may edify another.
> 1 Corinthians 7:15 But if the unbelieving depart, let him depart. A brother or a sister is not under bondage in such *cases:* but God hath called us to peace.
> 1 Corinthians 14:33 For God is not *the author* of confusion, but of peace, as in all churches of the saints.
> 2 Corinthians 13:11 Finally, brethren, farewell. Be perfect, be of good comfort, be of one mind, live in peace; and the God of love and peace shall be with you.
> Colossians 3:15 And let the peace of God rule in your hearts, to the which also ye are called in one body; and be ye thankful.

Proverbs 21:20 *There is* treasure to be desired and oil in the dwelling of the wise; but a foolish man spendeth it up.

Focus: This proverb contrasts the difference between the way the wise and the way the foolish view and handle wealth.

"There is treasure to be desired and oil in the dwelling of the wise." By diligence and care, wise men lay up wealth for their own current and future use, for their families, and for support of God's work. They are primarily interested in pleasing God with every aspect of their lives, which, in every regard, involves finances. They know that life is cyclical and that the different seasons of life will surely bring new and challenging circumstances. Sometimes there will be scarcity and difficult conditions, while at other times, there is plenty and ease of living. Stability of life and increase in wealth are normal byproducts from living wisely, and a person living wisely will spend wisely, and at the same time, depend on God for everything.

This verse repeats and emphasizes the warning of Proverbs 21:17 – "He that loveth pleasure shall be a poor man: he that *loveth* wine and oil shall not be rich." When a person *loves* pleasure so that it cripples his understanding and ability to meet responsibilities, he is choosing a path to poverty. He wastes money and only lives for the moment. He spends as if there were no tomorrow.

"Oil" is specifically mentioned because it was a valuable, measurable, and storable commodity that could be traded. Additionally, it was used for lighting, anointing and other Temple uses, as well as cooking. In 2 Kings 4:7, after the death of her husband, the widow, through a supernatural miracle, received a large amount of oil that was designated, first of all, to be used for paying debt and thereby preventing her sons from being sold as bondmen. After the debt was paid, she was free to use the oil to live on.

"But a foolish man spendeth it up." Just as stability of life and increase in wealth are normal byproducts for wise people, the opposite is true of the foolish who spend money on foolishness and do not store up for the future. An intentional divide between himself and God and His teachings causes the foolish man to have a distorted understanding of what is essential in life. He establishes priorities based on influence from others and the world system rather than Scripture.

A property owner was once talking to one of his tenants; and while trying to express the importance of taking care of the house, the landlord mentioned his large amount of investment. The foolish tenant replied, "If I had that kind of money, I wouldn't invest it. I'd have myself a good time and travel!" Such foolish talk is precisely the subject of this verse.

Even the humble dwelling of the righteous poor will have the blessings of God. The poor man who chooses righteousness will enjoy God's blessings with adequate provisions, plus he will enjoy the richness of God's word to guide him through this life.

> Deuteronomy 7:13 And he will love thee, and bless thee, and multiply thee: he will also bless the fruit of thy womb, and the fruit of thy land, thy corn, and thy wine, and thine oil, the increase of thy kine, and the flocks of thy sheep, in the land which he sware unto thy fathers to give thee.
> Psalm 112:1-3 Praise ye the LORD. Blessed *is* the man *that* feareth the LORD, *that* delighteth greatly in his commandments. His seed shall be mighty upon earth: the generation of the upright shall be blessed. Wealth and riches *shall be* in his house: and his righteousness endureth for ever.
> Proverbs 6:6-8 Go to the ant, thou sluggard; consider her ways, and be wise: Which having no guide, overseer, or ruler, Provideth her meat in the summer, and gathereth her food in the harvest.
> Proverbs 10:4-5 He becometh poor that dealeth with a slack hand: but the hand of the diligent maketh rich. He that gathereth in summer is a wise son: but he that sleepeth in harvest is a son that causeth shame.
> Proverbs 14:11 The house of the wicked shall be overthrown: but the tabernacle of the upright shall flourish.

Proverbs 21:21 He that followeth after righteousness and mercy findeth life, righteousness, and honour.

Focus: This proverb declares the benefits of pursuing righteousness and mercy.

"He that followeth after righteousness" habitually and perseveringly pursues being right and doing right with God and others. *To be in pursuit of righteousness* demonstrates a great desire to be godly, to follow God's commandments, to think, act, and specifically to live as God prescribes. To *follow after…mercy* is to habitually and perseveringly conduct oneself toward others in such ways as to demonstrate love, kindness, sympathy, and in some cases, forgiveness. **"Mercy"** is the aspect of God's love that causes Him to help the miserable person who may be so either because of breaking God's law or because of circumstances beyond his control. Because God is merciful, those who desire to be like Him will also be merciful.

A person who pursues righteousness and mercy will be rewarded with **"life, righteousness, and honour."**

(1) He will be rewarded with **"life"** to its fullest because his life pleases both God and man. *Unlike* the selfish person who only cares for himself, his thoughts and ways reach out to man with mercy and up to God with worship. He enjoys a truly happy life enhanced with peace because of his great trust in God. He is encouraged and enabled by God's presence and blessings that bring a measure of joy even in the darkest hours.

(2) He will be rewarded with **"righteousness"** because it is the goal being pursued and is a reward from God. He is right with God because he wants to be right with God, and he extends mercy because it is an aspect of being righteous. God gives him the desires of his heart.

(3) He will be rewarded with **"honour"** because he respects others and reveres God.

> Psalm 15:1-5 LORD who shall abide in thy tabernacle? who shall dwell in thy holy hill? He that walketh uprightly, and worketh righteousness, and speaketh the truth in his heart. He that backbiteth not with his tongue, nor doeth evil to his neighbour, nor taketh up a reproach against his neighbour. In whose eyes a vile person is contemned; but he honoureth them that fear the LORD. He that sweareth to his own hurt, and changeth not. He that putteth not out his money to usury, nor taketh reward against the innocent. He that doeth these things shall never be moved.
> Psalm 24:3-5 Who shall ascend into the hill of the LORD? or who shall stand in his holy place? He that hath clean hands, and a pure heart; who hath not lifted up his soul unto vanity, nor sworn deceitfully. He shall receive the blessing from the LORD, and righteousness from the God of his salvation.
> Proverbs 15:9 The way of the wicked is an abomination unto the LORD: but he loveth him that followeth after righteousness.
> Proverbs 8:18-21 Riches and honour *are* with me; *yea,* durable riches and righteousness. My fruit *is* better than gold, yea, than fine gold; and my revenue than choice silver. I lead in the way of righteousness, in the midst of the paths of judgment: That I may cause those that love me to inherit substance; and I will fill their treasures.
> Matthew 5:6 Blessed are they which do hunger and thirst after righteousness: for they shall be filled.
> Matthew 6:31-4 Therefore take no thought, saying, What shall we eat? or, What shall we drink? or, Wherewithal shall we be clothed? (For after all these things do the Gentiles seek:) for your heavenly Father knoweth that ye have need of all these things. But seek ye first the kingdom of God, and his righteousness; and all these things shall be added unto you. Take therefore no thought for the morrow: for the morrow shall take thought for the things of itself. Sufficient unto the day is the evil thereof.

Romans 2:7-11 To them who by patient continuance in well doing seek for glory and honour and immortality, eternal life: But unto them that are contentious, and do not obey the truth, but obey unrighteousness, indignation and wrath, Tribulation and anguish, upon every soul of man that doeth evil, of the Jew first, and also of the Gentile; But glory, honour, and peace, to every man that worketh good, to the Jew first, and also to the Gentile: For there is no respect of persons with God.

Proverbs 21:22 A wise *man* scaleth the city of the mighty, and casteth down the strength of the confidence thereof.

Focus: This proverb contrasts the strength of wisdom's strategy against anything man puts confidence in.

Wisdom in this verse is visualized as military strategy obtained directly from God. Such God-given wisdom gives a man the ability to overpower the strongest defenses of which an enemy is confident. **"A wise man scaleth the city of the mighty"** means that through wisdom's direction, the wise man can circumvent powerful defenses and ascend the city's *protective wall (literally or figuratively)*. Consequently, because of wisdom and not brute strength, he can ***cast down the strength of the confidence,*** meaning to strip them of their confidence in their robust defenses and powerful men.

A **"city of the mighty"** refers to a city of people who foolishly put their trust and confidence in the high walls instead of in the true "Mighty One," Jehovah. (Paul calls foolish people who trust in themselves "carnal" in 2 Corinthians 10:2-6 below.) People boast in the height of their walls, but a wise man who trusts in God can overcome obstacles, even unscalable walls, through God's leadership.

> "Sometimes more is done by prudence and wisdom, by art and cunning, by schemes and stratagems, than by power and force; especially in military affairs, and particularly in besieging and taking fortified cities; when one wise man, by his wisdom, may so order and manage things, as to be able, with a few under his command, to mount the walls of a city and take it, though defended by a mighty garrison in it."[559]

Proverbs 18:11 The rich mans wealth *is* his strong city, and as an high wall in his own conceit.

Ecclesiastes 9:13-18 This wisdom have I seen also under the sun, and it seemed great unto me: There was a little city, and few men within it; and there came a great king against it, and besieged it, and built great bulwarks against it: Now there was found in it a poor wise man, and he by his wisdom delivered the city; yet no man remembered that same poor man. Then said I, Wisdom is better than strength: nevertheless the poor man's wisdom is despised, and his words are not heard. The words of wise men are heard in quiet more than the cry of him that ruleth among fools. Wisdom is better than weapons of war: but one sinner destroyeth much good.

2 Corinthians 10:2-6 But I beseech you, that I may not be bold when I am present with that confidence, wherewith I think to be bold against some, which think of us as if we walked according to the flesh. For though we walk in the flesh, we do not war after the flesh: (For the weapons of our warfare are not carnal, but mighty through God to the pulling down of strong holds;) Casting down imaginations, and every high thing that exalteth itself against the knowledge of God, and bringing into captivity every thought to the obedience of Christ; And having in a readiness to revenge all disobedience, when your obedience is fulfilled.

Most importantly, wisdom can overcome the enemy because wisdom invokes God's intervention and direction. As observed earlier in the Book of Proverbs, wisdom also obtains wise counsel, moves cautiously, and disassociates from wicked people who would hinder the ability to function with excellence. Wisdom does not necessarily rely on physical strength, but instead relies on leadership from God. Be assured, when God involves Himself and supernatural events occur, the enemy will be filled with fear.

1 Samuel 25:32 And David said to Abigail, Blessed be the LORD God of Israel, which sent thee this day to meet me: And blessed be thy advice, and blessed be thou, which hast kept me this day from coming to shed blood, and from avenging myself with mine own hand.

Proverbs 24:5-6 A wise man *is* strong; yea, a man of knowledge increaseth strength. For by wise counsel thou shalt make thy war: and in multitude of counsellors there is safety.

Ecclesiastes 7:19 Wisdom strengtheneth the wise more than ten mighty men which are in the city.

Proverbs 21:23 Whoso keepeth his mouth and his tongue keepeth his soul from troubles.

Focus: This proverb declares the value of controlled speech.

One of the most profound benefits of having wisdom is that it leads the possessor to know when to speak and when to keep quiet. *Mouth and tongue* figuratively describe the words which they form. The Book of Proverbs devotes much of its content to warnings about the tongue, and the Book of James in the New Testament even gives the proper use of the tongue as a test for the soundness of an individual's faith – "If any man among you seem to be religious, and bridleth not his tongue, but deceiveth his own heart, this man's religion is vain." (James 1:26) Many verses either endorse controlling the tongue or illustrate by example the fact that careful selection of words keeps a wise person out of many troubles.

> Psalm 39:1 To the chief Musician, even to Jeduthun, A Psalm of David. I said, I will take heed to my ways, that I sin not with my tongue: I will keep my mouth with a bridle, while the wicked is before me.
> Proverbs 10:18-21 He that hideth hatred with lying lips, and he that uttereth a slander, is a fool. In the multitude of words there wanteth not sin: but he that refraineth his lips is wise. The tongue of the just is as choice silver: the heart of the wicked is little worth. The lips of the righteous feed many: but fools die for want of wisdom.
> Proverbs 12:13-14 The wicked is snared by the transgression of his lips: but the just shall come out of trouble. A man shall be satisfied with good by the fruit of his mouth: and the recompence of a man's hands shall be rendered unto him.
> Proverbs 13:2-3 A man shall eat good by the fruit of his mouth: but the soul of the transgressors shall eat violence. He that keepeth his mouth keepeth his life: but he that openeth wide his lips shall have destruction.
> Proverbs 14:3 In the mouth of the foolish is a rod of pride: but the lips of the wise shall preserve them.
> Proverbs 17:28 Even a fool, when he holdeth his peace, is counted wise: and he that shutteth his lips is esteemed a man of understanding.
> Proverbs 18:21 Death and life are in the power of the tongue: and they that love it shall eat the fruit thereof.
> James 1:19-20 Wherefore, my beloved brethren, let every man be swift to hear, slow to speak, slow to wrath: For the wrath of man worketh not the righteousness of God.
> James 3:2 For in many things we offend all. If any man offend not in word, the same is a perfect man, and able also to bridle the whole body. *[See also verses 3-13.]*

James greatly emphasizes the ***trouble*** aspect of this proverb when he writes, "Even so the tongue is a little member, and boasteth great things. Behold, how great a matter a little fire kindleth!" (James 3:5)

Proverbs 21:24 Proud *and* haughty scorner *is* his name, who dealeth in proud wrath.

Focus: This proverb identifies the major characteristics of a scorner.

"Proud *and* haughty scorner *is* his name." A **"name"** is a label, good or bad, that sets one person apart from another – not only for individual identification but often for representing a dominant characteristic. People often acquire a nickname that can be derogatory, accurately descriptive, or complimentary. In this proverb, the arrogant rebel against God and enemy of righteousness is labeled and thus identified as **"proud and haughty scorner."** He is thus a sneering, hateful, arrogant mocker held in very low esteem by God and avoided by good men.

"Who dealeth in proud wrath" describes how the scorner conducts all of his business and his personal life. Driven *not* by reason and justice but rather by intense hate and inability to tolerate opposition, he lashes out and goes into a rage when someone refuses to kowtow to his whims. Anyone with wisdom would immediately recognize him from his behavior and avoid him whenever possible. Thinking of himself as so much better than others (especially those who live righteously), he derides them. Because of his contempt for others, he does not hesitate to work at destroying them either by his words or by his actions.

The following is a list of Biblical characters who fit the category of ***proud and haughty scorners who acted with proud wrath.*** (1) *Sanballat and Tobiah*, who laughed Nehemiah to scorn and were filled with wrath (Nehemiah 2-6); (2) *Haman*, who hated the Jews, and being full of wrath, took decisive hateful steps to destroy the entire race (Esther 3-6); (3) *Nebuchadnezzar*, who insisted on himself being worshiped, and when three Jewish young men refused to bow down to his statue, had them thrown into a burning furnace (Daniel 3); (4) *Herod*, who became so angry at the wise men who didn't return and tell him where Jesus was, that he ordered the death of all children two years old and younger (Matthew 2:16); (5) *Pharaoh* refused to release the Jews and said, "Who is the LORD, that I should obey his voice?" (Exodus 5:2)

> Nehemiah 2:18-19 Then I told them of the hand of my God which was good upon me; as also the king's words that he had spoken unto me. And they said, Let us rise up and build. So they strengthened their hands for this good work. But when Sanballat the Horonite, and Tobiah the servant, the Ammonite, and Geshem the Arabian, heard it, they laughed us to scorn, and despised us, and said, What is this thing that ye do? will ye rebel against the king?

Esther 3:5-6 And when Haman saw that Mordecai bowed not, nor did him reverence, then was Haman full of wrath. And he thought scorn to lay hands on Mordecai alone; for they had shewed him the people of Mordecai: wherefore Haman sought to destroy all the Jews that were throughout the whole kingdom of Ahasuerus, even the people of Mordecai.

Daniel 3:19-20 Then was Nebuchadnezzar full of fury, and the form of his visage was changed against Shadrach, Meshach, and Abednego: therefore he spake, and commanded that they should heat the furnace one seven times more than it was wont to be heated. And he commanded the most mighty men that were in his army to bind Shadrach, Meshach, and Abednego, and to cast them into the burning fiery furnace.

Matthew 2:16 Then Herod, when he saw that he was mocked of the wise men, was exceeding wroth, and sent forth, and slew all the children that were in Bethlehem, and in all the coasts thereof, from two years old and under, according to the time which he had diligently enquired of the wise men.

Proverbs 21:25-26 The desire of the slothful killeth him; for his hands refuse to labour.
26.   He coveteth greedily all the day long: but the righteous giveth and spareth not.

Focus: This proverb contrasts the sin of the slothful with the virtue of the righteous.

"The desire of the slothful killeth him; for his hands refuse to labour." It is his overwhelming inordinate desire for rest that is killing this foolish person. He loves to sleep and is obsessed with satisfying the craving. **"His hands refuse to labor"** – not because they are paralyzed, but because he does not want to move them. He only wants to satisfy his craving for rest.

"For useful *labor* he has no heart. Meanwhile, with all his inactivity, he is a prey *all day long* to a *greedy covetousness;* tantalized with insatiable desires; while the hope of enjoyment, though not out of sight, yet, from want of exertion, is out of reach. Thus, dreaming of the end without mortification or godly exercise, he dies with his desires in his mouth; envying those, whose industrious diligence enables them to *give, and spare not.*"[560]

He wants to live comfortably, but **"his hands refuse to labor."** To say that *the slothful person's desire kills him* is a figure of speech that refers to the paralyzed work ethic within him. He is so "wise in his own conceit" that he devises pitiful, unbelievable excuses for not working.

Proverbs 20:4 The sluggard will not plow by reason of the cold; therefore shall he beg in harvest, and have nothing.

Proverbs 26:13-16 The slothful man saith, There is a lion in the way; a lion is in the streets. As the door turneth upon his hinges, so doth the slothful upon his bed. The slothful hideth his hand in his bosom; it grieveth him to bring it again to his mouth. The sluggard is wiser in his own conceit than seven men that can render a reason.

"He coveteth greedily all the day long: but the righteous giveth and spareth not." The life of **"the slothful"** can be characterized as a *downward spiral of unhappiness and sinful cravings* created by a perpetual *refusal to labor.* His desire is so intense that verse 25 describes it as *killing* or overwhelming him. He has a defeated spirit, discouraging and stifling any desire to labor. His unfulfilled desire overwhelms his heart with relentless, sinful *coveting.* Verse 26 stresses that his coveting is not sporadic, but rather he *covets greedily all day long*. His mind is occupied with his desires, having no place for God in his thoughts. He greedily seeks after the things that he lacks and desires them to the point that they are enlarged in his mind and worshiped by him.

Colossians 3:5-7 Mortify therefore your members which are upon the earth; fornication, uncleanness, inordinate affection, evil concupiscence, and covetousness, which is idolatry: For which things' sake the wrath of God cometh on the children of disobedience: In the which ye also walked some time, when ye lived in them.

1 Corinthians 6:9-10 Know ye not that the unrighteous shall not inherit the kingdom of God? Be not deceived: neither fornicators, nor idolaters, nor adulterers, nor effeminate, nor abusers of themselves with mankind, Nor thieves, nor covetous, nor drunkards, nor revilers, nor extortioners, shall inherit the kingdom of God.

Covetousness is a sin that often leads to more sins, such as lying to get the desired thing, or stealing. It involves human rationalization that seeks to find excuses for wanting what belongs to others.

David was not lazy, but he suffered long because he coveted another man's wife. That sin led to lying and murder (2 Samuel 11). The sword never departed from his house because, as 2 Samuel 12:10 states, "thou hast despised me *[God]* and hast taken the wife of Uriah the Hittite to be thy wife." Despite all the care God had given David, he surrendered to his selfish, fleshly desires rather than the will of God in this matter. In 2 Kings 5:20-27, Gehazi, Elisha's servant, lost his ministry and his health because of covetousness. In like manner, when Miriam and Aaron spoke covetously to Moses, saying, "Hath the Lord indeed spoken only by Moses? hath he not spoken by us?" (Numbers 12:2), God smote her with leprosy and left her outside the camp for seven days.

"The righteous" are opposite **"the slothful"** because they do not merely labor but labor with a desire to please God. Therefore, their work is blessed and is productive, giving them the ability to satisfy an innate desire to help others. While the covetous man *covets greedily all the day long,* the *righteous gives and spares not.*

> Luke 12:13-15 And one of the company said unto him, Master, speak to my brother, that he divide the inheritance with me. And he said unto him, Man, who made me a judge or a divider over you? And he said unto them, Take heed, and beware of covetousness: for a man's life consisteth not in the abundance of the things which he possesseth.
>
> 1 Timothy 6:6-9 But godliness with contentment is great gain. For we brought nothing into this world, and it is certain we can carry nothing out. And having food and raiment let us be therewith content. But they that will be rich fall into temptation and a snare, and into many foolish and hurtful lusts, which drown men in destruction and perdition. *[See also Romans 1:28-32 and Ephesians 5:1-4]*

Proverbs 21:27 The sacrifice of the wicked *is* abomination: how much more, *when* he bringeth it with a wicked mind?

Focus: This proverb declares God's attitude toward sacrifices of wicked people, especially when offered with an evil motive.

Verse 3 of this chapter establishes the fact that sacrifice was not acceptable without righteousness – "To do justice and judgment is more acceptable to the LORD than sacrifice" (Proverbs 21:3). This current verse enhances the depth of God's attitude when it states, **"The sacrifice of the wicked is *abomination*"** or morally disgusting. Furthermore, since he brings the same **"with a wicked** *[actively evil– hostile to God, guilty of sin against man and God. The "lawless ones."[561]]* **mind,"** he does so with a spirit of bribery, believing that God will somehow receive his gift and thereby endorse his evil acts. His sacrifice is complete hypocrisy, a sham. Through this despicable practice, he believes himself to have engaged God in sharing in his sinful acts by sharing the proceeds with Him.

> "The sacrifice of the sinner is abominable, as offered formally without repentance and faith; much more abominable, when he brings his offering to win, as it were, God's connivance in the sin which he commits and has no intention of renouncing . . . Such an outrage on God's purity and justice may well be called an abomination . . . The notion of propitiating the Deity by sharing with him the proceeds of sin is expressed in proverbial language. We have the homely saying, 'Steal the goose, and give the giblets in alms.'"[562]

Because the wicked person brings the sacrifice with a hypocritical mind, an ulterior motive, and an impenitent heart, **"the sacrifice of the wicked is an abomination."** The wicked man does not respect and honor God with his actions, nor is he obedient to His word; therefore, God never accepts anything **"the wicked"** sacrifices.

> Psalm 51:16-17 For thou desirest not sacrifice; else would I give it: thou delightest not in burnt offering. The sacrifices of God are a broken spirit: a broken and a contrite heart, O God, thou wilt not despise.
>
> Proverbs 15:8 The sacrifice of the wicked is an abomination to the LORD: but the prayer of the upright is his delight.
>
> Ecclesiastes 5:1 Keep thy foot when thou goest to the house of God, and be more ready to hear, than to give the sacrifice of fools: for they consider not that they do evil.
>
> Amos 5:21-24 I hate, I despise your feast days, and I will not smell in your solemn assemblies. Though ye offer me burnt offerings and your meat offerings, I will not accept them: neither will I regard the peace offerings of your fat beasts. Take thou away from me the noise of thy songs; for I will not hear the melody of thy viols. But let judgment run down as waters, and righteousness as a mighty stream.
>
> *[See also Isaiah 1:11-17; Jeremiah 6: 19-20; Matthew 23:14.]*

A primary illustration of the **"sacrifice of the wicked"** is found in the story of King Saul, who violated Scripture mandates by taking on the responsibilities of a priest and then excusing himself by lying. His animal sacrifices were made improperly and from a wicked heart. Notice the reprimand Samuel spoke for God, "Hath the LORD as great delight in burnt offerings and sacrifices, as in obeying the voice of the LORD? Behold, to obey is better than sacrifice, and to hearken than the fat of rams. For rebellion is as the sin of witchcraft, and stubbornness is as iniquity and idolatry. Because thou hast rejected the word of the LORD, he hath also rejected thee from being king." (1 Samuel 15:22-23)

Jesus gave Himself as the perfect, acceptable sacrifice for sin, thus fulfilling the law and *forever ending the need for Mosaic sacrifices.* Today, people may offer gifts *(not Mosaic sacrifices)* to the Lord as a demonstration of love for Him or give a gift to meet a need within the church or meet needs on a mission field. The early church had such generosity and love toward other believers that some of them sold their land and gave the proceeds to the apostles to distribute "unto every man according as he had need." (Acts 4:35) In a hypocritical demonstration of loving zeal for God and love for the brethren, Ananias and Sapphira made a type of "sacrifice of the wicked" and "lied to the Holy Ghost." (Acts 5:1-11) In order to be received of God, any offering given in the name of the Lord must be done with a pure heart, with honest motives, and with a desire to be pleasing in the eyes of the Lord. If a business person in any manner cheats his customers or defrauds for gain and then brings an offering *(substantial or not)* to the church as a false show of generosity, thinking that God will thereby overlook his evil conduct, he is doing so **"with a wicked mind."**

Proverbs 21:28 A false witness shall perish: but the man that heareth speaketh constantly.

Focus: This parable contrasts the brevity and doom of a lying witness and his lies with the longevity of the truthful witness and his truth.

"A false witness shall perish."   Because a liar is repulsive, both he and his words are eventually rejected. According to Proverbs 12:22 and 6:16, "lying lips" are an abomination to the LORD. Proverbs 19:28 states – "An ungodly witness scorneth judgment: and the mouth of the wicked devoureth iniquity. "A false witness that speaketh lies" is despised by the LORD. One of the Ten Commandments (Exodus 20:16) forbids that a man be a "false witness." He perjures himself by speaking fabricated lies from a wicked heart. Once people realize he is a "false witness," they no longer will trust his testimony in court or in private. Twice before, Proverbs has affirmed that the false witness will be punished:

Proverbs 19:5 A false witness shall not be unpunished, and he that speaketh lies shall not escape.

Proverbs 19:9 A false witness shall not be unpunished, and he that speaketh lies shall perish.

"Shall perish" means certain to *[die, be exterminated, destroyed]*; however, it does not imply that the false witness will die immediately. In the Book of Proverbs, God repeatedly speaks against perjury – giving a false witness in court to what one has seen or heard. "Both the false witness and the judge or others who followed his line will be destroyed. God punishes dishonesty!" [563]   (Proverbs 6:19; 12:17; 14:5; 25; 19:5, 9; 25:18)

"But the man that heareth speaketh constantly" refers to a *righteous witness* who is contrasted with the lying witness. He is one who cautiously weighs what he has heard or seen and is very careful to relay the truth. The righteous man is a **"man that heareth"** meaning that he carefully evaluates what he has heard and considers all aspects that *might* have caused him to misunderstand. He very cautiously testifies only to what he positively knows. The true witness is the person who perceives with his ears; and, because he loves God and seeks to obey His word, repeats what he has heard *without embellishment* to the court. Because he fears the Lord's disapproval as well as disapproval of godly people, he will not speak deceitfully. He speaks "the truth, the whole truth, and nothing but the truth."

He **"speaketh constantly"**   meaning that his testimony is respected and honored as the truth and is remembered and is carried as if on the wings of a bird to other people and perhaps to the next generation. His words resonate in the heart of those listening, and both he and his words are honored and remain in their memory.

The false witness is punished, and his words die, as does his reputation, his honor, and any respect he might hope to receive. The true witness obtains a good name or a reputation for truthfulness, whereas the liar obtains the name of "false witness." He is a liar.

Proverbs 12:17 He that speaketh truth sheweth forth righteousness: but a false witness deceit.

Proverbs 21:29 A wicked man hardeneth his face: but *as for* the upright, he directeth his way.

Focus: This proverb contrasts the wicked man's calloused rebellion against God with the upright man's confident submission to God's leadership.

"A wicked man hardeneth his face." According to the definition previously given in Proverbs 21:27, *a wicked man* is an actively evil person – hostile to God, guilty of sin against man and God. He is a member of the "lawless ones."[564]

Such a person **"hardeneth his face"** meaning that the wicked man "freezes" his face as an act of defiance. His hardened face is a sign of his hardened heart toward God. The Hebrew word *azaz* from which "hardeneth" was translated also translates as "impudent," which describes the hypocritical face of the adulterous woman who boldly declares that she has paid her vows to God. This brazen woman brought her dishonorably given but legitimate share of the sacrifice home to eat and subsequently used it as a part of her seduction plan for the simple, foolish young man. She was truly a sin-hardened woman, just as the wicked man in this proverb is a sin-hardened man. Their faces are both boldly disrespectful – impudent – hardened – symbolically declaring that they are intentionally following their own wicked way as opposed to that way of righteousness:

> Proverbs 7:13-14 So she caught him, and kissed him, and with an impudent face said unto him, I have peace offerings with me; this day have I payed my vows.

> "In his arrogance and hypocrisy a wicked person puts up a bold front. He tries to persuade people to believe him, often by deceit and lies."[565]

> "*A hardened face*, without shame or blushing for sin, is a fearful manifestation of a hardened heart. Cain standing boldly in the presence of his God, with his hands reeking with his brother's blood; Gehazi with his fearless lie; the Traitor, bearing to be pointed out by his Master, without visible emotion, then afterwards with unblushing effrontery kissing his sacred cheeks – how *hardened* must have been *their faces* in determined *wickedness!*"[566]

> Genesis 4:9 And the LORD said unto Cain, Where *is* Abel thy brother? And he said, I know not: *Am* I my brother's keeper?

> 2 Kings 5:25-27 But he went in, and stood before his master. And Elisha said unto him, Whence *comest thou,* Gehazi? And he said, Thy servant went no whither. And he said unto him, Went not mine heart *with thee,* when the man turned again from his chariot to meet thee? *Is it* a time to receive money, and to receive garments, and oliveyards, and vineyards, and sheep, and oxen, and menservants, and maidservants? The leprosy therefore of Naaman shall cleave unto thee, and unto thy seed for ever. And he went out from his presence a leper *as white* as snow.

> Matthew 26:48-49 Now he *[Judas Iscariot]* that betrayed him *[Jesus]* gave them a sign, saying, Whomsoever I shall kiss, that same is he: hold him fast. And forthwith he came to Jesus, and said, Hail, master; and kissed him.

These additional Scriptures also express the impudent, hardened sinner toward God: Proverbs 28:13-14, 29:1; Jeremiah 3:2-3, 5:3, 44:16-17; Ezekiel 2:4; Hebrews 3:7-13.

"But as for the upright, he directeth his way." The upright *[righteous]* are those whom God directs. Consequently, the peace of God will be reflected on their face rather than hardened disrespect. "The upright" gladly follow God Who directs and guards his steps.

> Psalm 119:59 I thought on my ways, and turned my feet unto thy testimonies.

> Proverbs 11:5 The righteousness of the perfect shall direct his way: but the wicked shall fall by his own wickedness.

> "This is rest indeed – to put ourselves in the Lord's hands, fearful of taking one step alone; carefully ordering our steps, lest by inadvertence, much more by willfulness, they should bring shame upon *his face*... Where the heart is set on duty, there will be seldom any great difficulty in discovering the path. Secret heavenly direction is engaged. An unfixed, unresolved mind gives great advantage to the enemy's assault. Here lies the contrast – The wicked man *hardens his face* against God's ordinances. The godly *directs his way* by them; not waiting in inactivity for miraculous leading, but improving those ordinary means, which throw light upon every step. Temporals, as well as spirituals; trifles, as well as important matters, are brought under the eye of our gracious God. Child-like confidence brings sunshine and acceptance, a brighter and more glorious privilege than the scepter of the universe."[567]

> Proverbs 3:5-6 Trust in the LORD with all thine heart; and lean not unto thine own understanding. In all thy ways acknowledge him, and he shall direct thy paths.

Proverbs 21:30 *There is* no wisdom nor understanding nor counsel against the LORD.

Focus: This proverb expresses the futileness of opposition against God.

Human **"wisdom"** falls hilariously short when attempting to challenge God, *especially in the area of wisdom.* Because **"understanding,"** like wisdom, is a mental ability gifted to man by his Creator, it is beyond ridiculous (in some ways even humorous) to imagine a human so challenging God. Considering the phrase, **"counsel against the LORD,"** – if collectively *every wicked person* out of over 7 billion on earth were to join together in opposition to God, their concerted efforts would be virtually nothing. The Bible records kings and individual people who thought they were wise enough or strong enough to overthrow the plans and counsels of God, but He brought their foolish schemes to nothing. God gave Abram the following prophecy of which He was in full control, and no amount of scheming or teaming together could defeat His plan.

> Genesis 15:12-14 And when the sun was going down, a deep sleep fell upon Abram; and, lo, an horror of great darkness fell upon him. And he said unto Abram, Know of a surety that thy seed shall be a stranger in a land that is not theirs, and shall serve them; and they shall afflict them four hundred years; And also that nation, whom they shall serve, will I judge: and afterward shall they come out with great substance.

Pharaoh devised two schemes to suppress the growth of the Hebrew nation that he held in slavery. First, he ordered hard labor, and second, he commanded the midwives to kill all the male babies at birth. God's plan for the nation of Israel and His plan for Moses would not be stopped by those wicked schemes or any other. The words of the Bible are very telling:

> Exodus 1:12 But the more they afflicted them, the more they multiplied and grew. And they were grieved because of the children of Israel.
> Exodus 1:17 But the midwives feared God, and did not as the king of Egypt commanded them, but saved the men children alive.
> Exodus 1:20 Therefore God dealt well with the midwives: and the people multiplied, and waxed very mighty.

Supernaturally saved alive, Moses, under God's plan, grew up in the house of Pharaoh (Exodus 2). He was educated by the Egyptians but made the personal choice to forsake all of Egypt's wealth and power and to follow God's leadership to the land of Midian. Forty years later, God instructed Moses from the burning bush, and he obeyed and returned to Egypt to lead the children of Israel out. Pharaoh's heart was hardened, and he refused to submit to God; consequently, God ultimately killed all the firstborn of Egypt and Pharaoh temporarily relented. The family of Abraham, God's chosen people, were finally released from Egypt to worship God in the wilderness. Pharaoh changed his wicked mind again and followed after Israel with his armies but was supernaturally destroyed in the Red Sea. He obviously thought that because of his intelligence plus huge numbers of people within his kingdom, mighty warriors, and chariots, he could defeat the plans of God. He could not accept that **"*There is* no wisdom nor understanding nor counsel against the LORD."**

> Exodus 14:26-28 And the LORD said unto Moses, Stretch out thine hand over the sea, that the waters may come again upon the Egyptians, upon their chariots, and upon their horsemen. And Moses stretched forth his hand over the sea, and the sea returned to his strength when the morning appeared; and the Egyptians fled against it; and the LORD overthrew the Egyptians in the midst of the sea. And the waters returned, and covered the chariots, and the horsemen, and all the host of Pharaoh that came into the sea after them; there remained not so much as one of them.

Balak's desire to curse Israel came to naught in Numbers 24:10 – "And Balak's anger was kindled against Balaam, and he smote his hands together: and Balak said unto Baalam, I called thee to curse mine enemies, and, behold, thou hast altogether blessed them these three times."

Ahab tried to escape God's judgment which involved the cutting off of his house by disguising himself and not allowing Jehoshaphat, the king of Judah, to put on a disguise. God overrode his wicked scheme through "a bow drawn at a venture" that killed the wicked king. (1Kings 22:30-35)

Sanballat and Tobiah tried to overthrow God's plan to rebuild the wall of Jerusalem after the Babylonian captivity. That did not work either. (Nehemiah 6:1-19; 7:1) Athaliah tried to destroy the house of David. Satan tried to tempt Jesus and keep Him from becoming the Saviour of mankind. All opposition against God is futile.

Proverbs 21:31 The horse *is* prepared against the day of battle: but safety *is* of the LORD.

Focus: This proverb is a declaration of God's sovereign protection for His people.

This verse carries on the idea of God's overarching control. Not only is puny man's wisdom, understanding, and counsel of no worth in the wicked's efforts to thwart God's plans; but no devices he invents or equipment he musters can be used to defeat Jehovah. ***Horses*** were "an emblem of military power and activity,"[568] but the Jews were early forbidden to use them.

> Deuteronomy 17:15-16 Thou shalt in any wise set *him* king over thee, whom the LORD thy God shall choose: *one* from among thy brethren shalt thou set king over thee: thou mayest not set a stranger over thee, which *is* not thy brother. But he shall not multiply horses to himself, nor cause the people to return to Egypt, to the end that he should multiply horses: forasmuch as the LORD hath said unto you, Ye shall henceforth return no more that way.

Later Solomon imported many horses from Egypt.

> 1 Kings 4:26 And Solomon had forty thousand stalls of horses for his chariots, and twelve thousand horsemen.
>
> 1 Kings 10:26 And Solomon gathered together chariots and horsemen: and he had a thousand and four hundred chariots, and twelve thousand horsemen, whom he bestowed in the cities for chariots, and with the king at Jerusalem.

At the time of the writing of this proverb, Solomon declares that a horse does not protect Israel – but **"safety is of the LORD."** Moreover, this proverb is in the spirit of orders given to Joshua when God said:

> "... Be not afraid because of them: for tomorrow about this time will I deliver them up all slain before Israel: thou shalt hough their horses, and burn their chariots with fire." (Joshua 11:6)

Breaking the tendon of the horse's lower leg was to "hough" it, and doing so rendered it useless for military purposes but still useful for all kinds of domestic work.[569] God would have Israel eliminate anything that would take the place of His demonstrative protection of His chosen people. Jehovah had promised to fight Israel's battles.

> Exodus 14:14 The LORD shall fight for you, and ye shall hold your peace.
>
> Deuteronomy 1:30 The LORD your God which goeth before you, he shall fight for you, according to all that he did for you in Egypt before your eyes ...
>
> 2 Chronicles 20:17 Ye shall not need to fight in this battle: set yourselves, stand ye still, and see the salvation of the LORD with you, O Judah and Jerusalem: fear not, nor be dismayed; to morrow go out against them: for the LORD will be with you.

Any country can strengthen its military machinery to the max, build the strongest defense imaginable, and recruit millions of troops only to discover that God is still in control of the outcomes. God is **"safety"** for those who walk with Him.

> Exodus 15:19 For the horse of Pharaoh went in with his chariots and with his horsemen into the sea, and the LORD brought again the waters of the sea upon them; but the children of Israel went on dry land in the midst of the sea.
>
> Psalm 3:3; 6-8 But thou, O LORD, art a shield for me; my glory, and the lifter up of mine head ... I will not be afraid of ten thousands of people, that have set themselves against me round about. Arise, O LORD; save me, O my God: for thou hast smitten all mine enemies upon the cheek bone; thou hast broken the teeth of the ungodly. Salvation belongeth unto the LORD: thy blessing is upon thy people. Selah.
>
> Psalm 20:7 Some trust in chariots, and some in horses: but we will remember the name of the LORD our God.
>
> Psalm 33:10-11 The LORD bringeth the counsel of the heathen to nought: he maketh the devices of the people of none effect. The counsel of the LORD standeth for ever, the thoughts of his heart to all generations.
>
> Psalm 33:16-20 There is no king saved by the multitude of an host: a mighty man is not delivered by much strength. An horse is a vain thing for safety: neither shall he deliver any by his great strength. Behold, the eye of the LORD is upon them that fear him, upon them that hope in his mercy; To deliver their soul from death, and to keep them alive in famine. Our soul waiteth for the LORD: he is our help and our shield.
>
> Isaiah 31:1 Woe to them that go down to Egypt for help; and stay on horses, and trust in chariots, because they are many; and in horsemen, because they are very strong; but they look not unto the Holy One of Israel, neither seek the LORD!
>
> Hosea 14:1-3 O Israel, return unto the LORD thy God; for thou hast fallen by thine iniquity. Take with you words, and turn to the LORD: say unto him, Take away all iniquity, and receive us graciously: so will we render the calves of our lips. Asshur shall not save us; we will not ride upon horses: neither will we say any more to the work of our hands, Ye are our gods: for in thee the fatherless findeth mercy.

Men may devise their foolish schemes, but only by trusting in God can a man be safe. Christ is the only refuge for the Christian. He is our **"safety** *[victory, salvation, help, deliverance]*."

> 1 Corinthians 15:57 But thanks be to God, which giveth us the victory through our Lord Jesus Christ.
>
> 1 John 5:4 For whatsoever is born of God overcometh the world: and this is the victory that overcometh the world, even our faith.
>
> *"But, after all, safety and salvation are of the Lord; he can save without armies, but armies cannot save without him; and therefore he must be sought to and trusted in for success, and when success is obtained he must have all the glory. When we are preparing for the day of battle our great concern must be to make God our friend and secure his favour."*[570]

CHAPTER TWENTY-TWO

> **Proverbs 22:1** A *good* name *is* rather to be chosen than great riches, *and* loving favour rather than silver and gold.

Focus: This proverb declares two things that are preferred to wealth.

A **"name,"** as used in this verse, indicates a person's reputation. All believers should desire to have a respected name among wise, godly men and, of course, with God. Children should be taught the value of a good name and encouraged to seek it from their earliest years.

"A good name" will be obtained if a person wisely adheres to the principles taught in Scripture. In previous years in the U.S., children typically remained near their families when they grew up. A community of people, beginning with parents or guardians and extending to other adults such as school teachers and church leaders, strongly influenced the child to work towards having a good name. Peers were even instrumental in influencing one another to have a good name. Instead of scorning their comments, children were generally respectful toward anyone who might confront them or inform their parents of deviant, foolish behavior that could taint their name and the family's name. Godly families still practice these same guidelines.

"A good name is rather to be chosen than great riches." A good name honors God and reflects obedience to His word. A person who has a respected name is favored by other people who are capable of providing benefits that can enhance his quality of life. Having a good name can serve to lift a person to a place of good counsel and good companions with whom to enjoy wonderful times.

In contrast with seeking "a good name," seeking **"great riches"** has the following negative consequences: it attracts false friends, fosters greedy selfishness, leads to a false sense of security that rejects God, and creates an environment that lacks tranquility, peace of mind, and comfort of the Holy Spirit.

> "We should be more careful to do that by which we may get and keep a good name than that by which we may raise and increase a great estate. Great riches bring great cares with them, expose men to danger, and add no real value to a man. A fool and a knave may have *great riches,* but *a good name* makes a man easy and safe, supposes a man wise and honest, redounds to the glory of God, and gives a man a greater opportunity of doing good. By great riches we may relieve the bodily wants of others, but by a good name we may recommend religion to them."[571]

"*And* loving favour rather than silver and gold." **"Loving favour"** involves loving acceptance, grace, or admiration. "Loving favour" is the high regard that God and people have for those with high moral character and who wisely live their lives. **"Silver and gold"** in the second half of this proverb and **"great riches"** in the first are similar expressions for wealth. When a person with a good name walks with God, he has the most important advantage of being personally associated with and blessed by God. No amount of wealth compares to the blessings of "a good name" and "loving favor."

> Proverbs 12:2 A good man obtaineth favour of the LORD: but a man of wicked devices will he condemn.
> 1 Samuel 2:26 And the child Samuel grew on, and was in favour both with the LORD, and also with men.
> 1 Samuel 25:25 Let not my lord, I pray thee, regard this man of Belial, even Nabal: for as his name is, so is he; Nabal is his name, and folly is with him: but I thine handmaid saw not the young men of my lord, whom thou didst send.
> 1 Kings 1:47 And moreover the king's servants came to bless our lord king David, saying, God make the name of Solomon better than thy name, and make his throne greater than thy throne. And the king bowed himself upon the bed.
> Ecclesiastes 7:1 A good name *is* better than precious ointment; and the day of death than the day of one's birth.
> Luke 2:52 And Jesus increased in wisdom and stature, and in favour with God and man.
> Acts 7:10 And delivered him *[Joseph]* out of all his afflictions, and gave him favour and wisdom in the sight of Pharaoh king of Egypt; and he made him governor over Egypt and all his house.

> **Proverbs 22:2** The rich and poor meet together: the LORD *is* the maker of them all.

Focus: This proverb expresses that by God's design all men meet on the common ground of humanity.

"The rich and poor meet together" as they interact throughout their public and private lives. Frequently, families will be comprised of both rich and poor, and likewise, cities have both. The wealthy can provide work opportunities for the poor, and the poor can provide necessary skills and labor for the rich. Regard for a person based on his wealth is disrespectful to him and to God, Who gives men various measures of ability and circumstance to get wealth. Disrespect for others because they lack wealth reveals an arrogant heart that will be resisted by God.

> "Their common humanity, their fatherhood in God, should make them regard one another as brethren, without distinction of rank or position: the rich should not despise the poor, the poor should not envy the rich, but all should live in love and harmony as one great family of God."[572]

> Proverbs 14:31 He that oppresseth the poor reproacheth his Maker: but he that honoureth him hath mercy on the poor.

> Proverbs 17:5 Whoso mocketh the poor reproacheth his Maker: *and* he that is glad at calamities shall not be unpunished.

Scripture records God's command to His chosen people to respect the needy by not fully reaping the corners of their fields and to intentionally leave the gleanings there for the poor, the fatherless, and the stranger. Furthermore, they were to leave some grapes on the vines for those same destitute persons.

> Leviticus 19:9-10 And when ye reap the harvest of your land, thou shalt not wholly reap the corners of thy field, neither shalt thou gather the gleanings of thy harvest. And thou shalt not glean thy vineyard, neither shalt thou gather *every* grape of thy vineyard; thou shalt leave them for the poor and stranger: I *am* the LORD your God.

People are born with various talents and different mental and physical abilities. **"The LORD is the maker of them all"** is a strong statement declaring that God created man; therefore, every man is a brother to the other.

> "There is great diversity in the several stations and circumstances of mankind. Yet the difference is mainly superficial, and the equality in all important matters manifest. *The rich and the poor*, apparently so remote from each other, *meet together*. All have the same birth. All enter the world naked, helpless, unconscious beings; all stand in the same natural relation to their God; dependent on him for their birth; the children of his Providence; the creatures of his moral government. All are subject to the same sorrow, sickness, infirmities, and temptations. At the gate of the invisible world the distinction of riches and poverty is dropped. All go to one place – alike having kindred with worms and corruption. And when they shall come forth from the long home at the final consummation, all – small as well as great – shall stand before God (Revelation 20:12).

> We *meet together* also on the same level as sinners. All are tainted with the same original corruption. 'All, like sheep, have' personally 'gone astray' (Isaiah 53:6). All need alike the same new birth to give them life, the same precious blood to cleanse them, the same robe of righteousness to cover them (Romans 3:21-22). It is in fact a common need, and a common salvation (Jude 1:3). In all these matters *the rich and the poor* are as one. 'God is no respecter of persons.' The difference appears only as the outward garment. Yet what a distance it makes! The one scarcely hears of or knows the other!

> And when redeemed into the family of God, is not every member of the family our brother? Here then *rich and poor* meet on equal standing at the same throne of grace, in the same spiritual body, at the same holy table. We communicate to each other the same blessed hopes, feel the same sympathies, and anticipate the same home."[573]

> Deuteronomy 8:17-18 And thou say in thine heart, My power and the might of mine hand hath gotten me this wealth. But thou shalt remember the LORD thy God: for it is he that giveth thee power to get wealth, that he may establish his covenant which he sware unto thy fathers, as it is this day.

> 1 Samuel 2:7 The LORD maketh poor, and maketh rich: he bringeth low, and lifteth up.

> Job 1:21 And said, Naked came I out of my mother's womb, and naked shall I return thither: the LORD gave, and the LORD hath taken away; blessed be the name of the LORD.

> Job 31:13-23 If I did despise the cause of my manservant or of my maidservant, when they contended with me; What then shall I do when God riseth up? and when he visiteth, what shall I answer him? Did not he that made me in the womb make him? and did not one fashion us in the womb? If I have withheld the poor from *their* desire, or have caused the eyes of the widow to fail; Or have eaten my morsel myself alone, and the fatherless hath not eaten thereof; (For from my youth he was brought up with me, as *with* a father, and I have guided her from my mother's womb); If I have seen any perish for want of clothing, or any poor without covering; If his loins have not blessed me, and *if* he were *not* warmed with the fleece of my sheep; If I have lifted up my hand against the fatherless, when I saw my help in the gate: *Then* let mine arm fall from my shoulder blade, and mine arm be broken from the bone. For destruction *from* God *was* a terror to me, and by reason of his highness I could not endure.

> Psalm 145:9 The LORD is good to all: and his tender mercies are over all his works.

> Malachi 2:10 Have we not all one father? hath not one God created us? why do we deal treacherously every man against his brother, by profaning the covenant of our fathers?

> 1 Timothy 6:2 And they that have believing masters, let them not despise them, because they are brethren; but rather do them service, because they are faithful and beloved, partakers of the benefit. These things teach and exhort.
>
> Revelation 20:12 And I saw the dead, small and great, stand before God; and the books were opened: and another book was opened, which is the book of life: and the dead were judged out of those things which were written in the books, according to their works.

Rich people who want to please God and enjoy the wealth that has come their way do not despise, ignore, or mistreat the poor; and poor people do not hate the rich. All are brothers – children of God.

Proverbs 22:3 A prudent *man* foreseeth the evil, and hideth himself: but the simple pass on, and are punished.

> Focus: This proverb contrasts a safety advantage of being prudent with a unsafe disadvantage of being simple. *(Proverbs 27:12 is identical to this proverb.)*

"A prudent man" is "cautious; circumspect; practically wise; careful of the consequences of enterprises, measures or actions; cautious not to act when the end is of doubtful utility, or probably impracticable."[574] Eight times the Book of Proverbs uses the Hebrew word for **"prudent"** to describe a characteristic of a wise person, and each time it is used in contrast either to the "fool" or to the **"simple."**

> Proverbs 12:16 A fool's wrath is presently known: but a prudent *man* covereth shame.
>
> Proverbs 12:23 A prudent man concealeth knowledge: but the heart of fools proclaimeth foolishness.
>
> Proverbs 13:16 Every prudent *man* dealeth with knowledge: but a fool layeth open *his* folly.
>
> Proverbs 14:8 The wisdom of the prudent *is* to understand his way: but the folly of fools *is* deceit.
>
> Proverbs 14:15 The simple believeth every word: but the prudent *man* looketh well to his going.
>
> Proverbs 14:18 The simple inherit folly: but the prudent are crowned with knowledge.
>
> Proverbs 22:3 A prudent *man* foreseeth the evil, and hideth himself: but the simple pass on, and are punished.
>
> Proverbs 27:12 A prudent *man* foreseeth the evil, *and* hideth himself; *but* the simple pass on, *and* are punished.

Prudence, in a good sense, is one of the characteristics of being wise and is here used as its synonym. **"A prudent man forseeth the evil, and hideth himself."** Evil people resemble rattlesnakes in that they typically *(though often unintentionally)* give warning before inflicting their wickedness. Their warnings include vicious words, telltale gestures *(body language)*, and devious behavior; and because approximately "55% of communication is body language, 38% is the tone of voice, and 7% is the actual words spoken,[575] the wise person astutely interprets *all* that he sees and hears thereby he foresees danger and establishes a way of escape. Sometimes evil suddenly barges in, leaving no way for the prudent person to avoid the situation, such as when a weapon is suddenly brandished. In those times, as in all times, the wise person relies on the principles of conduct that he has learned from Scripture and from other sagacious persons in order to minimize the danger.

> Proverbs 6:12-14 A naughty person, a wicked man, walketh with a froward mouth. He winketh with his eyes, he speaketh with his feet, he teacheth with his fingers; Frowardness *is* in his heart, he deviseth mischief continually; he soweth discord.
>
> Proverbs 6:16-19 These six *things* doth the LORD hate: yea, seven *are* an abomination unto him: A proud look, a lying tongue, and hands that shed innocent blood, An heart that deviseth wicked imaginations, feet that be swift in running to mischief, A false witness *that* speaketh lies, and he that soweth discord among brethren.

Joseph fled from Potiphar's wife when he realized her evil intention (Genesis 39: 7-12). David fled from Saul when he recognized his evil spirit and saw a javelin in his hand (1 Samuel 18-20). How many bad marriages or business partnerships or convictions for a felony would be avoided by *foreseeing evil and hiding?*

> 2 Corinthians 6:14 Be ye not unequally yoked together with unbelievers: for what fellowship hath righteousness with unrighteousness? and what communion hath light with darkness?

"But the simple pass on, and are punished." Simple people are unsettled in their views and are consequently easily influenced – like a child. He is naive and untaught; however, he is *not* one who cannot comprehend *or* a fool who despises wisdom. Instead, he is one whose exposure to life and wisdom has been limited, making him gullible. Simple persons are those of weak capacities and shallow understandings, and they are incautious and easily imposed upon.

Either the simple person does not recognize evil or evil people – or he sees the danger in his pathway but disregards it and proceeds. When he doesn't alter his course, he suffers the consequences and *is punished.* Simple people either do not have the years of experience or the will or mental capacity to recognize the subtleness of evil, and should the evil not be so subtle, they still may choose to dismiss their observation as unimportant.

> *"The simple,* who believe every word that flatters them, will believe none that warns them, and so they *pass on and are punished.* They venture upon sin, though they are told what will be in the end thereof; they throw themselves into trouble, notwithstanding the fair warning given them, and they repent their presumption when it is too late. See an instance of both these. Nothing is so fatal to precious souls as this, they will not take warning."[576]

> Exodus 9:21 And he that regarded not the word of the LORD left his servants and his cattle in the field. *[After being warned of God, he left them there to be destroyed by a severe hail from God. See also verses 18-20.]*

Proverbs 22:4 By humility *and* the fear of the LORD *are* riches, and honour, and life.

Focus: This proverb declares the rewards from having a proper evaluation of self and a proper attitude toward God.

Throughout the Book of Proverbs, **"the fear of the LORD"** is defined as an awesome respect for God rather than the kind of fear that causes one to be terrified. Furthermore, this verse specifically states that such a respectful attitude toward God is to be *coupled with* an attitude of personal **"humility"** in order to obtain *special rewards.* Repeatedly, the Scriptures state that God hates pride, and it follows that a modest opinion of self lays the groundwork for being in the will of God. As a result of the believer's clothing himself with humility and giving proper respect to God, He rewards him with **"riches, and honour, and life."** Only by God came **"life,"** and He only sustains the same. He alone can give *fullness of life* that retains joy even in the face of adversity, and it is God Who gives a person the power to get riches. (Deuteronomy 8:18) Honor from man without endorsement from God is only a tease, like an empty cloud in time of drought, for only God can truly lift a person up and give him worthwhile "honor." When a person comes to a spiritual understanding of the awesomeness of God, he will desire to minimize himself and have a similar humble reaction as did Isaiah in the following passage.

> Isaiah 6:5 Then said I, Woe is me! for I am undone; because I am a man of unclean lips, and I dwell in the midst of a people of unclean lips: for mine eyes have seen the King, the LORD of hosts.

Below are verses that enhance the understanding of this proverb.

> Deuteronomy 8:17-18 And thou say in thine heart, My power and the might of mine hand hath gotten me this wealth. But thou shalt remember the LORD thy God: for it is he that giveth thee power to get wealth, that he may establish his covenant which he sware unto thy fathers, as it is this day.
>
> Psalm 34:9 O fear the LORD, ye his saints: for there is no want to them that fear him. The young lions do lack, and suffer hunger: but they that seek the LORD shall not want any good thing.
>
> Psalm 112:1-3 Praise ye the LORD. Blessed *is* the man *that* feareth the LORD, *that* delighteth greatly in his commandments. His seed shall be mighty upon earth: the generation of the upright shall be blessed. Wealth and riches *shall be* in his house: and his righteousness endureth for ever.
>
> Proverbs 3:13,15 Happy is the man that findeth wisdom, and the man that getteth understanding . . . Length of days is in her right hand; and in her left hand riches and honour.
>
> Proverbs 15:33 The fear of the LORD is the instruction of wisdom; and before honour is humility.
>
> Proverbs 18:12 Before destruction the heart of man is haughty, and before honour is humility.
>
> Proverbs 21:21 He that followeth after righteousness and mercy findeth life, righteousness, and honour.
>
> Isaiah 33:6 And wisdom and knowledge shall be the stability of thy times, and strength of salvation: the fear of the LORD is his treasure.
>
> Luke 18:13-14 And the publican, standing afar off, would not lift up so much as his eyes unto heaven, but smote upon his breast, saying, God be merciful to me a sinner. I tell you, this man went down to his house justified rather than the other: for every one that exalteth himself shall be abased; and he that humbleth himself shall be exalted.
>
> John 10:10 The thief cometh not, but for to steal, and to kill, and to destroy: I am come that they might have life, and that they might have it more abundantly.
>
> Hebrews 11:6 But without faith *it is* impossible to please *him:* for he that cometh to God must believe that he is, and *that* he is a rewarder of them that diligently seek him.
>
> James 4:6, 10 But he giveth more grace. Wherefore he saith, God resisteth the proud, but giveth grace unto the humble . . . Humble yourselves in the sight of the Lord, and he shall lift you up.

Barnes elaborates on "riches and honour and life."

> "Might have it more abundantly – Literally, that they may have abundance, or that which abounds. The word denotes that which is not absolutely essential to life, but which is superadded to make life happy. They shall not merely have life – simple, bare existence – but they shall have all those superadded things which are needful to make that life eminently blessed and happy. It would be vast mercy to keep men merely from annihilation or hell; but Jesus will give them eternal joy, peace, the society of the blessed, and all those exalted means of felicity which are prepared for them in the world of glory."[577]

Proverbs 22:5 Thorns and snares are in the way of the froward: he that doth keep his soul shall be far from them.

Focus: This proverb stresses that trouble comes to those persons who resist God and that the righteous are separated from those same troubles.

In his walk, speech, and everyday life, a **"froward"** person is twisted, distorted, crooked, and perverted because he intentionally opposes God and makes himself a stranger to the commandments of God. **"Thorns"** symbolize the evil people and tragic situations (calamities) of life that cause one pain, and **"snares"** are symbolic of traps that are fallen into because of failing to heed instructions of wisdom. The **"way of the froward"** is the obstinate person's chosen hard path of life that involves unnecessary drama, unnecessary difficulties and dangers, and eventually destruction. It is a way or course of life selected by the froward, and the problems come because he has chosen the path away from God and His word. Proverbs 13:15 states, "...the way of transgressors *is* hard."

A **"soul"** is a living being, the man himself. A wise person **"doth keep his soul"** by guarding himself through wise decisions, choosing a path of life instructed by God, and steering away from the thorns and snares of life. He has an awesome respect for the LORD as taught in the previous proverb leading him to be humble, unlike the froward person who arrogantly disregards God. Life is easier and much more enjoyable when evil people and tragic situations are avoided.

> "The way of sin is vexatious and dangerous: *In the way of the froward,* that crooked way, which is contrary to the will and word of God, *thorns and snares are* found, thorns of grief for past sins and snares entangling them in further sin. He that makes no conscience of what he says and does will find himself hampered by that imaginary liberty, and tormented by his pleasures. Froward people, who are soon angry, expose themselves to trouble at every step. Every thing will fret and vex him that will fret and vex at every thing. . . . *He that keeps his soul,* that watches carefully over his own heart and ways, is *far from* those *thorns and snares,* for his way is both plain and pleasant."[578]

Joshua 23:11-13 Take good heed therefore unto yourselves, that ye love the LORD your God. Else if ye do in any wise go back, and cleave unto the remnant of these nations, even these that remain among you, and shall make marriages with them, and go in unto them, and they to you: Know for a certainty that the LORD your God will no more drive out any of these nations from before you; but they shall be snares and traps unto you, and scourges in your sides, and thorns in your eyes, until ye perish from off this good land which the LORD your God hath given you.

Job 18:5-8 Yea, the light of the wicked shall be put out, and the spark of his fire shall not shine. The light shall be dark in his tabernacle, and his candle shall be put out with him. The steps of his strength shall be straitened, and his own counsel shall cast him down. For he is cast into a net by his own feet, and he walketh upon a snare.

Psalm 11:5-7 The LORD trieth the righteous: but the wicked and him that loveth violence his soul hateth. Upon the wicked he shall rain snares, fire and brimstone, and an horrible tempest: this shall be the portion of their cup. For the righteous LORD loveth righteousness; his countenance doth behold the upright.

Proverbs 4:20-24 My son, attend to my words; incline thine ear unto my sayings. Let them not depart from thine eyes; keep them in the midst of thine heart. For they are life unto those that find them, and health to all their flesh. Keep thy heart with all diligence; for out of it are the issues of life. Put away from thee a froward mouth, and perverse lips put far from thee.

Proverbs 14:26-27 In the fear of the LORD is strong confidence: and his children shall have a place of refuge. The fear of the LORD is a fountain of life, to depart from the snares of death.

Proverbs 15:18-19 A wrathful man stirreth up strife: but he that is slow to anger appeaseth strife. The way of the slothful man is as an hedge of thorns: but the way of the righteous is made plain.

Proverbs 16:17 The highway of the upright is to depart from evil: he that keepeth his way preserveth his soul.

Proverbs 19:16 He that keepeth the commandment keepeth his own soul; but he that despiseth his ways shall die.

1 John 5:17-19 All unrighteousness is sin: and there is a sin not unto death. We know that whosoever is born of God sinneth not; but he that is begotten of God keepeth himself, and that wicked one toucheth him not. And we know that we are of God, and the whole world lieth in wickedness.

> **Proverbs 22:6** Train up a child in the way he should go: and when he is old, he will not depart from it.

Focus: This proverb stresses the consequential and enduring effect of training a child to live in a godly manner.

By instruction, reproof, and example, godly parents **"train up a child"** to think and act in ways taught by Scripture. Children learn by receiving positive *or* negative feedback through interacting with their parents and others. When what they have *heard* from their parents about righteousness is consistent with what they have *seen* in their parents, children enjoy peace and reinforcement; but when the two are inconsistent, they feel disturbed and are unsettled as to which way is right. Under either consistent or inconsistent example, the child is being trained – either to stability and Christianity or to instability and unrighteousness. (NOTE: Please see the similar Proverbs 22:15.)

The training is to be **"in the way he should go,"** which, without any doubt, means the way of the wise, the righteous, and the godly. The way he *should* go is not the way he *would* go if left to himself – a way described in the previous proverb as being full of thorns and snares wherein the froward walk, who are opposed to God.

> *"But this training must be practical.* The mere talk to *a child* about religion, without bringing it to bear upon his loose habits, and self-willed tempers, is utterly ineffective. None of us liveth to himself *alone*. We are all spreading around us an influence, whether for good or for evil. Here therefore in our families lies the responsibility of Christian consistency. If the child hears of godliness, and sees but wickedness, this is bringing him bread with one hand, and poison with the other; 'beckoning him with the hand to heaven, and at the same time taking him by the hand, and leading him in the way to destruction.' Who would receive even the choicest food from a leprous hand? Neglect is far better than inconsistency; forgetfulness, than contempt of principle. *A child* learns more by the eye than by the ear. Imitation is a far more powerful principle than memory. A well-trained child gladly looks to his parent's godliness as his model picture, to copy after. A wayward child eagerly seeks for the excuse of his own delinquency, and this discovery in parental example will harden him in infidelity and ungodliness."[579]

> John 10:10 The thief cometh not, but for to steal, and to kill, and to destroy: I am come that they might have life, and that they might have it more abundantly.
> Genesis 18:19 For I know him, that he will command his children and his household after him, and they shall keep the way of the LORD, to do justice and judgment; that the LORD may bring upon Abraham that which he hath spoken of him.
> Deuteronomy 6:6-7 And these words, which I command thee this day, shall be in thine heart: And thou shalt teach them diligently unto thy children, and shalt talk of them when thou sittest in thine house, and when thou walkest by the way, and when thou liest down, and when thou risest up.
> Ephesians 6:4 And, ye fathers, provoke not your children to wrath: but bring them up in the nurture and admonition of the Lord.
> 2 Timothy 3:14-17 But continue thou in the things which thou hast learned and hast been assured of, knowing of whom thou hast learned them; And that from a child thou hast known the holy scriptures, which are able to make thee wise unto salvation through faith which is in Christ Jesus. All scripture is given by inspiration of God, and is profitable for doctrine, for reproof, for correction, for instruction in righteousness: That the man of God may be perfect, throughly furnished unto all good works.
> *[See also Deuteronomy 4:9; 31:12-13 and Psalm 78:4-8]*

A parent who wants to "train up" a child properly must practice "tough love," which is a willingness to teach and do the tough (difficult) things out of a loving heart. Scripture declares that a believer should speak the truth in love (Ephesians 4:15) and as Ephesians 6:4 states "provoke not your children to wrath." The parent should *not* avoid training the child about dealing with sex and drugs, covetousness, hatred or disdain for others, and respect for God and others, because society frowns upon Biblical teaching. No matter how difficult to receive or share, truth needs to be communicated by love.

> Have you ever heard, or even said, 'this hurts me more than it hurts you' as a child is disciplined? When parents choose to do the hard work of disciplining a child, even when it inconveniences them or hurts them to have their child suffer negative consequences, that is tough love. Equally, it is tough love when a parent at times chooses not to rescue a child from negative consequences. Apart from love, discipline is selfish and can rapidly become abusive or neglectful. In love, and with God's wisdom, proper discipline can help train a child in the ways of God and will ultimately lead to better things (Hebrews 12:11). We discipline children because we care for them and want to equip them for life as an adult. We do the tough things because we love them."[580]

> Hebrews 12:11 Now no chastening for the present seemeth to be joyous, but grievous: nevertheless afterward it yieldeth the peaceable fruit of righteousness unto them which are exercised thereby.

When King David committed adultery and had his lover's husband killed, the prophet Nathan was the only one recorded in Scripture who confronted him about his sin (2 Samuel 12). Nathan spoke the truth to David in such a way that David became immediately repentant. Choosing to obey God and speak the truth (no matter the consequences) is tough love.

"And when he is old, he will not depart from it" – a statement totally understandable because no rational person who has been trained to walk in the way of wisdom with God; and has, *through experience,* enjoyed the blessings of a walk with God; and has thus avoided evil with all the accompanying sorrow throughout their childhood, youth and middle age, would leave this wonderful way of life and turn to evil **"when he is old."**

> Proverbs 22:7   The rich ruleth over the poor, and the borrower is servant to the lender.

> Focus: This proverb declares two potentially harsh, unbalanced and demeaning relationships that may exist because of differences in financial status.

This verse is a warning. A wise person should be financially dependent on God and independent of obligation to those who could potentially rule their lives. **"The rich ruleth over the poor,"** must have reminded the Jew of the Egyptian taskmasters who maliciously treated them in a rigorous, oppressive, or tyrannical manner. They were commanded to never treat their fellow Jew with such disrespect.

> Deuteronomy 24:18-22 But thou shalt remember that thou wast a bondman in Egypt, and the LORD thy God redeemed thee thence: therefore I command thee to do this thing. When thou cuttest down thine harvest in thy field, and hast forgot a sheaf in the field, thou shalt not go again to fetch it: it shall be for the stranger, for the fatherless, and for the widow: that the LORD thy God may bless thee in all the work of thine hands. When thou beatest thine olive tree, thou shalt not go over the boughs again: it shall be for the stranger, for the fatherless, and for the widow. When thou gatherest the grapes of thy vineyard, thou shalt not glean *it* afterward: it shall be for the stranger, for the fatherless, and for the widow. And thou shalt remember that thou wast a bondman in the land of Egypt: therefore I command thee to do this thing.

In Old Testament times, an unrighteous lender would *demand* that the borrower repay the money plus interest in violation of the Mosaic law. If the borrower could not pay his debt, he may have had no choice but to sell himself or his family to the lender to be a bond servant. Scripture relates the story of how Elisha, through a miracle of God, caused valuable oil to keep reproducing itself until all borrowed vessels were filled and thus prevented the widow's sons from being sold as bondmen because of the family's debt.

> 2 Kings 4:6-7 And it came to pass, when the vessels were full, that she said unto her son, Bring me yet a vessel. And he said unto her, There is not a vessel more. And the oil stayed. Then she came and told the man of God. And he said, Go, sell the oil, and pay thy debt, and live thou and thy children of the rest.

The Holy Spirit led Paul to write the following concerning debt: "Owe no man any thing, but to love one another: for he that loveth another hath fulfilled the law." (Romans 13:8) A borrower is at the mercy of his lender because he has received from the lender's assets and pledged his honor and his family name to repay the debt. The following warns of debt and explains the depth of agony involved in the words **"the borrower *is* servant to the lender."**

> "'Owe no man anything.' Keep out of debt. Avoid it as you would avoid war, pestilence, and famine. Hate it with a perfect hatred. Dig potatoes, break stones, peddle in tin wares, do anything that is honest and useful, rather than run into debt. As you value comfort, quiet, and independence, keep out of debt. As you value good digestion, a healthy appetite, a placid temper, a smooth pillow, pleasant dreams and happy wakings, keep out of debt. Debt is the hardest of all taskmasters; the most cruel of all oppressors. It is as a millstone about the neck. It is an incubus *[demon]* on the heart. It spreads a cloud over the whole firmament of man's being. It eclipses the sun; it blots out the stars; it dims and defaces the beautiful blue sky. It breaks the harmony of nature, and turns to dissonance all the voices of its melody. It furrows the forehead with premature wrinkles; it plucks the eye of its light. It drags the nobleness and kindness out of the port and bearing of a man; it takes the soul out of his laugh, and all stateliness and freedom from his walk. Come not, then, under its crushing dominion. But to love one another."[581]

Nehemiah led the Jews in a concerted, labor intense effort to rebuild the walls around Jerusalem. While this was happening, the poor laborers were being taken advantage of by the wealthy Jewish noblemen.

> Nehemiah 5:1-5 And there was a great cry of the people and of their wives against their brethren the Jews. For there were that said, We, our sons, and our daughters, *are* many: therefore we take up corn *for them,* that we may eat, and live. *Some* also there were that said, We have mortgaged our lands, vineyards, and houses, that we might buy corn, because of the dearth. There were also that said, We have borrowed money for the king's tribute, *and that upon* our lands and vineyards. Yet now our flesh *is* as the flesh of our brethren, our children as their children: and, lo, we bring into bondage our sons and our daughters to be servants,

and *some* of our daughters are brought unto bondage *already:* neither *is it* in our power *to redeem them;* for other men have our lands and vineyards.

Nehemiah's first response was anger at the wealthy Jewish nobles' "selfishness, greed, and insensitivity. Some people were hurting and suffering, and those who should have been the most compassionate (the nobles and officials) were most guilty of exploitation. "Though Nehemiah's anger was certainly righteous indignation, he did not take immediate action. Spending time reflecting on the problem enabled him to cool down, to see the facts in proper perspective, and to decide on a course of action."[582] After calming down, he rebuked the nobles, reminded them of the Bible's command against usury, called a large assembly of all the people, and asked the nobles:

> Nehemiah 5:11-12 Restore, I pray you, to them, even this day, their lands, their vineyards, their oliveyards, and their houses, also the hundredth *part* of the money, and of the corn, the wine, and the oil, that ye exact of them. Then said they, We will restore *them,* and will require nothing of them; so will we do as thou sayest. Then I called the priests, and took an oath of them, that they should do according to this promise.

Even though these Jewish workers went through these tribulations through no fault of their own, the events underscore man's greed and the borrower's helplessness. In an unusual turn, and through God's help and the wise leadership of Nehemiah, the situation was made into a victory. The circumstances also underscore the need for wisdom in borrowing money and care in following God's directives *before* an adverse situation arises.

Proverbs 22:8   He that soweth iniquity shall reap vanity: and the rod of his anger shall fail.

Focus: This proverb declares the empty, failing consequences for persons who do wickedly.

"He that soweth iniquity shall reap vanity." To commit acts that are wickedly wrong or are oppressing others is to *sow iniquity* (scatter seeds of wrongdoing and sin). A wicked sower **"shall reap vanity,"** indicating that he will reap *nothing good*. His harvest will be an "utter and eternal disappointment"[583] because his crop will resemble his scattered seed. Sin always produces trouble, and there is no way for a person to sow seeds of wickedness and reap a crop of pleasantness. It will be trouble, wickedness, misery, or sorrow in his life. "*Whatsoever a man soweth, that shall he also reap.*" (Galatians 6:7) He will not be blessed.

"And the rod of his anger shall fail." **"The rod"** symbolizes power and refers to whatever the sower of iniquity uses to cause trouble or harm to another person. This "rod" of oppression will not last. His time will come. "…He has ruled and smitten others angrily; this shall be taken from him; his authority shall fail, and he shall become subject to others, and be used in like manner…"[584] Perhaps this phrase refers to the previous proverb in which the rich take unmerciful and demanding advantage of the poor.

> Psalm 125:3 For the rod of the wicked shall not rest upon the lot of the righteous; lest the righteous put forth their hands unto iniquity.
> Isaiah 14:5-7 The LORD hath broken the staff of the wicked, *and* the sceptre of the rulers. He who smote the people in wrath with a continual stroke, he that ruled the nations in anger, is persecuted, *and* none hindereth. The whole earth is at rest, *and* is quiet: they break forth into singing.
> Isaiah 30:31 For through the voice of the LORD shall the Assyrian be beaten down, which smote with a rod.
> Job 4:8 Even as I have seen, they that plow iniquity, and sow wickedness, reap the same.
> Job 15:31 Let not him that is deceived trust in vanity: for vanity shall be his recompence.
> Hosea 10:13 Ye have plowed wickedness, ye have reaped iniquity; ye have eaten the fruit of lies: because thou didst trust in thy way, in the multitude of thy mighty men.
> Galatians 6:7-8 Be not deceived; God is not mocked: for whatsoever a man soweth, that shall he also reap. For he that soweth to his flesh shall of the flesh reap corruption; but he that soweth to the Spirit shall of the Spirit reap life everlasting.

Proverbs 22:9   He that hath a bountiful eye shall be blessed; for he giveth of his bread to the poor.

Focus: This proverb declares the reward for the benevolent-hearted person.

In the previous proverb, the law of sowing and reaping revealed that a wicked person reaps the reward of the wickedness that he sows. In this proverb, the righteous person, who generously sows to those in need, reaps the blessings of his kind and generous heart.

> 2 Corinthians 9:6-9 But this *I say,* He which soweth sparingly shall reap also sparingly; and he which soweth bountifully shall reap also bountifully. Every man according as he purposeth in his heart, *so let him give;* not grudgingly, or of necessity: for God loveth a cheerful giver. And God *is* able to make all grace abound toward you; that ye, always having all sufficiency in all *things,* may abound to every good work: (As it is written, He hath dispersed abroad; he hath given to the poor: his righteousness remaineth for ever.)

"He that hath a bountiful eye" is a generous person. In Proverbs 28:22, s **"bountiful eye"** is the opposite of an "evil eye." A "bountiful eye" sees the needs and hardships of others. Because of his kind, compassionate heart through which he sees the world **("bountiful eye")**, he wants to help those less fortunate; and, as applied in this proverb, he does so by giving "of his bread to the poor." (A person with **"an evil eye"** looks at another with envy or unmercifulness as he sees something he wants to take from the unsuspecting soul who managed to make it into his presence.)

> "What is a bountiful eye, and what is the blessing belonging to him who possesses it? The eye is a wonderful part of the curiously wrought human frame. But the term is used in Scripture in a moral point of view, and describes a peculiar state of the mind. Thus we read of the blinded eye, the enlightened eye, the single eye, the evil eye, all of which refer to the state of the mind or heart; and so does the term 'bountiful eye' . . . – one through which the soul looks in tender compassion – one that 'considers the cause of the poor' (Psalm 41:1) – one that compares and contrives – one that 'affects the heart,' stirs it up to feel, and moves the hand to minister. Such an eye looks in the right place to find appropriate objects. It does not shun misery, 'passing by' (like the priest and Levite) 'on the other side.' It looks through the right medium, even the love and compassion of God, and says, 'If God so loved us, we ought also to love one another.' 'What shall I render to the Lord for all His benefits toward me?' It looks to the right end, even the glory of God and the good of man; and looks for a right reward – not the approbation of man, but to please God. (*Christian Treasury*.)"[585]

Observe the use of "good" and "evil" eyes in the following verses.

> Deuteronomy 15:9 Beware that there be not a thought in thy wicked heart, saying, The seventh year, the year of release, is at hand; and thine eye be evil against thy poor brother, and thou givest him nought; and he cry unto the LORD against thee, and it be sin unto thee.
>
> Deuteronomy 28:56-57 The tender and delicate woman among you, which would not adventure to set the sole of her foot upon the ground for delicateness and tenderness, her eye shall be evil toward the husband of her bosom, and toward her son, and toward her daughter, And toward her young one that cometh out from between her feet, and toward her children which she shall bear: for she shall eat them for want of all things secretly in the siege and straitness, wherewith thine enemy shall distress thee in thy gates.
>
> Proverbs 23:6 Eat thou not the bread of him that hath an evil eye, neither desire thou his dainty meats: For as he thinketh in his heart, so is he: Eat and drink, saith he to thee; but his heart is not with thee.
>
> Proverbs 28:22 He that hasteth to be rich hath an evil eye, and considereth not that poverty shall come upon him.
>
> Matthew 20:15 Is it not lawful for me to do what I will with mine own? Is thine eye evil, because I am good?
>
> Luke 11:34-35 The light of the body is the eye: therefore when thine eye is single, thy whole body also is full of light; but when *thine eye* is evil, thy body also *is* full of darkness. Take heed therefore that the light which is in thee be not darkness.

Proverbs 22:10 Cast out the scorner, and contention shall go out; yea, strife and reproach shall cease.

Focus: This proverb specifies how to deal with a scorner and then specifies the rewards of such action.

The **"scorner,"** a proud, boastful mocker of righteousness and God, makes fun of sin, sneers at godliness, and laughs sarcastically at good men. He desires to bring others down while elevating himself. He is arrogant, having no apparent fear of God and no respect for others. There is little room for doubt that Noah, the preacher of righteousness, was scorned and mocked when he told the sinful population that God would destroy the world with a flood. Believers are always subject to be scorned and mocked for their righteousness and steadfast service to God.

> Proverbs 14:6-7 A scorner seeketh wisdom, and *findeth it* not: but knowledge *is* easy unto him that understandeth. Go from the presence of a foolish man, when thou perceivest not *in him* the lips of knowledge.
>
> Proverbs 21:23-24 Whoso keepeth his mouth and his tongue keepeth his soul from troubles. Proud and haughty scorner is his name, who dealeth in proud wrath.

Proverbs 26:20-21 Where no wood is, *there* the fire goeth out: so where *there is* no talebearer, the strife ceaseth. *As* coals *are* to burning coals, and wood to fire; so *is* a contentious man to kindle strife.

Proverbs 28:25 He that is of a proud heart stirreth up strife: but he that putteth his trust in the LORD shall be made fat.

Matthew 9:24 He said unto them, Give place: for the maid is not dead, but sleepeth. And they laughed him to scorn. *[Also see Mark 5:39-40, Luke 8: 52-55.]*

The counsel given in this proverb is to **"cast out the scorner,"** and the result will be that contention, strife and reproach (that he has produced) will go out with him. "Those that would secure the peace must exclude the scorner."[586]

"Chase away the scorner (Proverbs 1:22), the man who has no respect for things human or Divine, and the disputes and ill feeling which he caused will be ended; for 'where no wood is, the fire goeth out' (Proverbs 26:20). **Yea, strife and reproach shall cease.** The reproach and ignominy are those which the presence and words of the scorner bring with them; to have such a one in the company is a disgrace to all good men."[587]

Genesis 21:9-10 And Sarah saw the son of Hagar the Egyptian, which she had born unto Abraham, mocking. Wherefore she said unto Abraham, Cast out this bondwoman and her son: for the son of this bondwoman shall not be heir with my son, *even* with Isaac.

Nehemiah 4:1-2, 28 But it came to pass, that when Sanballat heard that we builded the wall, he was wroth, and took great indignation, and mocked the Jews. And he spake before his brethren and the army of Samaria, and said, What do these feeble Jews? will they fortify themselves? will they sacrifice? will they make an end in a day? will they revive the stones out of the heaps of the rubbish which are burned?... And one of the sons of Joiada, the son of Eliashib the high priest, was son in law to Sanballat the Horonite: therefore I chased him from me.

Psalm 101:5 Whoso privily slandereth his neighbour, him will I cut off: him that hath an high look and a proud heart will not I suffer.

Proverbs 26:20-21 Where no wood is, *there* the fire goeth out: so where *there is* no talebearer, the strife ceaseth. *As* coals *are* to burning coals, and wood to fire; so *is* a contentious man to kindle strife.

Titus 3:10-11 A man that is an heretick after the first and second admonition reject; Knowing that he that is such is subverted, and sinneth, being condemned of himself.

Proverbs 22:11 He that loveth pureness of heart, *for* the grace of his lips the king *shall be* his friend.

Focus: This proverb specifies a benefit of graceful speech stemming from a pure heart.

"He that loveth pureness of heart" is the person who has great affection for, and thus personally maintains, moral or ethical cleanliness. He lives a godly life and enjoys peace beyond explanation between himself and God; and, as much as is possible, he lives in peace and truthfulness with other people. Because his speech is opposite that of the previous proverb's scorner, who loves contention, strife and reproach, the **"grace of his lips"** is observed when he speaks appropriately and agreeably. His words are suitable, elegant, and with dignity.[588] His presence is like a sweet aroma rather than a scorner's stench, and he brings peace and pleasantness because his words are absent of flattery and a worldly lust for success at any cost. This man that **"loveth pureness of heart"** will be favored by God and man.

Having no reason for sensing any threat and knowing that his presence brings peace, **"the king shall be his friend."** His calm manners and carefully-chosen words will de-escalate an otherwise increasingly hostile situation. Because of the favor of God, there is likely to be associated with him a awareness of the presence of God.

Proverbs 16:13 Righteous lips are the delight of kings; and they love him that speaketh right.

Matthew 5:8 Blessed *are* the pure in heart: for they shall see God.

Luke 2:52 And Jesus increased in wisdom and stature, and in favour with God and man.

Romans 14:16-18 Let not then your good be evil spoken of: For the kingdom of God is not meat and drink; but righteousness, and peace, and joy in the Holy Ghost. For he that in these things serveth Christ *is* acceptable to God, and approved of men.

Proverbs 22:12 The eyes of the LORD preserve knowledge, and he overthroweth the words of the transgressor.

Focus: This proverb expresses the oversight and protection that God gives to Scripture.

Speaking symbolically of His Fatherly observation, evaluation, and concern, **"the eyes of the LORD"** are said to **"*preserve* knowledge"** in the first clause; and in the second, "He" (**"the LORD"**) is said to **"*overthrow* the words of the transgressors."** Because He "sees" and knows everything and consequently desires that His chosen people are knowledgeable concerning Himself, He takes action to preserve His word (Scripture). At the same time, He **"overthroweth"** *[subverts, turns upside down]* the **"words of the transgressor"** who opposes the word of God and everything He stands for. **"The transgressor"** represents the *wicked, deceitful, treacherous, unfaithful* men who have always opposed the Scriptures and God's people with their words. Specifically, the transgressor is the scorner (mentioned in verse 10) who is perpetually attempting to mock and defeat the word of God; but who is forever a loser overthrown by God.

> "The greatest truth that a person can possess with the mind or learn through experience is truth about God This cannot be gained by unaided human reason. It is acquired only as God shows Himself to people – in nature and conscience; in history or providence; and especially in the Bible.
>
> Mental knowledge by itself, as good as it may be, is inadequate; it is capable only of producing pride. Moral knowledge affects a person's will. It is knowledge of the heart, not the mind alone. The Book of Proverbs deals primarily with this kind of knowledge. Experiential knowledge is that gained through one's experience.
>
> The apostle Paul's wish for the church at Colosse was that they might increase in the 'knowledge of God.' (Colossians 1:10)"[589]
>
> Psalm 46:10 Be still, and know that I *am* God: I will be exalted among the heathen, I will be exalted in the earth.
>
> Proverbs 1:7 The fear of the LORD *is* the beginning of knowledge: *but* fools despise wisdom and instruction.
>
> Proverbs 2:1-6 My son, if thou wilt receive my words, and hide my commandments with thee; So that thou incline thine ear unto wisdom, *and* apply thine heart to understanding; Yea, if thou criest after knowledge, *and* liftest up thy voice for understanding; If thou seekest her as silver, and searchest for her as *for* hid treasures; Then shalt thou understand the fear of the LORD, and find the knowledge of God. For the LORD giveth wisdom: out of his mouth *cometh* knowledge and understanding.
>
> Proverbs 9:10 The fear of the LORD *is* the beginning of wisdom: and the knowledge of the holy *is* understanding.
>
> Proverbs 19:27 Cease, my son, to hear the instruction *that causeth* to err from the words of knowledge.
>
> Proverbs 23:12 Apply thine heart unto instruction, and thine ears to the words of knowledge.
>
> Proverbs 24:14 So *shall* the knowledge of wisdom *be* unto thy soul: when thou hast found *it,* then there shall be a reward, and thy expectation shall not be cut off.
>
> John 8:31-2 Then said Jesus to those Jews which believed on him, If ye continue in my word, *then* are ye my disciples indeed; And ye shall know the truth, and the truth shall make you free.
>
> Romans 1:19-20 Because that which may be known of God is manifest in them; for God hath shewed *it* unto them. For the invisible things of him from the creation of the world are clearly seen, being understood by the things that are made, *even* his eternal power and Godhead; so that they are without excuse. . .
>
> Romans 11:33 O the depth of the riches both of the wisdom and knowledge of God! how unsearchable *are* his judgments, and his ways past finding out!

The Preserver of knowledge is God Himself, Who works through His chosen men and women, who are described in verse 11 as *loving pureness of heart*. Throughout the ages, many have died protecting and preserving the word of God. Even though mankind is wicked, and Satan is running "to and fro" (Job 2:2) to blind men's minds to the truth, God has His wise and faithful men and women who stand endangering their lives and livelihoods to speak what they know of the truth. "The eyes of the LORD" see them, and He preserves these knowledgeable witnesses, and in the process, He keeps the knowledge of the truth available to the world.

In the Old Testament, when the knowledge of God Himself and His word seemed to be disappearing, 2 Chronicles records that a single copy of Scripture was found. Notice how the young Jewish king, Josiah reacted when "a book of the law of the LORD given by Moses" *was found* – obviously preserved by God.

> 2 Chronicles 34:19-21 And it came to pass, when the king had heard the words of the law, that he rent his clothes. And the king commanded Hilkiah, and Ahikam the son of Shaphan, and Abdon the son of Micah, and Shaphan the scribe, and Asaiah a servant of the king's, saying, Go, enquire of the LORD for me, and for them that are left in Israel and in Judah, concerning the words of the book that is found: for great is the wrath of the LORD that is poured out upon us, because our fathers have not kept the word of the LORD, to do after all that is written in this book.

In the New Testament, deceivers were overthrown as they tried to stop the word of God.

> Acts 13:9-12 Then Saul, (who also *is called* Paul,) filled with the Holy Ghost, set his eyes on him *[Elymas the sorcerer,]* And said, O full of all subtilty and all mischief, *thou* child of the devil, *thou* enemy of all righteousness, wilt thou not cease to pervert the right ways of the Lord? And now, behold, the hand of the Lord *is* upon thee, and thou shalt be blind, not seeing the sun for a season. And immediately there fell on him a mist and a darkness; and he went about seeking some to lead him by the hand. Then the deputy, when he saw what was done, believed, being astonished at the doctrine of the Lord.
>
> 2 Timothy 3:8 Now as Jannes and Jambres withstood Moses, so do these also resist the truth: men of corrupt minds, reprobate concerning the faith. But they shall proceed no further: for their folly shall be manifest unto all *men,* as theirs also was.

The Jewish scribes were first given the job of meticulously copying and preserving God's word. Through the voice of His mighty prophets and through the inspired words of the writers of the New Testament, the words were sent forth.

Then, after disciples were made around the world, the words and the knowledge of God had to be translated into the everyday language of the nations.

Men have given their lives to preserve the Scriptures.

> "Martin Luther was the first to translate the Bible into the vernacular, in his case, German. Gutenberg chose the Bible as the first product of his marvelous invention of movable type in 1455. For two centuries it was punishable by death to print the Bible in any language other than Latin, although the Old Testament existed in Hebrew and Greek. But under King James, a major effort created the translation known to most of the world."[590]

"The eyes of the LORD" watch the remnant faithfully teaching and preaching the word today. The true "church" is committed to its preservation (salt) and propagation (light). (Matthew 5:13-16) For this purpose, God is also preserving the church (born-again believers) on the earth "and the gates of hell shall not prevail against it." (Matthew 16:18)

> Jeremiah 20:9-11 Then I said, I will not make mention of him, nor speak any more in his name. But *his word* was in mine heart as a burning fire shut up in my bones, and I was weary with forbearing, and I could not *stay*. For I heard the defaming of many, fear on every side. Report, *say they,* and we will report it. All my familiars watched for my halting, *saying,* Peradventure he will be enticed, and we shall prevail against him, and we shall take our revenge on him. But the LORD *is* with me as a mighty terrible one: therefore my persecutors shall stumble, and they shall not prevail: they shall be greatly ashamed; for they shall not prosper: *their* everlasting confusion shall never be forgotten.
>
> 1 Thessalonians 2:4 But as we were allowed of God to be put in trust with the gospel, even so we speak; not as pleasing men, but God, which trieth our hearts.
>
> Romans 3:1 What advantage then hath the Jew? or what profit *is there* of circumcision? Much every way: chiefly, because that unto them were committed the oracles of God.
>
> 1 Timothy 6:20 O Timothy, keep that which is committed to thy trust, avoiding profane *and* vain babblings, and oppositions of science falsely so called:

Each modern-day believer must join God's army to preserve the word of truth by knowing the Bible well enough to resist the deception that will be foisted on the church in these last days. Ministers must not be afraid to preach the truth. "The eyes of the LORD" will watch over the churches who make much of God's word and the knowledge of God, who ignore profane and vain babbling, and who contend for the faith once delivered to the saints" (Jude 1:3), and who make disciples.

> Hosea 4:1, 6 Hear the word of the LORD, ye children of Israel: for the LORD hath a controversy with the inhabitants of the land, because *there is* no truth, nor mercy, nor knowledge of God in the land. ... My people are destroyed for lack of knowledge: because thou hast rejected knowledge, I will also reject thee, that thou shalt be no priest to me: seeing thou hast forgotten the law of thy God, I will also forget thy children.

Proverbs 22:13 The slothful *man* saith, *There is* a lion without, I shall be slain in the streets.

Focus: This proverb illustrates the ridiculous lame excuses of a slothful man.

"The slothful man" *[lazy, sluggish]* is so lazy that he *perhaps* hears a rumor or maybe dreams a dream that there is a lion "without" in the countryside. Therefore, he cannot go out of the house and into the fields to do any work. That story is not enough, so he embellishes his tale a little more when he conjures up a more fanciful tale about being "slain in the streets." "He talks of *a lion without,* but considers not his real danger from the devil, that *roaring lion,* which is in bed with him, and from his own slothfulness, which kills him."[591] Imagination is one of his enemies, along with fear, that adds to his cowardice. Proverbs 26 repeats this humorous thought and adds an additional description of "the slothful man."

> Proverbs 26:13-16 The slothful man saith, There is a lion in the way; a lion is in the streets. As the door turneth upon his hinges, so doth the slothful upon his bed. The slothful hideth his hand in his bosom; it grieveth him to bring it again to his mouth. The sluggard is wiser in his own conceit than seven men that can render a reason.

This Scripture humorously describes the lazy man and his preposterous imagination. Lazy people continually face failure and self-induced trouble and certainly do not represent the Father. Under the inspiration of the Holy Spirit, the Apostle John's wish for Gaius in 3 John 1:2 was "Beloved, I wish above all things that thou mayest prosper and be in health, even as thy soul prospereth."

> **Proverbs 22:14** The mouth of strange women *is* a deep pit: he that is abhorred of the LORD shall fall therein.

Focus: This proverb symbolically describes the beckoning, deceptive, sweet talk of a harlot as a trap whereby the fool (despised by God) is her victim.

"The mouth of strange women is a deep pit" is figurative language that describes the lying, flattering words of a harlot. A **"strange woman"** is "one that is not thy own, whether Jewess or heathen."[592] To listen to her deceit and to succumb to her charm is to fall into a **"deep pit"** from which most men don't escape. The **"mouth"** of the strange woman is specifically symbolic of her flattering talk but generally it refers to her entire wicked self because she is a conduit to hell.

This proverb warns of the extreme danger of succumbing to the harlot's seductive, deceitful, flattering lure. The simple soul who is enticed into her carefully disguised entrapment is blinded by the lust of his flesh and is a stranger to the wisdom of God. The unwise, the simple, and the foolish ones refuse the instruction of wisdom and follow the harlot's deceitful flattery into a well-designed pit, and fall even farther into the devil's grasp. Having turned away from God, the victim discovers that God has turned away from him in response to his foolish action. By satisfying his flesh, she can stupefy his mind and desensitize his conscience so that he prefers this satisfaction of the flesh to God. He has made a sad choice.

> Psalm 81:11-12 But my people would not hearken to my voice; and Israel would none of me. So I gave them up unto their own hearts' lust: *and* they walked in their own counsels.

The man engaged in harlotry has already sinned by refusing to heed God's Word. Furthermore, "The dire consequences of adultery are part of God's punishment in His wrath on sin."[593]

"He that is abhorred of the LORD shall fall therein." The man's previous rejection of God brought on the wrath of God, Who brought no restraints on the man to prevent him from falling into the harlot's trap. Therefore, he suffers the terrible tribulation that results from his willfulness in disobeying God.

> "...Namely, in a high and singular manner; who by his former impieties, and contempt of God and his grace, hath provoked God to leave him to his own heart's lusts, and to punish one sin with another; shall fall therein – And, without a miracle of grace, shall perish everlastingly."[594]
>
> Proverbs 1:29-33 For that they hated knowledge, and did not choose the fear of the LORD: They would none of my counsel: they despised all my reproof. Therefore shall they eat of the fruit of their own way, and be filled with their own devices. For the turning away of the simple shall slay them, and the prosperity of fools shall destroy them. But whoso hearkeneth unto me shall dwell safely, and shall be quiet from fear of evil.
>
> Proverbs 2:16-20 To deliver thee from the strange woman, even from the stranger which flattereth with her words; Which forsaketh the guide of her youth, and forgetteth the covenant of her God. For her house inclineth unto death, and her paths unto the dead. None that go unto her return again, neither take they hold of the paths of life. That thou mayest walk in the way of good men, and keep the paths of the righteous.
>
> Proverbs 23:27-28 For a whore is a deep ditch; and a strange woman is a narrow pit. She also lieth in wait as for a prey, and increaseth the transgressors among men.
>
> Proverbs 5:3 For the lips of a strange woman drop as an honeycomb, and her mouth is smoother than oil: But her end is bitter as wormwood, sharp as a twoedged sword. Her feet go down to death; her steps take hold on hell. Lest thou shouldest ponder the path of life, her ways are moveable, that thou canst not know them. Hear me now therefore, O ye children, and depart not from the words of my mouth. Remove thy way far from her, and come not nigh the door of her house: Lest thou give thine honour unto others, and thy years unto the cruel: Lest strangers be filled with thy wealth; and thy labours be in the house of a stranger; And thou mourn at the last, when thy flesh and thy body are consumed, And say, How have I hated instruction, and my heart despised reproof; And have not obeyed the voice of my teachers, nor inclined mine ear to them that instructed me!
>
> Proverbs 9:17-18 Stolen waters are sweet, and bread eaten in secret is pleasant. But he knoweth not that the dead are there; and that her guests are in the depths of hell.
>
> Ephesians 5:5 For this ye know, that no whoremonger, nor unclean person, nor covetous man, who is an idolater, hath any inheritance in the kingdom of Christ and of God.
>
> Revelation 21:7-8 He that overcometh shall inherit all things; and I will be his God, and he shall be my son. But the fearful, and unbelieving, and the abominable, and murderers, and whoremongers, and sorcerers, and idolaters, and all liars, shall have their part in the lake which burneth with fire and brimstone: which is the second death.

> **Proverbs 22:15** Foolishness *is* bound in the heart of a child; *but* the rod of correction shall drive it far from him.

Focus: This proverb declares that correction is necessary for removing foolishness from a child.

Every child is born with the inherited sin nature and thus with a proclivity toward **"foolishness."** His parents have the demanding, sometimes unpleasant responsibility of instructing, chastening, and disciplining so that their child learns to live respectably and honorably. *(NOTE: This proverb relates to Proverbs 22:6. Please see.)*

> "But *foolishness* is the mighty propensity to evil — imbibing wrong principles, forming bad habits, entering into an ungodly course. It means the very root and essence of sin in a fallen nature — the *folly* of being revolted from a God of love. It includes all the sins of which a child is capable — lying, deceit, willfulness, perverseness, want of submission to authority — a fearful aptness for evil, and revulsion against good. It is not the sheet of pure white paper; not the innocent, or even the tractable, creature, easily guided by proper means, that we have before us; but a little heart full of sin, containing all the seeds of future evil, multiplying to a fruitful harvest."[595]

Scriptures bear out the truth that **"foolishness is bound in the heart of a child."**

> Job 11:12 For vain man would be wise, though man be born like a wild ass's colt.
>
> Psalm 58:3 The wicked are estranged from the womb: they go astray as soon as they be born, speaking lies.
>
> Genesis 8:21 And the LORD smelled a sweet savour; and the LORD said in his heart, I will not again curse the ground any more for man's sake; for the imagination of man's heart is evil from his youth; neither will I again smite any more every thing living, as I have done.
>
> Isaiah 48:8 Yea, thou heardest not; yea, thou knewest not; yea, from that time that thine ear was not opened: for I knew that thou wouldest deal very treacherously, and wast called a transgressor from the womb.

"The rod of correction shall drive it far from him." The purpose of the **"rod"** is to displace foolishness and replace it with wisdom. People, young or old, usually do not change their behavior without experiencing some level of discomfort; consequently, the rod does not necessarily have to be representative of a physical spanking. The pain of discord, disapproval, or the loss of some pleasure can be much more painful than a physical spanking.

> Proverbs 3:11-12 My son, despise not the chastening of the LORD; neither be weary of his correction: For whom the LORD loveth he correcteth; even as a father the son in whom he delighteth.
>
> Proverbs 13:24 He that spareth his rod hateth his son: but he that loveth him chasteneth him betimes.
>
> Proverbs 19:18 Chasten thy son while there is hope, and let not thy soul spare for his crying.
>
> Proverbs 23:13-14 Withhold not correction from the child: for if thou beatest him with the rod, he shall not die. Thou shalt beat him with the rod, and shalt deliver his soul from hell.
>
> Proverbs 29:17 Correct thy son, and he shall give thee rest; yea, he shall give delight unto thy soul.
>
> Hebrews 12:5-6 And ye have forgotten the exhortation which speaketh unto you as unto children, My son, despise not thou the chastening of the Lord, nor faint when thou art rebuked of him: For whom the Lord loveth he chasteneth, and scourgeth every son whom he receiveth.

Proverbs was written to instruct the wise and those who desire to become wise. No godly parent has a heart to intentionally cause permanent damage (physical, emotional, psychological, or social) to any other individual, especially his own child. Just as the wise are to have an awesome respect for God, *(not a fear that causes trembling, shaking, and hiding),* children are to have the same awesome respect for their parents who rear the children for God until they become old enough to understand and become independently responsible. Because their love for their children never ceases, parents will always be in the background, ready to pray for, guide, and help. Children *should not be terrified of their parents.* They should not *have* a fear of their parents that causes trembling or shaking, or a desire to hide from them.

A reminder of the correct use of punishment comes from Ephesians. Parents are not to provoke their children to wrath by inconsistent discipline, petty rules resulting in impossible demands, harsh and rigorous usage, *or exhibiting anger*. When a child receives discipline from a parent having a temper fit, he perceives the parents' violent behavior as proper and is likely to duplicate the behavior when he becomes a parent. Children are *NEVER* to be abused physically, emotionally, or in any other manner. Wise parents understand how to discipline with love and kindness resulting in the child's respect for them and for the God they serve.

> Ephesians 6:4 And, ye fathers, provoke not your children to wrath: but bring them up in the nurture and admonition of the Lord.
>
> Colossians 3:21 Fathers, provoke not your children to anger, lest they be discouraged.

Furthermore, a child should never be punished without explaining why he is receiving punishment and how much he loves the child. Punishment is painful for both the child and the parent, but the child must realize that his punishment is an expression of parental love and concern.

> **Proverbs 22:16** He that oppresseth the poor to increase his *riches, and* he that giveth to the rich, *shall* surely *come* to want.

Focus: This proverb declares that retribution is certain to financial bullies of the poor and to bribers of the prosperous.

"He that oppresseth *[defrauds, extorts, exploits, does violence to]* **the poor to increase his riches"** does so through bullying such as depriving of wages or holding a monopolizing control. The rich bully knows that poor people seldom can oppose his strength of finances; and he certainly will not mind lying about the situation should he be called into question since he is indeed a thief at heart.

God instructs the believer about the proper treatment of **"the poor"** and explains what He, Himself, will do for the impoverished. In Deuteronomy 15:11, for example, God states, "For the poor shall never cease out of the land: therefore I command thee, saying, Thou shalt open thine hand wide unto thy brother, to thy poor, and to thy needy, in thy land." He wants the believer to take care of the poor – *not* oppress, wrong, exploit, do violence, deceive, or steal from them.

Some Biblical Warnings and Instructions against Mistreating the Poor

In the Law:

Exodus 22:21-27 Thou shalt neither vex a stranger, nor oppress him: for ye were strangers in the land of Egypt. Ye shall not afflict any widow, or fatherless child. If thou afflict them in any wise, and they cry at all unto me, I will surely hear their cry; And my wrath shall wax hot, and I will kill you with the sword; and your wives shall be widows, and your children fatherless. If thou lend money to any of my people that is poor by thee, thou shalt not be to him as an usurer, neither shalt thou lay upon him usury. If thou at all take thy neighbour's raiment to pledge, thou shalt deliver it unto him by that the sun goeth down: For that is his covering only, it is his raiment for his skin: wherein shall he sleep? and it shall come to pass, when he crieth unto me, that I will hear; for I am gracious.

Exodus 23:6 Thou shalt not wrest the judgment of thy poor in his cause. *[Also see Deuteronomy 24:14-15; 24:18-22.]*

In Psalms and Proverbs:

Psalm 12:5 For the oppression of the poor, for the sighing of the needy, now will I arise, saith the LORD; I will set *him* in safety *from him that* puffeth at him.

Proverbs 14:21 He that despiseth his neighbour sinneth: but he that hath mercy on the poor, happy *is* he.

Proverbs 14:31 He that oppresseth the poor reproacheth his Maker: but he that honoureth him hath mercy on the poor. *[Also see Proverbs 21:13; 22:22-23; 28:8; 28:27.]*

Warnings in The New Testament:

Galatians 2:9-10 And when James, Cephas, and John, who seemed to be pillars, perceived the grace that was given unto me, they gave to me and Barnabas the right hands of fellowship; that we should go unto the heathen, and they unto the circumcision. Only they would that we should remember the poor; the same which I also was forward to do.

James 2:2-4 For if there come unto your assembly a man with a gold ring, in goodly apparel, and there come in also a poor man in vile raiment; And ye have respect to him that weareth the gay clothing, and say unto him, Sit thou here in a good place; and say to the poor, Stand thou there, or sit here under my footstool: Are ye not then partial in yourselves, and are become judges of evil thoughts? *[Also see James 2:5-9.]*

"And he that giveth to the rich" with the intended purpose of ultimately *increasing his own riches* **"shall surely come to want."** His gift is a bribe. Obviously he acts for his own personal gain. Since the "rich" do not need his gift of money or goods, his giving to the rich purchases something favorable: he is buying influence, perhaps some honorable position, or even more riches in return.

Those who oppress the poor or give to the rich in order to get more wealth **"shall surely come to want."** God is the judge of when and how this retribution occurs. It may come in this lifetime through famine or pestilence or war or economic turndown or tragedy or some other form; and it will surely come at the Judgment when such devious and hateful persons face God.

Job 20:19-22 Because he hath oppressed and hath forsaken the poor; because he hath violently taken away an house which he builded not; Surely he shall not feel quietness in his belly, he shall not save of that which he desired. There shall none of his meat be left; therefore shall no man look for his goods. In the fulness of his sufficiency he shall be in straits: every hand of the wicked shall come upon him.

Zechariah 7:9-14 Thus speaketh the LORD of hosts, saying, Execute true judgment, and shew mercy and compassions every man to his brother: And oppress not the widow, nor the fatherless, the stranger, nor the poor; and let none of you imagine evil against his brother in your heart. But they refused to hearken, and pulled away the shoulder, and stopped their ears, that they should not hear. Yea, they made their hearts *as* an adamant stone, lest they should hear the law, and the words which the LORD of hosts hath sent in his spirit by the former prophets: therefore came a great wrath from the LORD of hosts. Therefore it is come to pass, *that* as he cried, and they would not hear; so they cried, and I would not hear, saith the LORD of hosts: But I scattered them with a whirlwind among all the nations whom they knew not. Thus the land was desolate after them, that no man passed through nor returned: for they laid the pleasant land desolate.

James 5:1-6 Go to now, ye rich men, weep and howl for your miseries that shall come upon you. Your riches are corrupted, and your garments are motheaten. Your gold and silver is cankered; and the rust of them shall be a witness against you, and shall eat your flesh as it were fire. Ye have heaped treasure together for the last days. Behold, the hire of the labourers who have reaped down your fields, which is of you kept back by fraud, crieth: and the cries of them which have reaped are entered into the ears of the Lord of sabaoth. Ye have lived in pleasure on the earth, and been wanton; ye have nourished your hearts, as in a day of slaughter. Ye have condemned and killed the just; and he doth not resist you.

Beginning here at Chapter 22:17 "to the end of chapter 24, he *[Solomon]* directs his speech to his son, his pupil, his reader, his hearer, speaking as to a particular person. Hitherto, for the most part, his sense was comprised in one verse, but here usually it is drawn out further." [596] It is of interest that the following paragraph (verses 17-21) concerning the value of being taught wisdom lies sandwiched between two cautions concerning abusing the poor.

> **Proverbs 22:17-21** Bow down thine ear, and hear the words of the wise, and apply thine heart unto my knowledge.
> 18. For *it is* a pleasant thing if thou keep them within thee; they shall withal be fitted in thy lips.
> 19. That thy trust may be in the LORD, I have made known to thee this day, even to thee.
> 20. Have not I written to thee excellent things in counsels and knowledge,
> 21. That I might make thee know the certainty of the words of truth; that thou mightest answer the words of truth to them that send unto thee?

Focus: This five-verse dialog gives reasons for heartfelt internalizing of wisdom to include pleasantness of life, a personal trusting relationship with God based on confidence of truth, and a ready ability to communicate those words of truth.

"Bow down thine ear, and hear the words of the wise" (verse 17a) is an earnest call (through the use of a word picture) that encourages the student of wisdom to pay undivided attention to the words of the wise. In this figurative illustration, he is to cup his hand behind his ears for better volume and block out all other conversations. "Pay close attention and learn this! Don't miss a word." This call of verse 17 strongly resembles the exhortation of Proverbs 5:1, "My son, attend unto my wisdom," *and* bow thine ear to my understanding" and Proverbs 4:20, "My son, attend to my words; incline thine ear unto my sayings."

"And apply thine heart unto my knowledge" (verse 17b) goes even farther by requesting that the listener engage his entire **"heart"** *[mind, emotion, will]* into the learning process so that this wisdom becomes embedded into the fabric of his mind. Thus, the listener becomes a person of wisdom.

Proverbs 1:5-6 A wise man will hear, and will increase learning; and a man of understanding shall attain unto wise counsels: To understand a proverb, and the interpretation; the words of the wise, and their dark sayings.

Proverbs 2:2-5 So that thou incline thine ear unto wisdom, and apply thine heart to understanding; Yea, if thou criest after knowledge, and liftest up thy voice for understanding; If thou seekest her as silver, and searchest for her as for hid treasures; Then shalt thou understand the fear of the LORD, and find the knowledge of God.

Proverbs 23:12 Apply thine heart unto instruction, and thine ears to the words of knowledge.

"An earnest exhortation to get wisdom and grace, by attending to *the words of the wise* men, both written and preached, the words of the prophets and priests, and particularly to that *knowledge* which Solomon in this book gives men of good and evil, sin and duty, rewards and punishments. To these *words,* to this *knowledge,* the ear must be *bowed down* in humility and serious attention and the heart *applied* by faith, and love, and close consideration. The ear will not serve without the heart."[597]

"For it is a pleasant *[agreeable, delightful, sweet]* **thing if thou keep them** *[words of the wise]* **within thee."** (verse 18a) Repeatedly, Proverbs has heralded the joy and ***pleasantness*** obtained by those who vigilantly **"keep"** *[give heed to, treasure up in memory, guard]* precious godly wisdom. Wisdom demands peace, produces clear thinking, adds value to life, and promotes confidence and a clear conscience. In summary, **"it is a pleasant thing"** *to keep wisdom within yourself.*

Proverbs 2:10 When wisdom entereth into thine heart, and knowledge is pleasant unto thy soul . . . *[See also verses 11-22.]*
Proverbs 3:17-18 Her ways are ways of pleasantness, and all her paths are peace. She is a tree of life to them that lay hold upon her: and happy is every one that retaineth her.
Proverbs 24:13-14 My son, eat thou honey, because it is good; and the honeycomb, which is sweet to thy taste: So shall the knowledge of wisdom be unto thy soul *[self, person; mind, emotions, will]*: when thou hast found it, then there shall be a reward, and thy expectation shall not be cut off.
Jeremiah 15:16 Thy words were found, and I did eat them; and thy word was unto me the joy and rejoicing of mine heart: for I am called by thy name, O LORD God of hosts.

The *pleasantness* of the wise stands in contrast to the terror of the foolish. As the previous verses of this chapter have shown, the wicked are forced to endure "thorns and snares" *[tribulation, heartaches, traps]* of their own making. Lost men have no peace or joy or clear thinking because they have no indwelling Christ; and, in their unpleasant wickedness, the elite, rich rule over and oppress the poor and make the poor their servants. The scorner causes strife and contention. The simple, ignorant men fall into the snare of the harlot and lose their marriages, their money, and their honor. All the wicked eventually give their souls over to Satan. *Not* desiring their children to be lost, godly parents want this pleasant life for their children, and they will exert themselves to teach this godly wisdom to them.

"They *[words of the wise]* **shall withal be fitted in thy lips."** (verse 18b) Because of being trained by godly wisdom, the wise develop joy and skill in speaking timely, properly, and effectively. When counsel is needed and requested, wisdom from God yields forth the right words at the right time with the right spirit and at the right place. As 1 Peter 3:15 states, "be ready always to give an answer to every man that asketh you a reason of the hope that is in you . . ."

Proverbs 8:6-9 Hear; for I will speak of excellent things; and the opening of my lips shall be right things. For my mouth shall speak truth; and wickedness is an abomination to my lips. All the words of my mouth are in righteousness; there is nothing froward or perverse in them. They are all plain to him that understandeth, and right to them that find knowledge.
Proverbs 10:21 The lips of the righteous feed many: but fools die for want of wisdom.
Proverbs 15:23 A man hath joy by the answer of his mouth: and a word spoken in due season, how good is it!
Proverbs 25:11-13 A word fitly spoken is like apples of gold in pictures of silver. As an earring of gold, and an ornament of fine gold, so is a wise reprover upon an obedient ear. As the cold of snow in the time of harvest, so is a faithful messenger to them that send him: for he refresheth the soul of his masters.
Luke 6:45 A good man out of the good treasure of his heart bringeth forth that which is good; and an evil man out of the evil treasure of his heart bringeth forth that which is evil: for of the abundance of the heart his mouth speaketh.

"That thy trust may be in the LORD, I have made known to thee this day, even to thee." (verse 19) Once a person *is personally gifted with wisdom from God*, he understands (because he is wise) that God has befriended and gifted him with something of far more value than great wealth. Wisdom from God proves to always be right in every aspect of life. Through experience the wise person knows that he can always trust the LORD. **"Have not I written to thee excellent things in counsels and knowledge, That I might make thee know the certainty of the words of truth."** (verses 20-21a) The wise individual is steadfast in his belief that the wisdom of God is excellent in every aspect. He can give good counsel because he has a knowledge of God and knowledge from God. He is positively certain that God's **"words of truth"** will stand any test.

"That thou mightest answer the words of truth to them that send unto thee?" (verse 21b) Confidence in God's "counsels and knowledge" comes through the experience of believing God and thus acting accordingly; therefore, it is imperative that godly wisdom is listened to, internalized, believed, and then practiced. Only then is the believer able to answer from **"the words of truth"** because it resonates within his heart.

"Knowledge is given us to do good with, that others may light their candle at our lamp, and that we may in our place serve our generation according to the will of God; and those who make conscience of keeping God's commandments will be best able to *give a reason of the hope that is in* them."[598]

Romans 10:14 How then shall they call on him in whom they have not believed? and how shall they believe in him of whom they have not heard? and how shall they hear without a preacher?
Romans 10:17 So then faith cometh by hearing, and hearing by the word of God.

Proverbs 22:22-23 Rob not the poor, because he *is* poor: neither oppress the afflicted in the gate:
23. For the LORD will plead their cause, and spoil the soul of those that spoiled them.

Focus: This two-verse proverb warns against abuse of the poor at the place of justice because God will personally advocate and retaliate in their behalf.

Two previous verses in this chapter (listed below) made the following points concerning the treatment of "the poor." (1) God made both rich and poor, and they meet each other on common ground (verse 2). (2) "The rich" are not to oppress the poor to increase their own wealth lest they come under the judgment of God (verse 16).

>Proverbs 22:2 The rich and poor meet together: the LORD is the maker of them all.
>Proverbs 22:16 He that oppresseth the poor to increase his riches, and he that giveth to the rich, shall surely come to want.

"Rob not the poor, because he is poor: neither oppress [*bruise, crush, humble*] **the afflicted in the gate."** To *rob the poor* simply because such robbery is easy is criminal enough but robbing him in the place of justice is even worse. **"Afflicted"** is here translated from a second Hebrew word for **"poor"** that expands the meaning to include *depressed in mind or circumstances, lowly, needy.* Because the **"afflicted"** are described as being **"in the gate,"** which was the designated place in a community where people came to obtain justice from the town leaders and ask for alms, this robbery is enlarged into a more heinous crime. One can only imagine the arrogance of those who considered themselves troubled by the poor and afflicted who just needed help to get through the day. "The words point to the special form of oppression of which unjust judges are the instruments."[599] To oppress the poor while they are pleading for justice "in the gate" multiplies the atrociousness of the crime and illustrates the cruelty of wicked minds. Such behavior raises the ire of God.

>"The oppressors will find him a just avenger. He will make reprisals upon them, will *spoil the souls of those that spoil them;* he will repay them in spiritual judgments, in curses to their souls. He that robs the poor will be found in the end a murderer of himself."[600]

"For the LORD will plead their cause, and spoil the soul of those that spoiled them." This verse declares that God is indeed the Helper of the helpless, and if someone takes advantage of the poor and helpless, God will take vengeance. Note that the man who would rob the poor, the widow, or the orphan is a coward because he takes from those who cannot defend themselves. The parable that Nathan told David after the king's sin with Bathsheba and Uriah illustrates God's disgust for those who oppress the poor (2 Samuel 12:1-4). The prophets continued to relate God's opinion of those who oppress the poor.

>Ezekiel 22:29-31 The people of the land have used oppression, and exercised robbery, and have vexed the poor and needy: yea, they have oppressed the stranger wrongfully. And I sought for a man among them, that should make up the hedge, and stand in the gap before me for the land, that I should not destroy it: but I found none. Therefore have I poured out mine indignation upon them; I have consumed them with the fire of my wrath: their own way have I recompensed upon their heads, saith the Lord GOD.
>Amos 5:12 For I know your manifold transgressions and your mighty sins: they afflict the just, they take a bribe, and they turn aside the poor in the gate from their right.
>Zechariah 7:9-10 Thus speaketh the LORD of hosts, saying, Execute true judgment, and shew mercy and compassions every man to his brother: And oppress not the widow, nor the fatherless, the stranger, nor the poor; and let none of you imagine evil against his brother in your heart.
>Malachi 3:5 And I will come near to you to judgment; and I will be a swift witness against the sorcerers, and against the adulterers, and against false swearers, and against those that oppress the hireling in his wages, the widow, and the fatherless, and that turn aside the stranger from his right, and fear not me, saith the LORD of hosts.

Proverbs 22:24-25 Make no friendship with an angry man; and with a furious man thou shalt not go:
25.   Lest thou learn his ways, and get a snare to thy soul.

Focus: This proverb (two verses) admonishes against friendship with a person who is known to have a furious nature and gives the reasons to avoid the same.

"Make no friendship with an angry man; and with a furious man thou shalt not go." *Friendships* are often difficult to obtain and challenging to turn away; however, if the potential friend's negative traits threaten peace, safety, and relationship with God, Scripture teaches to avoid the association. With such an angry person, **"thou shall not go,"** – "not take a walk with him, much less a journey; or shall not be frequently together."[601] An **"angry man"** and a **"furious man"** are the same in meaning as **"make no friendship"** and **"shalt not go"** are the same in meaning. Hence, the second clause repeats the first for emphasis. The *admonition* is to refuse friendship with a person who habitually does not control his temper. Associating with him is dangerous because the spirit of one person can easily rest upon another, especially where there is fondness. Bad habits are easily caught by friends.

"Lest thou learn his ways, and get a snare to thy soul." Though these angry responses are easy to produce, they have many severe and damaging repercussions (*snares*) that can entrap one for a lifetime, and sometimes eternally, as they lead a person farther away from God. When a believer copies the angry man's behavior, *his soul is snared* because he separates himself from other godly people, damages his personal relationship with God, and puts himself in the category of the foolish. Furthermore, foolish people, because they are void of wisdom, perpetuate their problems by continuing to make bad decisions. Spontaneously exhibiting an uncontrolled temper reveals a lack of personal control, a deficiency in communication skills, a disregard for peace, and (most important) a failed relationship with God.

> Proverbs 13:20 He that walketh with wise men shall be wise: but a companion of fools shall be destroyed.
>
> Proverbs 14:16, 17 A wise *man* feareth, and departeth from evil: but the fool rageth, and is confident. *He that is* soon angry dealeth foolishly: and a man of wicked devices is hated.
>
> Proverbs 14:29 *He that is* slow to wrath *is* of great understanding: but *he that is* hasty of spirit exalteth folly.
>
> Proverbs 16:32 *He that is* slow to anger *is* better than the mighty; and he that ruleth his spirit than he that taketh a city.
>
> Proverbs 18:6-7 A fool's lips enter into contention, and his mouth calleth for strokes. A fool's mouth *is* his destruction, and his lips *are* the snare of his soul.
>
> Proverbs 19:11 The discretion of a man deferreth his anger; and *it is* his glory to pass over a transgression.
>
> Proverbs 19:19 A man of great wrath shall suffer punishment: for if thou deliver *him,* yet thou must do it again.
>
> Proverbs 29:22 An angry man stirreth up strife, and a furious man aboundeth in transgression.
>
> 2 Corinthians 6:14 Be ye not unequally yoked together with unbelievers: for what fellowship hath righteousness with unrighteousness? and what communion hath light with darkness?

Proverbs 22:26-27 Be not thou *one* of them that strike hands, *or* of them that are sureties for debts.
27. If thou hast nothing to pay, why should he take away thy bed from under thee?

Focus: This proverb (two verses) instructs against cosigning and provides the reason why.

A **"surety"** is a person who foolishly guarantees ("**strikes hands**") to pay another person's debt if the person making the loan defaults in payment. Today this practice is known as ***cosigning***. The debtor is a person who does not have enough financial credibility to personally stand good for his own debt; thus, if he wants to secure a loan, he has to have additional credibility in the form of a surety or cosigner. The "surety" may be lured into this situation because of pity, or perhaps he is related to the debtor and is obligated to return a favor. He might be so simple, young, foolish, or ignorant as to not understand the severity of guaranteeing another person's debt. This proverb assumes that the surety himself would be placed in a severe financial strain if the borrower defaults and he has to pay, so much so that he might have to legally and honorably forfeit his own bed as payment. In the first line, there is a clear command from God saying, **"Be not thou one of them that strike hands, or of them that are sureties for debts."** In 21st century terms: "Do not cosign." Being a surety can be an act of ignorance of God's command, a failure to recognize the habitual bad behavior of those who lack financial credibility, or a lack of discretion.

> Proverbs 6:1-5 My son, if thou be surety for thy friend, if thou hast stricken thy hand with a stranger, Thou art snared with the words of thy mouth, thou art taken with the words of thy mouth. Do this now, my son, and deliver thyself, when thou art come into the hand of thy friend; go, humble thyself, and make sure thy friend. Give not sleep to thine eyes, nor slumber to thine eyelids. Deliver thyself as a roe from the hand of the hunter, and as a bird from the hand of the fowler.
>
> Proverbs 11:15 He that is surety for a stranger shall smart *for it:* and he that hateth suretiship is sure.
>
> Proverbs 17:18 A man void of understanding striketh hands, *and* becometh surety in the presence of his friend.
>
> Proverbs 20:16 Take his garment that is surety *for* a stranger: and take a pledge of him for a strange woman.

Please Note: *Giving* (NOT cosigning) to help those in need is *not to be compared to surety,* nor is taking care of parents, widows, or orphans. The Bible is very clear on this subject – "But if any provide not for his own, and specially for those of his own house, he hath denied the faith, and is worse than an infidel." (1 Timothy 5:8) Also, 1 John 3:17 states: " But whoso hath this world's good, and seeth his brother have need, and shutteth up his bowels *of compassion* from him, how dwelleth the love of God in him?" Giving out of one's resources is totally different from guaranteeing another person's debt.

Proverbs 22:28 Remove not the ancient landmark, which thy fathers have set.

Focus: This proverb is a direct command against a specific kind of theft (land).

"Remove not the ancient landmark" directly references the passage in Deuteronomy *(see below)* where the command was first given. "Moving a neighbor's boundary stone was equivalent to stealing his property. According to extra-Biblical literature, this was a widespread problem in the ancient Near East."[602] (Scripture mentions this subject at least 5 times, indicating its importance to God.)

> Deuteronomy 19:14 Thou shalt not remove thy neighbour's landmark, which they of old time have set in thine inheritance, which thou shalt inherit in the land that the LORD thy God giveth thee to possess it.
> Job 24:2-3 Some remove the landmarks; they violently take away flocks, and feed thereof. They drive away the ass of the fatherless, they take the widow's ox for a pledge.

The ancient landmark was that particular boundary stone whereby the corner of property was designated. Because it could easily be moved by an evil, greedy, covetous neighbor who intended to enlarge his own property by stealing some of his neighbor's, the command against doing so was firmly established by God.

> "The stone that divided one man's vineyard from his neighbour's was regarded as a sacred thing, on no account to be touched. This arrangement helped to perpetuate family holdings. It prevented the accumulation of large estates by the wealthy, and the alienation of the land from the poor. It guarded the weak from the oppression of the strong. It was a protection against deceit, error, and confusion. Ahab transgressed the Law in seeking to acquire Naboth's vineyard. It would be well if we could appreciate the spirit of the old Hebrew sanctity of the landmark."[603]
> Deuteronomy 27:17 Cursed be he that removeth his neighbour's landmark. And all the people shall say, Amen.
> Proverbs 23:10-11 Remove not the old landmark; and enter not into the fields of the fatherless: For their redeemer is mighty; he shall plead their cause with thee.
> Hosea 5:10 The princes of Judah were like them that remove the bound: therefore I will pour out my wrath upon them like water.

It is never right to take anything that belongs to someone else. This is a principle of life to the godly person because it violates the commandment "Thou shalt not steal" (Exodus 20:15).

Proverbs 22:29 Seest thou a man diligent in his business? he shall stand before kings; he shall not stand before mean *men*.

Focus: This proverb declares that being diligent in business is a good work ethic that advances one to higher levels of association.

"Seest thou a man" is a phrase used to point out a man whose behavior is to be observed, either good or bad. It means to look carefully and meditate upon a particular man's behavior, the way he carries himself, his dress, and his words. This phrase is found three times and only in the Book of Proverbs:

> Proverbs 22:29 Seest thou a man diligent in his business? he shall stand before kings; he shall not stand before mean *men*.
> Proverbs 26:12 Seest thou a man wise in his own conceit? *there is* more hope of a fool than of him.
> Proverbs 29:20 Seest thou a man *that is* hasty in his words? *there is* more hope of a fool than of him.

Verses 26:12 and 29:20 describe a man under observation who has developed poor character traits, and the teacher wants the student to note the foolish man's behavior and attitude and *refuse* to take on the same. In order to adopt his positive behavior, the student in this verse (22:29) is to observe the diligent man and take heed to his behavior – specifically, look at such a man **"in his business."**

"Diligent" means *quick, prompt, skilled,* and *ready*. Because the average person is satisfied with simply being mediocre, a person who handles his business with diligence will be observed by others and singled out as being far above average. Because of his excellent attitude and desire to enhance his abilities, the diligent worker would not seek to work with those who do not desire the same spirit of excellence. The shocking statement quoted below gives an illustration of what happens when a person doesn't practice diligence about life and work:

> Minimal effort will get you minimal results. Everything of real value will come through your effort. . . . 20% of people, at all organizational levels, do 80% of the work. And the 20% are above average performers because they exert above average effort, rather than just doing the minimum in order to "get by." . . . If you want to experience real . . . success, you will need to put in the effort necessary to be successful – nobody is going to simply hand you success . . . And since you are only as good as the people around you, you would be wise to put the effort into surrounding yourself with people who are also interested in success – otherwise their minimal effort will be detrimental to your performance.[604]

"He shall stand before kings" indicates that he shall *set or position oneself* or *present oneself* before kings. He shall be taken in service ("to serve or minister to another"[605]) of great leaders (kings, business leaders, governmental leaders). He shall be taken into their presence and receive favors of them. **"Mean"** men are described as *obscure* or *insignificant*.

> "A man thus export is fitted for any, even the highest situation, may well be employed in affairs of state, and enjoy the confidence of kings.. . . .An intellectual, clever, adroit man would never he satisfied with serving such masters; his ambition is higher; he knows that he is capable of better things."[606]

For example, Joseph and Daniel were slaves who were diligent about their business. Look at how they were advanced.

> Genesis 39:3-6; 42-44 And his master saw that the LORD was with him, and that the LORD made all that he did to prosper in his hand. And Joseph found grace in his sight, and he served him: and he made him overseer over his house, and all that he had he put into his hand. And it came to pass from the time that he had made him overseer in his house, and over all that he had, that the LORD blessed the Egyptian's house for Joseph's sake; and the blessing of the LORD was upon all that he had in the house, and in the field. And he left all that he had in Joseph's hand; and he knew not ought he had, save the bread which he did eat. And Joseph was a goodly person, and well favoured . . . And Pharaoh took off his ring from his hand, and put it upon Joseph's hand, and arrayed him in vestures of fine linen, and put a gold chain about his neck; And he made him to ride in the second chariot which he had; and they cried before him, Bow the knee: and he made him ruler over all the land of Egypt. And Pharaoh said unto Joseph, I am Pharaoh, and without thee shall no man lift up his hand or foot in all the land of Egypt.
> Daniel 1:3-4; 28 And the king spake unto Ashpenaz the master of his eunuchs, that he should bring certain of the children of Israel, and of the king's seed, and of the princes; Children in whom was no blemish, but well favoured, and skilful in all wisdom, and cunning in knowledge, and understanding science, and such as had ability in them to stand in the king's palace, and whom they might teach the learning and the tongue of the Chaldeans . . . So this Daniel prospered in the reign of Darius, and in the reign of Cyrus the Persian.

> *"Diligence*, even without godliness, is often the way to worldly advancement. Pharaoh chose Joseph's brethren, as '**men of activity**,' to be rulers of his cattle. Jeroboam owed his rise in Solomon's house to his "**industrious**" habits. But when a man 'serves the Lord in **fervency of spirit**,' thriftfully occupying his own talent for the day of reckoning; not only *the mean man*, but the mighty man of the world, will be too low for him. *He shall stand before* the King of kings with unspeakable honor, with unclouded acceptance –"Well done! **good and faithful servant**; enter thou into the joy of thy Lord."[607]

> Genesis 47:5-6 And Pharaoh spake unto Joseph, saying, Thy father and thy brethren are come unto thee: The land of Egypt *is* before thee; in the best of the land make thy father and brethren to dwell; in the land of Goshen let them dwell: and if thou knowest *any* men of activity among them, then make them rulers over my cattle.
> 1 Kings 11:28 And the man Jeroboam *was* a mighty man of valour: and Solomon seeing the young man that he was industrious, he made him ruler over all the charge of the house of Joseph.
> Matthew 25:19-23 After a long time the lord of those servants cometh, and reckoneth with them. And so he that had received five talents came and brought other five talents, saying, Lord, thou deliveredst unto me five talents: behold, I have gained beside them five talents more. His lord said unto him, Well done, *thou* good and faithful servant: thou hast been faithful over a few things, I will make thee ruler over many things: enter thou into the joy of thy lord. He also that had received two talents came and said, Lord, thou deliveredst unto me two talents: behold, I have gained two other talents beside them. His lord said unto him, Well done, good and faithful servant; thou hast been faithful over a few things, I will make thee ruler over many things: enter thou into the joy of thy lord. *[See also Luke 19:11-26.]*
> Romans 12:11 Not slothful in business; fervent in spirit; serving the Lord . . .

CHAPTER TWENTY-THREE

> **Chapter 23:1-3** When thou sittest to eat with a ruler, consider diligently what *is* before thee:
> 2 And put a knife to thy throat, if thou *be* a man given to appetite.
> 3. Be not desirous of his dainties: for they *are* deceitful meat.

Focus: This proverb (3 verses) is a warning against being deceived by powerful people and elaborate living.

"When thou sittest to eat with a ruler." (verse 1a) Wise warnings are given here to the person who associates with powerful people capable of either promoting *or* ruining their guests. The host may have ulterior motives, and he may be evaluating and tempting his guest. Verses 4-8 warn the young man against lusting after power and riches symbolized by the exquisite food. Responsibility lies within the guest to recognize what is happening and to prevent himself from being entrapped by some scheme that could potentially rob him of all the advantages of walking with God.

"Consider diligently what is before thee." (verse 1b) **"Consider diligently"** means to *become aware of by the senses to gain understanding.* The wise man is to observe all the people, the facilities, the food, and listen to the conversations. Utilizing his wisdom and spirit of excellence, he will behave properly and guard his relationship with God and men. He is astutely aware that *an appetite for the ruler's dainties* can be extremely dangerous, potentially causing him to abandon the wisdom that served to bring him to the table in the first place. He should predetermine not to become greedy and seek after that which solely satisfies the flesh, and also not to ever start down the road of living for pleasure. Wisdom prevents these adverse actions.

Every situation should be diligently and wisely evaluated by a believer in light of knowledge that he has been taught by Scripture and his godly parents. Also, sensitivity to Holy Spirit leadership is mandatory for the Christian, and good counsel is always in order.

> Psalm 141:3-4 Set a watch, O LORD, before my mouth; keep the door of my lips. Incline not my heart to *any* evil thing, to practise wicked works with men that work iniquity: and let me not eat of their dainties.
> Proverbs 14:35 The king's favour *is* toward a wise servant: but his wrath is *against* him that causeth shame.

> NOTE: Verses 3 and 6 address concerns about "dainties," and verses 1-8 speak of coveting after riches. If allowed, evil people will use their elaborate lifestyle, including food and drink, to establish deceitful, controlling relationships for personal gain and for abuse of their guests.

Every social environment has its own peculiarities with potential for challenging previously established standards of a believer who, through careless involvement, can have his views of right and wrong modified by unbelievers. Perpetually cautious, the wise man will guard his God-given principles and keenly observe his environment (especially noting other people's behavior, words, and body language) to avoid the many snares of life, and he will always be conscious of a proper relationship with God as well as with other people.

> "The wise man is guarding, in those verses (Proverbs 23:1-8), against two of the great leading sins of a fallen nature; the lust of the flesh, and the pride of life. The sin of luxury, and the deceitfulness of riches. And what multitudes among the sons of men are continually falling by their means. The Lord Jesus, in his unequaled manner, gives a caution against the surfeiting and drunkenness and cares of this life, lest the great day of account come in the midst of our enjoyment and find the soul unprepared."[608]
> Luke 21:34 And take heed to yourselves, lest at any time your hearts be overcharged with surfeiting, and drunkenness, and cares of this life, and *so* that day come upon you unawares.

"And put a knife to thy throat, if thou *be* a man given to appetite." (verse 2) But **"if thou *be* a man given to appetite"** *(for the ruler's dainties)* which certainly means *if* the person has a weakness in this area, then particular caution needs to be taken to avoid falling into such a trap. Should the guest sense any lustful yearning within himself for the ruler's **"dainties"** or sense that the ruler's pleasures would cause him to move away from being a wise, godly person, he will remember the expression **"put a knife to thy throat,"** a saying which is a deliberate exaggeration such as Jesus used to express the absolute seriousness of the situation.

> Matthew 5:29-30 And if thy right eye offend thee, pluck it out, and cast *it* from thee: for it is profitable for thee that one of thy members should perish, and not *that* thy whole body should be cast into hell. And if thy right hand offend thee, cut it off, and cast *it* from thee: for it is profitable for thee that one of thy members should perish, and not *that* thy whole body should be cast into hell.

> "The sin we are here warned against is luxury and sensuality, and the indulgence of the appetite in eating and drinking, a sin that most easily besets us . . . We ought to observe what is our own iniquity, and, if we find ourselves addicted to flesh-pleasing, we must not only stand upon our guard against temptations from without, but subdue the corruption within. Nature is desirous of food, and we are taught to pray for it, but it is lust that is desirous of dainties, and we cannot in faith pray for them, for frequently they are not food convenient for mind, body, or estate. They are deceitful meat, and therefore David, instead of praying for them, prays against them (Psalm 141:4). They are pleasant to the palate, but perhaps rise in the stomach, turn sour there, upbraid a man, and make him sick ... Why then should we covet that which will certainly cheat us?"

> Psalm 141:4 Incline not my heart to *any* evil thing, to practise wicked works with men that work iniquity: and let me not eat of their dainties.

Neither of these exaggerated statements *(in Proverbs or Matthew)* were meant to be acted out. They were given as memorable word pictures to fix in the hearers' minds the *graveness of the situations and the dangers* of not heeding the warnings. Be stern with self, refuse to yield to temptation, resist overindulgence.

"Be not desirous of his dainties: for they *are* deceitful meat." (verse 3) The **"ruler"** is presented in these Scriptures as being devious and one to be approached cautiously. The current warning about the deceitfulness of his elaborate lifestyle is symbolized by the exquisite meal. All of his dainties lure into a potential deep ditch, a snare, a trap. Along with the offer of such a fabulous and delicious meal comes a compelling and seductive comradery which has the potential of causing the godly person to disarm himself, take away the inhibitions of speech, and let down his standards of righteousness. People tend to "go along to get along" meaning they try to "fit in." Before long, *if* he ignores the warnings, the **"deceitful meat"** will have brought the wise man into the camp of fools, where he will reap the consequences.

> "The *dainties are deceitful meat*, sometimes from the insincerity of the host; always from the disappointment of the anticipated pleasure. (Ecclesiastes 2:10-11) To use them may be lawful. To *be desirous of them* is fearfully dangerous."[609]

> Ecclesiastes 2:10-11 And whatsoever mine eyes desired I kept not from them, I withheld not my heart from any joy; for my heart rejoiced in all my labour: and this was my portion of all my labour. Then I looked on all the works that my hands had wrought, and on the labour that I had laboured to do: and, behold, all *was* vanity and vexation of spirit, and *there was* no profit under the sun.

As a matter of application, every Christian should be aware of the dangers of having personal fellowship with the ungodly. To do business on the level with rulers can be honorable and blessed, but to have personal fellowship with the ungodly, regardless of their status, can become devastating to a walk with God. No king can possibly offer the same or even nearly the same rewards as the King of kings; therefore, cherish the relationship with the Saviour.

> 2 Corinthians 6:14 Be ye not unequally yoked together with unbelievers: for what fellowship hath righteousness with unrighteousness? and what communion hath light with darkness?

Chapter 23:4-5 Labour not to be rich: cease from thine own wisdom.
5. Wilt thou set thine eyes upon that which is not? for *riches* certainly make themselves wings; they fly away as an eagle toward heaven.

Focus: This proverb warns against the worldly wisdom of laboring for wealth and also establishes why doing so is foolish.

"Labour not to be rich: cease from thine own wisdom." Rather than laboring, "in an immoderate over anxious way and manner, to a weariness, as the word *[labour]* signifies, ... men should labour for durable riches, lay up treasure in heaven, seek those things which are above, and labour to be accepted of God."[610] Restraint is the common warning in the first eight verses of this chapter, and these two verses are part of a caution against the world's wisdom of striving to be rich. Everyone should have goals for his life, but establishing the goal **"to be rich"** is empty because: (1) It lacks any permanency, as described in verse 5; (2) It focuses on satisfying the flesh rather than God; and (3) It has no point of being fully satisfied; no place to say "that's enough" because the more riches a person acquires, the more he wants. It is that incessant desire for something that pulls a man away from God. It is covetousness – a sin specified by God in the Ten Commandments.

> "The man who concentrates all his wisdom, talents, and energy, who sacrifices all his peace . . .in the *labor after riches*, often has been at one stroke deprived of all, just when he supposed himself to be secure of all. Divine chastisement, indolence, extravagance, injustice, robbery, – bring to the lowest poverty. . . .Eternity is at the door; and naked shall we go out of the world, as we came into it. Yet even this palpable consciousness fails to teach men the lessons, to *cease from their own wisdom*, to seek true substance on earth, and in God's wisdom to lay up enduring 'treasures in heaven.'"

> 1 Timothy 6:8-11 And having food and raiment let us be therewith content. But they that will be rich fall into temptation and a snare, and *into* many foolish and hurtful lusts, which drown men in destruction and perdition. For the love of money is the root of all evil: which while some coveted after, they have erred from the faith, and pierced themselves through with many sorrows. But thou, O man of God, flee these things; and follow after righteousness, godliness, faith, love, patience, meekness.

Unlike spiritual wisdom that God gives for stability, strength, and spiritual development, this driving, relentless, slave-producing desire "to be rich" originates from **"thine own wisdom"** which comes totally from within a person. Carnal wisdom has no help from God, is unprotected by Him, and is easily defeated, leaving its victim frustrated and wondering what happened and why.

"Wilt thou set thine eyes upon that which is not? for *riches* certainly make themselves wings; they fly away as an eagle toward heaven." (verse 5) Potentially, all kinds of wealth can disappear quickly like a bird taking flight; however, when a person seeks to please God as a priority and through Godly wisdom gains wealth, it is accompanied by peace and comfort that only God can give.

The phrase **"certainly make"** in describing how riches seem to **"make themselves wings"** indicates that what was longed for and gazed at in desire and covetousness can be lost in a moment.[611] Getting wealth must not be a man's primary aim to which he devotes all his thoughts, desires, and work.

> Proverbs 28:20-22 A faithful man shall abound with blessings: but he that maketh haste to be rich shall not be innocent. To have respect of persons is not good: for for a piece of bread that man will transgress. He that hasteth to be rich hath an evil eye, and considereth not that poverty shall come upon him.
> John 6:27 Labour not for the meat which perisheth, but for that meat which endureth unto everlasting life, which the Son of man shall give unto you: for him hath God the Father sealed.
> 1 John 2:15-17 Love not the world, neither the things that are in the world. If any man love the world, the love of the Father is not in him. For all that is in the world, the lust of the flesh, and the lust of the eyes, and the pride of life, is not of the Father, but is of the world. And the world passeth away, and the lust thereof: but he that doeth the will of God abideth for ever.
> Matthew 6:19-21 Lay not up for yourselves treasures upon earth, where moth and rust doth corrupt, and where thieves break through and steal: But lay not up for yourselves treasures in heaven, where neither moth nor rust doth corrupt, and where thieves do not break through nor steal: For where your treasure is, there will your heart be also.
> Mark 4:18-19 And these are they which are sown among thorns; such as hear the word, And the cares of this world, and the deceitfulness of riches, and the lusts of other things entering in, choke the word, and it becometh unfruitful.

Chapter 23:6-8 Eat thou not the bread of *him that hath* an evil eye, neither desire thou his dainty meats:
7. For as he thinketh in his heart, so *is* he: Eat and drink, saith he to thee; but his heart *is* not with thee.
8. The morsel *which* thou hast eaten shalt thou vomit up, and lose thy sweet words.

Focus: This proverb (3 verses) warns against social interaction with evil people.

"Eat thou not the bread of *him that hath* an evil eye, neither desire thou his dainty meats." (verse 6) An **"evil eye"** reflects hatred or greed. According to this verse and the supporting verses below, **"evil eye"** meant its owner had a *wicked heart and hidden ungodly desires*. To say that a person had an "evil eye," therefore, was saying that he had *an evil heart with evil motives*. One has to deduct from the warning of this verse that the guest has previous knowledge of the evil condition of the host's heart before accepting a dining invitation. Setting aside or ignoring such insightful and helpful knowledge reveals a lack of godly wisdom. Perhaps the guest is tempted to ignore the threat so that he can obtain a personal favor or promotion, but he has confidence in the wrong person. He is foolishly gazing at evil and hoping to milk it for good. This proverb declares that the risk is not worth taking because the host has a devious motive behind his pernicious invitation. Because the host's heart is wicked, all that he does will be wicked.

Proverbs 28:20-22 *[See verse 4 for these verses.]*

Matthew 6:21-24 For where your treasure is, there will your heart be also. The light of the body is the eye: if therefore thine eye be single, thy whole body shall be full of light. But if thine eye be evil, thy whole body shall be full of darkness. If therefore the light that is in thee be darkness, how great is that darkness! No man can serve two masters: for either he will hate the one, and love the other; or else he will hold to the one, and despise the other. Ye cannot serve God and mammon.

Mark 7:20-23 And he said, That which cometh out of the man, that defileth the man. For from within, out of the heart of men, proceed evil thoughts, adulteries, fornications, murders, Thefts, covetousness, wickedness, deceit, lasciviousness, an evil eye, blasphemy, pride, foolishness: All these evil things come from within, and defile the man.

"For as he thinketh in his heart, so is he: Eat and drink, saith he to thee; but his heart is not with thee." (verse 7) His heart can't be with his guests because he is covetous and always thinks about personal gain. He uses his guests and other unsuspecting souls to satisfy his lust for power and possessions.

"The morsel which thou hast eaten shalt thou vomit up, and lose thy sweet words." (verse 8) **"Sweet words"** are those kind, unworthy, and perhaps *(though hopefully not)* untrue verbal praises of social politeness that mix in the stomach like poison with his delicious meat. Regurgitation, as described herein, is a literary exaggeration, which though distasteful, would be an easy erase of an evening of reckoning with poor judgment that never should have happened. Wise persons do not engage with people who have "an evil eye," and the wise do not flatter.

Deuteronomy 15:9 Beware that there be not a thought in thy wicked heart, saying, The seventh year, the year of release, is at hand; and thine eye be evil against thy poor brother, and thou givest him nought; and he cry unto the LORD against thee, and it be sin unto thee.

Deuteronomy 28:54-57 So that the man that is tender among you, and very delicate, his eye shall be evil toward his brother, and toward the wife of his bosom, and toward the remnant of his children which he shall leave: So that he will not give to any of them of the flesh of his children whom he shall eat: because he hath nothing left him in the siege, and in the straitness, wherewith thine enemies shall distress thee in all thy gates. The tender and delicate woman among you, which would not adventure to set the sole of her foot upon the ground for delicateness and tenderness, her eye shall be evil toward the husband of her bosom, and toward her son, and toward her daughter, And toward her young one that cometh out from between her feet, and toward her children which she shall bear: for she shall eat them for want of all things secretly in the siege and straitness, wherewith thine enemy shall distress thee in thy gates.

Proverbs 22:9 He that hath a bountiful eye shall be blessed; for he giveth of his bread to the poor.

Proverbs 23:9   Speak not in the ears of a fool: for he will despise the wisdom of thy words.

Focus: This proverb reveals why speaking wisdom to a fool is inappropriate.

Instruction concerning the inappropriateness of personal interaction with undesirable evil companions makes this proverb similar in theme to the last. Also, Proverbs advised in verse six above not to be a dinner guest of an evil person, and here the advice is **"Speak not in the ears of a fool."** Both cases involve speaking privately (**"in the ears"**) of evil people and erroneously expecting good to be produced. In order to obey this admonition, the student of wisdom will have had to have observed or heard enough from the foolish person to believe that speaking wisdom directly to him would surely bring a totally regretful response. Shun the person who has dedicated himself to sin, mocks all conversations about God, condemns the Scriptures as being false, and generally hates the idea of godliness. The reason given for not conversing with him is that **"he will despise the wisdom of thy words,"** and since such hate for the instruction of God is in his heart, he will likely act destructively in one fashion or another. It takes a sensitivity to the leadership of the Holy Spirit to know when to quit reaching out to such a person.

"Such was our Master's silence before Herod. If he would hear, there would be hope. But instead of being thankful for instruction, *he will despise the wisdom of thy words*, and take occasion from them only to scoff and blaspheme the more. Many doubtful cases, however, require much wisdom. And the safe rule will be, never to speak without prayer for divine guidance, and simplicity, and love."[612]

"We are here directed not to *cast pearls before swine* (Matthew 7:6) and not to expose things sacred to the contempt and ridicule of profane scoffers."[613]

Proverbs 1:7 The fear of the LORD *is* the beginning of knowledge: *but* fools despise wisdom and instruction.

Proverbs 9:7-8 He that reproveth a scorner getteth to himself shame: and he that rebuketh a wicked *man getteth* himself a blot. Reprove not a scorner, lest he hate thee: rebuke a wise man, and he will love thee.

Luke 23:8-9 And when Herod saw Jesus, he was exceeding glad: for he was desirous to see him of a long *season,* because he had heard many things of him; and he hoped to have seen some miracle done by him. Then he questioned with him in many words; but he answered him nothing.

Proverbs 23:10-11 Remove not the old landmark; and enter not into the fields of the fatherless:
11. For their redeemer *is* mighty; he shall plead their cause with thee.

Focus: This proverb warns against two specific acts of covetousness and gives God's response to such evil acts.

"Remove not the old landmark"(verse 10a) is a reminder and further explanation of two other Proverbs that have to do with stealing from the poor in one fashion or another.

Proverbs 22:22-23 Rob not the poor, because he is poor: neither oppress the afflicted in the gate: For the LORD will plead their cause, and spoil the soul of those that spoiled them.

Proverbs 22:28 – Remove not the ancient landmark, which thy fathers have set."

When the Israelites first came into the Promised Land, each tribe received an inheritance in the land, which was to be kept by the tribe and passed to the sons (and daughters) down through the ages. A boundary marker (**"old landmark"**) was set up to define the property bounds.

"The state of Palestine with regard to enclosures is very much the same now *[published in 1892]* as it has always been. Though gardens and vineyards are surrounded by dry stone walls or hedges of prickly pear, the boundaries of arable fields are marked by nothing but a little trench, a small cairn, or a single erect stone placed at certain intervals. It is manifest that a dishonest person could easily fill the gutter with earth, or remove these stones a few feet without much risk of detection and thus enlarge his own field by a stealthy encroachment on his neighbour's. – *Dr. Jamieson.*" [614]

First given in Deuteronomy, the command was to leave these precious and divinely-established landmarks alone:

Deuteronomy 19:14 Thou shalt not remove thy neighbour's landmark, which they of old time have set in thine inheritance, which thou shalt inherit in the land that the LORD thy God giveth thee to possess it.

Deuteronomy 27:17 Cursed *be* he that removeth his neighbour's landmark. And all the people shall say, Amen.

"And enter not into the fields of the fatherless" (verse 10b) did not mean that a person could not walk or ride onto another person's property to visit or to cross over the land to their own property. It meant instead that they were not to enter with ill intent to steal such things from the owner's personal property as crops, livestock, or equipment. (God regards orphans, widows, afflicted, and poor in the same category.)

Job 24:2-4 Some remove the landmarks; they violently take away flocks, and feed thereof. They drive away the ass of the fatherless, they take the widow's ox for a pledge. They turn the needy out of the way: the poor of the earth hide themselves together.

The significant threat for anyone moving a landmark or stealing from "the fatherless" was **"for their redeemer is mighty; he shall plead their cause with thee."** (verse 11) Like the widow, the "fatherless," were considered to be weak and without protection. If the orphan (or widow) had a related male (near kinsman or *goel*, a redeemer), he would take the person who violated these statutes before a judge or perhaps personally confront him. However, in the case of the defenseless orphan or widow, the LORD would take the place of their **"redeemer,"** and He would enact justice as He deemed necessary. The implication is that because He is **"mighty,"** His justice could be severe. *(See Proverbs 22:22-23 above.)*

Deuteronomy 10:17-18 For the LORD your God is God of gods, and Lord of lords, a great God, a mighty, and a terrible, which regardeth not persons, nor taketh reward: He doth execute the judgment of the fatherless and widow, and loveth the stranger, in giving him food and raiment.

Psalm 10:17-18 LORD, thou hast heard the desire of the humble: thou wilt prepare their heart, thou wilt cause thine ear to hear: To judge the fatherless and the oppressed, that the man of the earth may no more oppress.

Psalm 103:6 The LORD executeth righteousness and judgment for all that are oppressed.

Proverbs 15:25 The LORD will destroy the house of the proud: but he will establish the border of the widow.

> **Proverbs 23:12** Apply thine heart unto instruction, and thine ears to the words of knowledge.

Focus: This proverb teaches the importance of serious listening and taking to heart the teachings of God.

"Apply thine heart *[mind, emotions, will]* **unto instruction** *[chastisement, reproof, doctrine]*, **and thine ears to the words of knowledge."** Frequently, Proverbs repeats the importance of taking instruction to heart instead of having it "go in one ear and out the other." "The best taught and most advanced Christian will be most earnest in seeking more **instruction** and will most gladly sit at the feet of the Lord's ministers to hear **the words of knowledge**. Here lies the value of the Bible, as the one source of **instruction**, and the alone treasure-house of **the words of knowledge**."[615]

> "Observe the connection between the application of the heart and the ears. The heart open to sound advice or moral precept is yet shut to Christ and His doctrine. It is closed up in unbelief, prejudice, indifference, and the love of pleasure. A listless heart, therefore, produces a careless ear. But when the heart is graciously opened, softened, and enlightened, the attention of the ear is instantly fixed."[616]
>
> Psalm 19:8-11 The statutes of the LORD are right, rejoicing the heart: the commandment of the LORD is pure, enlightening the eyes. The fear of the LORD is clean, enduring for ever: the judgments of the LORD are true and righteous altogether. More to be desired are they than gold, yea, than much fine gold: sweeter also than honey and the honeycomb. Moreover by them is thy servant warned: and in keeping of them there is great reward.
>
> Psalm 119:18 Open thou mine eyes, that I may behold wondrous things out of thy law.
>
> Proverbs 2:2-5 So that thou incline thine ear unto wisdom, and apply thine heart to understanding; Yea, if thou criest after knowledge, and liftest up thy voice for understanding; If thou seekest her as silver, and searchest for her as for hid treasures; Then shalt thou understand the fear of the LORD, and find the knowledge of God.
>
> Proverbs 4:1-2 Hear, ye children, the instruction of a father, and attend to know understanding. For I give you good doctrine, forsake ye not my law.
>
> Proverbs 19:20 Hear counsel, and receive instruction, that thou mayest be wise in thy latter end.
>
> Proverbs 19:27 Cease, my son, to hear the instruction *that causeth* to err from the words of knowledge.
>
> Proverbs 22:17-19 Bow down thine ear, and hear the words of the wise, and apply thine heart unto my knowledge. For it is a pleasant thing if thou keep them within thee; they shall withal be fitted in thy lips. That thy trust may be in the LORD, I have made known to thee this day, even to thee.

> **Chapter 23:13-14** Withhold not correction from the child: for *if* thou beatest him with the rod, he shall not die.
> 14. Thou shalt beat him with the rod, and shalt deliver his soul from hell.

Focus: This proverb insists that child discipline must be consistent and purposeful.

The reader should understand that this Scripture is speaking to *wise parents who love God and love their children*. Being wise and loving, they desire to administer discipline properly. Wisdom will instruct, and love will demand to use the *minimum* force necessary to accomplish correction of a child. Unquestionably, the rod is not the first choice. Because people are given intellectual qualities, language is the most important means of communication and correction. Everyone should thank the Lord that He uses a soft voice of counsel and instruction before using the rod of correction.

For some children, all that is necessary is a loving word of correction given in the right spirit, at the right time, and at the right place. After a child demonstrates a determined willfulness not to be obedient, the parent should consider more severe correction. Finding fault continually or applying physical punishment for every minor misstep would cause the child to become calloused to correction, which would cause more delinquency. The child would begin to conceal his bad habits and become a hypocrite to his parents.

Also, note that the definition of **"rod"** is a general term for *a branch or twig used for punishing, writing, fighting, ruling, or walking.* Surely no wise person would think that the same size rod is used for all these purposes. A rod can be used symbolically for various kinds of discipline. Furthermore, discipline is intended to correct, *not* to vent anger, show authority, or simply punish; and it must be done consistently.

"He shall not die" is inserted into the instruction, *not* because the beating is severe enough that death might ensue; but because a child will typically learn to scream and carry on like he is dying after being told that a spanking is upcoming, even before any discipline is applied. Such learned acts of hypocrisy, though heart-rending, should not prevent necessary discipline. By no means did the Bible intend for parents to harm or inflict permanent damage, either physically, emotionally, or psychologically on a child.

The parent must remember that there is **purpose** in God's entrusting the child to the parent to rear. Not only can timely correction prevent an untimely death, but it shall **"deliver his soul from hell."** Think what would have been avoided if the parents mentioned below had lovingly and prayerfully corrected their children when they were young.

Eli's three sons – 1 Samuel 2:17, 23-25 Wherefore the sin of the young men was very great before the LORD: for men abhorred the offering of the LORD ... 1 Samuel 2:22-25 Now Eli was very old, and heard all that his sons did unto all Israel; and how they lay with the women that assembled *at* the door of the tabernacle of the congregation. And he said unto them, Why do ye such things? for I hear of your evil dealings by all this people. Nay, my sons; for *it is* no good report that I hear: ye make the LORD'S people to transgress. If one man sin against another, the judge shall judge him: but if a man sin against the LORD, who shall intreat for him? Notwithstanding they hearkened not unto the voice of their father, because the LORD would slay them ...

Samuel's three sons – 1 Samuel 3:13, 8:1-3 For I have told him that I will judge his house for ever for the iniquity which he knoweth; because his sons made themselves vile, and he restrained them not ... 1 Samuel 8:1-3 And it came to pass, when Samuel was old, that he made his sons judges over Israel. Now the name of his firstborn was Joel; and the name of his second, Abiah: *they were* judges in Beersheba. And his sons walked not in his ways, but turned aside after lucre, and took bribes, and perverted judgment.

David's sons – In addition to the death of Bathsheba's first son (2 Samuel 12:16–23) were the untimely deaths of three of his 19 named sons: *Amnon,* who was murdered by his half-brother, *Absalom* for raping Absalom's sister, Tamar (2 Samuel 12:16–23); Absalom who died while attempting to steal the kingdom (2 Samuel 18); and *Adonijah* who was executed shortly after David's death for trying to usurp the throne from Solomon (1 Kings 2:25). David's own sins lived out before his children, plus the lack of proper discipline exhibited in the rearing of Adonijah caused his children to have tribulation and face untimely deaths. Of Adonijah, Scripture states:

> 1 Kings 1:5-6 Then Adonijah the son of Haggith exalted himself, saying, I will be king: and he prepared him chariots and horsemen, and fifty men to run before him. And his father had not displeased him at any time in saying, Why hast thou done so? and he also was a very goodly man; and his mother bare him after Absalom.

Proper discipline results in the child having a greater love for parents and potentially for God. Mentioned often in the Book of Proverbs, "the fear of the LORD" means having an awesome respect for Him instead of a fearful, trembling, hate-to-think-about-what-He-is-going-to-do-to-me attitude. Likewise, children should have an awesome respect for their parents, *not* a fearful, trembling, hate-to-think-about-what-they-are-going-to-do-to-me. Children are much more likely to love God if they are raised in a consistently-loving environment rather than a hateful one.

> Proverbs 15:24 The way of life is above to the wise, that he may depart from hell beneath.
>
> 1 Corinthians 11:32 But when we are judged, we are chastened of the Lord, that we should not be condemned with the world.

Rearing a child requires much prayer and wisdom. Correction given with love and gently repeated when necessary, along with patient instruction, yields positive results. God did not instruct the neighbor, the grade school teacher, Sunday school teacher, babysitter, or the pastor to "Train up the child." (Proverbs 22:6) He gave that responsibility to the parents, and Scripture emphasizes here that *correction must not be withheld* even though giving proper discipline is inconvenient and heart-breaking at times. Still, it must be carried out *consistently with love that only a parent can give.* Even though every godly, wise parent desires only joy for their child, sometimes, there has to be a *little* pain to prevent the child from having pain later that is beyond measure. Such discipline is merciful and wise and demonstrative of love in action.

Chapter 23: 15-16 My son, if thine heart be wise, my heart shall rejoice, even mine.
16. Yea, my reins shall rejoice, when thy lips speak right things.

Focus: This proverb expresses the joy of a parent who observes godly wisdom in his child.

"My son, if thine heart be wise, my heart shall rejoice, even mine." (verse 15) Certainly, parents are proud and happy when their child is honored and praised for his abilities, talents, and financial independence. However, *a believer* can only fully and truly rejoice when his child exhibits a love for God and His word. Since the Bible was given by God primarily for believers, it is only natural that believing parents would rejoice over the child **"if thine heart be wise"** and **"when thy lips speak right things."**

> "His health, his comfort, his welfare, is inexpressibly dear to us. But while we watch over the casket, it is the jewel that we mainly value. The love of our child's soul is the life and soul of parental love. None but a parent knows the heart of a parent. None but a Christian parent knows the yearning anxiety, the many tears, prayers, and 'travailing in birth again' for the soul of a beloved child; or the fervor of joy and praise, when the first budding of heavenly *wisdom* bursts to view. The sight brings joy into the innermost depths of the bosom. Parents, who sympathize *not* with these sensations, and with whom Solomon's language is unfelt and uninteresting, realize neither their responsibilities nor their privileges."[617]

> Proverbs 4:1-8 Hear, ye children, the instruction of a father, and attend to know understanding. For I give you good doctrine, forsake ye not my law. For I was my father's son, tender and only *beloved* in the sight of my mother. He taught me also, and said unto me, Let thine heart retain my words: keep my commandments, and live. Get wisdom, get understanding: forget *it* not; neither decline from the words of my mouth. Forsake her not, and she shall preserve thee: love her, and she shall keep thee. Wisdom *is* the principal thing; *therefore* get wisdom: and with all thy getting get understanding. Exalt her, and she shall promote thee: she shall bring thee to honour, when thou dost embrace her.

"Yea, my reins shall rejoice, when thy lips speak right things." (verse 16) Note that **"heart"** in verse 15 and **"reins"** in verse 16 both refer to the parents' inner man, the seat of emotions and affections. When the child's **"lips speak right things** *[upright, straight, and equitable]*,**"** it is obvious that he is hearing and obeying God's word. When the child learns from parental teaching, he causes his parents (and everyone else who loves and is concerned about him) to rejoice. When the child speaks what is right with God, the parents and their entire support group know that he is obtaining wisdom; and when they say **"my reins shall rejoice,"** they describe inner thoughts of affection and rejoicing for the child's wisdom. (See Proverbs 23:22-25.)

> Proverbs 10:1 The proverbs of Solomon. A wise son maketh a glad father: but a foolish son is the heaviness of his mother.
>
> Proverbs 15:20 A wise son maketh a glad father: but a foolish man despiseth his mother.
>
> Proverbs 23:22-25 Hearken unto thy father that begat thee, and despise not thy mother when she is old. Buy the truth, and sell it not; also wisdom, and instruction, and understanding. The father of the righteous shall greatly rejoice: and he that begetteth a wise child shall have joy of him. Thy father and thy mother shall be glad, and she that bare thee shall rejoice.
>
> Proverbs 29:3 Whoso loveth wisdom rejoiceth his father: but he that keepeth company with harlots spendeth his substance.

Proverbs 23:17-18 Let not thine heart envy sinners: but *be thou* in the fear of the LORD all the day long.
18. For surely there is an end; and thine expectation shall not be cut off.

Focus: This proverb expresses the victorious conclusion as to why the fear of the LORD is preferred to envying sinners.

"My son" in verse 15 continues to be the *noun of direct address*. The child is to be aware that his being obedient to his parents and having a **"fear of the LORD** *[reverence for the LORD]*" will produce wonderful eternal results. He is ***not to be envious of sinners*** opposing godly teachings and who have no respect for God or His word. He is to keep in mind that **"there is an end"** *(of this life)* whereby justice from God will be pronounced and **"thine expectation"** *(of rewards and heaven)* **"shall not be cut off"** (will not end). The believer will be rewarded as promised.

> ". . .similar is David's counsel. He sets out the end, and shews how little reason we have to envy sinners, and what is the true path of duty and quietness. He was, however, himself, for a while shaken by this temptation. And though he did not envy sinners, so as to covet their worldly prosperity; yet comparing their condition with his own 'chastening,' 'it was too painful for the Psalmist until he went into the sanctuary of God. Then understood he their end,' and learned to rest in the assurance – 'Thine expectation shall not be cut off.' ... In this Christian walk with God, all is safe for eternity. The hope of the ungodly, the hypocrite, the worldling, shall perish. But thine expectation shall not be cut off. It is 'a hope that maketh not ashamed.' It is grounded upon 'the immutability of God's counsels,' and 'entereth into that within the vail.'"[618]

> Psalm 37:1-5 *A Psalm* **of David.** Fret not thyself because of evildoers, neither be thou envious against the workers of iniquity. For they shall soon be cut down like the grass, and wither as the green herb. Trust in the LORD, and do good; *so* shalt thou dwell in the land, and verily thou shalt be fed. Delight thyself also in the LORD; and he shall give thee the desires of thine heart. Commit thy way unto the LORD; trust also in him; and he shall bring *it* to pass.

Proverbs 3:31 Envy thou not the oppressor, and choose none of his ways.

Proverbs 19:23 The fear of the LORD *tendeth* to life: and *he that hath it* shall abide satisfied; he shall not be visited with evil.

Proverbs 24:1-4 Be not thou envious against evil men, neither desire to be with them. For their heart studieth destruction, and their lips talk of mischief. Through wisdom is an house builded; and by understanding it is established: And by knowledge shall the chambers be filled with all precious and pleasant riches.

Proverbs 24:13-14 My son, eat thou honey, because it is good; and the honeycomb, which is sweet to thy taste: So shall the knowledge of wisdom be unto thy soul: when thou hast found it, then there shall be a reward, and thy expectation shall not be cut off.

Proverbs 24:19-20 Fret not thyself because of evil *men,* neither be thou envious at the wicked; For there shall be no reward to the evil *man;* the candle of the wicked shall be put out.

Hebrews 10:35 Cast not away therefore your confidence, which hath great recompence of reward.

1 Corinthians 15:58 Therefore, my beloved brethren, be ye stedfast, unmoveable, always abounding in the work of the Lord, forasmuch as ye know that your labour is not in vain in the Lord.

Galatians 6:7-9 Be not deceived; God is not mocked: for whatsoever a man soweth, that shall he also reap. For he that soweth to his flesh shall of the flesh reap corruption; but he that soweth to the Spirit shall of the Spirit reap life everlasting. And let us not be weary in well doing: for in due season we shall reap, if we faint not.

Proverbs 23:19-21 Hear thou, my son, and be wise, and guide thine heart in the way.
20. Be not among winebibbers; among riotous eaters of flesh:
21. For the drunkard and the glutton shall come to poverty: and drowsiness shall clothe a man with rags.

Focus: This proverb provides the practical reasons to avoid the company of winebibbers and gluttons.

"Hear thou, my son" (verse 19a) is the introduction to a subsection that extends from verse 19 to verse 35. With the exhortations **"hear thou"** and **"hearken unto"** (verse 22), the father asks his son to listen intently to what he is saying. Only by listening to the father's counsels and applying them to his life can the son avoid unnecessary problems. With the same intent of *getting the attention of His listeners*, Jesus utilized the phrase "Who hath ears to hear, let him hear." (Matthew 11:15; 13:9) Thus, it should be apparent that the first step to obtaining wisdom and faith in God is accomplished by giving one's undivided attention with determination to hear and then obey wise instruction.

Romans 10:17 So then faith cometh by hearing, and hearing by the word of God.

Proverbs 1:5 A wise man will hear, and will increase learning; and a man of understanding shall attain unto wise counsels

"Be wise, and guide thine heart in the way." (verse 19b) Because the *noun of direct address* changes from **"child** *[naar – infancy to adolescence]"* in verse 13 to **"son** *[ben – a son as a builder of the family name]"* in verses 15 and 19 the subject matter is more directly related to an older adolescent who is maturing into adulthood. Verses 19 through 28 give exhortations to hear and be wise concerning specific situations to avoid, such as associations with drunkards, gluttons, or loose women. The failure to heed wise instruction leads a child or an adult to end up in "poverty" or a "deep pit." (This chapter further explores drunkenness in verses 29-35.)

The son's purpose in listening to his father is to gain the tremendous advantage of being led by wisdom – "I lead in the way of righteousness, in the midst of the paths of judgment: That I may cause those that love me to inherit substance; and I will fill their treasures." (Proverbs 8: 20-21) Wisdom obtained from the father will **"guide thine heart in the way."**

"By listening and heeding his father's instruction and desiring **the right path** (proper conduct), a **son is wise.** One way to stay on 'the right path' is to avoid drunkenness and gluttony. These two sins cause **drowsiness,** which results in laziness and poverty."[619]

Men seem to always have certain overwhelming besetting sins – particular temptations that lead them to submit to the demands of the flesh – such as drunkenness and gluttony. **"Be not among winebibbers; among riotous eaters of flesh"** (verse 20) is an order not to be among people with unrestrained, undisciplined conduct; specifically, those involved in excessive drinking of alcohol and unrestrained and aggressive consumption of food. **"Riotous eaters of flesh"** eat for the gratification of their own physical appetites with a total disregard for anything else – especially spiritual matters. *[***"Glutton"** (verse 21) *and* **"riotous eaters"** *are translated from the same Hebrew word which means worthless, vile, insignificant, to squander, and figuratively to be loose, morally worthless, or prodigal.]* To avoid being controlled by such addictions, the son was not to be in their company. Men who engage in excess drink and "riotous" eating are prone to heavy and excess sleeping, neglect of business, and laziness. Their excesses are expensive, habit-forming, and lead to physical, as well as, spiritual poverty. Both of these sins have adverse effects on the body, causing the health of the indulger to decline. Their interest is focused on the body and with little or none for the soul.

"Be not among winebibbers." "Winebibber" is another word for **"drunkard."** According to Proverbs 20:1, "wine is a mocker, and strong drink is raging: and whosoever is deceived thereby is not wise." The *personification of wine* pictures the alcoholic drink itself having human characteristics and thereby mocking the drinker, and then controlling his emotions to the point of making him rage out of control. Alcohol cannot mock or control emotion if one never takes the first drink, so the wise person knows to stay far back from the edge of that dangerous precipice. As alcohol takes more control of a person's brain due to excessive drinking, numerous sins occur. Depending on his level of intoxication, a drunkard becomes partially to fully unrestrained and capable of doing any act that his body will perform – including sexual perversion and other crimes. Hence, the admonishment is "be not among winebibbers." Excessive use of wine and strong drink has plagued mankind since the time of Noah.

> Genesis 9:20-24 And Noah began to be an husbandman, and he planted a vineyard: And he drank of the wine, and was drunken; and he was uncovered within his tent. And Ham, the father of Canaan, saw the nakedness of his father, and told his two brethren without. And Shem and Japheth took a garment, and laid it upon both their shoulders, and went backward, and covered the nakedness of their father; and their faces were backward, and they saw not their father's nakedness. And Noah awoke from his wine, and knew what his younger son had done unto him.
> Isaiah 5:11 Woe unto them that rise up early in the morning, that they may follow strong drink; that continue until night, till wine inflame them!
> Habakkuk 2:5 Yea also, because he transgresseth by wine, he is a proud man, neither keepeth at home, who enlargeth his desire as hell, and is as death, and cannot be satisfied, but gathereth unto him all nations, and heapeth unto him all people . . .

The Bible's instruction is to not be in the company of those who do not control *how much* food or drink goes into their mouth. Both evils result from lust: gluttony results from *lusting after food,* and alcoholism results from *lusting after drink*. In either case, other vital responsibilities are neglected – including the spiritual. Wisdom teaches control of every aspect of one's life, including speech, mannerisms, conduct, thinking, eating, and drinking. Wise people learn to be companions of other people who are wise because "iron sharpeneth iron." (Proverbs 27:17) Association with foolish people adversely affects good judgment.

> Proverbs 13:20 He that walketh with wise *men* shall be wise: but a companion of fools shall be destroyed.
> Proverbs 28:7 Whoso keepeth the law is a wise son: but he that is a companion of riotous men shameth his father.
> Romans 13:13-14 Let us walk honestly, as in the day; not in rioting and drunkenness, not in chambering and wantonness, not in strife and envying. But put ye on the Lord Jesus Christ, and make not provision for the flesh, to fulfil the lusts thereof.
> 1 Corinthians 10:31 Whether therefore ye eat, or drink, or whatsoever ye do, do all to the glory of God.
> Galatians 5:22-24 But the fruit of the Spirit is love, joy, peace, longsuffering, gentleness, goodness, faith, Meekness, temperance: against such there is no law. And they that are Christ's have crucified the flesh with the affections and lusts.
> Philippians 3:18-19 (For many walk, of whom I have told you often, and now tell you even weeping, that they are the enemies of the cross of Christ: Whose end is destruction, whose God is their belly, and whose glory is in their shame, who mind earthly things.)

"For the drunkard and the glutton shall come to poverty: and drowsiness shall clothe a man with rags." (verse 21) Verses 20 and 21 bring together foolish ways of life that destroy a person's reputation and reduce him to poverty – drinking to drunkenness, overeating excessively to riotousness, and excess sleeping and laziness brought on by either of the first two. Uncontrolled eating or drinking is foolishness. **"Drowsiness"** is sluggishness, and both uncontrolled drinking of alcohol and uncontrolled eating cause the brain to be sluggish. The number one priority then becomes sleep rather than productivity. Excessive sleep promotes laziness, neglect of physical and spiritual responsibilities, and an inability to make wise decisions. **"Poverty"** is the **typical result** of reveling, feasting, and continual overeating, drinking strong drink, and riotous living.

> Luke 15:11-18 And he said, A certain man had two sons: And the younger of them said to his father, Father, give me the portion of goods that falleth to me. And he divided unto them his living. And not many days after the younger son gathered all together, and took his journey into a far country, and there wasted his substance with riotous living. And when he had spent all, there arose a mighty famine in that land; and he began to be in want. And he went and joined himself to a citizen of that country; and he sent him into his fields to feed swine. And he would fain have filled his belly with the husks that the swine did eat: and no man gave unto him. And when he came to himself, he said, How many hired servants of my father's have bread enough and to spare, and I perish with hunger! I will arise and go to my father, and will say unto him, Father, I have sinned against heaven, and before thee . . .

It is of particular interest that this combination of winebibbing and gluttony is among the accusations leveled against the Lord Jesus Christ by the religious Jews. Maybe the Scripture-savvy Scribes and Pharisees had Proverbs 23 in mind when they thus *unjustly and inappropriately accused the Lord.* Pharisees, in particular believed themselves spiritually and morally superior. When Jesus came intermingling with the people, they became blind with rage, grasping at straws, desperately trying to find something wrong and to shut Him down.

> Matthew 11:18-19 For John came neither eating nor drinking, and they say, He hath a devil. The Son of man came eating and drinking, and they say, Behold a man gluttonous, and a winebibber, a friend of publicans and sinners. But wisdom is justified of her children.
>
> Hebrews 4:15 For we have not an high priest *[Jesus, the Son of God]* which cannot be touched with the feeling of our infirmities; but was in all points tempted like as *we are, yet* without sin.

Proverbs 23:22-25 Hearken unto thy father that begat thee, and despise not thy mother when she is old.
23. Buy the truth, and sell *it* not; *also* wisdom, and instruction, and understanding.
24. The father of the righteous shall greatly rejoice: and he that begetteth a wise *child* shall have joy of him.
25. Thy father and thy mother shall be glad, and she that bare thee shall rejoice.

Focus: This proverb (4 verses) stresses the effect on parents of a child who listens and learns from them, loves them, and longs for godly wisdom.

"Hearken *[perceive with the ear with the implication of obedience]* **unto thy father that begat thee, and despise not thy mother when she is old."** (verse 22) Wise children love their parents and *do not* disrespect them when old age has lessened their ability to move about and communicate. The command is first given in Exodus 20:12 – "Honour thy father and thy mother: that thy days may be long upon the land which the LORD thy God giveth thee." Both mother and father should be hearkened unto because: (1) They have parental rights that mandate a child (no matter his age) hear what they have to say – simply because they are his parents. (2) They have old age rights and deserve respect for their long lives – simply because they have valuable life experiences. Old age potentially brings loss of mental ability and impaired mobility, and these deficiencies sometimes result in difficult interpersonal communication. Nonetheless, children should treat their parents with dignity and respect by listening to their loving words. Parents should not have to spend their last days heartbroken and disrespected. Children should follow Biblical directives so that they do not have to face God with worthless excuses for improper foolish behavior toward their parents.

> "Respect was enjoined by the law to old age. What peculiar respect then, must be due to the silver locks of a father or a mother! –How incumbent the duty to smooth, by every affectionate and reverential attention and kindness, the declining path to the tomb of those who have been the guardians of your childhood and youth! –to strive to make them happy, instead of breaking their hearts by neglect and misconduct!"[620]
>
> Leviticus 19:32 Thou shalt rise up before the hoary head, and honour the face of the old man, and fear thy God: I *am* the LORD.
>
> Deuteronomy 5:16 Honour thy father and thy mother, as the LORD thy God hath commanded thee; that thy days may be prolonged, and that it may go well with thee, in the land which the LORD thy God giveth thee.

"Buy the truth, and sell it not; also wisdom, and instruction, and understanding." (verse 23) The teaching here to **"buy"** and ***not sell*** is pure figurative language incorporated to express great value. Truth, wisdom, instruction, and understanding can not be purchased with money–nor can they be sold for money any more than one can buy and sell brains, genius, or talent. They are not marketable. *As a figure of speech,* they can *only be bought* by first having a strong desire for them and then by expending effort and dedicating time, which is the most precious asset that a person possesses. *It is no loss* to spend significant portions of one's life to "buy" these invaluable gifts; on the contrary, it is a tremendous loss *not* to spend the time and effort to gain them. There is a price to pay, but it is not with money. Spending time, much prayer, study, and meditation in absorbing the word of God will cost hours and days leading perhaps into years that might otherwise be spent on *frivolous things* that have no lasting value. Discover God's view of right and wrong, and one will know the **truth.** Know TRUTH Himself, Jesus Christ, and one will have eternal life. Learn from His **instruction** (knowledge) and apply the same in thinking and acting. Thus, living under His approval, one will be wise. To utilize such **wisdom** in one's life reveals that he has **understanding.** *Sell not* these great assets from God for anything, not pleasure, power, or palace. Only a fool would exchange these for anything this sinful world has to offer.

Job 28:12-17 But where shall wisdom be found? and where is the place of understanding? Man knoweth not the price thereof; neither is it found in the land of the living. The depth saith, It is not in me: and the sea saith, It is not with me. It cannot be gotten for gold, neither shall silver be weighed for the price thereof. It cannot be valued with the gold of Ophir, with the precious onyx, or the sapphire. The gold and the crystal cannot equal it: and the exchange of it shall not be for jewels of fine gold.

Proverbs 2:1-5 My son, if thou wilt receive my words, and hide my commandments with thee; So that thou incline thine ear unto wisdom, and apply thine heart to understanding; Yea, if thou criest after knowledge, and liftest up thy voice for understanding; If thou seekest her as silver, and searchest for her as for hid treasures; Then shalt thou understand the fear of the LORD, and find the knowledge of God.

Proverbs 3:13-20 Happy *is* the man *that* findeth wisdom, and the man *that* getteth understanding. For the merchandise of it *is* better than the merchandise of silver, and the gain thereof than fine gold. She *is* more precious than rubies: and all the things thou canst desire are not to be compared unto her. Length of days *is* in her right hand; *and* in her left hand riches and honour. Her ways *are* ways of pleasantness, and all her paths *are* peace. She *is* a tree of life to them that lay hold upon her: and happy *is* every one that retaineth her. The LORD by wisdom hath founded the earth; by understanding hath he established the heavens. By his knowledge the depths are broken up, and the clouds drop down the dew.

Proverbs 17:16 Wherefore is there a price in the hand of a fool to get wisdom, seeing he hath no heart to it?

2 Timothy 2:15 Study to shew thyself approved unto God, a workman that needeth not to be ashamed, rightly dividing the word of truth.

"The father of the righteous shall greatly rejoice: and he that begetteth a wise child shall have joy of him. Thy father and thy mother shall be glad, and she that bare thee shall rejoice." (verses 24-25) When children are loved, protected, taught, provided for, prayed over, and directed in every aspect of their lives, they become, in an unexplainable manner, part of the very life of their parents. When all the preceding are acknowledged, one must realize that children play a direct role in the emotional well-being of their parents. To a large extent, the parents' happiness is directly related to the life of their children. A **"righteous"** child is right with God, thereby living according to God's will. His parents have no fear of his suffering, as does a fool. Because of his love for righteousness, the child positions himself in that particular place where God can bless him; and as he progresses in age, he will also progress in wisdom, giving him greater ability to comprehend the importance of his words and actions. When this happens, the parents can and will rejoice.

Proverbs 10:1 The proverbs of Solomon. A wise son maketh a glad father: but a foolish son is the heaviness of his mother.

Proverbs 23:26-35 My son, give me thine heart, and let thine eyes observe my ways.
27. For a whore *is* a deep ditch; and a strange woman *is* a narrow pit.
28. She also lieth in wait as *for* a prey, and increaseth the transgressors among men.
29. Who hath woe? who hath sorrow? who hath contentions? who hath babbling? who hath wounds without cause? who hath redness of eyes?
30. They that tarry long at the wine; they that go to seek mixed wine.
31. Look not thou upon the wine when it is red, when it giveth his colour in the cup, *when* it moveth itself aright.
32. At the last it biteth like a serpent, and stingeth like an adder.
33. Thine eyes shall behold strange women, and thine heart shall utter perverse things.
34. Yea, thou shalt be as he that lieth down in the midst of the sea, or as he that lieth upon the top of a mast.
35. They have stricken me, *shalt thou say, and* I was not sick; they have beaten me, *and* I felt *it* not: when shall I awake? I will seek it yet again.

Focus: This proverb (10 verses) expresses a call to the ways of wisdom to avoid the entrapment of the whore and the wretchedness of wine.

This extended section of chapter 23 (verses 26-35) discusses the two insidious traps that lure a man's heart away from God: adulterous women and love of wine. Both the lures promise pleasure but end in pain and impairment. Both trap their followers into a pit of poor judgment where understanding is darkened. Both separate men from God and secure them in their tenacious grasp.

> **Outline of Proverbs 23:26-35**
>
> I. Wisdom pleas for man's heart and heeding. (verse 26)
> II. Warnings about the whore:
>   A. She is a trap. (verse 27)
>   B. She is a patient pursuer of men (verse 28)
> III. Woeful results of over indulging in alcohol (verses 29-30)
>   A. Woe
>   B. Sorrow
>   C. Contentions
>   D. Babbling
>   E. Wounds
>   F. Redness of eye
> IV. Warning about alcohol (verses 31-35)
>   A. Red in cup, moves (verse 31)
>   B. Bites like a snake, stings like an adder (verse 32)
>   C. Breaks down inhibitions for the strange woman (verse 33)
>   D. Disarms the safety system (verse 34)
>   E. Deadens the senses and disables the will (verse 35)

"My son, give me thine heart, and let thine eyes observe my ways." (verse 26) The wise father/teacher makes this plea knowing that there is a life of success and happiness available if the young man listens and follows wisdom. If he would but open his understanding, he could observe the difference between following the solid values of God and chasing after the vaporous nonsense of this world. Wisdom asks for "thine heart" so that body, mind, and spirit can fully express righteousness.

> **"My son, give me thine heart.** – For that is the one gift alone worthy of acceptance which man can offer to God, and the only one which God will accept; an offering which man endeavors to keep for himself, substituting for it alms, unreal prayers, outward observances of religion, and obedience in matters of little moment."[621]

> "Certainly the heart is that which God especially requires, and calls for from every one of us; whatever we give, if we do not give him our hearts, it will not be accepted: he must be the chief object of our love. Our thoughts must dwell upon him; and on him, as our chief good and highest end, our most fervent affections must be placed. We must not think to divide our hearts between him and the world: he will have the whole heart, or no part of it."[622]

> Matthew 22:37 Jesus said unto him, Thou shalt love the Lord thy God with all thy heart, and with all thy soul, and with all thy mind.

> 1 John 2:15-17 Love not the world, neither the things that are in the world. If any man love the world, the love of the Father is not in him. For all that is in the world, the lust of the flesh, and the lust of the eyes, and the pride of life, is not of the Father, but is of the world. And the world passeth away, and the lust thereof: but he that doeth the will of God abideth for ever.

> **"Let thine eyes observe my ways**; keep closely to the paths of virtue which I teach thee, especially the path of purity, as the next verse shows."[623]

"For a whore *is* a deep ditch; and a strange woman *is* a narrow pit. She also lieth in wait as *for* a prey, and increaseth the transgressors among men." (verses 27-28) **"Whore"** and **"strange woman"** refer to evil women who use their bodies in an immoral manner. **"Deep ditch"** and **"narrow pit"** refer to the entrapment that these women set for their victims – a trap that is especially dangerous because it contains horrors that are well-disguised with beauty and pleasure, and escaping is extremely difficult. Proverbs 22:14 states "The mouth of strange women is a deep pit. . . ." and is now patiently waiting for her next casualty. Sooner or later a simple, foolish man will step into the pit as she **"increaseth the transgressors among men"** by encouraging them to sin and move farther away from God. She is the predator who causes her **"prey"** to transgress against God, his wife, parents, teacher, and righteous friends.

> Proverbs 2:18-19 For her house inclineth unto death, and her paths unto the dead. None that go unto her return again, neither take they hold of the paths of life.
>
> Proverbs 5:20 And why wilt thou, my son, be ravished with a strange woman, and embrace the bosom of a stranger?
>
> Proverbs 6:23-26 For the commandment is a lamp; and the law is light; and reproofs of instruction are the way of life: To keep thee from the evil woman, from the flattery of the tongue of a strange woman. Lust not after her beauty in thine heart; neither let her take thee with her eyelids. For by means of a whorish woman a man is brought to a piece of bread: and the adulteress will hunt for the precious life.
>
> Proverbs 7:4-5 Say unto wisdom, Thou art my sister; and call understanding thy kinswoman: That they may keep thee from the strange woman, from the stranger which flattereth with her words.

Proverbs 22:14 The mouth of strange women is a deep pit: he that is abhorred of the LORD shall fall therein.

"Who hath woe? who hath sorrow? who hath contentions? who hath babbling? who hath wounds without cause? who hath redness of eyes? They that tarry long at the wine; they that go to seek mixed wine." (verses 29-30) Drunkenness is another trap that takes people away from following God and is frequently a companion to the harlot. With six disturbing questions introduced by the interrogative pronoun **"who,"** these verses graphically call attention to the mental, social and physical problems from overindulging in alcohol.

"Who hath woe? Christians will have temptations and trials and may have chastisements but should not have to face *woes*. A **"woe"** is an extreme hurt brought on by one's own actions. It is the cry of despair of knowing what improper actions have caused, and it can also be the curse and despair brought upon those who disobey God's word. (See definition for "woe" – Hebrew word *'owy* below.)

> Isaiah 5:11-12; 21-25 Woe unto them that rise up early in the morning, that they may follow strong drink; that continue until night, till wine inflame them! And the harp, and the viol, the tabret, and pipe, and wine, are in their feasts: but they regard not the work of the LORD, neither consider the operation of his hands . . . Woe unto them that are wise in their own eyes, and prudent in their own sight! Woe unto them that are mighty to drink wine, and men of strength to mingle strong drink: Which justify the wicked for reward, and take away the righteousness of the righteous from him! Therefore as the fire devoureth the stubble, and the flame consumeth the chaff, so their root shall be as rottenness, and their blossom shall go up as dust: because they have cast away the law of the LORD of hosts, and despised the word of the Holy One of Israel. Therefore is the anger of the LORD kindled against his people, and he hath stretched forth his hand against them, and hath smitten them: and the hills did tremble, and their carcases were torn in the midst of the streets. For all this his anger is not turned away, but his hand is stretched out still.
>
> Isaiah 28:1-3 Woe to the crown of pride, to the drunkards of Ephraim, whose glorious beauty is a fading flower, which are on the head of the fat valleys of them that are overcome with wine! Behold, the Lord hath a mighty and strong one, which as a tempest of hail and a destroying storm, as a flood of mighty waters overflowing, shall cast down to the earth with the hand. The crown of pride, the drunkards of Ephraim, shall be trodden under feet . . .
>
> Isaiah 28:7-8 But they also have erred through wine, and through strong drink are out of the way; the priest and the prophet have erred through strong drink, they are swallowed up of wine, they are out of the way through strong drink; they err in vision, they stumble in judgment. For all tables are full of vomit and filthiness, so that there is no place clean.
>
> Habakkuk 2:5; 15-16 Yea also, because he transgresseth by wine, he is a proud man, neither keepeth at home, who enlargeth his desire as hell, and is as death, and cannot be satisfied, but gathereth unto him all nations, and heapeth unto him all people . . . Woe unto him that giveth his neighbour drink, that puttest thy bottle to him, and makest him drunken also, that thou mayest look on their nakedness! Thou art filled with shame for glory: drink thou also, and let thy foreskin be uncovered: the cup of the LORD'S right hand shall be turned unto thee, and shameful spewing shall be on thy glory.

"Who hath sorrow? Who hath woe?" "Sorrow" is translated from the Hebrew *'abowy,* meaning *want, oh! woe! (an exclamation of pain–indicates desire or uneasiness)*. **"Woe"** is translated from the Hebrew *'owy,* meaning *alas! oh!, (a passionate cry of grief or despair)*. "Sorrow" and "woe" are synonyms being repeated to give the effect of compounded and stacked sorrow on top of sorrow. The drunkard suffers, and if he has family, they suffer along with him; only, in some ways, their suffering is much greater than his. He lives with a constant debasement and guilt; and he looks at his family with immense self-reproach for what he is doing, even asking their forgiveness after every drunken bout. He faces the looks of his family for dishonoring them, impoverishing them – just small examples of the woes and sorrows which are without end and stacked one on top of the other.

"Who hath contentions?" The drunkard often has quarrels and lawsuits after partying. God created man as an intelligent being so that his mind would control his body. The drunkard loses this control; and while he still has a mind, it has relinquished control to this mocker with no reasoning ability, no respect for others, no desire for peace, and no conscience. Alcohol is often called "liquid courage" but would be better expressed as "solid catastrophe."

"Who hath babbling?" Alcoholics ramble on and on with nonsense. With his brain largely disabled and unable to evaluate his surroundings properly or reach reasonable conclusions, one of his most obvious impairments is inarticulate speech – babbling. Realizing the importance of appropriate communication, wise people are seriously concerned about every word spoken; and they speak with an intent to please God and not offend others. The drunk does not have the mental, physical, or spiritual ability to care.

"Who hath wounds without cause?" From empty words, many drunks advance to physical accidents and altercations. They stumble and fall and wake up with bruises and cuts from somewhere – but, from where, they do not remember. These are *not* wounds that have come from defending his country or protecting his family. A 2021 publication noted that "in 2019, 10,142 people died in alcohol-impaired driving crashes, accounting for 28% of all traffic-related deaths in the United States."[624]

"Who hath redness of eyes?" Bloodshot eyes are telltale signs of excessive consumption of alcohol that even naive people recognize. This physical trait occurs because alcohol swells the blood vessels in the eye, making them seem larger and in turn, making the eyes look redder.[625]

"They that tarry long at the wine; they that go to seek mixed wine." (verse 30) This statement answers the previous questions and identifies the poor soul suffering from all the penalties of excessive alcohol consumption identified in verse 29. Having a touch of sarcasm, **"they that go to seek mixed wine"** sets the alcoholic as a contradiction to the wise person who seeks after wisdom. The **"mixed wine"** is "not wine diluted and lowered with water, but made stronger and more inebriating, by the addition of more powerful ingredients, as honey, spices, myrrh, defrutum, opiates, etc."[626]

"Look not thou upon the wine when it is red, when it giveth his colour in the cup, when it moveth itself aright." (verse 31) This warning is against the prolonged, lustful looking at wine which would increase the appetite for it. As to the red color, the Bible refers to the wines of the Holy Land as "blood," a metaphor showing the remarkable resemblance between the color of red wine and blood. When wine is poured out of a container into a cup, it has a beautiful red color that appeals to the senses but is a snare that will cause addiction and loss of self-control. *[Note that the word for **"colour"** is the Hebrew 'ayin which means eye. The color and the sparkling of the wine are figuratively described as an eye that its victim cannot resist.]*

> Deuteronomy 32:14 Butter of kine, and milk of sheep, with fat of lambs, and rams of the breed of Bashan, and goats, with the fat of kidneys of wheat; and thou didst drink the pure blood of the grape.

When grapes are crushed, the abundant yeast in the grapes causes the process of fermentation to begin. In the absence of oxygen, the yeast reacts to the sugar in the grapes, and carbon dioxide and ethyl alcohol are produced. If oxygen is present, water is produced. The carbon dioxide gas begins to effervesce, resulting in bubbles *(sparkling wine*[627]*)* that give rise to the clause – **"when it moveth itself aright."**[51] The "sparkling" wine tantalizes the senses and causes people who are addictive to tarry and continue drinking for long periods.

"At the last it biteth like a serpent, and stingeth like an adder." (verse 32) After becoming sober, the drunkard feels results that are as devastating and painful as the wounds of a poisonous snake (**"serpent," "adder"**). It spreads its poison throughout the body, impairing the mind and damaging cells as it goes. In proportion to the amount consumed, alcohol can cause blackouts, headaches, nausea, and fatigue.

> "While alcohol doesn't kill brain cells, it can damage the dendrites, which are the branch-like ends of the brain cells. Dendrites are key for passing messages from one neuron to another, so a degradation of the dendrites can cause cognitive problems. Another brain disorder that alcoholics may develop is Wernicke-Korsakoff Syndrome. People with Wernicke-Korsakoff generally suffer from problems with memory, confusion, eye paralysis, and lack of muscle coordination. While this syndrome may lead to brain cell death, it is not because of the alcohol specifically–it's actually due to thiamine deficiency. Thiamine is an important B vitamin that's crucial to neuron health, and alcoholics may lack thiamine because consuming large quantities of alcohol can disrupt thiamine absorption in the body. Alcoholics may also be malnourished, which can additionally deplete thiamine reserves."[628]

"Thine eyes shall behold strange women, and thine heart shall utter perverse things." (verse 33) Sexual misconduct and intoxication are twins often seen together. Because the drunk's brain is impaired, his ability to make reasonable judgments is diminished. In a sober state, he might have enough character *not* to fixate on a harlot, whereas in a drunken state, he has a much greater probability of doing so. In a drunken state, a man will make perverse (froward) statements that he probably would never speak when sober. He is irrational, unrestrained, and unpredictable in conduct and speech.

> Genesis 19:32-36 Come, let us make our father drink wine, and we will lie with him, that we may preserve seed of our father. And they made their father drink wine that night: and the firstborn went in, and lay with her father; and he perceived not when she lay down, nor when she arose. And it came to pass on the morrow, that the firstborn said unto the younger, Behold, I lay yesternight with my father: let us make him drink wine this night also; and go thou in, and lie with him, that we may preserve seed of our father. And they made their father drink wine that night also: and the younger arose, and lay with him; and he perceived not when she lay down, nor when she arose. Thus were both the daughters of Lot with child by their father.

> Proverbs 31:4-5 It is not for kings, O Lemuel, it is not for kings to drink wine; nor for princes strong drink: Lest they drink, and forget the law, and pervert the judgment of any of the afflicted.

Isaiah 28:7-8 But they also have erred through wine, and through strong drink are out of the way; the priest and the prophet have erred through strong drink, they are swallowed up of wine, they are out of the way through strong drink; they err in vision, they stumble in judgment. For all tables are full of vomit and filthiness, so that there is no place clean.

"Yea, thou shalt be as he that lieth down in the midst of the sea, or as he that lieth upon the top of a mast." (verse 34) There is a double meaning to this verse. First, the drunk has no sense of stability; and not being able to walk a straight line, he staggers around with his mind so dizzy that he feels like the ground beneath him is rolling like the sea. Imagine the feeling of being at the top of a ship's rigging and swaying with the swells of the sea and rocking back and forth. Second, the inebriated one has no sense of danger. He is like a person senseless enough to lie down on the top of a mast, leaving himself likely to be thrown down to his death or like one who would lie down on the smooth surface of the sea, imagining it solid and able to support his body.

"They have stricken me, *shalt thou say,* **and I was not sick; they have beaten me,** *and* **I felt** *it* **not. I will seek it yet again."** (verse 35) This verse reflects the words of a drunk as he talks to himself – a common experience. He says that he was **"stricken"** (struck) by more than one person but **"was not sick,"** meaning that his brain did not recognize that his body had sustained injury. Then he said in this verse that the lack of brain activity went even farther as he was **"beaten"** and did not have any pain. Then, like the "dog returning to his own vomit," he returns to his own folly. (Proverbs 26:11) He says **"when shall I awake? I will seek it yet again."** At this point, strong wine has gained complete control. He is a slave to intoxicating wine.

CHAPTER TWENTY-FOUR

> **Proverbs 24:1-2** Be not thou envious against evil men, neither desire to be with them.
> 2. For their heart studieth destruction, and their lips talk of mischief.

Focus: This proverb warns not to envy or desire association with evil men and tells why.

To be **"envious against evil men"** is expressive of a desire to be like them in some manner, such as personality, appearance, or popularity. It could also include a desire to have some asset, such as personal property or real estate. Because they think and talk habitually of doing harm and wickedness, anything they possess is tainted by their sins. While such men cling to wickedness, evil also clings to them like an incurable lethal disease. Anything they possess has a stigma attached, and they should be shunned rather than sought-after.

"Evil men" are, figuratively speaking, those with a sin-diseased way of thinking that *studies destruction.* Because they constantly *study [ponder]* such violence as robbery, murder, and adultery, they are consumed with doing evil, **"Their lips talk of mischief."** Each time their mouth opens, it belches out wickedness from an evil heart. **"Mischief,"** at the time of the KJV translation, meant *trouble, wickedness, misery, pain, grief,* unlike the meaning of petty, childlike annoyance that it carries today.

Students of wisdom will maintain a proper close relationship with God and be content with and thankful for His gifts. They will also keep a proper distance from "evil men."

> Genesis 13:10-13 And Lot lifted up his eyes, and beheld all the plain of Jordan, that it *was* well watered every where, before the LORD destroyed Sodom and Gomorrah, *even* as the garden of the LORD, like the land of Egypt, as thou comest unto Zoar. Then Lot chose him all the plain of Jordan; and Lot journeyed east: and they separated themselves the one from the other. Abram dwelled in the land of Canaan, and Lot dwelled in the cities of the plain, and pitched *his* tent toward But the men of Sodom *were* wicked and sinners before the LORD exceedingly.
> Psalm 37:1-2 A Psalm of David. Fret not thyself because of evildoers, neither be thou envious against the workers of iniquity. For they shall soon be cut down like the grass, and wither as the green herb.
> Psalm 37:7 Rest in the LORD, and wait patiently for him: fret not thyself because of him who prospereth in his way, because of the man who bringeth wicked devices to pass.
> Psalm 73:2-9 But as for me, my feet were almost gone; my steps had well nigh slipped. For I was envious at the foolish, when I saw the prosperity of the wicked. For there are no bands in their death: but their strength is firm. They are not in trouble as other men; neither are they plagued like other men. Therefore pride compasseth them about as a chain; violence covereth them as a garment. Their eyes stand out with fatness: they have more than heart could wish. They are corrupt, and speak wickedly concerning oppression: they speak loftily. They set their mouth against the heavens, and their tongue walketh through the earth.
> Proverbs 1:15-16 My son, walk not thou in the way with them; refrain thy foot from their path: For their feet run to evil, and make haste to shed blood.
> Proverbs 3:31-33 Envy thou not the oppressor, and choose none of his ways. For the froward is abomination to the LORD: but his secret is with the righteous. The curse of the LORD is in the house of the wicked: but he blesseth the habitation of the just.
> Proverbs 13:20 He that walketh with wise *men* shall be wise: but a companion of fools shall be destroyed.
> Proverbs 23:17 Let not thine heart envy sinners: but be thou in the fear of the LORD all the day long.
> Proverbs 24:19-20 Fret not thyself because of evil men, neither be thou envious at the wicked; For there shall be no reward to the evil man; the candle of the wicked shall be put out.

> **Proverbs 24:3-4** Through wisdom is an house builded; and by understanding it is established:
> 4. And by knowledge shall the chambers be filled with all precious and pleasant riches.

Focus: This proverb specifies that wisdom, knowledge, and understanding are the cornerstones needed to build and establish a flourishing spiritual household.

"Through wisdom is an house builded." (verse 3) In the context of these two verses, **"house"** *[dwelling place or household, family]* represents the members of a family or the household, and *not* the physical structure. When parents raise their family so that every aspect of it pleases God, then the household will be built on wisdom. Wise parents have a proper relationship with God and have learned to be guided by His principles of life as taught in Scripture; consequently, every family member is taught how to be able to navigate through the challenges and opportunities of life in the most effective manner. They are taught to minimize evil influences and maximize godly outcomes. They learn to live "in the shadow of thy wings" (Psalm 17:8), where there is peace, power, protection, and provision.

> Joshua 24:15 And if it seem evil unto you to serve the LORD, choose you this day whom ye will serve; whether the gods which your fathers served that *were* on the other side of the flood, or the gods of the Amorites, in whose land ye dwell: but as for me and my house, we will serve the LORD.
>
> 2 Samuel 7:25-26 And now, O LORD God, the word that thou hast spoken concerning thy servant, and concerning his house, establish it for ever, and do as thou hast said. And let thy name be magnified for ever, saying, The LORD of hosts is the God over Israel: and let the house of thy servant David be established before thee.
>
> Proverbs 9:1 Wisdom hath builded her house, she hath hewn out her seven pillars . . .
>
> Proverbs 12:7 The wicked are overthrown, and are not: but the house of the righteous shall stand.
>
> Proverbs 14:1 Every wise woman buildeth her house: but the foolish plucketh it down with her hands.
>
> Isaiah 33:6 And wisdom and knowledge shall be the stability of thy times, and strength of salvation: the fear of the LORD is his treasure.
>
> Colossians 2:6-8 As ye have therefore received Christ Jesus the Lord, so walk ye in him: Rooted and built up in him, and stablished in the faith, as ye have been taught, abounding therein with thanksgiving. Beware lest any man spoil you through philosophy and vain deceit, after the tradition of men, after the rudiments of the world, and not after Christ.

"By understanding it *[household]* **is established."** "Understanding" enables a person to discern between "truth or falsehood, good or evil."[629] The entire Book of Proverbs involves understanding, not merely blind obedience. God communicates knowledge for understanding on an intellectual and spiritual basis, and He reasons with a man, as can be seen in Isaiah 1:18 and other Scriptures. Parents become wise by first having proper respect for God and consequently obeying His word and walking with Him. Wise parents understand the benefits and blessings of following God, and they understand the damnation and damage of following after the evil of this world and its fractured philosophy. They understand what their children really need to be successful in this life. Wise parents know God personally through His word and interaction, and they want their children to know Him.

> Isaiah 1:18 Come now, and let us reason together, saith the LORD: though your sins be as scarlet, they shall be as white as snow; though they be red like crimson, they shall be as wool.
>
> Matthew 7:24-27 Therefore whosoever heareth these sayings of mine, and doeth them, I will liken him unto a wise man, which built his house upon a rock: And the rain descended, and the floods came, and the winds blew, and beat upon that house; and it fell not: for it was founded upon a rock. And every one that heareth these sayings of mine, and doeth them not, shall be likened unto a foolish man, which built his house upon the sand: And the rain descended, and the floods came, and the winds blew, and beat upon that house; and it fell: and great was the fall of it.

Christ's parable (Matthew 7:24-27 above) shows what it means to be **"established."** Because the household is prepared properly in the word and wisdom of God, the teachings are ingrained in each one so that the trials and tribulations of life will not unmoor them, and the children will be able to grow without a constant threat of being destabilized. In addition to being provided with their physical needs of food, clothing, and shelter, they are taught and encouraged to gain knowledge of God and the world He created. The community will respect this household because the parents are wise and make proper provisions.

"And by knowledge shall the chambers be filled with all precious and pleasant riches." (verse 4) This **"knowledge"** of God gleaned from Scripture and from experience with Him produces proper respect for both God and fellow men. Such knowledge is foundational to a journey capable of producing "all precious and pleasant riches." "Thy word *is* a lamp unto my feet, and a light unto my path." (Psalm 119:105) God's word, first of all, guides a person to God; then, it teaches him to identify and stay away from wicked people and evil circumstances that would potentially destroy the fruitful gains of life. Such knowledge also teaches him about being rewarded by God for giving to God his first fruits and to the poor out of his blessed supply. It prevents improper or untimely speech that might incite unnecessary lawsuits or turn away profitable relationships. And it teaches him to be industrious rather than lazy, to avoid extravagance and too much leisure, and to treat everything he owns with respect knowing that God is ultimately the owner and provider of everything both tangible and intangible. All such wise living acts together to produce wealth.

> Job 20:19 Because he hath oppressed *and* hath forsaken the poor; *because* he hath violently taken away an house which he builded not; Surely he shall not feel quietness in his belly, he shall not save of that which he desired. There shall none of his meat be left; therefore shall no man look for his goods. In the fulness of his sufficiency he shall be in straits: every hand of the wicked shall come upon him. *When* he is about to fill his belly, *God* shall cast the fury of his wrath upon him, and shall rain *it* upon him while he is eating.

> Psalm 112:3 Wealth and riches *shall be* in his house: and his righteousness endureth for ever.

> Proverbs 8:18 Riches and honour *are* with me; *yea,* durable riches and righteousness.

> Proverbs 8:21 That I may cause those that love me to inherit substance; and I will fill their treasures.

> Proverbs 10:22 The blessing of the LORD, it maketh rich, and he addeth no sorrow with it.

> Proverbs 13:22 A good *man* leaveth an inheritance to his children's children: and the wealth of the sinner *is* laid up for the just.

> Proverbs 14:24 The crown of the wise *is* their riches: *but* the foolishness of fools *is* folly.

> Proverbs 22:4 By humility *and* the fear of the LORD *are* riches, and honour, and life.

Proverbs 24:5-6 A wise man *is* strong; yea, a man of knowledge increaseth strength.
6. For by wise counsel thou shalt make thy war: and in multitude of counsellors *there is* safety.

Focus: This proverb declares the kind of man who is strong and the source of knowledge that makes him stronger, capable, and safe.

"A wise man" trusts in God and relies on his **"knowledge"** of God's guiding principles. Through Jesus Christ, he has overcome Satan's strong hold on him, and he belongs to God. The more the wise man knows and follows God's leadership and way of thinking and doing, the wiser he becomes. This wisdom reflects itself in *strength of person* as he lives out what he knows best – a life lived for Christ. His strength reflects a *knowledge of God's greatness and of his own personal limitations*; while, at the same time projects a confidence that he will be victorious over situations and enemies. He reveals superior strength, not weakness, by asking counsel from other godly people.

"A wise man *is* strong." *The overwhelming characteristic of a wise man is his spiritual strength.* He does not have to shout or pound his fists on the table. He quietly speaks, and people listen. He has the strength of mind and character to reject evil and stand for righteousness. He will keep serving God regardless of the trials and tribulations he faces. The more knowledge he gains from the wise counsel of God's word and from wise counselors, the more other wise people respect his wisdom. Such knowledge is more powerful than physical strength, and no great work can be accomplished without it.

> "'**A wise man *is* strong.**' '…full of strength, because, however feeble in body, he is wise in counsel, firm in purpose, brave in conduct, thoroughly to be depended upon, and supported by his perfect trust in God."[630]

> "A wise man is strong, not in and of himself; he cannot think a good thought, nor do a good action, nor preserve himself from sin and Satan; but he is strong in Christ, and in the power of his might, and in his grace; and, through spiritual strength communicated to him, his heart is strengthened, and the work of grace in his heart; he is strengthened to exercise grace more strongly, to perform the duties of religion, to bear the cross of Christ, to withstand temptations, and to oppose his own corruptions."[631]

> Proverbs 1:7 The fear of the LORD *is* the beginning of knowledge: *but* fools despise wisdom and instruction.

> Proverbs 8:13-15 The fear of the LORD is to hate evil: pride, and arrogancy, and the evil way, and the froward mouth, do I hate. Counsel is mine, and sound wisdom: I am understanding; I have strength. By me kings reign, and princes decree justice.

> Proverbs 10:29 The way of the LORD is strength to the upright: but destruction shall be to the workers of iniquity.

> Proverbs 21:21-22 He that followeth after righteousness and mercy findeth life, righteousness, and honour. A wise man scaleth the city of the mighty, and casteth down the strength of the confidence thereof.

> Ecclesiastes 7:19 Wisdom strengtheneth the wise more than ten mighty men which are in the city.

> Ecclesiastes 9:17 The words of wise men are heard in quiet more than the cry of him that ruleth among fools.

> Isaiah 40:31 But they that wait upon the LORD shall renew their strength; they shall mount up with wings as eagles; they shall run, and not be weary; and they shall walk, and not faint.

> Colossians 1:10-11 That ye might walk worthy of the Lord unto all pleasing, being fruitful in every good work, and increasing in the knowledge of God; Strengthened with all might, according to his glorious power, unto all patience and longsuffering with joyfulness …

"For by wise counsel thou shalt make thy war *[a battle engagement, warfare]*: **and in multitude of counsellors there is safety** *[salvation, deliverance]*.**" "Wise counsel,"** as opposed to unwise, can advise from a righteous and unbiased perspective. However, that is not true of foolish counsel from those who see with prejudice and blindness toward the things of God. God does not help the person who denies him, consequently, he is limited to his own worldly wisdom and shortsightedness. His ungodly counsel, if taken, would be destructive, as King Rehoboam discovered when he took the counsel of the young, short-sighted, yes-men rather than the old, wise men. A wise leader wants to have understanding of every aspect of a situation in order to realize the best outcome, minimize damage, and protect people under his authority.

> 2 Chronicles 32:2-4 And when Hezekiah saw that Sennacherib was come, and that he was purposed to fight against Jerusalem, He took counsel with his princes and his mighty men to stop the waters of the fountains which were without the city: and they did help him. So there was gathered much people together, who stopped all the fountains, and the brook that ran through the midst of the land, saying, Why should the kings of Assyria come, and find much water?
>
> Proverbs 11:14 Where no counsel is, the people fall: but in the multitude of counsellors there is safety.
>
> Proverbs 15:22 Without counsel purposes are disappointed: but in the multitude of counsellors they are established.
>
> Proverbs 20:18 *Every* purpose is established by counsel: and with good advice make war.
>
> Luke 14:28-32 For which of you, intending to build a tower, sitteth not down first, and counteth the cost, whether he have sufficient to finish it? Lest haply, after he hath laid the foundation, and is not able to finish it, all that behold it begin to mock him, Saying, This man began to build, and was not able to finish. Or what king, going to make war against another king, sitteth not down first, and consulteth whether he be able with ten thousand to meet him that cometh against him with twenty thousand? Or else, while the other is yet a great way off, he sendeth an ambassage, and desireth conditions of peace.

Proverbs 24:7   Wisdom *is* too high for a fool: he openeth not his mouth in the gate.

Focus: This proverb categorizes the fool as lacking wisdom; consequently, his speech is muted when judgments are made in the gate.

"Wisdom is too high for a fool" because he opposes God and the teachings of God, the source of wisdom. He is perverse; therefore, to think in a godly manner is foreign to him. Wisdom, to the fool, is an unnecessarily complicated way of dealing with matters. It is weird, by his estimation. He is satisfied with the way he reasons and believes his folly is better than wisdom because his foolishness comes natural to him, straight from his wicked heart. Therefore, he need not expend any effort to reach the wise person's higher level because he believes that the wise person's level is actually lower than his. Because he associates with other fools, who reinforce and encourage his absurdity, he remains in a loop of foolishness. The more he eats from that table, the stronger fool he becomes.

> Proverbs 1:7 The fear of the LORD *is* the beginning of knowledge: *but* fools despise wisdom and instruction.
>
> Proverbs 12:15 The way of a fool *is* right in his own eyes: but he that hearkeneth unto counsel *is* wise.
>
> Proverbs 19:1 Better *is* the poor that walketh in his integrity, than *he that is* perverse in his lips, and is a fool.
>
> Proverbs 23:9 Speak not in the ears of a fool: for he will despise the wisdom of thy words.

"He openeth not his mouth in the gate." It was not because fools thought of themselves as not capable of speaking **"in the gate,"** but instead that they were not welcome or invited. The gate of the city was in the main opening of the city wall and was the place where wise leaders made important decisions. Because those leaders were aware that a fool had no wisdom to judge the rightness or wrongness of a situation, no wise man presiding in the gate would have asked counsel of the fool, and neither would he have sought the fool's judgment.

> 1 Corinthians 2:12-14 Now we have received, not the spirit of the world, but the spirit which is of God; that we might know the things that are freely given to us of God. Which things also we speak, not in the words which man's wisdom teacheth, but which the Holy Ghost teacheth; comparing spiritual things with spiritual. But the natural man receiveth not the things of the Spirit of God: for they are foolishness unto him: neither can he know *them,* because they are spiritually discerned.

Proverbs 24:8   He that deviseth to do evil shall be called a mischievous person.

Focus: This proverb defines a mischievous person as one who devises evil.

"He that deviseth *[weaves, fabricates, plots or contrives]* **to do evil**" is a man whose thoughts are so debased that all he thinks about is the evil he can accomplish. In the first few pages of Scripture, Satan himself is described as devising evil against humanity; therefore, anyone who devises evil is, in that aspect, like Satan.

> Genesis 3:1 Now the serpent was more subtil than any beast of the field which the LORD God had made. And he said unto the woman, Yea, hath God said, Ye shall not eat of every tree of the garden?
>
> Genesis 6:5 And GOD saw that the wickedness of man *was* great in the earth, and *that* every imagination of the thoughts of his heart *was* only evil continually.
>
> Psalm 36:1-4 To the chief Musician, *A Psalm* of David the servant of the LORD. The transgression of the wicked saith within my heart, *that there is* no fear of God before his eyes. For he flattereth himself in his own eyes, until his iniquity be found to be hateful. The words of his mouth *are* iniquity and deceit: he hath left off to be wise, *and* to do good. He deviseth mischief upon his bed; he setteth himself in a way *that is* not good; he abhorreth not evil.
>
> Proverbs 6:14 Frowardness *is* in his heart, he deviseth mischief continually; he soweth discord.
>
> Proverbs 24:1-2 Be not thou envious against evil men, neither desire to be with them. For their heart studieth destruction, and their lips talk of mischief.
>
> Romans 1:29-32 Being filled with all unrighteousness, fornication, wickedness, covetousness, maliciousness; full of envy, murder, debate, deceit, malignity; whisperers, Backbiters, haters of God, despiteful, proud, boasters, inventors of evil things, disobedient to parents, Without understanding, covenantbreakers, without natural affection, implacable, unmerciful: Who knowing the judgment of God, that they which commit such things are worthy of death, not only do the same, but have pleasure in them that do them.
>
> "To do evil is natural to men, all are prone to it; being conceived and born in sin, and, from the womb, more or less commit it: but for a man to sit down and contrive evil, as some men are inventors of evil things; contrive new sins, or at least new methods of sinning, such as new oaths, new games, new ways of tricking and deceiving men; and are always studying and devising ways and means of committing sin, and doing that which is evil in the sight of God and men."[632]

To say that a person who *devises to do evil* "**shall be called a mischievous person**" means literally that he is *defined and named* as being evil. Notice the use of "**shall be called**" (regarding the wise) in Proverbs 16:21–"The wise in heart shall be called prudent…" Compare that to how the scorner is named in Proverbs 21:24, which states – "Proud and haughty scorner is his name, who dealeth in proud wrath." People are known for their actions, good or bad.

"**Mischievous**" had a *much* stronger meaning in the seventeenth century than today. It meant *evil* then, while today, it means *to do things that are annoying in a playful manner*. In this verse, the word "mischievous" describes the man *devising* or plotting **to do evil**. "**A mischievous person**" (according to the Hebrew definition) is "literally, *lord of mischief, i.e.* owner, possessor of mischief."[633]

> "What a picture is here of human depravity, in its active working, its corrupt fountain, and its fearful end! Talent, imagination, active mind, is so debased, as to be all concentrated upon Satan's own work – *devising to do evil.* He was the first *deviser* (Genesis 3:1), and he practices his children, till he makes them, like himself, **masters of mischief**; contriving new modes of sinning, ways of trickery and deceit; like the degraded heathen, 'inventors of evil things.' (Romans 1:30) To do evil is the principle; *devising to do evil* is the energy, of his service. In this craft of evil, Balaam was *a mischievous person*. Abimelech has earned for himself the same reputation. (Judges 9:1-55) Jeroboam's subtle *mischief* has stamped his name with the black mark of reprobation –'who made Israel to sin. *[Ten times in Scripture]*' Jezebel, and others of less note, equally industrious in evil, will appear in the same ranks at the great day."[634]

"**A mischievous person**" has gained an evil reputation for himself. Mention his name, and his peers will immediately think of his evil behavior and words.

Proverbs 24:9 The thought of foolishness *is* sin: and the scorner *is* an abomination to men.

Focus: This proverb connects the scorner's sinful foolish thoughts as the root cause of his being despised by men.

The root of the scorner's sin is not youthful immaturity or ignorance, or even bad company. He sins because his corrupted mind delights in doing wrong; thus, others should observe him as a *source* of evil and not just an evildoer. The "**scorner**" hates anything associated with God, including the Scriptures. He openly makes fun of God's having any control or intervention in the life of men; he scoffs at the laws of God and the principles of righteousness; and he proudly speaks in his own conceit. He opposes, ridicules, talks against, and mocks those who stand with God as well as God

Himself. It is a shame that many righteous people lose their boldness in his presence, and it is also a shame that his continued scorning has thrown down many national laws based on the Bible. The scorner is truly an **"abomination to men"** meaning *[disgusting]* to them. No honorable person wants to hear his wicked words or be near his person. He is a threat to peace and justice, and to anything decent. He is a plaguelike source of evil to others. In the previous proverb (verse 8) and in Psalm 36:1-4, the evil person is evil because he thinks evil, produces evil, and is therefore known to be evil; and it is from such evil thinking that he becomes a scorner. Once the whole earth was filled with such evil people causing God to destroy all except Noah and his family.

> Genesis 6:5 And GOD saw that the wickedness of man was great in the earth, and that every imagination of the thoughts of his heart was only evil continually.
> Proverbs 12:5 The thoughts of the righteous are right: but the counsels of the wicked are deceit.

"Fools make a mock at sin" (Proverbs 14:9), indicating their light, flippant view of sin. The connection between foolishness and sin is driven home many times in the Book of Proverbs, and the relationship between the fool, foolishness, the scorner, and sin cannot be stated too often.

> Proverbs 21:24 Proud and haughty scorner is his name, who dealeth in proud wrath.
> Proverbs 22:10 Cast out the scorner, and contention shall go out; yea, strife and reproach shall cease.
> Proverbs 29:27 An unjust man *is* an abomination to the just: and *he that is* upright in the way *is* abomination to the wicked.

Proverbs 24:10-12 *If* thou faint in the day of adversity, thy strength *is* small.
11. If thou forbear to deliver *them that are drawn* unto death, and *those that are* ready to be slain;
12. If thou sayest, Behold, we knew it not; doth not he that pondereth the heart consider *it*? and he that keepeth thy soul, doth *not* he know *it*? and shall not he render to *every* man according to his works?

Focus: This proverb (three verses) declares that our omniscient and just God will hold accountable those who refuse to meet their moral obligations.

"If thou faint in the day of adversity, thy strength is small." (verse 10) A *"day of adversity"* is a day of anguish, distress, and tribulation. Such a day tests and reveals: (1) strength of character, (2) depth of trust in God and His word, (3) love for God and man, and (4) degree of courage. Every person faces adversity and is capable of *fainting* if his dependency is on self rather than on God and His promises. When this passage speaks of *fainting,* it is not referring to passing out from a lack of oxygen. Instead, it is the failure to bravely do the right thing because of being *fearful.*

> Job 4:3-5 Behold, thou hast instructed many, and thou hast strengthened the weak hands. Thy words have upholden him that was falling, and thou hast strengthened the feeble knees. But now it is come upon thee, and thou faintest; it toucheth thee, and thou art troubled.
> Ecclesiastes 7:14 In the day of prosperity be joyful, but in the day of adversity consider: God also hath set the one over against the other, to the end that man should find nothing after him.
> Isaiah 40:28-31 Hast thou not known? hast thou not heard, that the everlasting God, the LORD, the Creator of the ends of the earth, fainteth not, neither is weary? there is no searching of his understanding. He giveth power to the faint; and to them that have no might he increaseth strength. Even the youths shall faint and be weary, and the young men shall utterly fall: But they that wait upon the LORD shall renew their strength; they shall mount up with wings as eagles; they shall run, and not be weary; and they shall walk, and not faint.
> Ephesians 3:13 Wherefore I desire that ye faint not at my tribulations for you, which is your glory.
> Colossians 1:10-11 That ye might walk worthy of the Lord unto all pleasing, being fruitful in every good work, and increasing in the knowledge of God; Strengthened with all might, according to his glorious power, unto all patience and longsuffering with joyfulness...
> Hebrews 12:3-4 For consider him that endured such contradiction of sinners against himself, lest ye be wearied and faint in your minds. Ye have not yet resisted unto blood, striving against sin.
> Revelation 2:3 And hast borne, and hast patience, and for my name's sake hast laboured, and hast not fainted.
> Revelation 2:13 I know thy works, and where thou dwellest, even where Satan's seat is: and thou holdest fast my name, and hast not denied my faith, even in those days wherein Antipas was my faithful martyr, who was slain among you, where Satan dwelleth.

"If thou forbear to deliver them that are drawn unto death, and those that are ready to be slain." (verse 11) This verse steps up the intensity and seriousness of the ***day of adversity,*** making it a day when life or death is at stake. A person is not to restrain himself from intervening when he has knowledge of truth or is in a position of authority by proper wise action to prevent the death of an innocent person. Scripture gives many examples of people who spoke up for others or defended them at risk of their own lives, thus refusing to make excuses. Numerous Scriptures reveal that God is very concerned about those who can't help themselves, such as the poor, the widow, the disabled, and the orphaned. Now consider how much longer and more precious is eternal life than the physical. Consider also how much greater the eternal suffering in hell is compared to the temporary sufferings of this life. How much greater is the responsibility to apply every effort possible to warn the spiritually lost and keep them from hell.

> Genesis 37:21-22 And Reuben heard *it,* and he delivered him out of their hands; and said, Let us not kill him. And Reuben said unto them, Shed no blood, *but* cast him into this pit that *is* in the wilderness, and lay no hand upon him; that he might rid him out of their hands, to deliver him to his father again.
>
> Exodus 1:16-17 And he said, When ye do the office of a midwife to the Hebrew women, and see them upon the stools; if it be a son, then ye shall kill him: but if it be a daughter, then she shall live. But the midwives feared God, and did not as the king of Egypt commanded them, but saved the men children alive.
>
> 1 Samuel 19:4-6 And Jonathan spake good of David unto Saul his father, and said unto him, Let not the king sin against his servant, against David; because he hath not sinned against thee, and because his works *have been* to thee-ward very good: For he did put his life in his hand, and slew the Philistine, and the LORD wrought a great salvation for all Israel: thou sawest *it,* and didst rejoice: wherefore then wilt thou sin against innocent blood, to slay David without a cause? And Saul hearkened unto the voice of Jonathan: and Saul sware, *As* the LORD liveth, he shall not be slain.
>
> Psalm 82:3-4 Defend the poor and fatherless: do justice to the afflicted and needy. Deliver the poor and needy: rid them out of the hand of the wicked.
>
> Proverbs 31:8 Open thy mouth for the dumb in the cause of all such as are appointed to destruction.
>
> Isaiah 58:6-7 *Is* not this the fast that I have chosen? to loose the bands of wickedness, to undo the heavy burdens, and to let the oppressed go free, and that ye break every yoke? *Is it* not to deal thy bread to the hungry, and that thou bring the poor that are cast out to thy house? when thou seest the naked, that thou cover him; and that thou hide not thyself from thine own flesh?
>
> Ezekiel 33:8-9 When I say unto the wicked, O wicked man, thou shalt surely die; if thou dost not speak to warn the wicked from his way, that wicked man shall die in his iniquity; but his blood will I require at thine hand. Nevertheless, if thou warn the wicked of his way to turn from it; if he do not turn from his way, he shall die in his iniquity; but thou hast delivered thy soul.
>
> James 5:19-20 Brethren, if any of you do err from the truth, and one convert him; Let him know, that he which converteth the sinner from the error of his way shall save a soul from death, and shall hide a multitude of sins. *[See also Genesis 14:12-14; Jeremiah 38:8-11; and Luke 10:29-35.]*

"If thou sayest, Behold, we knew it not; doth not he that pondereth the heart consider *it*? and he that keepeth thy soul, doth *not* he know *it*? and shall not he render to *every* man according to his works?" (verse 12) "The tendency to hush up a wrong with a false plea of ignorance"[635] is denounced by this verse. Lying is wrong and doing so to escape some harmful personal repercussion is both evil and cowardly, especially when an innocent person depends on truthful testimony. How ridiculous for a person to claim that he is ignorant (when, in fact, he is not) to the omniscient God, Who searches the individual and knows him thoroughly, including when he sits down and gets up. The LORD understands his thoughts before he can mentally recognize that he is having such ideas. God is acquainted with every way, knows every word, and every thought.

> Psalm 139:1-4 O LORD, thou hast searched me, and known *me*. Thou knowest my downsitting and mine uprising, thou understandest my thought afar off. Thou compassest my path and my lying down, and art acquainted *with* all my ways. For *there is* not a word in my tongue, *but,* lo, O LORD, thou knowest it altogether.

"Doth not he that pondereth the heart consider *it*? For God to *ponder the heart* means that He balances every thought, motive, and desire a person has against truth.

> Genesis 4:9 And the LORD said unto Cain, Where *is* Abel thy brother? And he said, I know not: *Am* I my brother's keeper?
>
> 1 Samuel 16:7 But the LORD said unto Samuel, Look not on his countenance, or on the height of his stature; because I have refused him: for *the LORD seeth* not as man seeth; for man looketh on the outward appearance, but the LORD looketh on the heart.
>
> Psalm 44:21 Shall not God search this out? for he knoweth the secrets of the heart.
>
> Proverbs 21:2 Every way of a man *is* right in his own eyes: but the LORD pondereth the hearts.
>
> Jeremiah 17:10 I the LORD search the heart, *I* try the reins, even to give every man according to his ways, *and* according to the fruit of his doings.
>
> Romans 2:16 In the day when God shall judge the secrets of men by Jesus Christ according to my gospel.
>
> 1 Corinthians 4:5 Therefore judge nothing before the time, until the Lord come, who both will bring to light the hidden things of darkness, and will make manifest the counsels of the hearts: and then shall every man have praise of God.
>
> Hebrews 4:12-13 For the word of God *is* quick, and powerful, and sharper than any twoedged sword, piercing even to the dividing asunder of soul and spirit, and of the joints and marrow, and *is* a discerner of the thoughts and intents of the heart. Neither is there any creature that is not manifest in his sight: but all things *are* naked and opened unto the eyes of him with whom we have to do.

"And he that keepeth thy soul, doth *not* he know *it*?" (verse 12b) **"Keepeth the soul"** means that God preserves or guards a person's life. He alone determines whether or not a person lives. No man can do anything to a believer that God does not allow; consequently, the instruction is to have an awesome respect for God and abstain from fearing man who can only do what God permits. Adversity presents opportunity for a person to have faith in God, Who certainly does know of every circumstance of His children's lives.

"And shall not he render to *every* man according to his works?" (verse 12d) And the answer, of course, is "Yes." Every individual person will stand before God and give account for his/her works. Then God will **"render** *[recompense, repay]*" according to his works.

This passage (verses 10-12) deals specifically with works concerning fulfilling one's responsibility regarding *not fainting in the day of adversity* and thereby *delivering an innocent one from death*. These failed situations will be remembered at the "judgment seat of Christ" when the righteous will be judged (2 Corinthians 5:9-10) and also the "great white throne" where the ungodly will be judged. (Revelation 20:11-12)

> 2 Corinthians 5:9-10 Wherefore we labour, that, whether present or absent, we may be accepted of him. For we must all appear before the judgment seat of Christ; that every one may receive the things done in his body, according to that he hath done, whether it be good or bad.
>
> Revelation 20:11-12 And I saw a great white throne, and him that sat on it, from whose face the earth and the heaven fled away; and there was found no place for them. And I saw the dead, small and great, stand before God; and the books were opened: and another book was opened, which is *the book* of life: and the dead were judged out of those things which were written in the books, according to their works.

Proverbs 24:13-14 My son, eat thou honey, because *it is* good; and the honeycomb, *which is* sweet to thy taste:
14. So *shall* the knowledge of wisdom be unto thy soul: when thou hast found *it*, then there shall be a reward, and thy expectation shall not be cut off.

Focus: This proverb declares that wisdom will produce a guaranteed reward when the knowledge of wisdom is as sweet to the soul as honey is to the taste.

Once a person has tasted honey, he can never be convinced that it is other than sweet and good. Likewise, anyone who has **"the knowledge of wisdom"** can never be convinced that it is not good and sweet reaching into every aspect of his life – *into his soul*. The man who has experienced the rewards of wisdom knows that it provides the pleasure of being able to successfully face the complex challenges of life. Such wisdom produces a joyful walk with God and a productive and agreeable walk with other good men. All memories of godly wisdom are sweet and precious.

> "We should not ask a man whether honey was pleasant to the taste if he had never eaten it, and those are not qualified to bear witness concerning the spiritual enjoyment and benefit to be derived from the 'wisdom of God' who have not tested it. All those who have done so, whatever their condition in life, in whatever age they have lived, or whatever part of the world they have called their home, have agreed with David's testimony that it is '*more to be desired than gold, yea, than much fine gold: sweeter also than honey and the honey-comb*'" (Psalm 19:10)."[636]

To have a **"knowledge of wisdom"** is to study its doctrines until one has interwoven those instructions into the fabric of his mind. At that point every thought, word, and action is governed, not by the natural man but by the instructions of God. When this "knowledge of wisdom" is gained, **"there shall be a reward"** because the person with wisdom has a proper relationship with God and with good men. He is rewarded with quality life that involves an intimate, interactive relationship with God. They are truly close friends. **"Thy expectation shall not be cut off"** means the wise person's hope, as placed into his mind by God's word, will not be disappointed.

> Psalm 19:8-11 The statutes of the LORD are right, rejoicing the heart: the commandment of the LORD is pure, enlightening the eyes. The fear of the LORD is clean, enduring for ever: the judgments of the LORD are true and righteous altogether. More to be desired are they than gold, yea, than much fine gold: sweeter also than honey and the honeycomb. Moreover by them is thy servant warned: and in keeping of them there is great reward.
>
> Psalm 119:98-104 Thou through thy commandments hast made me wiser than mine enemies: for they are ever with me. I have more understanding than all my teachers: for thy testimonies are my meditation. I understand more than the ancients, because I keep thy precepts. I have refrained my feet from every evil way, that I might keep thy word. I have not departed from thy judgments: for thou hast taught me. How sweet are thy words unto my taste! yea, sweeter than honey to my mouth! Through thy precepts I get understanding: therefore I hate every false way.

Proverbs 23:18 For surely there is an end; and thine expectation shall not be cut off.

Proverbs 24:20 For there shall be no reward to the evil *man;* the candle of the wicked shall be put out.

Ezekiel 3:3 And he said unto me, Son of man, cause thy belly to eat, and fill thy bowels with this roll that I give thee. Then did I eat *it;* and it was in my mouth as honey for sweetness.

Matthew 16:27 For the Son of man shall come in the glory of his Father with his angels; and then he shall reward every man according to his works.

Colossians 3:23-24 And whatsoever ye do, do it heartily, as to the Lord, and not unto men; Knowing that of the Lord ye shall receive the reward of the inheritance: for ye serve the Lord Christ.

Revelation 22:12 And, behold, I come quickly; and my reward is with me, to give every man according as his work shall be.

Proverbs 24:15-16 Lay not wait, O wicked *man*, against the dwelling of the righteous; spoil not his resting place:
16. For a just *man* falleth seven times, and riseth up again: but the wicked shall fall into mischief.

Focus: This proverb is a warning to the wicked man that his plot to enact evil against the righteous will be unsuccessful and that he will himself fall into evil.

"Lay not wait, O wicked *man*, against the dwelling of the righteous; spoil not his resting place." There is a strong implication here of the wicked person going too far with his wicked endeavor against God's chosen. God seems to allow the wicked room enough to do his mischief in a public forum, perhaps as evidence collected for his day of judgment where he will certainly be held accountable, judged, and sentenced. But he goes too far when he extends himself to the point and place of disturbing that private place of peace and worship. The **"dwelling place of the righteous"** is his **"resting place."** It is the place of his altar where he prays and meets with God in a special way. It is also the place where he teaches his children the commandments of God and where he rests from his labor, so that on the next day, he can serve God to his fullest. When the wicked go there with their mischief, they go too far. When he *spoils* *[to be burly, powerful, ravages, ruins, destroys]* that place, he raises the ire of God. He touches "the apple of God's eye."

Revelation 20:11-12 And I saw a great white throne, and him that sat on it, from whose face the earth and the heaven fled away; and there was found no place for them. And I saw the dead, small and great, stand before God; and the books were opened: and another book was opened, which is *the book* of life: and the dead were judged out of those things which were written in the books, according to their works.

"For a just *man* falleth seven times, and riseth up again: but the wicked shall fall into mischief." The just or righteous man can *fall seven times* (numerous) and rise up again. **"Seven times,"** as used here, is a definite number that stands for, or symbolizes, the indefinite. Overcoming difficulty and evil attacks are part of the righteous person's victorious life. With the Lord's help, he picks himself up, dusts himself off, and goes about his business of serving God. The godly man is strengthened through his trials, and his godly life is made manifest to the world. Daniel (Daniel 6:1-28) and his three friends (Daniel 3:1-30) were strengthened because of their severe trial, and received a promotion from the king.

The *just and righteous* are reminded of God's care for them and of their proper conduct when tragedy strikes. A mental picture is drawn from this proverb of a righteous man, having been knocked down numerous times, rising up upon his knee, with the help of God, to stand once again firmly, calmly, and peacefully. As he stands upon his feet and looks in the distance, he sees the wicked offender running headlong into a pit of evil, inhabited by wicked, hateful people without conscience or mercy, where there is a prevailing spirit of fear, and all other wickedness, sponsored by the Devil he serves. The wicked man's evil life is a prelude, a taste of the Christless hell, where he will spend eternity.

"The teaching of the proverb warns men not to attack or plot against the righteous. They will lose their labor, 'Though the just man fall (not into sin, but into calamities), yet he riseth up.' The point of the teaching is not the liability of good men to err, but God's providential care over them… 'Seven times' is a certain for an uncertain number (compare Job 5:19). In contrast with this is the fate of the evildoers, who fall utterly even in a single distress."[637]

Job 5:19-22 He shall deliver thee in six troubles: yea, in seven there shall no evil touch thee. In famine he shall redeem thee from death: and in war from the power of the sword. Thou shalt be hid from the scourge of the tongue: neither shalt thou be afraid of destruction when it cometh. At destruction and famine thou shalt laugh: neither shalt thou be afraid of the beasts of the earth.

Psalm 7:11-16 God judgeth the righteous, and God is angry with the wicked every day. If he turn not, he will whet his sword; he hath bent his bow, and made it ready. He hath also prepared for him the instruments of death; he ordaineth his arrows against the persecutors. Behold, he travaileth with iniquity, and hath conceived mischief, and brought forth falsehood. He made a pit, and digged it, and is fallen into the ditch which he made. His mischief shall return upon his own head, and his violent dealing shall come down upon his own pate.

Psalm 9:16-17 The LORD is known by the judgment which he executeth: the wicked is snared in the work of his own hands. Higgaion. Selah. The wicked shall be turned into hell, and all the nations that forget God.

Psalm 34:19-22 Many *are* the afflictions of the righteous: but the LORD delivereth him out of them all. He keepeth all his bones: not one of them is broken. Evil shall slay the wicked: and they that hate the righteous shall be desolate. The LORD redeemeth the soul of his servants: and none of them that trust in him shall be desolate.

Psalm 37:9-13 For evildoers shall be cut off: but those that wait upon the LORD, they shall inherit the earth. For yet a little while, and the wicked shall not be: yea, thou shalt diligently consider his place, and it shall not be. But the meek shall inherit the earth; and shall delight themselves in the abundance of peace. The wicked plotteth against the just, and gnasheth upon him with his teeth. The Lord shall laugh at him: for he seeth that his day is coming.

Psalm 37:23-24 The steps of a good man are ordered by the LORD: and he delighteth in his way. Though he fall, he shall not be utterly cast down: for the LORD upholdeth him with his hand.

Psalm 37:39-40 But the salvation of the righteous is of the LORD: he is their strength in the time of trouble. And the LORD shall help them, and deliver them: he shall deliver them from the wicked, and save them, because they trust in him.

2 Corinthians 4:8-10 We are troubled on every side, yet not distressed; we are perplexed, but not in despair; Persecuted, but not forsaken; cast down, but not destroyed; Always bearing about in the body the dying of the Lord Jesus, that the life also of Jesus might be made manifest in our body.

Proverbs 24:17-18 Rejoice not when thine enemy falleth, and let not thine heart be glad when he stumbleth:
18. Lest the LORD see it, and it displease him, and he turn away his wrath from him.

Focus: This proverb (2 verses) is a command for the wise believer to control improper emotions in order to remain pleasing to God.

Believers are told to *control their emotions,* or God will stop exercising His wrath against their enemies *(personal enemies, not national enemies).* Jubilation by the believer over another person's suffering is a sin of disobedience that threatens the believer's spiritual well-being, his walk with God, and his further development of wisdom. Unchecked emotions, especially when reinforced and encouraged by similar emotions from other people, can strongly influence and overwhelm thinking that meets God's approval. Emotions can inappropriately drive a person's behavior and may also derail proper reasoning. To **"rejoice"** *when a personal enemy falls [cast down, fails]* or to be **glad when he stumbles** *[falters, staggers, or is made feeble]* leads to vindictiveness and from there to disrespect for humanity. God desires that every person fosters love in his heart and practices love toward his fellow man. Disregarding God's commandment and gravitating towards hostility is decidedly the wrong move. Hatred toward others is unacceptable, and so much so that God had rather cease His correction on one's personal enemy if a threat of such an attitude exists. Man must do everything possible to live in harmony with everyone, including his enemies, and leave wrath and vengeance with God.

Some may say this proverb contradicts the songs of victory sung by Miriam and the later victory song of Deborah and Barak. However, Miriam's song of rejoicing when Pharaoh's army was drowned in the Red Sea (Exodus 15) and Deborah and Barak's song when Sisera was killed (Judges 5) were *songs of praise to God* for His mighty acts of protection against a *national enemy. They were not songs of personal hate or vindictiveness.*

". . . Joy may be expressed at the fall of the public enemies of God and his people, as was by the Israelites at the destruction of Pharaoh and his host; and as will be by the church at the destruction of Antichrist, and which they are called upon to do (Revelation 18:20); partly on account of their own deliverance and safety, and chiefly because of the glory of God, and of his justice displayed therein; but as private revenge is not to be sought, nor acted, so joy at the calamity and ruin of a private enemy, or a man's own enemy, should not be expressed; but rather he is to be pitied and helped (Proverbs 25:21); for to love an enemy, and show regard to him, is the doctrine both of the Old and of the New Testament."[638]

Exodus 23:4-5 If thou meet thine enemy's ox or his ass going astray, thou shalt surely bring it back to him again. If thou see the ass of him that hateth thee lying under his burden, and wouldest forbear to help him, thou shalt surely help with him.

Leviticus 19:18 Thou shalt not avenge, nor bear any grudge against the children of thy people, but thou shalt love thy neighbour as thyself: I *am* the LORD.

Proverbs 25:21-22 If thine enemy be hungry, give him bread to eat; and if he be thirsty, give him water to drink: For thou shalt heap coals of fire upon his head, and the LORD shall reward thee.

Obadiah 1:12 But thou shouldest not have looked on the day of thy brother in the day that he became a stranger; neither shouldest thou have rejoiced over the children of Judah in the day of their destruction; neither shouldest thou have spoken proudly in the day of distress.

Matthew 5:43-48 Ye have heard that it hath been said, Thou shalt love thy neighbour, and hate thine enemy. But I say unto you, Love your enemies, bless them that curse you, do good to them that hate you, and pray for them which despitefully use you, and persecute you; That ye may be the children of your Father which is in heaven: for he maketh his sun to rise on the evil and on the good, and sendeth rain on the just and on the unjust. For if ye love them which love you, what reward have ye? do not even the publicans the same? And if ye salute your brethren only, what do ye more *than others?* do not even the publicans so? Be ye therefore perfect, even as your Father which is in heaven is perfect. *[See also Luke 6:27-31.]*

Scriptures below reveal the attitude of Job and David toward the actions of their enemies. The words of Jesus' prayer, concerning those who crucified Him are important for the Christian to evaluate and apply. "Father, forgive them for they know not what they do."

Job 31:29-30 If I rejoiced at the destruction of him that hated me, or lifted up myself when evil found him: Neither have I suffered my mouth to sin by wishing a curse to his soul.

Psalm 35:11-16 False witnesses did rise up; they laid to my charge *things* that I knew not. They rewarded me evil for good *to* the spoiling of my soul. But as for me, when they were sick, my clothing *was* sackcloth: I humbled my soul with fasting; and my prayer returned into mine own bosom. I behaved myself as though *he had been* my friend *or* brother: I bowed down heavily, as one that mourneth *for his* mother. But in mine adversity they rejoiced, and gathered themselves together: *yea,* the abjects gathered themselves together against me, and I knew *it* not; they did tear *me,* and ceased not: With hypocritical mockers in feasts, they gnashed upon me with their teeth.

2 Samuel 1:11-12 Then David took hold on his clothes, and rent them; and likewise all the men that *were* with him: And they mourned, and wept, and fasted until even, for Saul, and for Jonathan his son, and for the people of the LORD, and for the house of Israel; because they were fallen by the sword.

Luke 23:34-39 Then said Jesus, Father, forgive them; for they know not what they do. And they parted his raiment, and cast lots. And the people stood beholding. And the rulers also with them derided *him,* saying, He saved others; let him save himself, if he be Christ, the chosen of God. And the soldiers also mocked him, coming to him, and offering him vinegar, And saying, If thou be the king of the Jews, save thyself. And a superscription also was written over him in letters of Greek, and Latin, and Hebrew, THIS IS THE KING OF THE JEWS. And one of the malefactors which were hanged railed on him, saying, If thou be Christ, save thyself and us.

Proverbs 24:19-20 Fret not thyself because of evil *men*, neither be thou envious at the wicked;
20. For there shall be no reward to the evil *man*; the candle of the wicked shall be put out.

Focus: This proverb (2 verses) instructs the believer not to fret or be envious at the wicked and provides the reason why.

"Fretting" and **"envying"** each *result from focused thinking on an inappropriate area of concern*, such as the success of the wicked. Both envying and fretting promote ideas of dissatisfaction with the provisions and promises of God. Consequently, it is impossible to trust God for His oversight in one's life and to fret or envy at the same time. These undesirable emotions reveal a lack of faith in God and, if left unchecked, promote a divide in the relationship with Him. A wise person will intellectually corral and control his emotions, whereas an unwise one will allow his emotions to drive his actions.

"Fret *[be angry, burn, be displeased]* **not thyself because of evil *men*."** *Anger, burning and displeasure* work together to create fretting. The English word "fret" originated "... from the Old English word *freton* which means to devour like an animal. When you fret over something, it consumes your thoughts... you worry so much about something that it eats away at you."[639] Thus, fretting begins with anger, then burns within one's heart as he cannot get his mind out of a loop (thinking of little or nothing else), and then displeasure becomes his state of mind.

"Neither be thou envious *[provoke to jealous anger, cause jealousy]* **at the wicked.** Furthermore, **"envy"** is "wanting what someone else has and resenting them for having it."[640]

Psalm 37:1-2 A Psalm of David. Fret not thyself because of evildoers, neither be thou envious against the workers of iniquity. For they shall soon be cut down like the grass, and wither as the green herb.

Psalm 37:7-9 Rest in the LORD, and wait patiently for him: fret not thyself because of him who prospereth in his way, because of the man who bringeth wicked devices to pass. Cease from anger, and forsake wrath: fret not thyself in any wise to do evil. For evildoers shall be cut off: but those that wait upon the LORD, they shall inherit the earth.

The reason for not fretting or envying the wicked is that **"The candle of the wicked shall be put out."** They choose the darkness of evil that leads them to destruction rather than the godliness of light that leads to a walk with God now and to everlasting life later. To "fret" or "envy" a person with such destiny is unreasonable. "The lamp" and "the candle" are common metaphors referring to life and truth. "If a lamp in a Near Eastern tent went **out** at night, the surroundings were pitch dark, mindful of the darkness of death."[641] The light of the wicked will be absorbed by the darkness *(evil)* that he pursues, *and the evil man has no rewards from God* because he has *no relationship with Him.*

NOTE: Like Proverbs 23:5 which reminds the reader not "to set thine eyes upon that which is not," and warns not to labor for riches, this proverb declares not to worry or be jealous of a wicked man's seeming wealth. The believer may live in a humble home, but he's just a "pilgrim" here and God has prepared a glorious place for him when he has lived his life. The wicked man may live magnificently here, but *his candle will be put out* and he will face judgment and the second death. In God's eyes it is already so. God created man in His own image. If He knows His word is Truth, believers should believe it is so.

Job 18:5-6 Yea, the light of the wicked shall be put out, and the spark of his fire shall not shine. The light shall be dark in his tabernacle, and his candle shall be put out with him.

Luke 11:33-36 No man, when he hath lighted a candle, putteth *it* in a secret place, neither under a bushel, but on a candlestick, that they which come in may see the light. The light of the body is the eye: therefore when thine eye is single, thy whole body also is full of light; but when *thine eye* is evil, thy body also *is* full of darkness. Take heed therefore that the light which is in thee be not darkness. If thy whole body therefore *be* full of light, having no part dark, the whole shall be full of light, as when the bright shining of a candle doth give thee light.

"Take then the balance of eternity. Learn neither to overvalue the fancied sunshine of *the wicked*, nor to undervalue our own real happiness. *Envy not* his lot. Repine not at our own. Ours is far beyond his reach. His is far below our *envy*. 'His candle burneth; his prosperity flourisheth, until it hath kindled hell-fire; and then it is extinguished; whereas the lamp of the godly is put out here, to shine as a star in heaven.'"[642]

Numbers 16:26 And he spake unto the congregation, saying, Depart, I pray you, from the tents of these wicked men, and touch nothing of theirs, lest ye be consumed in all their sins.

Psalm 37:1-2 *[See this Scripture above.]*

Proverbs 3:31-32 Envy thou not the oppressor, and choose none of his ways. For the froward is abomination to the LORD: but his secret is with the righteous.

Proverbs 23:17-18 Let not thine heart envy sinners: but be thou in the fear of the LORD all the day long. For surely there is an end; and thine expectation shall not be cut off.

Proverbs 24:1-2 Be not thou envious against evil men, neither desire to be with them. For their heart studieth destruction, and their lips talk of mischief.

2 Corinthians 6:14-18 Be ye not unequally yoked together with unbelievers: for what fellowship hath righteousness with unrighteousness? and what communion hath light with darkness? And what concord hath Christ with Belial? or what part hath he that believeth with an infidel? And what agreement hath the temple of God with idols? for ye are the temple of the living God; as God hath said, I will dwell in them, and walk in them; and I will be their God, and they shall be my people. Wherefore come out from among them, and be ye separate, saith the Lord, and touch not the unclean thing; and I will receive you, And will be a Father unto you, and ye shall be my sons and daughters, saith the Lord Almighty.

Proverbs 24:21-22 My son, fear thou the LORD *and* the king: and meddle not with them that are given to change:
22. For their calamity shall rise suddenly; and who knoweth the ruin of them both?

Focus: This proverb (2 verses) instructs to have a respectful relationship with the LORD and the king and it tells the consequences that come to disrespectful rebels.

"My son, fear thou the LORD *and* the king." (verse 21a) **"My son"** continues to be the student of wisdom, and Scripture continues to provide reasons for the specific instructions that it gives. Supplying reasons for instruction gives the student an understanding of why he should obey the teaching. Parents who tell their children to stay away from certain people *WITHOUT* giving reasons are not completing the teaching process.

"Fear thou the LORD" comes first in the sentence to show precedence since it is the priority. Then comes the admonition to fear "the king" who was set up by "the LORD" as His earthly authority. Experience in life will reveal that those who do not *respect* elders and people in authority, will have the same disrespect for God. The rebel acts against *every* authority.

"And meddle not with them that are given to change." Wise people are cautious about their relationships; knowing that some relationships are helpful to quality living, while others are dangerous and threatening. People select friends, associates, and mentors whom they believe should have their confidence and respect. These unstable ones **"given to change"** are *rebels who have no respectful dread for God or any human authority.* They foolishly do not believe that anyone should have a right to establish statutes or laws or regulations. They refuse to obey God or man. Verse 22 gives the consequences of their behavior – *they will face sudden calamity and ruin.* Whoever intermixes with them (*meddles* with them) stands a possibility of receiving the same calamities. A wise person will take heed to the warning and disassociate himself from such disrespectful people.

Romans 13:1-4 Let every soul be subject unto the higher powers. For there is no power but of God: the powers that be are ordained of God. Whosoever therefore resisteth the power, resisteth the ordinance of God: and they that resist shall receive to themselves damnation. For rulers are not a terror to good works, but to the evil. Wilt thou then not be afraid of the power? do that which is good, and thou shalt have praise of the same: For he is the minister of God to thee for good. But if thou do that which is evil, be afraid; for he beareth not the sword in vain: for he is the minister of God, a revenger to execute wrath upon him that doeth evil.

David refused to rebel against Saul because Saul had been chosen and anointed of God for that time.

1 Samuel 24:6 And he said unto his men, The LORD forbid that I should do this thing unto my master, the LORD'S anointed, to stretch forth mine hand against him, seeing he *is* the anointed of the LORD.

Jesus communicated that He had no intention of usurping or opposing Caesar.

Matthew 22:17 Tell us therefore, What thinkest thou? Is it lawful to give tribute unto Caesar, or not? But Jesus perceived their wickedness, and said, Why tempt ye me, ye hypocrites? Shew me the tribute money. And they brought unto him a penny. And he saith unto them, Whose is this image and superscription? They say unto him, Caesar's. Then saith he unto them, Render therefore unto Caesar the things which are Caesar's; and unto God the things that are God's.

Under the leadership of the Holy Spirit, Peter, the Apostle, wrote the following:

1 Peter 2:13-14 Submit yourselves to every ordinance of man for the Lord's sake: whether it be to the king, as supreme; Or unto governors, as unto them that are sent by him for the punishment of evildoers, and for the praise of them that do well.

Scriptures are the authority for human behavior. Believers are to submit to leaders and laws of the land until those leaders or laws demand disobedience to the word of God. Such opposition to the commandment of God came up in Acts 5 when the religious leaders had Peter and the apostles arrested for preaching the truth about Jesus and the Crucifixion. The apostles were imprisoned, but an angel of the Lord freed them, and *in disobedience to human authority, but in obedience to God,* they went back and began preaching the word again. The jealous high priest had them arrested again. The apostles were not "rebels" who opposed because of foolish and obstinate hearts; they were simply obedient to the leadership of God.

Acts 5:28-29; 40-42 Saying, Did not we straitly command you that ye should not teach in this name? and, behold, ye have filled Jerusalem with your doctrine, and intend to bring this man's blood upon us. Then Peter and the other apostles answered and said, We ought to obey God rather than men ... when they had called the apostles, and beaten them, they commanded that they should not speak in the name of Jesus, and let them go. And they departed from the presence of the council, rejoicing that they were counted worthy to suffer shame for his name. And daily in the temple, and in every house, they ceased not to teach and preach Jesus Christ.

Shadrach, Meshach, and Abednego were not rebels but were obedient to God's word that commanded them not to bow down to or worship other gods. They, in obedience to God, respectfully refused to obey Nebuchadnezzar.

Exodus 20:3-5 Thou shalt have no other gods before me. Thou shalt not make unto thee any graven image, or any likeness *of any thing* that *is* in heaven above, or that *is* in the earth beneath, or that *is* in the water under the earth: Thou shalt not bow down thyself to them, nor serve them: for I the LORD thy God *am* a jealous God, visiting the iniquity of the fathers upon the children unto the third and fourth *generation* of them that hate me.

Daniel 3:14-18 Nebuchadnezzar spake and said unto them, Is it true, O Shadrach, Meshach, and Abednego, do not ye serve my gods, nor worship the golden image which I have set up? Now if ye be ready that at what time ye hear the sound of the cornet, flute, harp, sackbut, psaltery, and dulcimer, and all kinds of musick, ye fall down and worship the image which I have made; well: but if ye worship not, ye shall be cast the same hour into the midst of a burning fiery furnace; and who is that God that shall deliver you out of my hands? Shadrach, Meshach, and Abednego, answered and said to the king, O Nebuchadnezzar, we are not careful to answer thee in this matter. If it be so, our God whom we serve is able to deliver us from the burning fiery furnace, and he will deliver us out of thine hand, O king. But if not, be it known unto thee, O king, that we will not serve thy gods, nor worship the golden image which thou hast set up.

This proverb also states, **"meddle not with them that are given to change."** (verse 21b) These rebels have a particular desire to change leaders. Perhaps they want to take a leader's place themselves. They would prefer the notoriety of speaking against the leader, even a good leader. *(Should another leader be taken, these "given to changers" would most likely repeat their behavior.)*

"To be *given to change;* to undo all that has been done; to alter for the sake of altering; to be weary of the old, and captivated with the new, however untried; to make experiments upon modes of government – is a fearful hazard. It is losing the substance of real good in the dream of imaginary improvements."[643]

Men **"given to change"** can be seen in Korah's rebellion, Absalom's rebellion, and in the continued struggle for change in the kings of the Northern Kingdom. (See Chart of Kings in the Appendix.)

Numbers 16:3 And they *[Korah and many others]* gathered themselves together against Moses and against Aaron, and said unto them, Ye take too much upon you, seeing all the congregation are holy, every one of them, and the LORD is among them: wherefore then lift ye up yourselves above the congregation of the LORD?

"For their calamity shall rise suddenly; and who knoweth the ruin of them both?" (verse 22) When Absalom rebelled against David, a battle ensued in the forest of Ephraim near Mahanaim. Consequently, Absalom's losses in battle to David's army were horrific, and the rebellious son was killed in the process. In a frantic attempt to escape, Absalom rode his mule under an oak tree and had his head caught in the branches; then Joab and some of his attendants killed him with darts. (2Samuel 18)

God intervenes and punishes rebels in some instances. In the matter of the rebellion of Korah, Dathan, and Abiram, God opened up the ground beneath them. The earth swallowed up the men, their families and their possessions; and they were destroyed in front of the congregation. (Numbers 16)

Proverbs 16:14 The wrath of a king *is as* messengers of death: but a wise man will pacify it.

Proverbs 20:2 The fear of a king *is* as the roaring of a lion: *whoso* provoketh him to anger sinneth *against* his own soul.

Proverbs 24:23-26 These *things* also *belong* to the wise. *It is* not good to have respect of persons in judgment.
24. He that saith unto the wicked, Thou *art* righteous; him shall the people curse, nations shall abhor him:
25. But to them that rebuke *him* shall be delight, and a good blessing shall come upon them.
26. Every man shall kiss his lips that giveth a right answer.

Focus: This proverb (4 verses) addresses the evil of biased judgment (verse 23) and then contrasts how people react to such an unjust judge (verse 24) with how they react to a righteous one (verses 25-26).

Previous proverbs dealt with respect and obedience *from subjects upward* to those who bear rule. These verses deal with proper respect and honorable care *from rulers downward* to their subjects.

"These things also belong to the wise" (verse 23a) appears to be a link to Proverbs 22:17, where this section of the Book of Proverbs begins and continues to the last verse of this chapter. These four verses (23-26) deal specifically with the perversion of justice through prejudice (respect for some favored persons and disrespect for others).

"*It is* not good to have respect of persons in judgment." (verse 23b) **"*It is* not good"** refers to an absence of anything good. Specifically, "it is not good" to make judicial judgments *by preference rather than truth of circumstances.* The rich are not to be given preference over the poor *(or vice versa).* No category of person is to be given preference in judgment; and the principle extends from a judge in a courtroom, to a parent in the home, to leaders in the church. Respect everyone equally and judge according to truthful "merits of the cause,"[644] rather than by respect of persons. In our Bible, this well-known principle is found as early as Leviticus and as late as I Peter. Honest and fair treatment is a character trait of Jehovah God, who is known in all situations by His "judgment, justice, and equity." (Proverbs 1:3)

Leviticus 19:15 Ye shall do no unrighteousness in judgment: thou shalt not respect the person of the poor, nor honour the person of the mighty: but in righteousness shalt thou judge thy neighbour. (See also Deuteronomy 1:17 and 16:19)

Psalm 82:2-3 How long will ye judge unjustly, and accept the persons of the wicked? Selah. Defend the poor and fatherless: do justice to the afflicted and needy.

Proverbs 18:5 It is not good to accept the person of the wicked, to overthrow the righteous in judgment.

Proverbs 28:21 To have respect of persons is not good: for for a piece of bread that man will transgress.

John 7:24 Judge not according to the appearance, but judge righteous judgment.

1 Timothy 5:20-21 Them that sin rebuke before all, that others also may fear. I charge thee before God, and the Lord Jesus Christ, and the elect angels, that thou observe these things without preferring one before another, doing nothing by partiality.

James 2:3-3 And ye have respect to him that weareth the gay clothing, and say unto him, Sit thou here in a good place; and say to the poor, Stand thou there, or sit here under my footstool: Are ye not then partial in yourselves, and are become judges of evil thoughts?

1 Peter 1:17 And if ye call on the Father, who without respect of persons judgeth according to every man's work, pass the time of your sojourning here in fear:

"He that saith unto the wicked, Thou *art* righteous; him shall the people curse, nations shall abhor him." (verse 24) The evil of having respect for persons in judgment is the theme that continues from verse 23. Here in verse 24, the words "people" and "nations" indicate the setting is specifically public. For an ungodly, deceitful, unrighteous judge to say to any wicked person, **"thou art righteous;"** he is, in effect, declaring God's view of sin to be wrong. Such bold, arrogant prejudice toward the wicked is a defiance of God and should draw the ire of an entire nation! He has set himself above God! His legal declaration, which would have been previously trusted to be based on God's law and without prejudice, is now totally unworthy of even being heard. His action draws the ire of the public; and he is thereby branded as the unjust, wicked, prejudiced judge that he is. Because such miscarriages of justice open the gate for further opposition to godliness and breakdown of justice, **"Nations shall abhor him."** "Nations" rather than just individuals indicates that a general consensus of anger, rage, and indignation extends beyond individuals and families to whole groups of people. Such abhorrence has been inflamed because those same people know that one wicked judgment sets a precedent for additional crime to be acceptable; and also the people believe that the courts are no longer a place of honest, equal judgment where a fair trial can be given.

"But to them that rebuke him *[the wicked judge]* **shall be delight, and a good blessing shall come upon them."** (verse 25) If the judge had made proper and honest judgments, without prejudice for the wicked, he would have been a **"delight"** to the people, who would have pronounced **"a good blessing"** on him. They would have spoken kindly of him and probably prayed for God to bless and prosper him.

> Proverbs 17:15 He that justifieth the wicked, and he that condemneth the just, even they both are abomination to the LORD.
> Proverbs 18:5 It is not good to accept the person of the wicked, to overthrow the righteous in judgment.
> Proverbs 28:23 He that rebuketh a man afterwards shall find more favour than he that flattereth with the tongue.
> Isaiah 5:20 Woe unto them that call evil good, and good evil; that put darkness for light, and light for darkness; that put bitter for sweet, and sweet for bitter!
> Isaiah 5:23 Which justify the wicked for reward, and take away the righteousness of the righteous from him!
> Ezekiel 13:22 Because with lies ye have made the heart of the righteous sad, whom I have not made sad; and strengthened the hands of the wicked, that he should not return from his wicked way, by promising him life:

"*Every man* shall kiss *his* lips that giveth a right answer." (verse 26) *Kiss the (his) lips* is a symbolic expression for affection and approval. Kissing a person was also a sign of great respect and love. It is abhorrent that Judas betrayed Jesus with a kiss.

"A right *[straight]* **answer"** agrees (is straight) with God's word and therefore identifies righteousness as righteousness and evil as evil. "A right answer" is not twisted to agree with prejudice or a lie. People, as a rule, highly respect a person who approves the righteous and reproves the wicked; who does not give one person favor over another; and who, when called upon to testify, speaks truly, plainly, and pertinently on the topic he has been called to answer or judge.

In this verse, honest, straightforward words are so appreciated that the hearer gives an innocent, loving, appreciative kiss, adequately symbolizing heartfelt gratitude.

> Proverbs 15:23 A man hath joy by the answer of his mouth: and a word spoken in due season, how good is it!

Proverbs 24:27 Prepare thy work without, and make it fit for thyself in the field; and afterwards build thine house.

Focus: This proverb speaks of having a proper order in managing one's life (setting wise priorities).

This first clause **"prepare thy work without"** meaning outdoors **"in the field"** is set over against **"afterwards build thine house."** **"Make it fit for thyself"** means to make the field productive i.e., prepare the field for crops in order to make a living from it. **"House"** often means household or family, but the context of this proverb is specific to building the structure itself; though, an application can be made to building a family.

Peace of mind in a tent would be better than hunger, anxiety, and sleepless nights in a house because of spending too much energy in a misguided manner attempting to get luxury ahead of the practical. Establishing a proper order and setting priorities is done by the wise person who prays and trusts God to direct his thoughts. God will provide for His own, and thankfully He sometimes blesses despite impatience, ignorance, and illogical behavior. Still, there is a wise way to handle matters; and God will honor and bless the person seeking to be wise in handling his life. Problems that a godly person has to overcome are of much less magnitude, and the distance to the place of being blessed is much shorter when priorities are established with God's help and then followed. The foolish person who gets his priorities out of order (or fails to establish any at all) will soon face unnecessary setbacks, trials and hardships. This simple, memorable proverb can be applied to many areas of life where proper order is mandatory.

> Luke 14:28-30 For which of you, intending to build a tower, sitteth not down first, and counteth the cost, whether he have *sufficient* to finish *it*? Lest haply, after he hath laid the foundation, and is not able to finish *it*, all that behold *it* begin to mock him, Saying, This man began to build, and was not able to finish.

Proverbs 24:28-29 Be not a witness against thy neighbour without cause; and deceive *not* with thy lips.
29. Say not, I will do so to him as he hath done to me: I will render to the man according to his work.

Focus: This proverb teaches against testifying: (1) without cause, (2) without truth, and (3) without mercy *(with revenge)*.

Throughout Scripture, the godly are taught to guard their speech; and wise people are always careful to choose their words, the place they speak, to whom they speak, and how they speak. A proper relationship with God is dependent on a proper relationship with others, and speaking wisely is vital. Here in this proverb, the believer is given three specific rules:

(1) **"Be not a witness against thy neighbour without cause."** Don't start talking about someone when there is no reason to do so – without something profitable coming from it – unless you know that what you are saying is true *and* there is a clear call to testify it.[645] Idle speech is a pathway to problems. Frivolous matters, trivial concerns that may have occurred, but are not worthy of speaking, should be left off.
> Proverbs 3:30 Strive not with a man without cause, if he have done thee no harm.

(2) **"Deceive not with thy lips."** Don't deceive the judge or the jury or anyone else through directly stating something that is false or through a manner of speaking that would insinuate or imply testimony that could be misunderstood by the use of innuendos or hyperboles.[646] People often take insinuations or implications as truth.
> Exodus 20:16 Thou shalt not bear false witness against thy neighbour.
>
> Exodus 23:1 Thou shalt not raise a false report: put not thine hand with the wicked to be an unrighteous witness.
>
> 1 Kings 21:9-10 And she *[Jezebel]* wrote in the letters, saying, Proclaim a fast, and set Naboth on high among the people: And set two men, sons of Belial, before him, to bear witness against him, saying, Thou didst blaspheme God and the king. And then carry him out, and stone him, that he may die.
>
> Proverbs 14:5 A faithful witness will not lie: but a false witness will utter lies.
>
> Proverbs 19:9 A false witness shall not be unpunished, and he that speaketh lies shall perish.
>
> Matthew 26:59-61 Now the chief priests, and elders, and all the council, sought false witness against Jesus, to put him to death; But found none: yea, though many false witnesses came, yet found they none. At the last came two false witnesses, And said, This fellow said, I am able to destroy the temple of God, and to build it in three days.

(3) **"Say not, I will do so to him as he hath done to me: I will render to the man according to his work"** thereby seeking revenge so as to make him pay for whatever he did. Doing so is hateful and serves only harm to everyone. Mercy and truth are attributes of God and His children. Revenge and lies are attributes of Satan and his children.
> Vengeance is a choice for God to make "... and we must leave it to him, and not step into his throne, or take his work out of his hands. If we will needs be our own carvers, and judges in our own cause, we forfeit the benefit of an appeal to God's tribunal; therefore we must not avenge ourselves, because he has said, *Vengeance is mine.*"[647]
>
> Proverbs 20:22 Say not thou, I will recompense evil; but wait on the LORD, and he shall save thee.
>
> Romans 12:17-21 Recompense to no man evil for evil. Provide things honest in the sight of all men. If it be possible, as much as lieth in you, live peaceably with all men. Dearly beloved, avenge not yourselves, but rather give place unto wrath: for it is written, Vengeance is mine; I will repay, saith the Lord. Therefore if thine enemy hunger, feed him; if he thirst, give him drink: for in so doing thou shalt heap coals of fire on his head. Be not overcome of evil, but overcome evil with good.
>
> 1 Thessalonians 5:15 See that none render evil for evil unto any man; but ever follow that which is good, both among yourselves, and to all men.

> **Proverbs 24:30-34** I went by the field of the slothful, and by the vineyard of the man void of understanding;
> 31. And, lo, it was all grown over with thorns, and nettles had covered the face thereof, and the stone wall thereof was broken down.
> 32. Then I saw, *and* considered it well: I looked *upon it,* and received instruction.
> 33. *Yet* a little sleep, a little slumber, a little folding of the hands to sleep:
> 34. So shall thy poverty come *as* one that travelleth; and thy want as an armed man.

Focus: This parable (5 verses) is an object lesson depicting the personal tragedy that results from slothfulness.

If the believer is observant, discerning, and sensitive to being led by the Holy Spirit, he can learn much from such everyday occurrences as illustrated in these five verses. Wisdom teaches to observe and meditate on the conditions surrounding the successes and failures of others. Here Solomon paints a picture of an unkempt vineyard and its slothful owner – a parable tucked in among the proverbs.

"I went by the field of the slothful, and by the vineyard of the man void of understanding." The **"field"** is more than just a cleared area of land. Someone (more likely a family) has previously, with great care, exerted much energy and time to convert the **"field"** into a productive and valuable **"vineyard,"** complete with walls, in anticipation of annually reaping beautiful delicious grapes to be made into precious wine. But, there is something wrong! Those original proud, laborious owners are gone, and a **"slothful"** person now owns the vineyard. To give the reader a better understanding of the situation and of the owner, the writer further describes the slothfulness of the owner when he says it belongs to a man **"void of understanding."** He is empty-headed, lacking good judgment.

He is likely the owner by inheritance: a privilege of being born Jewish, particularly in the nation's early history. God gave each of the 12 tribes property to keep and maintain for life, forever; and if forfeited through debt or grievous circumstances, the land would even be returned to the family in the year of Jubilee (Leviticus 25: 8-22). The property was handed down from generation to generation. This current owner by inheritance is a person who is lazy and does not respect his tremendous gift of land, labor, love, and wealth.

"And, lo, it was all grown over with thorns, *and* nettles had covered the face thereof, and the stone wall thereof was broken down." (verse 31) This precious, valuable, life-sustaining, income-generating, joy-producing vineyard had not been hoed therefore allowing thorns and nettles to starve the precious grapevines of nutrition and block out sunshine. The carefully-built wall designed to retain precious topsoil, keep out varmints, and serve as a boundary for trespassers had not been repaired. It is crumbling from age and neglect. Obviously, this empty-headed sluggard has refused to expend any effort to maintain this valuable asset.

"Then I saw, *and* considered *it* well: I looked upon *it, and* received instruction." (verse 32) The reader can visualize Solomon stopping to gaze and analyze this overwhelming desolation. With fingers wrapped around his chin, silently praying for God's instruction, he gazes, muses, thinks, and learns. Solomon **"received instruction"** and was urged to greater care and diligence in his own life. Then he passed this understanding on to his students with the following words.

"*Yet* a little sleep, a little slumber, a little folding of the hands to sleep." (verse 33) The habits of slothfulness and the self-indulgence of laziness grow unexpectedly upon its clueless victims. Days and years have likely passed since the sluggard received this valuable piece of property. Hoeing the field and maintaining the wall were not nearly as necessary as sleep to his one-dimensional mind.

" So shall thy poverty come *as* one that travelleth; and thy want as an armed man." (verse 34) The descriptive word picture of a sleeping sluggard contained in verses 33-34 represents the conclusion of the matter and what Solomon has learned. He describes him as one who has found a patch of cool green grass and laid his irresponsible self down to fulfill his never-ending desire for sleep. With hands folded on his chest, he slumbers in total unawareness of impending danger. While the sluggard is in this state of unconsciousness, poverty pounces on him quickly and suddenly, as would an **"armed man"** (robber) or a traveling robber **("one that travelleth")**, and snatches away everything of value. So it is with the sluggard; no matter what asset he has somehow managed to acquire. The only certainty for him is that he will be overtaken by poverty which will occur suddenly and unexpectedly.

Proverbs 6:6-11 Go to the ant, thou sluggard; consider her ways, and be wise: Which having no guide, overseer, or ruler, Provideth her meat in the summer, and gathereth her food in the harvest. How long wilt thou sleep, O sluggard? when wilt thou arise out of thy sleep? Yet a little sleep, a little slumber, a little folding of the hands to sleep: So shall thy poverty come as one that travelleth, and thy want as an armed man.

Proverbs 10:4 He becometh poor that dealeth with a slack hand: but the hand of the diligent maketh rich.

Proverbs 13:4 The soul of the sluggard desireth, and hath nothing: but the soul of the diligent shall be made fat.

Proverbs 19:15 Slothfulness casteth into a deep sleep; and an idle soul shall suffer hunger.

Proverbs 20:4 The sluggard will not plow by reason of the cold; therefore shall he beg in harvest, and have nothing.

Proverbs 20:13 Love not sleep, lest thou come to poverty; open thine eyes, and thou shalt be satisfied with bread.

Proverbs 26:14 As the door turneth upon his hinges, so doth the slothful upon his bed.

Proverbs 27:23-27 Be thou diligent to know the state of thy flocks, and look well to thy herds. For riches are not for ever: and doth the crown endure to every generation? The hay appeareth, and the tender grass sheweth itself, and herbs of the mountains are gathered. The lambs are for thy clothing, and the goats are the price of the field. And thou shalt have goats' milk enough for thy food, for the food of thy household, and for the maintenance for thy maidens.

Ecclesiastes 10:18 By much slothfulness the building decayeth; and through idleness of the hands the house droppeth through.

2 Thessalonians 3:10 For even when we were with you, this we commanded you, that if any would not work, neither should he eat.

Hebrews 6:12 That ye be not slothful, but followers of them who through faith and patience inherit the promises.

SECTION III
(Chapters 25 -29)

Hezekiah was the 13th king of Judah, reigning from 726 BC to 697 BC, about 300 years after Solomon. The young 25-year-old King Hezekiah searched the inspired word of God for ways to establish his kingdom on righteousness and peace. He had witnessed the instability of wickedness that his father Ahaz's reign brought when he attempted to destroy all remembrance of God. Hezekiah was regretfully familiar with the spirit of fear that his father used to control the population.

No doubt the inspired word of God motivated him to action when he read – "Take away the dross from the silver and there shall come forth a vessel for the finer. Take away the wicked from before the king and his throne shall be established in righteousness." (Proverbs 25:4-5) He quickly cleansed the Temple, re-established the Passover, and collected tithes. (See 2 Chronicles 29-31)

Hezekiah relied on wisdom found in the proverbs of Solomon when the Assyrians invaded midway through his reign. The following are *some* of the guidelines that Hezekiah likely practiced for victory that are also named in Proverbs:

(1) Don't get in a hurry to have war.
   "Go not forth hastily to strive, lest thou know not what to do in the end thereof" (25:8)
(2) There is safety in trusting God for leadership.
   "The fear of man bringeth a snare: but whoso putteth his trust in the LORD shall be safe" (29:25)
   "Whoso walketh uprightly shall be saved: *but he that is* perverse in *his* ways shall fall at once." (28:18
(3) Insist on having wise men to carry forth negotiations.
   "He that sendeth a message by the hand of a fool cutteth off the feet, *and* drinketh damage." (26:6)
(4) Don't be concerned about a wicked opponent's cursing.
   "As the bird by wandering, as the swallow by flying, so the curse causeless shall not come." (26:2)
(5) Don't yield to evil people.
   "A righteous man falling down before the wicked *is as* a troubled fountain, and a corrupt spring." (25:26)
(6) Maintain good counsel.
   "Ointment and perfume rejoice the heart: so *doth* the sweetness of a man's friend by hearty counsel." (27:9)
(7) Don't think too highly of yourself.
   " Seest thou a man wise in his own conceit? there is more hope of a fool than of him." (26:12)

CHAPTER TWENTY-FIVE

> **Proverbs 25:1** These *are* also proverbs of Solomon, which the men of Hezekiah king of Judah copied out.

> **Who Was King Hezekiah?**
>
> Hezekiah was aware of God's acts in the past and believed in His involvement in daily events. 2 Kings states the following about Hezekiah:
>
> 2Kings 18:5 "He trusted in the Lord God of Israel, so that after him was none like him among all the kings of Judah, nor any that were before him, for he clave to the Lord, and departed not from following Him but kept His commandments."
>
> In the very first year and first month of his reign, the Lord put it "in his heart to make a covenant with the Lord God of Israel" (2 Chronicles 29). He opened and repaired the doors of the Lord's house which had been "shut up" and charged the Levites not to be negligent, but to "sanctify" the house and "carry forth the filthiness out of the holy place." He gave further instructions to light the lamps, burn incense, and offer burnt offerings as in former times. During the reign of his father, Ahaz, the Temple doors were closed, and idolatrous altars were set up in "every corner of Jerusalem." (2Chronicles 28:24). (From Robert Jamison, A. R. Fausset, David Brown, *A Commentary, Critical and Explanatory, on the Old and New Testaments*, 1871, e-Sword,12.0.1.)
>
> Wisely the youthful king turned to the word of God to guide his actions in undoing his father's evil. No doubt the Holy Spirit guided Hezekiah and "his men" to single out certain of Solomon's proverbs that he, and the Kingdom of Judah, would need. Perhaps the greatest significance of Hezekiah's choice of proverbs is reflected in the way that these truths addressed his circumstances. Many of them speak of ways in which a kingdom is preserved and prolonged. During his thirty-year reign, he would need wisdom to lead and wisdom to reform the nation. He had a strong desire to cleanse the land of idolatry and re-establish God's rights over the nation. Within just a matter of days, he cleansed the Temple, celebrated the Passover, and collected the tithes for the Lord (2 Chronicles 29-31). Hezekiah's reign was characterized by a deep desire for justice, integrity, and godly administration. *[Hezekiah's story is told in 2 Kings 16:20-20:21; 2 Chronicles 28:27-32:33; and Isaiah 36:1-39:8. He is also mentioned in Proverbs 25:1; Isaiah 1:1; Jeremiah 15:4; 26:18-19; Hosea 1:1; and Micah 1:1.]*

It is obvious from Scripture that Hezekiah wanted to be wise and please the Lord. Being faced with the task of leading Judah to recover their worship of God (after his father Ahaz's wicked leadership), Hezekiah sought to properly **"copy out"** some of Solomon's proverbs that were previously not compiled. These proverbs were gleaned either from Solomon's other writings or directly from individuals (oral tradition). The **"also"** in this first verse of Proverbs 25, probably refers to the proverbs given in chapters 10:17 through 24:22. Note how these proverbs, which became chapters 25 through 29, relate to the king and his leadership, as well as to the citizens of Judah and their need for wisdom, integrity, and righteousness in daily living.

Proverbs 25 actually starts with verse 2 while verse 1 serves as an introduction. It was most likely written by one of the copiers identified as **"men of Hezekiah."** The exact function of these men is not known, but they likely were his scribes.

> **Proverbs 25:2** *It is* the glory of God to conceal a thing: but the honour of kings *is* to search out a matter.

Focus: This proverb contrasts how God and man are both honored according to their relationship with knowledge.

NOTE: **"Glory"** and **"honour"** are synonyms translated from the same Hebrew word, and **"Thing"** and **"matter"** are also synonyms.

"It is the glory of God to conceal a thing." The *"glory of God" is observable* in His entire creation – in the sheer massiveness of the universe – in the microscopic elements – in the complexity of the electronics of the human brain – in just the concept of human thought – in life itself – and in all the other aspects of creation that are beyond explanation or observation. He has favored the human race by allowing man to understand just a speck of what He knows. Therefore, when intelligent, spiritual men recognize that God is bigger in every imaginable and unimaginable way, they have to agree that **"it is the glory of God to conceal a thing."** Obviously, Eve refused to accept the fact that it was God's glory to conceal a complete understanding of why He didn't want her and Adam to partake of the fruit of the forbidden tree. She insisted on knowing what God had concealed for her own good. (Genesis 3)

> Deuteronomy 29:29 The secret things belong unto the LORD our God: but those things which are revealed belong unto us and to our children for ever, that we may do all the words of this law.
>
> Job 11:7-9 Canst thou by searching find out God? canst thou find out the Almighty unto perfection? *It is* as high as heaven; what canst thou do? deeper than hell; what canst thou know? The measure thereof *is* longer than the earth, and broader than the sea.
>
> Isaiah 45:15 Verily thou *art* a God that hidest thyself, O God of Israel, the Saviour.
>
> Mark 4:10-12 And when he was alone, they that were about him with the twelve asked of him the parable. And he said unto them, Unto you it is given to know the mystery of the kingdom of God: but unto them that are without, all *these* things are done in parables: That seeing they may see, and not perceive; and hearing they may hear, and not understand; lest at any time they should be converted, and *their* sins should be forgiven them.
>
> Romans 1:19-23 Because that which may be known of God is manifest in them; for God hath shewed *it* unto them. For the invisible things of him from the creation of the world are clearly seen, being understood by the things that are made, *even* his eternal power and Godhead; so that they are without excuse: Because that, when they knew God, they glorified *him* not as God, neither were thankful; but became vain in their imaginations, and their foolish heart was darkened. Professing themselves to be wise, they became fools, And changed the glory of the uncorruptible God into an image made like to corruptible man, and to birds, and fourfooted beasts, and creeping things.
>
> Romans 11:33 O the depth of the riches both of the wisdom and knowledge of God! how unsearchable are his judgments, and his ways past finding out!

"But the honour of kings *is* to search out a matter." Unlike God, Who knows all things, kings are charged with the duty of solving issues of justice brought before them and of keeping the nation safe (among many other responsibilities). It is their honor "**to search out a matter;**" however, they must always make judgments based on limited information. Because a wise, righteous king knows that his knowledge is always limited, he relies on God to give spiritual and physical guidance. It is God's glory that He does not need to search out a matter because He already knows the answer. However, it is the honor of wise kings "by all the methods of enquiry, to search out or investigate the matters that are brought before them, to take pains in examining offenders, that they may discover their designs and bring to light the hidden works of darkness, not to give judgment hastily or till they have weighed things, nor to leave it wholly to others to examine things, but to see with their own eyes."[648]

Wise kings who desire to uncover truth in order to make proper and good judgments must have a working knowledge of the Scriptures *PLUS* a personal relationship with God. Any king can **"search out a matter"** best when God and His word guide him. Thus, he will be able to lead properly. The personified wisdom in Proverbs 8:14 stated: "Counsel is mine, and sound wisdom: I am understanding; I have strength."

The idea of *searching* connects this proverb to the next one. Solomon compares man's limited knowledge with God's infinite, boundless, immeasurable knowledge.

Proverbs 25:3 The heaven for height, and the earth for depth, and the heart of kings *is* unsearchable.

> Focus: This proverb utilizes the well-known truth that the vastness of God's creation is undiscoverable to express the truth that the heart of kings is also beyond discovery – both are unsearchable.

"The heart of kings *is* unsearchable" (not searchable). Something that can be searched out ("the honour of kings *is* to search out a matter."– verse 2) is obviously the opposite of something that can't be searched out. Almost any adult can testify that it is impossible to discover the height of heaven or precisely the depth of earth. The Bible gives such common facts to comparatively illustrate how difficult it is to know the heart of a king. Wise kings will seek counsel from other men and God's word, yet the king's inward thoughts and purposes are rarely discoverable to others. Imagine the shock of the bystanders when King Solomon called for a sword with which to divide the living child between the two mothers, each claiming the child belonged to her (1Kings 3:25). Probably the observers thought it was a ridiculous, even brutal, and an ungodly decision. Later, after the true mother identified herself, Israel feared the king because they saw God was with him (1Kings 3:28) and steering the deep thoughts of his heart to produce wisdom. It is doubtful that Solomon ever revealed all the information he had gleaned about these two women and their circumstances, personalities, and character before suggesting such drastic action as cutting the baby in half. Just as God must be trusted to do the best for His people, leadership that He installs needs to be trusted by the population to make right decisions.

God requires that men exercise great effort to learn of Him, but He also has secrets which he only reveals to His friends (those that love and trust Him). Kings also hide some of their knowledge from their subjects. A wise king conscientiously conceal matters that do not need to be made public, especially in sensitive matters of national security.

> "The contrast between the glory of God and that of the king lies in this—that whereas both God and the king desire man's welfare, the former promotes this by making him feel his ignorance and littleness and entire dependence upon this mysterious Being whose nature and designs mortals cannot understand; the latter advances the good of his subjects by giving them confidence in his zeal and power to discover truth, and using his knowledge for their benefit."[649]

Proverbs 25:4-5 Take away the dross from the silver, and there shall come forth a vessel for the finer.
5. Take away the wicked *from* before the king, and his throne shall be established in righteousness.

Focus: This proverb (2 verses) illustrates the necessity of removing wicked individuals in order to establish a righteous authority.

Removing of dross (the unusable impurities) from silver is done so in order to leave the purer silver that is then ready **"for the finer"** (A "finer" is the craftsman who has the artistry and aptitude to cast pure silver into a beautiful, serviceable instrument). A silversmith heats his metal until the worthless **"dross"** floats to the top and is scraped away from the pure silver; likewise, a wise and responsible king knows that wicked people must be removed from his presence. Such a separation is important because a wise king knows that the wicked counselor has the potential, through personal persuasion, to corrupt laws, justice, and good judgment. Their poison could spread to the entire kingdom. **"His throne shall be established in righteousness"** when he removes them. Such action is the leader's responsibility: he must have enough discernment to recognize evil people, and he also must possess the strength and courage to remove them. Righteousness encourages the presence, protection, and provisions of God. On the other hand, wickedness guarantees a separation from God; and it is far better to go through the struggle of separating from wicked people than to separate from God.

> Proverbs 16:12 *It is* an abomination to kings to commit wickedness: for the throne is established by righteousness.
>
> Proverbs 20:8 A king that sitteth in the throne of judgment scattereth away all evil with his eyes.
>
> Psalm 1:4-6 The ungodly *are* not so: but *are* like the chaff which the wind driveth away. Therefore the ungodly shall not stand in the judgment, nor sinners in the congregation of the righteous. For the LORD knoweth the way of the righteous: but the way of the ungodly shall perish.

In a comparable action, Proverbs 20:26 states, "A wise king scattereth the wicked, and bringeth the wheel over them." Sometimes a wagon wheel would be brought over the grain on the threshing floor to separate the chaff or trash from the grain. Then a winnowing fan would toss the worthless chaff up in the air where the winds would blow it away from the threshing floor.

Proverbs 25:6-7 Put not forth thyself in the presence of the king, and stand not in the place of great *men*:
7. For better *it is* that it be said unto thee, Come up hither; than that thou shouldest be put lower in the presence of the prince whom thine eyes have seen.

Focus: This proverb suggests an act of humility that is preferred to a consequence of arrogance.

Counsel from Scripture to the hearer of wisdom is this – a wise person *does not pretend* to be of higher status than he actually is. Self-promotion and egotism are ugly and repugnant traits that often draw a reaction that demotes the poor egotist back to his appropriate level. It is better to be *humble* than to be *humbled* in front of the **"prince whom thine eyes have seen"** or before the "prince" that was boldly intruded upon.

> Exodus 3:11 And Moses said unto God, Who *am* I, that I should go unto Pharaoh, and that I should bring forth the children of Israel out of Egypt?
>
> 1 Samuel 15:17 And Samuel said, When thou *wast* little in thine own sight, *wast* thou not *made* the head of the tribes of Israel, and the LORD anointed thee king over Israel?
>
> 1 Samuel 18:18 And David said unto Saul, Who *am* I? and what *is* my life, *or* my father's family in Israel, that I should be son in law to the king?
>
> Psalm 131:1 LORD, my heart is not haughty, nor mine eyes lofty: neither do I exercise myself in great matters, or in things too high for me.
>
> Proverbs 25:27 *It is* not good to eat much honey: so *for men* to search their own glory *is not* glory.
>
> Proverbs 27:2 Let another man praise thee, and not thine own mouth; a stranger, and not thine own lips.
>
> Jeremiah 1:6 Then said I, Ah, Lord GOD! behold, I cannot speak: for I *am* a child.
>
> Amos 7:14-15 Then answered Amos, and said to Amaziah, I *was* no prophet, neither *was* I a prophet's son; but I *was* an herdman, and a gatherer of sycomore fruit: And the LORD took me as I followed the flock, and the LORD said unto me, Go, prophesy unto my people Israel. *[See also 1 Samuel 9:20-22 concerning Saul.]*

It is better for the ruler to select a person to be raised to a higher level – **"Come up hither"** – than for a man to elevate himself and improperly take a higher position. Jesus gave a parable that effectively illustrates this proverb.

> Luke 14:7-11 And he put forth a parable to those which were bidden, when he marked how they chose out the chief rooms; saying unto them, When thou art bidden of any *man* to a wedding, sit not down in the highest room; lest a more honourable man than thou be bidden of him; And he that bade thee and him come and say to thee, Give this man place; and thou begin with shame to take the lowest room. But when thou art bidden, go and sit down in the lowest room; that when he that bade thee cometh, he may say unto thee, Friend, go up higher: then shalt thou have worship in the presence of them that sit at meat with thee. For whosoever exalteth himself shall be abased; and he that humbleth himself shall be exalted.

Proverbs 25:8-10 Go not forth hastily to strive, lest *thou know not* what to do in the end thereof, when thy neighbour hath put thee to shame.
9. Debate thy cause with thy neighbour *himself;* and discover not a secret to another:
10. Lest he that heareth *it* put thee to shame, and thine infamy turn not away.

Focus: This proverb (3 verses) teaches how to properly interact with others in the face of budding strife, so as to prevent severe personal damage.

These three verses form rules of wise conduct that, if followed, will prevent unnecessary ill feelings, sleepless nights, confusion, shamefulness, and loss of friendship, not to mention unnecessary cost, should the conflict end in litigation.

"Go not forth hastily to strive, lest *thou know not* what to do in the end thereof, when thy neighbour hath put thee to shame." (verse 8) **"Strive"** here means to instigate a contention or a quarrel. ***Going forth hastily to strive*** is foolish behavior that reveals immature thinking and a lack of foresight, and such hot-headed, emotion-driven behavior is invariably regretted in the end. Wisdom mandates that a wise person take time to evaluate, investigate, and communicate – and he should do so with an attitude of seeking a peaceful solution NOT with an attitude of revenge or igniting the situation. People often realize that their first thoughts about a situation or a person were not accurate and that their view was clouded by their own preconceived notions or incomplete information. It is best to deal with every matter in a thoughtful, kind, mature, and Christ-like manner rather than rushing off to shamefully regret an unnecessary conflict that only brings defeat (especially if such strife ends in an expensive court case).

"Shame" comes most often in the form of learning that family, friends, and neighbors *have lost respect for the hasty one's ability to demonstrate good judgment*. Also, that hasty person will probably not only experience a loss of an otherwise good relationship, but also financial or property loss and the confusion of ***not knowing what to do in the end***.

> Proverbs 14:29 He that is slow to wrath is of great understanding: but he that is hasty of spirit exalteth folly.
>
> Proverbs 29:20 Seest thou a man that is hasty in his words? there is more hope of a fool than of him.

Strife should be avoided, not sought. Paul stated in Romans 12:8, "If it be possible, as much as lieth in you, live peaceable with all men."

Genesis 13:8-9 And Abram said unto Lot, Let there be no strife, I pray thee, between me and thee, and between my herdmen and thy herdmen; for we *be* brethren. *Is* not the whole land before thee? separate thyself, I pray thee, from me: if *thou wilt take* the left hand, then I will go to the right; or if *thou depart* to the right hand, then I will go to the left.

Proverbs 17:14 The beginning of strife *is as* when one letteth out water: therefore leave off contention, before it be meddled with.

"Debate thy cause with thy neighbour *himself;* and discover not a secret to another: Lest he that heareth *it* put thee to shame, and thine infamy turn not away." (verses 9-10) These verses imply that the "neighbor" is actually someone close rather than just some associate, as is often the meaning of "neighbor." It also implies that a private conversation between these neighbors has been regretfully made public. To ***debate a cause*** means to contend or plead a position or belief. The advice given here is to have such a contest of ideas with another in private, where it belongs, rather than to make the strife public. Furthermore, the debate should be held with a spirit of reconciliation, *not* aggression. Problems escalate when there is a failure to safeguard secrets shared between people because of their time spent together and their mutual trust. Making those entrusted secrets ***known to others***, especially for personal gain or vengeance, demonstrates a failure of good judgment, a breakdown of good character, and a loss of dignity. The irresponsibly-talking neighbor will be ***infamously*** characterized as a betrayer of confidence, and his reputation will be marred. **"Thine infamy turn not away"** declares that his foolish actions producing the shame and loss of good reputation will not go away for many years or his lifetime.

Proverbs 11:13 A talebearer revealeth secrets: but he that is of a faithful spirit concealeth the matter.

Proverbs 20:19 He that goeth about *as* a talebearer revealeth secrets: therefore meddle not with him that flattereth with his lips.

Matthew 18:15-20 Moreover if thy brother shall trespass against thee, go and tell him his fault between thee and him alone: if he shall hear thee, thou hast gained thy brother.

This proverb (verses 8-10) is specifically a warning for believers to act wisely concerning strife. When wise communication breaks down and resolve fails, personal strife can quickly escalate and move into a public courtroom. In the courtroom, a small matter becomes large, expensive, embarrassing, and often an unnecessary development. **"Go not forth hastily to strive."**

Proverbs 25:11 A word fitly spoken *is like* apples of gold in pictures of silver.

Focus: This proverb expresses the beauty of speaking wisely.

"A word fitly spoken" is a word that is spoken at the right time, at the right place, and in the right spirit. Such a word might even be in the form of a rebuke. In contrast with the beauty of wise speaking is the ugliness of a talebearer's ill-spoken, irresponsible words (as discussed in previous verses from this chapter).

Hatefully-spoken words are ugly and hang heavy on the heart, bringing grief and sorrow in contrast with loving words that bring relief and joy. Words can prick the heart with pain or medicate the heart with soothing relief; however, the most soothing words can pierce the soul when spoken in the wrong spirit or at the wrong time. Words flood the air space, but only a few are **"fitly spoken."** The best words are expensive because choosing them costs the speaker time, thought, consideration, and suppression of ego.

Ultimately, the most beautiful and valuable words of truth, goodness, and salvation come from the Scriptures, especially those of Jesus. His words are priceless, soothing, encouraging, edifying, and strengthening. They deliver blessed hope. Additionally, His words of rebuke are beneficial in changing the wrong direction of a person's life.

Dedicated, charitable Christians learn to be sensitive to the Holy Spirit, who will guide their speech and their actions. The King James Bible translators originally placed this note in the margin next to this verse: "spoken upon his wheels."[650] In other words, the "word fitly spoken" was not forced or dragged but rolling along smoothly.

Scripture gives these additional thoughtful guidelines for speaking properly.

Proverbs 12:25 Heaviness in the heart of man maketh it stoop: but a good word maketh it glad.

Proverbs 15:23 A man hath joy by the answer of his mouth: and a word *spoken* in due season, how good *is it!*

Proverbs 27:5 Open rebuke *is* better than secret love.

Believers are also encouraged to speak words of encouragement or offer comfort in time of sorrow or tribulation.

> 2 Corinthians 1:3-4 Blessed *be* God, even the Father of our Lord Jesus Christ, the Father of mercies, and the God of all comfort; comforteth us in all our tribulation, that we may be able to comfort them which are in any trouble, by the comfort wherewith we ourselves are comforted of God.
> Colossians 4:7-8 All my state shall Tychicus declare unto you, *who is* a beloved brother, and a faithful minister and fellowservant in the Lord: Whom I have sent unto you for the same purpose, that he might know your estate, and comfort your hearts;
> 1Thessalonians 5:11 Wherefore comfort yourselves together, and edify one another, even as also ye do.
> Romans 14:19 Let us therefore follow after the things which make for peace, and things wherewith one may edify another.
> 1Thessalonians 5:14-15 Now we exhort you, brethren, warn them that are unruly, comfort the feebleminded, support the weak, be patient toward all *men*. See that none render evil for evil unto any *man;* but ever follow that which is good, both among yourselves, and to all men.

Proverbs 25:12 *As* an earring of gold, and an ornament of fine gold, *so is* a wise reprover upon an obedient ear.

Focus: This proverb testifies that words of reproof are beautiful and valuable when wisely spoken and properly received.

Continuing with the topic of the wise use of words from verse 11, Solomon advances from a general conversation to one involving reproof, which increases the potential for discord to develop. Even though properly given, reproof is not always taken well; however, the conversation involving reproof is made beautiful and valuable when the reprover is wise, and the listener is obedient. The two conversationalists of this verse are represented as a **"wise reprover"** (speaker) and **"an obedient ear"** (listener). Had the listener been foolish, the communication would have never happened or resulted in reactionary strife since a fool refuses to be corrected. When a wise person corrects another wise person, the entire conversation reflects value, honor, grace, and beauty, as does **"an earring of gold and an ornament of fine gold."**

> Psalm 141:5 Let the righteous smite me; *it shall be* a kindness: and let him reprove me; *it shall be* an excellent oil, *which* shall not break my head: for yet my prayer also *shall be* in their calamities.
> Proverbs 1:8-9 My son, hear the instruction of thy father, and forsake not the law of thy mother: For they *shall be* an ornament of grace unto thy head, and chains about thy neck.
> Proverbs 9:7-8 He that reproveth a scorner getteth to himself shame: and he that rebuketh a wicked *man getteth* himself a blot. Reprove not a scorner, lest he hate thee: rebuke a wise man, and he will love thee.
> Proverbs 15:31-32 The ear that heareth the reproof of life abideth among the wise. He that refuseth instruction despiseth his own soul: but he that heareth reproof getteth understanding.
> Proverbs 27:6 Faithful *are* the wounds of a friend; but the kisses of an enemy *are* deceitful.

Both Scripture and the Holy Spirit reprove the believer, making him suitable for a closer walk with God and providing wisdom to the things of this world. How beautiful are the results that God obtains from **"an obedient ear"** of a wise Christian who esteems God's loving rebuke as honorable and full of grace and beauty. Such a Christian is totally receptive to His word and the Holy Spirit. Any sinner having a repentant heart and an obedient ear will discover God's rebuke to be more beautiful than the gold and silver that could have previously been his god.

> Psalm 119:127-128 Therefore I love thy commandments above gold; yea, above fine gold. Therefore I esteem all *thy* precepts *concerning* all *things to be* right; *and* I hate every false way.
> John 16:7-11 Nevertheless I tell you the truth; It is expedient for you that I go away: for if I go not away, the Comforter will not come unto you; but if I depart, I will send him unto you. And when he is come, he will reprove the world of sin, and of righteousness, and of judgment: Of sin, because they believe not on me; Of righteousness, because I go to my Father, and ye see me no more; Of judgment, because the prince of this world is judged.
> 2 Timothy 3:16-17 All scripture *is* given by inspiration of God, and *is* profitable for doctrine, for reproof, for correction, for instruction in righteousness: That the man of God may be perfect, throughly furnished unto all good works.
> 2 Timothy 4:2-4 Preach the word; be instant in season, out of season; reprove, rebuke, exhort with all longsuffering and doctrine. For the time will come when they will not endure sound doctrine; but after their own lusts shall they heap to themselves teachers, having itching ears; And they shall turn away *their* ears from the truth, and shall be turned unto fables.
> Hebrews 4:12 For the word of God *is* quick, and powerful, and sharper than any twoedged sword, piercing even to the dividing asunder of soul and spirit, and of the joints and marrow, and *is* a discerner of the thoughts and intents of the heart.

> **Proverbs 25:13** As the cold of snow in the time of harvest, *so is* a faithful messenger to them that send him: for he refresheth the soul of his masters.

Focus: This proverb explains the delightful, refreshing value of a faithful messenger.

Clearly, the understanding of this proverb is that a **"faithful messenger"** refreshes his **"masters"** *(owners or senders)* like **"the cold of snow"** would refresh a person working in the heat of harvest time. Just as snow is an extreme rarity at harvest time, a **"faithful messenger"** is a rarity because he faithfully does and says exactly what his master expects. He delivers the message on time, in the designated place, to the proper intended receiver, and precisely as it was relayed to him. He is faithful not to change the message in any regard, thus keeping its intended purpose and consequences. The "faithful messenger" is refreshing to his master because he is comforting, reliable, and a rarity. People who show themselves faithful in the transaction of business, the execution of commands, or the discharge of official duties are indeed refreshing.

Egotistical men tend to distort the message to benefit their personal cause. They make themselves look good at the expense of the truth. Notice the descriptions of the *un*faithful messenger:

> Proverbs 10:26 As vinegar to the teeth, and as smoke to the eyes, so is the sluggard to them that send him.
> Proverbs 13:17 A wicked messenger falleth into mischief: but a faithful ambassador *is* health.
> Proverbs 26:6 He that sendeth a message by the hand of a fool cutteth off the feet, *and* drinketh damage.

Master of all masters is God Himself, Who chooses and calls certain men to carry His message to peoples of all nations. Their duty is to relay God's word exactly as the Holy Spirit gives it. The **"faithful messenger"** who responsibly delivers the inerrant message of truth is, without doubt, pleasing to God. Paul had several things to say about God's messenger of truth:

> Romans 10:15 And how shall they preach, except they be sent? as it is written, How beautiful are the feet of them that preach the gospel of peace, and bring glad tidings of good things!
> Philippians 2:25-30 Yet I supposed it necessary to send to you Epaphroditus, my brother, and companion in labour, and fellowsoldier, but your messenger, and he that ministered to my wants. For he longed after you all, and was full of heaviness, because that ye had heard that he had been sick. For indeed he was sick nigh unto death: but God had mercy on him; and not on him only, but on me also, lest I should have sorrow upon sorrow. I sent him therefore the more carefully, that, when ye see him again, ye may rejoice, and that I may be the less sorrowful. Receive him therefore in the Lord with all gladness; and hold such in reputation: Because for the work of Christ he was nigh unto death, not regarding his life, to supply your lack of service toward me.
> 1 Timothy 1:12 And I thank Christ Jesus our Lord, who hath enabled me, for that he counted me faithful, putting me into the ministry;
> 2 Timothy 2:1-2 Thou therefore, my son, be strong in the grace that is in Christ Jesus. And the things that thou hast heard of me among many witnesses, the same commit thou to faithful men, who shall be able to teach others also.

> **Proverbs 25:14** Whoso boasteth himself of a false gift *is like* clouds and wind without rain.

Focus: This proverb describes the hollow character of a boastful liar and the failed expectancy of those who believe him.

A person who ***boasts himself of a false gift*** *[a present, a gift, or a reward]* prevaricates. The liar tells others that he *has given something* (money, possession, time), when in fact he has done no such thing. Alternately, he may have lied about what he *will give* when he has no such intention; however, he proudly proclaims his gift. Furthermore, by way of application, he may be trying to convince his audience that he has some greatly needed talent or skill when he does not. This ***boaster*** makes a show, is clamorously foolish, and makes a fool of himself.

The second half of this verse completes the lesson of the proverb by illustrating the proud boaster's lying through the use of a simile. He is **"*like* clouds and wind without rain."** Think of the extreme disappointment of hot, exhausted farmers out in their fields watching the clouds gather and feeling the cool breeze gently drying the sweat from their faces. With great expectation, they lean on their hoe handles, waiting for the cool drops of refreshing rain–only there is no rain, the clouds are empty and the wind is soon gone. What a feeling of mockery and betrayal! This is the disappointment of one who promises much and gives nothing. The marginal note of the KJV says the boaster promises "in a gift of falsehood."[651]

> Malachi 1:13-14 Ye said also, Behold, what a weariness *is it!* and ye have snuffed at it, saith the LORD of hosts; and ye brought *that which was* torn, and the lame, and the sick; thus ye brought an offering: should I accept this of your hand? saith the LORD. But cursed *be* the deceiver, which hath in his flock a male, and voweth, and sacrificeth unto the Lord a corrupt thing: for I *am* a great King, saith the LORD of hosts, and my name *is* dreadful among the heathen.
>
> Acts 5:1-3 But a certain man named Ananias, with Sapphira his wife, sold a possession, And kept back *part* of the price, his wife also being privy *to it,* and brought a certain part, and laid *it* at the apostles' feet. But Peter said, Ananias, why hath Satan filled thine heart to lie to the Holy Ghost, and to keep back *part* of the price of the land?

Proverbs 25:15 By long forbearing is a prince persuaded, and a soft tongue breaketh the bone.

Focus: This proverb expresses the effectiveness of patient and gentle communication specifically with a leader *(prince)*.

"By long forbearing is a prince persuaded." Noah Webster defines **"forbearing"** as "a ceasing or restraining from action; patience; long suffering."[652] A "prince" is one in authority who also has enough power to cause an aggressor considerable damage. Waiting until the situation is right (right time, right place, right spirit) before pressing a matter is a needed attribute for anyone trying to persuade another person (especially a leader). Patience is valuable to prevent harmful and unnecessary repercussions. Under normal life situations, where people are not being motivated by evil, a combination of patience and gentle words is more powerful to persuade than a whole conglomeration of aggressive, thunderous demands.

"A soft tongue breaketh the bone" is a statement that utilizes the figure of speech called *hyperbole* (an exaggerated statement not meant to be taken literally). Here it effectively and humorously expresses the truth that gentle communication is powerful. **"A soft tongue"** or a quietly-spoken, meek, and humble word will soften the hardened heart. Previously, in Proverbs 15:1, the reader was given a rule for gentleness – "A soft answer turneth away wrath: but grievous words stir up anger."

This lesson in Proverbs is substantiated by Old Testament examples such as Abigail's pleading with David when he was enraged, and also, David's avoidance of Soul during his violent temper episodes. In addition, the Gospels tell of how Jesus dealt ever so patiently and gently with Peter. Wise people understand that often patience, along with properly spoken words, can be more effective and more powerful (and without collateral damage) than strong-arm tactics.

> 1 Samuel 25:23-25 And when Abigail saw David, she hasted, and lighted off the ass, and fell before David on her face, and bowed herself to the ground, And fell at his feet, and said, Upon me, my lord, *upon* me *let this* iniquity *be:* and let thine handmaid, I pray thee, speak in thine audience, and hear the words of thine handmaid. Let not my lord, I pray thee, regard this man of Belial, *even* Nabal: for as his name *is,* so *is* he; Nabal *is* his name, and folly *is* with him: but I thine handmaid saw not the young men of my lord, whom thou didst send.
>
> Proverbs 16:14 The wrath of a king *is as* messengers of death: but a wise man will pacify it.
>
> Ecclesiastes 10:4 If the spirit of the ruler rise up against thee, leave not thy place; for yielding pacifieth great offences.
>
> Romans 2:4 Or despisest thou the riches of his goodness and forbearance and longsuffering; not knowing that the goodness of God leadeth thee to repentance?
>
> James 1:18-20 Of his own will begat he us with the word of truth, that we should be a kind of firstfruits of his creatures. Wherefore, my beloved brethren, let every man be swift to hear, slow to speak, slow to wrath: For the wrath of man worketh not the righteousness of God.

Proverbs 25:16 Hast thou found honey? eat so much as is sufficient for thee, lest thou be filled therewith, and vomit it.

Focus: This proverb illustrates the importance of moderation.

It is admirable, necessary, and safe to control one's consumption or utilization of anything, especially those things that are likely to be overdone because they bring pleasure. To love to take vacations is fine until doing so robs one of the ability to maintain family and home. To love collectibles, such as teddy bears, is harmless until one no longer has a place to sit or a bed to sleep on. Note the comparison of honey to searching for one's praise in verse 27– "*It is* not good to eat much honey: so *for men* to search their own glory *is not* glory."

> "'*Hast thou found honey?*' – Which, in those parts, was often found in woods or fields. By honey, he understands not only all delicious meats, but all present and worldly delights, which we are here taught to use with moderation: for as honey, moderately taken, strengthens the body and prolongs life, but, if taken to excess, disturbs the stomach, and turns the pleasure into pain; so it is with earthly satisfactions and pursuits. Moderately used they are refreshing and useful; immoderately, they produce disgust, or are accompanied with guilt and followed by trouble."[653]

> Luke 21:34 And take heed to yourselves, lest at any time your hearts be overcharged with surfeiting, and drunkenness, and cares of this life, and *so* that day come upon you unawares.
> Philippians 4:5 Let your moderation be known unto all men. The Lord is at hand.

Proverbs 25:17 Withdraw thy foot from thy neighbour's house; lest he be weary of thee, and *so* hate thee.

Focus: This proverb advises why visiting others should be done in moderation.

As explained about honey in the previous verse, too much of almost anything can cause a problem. Initially, visits to the neighbor's house (nearby or far away) may be as enjoyable as honey, but visiting too frequently can cause loathing. [*KJV Notes* states **"weary of thee"** also means "full of thee"[654] like eating too much honey.] The neighbor's love could turn to disgust.

A wise person will always respect the other person's privacy and personal space. To avoid becoming a nuisance, he will avoid visiting too often and visit only enough so that the visits are valued and respected. A modern-day proverb resembling verse 17 is "Familiarity breeds contempt."

There is an exception to this rule: God will never tire of visits from His children, so there is no need to restrain our visits with Him. The more we are with Him, the better the relationship.

> Proverbs 8:34-35 Blessed *is* the man that heareth me *[personified wisdom]*, watching daily at my gates, waiting at the posts of my doors. For whoso findeth me findeth life, and shall obtain favour of the LORD.

Proverbs 25:18 A man that beareth false witness against his neighbour *is* a maul, and a sword, and a sharp arrow.

Focus: This proverb declares that a false witness has a destructive mouth that equates to dangerous lethal weapons.

A liar always causes damage, especially a liar testifying in court. The liar himself becomes a weapon of war when he lies against his neighbor *[brother, companion, friend, husband, acquaintance, or lover]*. To say that the liar is a walking sword is bad enough; but to identify him as a maul, *and* a sword, *and* a sharp arrow is to triple down and consider him a severe threat to humanity. "Giving false testimony in court against a neighbor can crush, divide, or pierce like a club... sword, or... arrow. Lying can wound a person's character and even destroy his life as effectively as weapons."[655]

The liar is not envisioned as one making poor judgment and in need of pity. With his lying, he is seen only as a weapon capable of inflicting severe bruising, cutting, and piercing to the heart. He wounds a person's character, destroys lives, and is dangerous.

> NOTE: Hatred is often a factor in the behavior of the false witness, but much is taught in Scripture that forbids the righteous to hate others, even the false witness. Two facts should be remembered by the believer forced to deal with a false witness: humanity, even in its worst, most sinful form, is always to be respected since man was made in the image of God; and God must enact vengeance, not man.

> Psalm 120:1-2 A Song of degrees. In my distress I cried unto the LORD, and he heard me. Deliver my soul, O LORD, from lying lips, *and* from a deceitful tongue.

Proverbs 6:16-19 These six *things* doth the LORD hate: yea, seven *are* an abomination unto him: A proud look, a lying tongue, and hands that shed innocent blood, An heart that deviseth wicked imaginations, feet that be swift in running to mischief, A false witness *that* speaketh lies, and he that soweth discord among brethren.

"*False witness* is universally condemned. But where, save in the word of God, are its true character and deep aggravation of guilt adequately set forth? What a picture is here of cruelty and malice – nay – even of intentional murder! Three murderous instruments are before us, identifying the sixth and ninth commandments. The tongue, intended as 'a tree of life,' becomes a weapon of death. Who can bear the sin involved in this fearful perversion? Often does the open perjury, as *a sword and sharp arrow*, pierce the fountain of life. And little better are those calumnies and unkind insinuations — all breaches of charity — uttered so freely in common conversation. 'Consider, ye that deal in such conversation, whether you could think of treating the objects of your defamatory discourse, as Jael did Sisera, or as Joab did Abner. Would you shrink with horror at the thought of beating out your neighbor's brains with an hammer, or of piercing his bowels with *a sword, or a sharp arrow?* Why then do you indulge in the like barbarity; destroying as far as you can that reputation, which is dear to men as their life, and wounding all their best interests, by mangling their character? Other injuries a man may wear away or outlive. But defamation, notwithstanding all retrieving circumstances to heal the wound, too often leaves a scar to the dying day."[656]

Genesis 39:14-20 *[Potiphar's wife's lies about Joseph cost him time in prison]* And she spake unto him *[Potiphar]* according to these words, saying, The Hebrew servant, which thou hast brought unto us, came in unto me to mock me: And it came to pass, as I lifted up my voice and cried, that he left his garment with me, and fled out. And it came to pass, when his master heard the words of his wife, which she spake unto him, saying, After this manner did thy servant to me; that his wrath was kindled. And Joseph's master took him, and put him into the prison, a place where the king's prisoners *were* bound: and he was there in the prison.

1 Kings 21:10-13 And set two men, sons of Belial, before him *[Naboth]*, to bear witness against him, saying, Thou didst blaspheme God and the king. And *then* carry him out, and stone him, that he may die. And the men of his city, *even* the elders and the nobles who were the inhabitants in his city, did as Jezebel had sent unto them, *and* as it *was* written in the letters which she had sent unto them. They proclaimed a fast, and set Naboth on high among the people. And there came in two men, children of Belial, and sat before him: and the men of Belial witnessed against him, *even* against Naboth, in the presence of the people, saying, Naboth did blaspheme God and the king. Then they carried him forth out of the city, and stoned him with stones, that he died.

Psalm 50:19-20 Thou givest thy mouth to evil, and thy tongue frameth deceit. Thou sittest *and* speakest against thy brother; thou slanderest thine own mother's son.

Proverbs 12:17-18 *He that* speaketh truth sheweth forth righteousness: but a false witness deceit. There is that speaketh like the piercings of a sword: but the tongue of the wise *is* health.

Proverbs 15:4 A wholesome tongue *is* a tree of life: but perverseness therein *is* a breach in the spirit.

Jeremiah 9:3-9 And they bend their tongues *like* their bow *for* lies: but they are not valiant for the truth upon the earth; for they proceed from evil to evil, and they know not me, saith the LORD. Take ye heed every one of his neighbour, and trust ye not in any brother: for every brother will utterly supplant, and every neighbour will walk with slanders. And they will deceive every one his neighbour, and will not speak the truth: they have taught their tongue to speak lies, *and* weary themselves to commit iniquity. Thine habitation *is* in the midst of deceit; through deceit they refuse to know me, saith the LORD. Therefore thus saith the LORD of hosts, Behold, I will melt them, and try them; for how shall I do for the daughter of my people? Their tongue *is as* an arrow shot out; it speaketh deceit: *one* speaketh peaceably to his neighbour with his mouth, but in heart he layeth his wait. Shall I not visit them for these *things?* saith the LORD: shall not my soul be avenged on such a nation as this?

Matthew 26:59-60 Now the chief priests, and elders, and all the council, sought false witness against Jesus, to put him to death; But found none: yea, though many false witnesses came, *yet* found they none. At the last came two false witnesses.

Proverbs 25:19 Confidence in an unfaithful man in time of trouble *is like* a broken tooth, and a foot out of joint.

Focus: This proverb describes the *personal agony* that results from placing confidence in an unfaithful man in times of distress.

"Confidence" means *trust, refuge, security*. An **"unfaithful man"** is one who *acts treacherously, deceitfully, who deals faithlessly*. There is no confidence to be had **"in an unfaithful man in time of trouble;"** such as when the wheel has come off the wagon and it's too heavy and cumbersome for one person to repair; or as when there's an accident and someone is needed to go for help; or as when rain is coming and the hay has to be put in the barn quickly. In such times, the unfaithful man is *useless,* and *not only useless but personally painful*. The person who places confidence in him to render aid will feel the total pain of disappointment and disability, as though he had **"a broken tooth and a foot out of joint."**

Job 6:14-17 To him that is afflicted pity *should be shewed* from his friend; but he forsaketh the fear of the Almighty. My brethren have dealt deceitfully as a brook, *and* as the stream of brooks they pass away; Which are blackish by reason of the ice, *and* wherein the snow is hid: What time they wax warm, they vanish: when it is hot, they are consumed out of their place.

Psalm 55:12-14 For *it was* not an enemy *that* reproached me; then I could have borne *it:* neither *was it* he that hated me *that* did magnify *himself* against me; then I would have hid myself from him: But *it was* thou, a man mine equal, my guide, and mine acquaintance. We took sweet counsel together, *and* walked unto the house of God in company.

Psalm 118:8-9 *It is* better to trust in the LORD than to put confidence in man. *It is* better to trust in the LORD than to put confidence in princes.

Psalm 146:3-4 Put not your trust in princes, *nor* in the son of man, in whom *there is* no help. His breath goeth forth, he returneth to his earth; in that very day his thoughts perish.

Proverbs 17:17 A friend loveth at all times, and a brother is born for adversity.

Isaiah 36:5-6 I say, *sayest thou,* (but *they are but* vain words) *I have* counsel and strength for war: now on whom dost thou trust, that thou rebellest against me? Lo, thou trustest in the staff of this broken reed, on Egypt; whereon if a man lean, it will go into his hand, and pierce it: so *is* Pharaoh king of Egypt to all that trust in him.

Matthew 26:55-6 In that same hour said Jesus to the multitudes, Are ye come out as against a thief with swords and staves for to take me? I sat daily with you teaching in the temple, and ye laid no hold on me. But all this was done, that the scriptures of the prophets might be fulfilled. Then all the disciples forsook him, and fled.

2 Timothy 4:16 At my first answer no man stood with me, but all *men* forsook me: *I pray God* that it may not be laid to their charge.
[See also Jeremiah 17:5-7; Acts 15:37-40]

Proverbs 25:20 *As* he that taketh away a garment in cold weather, *and as* vinegar upon nitre, so *is* he that singeth songs to an heavy heart.

Focus: This proverb describes the inappropriateness of singing songs to a person in a severe stage of grief.

In order to emphasize that ***singing songs to a heavy heart*** is harmful, the teacher of wisdom first names two separate acts well-known to be harmful. ***(1) Taking away a garment in cold weather*** was sure to cause discomfort and might even cause the owner to freeze to death. **(2)** ***Putting vinegar upon nitre*** caused the nitre to bubble (effervesce) and become useless. With these two acts listed as well-known wrongdoings, the case was made that it is also unwise and harmful to ***sing songs to a heavy heart***.

NOTE: Nitre was thought to have been used during Old Testament times as a cleaning agent, and in cooking, and bread making.[657] In recent times, it has been used as a chief agent in gunpowder and also as fertilizer.[658] Regardless of the specific use, pouring vinegar upon it is destructive.

Because every stage of a **"heavy heart"** *[a grievous, displeased, sad feeling from bad circumstances, depression[659]]* is not the same, a wise person will be sensitive to the level of grief and evaluate whether or not he should even speak to the grieving person. Sometimes it is best to simply walk up and stand beside him, saying nothing. To sing to a severely depressed person would be unwise and cruel. Paul stated that the believer is to "weep with those that weep." (Romans 12:15) At a lesser stage of grief, both words and song would be welcome; however, at all stages, when a person is distressed and heavy-hearted, he needs help from someone sensitive, sympathetic, and consoling. This verse implies that the "heavy heart" is in the deepest, grieving level and that a song would be considered insensitive and perhaps mocking of the sufferer's distress.

Job 2:11-13 Now when Job's three friends heard of all this evil that was come upon him, they came every one from his own place; Eliphaz the Temanite, and Bildad the Shuhite, and Zophar the Naamathite: for they had made an appointment together to come to mourn with him and to comfort him. And when they lifted up their eyes afar off, and knew him not, they lifted up their voice, and wept; and they rent every one his mantle, and sprinkled dust upon their heads toward heaven. So they sat down with him upon the ground seven days and seven nights, and none spake a word unto him: for they saw that *his* grief was very great.

Job 16:1-5 Then Job answered and said, I have heard many such things: miserable comforters *are* ye all. Shall vain words have an end? or what emboldeneth thee that thou answerest? I also could speak as ye *do:* if your soul were in my soul's stead, I could heap up words against you, and shake mine head at you. *But* I would strengthen you with my mouth, and the moving of my lips should assuage *your grief.*

Job 30:31 My harp also is *turned* to mourning, and my organ into the voice of them that weep.

Psalm 137:1-4 By the rivers of Babylon, there we sat down, yea, we wept, when we remembered Zion. We hanged our harps upon the willows in the midst thereof. For there they that carried us away captive required of us a song; and they that wasted us *required of us* mirth, *saying,* Sing us *one* of the songs of Zion. How shall we sing the LORD'S song in a strange land?

Ecclesiastes 3:1,4 To every *thing there is* a season, and a time to every purpose under the heaven:...A time to weep, and a time to laugh; a time to mourn, and a time to dance.

Daniel 6:18 Then the king went to his palace, and passed the night fasting: neither were instruments of musick brought before him: and his sleep went from him.

Romans 12:15 Rejoice with them that do rejoice, and weep with them that weep.

Hebrews 13:3 Remember them that are in bonds, as bound with them; *and* them which suffer adversity, as being yourselves also in the body.

This proverb is another reminder that believers are to have the right spirit and choose the right time and right place when they say or "sing" anything – a choice that requires wisdom and discernment.

Proverbs 25:21-22 If thine enemy be hungry, give him bread to eat; and if he be thirsty, give him water to drink:
22.   For thou shalt heap coals of fire upon his head, and the LORD shall reward thee.

Focus: This proverb (two verses) teaches the righteous method for a wise person to deal with a *personal enemy*.

A person regarded as a *personal **enemy*** demonstrates hate through such actions as making personal derogatory comments, scorning, cursing, lying about, stealing from, or using any other way to attempt to inflict physical or psychological injury. A personal enemy is *not* the same as a national war-time enemy.

The first two clauses of this verse, **"If thine enemy be hungry, give him bread to eat; and if he be thirsty, give him water to drink,"** are straightforward and need no explanation. Such an act of kindness has a consequence stated in the third clause, **"for thou shalt heap coals of fire upon his head." "Coals of fire"** is first mentioned in Leviticus 16:12 concerning one of the prescribed actions of the high priest on the Day of Atonement, "And he shall take a censer full of burning coals of fire from off the altar before the LORD, and his hands full of sweet incense beaten small, and bring it within the veil." The purpose of the high priest putting incense on the coals of fire was to fill the Holy of Holies with the smoke of the incense, which serves as a thin veil between himself and the presence of the Lord, thereby keeping him from dying – "And he *[God]* said, Thou canst not see my face: for there shall no man see me, and live." (Exodus 33:20) Also, the smoke ascended up to God as a sweet-smelling savor meeting His approval for Israel's obedience in performing the sacrifices as instructed. Likewise, just as these named acts are acceptable to God, acts of kindness towards an enemy are also acceptable to God as acts of humble obedience.

By giving food and water to an enemy, one proves that he had rather follow God's directives and be pleasing to Him than to satisfy the fleshly desire for vengeance. Since his acts of kindness are toward someone who is his enemy, the acts done for the enemy will be like incense poured onto **"coals of fire,"** creating a smoke of sweet savor rising to the throne room of God. God will be pleased with his behavior and accept his acts of kindness, forgiveness, and grace, **"and the LORD shall reward thee."** God rewards man in many ways both now and at the judgment seat of Christ.

> "We are not bound to trust our enemies; but we are bound to forgive them. And yet too often our 'love' to them is only ceasing to quarrel with them. If we put off revenge, as inconsistent with our Christian name; yet do we 'put on, as the elect of God, bowels of mercies?...660
>
> Proverbs 24:29 Say not, I will do so to him as he hath done to me: I will render to the man according to his work.
>
> 2 Corinthians 5:10 For we must all appear before the judgment seat of Christ; that every one may receive the things *done* in *his* body, according to that he hath done, whether *it be* good or bad.
>
> Ephesians 4:31-32 Let all bitterness, and wrath, and anger, and clamour, and evil speaking, be put away from you, with all malice: And be ye kind one to another, tenderhearted, forgiving one another, even as God for Christ's sake hath forgiven you.
>
> Colossians 3:12-13 Put on therefore, as the elect of God, holy and beloved, bowels of mercies, kindness, humbleness of mind, meekness, longsuffering; Forbearing one another, and forgiving one another, if any man have a quarrel against any: even as Christ forgave you, so also *do* ye.
>
> Hebrews 11:6 But without faith *it is* impossible to please *him:* for he that cometh to God must believe that he is, and *that* he is a rewarder of them that diligently seek him.

Paul gives a direct reference to this proverb with regard to vengeance:

> Romans 12:19-21 Dearly beloved, avenge not yourselves, but *rather* give place unto wrath: for it is written, Vengeance *is* mine; I will repay, saith the Lord. Therefore if thine enemy hunger, feed him; if he thirst, give him drink: for in so doing thou shalt heap coals of fire on his head. Be not overcome of evil, but overcome evil with good.

These verses from the gospels also give understanding to God's expectations and rewards for His children pursuing peaceful relationships:

Matthew 5:11-12 Blessed are ye, when *men* shall revile you, and persecute *you,* and shall say all manner of evil against you falsely, for my sake. Rejoice, and be exceeding glad: for great *is* your reward in heaven: for so persecuted they the prophets which were before you.

Matthew 5:44-48 But I say unto you, Love your enemies, bless them that curse you, do good to them that hate you, and pray for them which despitefully use you, and persecute you; That ye may be the children of your Father which is in heaven: for he maketh his sun to rise on the evil and on the good, and sendeth rain on the just and on the unjust. For if ye love them which love you, what reward have ye? do not even the publicans the same? And if ye salute your brethren only, what do ye more *than others?* do not even the publicans so? Be ye therefore perfect, even as your Father which is in heaven is perfect.

Luke 6:22 Blessed are ye, when men shall hate you, and when they shall separate you *from their company,* and shall reproach *you,* and cast out your name as evil, for the Son of man's sake. Rejoice ye in that day, and leap for joy: for, behold, your reward *is* great in heaven: for in the like manner did their fathers unto the prophets.

Luke 6:27 But I say unto you which hear, Love your enemies, do good to them which hate you …

Luke 6:35 But love ye your enemies, and do good, and lend, hoping for nothing again; and your reward shall be great, and ye shall be the children of the Highest: for he is kind unto the unthankful and *to* the evil.

Also, in Proverbs 24, there is a warning about the believer's attitude in regard to the "enemy."

Proverbs 24:17-18   Rejoice not when thine enemy falleth, and let not thine heart be glad when he stumbleth: Lest the LORD see *it,* and it displease him, and he turn away his wrath from him.

Hate is *never* to be a part of the Christian's life *nor* is vengeance *nor* is *a glad heart when the enemy stumbles.*

Proverbs 25:23 The north wind driveth away rain: so *doth* an angry countenance a backbiting tongue.

Focus: This proverb instructs as to how to stop backbiting talk without saying a word.

"The north wind driveth away rain" refers to rain from clouds coming off the Mediterranean Sea, likely originating out of the west/northwest. "Fair weather cometh out of the north: with God *is* terrible majesty." (Job 37:22)

"An angry countenance" is an effective means of communicating disapproval. A parent's *look of disapproval* can melt the heart of a good-hearted child who was seeking approval for his improper words or actions. Also, such a look can break the heart of an adult, as did Jesus' look to Peter.

Luke 22:60-62 And Peter said, Man, I know not what thou sayest. And immediately, while he yet spake, the cock crew. And the Lord turned, and looked upon Peter. And Peter remembered the word of the Lord, how he had said unto him, Before the cock crow, thou shalt deny me thrice. And Peter went out, and wept bitterly.

"A backbiting tongue" describes the words of a person who *privately, secretly*, or *maliciously* tells information that damages another's reputation. The information may even be true, yet still damaging. Flimsy excuses for backbiting include: "I was just reacting to a bad experience," or "I was attempting to get the advantage over a hostile situation." Because even good and pleasant conversation can turn to backbiting as quickly as the next thought can come, regretful incidences of backbiting occur in almost everyone's life. Backbiting would not be so common if there were not so many perked ears.

Psalm 101:5 Whoso privily slandereth his neighbour, him will I cut off: him that hath an high look and a proud heart will not I suffer.

"An angry countenance" instantly reveals heartfelt displeasure and has the piercing effect of silencing an evil, slanderous conversation.

Proverbs 25:24 *It is* better to dwell in the corner of the housetop, than with a brawling woman and in a wide house.

Focus: This proverb expresses the misery that a brawling woman can cause.

NOTE: This verse repeats Proverbs 21:9, except this verse has "the corner of the housetop" rather than "a corner of the housetop." Commentary notes are identical for both verses.

***"It is* better to dwell in a corner of the housetop."** Homes in Israel (and in any other country) have the potential for peace and an enjoyable marriage when both husband and wife are focused on pleasing God. Jewish families were expected to submit to God's doctrine on wise living, but obviously, from this verse, both husband and wife did not always do so.

In Solomon's days, houses were built with a flat roof, and protection from falling off was provided by building a battlement (wall) around the top perimeter. This roof was open to the sun and rain, but people would go up for different reasons, including retirement for the day while taking in the evening beauty, or perhaps to sleep, study, meditate, or pray – but in this case, to escape strife from a hostile spouse. On such a rooftop, against the safety wall the Shunammite woman and her husband provided a room for Elisha on the occasions that he passed that way. "Let us make a little chamber, I pray thee, on the wall; and let us set for him there a bed, and a table, and a stool, and a candlestick: and it shall be, when he cometh to us, that he shall turn in thither." (2 Kings 4:10)

"Than with a brawling woman in a wide house." A **"wide"** *[company, society]* is specifically a house large enough to accommodate more than one family, making the escape to "a corner of the housetop," an even greater sacrifice than such an escape would have been from a normal-sized home. Exchanging comfortable spacious rooms with human fellowship for a small corner of isolation (not mentioning having to deal with the weather elements) speaks of just how dire was the situation. However, such action is certainly a desirable alternative to contending with **"a brawling woman."** **"Brawling"** describes her as being contentious and causing strife by which she relentlessly drives out peace *and her husband.*

> Proverbs 19:13 A foolish son is the calamity of his father: and the contentions of a wife are a continual dropping.
> Proverbs 12:4 A virtuous woman is a crown to her husband: but she that maketh ashamed is as rottenness in his bones.
> Proverbs 21:9 It is better to dwell in a corner of the housetop, than with a brawling woman and in a wide house. *[Same as Proverbs 25:24.]*
> Proverbs 27:15-16 A continual dropping in a very rainy day and a contentious woman are alike. Whosoever hideth her hideth the wind, and the ointment of his right hand, which bewrayeth itself.
> Proverbs 15:16-17 Better is little with the fear of the LORD than great treasure and trouble therewith. Better is a dinner of herbs where love is, than a stalled ox and hatred therewith.
> Proverbs 17:1 Better is a dry morsel, and quietness therewith, than an house full of sacrifices with strife.

Proverbs 25:25 *As* cold waters to a thirsty soul, so *is* good news from a far country.

Focus: This proverb depicts the refreshing satisfaction that accompanies sought- after good news.

Notice how this proverb continues the idea given in Proverbs 25:13 – "As the cold of snow in the time of harvest, *so is* a faithful messenger to them that send him: for he refresheth the soul of his masters" and Proverbs 15:30 – "The light of the eyes rejoiceth the heart: and a good report maketh the bones fat."

Communication did not come immediately in those early days as it does today. There were no telephones, no telegraph, and certainly not satellite-reflected, instantaneous news from almost anywhere on earth to almost anywhere else on earth. Texting, cell phones, Internet, and televisions did not exist. Ships were slow, and the information by word of mouth or by letter was often fragmented incomplete information. Nevertheless, **"good news"** that came when a person had been waiting with bated breath to hear from a friend or family member in another country was indeed refreshing.

> Genesis 45:25-28 And they went up out of Egypt, and came into the land of Canaan unto Jacob their father, And told him, saying, Joseph *is* yet alive, and he *is* governor over all the land of Egypt. And Jacob's heart fainted, for he believed them not. And they told him all the words of Joseph, which he had said unto them: and when he saw the wagons which Joseph had sent to carry him, the spirit of Jacob their father revived: And Israel said, *It is* enough; Joseph my son *is* yet alive: I will go and see him before I die.
> Proverbs 13:12 Hope deferred maketh the heart sick: but *when* the desire cometh, *it is* a tree of life.
> Proverbs 15:30 The light of the eyes rejoiceth the heart: *and* a good report maketh the bones fat.

"Good tidings," or **"good news,"** is used twelve times in the Bible. Two of those "good tidings" are listed below:

> Luke 2:10 And the angel said unto them, Fear not: for, behold, I bring you good tidings of great joy, which shall be to all people.
> 1Thessalonians 3:6 But now when Timotheus came from you unto us, and brought us good tidings of your faith and charity, and that ye have good remembrance of us always, desiring greatly to see us, as we also *to see* you: Therefore, brethren, we were comforted over you in all our affliction and distress by your faith: For now we live, if ye stand fast in the Lord.

By way of application, how much more wonderful than any other news is the good news that Jesus Christ has paid the penalty for our sins.

> "Such is the Gospel; it is good news, and glad tidings of good things; it brings the good news of the grace, and favour, and good will of God to men; of his appointment and provision of a Saviour for them; of the incarnation of Christ; of salvation being wrought out by him for the chief of sinners, which is free, full, and for ever; and of peace, pardon, righteousness, and eternal life, through him, And this comes 'from a far country'; from heaven, the better country than Canaan, which was a type of it, or any country in this world, and which is afar from hence; the Gospel comes from God in heaven, and it is a report concerning that; it is good news to saints, of an estate they have there, an inheritance, a house, a city and kingdom prepared for them there: this news is brought by the prophets of the Old Testament, who diligently inquired of salvation by Christ; by the angels at Christ's incarnation; by John the Baptist, the forerunner of Christ; by Christ himself, who was anointed to preach good tidings to the meek; and by his apostles, and all the faithful ministers of the word: and the message they bring is good news; not to carnal and self-righteous persons, but to sensible sinners; and to them it is as cold waters to a weary or thirsty soul; it assuages the heat of the law, and the wrath that works in the conscience; it quenches the thirst of carnal things, and after a man's own righteousness; it revives and refreshes his weary drooping spirits, and fills him with a joy unspeakable and full of glory; as Jacob's spirits were revived on hearing the good news of Joseph, Genesis 45:26."[661]

Isaiah 52:7 How beautiful upon the mountains are the feet of him that bringeth good tidings, that publisheth peace; that bringeth good tidings of good, that publisheth salvation; that saith unto Zion, Thy God reigneth!

Romans 10:15 And how shall they preach, except they be sent? as it is written, How beautiful are the feet of them that preach the gospel of peace, and bring glad tidings of good things!

Proverbs 25:26 A righteous man falling down before the wicked *is as* a troubled fountain, and a corrupt spring.

Focus: This proverb depicts the shocking and disastrous impact on others when a righteous man yields himself to wicked people or complies with their sinful behavior.

A **righteous** man is at peace with God. His relationship with God is reflected in his honest conduct, calm speech, godly character, and his total lifestyle of walking with God. Other believers anchor in him, drawing strength and calmness as he lives out God's standard of holiness. Proverbs 10:11 describes his wisdom by saying that his mouth "is a well of life." When such a person *falls down* [yields to, cringes[662]] **before** the wicked for any reason, the consequence to those who relied on him for an example, anchor, and guidance is severe emotional disappointment and spiritual turbulence. The Ancient Hebrew pictograph of a **"righteous man falling down"** is described by Jeff Benner as a green branch that contains water and is flexible. It can be bent into any shape and then left to dry in that shape.[663] So is a man who falls down to the wicked. He can no longer stand erect, eyes glistening, voice strong, as a testimony of a choice, sturdy vessel for God. Instead, he has "conformed to this world." (Romans 12:2)

Those who once considered him a faithful and trusted source of spiritual strength like a peaceful, pure, good, life-giving water source now find **"a troubled fountain"** or "corrupt spring" – agitated, filthy, and unfit to drink. Righteous men are expected to draw their strength, motivation, and direction from God, not to succumb to fear, fatigue, finances, females, false prophets, or any other form of allurement that could cause a person *to bow in humiliation before the wicked*. He cannot allow himself to be lured or even terrified into any of their awful, rebellious, God-dishonoring conduct. He cannot pity them for their weaknesses, excuse their sins, and neither can he display a hateful, overbearing spirit. He must be humble and remain strong at the same time.

2 Samuel 12:9 Wherefore hast thou *[David]* despised the commandment of the LORD, to do evil in his sight? thou hast killed Uriah the Hittite with the sword, and hast taken his wife *to be* thy wife, and hast slain him with the sword of the children of Ammon.

1 Kings 11:6-8 And Solomon did evil in the sight of the LORD, and went not fully after the LORD, as *did* David his father. Then did Solomon build an high place for Chemosh, the abomination of Moab, in the hill that *is* before Jerusalem, and for Molech, the abomination of the children of Ammon. And likewise did he for all his strange wives, which burnt incense and sacrificed unto their gods.

2 Kings 18:15-16 And Hezekiah gave *him [Sennacherib king of Assyria]* all the silver that was found in the house of the LORD, and in the treasures of the king's house. At that time did Hezekiah cut off *the gold from* the doors of the temple of the LORD, and *from* the pillars which Hezekiah king of Judah had overlaid, and gave it to the king of Assyria.

Proverbs 10:11 The mouth of a righteous *man is* a well of life: but violence covereth the mouth of the wicked.

Proverbs 10:25 As the whirlwind passeth, so *is* the wicked no *more:* but the righteous *is* an everlasting foundation.

Proverbs 10:28 The hope of the righteous *shall be* gladness: but the expectation of the wicked shall perish.

Proverbs 10:30 The righteous shall never be removed: but the wicked shall not inhabit the earth.

Proverbs 12:3 A man shall not be established by wickedness: but the root of the righteous shall not be moved.

Proverbs 12:7 The wicked are overthrown, and *are* not: but the house of the righteous shall stand.

Proverbs 14:19 The evil bow before the good; and the wicked at the gates of the righteous.

Ezekiel 32:2 Son of man, take up a lamentation for Pharaoh king of Egypt, and say unto him, Thou art like a young lion of the nations, and thou *art* as a whale in the seas: and thou camest forth with thy rivers, and troubledst the waters with thy feet, and fouledst their rivers.

Matthew 26:69, 74 Now Peter sat without in the palace: and a damsel came unto him, saying, Thou also wast with Jesus of Galilee. But he denied before *them* all, saying, I know not what thou sayest . . . Then began he to curse and to swear, *saying,* I know not the man. And immediately the cock crew.

2 Timothy 4:10 For Demas hath forsaken me, having loved this present world, and is departed unto Thessalonica; Crescens to Galatia, Titus unto Dalmatia.

Proverbs 25:27 *It is* not good to eat much honey: so *for men* to search their own glory *is not* glory.

Focus: This proverb illustrates the repugnancy of self-induced glory.

Most men like to hear their own name spoken in praise, and hearing their name praised is like enjoying the sweetness of honey; but the ill effects of too much, in both cases, are repugnant. It is especially repugnant when the individual elicits praise.

Proverbs 25:16 Hast thou found honey? eat so much as is sufficient for thee, lest thou be filled therewith, and vomit it.

"... there is an extreme; and to that extreme Solomon here refers. There is such a thing as vain glory. There is such a thing as a person's indulging an insatiable appetite for applause and honour. There is such a thing as 'searching it out,' looking ever after it, eager to get it, and touchily jealous of every omission to bestow it and every deficiency in its amount; exploring for it in every possible direction; listening with an ear on the alert to catch every breathing of adulation; fishing for praise; throwing out hints to draw it forth; eulogizing others, to tempt a return; saying things in disparagement of oneself, for the sake of having them contradicted,-things which, said by another, would stir the hottest of his blood . . . A man's honour should rather come to him, than be eagerly solicited and searched for. It should not be made his object. If we follow the example of Jesus, we shall seek God's glory as our first and constant aim, not our own. And this is the way to true glory; for He says – 'him that honoureth me I will honour.'"[664]

Better that a man should privately seek God's approval than to encourage honor and recognition from others. If others give praise, it should not be because it was sought after.

Proverbs 20:6 Most men will proclaim every one his own goodness: but a faithful man who can find?

Proverbs 27:2 Let another man praise thee, and not thine own mouth; a stranger, and not thine own lips.

Luke 18:10-14 Two men went up into the temple to pray; the one a Pharisee, and the other a publican. The Pharisee stood and prayed thus with himself, God, I thank thee, that I am not as other men *are,* extortioners, unjust, adulterers, or even as this publican. I fast twice in the week, I give tithes of all that I possess. And the publican, standing afar off, would not lift up so much as *his* eyes unto heaven, but smote upon his breast, saying, God be merciful to me a sinner. I tell you, this man went down to his house justified *rather* than the other: for every one that exalteth himself shall be abased; and he that humbleth himself shall be exalted.

John 5:44 How can ye believe, which receive honour one of another, and seek not the honour that *cometh* from God only?

John 7:18 He that speaketh of himself seeketh his own glory: but he that seeketh his glory that sent him, the same is true, and no unrighteousness is in him.

John 12:43 For they loved the praise of men more than the praise of God.

Roman 12:10 *Be* kindly affectioned one to another with brotherly love; in honour preferring one another . . .

1 Corinthians 15:9 For I am the least of the apostles, that am not meet to be called an apostle, because I persecuted the church of God.

Galatians 5:26 Let us not be desirous of vain glory, provoking one another, envying one another.

Philippians 2:3 *Let* nothing *be done* through strife or vainglory; but in lowliness of mind let each esteem other better than themselves.

1 Peter 5:5 Likewise, ye younger, submit yourselves unto the elder. Yea, all *of you* be subject one to another, and be clothed with humility: for God resisteth the proud, and giveth grace to the humble.

Proverbs 25:28 He that *hath* no rule over his own spirit *is like* a city *that is* broken down, *and* without walls.

Focus: This proverb compares the lack of self-control to an overrun, defenseless city.

"Without walls" clarifies the meaning of the phrase **"a city that is broken down."** In those early cities, walls were the primary defense. The size and complexity of the wall depended on several factors, including the severity of the threat and the extent of desire for safety. Some city walls had moats around them and were high enough to prevent scaling, guarded by sentries, and wide enough to run chariots atop. They prevented, or at least deterred, unwanted encroachment by enemies. Likewise, a wise man of character establishes Scriptural rules of behavior to prevent anyone from gaining control of his temperament and forcing an unrestrained emotional reaction from him. *He rules his own spirit because he is a person of self-control.* Wise men learn *to act* on what they know is right to control themselves in volatile situations rather than *to react* and have situations erupt out of control. Someone suggested that 90 percent of our problems are caused by spontaneous *reactions* to situations rather than thinking, gathering facts, asking God for help, and then *acting* in an intelligent reasonable manner.

A man who has **"no rule** *[no restraint or control]* **over his own spirit"** allows his emotions to control his behavior, especially in anger. He "feels" rather than "thinks," and he has no godly principles to live by. Temptation beckons, and he responds. Bad thoughts come, and he entertains them. If someone irritates him, he dives into a fight without thought. *The wall of his soul is flattened, and enemies come in and jerk him whichever way they desire.*

Satan easily takes advantage of such a person. By throwing the slightest spark into his combustible spirit, Satan can inspire him to sin and make him the unconscious instrument of his evil purposes. By indulging in an angry spirit, a man "gives place" to the devil. His spiritual state is continually in imminent danger. His soul is exposed to every assault of the enemy and is in peril of being overrun, **"like a city that is broken down,** *and* **without walls."**

> 1 Samuel 20:30 Then Saul's anger was kindled against Jonathan, and he said unto him, Thou son of the perverse rebellious *woman*, do not I know that thou hast chosen the son of Jesse to thine own confusion, and unto the confusion of thy mother's nakedness?
>
> 1 Samuel 25:17 Now therefore know and consider what thou wilt do; for evil is determined against our master, and against all his household: for he *is such* a son of Belial, that *a man* cannot speak to him.
>
> Proverbs 16:32 *He that is* slow to anger *is* better than the mighty; and he that ruleth his spirit than he that taketh a city.
>
> Proverbs 22:24 Make no friendship with an angry man; and with a furious man thou shalt not go:
>
> Romans 12:19 Dearly beloved, avenge not yourselves, but *rather* give place unto wrath: for it is written, Vengeance *is* mine; I will repay, saith the Lord.
>
> Ephesians 4:27 Neither give place to the devil.
>
> 1 Timothy 2:8 I will therefore that men pray every where, lifting up holy hands, without wrath and doubting.

CHAPTER TWENTY-SIX

> **Proverbs 26:1** As snow in summer, and as rain in harvest, so honour is not seemly for a fool.

Focus: This proverb declares the inappropriateness of honoring the fool.

To the Hebrew, **"Snow in summer"** or **"rain in harvest"** would perhaps have been considered supernatural or even a curse – very strange, to say the least, and potentially damaging to their crops. Either situation would have been shocking, a great surprise to see, in addition to being destructive. People would have wondered if God were trying to tell them of their errors.

> 1 Samuel 12:16-17 Now therefore stand and see this great thing, which the LORD will do before your eyes. *Is it* not wheat harvest to day? I will call unto the LORD, and he shall send thunder and rain; that ye may perceive and see that your wickedness *is* great, which ye have done in the sight of the LORD, in asking you a king.

Using these weird weather happenings to illustrate inappropriateness, Solomon moves on to say that **honoring a fool** is also an inappropriate event. Doing so is like putting whipped cream on an onion. To honor a fool is **"not seemly"** *[not suitable]*; and, except for verse 2, the first twelve verses of this chapter describe interactions with a fool that reinforce the absolute inappropriateness of giving him honor.

> **"So honour is not seemly for a fool:"** for a wicked man; such should not be favoured by kings, and set in high places of honour and trust . . . and they are as hurtful and pernicious, since they discourage virtue and encourage vice, and hinder the prosperity of the commonwealth; such vile persons are contemned in the eyes of good men, and are disregarded of God . . .[665]

Scriptures declare the following various characteristics of a fool. He has no godly wisdom, is void of understanding (empty-headed), wise in his own conceit, and is a liar. He does not listen to counsel or regard reproof, and his actions show that he enjoys strife. There are forty-one verses about the fool in Proverbs and sixty-nine in all of the Bible. Below are a few descriptive verses.

> Psalm 14:1 The fool hath said in his heart, *There is* no God. They are corrupt, they have done abominable works, *there is* none that doeth good.
> Proverbs 10:10 He that winketh with the eye causeth sorrow: but a prating fool shall fall.
> Proverbs 10:13 In the lips of him that hath understanding wisdom is found: but a rod *is* for the back of him that is void of understanding.
> Proverbs 10:18 He that hideth hatred *with* lying lips, and he that uttereth a slander, *is* a fool.
> Proverbs 10:23 *It is* as sport to a fool to do mischief: but a man of understanding hath wisdom.
> Proverbs 12:15 The way of a fool *is* right in his own eyes: but he that hearkeneth unto counsel *is* wise.
> Proverbs 13:16 Every prudent *man* dealeth with knowledge: but a fool layeth open *his* folly.
> Proverbs 14:3 In the mouth of the foolish *is* a rod of pride: but the lips of the wise shall preserve them.
> Proverbs 14:16 A wise *man* feareth, and departeth from evil: but the fool rageth, and is confident.
> Proverbs 15:5 A fool despiseth his father's instruction: but he that regardeth reproof is prudent.
> Proverbs 19:10 Delight is not seemly for a fool; much less for a servant to have rule over princes.
> Proverbs 20:3 *It is* an honour for a man to cease from strife: but every fool will be meddling.
> Proverbs 26:12 Seest thou a man wise in his own conceit? *there is* more hope of a fool than of him.

"Over the last century or so, we have witnessed a fair amount of honor lavished upon atheistic scientists such as Linus Pauling, Charles Darwin, and Sigmund Freud. Given another hundred years or so, the world may come to fully understand the true extent of their errors (even in their so-called scientific discoveries). The unabashed, enthusiastic endorsement of these fools on the part of the reigning scientific establishment may prove to be far more destructive than any of us could imagine . . . "[666] (Article is dated 26 April 2018.)

"Honor is not seemly for a fool" because he, first of all, does not deserve it. His folly is only increased through this form of approval. If such honor gives him authority, he will undoubtedly use it to discourage righteousness, give credibility to evil, and gather other fools around himself to further strengthen his destructive acts. His work hinders the blessing of God, quality of life, and justice. Wise people shun him.

Proverbs 26:2 As the bird by wandering, as the swallow by flying, so the curse causeless shall not come.

Focus: This proverb utilizes a bird's erratic flight to illustrate the ineffectiveness of a causeless curse.

A **"curse"** is "a prayer for injury, harm, or misfortune to befall another."[667] A **"causeless"** *[undeserved, without cause]* curse is like a wandering bird or a flying swallow that darts about overhead but never lights – **"the curse causeless shall not come."**

> "The folly of passion . . . makes men scatter *causeless curses,* wishing ill to others upon presumption that they are bad and have done ill, when either they mistake the person or misunderstand the fact, or they call evil good and good evil. Give honour to a fool, and he thunders out his anathemas against all that he is disgusted with, right or wrong. Great men, when wicked, think they have a privilege to keep those about them in awe, by cursing them, and swearing at them, which yet is an expression of the most impotent malice and shows their weakness as much as their wickedness.
>
> The safety of innocency – He that is cursed without cause, whether by furious imprecations or solemn anathemas, the curse shall do him no more harm than the bird that flies over his head, than Goliath's curses did to David, 1Samuel 17:43. It will fly away like the sparrow or the wild dove, which go nobody knows where, till they return to their proper place, as the curse will at length return upon the head of him that uttered it."[668]

Following are Biblical instances of causeless curses that had no effect.

1. Balak, king of Moab, hired the wicked prophet Balaam to curse the nation of Israel. God would not honor his evil request, and the curse was powerless.

   Numbers 22:5-6 He *[King Balak]* sent messengers therefore unto Balaam the son of Beor to Pethor, which *is* by the river of the land of the children of his people, to call him, saying, Behold, there is a people come out from Egypt: behold, they cover the face of the earth, and they abide over against me: Come now therefore, I pray thee, curse me this people; for they *are* too mighty for me: peradventure I shall prevail, *that* we may smite them, and *that* I may drive them out of the land: for I wot that he whom thou blessest *is* blessed, and he whom thou cursest is cursed.

2. Goliath's and Shimei's curses did not harm David, nor did the curse of Jeremiah's enemies.

   1 Samuel 17:43 And the Philistine said unto David, *Am* I a dog, that thou comest to me with staves? And the Philistine cursed David by his gods.

   2Samuel 16:11-12 And David said to Abishai, and to all his servants, Behold, my son, which came forth of my bowels, seeketh my life: how much more now *may this* Benjamite *do it?* let him alone, and let him curse; for the LORD hath bidden him. It may be that the LORD will look on mine affliction, and that the LORD will requite me good for his cursing this day.

   Jeremiah 15:10 Woe is me, my mother, that thou hast borne me a man of strife and a man of contention to the whole earth! I have neither lent on usury, nor men have lent to me on usury; *yet* every one of them doth curse me. The LORD said, Verily it shall be well with thy remnant; verily I will cause the enemy to entreat thee *well* in the time of evil and in the time of affliction.

The following are Biblical examples of righteous curses with just cause.

1. Jotham's curse came upon Abimelech and the men of Shechem because it was righteous.

   Judges 9:55-57 And when the men of Israel saw that Abimelech was dead, they departed every man unto his place. Thus God rendered the wickedness of Abimelech, which he did unto his father, in slaying his seventy brethren: And all the evil of the men of Shechem did God render upon their heads: and upon them came the curse of Jotham the son of Jerubbaal.

2. Elisha's curse came to the young mockers of Bethel because it was righteous.

   2Kings 2:23-24 And he went up from thence unto Bethel: and as he was going up by the way, there came forth little children out of the city, and mocked him, and said unto him, Go up, thou bald head; go up, thou bald head. And he turned back, and looked on them, and cursed them in the name of the LORD. And there came forth two she bears out of the wood, and tare forty and two children of them.

3. Joshua's curse came upon Jericho because the reason for the curse was righteous.

   Joshua 6:26 And Joshua adjured *them* at that time, saying, Cursed *be* the man before the LORD, that riseth up and buildeth this city Jericho: he shall lay the foundation thereof in his firstborn, and in his youngest *son* shall he set up the gates of it.

   1Kings 16:34 In his days did Hiel the Bethelite build Jericho: he laid the foundation thereof in Abiram his firstborn, and set up the gates thereof in his youngest *son* Segub, according to the word of the LORD, which he spake by Joshua the son of Nun.

4. The LORD's curse is upon the wicked. His curse is certainly righteous, but there is no fear of impending judgment for those whose sins are forgiven.
   Proverbs 3:33 The curse of the LORD *is* in the house of the wicked: but he blesseth the habitation of the just.
   Romans 8:1 *There is* therefore now no condemnation to them which are in Christ Jesus, who walk not after the flesh, but after the Spirit.
   John 3:17-18 For God sent not his Son into the world to condemn the world; but that the world through him might be saved. He that believeth on him is not condemned: but he that believeth not is condemned already, because he hath not believed in the name of the only begotten Son of God.

Christians need never fear curses from others and should have such peace and mercy enough to pray for those who curse them.
   Matthew 5:44 But I say unto you, Love your enemies, bless them that curse you, do good to them that hate you, and pray for them which despitefully use you, and persecute you; That ye may be the children of your Father which is in heaven: for he maketh his sun to rise on the evil and on the good, and sendeth rain on the just and on the unjust.

Proverbs 26:3   A whip for the horse, a bridle for the ass, and a rod for the fool's back.

Focus: This proverb compares the necessary methods of controlling animals with the method necessary for controlling a fool.

Men are not typically compared to obstinate animals, as in this proverb, because man was created with a higher intellect. However, it is not the **"fool's"** intellect that is in question, but his silliness, arrogance, and stubbornness. A whip is an instrument that some use on a stubborn horse, and the bridle is used to control the obstinate donkey. A fool has to be treated harshly because of his unwillingness to conduct himself in a manner that allows honorable and peaceful communication. Because of his self-conceited rebellion, pain and restraint *regretfully* replace words. A "rod" is an actual instrument of correction, but is also symbolic for other means of correction.
   Psalm 32:8-9 I will instruct thee and teach thee in the way which thou shalt go: I will guide thee with mine eye. Be ye not as the horse, or as the mule, which have no understanding: whose mouth must be held in with bit and bridle, lest they come near unto thee.
   Proverbs 10:13 In the lips of him that hath understanding wisdom is found: but a rod is for the back of him that is void of understanding.
   Proverbs 14:3 In the mouth of the foolish is a rod of pride: but the lips of the wise shall preserve them.
   Proverbs 19:29 Judgments are prepared for scorners, and stripes for the back of fools.

Proverbs 26: 4-5   Answer not a fool according to his folly, lest thou also be like unto him.
5. Answer a fool according to his folly, lest he be wise in his own conceit.

Focus: This two-verse proverb teaches the risk of answering a fool and the proper reasoning and timing to take such a risk.

In order to understand the instruction of this seemingly contradictory proverb, the reader must understand the meaning of **"folly"** *[silliness, foolishness]*. Folly within a person causes him to talk and act in a way that challenges good sense and sound reasoning. He is likely to be irrational in both thought and action. Anyone attempting to communicate with such a volatile person must understand the danger involved. **"Answer not a fool"** (verse 4) *if* responding will draw the believer into the folly that the fool is demonstrating, or in other words, **"lest thou also be like unto him."** If the fool is screaming in a rage, a wise person will not engage in a conversation with him because doing so might regretfully result in responsive screaming. If the fool brags or exaggerates the truth or ridicules others, the wise will remove himself and not be drawn into "like" communication.

Answering a fool (verse 5) is a proper response *if* responding can prevent him from becoming **"wise in his own conceit,"** meaning *wise in his own mind.* Self-conceit gives him energy, boldness, and false confidence that fuels his irrational conversation. With enlarged self-conceit, he thus strongly believes that his folly is right. His foolishness might be blaspheming God or guiding people to do evil acts that present danger to the young and impressionable. In that case, he should be challenged with the strength of wisdom. A wise, challenging response could prevent the spread of his mischief.

> "Silence may sometimes be mistaken for defeat. Unanswered words may be deemed unanswerable, and *the fool* become arrogant, more and more *wise in his own conceit*. An *answer* therefore may be called for; yet not in folly, but to folly; not in his foolish manner, but in the manner which his foolishness required; *not according to his folly*, but according to thine own wisdom. Yet here, our words would be sharp as rods. The fool's back needs them. Such was Job's answer to his wife; grave, convincing, silencing – 'Thou speakest as one of *the foolish* women speaketh. What! shall we receive good at the hand of God, and shall we not receive evil?' (Job 2:9-10) Oh! for wisdom to govern the tongue; to discover 'the time to keep silence, and the time to speak' (Ecclesiastes 3:7); most of all to suggest the 'word fitly spoken' (Proverbs 15:23; 25:11) for effective reproof! How instructive is the pattern of our great Master! His silence and his answers were equally worthy of Himself. The former always conveyed a dignified rebuke. The latter issued in the confusion of his captious enemies."[669]

Proverbs 23:9 Speak not in the ears of a fool: for he will despise the wisdom of thy words.

Proverbs 29:9 *If* a wise man contendeth with a foolish man, whether he rage or laugh, *there is* no rest.

Ecclesiastes 3:7 A time to rend, and a time to sew; a time to keep silence, and a time to speak…

Isaiah 5:21 Woe unto *them that are* wise in their own eyes, and prudent in their own sight!

John 8:3-7 And the scribes and Pharisees brought unto him a woman taken in adultery; and when they had set her in the midst, They say unto him, Master, this woman was taken in adultery, in the very act. This they said, tempting him, that they might have to accuse him. But Jesus stooped down, and with *his* finger wrote on the ground, *as though he heard them not.* So when they continued asking him, he lifted up himself, and said unto them, He that is without sin among you, let him first cast a stone at her.

Luke 20:8 And Jesus said unto them, Neither tell I you by what authority I do these things.

Colossians 4:6 Let your speech *be* alway with grace, seasoned with salt, that ye may know how ye ought to answer every man.

1 Peter 3:9-11 Not rendering evil for evil, or railing for railing: but contrariwise blessing; knowing that ye are thereunto called, that ye should inherit a blessing. For he that will love life, and see good days, let him refrain his tongue from evil, and his lips that they speak no guile: Let him eschew evil, and do good; let him seek peace, and ensue it.

Proverbs 26:6 He that sendeth a message by the hand of a fool cutteth off the feet, *and* drinketh damage.

Focus: This proverb, by use of hyperboles, expresses the severity of personal damage that can result from trusting a fool to responsibly carry out an important matter.

Sending a message by the hand of a fool is a dangerous act of misplaced trust. The repercussions of such an act are expressed in exaggerated terms **(cutting off the feet)** to enhance the understanding of this seriously bad decision. **Cutting off the** (the sender's) **feet** expresses the idea that the sender will suffer severe consequences. In order to adequately express the severity of this mistake, the proverb further states that the sender *drinks damage*.

> "*Drinking,* it must be observed, in the Scriptures, frequently signifies the doing or receiving of any thing *plentifully,* as they who multiply sins are said to *drink iniquity like water,* and they who are greatly afflicted are commonly said to *drink the cup of sorrow.*"[670]

In a day when the primary mode of transportation was walking, **cutting off the feet** was equivalent to cutting off almost all means of mobility. Indeed, one would have no longer been able to care for himself; and in addition to being immobile, he would have destroyed his business, created unnecessary severe pain, and probably made himself into a beggar.

To say that a person trusting a fool **"drinketh damage"** is another hyperbole that gives a word picture of a person pulling his head back in a sword swallowing position, opening his mouth as wide open as possible, and pouring in "damage." Examples of damage from trusting the fool might be: loss of a good reputation, decreased business, destroyed relationships, and possibly financial insolvency. Imagine what would happen if the foolish messenger were carrying a message of diplomatic importance to another country.

The fool has an opposite value system from the wise; consequently, he proves to be absolutely unreliable when trusted. He does not comprehend the importance of situations or the value of relationships as does the wise person; consequently, destruction dogs him.

Proverbs 26:7 The legs of the lame are not equal: so *is* a parable in the mouth of fools.

Focus: This proverb expresses the extreme awkwardness of a fool trying to utilize the wisdom of a parable.

The fool of verse 6 cannot be trusted with a message, and the fool of verse 7 cannot be trusted to speak a parable. He bungles everything he tries to do because he has refused wisdom.

"The legs of the lame are not equal," making it obvious to every onlooker that his legs are defective. He cannot walk in a normal fashion, if at all. If he were to attempt to dance, every observer would notice the difficulty, the awkwardness, and the painful struggle.

"So is a parable in the mouth of fools," means that the fool's reasoning ability and understanding are obviously defective, *like* the lame man's legs are defective. In comparing the speaking of a parable by a fool to the defective legs of a lame man, this verse reveals that a fool *[dullard, silly person]* shows his ignorance, inability, and wickedness when he tries to talk about or explain the mystery of a parable. The entire picture is one of dysfunction. The ungodly fool tries to express godly wisdom from a sinful heart, defective reasoning, and without understanding.

> "A fool fails in the exhibition; he misses the point of the wise saying which he produces; it falls lame from his mouth, affords no instruction to others, and makes no way with its hearers."[671]
>
> Psalm 64:8 So they shall make their own tongue to fall upon themselves: all that see them shall flee away.
>
> Proverbs 17:7 Excellent speech becometh not a fool: much less do lying lips a prince.
>
> Proverbs 26:9 *As* a thorn goeth up into the hand of a drunkard, so *is* a parable in the mouth of fools.

Proverbs 26:8 As he that bindeth a stone in a sling, so *is* he that giveth honour to a fool.

Focus: This proverb compares the throwing away of honor by placing it on a fool to flinging away of a stone with a slingshot.

To bind **"a stone in a sling"** means firmly fixing a chosen stone into a slingshot pouch. The stone is then bound into the material by folding it over the stone, thus creating a pocket for the stone. Both ends of the sling's two strings are then grasped with one hand and swung in a circular motion until the desired momentum is reached. Then, one of the strings is released at the correct position of the circular swing, whereby the stone will fly towards the target. If the stone fails to strike the target, it is unlikely to be found again, joining other undiscoverable stones.

Honoring a fool is like placing a stone into a sling. Both the stone and the honor are thrown away, never to be recovered. Like the stone thrust from the sling, the fool and the honor heaped on him soon part company, and they are seen no more together. Remember the words of Romans 13:7 – "Render therefore to all their dues: tribute to whom tribute *is due;* custom to whom custom; fear to whom fear; honour to whom honour." Honor certainly does not belong to a fool.

> Proverbs 26:1 As snow in summer, and as rain in harvest, so honour is not seemly for a fool.

Honor ceases to sparkle after being placed on a fool's head, and afterward no deserving person would want the tarnished crown. To prevent unnecessary damage within the church, Paul instructed Timothy in 1 Timothy 5:22 – "Lay hands suddenly on no man, neither be partaker of other men's sins: keep thyself pure."

Proverbs 26:9 *As* a thorn goeth up into the hand of a drunkard, so *is* a parable in the mouth of fools.

Focus: This proverb expresses the insensitivity that a fool has to the wisdom of a parable.

A **"drunkard"** is daily dedicated to alcohol consumption and remains in an impaired mental state. He is barely sensitive to pain and probably will only moderately feel the pain of a thorn as it is forced up into his hand; but if drunk enough, he would not have the mental faculties to respond or remember the event. The definition of the Hebrew word for "thorn" also includes the *thornbush.* Imagine a drunkard wielding a large thorn, or worse, a thornbush, like a weapon. The skin tears might not be very painful at the time, and he probably would not remember doing it, except for the cuts and dried blood. Barnes writes: "As such a weapon so used may do mischief to the man himself or to others, so may the sharp, keen-edged proverb when used by one who does not understand it."[672]

A fool, like the drunkard, is dedicated, not necessarily to alcohol, but to folly. He is insensitive and annoyed with wisdom. Though he hears "a parable," his state of spiritual stupor causes him to dismiss the same. He can neither respond properly, nor understand, nor retain it in his memory; and certainly cannot speak the same.

> "...A fool handling the maxims of wisdom is like a drunken man handling thorns. The drunkard, not knowing what he is about, lays hold of them rashly and recklessly, and thus wounds himself: – so the fool wounds himself by his manner of using the sayings of the wise. He confirms his reputation for folly; he exposes himself to pity or scorn; or even, inadvertently, from not at all perceiving how the use he is making of some one of them recoils upon himself, he pronounces his own verdict of culpability and condemnation; or still further, when attempting to bring a proverbial or pithy saying to bear on the support of his own cause, he blunders, by the misapplication of it, into a conclusion the very opposite of what he intended. He lays down principles that, in the eyes of every one who hears him, go to condemn himself, without his being in the least degree sensible of it. The thorn, ere he is aware, has 'gone up into his hand,' and the pain and the blood discover to him his folly."[673]

Proverbs 26:10 The great *God* that formed all *things* both rewardeth the fool, and rewardeth transgressors.

Focus: This proverb supports the fact that since God created all things, He is justified in determining the appropriate retribution for those who oppose Him.

This first clause, **"the great *God* that formed all *things*,"** reiterates the historical truth of creation taken initially from the first few pages of Scripture. *"God"* is in italics showing that "God" was not specified in the Hebrew text of this verse and was added by the King James translators. Only God **"formed all *things*;"** consequently, the translation makes perfect sense and is reliably accurate.

> Genesis 1:1 In the beginning God created the heaven and the earth.
> Colossians 1:16 For by him were all things created, that are in heaven, and that are in earth, visible and invisible, whether *they be* thrones, or dominions, or principalities, or powers: all things were created by him, and for him . . .
> Revelation 4:11 Thou art worthy, O Lord, to receive glory and honour and power: for thou hast created all things, and for thy pleasure they are and were created. *[See also Exodus 20:11; 2 Chronicles 2:12; Nehemiah 9:6; Psalm 33:9, 102:25, 124:8; 148:5; Proverbs 8:23-32; Isaiah 40:26, 40:28; Jeremiah 10:11, 27:5, 32:17, 51:15; John 1:1-3; Acts 14:15; 17:24; Romans 1:25; Ephesians 3:9; Colossians 1:16-17; Hebrews 1:2, 1:10, 11:3; 1 Peter 4:19.]*

God **"both rewardeth the fool, and rewardeth transgressors."** The primary difference between "the fool" and "transgressors" is that "the fool" blatantly opposes God and godly wisdom, while "transgressors" specifically oppose and violate the commandments of God. They both choose the bad path of opposing God and ultimately earn an appropriately bad reward. Nonetheless, God graciously allows mankind the freedom to believe and trust Him or to reject Him and His word. **"Rewards"** is translated from the Hebrew *sakar [to hire, to earn wages]*. God pays "the fool" and "transgressors" according to their wicked labor. Men are punished by God for their sins.

> Psalm 28:4-5 Give them according to their deeds, and according to the wickedness of their endeavours: give them after the work of their hands; render to them their desert. Because they regard not the works of the LORD, nor the operation of his hands, he shall destroy them, and not build them up.
> Psalm 62:12 Also unto thee, O Lord, *belongeth* mercy: for thou renderest to every man according to his work.
> Psalm 91:8 Only with thine eyes shalt thou behold and see the reward of the wicked.
> Matthew 16:27 For the Son of man shall come in the glory of his Father with his angels; and then he shall reward every man according to his works.
> Romans 2:5 But after thy hardness and impenitent heart treasurest up unto thyself wrath against the day of wrath and revelation of the righteous judgment of God; Who will render to every man according to his deeds: . . .
> Revelation 2:23 And I will kill her children with death; and all the churches shall know that I am he which searcheth the reins and hearts: and I will give unto every one of you according to your works.
> Revelation 20:11-15 And I saw a great white throne, and him that sat on it, from whose face the earth and the heaven fled away; and there was found no place for them. And I saw the dead, small and great, stand before God; and the books were opened: and another book was opened, which is the book of life: and the dead were judged out of those things which were written in the books, according to their works. And the sea gave up the dead which were in it; and death and hell delivered up the dead which were in them: and they were judged every man according to their works. And death and hell were cast into the lake of fire. This is the second death. And whosoever was not found written in the book of life was cast into the lake of fire.

Revelation 22:12 And, behold, I come quickly; and my reward is with me, to give every man according as his work shall be. *[See also Ecclesiastes 12:14; Isaiah 65:12; 66:4; Jeremiah 17:10; 32:19.]*

One of God's characteristics is that he is equitable, and He will certainly reward mankind in an equitable fashion. (Proverbs 1:3)

Proverbs 26:11 As a dog returneth to his vomit, so a fool returneth to his folly.

Focus: This proverb illustrates the fool's nonsense that leads him to keep repeating the sins that define him as a fool.

A dog returns to his vomit because he obviously views it as a food source and cannot discern the difference between it and fresh, good food. He does not understand that something within that vomit likely made him sick. Likewise, the ***fool returns to his folly*** because he does not have the discernment to know the difference between good behavior and that which is corrupted. He does not know that his foolish, corrupted acts, which identify him as a fool, keep making him more the fool. Throughout the Book of Proverbs, his foolish actions are variously described as uncontrolled speaking, lying, slandering, producing mischief *(wickedness)*, refusing counsel, behaving egocentrically, fearlessly associating with evil, despising his father's instruction, lacking understanding, starting contention, meddling, and despising wisdom.

The Apostle Peter referred to this proverb to illustrate the foolishness of someone who has been introduced to the "way of righteousness" but returns to the "the pollutions of the world:"

2 Peter 2:20-22 For if after they have escaped the pollutions of the world through the knowledge of the Lord and Saviour Jesus Christ, they are again entangled therein, and overcome, the latter end is worse with them than the beginning. For it had been better for them not to have known the way of righteousness, than, after they have known *it,* to turn from the holy commandment delivered unto them. But it is happened unto them according to the true proverb, The dog *is* turned to his own vomit again; and the sow that was washed to her wallowing in the mire.

The following verses also exemplify the truth of this proverb.

Ruth 1:14-15 And they lifted up their voice, and wept again: and Orpah kissed her mother in law; but Ruth clave unto her. And she said, Behold, thy sister in law is gone back unto her people, and unto her gods: return thou after thy sister in law.

Psalm 85:8 I will hear what God the LORD will speak: for he will speak peace unto his people, and to his saints: but let them not turn again to folly.

Proverbs 23:35 They have stricken me, *shalt thou say, and* I was not sick; they have beaten me, *and* I felt *it* not: when shall I awake? I will seek it yet again.

John 5:14 Afterward Jesus findeth him in the temple, and said unto him, Behold, thou art made whole: sin no more, lest a worse thing come unto thee.

Proverbs 26:12 Seest thou a man wise in his own conceit? there is more hope of a fool than of him.

Focus: This proverb declares the extreme difficulty of a prideful, arrogant person becoming wise.

"Seest thou a man" is part of a question used in this proverb (and two others listed below) to call attention to a specific man; so that his behavior, and the consequences of his behavior, can be closely studied. The wise man is to observe the other person, compare his behavior to his own, and learn to do right.

Proverbs 22:29 Seest thou a man diligent in his business? he shall stand before kings; he shall not stand before mean men.
Proverbs 29:20 Seest thou a man that is hasty in his words? there is more hope of a fool than of him.

People who learn by observation can progress much faster than those who must suffer in order to learn.

"Wise in his own conceit" identifies the *overwhelming characteristic of arrogance* specific to this man under observation. His supreme weakness is believing that his personal abilities are much greater than they actually are. He has an unqualified, egocentric opinion of himself, and he is blinded to any idea that he needs counsel to make wise decisions. His pride causes him to believe that he is as capable and *as smart* as anyone (or everyone) including God. Therefore he slams the door to improvement and success and ultimately to repentance. Arrogant people believe themselves to be above repentance.

Because he imagines himself perfect and needing no improvement or guidance from Jehovah, **"there is more hope of a fool than of him."** His arrogant attitude concerning his own greatness is as comical as an overconfident 4-pound Chihuahua strutting around challenging a 130-pound Rottweiler. Such pride causes God to resist him, for "God resisteth the proud, but giveth grace to the humble" (James 4:6). The more prideful he becomes, the greater the distance he puts between himself and God. At some point, God will allow him to go his own way as He did Cain. (Genesis 4:3-13) Cain had been raised in a home that knew God, and his parents had instructed him in God's ways, but he rejected the instruction because he was **"wise in his own conceit."** His hardened mind disavowed God's instructions and followed only what he wanted to be true, causing him to digress to the point of *no hope*, nothing to look forward to – only judgment.

Even a fool can have hope *if* he feels enough pain and turns from his folly. Being *"wise in his own conceit"* caused enormous problems for the Prodigal Son of Luke 15:11-24, as it did for the lukewarm church of the Laodiceans, who received warning from the Lord about their pride.

> Luke 15:16-19 And he would fain have filled his belly with the husks that the swine did eat: and no man gave unto him. And when he came to himself, he said, How many hired servants of my father's have bread enough and to spare, and I perish with hunger! I will arise and go to my father, and will say unto him, Father, I have sinned against heaven, and before thee, And am no more worthy to be called thy son: make me as one of thy hired servants.
>
> Revelation 3:17 Because thou sayest, I am rich, and increased with goods, and have need of nothing; and knowest not that thou art wretched, and miserable, and poor, and blind, and naked: I counsel thee to buy of me gold tried in the fire, that thou mayest be rich; and white raiment, that thou mayest be clothed, and that the shame of thy nakedness do not appear; and anoint thine eyes with eyesalve, that thou mayest see.

Proverbs 26:13-16 The slothful *man* saith, *There is* a lion in the way; a lion *is* in the streets.
14. *As* the door turneth upon his hinges, so *doth* the slothful upon his bed.
15. The slothful hideth *his* hand in his bosom; it grieveth him to bring it again to his mouth.
16. The sluggard *is* wiser in his own conceit than seven men that can render a reason.

Focus: This set of proverbs (4 verses) utilizes the figure of speech known as hyperbole *[a deliberate exaggeration used for effect]* to deliver a comprehensive view of the sluggard's mindset.

"Slothful" and **"sluggard"** are translated from the same Hebrew word, which means *sluggish or lazy.* Proverbs speaks of the "slothful" eight times and the "sluggard" six times. None of the verses paint a picture of the lazy man in a favorable light.

"The slothful man saith, There is a lion in the way; a lion is in the streets." (verse 13) This verse (very similar to Proverbs 22:13, "The slothful man saith, There is a lion without, I shall be slain in the streets") shows that the "sluggard" is fantasizing about dangers in the street and using that fantasy as an excuse for not going outside. He is lying to himself so that he will not have to work.

> Psalm 104:20-23 Thou makest darkness, and it is night: wherein all the beasts of the forest do creep *forth*. The young lions roar after their prey, and seek their meat from God. The sun ariseth, they gather themselves together, and lay them down in their dens. Man goeth forth unto his work and to his labour until the evening.
>
> Proverbs 15:19 The way of the slothful man is as an hedge of thorns: but the way of the righteous is made plain.

"As the door turneth upon his hinges, so doth the slothful upon his bed." (verse 14) Since the plan for his life is to do nothing, his bed is the best place to succeed. The door's hinges have one part attached to a door jamb and its opposite part to the door's edge, thereby keeping the door in place. Likewise, the slothful person seems hinged to his bed as he turns from side to side.

> Proverbs 6:9-11 How long wilt thou sleep, O sluggard? when wilt thou arise out of thy sleep? Yet a little sleep, a little slumber, a little folding of the hands to sleep: So shall thy poverty come as one that travelleth, and thy want as an armed man.
>
> Proverbs 19:15 Slothfulness casteth into a deep sleep; and an idle soul shall suffer hunger.
>
> Proverbs 24:30-34 I went by the field of the slothful, and by the vineyard of the man void of understanding; And, lo, it was all grown over with thorns, and nettles had covered the face thereof, and the stone wall thereof was broken down. Then I saw, and considered it well: I looked upon it, and received instruction. Yet a little sleep, a little slumber, a little folding of the hands to sleep: So shall thy poverty come as one that travelleth; and thy want as an armed man.

"**The slothful hideth his hand in his bosom; it grieveth him to bring it again to his mouth.**" (verse 15) In this comical proverb *(as in Proverbs 19:24)*, the **"slothful man"** is pictured as being so incredibly lazy, that when he reaches down to get some food out of his bowl, held dearly close to his bosom, he does not have enough energy and willpower to pick up his hand and bring it to his mouth. Since the outer Hebrew garment had no sleeves, the lazy man's hands and arms might have been covered with the robe's folds, and he was grieved because disentangling himself to eat involved too much effort. The Scripture ridicules the slothful person using sarcasm and hyperbole.

Proverbs 19:24 A slothful *man* hideth his hand in *his* bosom, and will not so much as bring it to his mouth again.

"**The sluggard is wiser in his own conceit than seven men that can render a reason.**" (verse 16) "**The sluggard**" has been described in previous verses as being too lazy to get up in the morning and lacking enough energy to bring his hand to his mouth to eat. He is "**wiser in his own conceit** *[in his own eyes]*," believing that his behavior is wiser than everyone else's. He spurns the industriousness of his successful neighbors, determining in his mind that they are the fools for even thinking that work is more important than rest. In his own mind, he proves again that he is justified by staying in bed! "... By his idleness, he avoids those troubles and dangers to which other men, by their activity, expose themselves, forgetting, in the mean time, what reproach and loss are brought upon him by his slothfulness."[674]

"**Than seven men that can render a reason**" refers to men *who can understand enough to give a reason for their hard work*. The number "**seven**" is representative of completion. The addition of the word "**than**" before it also implies that it is a definite number used for the indefinite.[675] In other words, the sluggard considers himself wiser than an indefinite number of other men who give reasons for their wise, industrious, and productive lifestyles. He thinks he is the wisest of all.

Proverbs 26:12 Seest thou a man wise in his own conceit? there is more hope of a fool than of him.

Proverbs 26:17 He that passeth by, *and* meddleth with strife *belonging* not to him, *is like* one that taketh a dog by the ears.

Focus: This proverb illustrates the potential personal injury that a wayfarer can sustain by involving himself with strife that is none of his concern.

"**He that passeth by, and meddleth with strife belonging not to him**" describes a traveler who happens to travel near enough an argument that it attracts his attention. In his foolishness, he decides to interject himself into this private (though public enough to be noticed by a passer-by) disagreement between two people he may or may not know personally. He does not know what started the strife or who is at fault, and he has no solutions to offer; yet, he determines to intervene. He is *meddling.*

He "**is like one that taketh a dog by the ears.**" For a person to grab a dog by the ears, he must have some idea of taking control of the animal. However, grabbing his ears will infuriate the animal and cause him to become aggressive and go on the attack. Once the grasp is made, there remains no good exit plan – no way to get away without receiving damage from sharp canines, either to skin or clothing. *If* the ear grabber holds on, he is bound to keep holding so that the dog cannot reach around and bite with his teeth; and if the ear grabber turns loose, the dog might be mad enough to inflict multiple wounds. Worse than that, the animal could summons his siblings to help, and then there would be more dogs in the fight than can be beaten off. There is nothing to be gained by grabbing a dog by the ears. Likewise, there is no good reason for a person to inject himself into a dispute where he has no business and where he cannot expect anything but *unnecessary* trouble.

Jehoshaphat, king of Judah, volunteered to involve himself and his nation in strife that did not belong to him and was almost killed.

1 Kings 22:4; 22:32-34 And he said unto Jehoshaphat, Wilt thou go with me to battle to Ramothgilead? And Jehoshaphat said to the king of Israel, I am as thou art, my people as thy people, my horses as thy horses . . . And it came to pass, when the captains of the chariots saw Jehoshaphat, that they said, Surely it is the king of Israel. And they turned aside to fight against him: and Jehoshaphat cried out. And it came to pass, when the captains of the chariots perceived that it was not the king of Israel, that they turned back from pursuing him. And a certain man drew a bow at a venture, and smote the king of Israel between the joints of the harness: wherefore he said unto the driver of his chariot, Turn thine hand, and carry me out of the host; for I am wounded.

Proverbs 20:3 *It is* an honour for a man to cease from strife: but every fool will be meddling.

Proverbs 25:8 Go not forth hastily to strive, lest thou know not what to do in the end thereof, when thy neighbour hath put thee to shame.

2 Timothy 2:23-24 But foolish and unlearned questions avoid, knowing that they do gender strifes. And the servant of the Lord must not strive; but be gentle unto all *men,* apt to teach, patient.

When invited into a dispute over an inheritance, Jesus excused Himself.

Luke 12:13-14 And one of the company said unto him, Master, speak to my brother, that he divide the inheritance with me. And he said unto him, Man, who made me a judge or a divider over you?

Other Scripture, such as the story of the Good Samaritan, provides an understanding that there is a proper time for involvement in situations where merciful help is both needed and appreciated.

Luke 10:30-37 And Jesus answering said, A certain *man* went down from Jerusalem to Jericho, and fell among thieves, which stripped him of his raiment, and wounded *him,* and departed, leaving *him* half dead. And by chance there came down a certain priest that way: and when he saw him, he passed by on the other side. And likewise a Levite, when he was at the place, came and looked *on him,* and passed by on the other side. But a certain Samaritan, as he journeyed, came where he was: and when he saw him, he had compassion *on him, And went to him,* and bound up his wounds, pouring in oil and wine, and set him on his own beast, and brought him to an inn, and took care of him. And on the morrow when he departed, he took out two pence, and gave *them* to the host, and said unto him, Take care of him; and whatsoever thou spendest more, when I come again, I will repay thee. Which now of these three, thinkest thou, was neighbour unto him that fell among the thieves? he said, He that shewed mercy on him. Then said Jesus unto him, Go, and do thou likewise.

Proverbs 26:18-19 As a mad *man* who casteth firebrands, arrows, and death,
19. So *is* the man *that* deceiveth his neighbour, and saith, Am not I in sport?

Focus: This proverb compares the devastation that a liar causes to the devastation that weapons of war cause in the hands of a mad man.

A **"mad *man*"** can be irrational, insane, uncontrollable, recklessly indiscriminate, and violently destructive – and so can a foolish, loose-tongued, dangerously deceptive neighbor. **"Firebrands, arrows, and death"** together represent an arsenal of lethal weapons. **"Firebrands"** are used to set objects ablaze. **"Arrows"** are intended to pierce the body bringing severe injury and possible death. ***To cast death*** is a figure of speech that expresses the intensity of the mad man's desire to inflict harm.

NOTE: In the previous chapter, the words of the false witness against his neighbor are also described as weapons of war, "a maul, and a sword, and a sharp arrow." (Proverbs 25:19)

"So is the man that deceiveth his neighbor *[an associate--more or less close],***"** is a clause that identifies the deceptive person as a **"mad man"** and places him in the same category as one who casts **"firebrands, arrows, and death."** His wicked heart devises and carries out a devilish plot utilizing deception as a weapon to cause destruction and make his neighbor suffer.

If the evil, deceiving one were to convince his neighbor that his healthy flock of sheep has the beginning of a contagious disease, and if the unsuspecting neighbor reacts by destroying that "diseased" portion of his flock, the deceiver will cause severe damage to his neighbor's livelihood. Truth will eventually come to light, and the deceiver will have to spew out his second lie, his cover-up lie, **"am not I in sport?"** These false words in no way exonerate the villain. He plotted evil against his neighbor to cause him serious injury. Though the injury did not come directly from a physical weapon such as firebrands and arrows; non-the-less, the injury to his neighbor is substantial.

Proverbs 10:23 It *is* as sport to a fool to do mischief: but a man of understanding hath wisdom.

Proverbs 14:9 Fools make a mock at sin: but among the righteous *there is* favour.

Proverbs 15:21 Folly *is* joy to *him that is* destitute of wisdom: but a man of understanding walketh uprightly.

Jeremiah 9:3-6 And they bend their tongues *like* their bow *for* lies: but they are not valiant for the truth upon the earth; for they proceed from evil to evil, and they know not me, saith the LORD. Take ye heed every one of his neighbour, and trust ye not in any brother: for every brother will utterly supplant, and every neighbour will walk with slanders. And they will deceive every one his neighbour, and will not speak the truth: they have taught their tongue to speak lies, *and* weary themselves to commit iniquity. Thine habitation *is* in the midst of deceit; through deceit they refuse to know me, saith the LORD.

> **Proverbs 26:20** Where no wood is, *there* the fire goeth out: so where *there is* no talebearer, the strife ceaseth.

Focus: This proverb identifies a source of strife and how to put an end to it.

A talebearer speaks inflammatory words with an ulterior motive of stirring up strife to advance himself. He tells inappropriate stories that may be false *or* true, but either way, they should not be told. A talebearer quickly starts strife by telling one individual that another said something evil about him. Perhaps he may tell something improper that happened in the other person's childhood that would have been best unsaid. A talebearer finds delight in whispering these tales, causing injury, division, and strife. He belittles those he considers competitors and sets people against each other. The talebearer likes to tell tales to suggest ill will or to disclose bad situations that exist between people, and he is malicious in creating mutual anger and causing friends to become enemies.

Just as removing wood from the fire stops the fire, removing the talebearer stops the strife. Proverbs 25:23 clearly states another appropriate action to remove the influence of the talebearer – "The north wind driveth away rain: so *doth* an angry countenance a backbiting tongue." A stern, angry frown will alert the talebearer that his words are inappropriate and unwanted.

Proverbs 20:19 He that goeth about *as* a talebearer revealeth secrets: therefore meddle not with him that flattereth with his lips.

> **Proverbs 26:21** *As* coals *are* to burning coals, and wood to fire; so *is* a contentious man to kindle strife.

Focus: This proverb declares that a contentious man starts and keeps strife hot with the same effectiveness that fuel keeps a fire going.

The **"contentious man"** is more obvious and easily recognized than the talebearer in the previous verse because he openly (rather than secretly) causes strife. He **kindles** *[incites, inflames]* **strife**. Wherever he shows up, there is likely to be an argument. Believing that he can hold his own with anyone, he enjoys a brawl; and having a chip on his shoulder, he struts around inviting someone to knock it off. He is a wrathful, faultfinding, irritating person who kindles strife with provoking words and deeds. His contemptuous look and haughty spirit will be enough to exacerbate, if not ignite trouble – to **"kindle strife."** Without the "contentious man" appearing on the scene to stir up disagreements, there would likely be peace.

Godly people desiring to be at peace with everyone learn to filter their words and control their actions.

2 Samuel 20:1 And there happened to be there a man of Belial, whose name *was* Sheba, the son of Bichri, a Benjamite: and he blew a trumpet, and said, We have no part in David, neither have we inheritance in the son of Jesse: every man to his tents, O Israel.

Proverbs 15:18 A wrathful man stirreth up strife: but *he that is* slow to anger appeaseth strife.

Proverbs 16:27-28 An ungodly man diggeth up evil: and in his lips there is as a burning fire. A froward man soweth strife: and a whisperer separateth chief friends.

Proverbs 22:10 Cast out the scorner, and contention shall go out; yea, strife and reproach shall cease.

Proverbs 29:22 An angry man stirreth up strife, and a furious man aboundeth in transgression.

Romans 2:5-11 But after thy hardness and impenitent heart treasurest up unto thyself wrath against the day of wrath and revelation of the righteous judgment of God; Who will render to every man according to his deeds: To them who by patient continuance in well doing seek for glory and honour and immortality, eternal life: But unto them that are contentious, and do not obey the truth, but obey unrighteousness, indignation and wrath, Tribulation and anguish, upon every soul of man that doeth evil, of the Jew first, and also of the Gentile; But glory, honour, and peace, to every man that worketh good, to the Jew first, and also to the Gentile: For there is no respect of persons with God.

> **Proverbs 26:22** The words of a talebearer *are* as wounds, and they go down into the innermost parts of the belly.

Focus: This proverb (identical to Proverbs 18:8) expresses the severe damage that talebearing causes.

Like a delicious morsel of food is delightful to eat, the talebearer's lips speak words that are delightful for some people to hear. His words are like sharp knives creating wounds. They are words of discord and strife piercing everyone who "tastes" his concoction. All are harmed – the talebearer, the listener, and the one spoken about. Reputations are ruined, friendships destroyed, feuds initiated, clear consciences made into troubled minds, and peace made into war. God detests the talebearer, and wise people dodge him or show him an angry countenance when he leans to whisper his malicious words.

> Leviticus 19:16 Thou shalt not go up and down *as* a talebearer among thy people: neither shalt thou stand against the blood of thy neighbour: I *am* the LORD.
> Psalm 50:19-20 Thou givest thy mouth to evil, and thy tongue frameth deceit. Thou sittest and speakest against thy brother; thou slanderest thine own mothers son.
> Psalm 52:2 Thy tongue deviseth mischiefs; like a sharp razor, working deceitfully.
> Proverbs 12:18 There is that speaketh like the piercings of a sword: but the tongue of the wise *is* health.
> Proverbs 16:28 A froward man soweth strife: and a whisperer separateth chief friends.
> Proverbs 17:9 He that covereth a transgression seeketh love; but he that repeateth a matter separateth *very* friends.
> 1 Corinthians 13:6 Rejoiceth not in iniquity, but rejoiceth in the truth.

Proverbs 26:23   Burning lips and a wicked heart *are like* a potsherd covered with silver dross.

Focus: This proverb describes the worthlessness and hypocrisy of pleasant words derived from a wicked heart.

"Burning lips" is a term that describes "lips glowing with affection, uttering warm words of love."[676] This kind of speech is normally considered valuable and is well-received; however, when spoken hypocritically from a wicked heart, it is disgusting and as worthless as a broken piece of pottery. The hypocrite's "burning lips" may trick his listener into believing his lies, like silver dross covering a potsherd can fool the onlooker into believing he has found a piece of solid silver. However, eventually, the hypocrite will be discovered, his words proven to be lies, and his wicked heart revealed. Joseph's brothers pictured this blatant hypocrisy when they, "rose up to comfort their father" after secretly selling their brother into slavery. Saul was another hypocrite. He pretended to honor David by giving David his daughter Michal to wed, but secretly the marriage was designed by Saul to become David's specially arranged personal disaster. Furthermore, so sad to say, it was later David who hypocritically honored Uriah the Hittite as a messenger, while plotting his death.

> 2 Samuel 15:4-6 Absalom said moreover, Oh that I were made judge in the land, that every man which hath any suit or cause might come unto me, and I would do him justice! And it was so, that when any man came nigh to him to do him obeisance, he put forth his hand, and took him, and kissed him. And on this manner did Absalom to all Israel that came to the king for judgment: so Absalom stole the hearts of the men of Israel.
> 2 Samuel 20:9-10 And Joab said to Amasa, *Art* thou in health, my brother? And Joab took Amasa by the beard with the right hand to kiss him. But Amasa took no heed to the sword that *was* in Joab's hand: so he smote him therewith in the fifth *rib,* and shed out his bowels to the ground, and struck him not again; and he died. So Joab and Abishai his brother pursued after Sheba the son of Bichri.
> Psalm 55:21 The words of his mouth were smoother than butter, but war was in his heart: his words were softer than oil, yet were they drawn swords.
> Proverbs 10:18 He that hideth hatred *with* lying lips, and he that uttereth a slander, *is* a fool.
> Proverbs 10:20 The tongue of the just is as choice silver: the heart of the wicked is little worth.
> Proverbs 26:24-26 He that hateth dissembleth with his lips, and layeth up deceit within him; When he speaketh fair, believe him not: for *there are* seven abominations in his heart. *Whose* hatred is covered by deceit, his wickedness shall be shewed before the *whole* congregation.
> Proverbs 29:5 A man that flattereth his neighbour spreadeth a net for his feet.

Secret, deceitful words are well-known to God, Who sees the wicked heart.

> Jeremiah 17:9-10 The heart *is* deceitful above all *things,* and desperately wicked: who can know it? I the LORD search the heart, *I* try the reins, even to give every man according to his ways, *and* according to the fruit of his doings.
> Hebrews 4:12-13 For the word of God is quick, and powerful, and sharper than any twoedged sword, piercing even to the dividing asunder of soul and spirit, and of the joints and marrow, and is a discerner of the thoughts and intents of the heart. Neither is there any creature that is not manifest in his sight: but all things are naked and opened unto the eyes of him with whom we have to do.
> Luke 12:2-3 For there is nothing covered, that shall not be revealed; neither hid, that shall not be known. Therefore whatsoever ye have spoken in darkness shall be heard in the light; and that which ye have spoken in the ear in closets shall be proclaimed upon the housetops.

Verses 24-28 continue describing the hypocrite, the liar. A believer should *not* be fooled by a man's inconsistent fair appearance of godliness. It takes time and experience for hearts to be revealed.

> **Proverbs 26:24-26** He that hateth dissembleth with his lips, and layeth up deceit within him;
> 25. When he speaketh fair, believe him not: for *there are* seven abominations in his heart.
> 26. *Whose* hatred is covered by deceit, his wickedness shall be shewed before the *whole* congregation.

Focus: This proverb (3 verses) warns against believing a hateful hypocrite who will eventually be exposed.

"He that hateth dissembleth with his lips." (verse 24a) ***The hater*** has his mind set to **dissemble** *[disguise or misconstrue]*. His dissembling is smooth talk (flattering lies) designed to disguise hate. He pretends friendship with his lips, but his heart hates. He talks like he is the person's best friend and pretends love and kindness, but he is planning evil in his heart. "He carries himself like another man."[677] The warning is for the believer not to be fooled when a man speaks flattering words, for he wants to gain control of his victim's heart and will. Satan spoke smoothly to Eve, but he had a devious purpose in his heart – he wanted to trick her into disbelieving God. Satan used the adulteress of Proverbs 7 to flatter the simple youth and lead him down the path to sin and hell. The flatterer usually has an ulterior motive that bodes ill for the person being flattered. *(NOTE: He that hates is a personal enemy.)*

The hater (the **dissembler**) **"layeth up deceit within him"** (verse 24b), indicating that he keeps mischief hidden in his heart until he can carry out his thoughts.

"When he speaketh fair, believe him not." (verse 25a) The wise person does not believe every word, *especially* words from a person who has a life that demonstrates hate. When the hypocrite's words suddenly become **"fair"** *[gracious, favorable]* and excessive in praise, the wise one is even more alerted. The hypocrite's previous acts and words must be remembered, and his body language watched to determine the truth. Like a rattlesnake that rattles its tail before he strikes, the hypocrite will inadvertently say something or act in such a way that reveals his wicked heart. This wicked hypocrite is adept at speaking words enjoyable to hear to cover his multitude of wicked purposes, schemes, and designs planned against his victim. He simply waits until the right time to execute his abominable acts against God and men.[678]

"For *there are* seven abominations in his heart." (verse 25b) The **"seven abominations** *[things morally disgusting]*" indicate "a great variety of base and wicked designs."[679]

"*Whose* hatred is covered by deceit, his wickedness shall be shewed before the *whole* congregation." (verse 26) He lies to cover up his hatred, but eventually, everyone recognizes the hypocrite for what he is. The dissembler's evil intent will be made manifest.

> Psalm 28:3 Draw me not away with the wicked, and with the workers of iniquity, which speak peace to their neighbours, but mischief *is* in their hearts.
> Proverbs 14:15 The simple believeth every word: but the prudent *man* looketh well to his going.
> Matthew 22:15 Then went the Pharisees, and took counsel how they might entangle him in *is* talk. *[See also verses 16-22.]*
> Luke 20:20-23 And they watched *him,* and sent forth spies, which should feign themselves just men, that they might take hold of his words, that so they might deliver him unto the power and authority of the governor. And they asked him, saying, Master, we know that thou sayest and teachest rightly, neither acceptest thou the person *of any,* but teachest the way of God truly: Is it lawful for us to give tribute unto Caesar, or no? But he perceived their craftiness, and said unto them, Why tempt ye me?

> **Proverbs 26:27** Whoso diggeth a pit shall fall therein: and he that rolleth a stone, it will return upon him.

Focus: This proverb specifies that men become victims to their own entrapments – sin has its own retribution.

Pits have been a standard method of capturing enemies for centuries. An unescapable deep pit was dug along an enemy's known pathway, and the opening was disguised with lightly-supported substances such as cut tree branches, dirt, leaves, and brush. Once the enemy fell into such a trap, his life expectancy was short. Another method of physically destroying an enemy in times past was to scotch a large **"stone"** (a boulder) at the top of a hill to release it at an opportune time, thereby mowing down the enemy. Sometimes those same stones were somehow released unexpectedly and uncontrollably rolled upon the one setting the stone.

Wicked people often fall into the traps they set for others because hate blinds their minds so that they make egregious mistakes, greed causes them to extend past the point of safety, or the judgment of God is exercised through providence.

> Psalm 9:15-16 The heathen are sunk down in the pit that they made: in the net which they hid is their own foot taken. The LORD is known by the judgment which he executeth: the wicked is snared in the work of his own hands. Higgaion. Selah.
> Psalm 57:6 They have prepared a net for my steps; my soul is bowed down: they have digged a pit before me, into the midst whereof they are fallen themselves. Selah.
> Proverbs 1:17-19 Surely in vain the net is spread in the sight of any bird. And they lay wait for their own blood; they lurk privily for their own lives. So are the ways of every one that is greedy of gain; which taketh away the life of the owners thereof.
> Proverbs 28:10 Whoso causeth the righteous to go astray in an evil way, he shall fall himself into his own pit: but the upright shall have good things in possession.
> Galatians 6:7-10 Be not deceived; God is not mocked: for whatsoever a man soweth, that shall he also reap. For he that soweth to his flesh shall of the flesh reap corruption; but he that soweth to the Spirit shall of the Spirit reap life everlasting. And let us not be weary in well doing: for in due season we shall reap, if we faint not. As we have therefore opportunity, let us do good unto all *men,* especially unto them who are of the household of faith. *[See also Psalm 7:11-16; 35:7-8; 57:6.]*

There are three prominent examples of the truth of this proverb found in the Bible: Jacob deceived his father through the use of a kid of goats in Genesis 27; he himself was deceived through the use of a kid in Genesis 37; David had a man killed with a sword and was punished by the sword never leaving his house in 2 Samuel 11 and 12; and Haman was destroyed on a gallows he had prepared for someone else.

> Genesis 27:21-3 And Isaac said unto Jacob, Come near, I pray thee, that I may feel thee, my son, whether thou *be* my very son Esau or not. And Jacob went near unto Isaac his father; and he felt him, and said, The voice *is* Jacob's voice, but the hands *are* the hands of Esau. And he discerned him not, because his hands were hairy, as his brother Esau's hands: so he blessed him. *[See also Genesis 27:9-19.]*
> Genesis 37:31-32 And they took Joseph's coat, and killed a kid of the goats, and dipped the coat in the blood; And they sent the coat of many colours, and they brought it to their father; and said, This have we found: know now whether it be thy son's coat or no.
> 2 Samuel 12:9-10 Wherefore hast thou despised the commandment of the LORD, to do evil in his sight? thou hast killed Uriah the Hittite with the sword, and hast taken his wife to be thy wife, and hast slain him with the sword of the children of Ammon. Now therefore the sword shall never depart from thine house; because thou hast despised me, and hast taken the wife of Uriah the Hittite to be thy wife. *[See also 2 Samuel 11:14-15.]*
> Esther 7:10 So they hanged Haman on the gallows that he had prepared for Mordecai. Then was the king's wrath pacified.

Proverbs 26:28 A lying tongue hateth *those that are* afflicted by it; and a flattering mouth worketh ruin.

Focus: This proverb specifies the truth that when someone is injured through a direct lie or a flattering lie, the lie is driven by hate for the victim.

A lying tongue hates those that are afflicted [crushed, oppressed, injured] *by it.* A person who inflicts injury on another with his slanderous lies does so from a heart of hate. He intentionally makes his enemy a victim. A person who loves another will be careful not to say anything that would injure, but the opposite is true of a liar. He that lies about another, causing him injury, is venting the steam of hate through lying lips.

A flattering mouth works ruin, "both to itself and to the persons flattered by it."[680] Flattery is a lie; only the words are spoken smoothly to give the appearance of a compliment; nonetheless, these lies are motivated by hate and are potentially destructive. The flatterer purposes to win over the other person for personal gain when he fawns over him and lavishes praise which may or may not be believable. Our first parents fell prey to the flattery of "ye shall be as gods," only to be ruined. "Flattery is the snare; ruin is the end."[681]

> NOTE: Proverbs speaks of flattery that comes from a heart of hate but there is also flattery that is spoken as a matter of convenience, rather than from a heart of hate. It is done to escape an immediately bad situation; such as when someone is, more or less, asking for a compliment, when none is due. Such flattery, if given, is still a lie and likely to result in future problems. It is certainly best to tell the truth, keep quiet, or change the subject.

> Psalm 5:9 For there is no faithfulness in their mouth; their inward part is very wickedness; their throat is an open sepulchre; they flatter with their tongue.

Proverbs 6:23-24 For the commandment *is* a lamp; and the law *is* light; and reproofs of instruction *are* the way of life: To keep thee from the evil woman, from the flattery of the tongue of a strange woman.

Proverbs 7:21-23 With her much fair speech she caused him to yield, with the flattering of her lips she forced him. He goeth after her straightway, as an ox goeth to the slaughter, or as a fool to the correction of the stocks;   Till a dart strike through his liver; as a bird hasteth to the snare, and knoweth not that it *is* for his life.

Proverbs 20:19 He that goeth about as a talebearer revealeth secrets: therefore meddle not with him that flattereth with his lips.

Proverbs 25:23 The north wind driveth away rain: so doth an angry countenance a backbiting tongue.

Proverbs 29:5 A man that flattereth his neighbour spreadeth a net for his feet.

Luke 20:20-23 And they watched *him,* and sent forth spies, which should feign themselves just men, that they might take hold of his words, that so they might deliver him unto the power and authority of the governor. And they asked him, saying, Master, we know that thou sayest and teachest rightly, neither acceptest thou the person *of any,* but teachest the way of God truly: Is it lawful for us to give tribute unto Caesar, or no? But he perceived their craftiness, and said unto them, Why tempt ye me?

Phillip Henry wrote the following in his *Life*[682]:

Be as much troubled by unjust praises as by unjust slanders.

CHAPTER TWENTY-SEVEN

In the first six verses of this section, every two verses form a pair of related proverbs. The first pair is directed toward unbecoming boasting. Verses 3 and 4 deal with the problems of wrath, while 5 and 6 explain the value of rebuke, which may sting in the beginning but which could be very profitable for the wise.

> **Proverbs 27:1** Boast not thyself of tomorrow; for thou knowest not what a day may bring forth.

Focus: This proverb declares the absurdity of boasting about the future.

"Boast not thyself of tomorrow." The Hebrew words for "boast" and "praise" in verses 1 and 2 are translated from the same root word, which means to make a show, hence to be proud and clamorously foolish. A person's boasting about tomorrow, expounding on what he will do in the future, or boasting about his abilities or finances is demonstrative pride and foolishness since he does not know what will survive the moment, much less be functioning tomorrow. The nature of pride is to make its host look foolish. This personal boasting is unacceptable, as explained in the second clause.

"For thou knowest not what a day may bring forth," whether good or bad. Man has a curtain over his eyes concerning his personal future, except for the eternal heaven God promised to the redeemed and eternal hell to the lost. Finite man does not have the power to know the future. In addition, boasting himself of tomorrow is a false hope, evidence of misplaced trust that allows a person to believe that he has plenty of time to be reconciled with God.

> Proverbs 16:9 A man's heart deviseth his way: but the LORD directeth his steps.
>
> Proverbs 19:21 *There are* many devices in a man's heart; nevertheless the counsel of the LORD, that shall stand.
>
> Matthew 6:31-34 Therefore take no thought, saying, What shall we eat? or, What shall we drink? or, Wherewithal shall we be clothed? (For after all these things do the Gentiles seek:) for your heavenly Father knoweth that ye have need of all these things. But seek ye first the kingdom of God, and his righteousness; and all these things shall be added unto you. Take therefore no thought for the morrow: for the morrow shall take thought for the things of itself. Sufficient unto the day *is* the evil thereof.
>
> Luke 12:16-20 And he spake a parable unto them, saying, The ground of a certain rich man brought forth plentifully: And he thought within himself, saying, What shall I do, because I have no room where to bestow my fruits? And he said, This will I do: I will pull down my barns, and build greater; and there will I bestow all my fruits and my goods. And I will say to my soul, Soul, thou hast much goods laid up for many years; take thine ease, eat, drink, and be merry. But God said unto him, Thou fool, this night thy soul shall be required of thee: then whose shall those things be, which thou hast provided?
>
> James 4:13-17 Go to now, ye that say, To day or to morrow we will go into such a city, and continue there a year, and buy and sell, and get gain: Whereas ye know not what shall be on the morrow. For what is your life? It is even a vapour, that appeareth for a little time, and then vanisheth away. For that ye ought to say, If the Lord will, we shall live, and do this, or that. But now ye rejoice in your boastings: all such rejoicing is evil. Therefore to him that knoweth to do good, and doeth it not, to him it is sin.

> **Proverbs 27:2** Let another man praise thee, and not thine own mouth; a stranger, and not thine own lips.

Focus: This proverb declares the proper route for praise to come to an individual.

"Let another man praise thee, and not thine own mouth." Verse 1 cautions a person about boasting about *what he will do,* while verse 2 cautions him about boasting *about himself or his own actions or accomplishments.* While it is proper to respect human intelligence, beauty, and ability; for the very reason that God created man in His own image, it is generally wrong to praise self to others. Man is "fearfully and wonderfully made," but self-praise, *which is demonstrative pride,* is ugly, counter-productive, unbecoming to godly character, and disapproved by God and good men.

"Another man," the**"** **stranger** *[unknown, unfamiliar]"* in this verse, refers to *anyone but oneself.* It would be more palatable for a newly introduced person (a total stranger) to give praise. **"Not thine own lips"** restates the fact that a person's mouth is *not* to speak words of praise about himself.

> "We must do that which is commendable, for which even strangers may praise us. Our *light* must *shine before men,* and we must do good works that may be seen, though we must not do them on purpose that they may be seen. Let our own works be such as will praise us, even *in the gates*... When we have done it we must not commend ourselves, for that is an evidence of pride, folly, and self-love, and a great lessening to a man's reputation. Every one will be forward to run him down that cries himself up. There may be a just occasion for us to vindicate ourselves, but it does not become us to applaud ourselves."[683]

In many verses, wisdom teaches the opposite of self-praise – humility. Having a desire to please God, wise people thus perform their work and otherwise live their lives with humility striving for a spirit of excellence. When people know their abilities are a gift from God, they can then accept praise with a thankful heart. Praise will not puff them up to become haughty. There are occasions when a person has to humbly defend himself as in a court of law (or to keep from getting dragged into one) but, if possible, even such defense should be made by others.

> "'St. Paul was put upon it, to speak of himself more than he chose to do; and when he speaks of things concerning himself, he puts in ever and anon, 'I speak as a fool' – intimating, that unless there be very great cause, whoever talks much of himself, talks like a fool." (2 Corinthians 11:5-12; 12:11)[684]

> "To be commended by others, by any but a man's self, is to his credit and reputation; but nothing more hurtful to it than self-commendation; see 2Corinthians 10:18; in some cases it is right for a man indeed to commend himself, when the glory of God, the credit of religion, the cause of truth and self-vindication, require it; as the prophet Samuel, the Apostle Paul, and others, have been obliged to do, 1Samuel 12:3."[685]

> "'Praise'– says an old expositor – 'is a comely garment. But though thyself doth wear it, *another* must put it on, or else it will never sit well about thee. Praise is sweet music, but it is never tuneable in *thine own mouth*. If it cometh from the mouth of *another*, it soundeth most tuneably in the ears of all that hear it. Praise is a rich treasure, but it will never make thee rich, unless *another* tell the same.'"[686]

1 Samuel 12:3 Behold, here I *am:* witness against me before the LORD, and before his anointed: whose ox have I taken? or whose ass have I taken? or whom have I defrauded? whom have I oppressed? or of whose hand have I received *any* bribe to blind mine eyes therewith? and I will restore it you.

Proverbs 25:16 ... 27 Hast thou found honey? eat so much as is sufficient for thee, lest thou be filled therewith, and vomit it. . . . It is not good to eat much honey: so for men to search their own glory is not glory.

Matthew 23:12 And whosoever shall exalt himself shall be abased; and he that shall humble himself shall be exalted.

1 Corinthians 13:4-6 Charity suffereth long, and is kind; charity envieth not; charity vaunteth not itself, is not puffed up, Doth not behave itself unseemly, seeketh not her own, is not easily provoked, thinketh no evil; Rejoiceth not in iniquity, but rejoiceth in the truth . . .

2 Corinthians 10:12 ... 18 For we dare not make ourselves of the number, or compare ourselves with some that commend themselves: but they measuring themselves by themselves, and comparing themselves among themselves, are not wise . . . For not he that commendeth himself is approved, but whom the Lord commendeth.

2Corinthians 11:12 But what I do, that I will do, that I may cut off occasion from them which desire occasion; that wherein they glory, they may be found even as we. *[See Paul's total defense of himself in 2 Corinthians 11:5-13.]*

Philippians 2:3-5 Let nothing be done through strife or vainglory; but in lowliness of mind let each esteem other better than themselves. Look not every man on his own things, but every man also on the things of others. Let this mind be in you, which was also in Christ Jesus...

1 Thessalonians 5:11 Wherefore comfort yourselves together, and edify one another, even as also ye do.

James 4:6 But he giveth more grace. Wherefore he saith, God resisteth the proud, but giveth grace unto the humble.

1 Peter 5:5 Likewise, ye younger, submit yourselves unto the elder. Yea, all of you be subject one to another, and be clothed with humility: for God resisteth the proud, and giveth grace to the humble.

Proverbs 27:3   A stone *is* heavy, and the sand weighty; but a fool's wrath *is* heavier than them both.

Focus: This proverb describes the grievously wearisome burden of dealing with a fool's wrath.

In this 21st century of numerous industrialized countries, large stones and sand are seldom carried by hand. However, to anyone who has ever had the difficult task of doing so, the words **"heavy"** and **"weighty"** bring back memories of hardship, strain, sweat, frustration, and pain. The Bible declares that lifting a big rock or a heavy sack of sand is much easier than the difficulty of dealing with **"a fool's wrath."** In contrast to the simple but arduous physical challenges brought on by the moving of these objects is the emotional, psychological, and perhaps even physical challenges that the ungoverned wrath of a fool can cause. Because he can be excessively cruel and oppressive, the fool can cause severe grief. He has no regard for the damage he causes, and no amount of reasoning will tamp down or move him away from his violently reckless explosions of nonsense. "A fool's wrath is unreasonable and excessive."[687] It is often impossible to determine what initiated his wrath, how far out it will reach, and when it will stop. The wise person will stay as far away from him as possible, for his wrath seems to be so incredibly "weighty" in his soul where it is permanently lodged.

> Genesis 49:5-7 Simeon and Levi *are* brethren; instruments of cruelty *are in* their habitations. O my soul, come not thou into their secret; unto their assembly, mine honour, be not thou united: for in their anger they slew a man, and in their selfwill they digged down a wall. Cursed *be* their anger, for *it was* fierce; and their wrath, for it was cruel: I will divide them in Jacob, and scatter them in Israel.
>
> Esther 3:5-6 And when Haman saw that Mordecai bowed not, nor did him reverence, then was Haman full of wrath. And he thought scorn to lay hands on Mordecai alone; for they had shewed him the people of Mordecai: wherefore Haman sought to destroy all the Jews that *were* throughout the whole kingdom of Ahasuerus, *even* the people of Mordecai.
>
> Proverbs 12:16 A fool's wrath is presently known: but a prudent *man* covereth shame.
>
> Proverbs 17:12 Let a bear robbed of her whelps meet a man, rather than a fool in his folly.
>
> Proverbs 18:6 A fool's lips enter into contention, and his mouth calleth for strokes.
>
> Proverbs 19:19 A man of great wrath shall suffer punishment: for if thou deliver *him,* yet thou must do it again.
>
> Matthew 2:16 Then Herod, when he saw that he was mocked of the wise men, was exceeding wroth, and sent forth, and slew all the children that were in Bethlehem, and in all the coasts thereof, from two years old and under, according to the time which he had diligently enquired of the wise men.

Proverbs 27:4   Wrath *is* cruel, and anger *is* outrageous; but who *is* able to stand before envy?

Focus: This proverb declares that man can endure anger and wrath, but none can stand against envy.

"Wrath *is* cruel *[fierce]***, and anger *is* outrageous** *[a deluge (literally or figuratively), downpour, overflowing]*.**" "Wrath"** and **"anger"** are emotional overflowings that often express themselves openly for all to see through conspicuous facial expressions, tone of voice, and possibly violence and profanity. In fact, the Hebrew definition of "anger" refers to the nostrils, nose, or face partly because of the anger evident in flaring nostrils and from rapid breathing produced by passion. Because they exemplify an *enraged human nature*, anger and wrath are usually forbidden by Scripture – the specific exceptions are the "righteous" anger of kings against the wicked and believers against sin. Both anger and wrath are usually provoked by a perceived wrong from one person and consequently overflow to affect everyone nearby.

> Psalm 37:8 Cease from anger, and forsake wrath: fret not thyself in any wise to do evil.
>
> Proverbs 12:16 A fool's wrath is presently known: but a prudent *man* covereth shame.
>
> "...like the breaking in of the sea, or a flood of mighty waters, which know no bounds, and there is no stopping them: so cruel and outrageous were the wrath and anger of Simeon and Levi, in destroying the Shechemites; of Pharaoh, in making the Israelites to serve with hard bondage, and ordering their male children to be killed and drowned; and of Herod, in murdering the infants in and about Bethlehem."[688]
>
> Genesis 49:5-7 Simeon and Levi are brethren; instruments of cruelty are in their habitations. O my soul, come not thou into their secret; unto their assembly, mine honour, be not thou united: for in their anger they slew a man, and in their self will they digged down a wall. Cursed be their anger, for it was fierce; and their wrath, for it was cruel: I will divide them in Jacob, and scatter them in Israel.
>
> Proverbs 14:29 *He that is* slow to wrath *is* of great understanding: but *he that is* hasty of spirit exalteth folly.

Sometimes anger and wrath can be softened.

> Proverbs 15:1 A soft answer turneth away wrath: but grievous words stir up anger.
>
> Proverbs 21:14 A gift in secret pacifieth anger: and a reward in the bosom strong wrath.

"But who *is* able to stand before envy?" Unlike wrath and anger, **"envy"** seemingly has no provoking cause, may not be apparent to others, and quietly bubbles beneath the surface. At the same time, it secretly contrives the ruin of its enemy. Envy can be described as *a strong emotion of resentment for another person because of some quality or thing that he possesses*.

"Envy" is like jealousy in that both cause anger. However, envy should be distinguished from jealousy – "We are *jealous* of our own; we are *envious* of another man's possessions. *Jealousy fears to lose what it has*; *envy* is pained at seeing another have."[689] For example, a jealous man may perceive that his wife is ignoring him or giving too much attention to another. *(Notice the husband's jealousy in Proverbs 6:32-35 below.)* **An envious man wants another man's wife. Both envy and jealousy resolutely seek to take possession of or keep what the mind is coveting, and both create seething anger.**

> Proverbs 6:32-35 But whoso committeth adultery with a woman lacketh understanding: he *that* doeth it destroyeth his own soul. A wound and dishonour shall he get; and his reproach shall not be wiped away. For jealousy *is* the rage of a man: therefore he will not spare in the day of vengeance. He will not regard any ransom; neither will he rest content, though thou givest many gifts.

The extreme power of **"envy"** is emphasized with the question, **"who *is* able to stand before envy?"**

> "All mankind in Adam fell before the envy of Satan; for it was through the envy of the devil that sin and death came into the world ... Abel could not stand before the envy of Cain; nor Joseph before the envy of his brethren; nor Christ before the envy of the Jews, his bitter enemies; and, where it is, there is confusion and every evil work, James 3:14. An envious man is worse than an angry and wrathful man; his wrath and anger may be soon over, or there may be ways and means of appeasing him; but envy continues and abides, and works insensibly."[690]

> Isaiah 14:12-14 How art thou fallen from heaven, O Lucifer, son of the morning! *how* art thou cut down to the ground, which didst weaken the nations! For thou hast said in thine heart, I will ascend into heaven, I will exalt my throne above the stars of God: I will sit also upon the mount of the congregation, in the sides of the north: I will ascend above the heights of the clouds; I will be like the most High.

> Acts 7:9 And the patriarchs, moved with envy, sold Joseph into Egypt: but God was with him,

Seemingly, envy feeds on itself and is ready to work ruin for its victim at a chosen and convenient time when the most damage can be inflicted. Envy has little or no mercy, and there seems to be no defense because the victim does not know it exists or when it will cause ruin in his life. Therefore there is *no use in pleading for mercy, no way to appease, and nothing but destruction left in its path.*

> "*Wrath is cruel* – And doth many barbarous things; and *anger is outrageous* – Often depriving a man of the proper use of his reason, and hurrying him into many mischiefs and miseries; *but who is able to stand before envy?* – Envy is worse than both of them, 1st, Because it is more unjust and unreasonable, as not being caused by any provocation, as wrath and anger are; but proceeding from mere malignity of mind, whereby a man is grieved for another man's happiness, in which he ought to rejoice; 2d, Because it is more deeply rooted and implacable, whereas the other passions are commonly allayed; and, 3d, Because it is more secret and indiscernible, and therefore the mischievous effects of it are hardly avoidable, whereas wrath and anger discover themselves, and so forewarn and forearm a man against danger."[691]

> Proverbs 14:30 A sound heart *is* the life of the flesh: but envy the rottenness of the bones.

> Romans 1:28-32 And even as they did not like to retain God in their knowledge, God gave them over to a reprobate mind, to do those things which are not convenient; Being filled with all unrighteousness, fornication, wickedness, covetousness, maliciousness; full of envy, murder, debate, deceit, malignity; whisperers, Backbiters, haters of God, despiteful, proud, boasters, inventors of evil things, disobedient to parents, Without understanding, covenantbreakers, without natural affection, implacable, unmerciful: Who knowing the judgment of God, that they which commit such things are worthy of death, not only do the same, but have pleasure in them that do them.

In the New Testament, envy was often the source of cruelty to Jesus and to His followers.

> Matthew 27:17-18 Therefore when they were gathered together, Pilate said unto them, Whom will ye that I release unto you? Barabbas, or Jesus which is called Christ? For he knew that for envy they had delivered him.

> Acts 13:45 But when the Jews saw the multitudes, they were filled with envy, and spake against those things which were spoken by Paul, contradicting and blaspheming.

> Acts 17:5 But the Jews which believed not, moved with envy, took unto them certain lewd fellows of the baser sort, and gathered a company, and set all the city on an uproar, and assaulted the house of Jason, and sought to bring them out to the people.

Christians are warned to guard against the sin of envy, which shows itself in various forms. Envy can be born out of strife whereby foolish persons contend for preeminence. James 3:14-16 links it to self-seeking and selfish ambition, "But if ye have bitter envying and strife in your hearts, glory not, and lie not against the truth. This wisdom descendeth not from above, but *is* earthly, sensual, devilish. For where envying and strife *is,* there *is* confusion and every evil work."

> Romans 13:13 Let us walk honestly, as in the day; not in rioting and drunkenness, not in chambering and wantonness, not in strife and envying.

> 1 Timothy 6:3-5 If any man teach otherwise, and consent not to wholesome words, even the words of our Lord Jesus Christ, and to the doctrine which is according to godliness; He is proud, knowing nothing, but doting about questions and strifes of words, whereof cometh envy, strife, railings, evil surmisings, Perverse disputings of men of corrupt minds, and destitute of the truth, supposing that gain is godliness: from such withdraw thyself.

> 1 Peter 2:1-2 Wherefore laying aside all malice, and all guile, and hypocrisies, and envies, and all evil speakings, As newborn babes, desire the sincere milk of the word, that ye may grow thereby.

> **Proverbs 27:5** Open rebuke *is* better than secret love.

Focus: This proverb reveals God's preference of open rebuke to secret love.

The terms **"open"** *[reveal, publish, uncover]* and **"rebuke"** *[correct, chastise]* are combined to form the phrase **"open rebuke,"** which means to tell someone their fault or sin *to their face*. "Open rebuke" contrasts with **"secret love,"** which, in this context, is love that never reveals itself through an open rebuke. Love that is strong enough to rebuke is willing to pay a possible high price in order to help the other person. The rebuke may create hard feelings and cost the loss of friendship but save the other person from disaster. A love that refuses to help prevent a friend from significant losses, through open rebuke when necessary, fails to pass the test of being genuine.

The Mosaic law prescribed such a close brotherhood between members of the Jewish nation that each was his brother's keeper. Leviticus 19:17 commands, "Thou shalt not hate thy brother in thine heart: thou shalt in any wise rebuke thy neighbour *[friend, another person]*, and not suffer sin upon him." Hate for another (secret or open) was strictly prohibited. If one saw another person coming to ruin, he was ordered by God to rebuke him, thus preventing him from damage. A failure to rebuke him would reveal an absence of love, and having such a disregard for his safety and well-being would be considered hate. Likewise, the Christian should prove his love for his fellow man, made in the image of God, and give "open rebuke" where needed.

> "What is the friend, who will be a real blessing to my soul? Is it one, that will humor my fancies, and flatter my vanity? Is it enough, that he loves my person, and would spend his time and energies in my service? This comes far short of my requirement. I am a poor, straying sinner, with a wayward will and a blinded heart; going wrong at every step. The friend for my case is one, who will watch over me with *open rebuke;* but a reprover, when needful; not a flatterer. The genuineness of friendship without this mark is more than doubtful; its usefulness utterly paralyzed. That *secret love,* that dares not risk a *faithful wound,* and spares *rebuke,* rather than inflict pain, judged by God's standard, is hatred. Far better the wound should be probed than covered. *Rebuke,* kindly, considerately, and prayerfully administered, cements friendship, rather than loosens it."[692]

> Psalm 141:5 Let the righteous smite me; *it shall be* a kindness: and let him reprove me; *it shall be* an excellent oil, *which* shall not break my head: for yet my prayer also *shall be* in their calamities.

"Open rebuke" *does not mean* to rebuke before a crowd of people. Such action is *very seldom* the right thing to do. Instead, he is to love someone enough to scold them face-to-face, and such chastisement is a privilege that close friendship enjoys. It is also somewhat risky since it might inadvertently result in the friend's being permanently offended. Only a person of character, having true genuine love and self-denial, will be willing to perform such a task. A true loving friend is willing to risk having personal issues in order to save the friend from unnecessary problems.

God may urge someone, who loves God and mankind, to rebuke a person who is not a personal friend but is about to ruin himself. Taking such action requires absolute trust that God is guiding him and that he is doing the right thing.

> Proverbs 17:17 A friend loveth at all times, and a brother is born for adversity.
>
> Proverbs 25:11-12 A word fitly spoken *is like* apples of gold in pictures of silver. *As* an earring of gold, and an ornament of fine gold, *so is* a wise reprover upon an obedient ear.
>
> Proverbs 28:23 He that rebuketh a man afterwards shall find more favour than he that flattereth with the tongue.
>
> Proverbs 29:17 Correct thy son, and he shall give thee rest; yea, he shall give delight unto thy soul.
>
> Matthew 18:15 Moreover if thy brother shall trespass against thee, go and tell him his fault between him and thee alone: if he shall hear thee, thou hast gained thy brother.
>
> Luke 17:1-4 Then said he unto the disciples, It is impossible but that offences will come: but woe *unto him,* through whom they come! It were better for him that a millstone were hanged about his neck, and he cast into the sea, than that he should offend one of these little ones. Take heed to yourselves: If thy brother trespass against thee, rebuke him; and if he repent, forgive him. And if he trespass against thee seven times in a day, and seven times in a day turn again to thee, saying, I repent; thou shalt forgive him.
>
> Galatians 2:14 But when I saw that they walked not uprightly according to the truth of the gospel, I said unto Peter before *them* all, If thou, being a Jew, livest after the manner of Gentiles, and not as do the Jews, why compellest thou the Gentiles to live as do the Jews?

> **Proverbs 27:6** Faithful *are* the wounds of a friend; but the kisses of an enemy *are* deceitful.

Focus: This proverb contrasts the faithful wounds of a friend with an enemy's fraudulent acts of flattery.

As observed in the last verse, **"an enemy"** *[one who hates]*; and **"a friend"** *[one who loves, has affection for]* take two different courses of action against others. As discussed in verse 5, **"wounds of a friend"** are rebukes from a person who loves another enough to overcome inhibitions and is willing to take the consequences from the *wounding act of loving rebuke*. Although pain for the rebuke may be felt sharply for the present time, such rebukes are valuable and faithful, being spoken entirely for the other's benefit and intended only for his good. The rebuke is strictly truth, containing nothing devious nor originating from any sly motive. Such a **"wound"** by **"a friend"** is **"faithful"** *[supporting, nourishing, reliable]* and beneficial to the good of his friend, and ultimately, the relationship between the two.

The **"kisses of an enemy"** can be overly-abundant, in addition to being hypocritical and flattering. These kisses are "deceitful" because they conceal secret hate, as indicated by the kiss of Judas. **"Kisses of an enemy"** may seem a relief for the moment in that there is temporary peace, but they are **"deceitful,"** wretched, and disgusting. Such a hypocritical gesture of love is intended to produce a perception of valuable and faithful friendship but is actually hateful and potentially harmful. **"Kisses"** here should be understood as *real* kisses; however, the term may be any *symbolic* gesture of love, including fraudulent flattering acts, such as gifts designed to woo a person into a compromised and weakened position.

> Psalm 41:9 Yea, mine own familiar friend, in whom I trusted, which did eat of my bread, hath lifted up his heel against me.
>
> Psalm 141:5 Let the righteous smite me; *it shall be* a kindness: and let him reprove me; *it shall be* an excellent oil, *which* shall not break my head: for yet my prayer also *shall be* in their calamities.
>
> Proverbs 9:8 Reprove not a scorner, lest he hate thee: rebuke a wise man, and he will love thee.
>
> Ecclesiastes 7:5 It is better to hear the rebuke of the wise, than for a man to hear the song of fools.
>
> Matthew 26:48-50 Now he that betrayed him gave them a sign, saying, Whomsoever I shall kiss, that same is he: hold him fast. And forthwith he came to Jesus, and said, Hail, master; and kissed him. And Jesus said unto him, Friend, wherefore art thou come? Then came they, and laid hands on Jesus, and took him.
>
> Luke 20:20-23 And they watched *him,* and sent forth spies, which should feign themselves just men, that they might take hold of his words, that so they might deliver him unto the power and authority of the governor. And they asked him, saying, Master, we know that thou sayest and teachest rightly, neither acceptest thou the person *of any,* but teachest the way of God truly: Is it lawful for us to give tribute unto Caesar, or no? But he perceived their craftiness, and said unto them, Why tempt ye me?
>
> Revelation 3:19 As many as I love, I rebuke and chasten: be zealous therefore, and repent.

Proverbs 27:7   The full soul loatheth an honeycomb; but to the hungry soul every bitter thing is sweet.

> Focus: This proverb declares that a person's attitude toward a thing is greatly influenced by how much of it he possesses.

To fail to appreciate something abundant in supply is a characteristic of humanity. A **"full soul"** is someone who has eaten to capacity. He does not want even one more bite of food – not even the delicious honeycomb. The abundance of food (and almost anything else) tends to *affect the typical person's attitude*. Rather than giving value to and yearning after the thing, he now loathes it because of having it in abundance.

The prime example of **loathing** food is illustrated in the Israelites' desire in the wilderness. They loathed the manna God had provided for them, and they wept because they did not have meat – "Who shall give us flesh to eat?" (Numbers 11:4) They had all the food they could eat, but they tired of it. They were ungrateful for the food that God had provided and for what God had done in freeing them from bondage.

> NOTE: "For 'loathes' the Hebrew is literally 'treads upon,' 'tramples underfoot,' which is the expression of the greatest disgust and contempt;... the well-fed man will not stoop to pick up the comb which may have dropped in his path from some tree or rock... Self-restraint increases enjoyment; over-indulgence produces satiety, fatigue, and indolence.[693]

The **"hungry soul"** is the opposite of the **"full soul."** He yearns for just one bite of food, any food, especially the honeycomb. He will bless God for the simple food set before him, whereas the rich feel the best dainties are hardly worth thanking Him for. Mary, the mother of Jesus, who was "highly favored of God," said with gratitude, "He hath filled the hungry with good things; and the rich he hath sent empty away." (Luke 1:53) When he had wasted all his inheritance, the prodigal was so hungry that "he would fain have filled his belly with the husks that the swine did eat." (Luke 15:16)

Riches often produce an attitude of ingratitude, and those who possess abundance often turn their noses up at even the best of things. Scripture supports the fact that God knows all things including men's attitudes. He will often interact with man accordingly. Having a "hateful spirit" toward God's blessings will certainly bring His disapproval. Jesus said that the physical wealth of the Laodicean church had blinded their spiritual understanding and made them loath true spiritual riches: Revelation 3:17 "Because thou sayest, I am rich, and increased with goods, and have need of nothing; and knowest not that thou art wretched, and miserable, and poor, and blind, and naked…"

> Numbers 21:5 And the people spake against God, and against Moses, Wherefore have ye brought us up out of Egypt to die in the wilderness? for *there is* no bread, neither *is there any* water; and our soul loatheth this light bread.
>
> Luke 18:24 And when Jesus saw that he *[rich young ruler]* was very sorrowful, he said, How hardly shall they that have riches enter into the kingdom of God!

"The full soul loatheth an honeycomb… may be… applied to a self-sufficient man, that is full of himself: of his own wisdom and knowledge in divine things; of his strength, and the power of his free will; of his purity, holiness, goodness, and righteousness; who loathes the Gospel,… which makes him out an arrant fool, blows a blast on all his goodness and goodliness, strips the creature of his righteousness, and excludes boasting; **but to the hungry soul every bitter thing is sweet**… And so is the Gospel, and every doctrine of it, to a sensible sinner; that is in want, and knows its wants, and has desires after spiritual things created in it; hungers and thirsts after the word and ordinances; after Christ, the bread of life; after the blessings of grace in him; particularly after the pardon of sin, and justifying righteousness and salvation by him; and after more knowledge of him, and communion with him… This may also be applied to the hearing of the word; where and when there is plenty of means, men grow weary of the word, sick of it, and surfeit upon it and loath it; or, however, are very curious and nice, and cannot take up with plain preaching, but must have something suited to their palate, dressed up in a very elegant manner: but when the word of the Lord is precious or rare, and where there are few opportunities of hearing it, sensible souls, that have spiritual appetites, are glad of it; and it is sweet unto them, though not so nicely dressed and though brought to them in a homely manner."[694]

Proverbs 27:8 As a bird that wandereth from her nest, so *is* a man that wandereth from his place.

Focus: This proverb expresses the shock that occurs when a man roves from his place of responsibility.

According to Cornell Lab of Ornithology @ celebrateurbanbirds.org, birds build nests to lay eggs and have baby birds. Once the young are hatched and flying, the nest is no longer used. After that, birds do not return to their nests as humans do to their homes and beds. The nest is temporary and not a permanent home, but when the nest is in use, the parent birds have specific family responsibilities.

When a bird ***wanders from her nest***, she has deserted her responsibilities of protecting and providing for her young. This occurrence would be shocking, unexpected, and contrary to her God-given instincts. A man's leaving his responsibilities of protecting and providing for his family is even more shocking, unexpected, and contrary to his God-given instincts.

The impact of a ***man's wandering from his place*** is illustrated by Elimelech and his family's story in the Book of Ruth. When a famine came in Bethlehem-judah *["house of bread" and "praise"]*, Elimelech *[my God is King]* took his wife Naomi *["pleasant"]* and two sons, Mahlon *[sick]* and Chilion *[pining]*, to the heathen country of Moab (*contemptuously called God's "washpot" in Psalm 60:8; 108:9*). The two sons consequently chose heathen wives in Moab. Then Elemelech and the two sons died there in Moab, leaving Naomi with two daughters-in-law. Elimelech had dangerously chosen to wander away from the house of God, which was his place, and the place where God had promised to protect and provide.

As punishment for murdering his brother, God forced Cain out of his place. His punishment included a curse from God, a weakening in the response of the earth to his labor, and to be a "fugitive and a vagabond…in the earth." Cain did not voluntarily wander from his "nest," but rather was forced out if it by God.

> Genesis 4:10-12 And he said, What hast thou done? the voice of thy brother's blood crieth unto me from the ground. And now *art* thou cursed from the earth, which hath opened her mouth to receive thy brother's blood from thy hand; When thou tillest the ground, it shall not henceforth yield unto thee her strength; a fugitive and a vagabond shalt thou be in the earth.
>
> Proverbs 21:16 The man that wandereth out of the way of understanding shall remain in the congregation of the dead.
>
> Isaiah 16:2 For it shall be, *that,* as a wandering bird cast out of the nest, *so* the daughters of Moab shall be at the fords of Arnon.
>
> Luke 15:13 And not many days after the younger son gathered all together, and took his journey into a far country, and there wasted his substance with riotous living.
>
> 1 Timothy 5:8 But if any provide not for his own, and specially for those of his own house, he hath denied the faith, and is worse than an infidel.

> **Proverbs 27:9** Ointment and perfume rejoice the heart: so *doth* the sweetness of a man's friend by hearty counsel.

Focus: This proverb compares the refreshment and comfort derived from a sweet aroma to the joy of a friend's hearty counsel.

The joyful experience of receiving much needed hearty counsel from a true loving friend is compared with the pleasant experience of inhaling the delightful fragrance of ointment or perfume. Hearty counsel gives a person joy because of knowing that his friend has given him good advice. Preaching of the Scripture is "hearty counsel" to the Christian and makes his heart jubilant.

> "**Ointment and perfume** - Anointing the head and various parts of the body with aromatic oil is frequent in the East, and fumigating the beards of the guests at the conclusion of an entertainment is almost universal; as is also sprinkling rose-water, and water highly odoriferous. Two of the curious vessels which are used for this purpose are now before me; they hold some quarts each, and are beautifully inlaid with silver in the form of sprigs, leaves, etc."[695]

Moses was distraught and overburdened with his responsibilities when his father-in-law Jethro gave him "hearty counsel." (See Exodus 18:14-24.)

> 1 Samuel 23:16 And Jonathan Saul's son arose, and went to David into the wood, and strengthened his hand in God.
>
> Psalm 133:1-2 Behold, how good and how pleasant it is for brethren to dwell together in unity! It is like the precious ointment upon the head, that ran down upon the beard, even Aaron's beard: that went down to the skirts of his garments . . .
>
> Proverbs 15:23 A man hath joy by the answer of his mouth: and a word *spoken* in due season, how good *is it!*
>
> Proverbs 16:24 Pleasant words *are as* an honeycomb, sweet to the soul, and health to the bones.

> **Proverbs 27:10** Thine own friend, and thy father's friend, forsake not; neither go into thy brother's house in the day of thy calamity: *for* better *is* a neighbour *that is* near than a brother far off.

Focus: This proverb expresses (1) a duty of maintaining family and personal friendships and (2) the immediate value of a nearby friend.

"Thine own friend, and thy father's friend, forsake not." Friendships developed due to affection are authentic. When that respected friendship is second generation, passed on from a parent, the friendship will have been well proven through time and circumstance; hence, the admonition "thine own friend, and thy father's friend, forsake not." These should be kept close and valued even though there is an age difference.

Jonathan was much closer to David than he was to any of his brothers. Jesus was much closer to His disciples than his stepbrothers and stepsisters. Solomon cultivated the prized friendship with his father's friend Hiram (1 Kings 5:1-10), but his son Rehoboam foolishly failed to see the value of his father's friends. He forsook their wise counsel and ultimately destroyed the unity of his kingdom. (1 Kings 12:6-19)

> Proverbs 17:17 A friend loveth at all times, and a brother is born for adversity.
>
> Proverbs 18:24 A man *that hath* friends must shew himself friendly: and there is a friend *that* sticketh closer than a brother.

"Neither go into thy brother's house in the day of thy calamity: *for* better *is* a neighbour *that is* near than a brother far off." There is a definite advantage to having a faithful, true, nearby neighbor *[a resident, fellow citizen]* who is that lifetime friend who sticks closer than a brother. He is willing and eager to help in times of trouble because the relationship is based on affection, attraction, and experience. He contrasts with a brother *[relative, kinship]* who lives far away and has a distant personal relationship that may exist strictly because of being kin. Blood relationships are brought about involuntarily through birth and often fail to meet the test of true friendships.

> **Proverbs 27:11** My son, be wise, and make my heart glad, that I may answer him that reproacheth me.

Focus: This proverb encourages wise behavior of the student for two specific reasons.

"**My son**" (used as a noun of direct address in 23 verses in Proverbs) is an affectionate term for a child, student, follower, or disciple; and it can refer to a believer in God. The Hebrew term for "My son" is *ben*, which means "the house continues," and is a description of the one who continues the house (family line) into the next generation.[696] The house to be continued in Proverbs is the house of *faith in God*. Those being addressed as "my son" or "ye children" are those who will believe in God, keep His word, and trust in His promises. In Proverbs, the seed being carried forward is the seed of faith in God, *not* the seed of humanity. The idea of passing on the seed of faith is illustrated by the earthly father teaching his children. *(NOTE: This is the only time "my son" is used in Proverbs 25-29.)*

Along with Proverbs 10:1, 15:20, 23:15, and 23:24, this verse expresses that when the student becomes wise, he is a source of joy to his instructor. The wise student brings him joy because not only are his teachings proved superior, but he is also glad that he has invested his time and energy into the "son" and glad that the "son" takes to heart all that is taught. Nevertheless, there are always critics who want to bring **reproach** (strong accusations against the teacher's teaching or methods) by saying he is too strict, that he causes the poor student to miss out on all the fun that other children have, that he is curtailing the student's social or emotional development, or that he is preventing the student from experiencing all of life. A *glad hearted teacher's* answer (though probably best not spoken) might be, "Observe, if you will, of 'my son' and take note that he is quite wise, successful, and blessed of God. Compare him to others lacking the discipline of wise teachings. He makes me glad!"

In an expression of the truth of this great proverb, John said to Gaius: "I have no greater joy than to hear that my children walk in truth." (3 John 1:4) Similar proverbs include the following:

> Proverbs 10:1 The proverbs of Solomon. A wise son maketh a glad father: but a foolish son *is* the heaviness of his mother.
>
> Proverbs 12:8 A man shall be commended according to his wisdom: but he that is of a perverse heart shall be despised.
>
> Proverbs 15:2 The tongue of the wise useth knowledge aright: but the mouth of fools poureth out foolishness.
>
> Proverbs 15:20 A wise son maketh a glad father: but a foolish man despiseth his mother.
>
> Proverbs 23:15 My son, if thine heart be wise, my heart shall rejoice, even mine.
>
> Proverbs 23:24 The father of the righteous shall greatly rejoice: and he that begetteth a wise child shall have joy of him.
>
> Proverbs 29:3 Whoso loveth wisdom rejoiceth his father: but he that keepeth company with harlots spendeth his substance.

Unfortunately, some parents cannot be glad over their adult children's behavior. Levi and Simeon were a reproach to their father, Jacob, who was a deceiver and a manipulator himself. Simeon and his brother Levi had tricked the Hivites of Shechem and massacred all the males because one of them had raped Dinah, their sister. Likewise, the sons of the high priest Eli were a reproach to Eli and to God. Therefore, neither of these two fathers could say that their offspring were wise and lived in a manner respected by God and good men.

> Genesis 34:30 And Jacob said to Simeon and Levi, Ye have troubled me to make me to stink among the inhabitants of the land, among the Canaanites and the Perizzites: and I being few in number, they shall gather themselves together against me, and slay me; and I shall be destroyed, I and my house.
>
> 1 Samuel 2:12 Now the sons of Eli were sons of Belial; they knew not the LORD. And the priests' custom with the people was, that, when any man offered sacrifice, the priest's servant came, while the flesh was in seething, with a fleshhook of three teeth in his hand; And he struck it into the pan, or kettle, or caldron, or pot; all that the fleshhook brought up the priest took for himself. So they did in Shiloh unto all the Israelites that came thither. Also before they burnt the fat, the priest's servant came, and said to the man that sacrificed, Give flesh to roast for the priest; for he will not have sodden flesh of thee, but raw. And if any man said unto him, Let them not fail to burn the fat presently, and then take as much as thy soul desireth; then he would answer him, Nay; but thou shalt give it me now: and if not, I will take it by force. Wherefore the sin of the young men was very great before the LORD: for men abhorred the offering of the LORD.
>
> 1 Samuel 3:13 For I *[the LORD]* have told him *[Eli]* that I will judge his house for ever for the iniquity which he knoweth; because his sons made themselves vile, and he restrained them not.

Proverbs 27:12 A prudent *man* foreseeth the evil, *and* hideth himself; *but* the simple pass on, *and* are punished.

> Focus: This proverb contrasts a safety advantage of being prudent with an unsafe disadvantage of being simple. *(Proverbs 22:3 is identical to this proverb.)*

"**A prudent man**" is "cautious; circumspect; practically wise; careful of the consequences of enterprises, measures or actions; cautious not to act when the end is of doubtful utility, or probably impracticable."[697] Eight times the Book of Proverbs uses the Hebrew word for "**prudent**" to describe a characteristic of a wise person, and each time it is used in contrast either to the "fool" or to the "**simple.**"

Proverbs 12:16 A fool's wrath is presently known: but a prudent *man* covereth shame.
Proverbs 12:23 A prudent man concealeth knowledge: but the heart of fools proclaimeth foolishness.
Proverbs 13:16 Every prudent *man* dealeth with knowledge: but a fool layeth open *his* folly.
Proverbs 14:8 The wisdom of the prudent *is* to understand his way: but the folly of fools *is* deceit.
Proverbs 14:15 The simple believeth every word: but the prudent *man* looketh well to his going.
Proverbs 14:18 The simple inherit folly: but the prudent are crowned with knowledge.
Proverbs 22:3 A prudent *man* foreseeth the evil, and hideth himself: but the simple pass on, and are punished.
Proverbs 27:12 A prudent *man* foreseeth the evil, *and* hideth himself; *but* the simple pass on, *and* are punished.

Prudence, in a good sense, is one of the characteristics of being wise and is here used as its synonym. **"A prudent man forseeth the evil, and hideth himself."** Evil people resemble rattlesnakes in that they typically *(though often unintentionally)* give warning before inflicting their wickedness. Their warnings include vicious words, telltale gestures *(body language)*, and devious behavior; and because approximately "55% of communication is body language, 38% is the tone of voice, and 7% is the actual words spoken,"[698] the wise person astutely interprets ***all*** that he sees and hears thereby he foresees danger and establishes a way of escape. Sometimes evil suddenly barges in, leaving no way for the prudent person to avoid the situation, such as when a weapon is suddenly brandished. In those times, as in all times, the wise person relies on the principles of conduct that he has learned from Scripture and from other sagacious persons in order to minimize the danger.

Proverbs 6:12-14 A naughty person, a wicked man, walketh with a froward mouth. He winketh with his eyes, he speaketh with his feet, he teacheth with his fingers; Frowardness *is* in his heart, he deviseth mischief continually; he soweth discord.

Proverbs 6:16-19 These six *things* doth the LORD hate: yea, seven *are* an abomination unto him: A proud look, a lying tongue, and hands that shed innocent blood, An heart that deviseth wicked imaginations, feet that be swift in running to mischief, A false witness *that* speaketh lies, and he that soweth discord among brethren.

Joseph fled from Potiphar's wife when he realized her evil intention (Genesis 39: 7-12). David fled from Saul when he recognized his evil spirit and saw a javelin in his hand (1 Samuel 18-20). How many bad marriages or business partnerships or convictions for a felony would be avoided by *foreseeing evil and hiding?*

2 Corinthians 6:14 Be ye not unequally yoked together with unbelievers: for what fellowship hath righteousness with unrighteousness? and what communion hath light with darkness?

"But the simple pass on, and are punished." Simple people are unsettled in their views and are consequently easily influenced – like a child. He is naive and untaught; however, he is *not* one who cannot comprehend *or* a fool who despises wisdom. Instead, he is one whose exposure to life and wisdom has been limited, making him gullible. Simple persons are those of weak capacities and shallow understandings, and they are incautious and easily imposed upon.

Either the simple person does not recognize evil or evil people – or he sees the danger in his pathway but disregards it and proceeds. When he doesn't alter his course, he suffers the consequences and ***is punished.*** Simple people either do not have the years of experience or the will or mental capacity to recognize the subtleness of evil, and should the evil not be so subtle, they still may choose to dismiss their observation as unimportant.

"The simple, who believe every word that flatters them, will believe none that warns them, and so they *pass on and are punished.* They venture upon sin, though they are told what will be in the end thereof; they throw themselves into trouble, notwithstanding the fair warning given them, and they repent their presumption when it is too late. See an instance of both these. Nothing is so fatal to precious souls as this, they will not take warning."[699]

Exodus 9:21 And he that regarded not the word of the LORD left his servants and his cattle in the field. *[After being warned of God, he left them there to be destroyed by a severe hail from God. See also verses 18-20.]*

Proverbs 27:13 Take his garment that is surety for a stranger, and take a pledge of him for a strange woman.

Focus: This proverb teaches that extra precautionary measures are necessary when dealing with a foolhardy person. (This proverb is identical to Proverbs 20:16.)

A **"surety"** is a person who verifies to a money lender that he will stand good for the debt of someone other than himself (should that someone not be able to pay the specified debt). Today, such a person is called a cosigner. The person who becomes a surety mingles his finances with another person. In this case, the verse describes the *someone else* as a person whom he barely knows (**"stranger"**) and advances in the second clause to identify her as an adulterous woman (**"strange woman"**). The danger of cosigning is stressed in several other passages in Proverbs, and Proverbs 27:13 is the same as this verse.

> Proverbs 6:1-5 My son, if thou be surety for thy friend, if thou hast stricken thy hand with a stranger, Thou art snared with the words of thy mouth, thou art taken with the words of thy mouth. Do this now, my son, and deliver thyself, when thou art come into the hand of thy friend; go, humble thyself, and make sure thy friend. Give not sleep to thine eyes, nor slumber to thine eyelids. Deliver thyself as a roe from the hand of the hunter, and as a bird from the hand of the fowler.
>
> Proverbs 11:15 He that is surety for a stranger shall smart for it: and he that hateth suretiship is sure.
>
> Proverbs 17:18 A man void of understanding striketh hands, and becometh surety in the presence of his friend.
>
> Proverbs 22:26-27 Be not thou one of them that strike hands, or of them that are sureties for debts. If thou hast nothing to pay, why should he take away thy bed from under thee?
>
> Proverbs 27:12-13 A prudent *man* foreseeth the evil, *and* hideth himself; *but* the simple pass on, *and* are punished. Take his garment that is surety for a stranger, and take a pledge of him for a strange woman.

In case the debt is not paid, the item held for collateral, is a **"garment"** in the first clause. In the second clause garment is substituted for the general term **"pledge."**   Both sides of the proverb stress that a man who will make himself responsible for the debt of someone only slightly known to himself is foolish and unreliable. So much so that in order for the lender to secure repayment of such a loan, he will be justified in holding the surety's garment (***not** the garment of the person receiving the loan*) until the debt is paid. Holding a poor person's garment overnight was forbidden by the Mosaic law, but if the person being responsible ("surety") for a stranger's debt is that blatantly *(not poor)* foolish, then holding his garment until the debt is paid, appears to be justified. Additionally, a person who would stand good for the debt of a "strange woman" is so foolish that the person making the loan is justified in taking something of substantial value ("pledge"). The implication (by repeating the phrase only with different words) is that the **"pledge"** goes beyond the value of a garment because the risk increases with the introduction of a harlot into the equation.

> "Two sorts of persons are here spoken of that are ruining their own estates, and will be beggars shortly, and therefore are not to be trusted with any good security: 1. Those that will be bound for any body that will ask them, that entangle themselves in rash suretiship to oblige their idle companions; they will break at last, nay, they cannot hold out long; these waste by wholesale. 2. Those that are in league with abandoned women, that treat them, and court them, and keep company with them. They will be beggars in a little time; never give them credit without good pledge. Strange women have strange ways of impoverishing men to enrich themselves."[700]

NOTE: The reason the Law prohibited taking a garment for a pledge was *to protect the poor and unfortunate who were forced to borrow out of necessity*; however, Proverbs 20:16 and 27:13 describe a foolish man, not a poor one, who involves himself with "a strange woman."

> Exodus 22:26-27 If thou at all take thy neighbour's raiment to pledge, thou shalt deliver it unto him by that the sun goeth down: For that is his covering only, it is his raiment for his skin: wherein shall he sleep? and it shall come to pass, when he crieth unto me, that I will hear; for I am gracious.

Proverbs 27:14 He that blesseth his friend with a loud voice, rising early in the morning, it shall be counted a curse to him.

Focus: This proverb expresses the negative effect of ostentatious flattery.

To bless **someone** is an act that usually refers to giving praise and thanks, but the **"loud voice"** and *early morning* time indicates an ulterior motive, and the action is subject to suspicion. Flattery that is disguised as praise is despised rather than appreciated. Any astute person would recognize that such a blatant adulation that is being heaped on him is for the purpose of getting attention. The loud-voiced hypocritical one believes that his **"rising early in the morning"** will show a zeal that he has for scattering blessings on his **"friend"** *[an associate (more or less close), a neighbor, a fellow citizen]*, but actually, he is manifesting his selfishness.

Rather than being received as a positive effect on the relationship, this foolish, ill-timed, tactless, insistent behavior is **"counted a curse"** as nuisances usually are. Good relationships are built instead on such attributes as agreeableness, transparency, honesty, politeness, and sincerity without rudeness.

Proverbs 27:15-16 A continual dropping in a very rainy day and a contentious woman are alike.
  16.   Whosoever hideth her hideth the wind, and the ointment of his right hand, which bewrayeth itself.

Focus: This proverb describes the contentious woman's miserable characteristics inescapable, persistently quarrelsome, and obvious.

"A continual dropping in a very rainy day" describes rain that keeps on and on, not letting up. It is far beyond a pleasant light rain that produces joy – such heavy rain drives everyone indoors – and, in this verse, only to discover a leaking roof. Then that drip, drip, drip reminds the father of a growing problem with the roof, which certainly will not heal itself, but only gets worse as the day proceeds; and the **"continual dropping"** is most irritating and miserable.

Likewise, having a history of producing unsettling noise through her persistent striving, **"a contentious woman"** *[apt to contend; given to angry debate; quarrelsome; perverse[701]]* is a source of misery. She corners him, never letting up, always pounding him with quarrelsome words like the incessant drops of rain from the leaky roof. Any attempt to corral or contain her, to help control her passions, or to reduce the contention, is like trying to **hide the wind** or contain the odor that permeates an area when a person rubs perfumed **"ointment"** onto **"his right hand."** The odor becomes part of his hand and **"bewrayeth itself"** or *self-proclaims its presence*. Everyone can smell it. The odor can't be suppressed; and neither can the contentious woman, even by the strongest of acceptable methods. Not only can the faults of the contentious woman not be hidden or checked, but also she is as much a part of him as his right hand. A respectable man would want his neighbors and friends to be ignorant of his miserable home life, but she exhibits her contentious behavior for all to see. She is her husband's torment and her own shame.[702]

> Proverbs 19:13 A foolish son *is* the calamity of his father: and the contentions of a wife *are* a continual dropping.
>
> Proverbs 21:9 *It is* better to dwell in a corner of the housetop, than with a brawling woman in a wide house. *[Also, 25:24]*
>
> Proverbs 21:19 *It is* better to dwell in the wilderness, than with a contentious and an angry woman.

Proverbs 27:17 Iron sharpeneth iron; so a man sharpeneth the countenance of his friend.

Focus: This proverb expresses the positive influence a friend has on his friend.

As is commonly known, ***iron sharpens iron,*** meaning that when a piece of iron is rubbed against another piece of iron, rust and stains are knocked off, dents are smoothed out, and a sharp edge is intentionally created. Just as these drastic physical changes occur with iron, so *drastic mental and emotional changes can occur when two friends speak candidly and lovingly to one another*. One friend may knock down thoughts of defeat, thereby boosting his friend's energy and giving hope. Perhaps one friend is able to challenge the other friend to attempt something he thought he could not do. The iron file can sharpen the iron blade, making it sharper and more useful. A wise friend quickens his friend's "ingenuity, enlivens his affections, strengthens his judgment, excites him to virtuous and useful actions, and makes him, in all respects, a better man."[703]

Interactions with a friend can be reminders of the love, faithfulness, experiences, and fruitful conversations of the past. Even more profound is the effect when one friend speaks the words of Scripture to his friend causing him to remember God's great work and promises. Scripture is a tool of the Holy Spirit that He uses to produce "joy unspeakable."

> "In the sympathies of friendship, when the mind is dull, and the countenance overcast, a word from a friend puts an edge upon the blunted energy, and exhilarates the countenance. (Job 4:3-4) The commanding word in the field of battle puts a keen edge upon *the iron*. (2Samuel 10:11-13) The mutual excitation for evil is a solemn warning against 'evil communications.' But most refreshing is it, when, as in the dark ages of the Church, 'they that feared the LORD spake often one to another.' (Malachi 3:16) *Sharpening* indeed must have been the intercourse at Emmaus, when 'the hearts of the disciples burned within them.' The Apostle was often so invigorated by *the countenance of his friends*, that he longed to be 'somewhat filled with their company.' Upon this principle – 'Two are better than one' – our Lord sent his first preachers to their work. And the first Divine ordination in the Christian Church was after this precedent. (Acts 13:2-4)"[704]
>
> 1 Samuel 23:16 And Jonathan Saul's son arose, and went to David into the wood, and strengthened his hand in God.
>
> Job 4:3-4 Behold, thou hast instructed many, and thou hast strengthened the weak hands. Thy words have upholden him that was falling, and thou hast strengthened the feeble knees.
>
> Proverbs 13:20 He that walketh with wise *men* shall be wise: but a companion of fools shall be destroyed.
>
> Proverbs 27:9 Ointment and perfume rejoice the heart: so *doth* the sweetness of a man's friend by hearty counsel.
>
> Isaiah 35:3-4 Strengthen ye the weak hands, and confirm the feeble knees. Say to them *that are* of a fearful heart, Be strong, fear not: behold, your God will come *with* vengeance, *even* God *with* a recompence; he will come and save you.
>
> Acts 28:15 And from thence, when the brethren heard of us, they came to meet us as far as Appii forum, and The three taverns: whom when Paul saw, he thanked God, and took courage.

Titus 1:7-8 For a bishop must be blameless, as the steward of God; not selfwilled, not soon angry, not given to wine, no striker, not given to filthy lucre; But a lover of hospitality, a lover of good men, sober, just, holy, temperate . . .

Proverbs 27:18 Whoso keepeth the fig tree shall eat the fruit thereof: so he that waiteth on his master shall be honoured.

Focus: This proverb teaches that faithfulness to perform duties has rewards.

Keeping or maintaining a **"fig tree"** involves cultivating, planting, digging around, fertilizing, pruning, and protecting. The farmer receives rewards for his labor when he eats the delicious and very nutritious fruit. In like manner, the servant who faithfully performs his duties to make sure that his master is properly cared for and productive (fruitful) **"shall be honored"** (rewarded), as was Deborah. She served Isaac's wife Rebekah (Genesis 35:8) and was honored in her death. Elisha was honored with a double portion of Elijah's spirit for his devoted service. (2 Kings 2:9-14) The greatest of all honors comes from Jesus, Who promises honor to His servants because of what they do for Him – "If any man serve me, let him follow me; and where I am, there shall also my servant be: if any man serve me, him will my Father honour." (John 12:26)

> Genesis 39:2-6 And the LORD was with Joseph, and he was a prosperous man; and he was in the house of his master the Egyptian. And his master saw that the LORD *was* with him, and that the LORD made all that he did to prosper in his hand. And Joseph found grace in his sight, and he served him: and he made him overseer over his house, and all *that* he had he put into his hand. And it came to pass from the time *that* he had made him overseer in his house, and over all that he had, that the LORD blessed the Egyptian's house for Joseph's sake; and the blessing of the LORD was upon all that he had in the house, and in the field. And he left all that he had in Joseph's hand; and he knew not ought he had, save the bread which he did eat. And Joseph was *a* goodly *person,* and well favoured.
>
> 2 Kings 2:9-10 And it came to pass, when they were gone over, that Elijah said unto Elisha, Ask what I shall do for thee, before I be taken away from thee. And Elisha said, I pray thee, let a double portion of thy spirit be upon me. And he said, Thou hast asked a hard thing: *nevertheless,* if thou see me *when I am* taken from thee, it shall be so unto thee; but if not, it shall not be *so.*
>
> Matthew 25:22-23 He also that had received two talents came and said, Lord, thou deliveredst unto me two talents: behold, I have gained two other talents beside them. His lord said unto him, Well done, good and faithful servant; thou hast been faithful over a few things, I will make thee ruler over many things: enter thou into the joy of thy lord.

Proverbs 27:19 As in water face *answereth* to face, so the heart of man to man.

Focus: This proverb declares that men have a common heart-to-heart understanding of each other that is as obvious and detectable as a mirror reflection.

Every normal person can look at himself in a mirror and recognize his own face. He can also look at another person and know the commonality of their individual hearts (mind, emotions, and will). A child looks at another child and understands the other child's dependency on his parents. A mother can look at another mother and understand the emotions, pain and joy of childbearing. A father can look at another father and understand his protective instinct for his child. There are many common likes and dislikes, sorrows and joys, victories and defeats. People love to be loved, prefer joy to sorrow, appreciate a day of rest, like to be treated honestly and fairly, appreciate justice, and enjoy respect from others. *So the heart of one man knows that another person's heart is very much the same as his own.*

> Psalm 33:13-15 The LORD looketh from heaven; he beholdeth all the sons of men. From the place of his habitation he looketh upon all the inhabitants of the earth. He fashioneth their hearts alike; he considereth all their works.

Wise people realize that every individual has a common need for salvation.

> Romans 3:23 For all have sinned, and come short of the glory of God.
>
> 2 Corinthians 5:17 Therefore if any man *be* in Christ, he is a new creature: old things are passed away; behold, all things are become new.

Proverbs 27:20 Hell and destruction are never full; so the eyes of man are never satisfied.

Focus: This proverb declares man's insatiable appetite for more of everything.

"Hell and destruction are never full." **"Hell"** is translated *from the Hebrew word* sheol, *which is* "... *generally used as the place to which the souls of the dead are consigned – the receptacle of all departed spirits, whether good or bad.*"[705] **"Destruction"** is translated *from the Hebrew* 'abaddon, *which means place of destruction, ruin. It is* "*the place and state of the damned, of which men know nothing but by Divine revelation.*"[706] "*Abaddon is the lowest depth of hell, the 'abyss'* [Greek abussos] *of Luke 8:31; Revelation 9:2, 20:1.*"[707] Hell and destruction always want another person, another victim.

> "Death is insatiable. The first death, the second death, both are so. The grave is not clogged with the multitude of dead bodies that are daily thrown into it, but is still an open sepulchre, and cries, *Give, give*. Hell also has enlarged itself, and still has room for the damned spirits that are committed to that prison."[708]

Proverbs 5:5 Her feet go down to death; her steps take hold on hell.

Proverbs 7:27 Her house *is* the way to hell, going down to the chambers of death.

Matthew 13:28-30; 38-42 He said unto them, An enemy hath done this. The servants said unto him, Wilt thou then that we go and gather them up? But he said, Nay; lest while ye gather up the tares, ye root up also the wheat with them. Let both grow together until the harvest: and in the time of harvest I will say to the reapers, Gather ye together first the tares, and bind them in bundles to burn them: but gather the wheat into my barn ... The field is the world; the good seed are the children of the kingdom; but the tares are the children of the wicked *one;* The enemy that sowed them is the devil; the harvest is the end of the world; and the reapers are the angels. As therefore the tares are gathered and burned in the fire; so shall it be in the end of this world. The Son of man shall send forth his angels, and they shall gather out of his kingdom all things that offend, and them which do iniquity; And shall cast them into a furnace of fire: there shall be wailing and gnashing of teeth.

Just as **"Hell and Destruction are never full,"** the eyes of man are never satisfied. **"Full"** and **"satisfied"** have the same meaning. People constantly want to see and own new things.

> "Man is always seeking for what he can never find, satisfaction in earthly things. He toils after his object, and when he has grasped it, he toils still; the possessor of abundance, not of happiness. His best efforts only bring him a meager enjoyment, not deserving the name. The summit of ambition, when reached, is not his resting-place; only the point, whence he stretches after something higher. All the affections of fallen man are filled with unquenched thirst. He may fancy his desires to be moderate. He may set bounds to them, and flatter himself, that he shall never overpass them. But give him a world, and, like the far-famed conqueror, he will weep for another, and sink at last into a wretched eternity of unsatisfied desires."[709]

Proverbs 15:11 Hell and destruction are before the LORD: how much more then the hearts of the children of men?

Proverbs 23:4-5 Labour not to be rich: cease from thine own wisdom. Wilt thou set thine eyes upon that which is not? for *riches* certainly make themselves wings; they fly away as an eagle toward heaven.

Proverbs 30:15-16 The horseleach hath two daughters, crying, Give, give. There are three things that are never satisfied, yea, four things say not, It is enough: The grave; and the barren womb; the earth that is not filled with water; and the fire that saith not, It is enough.

Ecclesiastes 1:8 All things are full of labour; man cannot utter it: the eye is not satisfied with seeing, nor the ear filled with hearing.

Ecclesiastes 2:9-10 So I was great, and increased more than all that were before me in Jerusalem: also my wisdom remained with me. And whatsoever mine eyes desired I kept not from them, I withheld not my heart from any joy; for my heart rejoiced in all my labour: and this was my portion of all my labour.

Ecclesiastes 5:10 He that loveth silver shall not be satisfied with silver; nor he that loveth abundance with increase: this *is* also vanity.

Isaiah 5:13-14 Therefore my people are gone into captivity, because they have no knowledge: and their honourable men are famished, and their multitude dried up with thirst. Therefore hell hath enlarged herself, and opened her mouth without measure: and their glory, and their multitude, and their pomp, and he that rejoiceth, shall descend into it.

Habakkuk 2:5 Yea also, because he transgresseth by wine, he is a proud man, neither keepeth at home, who enlargeth his desire as hell, and is as death, and cannot be satisfied, but gathereth unto him all nations, and heapeth unto him all people:

1 John 2:16 For all that *is* in the world, the lust of the flesh, and the lust of the eyes, and the pride of life, is not of the Father, but is of the world.

Proverbs 27:21 *As* the fining pot for silver, and the furnace for gold; so *is* a man to his praise.

Focus: This proverb depicts man's heart as an implement (fining pot, furnace) testing praise for impurities.

Both the **"fining pot"** [*"A melting pot" so tempered as to endure extreme heat without melting it. It is used for melting ores or metals.*[710]] and the **"furnace"** [*refining furnace or pot*] are implements used to heat metal to a high enough temperature to cause the dross (trash) to rise to the top where it can be separated from the valuable and pure metal. The praise a person receives often contains an impurity called "flattery," which needs to be separated from genuine praise and rejected, and it is the test of a man's character to see if he can separate it.

When the person gloats over praise, genuine or otherwise, he reveals arrogance and pride. If he accepts the praise modestly, he is revealing humility. A wise man knows to accept honest praise humbly so that he can honor God with whatever ability he might possess. In 1 Corinthians 4, the apostle Paul doubtless had in his mind the teachers in the church of Corinth, and intended to show them that there was no occasion of pride or preeminence. As God had given to them all that they possessed, nothing could be the occasion of boasting or self-confidence. A wise person knows that everything he is or accomplishes is due to the blessings of God. (Those blessings can certainly be enhanced by diligence and wisdom, but God is always the source of every ability.)

> 1 Corinthians 4:7 For who maketh thee to differ *from another*? and what hast thou that thou didst not receive? now if thou didst receive *it*, why dost thou glory, as if thou hadst not received *it*?

> "As the crucible brings all impurities to the surface, so public opinion drags forth all that is bad in a man, and he who stands this test is generally esteemed. Certainly praise is a stimulus to exertion, an incentive to try to make one's self worthy of the estimation in which one is held, especially if he purifies it from the dross and earthliness mixed with it, and takes to himself only what is genuine and just. But public opinion is very commonly false and is always a very unsafe criterion of moral excellence… 'So let a man be to his praise,' *i.e.* to the mouth which praises him; let him test this commendation, to see what it is worth, before he accepts it as his due.'"[711]

> Proverbs 17:3 The fining pot is for silver, and the furnace for gold: but the LORD trieth the hearts.

> Proverbs 25:4 Take away the dross from the silver, and there shall come forth a vessel for the finer.

> Proverbs 25:27 It is not good to eat much honey: so for men to search their own glory is not glory.

Proverbs 27:22 Though thou shouldest bray a fool in a mortar among wheat with a pestle, *yet* will not his foolishness depart from him.

Focus: This proverb expresses the idea that foolishness cannot be separated from a fool.

A **"mortar"** refers to a bowl made out of a hard substance such as stone, and a **"pestle"** is a hard club-shaped tool with a blunt end. Wheat is pounded and ground *(brayed)* in the mortar to effectively separate impurities and husks from the grain. This process illustrates the beating effect of tribulation that comes to an arrogant, hardened, perverse foolish person. Braying the fool in the mortar of trouble will not remove the foolishness from him because foolishness has become part of who he is. He usually brings these problems upon himself because he ignores God's word and His plan for his life. He should observe the calamities and question himself; but, being a fool, he thinks his actions are right.

Folly sticks to the fool until his last breath regardless of teaching, experiences, and punishment because the fool despises wisdom. He mocks when found guilty, and he is quarrelsome and licentious.

> Isaiah 9:13 For the people turneth not unto him that smiteth them, neither do they seek the LORD of hosts.

> Jeremiah 13:23 Can the Ethiopian change his skin, or the leopard his spots? *then* may ye also do good, that are accustomed to do evil.

Proverbs 27:23-27 Be thou diligent to know the state of thy flocks, *and* look well to thy herds.
24. For riches *are* not for ever: and doth the crown *endure* to every generation?
25. The hay appeareth, and the tender grass sheweth itself, and herbs of the mountains are gathered.
26. The lambs *are* for thy clothing, and the goats *are* the price of the field.
27. And *thou shalt have* goats' milk enough for thy food, for the food of thy household, and *for* the maintenance for thy maidens.

Focus: This proverb (5 verses) teaches the importance of having diligent *oversight* of one's livelihood.

Previously, Proverbs 24:30-34 graphically discussed the consequences of laziness concerning the sluggard's not caring for his vineyard. These current verses stress the importance of making every aspect of the farm productive.

"Be thou diligent to know the state of thy flocks, and look well to thy herds." (verse 23) The first and second clause of verse 23 makes the same point with different words; thus, doubling down on the importance of *personal oversight*. It is difficult to distinguish between a flock and a herd, but in general, a **herd** refers to a grouping of some four-legged animals, and a *flock* refers to a group of sheep, goats, or birds. The point of the proverb is that the owner is to personally look after and ascertain the condition of his animals; in fact, **"to know"** and to **"look well"** (or "set thy heart"[712]) imply that he should know them well enough to recognize them individually.

> Genesis 31:38-40 This twenty years *have* I *been* with thee; thy ewes and thy she goats have not cast their young, and the rams of thy flock have I not eaten. That which was torn *of beasts* I brought not unto thee; I bare the loss of it; of my hand didst thou require it, *whether* stolen by day, or stolen by night. *Thus* I was; in the day the drought consumed me, and the frost by night; and my sleep departed from mine eyes.
>
> Psalm 7:70-71 He chose David also his servant, and took him from the sheepfolds: From following the ewes great with young he brought him to feed Jacob his people, and Israel his inheritance

"For riches *are* not for ever: and doth the crown *endure* to every generation?" (verse 24) This verse addresses the fact that the **"riches"** of an individual and royal authority only belong to a person for a period of time. When the person is a steward over the riches or the throne, he is to be constantly taking the oversight. There is no instruction here about being or becoming rich, only about proper care and diligent awareness; however, wealth typically increases with God's blessings and proper supervision. A person's life span on earth is limited; consequently, wealth and the throne change ownership with time.

"The hay appeareth, and the tender grass sheweth itself, and herbs of the mountains are gathered. The lambs *are* for thy clothing, and the goats *are* the price of the field. And *thou shalt have* goats' milk enough for thy food, for the food of thy household, and *for* the maintenance for thy maidens." (verses 25-27) These verses stress *the provisions of God and His order of nature* while *the theme of personal responsibility and oversight is continued*. God set in order a regular seasonal progression for the necessities of man and beast. There is a certain time when ripe hay can be cut down to provide fodder for animals. When tender grass pops up in the spring, the wise farmer knows it is time to send his lambs to feed in the mountains, saving his home pasture. Lambs also eat the fresh herbs of the mountains, and a variety of herbs are gathered for medicinal uses at home. Flocks and herds provide clothing (the sheep's wool is spun into yarn which will be woven into cloth); the sale of the goats that have been tenderly cared for provides money to buy another field; goats' milk is used for nutritious food. God's provisions are replaced seasonally, while riches are spent and may not be replaced.

A wise man discovers that God has an order established in nature, and he learns to labor in coordination with that order and with God personally so that he can effectively do his part. God will aid the wise person in making his life both enjoyable and productive as he cares for God's provisions, works hard, and gives proper attentive care to what has been made available.

Although this Scripture deals with a small farm, application can be made to whatever source of livelihood a person has. Wise people do not allow their investments to go without personal care and oversight, thereby minimizing the risk of failure. Once the livelihood source gets beyond being small, the owner is forced to supervise the supervisors. Scripture often stresses that believers are to be good stewards of what God has entrusted to their care – an oversight that involves both physical and spiritual attention.

CHAPTER TWENTY-EIGHT

Introduction:

Chapter Twenty-Eight contains the third set of Solomon's proverbs copied out by Hezekiah's men. Because Solomon desired greatly for the people of the nation of Israel to follow God, the Holy Spirit used him to contrast the actions, fruits, and rewards of the ungodly with the actions, fruits, and rewards of the spiritual man who walks in the "fear of the LORD." The blessings of walking with God are contrasted with the problems that beset the way of the ungodly and the judgment that awaits them.

> **Proverbs 28:1** The wicked flee when no man pursueth: but the righteous are bold as a lion.

Focus: This proverb contrasts the behavior of the fearful wicked with that of the emboldened righteous.

"The wicked flee when no man pursueth" because: (1) Their conscience condemns them, and they are afraid of being caught for their evil deeds. (2) They are fearful of the judgments of God, knowing that He is against them. (3) They distrust everyone and believe that all people are as wicked as themselves and will thus do the same wicked things to them as they have done to others. (4) They imagine the worst because their minds think on evil continually. (5) They trust in the things that are always changing rather than in God, Who never changes. (6) They can have no invitation to pray to God for supernatural help until they first trust Him as Lord. (7) They have no godly wisdom and must rely solely on the wisdom of this world. (8) They imagine evil approaching them because God places a supernatural fear in their heart.

Adam and Eve fled and hid from God after proving their disbelief in His word. (Genesis 3:8) "Two kings of the Amorites" fled from hornets that God supernaturally sent as instruments of war. (Joshua 24:12) By word of mouth, God put a supernatural fear into the hearts of the enemies of Israel to cause them to "tremble and be in anguish." (Deuteronomy 2:25; Exodus 15:14-16) God supernaturally caused the Syrians to imagine hearing "a noise of chariots, and a noise of horses, even the noise of a great host" and then to flee in great fear. (2 Kings 7:6-7)

> Genesis 3:8 And they heard the voice of the LORD God walking in the garden in the cool of the day: and Adam and his wife hid themselves from the presence of the LORD God amongst the trees of the garden.
> Exodus 15:14-16 The people shall hear, *and* be afraid: sorrow shall take hold on the inhabitants of Palestina. Then the dukes of Edom shall be amazed; the mighty men of Moab, trembling shall take hold upon them; all the inhabitants of Canaan shall melt away. Fear and dread shall fall upon them; by the greatness of thine arm they shall be *as* still as a stone; till thy people *[Jews]* pass over, O LORD, till the people pass over, which thou hast purchased.
> Leviticus 26:36 And upon them that are left *alive* of you I will send a faintness into their hearts in the lands of their enemies; and the sound of a shaken leaf shall chase them; and they shall flee, as fleeing from a sword; and they shall fall when none pursueth.
> Deuteronomy 2:25 This day will I begin to put the dread of thee and the fear of thee upon the nations *that are* under the whole heaven, who shall hear report of thee, and shall tremble, and be in anguish because of thee.
> Deuteronomy 28:7 The LORD shall cause thine enemies that rise up against thee to be smitten before thy face: they shall come out against thee one way, and flee before thee seven ways.
> Deuteronomy 28:25 The LORD shall cause thee to be smitten before thine enemies: thou shalt go out one way against them, and flee seven ways before them: and shalt be removed into all the kingdoms of the earth.
> Joshua 24:12 And I sent the hornet before you, which drave them out from before you, even the two kings of the Amorites; but not with thy sword, nor with thy bow.
> 2 Kings 7:6-7 For the Lord had made the host of the Syrians to hear a noise of chariots, and a noise of horses, even the noise of a great host: and they said one to another, Lo, the king of Israel hath hired against us the kings of the Hittites, and the kings of the Egyptians, to come upon us. Wherefore they arose and fled in the twilight, and left their tents, and their horses, and their asses, even the camp as it was, and fled for their life.

Psalm 53:5 There were they in great fear, *where* no fear was: for God hath scattered the bones of him that encampeth *against* thee: thou hast put *them* to shame, because God hath despised them.

Jeremiah 20:4 For thus saith the LORD, Behold, I will make thee a terror to thyself, and to all thy friends: and they shall fall by the sword of their enemies, and thine eyes shall behold *it:* and I will give all Judah into the hand of the king of Babylon, and he shall carry them captive into Babylon, and shall slay them with the sword.

Titus 1:15 Unto the pure all things *are* pure: but unto them that are defiled and unbelieving *is* nothing pure; but even their mind and conscience is defiled.

"But the righteous are bold as a lion" because: (1) They have the witness of a clear conscience. (Acts 24:16) (2) They trust in God and are confident that "all things work together for good to them that love God." (Romans 8:2) (3) They are confident that God loves and favors them. (Psalm 1:3; 139:7-13) (4) They are fully persuaded that God is good for all His promises to them. (2 Corinthians 1:20) (5) They have great strength from having been with Jesus. (Acts 4:13) (6) They have the comforting presence of the Holy Spirit to give them peace. (Acts 4:29-31) (7) They have the consoling word of God saying that He will protect and guide them. (Isaiah 54:14, 17) (8) They have peace from godly wisdom that is always accurate in approach and solution. (Ecclesiastes 8:1) (9) They have been given by God a spirit "of power and of love and of a sound mind." (2 Timothy 1:7)

Psalm 1:3 And he shall be like a tree planted by the rivers of water, that bringeth forth his fruit in his season; his leaf also shall not wither; and whatsoever he doeth shall prosper.

Psalm 139:7-13 Whither shall I go from thy spirit? or whither shall I flee from thy presence? If I ascend up into heaven, thou *art* there: if I make my bed in hell, behold, thou art there. *If* I take the wings of the morning, *and* dwell in the uttermost parts of the sea; Even there shall thy hand lead me, and thy right hand shall hold me. If I say, Surely the darkness shall cover me; even the night shall be light about me. Yea, the darkness hideth not from thee; but the night shineth as the day: the darkness and the light *are* both alike *to thee*. For thou hast possessed my reins: thou hast covered me in my mother's womb.

Ecclesiastes 8:1 Who *is* as the wise *man?* and who knoweth the interpretation of a thing? a man's wisdom maketh his face to shine, and the boldness of his face shall be changed.

Isaiah 54:14 In righteousness shalt thou be established: thou shalt be far from oppression; for thou shalt not fear: and from terror; for it shall not come near thee.

Isaiah 54:17 No weapon that is formed against thee shall prosper; and every tongue that shall rise against thee in judgment thou shalt condemn. This is the heritage of the servants of the LORD, and their righteousness is of me, saith the LORD.

Jeremiah 29:11 For I know the thoughts that I think toward you, saith the LORD, thoughts of peace, and not of evil, to give you an expected end.

Acts 4:13 Now when they saw the boldness of Peter and John, and perceived that they were unlearned and ignorant men, they marvelled; and they took knowledge of them, that they had been with Jesus.

Acts 4:29-31 And now, Lord, behold their threatenings: and grant unto thy servants, that with all boldness they may speak thy word, By stretching forth thine hand to heal; and that signs and wonders may be done by the name of thy holy child Jesus. And when they had prayed, the place was shaken where they were assembled together; and they were all filled with the Holy Ghost, and they spake the word of God with boldness.

Romans 8:28 And we know that all things work together for good to them that love God, to them who are the called according to *his* purpose.

2 Corinthians 1:20 For all the promises of God in him *are* yea, and in him Amen, unto the glory of God by us.

2 Timothy 1:7 For God hath not given us the spirit of fear; but of power, and of love, and of a sound mind.

1 Peter 5:8-9 Be sober, be vigilant; because your adversary the devil, as a roaring lion, walketh about, seeking whom he may devour: Whom resist stedfast in the faith, knowing that the same afflictions are accomplished in your brethren that are in the world.

Below are some of the men and women known for their bold faith in God.

Noah – Hebrews 11:7 "By faith Noah, being warned of God of things not seen as yet, moved with fear, prepared an ark to the saving of his house; by the which he condemned the world, and became heir of the righteousness which is by faith."

Abraham – Hebrews 11:8 -10 "By faith Abraham, when he was called to go out into a place which he should after receive for an inheritance, obeyed; and he went out, not knowing whither he went. By faith he sojourned in the land of promise, as in a strange country, dwelling in tabernacles with Isaac and Jacob, the heirs with him of the same promise: For he looked for a city which hath foundations, whose builder and maker is God."

Moses – Hebrews 11:24-28 "By faith Moses, when he was come to years, refused to be called the son of Pharaoh's daughter; Choosing rather to suffer affliction with the people of God, than to enjoy the pleasures of sin for a season; Esteeming the reproach of Christ greater riches than the treasures in Egypt: for he had respect unto the recompence of the reward. By faith he forsook Egypt, not fearing the wrath of the king: for he endured, as seeing him who is invisible. Through faith he kept the passover, and the sprinkling of blood, lest he that destroyed the firstborn should touch them."

Rahab – Hebrews 11:31 "By faith the harlot Rahab perished not with them that believed not, when she had received the spies with peace."

Shadrach, Meshach, and Abednego **boldly stood up for Jehovah** – Daniel 3:16-18 "Shadrach, Meshach, and Abednego, answered and said to the king, O Nebuchadnezzar, we are not careful to answer thee in this matter. If it be so, our God whom we serve is able to deliver us from the burning fiery furnace, and he will deliver us out of thine hand, O king. But if not, be it known unto thee, O king, that we will not serve thy gods, nor worship the golden image which thou hast set up."

Others boldly faced death for Jehovah – Hebrews 11:33-38 "Who through faith subdued kingdoms, wrought righteousness, obtained promises, stopped the mouths of lions, Quenched the violence of fire, escaped the edge of the sword, out of weakness were made strong, waxed valiant in fight, turned to flight the armies of the aliens. Women received their dead raised to life again: and others were tortured, not accepting deliverance; that they might obtain a better resurrection: And others had trial of cruel mockings and scourgings, yea, moreover of bonds and imprisonment: They were stoned, they were sawn asunder, were tempted, were slain with the sword: they wandered about in sheepskins and goatskins; being destitute, afflicted, tormented; (Of whom the world was not worthy:) they wandered in deserts, and in mountains, and in dens and caves of the earth."

Proverbs 28:2   For the transgression of a land many *are* the princes thereof: but by a man of understanding *and* knowledge the state *thereof* shall be prolonged.

Focus: This proverb declares transgression is a cause of instability and turnover in governmental leadership, but a man of understanding and knowledge will provide stability.

"For the transgression of a land many *are* the princes thereof." Because Israel was God's chosen people, she was established by God with the intent that she would follow His commandments and be subject to His will in all areas of leadership and operation. However, Israel often rebelled against God and demanded her own way. **"Transgression,"** as used in this verse, is specifically rebellion *[a revolt]* that pulls away from the authority of God and His laws. Figuratively speaking, the transgression is said to be **"of a land." "A land,"** per se, cannot rebel or revolt; therefore, it is a figure of speech representing the people of a nation (Israel). When a nation sets its mind on rebelling against God and thereby allows open sin, lawlessness, apostasy, and other degrading conduct to exist, that country becomes subject to being overthrown by power-hungry individuals seeking superiority.

Such **"transgression"** by Israel always resulted in the loss of God's providential care, which caused instability and defeat. Through greed for power, princes were removed from their place of authority; and other persons, often persons of other rebellious families, took over the throne. Such frequent changes were seldom for the better and were usually accompanied by blood and slaughter and additional heavy taxes.

Jeroboam took ten of the twelve tribes of Israel from Rehoboam *(the rightful but foolish heir to Solomon's throne)* and then transgressed the commandments of God by instituting golden calf worship in his Northern Kingdom. He established a precedent of transgression against God that resulted in many future rebellious rulers being killed and their thrones taken by others. *(See the chart of the Kings of Israel in the Appendix.)* All the kings of the Northern Kingdom were evil, and during the times of Israel's Divided Kingdom, *there were* **many princes**. When a nation is led by a leader who is rebellious against God and His laws, the result will be instability and frequent turnover of leadership. Interestingly, seven of the nineteen kings of Israel's Northern Kingdom were murdered by individuals who killed the king and took the throne. The following excerpt summarizes what happens when God punishes His people.

"National sins bring national disorders and the disturbance of the public repose: '**For the transgression of a land**,' and a general defection from God and religion to idolatry, profaneness, or immorality, '**many are the princes thereof**,' many at the same time pretending to the sovereignty and contending for it, by which the people are crumbled into parties and factions, biting and devouring one another, or many successively, in a little time, one cutting off another . . . or soon cut off by the hand of God or of a foreign enemy . . . "[713]

Leviticus 26:13-17 I am the LORD your God, which brought you forth out of the land of Egypt, that ye should not be their bondmen; and I have broken the bands of your yoke, and made you go upright. But if ye will not hearken unto me, and will not do all these commandments; And if ye shall despise my statutes, or if your soul abhor my judgments, so that ye will not do all my commandments, but that ye break my covenant: I also will do this unto you; I will even appoint over you terror, consumption, and the burning ague, that shall consume the eyes, and cause sorrow of heart: and ye shall sow your seed in vain, for your enemies shall eat it. And I will set my face against you, and ye shall be slain before your enemies: they that hate you shall reign over you; and ye shall flee when none pursueth you.

Proverbs 11:11 By the blessing of the upright the city is exalted: but it is overthrown by the mouth of the wicked.

Isaiah 3:1-4 For, behold, the Lord, the LORD of hosts, doth take away from Jerusalem and from Judah the stay and the staff, the whole stay of bread, and the whole stay of water, The mighty man, and the man of war, the judge, and the prophet, and the prudent, and the ancient, The captain of fifty, and the honourable man, and the counsellor, and the cunning artificer, and the eloquent orator. And I will give children to be their princes, and babes shall rule over them.

Hosea 8:4 They have set up kings, but not by me: they have made princes, and I knew *it* not: of their silver and their gold have they made them idols, that they may be cut off.

"But by a man of understanding and knowledge the state thereof shall be prolonged." "A man of understanding and knowledge" is a wise leader. Unlike the conditions of the Northern Kingdom of Israel, which suffered from instability and continual change of leadership, the conditions in Judah were much better due to wise leaders' bringing more stability in the operation and in the leadership. **"The state thereof"** means the physical condition which is directly related to the spiritual, especially with Israel. When her spiritual relationship with God was proper, her physical state was also proper. Conditions change when a man of integrity takes the throne following a wicked leader. A godly man will bring stability that will be maintained if the country will follow his leading. If the man "of understanding and knowledge" be the ruler, counselor to the ruler, or a wise man in the kingdom, he will *(if allowed)* lead the country in the ways of God. His righteous leadership will guarantee the ***prolonging*** of stability because of the protection and provisions as promised by God. "Order ... is maintained in a nation by good rulers who have insight and knowledge about how to govern."[714]

Exodus 18:21 Moreover thou shalt provide out of all the people able men, such as fear God, men of truth, hating covetousness; and place such over them, to be rulers of thousands, and rulers of hundreds, rulers of fifties, and rulers of tens...

Isaiah 33:6 And wisdom and knowledge shall be the stability of thy times, and strength of salvation: the fear of the LORD is his treasure.

1 Timothy 2:1-2 I exhort therefore, that, first of all, supplications, prayers, intercessions, and giving of thanks, be made for all men; For kings, and for all that are in authority; that we may lead a quiet and peaceable life in all godliness and honesty.

Proverbs 28:3 A poor man that oppresseth the poor *is like* a sweeping rain which leaveth no food.

Focus: This proverb describes a shocking contradiction of expected conduct.

"Rain" is expected to bring vitality. Without it, seeds and plants fail; and if the dryness is severe enough, famine results. Joyfully, when there is rain, there is hope, but if the shower becomes a **"sweeping rain"** that washes away the seed and drowns existing crops, then *hope turns to despair.* Likewise, the poor experience a joyful expectation of relief when a **"poor man"** is raised to a position of authority. Because of his own previous hardships from impoverishment, he is naturally expected to sympathetically bring relief and vitality. If, instead, he brings sweeping terror and oppresses those who expected to get help, he will turn *hope into horror.* He becomes a terror, a disaster.

"A poor man" who is not a believer is likely to be predominately selfish, and if raised to a position of authority, he will take what he can get from any available source, and **"the poor"** are the easiest targets. In most cases, other poor people soon discover that he is the worst oppressor of all because he takes away their last morsel of food like the powerful rain, which washes even the seeds out of the ground.

Matthew 18:23-35 Therefore is the kingdom of heaven likened unto a certain king, which would take account of his servants. And when he had begun to reckon, one was brought unto him, which owed him ten thousand talents. But forasmuch as he had not to pay, his lord commanded him to be sold, and his wife, and children, and all that he had, and payment to be made. The servant therefore fell down, and worshipped him, saying, Lord, have patience with me, and I will pay thee all. Then the lord of that servant was moved with compassion, and loosed him, and forgave him the debt. But the same servant went out, and found one of his fellowservants, which owed him an hundred pence: and he laid hands on him, and took him by the throat, saying, Pay me that thou owest. And his fellowservant fell down at his feet, and besought him, saying, Have patience with me, and I will pay thee all. And he would not: but went and cast him into prison, till he should pay the debt. So when his fellowservants saw what was done, they were very sorry, and came and told unto their lord all that was done. Then his lord, after that he had called him, said unto him, O thou wicked servant, I forgave thee all that debt, because thou desiredst me: Shouldest not thou also have had compassion on thy fellowservant, even as I had pity on thee? And his lord was wroth, and delivered him to the tormentors, till he should pay all that was due unto him. So likewise shall my heavenly Father do also unto you, if ye from your hearts forgive not every one his brother their trespasses.

Romans 1:28; 32 And even as they did not like to retain God in *their* knowledge, God gave them over to a reprobate mind, to do those things which are not convenient ... Who knowing the judgment of God, that they which commit such things are worthy of death, not only do the same, but have pleasure in them that do them.

> **Proverbs 28:4** They that forsake the law praise the wicked: but such as keep the law contend with them.

Focus: This proverb contrasts those who forsake the law with those who keep it.

"They that forsake the law" are those who oppose it, live in opposition to it, find it objectionable, and certainly do not have a desire to obey it. Naturally, they will **"praise the wicked"** since they are themselves wicked and have forsaken God's law. They associate with other wicked persons who approve of their godless lifestyle; they find pleasure in giving credibility to each other and in supporting the ongoing wickedness and opposition to God.

> Romans 1:28; 32 And even as they did not like to retain God in *their* knowledge, God gave them over to a reprobate mind, to do those things which are not convenient... Who knowing the judgment of God, that they which commit such things are worthy of death, not only do the same, but have pleasure in them that do them.

"But such as keep the law contend with them." God's law governs the way those who love God and His law think and live. If they remain silent, their very lifestyle contends with the ungodly and brings condemnation and anguish of conscience upon them. Thus did Noah condemn the ungodly through his habits of life and also through his preaching of righteousness. Every Christian has a responsibility to contend (where and when appropriate) with those who forsake the law of God, speak out against evil, put evil doers to shame, and to be as bold as a lion *yet as meek as our Lord*. The godly and the ungodly live opposite lifestyles. Those works that the godly find pleasurable, the wicked find objectionable, and vice versa; consequently, they **"contend with"** each other. Nehemiah is an example of one who struggled, in what appears to be an excessive manner, with those who opposed keeping the law.

> Nehemiah 13:17 Then I contended with the nobles of Judah, and said unto them, What evil thing is this that ye do, and profane the sabbath day?
> Nehemiah 13:24-25 And their children spake half in the speech of Ashdod, and could not speak in the Jews' language, but according to the language of each people. And I contended with them, and cursed them, and smote certain of them, and plucked off their hair, and made them swear by God, saying, Ye shall not give your daughters unto their sons, nor take their daughters unto your sons, or for yourselves.

Christians today are not under the Mosaic law but under grace, and though expected to stand up for the faith, they are not to strive *(fight, make war)*. "And the servant of the Lord must not strive: but be gentle unto all *men*, apt to teach, patient, In meekness instructing those that oppose themselves; if God peradventure will give them repentance to the acknowledging of the truth; And *that* they may recover themselves out of the snare of the devil, who are taken captive by him at his will." (2 Timothy 2:24-26)

The Bible commands the believer to "contend for the faith" only with the leadership of the Holy Spirit. who produces "love, joy, peace, longsuffering, gentleness, goodness, faith, meekness, temperance: against such there is no law." When these excellent qualities are present, opposition honors God and respects His created humanity.

> Proverbs 24:23-25 These *things* also *belong* to the wise. *It is* not good to have respect of persons in judgment. He that saith unto the wicked, Thou *art* righteous; him shall the people curse, nations shall abhor him: But to them that rebuke *him* shall be delight, and a good blessing shall come upon them.
> Jude 1:3 Beloved, when I gave all diligence to write unto you of the common salvation, it was needful for me to write unto you, and exhort you that ye should earnestly contend for the faith which was once delivered unto the saints.

> **Proverbs 28:5** Evil men understand not judgment: but they that seek the LORD understand all *things*.

Focus: This proverb contrasts those who do not understand godly opinion of right and wrong (judgment) with those who do.

"Evil men understand not judgment" because their minds are consumed with wickedness and doing evil. The more evil they think about and do, the more their minds lust for the same, until thinking righteously is entirely foreign, rendering them unable to understand the difference between right and wrong **("judgment")**. **"Evil men"** will not allow the word of God nor the Spirit of God to influence their thinking because they are prejudiced against the things of God.

> Psalm 92:6 A brutish man knoweth not; neither doth a fool understand this.
> Proverbs 1:7 The fear of the LORD is the beginning of knowledge: but fools despise wisdom and instruction.

Proverbs 1:29-30 For that they hated knowledge, and did not choose the fear of the LORD: They would none of my counsel: they despised all my reproof.

Proverbs 2:11-15 Discretion shall preserve thee, understanding shall keep thee: To deliver thee from the way of the evil man, from the man that speaketh froward things; Who leave the paths of uprightness, to walk in the ways of darkness; Who rejoice to do evil, and delight in the frowardness of the wicked; Whose ways are crooked, and they froward in their paths . . .

Jeremiah 4:22 For my people is foolish, they have not known me; they are sottish children, and they have none understanding: they are wise to do evil, but to do good they have no knowledge.

Jeremiah 8:7 Yea, the stork in the heaven knoweth her appointed times; and the turtle and the crane and the swallow observe the time of their coming; but my people know not the judgment of the LORD.

Ephesians 4:17-19 This I say therefore, and testify in the Lord, that ye henceforth walk not as other Gentiles walk, in the vanity of their mind, Having the understanding darkened, being alienated from the life of God through the ignorance that is in them, because of the blindness of their heart: Who being past feeling have given themselves over unto lasciviousness, to work all uncleanness with greediness.

2 Thessalonians 2:11-12 And for this cause God shall send them strong delusion, that they should believe a lie: That they all might be damned who believed not the truth, but had pleasure in unrighteousness.

"But they that seek the LORD" are the godly, the righteous, those who want to know more about God, who believe Him to be right. They seek his wisdom, knowledge and understanding.

Psalm 25:14 The secret of the LORD is with them that fear him; and he will shew them his covenant.

Proverbs 9:9-10 Give instruction to a wise man, and he will be yet wiser: teach a just man, and he will increase in learning. The fear of the LORD is the beginning of wisdom: and the knowledge of the holy is understanding.

Mark 4:11-12 And he said unto them, Unto you it is given to know the mystery of the kingdom of God: but unto them that are without, all these things are done in parables: That seeing they may see, and not perceive; and hearing they may hear, and not understand; lest at any time they should be converted, and their sins should be forgiven them.

"Understand all things" does not mean that those who seek the Lord will know all things possible to know but rather *all things that God views as right*. Only God Himself understands everything. The more a person seeks after the Lord and studies His word and draws close to Him, the more he will know what is right and wrong in this life. *Christians know how to live right and to do right because they are taught by God's word and led by the Holy Spirit.* (1 John 2:20, 27)

Psalm 111:10 The fear of the LORD *is* the beginning of wisdom: a good understanding have all they that do *his commandments:* his praise endureth for ever.

John 7:16-17 Jesus answered them, and said, My doctrine is not mine, but his that sent me. If any man will do his will, he shall know of the doctrine, whether it be of God, or *whether* I speak of myself.

1 Corinthians 2:12-16 Now we have received, not the spirit of the world, but the spirit which is of God; that we might know the things that are freely given to us of God. Which things also we speak, not in the words which man's wisdom teacheth, but which the Holy Ghost teacheth; comparing spiritual things with spiritual. But the natural man receiveth not the things of the Spirit of God: for they are foolishness unto him: neither can he know *them,* because they are spiritually discerned. But he that is spiritual judgeth all things, yet he himself is judged of no man. For who hath known the mind of the Lord, that he may instruct him? But we have the mind of Christ.

1 John 2:20 But ye have an unction from the Holy One, and ye know all things.

1 John 2:27 But the anointing which ye have received of him abideth in you, and ye need not that any man teach you: but as the same anointing teacheth you of all things, and is truth, and is no lie, and even as it hath taught you, ye shall abide in him.

Proverbs 28:6 Better *is* the poor that walketh in his uprightness, than *he that is* perverse *in his* ways, though he *be* rich.

Focus: This proverb contrasts the value of poverty accompanied by uprightness with the value of wealth accompanied by perverseness.

The man who **"walketh in his uprightness"** lives according to the instructions of God's word, while the **"perverse in his ways"** willfully opposes God and His teachings. A perverse, froward person inflicts controversy, opposition, and damage to the work of God and to the good of man. Additionally, the perverse worldly view (opposite God's view) believes that it is better to be rich and perverse than poor and righteous. People who are perverse in their ways often have two ways and two faces, so that they can pretend to be holy when it benefits them. Wealth is their goal, not righteousness.

"The poor that walketh in his uprightness" is **"better"** because he is God's friend and not an enemy like the ungodly. He is also better because he is an example to those who guide their family and friends by both lifestyle and words. God delights in the upright person. Because of a lack of wealth, dishonesty can be a great temptation to the poor; thus, for the poor to rise to the level of walking in uprightness seems more difficult than for the average person who is not struggling for daily needs. "Two *things* have I required of thee; deny me *them* not before I die: Remove far from me vanity and lies: give me neither poverty nor riches; feed me with food convenient for me: Lest I be full, and deny *thee,* and say, Who *is* the LORD? or lest I be poor, and steal, and take the name of my God *in vain."* (Proverbs 30:7-9)

> Proverbs 11:20 They that are of a froward heart *are* abomination to the LORD: but *such as are* upright in *their* way *are* his delight.
>
> Proverbs 12:22 Lying lips *are* abomination to the LORD: but they that deal truly *are* his delight.
>
> Proverbs 15:16 Better is little with the fear of the LORD than great treasure and trouble therewith.
>
> Proverbs 16:8 Better is a little with righteousness than great revenues without right.
>
> Proverbs 19:1 Better *is* the poor that walketh in his integrity, than *he that is* perverse in his lips, and is a fool.

Proverbs 28:7 Whoso keepeth the law *is* a wise son: but he that is a companion of riotous *men* shameth his father.

Focus: This proverb contrasts the effect that a wise son has on his father with the effect that a foolish son has.

"Whoso keepeth the law" in the first clause is contrasted with **"companion of riotous *men*"** in the second. One maintains companionship *with the law of God and walks uprightly,* while the other maintains companionship with *vile, loose-living, foolish people.* One lives a life that produces admiration because of his wisdom, while the other lives a life that produces shame because of foolishness. Also translated as "gluttony in Proverbs 23:20, **"riotous"** is translated from a Hebrew word that means worthless, vile, and prodigal. Consequently, the word is usually associated with excessive drinking and gluttony. The prodigal son wasted his inheritance with riotous living. The foolish son chooses to be **"a companion of riotous *men*,"** who are those prone to be free from any restraints or guidelines of the word of God. He learns their low values, picks up their foul language, takes their ungodly counsel, and acts like a fool. He lives a lifestyle that God and good men oppose and thus brings shame to his father.

> Proverbs 20:1 Wine *is* a mocker, strong drink *is* raging: and whosoever is deceived thereby is not wise.
>
> Proverbs 23:20-21 Be not among winebibbers; among riotous eaters of flesh: For the drunkard and the glutton shall come to poverty: and drowsiness shall clothe *a man* with rags.
>
> Proverbs 23:29-33 Who hath woe? who hath sorrow? who hath contentions? who hath babbling? who hath wounds without cause? who hath redness of eyes? They that tarry long at the wine; they that go to seek mixed wine. Look not thou upon the wine when it is red, when it giveth his colour in the cup, *when* it moveth itself aright. At the last it biteth like a serpent, and stingeth like an adder. Thine eyes shall behold strange women, and thine heart shall utter perverse things.

In Deuteronomy, Moses told the people of Israel that their obedience to Jehovah's laws would cause the nations to respect Israel and call it a "wise" and "great nation." Certainly, this could be applied to any person who chooses God's word as a companion.

> Deuteronomy 4:5-6 Behold, I have taught you statutes and judgments, even as the LORD my God commanded me, that ye should do so in the land whither ye go to possess it. Keep therefore and do them; for this is your wisdom and your understanding in the sight of the nations, which shall hear all these statutes, and say, Surely this great nation is a wise and understanding people.

Keeping the law correlates to the fear of God, and the fear of God is the beginning of wisdom. He is a wise son who chooses to stay away from those that indulge in riotous living. A son who "keepeth the law" will certainly choose companions who do the same.

Proverbs 28:8 He that by usury and unjust gain increaseth his substance, he shall gather it for him that will pity the poor.

Focus: This proverb states that gain from forbidden, abusive financial practices will be redistributed.

During Solomon's era, **"usury,"** as used in this verse, was *any interest* charged on a debt to a fellow Jew; however, later, it came to mean gain acquired by charging *too much* interest. Leviticus 25:36-37 provides a clear mandate against "usury" and "unjust gain" when it states, "Take thou no usury of him, or increase: but fear thy God; that thy brother may live with thee. Thou shalt not give him thy money upon usury, nor lend him thy victuals for increase."

"The Jews were forbidden by the law of Moses to take interest from their brethren, but were permitted to take it from foreigners. The prohibition grew out of the agricultural status of the people, in which ordinary business loans were not needed. And loans as were required should be made only as to friends and brothers in need."[715]

The admonition was against abusive, unmerciful practices that disobeyed God's law against Hebrew brethren and disrespected the poor. **"Unjust gain"** can also be acquired by other deceitful or improper means, such as using a false weight. Because godly people depend on God for wealth, they are never to abuse or take advantage of others, especially the poor.

> Exodus 22:25 If thou lend money to *any of* my people *that is* poor by thee, thou shalt not be to him as an usurer, neither shalt thou lay upon him usury.
> Deuteronomy 23:19-20 Thou shalt not lend upon usury to thy brother; usury of money, usury of victuals, usury of any thing that is lent upon usury: Unto a stranger thou mayest lend upon usury; but unto thy brother thou shalt not lend upon usury: that the LORD thy God may bless thee in all that thou settest thine hand to in the land whither thou goest to possess it.
> Leviticus 25:35-36 And if thy brother be waxen poor, and fallen in decay with thee; then thou shalt relieve him: yea, though he be a stranger, or a sojourner; that he may live with thee. Take thou no usury of him, or increase: but fear thy God; that thy brother may live with thee.
> Leviticus 25:14 And if thou sell ought unto thy neighbour, or buyest ought of thy neighbour's hand, ye shall not oppress one another ...

"He shall gather it for him that will pity the poor." The one that oppresses through usury might have the unjust gain for a little while, but the riches eventually shall fall into the hands of one who will make a better use of them. *Justice eventually overtaking injustice* as described in verse 8 is a common theme in Scripture. And since God is not only just but all powerful, He will take the oversight to ensure that His proclamation remains true.

> Job 27:13, 16-17 This is the portion of a wicked man with God, and the heritage of oppressors, which they shall receive of the Almighty ... Though he heap up silver as the dust, and prepare raiment as the clay; He may prepare it, but the just shall put it on, and the innocent shall divide the silver.
> Proverbs 11:24 There is that scattereth, and yet increaseth; and there is that withholdeth more than is meet, but it tendeth to poverty.
> Proverbs 13:22 A good man leaveth an inheritance to his children's children: and the wealth of the sinner is laid up for the just.
> Proverbs 22:16 He that oppresseth the poor to increase his *riches, and* he that giveth to the rich, *shall* surely *come* to want.
> Ecclesiastes 2:26 For God giveth to a man that is good in his sight wisdom, and knowledge, and joy: but to the sinner he giveth travail, to gather and to heap up, that he may give to him that is good before God. This also is vanity and vexation of spirit.
> Ezekiel 18:13 Hath given forth upon usury, and hath taken increase: shall he then live? he shall not live: he hath done all these abominations; he shall surely die; his blood shall be upon him.

Proverbs 28:9 He that turneth away his ear from hearing the law, even his prayer *shall be* abomination.

Focus: This proverb declares that a man's rejection of God's law is met with God's rejection of the man – even his prayers.

To turn **"away his ear from hearing the law"** is to block the word of God from entering the mind. Some refuse to be where the word of God is being explained (church, Bible study) and purposefully avoid any association with Scripture. They will not read nor hear the Bible for fear they should come under its influence and persuasion. Others may reject His word, calling it illegitimate in its writing, inappropriate for today's world, or inaccurate. Some may not want anything to do with God Himself. Whatever the reason given by the rejecter, his refusing to give ear to Scripture results in God's refusing to give ear to him because such refusal to hear is rebellion to the God who created him in His own image to worship, serve Him, and to fellowship with Him. How then "... Shall the clay say to him that fashioneth it, What makest thou? Or thy work, He hath no hands?" (Isaiah 45:9)

> 1 Samuel 15:22-23 And Samuel said, Hath the LORD as great delight in burnt offerings and sacrifices, as in obeying the voice of the LORD? Behold, to obey is better than sacrifice, and to hearken than the fat of rams. For rebellion is as the sin of witchcraft, and stubbornness is as iniquity and idolatry. Because thou hast rejected the word of the LORD, he hath also rejected thee from being king.
> Proverbs 15:8-9 The sacrifice of the wicked is an abomination to the LORD: but the prayer of the upright is his delight. The way of the wicked is an abomination unto the LORD: but he loveth him that followeth after righteousness.
> Isaiah 59:1-2 Behold, the LORD'S hand is not shortened, that it cannot save; neither his ear heavy, that it cannot hear: But your iniquities have separated between you and your God, and your sins have hid his face from you, that he will not hear.

When a man despises God's word, he will be abhorred and rejected by God. God will reject his prayers, and he will also face unnecessary problems and tribulations in this life. After this life, he will face God in the judgment, be weighed in the balance of God's justice, and be found wanting. Every man needs God's help, whether he knows it or not.

Proverbs 13:15 Good understanding giveth favour: but the way of transgressors *is* hard.

Jeremiah 6:19 Hear, O earth: behold, I will bring evil upon this people, even the fruit of their thoughts, because they have not hearkened unto my words, nor to my law, but rejected it.

Zechariah 7:11-13 But they refused to hearken, and pulled away the shoulder, and stopped their ears, that they should not hear. Yea, they made their hearts as an adamant stone, lest they should hear the law, and the words which the LORD of hosts hath sent in his spirit by the former prophets: therefore came a great wrath from the LORD of hosts. Therefore it is come to pass, that as he cried, and they would not hear; so they cried, and I would not hear, saith the LORD of hosts . . .

2 Timothy 4:3-4 For the time will come when they will not endure sound doctrine; but after their own lusts shall they heap to themselves teachers, having itching ears; And they shall turn away their ears from the truth, and shall be turned unto fables.

Proverbs 28:10 Whoso causeth the righteous to go astray in an evil way, he shall fall himself into his own pit: but the upright shall have good *things* in possession.

Focus: This proverb contrasts the consequence of an evil entrapper of the righteous with the consequence of the upright.

Whoever causes the righteous to go astray in an evil way, he shall fall himself into his own pit. Throughout Scriptures, a major recurring theme is that God has special, personal, and direct oversight of those in alignment with Him and His word, His thinking, and His laws. These are the **"righteous,"** the believers, the born-again Christians. God speaks to them through His word and sometimes directly. He sent His Son to pay the price of their sins, and then He sent the Holy Spirit to guide and comfort them. He has a very special interest in the **"righteous"** who have chosen to spend eternity with Him. They are further identified throughout Scripture as the wise, the redeemed, the children of God, and the sons of God. They are sinners saved by the grace of God.

When a person *employs evil to cause the righteous to go astray*, he causes the **"righteous"** to fall into some sin and evil opposed by God. This verse clearly states that whoever is so led by Satan and follows through with such an evil act of entrapment shall do so at the expense of God's reprisal resulting in the evil one himself falling into the very trap that he set. Throughout history, evil people have attempted to deceive God's people and to entice them into doctrinal errors or physical immoralities. These evil men even appear in the assemblies of believers around the world. Jesus makes this statement in Matthew 24:24 – "For there shall arise false Christs, and false prophets, and shall shew great signs and wonders; insomuch that, if it were possible, they shall deceive the very elect."

Psalm 7:15-16 He made a pit, and digged it, and is fallen into the ditch which he made. His mischief shall return upon his own head, and his violent dealing shall come down upon his own pate.

Proverbs 26:27 Whoso diggeth a pit shall fall therein: and he that rolleth a stone, it will return upon him.

Acts 13:8 But Elymas the sorcerer (for so is his name by interpretation) withstood them, seeking to turn away the deputy from the faith.

Romans 16:17-18 Now I beseech you, brethren, mark them which cause divisions and offences contrary to the doctrine which ye have learned; and avoid them.   For they that are such serve not our Lord Jesus Christ, but their own belly; and by good words and fair speeches deceive the hearts of the simple.

2 Corinthians 11:3-4 But I fear, lest by any means, as the serpent beguiled Eve through his subtilty, so your minds should be corrupted from the simplicity that is in Christ. For if he that cometh preacheth another Jesus, whom we have not preached, or if ye receive another spirit, which ye have not received, or another gospel, which ye have not accepted, ye might well bear with him.

2 Corinthians 11:13-15   For such are false apostles, deceitful workers, transforming themselves into the apostles of Christ. And no marvel; for Satan himself is transformed into an angel of light. Therefore it is no great thing if his ministers also be transformed as the ministers of righteousness; whose end shall be according to their works.

Revelation 2:14   But I have a few things against thee, because thou hast there them that hold the doctrine of Balaam, who taught Balac to cast a stumblingblock before the children of Israel, to eat things sacrificed unto idols, and to commit fornication.

"But the upright *[righteous]* **shall have good things in possession."** They are **"upright"** because they are forgiven, not sinless. Because they are human, they can and will make mistakes and perhaps fall into an evil trap; but because they are wise and seek to please God, they will ask for forgiveness and be restored into good standing with God. "If we confess our sin, he is faithful and just to forgive us *our* sins, and to cleanse us from all unrighteousness" (1 John 1:9). Because he has sinned and found repentance, the true believer who desires above all things to please God will be humbled and watchful in the future and strengthened in his faith. "He shall be abundantly rewarded by God's grace and protection, by the comfort of a conscience at rest, and by prosperity in his worldly concerns – an adumbration of the eternal recompense awaiting him in the life to come."⁷¹⁶ Then he **"shall have good things in possession"** meaning that God is rewarding him and shall reward him. As Proverbs 3:35 states, "The wise shall inherit glory: but shame shall be the promotion of fools."

> Deuteronomy 7:12-15 Wherefore it shall come to pass, if ye hearken to these judgments, and keep, and do them, that the LORD thy God shall keep unto thee the covenant and the mercy which he sware unto thy fathers: And he will love thee, and bless thee, and multiply thee: he will also bless the fruit of thy womb, and the fruit of thy land, thy corn, and thy wine, and thine oil, the increase of thy kine, and the flocks of thy sheep, in the land which he sware unto thy fathers to give thee. Thou shalt be blessed above all people: there shall not be male or female barren among you, or among your cattle. And the LORD will take away from thee all sickness, and will put none of the evil diseases of Egypt, which thou knowest, upon thee; but will lay them upon all them that hate thee.
>
> Psalm 37:25-26 I have been young, and *now* am old; yet have I not seen the righteous forsaken, nor his seed begging bread. *He is* ever merciful, and lendeth; and his seed *is* blessed.
>
> Proverbs 10:3 The LORD will not suffer the soul of the righteous to famish: but he casteth away the substance of the wicked.
>
> Proverbs 15:6 In the house of the righteous is much treasure: but in the revenues of the wicked is trouble.
>
> Matthew 6:33 But seek ye first the kingdom of God, and his righteousness; and all these things shall be added unto you.
>
> 1 Corinthians 2:9 But as it is written, Eye hath not seen, nor ear heard, neither have entered into the heart of man, the things which God hath prepared for them that love him.
>
> 1 Peter 1:3-4 Blessed be the God and Father of our Lord Jesus Christ, which according to his abundant mercy hath begotten us again unto a lively hope by the resurrection of Jesus Christ from the dead, To an inheritance incorruptible, and undefiled, and that fadeth not away, reserved in heaven for you, Who are kept by the power of God through faith unto salvation ready to be revealed in the last time.

Proverbs 28:11   The rich man *is* wise in his own conceit; but the poor that hath understanding searcheth him out.

Focus: This proverb teaches that a godly, wise person, though poor, sees through the rich person's overestimation of himself.

"The rich man is wise in his own conceit *[in his own eyes]*" because of his accumulated wealth. Because he has a divinely-enlightened mind, which is true **"understanding** *[part of wisdom, awareness through the senses, discernment. The power to distinguish right from wrong, truth from falsehood.⁷¹⁷]*,**"** the poor man **"searcheth him out."** In other words, the poor man examines the rich man's actions and words, makes an accurate evaluation of his level of wisdom, and sees the rich man for the fool he is.

The phrase **"wise in his own conceit"** appears in the Bible four times, including this proverb, and each time it is in the Book of Proverbs.

> Proverbs 26:5 Answer a fool according to his folly, lest he be wise in his own conceit.
>
> Proverbs 26:12 Seest thou a man wise in his own conceit? there is more hope of a fool than of him.
>
> Proverbs 26:16 The sluggard is wiser in his own conceit than seven men that can render a reason.

Even though "the rich man" arrogantly believes that his *wisdom* alone is the reason for his success, Scripture teaches otherwise.

> Ecclesiastes 10:1 Dead flies cause the ointment of the apothecary to send forth a stinking savour: so doth a little folly him that is in reputation for wisdom and honour.
>
> Revelation 3:14 Because thou sayest, I am rich, and increased with goods, and have need of nothing; and knowest not that thou art wretched, and miserable, and poor, and blind, and naked . . .

"A rich man thinks so highly of his position, is so flattered by parasites, and deems himself placed so immeasurably above social inferiors, that he learns to consider himself possessed of other qualifications, even mental and intellectual gifts, with which wealth has no concern. This purse-proud arrogance which looks upon financial skill and sharpness in bargaining as true wisdom, is confined to no age or country." ⁷¹⁸

But the poor that hath understanding searches him out means that the poor person meditates on his words and body language to understand the full meaning of his communication and the character of his person. He thus intimately evaluates "the rich man," and based on his words and behavior, *"the poor"* conclude that **"the rich man"** has drastically overestimated himself.

> Proverbs 19:1 Better *is* the poor that walketh in his integrity, than *he that is* perverse in his lips, and is a fool.

Proverbs 28:12   When righteous *men* do rejoice, *there is* great glory: but when the wicked rise, a man is hidden.

Focus: This proverb contrasts the rejoicing of righteous people living under godly leadership with their hiding under ungodly leadership.

"When righteous *men* do rejoice, *there is* great glory." Righteous men rejoice under godly leadership because they are free to openly express their views of God and of right and wrong – views reflected in every area of social and political life. **"There is great glory"** describes the righteous, who are beaming with happiness because they have regained their freedom when oppression by the wicked has ceased. They can rejoice and praise God.

> Esther 8:15-16 And Mordecai went out from the presence of the king in royal apparel of blue and white, and with a great crown of gold, and with a garment of fine linen and purple: and the city of Shushan rejoiced and was glad. The Jews had light, and gladness, and joy, and honour.
>
> Proverbs 11:10 When it goeth well with the righteous, the city rejoiceth: and when the wicked perish, there is shouting.
>
> Proverbs 29:2 When the righteous are in authority, the people rejoice: but when the wicked beareth rule, the people mourn.

"But when the wicked rise *[become established or come into power]*,**"** the righteous are forced into hiding to escape persecution and danger to themselves, their families, and their property. The wicked oppress the righteous when they gain control of a country. This state of affairs is mentioned several times in the Bible, including the last verse of this chapter which states, "When the wicked rise, men hide themselves: but when they perish, the righteous increase." (Proverbs 28:28)

> 1 Kings 18:13 Was it not told my lord what I did when Jezebel slew the prophets of the LORD, how I hid an hundred men of the LORD'S prophets by fifty in a cave, and fed them with bread and water?
>
> Job 24:1-4 Why, seeing times are not hidden from the Almighty, do they that know him not see his days? Some remove the landmarks; they violently take away flocks, and feed thereof. They drive away the ass of the fatherless, they take the widow's ox for a pledge. They turn the needy out of the way: the poor of the earth hide themselves together.

The first wonderful illustrations of the righteous being in control, the people rejoicing, and glory being all around are seen when David assumes the throne in Jerusalem, when the ark is returned to the people of God, and when Solomon builds the Temple for the glory and honor of Jehovah. The greatest illustration of the righteous rejoicing will unfold when Christ returns victoriously as King of kings and Lord of lords. Evil men will control the earth no more, and Christians will rejoice forever in the light of His glorious kingdom.

Christians have suffered persecution under the rule of the unrighteous. In 2021, persecution was obvious. According to an article on christianpost.com, "One-hundred percent of Christians in 21 countries around the world experience persecution for their faith in Christ as over 215 million Christians faced "high levels" of persecution in the last year, a leading human rights watchdog group reports . . . The top 21 countries on the list included in this order: North Korea, Somalia, Afghanistan, Pakistan, Sudan, Syria, Iraq, Iran, Yemen, Eritrea, Libya, Nigeria, Maldives, Saudi Arabia, India, Uzbekistan, Vietnam, Kenya, Turkmenistan, Qatar, and Egypt."[719]

A recent 2012 joint report by the Texas-based Liberty Institute and the Washington-based Family Research Counsel indicates that anti-Christian persecution is on the rise in the U.S. and that government agencies are involved in trying to push Christian expression out the door. They report that since the 1960s, the attacks have picked up speed. Violations listed in the joint report include:

- "A federal judge threatened "incarceration" to a high school valedictorian unless she removed references to Jesus from her graduation speech.
- City officials prohibited senior citizens from praying over their meals, listening to religious messages or singing gospel songs at a senior activities center.
- A public school official physically lifted an elementary school student from his seat and reprimanded him in front of his classmates for praying over his lunch.
- Following U.S. Department of Veterans Affairs policies, a federal government official sought to censor a pastor's prayer, eliminating references to Jesus, during a Memorial Day ceremony honoring veterans at a national cemetery.
- Public school officials prohibited students from handing out gifts because they contained religious messages.
- A public school official prevented a student from handing out flyers inviting her classmates to an event at her church.
- A public university's law school banned a Christian organization because it required its officers to adhere to a statement of faith that the university disagreed with.
- The U.S. Department of Justice argued before the Supreme Court that the federal government can tell churches and synagogues which pastors and rabbis it can hire and fire.
- The State of Texas sought to approve and regulate what religious seminaries can teach.
- Through the Patient Protection and Affordable Care Act, also known as Obamacare, the federal government is forcing religious organizations to provide insurance for birth control and abortion-inducing drugs in direct violation of their religious beliefs.
- The U.S. Department of Veterans Affairs banned the mention of God from veterans' funerals, overriding the wishes of the deceased's families.
- A federal judge held that prayers before a state House of Representatives could be to Allah but not to Jesus."[720]

> **Proverbs 28:13** He that covereth his sins shall not prosper: but whoso confesseth and forsaketh *them* shall have mercy.

Focus: This proverb contrasts the loss that comes from covering up sins with the gain that comes from confessing and forsaking them.

"He that covereth *[conceals or hides]* **his sins shall not prosper."** People attempt to cover their sins in several ways, including lying and becoming a hypocrite, blaming others, blaming God, or blaming their sinful nature derived from Adam. They also blame their parents for the way they were raised, or they balance their good works against their sin, declaring it as nothing in proportion to the good they have done. Some hide behind a belief that since they have confessed Jesus as Savior, they are free to commit any sin they please. Several biblical characters come to mind when one thinks of those who attempted to cover their sins.

(1) Adam and Eve disobeyed God's command and then tried to avoid Him after they had sinned.

> Genesis 3:8 And they heard the voice of the LORD God walking in the garden in the cool of the day: and Adam and his wife hid themselves from the presence of the LORD God amongst the trees of the garden.
> Genesis 3:12-13 And the man said, The woman whom thou gavest to be with me, she gave me of the tree, and I did eat. And the LORD God said unto the woman, What is this that thou hast done? And the woman said, The serpent beguiled me, and I did eat.

(2) David tried to keep silent about his sin, only to find that his conscience tormented him.

> Psalm 32:3-5 When I kept silence, my bones waxed old through my roaring all the day long. For day and night thy hand was heavy upon me: my moisture is turned into the drought of summer. Selah. I acknowledged my sin unto thee, and mine iniquity have I not hid. I said, I will confess my transgressions unto the LORD; and thou forgavest the iniquity of my sin. Selah.

(3) Cain attempted to avoid answering God after he murdered his brother. He also lied, and tried to avoid admitting his guilt.

> Genesis 4:9 And the LORD said unto Cain, Where *is* Abel thy brother? And he said, I know not: *Am* I my brother's keeper?
> Genesis 4:13 And Cain said unto the LORD, My punishment *is* greater than I can bear.

(4) Joseph's brothers lied to their father after they abducted, abused, and sold Joseph into slavery only, to suffer years of grief and sorrow.

> Genesis 37:31-32 And they took Joseph's coat, and killed a kid of the goats, and dipped the coat in the blood; And they sent the coat of *many* colours, and they brought *it* to their father; and said, This have we found: know now whether it *be* thy son's coat or no.
> Genesis 42:21 And they said one to another, We *are* verily guilty concerning our brother, in that we saw the anguish of his soul, when he besought us, and we would not hear; therefore is this distress come upon us.

(5) Saul lied to Samuel and attempted to blame the people for his sins of turning back from following God and for failing to perform God's commandments.

> 1 Samuel 15:14;24 And Samuel said, What meaneth then this bleating of the sheep in mine ears, and the lowing of the oxen which I hear?. . . And Saul said unto Samuel, I have sinned: for I have transgressed the commandment of the LORD, and thy words: because I feared the people, and obeyed their voice.

(6) During the days of Jesus, Pharisees were the epitome of hypocrisy because they appeared to be righteous while seeking vain glory; they were full of pride and hate; they oppressed the widows and the fatherless; prayed long, showy prayers; and practiced extortion and excess.

> Matthew 23:27-28 Woe unto you, scribes and Pharisees, hypocrites! for ye are like unto whited sepulchres, which indeed appear beautiful outward, but are within full of dead men's bones, and of all uncleanness. Even so ye also outwardly appear righteous unto men, but within ye are full of hypocrisy and iniquity.

"But whoso confesseth and forsaketh *them* shall have mercy." When men confess and forsake their sins rather than attempting to cover them, God reciprocates with extended mercy in the form of forgiveness. As a benefit, men experience a peace beyond all understanding.

> "The conditions of freedom are confession and amendment, confession to God of sins against Him, to men of sins against them. The teaching of ethical wisdom on this point is identical with that of psalmist, prophet, apostles, and our Lord Himself."[721]
>
> Isaiah 1:16-20 Wash you, make you clean; put away the evil of your doings from before mine eyes; cease to do evil; Learn to do well; seek judgment, relieve the oppressed, judge the fatherless, plead for the widow. Come now, and let us reason together, saith the LORD: though your sins be as scarlet, they shall be as white as snow; though they be red like crimson, they shall be as wool. If ye be willing and obedient, ye shall eat the good of the land: But if ye refuse and rebel, ye shall be devoured with the sword: for the mouth of the LORD hath spoken it.
> Isaiah 55:6-7 Seek ye the LORD while he may be found, call ye upon him while he is near: Let the wicked forsake his way, and the unrighteous man his thoughts: and let him return unto the LORD, and he will have mercy upon him; and to our God, for he will abundantly pardon.

Ezekiel 18:20-22 The soul that sinneth, it shall die. The son shall not bear the iniquity of the father, neither shall the father bear the iniquity of the son: the righteousness of the righteous shall be upon him, and the wickedness of the wicked shall be upon him. But if the wicked will turn from all his sins that he hath committed, and keep all my statutes, and do that which is lawful and right, he shall surely live, he shall not die. All his transgressions that he hath committed, they shall not be mentioned unto him: in his righteousness that he hath done he shall live.

Hosea 5:15 I will go and return to my place, till they acknowledge their offence, and seek my face: in their affliction they will seek me early.

1 John 1:7-9 But if we walk in the light, as he is in the light, we have fellowship one with another, and the blood of Jesus Christ his Son cleanseth us from all sin. If we say that we have no sin, we deceive ourselves, and the truth is not in us. If we confess our sins, he is faithful and just to forgive us our sins, and to cleanse us from all unrighteousness.

Proverbs 28:14 Happy *is* the man that feareth alway: but he that hardeneth his heart shall fall into mischief.

Focus: This proverb contrasts the two opposite ways that people regard evil.

"Happy is the man that feareth alway." When a man is **"alway"** *[constantly]* fearful of what **"mischief"** *[evil]* can do to him, he will stay far enough away to keep from falling into its grip. To remain close to God and away from evil is to remain **"happy."**

> "Happy is the man who always keeps up in his mind a holy awe and reverence of God, his glory, goodness, and government, who is always afraid of offending God and incurring his displeasure, who keeps conscience tender and has a dread of the appearance of evil, who is always jealous of himself, distrustful of his own sufficiency, and lives in expectation of troubles and changes, so that, whenever they come, they are no surprise to him. He who keeps up such a fear as this will live a life of faith and watchfulness, and therefore happy is he, blessed and holy."[722]

When a person **"hardeneth his heart"** *[becomes obstinate]*, thereby casting off the fear that would have kept him at a safe distance from evil, he **"shall fall into mischief."** Such a man is foolish, refusing to give ear to the teachings of Scripture, to his conscience, to the counsel of wise friends, or even to the warnings of past experience. He loses the peace, power, provisions, and protection of God and joins the ranks of the miserably evil.

Exodus 8:13-15 And the LORD did according to the word of Moses; and the frogs died out of the houses, out of the villages, and out of the fields. And they gathered them together upon heaps: and the land stank. But when Pharaoh saw that there was respite, he hardened his heart, and hearkened not unto them; as the LORD had said.

Proverbs 14:16 A wise man feareth, and departeth from evil: but the fool rageth, and is confident.

Proverbs 17:20 He that hath a froward heart findeth no good: and he that hath a perverse tongue falleth into mischief.

Proverbs 29:1 He, that being often reproved hardeneth *his* neck, shall suddenly be destroyed, and that without remedy.

Proverbs 28:15 *As* a roaring lion, and a ranging bear; *so is* a wicked ruler over the poor people.

Focus: This proverb describes the poor's fear of a tyrannical, wicked ruler.

The Bible compares the wicked king to two wild beasts who strike fear in the heart of a man – **" a roaring lion, and a ranging bear."** Capable of being heard for miles, the mighty *roaring of a lion* frightens away intruders and is demonstrative of his tremendous physical power. When **"a ranging bear"** runs about searching for food, his agitated darting movements coupled with his great size and powerful claw-filled paws are a severe threat to anyone who crosses his path.

Previously in Proverbs, "the king's wrath" and "the fear of the king" were compared to the roaring lion. Peter warns that the devil is like a "roaring lion." Like a mighty lion or bear, "a wicked ruler" threatens cruelty and devastation. The wicked king keeps the "poor people" in fear because they have little defense, and they do not know when the wicked ruler will come near.

Proverbs 19:12 The king's wrath *is* as the roaring of a lion; but his favour *is* as dew upon the grass.

Proverbs 20:2 The fear of a king *is* as the roaring of a lion: *whoso* provoketh him to anger sinneth *against* his own soul.

1 Peter 5:8 Be sober, be vigilant; because your adversary the devil, as a roaring lion, walketh about, seeking whom he may devour:

"So is a wicked ruler over the poor people." This verse expands on the truth from verse 12 that a wicked king causes fear – "When righteous *men* do rejoice, *there is* great glory: but when the wicked rise, a man is hidden." Making their lives as miserable and uncertain as possible, the despotic ruler threatens those under his authority, thereby keeping them under his control. He is powerful, heartless, and unrestrained, and he makes his authority known publically and unashamedly by snatching away property and *if he wants to*, the life of those opposing him. The **"wicked ruler"** is hostile to God's laws and teachings about the poor and behaves himself inhumanly because he is ungodly. Because of their lack of training, lack of associations in upper levels of society, and inability to pay, **"the poor people** *[low, weak, needy]*" of any kingdom are the most vulnerable. Proverbs has taught much about God's view of **"the poor,"** mentioning them six times in this chapter and twenty-nine times in the Book of Proverbs. God's compassion for the poor is exemplified in this early commandment to man, "Thou shalt open thine hand wide unto thy brother, to thy poor, and to thy needy, in thy land. (Deuteronomy 15:11)

The psalmist asks for God's protection from such wicked oppressors.

> Psalm 17:8-12 Keep me as the apple of the eye, hide me under the shadow of thy wings, From the wicked that oppress me, *from* my deadly enemies, *who* compass me about. They are inclosed in their own fat: with their mouth they speak proudly. They have now compassed us in our steps: they have set their eyes bowing down to the earth; Like as a lion *that* is greedy of his prey, and as it were a young lion lurking in secret places.

Proverbs 28:16 The prince that wanteth understanding *is* also a great oppressor: *but* he that hateth covetousness shall prolong *his* days.

Focus: This proverb declares that a foolish, covetous prince oppresses his people and thereby shortens his days in authority.

"The prince *[leader]* **that wanteth** *[in need of, lacking]* **understanding is also a great oppressor** *[extortionist, defrauder]*." The tyrannical prince is a "great oppressor" *for the very reason that* he lacks understanding, and one who lacks understanding is foolish. He cruelly takes advantage of others.

The second clause, **"but he that hateth covetousness shall prolong *his* days"** indicates that his lack of understanding (his foolishness) manifests itself in covetousness that operates through oppression. The violence he exercises is serving to shorten his days as a leader because of rebellion by the people under his authority and likely the judgment by God. Timothy rightly wrote, "For the love of money is the root of all evil: which while some coveted after, they have erred from the faith, and pierced themselves through with many sorrows." (1 Timothy 6:10)

In this verse, **"covetousness"** is translated from the Hebrew *betsa'* *[unjust gain through violence]*. All Scriptural usages of "covetousness" do not include the "gain by violence" aspect. But, in this verse, the oppressive prince obtains something from others by intimidation, force, or illegal means.[723] He uses his position of power to oppress others by illegally confiscating that for which he improperly yearns. Alienation is a natural human response toward an oppressor, and a "great oppressor" will be greatly resisted by men and God. Those under his authority who resist and alienate themselves from the prince could potentially have otherwise given him honor. He also could have enjoyed God's favor rather than His wrath.

"But he that hateth covetousness shall prolong *his* days." If he would *hate covetousness*, rather than love it, he would potentially have enjoyed God's approval, the people's love, and peace and satisfaction in his own heart and mind. Those under his authority would defend and pray for him because of his kindness and justice; thus, "prolong his days" as a leader and perhaps on earth as well. Solomon stated this premise in Proverbs 15:27 – "He that is greedy of gain troubleth his own house; but he that hateth gifts shall live." Choosing leaders who hate covetousness is wise, because these men and women of integrity will *not* be greedy of others' wealth and possessions and their loyalty will not be bought by other evil men. Moses was told to pick out men "hating covetousness." Isaiah spoke of men who "despiseth the gain of oppressions."

> Exodus 18:21 Moreover thou shalt provide out of all the people able men, such as fear God, men of truth, hating covetousness; and place such over them, to be rulers of thousands, and rulers of hundreds, rulers of fifties, and rulers of tens . . .
> Isaiah 33:15-17 He that walketh righteously, and speaketh uprightly; he that despiseth the gain of oppressions, that shaketh his hands from holding of bribes, that stoppeth his ears from hearing of blood, and shutteth his eyes from seeing evil; He shall dwell on high: his place of defence shall be the munitions of rocks: bread shall be given him; his waters shall be sure. Thine eyes shall see the king in his beauty: they shall behold the land that is very far off.

Jeremiah 8:10 Therefore will I give their wives unto others, *and* their fields to them that shall inherit *them:* for every one from the least even unto the greatest is given to covetousness, from the prophet even unto the priest every one dealeth falsely.

Micah 2:1 Woe to them that devise iniquity, and work evil upon their beds! when the morning is light, they practise it, because it is in the power of their hand. And they covet fields, and take them by violence; and houses, and take them away: so they oppress a man and his house, even a man and his heritage.

Wicked Ahab, king of Israel, and his queen Jezebel coveted the vineyard of Naboth; and when Naboth refused to part with it, Jezebel arranged to take it by force. She had Naboth falsely accused and killed. However, the oppressive actions that began in their covetous hearts resulted in both dying in a violent manner through the judgment of God.

1 Kings 21:17-21; 23 And the word of the LORD came to Elijah the Tishbite, saying, Arise, go down to meet Ahab king of Israel, which is in Samaria: behold, he is in the vineyard of Naboth, whither he is gone down to possess it. And thou shalt speak unto him, saying, Thus saith the LORD, Hast thou killed, and also taken possession? And thou shalt speak unto him, saying, Thus saith the LORD, In the place where dogs licked the blood of Naboth shall dogs lick thy blood, even thine. And Ahab said to Elijah, Hast thou found me, O mine enemy? And he answered, I have found thee: because thou hast sold thyself to work evil in the sight of the LORD. Behold, I will bring evil upon thee, and will take away thy posterity … And of Jezebel also spake the LORD, saying, The dogs shall eat Jezebel by the wall of Jezreel.

Jesus and the New Testament writers often warned believers about covetousness (with or without violence).

Mark 7:20-23 And he said, That which cometh out of the man, that defileth the man. For from within, out of the heart of men, proceed evil thoughts, adulteries, fornications, murders, Thefts, covetousness, wickedness, deceit, lasciviousness, an evil eye, blasphemy, pride, foolishness: All these evil things come from within, and defile the man.

Luke 12:15 And he said unto them, Take heed, and beware of covetousness: for a man's life consisteth not in the abundance of the things which he possesseth.

Luke 16:10-14 He that is faithful in that which is least is faithful also in much: and he that is unjust in the least is unjust also in much. If therefore ye have not been faithful in the unrighteous mammon, who will commit to your trust the true riches? And if ye have not been faithful in that which is another man's, who shall give you that which is your own? No servant can serve two masters: for either he will hate the one, and love the other; or else he will hold to the one, and despise the other.Ye cannot serve God and mammon. And the Pharisees also, who were covetous, heard all these things: and they derided him. *[See also Romans 1:28-32, 13:8; I Corinthians 5:9-11, 6:9-10; I Timothy 3:3-5; II Timothy 3:1-5; II Peter 2:1-3; 2:14.]*

Proverbs 28:17 A man that doeth violence to the blood of any person shall flee to the pit; let no man stay him.

Focus: This proverb prescribes proper action toward a known murderer.

Under Old Testament Mosaic law, when someone took a life inadvertently, he was to be given mercy; and the law provided safe refuge in one of the Cities of Refuge for him. Also, Proverbs 24:11-12 declared that innocent persons, falsely accused, were to be rescued. However, when a person did **"violence to the blood of any person"** and thereby willfully took a life, he was to **"flee to the pit"** meaning the place where his deceased body will remain. Such *fleeing* could have been hastened by his inescapable terrorizing conscience, or by the judicial system, or by the direct judgment of God.[724] **"Let no man stay him"** meant not to interfere by support in one manner or the other, but to allow the process of whatever was taking him down to take its course.

Genesis 9:6 Whoso sheddeth man's blood, by man shall his blood be shed: for in the image of God made he man.

Exodus 21:13 And if a man lie not in wait, but God deliver him into his hand; then I will appoint thee a place whither he shall flee. But if a man come presumptuously upon his neighbour, to slay him with guile; thou shalt take him from mine altar, that he may die.

Deuteronomy 19:9-12 If thou shalt keep all these commandments to do them, which I command thee this day, to love the LORD thy God, and to walk ever in his ways; then shalt thou add three cities more for thee, beside these three: That innocent blood be not shed in thy land, which the LORD thy God giveth thee for an inheritance, and so blood be upon thee. But if any man hate his neighbour, and lie in wait for him, and rise up against him, and smite him mortally that he die, and fleeth into one of these cities: Then the elders of his city shall send and fetch him thence, and deliver him into the hand of the avenger of blood, that he may die. *[See also Numbers 35:31-34; 2 Samuel 3:27-30; 2 Kings 9:25-26.]*

Proverbs 28:18 Whoso walketh uprightly shall be saved: *but he that is* perverse in *his* ways shall fall at once.

Focus: This proverb specifies that divine protection is provided to the upright but none to the perverse.

Along with others, this proverb declares that God has a special interest and protection for **"whoso walketh uprightly,"** meaning those who live according to divine instruction. Walking close to God, in and of itself, keeps a person away from dangerous places and perverse people. It gives a person wisdom to govern his tongue and to corral his feet. In addition, God promises here that he **"shall be saved"** *[delivered, liberated, safe, rescued]*. God defeats plots against him, deflects arrows that shoot at him, and provides a hiding place when necessary – sometimes in plain sight. The upright is kept sure and safe from sin and its ramifications, from the wicked who hate righteousness, and from the curse of the Law, from God's wrath to come, and from Hell.

"*He that is* perverse in *his* ways shall fall at once" shows that the perverse, who have chosen to be obstinate against God, are allowed by God to live separated from His protection. The perverse man is "not straightforward, but vacillates between right and wrong, or pretends to be pursuing one path while he is really taking another."[725] He is not at all safe but is exposed to the effects of sin and those people who love sin, to the curses of the Law, to God's wrath to come, and to Hell. He **"shall fall at once,"** meaning suddenly into one of the traps he has set for others; or into the hands of his wicked, hypocritical friends; or into the hateful arms of his father, the Devil.

> Psalm 84:11 For the LORD God is a sun and shield: the LORD will give grace and glory: no good thing will he withhold from them that walk uprightly.
> Psalm 119:105 NUN. Thy word is a lamp unto my feet, and a light unto my path.
> Proverbs 1:32-33 For the turning away of the simple shall slay them, and the prosperity of fools shall destroy them. But whoso hearkeneth unto me shall dwell safely, and shall be quiet from fear of evil.
> Proverbs 2:10-15 When wisdom entereth into thine heart, and knowledge is pleasant unto thy soul; Discretion shall preserve thee, understanding shall keep thee: To deliver thee from the way of the evil man, from the man that speaketh froward things; Who leave the paths of uprightness, to walk in the ways of darkness; Who rejoice to do evil, and delight in the frowardness of the wicked; Whose ways are crooked, and they froward in their paths . . .
> Proverbs 3:21-26 My son, let not them depart from thine eyes: keep sound wisdom and discretion: So shall they be life unto thy soul, and grace to thy neck. Then shalt thou walk in thy way safely, and thy foot shall not stumble. When thou liest down, thou shalt not be afraid: yea, thou shalt lie down, and thy sleep shall be sweet. Be not afraid of sudden fear, neither of the desolation of the wicked, when it cometh. For the LORD shall be thy confidence, and shall keep thy foot from being taken.
> Proverbs 10:9 He that walketh uprightly walketh surely: but he that perverteth his ways shall be known.
> Proverbs 11:3 The integrity of the upright shall guide them: but the perverseness of transgressors shall destroy them.
> Proverbs 17:20 He that hath a froward heart findeth no good: and he that hath a perverse tongue falleth into mischief.
> Proverbs 18:10 The name of the LORD *is* a strong tower: the righteous runneth into it, and is safe.
> Proverbs 28:6 Better is the poor that walketh in his uprightness, than he that is perverse in his ways, though he be rich.
> Proverbs 28:26 He that trusteth in his own heart is a fool: but whoso walketh wisely, he shall be delivered.

Proverbs 28:19 He that tilleth his land shall have plenty of bread: but he that followeth after vain *persons* shall have poverty enough.

Focus: This proverb contrasts the diligent, righteous person with the delinquent, evil person.

"Plenty of bread" is here contrasted with **"poverty enough."** (The text even uses the same Hebrew word *saba'* for **"plenty"** and **"enough."**) This wordplay seems to be sarcasm that puts down those foolish ones who seek after the empty pipe dreams that other foolish people keep before themselves to avoid being diligent about their business.

Contrasting the wise with the foolish, this proverb is another that emphasizes the honorable and productive characteristic of wisdom that lead a person to diligent work *versus* the shameful and debilitating characteristic of foolishness that leads to ignoring responsibilities and following after **"vain *persons*."** Wisdom teaches the personal responsibility of following the laws of God. Foolish people often have a crowd mentality believing that the large number of people acting in a given manner somehow justifies their action. These foolish ones do not adequately help themselves, nor do they contribute to the betterment of society. Excluding situations that reduce the ability to be productive such as; a breakdown of health, national disasters, and war, a wise person in an otherwise healthy environment should produce a comfortable living from his wise and diligent labor. If a person **"tilleth his land"** *(works at producing a crop),* he should reap a crop and enjoy the proceeds from it. On the other hand, if a person **"followeth after vain persons,"** rather than taking care of his business, he will *produce poverty* rather than provision. Notice also the following:

> Proverbs 13:20 He that walketh with wise men shall be wise: but a companion of fools shall be destroyed.

Proverbs 13:23 Much food is in the tillage of the poor: but there is that is destroyed for want of judgment.

In the parable of the Prodigal Son given by Jesus (Luke 15:11-24), the foolish son decided to vacate all his responsibilities and duties as a son and engage in **"riotous living,"** which no doubt had to be carried out with other renegades. Except for his repentance followed by his father's forgiveness, he would have spent the remainder of his life struggling in poverty.

Proverbs 28:20 A faithful man shall abound with blessings: but he that maketh haste to be rich shall not be innocent.

Focus: This proverb contrasts the reward for faithfulness with the punishment for greed.

"A faithful man [*firm, steadfast, steady*] **shall abound with blessings."** A **"blessing"** "involves providing something of value to another. God 'blesses' us by providing for our needs and we in turn 'bless' God by giving him of ourselves as his servants."[726] A man of faithfulness would prefer to be poor by providence than be rich by sin.[727] Other people can depend on the faithful man to always be honest because he steadfastly lives his life according to Scripture. He *believes that God rewards* the person who trusts in Him by following His commandments, and he ***waits for God*** to reward him according to His will and His personal desire for him.

> Psalm 68:19 Blessed be the Lord, who daily loadeth us with benefits, even the God of our salvation. Selah.
>
> Proverbs 8:32-4 Now therefore hearken unto me, O ye children: for blessed are they that keep my ways. Hear instruction, and be wise, and refuse it not. Blessed is the man that heareth me, watching daily at my gates, waiting at the posts of my doors.
>
> Proverbs 10:22 The blessing of the LORD, it maketh rich, and he addeth no sorrow with it.
>
> Proverbs 20:7 The just man walketh in his integrity: his children are blessed after him.
>
> Hebrews 11:6 But without faith *it is* impossible to please *him:* for he that cometh to God must believe that he is, and *that* he is a rewarder of them that diligently seek him.

"But he that maketh haste to be rich shall not be innocent [*exempt from punishment, having a clean record*]**."** In contrast to the faithful man is the man of unfaithfulness who prefers to be rich and is willing to sin against God and man to achieve his goal. A man who is unfaithful to God goes his own way trusting in getting rich by whatever means he can. His principles of greed are his own, and he is not concerned with being obedient to God or giving honor to other men. He believes in himself and ***makes haste*** to follow his own schemes to get wealth. He **"shall not be innocent"** because he opposes the commandments of God, refuses to wait on Him, and is overtaken with greed. He is known by people for the crook that he is, for living a life of unrest, for not trusting anyone, and for not being trusted. One rushing for wealth has wrong priorities and ultimately abuses laws and people; thus, he shall stand before God as guilty *and will be punished* – he "shall not be innocent."

> Proverbs 10:6-8 Blessings are upon the head of the just: but violence covereth the mouth of the wicked. The memory of the just is blessed: but the name of the wicked shall rot. The wise in heart will receive commandments: but a prating fool shall fall.
>
> Proverbs 13:11 Wealth *gotten* by vanity shall be diminished: but he that gathereth by labour shall increase.
>
> Proverbs 20:21 An inheritance *may be* gotten hastily at the beginning; but the end thereof shall not be blessed.
>
> Proverbs 23:4 Labour not to be rich: cease from thine own wisdom.
>
> 1 Timothy 6:9-11 But they that will be rich fall into temptation and a snare, and into many foolish and hurtful lusts, which drown men in destruction and perdition. For the love of money is the root of all evil: which while some coveted after, they have erred from the faith, and pierced themselves through with many sorrows. But thou, O man of God, flee these things; and follow after righteousness, godliness, faith, love, patience, meekness.

Proverbs 28:21 To have respect of persons *is* not good: for for a piece of bread *that* man will transgress.

Focus: This proverb declares that favoritism is wrong and that a man given to it will sell out for little or nothing.

"To have respect of persons" means *giving someone an inequitable advantage* over another based on something other than merit. In other words, "respect of persons" is showing favoritism or partiality to one person over another. Such "respect of persons" is often reflected in court judgments. Outside the courtroom, it also shows up in giving rewards, honors, jobs, and positions of importance. It is also reflected in prejudice against other people because of their race, religion, national origin, financial status, handicap, or appearance. An inequitable advantage could be given to someone because of that person's wealth, long-time friendship, or perhaps membership in the same club or organization. It could also come about because of having received that person's previous favor or a bribe, as shown in the second clause of this proverb. To practice such injustice is a dishonest preference showing a lack of good judgment and conscience.

The second part of this proverb expands from simply showing partiality to doing so by receiving a bribe. An individual who receives a bribe will need only **"a piece of bread"** *(very little)* to induce him to commit sins or to **"transgress** *[to break away (from just authority), or to sin]."* Anyone showing "respect of persons" is a transgressor or sinner. (See also James 2:8-9 below.)

> Leviticus 19:15 Ye shall do no unrighteousness in judgment: thou shalt not respect the person of the poor, nor honour the person of the mighty: *but* in righteousness shalt thou judge thy neighbour.
> Deuteronomy 1:17 Ye shall not respect persons in judgment; *but* ye shall hear the small as well as the great; ye shall not be afraid of the face of man; for the judgment *is* God's: and the cause that is too hard for you, bring *it* unto me, and I will hear it.
> Deuteronomy 16:19 Thou shalt not wrest judgment; thou shalt not respect persons, neither take a gift: for a gift doth blind the eyes of the wise, and pervert the words of the righteous.
> Proverbs 17:15 He that justifieth the wicked, and he that condemneth the just, even they both *are* abomination to the LORD.
> Proverbs 24:23-25 These things also belong to the wise. It is not good to have respect of persons in judgment. He that saith unto the wicked, Thou art righteous; him shall the people curse, nations shall abhor him: But to them that rebuke him shall be delight, and a good blessing shall come upon them.
> Matthew 22:36-40 Jesus said unto him, Thou shalt love the Lord thy God with all thy heart, and with all thy soul, and with all thy mind. This is the first and great commandment. And the second *is* like unto it, Thou shalt love thy neighbour as thyself. On these two commandments hang all the law and the prophets.
> James 2:8-9 If ye fulfil the royal law according to the scripture, Thou shalt love thy neighbour as thyself, ye do well: But if ye have respect to persons, ye commit sin, and are convinced of the law as transgressors.
> Romans 2:11 For there is no respect of persons with God.
> James 2:1-4 My brethren, have not the faith of our Lord Jesus Christ, *the Lord* of glory, with respect of persons. For if there come unto your assembly a man with a gold ring, in goodly apparel, and there come in also a poor man in vile raiment; And ye have respect to him that weareth the gay clothing, and say unto him, Sit thou here in a good place; and say to the poor, Stand thou there, or sit here under my footstool: Are ye not then partial in yourselves, and are become judges of evil thoughts?

> **NOTE:** There are 6 **"not good"** sayings in the Book of Proverbs with 28:21 being the last. An act that is "not good" is very bad and sinful.
> Proverbs 17:26 Also to punish the just *is* not good, *nor* to strike princes for equity.
> Proverbs 18:5 It is not good to accept the person of the wicked, to overthrow the righteous in judgment.
> Proverbs 19:2 Also, *that* the soul *be* without knowledge, *it is* not good; and he that hasteth with *his* feet sinneth.
> Proverbs 24:23 These *things* also *belong* to the wise. *It is* not good to have respect of persons in judgment.
> Proverbs 25:27 *It is* not good to eat much honey: so *for men* to search their own glory *is not* glory.
> Proverbs 28:21 To have respect of persons is not good: for for a piece of bread that man will transgress.

Proverbs 28:22 He that hasteth to be rich *hath* an evil eye, and considereth not that poverty shall come upon him.

Focus: This proverb declares that bad character (an evil eye) is the driver behind racing to be rich and, at the same time, a blinder to the future.

"He that hasteth to be rich *hath* an evil eye." *("Hasteth" to be rich implies that he is pushed on by his desires to get riches by right or wrong.*[728]*)* The human eye reflects emotions that can be seen when a person has sorrow enough or sometimes joy enough to cause him to tear up. Mercy and kindness can also be seen in the eye; but an **"evil eye"** reflects hatred, deceit, and covetousness. The **"evil eye"** came to be a term that meant its owner had *a wicked heart and hidden ungodly desires* that the wise person could perceive. An overwhelming, single-minded intent to get rich quickly can conquer a person's heart and mind causing him to disregard any intentions to please God and abort any sympathy for others. When this happens, it will be reflected in his eye as an "evil eye," which is actually, in the long run, driving him toward "poverty" rather than prosperity.

> "The man of evil eye *(Proverbs 23:6)* is the envious and covetous man; such a one tries to improve his position and raise himself speedily to the height of him whom he envies, and is quite unscrupulous as to the means which he uses to effect his purpose, and keeps all that he gains selfishly to himself. And yet he is really blind to his own best interests."[729]

> **Note the use of "evil eye" throughout the Scriptures**
>
> Deuteronomy 15:9 Beware that there be not a thought in thy wicked heart, saying, The seventh year, the year of release, is at hand; and thine eye be evil against thy poor brother, and thou givest him nought; and he cry unto the LORD against thee, and it be sin unto thee.
>
> Deuteronomy 28:54 *So that* the man *that is* tender among you, and very delicate, his eye shall be evil toward his brother, and toward the wife of his bosom, and toward the remnant of his children which he shall leave . . .
>
> Deuteronomy 28:56 The tender and delicate woman among you, which would not adventure to set the sole of her foot upon the ground for delicateness and tenderness, her eye shall be evil toward the husband of her bosom, and toward her son, and toward her daughter,
>
> Proverbs 23:6 Eat thou not the bread of *him that hath* an evil eye, neither desire thou his dainty meats . . .
>
> Proverbs 28:22 He that hasteth to be rich *hath* an evil eye, and considereth not that poverty shall come upon him.
>
> Matthew 6:23 But if thine eye be evil, thy whole body shall be full of darkness. If therefore the light that is in thee be darkness, how great *is* that darkness!
>
> Matthew 20:15 Is it not lawful for me to do what I will with mine own? Is thine eye evil, because I am good?
>
> Mark 7:22 Thefts, covetousness, wickedness, deceit, lasciviousness, an evil eye, blasphemy, pride, foolishness . . .
>
> Luke 11:34 The light of the body is the eye: therefore when thine eye is single, thy whole body also is full of light; but when *thine eye* is evil, thy body also *is* full of darkness.

He "considereth not that poverty shall come upon him." His "evil eye" will reveal that he is un-welcoming toward God's word, uncharitable to the poor, and unethical in his business methods. Eventually, he becomes so isolated from God and other people that he is spiritually and socially impoverished, whether his physical wealth remains or not. How great is the man's poverty when the only friend he has is his wealth, the only enjoyment is to count his coins, the only communication with God is a request for more wealth, and his single hope is never satisfied. In addition, his riches may take wings and leave him in ashes.

> Proverbs 28:20 A faithful man shall abound with blessings: but he that maketh haste to be rich shall not be innocent.

Throughout Scripture, God condemns improperly gained wealth.

> Proverbs 11:24-25 There is that scattereth, and yet increaseth; and *there is* that withholdeth more than is meet, but *it tendeth* to poverty. The liberal soul shall be made fat: and he that watereth shall be watered also himself.
>
> Proverbs 13:11 Wealth *gotten* by vanity shall be diminished: but he that gathereth by labour shall increase.
>
> Proverbs 23:4-5 Labour not to be rich: cease from thine own wisdom. Wilt thou set thine eyes upon that which is not? for *riches* certainly make themselves wings; they fly away as an eagle toward heaven.
>
> 1 Timothy 6:9-10 But they that will be rich fall into temptation and a snare, and *into* many foolish and hurtful lusts, which drown men in destruction and perdition. For the love of money is the root of all evil: which while some coveted after, they have erred from the faith, and pierced themselves through with many sorrows.

Proverbs 28:23 He that rebuketh a man afterwards shall find more favour than he that flattereth with the tongue.

Focus: This proverb specifies the advantage of a loving rebuke over lying flattery.

In this proverb, ***he that rebukes a man*** contrasts with ***he that flatters with the tongue***. The lesson to be learned is that the person who chooses the most *difficult path of being truthful* and of being a true friend (by giving a helpful rebuke) will afterward have more **"favor"** than the man who chooses the *low road of flattery*. Flattery is disingenuous and strokes the ego while telling a person what he wants to hear.

Rebuke means to correct, to reason together, "to reprove him for his faults."[730] ***Flattery*** means to be smooth, slippery, or deceitful. Rebuke and flattery have two entirely different purposes. The rebuker loves or at least has a great deal of respect for the other person and tries to help him correct a fault. The deceitful flatterer gives false words of seeming praise to obtain selfish desires. In speaking of ungodly men, Jude makes the statement:

> Jude 1:16 These are murmurers, complainers, walking after their own lusts; and their mouth speaketh great swelling words, having men's persons in admiration because of advantage.

Praise has a proper place and can be most helpful; but it *can also metastasize into **flattery*** if it becomes excessive. It can be useful as an expression of appreciation and as an encouragement to continue positive behavior. In contrast, ***flattery*** is calculative, manipulative, and a form of hypocrisy. Children are sometimes praised ***excessively*** for good behavior or accomplishments. However, when such worthy praise reaches the stage of excess, it ceases to be praise and becomes flattery, which is likely to eventually produce pride and improper behavior.

A loving believer will always strive to speak the truth because love rejoices in the truth (1 Corinthians 13:6); however, truth is not always soothing or acceptable, especially when it comes in the form of a stinging rebuke. Deception is not proper for the Christian (John 14:6). Similar to the way praise can morph into flattery, excessive rebuke with improper motive becomes a means of putting another down.

A good and proper rebuke brings to the conscience damaging faults. It can stop bad decisions, modify bad behavior, change the way a person thinks, and consequently strengthen a permanent lifetime friendship. To rebuke a friend takes courage, selflessness, a high regard for truth and love, as well as a willingness to suffer loss should it be received improperly. *A proper rebuke* is given in a delicate, sensitive, and affectionate manner. The doctor who cuts into an infected, purulent wound may not be immediately appreciated because of the pain; but later, as the running sore heals, he will surely be thanked.

> Proverbs 6:23 For the commandment *is* a lamp; and the law *is* light; and reproofs of instruction *are* the way of life: To keep thee from the evil woman, from the flattery of the tongue of a strange woman.
> Proverbs 9:7-8 He that reproveth a scorner getteth to himself shame: and he that rebuketh a wicked man getteth himself a blot. Reprove not a scorner, lest he hate thee: rebuke a wise man, and he will love thee.
> Proverbs 24:24-25 He that saith unto the wicked, Thou art righteous; him shall the people curse, nations shall abhor him: But to them that rebuke him shall be delight, and a good blessing shall come upon them.
> Proverbs 27:5-6 Open rebuke is better than secret love. Faithful are the wounds of a friend; but the kisses of an enemy are deceitful.
> Proverbs 29:5 A man that flattereth his neighbour spreadeth a net for his feet.
> Ecclesiastes 7:5 It is better to hear the rebuke of the wise, than for a man to hear the song of fools.

Love never flatters others, and wisdom never desires to be flattered. However, because sin is neither loving nor wise, humans are often tempted to manipulate others with flattery and rebuke – as well as to enjoy being flattered.

Thinking they could catch Jesus in His words, the Pharisees tried to trick the Master by flattering Him beforehand. They were a picture of Psalm 5:9 – "For there is no faithfulness in their mouth; their inward part is very wickedness; their throat is an open sepulchre; they flatter with their tongue."

> Mark 12:13-17 "And they send unto him certain of the Pharisees and of the Herodians, to catch him in his words. And when they were come, they say unto him, Master, we know that thou art true, and carest for no man: for thou regardest not the person of men, but teachest the way of God in truth: Is it lawful to give tribute to Caesar, or not? Shall we give, or shall we not give? But he, knowing their hypocrisy, said unto them, Why tempt ye me? bring me a penny, that I may see it. And they brought it. And he saith unto them, Whose is this image and superscription? And they said unto him, Caesar's. And Jesus answering said unto them, Render to Caesar the things that are Caesar's, and to God the things that are God's. And they marvelled at him.

Their flattering words about Jesus ***contained*** truth, but these wicked men did not believe their own words, and they were trying to entrap him. They were looking for their own personal gain and advantage.

> Psalm 5:8-9 Lead me, O LORD, in thy righteousness because of mine enemies; make thy way straight before my face. For there is no faithfulness in their mouth; their inward part is very wickedness; their throat is an open sepulchre; they flatter with their tongue.
> Psalm 36:1-2 The transgression of the wicked saith within my heart, that there is no fear of God before his eyes. For he flattereth himself in his own eyes, until his iniquity be found to be hateful.
> Proverbs 2:11-12, 16-17 Discretion shall preserve thee, understanding shall keep thee: To deliver thee from the way of the evil man, from the man that speaketh froward things;. . . To deliver thee from the strange woman, even from the stranger which flattereth with her words; Which forsaketh the guide of her youth, and forgetteth the covenant of her God.
> Proverbs 7:4-5 Say unto wisdom, Thou art my sister; and call understanding thy kinswoman: That they may keep thee from the strange woman, from the stranger which flattereth with her words.
> Proverbs 28:23 He that rebuketh a man afterwards shall find more favour than he that flattereth with the tongue.
> Proverbs 29:5 A man that flattereth his neighbour spreadeth a net for his feet.

One man who succumbed to insincere flattery was Herod Agrippa I, who ruled Galilee and Perea for the Roman Empire. He loved to be flattered. One day he dressed in his royal robes and gave an oration to the people of Tyre and Sidon, who were seeking peace. The Bible records the end of this proud ruler:

Acts 12:22-23 And the people gave a shout, saying, It is the voice of a god, and not of a man. And immediately the angel of the Lord smote him, because he gave not God the glory: and he was eaten of worms, and gave up the ghost.

> **Proverbs 28:24** Whoso robbeth his father or his mother, and saith, *It is* no transgression; the same *is* the companion of a destroyer.

Focus: This proverb categorizes a self-excusing parent robber.

A person who will rob his parents and say that he has done no wrong is to be considered in the same category as one known to destroy lives – **"companion of a destroyer."** He is like a ruthless robbing gang member. Being vile, destructive, and without conscience toward his parents, he is the same as any other thief; only the heartlessness of a parent robber is worse since he defies the natural innate desire to love, respect, protect, and honor his parents.

One of the last things on the mind of Jesus as He was being crucified was the care of his precious earthly mother. Lovingly and with great agony from the cross, he handed over the care of His mother to the Apostle John when he said to His mother, "Woman, behold thy son!" and then to John, "Behold thy mother!" (John 19:26) The antithesis of such rich godly love and responsibility is one who would be destructive to his parents in any form. Parent robbery can occur in several ways: open theft, secret theft, fraud, or debt in the parent's name, or failure to meet their needs in their old age when one has such capacity.

Jesus had the following to say to the scribes and Pharisees who claimed, by their tradition (in opposition to Scripture), that they were giving to the temple's treasury and ignoring the great need of the parents. Jesus *did not condemn* the practice of giving to God because, in Mark 12:44, He commended the poor widow who gave all of her living, but *He did condemn the practice of giving to God and then using the gift as an excuse* for not helping one's parents. *The scribes and Pharisees permitted a man to rob his parents* of their basic needs by not caring for them if the child did it in the name of God. To "honor thy father and mother" includes providing for their needs when they are old and in distress. "Whoso curseth father or mother" included a refusal to obey them, to provide for them, or even to speak in anger to them.[731]

Mark 7:9-13 And he said unto them, Full well ye reject the commandment of God, that ye may keep your own tradition. For Moses said, Honour thy father and thy mother; and, Whoso curseth father or mother, let him die the death: But ye say, If a man shall say to his father or mother, It is Corban, that is to say, a gift, by whatsoever thou mightest be profited by me; he shall be free. And ye suffer him no more to do ought for his father or his mother; Making the word of God of none effect through your tradition, which ye have delivered: and many such like things do ye.

The statement **"it is no transgression"** *(sin)* indicates that the rebellious son took money or property from his parents and that his twisted mind justified his action. Perhaps he deluded himself by saying that it would have become his regardless after their demise. Such improper thinking is difficult to fully grasp because families were quite large in those days, and it is questionable which property would be his and which his siblings. It is also doubtful that the thief would have told his siblings that he had stolen from his parents and then ask them to deduct the amount from his share of the property. He was a thief, a destroyer.

Proverbs 19:26 He that wasteth *his* father, *and* chaseth away *his* mother, *is* a son that causeth shame, and bringeth reproach.

Proverbs 20:21 An inheritance *may be* gotten hastily at the beginning; but the end thereof shall not be blessed.

1 Timothy 6:9-11 But they that will be rich fall into temptation and a snare, and into many foolish and hurtful lusts, which drown men in destruction and perdition. For the love of money is the root of all evil: which while some coveted after, they have erred from the faith, and pierced themselves through with many sorrows.

> **Proverbs 28:25** He that is of a proud heart stirreth up strife: but he that putteth his trust in the LORD shall be made fat.

Focus: This proverb contrasts the results of arrogance *(stirs up strife)* with trusting in God (made fat – content).

"He that is of a proud heart stirreth up strife *[quarrels, strife]*." Believing that he has the answer to every problem and is easily offended when other men do not recognize his imagined superiority, the "proud heart" is one who flatters himself and excessively loves himself. Pride is the poison that suppresses faith in God, the catalyst that initiates strife, and the ugly on the face of an otherwise attractive person. It lays down the pavement for a walk of misery full of discontentment and arguments with both men and God.

Proverbs 13:10 Only by pride cometh contention: but with the well advised is wisdom.

Proverbs 21:23-24 Whoso keepeth his mouth and his tongue keepeth his soul from troubles. Proud and haughty scorner is his name, who dealeth in proud wrath.

"But he that putteth his trust in the LORD shall be made fat" showing not only that the person of faith in God is the opposite character of one who stirs up strife; but he also lives at peace, satisfied, and content **("made fat")**. He does not keep a fight going, doesn't think too highly of himself, and has "the peace of God which passeth all understanding." Even if not so attractive physically, he has a beautiful spirit which others find calming, nonthreatening, and pleasant.

> "Those make themselves fat, and always easy, that live in a continual dependence upon God and his grace: *He who puts his trust in the Lord,* who, instead of struggling for himself, commits his cause to God, *shall be made fat.* He saves the money which others spend upon their pride and contentiousness; he enjoys himself, and has abundant satisfaction in his God; and thus his soul dwells at ease, and he is most likely to have plenty of outward good things. None live so easily, so pleasantly, as those who live by faith."[732]

Psalm 84:11 For the LORD God *is* a sun and shield: the LORD will give grace and glory: no good *thing* will he withhold from them that walk uprightly.

Proverbs 15:18 A wrathful man stirreth up strife: but he that is slow to anger appeaseth strife.

Proverbs 15:30 The light of the eyes rejoiceth the heart: and a good report maketh the bones fat.

Philippians 4:6-7 Be careful for nothing; but in every thing by prayer and supplication with thanksgiving let your requests be made known unto God. And the peace of God, which passeth all understanding, shall keep your hearts and minds through Christ Jesus.

1 Thessalonians 4:1 Furthermore then we beseech you, brethren, and exhort *you* by the Lord Jesus, that as ye have received of us how ye ought to walk and to please God, *so* ye would abound more and more.

Proverbs 28:26 He that trusteth in his own heart is a fool: but whoso walketh wisely, he shall be delivered.

Focus: This proverb contrasts the foolish person full of ego with the wise, humble person.

He that trusts in his own heart is a fool. A proud man *is* such because he believes himself to be totally sufficient and able to solve any problem or issue that comes his way. He consequently does not rely on God's help to live his life. Believing such foolishness is not only an open display of ignorance but is also potentially damning. Separation from God would be serious enough, but to be struggling through this life being resisted by God is indeed more than difficult and reveals the *heart of a fool who will not escape the severe judgment of God.* To believe that the creature has more ability than the Creator is seriously foolish, but add to that God's resistance, and the proud one has thus written himself a prescription for pure agony. He ***stirs up trouble*** just as surely as one who stirs up a hornet's nest, only the effects are much more severe and longer lasting than mere stings though there be many of them. "God resisteth the proud, but giveth grace unto the humble." (James 4:6 and 1Peter 5:5)

> "The wise man *[Solomon]* awfully illustrates his own Proverb. It must have been some bitter root of self-confidence, that prostrated his wondrous wisdom in the lowest degradation.

1 Kings 11:1-8 And Solomon did evil in the sight of the LORD, and went not fully after the LORD, as *did* David his father. Then did Solomon build an high place for Chemosh, the abomination of Moab, in the hill that *is* before Jerusalem, and for Molech, the abomination of the children of Ammon. And likewise did he for all his strange wives, which burnt incense and sacrificed unto their gods.

> "...Peter also – how did he *befool* himself in his *trust!* Presuming upon 'the willingness of the spirit,' and forgetting his Lord's most needful caution against 'the weakness of the flesh;' though named a Rock, he fell as a reed before the first breath of temptation. Had not the everlasting arms been underneath, it would have been the fall of Judas into the depths of hell. An instructive lesson to shew us, that all dependence upon feelings, impulse, native strength, sincere purpose or conviction – is vain confidence. Sad experience has convinced us of this. Yet in the blindness of our folly, we are ever ready to *trust* again, if the Lord prevent not, to our ruin."[733]

"But whoso walketh wisely, he shall be delivered." The blessing for the person who ***walks wisely*** (meaning one who humbly trusts in God – which trust is the character of the wise man[734]) is that **"he shall be delivered."** The wise man who knows he needs divine help and seeks the counsel of God and wise men ***will be delivered*** from the dangers and mischief that the fool encounters, both in this life and at the Judgment. Christians have little faith in self and much faith in God because they know that "...man is born unto trouble, as the sparks fly upward." (Job 5:7)

2 Samuel 22:1-4 And David spake unto the LORD the words of this song in the day *that* the LORD had delivered him out of the hand of all his enemies, and out of the hand of Saul: And he said, The LORD *is* my rock, and my fortress, and my deliverer; The God of my rock; in him will I trust: *he is* my shield, and the horn of my salvation, my high tower, and my refuge, my saviour; thou savest me from violence. I will call on the LORD, *who is* worthy to be praised: so shall I be saved from mine enemies.

Job 28:28 And unto man he said, Behold, the fear of the Lord, that *is* wisdom; and to depart from evil *is* understanding.

Proverbs 3:5-6 Trust in the LORD with all thine heart; and lean not unto thine own understanding. In all thy ways acknowledge him, and he shall direct thy paths.

Proverbs 14:3 In the mouth of the foolish is a rod of pride: but the lips of the wise shall preserve them.

Jeremiah 9:23-24 Thus saith the LORD, Let not the wise *man* glory in his wisdom, neither let the mighty *man* glory in his might, let not the rich *man* glory in his riches: But let him that glorieth glory in this, that he understandeth and knoweth me, that I *am* the LORD which exercise lovingkindness, judgment, and righteousness, in the earth: for in these *things* I delight, saith the LORD.

Ephesians 2:8-10 For by grace are ye saved through faith; and that *not of yourselves:it is* the gift of God: Not of works, lest any man should boast. For we are his workmanship, created in Christ Jesus unto good works, which God hath before ordained that we should walk in them.

Proverbs 28:27   He that giveth unto the poor shall not lack: but he that hideth his eyes shall have many a curse.

Focus: This proverb contrasts the reward to those who help the poor with the curse to those who refuse to help them.

"He that giveth unto the poor shall not lack." No doubt, people should prepare for difficult times, but not so much as to disobey the commandments of God and refuse to help those in need. The righteous person knows that God's commandments are superior to human logic and that being obedient to Him produces more, saves more, and causes more enjoyment. Security is in God for the Christian, not in self or in provisions. This proverb is one among several in which the wise are told that the giver **"shall not lack"** in giving to the poor. It is undoubtedly God's business how He makes giving turn into receiving. Furthermore, the righteous do not need God to explain how it happens, they just obey God and expect Him to keep His end of the bargain – which He always does.

"But he that hideth his eyes shall have many a curse." Scripture was written to the Jews who were certainly aware of God's commands and were expected to obey them or suffer the consequences. Even though they *may* have read the many Scriptural mandates to care for the poor and heard the many testimonies of God's supernatural provisions, some still cannot trust God. Those spiritually-anemic and doubting souls are identified as the ones who *hide* their **"eyes"** to provide themselves with an excuse for not obeying God, but the consequence of their action is that they **"shall have many a curse."** Those curses might come in the form of holes in pockets and otherwise unexplained losses that make riches that seemed so secure suddenly take wings and fly away.

Deuteronomy 15:9-11 Beware that there be not a thought in thy wicked heart, saying, The seventh year, the year of release, is at hand; and thine eye be evil against thy poor brother, and thou givest him nought; and he cry unto the LORD against thee, and it be sin unto thee. Thou shalt surely give him, and thine heart shall not be grieved when thou givest unto him: because that for this thing the LORD thy God shall bless thee in all thy works, and in all that thou puttest thine hand unto. For the poor shall never cease out of the land: therefore I command thee, saying, Thou shalt open thine hand wide unto thy brother, to thy poor, and to thy needy, in thy land.

Deuteronomy 24:14-15 Thou shalt not oppress an hired servant that is poor and needy, whether he be of thy brethren, or of thy strangers that are in thy land within thy gates: At his day thou shalt give him his hire, neither shall the sun go down upon it; for he is poor, and setteth his heart upon it: lest he cry against thee unto the LORD, and it be sin unto thee.

Psalm 41:1-3 To the chief Musician, A Psalm of David. Blessed is he that considereth the poor: the LORD will deliver him in time of trouble. The LORD will preserve him, and keep him alive; and he shall be blessed upon the earth: and thou wilt not deliver him unto the will of his enemies. The LORD will strengthen him upon the bed of languishing: thou wilt make all his bed in his sickness.

Proverbs 11:24-26 There is that scattereth, and yet increaseth; and there is that withholdeth more than is meet, but it tendeth to poverty. The liberal soul shall be made fat: and he that watereth shall be watered also himself. He that withholdeth corn, the people shall curse him: but blessing shall be upon the head of him that selleth it.

Proverbs 14:21 He that despiseth his neighbour sinneth: but he that hath mercy on the poor, happy *is* he.

Proverbs 14:31 He that oppresseth the poor reproacheth his Maker: but he that honoureth him hath mercy on the poor.

Proverbs 19:17 He that hath pity upon the poor lendeth unto the LORD; and that which he hath given will he pay him again.

Proverbs 21:13 Whoso stoppeth his ears at the cry of the poor, he also shall cry himself, but shall not be heard.

Proverbs 21:26 He coveteth greedily all the day long: but the righteous giveth and spareth not.

Proverbs 22:9 He that hath a bountiful eye shall be blessed; for he giveth of his bread to the poor.

Proverbs 29:7 The righteous considereth the cause of the poor: *but* the wicked regardeth not to know *it.*

2 Corinthians 9:6-10 But this I say, He which soweth sparingly shall reap also sparingly; and he which soweth bountifully shall reap also bountifully. Every man according as he purposeth in his heart, so let him give; not grudgingly, or of necessity: for God loveth

a cheerful giver. And God is able to make all grace abound toward you; that ye, always having all sufficiency in all things, may abound to every good work: (As it is written, He hath dispersed abroad; he hath given to the poor: his righteousness remaineth for ever. Now he that ministereth seed to the sower both minister bread for your food, and multiply your seed sown, and increase the fruits of your righteousness)...

Proverbs 28:28 When the wicked rise, men hide themselves: but when they perish, the righteous increase.

Focus: This proverb declares the effect of the rise and fall of wicked leadership on the righteous.

The thought of **"when the wicked rise, men hide themselves"** is very similar to verse 12 which states, "When righteous *men* do rejoice, *there is* great glory: but when the wicked rise, a man is hidden." **"When the wicked rise"** is expressive of the fact that wicked people are lifted to a position of authority and power, especially politically, to a government position where they are commissioned to use their corrupt judgment and power. **"Wicked"** people are opposed to the teaching of the Bible. Such a person will believe that the word of God is out of date, and the people of God are a threat that needs to be controlled, if not exterminated. Hitler was an extreme example, though many would do the same ungodly and unthinkable crimes that he did if they could get by with it. They begin by having laws passed that are opposed to the Scriptures and proceed to punish Christians for being in opposition to their ungodly laws and leadership. Christians eventually are forced to go into hiding to prevent being imprisoned or killed.

"But when they perish, the righteous increase." A 2019 headline on cbnnews.com blared, "Christians 'Standing in the Way' of China's Xi Jinping's Totalitarian Rule." God-fearing people always stand in opposition to God-hating regimes, and fundamental Bible-believing Christians in China have to meet secretly in homes or in the woods away from others. They hide themselves because of wicked rulers who will eventually die, and **"when they perish,"** persecuted believers may come out of hiding and worship openly. If Xi Jinping were to die, and a non-Communist, righteous person were to assume control, Christians would be free to worship and be a strong positive influence in society. It can then be said that **"the righteous increase"** in number, in voice, in authority, and in the message that "Jesus saves."

1 Kings 18:13 Was it not told my lord what I did when Jezebel slew the prophets of the LORD, how I hid an hundred men of the LORD'S prophets by fifty in a cave, and fed them with bread and water?

Esther 8:15-16 And Mordecai went out from the presence of the king in royal apparel of blue and white, and with a great crown of gold, and with a garment of fine linen and purple: and the city of Shushan rejoiced and was glad. The Jews had light, and gladness, and joy, and honour.

Proverbs 11:10 When it goeth well with the righteous, the city rejoiceth: and when the wicked perish, there is shouting.

Proverbs 29:2 When the righteous are in authority, the people rejoice: but when the wicked beareth rule, the people mourn.

Acts 9:31 Then had the churches rest throughout all Judaea and Galilee and Samaria, and were edified; and walking in the fear of the Lord, and in the comfort of the Holy Ghost, were multiplied. *[This took place after Paul was saved on the road to Damascus.]*

CHAPTER TWENTY-NINE

Chapter 29 completes the section copied out by the men of Hezekiah. (Chapters 25-29) See Chapter 25 for additional information on King Hezekiah and this section of Proverbs.

> **Proverbs 29:1** He, that being often reproved hardeneth *his* neck, shall suddenly be destroyed, and that without remedy.

Focus: This proverb describes the result of a rebellious person's refusal to be corrected.

"He, that being often reproved hardeneth his neck" describes a person who is often corrected but refuses to accept such correction. ***Reproofs*** may come through Scriptural teachings, Holy Spirit conviction, friends, teachers, sermons, or from disastrous events allowed by the providence of God. Rather than properly respond to reproofs with gladness that he is being helped, the unwise person will bow up with resistance.

"Hardeneth his neck" is a metaphor concerning burden animals, such as the oxen, mule, or horse, whose refusal to submit to a yoke renders them uncontrollable. Jesus carried the metaphor forward in the New Testament when He instructed His followers to submit to the wisdom of His teaching and thereby learn to live in a peaceful, effective, and loving manner. Matthew 11:28-30 "Come unto me, all *ye* that labour and are heavy laden, and I will give you rest. Take my yoke upon you, and learn of me; for I am meek and lowly in heart: and ye shall find rest unto your souls. For my yoke *is* easy, and my burden is light." Living according to the teachings of Jesus, which is wisdom in its purest form, is restful, easy, and light; while the way of the fool is anxious, difficult, and oppressive. Because of being relentlessly rebellious and consistently incorrigible, the rebel's outcome is that he **"shall suddenly be destroyed,"** which means he will be wrecked or broken in pieces like a potter's vessel that can never be put back together. Once the rebel has completely and finally refused the way of God, he will have set himself aside on a dark path. The voice of personified wisdom cried out in Proverbs 1:24-31 against this man who has been **"often reproved."**

> Proverbs 1:24-31 Because I have called, and ye refused; I have stretched out my hand, and no man regarded; But ye have set at nought all my counsel, and would none of my reproof: I also will laugh at your calamity; I will mock when your fear cometh; When your fear cometh as desolation, and your destruction cometh as a whirlwind; when distress and anguish cometh upon you. Then shall they call upon me, but I will not answer; they shall seek me early, but they shall not find me: For that they hated knowledge, and did not choose the fear of the LORD: They would none of my counsel: they despised all my reproof. Therefore shall they eat of the fruit of their own way, and be filled with their own devices.

"And that without remedy" is a heartrending phrase to those who know that God has deadlines which seal one's doom when crossed. There is no healing for the disease of obstinance and rejection of God at this point. These have totally rejected the offer of forgiveness, and God certainly will not have Heaven populated with rebellion. The classic example of people who "hardeneth" their neck and were destroyed without remedy is found in Genesis 6. This chapter describes a world whose mind was on evil continually.

> Genesis 6:5-8 And GOD saw that the wickedness of man *was* great in the earth, and *that* every imagination of the thoughts of his heart *was* only evil continually. And it repented the LORD that he had made man on the earth, and it grieved him at his heart. And the LORD said, I will destroy man whom I have created from the face of the earth; both man, and beast, and the creeping thing, and the fowls of the air; for it repenteth me that I have made them. But Noah found grace in the eyes of the LORD.
>
> Proverbs 5:12-13 And say, How have I hated instruction, and my heart despised reproof; And have not obeyed the voice of my teachers, nor inclined mine ear to them that instructed me!
>
> Proverbs 6:12-15 A naughty person, a wicked man, walketh with a froward mouth. He winketh with his eyes, he speaketh with his feet, he teacheth with his fingers; Frowardness *is* in his heart, he deviseth mischief continually; he soweth discord. Therefore shall his calamity come suddenly; suddenly shall he be broken without remedy.
>
> Proverbs 10:17 He *is in* the way of life that keepeth instruction: but he that refuseth reproof erreth.
>
> Proverbs 12:1 Whoso loveth instruction loveth knowledge: but he that hateth reproof *is* brutish.

Proverbs 15:10 Correction *is* grievous unto him that forsaketh the way: *and* he that hateth reproof shall die.

Proverbs 29:15 The rod and reproof give wisdom: but a child left *to himself* bringeth his mother to shame.

Isaiah 55:6-7 Seek ye the LORD while he may be found, call ye upon him while he is near: Let the wicked forsake his way, and the unrighteous man his thoughts: and let him return unto the LORD, and he will have mercy upon him; and to our God, for he will abundantly pardon.

John 3:19-21 And this is the condemnation, that light is come into the world, and men loved darkness rather than light, because their deeds were evil. For every one that doeth evil hateth the light, neither cometh to the light, lest his deeds should be reproved. But he that doeth truth cometh to the light, that his deeds may be made manifest, that they are wrought in God.

2 Thessalonians 2:10-12 And with all deceivableness of unrighteousness in them that perish; because they received not the love of the truth, that they might be saved. And for this cause God shall send them strong delusion, that they should believe a lie: That they all might be damned who believed not the truth, but had pleasure in unrighteousness.

Revelation 20:15 And whosoever was not found written in the book of life was cast into the lake of fire.

Proverbs 29:2   When the righteous are in authority, the people rejoice: but when the wicked beareth rule, the people mourn.

Focus: This proverb contrasts the joyous effect that righteous leaders have on a population with the sad effect that wicked leaders have.

"When the righteous are in authority," they exercise godly leadership, in part, by holding wicked people accountable for their hateful, malicious deeds. When laws are written, the righteous also work to ensure that these laws reflect the wisdom of God and that such laws are enforced. Because they hold themselves accountable to God, rely on His word for direction, and are guided by the Holy Spirit, "the righteous" have opposite standards to "the wicked." Godly leaders are not subject to bribes or flattery; and they attempt to treat all men equally despite economic status, culture, religion, education, race, and sex, or any other difference. Men are thus held accountable for their evil doings and punished appropriately.

Because of their opposition to God, His people, His wisdom, and His church, wickedness abounds when **"the wicked beareth rule."** Wickedness is not only encouraged but is the driving force behind their governmental procedures and laws. Because the righteous population is persecuted and suffers at the hand of wicked leaders, they have reasons to **"mourn."**

> "'**The people mourn**' or 'groan'. . . under their tyranny and oppression, and because of the sad state of things; the number of good men is lessened, being cut off, or obliged to flee; wicked men and wickedness are encouraged and promoted; heavy taxes are laid upon them, and exorbitant demands made and cruelty, injustice, and arbitrary power exercised; and no man's person and property safe." [735]

David's prayer for Solomon illustrates what God expects for a righteous king.

Psalm 72:1-7 A Psalm for Solomon. Give the king thy judgments, O God, and thy righteousness unto the king's son. He shall judge thy people with righteousness, and thy poor with judgment. The mountains shall bring peace to the people, and the little hills, by righteousness. He shall judge the poor of the people, he shall save the children of the needy, and shall break in pieces the oppressor. They shall fear thee as long as the sun and moon endure, throughout all generations. He shall come down like rain upon the mown grass: as showers that water the earth. In his days shall the righteous flourish; and abundance of peace so long as the moon endureth.

In contrast, Isaiah details the actions of wicked rulers. When the ungodly are in leadership places, they are less restrained and emboldened to carry forth their individual hatefulness. Proverbs mentions the reaction to the wicked's rule in several verses.

Isaiah 59:2-8 But your iniquities have separated between you and your God, and your sins have hid *his* face from you, that he will not hear. For your hands are defiled with blood, and your fingers with iniquity; your lips have spoken lies, your tongue hath muttered perverseness. None calleth for justice, nor *any* pleadeth for truth: they trust in vanity, and speak lies; they conceive mischief, and bring forth iniquity. They hatch cockatrice' eggs, and weave the spider's web: he that eateth of their eggs dieth, and that which is crushed breaketh out into a viper. Their webs shall not become garments, neither shall they cover themselves with their works: their works *are* works of iniquity, and the act of violence *is* in their hands. Their feet run to evil, and they make haste to shed innocent blood: their thoughts *are* thoughts of iniquity; wasting and destruction *are* in their paths. The way of peace they know not; and *there is* no judgment in their goings: they have made them crooked paths: whosoever goeth therein shall not know peace.

Proverbs 11:10 When it goeth well with the righteous, the city rejoiceth: and when the wicked perish, *there is* shouting.

Proverbs 28:12 When righteous *men* do rejoice, *there is* great glory: but when the wicked rise, a man is hidden.

Proverbs 28:15-16 *As* a roaring lion, and a ranging bear; *so is* a wicked ruler over the poor people. The prince that wanteth understanding *is* also a great oppressor: *but* he that hateth covetousness shall prolong his days.

Proverbs 28:28 When the wicked rise, men hide themselves: but when they perish, the righteous increase.

Therefore godly people should, as much as possible, be engaged in and influence politics to ensure that righteous people are selected to hold leadership roles. "For religion to withdraw from politics is to hand that important region of life over to the devil."[736]

> **Proverbs 29:3** Whoso loveth wisdom rejoiceth his father: but he that keepeth company with harlots spendeth *his* substance.

Focus: This proverb contrasts a father's joy caused by a wise son's behavior with a father's grief from a foolish son's behavior.

"Whoso loveth wisdom rejoiceth his father." From the time their children are born, *wise parents* start teaching them Scripture's wisdom. The purpose of their labor is to teach their offspring to live an independent successful life under the blessings of God, stay out of the entrapments of evil people whose father is Satan, and enjoy a godly life. For a godly person's child to grow to maturity *loving wisdom* is not only a source of rejoicing, but also a great reward for the parents' years of relentless and painstaking effort.

The character of persons that an individual *keeps company with* reflects his ability to understand life. Because the wise son loves wisdom, other wise people *(not harlots)* become his trusted companions. His life is altered to some level by these influential "friends." Associates have a way of swaying each other's values, ways of thinking, and attitudes toward God and His commandments. In contrast to foolish sons who continually produce bad news, wise sons produce positive, encouraging, and hopeful emotions within their parents; thus causing the father to rejoice. Wisdom teaches a person to conduct himself appropriately and productively to increase both joy and substance.

> Proverbs 10:1 The proverbs of Solomon. A wise son maketh a glad father: but a foolish son is the heaviness of his mother.
> Proverbs 15:20 A wise son maketh a glad father: but a foolish man despiseth his mother.
> Proverbs 23:15 My son, if thine heart be wise, my heart shall rejoice, even mine.
> Proverbs 23:24 The father of the righteous shall greatly rejoice: and he that begetteth a wise child shall have joy of him.
> Proverbs 24:4 And by knowledge shall the chambers be filled with all precious and pleasant riches.
> Proverbs 27:11 My son, be wise, and make my heart glad, that I may answer him that reproacheth me.

"But he that keepeth company with harlots spendeth *his* substance." Association with harlots reveals a distinct lack of wisdom and self-control. Moral ruin and financial destruction are companions that often travel like contagious diseases on the backs of ungodly people.

The second clause of this proverb could stand as a thesis sentence for the story of the prodigal son of Luke 15. The prodigal son wasted his inheritance with riotous living. A foolish son chooses to be **"a companion of riotous *men*,"** who are those prone to be free from any restraints or guidelines of the word of God. Consequently, the word **"riotous"** is usually associated with excessive drinking and gluttony. The prodigal son of Luke 15 wasted his inheritance (**"substance"**) with riotous living. Such a rebel learns other riotous men's low values, picks up their foul language, takes their ungodly counsel, and acts like a fool. He lives a lifestyle that God and good men oppose and thus brings shame to his father.

Sexual misconduct and intoxication are twins often seen together. Because the drunk's brain is impaired, his ability to make reasonable judgments is diminished. In a sober state, he might have enough character *not* to fixate on a harlot, whereas in a drunken state, he has a much greater probability of doing so.

The harlot of Proverbs 7 lures the young man through fleshly lusts that overwhelm and conquer his thinking. Because his mind is captured by the pleasure of lust, his brain is put in a loop thinking only of pleasure. All the benefits of the years of training by his dear parents stand in jeopardy. He is likely to lose the good things that righteous living provides such as peace, a sound mind, and wealth (all of which can be considered as his **"substance"**). He has become a fool, disgraces his parents, and condemns his own soul.

> Proverbs 5:5-13 Her feet go down to death; her steps take hold on hell. Lest thou shouldest ponder the path of life, her ways are moveable, that thou canst not know them. Hear me now therefore, O ye children, and depart not from the words of my mouth. Remove thy way far from her, and come not nigh the door of her house: Lest thou give thine honour unto others, and thy years unto the cruel: Lest strangers be filled with thy wealth; and thy labours be in the house of a stranger; And thou mourn at the last,

when thy flesh and thy body are consumed, And say, How have I hated instruction, and my heart despised reproof; And have not obeyed the voice of my teachers, nor inclined mine ear to them that instructed me!

Proverbs 21:20 There is treasure to be desired and oil in the dwelling of the wise; but a foolish man spendeth it up.

Proverbs 28:7 Whoso keepeth the law *is* a wise son: but he that is a companion of riotous men shameth his father.

Luke 15:13 And not many days after the younger son gathered all together, and took his journey into a far country, and there wasted his substance with riotous living.

Wisdom is a guide that will keep a young man away from harlots and adulterers.

Proverbs 2:16-18 To deliver thee from the strange woman, even from the stranger which flattereth with her words; Which forsaketh the guide of her youth, and forgetteth the covenant of her God. For her house inclineth unto death, and her paths unto the dead.

Proverbs 6:32-33 But whoso committeth adultery with a woman lacketh understanding: he that doeth it destroyeth his own soul. A wound and dishonour shall he get; and his reproach shall not be wiped away.

Proverbs 29:4   The king by judgment establisheth the land: but he that receiveth gifts overthroweth it.

Focus: This proverb contrasts the effect on a country that fair and equitable judgments have with the effect that judgments by bribery have.

The king by judgment establishes the land. By **"judgment"** is meant "a right and godly opinion reached after discerning and consideration."[737] ("The teaching of Proverbs is to lead us to pass a right sentence upon human actions, whether our own or anothers."[738]) Therefore, a godly judgment is judgment that is wise, fair, and equitable. Justice and judgment bring a nation stability and joy (Proverbs 29: 2, 14).

To establish the land is a phrase that speaks of stability within the population. It is a stability that is generated through godly, fundamental methods of leadership. A king governs and stabilizes the people, not the **"land"** per se. "Land" is used here symbolically to represent a nation *(Israel)* and is similar to the use in John 3:16 of the word "world." "For God so loved the world" meaning His entire creation but primarily the people of the world. Jesus' love was and is for the people of the world whom He provided redemption by his vicarious death. (Sad to say, everyone doesn't believe to salvation.) When the people of a land are "established," they are settled in their minds and comfortable with the way leadership is functioning and believe that the laws are fair and equitable.

2 Chronicles 9:7-8 Happy are thy men *[those men under Solomon's righteous rule]*, and happy are these thy servants, which stand continually before thee, and hear thy wisdom. Blessed be the LORD thy God, which delighted in thee to set thee on his throne, to be king for the LORD thy God: because thy God loved Israel, to establish them for ever, therefore made he thee king over them, to do judgment and justice.

Psalm 89:14 Justice and judgment are the habitation of thy throne: mercy and truth shall go before thy face.

Psalm 97:2 Clouds and darkness are round about him: righteousness and judgment are the habitation of his throne.

Proverbs 16:10-13 A divine sentence is in the lips of the king: his mouth transgresseth not in judgment. A just weight and balance are the LORD'S: all the weights of the bag are his work. It is an abomination to kings to commit wickedness: for the throne is established by righteousness. Righteous lips are the delight of kings; and they love him that speaketh right.

Proverbs 29:14 The king that faithfully judgeth the poor, his throne shall be established for ever.

Isaiah 9:7 Of the increase of his government and peace there shall be no end, upon the throne of David, and upon his kingdom, to order it, and to establish it with judgment and with justice from henceforth even for ever. The zeal of the LORD of hosts will perform this.

But he that receiveth gifts overthrows *[pulls down in pieces, breaks, destroys]* ***it.*** Justice and equity become extinct when a leader receives gifts (bribes) for judgments. For a land to be thus overthrown by corrupt judgments means that the people will become unstable and fearful, lacking trust in any judgment by its judges or even any information given by governmental leadership. When leadership is covetous and receives **"gifts"** or bribes, the leadership is no longer impartial with judgments and has thus put justice up for sale; hence, the people become unstable, the laws ineffective, and the courtroom unfair. At such a point, the nation is in a turmoil rather than being established. If permitted, there will likely be protests and riots in the streets. Partiality and injustice make the best laws invalid.

Isaiah 59:14 And judgment is turned away backward, and justice standeth afar off: for truth is fallen in the street, and equity cannot enter.

Amos 5:12 For I know your manifold transgressions and your mighty sins: they afflict the just, they take a bribe, and they turn aside the poor in the gate *from their right.*

Acts 24:25-27 And as he reasoned of righteousness, temperance, and judgment to come, Felix trembled, and answered, Go thy way for this time; when I have a convenient season, I will call for thee. He hoped also that money should have been given him of Paul, that he might loose him: wherefore he sent for him the oftener, and communed with him. But after two years Porcius Festus came into Felix' room: and Felix, willing to shew the Jews a pleasure, left Paul bound.

Proverbs 29:5 A man that flattereth his neighbour spreadeth a net for his feet.

Focus: This proverb describes an intended purpose and result of flattering a neighbor.

"**Flatterers** put men off their guard, which betrays them into foolish conduct."[739] **Flattering** *[dividing, plundering, deceiving, figuratively – to be smooth]*" is the technique that is used to deceive the neighbor into believing his abilities are greater than they actually are, and he consequently begins to make foolish, unwise decisions based on his misconception. The flatterer may be attempting to get revenge or inflict injury when he flatters the recipient with words that convince him that he certainly will not need to pay for help during the harvest. Consequently, because of a false opinion of his abilities, the neighbor refuses to get help, an action that causes him to lose a portion of his crop. As another example, perhaps the recipient is having financial difficulty, and the neighbor flatters him with words that convince him to keep doing the same things that got him into the difficulty. He suffers bankruptcy because he believes the flattery. Flattery under the pretense of kindness is not only an act of foolishness; it is a lie that causes its victim to become ensnared in a misconception of himself.

> "There is no flattery of which it can be truly said that it is harmless. . . Solomon does not refer solely to the intention of the flatterer; he refers also to the tendency of the flattery . . . Injury may be done, and many a time is done, when no harm is meant to the party, and when there is no interest of our own to serve. And there is no little guilt on the part of those, who, seeing vanity to be a man's failing, set themselves of purpose to feed it, – pouring into the ear, merely in the way of an amusing experiment . . . The experiment is a cruel one. But it has another and a more direct ingredient of evil-falsehood. You cannot flatter thus without lying . . . "[740]
>
> Psalm 12:2 They speak vanity every one with his neighbour: with flattering lips and with a double heart do they speak.
>
> Proverbs 7:10; 21-23 And, behold, there met him a woman with the attire of an harlot, and subtil of heart . . . With her much fair speech she caused him to yield, with the flattering of her lips she forced him. He goeth after her straightway, as an ox goeth to the slaughter, or as a fool to the correction of the stocks; Till a dart strike through his liver; as a bird hasteth to the snare, and knoweth not that it is for his life.
>
> Proverbs 20:19 He that goeth about as a talebearer revealeth secrets: therefore meddle not with him that flattereth with his lips.
>
> Proverbs 26:24-28 He that hateth dissembleth with his lips, and layeth up deceit within him; When he speaketh fair, believe him not: for there are seven abominations in his heart. Whose hatred is covered by deceit, his wickedness shall be shewed before the whole congregation. Whoso diggeth a pit shall fall therein: and he that rolleth a stone, it will return upon him. A lying tongue hateth those that are afflicted by it; and a flattering mouth worketh ruin.

Proverbs 29:6 In the transgression of an evil man *there is* a snare: but the righteous doth sing and rejoice.

Focus: This proverb contrasts the sadness and lamenting of evil men (because of their snare-laden transgressions) with the singing and rejoicing of the righteous.

"**In the transgression of an evil man there is a snare** *[bait, lure]*." **Evil men transgress** or rebel against God and His commandments. Their transgression serves to bind them to dreadful horrors and inevitable ruin. Evil men foolishly oppose God's wise and righteously-designed order in which this world was set to operate. Because they hate the Creator's design, they go another way, an inferior way filled with traps. *Transgression against God is within itself a snare* because it causes its host to oppose the honorable laws of man and the commandments of God. For a person to think that he can oppose God and have no consequence is foolishness and contrary to Scripture. He is like a chained dog thinking he is free until he slams himself against the end of his chain. Sin and disaster are links that make up the chain of sin, jerking its captive back under its horrible control.

> Job 18:5 -18 Yea, the light of the wicked shall be put out, and the spark of his fire shall not shine. The light shall be dark in his tabernacle, and his candle shall be put out with him. The steps of his strength shall be straitened, and his own counsel shall cast him down. For he is cast into a net by his own feet, and he walketh upon a snare. The gin shall take him by the heel, and the robber shall prevail against him. The snare is laid for him in the ground, and a trap for him in the way. Terrors shall make him afraid on every side, and shall drive him to his feet. His strength shall be hunger bitten, and destruction shall be ready at his side. It shall devour the strength of his skin:

even the firstborn of death shall devour his strength. His confidence shall be rooted out of his tabernacle, and it shall bring him to the king of terrors. It shall dwell in his tabernacle, because it is none of his: brimstone shall be scattered upon his habitation. His roots shall be dried up beneath, and above shall his branch be cut off. His remembrance shall perish from the earth, and he shall have no name in the street. He shall be driven from light into darkness, and chased out of the world.

Proverbs 5:22 His own iniquities shall take the wicked himself, and he shall be holden with the cords of his sins.

Proverbs 11:5 The righteousness of the perfect shall direct his way: but the wicked shall fall by his own wickedness.

Proverbs 12:13 The wicked is snared by the transgression of his lips: but the just shall come out of trouble.

Proverbs 21:12 The righteous man wisely considereth the house of the wicked: but God overthroweth the wicked for their wickedness.

Isaiah 65:14-15 Behold, my servants shall sing for joy of heart, but ye *[those who forsake the LORD]* shall cry for sorrow of heart, and shall howl for vexation of spirit. And ye shall leave your name for a curse unto my chosen: for the Lord GOD shall slay thee, and call his servants by another name...

John 3:17-18 For God sent not his Son into the world to condemn the world; but that the world through him might be saved. He that believeth on him is not condemned: but he that believeth not is condemned already, because he hath not believed in the name of the only begotten Son of God.

But the righteous sing and rejoice. Wisdom and godliness drive the behavior of the righteous who **"sing"** because of the freedom to live without fear of reprisal for evil and who **"rejoice"** in being forgiven, assured "of present safety and eternal happiness."[741] The Christian rejoices in his standing with Jesus, his pardon of sin, his relationship with the Trinity, the many promises of the Bible, peace of mind, hope of Heaven, delight of Christian fellowship, the guiding voice of God throughout his life, and in knowing right from wrong. The Christian's song is built on the solid foundation of freedom from condemnation. Believers even sing in the face of severe adversity, as did Paul and Silas while in prison. Having great freedom, the righteous delight to sing about their blessings; but the transgressor has a snare rather than a song. He always slams against the end of the Devil's chain.

Psalm 16:11 Thou wilt shew me the path of life: in thy presence is fulness of joy; at thy right hand there are pleasures for evermore.

Psalm 27:4-6 One thing have I desired of the LORD, that will I seek after; that I may dwell in the house of the LORD all the days of my life, to behold the beauty of the LORD, and to enquire in his temple. For in the time of trouble he shall hide me in his pavilion: in the secret of his tabernacle shall he hide me; he shall set me up upon a rock. And now shall mine head be lifted up above mine enemies round about me: therefore will I offer in his tabernacle sacrifices of joy; I will sing, yea, I will sing praises unto the LORD.

Proverbs 3:13, 17 Happy is the man that findeth wisdom, and the man that getteth understanding.. Her ways *[Wisdom's ways]* are ways of pleasantness, and all her paths are peace.

Proverbs 31:25 Strength and honour are her *[wise woman's]* clothing; and she shall rejoice in time to come.

1 Peter 1:8-9 Whom having not seen, ye love; in whom, though now ye see *him* not, yet believing, ye rejoice with joy unspeakable and full of glory: Receiving the end of your faith, *even* the salvation of *your* souls.

1 John 1:4 And these things write we unto you, that your joy may be full.

Proverbs 29:7   The righteous considereth the cause of the poor: *but* the wicked regardeth not to know *it.*

Focus: This proverb contrasts the attitude of the righteous with the attitude of the wicked concerning fair judgment of the poor.

"The righteous*[lawful, correct, just]* **considereth** *[to ascertain by seeing, acknowledge]* **the cause***[plea, legal suit]* **of the poor." "The righteous"** agree with God and love His commandments; consequently, they live by and treat others in a manner that reflects God's values and principles. Scripture repeatedly teaches that all men are to be treated equally in judgments. Righteous people believe the Scriptures and understand that God expects them to have a fair and equitable attitude toward everyone, especially **"the poor." "Cause of the poor"** describes the poor person's plea for a good, fair judgment, especially from a judge.

The wicked regardeth *[to become aware of by the senses, to understand, to know]* **not to know** *[to understand, to know, to discern]* **it."** When the poor presents his plea before the judge, the wicked judge *chooses* to ignore the plight of the poor. They *have no regard for the cause of the poor.* They give it no consideration because they believe that the poor are beneath them, do not deserve justice, and cannot do anything to help them in return. Therefore when the poor attempt to advance their **"cause,"** it is ignored (disregarded).

Job 29:16 I was a father to the poor: and the cause which I knew not I searched out.

Psalm 41:1 To the chief Musician, A Psalm of David. Blessed is he that considereth the poor: the LORD will deliver him in time of trouble.

Psalm 82:2-4 How long will ye judge unjustly, and accept the persons of the wicked? Selah. Defend the poor and fatherless: do justice to the afflicted and needy. Deliver the poor and needy: rid them out of the hand of the wicked.

Proverbs 19:17 He that hath pity upon the poor lendeth unto the LORD; and that which he hath given will he pay him again.

Proverbs 21:13 Whoso stoppeth his ears at the cry of the poor, he also shall cry himself, but shall not be heard.

Proverbs 28:5 Evil men understand not judgment: but they that seek the LORD understand all *things*.

Luke 18:2-5 Saying, here was in a city a judge, which feared not God, neither regarded man: and there was a widow in that city; and she came unto him, saying, Avenge me of mine adversary. And he would not for a while: but afterward he said within himself, Though I fear not God, nor regard man; yet because this widow troubleth me, I will avenge her, lest by her continual coming she weary me.

Acts 24:25-27 And as he reasoned of righteousness, temperance, and judgment to come, Felix trembled, and answered, Go thy way for this time; when I have a convenient season, I will call for thee. He hoped also that money should have been given him of Paul, that he might loose him: wherefore he sent for him the oftener, and communed with him. But after two years Porcius Festus came into Felix' room: and Felix, willing to shew the Jews a pleasure, left Paul bound.

Proverbs 29:8   Scornful men bring a city into a snare: but wise *men* turn away wrath.

Focus: This proverb contrasts the effects that scornful men have on a city with the effects that wise men have.

"Scornful men" express disdain, blowing out arrogant language and elevating themselves above other men and even above God. In fact, they mock God and the people who serve Him. Scorners are proud, braggers, and unbridled; and their language is incendiary, dragging the city into an entrapment (**"snare"**) of reprisal from both men and God. They have no leadership from God and are dangerous to the public. Since they are ungodly, they will do business illegally, and scorn at laws. Their actions prove that they believe themselves above the law. Their word means nothing, and they will quickly side with others who oppose the teachings of God. All that the scorners do causes discord and confusion.

"... those who despise and scoff at all things great and high, whether sacred or profane. These are the persons who raise rebellion in a country and excite opposition to constituted authority. . . These scorners excite the populace to acts of fury, when all respect for piety and virtue is lost; they fan the passions of the fickle people, and lead them to civil discord and dangerous excesses."[742]

Proverbs 21:23-24 Whoso keepeth his mouth and his tongue keepeth his soul from troubles. Proud and haughty scorner is his name, who dealeth in proud wrath.

James 3:5-6 Even so the tongue is a little member, and boasteth great things. Behold, how great a matter a little fire kindleth! And the tongue is a fire, a world of iniquity: so is the tongue among our members, that it defileth the whole body, and setteth on fire the course of nature; and it is set on fire of hell.

"But wise men turn away wrath" by having a love for God and other men. Truthfulness is highly regarded, while law and order is not only respected but decidedly supported. Through well-chosen words, their speech reveals respect and honor where it is due, calming otherwise inflammatory situations. All that they do is exactly opposite the scorner.

"Who are the men that are the blessings of a land – the wise men who by promoting religion, which is true wisdom, turn away the wrath of God, and who, by prudent counsels, reconcile contending parties and prevent the mischievous consequences of divisions.

Proud and foolish men kindle the fires which wise and good men must extinguish."[743]

Proverbs 11:11 By the blessing of the upright the city is exalted: but it is overthrown by the mouth of the wicked.

Proverbs 15:1 A soft answer turneth away wrath: but grievous words stir up anger.

Scripture cites several examples of wise men turning away the wrath of God, including Moses (Exodus 32:10-14, Deuteronomy 9:12-29), Phinehas (Numbers 25: 6-11), David (2 Samuel 24:10-19), and Amos (Amos 6:14-7:6). Jonah warned Ninevah of the wrath of God, and Ezekiel records God's searched for a man to turn away His wrath.

Jonah 3:4-10 And Jonah began to enter into the city a day's journey, and he cried, and said, Yet forty days, and Nineveh shall be overthrown. So the people of Nineveh believed God, and proclaimed a fast, and put on sackcloth, from the greatest of them even to the least of them. word came unto the king of Nineveh, and he arose from his throne, and he laid his robe from him, and covered him with sackcloth, and sat in ashes. And he caused it to be proclaimed and published through Nineveh by the decree of the king and his nobles, saying, Let neither man nor beast, herd nor flock, taste any thing: let them not feed, nor drink water: But let man and beast be covered with sackcloth, and cry mightily unto God: yea, let them turn every one from his evil way, and from the violence that is in their hands. Who can tell if God will turn and repent, and turn away from his fierce anger, that we perish not? And God saw their works, that they turned from their evil way; and God repented of the evil, that he had said that he would do unto them; and he did it not.

Ezekiel 22:29-31 The people of the land have used oppression, and exercised robbery, and have vexed the poor and needy: yea, they have oppressed the stranger wrongfully. And I sought for a man among them, that should make up the hedge, and stand in the gap before me for the land, that I should not destroy it: but I found none. Therefore have I poured out mine indignation upon them; I have consumed them with the fire of my wrath: their own way have I recompensed upon their heads, saith the Lord GOD.

Proverbs 29:9 *If* a wise man contendeth with a foolish man, whether he rage or laugh, *there is* no rest.

Focus: This proverb warns of the futility of a wise person contending with a foolish one.

"If a wise man contendeth with a foolish man," whether the controversy is in a court of law (as **"contendeth"** would indicate) or in a social setting, the wise man will not have any **"rest."** There is no reasoning with the foolish man who lives his life by evil notions of disinformation rather than truth. Because his basis of understanding is established on humanistic philosophy rather than Scripture, **"a foolish man"** is opposed to **"a wise man."** The foolish man has no confidence or even belief in God, Heaven or Hell; and he will likely believe that the Scriptures are useless – even a hoax.

"Whether he rage or laugh, there is no rest." To attempt to reason with "a foolish man" from a basis of godly wisdom is futile and only leads to unrest. By displaying his opposition through **raging or laughing**, his reaction will be mockery. There is no common ground for reasoning because the basis for understanding is as far separated as Heaven and Hell. "He that fights with a dunghill, whether he be conqueror or conquered, is sure to be defiled."[744]

> Proverbs 14:16 A wise man feareth, and departeth from evil: but the fool rageth, and is confident.
>
> Matthew 11:16-19 "But whereunto shall I liken this generation? It is like unto children sitting in the markets, and calling unto their fellows, and saying, We have piped unto you, and ye have not danced; we have mourned unto you, and ye have not lamented. For John came neither eating nor drinking, and they say, He hath a devil. The Son of man came eating and drinking, and they say, Behold a man gluttonous, and a winebibber, a friend of publicans and sinners. But wisdom is justified of her children."

Proverbs 29:10 The bloodthirsty hate the upright: but the just seek his soul.

Focus: This proverb contrasts the ungodly's murderous hatred for the righteous with the godly's preserving love for them.

"Bloodthirsty," a term that only occurs in Proverbs 29:10, is identified in the margin of the 1611 King James Bible as "men of blood."[745] These criminals are those whose hate for the **"upright"** is so intense that they are eager to kill them for no reason other than the fact that the righteous (by their very existence) bring condemnation to their own wicked conscience.

"The upright" and the **"just"** are terms that identify those who are aligned with God – the righteous. Hateful, ungodly men desire to kill the godly, but the righteous **"seek"** to secure the righteous, to bring them to safety. King Saul would have killed David, but Jonathan prevented the catastrophe. (1 Samuel 19:1-20:42) Queen Jezebel would have drained the blood of all the prophets of the LORD, but Obadiah "hid them in a cave, and fed them with bread and water." (1 Kings 18:4-5) The princes of King Zedekiah would have killed Jeremiah, but Ebedmelech and 30 others drew him out of the pit. (Jeremiah 38:7-13) Herod would have killed Peter, but the church prayed, and he was released. (Acts 12:1-18). The Apostle Paul, in Damascus, would have been taken captive by the governor under Aretas and killed by the Jews, but good men helped him escape down the wall in a basket. (2 Corinthians 11:32-33).

> "The bloodthirsty hate the upright. (Hebrews 11:36-37) Their innocency was the only ground of hatred; and, on the threatened apprehension of any outbreak of evil, the swelling cry of the bloodthirsty multitude was – 'The Christians to the lions!' The next picture downward in the annals of the Church is not less illustrative – 'I saw the woman' – awful sight! – 'drunken with the blood of the saints, and with the blood of the martyrs of Jesus.' (Revelation 17:6) We cannot doubt but the fierce elements of the cruelty still lie in slumbering concealment. Nothing but the Gospel can kill the principle. Everything short of this only chains down the violence. In a softer mold it still retains all its substance and power, and waits only for the removal of present restraints to develop the same bloodthirsty hatred as ever."[746]

On the first few pages of Scripture this hatred of the wicked for the righteous began and continues throughout recorded history. It will end only with the righteous being eternally separated from the wicked.

> Genesis 3:15 And I will put enmity between thee and the woman, and between thy seed and her seed; it shall bruise thy head, and thou shalt bruise his heel.

Genesis 4:8 And Cain talked with Abel his brother: and it came to pass, when they were in the field, that Cain rose up against Abel his brother, and slew him. *[1 John 3:12 Not as Cain, who was of that wicked one, and slew his brother. And wherefore slew he him? Because his own works were evil, and his brother's righteous.]*

Matthew 23:29-35 Woe unto you, scribes and Pharisees, hypocrites! because ye build the tombs of the prophets, and garnish the sepulchres of the righteous, and say, If we had been in the days of our fathers, we would not have been partakers with them in the blood of the prophets. Wherefore ye be witnesses unto yourselves, that ye are the children of them which killed the prophets. Fill ye up then the measure of your fathers. Ye serpents, ye generation of vipers, how can ye escape the damnation of hell? Wherefore, behold, I send unto you prophets, and wise men, and scribes: and some of them ye shall kill and crucify; and some of them shall ye scourge in your synagogues, and persecute them from city to city: That upon you may come all the righteous blood shed upon the earth, from the blood of righteous Abel unto the blood of Zacharias son of Barachias, whom ye slew between the temple and the altar.

Matthew 24:9 Then shall they deliver you up to be afflicted, and shall kill you: and ye shall be hated of all nations for my name's sake. *[See also Matthew 10:22, 13:13; Luke 21:17.]*

Hebrews 11:36-37 And others had trial of cruel mockings and scourgings, yea, moreover of bonds and imprisonment: They were stoned, they were sawn asunder, were tempted, were slain with the sword: they wandered about in sheepskins and goatskins; being destitute, afflicted, tormented. . .

Revelation 11:9-10 And they of the people and kindreds and tongues and nations shall see their dead bodies three days and an half, and shall not suffer their dead bodies to be put in graves. And they that dwell upon the earth shall rejoice over them, and make merry, and shall send gifts one to another; because these two prophets tormented them that dwelt on the earth.

Revelation 17:6 And I saw the woman drunken with the blood of the saints, and with the blood of the martyrs of Jesus: and when I saw her, I wondered with great admiration.

Proverbs 29:11 A fool uttereth all his mind: but a wise *man* keepeth it in till afterwards.

Focus: This proverb declares that unfiltered talk is a characteristic of the fool and that restrained talk is a characteristic of the wise.

"A fool uttereth all his mind" – all at once, unnecessarily, at the wrong time, without caution or forethought, and usually with the wrong spirit. This proverb is another warning against being hasty with words and speaking without thinking. Passion, especially anger, needs a lid; so it does not vent through the lips.

Because of his training, a **"wise"** person will control his passion and consequently his speech by deciding when, where and how he can best address every situation. Thus, He makes sure that he is acting on what he knows is right, rather than being drawn into a hasty, thoughtless, reaction that will probably be improper. At the correct time, a wise man will voice his selected thoughts or choose to remain silent. He will have had time to properly assimilate facts, gain insight and pray for God's leadership. The believer should remember that there is a "Right time, right place, and a right spirit" to speak, especially about matters that need to be handled delicately.

The fool, however, follows a pattern of speaking known as "stream of consciousness." Thus, whatever passion he feels, drives his speech; and since he has no filter for his words, he vents his every thought. He takes no time to control his passion, measure his words or consider the ramifications of his utterance.

"'There is a time for everything' – the wise man elsewhere writes – 'a time to keep silence, and a time to speak.' (Ecclesiastes 3:7) It is a mark of true wisdom to discern the times. (Ecclesiastes 8:5) Indeed the discipline, or the want of discipline, upon the 'little member,' (James 3:5) is a sound test of character. The man, who speaks hastily and with conceit, will be put to shame in his folly (Proverbs 18:3). He might have been 'counted' wise in his silence (Proverbs 17:28). But silence is beyond his power – He uttereth all his mind – tells all he knows, thinks, or intends, and runs on, until he has 'poured out all his foolishness' (Proverbs 15:2). It is sometimes thought a proof of honesty to utter all our mind. But it is rather a proof of folly. For how many things it would be far better never to speak; indeed to suppress in the very thought! (Proverbs 30:32) How much of 'foolish talking and jesting' (Ephesians 5:4); how many angry, detracting, uncharitable words do we utter, because we have neglected to watch, or rather to entreat 'the LORD to set a watch upon, our lips,' as the door of our hearts!(Psalm 141:3) And what wrong judgments we often pass upon men's actions, because we utter all our mind as it were in one breath, without pondering, or perhaps without materials to form a correct judgment!"[747]

Judges 16:17 That he *[Samson]* told her all his heart, and said unto her, There hath not come a razor upon mine head; for I have been a Nazarite unto God from my mother's womb: if I be shaven, then my strength will go from me, and I shall become weak, and be like any other man.

Psalm 141:3 Set a watch, O LORD, before my mouth; keep the door of my lips.

Proverbs 12:16 A fool's wrath is presently known: but a prudent man covereth shame.

Proverbs 10:12 Hatred stirreth up strifes: but love covereth all sins.

Proverbs 12:23 A prudent man concealeth knowledge: but the heart of fools proclaimeth foolishness.

Proverbs 14:33 Wisdom resteth in the heart of him that hath understanding: but that which is in the midst of fools is made known.

Proverbs 15:2 The tongue of the wise useth knowledge aright: but the mouth of fools poureth out foolishness.

Proverbs 15:28 The heart of the righteous studieth to answer: but the mouth of the wicked poureth out evil things.

Proverbs 17:28 Even a fool, when he holdeth his peace, is counted wise: and he that shutteth his lips is esteemed a man of understanding.

Proverbs 18:13 He that answereth a matter before he heareth it, it is folly and shame unto him.

Proverbs 29:20 Seest thou a man that is hasty in his words? there is more hope of a fool than of him.

Proverbs 30:32 If thou hast done foolishly in lifting up thyself, or if thou hast thought evil, lay thine hand upon thy mouth.

Ecclesiastes 3:7 A time to rend, and a time to sew; a time to keep silence, and a time to speak;

Ecclesiastes 8:5 Whoso keepeth the commandment shall feel no evil thing: and a wise man's heart discerneth both time and judgment.

Ephesians 5:3-4 But fornication, and all uncleanness, or covetousness, let it not be once named among you, as becometh saints; Neither filthiness, nor foolish talking, nor jesting, which are not convenient: but rather giving of thanks.

James 3:5 Even so the tongue is a little member, and boasteth great things. Behold, how great a matter a little fire kindleth!

Proverbs 29:12 If a ruler hearken to lies, all his servants *are* wicked.

Focus: This proverb declares the disastrous consequence that follows when a foolish ruler gives credence to lies.

This is another maxim of wisdom bearing reference to the character and conduct of men in leadership. If the king **harkens** *[pays attention, listens]* to lies by giving them credibility as though they were truth, he will encourage his servants to lie. If wise people will not voluntarily vacate such an evil environment, they will likely be driven away, being in ill favor with the others. For a king to give credence to lies indicates that he encourages people to say only those things that he desires to hear, including flattery, slander, and deceitful reports of the condition of the kingdom – all of which will lead to his ultimate ruin. For a king to **"hearken to lies"** and thus create an environment of deception would encourage **all his servants to become wicked,** and he would be ultimately surrounded by wickedness. No one could be trusted for anything under such conditions. If we had not witnessed this egregious governmental situation in the United States, it would be difficult to imagine any organization, especially a kingdom, operating with any efficiency after having depleted itself of honesty and surrounded the leadership with deceitful people.

King Ahab preferred the 400 lying prophets that surrounded him to the one who told the truth, and it brought him to disaster. The one godly prophet in Ahab's court, Micaiah, was hated because he always told the truth. Moreover, because of being a godly prophet among the wicked majority of 400 liars, he was mocked, confined to jail, and fed only enough to keep him alive.

1 Kings 22:13-14 And the messenger that was gone to call Micaiah spake unto him, saying, Behold now, the words of the prophets declare good unto the king with one mouth: let thy word, I pray thee, be like the word of one of them, and speak that which is good. And Micaiah said, As the LORD liveth, what the LORD saith unto me, that will I speak.

David had a philosophy that encouraged the righteous men to prevail around him:

Psalm 101:4-8 A froward heart shall depart from me: I will not know a wicked person. Whoso privily slandereth his neighbour, him will I cut off: him that hath an high look and a proud heart will not I suffer. Mine eyes shall be upon the faithful of the land, that they may dwell with me: he that walketh in a perfect way, he shall serve me. He that worketh deceit shall not dwell within my house: he that telleth lies shall not tarry in my sight. I will early destroy all the wicked of the land; that I may cut off all wicked doers from the city of the LORD.

Proverbs 29:13 The poor and the deceitful man meet together: the LORD lighteneth both their eyes.

Focus: This proverb reveals the fact that all men meet together on common ground with a God-given common ability to perceive God.

"The poor and the deceitful man meet together." This verse has some similarity to Proverbs 22:2 – "The rich and poor meet together: the LORD is the maker of them all." Both proverbs declare that the poor meet with those who are not poor for everyday life. One states "the LORD is the maker of them all" and the other "the LORD lighteneth both their eyes." "That is to say, all intelligence is a divine gift, whether it be used in righteousness or in wickedness."[748]

Ephesians 1:17-18 That the God of our Lord Jesus Christ, the Father of glory, may give unto you the spirit of wisdom and revelation in the knowledge of him: The eyes of your understanding being enlightened; that ye may know what is the hope of his calling, and what the riches of the glory of his inheritance in the saints ...

A **"deceitful man"** gains wealth by dishonest, injurious means. The KJV 1611 marginal notes read "the usurer" as an alternative to "the deceitful man."[749] Usury was the form of oppression that the poor suffered from the most. The **"deceitful man"** oppresses or breaks down the poor by overcharging interest or by using any other possible advantage. **"The poor"** is humble, whereas the **"deceitful man"** is proud. One is honest, the other deceitful. One lives in meager circumstances, the other in wealth.

One commonality shared between "the poor" man and "the deceitful man" is that they are each given life, intelligence, and an ability to perceive God for **"the LORD lighteneth both their eyes."** "Both rich and poor, the oppressor and the oppressed, owe their light and life to God; He makes the sun rise on the evil and on the good; He sends rain on the just and the unjust; He is the Father, Ruler, and Judge of all. Here is comfort for the poor, that he has a tender Father who watches over him; here is a warning for the rich, that he will have to give an account of his stewardship."[750] Despite his financial means, each man has to choose between godliness or wickedness: each individual can either live under divine favor or outside God's providential care. God **"lighteneth both their eyes"** with intelligence, but every man chooses whether he will follow God or not. Each chooses his own destiny. Some choose to go away from God because Satan has been allowed to remove the truth from their heart, others because they have no depth of concern, and yet others because the "care of this world and the deceitfulness of riches" has a greater lure than the truth of God's word. (Matthew 13:22)

Psalm 13:3-6 Consider *and* hear me, O LORD my God: lighten mine eyes, lest I sleep the *sleep of* death; Lest mine enemy say, I have prevailed against him; *and* those that trouble me rejoice when I am moved. But I have trusted in thy mercy; my heart shall rejoice in thy salvation. I will sing unto the LORD, because he hath dealt bountifully with me.

John 1:4-5 In him was life; and the life was the light of men. And the light shineth in darkness; and the darkness comprehended it not.

Acts 10:34 Then Peter opened his mouth, and said, Of a truth I perceive that God is no respecter of persons: But in every nation he that feareth him, and worketh righteousness, is accepted with him.

Acts 26:18 To open their eyes, *and* to turn *them* from darkness to light, and *from* the power of Satan unto God, that they may receive forgiveness of sins, and inheritance among them which are sanctified by faith that is in me.

2 Corinthians 4:4 In whom the god of this world hath blinded the minds of them which believe not, lest the light of the glorious gospel of Christ, who is the image of God, should shine unto them.

Ephesians 4:17-19 This I say therefore, and testify in the Lord, that ye henceforth walk not as other Gentiles walk, in the vanity of their mind, Having the understanding darkened, being alienated from the life of God through the ignorance that is in them, because of the blindness of their heart: Who being past feeling have given themselves over unto lasciviousness, to work all uncleanness with greediness.

Proverbs 29:14 The king that faithfully judgeth the poor, his throne shall be established for ever.

Focus: This proverb promises God's blessing on a king who judges the poor with fairness.

"The king that faithfully judgeth the poor." No Scripture suggests that favor in legal judgments be given to anyone, rich or poor; each is supposed to be treated equitably. However, **"the poor"** are often despised, neglected, or dismissed because of their lack of ability or influence due to poverty or unappreciated social status. Therefore, the duty of a king is:

"to judge faithfully between man and man, and to determine all causes brought before them, according to truth and equity, particularly to take care of *the poor,* not to countenance *[favor or honor]* them in an unjust cause for the sake of their poverty (Exodus 23:3), but to see that their poverty do not turn to their prejudice if they have a just cause. The rich will look to themselves, but *the poor* and needy the prince must *defend* (Psalm 82:3) and plead for (Proverbs 31:9)."[751]

"His throne shall be established for ever." When a judge-king is acceptable in the sight of God and honorable in the sight of the people, he gains the favor of both. He will be supernaturally and humanly supported, encouraged, and maintained. **"For ever"** obviously means God will supernaturally intervene to keep him on the throne for an extended time, along with the understanding that God will keep a family successor on his throne. Kings who do not care about pleasing God or the people set about to establish their throne through oppression, for which they are doomed by God (rather than established by Him) and distanced by the people (rather than supported by them).

Proverbs 16:12 It is an abomination to kings to commit wickedness: for the throne is established by righteousness.

Jeremiah 22:3-4 Thus saith the LORD; Execute ye judgment and righteousness, and deliver the spoiled out of the hand of the oppressor: and do no wrong, do no violence to the stranger, the fatherless, nor the widow, neither shed innocent blood in this place. For if ye do this thing indeed, then shall there enter in by the gates of this house kings sitting upon the throne of David, riding in chariots and on horses, he, and his servants, and his people.
[Many other Scriptures teach of equity in judgment including, but not limited to: Leviticus 19:15; Psalm 72:2, 12-14; Psalm 82:1-4; Proverbs 1:1-3; Isaiah 1:17; Jeremiah 22:13-17; Ezekiel 18:17; Micah 3:9-11.]

Proverbs 29:15 The rod and reproof give wisdom: but a child left *to himself* bringeth his mother to shame.

Focus: This proverb contrasts the consequence of disciplining a child with the consequence of failing to discipline.

"The rod and reproof give wisdom." If a child is successfully disciplined (with "rod" and "reproof"), the correction will bring forth or **"give"** wisdom. The understanding of this verse is that discipline is being given with the goal of producing wisdom, *not* simply changing behavior that is annoying. Through discipline, a child is taught love and respect for the authority and will of his parents. If he is so trained, he will most likely love and respect the authority and will of God. Parents are representatives of God's authority and God's will. Children who do not respect and honor their parents are not likely, as adults, to respect and honor God.

Wise parents know to use the least amount of force and to minimize pain to accomplish any task, and the discipline of a child is no different. If talking to a child will correct his behavior, certainly, there is no need to be harsh or punish him in any other way. When **"reproof"** alone doesn't accomplish the task, then the **"rod"** becomes necessary, but the "rod" should never be used alone without "rebuke." Such "rebuke" must involve explaining why he is being disciplined and what proper behavior is expected in the future. Also, a "rod" can be symbolic of discipline rather than simply a switch.

"A child left to himself" will have regard only for his own will and his own authority, rather than that of his parents; and since he does not know right from wrong, he will likely follow the dictates of whatever his childish and worldly mind reasons to be correct.

To leave **"a child to himself"** is to leave him to the dictates of his flesh, a condition which becomes anything he can think to do without restraint. Galatians chapter 5 provides an understanding of what a human being will do without restraint. Any of the following behaviors would bring **"shame"** to a mother.

> Galatians 5:19-21 Now the works of the flesh are manifest, which are these; Adultery, fornication, uncleanness, lasciviousness, Idolatry, witchcraft, hatred, variance, emulations, wrath, strife, seditions, heresies, Envyings, murders, drunkenness, revellings, and such like: of the which I tell you before, as I have also told you in time past, that they which do such things shall not inherit the kingdom of God.

But, if the child is taught to seek wisdom he can have a totally different life. Proverbs 9:10 declares, "The fear of the LORD is the beginning of wisdom: and the knowledge of the holy is understanding;" therefore, teaching a child to place himself under the will and authority of his parents, and subsequently of God, will give him the capacity to live with the following attributes which produce no "shame" but rather joy and gladness and thankfulness and pride of parenthood.

> Galatians 5:22-23 But the fruit of the Spirit is love, joy, peace, longsuffering, gentleness, goodness, faith, meekness, temperance: against such there is no law.

Consider the following verses that speak of parental discipline or the lack thereof:

> 1 Samuel 3:11-14 And the LORD said to Samuel, Behold, I will do a thing in Israel, at which both the ears of every one that heareth it shall tingle. In that day I will perform against Eli all things which I have spoken concerning his house: when I begin, I will also make an end. For I have told him that I will judge his house for ever for the iniquity which he knoweth; because his sons made themselves vile, and he restrained them not. And therefore I have sworn unto the house of Eli, that the iniquity of Eli's house shall not be purged with sacrifice nor offering for ever.
> 1 Kings 1:5-6 Then Adonijah the son of Haggith exalted himself, saying, I will be king: and he prepared him chariots and horsemen, and fifty men to run before him. And his father had not displeased him at any time in saying, Why hast thou done so? and he also was a very goodly man; and his mother bare him after Absalom. *[David was his father.]*
> Proverbs 6:20-23 My son, keep thy father's commandment, and forsake not the law of thy mother: Bind them continually upon thine heart, and tie them about thy neck. When thou goest, it shall lead thee; when thou sleepest, it shall keep thee; and when thou awakest, it shall talk with thee. For the commandment is a lamp; and the law is light; and reproofs of instruction are the way of life…
> Proverbs 13:24 He that spareth his rod hateth his son: but he that loveth him chasteneth him betimes.

Proverbs 17:21 He that begetteth a fool doeth it to his sorrow: and the father of a fool hath no joy.

Proverbs 17:25 A foolish son is a grief to his father, and bitterness to her that bare him.

Proverbs 22:6 Train up a child in the way he should go: and when he is old, he will not depart from it.

Proverbs 22:15 Foolishness is bound in the heart of a child; but the rod of correction shall drive it far from him.

Proverbs 23:13-15 Withhold not correction from the child: for if thou beatest him with the rod, he shall not die. Thou shalt beat him with the rod, and shalt deliver his soul from hell. My son, if thine heart be wise, my heart shall rejoice, even mine.

Ephesians 6:4 And, ye fathers, provoke not your children to wrath: but bring them up in the nurture and admonition of the Lord.

Hebrews 12:6-11 For whom the Lord loveth he chasteneth, and scourgeth every son whom he receiveth. If ye endure chastening, God dealeth with you as with sons; for what son is he whom the father chasteneth not? But if ye be without chastisement, whereof all are partakers, then are ye bastards, and not sons. Furthermore we have had fathers of our flesh which corrected us, and we gave them reverence: shall we not much rather be in subjection unto the Father of spirits, and live? For they verily for a few days chastened us after their own pleasure; but he for our profit, that we might be partakers of his holiness. Now no chastening for the present seemeth to be joyous, but grievous: nevertheless afterward it yieldeth the peaceable fruit of righteousness unto them which are exercised thereby.

Proverbs 29:16 When the wicked are multiplied, transgression increaseth: but the righteous shall see their fall.

Focus: This proverb declares that there is a relationship between the number of wicked people and the magnitude of transgression – "but the righteous shall see their fall."

"When the wicked are multiplied, transgression increaseth." Since sin is the evidence of wickedness, the meaning of the first clause is that when wicked people become more numerous, transgressions against God increase. As transgressions become more numerous, the wicked's sins grow more acceptable to themselves. Through acceptance by this new majority, evil people manage to get elevated to positions of authority; but, as the second clause states, **"the righteous shall see their fall."** Because they develop a false sense that there is "strength in numbers," wicked people embolden other wicked people to sin, never recognizing that numbers are insignificant against the judgment of God. In addition, wicked people have a way of thinking and acting that opposes God and good sense because of their profound willful self-destructive ignorance of God. A mind set that is against goodness and fairness and full of deceitfulness, greediness, and covetousness, will eventually lead to in-fighting among their evil selves. Eventually, God will take the wicked into destruction. The upright will have the privilege of seeing His judgment against them. From the safety of the ark, Noah observed the wicked being destroyed in the flood. Moses and all of Israel saw the Egyptians dead on the shores of the Red sea. Abraham observed the "smoke of the country" (Genesis 19:28) as Sodom and Gomorrah "went up as the smoke of a furnace." If the wicked were not stopped, the world would be overrun by them.

Genesis 6:5-7 And GOD saw that the wickedness of man as great in the earth, and that every imagination of the thoughts of his heart was only evil continually. And it repented the LORD that he had made man on the earth, and it grieved him at his heart. And the LORD said, I will destroy man whom I have created from the face of the earth; both man, and beast, and the creeping thing, and the fowls of the air; for it repenteth me that I have made them.

Genesis 11:8-9 So the LORD scattered them abroad from thence upon the face of all the earth: and they left off to build the city. Therefore is the name of it called Babel; because the LORD did there confound the language of all the earth: and from thence did the LORD scatter them abroad upon the face of all the earth.

Genesis 18:23 And Abraham drew near, and said, Wilt thou also destroy the righteous with the wicked?

Genesis 19:28 And he looked toward Sodom and Gomorrah, and toward all the land of the plain, and beheld, and, lo, the smoke of the country went up as the smoke of a furnace.

Psalm 37:34-36 Wait on the LORD, and keep his way, and he shall exalt thee to inherit the land: when the wicked are cut off, thou shalt see it. I have seen the wicked in great power, and spreading himself like a green bay tree. Yet he passed away, and, lo, he was not: yea, I sought him, but he could not be found.

Isaiah 66:24 And they shall go forth, and look upon the carcases of the men that have transgressed against me: for their worm shall not die, neither shall their fire be quenched; and they shall be an abhorring unto all flesh.

Hosea 4:7 As they were increased, so they sinned against me: therefore will I change their glory into shame.

Proverbs 29:17 Correct thy son, and he shall give thee rest; yea, he shall give delight unto thy soul.

Focus: This proverb declares two parental benefits from administering child discipline.

When the child is young, **"correct thy son"** to prevent improper conduct from becoming his accepted way of life. Without correction, a child will follow the dictates of unregulated human nature. Such a child has the potential to produce many sinful habits, including sexual promiscuity, theft, lies, and disrespect for parents, God, and other people. He potentially may disregard any authority, develop poor work ethics, foster uncontrolled anger, covetousness, and other conduct as described in Galatians 5:19-21. Any and all of the aforementioned acts of misconduct cause a godly parent to suffer sleepless nights, to withdraw from friends and family, to suffer embarrassment, and to endure overall discomfort in life. In severe cases, as the child advances in age and size, his parents may even fear for their own personal safety. When a child behaves in a godly, honorable fashion, he delivers a tremendous **"gift"** to his parents; and that gift is **"rest,"** a relaxed state of mind which comes from being at peace. Parents who trust their child to act in a wise manner are able to sleep at night, to be free from concern of hearing bad reports about their child when meeting with friends and family, and to be proud of their child rather than embarrassed. Such enjoyable conditions do indeed constitute **delight and rest unto the parent's soul**.

> "**Observe how the objection of parental weakness is anticipated.** 'If I put my son to pain, will he not hate me?' No – when 'left to himself,' he was a deep and anxious trouble. Now he shall give thee rest. Before – he 'brought thee to shame.' (Proverbs 29:15) Now he shall give delight to thy soul. The momentary feelings of the child under correction will give way to the conviction of the parent's wisdom and regard for his profit. (Hebrews 12:9) **Yet the rule against discouragement would not have been repeated, had there not been some parental evil to be corrected.** ... Children claim a considerate treatment. They must not be driven by brute force. Authority must be tempered with love. The grounds of extraordinary commands should be explained to them. What is good should be liberally commended. The best construction should be put upon defective efforts. The distinction should be carefully drawn between weakness and willfulness, between heedlessness and obstinacy. Home should be gladdened with the invigorating joy of spring, and replete with every wholesome indulgence. Every attempt should be made to gain confidence, so that the child, instead of a cold trembling reserve, should run into our arms. But in this glowing atmosphere, forget not God's rule. The completeness of discipline is the father's firmness combined with the mother's tenderness; each infusing into the other the quality of each. A wise parent will put his seal to the testimony, that this well-disciplined education is the surest means of securing the children's affection, gratitude, and reverence."[752]

Both King David and the prophet Samuel must have suffered much unrest because of the vile conduct of their children.

> 1 Samuel 3:13 For I have told him *[Samuel]* that I will judge his house for ever for the iniquity which he knoweth; because his sons made themselves vile, and he restrained them not.
> 1 Kings 1:5-6 Then Adonijah the son of Haggith exalted himself, saying, I will be king: and he prepared him chariots and horsemen, and fifty men to run before him. And his father had not displeased him at any time in saying, Why hast thou done so? and he also was a very goodly man; and his mother bare him after Absalom.
> Proverbs 23:13-15 Withhold not correction from the child: for if thou beatest him with the rod, he shall not die. Thou shalt beat him with the rod, and shalt deliver his soul from hell. My son, if thine heart be wise, my heart shall rejoice, even mine.

Proverbs 29:18 Where *there is* no vision, the people perish: but he that keepeth the law, happy *is* he.

Focus: This proverb contrasts the unhappy consequence of having no direct instruction from God with happiness from keeping the instructions from God.

"Where *there is* no vision, the people perish." Used in this verse to express *revelation that comes from God,* the full meaning of **"vision"** is understood when "vision" is compared to **"keepeth the law"** in the second half of the verse. Opposite to *keeping the law* is NOT keeping the law. Specifically, *the law is not kept* because of **not having a vision** – not having a revelation or communication from God. The people have "no vision" because the law of God (word of God) is not being proclaimed, not being preached or prophesied as preaching is termed in Romans and 1 Corinthians.

> Romans 12:6 Having then gifts differing according to the grace that is given to us, whether prophecy, let us prophesy according to the proportion of faith ...
> 1 Corinthians 14:4 He that speaketh in an unknown tongue edifieth himself; but he that prophesieth edifieth the church.

Preaching is proclaiming the word of God truthfully, unafraid, unashamed, under the anointing of the Holy Spirit, as God intended it to be done. There is no vision where preaching has become teaching of cold, dead facts. Where emotion is substituted for preaching, there is no vision. Where psychology is substituted for preaching, there is no vision. Where anything is substituted for the truth of God's word, there is no vision – and the people perish. Spiritually the poor church becomes unhappy, and spiritually, they die. The people go backward, leave their first love, quit praying, cease living for God, and become like the world. They *fail to keep the law of God*. Albert Barnes in his commentary on Hebrews 4:12 wrote:

> "The 'Word of God' is 'what God speaks' - whether it be a promise or a threatening; whether it be Law or gospel; whether it be a simple declaration or a statement of a doctrine. The idea here is, that what 'God had said' is suited to detect hypocrisy and to lay open the true nature of the feelings of the soul, so that there can be no escape for the guilty."

Hebrews 4:12 For the word of God is quick, and powerful, and sharper than any twoedged sword, piercing even to the dividing asunder of soul and spirit, and of the joints and marrow, and is a discerner of the thoughts and intents of the heart.

Receiving vision is receiving communication from God, the law of God (the word of God). It is not a product of a speaker's intelligence or his imagination, but it is a working of the Holy Spirit from the heart of God to the heart of man that results in compelling obedience. Receiving a vision from God is receiving God's code of conduct for living and for dying. It is that which sustains spiritual life and greatly enhances physical life. A happy person is one who hears from God and is obedient to His word. Where there is vision, there is an ability to "see" the things of God. Such vision strengthens love for Jesus, builds a robust platform of trust in Him, and opens the conduit of prayer. Furthermore, without the work of the Holy Spirit in conjunction with the word of God, there is no vision – no direct communication from God.

> Luke 4:18-19 The Spirit of the Lord is upon me, because he hath anointed me to preach the gospel to the poor; he hath sent me to heal the brokenhearted, to preach deliverance to the captives, and recovering of sight to the blind, to set at liberty them that are bruised, To preach the acceptable year of the Lord.
> John 14:26-27 But the Comforter, *which is* the Holy Ghost, whom the Father will send in my name, he shall teach you all things, and bring all things to your remembrance, whatsoever I have said unto you. Peace I leave with you, my peace I give unto you: not as the world giveth, give I unto you. Let not your heart be troubled, neither let it be afraid.
> John 15:6-11 If a man abide not in me, he is cast forth as a branch, and is withered; and men gather them, and cast *them* into the fire, and they are burned. If ye abide in me, and my words abide in you, ye shall ask what ye will, and it shall be done unto you. Herein is my Father glorified, that ye bear much fruit; so shall ye be my disciples. As the Father hath loved me, so have I loved you: continue ye in my love. If ye keep my commandments, ye shall abide in my love; even as I have kept my Father's commandments, and abide in his love. These things have I spoken unto you, that my joy might remain in you, and *that* your joy might be full.
> John 16:13 Howbeit when he, the Spirit of truth, is come, he will guide you into all truth: for he shall not speak of himself; but whatsoever he shall hear, *that* shall he speak: and he will shew you things to come.
> 1 Corinthians 2:1-5 And I, brethren, when I came to you, came not with excellency of speech or of wisdom, declaring unto you the testimony of God. For I determined not to know any thing among you, save Jesus Christ, and him crucified. And I was with you in weakness, and in fear, and in much trembling. And my speech and my preaching was not with enticing words of man's wisdom, but in demonstration of the Spirit and of power: That your faith should not stand in the wisdom of men, but in the power of God.
> 1 Corinthians 2:10-16 But God hath revealed them unto us by his Spirit: for the Spirit searcheth all things, yea, the deep things of God. For what man knoweth the things of a man, save the spirit of man which is in him? even so the things of God knoweth no man, but the Spirit of God. Now we have received, not the spirit of the world, but the spirit which is of God; that we might know the things that are freely given to us of God. Which things also we speak, not in the words which man's wisdom teacheth, but which the Holy Ghost teacheth; comparing spiritual things with spiritual. But the natural man receiveth not the things of the Spirit of God: for they are foolishness unto him: neither can he know them, because they are spiritually discerned. But he that is spiritual judgeth all things, yet he himself is judged of no man. For who hath known the mind of the Lord, that he may instruct him? But we have the mind of Christ.

During the time of Eli (I Samuel 3:1), "the word of the Lord was precious in those days," meaning that God's gift of revealing His will was rare. In addition, *"there was no open vision,"* meaning that there was nothing from God that was made public, which was critical to the Spiritually-founded and Spiritually-guided nation of Israel. They did not have the mind of God to guide them. Consequently, Israel was in a state of confusion, sinfulness, and rebellion.

The words of Chronicles are even more profound. In King Asa's day (2 Chronicles 15:3), the Bible states, "Now for a long season Israel hath been without the true God, and without a teaching priest, and without law," meaning that Israel did not have the law, the word of God, proclaimed to them authoritatively. The miserable consequences of not receiving God and His word are expressed in the words, **"the people perish,"** the meaning described in 2 Chronicles 15:5-6 follows: "And in those times there was no peace to him that went out, nor to him that came in, but great vexations were upon all the inhabitants of the countries. And nation was destroyed of nation, and city of city: for God did vex them with all adversity."

"But he that keepeth the law, happy is he" – a condition Asa apparently recognized as missing and went about to correct, for 2 Chronicles 15:2b, 7-8, 19 states, "…The LORD *is* with you, while ye be with him; and if ye seek him, he will be found of you; but if ye forsake him, he will forsake you. … Be ye strong therefore, and let not your hands be weak: for your work shall be rewarded. And when Asa heard these words, and the prophecy of Azariah the prophet, he took courage, and put away the abominable idols out of all the land of Judah and Benjamin, and out of the cities which he had taken from mount Ephraim, and renewed the altar of the LORD, that was before the porch of the LORD … And there was no more war unto the five and thirtieth year of the reign of Asa."

God had, in fact, prophesied the departure of His glory well in advance. Back in Deuteronomy 31:17-18, He had warned: "Then My anger shall be aroused against them in that day, and I will forsake them, and I will hide My face from them, and they shall be devoured. And many evils and troubles shall befall them, so that they will say in that day, "Have not these evils come upon us because our God is not among us?" In Hosea 9:12, God proclaimed, " . . . woe also to them when I depart from them!"

> Amos 8:11-12 Behold, the days come, saith the Lord GOD, that I will send a famine in the land, not a famine of bread, nor a thirst for water, but of hearing the words of the LORD: And they shall wander from sea to sea, and from the north even to the east, they shall run to and fro to seek the word of the LORD, and shall not find it.
> 2 Timothy 4:3-4 For the time will come when they will not endure sound doctrine; but after their own lusts shall they heap to themselves teachers, having itching ears; And they shall turn away their ears from the truth, and shall be turned unto fables.

Proverbs 29:19 A servant will not be corrected by words: for though he understand he will not answer.

Focus: This proverb gives insight into the heart of a servant who is serving under bondage.

A **"servant"** who **"will not be corrected by words"** believes that he is being abused and therefore serves under bondage. He hates being a servant; and everything about him resents and rejects being instructed as to a correct way of acting, working, thinking, or responding. He feels out of place and believes that he does not belong where he is being forced to labor; consequently, he does everything possible to oppose **"for though he understand he will not answer."** He has no respect for his master, dishonors him, and refuses to answer either by word or deed. He sulks, stiffens up, and is constantly in sullen discord.

By way of example, when a person is coerced to be part of a local assembly of Christians but has never been born again, he will not willingly submit to the *correction by the word of God*. He is not an obedient born-again child of God and is forever obstinate.

> Luke 6:44-46 For every tree is known by his own fruit. For of thorns men do not gather figs, nor of a bramble bush gather they grapes. A good man out of the good treasure of his heart bringeth forth that which is good; and an evil man out of the evil treasure of his heart bringeth forth that which is evil: for of the abundance of the heart his mouth speaketh. And why call ye me, Lord, Lord, and do not the things which I say?
> Romans 8:14-15 For as many as are led by the Spirit of God, they are the sons of God. For ye have not received the spirit of bondage again to fear; but ye have received the Spirit of adoption, whereby we cry, Abba, Father.

Proverbs 29:20 Seest thou a man *that is* hasty in his words? *there is* more hope of a fool than of him.

Focus: This proverb identifies the desperate situation of a man who refuses to give time and consideration before giving an answer.

"Seest thou a man" is a phrase used three times in Proverbs to indicate that the behavior of a particular person is worthy of observation and study. His life will provide important lessons either positively or negatively. People who learn by observation are wise and able to progress much faster than those who must suffer to absorb the same instruction. The wise observer should learn from the mistakes of others, and change the way of his life.

> Proverbs 22:29 Seest thou a man diligent in his business? he shall stand before kings; he shall not stand before mean men.
> Proverbs 26:12 Seest thou a man wise in his own conceit? there is more hope of a fool than of him.
> Proverbs 29:20 Seest thou a man that is hasty in his words? there is more hope of a fool than of him.

A person who is **"hasty in his words"** speaks thoughtlessly and spontaneously. He is obviously overconfident. This descriptive phrase could describe most young persons who have not yet learned to exercise caution in responding to situations, but here it reflects someone who should know better. The hasty person is dominated by pride, arrogance, and a belief that there is no need for counsel or review of facts, or even taking a second look. In other words, he believes himself brilliant, not needing counsel or scrutiny, and capable of responding to every situation immediately.

> Proverbs 15:28 The heart of the righteous studieth to answer: but the mouth of the wicked poureth out evil things.

Proverbs 21:5 The thoughts of the diligent tend only to plenteousness; but of every one that is hasty only to want.

Proverbs 29:11 A fool uttereth all his mind: but a wise man keepeth it in till afterwards.

Ecclesiastes 5:2 Be not rash with thy mouth, and let not thine heart be hasty to utter any thing before God: for God is in heaven, and thou upon earth: therefore let thy words be few.

James 1:19-20 Wherefore, my beloved brethren, let every man be swift to hear, slow to speak, slow to wrath: For the wrath of man worketh not the righteousness of God.

James 3:5-8 Even so the tongue is a little member, and boasteth great things. Behold, how great a matter a little fire kindleth! And the tongue *is* a fire, a world of iniquity: so is the tongue among our members, that it defileth the whole body, and setteth on fire the course of nature; and it is set on fire of hell. For every kind of beasts, and of birds, and of serpents, and of things in the sea, is tamed, and hath been tamed of mankind: But the tongue can no man tame; *it is* an unruly evil, full of deadly poison.

"There is more hope of a fool than of him," meaning there is "more hope" that a "fool" will become wise and able to properly respond to the matters of life and to have a relationship with God. "There is more hope" because perhaps the *dullness* of a fool will cause him to be slower to answer, thereby giving him a chance to have *some* measure of thinking, surveying, and reasoning before answering. There is some *very minimum* amount of hope that the fool will progress in his understanding and that somehow he will receive instruction and listen to reason. "The hasty and ill-advised speaker consults no one, takes no thought before he speaks, nor reflects on the effect of his words; such a man it is almost impossible to reform"[753] "More hope than a fool" occurs in the above-quoted Proverbs 26:12, which advises that the person of pride is nearly hopeless. Here in Proverbs 29:20, the impulsive speaker is in the same condition. Although the verses have different introductory subjects, both have arrogance as the same root which causes multiple problems.

> **Proverbs 29:21** He that delicately bringeth up his servant from a child shall have him become *his* son at the length.

Focus: This proverb specifies the consequence of rearing a servant as though he were a family member.

If a servant is given favors such as would typically be given to an offspring, he will (at length) come to expect, or perhaps demand, that those same favors continue. When a **"servant"** is treated like a **"son"** *from his childhood*, he begins to think that he is a son. Because actions speak much louder than words, it would violate human nature for him to think otherwise. To attempt to make him believe that he should be treated as a servant (after treating him as a son) would be extremely difficult and cause emotional pain and mental anguish. On the other hand, if the purpose of treating the servant like a son is to indeed make him a son, the mission will be accomplished.

All branches of the American military understand this principle of serving by rank and have specific rules involving the privileges of officers versus privileges of enlisted personnel and interaction between the two groups. They also have specific rules regarding the privileges of higher-ranking flag officers versus those of lower-ranking officers.

Proverbs 30:21-23 For three things the earth is disquieted, and for four which it cannot bear: For a servant when he reigneth; and a fool when he is filled with meat; For an odious woman when she is married; and an handmaid that is heir to her mistress.

"It is an imprudent thing in a master to be too fond of a servant, to advance him too fast, and admit him to be too familiar with him, to suffer him to be over-nice and curious in his diet, and clothing, and lodging, and so to bring him up delicately, because he is a favourite, and an agreeable servant; it should be remembered that he is a servant, and, by being thus indulged, will be spoiled for any other place. ... It is an ungrateful thing in a servant, but what is very common, to behave insolently because he has been used tenderly. The humble prodigal thinks himself unworthy *to be called a son*, and is content to be a servant; the pampered slave thinks himself too good to be called *a servant*, and will be *a son at the length*, will take his ease and liberty, will be on a par with his master, and perhaps pretend to the inheritance. Let masters *give their servants that which is equal* and fit for them, and neither more nor less. This is very applicable to the body, which is a servant to the soul; those that *delicately bring up* the body, that humour it, and are over-tender of it, will find that at length it will forget its place, and *become a son*, a master, a perfect tyrant."[754]

Outside the interpretation of this Scripture, it should be noted in the following Scriptures that God certainly and specifically did intend for those who were servants of sin and afterwards became "born again" to become His children. From the time they are "born again" as spiritual babes, He treats them as His very own, giving them special favors all their lives and then taking them home to heaven to live with Him for eternity. He expects these previous slaves of sin to act and live like His children – for they are.

John 1:12 But as many as received him, to them gave he power to become the sons of God, *even* to them that believe on his name...

John 15:14-15 Ye are my friends, if ye do whatsoever I command you. Henceforth I call you not servants; for the servant knoweth not what his lord doeth: but I have called you friends; for all things that I have heard of my Father I have made known unto you.

Romans 8:16-17 The Spirit itself beareth witness with our spirit, that we are the children of God: And if children, then heirs; heirs of God, and joint-heirs with Christ; if so be that we suffer with *him,* that we may be also glorified together.

Romans 8:21 Because the creature itself also shall be delivered from the bondage of corruption into the glorious liberty of the children of God.

Romans 9:7-8 Neither, because they are the seed of Abraham, *are they* all children: but, In Isaac shall thy seed be called. That is, They which are the children of the flesh, these *are* not the children of God: but the children of the promise are counted for the seed.

James 2:23 And the scripture was fulfilled which saith, Abraham believed God, and it was imputed unto him for righteousness: and he was called the Friend of God.

1 John 3:1 Behold, what manner of love the Father hath bestowed upon us, that we should be called the sons of God: therefore the world knoweth us not, because it knew him not.

1 John 3:2 Beloved, now are we the sons of God, and it doth not yet appear what we shall be: but we know that, when he shall appear, we shall be like him; for we shall see him as he is.

Proverbs 29:22 An angry man stirreth up strife, and a furious man aboundeth in transgression.

Focus: This proverb describes the consequences of an angry man's actions.

A wise man *will not* be negatively labeled as an **"angry man"** and *certainly not* **"a furious man."** For a person to come *under the influence of wrath* is, in some ways, similar to a person who comes under the influence of drugs – both influences negatively affect his ability to think properly and prevent him from making sound judgments. The **"angry man"** behaves like anger is his best friend, his confidant, and his agency of power. By being angry, he gives the impression that he believes that he can "get the jump" on every situation and be in control; when actually, he is out of control. He *stirs up strife* with his family, friends, neighbors, work associates, or even strangers who have no intention of being contentious. He is set to "go off" at any moment. To be near him is to be ill at ease. If he proceeds with such conduct, allowing his anger to drive out all good judgment, he may become **"furious,"** causing his mind to become blinded by anger. In such a state, he may cause such *transgressions* as permanently damaging another's emotional well-being, causing bodily injury, or even committing murder. He is like a hurricane blowing down everything in its path.

Wise, godly people learn to live by biblical truths and come *under the influence of the Holy Spirit,* Who teaches and produces love, joy, peace, longsuffering, gentleness, goodness, faith, meekness, and temperance within the believer.

The Bible speaks of one proper time when a wise person can use a fully-controlled "angry countenance" (not foolish anger). "The north wind driveth away rain: so doth an angry countenance a backbiting tongue." (Proverbs 25:23)

Proverbs 10:11-12 The mouth of a righteous man is a well of life: but violence covereth the mouth of the wicked. Hatred stirreth up strifes: but love covereth all sins.

Proverbs 15:18 A wrathful man stirreth up strife: but he that is slow to anger appeaseth strife.

Proverbs 17:19 He loveth transgression that loveth strife: and he that exalteth his gate seeketh destruction.

Proverbs 19:11 The discretion of a man deferreth his anger; and it is his glory to pass over a transgression.

Proverbs 22:24 Make no friendship with an angry man; and with a furious man thou shalt not go...

Proverbs 26:21 As coals are to burning coals, and wood to fire; so is a contentious man to kindle strife.

Proverbs 28:25 He that is of a proud heart stirreth up strife: but he that putteth his trust in the LORD shall be made fat.

Proverbs 30:33 Surely the churning of milk bringeth forth butter, and the wringing of the nose bringeth forth blood: so the forcing of wrath bringeth forth strife.

Ephesians 4:26-27 Be ye angry, and sin not: let not the sun go down upon your wrath: Neither give place to the devil.

Ephesians 4:31-32 Let all bitterness, and wrath, and anger, and clamour, and evil speaking, be put away from you, with all malice: And be ye kind one to another, tenderhearted, forgiving one another, even as God for Christ's sake hath forgiven you.

James 1:19-20 Wherefore, my beloved brethren, let every man be swift to hear, slow to speak, slow to wrath: For the wrath of man worketh not the righteousness of God.

James 3:16 For where envying and strife is, there is confusion and every evil work.

Colossians 3:5-8 Mortify therefore your members which are upon the earth; fornication, uncleanness, inordinate affection, evil concupiscence, and covetousness, which is idolatry: For which things' sake the wrath of God cometh on the children of disobedience: In the which ye also walked some time, when ye lived in them. But now ye also put off all these; anger, wrath, malice, blasphemy, filthy communication out of your mouth.

> **Proverbs 29:23** A man's pride shall bring him low: but honour shall uphold the humble in spirit.

Focus: This proverb warns about the damaging effect of pride and declares the reward for humility.

"A man's pride shall bring him low." As revealed in many verses throughout the Bible, pride *[arrogance, haughtiness]* is unquestionably despised by God and is repugnant to men – even to other proud men. Because pride drives a person toward self-aggrandizement, he overvalues himself and perhaps his power, wealth, rank, and honor. Because of his inflated view of self, other people are not overly sympathetic when his balloon of pride is popped, and he is ***brought low.*** Observe from life how often that high rung toward the top of the "ladder of success" is missing and the poor, proud, rapid-climbing soul, missing the step, begins a free fall, ultimately finding himself bruised, battered, and humiliated back at the bottom. A man should strive to exhibit a spirit of excellence and be his best for God, but pride blinds a man and prevents him from receiving help from his Creator, Who is actually resisting the man of pride.

"Honour shall uphold the humble in spirit." Humble people do not seek honor; but by wise living, honor is bestowed upon them and becomes an element of strength, giving them admiration from others and a solid, respected platform from which to be heard. Humble people oftentimes are lifted further by God as they ultimately find their lives being guided by the King of kings. They are the poor in spirit who are blessed and enjoy living in the kingdom of heaven. (Matthew 5:3; 18:4) The outcome is much better and more rewarding for the one who has a humble spirit and is thus lifted up by God.

- 2 Chronicles 33:10-13 And the LORD spake to Manasseh, and to his people: but they would not hearken. Wherefore the LORD brought upon them the captains of the host of the king of Assyria, which took Manasseh among the thorns, and bound him with fetters, and carried him to Babylon. And when he was in affliction, he besought the LORD his God, and humbled himself greatly before the God of his fathers, And prayed unto him: and he was intreated of him, and heard his supplication, and brought him again to Jerusalem into his kingdom. Then Manasseh knew that the LORD he was God.
- 2 Chronicles 33:23-24 And humbled not himself before the LORD, as Manasseh his father had humbled himself; but Amon trespassed more and more. And his servants conspired against him, and slew him in his own house.
- Job 40:12 Look on every one *that is* proud, *and* bring him low; and tread down the wicked in their place.
- Psalm 10:2 The wicked in *his* pride doth persecute the poor: let them be taken in the devices that they have imagined.
- Proverbs 14:3 In the mouth of the foolish *is* a rod of pride: but the lips of the wise shall preserve them.
- Proverbs 15:33 The fear of the LORD is the instruction of wisdom; and before honour is humility.
- Proverbs 16:18-19 Pride *goeth* before destruction, and an haughty spirit before a fall. Better *it is to be* of an humble spirit with the lowly, than to divide the spoil with the proud.
- Proverbs 18:12 Before destruction the heart of man is haughty, and before honour is humility.
- Proverbs 25:6-7 Put not forth thyself in the presence of the king, and stand not in the place of great *men:* For better *it is* that it be said unto thee, Come up hither; than that thou shouldest be put lower in the presence of the prince whom thine eyes have seen.
- Isaiah 2:11-12; 17 The lofty looks of man shall be humbled, and the haughtiness of men shall be bowed down, and the LORD alone shall be exalted in that day. For the day of the LORD of hosts shall be upon every one that is proud and lofty, and upon every one that is lifted up; and he shall be brought low … And the loftiness of man shall be bowed down, and the haughtiness of men shall be made low: and the LORD alone shall be exalted in that day.
- Isaiah 57:15 For thus saith the high and lofty One that inhabiteth eternity, whose name *is* Holy; I dwell in the high and holy *place,* with him also *that is* of a contrite and humble spirit, to revive the spirit of the humble, and to revive the heart of the contrite ones.
- Daniel 5:20-21 But when his heart was lifted up, and his mind hardened in pride, he was deposed from his kingly throne, and they took his glory from him: And he was driven from the sons of men; and his heart was made like the beasts, and his dwelling was with the wild asses: they fed him with grass like oxen, and his body was wet with the dew of heaven; till he knew that the most high God ruled in the kingdom of men, and that he appointeth over it whomsoever he will.
- Matthew 5:3 Blessed *are* the poor in spirit: for theirs is the kingdom of heaven.
- Matthew 18:4 Whosoever therefore shall humble himself as this little child, the same is greatest in the kingdom of heaven.
- Matthew 23:5-12 But all their works they do for to be seen of men: they make broad their phylacteries, and enlarge the borders of their garments, And love the uppermost rooms at feasts, and the chief seats in the synagogues, And greetings in the markets, and to be called of men, Rabbi, Rabbi. But be not ye called Rabbi: for one is your Master, *even* Christ; and all ye are brethren. And call no *man* your father upon the earth: for one is your Father, which is in heaven. Neither be ye called masters: for one is your Master, *even* Christ. But he that is greatest among you shall be your servant. And whosoever shall exalt himself shall be abased; and he that shall humble himself shall be exalted.
- Luke 14:11 For whosoever exalteth himself shall be abased; and he that humbleth himself shall be exalted. *[See also Luke 18:14; 1 Peter 5:5.]*
- Acts 12:21-23 And upon a set day Herod, arrayed in royal apparel, sat upon his throne, and made an oration unto them. And the people gave a shout, saying, It is the voice of a god, and not of a man. And immediately the angel of the Lord smote him, because he gave not God the glory: and he was eaten of worms, and gave up the ghost.

James 4:6-10 But he giveth more grace. Wherefore he saith, God resisteth the proud, but giveth grace unto the humble. Submit yourselves therefore to God. Resist the devil, and he will flee from you. Draw nigh to God, and he will draw nigh to you. Cleanse your hands, ye sinners; and purify your hearts, ye double minded. Be afflicted, and mourn, and weep: let your laughter be turned to mourning, and your joy to heaviness. Humble yourselves in the sight of the Lord, and he shall lift you up.

1 Peter 5:6 Humble yourselves therefore under the mighty hand of God, that he may exalt you in due time.

Proverbs 29:24 Whoso is partner with a thief hateth his own soul: he heareth cursing, and bewrayeth *it* not.

Focus: This proverb declares serious consequences from having a partnership with a thief.

"Whoso is partner with a thief hateth his own soul." For a person to have dealings with a thief so as to cover up his deeds, to aid him in some manner, or to knowingly receive his stolen property, necessitates that he is cooperating with a person who is transgressing against God and His laws. Any wise person will know that having such a relationship with a thief places him in the category as an accomplice; thereby outside the protection of God, in the radar of civil authorities, and possibly subject to an avenger. By having such a relationship, he willingly and willfully subjects himself to imminent danger. By his actions, he is disregarding his own well being and safety and gives the appearance as though he **hates his own soul.**

"He heareth cursing, and bewrayeth it not" is a statement indicating that the person who is **"partner with a thief"** is presently before a judge and placed under an oath to tell the truth. The judge declares a curse on him if he fails to tell the truth. He hears the judges charge and potential curse but refuses to tell the truth. ***"Cursing"*** is from the Hebrew word translated "swearing" in Leviticus 5:1 "And if a soul sin, and hear the voice of swearing, and *is* a witness, whether he hath seen or known *of it;* if he do not utter *it,* then he shall bear his iniquity." Thus, we understand that the voice of "cursing" and that of "swearing" refer to being sworn under oath to tell the truth, as in a court of law.[755]

> "When a theft was committed, the person wronged or the judge pronounced an imprecation *[curse, adjuration]* on the thief and on any one who was privy to the crime, and refrained from giving information; a witness who saw and knew of it, and was silent under this formal adjuration, has to bear his iniquity; he is not only an accomplice of a criminal, he is also a perjurer; one sin leads to another."[756]

"Bewrayeth" *[to manifest, to bring forth or tell what one knows]* is used only three times in Scripture. In the verse at hand, it refers to a man who will not reveal the truth in court because he is **"partner with a thief."** In Proverbs 27:16 it refers to a husband attempting to conceal the fact that his wife is contentious, and in Matthew 26:73 it refers to the accent of Peter's speech revealing that he was a Galilean who was with Christ, though he lied and denied the same.

> Proverbs 27:16 Whosoever hideth her hideth the wind, and the ointment of his right hand, *which* bewrayeth *itself.*
> Proverbs 29:24 Whoso is partner with a thief hateth his own soul: he heareth cursing, and bewrayeth *it* not.
> Matthew 26:73 And after a while came unto *him* they that stood by, and said to Peter, Surely thou also art *one* of them; for thy speech bewrayeth thee.

Proverbs 29:25 The fear of man bringeth a snare: but whoso putteth his trust in the LORD shall be safe.

Focus: This proverb contrasts the snare that comes to a person who has a fear of man with the safety enjoyed by one who has trust in the LORD.

"The fear of man bringeth a snare *[a noose, trap, bait both literally and figuratively]*.**"** It places a person on a path outside the direct leadership of God and consequently subjects him to devastation caused by making fear-based decisions. Satan easily sets traps for people who forsake the leadership of God. Actions based on the fear of man are erratic, unstable, and unsafe. (When a preacher becomes afraid to preach the truth because he fears disapproval of a congregation, he falls into the pit of being an unfaithful messenger where neither God nor man will give him honor.)

> Genesis 26:7 And the men of the place asked him of his wife; and he said, She is my sister: for he feared to say, She is my wife; lest, said he, the men of the place should kill me for Rebekah; because she was fair to look upon.
> Exodus 32:21-24 And Moses said unto Aaron, What did this people unto thee, that thou hast brought so great a sin upon them? And Aaron said, Let not the anger of my lord wax hot: thou knowest the people, that they are set on mischief. For they said unto me, Make us gods, which shall go before us: for as for this Moses, the man that brought us up out of the land of Egypt, we wot not what is become of him. And I said unto them, Whosoever hath any gold, let them break it off. So they gave it me: then I cast it into the fire, and there came out this calf.

1 Samuel 15:24 And Saul said unto Samuel, I have sinned: for I have transgressed the commandment of the LORD, and thy words: because I feared the people, and obeyed their voice.

Matthew 26:69-74 Now Peter sat without in the palace: and a damsel came unto him, saying, Thou also wast with Jesus of Galilee. But he denied before them all, saying, I know not what thou sayest. And when he was gone out into the porch, another maid saw him, and said unto them that were there, This fellow was also with Jesus of Nazareth. And again he denied with an oath, I do not know the man. And after a while came unto him they that stood by, and said to Peter, Surely thou also art one of them; for thy speech bewrayeth thee. Then began he to curse and to swear, saying, I know not the man. And immediately the cock crew.

John 9:20-22 His parents answered them and said, We know that this is our son, and that he was born blind: But by what means he now seeth, we know not; or who hath opened his eyes, we know not: he is of age; ask him: he shall speak for himself. These words spake his parents, because they feared the Jews: for the Jews had agreed already, that if any man did confess that he was Christ, he should be put out of the synagogue.

Galatians 2:11-12 But when Peter was come to Antioch, I withstood him to the face, because he was to be blamed. For before that certain came from James, he did eat with the Gentiles: but when they were come, he withdrew and separated himself, fearing them which were of the circumcision.

Matthew 10:28 And fear not them which kill the body, but are not able to kill the soul: but rather fear him which is able to destroy both soul and body in hell.

"But whoso putteth his trust in the LORD shall be safe." People are motivated to action by faith placed somewhere – either in God or in something/someone they trust. When men choose to place their trust in the Creator rather than the created, they will have chosen the source and the protective strength of God whereby "all things consist." (Colossians 1:17) With God, safety exists. When a person trusts in God, he gains a high place above his circumstances. ***Trusting in the LORD*** gets stronger through experiences; and as a person enjoys victory over trials, knowing that God has intervened, his faith grows, and his trust becomes stronger.

Psalm 18:2-3 The LORD is my rock, and my fortress, and my deliverer; my God, my strength, in whom I will trust; my buckler, and the horn of my salvation, and my high tower. I will call upon the LORD, who is worthy to be praised: so shall I be saved from mine enemies.

Psalm 20:7 Some trust in chariots, and some in horses: but we will remember the name of the LORD our God.

Psalm 37:3 Trust in the LORD, and do good; so shalt thou dwell in the land, and verily thou shalt be fed.

Psalm 118:8 It is better to trust in the LORD than to put confidence in man.

Proverbs 29:26 Many seek the ruler's favour; but *every* man's judgment *cometh* from the LORD.

Focus: This proverb declares that many people have misplaced trust because they misunderstand the true source of man's judgment.

In verse 25, a "fear of man" replaced trust in God. In this verse seeking the favor of a ruler replaces seeking the favor of God. **"Many seek the ruler's favour,"** not understanding that God is actually in control of every verdict. If the process of seeking a ruler's personal favor involves flattery or bribery of any kind, both the results and the process are sure to displease the LORD. It would be much safer and the outcome more satisfying to simply trust God to help in ways that man cannot. It is always best to wisely conduct oneself in a manner that pleases God. Our omniscient and omnipotent God can open eyes blinded to the truth, and He has the ability to change men's minds by giving them thoughts or removing thoughts. It would be best to simply trust God to help in every way and in every situation and be obedient to Him because **"every man's judgment cometh from the LORD."**

2 Kings 6:26-27 And as the king of Israel was passing by upon the wall, there cried a woman unto him, saying, Help, my lord, O king. And he said, If the LORD do not help thee, whence shall I help thee? out of the barnfloor, or out of the winepress?

Psalm 27:7-8 Hear, O LORD, *when* I cry with my voice: have mercy also upon me, and answer me. *When thou saidst,* Seek ye my face; my heart said unto thee, Thy face, LORD, will I seek.

Psalm 37:5-7 Commit thy way unto the LORD; trust also in him; and he shall bring it to pass. And he shall bring forth thy righteousness as the light, and thy judgment as the noonday. Rest in the LORD, and wait patiently for him: fret not thyself because of him who prospereth in his way, because of the man who bringeth wicked devices to pass.

Proverbs 16:33 The lot is cast into the lap; but the whole disposing thereof is of the LORD.

Proverbs 19:6 Many will intreat the favour of the prince: and every man *is* a friend to him that giveth gifts.

Proverbs 21:1 The king's heart is in the hand of the LORD, as the rivers of water: he turneth it whithersoever he will.

Proverbs 29:27 An unjust man *is* an abomination to the just: and *he that is* upright in the way *is* abomination to the wicked.

Focus: This proverb declares that the righteous and the wicked find each other extremely disgusting.

The truth of the second half of this Proverb – **"and *he that is* upright in the way is abomination to the wicked"** – is illustrated in the first few pages of Scripture when Cain killed Abel. 1 John 3:12 plainly declares the reason for Abel's murder, "Not as Cain, *who* was of that wicked one, and slew his brother. And wherefore slew he him? Because his own works were evil, and his brother's righteous." The epitome of illustrations is found in the crucifixion of Jesus. Those who demanded that Jesus be crucified were a picture of unjust mankind while Jesus was purely righteous, without sin. Christians see an enemy of God in the lifestyle of the ungodly because they oppose truth, wisdom, morality, and holiness. On the other hand, ungodly people see the person who lives according to the instructions of God as an adversary who condemns the evil man's own wicked lifestyle and his ungodly plots.

Because the "unjust man" is a slave to Satan and the "upright" man is a servant to God, their differing views of right and wrong are in constant conflict. Christians are taught to never hate anyone; rather to always live in a manner that exemplifies the spirit of forgiveness. Christians are to abhor the ungodly person's *ways* but always season such thoughts with pity.

> Genesis 3:14-15 And the LORD God said unto the serpent, Because thou hast done this, thou art cursed above all cattle, and above every beast of the field; upon thy belly shalt thou go, and dust shalt thou eat all the days of thy life: And I will put enmity between thee and the woman, and between thy seed and her seed; it shall bruise thy head, and thou shalt bruise his heel.
>
> Psalm 37:12-13 The wicked plotteth against the just, and gnasheth upon him with his teeth. The Lord shall laugh at him: for he seeth that his day is coming.
>
> Proverbs 8:7 For my mouth shall speak truth; and wickedness is an abomination to my lips. All the words of my mouth are in righteousness; there is nothing froward or perverse in them.
>
> Proverbs 29:10 The bloodthirsty hate the upright: but the just seek his soul.
>
> John 17:14 I have given them thy word; and the world hath hated them, because they are not of the world, even as I am not of the world.
>
> Romans 8:5-8 For they that are after the flesh do mind the things of the flesh; but they that are after the Spirit the things of the Spirit. For to be carnally minded is death; but to be spiritually minded is life and peace. Because the carnal mind is enmity against God: for it is not subject to the law of God, neither indeed can be. So then they that are in the flesh cannot please God.
>
> 2 Corinthians 6:14 Be ye not unequally yoked together with unbelievers: for what fellowship hath righteousness with unrighteousness? and what communion hath light with darkness?

SECTION IV
(Chapters 30-31)

Though other persons are identified and discussed, these last two chapters of Proverbs concentrate on two main characters. In Chapter 30, Agur is the wise man who speaks wisdom to his two students. In Chapter 31, the wise woman who doesn't speak directly but is *spoken about* in detail is "the Virtuous Woman." There is no relationship between these last two chapters nor between these two individuals; however, the two chapters are considered in one section because these two main characters are representative of wisdom taught throughout the other 29 chapters of Proverbs. In a manner of speaking, they represent the embodiment of wisdom and thus form concluding examples to this precious, priceless portion of the word of God. King Lemuel is a third lesser character of this section whose mother sternly reminds him of two moral weaknesses that he must not yield to, lest he becomes a fool.

Agur is a picture of humility and godly wisdom as he expressly recognizes God's design in all of creation. He provides an example of a wise person who views God's creative wisdom through the different aspects of earth's scientific marvels and her many creatures. He teaches through his thoughts of amazing discoveries.

The "Virtuous Woman" is also a picture of humility and godly wisdom, only she is the physical expression of wisdom in every aspect of her life. Her interaction with family, servants, and community shows how wisdom shapes and blesses the life of an individual surrendered to God's instructions. She demonstrates both a life lived through wisdom and the blessings granted to a person of wisdom.

Just as Agur is stunned in a world full of God's wisdom, the "Virtuous Woman" stuns the people around her with her manifestation of a life fully expressive of God's wisdom. Agur's words depict a man enamored with the wisdom of every element of God's creation, and "the Virtuous Woman" lives a life that exemplifies the benefits of knowing how to function most effectively through thinking and acting in ways that are in total agreement with God. Her life is a premium example of a woman who is wholly surrendered to God. Her everyday life activities provide a living example of how a wise woman lives.

Both Agur and the "Virtuous Woman" have been transformed by godly wisdom so that they understand and function in a manner that simultaneously expresses humility and honor.

CHAPTER THIRTY

Outline of Agur's Wisdom Discourse in Chapter 30

I. Agur Humbly Introduces Himself   verses 1-3
  A. More brutish than any man
  B. Have not the understanding of a man
  C. Have not learned Wisdom
  D. Have not the knowledge of the holy
II. Extols God   verse 4
  A. Who has ascended up to Heaven
  B. Who has gathered the wind in his fists
  C. Who hath bound the waters in a garment
  D. Who hath established all the ends of the earth
  E. What is his name and his son's name
III. Extols God and word of God   verses 5-6
  A. His word is pure
  B. He is a shield to those who trust Him
  C. Warning – Add not to His words
IV. Prays for Purity and a Pleasant Life   verses 7-9
  A. Remove from me vanity and lies
  B. Give me neither poverty nor riches
  C. Warning – too little or too much brings the temptation to sin
V. Cautions Against Mistreatment of Servants   verse 10
VI. Identifies Four Wicked Generations   verses 11-14
  A. Disrespectful
  B. Hypocritical
  C. Arrogant
  D. Oppressive
VII. Names Four Things That are Insatiable   verses 15-16
  A. Grave
  B. Barren Womb
  C. Earth
  D. Fire
VIII. Warns Against Mistreatment of Parents   verse 17
IX. Names Four Ways That are Wonderful   verses 18-19
  A. Eagle in the Air
  B. Serpent upon a rock
  C. Ship in the midst of the sea
  D. Man with a maid
X. Names the Way that a Wicked Adulterous Woman Excuses Herself   verse 20
XI. Names Four Things That are Intolerable   verses 21-23
  A. Servant when he reigneth
  B. Fool filled with meat
  C. Odious woman, when married
  D. Handmaid that is heir to her mistress
XII. Names Four Things That are Little but Exceedingly Wise   verses 24-28
  A. Ants are weak but make preparations for winter
  B. Conies are feeble but make houses in rocks
  C. Locusts have no king but are highly organized
  D. Spiders live in king's palaces
XIII. Names Four Things that are Comely in Going   verses 29-31
  A. Lion is strongest and fearless
  B. Greyhound
  C. He goat
  D. King against whom there is no rising up
XIV. Identifies Shamefulness in Being Foolish   verse 32
XV. Identifies Strife with Forcing of Wrath   verse 33
  A. Churning of milk brings forth butter
  B. Wringing of nose brings forth blood
  C. Forcing of wrath brings forth strife

Proverbs 30:1-3   The words of Agur the son of Jakeh, *even* the prophecy: the man spake unto Ithiel, even unto Ithiel and Ucal,
  2. Surely I *am* more brutish than *any* man, and have not the understanding of a man.
  3. I neither learned wisdom, nor have the knowledge of the holy.

These first three verses provide insight into Agur's humble frame of mind (emptied of self). His humility opened the door for God to fill him with wisdom, knowledge, and understanding.

"The words of Agur the son of Jakeh, *even* the prophecy: the man spake unto Ithiel, even unto Ithiel and Ucal" (verse 1) In this first verse, which may be considered the title of this short section of inspired writing, four people are named: Agur, Jakeh, Ithiel, and Ucal. **Agur's** name signifies *"collector."*[757] **Jakeh** (*the obedient one*) is Agur's father; "**Ithiel** signifies *God with me ... Ucal* signifies *the Mighty One."*[758] Other than what is written in this verse, no biographical facts are known about Agur, Ithiel, or Ucal; and speculation never reaches a reliable conclusion.

The phrase ***"even* the prophecy"** informs the reader that Agur *received an utterance from God with a burden to deliver the same to others,* and he speaks that prophecy to Ithiel and Ucal. **"Prophecy"** in this chapter and the next may be defined as "... instruction, a declaration of things useful and profitable; likewise, "preaching in the New Testament is called prophesying (1 Corinthians 14:1). This Book of Proverbs is a part of the word of God, of the prophecy which came not by the will of man, but by the inspiration of God (2 Peter 1:19). The excellent, good man Agur, was divinely inspired."[759] The chapter contains no prediction of future events except for the reference in verse 4 to the Son of God in the clause "and what *is* his son's name, if thou canst tell?"

> 1 Corinthians 14:1 Follow after charity, and desire spiritual *gifts,* but rather that ye may prophesy.
>
> 2 Peter 1:19-21 We have also a more sure word of prophecy; whereunto ye do well that ye take heed, as unto a light that shineth in a dark place, until the day dawn, and the day star arise in your hearts: Knowing this first, that no prophecy of the scripture is of any private interpretation. For the prophecy came not in old time by the will of man: but holy men of God spake *as they were* moved by the Holy Ghost.

"Surely I *am* more brutish than *any* man, and have not the understanding of a man." (verse 2) Agur has a humble opinion of himself and declares that he does not have "**the understanding of a man**;" but his writing, as dictated by the Holy Spirit, indicates that he was undoubtedly made aware by the Holy Spirit of various generations of people (verses 11-14) and of the anxieties caused by improper roles of people (verses 22-23). He had insight that he attributes NOT to his own native ability. He believed himself to be **"brutish"** ("dull-minded like an animal"[760]) because he recognized that his knowledge of God was slight. Arrogant people, who believe that their knowledge is much greater than it is, fail to recognize that no one will have a perfect knowledge of God until the Messiah sets up His kingdom on earth. Isaiah 11:19 states, "... for the earth shall be full of the knowledge of the LORD, as the waters cover the sea." Agur is not lifted up in pride because of what he knows; instead, he realizes that there is a massive amount of information he does NOT know. Humble men, like Agur, learn to say how little they know rather than how much. Furthermore, when an honest person evaluates his own heart, he must conclude himself to be base and relatively ignorant, and sinful. Otherwise, he would not learn to depend on the leadership of God, would not stand in awe of God's magnificence, and would not be of use to God.

Notice that David had almost the same thoughts as Agur and came to a positive conclusion:

> Psalm 73:22-24 So foolish *was* I, and ignorant: I was *as* a beast before thee. Nevertheless I *am* continually with thee: thou hast holden *me* by my right hand. Thou shalt guide me with thy counsel, and afterward receive me *to* glory.

> "'*Surely I am more brutish than any man!'* Whoever knows his own heart, knows that of himself, that he can hardly conceive of any one else being so degraded as himself. Add to which – it is the child of God comparing himself with his perfect standard. And in the perception of his own short-comings, the most discerning clear-sighted penitent feels, that he can never abase himself as he ought before his God – He would lie low, lower still, infinitely lower, in the dust. Holy Paul, comparing himself with the spirituality of the perfect law, exclaims – 'I am carnal, sold under sin.' (Romans 7:14) Isaiah, in the presence of a holy God cries out –'Woe is me, for I am undone; because I am a man of unclean lips.' (Isaiah 6:5) Job in the manifestation of the power of God sinks into absolute nothingness and unworthiness. (Job 40:4; 42:6) . . . The nearer our contemplation of God, the closer our communion with him, the deeper will be our self-abasement before him; like the winged seraphs 'before the throne, who with twain cover their faces, and with twain cover their feet.' (Isaiah 6:2) Well, therefore, may the wisest and holiest of men, though 'renewed in knowledge after the image of him that created him' (Colossians 3:10), take up the humiliating confession – *'Surely I am more brutish than any man'* – Genuine humility is the only path of wisdom. Unless a man stoops, he can never enter the door. He must become 'a fool, that he may be wise.' And when he is humbled in his shame, then let him see the house of his God in its breadth and length (Ezekiel 44:5); enjoying clearer, and panting still for clearer manifestations of the incomprehensible God."[761]

"I neither learned wisdom, nor have the knowledge of the holy." (verse 3) Continuing with a humble spirit and with an apparent undeterred goal of receiving wisdom, knowledge, and understanding from God, Agur declares that he did not learn wisdom, nor does he have (within himself) the knowledge of God. Certainly, he is right. Such wisdom and knowledge and understanding come from God. His thoughts were genuine and inspired by God. His writing causes the astute reader to realize, or at least observe, as much as possible, the complexities of God and His Creation. Also, his writing makes one realize just how simple the understanding of man is when compared to that of God. Agur made it clear that God has a Son, Who the New Testament reveals as Jesus Christ; and he also expressed the great value of God's word. As is true of all of the Book of Proverbs, this chapter was meant to be pondered, studied, examined, and learned from. It stands miles above that of a cursory read. As far as Agur's wisdom, knowledge, and understanding are concerned, when God calls a man, He also qualifies and personally teaches him.

> "The natural man, the natural powers, perceive not, nay, they *receive not, the things of the Spirit of God.* Some suppose Agur to be asked, as Apollo's oracle was of old, *Who was the wisest man?* The answer is, *He that is sensible of his own ignorance,* especially in divine things... *All that I know is that I know nothing."*[762]

1 Corinthians 2:9-14 But as it is written, Eye hath not seen, nor ear heard, neither have entered into the heart of man, the things which God hath prepared for them that love him. But God hath revealed *them* unto us by his Spirit: for the Spirit searcheth all things, yea, the deep things of God. For what man knoweth the things of a man, save the spirit of man which is in him? even so the things of God knoweth no man, but the Spirit of God. Now we have received, not the spirit of the world, but the spirit which is of God; that we might know the things that are freely given to us of God. Which things also we speak, not in the words which man's wisdom teacheth, but which the Holy Ghost teacheth; comparing spiritual things with spiritual. But the natural man receiveth not the things of the Spirit of God: for they are foolishness unto him: neither can he know *them,* because they are spiritually discerned.

> **Proverbs 30:4** Who hath ascended up into heaven, or descended? who hath gathered the wind in his fists? who hath bound the waters in a garment? who hath established all the ends of the earth? what *is* his name, and what *is* his son's name, if thou canst tell?

Verse one presented a mental image of Agur speaking to Ithiel and Ucal, *perhaps* atop a huge flat rock with a canopy of blue skies and white clouds. God's creation is in panoramic view, while Agur clearly testifies that his instruction is not coming from human wisdom. Intrigued, they listen carefully, waiting for him to share spiritual food, and this he does by asking five rhetorical questions, the answers to which were obvious.

Jesus used the same method of instruction in the Temple with the learned doctors. Using questions and answers was a typical method of learning for the Jews. Notice the example of the 12-year-old Jesus participating in a session in the Temple with the learned doctors.

> Luke 2:46-47 And it came to pass, that after three days they found him in the temple, sitting in the midst of the doctors, both hearing them, and asking them questions. And all that heard him were astonished at his understanding and answers.

"Who hath ascended up into heaven, or descended?" Certainly, Agur, unwittingly, is speaking of Jesus; and the Holy Spirit has directed his thinking and thus his words. Looking back from the 21st century, the Christian can unmistakably understand the question and knows the answer.

Such travel between the third heaven and earth is *not possible directly in an earthly body* or even in a spaceship. God has confined man to earth and to a minuscule portion of the second heaven and none of the third until he will be given a celestial body at the resurrection. Four exceptions recorded in Scripture include Old Testament saints Enoch and Elijah. Paul speaks of "visions and revelations" in the New Testament and says that he was caught up "to the third heaven." Also, Paul describes the physical and spiritual changes that will equip the born-again child of God for making such a trip at the resurrection in First Corinthians 15. Jesus, of course, came to earth from heaven and went back to heaven.

John Gill wrote the following comments concerning this first question of Agur.

> "Who is it 'That has been thither to fetch knowledge of God and divine things, and has returned to communicate it. Enoch was taken up to heaven before this time: and Elijah, as is very probable, after; but neither of them returned again, to inform mortals what was to be seen, known, and enjoyed there: since, the Apostle Paul was caught up into the third heaven, and came back again; but then the things he heard were such as it was not lawful for a man to utter: and indeed, since the coming of Christ there is no need of any further revelation to be made nor of any such expedition, in order to obtain it, Romans 10:6 . . . he lay in the bosom of the Father, and was privy to his whole mind and will; he descended from heaven to earth not by local motion, but, by assumption of nature; and when he had made known his Father's will, and done his work, he ascended far above all heavens, and received gifts for men; to fill his churches and ministers with them, in order to communicate and improve spiritual and divine knowledge; and therefore, with great propriety and pertinence, he applies these words to himself, John 3:13."[763]

> Genesis 5:21-24 And Enoch lived sixty and five years, and begat Methuselah: And Enoch walked with God after he begat Methuselah three hundred years, and begat sons and daughters: And all the days of Enoch were three hundred sixty and five years: And Enoch walked with God: and he *was* not; for God took him.
> Matthew 17:1-3 And after six days Jesus taketh Peter, James, and John his brother, and bringeth them up into an high mountain apart, And was transfigured before them: and his face did shine as the sun, and his raiment was white as the light. And, behold, there appeared unto them Moses and Elias talking with him.
> John 3:13 And no man hath ascended up to heaven, but he that came down from heaven, *even* the Son of man which is in heaven.
> Romans 10:6-7 But the righteousness which is of faith speaketh on this wise, Say not in thine heart, Who shall ascend into heaven? (that is, to bring Christ down *from above:*) Or, Who shall descend into the deep? (that is, to bring up Christ again from the dead.)
> 2 Corinthians 12:1-4 It is not expedient for me doubtless to glory. I will come to visions and revelations of the Lord. I knew a man in Christ above fourteen years ago, (whether in the body, I cannot tell; or whether out of the body, I cannot tell: God knoweth;) such an one caught up to the third heaven. And I knew such a man, (whether in the body, or out of the body, I cannot tell: God knoweth;) How that he was caught up into paradise, and heard unspeakable words, which it is not lawful for a man to utter.
> Ephesians 4:9-10 (Now that he ascended, what is it but that he also descended first into the lower parts of the earth? He that descended is the same also that ascended up far above all heavens, that he might fill all things.)

"Who hath gathered the wind in his fists?" This question calls to mind the only Son of God, Jesus, as He stilled the storm, manifesting His deity once again. Jesus had said many times that He and the Father are One, each part of the Trinity.

> "Not any mere creature; not any man or set of men; it is not in the power of any, either men or angels, to restrain or let loose the winds at pleasure; nor has Satan, though called the prince of the power of the air, that is, of the devils in the air, any such command of them; none but he that made them can command them to blow, or be still; even he who brings them out of his treasures, and his own son, whom the wind and seas obeyed; see Psalm 135:7."[764]

Job 38:4-13 Where wast thou when I laid the foundations of the earth? declare, if thou hast understanding. Who hath laid the measures thereof, if thou knowest? or who hath stretched the line upon it? Whereupon are the foundations thereof fastened? or who laid the corner stone thereof; When the morning stars sang together, and all the sons of God shouted for joy? Or *who* shut up the sea with doors, when it brake forth, *as if* it had issued out of the womb? When I made the cloud the garment thereof, and thick darkness a swaddlingband for it, And brake up for it my decreed *place,* and set bars and doors, And said, Hitherto shalt thou come, but no further: and here shall thy proud waves be stayed? Hast thou commanded the morning since thy days; *and* caused the dayspring to know his place; That it might take hold of the ends of the earth, that the wicked might be shaken out of it? *[NOTE: this passage uses the metaphor of the cloud being the garment that holds the rain water as Agur did in verse 4.]*

Psalm 135:7 He causeth the vapours to ascend from the ends of the earth; he maketh lightnings for the rain; he bringeth the wind out of his treasuries.

Isaiah 40:12 Who hath measured the waters in the hollow of his hand, and meted out heaven with the span, and comprehended the dust of the earth in a measure, and weighed the mountains in scales, and the hills in a balance?

Mark 4:37-39 And there arose a great storm of wind, and the waves beat into the ship, so that it was now full. And he was in the hinder part of the ship, asleep on a pillow: and they awake him, and say unto him, Master, carest thou not that we perish? And he arose, and rebuked the wind, and said unto the sea, Peace, be still. And the wind ceased, and there was a great calm.

"Who hath bound the waters in a garment?"

> "The waters are the clouds which cover the vault of heaven, and are held, as it were, in a garment, so that, in spite of the weight which they contain, they fall not upon the earth. As Job says Job 26:8, 'He bindeth up the waters in his thick clouds; and the cloud is not rent under them.' And again, (Job 38:37) 'Who can number the clouds by wisdom? or who can pour out the bottles of heaven?' So the psalmist, 'Thou coveredst it *[the earth]* with the deep as *with* a garment: the waters stood above the mountains.'(Psalm 104:6)"[765]

"Who hath established all the ends of the earth? What *is* his name, and what *is* his son's name, if thou canst tell?" God as Creator spoke the world into existence and populated it, and alongside Him was the Holy Spirit and His Son, the Co-creator. Who is also known for His wisdom and *as* "the power of God and the wisdom of God" (1 Corinthians 1:24). As genuine Christians do, Agur longs to know more about God and His son.

Job 38:4-6 Where wast thou when I laid the foundations of the earth? declare, if thou hast understanding. Who hath laid the measures thereof, if thou knowest? or who hath stretched the line upon it? Whereupon are the foundations thereof fastened? or who laid the corner stone thereof...

Jeremiah 51:15 He hath made the earth by his power, he hath established the world by his wisdom, and hath stretched out the heaven by his understanding.

John 1:1 In the beginning was the Word, and the Word was with God, and the Word was God.

John 10:30 I and *my* Father are one.

John 14:7-9 If ye had known me, ye should have known my Father also: and from henceforth ye know him, and have seen him. Philip saith unto him, Lord, shew us the Father, and it sufficeth us. Jesus saith unto him, Have I been so long time with you, and yet hast thou not known me, Philip? he that hath seen me hath seen the Father; and how sayest thou *then,* Shew us the Father?

Colossians 1:13-18 . . . and hath translated *us* into the kingdom of his dear Son: In whom we have redemption through his blood, *even* the forgiveness of sins: Who is the image of the invisible God, the firstborn of every creature: For by him were all things created, that are in heaven, and that are in earth, visible and invisible, whether *they be* thrones, or dominions, or principalities, or powers: all things were created by him, and for him: And he is before all things, and by him all things consist. And he is the head of the body, the church: who is the beginning, the firstborn from the dead; that in all *things* he might have the preeminence.

Revelation 19:13 And he *was* clothed with a vesture dipped in blood: and his name is called The Word of God.

Proverbs 30:5-6 Every word of God *is* pure: he *is* a shield unto them that put their trust in him.
6. Add thou not unto his words, lest he reprove thee, and thou be found a liar.

Perhaps the reader will still have a mental image from verse one of the prophet Agur standing graciously and powerfully yet unpretentiously before his two eager students, Ithiel and Ucal. He humbly labeled himself (verses 2 and 3) as inadequate, lacking innate wisdom, knowledge, and understanding: a description that any godly, wise man exposed to the marvelous greatness of God would tend to believe about himself. Explosive questions in verse 4 turn the minds of Ithiel and Ucal to the greatness of the Creator and His Son, emphasizing the severe lacking in man's innate ability to comprehend God. From that scene of deep thought about the great Creator, Agur moves to speak about *God's pure word* (verses 5 and 6).

"Every word of God *is* pure: he *is* a shield unto them that put their trust in him." (verse 5) Agur declares emphatically and prophetically that "every word of God is pure," leaving no room for suggesting otherwise or questioning this great statement of truth. There are NO impurities in the word of God. It is like one hundred percent pure gold, having absolutely no dross or alloy. It is perfect, containing no errors, no misstatements, no false claims, nothing insincere, no possibility of failure in any regard. It is pure truth. and every word can be trusted completely as it reveals God to the reader. Seemingly in the same breath, Agur declares, "he is a shield unto them that put their trust in him," making Ithiel and Ucal, and every sincere reader, understand that *there is a wonderful relationship between God and that person who trusts in Him and believes that His word can be fully relied upon.* When a person lives according to His word, he gains experiences with God that provide personal proof that God *shields* and protects those who walk with Him. There is a bond, a relationship, a partnership, and a divine protection with God where there is "trust in him."

"Add thou not unto his words, lest he reprove thee, and thou be found a liar." *(*verse 6) Agur then warns Ithiel and Ucal that altering His word to "add" to it is dangerous and leads to being *reproved* and being "found a liar." To "add" to the word of God is to make it say anything that it does not say. It would be far better to say, "I don't know what that verse says," than to declare speculations that listeners misunderstand for truth. To be "found a liar" may sound harsh to the human ear, but God obviously intends for men to have the same humble spirit that Agur had and to simply proclaim God's word as it is. Someone once said, *"The word of God is like a lion. You don't have to defend it. Just open the gate and it will defend itself."*

> Deuteronomy 12:32 What thing soever I command you, observe to do it: thou shalt not add thereto, nor diminish from it.
>
> Deuteronomy 29:29 The secret *things belong* unto the LORD our God: but those *things which are* revealed *belong* unto us and to our children for ever, that *we* may do all the words of this law.
>
> 2 Samuel 22:31 *As for* God, his way *is* perfect; the word of the LORD *is* tried: he *is* a buckler to all them that trust in him.
>
> Psalm 12:6 The words of the LORD *are* pure words: *as* silver tried in a furnace of earth, purified seven times.
>
> Psalm 119:140 Thy word *is* very pure: therefore thy servant loveth it.
>
> Matthew 22:29 Jesus answered and said unto them, Ye do err, not knowing the scriptures, nor the power of God.
>
> 2Corinthians 2:17 For we are not as many, which corrupt the word of God: but as of sincerity, but as of God, in the sight of God speak we in Christ. Therefore seeing we have this ministry, as we have received mercy, we faint not; But have renounced the hidden things of dishonesty, not walking in craftiness, nor handling the word of God deceitfully; but by manifestation of the truth commending ourselves to every man's conscience in the sight of God.
>
> 2Timothy 3:16-17 All scripture *is* given by inspiration of God, and *is* profitable for doctrine, for reproof, for correction, for instruction in righteousness: That the man of God may be perfect, throughly furnished unto all good works.
>
> Revelation 22:18-19 For I testify unto every man that heareth the words of the prophecy of this book, If any man shall add unto these things, God shall add unto him the plagues that are written in this book: And if any man shall take away from the words of the book of this prophecy, God shall take away his part out of the book of life, and out of the holy city, and *from* the things which are written in this book.

Proverbs 30:7-9 Two *things* have I required of thee; deny me *them* not before I die:
    8. Remove far from me vanity and lies: give me neither poverty nor riches; feed me with food convenient for me:
    9. Lest I be full, and deny *thee,* and say, Who *is* the LORD? or lest I be poor, and steal, and take the name of my God in vain.

Since verse 1, Agur has spoken to his two listeners, Ithiel and Ucal. In verses 1-3, Agur declared himself brutish and unlearned; then in verse 4, he presented questions that demanded honor to the creative glory and magnificence of God and His Son. In verses 5 and 6, he echoed the Scriptural truth that the word of God is pure, that God is a shield to those who trust Him, and that there is danger in adding to His word. In verses 7-9, Agur allows his audience to listen as he lays open his heart to God in prayer, asking God to give him a life demonstrative of a marvelously protected and trusting relationship.

It appears that the two previous verses inspire this prayer of verses 7-9, whereby Agur reveals his honorable and humble motive of maintaining a good and proper relationship with God. The prayer reflects an expansion of his humble words about himself in verses 1-3 showing that he has a wise distrust in his human ability. Agur obviously desires to *remain behind*

God's shield of protection that is only established by a trusting relationship. He certainly would also like to be known as being *truthful* and never having to be reproved by God.

The statement, **"two things have I required of thee,"** without doubt, was NOT a mandate that Agur was placing on God (something which would have been pure foolishness and totally inconsistent with his view of God as expressed in verse 4); but rather it is Agur's way of wording a request for God's help because of what he knew would be "required" *IF* he were going to be able to maintain a proper dependent, servant relationship with God. The additional request he made was to **"deny me *them* not before I die,"** meaning "grant me these two things for the rest of my life."[766]

> James 4:3 We ask, and receive not, because ye ask amiss, that ye may consume *it* upon your lusts.
> Romans 8:26-27 Likewise the Spirit also helpeth our infirmities: for we know not what we should pray for as we ought: but the Spirit itself maketh intercession for us with groanings which cannot be uttered. And he that searcheth the hearts knoweth what *is* the mind of the Spirit, because he maketh intercession for the saints according to *the will of* God.

"Remove far from me vanity and lies: Give me neither poverty nor riches; feed me with food convenient for me: Lest I be full, and deny *thee,* and say, Who *is* the LORD? or lest I be poor, and steal, and take the name of my God in vain." (verses 8 and 9) Much of life can be empty and worthless **"vanity,"** which includes false lives, false appearances of happiness, and fruitless expectations. Agur does not want his heart set on such vanity. He yearns for a close relationship with God that yields a life that is "solid, true, durable, and eternal."[767]

Most of humanity lives to satisfy the demands of the flesh with **"vanity and lies;"** consequently, civilization has to have strict laws to keep order. Without such laws and enforcement, only the strongest would survive. When man has a relationship with God, he becomes responsible to the Judge of the universe and follows His guidelines and the Holy Spirit to govern his conduct. A trusting relationship with God, resulting in a walk with Him, leads one away from such *emptiness and distortion of truth.*

> Psalm 119:29 Remove from me the way of lying: and grant me thy law graciously.
> Psalm 119:37 Turn away mine eyes from beholding vanity; *and* quicken thou me in thy way.
> Jonah 2:8 They that observe lying vanities forsake their own mercy.
> 1 John 2:15-17 Love not the world, neither the things *that are* in the world. If any man love the world, the love of the Father is not in him. For all that *is* in the world, the lust of the flesh, and the lust of the eyes, and the pride of life, is not of the Father, but is of the world. And the world passeth away, and the lust thereof: but he that doeth the will of God abideth for ever.

"Give me neither poverty nor riches." For Agur to keep this cherished and protected relationship with God, he asked for God to give him *a financially-balanced life* so that he would not be lured away from God by desires or extreme need. He asked to be placed in the middle with **"neither poverty nor riches"** for the honorable purpose of remaining right with God.

"Feed me with food convenient for me." For the same reason as above, he asked that his food be "convenient," that is, that which God wanted for him to have, whereby he did not have to worry where the next meal would be coming from nor have the extreme dainties such as kings have so that he began to *"live to eat rather than eat to live."* It was a matter of trust. Food represented provision for living and he dreaded that too much would cause him to **"be full, and deny"** God. No doubt, he had seen some who had so much provision that they felt *no* need to have a relationship with God or ask Him for anything, resulting in the condemnatory statement **"Who is the LORD?"** If Agur had denied God in his action and speech, he would have proven that his testimony was in vain. Not having enough provisions could result in poverty that encouraged a man to **"steal, and take the name of God in vain."** Such poverty results in misery and motivates some men to believe that if there were a God, He would help them; and since they are not being assisted, they "take the name of God in vain." *Agur's honorable desire was to stay far away from anything interfering with a proper relationship with God.*

> Exodus 16:18 And when they did mete *it* with an omer, he that gathered much had nothing over, and he that gathered little had no lack; they gathered every man according to his eating.
> Deuteronomy 8:12-14 Lest *when* thou hast eaten and art full, and hast built goodly houses, and dwelt *therein; And when* thy herds and thy flocks multiply, and thy silver and thy gold is multiplied, and all that thou hast is multiplied; Then thine heart be lifted up, and thou forget the LORD thy God, which brought thee forth out of the land of Egypt, from the house of bondage;
> Deuteronomy 32:15 But Jeshurun *[a symbolic name for Israel]* waxed fat, and kicked: thou art waxen fat, thou art grown thick, thou art covered *with fatness;* then he forsook God *which* made him, and lightly esteemed the Rock of his salvation.
> Matthew 6:11 Give us this day our daily bread.
> Mark 10:23-25 And Jesus looked round about, and saith unto his disciples, How hardly shall they that have riches enter into the kingdom of God! And the disciples were astonished at his words. But Jesus answereth again, and saith unto them, Children, how hard is it for them that trust in riches to enter into the kingdom of God! It is easier for a camel to go through the eye of a needle, than for a rich man to enter into the kingdom of God.

> Philippians 4:10-13 But I rejoiced in the Lord greatly, that now at the last your care of me hath flourished again; wherein ye were also careful, but ye lacked opportunity. Not that I speak in respect of want: for I have learned, in whatsoever state I am, *therewith* to be content. I know both how to be abased, and I know how to abound: every where and in all things I am instructed both to be full and to be hungry, both to abound and to suffer need. I can do all things through Christ which strengtheneth me.
>
> 1 Timothy 6:6-10 But godliness with contentment is great gain. For we brought nothing into *this* world, *and it is* certain we can carry nothing out. And having food and raiment let us be therewith content. But they that will be rich fall into temptation and a snare, and *into* many foolish and hurtful lusts, which drown men in destruction and perdition. For the love of money is the root of all evil: which while some coveted after, they have erred from the faith, and pierced themselves through with many sorrows.

Proverbs 30:10 Accuse not a servant unto his master, lest he curse thee, and thou be found guilty.

"Accuse not a servant unto his master." The translators' note in the margin of the Bible reads, "Hurt not with thy tongue."[768] **"Accuse,"** as used here, means to make accusations such as are slanderous and meant to harm, rather than to accuse of doing something whereby the servant needs to be corrected for safety or another benefit. Scriptural instructions, such as this verse, clearly protect those of lesser positions, like a servant. Servants are to be kept from additional hardships to their already difficult life, especially those hardships brought on by falsifications of others.

"Lest he curse thee *[to make vile, to be of little account, insignificant]*,**" and thou be found guilty"** (of speaking vile words, thus lying and having little character). The reactionary **"curse"** (as defined above by the Hebrew word *qalal*) from the servant is simply the exposing of his accuser's lie within his slanderous accusation; and consequently, his accuser's *lesser character*. People are not likely to make false accusations unless they believe that they will get some personal gain from doing so. Such behavior is indeed indicative of bad character.

> Titus 3:2-3 To speak evil of no man, to be no brawlers, *but* gentle, shewing all meekness unto all men. For we ourselves also were sometimes foolish, disobedient, deceived, serving divers lusts and pleasures, living in malice and envy, hateful, *and* hating one another.

Proverbs 30:11-14 *There is* a generation *that* curseth their father, and doth not bless their mother.
12. *There is* a generation *that are* pure in their own eyes, and *yet* is not washed from their filthiness.
13. There is a generation, O how lofty are their eyes! and their eyelids are lifted up.
14. *There is* a generation, whose teeth *are as* swords, and their jaw teeth *as* knives, to devour the poor from off the earth, and the needy from *among* men.

Agur started this discourse with a very humble view of himself. He then discussed the greatness of the Creator and His Son, followed by the purity of God's word. Then he spoke about his own desire for a proper walk with God. Verse 10 discussed an individual whose low character was manifested through the "curse" of a servant. Now Agur turns his attention to four categorically wicked generations of people who describe classes of people belonging to every century, who will be dominant in the last days before our Lord returns. (2 Timothy 3:1-5) These classes of people are abominable to both God and good men.

"*There is* a generation *that* curseth their father, and doth not bless their mother." (verse 11) The *disrespectful generation* who "curseth" their father and refuses to "bless their mother" do so because they *only* have respect for themselves. It is pitiful to observe how the ungodly person thinks of himself as irreproachable, not understanding his own depravity. Only the convicting power of the Holy Spirit coupled with the word of God can reach his dark heart. If the offspring of this generation were to show respect for their parents, doing so would be an admission that their parents were correct in their chastisements. So, the rebellious youths show a disrespect for them. It is not natural for children to curse their fathers and to turn away from their mother's tenderness and love. These will have no respect or relationship with God because they have none with their godly parents. This generation spoken of in verse 11, does not "salute, thank, or praise" their parents; they rather berate them. The following verses show that God expects children to respect and honor their parents:

> Exodus 20:12 Honour thy father and thy mother: that thy days may be long upon the land which the LORD thy God giveth thee.
>
> Leviticus 20:9 For every one that curseth his father or his mother shall be surely put to death: he hath cursed his father or his mother; his blood *shall be* upon him.
>
> Proverbs 23:22 Hearken unto thy father that begat thee, and despise not thy mother when she is old.

Proverbs 30:17 The eye *that* mocketh at *his* father, and despiseth to obey *his* mother, the ravens of the valley shall pick it out, and the young eagles shall eat it.

Ephesians 6:1 Children, obey your parents in the Lord: for this is right.

Colossians 3:20 Children, obey *your* parents in all things: for this is well pleasing unto the Lord.

2 Timothy 3:1-5 This know also, that in the last days perilous times shall come. For men shall be lovers of their own selves, covetous, boasters, proud, blasphemers, disobedient to parents, unthankful, unholy, Without natural affection, trucebreakers, false accusers, incontinent, fierce, despisers of those that are good, Traitors, heady, highminded, lovers of pleasures more than lovers of God; Having a form of godliness, but denying the power thereof: from such turn away.

Jesus condemned the Pharisees for allowing men to use a religious excuse to avoid providing for their parents. Notice how religious leaders encouraged a sinful practice condemned by God to be acceptable to the people of the nation.

Mark 7:10-13 For Moses said, Honour thy father and thy mother; and, Whoso curseth father or mother, let him die the death: But ye say, If a man shall say to his father or mother, *It is* Corban, that is to say, a gift, by whatsoever thou mightest be profited by me; *he shall be free*. And ye suffer him no more to do ought for his father or his mother; Making the word of God of none effect through your tradition, which ye have delivered: and many such like things do ye.

NOTE: **"Corban"** *[is a Greek word "of Hebrew and Chaldee origin"]* used to refer to a gift devoted to God. It was a dedicatory formula pronounced over money and property donated to the temple and its service by an inviolable vow. If a son declared that the resources needed to support his aging parents were "Corban" then, according to tradition, he was exempt from the command of God (Exodus 20:12), and his parents were legally excluded from any claim on him. This made the tenth commandment of no effect, to the point that aging parents were refused any help, including food.[769]

"There is a generation *that are* pure in their own eyes, and *yet* is not washed from their filthiness." (verse 12) This ***hypocritical generation*** measures their own spirituality against themselves rather than against God's standard; consequently, they never see a need for repentance. They see themselves as morally or ethically free of sin – **"pure in their own eyes."** They are **"not washed from their filthiness;"** however, they visualize themselves as being so. Israelites often served God outwardly in rituals, but they often had no personal relationship with Him.

Proverbs 16:2 All the ways of a man *are* clean in his own eyes; but the LORD weigheth the spirits.

Proverbs 20:9 Who can say, I have made my heart clean, I am pure from my sin?

Matthew 23:25-26 Woe unto you, scribes and Pharisees, hypocrites! for ye make clean the outside of the cup and of the platter, but within they are full of extortion and excess. *Thou* blind Pharisee, cleanse first that *which is* within the cup and platter, that the outside of them may be clean also.

2 Timothy 3:5 Having a form of godliness, but denying the power thereof: from such turn away.

Titus 3:5 Not by works of righteousness which we have done, but according to his mercy he saved us, by the washing of regeneration, and renewing of the Holy Ghost …

Revelation 1:5 And from Jesus Christ, who is the faithful witness, and the first begotten of the dead, and the prince of the kings of the earth. Unto him that loved us, and washed us from our sins in his own blood …

"There is a generation, O how lofty are their eyes! and their eyelids are lifted up." (verse 13) The ***arrogant generation*** believes in their personal superiority, reflected in the haughty lifting up (loftiness) of **"their eyes."** Their faces are boldly arrogant, without humility, indicating a disregard for both God and men. God resists these proud people.

Proverbs 3:7 Be not wise in thine own eyes: fear the LORD, and depart from evil.

Proverbs 12:15 The way of a fool *is* right in his own eyes: but he that hearkeneth unto counsel *is* wise.

Isaiah 57:15 For thus saith the high and lofty One that inhabiteth eternity, whose name *is* Holy; I dwell in the high and holy *place*, with him also *that is* of a contrite and humble spirit, to revive the spirit of the humble, and to revive the heart of the contrite ones.

James 4:6 But he giveth more grace. Wherefore he saith, God resisteth the proud, but giveth grace unto the humble. *[Also see 1 Peter 5:5.]*

"There is a generation, whose teeth *are as* swords, and their jaw teeth *as* knives, to devour the poor from off the earth, and the needy from *among* men." (verse 14) Because it is driven as much by covetousness as by hate, this generation's viciousness is difficult for the child of God to measure. He can scarcely paint the full depth of the color of their evil, vicious heart. As much as this particular generation desires the little that *the poor and needy* possess, they mostly want to vent their Satanically-driven hate. They are oppressive, without pity, and certainly without respect or regard for the poor. They are like animals ripping up their prey. The two very expressive similes describe the viciousness of their evil heart with which they hate – **"teeth *are as* swords, and their jaw teeth *as* knives."**

Psalm 10:7-11 His mouth is full of cursing and deceit and fraud: under his tongue *is* mischief and vanity. He sitteth in the lurking places of the villages: in the secret places doth he murder the innocent: his eyes are privily set against the poor. He lieth in wait secretly as a lion in his den: he lieth in wait to catch the poor: he doth catch the poor, when he draweth him into his net. He croucheth, *and* humbleth himself, that the poor may fall by his strong ones. He hath said in his heart, God hath forgotten: he hideth his face; he will never see *it*.

Psalm 14:4 Have all the workers of iniquity no knowledge? who eat up my people as they eat bread, and call not upon the LORD.

Psalm 52:2 Thy tongue deviseth mischiefs; like a sharp razor, working deceitfully.

Psalm 57:4 My soul is among lions: and I lie even among them that are set on fire, even the sons of men, whose teeth are spears and arrows, and their tongue a sharp sword.

Amos 8:4-7 Hear this, O ye that swallow up the needy, even to make the poor of the land to fail, Saying, When will the new moon be gone, that we may sell corn? and the sabbath, that we may set forth wheat, making the ephah small, and the shekel great, and falsifying the balances by deceit? That we may buy the poor for silver, and the needy for a pair of shoes; *yea,* and sell the refuse of the wheat? The LORD hath sworn by the excellency of Jacob, Surely I will never forget any of their works.

> **Proverbs 30: 15-16** The horseleach hath two daughters, *crying,* Give, give. There are three *things that* are never satisfied, *yea,* four *things* say not, *It is* enough:
> 16. The grave; and the barren womb; the earth *that* is not filled with water; and the fire *that* saith not, *It is* enough.

Having spoken of immeasurable, vicious hatred coupled with insatiable greed and covetousness in verse 14, Agur proceeds in verses 15 and 16 to further identify the *foolish human trait of lustful dissatisfaction.* First, he compares it with an obnoxious blood-sucking worm, **"the horseleach,"** and then by listing well-known things that are commonly known to never reach satisfaction: the grave, the childless woman, and fire.

"The horseleach hath two daughters, *crying,* Give, give." (verse 15a) Because of how it functions, the "horseleach" (used this once in Scripture) symbolizes dissatisfaction and covetousness. It is a small two-headed (one on each end) blood-sucking worm that gets into the nose of a horse and is difficult to remove, and it soon reproduces more little blood-suckers – **"two daughters"** crying out **"give, give."**

Next, Agur names four insatiable things in life to further exemplify dissatisfaction and covetousness.

"There are three *things that* are never satisfied, *yea,* four *things* say not, *It is* enough." (verse 15b)

NOTE: This sentence utilizes a literary tool known as *graded numerical sequence* which is also used in the books of Job and Amos. By giving one number followed by another larger number, one gets the truthful impression that there are more of this type of insatiable things, but that only four are being listed in this verse. *(See also Proverbs 6:16; Proverbs 30:15, Proverbs 30:18; Proverbs 30:21; and Proverbs 30:29 for other examples.)*

(1) The Hebrew word *Sheol* is translated as **"the grave** *[underworld, grave, hell, pit, Old Testament designation for the abode of the dead: the place of no return; righteous not abandoned to it]*" in Proverbs 1:12 and 30:16. Multitudes have gone to the grave, but still it is not satisfied.

> Genesis 3:19 In the sweat of thy face shalt thou eat bread, till thou return unto the ground; for out of it wast thou taken: for dust thou *art,* and unto dust shalt thou return.
>
> Ecclesiastes 3:20 All go unto one place; all are of the dust, and all turn to dust again.
>
> Romans 5:12 Wherefore, as by one man sin entered into the world, and death by sin; and so death passed upon all men, for that all have sinned . . .
>
> Revelation 21:4 And God shall wipe away all tears from their eyes; and there shall be no more death, neither sorrow, nor crying, neither shall there be any more pain: for the former things are passed away.

(2) **"The Barren Womb"** - God, the Creator, has placed inside the heart of woman a yearning to have children, and then He promised His nation of Israel in Deuteronomy 7:14 that He would bless them in that none would be barren. When a woman, such as Rachael or Hannah, was barren, they considered themselves cursed or punished by God for wrongdoing.

> Genesis 30:1 And when Rachel saw that she bare Jacob no children, Rachel envied her sister; and said unto Jacob, Give me children, or else I die.
>
> Deuteronomy 7:14 Thou shalt be blessed above all people: there shall not be male or female barren among you, or among your cattle.
>
> 1 Samuel 1:11 And she vowed a vow, and said, O LORD of hosts, if thou wilt indeed look on the affliction of thine handmaid, and remember me, and not forget thine handmaid, but wilt give unto thine handmaid a man child, then I will give him unto the LORD all the days of his life, and there shall no razor come upon his head.
>
> Psalm 127:3 Lo, children *are* an heritage of the LORD: *and* the fruit of the womb *is his* reward.

(3) **"The Earth that is not filled with water."** - When the earth is dry, it especially thirsts for rain, but as soon as one rain is past, it readies for the next.

(4) **"The Fire** - If fuel is in the proper condition (dry wood) and there is oxygen, a fire will keep consuming fuel until there is no more available.

> **Proverbs 30:17** The eye *that* mocketh at *his* father, and despiseth to obey *his* mother, the ravens of the valley shall pick it out, and the young eagles shall eat it.

Shocking and attention-getting, this proverb contains two figures of speech. First, the entire verse is a figure of speech known as hyperbole; and second, within the hyperbole, is a synecdoche. Hyperbole uses *obvious and intentional exaggeration* to grab attention effectively. In contrast, the synecdoche uses a part of something to represent the whole. (In this case, the eye represents the entire person.) No Christian would ever encourage or even want to have a mental picture of this horrible depiction of the consequence of rebellion. The whole intent of the verse is to dramatically illustrate the severity of mocking one's father or hating to obey one's mother.

> "'**The eye**' is named as the mind's instrument for expressing scorn and insubordination; it is the index to the inner feeling; and look may be as sinful as action. **And despiseth to obey his mother**; i.e., holds obedience to his mother to be a thing of no importance whatever."[770]

"The ravens of the valley shall pick it out, and the young eagles shall eat it." Such an egregious and horrific penalty was NOT part of the Mosaic law and is certainly not part of current law in civilized countries. Agur seems to be expounding on verse 11, where he stated, "There is a generation that curseth their father, and doth not bless their mother," and this verse is given as a greatly exaggerated but fierce warning that expresses how terrible is the offense. No doubt, many criminals who have made their own lives a catastrophe and their parents' lives sorrow and shame would attest to the fact that their entire miserable life started with disrespect for their parents. Since burial is the last act of respect for a person, this proverb depicts disrespect for the rebel through refusal to honor him with burial.

> Leviticus 20:9 For every one that curseth his father or his mother shall be surely put to death: he hath cursed his father or his mother; his blood shall be upon him.
> Proverbs 20:20 Whoso curseth his father or his mother, his lamp shall be put out in obscure darkness.
> Proverbs 23:22 Hearken unto thy father that begat thee, and despise not thy mother when she is old.
> Mark 7:9-13 And he said unto them, Full well ye reject the commandment of God, that ye may keep your own tradition. For Moses said, Honour thy father and thy mother; and, Whoso curseth father or mother, let him die the death: But ye say, If a man shall say to his father or mother, *It is* Corban, that is to say, a gift, by whatsoever thou mightest be profited by me; *he shall be free*. And ye suffer him no more to do ought for his father or his mother; Making the word of God of none effect through your tradition, which ye have delivered: and many such like things do ye. *[See page 574 for a detailed explanation of "Corban."]*

> **Proverbs 30:18-20** There be three *things which* are too wonderful for me, yea, four which I know not:
> 19. The way of an eagle in the air; the way of a serpent upon a rock; the way of a ship in the midst of the sea; and the way of a man with a maid.
> 20. Such *is* the way of an adulterous woman; she eateth, and wipeth her mouth, and saith, I have done no wickedness.

Agur described the greatness of the Creator in verse 3, and afterward, he wrote about the interactions of men with other men and with God. His writing describes astonishment at his own inabilities and those of others, especially those who wilfully sin, as described in verses 11-14, and the lack of satisfaction in verses 15-16. The chapter, as a whole, describes an amazed Agur spinning around, looking at all of God's wonderful creation. He is enamored with the wisdom of creation and the wonder of the creatures, yet stunned by men's foolishness.

These three verses (18-20) are a pictorial description of his bewilderment. He observes the **"eagle in the air,"** the **"serpent upon a rock," "a ship in the midst of the sea," "the way of a man with a maid"** (the description of a man's affectionately courting a woman), and the disgusting description of **"the way of an adulterous woman"** who is consumed with lust rather than love. Movements through air, land, and sea are all observed with amazement because these movements only momentarily leave a disturbance of the elements. But behind the "adulterous woman" is a wake of terror, heartache, and disaster. The **"way"** or manner that an eagle gets the invisible air under his wings and effortlessly glides seemingly forever; then suddenly, from tremendous height, with keen eyesight, spots dinner running along the ground. With spectacular grace and seeing astonishingly well from high in the air, he will dive and swoop down with tremendous accuracy and great strength of talons and wings to fulfill his desire for a meal. The way of an eagle is just **"too wonderful!"** And then, there is the snake smoothly gliding over a rock with no legs and no feet. It is just amazing to watch!! Agur then takes the reader's attention to the sea where a ship is able to navigate through the water with majesty.

In proportion to the size of a ship, a very small rudder guides the large vessel through the sea. Finally, Agur turns to man, whom God created to fellowship with Him. The **"way"** or manner that a young man courts and treats a maid so as to win her heart is as majestic and pure and honorable as an eagle gliding through the air or a serpent across a rock. All of this observation is astounding!! It is wonderful! It reveals the wisdom of God!

Then, in disgust, verse 20 describes the **"wickedness"** of **"an adulterous woman."** Her self-righteous manner disrupts the wonder, the magic, the purity and innocence of God's marvelous creation. Furthermore, she represents the *lure of sin* that takes man into territory away from the grandeur, the magnificence, and pleasurable walk with God. She **"wipeth her mouth, and saith, I have done no wickedness."** My, what foolishness engulfs a man, what sin poisons his thinking to cause him to leave the pleasantness and beauty and joy of **"the way of a man with a maid"** and embrace the destructive, damning, and dooming forces of evil that engulf the adulteress and take him away from God and into the grip of Satan.

> Job 42:3 Who is he that hideth counsel without knowledge? therefore have I uttered that I understood not; things too wonderful for me, which I knew not.
> Psalm 139:14 I will praise thee; for I am fearfully *and* wonderfully made: marvellous *are* thy works; and that my soul knoweth right well.
> Proverbs 5:3-5 For the lips of a strange woman drop as an honeycomb, and her mouth *is* smoother than oil: But her end is bitter as wormwood, sharp as a twoedged sword. Her feet go down to death; her steps take hold on hell.

Proverbs 30:21-23 For three *things* the earth is disquieted, and for four *which* it cannot bear:
22. For a servant when he reigneth; and a fool when he is filled with meat;
23. For an odious *woman* when she is married; and an handmaid that is heir to her mistress.

"The earth is disquieted" is a phrase meaning that the people of the earth are perturbed. To imply that every person on the earth is upset over the matters mentioned is a hyperbole – an exaggeration that is easily recognized as a figure of speech. Agur continues using *figures of speech* in these three verses to declare situations that upset and disrupt normal order. Using the word **"earth"** to represent the people rather than the planet is a figure of speech known as metonymy. **"For three things"** – **"and for four"** is a literary style known as *graded numerical sequence*, employed again in this chapter to draw attention to similar items and emphasize that the number of these types of situations identified are more in number than listed, but only these four are mentioned:

(1) **"A servant when he reigneth"** is disruptive to normal order and causes much disturbance because the "servant," having been suddenly installed in a place of power and leadership, is untrained and unqualified. He will not understand the use of power and possibly crush situations and, consequently, people by overreaching. In other situations that demand to be suppressed quickly, he will wait too long, letting them get out of hand. He also will not understand the principles of leadership that take years to grasp and develop since one usually learns them slowly when climbing gradually up the ladder of success. There are exceptions, such as Joseph in the Book of Genesis, but he was properly placed in a reigning position from a servant position because of godly wisdom and God's providence.

(2) **"A fool when he is filled with meat"** is disruptive and causes much disturbance because the **"fool"** is a senseless, vile, wicked person, who being fully satisfied with food, is likely to be even more boisterous and demanding with his folly. His riotous conduct does not justify being made comfortable with plenty to eat, because he already rages senselessly.

(3) **"An odious woman when she is married"** is disruptive and causes much disturbance because the **"odious"** *[hateful]* woman is not content creating problems where there would otherwise be none. The home should be a place of peace where family members love and protect each other and where there is rest and comfort; however, an "odious" woman destroys rather than builds, therefore making the home a place of agitation rather than tranquility.

(4) **"An handmaid that is heir to her mistress"** - despite how she becomes heir, the handmaid is disruptive and causes much disturbance. Such elevation can be accomplished in several ways, including inheritance after the mistress's death, marriage to her mistress's husband after her death, or displacement through insurrection. Now

that she is suddenly in charge of everything previously belonging to **"her mistress,"** she will probably not handle the complex job successfully. Typically a slave girl will not have been taught any leadership duties and responsibilities, such as organizing the household, managing finances, or organizing workers. In addition there is likely to be great jealousy and disdain from other servants who refuse to view her as their leader since she was for a long time their equal. All the household would be uprooted, discomforted, embarrassed, and perhaps dispersed.

Proverbs 19:10 Delight is not seemly for a fool; much less for a servant to have rule over princes.

Proverbs 28:3 A poor man that oppresseth the poor *is like* a sweeping rain which leaveth no food.

Lamentations 5:8 Servants have ruled over us: *there is* none that doth deliver *us* out of their hand.

Isaiah 3:4-5 And I will give children *to be* their princes, and babes shall rule over them. And the people shall be oppressed, every one by another, and every one by his neighbour: the child shall behave himself proudly against the ancient, and the base against the honourable.

Proverbs 30:24-28 There be four *things which are* little upon the earth, but they *are* exceeding wise:
25. The ants *are* a people not strong, yet they prepare their meat in the summer;
26. The conies *are but* a feeble folk, yet make they their houses in the rocks;
27. The locusts have no king, yet go they forth all of them by bands;
28. The spider taketh hold with her hands, and is in kings' palaces.

"There be four *things which are* little upon the earth, but they *are* exceeding wise." Agur now describes four creatures that demand respect for ingenuity reflective of their God-given instinct. Wise men will observe God's creatures, learning from them and thus becoming yet wiser, particularly concerning: (1) making adequate preparation for the future as do ants, (2) overcoming weakness through the use of strongholds as does the coney, (3) exercising order and discipline as do the bands of locusts, and (4) being diligent and efficient with God-given talents to be able to function in a great variety of places as does the spider.

(1) **"The ants *are* a people not strong, yet they prepare their meat in the summer."** Barnes writes, "The ants may truly be called a *people*, as they have houses, towns, public roads, etc.; and show their wisdom and prudence by preparing their meat in due season."[771] Previously, Proverbs describes the wisdom of the ants and how "they prepare their meat in the summer."

Proverbs 6:6-8 Go to the ant, thou sluggard; consider her ways, and be wise: Which having no guide, overseer, or ruler, Provideth her meat in the summer, *and* gathereth her food in the harvest.

They are considered wise because they do not need any "guide, overseer, or ruler." The ants work diligently to gather food in the summer in preparation for winter. They do not need anyone to tell them about the looming need or how to prepare. Human beings who cannot comprehend and prepare for the future needs of the regular cycles of life, such as weather seasons and aging, have little wisdom. Even the tiny ant could teach this wisdom, should there be a willingness to learn.

Proverbs 10:5 He that gathereth in summer *is* a wise son: *but* he that sleepeth in harvest *is* a son that causeth shame.

(2) **"The conies *are but* a feeble folk, yet make their houses in the rocks."** The coney cannot dig because of its soft, tender feet; so it builds its houses in the holes and rocks.[772] It is a furry little creature that looks like a groundhog and is about the size of a rabbit. God placed the conies in the exact habitat where they could easily navigate the rocky outcrops and yet be camouflaged for defense.

Psalm 104:18 The high hills *are* a refuge for the wild goats; *and* the rocks for the conies.

"The conies make theirs in the rocks, to cure *[sic]* themselves from their more potent enemies; and thus what they want in strength is made up in sagacity, and by their wise conduct they provide for their safety and protection. These are an emblem of the people of God, who are a weak and feeble people, unable of themselves to perform spiritual duties, to exercise grace, to withstand the corruptions of their nature, resist the temptations of Satan, bear up under afflictive providences, and grapple with spiritual enemies, or defend themselves from them: but such heavenly wisdom is given them, as to betake themselves for refuge and shelter to Christ, the Rock of Israel; the Rock of salvation, the Rock that is higher than they; a strong one, on which the church is built, and against which the gates of hell cannot prevail: and here they are safe from the storms of divine wrath, and the avenging justice of God; from the rage and fury of men, and the fiery darts of Satan; here they dwell safely and delightfully, and have all manner of provision at hand for them; they are the inhabitants of that Rock, who have reason to sing indeed!"[773]

(3) **"The locusts have no king, yet go they forth all of them by bands."** With no king or leader to command them, the locusts, which at times travel in swarms, have such good order, discipline, and direction that one would think someone were calling cadence. God brought a plague of locusts to Egypt, destroying the crops and even coming into the houses. "Joel speaks of them as a well-ordered army, as it were men of war, marching every one on his ways, not entangling their ranks, walking everyone in his path."[774] Good organization multiplies effectiveness; but becoming orderly and exercising discipline (for many humans) takes too much desire, effort, foresight, and time to develop the necessary skills.

> Joel 2:7-9 They shall run like mighty men; they shall climb the wall like men of war; and they shall march every one on his ways, and they shall not break their ranks: Neither shall one thrust another; they shall walk every one in his path: and *when* they fall upon the sword, they shall not be wounded. They shall run to and fro in the city; they shall run upon the wall, they shall climb up upon the houses; they shall enter in at the windows like a thief.

(4) **"The spider taketh hold with her hands, and is in kings' palaces."** Hundreds of different species of spiders are found in the Holy Land, and many live in king's palaces and the houses of ordinary people.

> In 2004 a team of scientists from Germany and Sweden discovered that a spider "taking hold" of the ceiling with her eight spider legs ("hands") can hold over 170 times her own body weight.
>
> The team used a scanning electron microscope to make images of the foot of a jumping spider... There is a tuft of hairs on the bottom of the spider's leg, and each individual hair is covered in more hairs. These smaller hairs are called setules, and they are what makes the spider stick.
>
> ... the force these spiders use to stick to surfaces is the van der Waals force, which acts between individual molecules that are within a nanometer of each other (a nanometer is about ten thousand times smaller than the width of a human hair). The team used a technique called Atomic Force Microscopy (AFM) to measure this force. The flexible contact tips of the setules are triangular, and they have an amazingly high adhesive force on the underlying surface.[775]

It took scientists a long time to discover how a spider can **"take hold with her hands."** Solomon certainly did not know how the spider could cling to ceilings and walls, but he watched the arachnids and learned from them. God intends for wise men to learn from both His word and His works of Creation. Though very small, these creatures are diligent in making their own provisions, producing perfectly designed webs (without even one day in a college engineering class), and acting wisely to secure their own safety. A person can also observe and learn patience from the spider as it waits for its prey.

Proverbs 30:29-31   There be three *things* which go well, yea, four are comely in going:
30.   A lion *which is* strongest among beasts, and turneth not away for any;
31.   A greyhound; an he goat also; and a king, against whom *there is* no rising up.

Agur characterizes the king in these three verses by comparing his stateliness and power to three beautiful, admired animals. As stated in verse 29, his purpose is to call attention to the fact that these animals are **"comely in going"** – *just like a king*. They all have appearances that are viewed as noble, and all have dignity in their demeanor. Especially noted by Agur is the power of the lion, which faces down his enemies (**"turneth not away for any"**). When such power (**"strongest among beasts"**) is identified in a king, it serves to deter rebellion, for against such strength, **"there is no rising up."** Also, by simply specifying the fact that the **"greyhound"** and the **"he goat"** are **"comely in going,"** Agur means only to draw attention to that characteristic of powerful, graceful appearance. Such stateliness and strength define these animals as leaders, and so it is with the wise king who gains the respect of the people through similar grace and strength. (This is the final example of graded numerical sequence in this chapter. See verse 15 above.)

(1) **"A lion *which is* strongest among beasts, and turneth not away for any."** (verse 30) As a symbol of strength, dignity, ferocity, and power, the lion is on the ensign *[according to rabbinical tradition]* of the tribe of Judah, and our Savior is identified Scripturally as "The Lion of the Tribe of Judah."

> Genesis 49:8-10 Judah, thou *art he* whom thy brethren shall praise: thy hand *shall be* in the neck of thine enemies; thy father's children shall bow down before thee. Judah *is* a lion's whelp: from the prey, my son, thou art gone up: he stooped down, he couched as a lion, and as an old lion; who shall rouse him up? The sceptre shall not depart from Judah, nor a lawgiver from between his feet, until Shiloh come; and unto him *shall* the gathering of the people *be*.
>
> Revelation 5:5 And one of the elders saith unto me, Weep not: behold, the Lion of the tribe of Juda, the Root of David, hath prevailed to open the book, and to loose the seven seals thereof.

> "The Asiatic lion (*Panthera leo persica*) was once common in Israel but has been extinct since the end of the 19th century, due largely to unchecked hunting under Ottoman rule... The writers of 37 of the Bible's 66 books mention the lion and its

reputation some 157 times ... Man is filled with admiration for the lion's majestic gait. The unparalleled might of the lion provokes respect: 'What is stronger than a lion?' (Judges 14:18). The courage and bravery of the lion is also spoken of: 'He also that is valiant, whose heart is as the heart of a lion ...' (2 Samuel 17:10). The lion is fearless of man even 'when a multitude of shepherds is called forth against him' (Isaiah 31:4). Lions decorated Solomon's temple – the bases were ornamented by moldings of lions (1 Kings 7:29, 36) while 12 statues of lions were put on the stairs leading to Solomon's throne (1Kings10:19,20)."[776]

" A male lion's roar can be heard by humans up to 5 miles away ... They are very strong and can carry off a complete buffalo carcass ... The lion's blow is one of the most powerful forces in nature, which provides the basis for the Hebrew word *layish*, meaning a crushing blow."[777]

Like the lion, the way the king carries himself is indicative of his strength, his bravery, his previous victories, and his confidence. The lion **"turneth not away"** from any pursuer or any foe, but faces them in conflict because he is not afraid – he *is* the "King of Beasts."

Proverbs 20:2 The fear of a king *is* as the roaring of a lion: *whoso* provoketh him to anger sinneth *against* his own soul.

(2) **"A greyhound."** (verse 31) **"Greyhound"** is translated from two Hebrew words that, taken together, describe a very slender animal, tightly girt around the waist, and very fleet. The greyhound hunts by sight rather than scent, has great speed, is agile in running, and has a proud, aloof appearance. This Egyptian dog has a very stately demeanor and was raced by ancient Egyptians.[778]

(3) **"An he goat."** (verse 31) A Bible-land shepherd looks after the goats much as he would care for a flock of sheep. Sometimes the goats belong to one flock along with the sheep, and in this case, it is usually a he-goat that is the special leader of the whole. The he goat walking proudly at the head of the flock represents leadership ability and symbolizes the flock's guide and protector.

Jeremiah 50:8 Remove out of the midst of Babylon, and go forth out of the land of the Chaldeans, and be as the he goats before the flocks.

(4) **"And a king, against whom *there is* no rising up."** (verse 31) A wise king, who walks in the light of Scripture, would be identified with the graceful, powerful appearance of these creatures. He would be strong because of God's presence, and he would be a loving protector of the people. Because of the leadership of God in his life, a wise king would be revered by the citizens.

Like the he-goat, the king is the flock's guide and protector. Unafraid and strong physically, the lion is symbolic of strength and confidence like any king or leader should be; and the greyhound symbolizes gracefulness, speed and purposefulness as he hunts – he is single-minded. These three traits are very admirable and noteworthy in a king. Weakness is shown in leaders who are afraid and negotiate with an enemy, who have their minds divided constantly between business and pleasure, and who are unconcerned for the needs and protection of their citizens. A godly king will guide the people in the right direction and support the law.

Proverbs 30:32 If thou hast done foolishly in lifting up thyself, or if thou hast thought evil, *lay* thine hand upon thy mouth.

Laying a hand on one's mouth is common body language today, and obviously was when Agur wrote this proverb. Humorous to watch, this unspoken signal has the same meaning that it did in Solomon's day: "I need to shut my mouth!" The need to be quiet could be based on one of two things:

(1) A foolish act such as **"lifting up thyself"** is to be prideful, a character trait that often manifests itself with improper words. Agur's advice is to block those damaging words by covering one's mouth with the hand. (It would indeed take a sagacious king to take on all the characteristics of the lion, greyhound, and he goat from verses 29-31 and NOT be full of pride.)

(2) A foolish thought that is perhaps evil causes a believer to **"lay thine hand upon thy mouth"** to keep those thoughts from being vocalized and causing harm. Job used the expression a couple of times – once when talking to his fair-weather friends and second when speaking to God after being shown his error.

Judges 18:19 And they said unto him, Hold thy peace, lay thine hand upon thy mouth, and go with us, and be to us a father and a priest: is it better for thee to be a priest unto the house of one man, or that thou be a priest unto a tribe and a family in Israel?

Job 21:5 Mark me, and be astonished, and lay *your* hand upon *your* mouth.

Job 40:4 Behold, I am vile; what shall I answer thee? I will lay mine hand upon my mouth.

> **Proverbs 30:33** Surely the churning of milk bringeth forth butter, and the wringing of the nose bringeth forth blood: so the forcing of wrath bringeth forth strife.

By the time a person has reached adulthood, he should have realized, through experience or observation, that even a person known to be peaceable, *if pressured enough*, will eventually strike back. It is as natural a process as producing butter from churned milk and blood from a twisted nose.

> **"Churning … wringing … forcing** - In the Hebrew text it is one and the same word. 'The pressure of milk produces curds, the pressure of the nose produces blood, the pressure of wrath (i. e., brooding over and, as it were, condensing it) produces strife.'"[779]

Butter is eventually extracted from milk by the intentional process of persistent churning. In ancient Israel, "cheese was made by placing milk in a bag made out of animal skin. The bag was hung out in the sun and pushed back and forth. The bag's skin of the bag contained an enzyme that, when heated and shaken, caused the milk to sour and separate into its two parts, fat (curds or cheese) and water (whey). The whey could be drunk and the curds eaten or stored for future consumption. The cheese has a buttery texture and flavor."[780] This process does not happen unwittingly or instantaneously but is a purposeful act. Just as making butter is an intentional act, to grab a person by the nose and twist it is an intentional act that will bring forth blood given that there is enough pressure applied and the nose twisted far enough. Agur closes out his writing by illustrating the fact that strife is **"brought forth"** (drawn from a person) as a result of forcing him to become angry – a purposeful act carried out intentionally through foolishness or unintentionally through ignorance.

> 2Corinthians 13:11 Finally, brethren, farewell. Be perfect, be of good comfort, be of one mind, live in peace; and the God of love and peace shall be with you.
>
> Galatians 5:22-23 But the fruit of the Spirit is love, joy, peace, longsuffering, gentleness, goodness, faith, Meekness, temperance: against such there is no law.
>
> Philippians 4:7 And the peace of God, which passeth all understanding, shall keep your hearts and minds through Christ Jesus.
>
> James 3:16-18 For where envying and strife *is*, there *is* confusion and every evil work. But the wisdom that is from above is first pure, then peaceable, gentle, *and* easy to be intreated, full of mercy and good fruits, without partiality, and without hypocrisy. And the fruit of righteousness is sown in peace of them that make peace.

CHAPTER THIRTY-ONE

> **CHAPTER 31:1** The words of king Lemuel, the prophecy that his mother taught him.

In the previous chapter, the heart of a man who loved God and believed His word was presented. This chapter shows the life and whole-hearted dedication of a godly woman. Both chapters are a fitting summation of the teachings of the Book of Proverbs revealing how blessed believers would be if they followed these two examples.

"The words of king Lemuel." Nothing is known about Lemuel other than what is written in verses 1 and 4 of this chapter; however, notice that "king" is not capitalized before Lemuel in verse one. (Ordinarily, a title before a name is capitalized, such as "Queen Mary.") **"Lemuel,"** which signifies "one *of* or *from God* or belonging to God,"[781] is similar to the meaning of **Jedidiah** ("beloved of God"), a name for Solomon given to him by God through the prophet Nathan. Like "Lemuel," Jedidiah is also found only in one chapter of the Bible.

> 2 Samuel 12:25 And he sent by the hand of Nathan the prophet; and he called his name Jedidiah, because of the LORD.

> "The idea is this: Nathan came to David according to Jehovah's instructions, and gave Solomon the name *Jedidiah* for Jehovah's sake, i.e., because Jehovah loved him. The giving of such a name was a practical declaration on the part of Jehovah that He loved Solomon ...*Jedidiah*, therefore, was not actually adopted as Solomon's name."[782]

In the Book of Ecclesiastes, Solomon calls himself "the Preacher" *[which means "collector (of sentences), preacher, public speaker, speaker in an assembly]. Solomon apparently liked to use names for himself, other than Solomon, in his writings.* Notice that the Apostle John also maintains this practice of not naming himself in the Gospel of John (19:6, 21:7, 21:20), where he calls himself "the disciple whom Jesus loved." He calls himself "the elder" in 2nd and 3rd John but identifies himself by his name "John" in Revelation 1:1.

"The prophecy that his mother taught him." In this verse, **"prophecy"** was "an utterance" delivered because of the burdened mother's foresight of sins that her son would face or is facing. Webster gives the first definition of "prophecy" as "a declaration of something to come"; but cites Proverbs 31 specifically as having a secondary meaning: "preaching; public interpretation of Scripture; exhortation or instruction. Proverbs 31."[783]

The word **"prophecy"** is used only twice in the Book of Proverbs (Proverbs 30:1; 31:1), and both times with the same meaning of "an utterance" rather than a foretelling of future events. The queen mother's prophecy or burden comprises the first nine verses of this chapter. There can be no argument that the loving mother's burden for her son, resulting in warnings contained in these nine verses, portrays a cherished and beloved lady (and queen mother) who is totally opposite of the "strange woman" seen throughout the Book of Proverbs, who ruins the lives of her victims and often brings them to poverty. The queen mother's instruction is in total agreement with Solomon's purpose for the Book of Proverbs.

> Proverbs 1:2-4 To know wisdom and instruction; to perceive the words of understanding; To receive the instruction of wisdom, justice, and judgment, and equity; To give subtilty to the simple, to the young man knowledge and discretion.

The Book of Proverbs usually pictures a father addressing his sons. Solomon often referred to the learners as "My son" and "Ye children." Twice, however, the father refers to the mother's instruction:

> Proverbs 1:8-9 My son, hear the instruction of thy father, and forsake not the law of thy mother: For they *shall be* an ornament of grace unto thy head, and chains about thy neck.
> Proverbs 6:20-21 My son, keep thy father's commandment, and forsake not the law of thy mother: Bind them continually upon thine heart, *and* tie them about thy neck.

There are no greater or more effective teachers than godly and loving parents, especially a mother who begins instruction with the baby in her arms. Notice the meticulous learning process described in Isaiah 28:10 – "For precept must be upon precept, precept upon precept; line upon line, line upon line; here a little, and there a little."

> **Proverbs 31:2** What, my son? and what, the son of my womb? and what, the son of my vows?

Something is wrong! By repeatedly asking **"What?"** the mother was declaring in today's language "What in the world is going on with you?" There is no way of knowing the son's age; however, the reader cannot be wrong in assuming that he is old enough to be taught the mature subjects of women and wine. But before addressing his foolish behavior in these areas, the mother proclaims her *right to interfere* by asserting the facts that he is **her son, the son of her womb and the son of her vows.** She gets his attention with this verse and then in verses 3 through 9 addresses the issues specifically. Obviously the son has "lost his compass." He is not thinking and acting with the wisdom previously instilled within him by his mother and father, but rather is behaving as a fool who has laid aside proper relationships with both women and wine; and his ability to make good judgments is questionable.

Because of the Lord's favor, she knew king Lemuel must exercise wisdom in every aspect of his life!!

> Deuteronomy 7:6-8 For thou *art* an holy people unto the LORD thy God: the LORD thy God hath chosen thee to be a special people unto himself, above all people that *are* upon the face of the earth. The LORD did not set his love upon you, nor choose you, because ye *were* more in number than any people; for ye were the fewest of all people: But because the LORD loved you, and because he would keep the oath which he had sworn unto your fathers, hath the LORD brought you out with a mighty hand, and redeemed you out of the house of bondmen, from the hand of Pharaoh king of Egypt.

"The son of my womb" indicates he was her son, not by adoption, but the one birthed in her womb, and brought forth with the agony of childbirth. He was raised with tender care; and therefore it was her duty to give admonitions, and his to receive them; and what she spoke was from sincere and fervent affection for him, which she believed he would not despise.[784]

> "The question, which is at the same time a call, is like a deep sigh from the heart of the mother concerned for the welfare of her son, who would say to him what is beneficial, and say it in words which strike and remain fixed. He is indeed her dear son, the son whom she carries in her heart, the son for whom with vows of thanksgiving she prayed to God; and as he was given her by God, so to His care she commits him."[785]

"The son of my vows." Parents often make private, verbal and non-verbal, promises both to God and to individuals, and these vows may or may not be known to others while all is known to God. Being a godly woman, she desperately wanted her son to be wise, to have the mind of God.

> 2 Samuel 12:24-25 And David comforted Bathsheba his wife, and went in unto her, and lay with her: and she bare a son, and he called his name Solomon: and the LORD loved him. And he sent by the hand of Nathan the prophet; and he called his name Jedidiah, because of the LORD.

> **Proverbs 31:3** Give not thy strength unto women, nor thy ways to that which destroyeth kings.

Verses 3-9 contain the burden or "prophecy" on the subjects that Lemuel's mother believes could be his downfall. Such wisdom as she imparts to him is important to a godly person but not to the fool. She deals with two sins spoken of many times in Proverbs: women and wine.

"Give not thy strength unto women." The strength of a person is determined at the primary level by his thoughts. For a king to give his **strength to women** would mean that he would concentrate on women and fail to think about the important matters of being a godly king. Sooner or later, to whatever a person gives his thoughts, he also devotes his actions or **"ways."** Since Lemuel's mother, by experience and observation, knew the disruptive and destructive power of lust, her admonition is to not fall into the trap and thereby lose his strength of person.

Solomon himself had learned this great truth through negative experience and observation. *(See Time Line of Solomon's Life in the Appendix.)* Therefore, he admonished others throughout the Book of Proverbs to avoid having body and mind commandeered by the adulterous woman who entraps a simple man so that he never turns to God. Many men have become weaklings because of having had their minds and bodies taken into captivity by evil women.

Like every person desiring to be wise, the godly king should concentrate on the teachings of God, and He will lead in the way of righteousness. Lust has a way of filling one's mind and crowding out good thoughts.

Matthew Henry's interpretation of the mother's plea is paraphrased here:

> "'Give not thy strength unto women,' unto strange women. Her son must neither be soft and effeminate, nor spend his time in a vain conversation with women when he should be getting knowledge and despatching business, nor employ his mind (which is the strength of the soul) in courting and complimenting when he should employ his mind in the affairs of the government. Shun all adultery, fornication, and lasciviousness, which waste the strength of the body, and bring into it dangerous diseases. Remember what gave such a shock to the kingdom of David himself, in the matter of Uriah. Let the sufferings of others be your warning. Are those fit to govern others that are themselves slaves to their own lusts? It makes them unfit for business, and fills their court with the basest and worst of animals. Let none give their strength to that which destroys souls."[786]

> Nehemiah 13:26 Did not Solomon king of Israel sin by these things? yet among many nations was there no king like him, who was beloved of his God, and God made him king over all Israel: nevertheless even him did outlandish women cause to sin.

"Nor thy ways to that which destroyeth kings" is an introductory phrase for the upcoming verses that deal specifically with the abuse of alcohol and fixation on women. The king is, in verse three, receiving instruction from his mother on two things that will turn a sound mind into plastic and lead to destruction.

Proverbs 31:4-9   *It is* not for kings, O Lemuel, *it is* not for kings to drink wine; nor for princes strong drink:
5. Lest they drink, and forget the law, and pervert the judgment of any of the afflicted.
6. Give strong drink unto him that is ready to perish, and wine unto those that be of heavy hearts.
7. Let him drink, and forget his poverty, and remember his misery no more.
8. Open thy mouth for the dumb in the cause of all such as are appointed to destruction.
9. Open thy mouth, judge righteously, and plead the cause of the poor and needy.

Verses 4-9 comprise a single paragraph with the theme being that those responsible for making right (*righteous*) legal judgments are not to have their reasoning diminished by **"strong drink."** **"*It is* not for kings, O Lemuel, *it is* not for kings to drink wine; nor for princes strong drink: Lest they drink, and forget the law, and pervert the judgment of any of the afflicted."** (verses 4 and 5) These verses constitute a single sentence emphasizing that those in leadership (**"kings"** and **"princes"**), who are charged with the duty of making judgments in legal matters are to maintain clarity of thought so that they never misstate or misunderstand **"the law"** as it applies to situations brought before them. Because of that mandated clarity of thought and understanding of **"the law,"** *neither* **"wine"** or **"strong drink"** *is for them*. The following are examples from Scripture of leaders who foolishly yielded themselves to alcohol and suffered the consequences.

Elah - 1Kings 16:8-10 In the twenty and sixth year of Asa king of Judah began Elah the son of Baasha to reign over Israel in Tirzah, two years. And his servant Zimri, captain of half his chariots, conspired against him, as he was in Tirzah, drinking himself drunk in the house of Arza steward of his house in Tirzah. And Zimri went in and smote him, and killed him, in the twenty and seventh year of Asa king of Judah, and reigned in his stead.

Benhadad - 1Kings 20:16 And they went out at noon. But Benhadad was drinking himself drunk in the pavilions, he and the kings, the thirty and two kings that helped him.

Belshazzar - Daniel 5:1-4 Belshazzar the king made a great feast to a thousand of his lords, and drank wine before the thousand. Belshazzar, whiles he tasted the wine, commanded to bring the golden and silver vessels which his father Nebuchadnezzar had taken out of the temple which *was* in Jerusalem; that the king, and his princes, his wives, and his concubines, might drink therein. Then they brought the golden vessels that were taken out of the temple of the house of God which *was* at Jerusalem; and the king, and his princes, his wives, and his concubines, drank in them. They drank wine, and praised the gods of gold, and of silver, of brass, of iron, of wood, and of stone.

Ahasuerus' unseemly conduct to Vashti was doubtless caused by drinking. (Esther 1:9-11)

Herod ordered John the Baptist's murder at an ungodly feast. (Mark 6:21-28) The feast was surely (though not specified in Scripture) brought to a frenzy by the use of alcohol.

Priest and prophet "err through strong drink." (Isaiah 28:7; 56:12) A wise veto therefore is Scripturally established for the leader of the local church – he must be "not given to wine" (1Timothy 3:3; Titus 1:7).

Specifically mentioned in these verses (4-9) are the "**afflicted**," who were previously identified as the poor, the widow, the orphan, and anyone who could not defend himself. These especially need the protection of magistrates and judges whose understanding will not be perverted by an inebriated judge.

During the time of Solomon, the phrase **"the law"** spoke specifically of the law of Moses as it was the Hebrew justice system. The point of this passage is that drinking alcohol distorts good judgment. If the person drinking is in position to give a judgment concerning the guilt or innocence, well-being, and future of someone else, the judge should not have his judgment distorted because alcohol has confused and blinded him about the law – "**Lest they drink, and forget the law, and pervert the judgment of any of the afflicted.**"

"**Give strong drink unto him that is ready to perish, and wine unto those that be of heavy hearts. Let him drink, and forget his poverty, and remember his misery no more.**" (verses 6-7) At first glance, these two verses seem to take a diversion from the theme of the paragraph (strong drink is not for kings or princes), but after reading all six verses, one understands that they constitute a form of *irony* (which may be sarcasm) used to illustrate the travesty committed when "**kings**" and "**princes**" allow themselves to be duped by alcohol. The resulting corrupt judicial decisions leave the *afflicted* who is "**ready to perish**" and of *a heavy heart* with only one recourse. He is to (not seriously, but ironically speaking) copy the besotted judge and drink himself drunk to "**forget his poverty**" and "**remember his misery no more.**" The two verses seem to be pure irony intending to jar judges' thinking. Some other Biblical uses of irony, in the form of sarcasm, are listed below.

> 2 Samuel 6:20 Then David returned to bless his household. And Michal the daughter of Saul came out to meet David, and said, How glorious was the king of Israel to day, who uncovered himself to day in the eyes of the handmaids of his servants, as one of the vain fellows shamelessly uncovereth himself!
>
> 1 Kings 18:27 And it came to pass at noon, that Elijah mocked them, and said, Cry aloud: for he is a god; either he is talking, or he is pursuing, or he is in a journey, or peradventure he sleepeth, and must be awaked.
>
> 1 Kings 22:15-16 So he came to the king. And the king said unto him, Micaiah, shall we go against Ramothgilead to battle, or shall we forbear? And he answered him, Go, and prosper: for the LORD shall deliver it into the hand of the king. And the king said unto him, How many times shall I adjure thee that thou tell me nothing but *that which is* true in the name of the LORD?
>
> Matthew 7:3 And why beholdest thou the mote that is in thy brother's eye, but considerest not the beam that is in thine own eye?
>
> Matthew 23:24 *Ye* blind guides, which strain at a gnat, and swallow a camel.
>
> John 1:46 And Nathanael said unto him, Can there any good thing come out of Nazareth? Philip saith unto him, Come and see.
>
> "Drunkenness opens all the sanctuaries of nature, and discovers the nakedness of the soul, all its weaknesses and follies; it multiplies sins and discovers them; it makes a man incapable of being a private friend or a public counselor. It taketh a man's soul into slavery and imprisonment more than any vice whatsoever, because it disarms a man of all his reason and his wisdom, whereby he might be cured, and, therefore, commonly it grows upon him with age; a drunkard being still more a fool and less a man."[787]

Please note several rebuking passages from Proverbs concerning alcohol.

> Proverbs 20:1 Wine is a mocker, strong drink is raging: and whosoever is deceived thereby is not wise.
>
> Proverbs 21:17 He that loveth pleasure shall be a poor man: he that loveth wine and oil shall not be rich.
>
> Proverbs 23:29-35 Who hath woe? who hath sorrow? who hath contentions? who hath babbling? who hath wounds without cause? who hath redness of eyes? They that tarry long at the wine; they that go to seek mixed wine. Look not thou upon the wine when it is red, when it giveth his colour in the cup, when it moveth itself aright. At the last it biteth like a serpent, and stingeth like an adder. Thine eyes shall behold strange women, and thine heart shall utter perverse things. Yea, thou shalt be as he that lieth down in the midst of the sea, or as he that lieth upon the top of a mast. They have stricken me, shalt thou say, and I was not sick; they have beaten me, and I felt it not: when shall I awake? I will seek it yet again.

"**Open thy mouth for the dumb in the cause of all such as are appointed to destruction. Open thy mouth, judge righteously, and plead the cause of the poor and needy.**" (verses 8-9) These verses return to the central theme of *making righteous judgments* with another mandate to *speak up with righteous clarity*. Stated twice for emphasis, "**open thy mouth**" demands that the "**dumb**" (those who cannot speak for themselves) and the "**poor and needy**" are properly represented. The age-old problem of the rich getting special care and the poor getting shoved aside is opposed by God in numerous Scripture references. The judge, who is among the "**princes**," is to speak "**righteously**" for those who cannot speak for themselves and are at the court's mercy. They are to be given proper and honest judgment by a sober and godly prince.

The command to "**judge righteously**" is close to God's heart and is found in several places in Scripture:

> Leviticus 19:15 Ye shall do no unrighteousness in judgment: thou shalt not respect the person of the poor, nor honour the person of the mighty: but in righteousness shalt thou judge thy neighbour.

Deuteronomy 1:16-17 And I charged your judges at that time, saying, Hear the causes between your brethren, and judge righteously between every man and his brother, and the stranger that is with him. Ye shall not respect persons in judgment; but ye shall hear the small as well as the great; ye shall not be afraid of the face of man; for the judgment is God's: and the cause that is too hard for you, bring it unto me, and I will hear it.

Job 29:12-16 Because I delivered the poor that cried, and the fatherless, and him that had none to help him. The blessing of him that was ready to perish came upon me: and I caused the widow's heart to sing for joy. I put on righteousness, and it clothed me: my judgment was as a robe and a diadem. I was eyes to the blind, and feet was I to the lame. I was a father to the poor: and the cause which I knew not I searched out.

Isaiah 1:17 Learn to do well; seek judgment, relieve the oppressed, judge the fatherless, plead for the widow.

Jeremiah 22:16 He judged the cause of the poor and needy; then it was well with him: was not this to know me? saith the LORD.

John 7:24 Judge not according to the appearance, but judge righteous judgment.

INTRODUCTION TO VERSES 10-31:

Verses 10 through 31 of this insightful chapter provide a beautiful poem that shows the benefits of marrying **"a virtuous woman."** Although the queen mother had previously (verse 3) admonished her son *against giving his strength to women*, this portion of the chapter describes a woman to whom he can and should give his strength – *if he can find and marry her*. Such an excellent example is she that the descriptive verses were put into Hebrew acrostic form, "each beginning with a consecutive letter of the Hebrew alphabet: Proverbs 31:10 (*aleph*); 31:11 (*beth*); 31:12 (*gimel*) and so on to the end of the chapter, the last verse of which has the letter (*tau*)."[788] *Pulpit Commentary* and others believe that the acrostic form was used to facilitate memorization, as were some of the Psalms and parts of Lamentations.

This beautiful portion of Scripture encourages men to seek more than a pretty face when they look for a wife. It contains the identifying traits of a woman who fears the Lord; while, at the same time, teaches ladies to be their best for God. It provides Scriptural evidence that a lady *can* utilize her talents by putting them to the use that God intended. Also, these verses comprise a Scriptural example showing that a lady can be a *"keeper at home"* and, at the same time, a business woman for the good of the household. This Scripture "praises the everyday achievements of a wealthy Jewish wife – a woman who keeps her household functioning day and night by buying, trading, investing, planting, sewing, spindling, managing servants, extending charity, providing food for the family, and preparing for each season."[789] Her actions are evidence of wisdom founded on an awesome respect for God. She loves and respects her husband, respectfully interacts with all ranks of people, and she wisely understands the relationship of God's creation to her life. She has a personal relationship with God.

The weekly Jewish Sabbath (*Shabbath* - Day of Rest - Exodus 16:23) begins with supper Friday at sundown and ends Saturday at sundown. Before the opening *Shabbath* prayer said for the meal, many modern Jewish families chant, sing or recite the *Eshet Hayhil [which the King James Bible translates into "a virtuous woman," and Israelis translate "woman of valor"]* in honor of the wife or mother or *Eshet Hayhil's* in general.[790] Not only is the family praising the woman, but the husband is encouraging her to live a purposeful life that would reflect the Lord. Where her life matched the traits sung about in the poem, she was encouraged. In areas where she was lacking, she was exhorted. Along with the weekly hearing of the poem, the family was reminded of the value and joy a godly woman can bring to their lives and to their home.

> Go to https://www.youtube.com/watch?v=yh-JCjOraTs to hear a rendition of the *Eshet Hayhil* in Hebrew.

Proverbs 31:10 *Aleph* Who can find a virtuous woman? for her price *is* far above rubies.

"Who can find a virtuous woman?" "'Virtuous woman' is translated from the Hebrew expression *ishshah chayil* which means "woman of force," "woman of valor," "virtuous woman." (NOTE: Adam Clark and others refer to the "virtuous woman" as "*esheth chayil*."[791]) The expression combines the ideas of moral goodness and bodily vigor and activity.[792]

NOTE: Over the centuries, the meaning of the word "virtuous" has narrowed considerably. According to the Internet dictionary, Mirriam-webster.com, the meaning of "virtuous" is "conforming to a high standard of morality, righteous." Obviously, the current meaning inadequately represents only a portion of the original definition that includes power and bodily strength. (See additional NOTE for more detail on page 598.)

The Bible names one woman specifically as an *eshet hayhil*. In Ruth 3:11, Boaz describes Ruth, " And now, my daughter, fear not; I will do to thee all that thou requirest: *for all the city of my people doth know that thou art a virtuous woman [eshet hayhil]."*

The *representation* of the virtuous woman presented in Proverbs 31 is *upright, God-fearing, economical, wise, strong, profitable to her husband, and careful for her family.* Previous verses in Proverbs gave characteristics of a wise woman, but none of the details contained in this chapter.

> Proverbs 12:4 A virtuous woman *is* a crown to her husband: but she that maketh ashamed *is* as rottenness in his bones.
> Proverbs 18:22 Whoso findeth a wife findeth a good thing, and obtaineth favour of the LORD.
> Proverbs 19:24 House and riches are the inheritance of fathers: and a prudent wife is from the LORD.
> Proverbs 14:1 Every wise woman buildeth her house: but the foolish plucketh it down with her hands.

The question of who can find a virtuous woman does not suggest that such women are nonexistent; but that they should be admired because they, like virtuous, noble, strong, God-fearing, industrious men, are rare and precious.

"For her price *is* far above rubies." Like the wisdom she epitomizes, the *eshet chayil* is more valuable than rubies. Notice how "wisdom" is described in the Book of Proverbs with the same word that describes the value of this God-fearing woman.

> Proverbs 3:13-15 Happy *is* the man *that* findeth wisdom, and the man *that* getteth understanding. For the merchandise of it *is* better than the merchandise of silver, and the gain thereof than fine gold. She *is* more precious than rubies: and all the things thou canst desire are not to be compared unto her.
> Proverbs 8:11 For wisdom is better than rubies; and all the things that may be desired are not to be compared to it.

> "Let a man ask himself what would be the worth to his heart, to his home, to his children, to society, of such a woman as is described here... the woman that every woman would be if she only feared God, loved His word, imbibed His Spirit, and molded her character upon His most blessed teachings..."

> The Bible, which is the great reservoir of the rights of man is also the storehouse of the rights of woman. Woman's Magna Charta is the word of God. It teaches us to honour woman; it warns every man that if he degrades woman he degrades himself, and that everywhere man rises as he lifts woman up.... It is not every woman whose price is "far above rubies."

> ... The husband is the head of the household; but a wife's position does not imply inferiority. She is her husband's companion in life and for life, to be regarded by him as his equal. The husband is the bread-winner, the wife is the bread-keeper and distributor. In all the affairs of domestic life the wife should maintain her position and influence. She should insure her authority by proving her ability to do what the office of a wife demands.

> Never for a moment permit your husband to feel that he may not trust the concerns of home to your care. Act in such a way that instinctively he will know his property, his honour, his happiness, are safe in your hands." [793]

To the Hebrew, the word **"price"** meant value as well as the cost of merchandise. This passage is not implying that a wife is a costly purchase for a man (in fact, the bride's family usually gave a dowery to her husband); but it is a beautiful expression of how much a "virtuous woman" is really worth to her husband and children. Certainly the godly woman who loves the Lord and takes care of the family is valued "far above rubies," just as wisdom has immeasurable value. *(See verses above.)*

Proverbs 31:11 ***Beth*** The heart of her husband doth safely trust in her, so that he shall have no need of spoil.

---

*This verse introduces the remainder of the chapter, which details the reasons for her husband's "**trust in her**."* The positive results of living wisely, as directed by God, are manifest in her life. **"Trust"** lies primarily in the fact that she is full of wisdom. The virtuous woman's life pleases God, and produces gain (in every manner); therefore, she can be trusted, and there is **"no need of spoil"** or plunder such as by taking property from others. Even if her husband were called to be part of an army to defend the nation, he would need to take no "spoil" from the enemy. He already has more of everything than he can use – thanks to God-given wisdom acted out through both himself and his virtuous wife. Matthew Henry speaks about the trust her husband has in her:

> "She conducts herself so that he may repose an entire confidence in her. He trusts in her chastity, which she never gave him the least occasion to suspect or to entertain any jealousy of; she is not morose and reserved, but modest and grave, and has all the marks of virtue

in her countenance and behaviour; her husband knows it, and therefore his *heart doth safely trust in her;* he is easy, and makes her so. He trusts in her conduct, that she will speak in all companies, and act in all affairs, with prudence and discretion, so as not to occasion him either damage or reproach. He trusts in her fidelity to his interests, and that she will never betray his counsels nor have any interest separate from that of his family. When he goes abroad, to attend the concerns of the public, he can confide in her to order all his affairs at home, as well as if he himself were there. She is a good wife that is fit to be trusted, and he is a good husband that will leave it to such a wife to manage for him." [794]

> **Proverbs 31:12** *Gimel* She will do him good and not evil all the days of her life.

"She will do him good" refers to every action of the virtuous woman. The virtuous woman **"will do"** her husband **"good"** by dealing bountifully with him and pursuing his best interests. Her life is the picture of the "help meet" (or helper corresponding to him) that God intended woman to be.

Proverbs 18:22 *Whoso* findeth a wife findeth a good *thing,* and obtaineth favour of the LORD.

Because he and she are so reflective of each other, *whatever she says or does affects him*: an effect which may be physical, psychological, emotional, financial, or spiritual. Once married, neither husband nor wife is ever an individual again in the sense that they were before marriage. His actions reflect on her as much as hers reflect on him. People often repeat the saying, "the man is the head of the house, but the wife is the neck that turns the head." That may sound humorous, but the fact is that whether or not the wife is content has an overwhelming effect on his satisfaction with her and with his own life in general. A companion quip is "If Mamma ain't *[sic]* happy, ain't *[sic]* nobody happy," and this saying is also humorous but absolutely true. Every wife would probably add "If Poppa ain't *[sic]* happy, ain't *[sic]* nobody happy," thus reflecting their closeness. A godly woman will always strive to do her husband good.

Genesis 2:18 And the LORD God said, *It is* not good that the man should be alone; I will make him an help meet for him.
Genesis 2:23-24 And Adam said, This *is* now bone of my bones, and flesh of my flesh: she shall be called Woman, because she was taken out of Man. Therefore shall a man leave his father and his mother, and shall cleave unto his wife: and they shall be one flesh.
Genesis 3:6 And when the woman saw that the tree *was* good for food, and that it *was* pleasant to the eyes, and a tree to be desired to make *one* wise, she took of the fruit thereof, and did eat, and gave also unto her husband with her; and he did eat.

Being identified as a **"virtuous woman"** signifies, within the meaning of the phrase, that she will **"do him good."** Because she is a wise child of God, she thinks good; therefore, she acts good. She has good motives and good intentions. *She will not do him evil* because she is opposed to evil. Should evil thoughts enter her heart, she will immediately oppose them *because she fears God*. And it is her awesome respect for God that laid the foundation for her to excel in being wise and consequently a "virtuous woman." She will never intentionally harm anyone, especially her husband.

Proverbs 31:26 She openeth her mouth with wisdom; and in her tongue *is* the law of kindness.
Proverbs 31:30 Favour *is* deceitful, and beauty *is* vain: *but* a woman *that* feareth the LORD, she shall be praised.

Because she is dedicated to God, she behaves in a manner that ensures that God is pleased with her actions, words, and thoughts. Her husband is the benefactor of being married to a dedicated woman of God. She is **"good"** for his peaceful home and his peace of mind. She interacts with everyone in a godly fashion so that he always knows that she has communicated righteously. She knows the importance of being honorable in every manner, including how she appropriately dresses herself and her children. She equally ensures that her husband has proper and adequate attire. She is good for him because she is prudently working *with* him to make certain that their reputations remain high in all matters of their lives. Because her walk with God is *not* temporary, "**she will do him good and not evil all the days of her life.**" She is not fickle but stable, living her life according to the principles laid out by the word of God. Her husband trusts her today, tomorrow, and for the duration of his life. She is indeed a wise and "a virtuous woman."

The "virtuous woman" stands in sharp contrast to the adulterous woman so often mentioned in Proverbs.

Proverbs 2:16-19 To deliver thee from the strange woman, *even* from the stranger *which* flattereth with her words; Which forsaketh the guide of her youth, and forgetteth the covenant of her God. For her house inclineth unto death, and her paths unto the dead. None that go unto her return again, neither take they hold of the paths of life.
Proverbs 5:3-13 For the lips of a strange woman drop *as* an honeycomb, and her mouth *is* smoother than oil: But her end is bitter as wormwood, sharp as a twoedged sword. Her feet go down to death; her steps take hold on hell. Lest thou shouldest ponder the path of life, her ways are moveable, *that* thou canst not know *them*. Hear me now therefore, O ye children, and depart not from the words of my mouth. Remove thy way far from her, and come not nigh the door of her house: Lest thou give thine honour unto others, and thy years unto the cruel: Lest strangers be filled with thy wealth; and thy labours *be* in the house of a stranger; And

thou mourn at the last, when thy flesh and thy body are consumed, And say, How have I hated instruction, and my heart despised reproof; And have not obeyed the voice of my teachers, nor inclined mine ear to them that instructed me!

Proverbs 23:27-8 For a whore *is* a deep ditch; and a strange woman *is* a narrow pit. She also lieth in wait as *for* a prey, and increaseth the transgressors among men.

Proverbs 19:13 A foolish son *is* the calamity of his father: and the contentions of a wife *are* a continual dropping.

Proverbs 21:19 *It is* better to dwell in the wilderness, than with a contentious and an angry woman.

Proverbs 22:14 The mouth of strange women *is* a deep pit: he that is abhorred of the LORD shall fall therein.

Proverbs 23:27-28 For a whore *is* a deep ditch; and a strange woman *is* a narrow pit. She also lieth in wait as *for* a prey, and increaseth the transgressors among men.

Proverbs 31:13 ***Daleth*** She seeketh wool, and flax, and worketh willingly with her hands.

Throughout this chapter, the "virtuous woman" is identified as wealthy, thus indicating that she would not have to **work with her hands** but obviously has **"willingly"** chosen otherwise. The work of her hands is honorable and rewarding. It *exemplifies* the expected *standard of excellence* for all the family and workers of her household. She *enjoys* the God-given physical and mental abilities whereby she can accomplish desirable goals. Profitable labor is valuable to a wise person because it is a *manifestation of learned wisdom*. She is diligent about her work and life and not slothful like the fool that Solomon spoke about. With excellence, she and her workers produce their own items necessary to carry on life, and excess items are sold for profit. Having exercised wisdom in every aspect of production, she has goods to trade and money to buy in the marketplaces. "She maketh fine linen, and selleth *it;* and delivereth girdles unto the merchant" (verse 24). A proud person probably would not work **"willingly"** *(with pleasure and delight)* with her hands because she would feel that physical work is beneath her. However, the virtuous woman proves that she is not proud, or else she would be resisted by God rather than favored by Him. (James 4:6)

"Wool and flax" were two valuable raw materials used to produce a variety of necessary items, including: linen for clothing, garments for the priests, and the attire of the saints.[795] In addition, flax was used for food and for flaxseed oil *(also called linseed oil)*. **Wool** was primarily used for outer garments.[796] It is also symbolic of whiteness and purity.

Proverbs 31:14 ***Hey*** She is like the merchants' ships; she bringeth her food from afar.

"Merchants' ships" bring loads of food from distant places, and she resembles them as she travels back from market with her wagons laden with traded and purchased goods. Her overflowing cargo is reminiscent of a ship sailing the seas with a full load. ***Like the merchants' ships,*** there is something majestic and powerful about the way she carries on her wise and holy life. God obviously blesses her with abundance.

Proverbs 31:15 ***Waw*** She riseth also while it is yet night, and giveth meat to her household, and a portion to her maidens.

The "virtuous woman" reveals strength of character, diligence, and an industrious lifestyle throughout these descriptive verses. Relentless in fulfilling her *self-imposed responsibilities*, she always performs with a spirit of excellence, always operates at a high energy level, and always is productive and profitable. It would be impossible for anyone to place demands on her that would be greater than she places on herself, so **"rising before daylight"** is of no surprise. Doing so matches her character. She could assign the tasks of feeding her household to one of her maidens, but she feels it is her privilege and her honor to have a wonderful family and to personally meet their physical needs. She enjoys the task, though it requires self-sacrifice. Providing her great joy, her children, and her husband are gifts from God. She enjoys seeing them around the table and feels honored to have prepared for them.

After the personal time of family breakfast, she turns to give **"a portion to her maidens,"** meaning that she assigns them their portion of work for the day and gives them their portion of food. She has likely considered the next day's work before going to bed and has formulated a plan. The day has started wisely. It will be pleasant, productive, and, most importantly, blessed by God.

> Proverbs 10:4 He becometh poor that dealeth *with* a slack hand: but the hand of the diligent maketh rich.
>
> Proverbs 12:24 The hand of the diligent shall bear rule: but the slothful shall be under tribute.
>
> Proverbs 12:27 The slothful *man* roasteth not that which he took in hunting: but the substance of a diligent man *is* precious.
>
> Proverbs 13:4 The soul of the sluggard desireth, and *hath* nothing: but the soul of the diligent shall be made fat.
>
> Proverbs 21:5 The thoughts of the diligent *tend* only to plenteousness; but of every one *that is* hasty only to want.
>
> Proverbs 22:29 Seest thou a man diligent in his business? he shall stand before kings; he shall not stand before mean *men*.
>
> Proverbs 27:23 Be thou diligent to know the state of thy flocks, *and* look well to thy herds.
>
> Luke 12:42 And the Lord said, Who then is that faithful and wise steward, whom *his* lord shall make ruler over his household, to give *them their* portion of meat in due season?

Proverbs 31:16 *Zayin*;   verse *17* *Heth*;   verse *18* *Teth*

16. She considereth a field, and buyeth it: with the fruit of her hands she planteth a vineyard.
17. She girdeth her loins with strength, and strengtheneth her arms.
18. She perceiveth that her merchandise *is* good: her candle goeth not out by night.

Verses 16-18 stress first the mental and then the physical strength that the virtuous woman exercised in adding an additional aspect of a business to her already heavy self-imposed workload. **Considering a field** involves more than a cursory evaluation. *Location* can be a serious issue, especially if excessive traveling is required for working the field or if it is near something like a city dump or someone who is disagreeable, making the property undesirable. *The soil type* can be good for some crops and bad for others. *Topography* has to be considered as to whether the land is flat or has hills and valleys – how much of it is valuable to grow crops is also important. *Water* available for irrigation is another serious consideration, and also, is the land prone to seasonal *flooding*? *The property's type of existing growth* will determine how much labor is involved in clearing the land and preparing it for the desired crop.

Since she is a "hands-on" person, this virtuous lady had to consider if she could devote the time to the many facets of making the property profitable. Then she had to consider if she had the business acumen to profitably culminate the purchase and the physical strength to ready the field, then plant it, work it, and finally harvest the grapes.

With all the above considerations, the wise and virtuous woman would have prayed and waited on God to see if He would give her peace of mind before purchasing the property. Her husband would also have to agree, and she would additionally have considered valuable outside counsel.

In other words, she prudently considers the price and actual value of the property, the purpose for which she would use it, and how productive it would be. She is not hasty in her decision because she knows what can happen if a decision is made hastily.

> Proverbs 19:2 Also, that the soul be without knowledge, it is not good; and he that hasteth with his feet sinneth.
>
> Proverbs 21:5 The thoughts of the diligent tend only to plenteousness; but of every one that is hasty only to want.

". . . and buyeth it." Being wealthy, as the virtuous woman was, she probably did not have to consider too deeply whether or not she had the money to spare. The consideration would be more on the line of "does God want me to have this, and will purchasing this property provide a good return of investment?"

> NOTE: Citing Proverbs 31, some commentators believe that "The rights of women in traditional Judaism are much greater than they were in the rest of Western civilization until the 20th century. Women had the right to buy, sell, and own property, and make their own contracts – rights which women in Western countries (including the U.S.) did not have until about 100 years ago... Proverbs 31:10-31 speaks repeatedly of business acumen as a trait to be prized in women (verses 11, 13, 16, and 18 especially)."[797]

However, other Scriptures seem to indicate that women had few rights after the fall. Probably what is true today was true nearly 3,000 years ago: a righteous man loved his wife and treated her with dignity and respect, honoring her for her skills and individuality. The godly man encouraged his wife to use her talents and enjoy life. In contrast, the foolish and ungodly husband would have made the household miserable and dysfunctional by suppressing her freedom and productivity.

"With the fruit of her hands she planteth a vineyard." No doubt, she had money that she had personally earned to buy the land and the rootings of the grapevines. This money was the reward or **"fruit"** of her diligence. The work she accomplished by clearing and planting the land was also the **"fruit of her hands."** She was wealthy, and she had the help of her maidens for this task, but the reader should consider her leadership qualities employed in having such a contented workforce. Some people are not leaders, and their workers have no respect for them, resulting in their workers and staff not being diligent about their work.

The phrase **"girdeth her loins with strength"** is a figure of speech called an *idiom* or *idiomatic expression*. Idioms are fixed expressions with a nonliteral meaning which cannot be deduced from the combined meaning of its actual words. **"Girdeth"** means to put on as a belt or armor. Perhaps this is a reference to Psalm 18:32 – "*It is* God that girdeth me with strength, and maketh my way perfect." and Psalm 93:1– "The LORD reigneth, he is clothed with majesty; the LORD is clothed with strength, *wherewith* he hath girded himself: the world also is stablished, that it cannot be moved."

> "Note: The *girdle* was a necessary part of the eastern dress: it *strengthened* and *supported* the loins; served to *confine* the *garments* close to the body; and to tuck them in when journeying. The *strength* of God was to his *soul* what the girdle was to the body."[798]

Because she had a great personal desire to purchase the property, plant the vineyard, and make it profitable, **"she girdeth her loins with strength, and strengtheneth her arms."** Both phrases "She girdeth her loins with strength" and "*she* strengtheneth her arms," constitute a double preparation and a double declaration of intent to accomplish her goals. She boldly made up her mind, beyond question, that her body would cooperate with her desire to do the work. She would meet the demands with will power.

"Strength," in verse seventeen, is the kind of strength that begins as *motivation in an individual's mind*. A lady who is seeking to please God in every fiber of her being will see the work at hand, the blessings to be obtained from doing the work, the exhaustion that will result from the labor, and the disappointments that she would face if the work is not accomplished. She sees the grime and backbreaking labor involved in planting the vineyard. She remembers how tired she was after staying up most of the night spinning the yarn, preparing the cloth, and making it into girdles to use as barter with the merchants. She learned that it was difficult to inspire her children to learn about God, to teach them to study, to teach them to work, and to teach them to "gird their arms (mind, body, soul) for the work that they would do now and in the future.

> 2Samuel 22:33 God *is* my strength *and* power: and he maketh my way perfect. *[See also Psalm 18:32.]*
> 1Chronicles 16:11 Seek the LORD and his strength, seek his face continually.
> 1Chronicles 16:27 Glory and honour are in his presence; strength and gladness *are* in his place.
> Nehemiah 8:10 Then he said unto them, Go your way, eat the fat, and drink the sweet, and send portions unto them for whom nothing is prepared: for *this* day *is* holy unto our Lord: neither be ye sorry; for the joy of the LORD is your strength.
> Psalm 18:2 The LORD *is* my rock, and my fortress, and my deliverer; my God, my strength, in whom I will trust; my buckler, and the horn of my salvation, *and* my high tower.
> Psalm 19:14 Let the words of my mouth, and the meditation of my heart, be acceptable in thy sight, O LORD, my strength, and my redeemer. *[See also Psalm 22:19; 27:1; 28:7; 29:11; 31:4;46:1; 62:7; 68:35;71:16; 73:26;105:4; 118:14; plus Proverbs 10:29; 24:5; 24:10; plus Isaiah 12:2;17:10; 26:4; 40:29;40:31; 49:4; plus Habakkuk 3:19, 2 Corinthians 12:9, Hebrews 11:11 and Revelation 3:8.]*

Only the "fear of the Lord" and the wisdom He provides when the believer turns to Him can give this great measure of strength.

"She perceiveth that her merchandise *is* good *[pleasant, agreeable, appropriate]*." Imagine God looking at His Creation" and calling it "Good." She has done and continues to do all the right things to ensure that what she has to sell is excellent. By God's grace, she has worked with a spirit of excellence.

"Her candle goeth not out by night" is an additional statement supporting the fact that she labors until the work is accomplished.

Proverbs 31:19   *Yod*   She layeth her hands to the spindle, and her hands hold the distaff.

Verse 19 provides an additional example of the industriousness of the virtuous woman, who is more than hard-working; she is also an example and guide to her family and her maidens. By her own example, she teaches them to live and to work wisely.

> "The spindle and distaff are the most ancient of all the instruments used for spinning, or making thread. The spinning-wheel superseded them in these countries; but still they were in considerable use till spinning machinery superseded both them and the spinning-wheels in general."[799]
>
> The distaff is "A stick on which flax or wool was wound ready for hand-spinning before the spinning-wheel came into use. It was held under the left arm, or stuck in the girdle, of the spinner. The fibers were drawn from it and twisted by the thumb and forefinger of the right hand. The thread so spun was wound on an oval reel, generally provided at its thickest part with a ring hanging from the thread and turning with it during spinning in order to ensure regularity of the movement. In Israel the use of the distaff was deemed the "wisdom" of women, (Yoma, 66b) and the articles manufactured were sold even in foreign countries."[800]

> To see a video of this operation go to https://www.youtube.com/watch?v=tQYdmRw-gHM]

It was customary for all the Jews, no matter what station in life, to have a handcraft or trade that they could use in times of necessity. As children, they were taught another trade. The learned Apostle Paul was trained to make tents – a trade he used to make money to support his ministry. Some wealthy children might have thought themselves "too good" to pick up the spindle and distaff. Certainly, the "virtuous woman" did not think it beneath her station to ***lay her hands to the spindle and distaff.*** She was eager to apply herself to work that would benefit her husband, her family, and others. Her work ethic is additional evidence that she was a "virtuous woman."

Proverbs 31:20   ***Kaph***   She stretcheth out her hand to the poor; yea, she reacheth forth her hands to the needy.

With the gesture of ***stretching out her hand***, she is expressing sympathy and readiness to help the poor – not just give the gift that is in her hand. Symbolically, the gesture says that her strong hand is able to help. The second clause, **"yea, she reacheth forth her hands to the needy,"** is a gesture whereby both hands are extended so that they can be grasped. *This verse is a word picture of sympathy reaching out to misery and poverty.* Without sympathy and willingness to help the poor, the trustworthiness and industriousness described through this chapter, and all of her work and productivity, might be of great value to her husband but not to God.[801]

Helping the poor is a commandment of God and an often-repeated, important theme in Scripture. Below is a sampling of Bible passages that address reaching out to the poor and needy.

> Deuteronomy 26:12-14 When thou hast made an end of tithing all the tithes of thine increase the third year, *which is* the year of tithing, and hast given *it* unto the Levite, the stranger, the fatherless, and the widow, that they may eat within thy gates, and be filled; Then thou shalt say before the LORD thy God, I have brought away the hallowed things out of *mine* house, and also have given them unto the Levite, and unto the stranger, to the fatherless, and to the widow, according to all thy commandments which thou hast commanded me: I have not transgressed thy commandments, neither have I forgotten them: I have not eaten thereof in my mourning, neither have I taken away *ought* thereof for *any* unclean *use,* nor given *ought* thereof for the dead: *but* I have hearkened to the voice of the LORD my God, *and* have done according to all that thou hast commanded me.
>
> Proverbs 19:17 He that hath pity upon the poor lendeth unto the LORD; and that which he hath given will he pay him again.
>
> Proverbs 22:9 He that hath a bountiful eye shall be blessed; for he giveth of his bread to the poor.
>
> Matthew 5:42 Give to him that asketh thee, and from him that would borrow of thee turn not thou away.
>
> Matthew 25:34-40 Then shall the King say unto them on his right hand, Come, ye blessed of my Father, inherit the kingdom prepared for you from the foundation of the world: For I was an hungred, and ye gave me meat: I was thirsty, and ye gave me drink: I was a stranger, and ye took me in: Naked, and ye clothed me: I was sick, and ye visited me: I was in prison, and ye came unto me. Then shall the righteous answer him, saying, Lord, when saw we thee an hungred, and fed *thee?* or thirsty, and gave *thee* drink? When saw we thee a stranger, and took *thee* in? or naked, and clothed *thee?* Or when saw we thee sick, or in prison, and came unto thee? And the King shall answer and say unto them, Verily I say unto you, Inasmuch as ye have done it unto one of the least of these my brethren, ye have done it unto me.
>
> James 5:1-4 Go to now, *ye* rich men, weep and howl for your miseries that shall come upon you. Your riches are corrupted, and your garments are motheaten. Your gold and silver is cankered; and the rust of them shall be a witness against you, and shall eat your flesh as it were fire. Ye have heaped treasure together for the last days. Behold, the hire of the labourers who have reaped down

your fields, which is of you kept back by fraud, crieth: and the cries of them which have reaped are entered into the ears of the Lord of sabaoth.

1John 3:17 But whoso hath this world's good, and seeth his brother have need, and shutteth up his bowels *of compassion* from him, how dwelleth the love of God in him?

Proverbs 31:21 *Lamed* She is not afraid of the snow for her household: for all her household *are* clothed with scarlet.

This verse speaks of the wisdom that the virtuous woman had in making proper preparations for the difficult time of winter (symbolized by the word "**snow**"). "**She is not afraid of the snow**" does not mean that she is not afraid of the snow itself as an element of weather; rather, it means that she is not afraid of the challenges to her family brought on by freezing conditions. She makes plans to meet those challenges. During winter, immobility for extended periods mandated that preparations be properly completed beforehand. This is another example of the virtuous woman's work being done with wisdom, to completion, and with a spirit of excellence. She prepares wisely, and trusts God for guidance.

"**For all her household *are* clothed with scarlet.**" Since dying is the final process in making a garment, if the coats had been undyed, they would *not* have had the completeness that the dying (**"scarlet"**) indicates. This process also indicated that the cloth had been deemed worthy of dying, and no expense had been spared. Dyeing large outer garments would have been difficult, painstaking, labor intense, and time-consuming, thus illustrating her patience and strong desire to be well-prepared for the cold. Also, she has provided all the household beautiful, expensive outer garments that they are proud to wear. No doubt they were admired by others in the community.

> NOTE: The word **"scarlet"** is used 43 times in the Old Testament, primarily for the materials used in constructing the tabernacle and the temple, as Exodus 26:1 illustrates. The scarlet cloth had a distinct color with symbolic meaning in the Temple and also in describing salvation. As seen in Isaiah 1:18, **"wool"** represents the purity resulting when sins are forgiven. The marginal notes of the King James Bible also indicate "double garments."[802]
>
> Exodus 26:1 Moreover thou shalt make the tabernacle *with* ten curtains *of* fine twined linen, and blue, and purple, and scarlet: *with* cherubims of cunning work shalt thou make them.
>
> Joshua 2:18-21 Behold, *when* we come into the land, thou shalt bind this line of scarlet thread in the window which thou didst let us down by: and thou shalt bring thy father, and thy mother, and thy brethren, and all thy father's household, home unto thee. And it shall be, *that* whosoever shall go out of the doors of thy house into the street, his blood *shall be* upon his head, and we *will be* guiltless: and whosoever shall be with thee in the house, his blood *shall be* on our head, if *any* hand be upon him.
>
> Isaiah 1:18 Come now, and let us reason together, saith the LORD: though your sins be as scarlet, they shall be as white as snow; though they be red like crimson, they shall be as wool.

Proverbs 31:22 *Mem* She maketh herself coverings of tapestry; her clothing *is* silk and purple.

With a pure heart and honest intentions approved by God, this godly woman decorated her bed with an elaborate tapestry throw, probably made of wool and ornamented with elaborate stitching. In making her family's bed coverings, she further showed her industriousness and a desire to please God and her husband. Godly people can enjoy the beauty and quality of God's marvelous provisions with joy and peace. In contrast to the virtuous woman's righteous behavior, the adulteress is said to entice the simple youth, without wisdom, to come to her beautifully decorated, but licentious, bedroom while her husband is out of town (Proverbs 7:16). What the virtuous woman uses to please her husband and God, the vulgar woman uses as another ploy to attract the foolish young man and further condemn herself with God.

> Proverbs 7:16 I *[adulteress]* have decked my bed with coverings of tapestry, with carved *works,* with fine linen of Egypt

"**Her clothing *is* silk and purple.**" According to Nelson's *Bible Dictionary*: "From the earliest times, trade existed between India and China on the one hand and India and the Mesopotamian valley on the other. So it is possible that Solomon's extensive trade could have brought silk to Israel."[803] Also, the term "fine linen" in Scripture refers to sheer, often almost translucent material of the expensive, finely woven linen worn by royal and wealthy people or the priests of the Temple. It is a glittering white color. The virtuous woman's clothing is attractive and fine-looking, representing her beautiful life and continual walk with God. Verse 25 states, "strength and honor are her clothing," [804] and thus her clothing reflects her character.

"Purple" material was used in the furnishings of the Tabernacle and the Temple. It was also used for king's clothing, the priests' garments, and for the wealthy's clothing. The most precious ancient dye, purple was made from the "murex shellfish found in the Mediterranean Sea. A total of 250,000 mollusks were required to make one ounce of the dye, which partly accounts for its great price. It was highly valued within the nation of Israel.[805]

> Exodus 26:1 Moreover thou shalt make the tabernacle *with* ten curtains *of* fine twined linen, and blue, and purple, and scarlet: *with* cherubims of cunning work shalt thou make them.

Proverbs 31:23 *Nun*   Her husband is known in the gates, when he sitteth among the elders of the land.

The phrases of this verse indicate that the virtuous woman's husband takes part in the judgment of legal cases in the gate of the city. Starting with the established truth, "a virtuous woman *is* a crown to her husband" (Proverbs 12:4), there can be no question that part of the reason **"her husband is known in the gates"** and *sits* **"among the elders"** is that his wife has a history of handling herself wisely in every manner possible. Indeed, he is known as "her husband" – as the virtuous woman's husband, with all her honor and dignity reflecting on him. Because she takes care of the merchandising, maidens, vineyard, meals, and clothing, he would certainly have more time to be available as an elder of the city. She honors her husband's leadership and edifies him personally. Because of their wise living, the couple *(as a couple)* would be recognized and appreciated by the city's population as having godly wisdom and being trustworthy.

Proverbs 31:24 *Samek*   She maketh fine linen, and selleth *it;* and delivereth girdles unto the merchant.

"Fine linen" refers to fine undergarments or shirts worn next to the body or as an outer wrapper. In the East, these are often made of a delicate and elegant texture which can be compared to transparent gauze. Fine linen was worn by persons of rank, especially the ladies. " **'Girdles'** were necessary articles of attire with the flowing robes of Eastern dress. The common kind was made of leather, as is the use at the present day; but a more costly article was of linen curiously worked in gold and silver thread, and studded with jewels and gold."[806]

The virtuous woman was able to produce more than her family needed and sell the surplus at the marketplace because, in her godly wisdom, she was energetic, industrious, of an excellent spirit, and keen about finances.

Proverbs 31:25 *Ayin*   Strength and honour are her clothing; and she shall rejoice in time to come.

In verse 17, the virtuous woman is described as girding **"her loins with strength."** In this current verse, **"Strength and honour"** are used symbolically as **"her clothing"** to describe her overwhelming character traits.

This statement reminds the reader of Proverbs 1:8-9: " My son, hear the instruction of thy father, and forsake not the law of thy mother: For they *shall be* an ornament of grace unto thy head, and chains about thy neck." To retain the instruction of one's father and the law of one's mother meant for their teachings to be obvious in the communication and conduct of the child. Obedient behavior gives the child dignity, honor and respect from family, friends and acquaintances. His life reflects the godly teachings of his parents and their teachings are as obvious as an ornament of grace around his head and decorative chains about his neck.

Likewise, the virtuous woman has the teachings of the word of God so deeply ingrained in her heart, life, and character that **"strength and honour"** are as obvious as outer garments.

People are often characterized with one or two words by others. Sad to say, when people are evil, such identifying words might reflect that character as "liar" or "cheat." For the godly person, those descriptive words can be such words as "godly lady" or "gracious lady." When the virtuous lady was approached or thought of by others, she was characterized with the words **"strength and honor."** She was honorable and made decisive steps to retain that honor in all her dealings both when conducting business and when dealing personally with individuals.

In addition, she was a godly, righteous person who sagaciously prepared for the future, both physically and spiritually. Furthermore, she **"shall rejoice in time to come"** or in the future, because of those preparations. She is confident that she has made adequate preparations for her household. The family has been brought up to honor God. They have both appropriate winter and summer clothing and adequate food. She is like the ant that the Book of Proverbs has already described.

> Proverbs 6:6-8 Go to the ant, thou sluggard; consider her ways, and be wise: Which having no guide, overseer, or ruler, Provideth her meat in the summer, *and* gathereth her food in the harvest.
> Proverbs 30:25 The ants *are* a people not strong, yet they prepare their meat in the summer . . .

She can look back over a life well-spent for the glory of God. She radiates confidence in God's promises that His providence and protection will be there during times of calamity and difficulties. She knows that she will rest with Him in the eternal home He has provided for those who serve Him. She is rejoicing!

> Job 5:19-22 He shall deliver thee in six troubles: yea, in seven there shall no evil touch thee. In famine he shall redeem thee from death: and in war from the power of the sword. Thou shalt be hid from the scourge of the tongue: neither shalt thou be afraid of destruction when it cometh. At destruction and famine thou shalt laugh: neither shalt thou be afraid of the beasts of the earth.
> Psalm 104:1 Bless the LORD, O my soul. O LORD my God, thou art very great; thou art clothed with honour and majesty.
> Psalm 112:7 He shall not be afraid of evil tidings: his heart is fixed, trusting in the LORD.

Proverbs 31:26 *Pey* She openeth her mouth with wisdom; and in her tongue *is* the law of kindness.

So much has already been written in the Book of Proverbs about the words of a person's mouth broadcasting the presence or the absence of wisdom, that it would be difficult to mention only some of the verses. (Fifty-three verses contain the word **"wisdom."**)

She would *not* be wise if her mouth were always in motion with frivolous or hurtful conversation; but when she does open her mouth to speak, she has something appropriate to say. She speaks in a discreet and prudent manner; she does not gossip, flatter, talk of trifling matters, or run others down because **"in her tongue *is* the law of kindness."** With deliberation, she has established rules for her speech so that unkind words are corralled and swallowed.

> "This *['law of kindness']* is the most distinguishing excellence of this woman. There are very few of those who are called managing women who are not lords over their husbands, tyrants over their servants, and insolent among their neighbors. But this woman, with all her eminence and excellence, was of a meek and quiet spirit. Blessed woman!"[807]

Proverbs 31:27 *Tsade* She looketh well to the ways of her household, and eateth not the bread of idleness.

"She looketh well to the ways of her household" indicates that she personally superintends everything done under her oversight. Her instruction is well-spoken and received, consequently the children and the servants respectfully follow the directives. If she does not physically see a deviating step, she senses it; and deals immediately with any deviation from the principles the family have been trained to live by. No serving maiden would have the astuteness that she has concerning what is right for her family, and she will not leave the oversight of this most important matter to anyone.

> Genesis 18:19 For I know him, that he will command his children and his household after him, and they shall keep the way of the LORD, to do justice and judgment; that the LORD may bring upon Abraham that which he hath spoken of him.

Joshua 24:15 And if it seem evil unto you to serve the LORD, choose you this day whom ye will serve; whether the gods which your fathers served that *were* on the other side of the flood, or the gods of the Amorites, in whose land ye dwell: but as for me and my house, we will serve the LORD.

Proverbs 14:1 Every wise woman buildeth her house: but the foolish plucketh it down with her hands.

2 Timothy 1:5 When I call to remembrance the unfeigned faith that is in thee, which dwelt first in thy grandmother Lois, and thy mother Eunice; and I am persuaded that in thee also.

To eat the **"Bread of idleness"** would mean that her life would be sustained by inactivity brought about by laziness, which has been proved in this chapter *not* to be true. (Bread is that which sustains life.) Instead, she consumes the bread of diligence; and her rich, godly life is maintained by such activity. Idleness has not been a factor in any part of her life. Her children all know that she is astute, never lazy, and never procrastinates. Misbehavior and deviations from acceptable standards are dealt with promptly and properly. She stands guard, ensuring that her household is following the ways of the Lord, the wise path.

Proverbs 10:4-5 He becometh poor that dealeth with a slack hand: but the hand of the diligent maketh rich. He that gathereth in summer is a wise son: but he that sleepeth in harvest is a son that causeth shame.

Proverbs 12:24 The hand of the diligent shall bear rule: but the slothful shall be under tribute.

Proverbs 13:4 The soul of the sluggard desireth, and hath nothing: but the soul of the diligent shall be made fat.

Proverbs 19:15 Slothfulness casteth into a deep sleep; and an idle soul shall suffer hunger.

Proverbs 20:4 The sluggard will not plow by reason of the cold; therefore shall he beg in harvest, and have nothing.

Proverbs 24:30-34 I went by the field of the slothful, and by the vineyard of the man void of understanding; And, lo, it was all grown over with thorns, and nettles had covered the face thereof, and the stone wall thereof was broken down. Then I saw, and considered it well: I looked upon it, and received instruction. Yet a little sleep, a little slumber, a little folding of the hands to sleep: So shall thy poverty come as one that travelleth; and thy want as an armed man.

Ecclesiastes 10:18 By much slothfulness the building decayeth; and through idleness of the hands the house droppeth through.

1 Corinthians 15:58 Therefore, my beloved brethren, be ye stedfast, unmoveable, always abounding in the work of the Lord, forasmuch as ye know that your labour is not in vain in the Lord.

Proverbs 31:28 *Koph*   Her children arise up, and call her blessed; her husband *also,* and he praiseth her.

Because she has consistently led her family, her children exhibit virtuous habits such as orderliness in their lives, thankfulness, and respectfulness. She has taught and modeled the "fear of the Lord" before them and the discipline of work. In addition she has shown respect for her husband and has given her children reason to respect her. "Her children arise up" indicates that they eagerly stand up and take every opportunity to "call her blessed." They realize that God has honored her with favor for her wise living. She is indeed blessed of God.

Being an honorable and honest man who appreciates his wife in every regard, her husband gives her credit for her great accomplishments and for making him **"known in the gates."** He makes sure that he properly *praises her.* She has been obedient to God, intentionally and carefully placing herself and her family under God's rewarding promises, and He has made her prosper accordingly.

"Proverbs 31:28-29 give the eulogium *[praise for the dead]* pronounced by children and husband. The former 'rise up' as in reverence; the latter declares her superiority to all women, with the hyperbolical language natural to love. Happy the man who, after long years of wedded life, can repeat the estimate of his early love with the calm certitude born of experience!"[808]

Proverbs 31:29 *Resh*   Many daughters have done virtuously, but thou excellest them all.

This virtuous wife excels in all the areas she puts her hand and heart to. She devotes time, energy, and skill to achieve excellence in every work for her family. Because of her great love for the Lord, she always does her best. She has no thought of being average or mediocre.

Today, virtuous means self-righteous, good, and chaste,[809] but in the 17th century, it meant strength and power and efficiency. The "virtuous woman" was an example of *godly wisdom in motion*, and she **excelled** because SHE WAS A POWERFUL EXAMPLE OF GODLY WISDOM.

> NOTE "***Chayil*** or *hayhil* (pronounced *khah'-yil*), means probably a force, whether of men, means, or other resources; an army, wealth, virtue, valor, strength, ability, activity, goods, might, power, riches, and worthy. *Brown-Driver-Briggs* adds "efficiency" to the definition. In the five times *chayhil [Strong's number H2428]* is used in the Book of Proverbs it is translated "virtuous" in 12:4 and 31:10; "virtuously" in 31:29; "strength" in 31:3; and "wealth" in 13:22.
>
> "Thou hast ascended above the whole of them – thou hast carried every duty, every virtue, and every qualification and excellency, to a higher perfection, than any of whom we have ever read or heard."[810]

The following is a summary of the qualities of the virtuous woman as given in verses 1-29.

(1) IS TRUSTED by her husband to not only be frugal and hard-working (verse 27b), but to develop her BUSINESS ACUMEN (buying and planting a vineyard and selling merchandise (verses 16-18 and 24) that helps to bring financial well-being to the household. (verse 11) The reasons for trusting her are given in the remainder of the chapter.
(2) DOES HER HUSBAND GOOD (verse 12) which implies that she is respectful to him, seeks his best interests, tries to please him, DECORATES to please him (verse 22).
(3) IS DILIGENT – works willingly (verses 13-15).
(4) HAS SPIRITUAL, MENTAL, AND PHYSICAL STRENGTH. She realizes the labor she has before her and develops her physical strength to handle it. (verses 16-18)
(5) GIVES TO THE POOR AND NEEDY. (verse 20)
(6) MAKES PLANS for future events (verse 21) and for proper and tastefully made clothing. (verse 22)
(7) RESPECTS her husband as do the elders in the gate. (verse 23)
(8) PRACTICES WISDOM. (verse 26)
(9) WATCHES OVER the speech and ways of the children and maidens to make sure they are following her Biblical teachings. (verse 27a)

Proverbs 31:30 **Sin, Shin** Favour *is* deceitful, and beauty *is* vain: *but* a woman *that* feareth the LORD, she shall be praised.

"Favour," originating because of a shapely body, status, relationship, or charming personality, **"is deceitful."** None of those attributes will give a woman the foundation for building a quality life or a praise-worthy long-term honorable relationship – and certainly not a family.

There is no solid foundation in **"beauty"** to build a life on, and it fades away with time. Also, sickness will impair the beauty of the face, as does suffering. Infatuation over beauty can quickly turn to dislike, disloyalty, dishonesty, or discontentment.

The solid foundation for quality living is the ***fear of God.*** That awesome respect for God puts a person on the right path to learn and live by God's direction and consequently be positioned where God can and will bless abundantly. Because the virtuous woman chooses the "fear of the Lord" as her steering mechanism for life, ***she shall be praised*** by God and everyone who knows her.

Proverbs 31:31 **Taw** Give her of the fruit of her hands; and let her own works praise her in the gates.

"Give her the fruit of her hands." **"Fruit of her hands"** is a phrase first introduced in verse 16 and restated here to describe that which she has produced with her life. **"Give her"** from God, directly and through others, the same as she has given – "the fruit of her hands." Let all the blessings that she has bestowed upon her family, friends, neighbors, and business acquaintances redound to her. Her excellent life deserves the same treatment that she gives to others. **"The fruit"** results from her entire presentation of herself as a wise woman, a righteous woman, a virtuous woman, a sympathetic woman, and a diligent woman. It includes all of her works, her words, and her willingness to help others and her whole family. **"Her hands"** are symbolic of her entire person.

"And let her own works praise her in the gates." She will receive *praise* **"in the gates"** because the entire community observes all the good that she does. Because she has affected everyone for good, the leaders will speak of her "in the gates," where her husband is known (verse 23). These statements compare easily to what Boaz said of Ruth, "for all the city of my people doth know that thou art a virtuous woman." (Ruth 3:11)

> The virtues of a noble wife are those that are extolled throughout the Book of Proverbs: hard work, wise investments, good use of time, planning ahead, care for others, respect for one's spouse, ability to share godly values with others, wise counsel, and godly fear. As Proverbs has stated repeatedly, these are qualities that lead to honor, praise, success, personal dignity, worth, and enjoyment of life. In the face of the adulteress' temptations mentioned often in Proverbs, it is fitting that the book concludes by extolling a virtuous wife. Young men and others can learn from this noble woman. By fearing God, they can live wisely and righteously. *That* is the message of Proverbs.[811]

> Psalm 128:1-6 A Song of degrees. Blessed *is* every one that feareth the LORD; that walketh in his ways. For thou shalt eat the labour of thine hands: happy *shalt* thou *be,* and *it shall be* well with thee. Thy wife *shall be* as a fruitful vine by the sides of thine house: thy children like olive plants round about thy table. Behold, that thus shall the man be blessed that feareth the LORD. The LORD shall bless thee out of Zion: and thou shalt see the good of Jerusalem all the days of thy life. Yea, thou shalt see thy children's children, *and* peace upon Israel.

ENDNOTES

NOTE: Unless otherwise stated, all Hebrew definitions are from BTSCTVM+, a combination of Francis Brown, R. Driver, and Charles Briggs, *The Brown-Driver-Briggs Hebrew and English Lexicon*, Joseph Thayer, *Greek-English Lexicon of the New Testament: Coded with Strong's Concordance Numbers*, and James Strong, *Exhaustive Concordance Of The Bible: Dictionary of the Hebrew Bible and the Greek Testament*, 1890, e-Sword 12.1.0.

Chapter 1

1. Charles Bridges, *Commentary on Proverbs*, 1906, e-Sword, 12.0.1.
2. Ralph Wardlaw, *Lectures on the Book of Proverbs*, 3 Vols, edited by his son, J.S. Wardlaw, 1838-1844, e-Sword 12.0.1.
3. Albert Barnes, *Notes on the Bible*, 1847-1885, e-Sword, 12.0.1.
4. Robert Jamison, A. R. Fausset, David Brown, *A Commentary, Critical and Explanatory, on the Old and New Testaments*, 1871, e-Sword, 12.0.1.
5. Ronald F. Youngblood, General Editor; General Editor of Original Edition: Herbert Lockyer, Sr., *Nelson's New Illustrated Bible Dictionary*, Thomas Nelson Publishers: 1986, 1995, e-Sword 12.0.1.
6. Noah Webster, *Dictionary of American English*, 1828, e-Sword 11.2.2.
7. H. D. M. Spence and Joseph S. Exell, *The Pulpit Commentary*, 1897, e-Sword, 12.0.1.
8. Barnes, *Notes*.
9. Joseph Benson, *Commentary on the Old and New Testaments*, 1857, e-Sword 12.0.1.
10. Barnes, *Notes*.
11. Charles John Ellicott, Ed., *A Bible Commentary for English Readers*, J. W. Nutt, "Proverbs," e-Sword, 12.0.1.
12. Webster, *1828 Dictionary*.
13. John F. Walvoord and Roy B. Zuck, *The Bible Knowledge Commentary*, e-Sword, 12.0.1.
14. Jeff A. Benner, "Parent Roots of Hebrew Words," as published in http://www.ancient-hebrew.org/vocabulary_parent.html.
15. Peter Pett, *Commentary Series on the Bible*, 2013, e-Sword 12.0.1.
16. Barnes, *Notes*.
17. Walvoord and Zuck, *BKC*.
18. John Gill, *Exposition of the Bible*, 1746-1766, 1816, e-Sword 12.0.1.
19. Spence and Exell, *Pulpit Commentary*.
20. Youngblood, Nelson's Dictionary.
21. Matthew Poole, *Commentary*, 1853, e-Sword 11.1.0
22. Wardlaw, *Lectures*.

Chapter 2

23. Spence and Exell, *Pulpit Commentary*.
24. Spence and Exell, *Pulpit Commentary*.
25. Pett, *Commentary*.
26. Matthew Henry, *Commentary on the Whole Bible*, 1708-1714, e-Sword 12.0.1.
27. Spence and Exell, *Pulpit Commentary*.
28. Spence and Exell, *Pulpit Commentary*.
29. Barnes, *Notes*.
30. Walvoord and Zuck, *BKC*.
31. Barnes, *Notes*.

Chapter 3

32. Benner, "Parent Roots of Hebrew Words," as published in http://www.ancient-hebrew.org/vocabulary_parent.html.
33. Spence and Exell, *Pulpit Commentary*.
34. Spence and Exell, *Pulpit Commentary*.
35. Webster, *1828 Dictionary*.
36. Youngblood, *Nelson's Dictionary*.
37. Barnes, *Notes*.
38. Spence and Excell, *Pulpit Commentary*.
39. Barnes, *Notes*.
40. Spence and Exell, *Pulpit Commentary*.
41. Hastings, James, Editor, *Great Texts of the Bible*, 1911-1916, e-Sword 12.0.1.
42. Hastings, *Great Texts*.
43. James Nesbit, Compiler and Editor, *The Church Pulpit Commentary*, (12 Vol.), 1908, e-Sword 12.0.1.
44. Gill, *Exposition*.
45. Spence and Exell, *Pulpit Commentary*.
46. Gill, *Exposition*.
47. https://sciencing.com/what-functions-umbilical-cord-4672809.html
48. https://www.medicalnewstoday.com/articles/285666.php.
49. Spence and Exell, *Pulpit Commentary*.
50. Spence and Exell, *Pulpit Commentary*.
51. Spence and Exell, *Pulpit Commentary*.
52. https://www.apmex.com/what-is-fine-gold
53. Henry, *Commentary*.
54. Spence and Exell, *Pulpit Commentary*.
55. Bridges, *Commentary*.
56. Spence and Exell, *Pulpit Commentary*.
57. Webster, *1828 Dictionary*.
58. Spence and Exell, *Pulpit Commentary*.
59. Henry, *Commentary*.
60. Charles Haddon Spurgeon, *Treasury of David*, 1869-1885, (from Psalm 121:3), e-Sword 12.0.1.
61. Barnes, *Notes*.
62. Barnes, *Notes*.

Chapter 4

63. Poole, *Commentary*.
64. Ellicott, Editor, J. W. Nutt, "Proverbs," *Commentary*.
65. Joseph Exell, Editor, W. Harris, *Proverbs*, in *The Preachers Complete Homiletical Commentary*, 1892, e-Sword 11.1.0.
66. Exell, Editor, Harris, "Proverbs", *Homiletical Commentary*.
67. Exell, Editor, Harris, "Proverbs", *Homiletical Commentary*.
68. Poole, *Commentary*.
69. Spence and Exell, *Pulpit Commentary*.
70. Spence and Exell, *Pulpit Commentary*.
71. Exell, Editor, Harris, "Proverbs", *Homiletical Commentary*.
72. Exell, *Illustrator*.
73. Spence and Exell, *Pulpit Commentary*.
74. Bridges, *Commentary*.
75. Exell, Editor, Harris, "Proverbs", *Homiletical Commentary*.
76. Spence and Exell, *Pulpit Commentary*.
77. Poole, *Comentary*.

Chapter 5

78. Barnes, *Notes*.
79. Adam Clarke, *Commentary on the Bible*, 1810-1826, e-Sword 12.0.1.
80. Walvoord and Zuck, *BKC*.
81. Spence and Exell, *Pulpit Commentary*.
82. Clarke, *Commentary*.
83. Henry, *Commentary*.
84. Jamison, Fausset, Brown, *Commentary*.
85. Clarke, *Commentary*.
86. Webster, *1828 Dictionary*.
87. Walvoord and Zuck, *BKC*.
88. Clarke, *Commentary*.
89. Gill, *Exposition*.
90. Walvoord and Zuck, *BKC*.
91. Gill, *Exposition*.
92. Spence and Exell, *Pulpit Commentary*.
93. Gill, *Exposition*.
94. Benson, *Commentary*.
95. Poole, *Commentary*.
96. Spence and Exell, *Pulpit Commentary*.
97. Benson, *Commentary*.
98. Clarke, *Commentary*.
99. Jeff A. Benner, *Ancient Hebrew Lexicon of the Bible*, 2006, e-Sword 12.0.1.
100. Spence and Exell, *Pulpit Commentary*.

Chapter 6

101. Poole, *Commentary*.
102. Bridges, *Commentary*.
103. Bridges, *Commentary*.
104. Bridges, *Commentary*.
105. Spence and Exell, *Pulpit Commentary*.
106. Spence and Exell, *Pulpit Commentary*.
107. Bridges, *Commentary*.
108. Bridges, *Commentary*.
109. Wardlaw, *Lectures*.
110. Gill, *Exposition*.
111. Spence and Exell, *Pulpit Commentary*.
112. Spence and Exell, *Pulpit Commentary*.
113. Bridges, *Commentary*.
114. Bridges, *Commentary*.
115. Spence and Exell, *Pulpit Commentary*.
116. Bridges, *Commentary*.
117. Spence and Exell, *Pulpit Commentary*.
118. *Merriam-Webster's Collegiate Dictionary*, Version 3, Springfield, Massachusetts: 2003.

Chapter 7

119. Matthew Henry, abridgment by George Burder and John Hughes, *Concise Commentary on the Whole Bible*, 1811, e-Sword 12.01.
120. Clarke, *Commentary*.
121. Clarke, *Commentary*.
122. Gill, *Exposition*.
123. Benson, *Commentary*.
124. Gill, *Exposition*.
125. Clarke, *Commentary*.
126. Spence and Exell, *Pulpit Commentary*.

127. Benson, *Commentary*.
128. Gill, *Exposition*.
129. Benson, *Commentary*.
130. Clarke, *Commentary*.

Chapter 8

131. William Robertson Nicoll and R.F. Horton, *Expositors Bible Commentary*, 1890-1891, e-Sword 12.0.1.
132. Henry, *Commentary*.
133. Spence and Exell, *Pulpit Commentary*.
134. Poole, *Commentary*.
135. Wardlaw, *Lectures*.
136. Bridges, *Commentary*.
137. Bridges, *Commentary*.
138. Spence and Exell, *Pulpit Commentary*.
139. Spence and Exell, *Pulpit Commentary*. Clarke, *Commentary*.
140. Henry, *Commentary*.
141. Benson, *Commentary*.
142. Spence and Exell, *Pulpit Commentary*.
143. Jamison, Fausset, Brown, *Commentary*.
144. Wardlaw, *Lectures*.

Chapter 9

145. Nicoll and Horton, *Expositors Bible Commentary*.
146. Johann Carl Friedrich Kiel and Franz Delitzsch, *Commentary on the Old Testament*, 1866-1891, e-Sword 12.0.1.
147. Walvoord and Zuck, *BKC*.
148. Benson, *Commentary*.
149. Nicoll and Horton, *Expositors Bible Commentary*.
150. Nicoll and Horton, *Expositors Bible Commentary*.
151. Jamison, Fausset, Brown, *Commentary*.
152. Spence and Exell, *Pulpit Commentary*.
153. Bridges, *Commentary*.
154. Barnes, *Notes*.
155. Spence and Excell, *Pulpit Commentary*.
156. Spence and Exell, *Pulpit Commentary*.

Chapter 10

157. Spence and Exell, *Pulpit Commentary*.
158. Poole, *Commentary*.
159. Poole, *Commentary*.
160. Bridges, *Commentary*.
161. E. W. Bullinger, *The Companion Bible*, 1909-1922, e-Sword 12.0.1.
162. Webster, *1828 Dictionary*.
163. Bridges, *Commentary*.
164. Pett, *Commentary*.
165. Bridges, *Commentary*.
166. James Orr, *International Standard Bible Encyclopedia*, 1915, 1939, e-Sword 12.0.1.
167. Poole, *Commentary*.
168. Gill, *Exposition*.
169. Walvoord and Zuck, *BKC*.
170. Henry, *Commentary*.
171. Pett, *Commentary*.
172. Spence and Exell, *Pulpit Commentary*.

Chapter 11

173. Clarke, *Commentary*.
174. Spence and Exell, *Pulpit Commentary*.
175. Webster, *1828 Dictionary*.
176. Spence and Exell, *Pulpit Commentary*.
177. Gill, *Exposition*.
178. Barnes, *Notes*.
179. Spence and Exell, *Pulpit Commentary*.
180. Clarke, *Commentary*.
181. Benson, *Commentary*.
182. Bridges, *Commentary*.
183. Henry, *Commentary*.
184. Calvin George, *KJV Marginal Notes*, (In honor of the 400th Anniversary of the Authorized Version 1611-2011), e-Sword 12.0.1.
185. Webster, *1828 Dictionary*.

Chapter 12

186. Walvoord and Zuck, *BKC*.
187. Bridges, *Commentary*.
188. Spence and Exell, *The Pulpit Commentary*.
189. Spence and Excell, *Pulpit Commentary*.
190. Exell, Editor, Harris, "Proverbs", *Homiletical Commentary*.
191. Wardlaw, *Lectures*.
192. Barnes, *Notes*.
193. Benson, *Commentary*.
194. Exell, Editor, Harris, "Proverbs", *Homiletic Commentary*.
195. Exell, Editor, Harris, "Proverbs", *Homiletical Commentary*.
196. Poole, *Commentary*.
197. Benson, *Commentary*.
198. Exell, Editor, Harris, "Proverbs", *Homiletical Commentary*.
199. Henry, *Commentary*.
200. Pett, *Commentary*.
201. Benson, *Commentary*.
202. Walvoord and Zuck, *BKC*.
203. Wardlaw, *Lectures*.
204. Walvoord and Zuck, *Commentary*.
205. Spence and Exell, *Pulpit Commentary*.
206. Pett, *Commentary*.
207. Barnes, *Notes*.
208. https://www.bible-history.com/biblestudy/marriage.html
209. Spence and Exell, *Pulpit Commentary*.
210. Gill, *Exposition*.
211. Clarke, *Commentary*.
212. Barnes, *Notes*.
213. Bridges, *Commentary*.
214. Spence and Exell, *Pulpit Commentary*.
215. Webster, *1828 Dictionary*.
216. Spence and Exell, *Pulpit Commentary*.
217. Bridges, *Commentary*.
218. Wardlaw, *Lectures*.
219. Bridges, *Commentary*.
220. Gill, *Exposition*.
221. W. Harris, *The Preacher's Complete Homiletic Commentary on the Book of Proverbs*, 1892, e-Sword 12.0.1
222. Clarke, *Commentary*.
223. Henry, *Commentary*.
224. Webster, *1828 Dictionary*.
225. Webster, *1828 Dictionary*.
226. Exell, Editor, Harris, "Proverbs", *Homiletical Commentary*.
227. Bridges, *Commentary*.
228. Webster, *Dictionary*.
229. Bridges, *Commentary*.

Chapter 13

230. Webster, *1828 Dictionary*.
231. Gill, *Exposition*.
232. Wardlaw, *Lectures*.
233. W. E. Vine, Merrill F. Unger, William White, Jr., *Vine's Complete Expository Dictionary of Old Testament Words*, Nashville: Thomas Nelson Publisher, 1968, 1908, 1985, 1986, e-Sword 12.0.1.
234. Henry, *Commentary*.
235. Bridges, *Commentary*.
236. Barnes, *Notes*.
237. Webster, *1828 Dictionary*.
238. Barnes, *Notes*.
239. Pett, *Commentary*.
240. Gill, *Exposition*.
241. Bridges, *Commentary*.
242. Exell, *Illustrator*.
243. Spence and Exell, *Pulpit Commentary*.
244. Henry, *Commentary*.
245. Bridges, *Commentary*.
246. Bridges, *Commentary*.
247. Benson, *Commentary*.
248. Henry, abridgment by Burder and Hughes, *Concise Commentary*.
249. Bridges, *Commentary*.
250. Webster, *1828 Dictionary*.
251. Exell, Editor, Harris, "Proverbs", *Homiletical Commentary*.
252. Walvoord and Zuck, *BKC*.
253. Benson, *Commentary*.
254. Spence and Exell, *Commentary*.
255. Henry, *Commentary*.
256. Henry, *Commentary*.
257. Exell, Editor, *The Biblical Illustrator*.
258. J.J.S. Perowne, Editor, *The Cambridge Bible for Schools and Colleges*, 1882-1921, e-Sword, 12.0.1.
259. Johann Carl Friedrich Kiel and Franz Delitzsch, *Commentary on the Old Testament*, 1866-1891, e-Sword 12.0.1.
260. Bridges, *Commentary*.
261. W. Robertson Nicoll, Editor, *Sermon Bible Commentary*, 1888-1893, e-Sword, 12.0.1.
262. Exell, Editor, Harris, "Proverbs", *Homiletical Commentary*.
263. Clarke, *Commentary*.
264. Spence and Exell, *Pulpit Commentary*.
265. Bridges, *Commentary*.
266. Exell, Editor, Harris, "Proverbs", *Homiletical Commentary*.
267. Bridges, *Commentary*.
268. Wardlaw, *Lectures*.

Chapter 14

269. Spence and Exell, *Pulpit Commentary*.
270. Exell, *Illustrator*.
271. Bridges, *Commentary*.
272. Exell, Editor, Harris, "Proverbs", *Homiletical Commentary*.
273. Gill, *Exposition*.
274. Henry, *Commentary*.
275. Ellicott, Editor, J. W. Nutt, "Proverbs," *Commentary*.
276. Bridges, *Commentary*.
277. Henry, *Commentary*.
278. Webster, *1828 Dictionary*.
279. Exell, *Illustrator*.
280. Spence and Exell, *Pulpit Commentary*.
281. Spence and Exell, *Pulpit Commentary*.
282. Kiel and Delitzsch, *Commentary*.
283. Adam Clarke, *Commentary on the Bible*, 1810-1826, e-Sword 12.0.1.
284. Gill, *Exposition*.
285. Exell, *Illustrator*.
286. Bridges, *Commentary*.
287. Benson, *Commentary*.
288. Bridges, *Commentary*.
289. Benson, *Commentary*.
290. Henry, *Commentary*.
291. Bridges, *Commentary*.
292. Barnes, *Notes*.
293. Youngblood, *Dictionary*.
294. Benson, *Commentary*.
295. Henry, *Commentary*.
296. Gill, *Exposition*.
297. Henry, *Commentary*.
298. Spence and Exell, *Pulpit Commentary*.
299. Barnes, *Notes*.
300. Barnes, *Notes*.
301. Youngblood, *Nelson's Dictionary*.

302. https://www.mayoclinic.org/healthy-lifestyle/stress-management/in-depth/stress-symptoms/art-20050987
303. Walvoord and Zuck, *BKC*.
304. Exell, *Illustrator*.
305. Bullinger, *Companion Bible*.
306. Poole, *Commentary*.
307. Gill, *Exposition*.
308. Spence and Exell, *Pulpit Commentary*.
309. Pett, *Commentary*.

Chapter 15

310. Gill, *Exposition*.
311. Benson, *Commentary*.
312. Henry, *Commentary*.
313. Henry, *Commentary*.
314. Henry, *Commentary*.
315. Bridges, *Commentary*.
316. Bridges, *Commentary*.
317. Henry, abridgment by Burder and Hughes, *Concise Commentary*.
318. Bridges, *Commentary*.
319. Spence and Exell, *Pulpit Commentary*.
320. Poole, *Commentary*.
321. Spence and Exell, *Pulpit Commentary*.
322. Henry, *Commentary*.
323. Spence and Exell, *Pulpit Commentary*.
324. Harris, *Preacher's Complete Homiletic Commentary*.
325. Bridges, *Commentary*.
326. Wardlaw, *Lectures*.
327. Harris, *Preacher's Commentary*.
328. Albert Barnes, *Notes on the Bible*, 1847-1885, e-Sword, 12.0.1.
329. Bridges, *Commentary*.
330. John Gill, *Exposition*.
331. Walvoord and Zuck, *BKC*.
332. Wardlaw, *Lectures*.
333. John Gill, *Exposition*.
334. Barnes, *Notes*.
335. Bridges, *Commentary*.
336. Henry, *Commentary*.
337. Barnes, *Notes*.
338. Henry, *Commentary*.
339. Henry, *Commentary*.
340. Benson, *Commentary*.
341. Bridges, *Commentary*.
342. Bridges, *Commentary*.
343. Bridges, *Commentary*.
344. John Gill, *Exposition*.
345. Henry, *Commentary*.
346. Exell, Editor, Harris, "Proverbs", *Homiletical Commentary*.
347. https://www.medicalnewstoday.com/articles/285666.php.
348. Bridges, *Commentary*.
349. Henry, *Concise Commentary*.
350. John Gill, *Exposition*.
351. John Gill, *Exposition*.
352. Exell, Editor, Harris, "Proverbs", *Homiletical Commentary*.

Chapter 16

353. Wardlaw, *Lectures*.
354. Henry, *Commentary*.
355. Bridges, *Commentary*.
356. Barnes, *Notes*.
357. John Gill, *Exposition*.
358. Bullinger, *Companion Bible*.
359. Harris, *Preacher's Complete Homiletic Commentary*.
360. Gill, *Exposition*.
361. https://bible.org/question/what-purpose-did-god-create-world, January 1, 2001.
362. Benson, *Commentary*.
363. Youngblood, *Nelson's Dictionary*.
364. Benson, *Commentary*.
365. Henry, *Commentary*.
366. Bridges, *Commentary*.
367. Bridges, *Commentary*.
368. Henry, *Commentary*.
369. Wardlaw, *Lectures*.
370. Barnes, *Notes*.
371. Youngblood, *Nelson's Dictionary*.
372. Pett, *Commentary*.
373. Wardlaw, *Lectures*.
374. Whedon, *Commentary*.
375. Barnes, *Notes*.
376. Kiel and Delitzsch, *Commentary*.
377. C.S. Lewis, *Mere Christianity* (New York: Simon & Schuster Touchstone edition, 1996), pp. 109, 111.
378. Bridges, *Commentary*.
379. Henry, *Commentary*.
380. Wardlaw, *Lectures*.
381. Gill, *Exposition*.
382. Spence and Exell, *Pulpit Commentary*.
383. Ellicott, Editor, J. W. Nutt, "Proverbs," *Commentary*.
384. Barnes, *Notes*.
385. Henry, *Commentary*.
386. Kiel and Delitzsch, *Commentary*.
387. Spence and Exell, *Pulpit Commentary*.
388. Clarke, *Commentary*.
389. Walvoord and Zuck, *BKC*.
390. Barnes, *Notes*.
391. Henry, *Commentary*.
392. Spence and Exell, *Pulpit Commentary*.
393. Spence and Exell, *Pulpit Commentary*.
394. Spence and Exell, *Pulpit Commentary*.
395. Spence and Exell, *Pulpit Commentary*.
396. Clarke, *Commentary*.
397. https://www.gotquestions.org/casting-lots.html
398. Youngblood, *Nelson's Dictionary*.
399. Bridges, *Commentary*.

Chapter 17

400. Benson, *Commentary*.
401. Spence and Exell, *Pulpit Commentary*.
402. Henry, *Commentary*.
403. Exell, Editor, Harris, "Proverbs", *Homiletical Commentary*.
404. Spence and Exell, *Pulpit Commentary*.
405. Barnes, *Notes*.
406. Pett, *Commentary*.
407. Kiel and Delitzsch, *Commentary*.
408. Henry, *Commentary*.
409. Pett, *Commentary*.
410. Walvoord and Zuck, *BKC*.
411. Barnes, *Notes*.
412. Bridges, *Commentary*.
413. Bridges, *Commentary*.
414. Pett, *Commentary*.
415. Bridges, *Commentary*.
416. Exell, Editor, Harris, "Proverbs", *Homiletical Commentary*.
417. Barnes, *Notes*.
418. Barnes, *Notes*.
419. Exell, *Illustrator*.
420. Walvoord and Zuck, *BKC*.
421. Bridges, *Commentary*.
422. Bridges, *Commentary*.
423. Wardlaw, *Lectures*.
424. Bridges, *Commentary* Spence and Exell, *Pulpit Commentary*.
425. Clarke, *Commentary*.
426. Perverse. Retrieved from https://www.dictionary.com/browse/perverse
427. Walvoord and Zuck, *BKC*.
428. Wardlaw, *Lectures*.
429. https://inspiredspine.com/signs-dried-spinal-disc/
430. Walvoord and Zuck, *BKC*.
431. Bridges, *Commentary*.
432. Spence and Exell, *Pulpit Commentary*.
433. Bridges, *Commentary*.
434. Wardlaw, *Lectures*.

Chapter 18

435. Bridges, *Commentary*.
436. Gill, *Exposition*.
437. Spence and Exell, *Pulpit Commentary*.
438. Spence and Exell, *Pulpit Commentary*.
439. Spence and Exell, *Pulpit Commentary*.
440. Henry, *Commentary*.
441. Bullinger, *Companion Bible*.
442. Bridges, *Commentary*.
443. Exell, Editor, Harris, "Proverbs", *Homiletical Commentary*.
444. Bridges, *Commentary*.
445. Spence and Exell, *Pulpit Commentary*.
446. Lewis, *Mere Christianity*.
447. Bridges, *Commentary*.
448. Benson, *Commentary*.
449. Bridges, *Commentary*.
450. Jamison, Fausset, Brown, *Commentary*.
451. Spence and Exell, *Pulpit Commentary*.
452. Spence and Exell, *Pulpit Commentary*.
453. Henry, *Commentary*.
454. Benson, *Commentary*.
455. Pett, *Commentary*.
456. Spence and Exell, *Pulpit Commentary*.
457. Walvoord and Zuck, *BKC*.
458. Clarke, *Commentary*.
459. Barnes, *Notes*.
460. Spence and Exell, *Pulpit Commentary*.

Chapter 19

461. Bridges, *Commentary*.
462. Harris, *Preacher's Complete Homiletic Commentary*.
463. Bridges, *Commentary*.
464. Barnes, *Notes*.
465. Spence and Exell, *Pulpit Commentary*.
466. Barnes, *Notes*.
467. Wardlaw, *Lectures*.
468. Barnes, *Notes*.
469. Wardlaw, *Lectures*.
470. Bridges, *Commentary*.
471. Walvoord and Zuck, *BKC*.
472. Exell, Editor, Harris, "Proverbs", *Homiletical Commentary*.
473. Barnes, *Notes*.
474. Henry, *Commentary*.
475. Spence and Exell, *Pulpit Commentary*.
476. Bridges, *Commentary*.
477. Gill, *Exposition*.
478. Bridges, *Commentary*.
479. Wardlaw, *Lectures*.
480. Webster, *1828 Dictionary*.
481. Benson, *Commentary*.
482. Henry, *Commentary*.
483. Bridges, *Commentary*.
484. Henry, *Commentary*.

485. Spence and Exell, *Pulpit Commentary*.
486. Kiel and Delitzsch, *Commentary*.
487. College Press Bible Textbook Series, David Hunt, "Pondering the Proverbs," 1983, e-Sword 12.0.1.
488. Benson, *Commentary*.

Chapter 20

489. Benson, *Commentary*.
490. Benson, *Commentary*.
491. Walvoord and Zuck, *BKC*.
492. Benson, *Commentary*.
493. Henry, *Commentary*.
494. Barnes, *Notes*.
495. Spence and Exell, *Pulpit Commentary*.
496. Henry, *Commentary*.
497. Gill, *Exposition*.
498. Benson, *Commentary*.
499. Alexander MacLaren, *Expositions of Holy Scripture*, 1904-1910, e-sword 12.0.1.
500. Kiel and Delitzsch, *Commentary*.
501. Spence and Exell, *Pulpit Commentary*.
502. Gill, *Exposition*.
503. Bullinger, *Companion Bible*.
504. Bullinger, *Companion Bible*.
505. Henry, *Commentary*.
506. Bridges, *Commentary*.
507. Henry, *Commentary*.
508. Henry, *Commentary*.
509. Henry, *Commentary*.
510. Barnes, *Notes*.
511. Bridges, *Commentary*.
512. Bridges, *Commentary*.
513. Henry, *Commentary*.
514. Henry, *Commentary*.
515. Henry, *Commentary*.
516. Spence and Exell, *Pulpit Commentary*.
517. Spence and Exell, *Pulpit Commentary*.
518. Benson, *Commentary*.
519. Spence and Exell, *Pulpit Commentary*.
520. Henry, *Commentary*.
521. Spence and Exell, *Pulpit Commentary*.
522. Bridges, *Commentary*.
523. Spence and Exell, *Pulpit Commentary*.
524. Spence and Exell, *The Pulpit Commentary*.
525. Henry, *Commentary*.
526. Hastings, *Great Texts*.
527. Youngblood, *Nelson's Dictionary*.
528. Henry, *Commentary*.
529. George, *KJV Marginal Notes*.

Chapter 21

530. Daniel Whedon, *Commentary on the Old and New Testaments*, published 1874-1909, e-Sword 11.2.2.
531. Spence and Exell, *Pulpit Commentary*.
532. Gill, *Exposition*.
533. Spence and Exell, *Pulpit Commentary*.
534. Webster, *1828 Dictionary*.
535. Spence and Exell, *Pulpit Commentary*.
536. Spence and Exell, *Pulpit Commentary*.
537. Barnes, *Notes*.
538. Exell, Editor, Harris, "Proverbs", *Homiletical Commentary*.
539. Bridges, *Commentary*.
540. Exell, Editor, Harris, "Proverbs", *Homiletical Commentary*.
541. Henry, *Commentary*.
542. Kiel and Delitzsch, *Commentary*.
543. Benson, *Commentary*.
544. Webster, *1828 Dictionary*.
545. Henry, *Commentary*.
546. Bridges, *Commentary*.
547. Bridges, *Commentary*.
548. Henry, *Commentary*.
549. Henry, *Commentary*.
550. Bullinger, *Companion Bible*.
551. Bridges, *Commentary*.
552. Bridges, *Commentary*.
553. Spence and Exell, *Pulpit Commentary*.
554. Spence and Exell, *Pulpit Commentary*.
555. Spence and Exell, *Pulpit Commentary*.
556. Spence and Exell, *Pulpit Commentary*.
557. Spence and Exell, *Pulpit Commentary*.
558. Spence and Exell, *Pulpit Commentary*.
559. Gill, *Exposition*.
560. Bridges, *Commentary*.
561. Bullinger, *Companion Bible*.
562. Spence and Exell, *Pulpit Commentary*.
563. Walvoord and Zuck, *BKC*.
564. Bullinger, *Companion Bible*.
565. Walvoord and Zuck, *BKC*.
566. Bridges, *Commentary*.
567. Bridges, *Commentary*.
568. Spence and Exell, *Pulpit Commentary*.
569. College Press Bible Textbook Series, David Hunt, "Pondering the Proverbs."
570. Henry, *Commentary*.

Chapter 22

571. Henry, *Commentary*.
572. Spence and Exell, *Pulpit Commentary*.
573. Bridges, *Commentary*.
574. Webster, *1828 Dictionary*.
575. https://www.psychologytoday.com/us/blog/beyond-words/201109/is-nonverbal-communication-numbers-game
576. Henry, *Commentary*.
577. Barnes, *Notes*.
578. Henry, *Commentary*.
579. Bridges, *Commentary*.
580. www.CompellingTruth.org
581. M. A. Cannon, "The Avoidance of Debt" as quoted in Joseph S. Exell, *The Biblical Illustrator*, 1900, e-Sword 12.0.1.
582. Walvoord and Zuck, *BKC*.
583. Bridges, *Commentary*.
584. Gill, *Exposition*.
585. Exell, *Illustrator*.
586. Henry, *Commentary*.
587. Spence and Exell, *Pulpit Commentary*.
588. Webster, *1828 Dictionary*.
589. Youngblood, *Nelson's Dictionary*.
590. https://museumofprinting.org/news-and-events/gutenberg-and-the-history-of-the-printed-bible/
591. Henry, *Commentary*.
592. Clarke, *Commentary*.
593. Walvoord and Zuck, *BKC*.
594. Benson, *Commentary*.
595. Bridges, *Commentary*.
596. Barnes, *Notes*.
597. Barnes, *Notes*.
598. Henry, *Commentary*.
599. Barnes, *Notes*.
600. Henry, *Commentary*.
601. Gill, *Exposition*.
602. Barnes, *Notes*.
603. Spence and Exell, *Pulpit Commentary*.
604. Jim Gilcrest as quoted on https://blog.bpir.com/human-resources/how-much-effort-do-you-put-into-your-work/ January 15, 2014.
605. Spence and Exell, *Pulpit Commentary*.
606. Spence and Exell, *Pulpit Commentary*.
607. Bridges, *Commentary*.

Chapter 23

608. Robert Hawker, *Poor Man's Commentary*, 1805, e-Sword 12.0.1.
609. Bridges, *Commentary*.
610. Gill, *Exposition*.
611. Spence and Exell, *Pulpit Commentary*.
612. Bridges, *Commentary*.
613. Henry, *Commentary*.
614. Exell, Editor, Harris, "Proverbs", *Homiletical Commentary*.
615. Bridges, *Commentary*.
616. Bridges, *Commentary*.
617. Bridges, *Commentary*.
618. Bridges, *Commentary*.
619. Walvoord and Zuck, *BKC*.
620. Wardlaw, *Lectures*.
621. Ellicott, Editor, J. W. Nutt, "Proverbs," *Commentary*.
622. Benson, *Commentary*.
623. Exell, Editor, Harris, "Proverbs", *Homiletical Commentary*.
624. https://www.iii.org/fact-statistic/facts-statistics-alcohol-impaired-driving
625. https://www.medicaldaily.com/alcohol-and-your-eyes-6-ways-excessive-drinking-can-impair-your-vision-406993
626. Timothy S. Morton, *The Treasury of Scripture Knowledge*, enhanced, 2010-2014, e-Sword 12.0.1
627. Summarized from https://www.thoughtco.com/what-is-fermentation-608199.
628. https://www.brainhq.com/brain-resources/cool-brain-facts-myths/brain-mythology/brain-myth-alcohol-kills-brain-cells

Chapter 24

629. Webster, *1828 Dictionary*.
630. Spence and Exell, *Pulpit Commentary*.
631. Gill, *Exposition*.
632. Gill, *Exposition*.
633. Spence and Exell, *Pulpit Commentary*.
634. Bridges, *Commentary*.
635. Barnes, *Notes*.
636. Exell, Editor, Harris, "Proverbs", *Homiletical Commentary*.
637. Barnes, *Notes*.
638. Gill, *Exposition*.
639. https://www.vocabulary.com/dictionary/fret
640. https://www.vocabulary.com/dictionary/envy
641. Walvoord and Zuck, *BKC*.
642. Bridges, *Commentary*.
643. Bridges, *Commentary*.
644. Benson, Commentary.
645. Henry, *Commentary*.
646. Henry, *Commentary*.
647. Henry, *Commentary*.

Chapter 25

648. Henry, *Commentary*.
649. Spence and Exell, *Pulpit Commentary*.
650. George, *KJV Marginal Notes*.
651. George *KJV Marginal Notes*.
652. Webster, *1828 Dictionary*.
653. Benson, *Commentary*.
654. George, *KJV Marginal Notes*.
655. Walvoord and Zuck, *BKC*.
656. Bridges, *Commentary*.
657. Spence and Exell, *Pulpit Commentary*.
658. https://en.wikipedia.org/wiki/Niter
659. Benner, *Hebrew Lexicon*.
660. Bridges, *Commentary*.
661. Gill, *Exposition*.
662. Barnes, *Notes*.

663. Benner, *Hebrew Lexicon*.
664. Wardlaw, *Lectures*.

Chapter 26
665. Gill, *Exposition*.
666. https://www.generations.org/devotionals/481
667. Youngblood, *Nelson's Dictionary*.
668. Gill, *Exposition*.
669. Bridges, *Commentary*.
670. Benson, *Commentary*.
671. Spence and Exell, *Pulpit Commentary*.
672. Barnes, *Notes*.
673. Wardlaw, *Lectures*.
674. Benson, *Commentary*.
675. Barnes, *Notes*.
676. Barnes, *Notes*.
677. Poole, *Commentary*.
678. Gill, *Exposition*.
679. Benson, *Commentary*.
680. Gill, *Exposition*.
681. Bridges, *Commentary*.
682. https://gracequotes.org/author-quote/philip-henry/

Chapter 27
683. Henry, *Commentary*.
684. Whichcote's *Sermons* as quoted in Charles Bridges, *Commentary on Proverbs*, 1906, e-Sword, 12.0.1.
685. Gill, *Exposition*.
686. Bridges, *Commentary*.
687. Robert Jamison, A. R. Fausset, David Brown, *A Commentary, Critical and Explanatory, on the Old and New Testaments*, 1871, e-Sword, 12.0.1.
688. Gill, *Exposition*.
689. Crabb's *English Synonyms* as quoted in James Orr, *International Standard Bible Encyclopedia*, 1915, 1939, e-Sword 12.0.1.
690. Gill, *Exposition*.
691. Benson, *Commentary*.
692. Bridges, *Commentary*.
693. Spence and Exell, *Pulpit Commentary*.
694. John Gill, *Exposition*.
695. Clarke, *Commentary*.
696. Benner, "Parent Roots of Hebrew Words," as published in http://www.ancient-hebrew.org/vocabulary_parent.html.
697. Webster, *1828 Dictionary*.
698. https://www.psychologytoday.com/us/blog/beyond-words/201109/is-nonverbal-communication-numbers-game
699. Henry, *Commentary*.
700. Henry, *Commentary*.
701. Webster, *1828 Dictionary*.
702. Bridges, *Commentary*.
703. Benson, *Commentary*.
704. Bridges, *Commentary*.
705. Spence and Exell, *Pulpit Commentary*.
706. Poole, *Commentary*.
707. Spence and Exell, *Pulpit Commentary*.
708. Henry, *Commentary*.
709. Bridges, *Commentary*.
710. Webster, *1828 Dictionary*.
711. Spence and Exell, *Pulpit Commentary*.
712. George, *KJV Marginal Notes*.

Chapter 28
713. Henry, *Commentary*.
714. Walvoord and Zuck, *BKC*.
715. William Smith, *Smith's Bible Dictionary*, 1863, 12.0.1.
716. Spence and Exell, *Pulpit Commentary*.
717. Barnes, *Notes*.
718. Spence and Exell, *Pulpit Commentary*.
719. https://www.christianpost.com/news/100-percent-of-christians-face-persecution-in-21-countries-open-doors-world-watch-list-2017-172850/
720. https://www.wnd.com/2012/09/persecution-of-christians-on-rise-in-u-s/
721. Barnes, *Notes*.
722. Barnes, *Notes*.
723. Webster, *1828 Dictionary*.
724. Bridges, *Commentary*.
725. Spence and Exell, *Pulpit Commentary*.
726. Jeff Benner, *Ancient Hebrew Word Meanings*, as quoted on https://nuggets4u.files.wordpress.com/2013/04/ancient-hebrew-word-meanings.doc.
727. Bridges, *Commentary*.
728. Benson, *Commentary*.
729. Spence and Exell, *Pulpit Commentary*.
730. Benson, *Commentary*.
731. Barnes, *Notes*.
732. Henry, *Commentary*.
733. Bridges, *Commentary*.

Chapter 29
734. Henry, *Commentary*.
735. Gill, *Exposition*.
736. Spence and Exell, *Pulpit Commentary*.
737. Spence and Exell, *Pulpit Commentary*.
738. Barnes, *Notes*.
739. Henry, abridgment by Burder and Hughes, *Concise Commentary*.
740. Wardlaw, *Lectures*.
741. Poole, *Commentary*.
742. Spence and Exell, *Pulpit Commentary*.
743. Henry, *Commentary*.
744. Henry, *Commentary*.
745. George, *KJV Marginal Notes*.
746. Bridges, *Commentary*
747. Bridges, *Commentary*.
748. G. Campbell Morgan, *Exposition on the Whole Bible*, 2002 by Michael Andrews. *[actually produced in 1959 after his death]*
749. George, *KJV Marginal Notes*.
750. Spence and Exell, *Pulpit Commentary*.
751. Henry, *Commentary*
752. Bridges, *Commentary*.
753. Spence and Exell, *Pulpit Commentary*.
754. Henry, *Commentary*.
755. Kiel and Delitzsch, *Commentary*.
756. Spence and Exell, *Pulpit Commentary*.

Chapter 30
757. Henry, *Commentary*.
758. Henry, *Commentary*.
759. Gill, *Exposition*.
760. Walvoord and Zuck, *BKC*.
761. Bridges, *Commentary*.
762. Henry, *Commentary*.
763. Gill, *Exposition*.
764. Gill, *Exposition*.
765. Spence and Exell, *Pulpit Commentary*.
766. Spence and Excell, *Pulpit Commentary*.
767. Clarke, *Commentary*.
768. George, *KJV Marginal Notes*.
769. Walvoord and Zuck, *BKC*.
770. Spence and Exell, *Pulpit Commentary*.
771. Barnes, *Notes*.
772. Barnes, *Notes*.
773. Gill, *Exposition*.
774. Spence and Exell, *Pulpit Commentary*.
775. https://www.sciencedaily.com/releases/2004/04/040426054407.htm
776. https://www.academia.edu/1189718/The_Lion_and_the_Leopard_in_the_Bible
777. https://www.wayoflife.org/reports/the-lion.php
778. Youngblood, *Nelson's Dictionary*.
779. Barnes, *Notes*.
780. Benner, *Hebrew Lexicon*.

Chapter 31
781. Poole, *Commentary*.
782. Kiel and Delitzsch, *Commentary*.
783. Webster, *1828 Dictionary*.
784. Pool, *Commentary*.
785. Kiel and Delitzsch, *Commentary*.
786. Henry, *Commentary*.
787. Jeremy Taylor, *The rule and exercises of Holy Living*, (Philadelphia: J.W. Bradley, 1.860) p. 100.
788. Clarke, *Commentary*.
789. https://rachelheldevans.com/blog/3-things-you-might-not-know-about-proverbs-31
790. https://hebrew4christians.com/Blessings/Shabbat_Blessings/Eshet_Chayil/eshet_chayil.html
791. Clarke, *Commentary*.
792. Spence and Exell, *Pulpit Commentary*.
793. Exell, *Illustrator*.
794. Henry, *Commentary*.
795. Andrew Robert Fausset, *Fausset's Bible Dictionary*, 1888, e-Sword 12.0.1.
796. Orr, *ISBE*.
797. http://www.jewfaq.org/women.htm
798. Jerome H. Smith, *The Ultimate Cross-Reference Treasury*, (Nashville: Thomas Nelson, Inc.), e-Sword, 12.0.1.
799. Clarke, *Commentary*.
800. *1901 Jewish Encyclopedia* as quoted on www.studylight.org/encyclopedias/tje/d/distaff.html.
801. Kiel and Delitzsch, *Commentary*.
802. George, *KJV Marginal Notes*.
803. Youngblood, *Nelson's Dictionary*.
804. https://www.biblegateway.com/resources/encyclopedia-of-the-bible/Linen.
805. Youngblood, *Nelson's Dictionary*.
806. Spence and Exell, *Pulpit Commentary*..
807. Clarke, *Commentary*.
808. MacLaren, *Expositions*.
809. *https://www.freethesaurus.com/virtuous*
810. Clarke, *Commentary*.
811. Walvoord and Zuck, *BKC*.

APPENDIX

KINGS OF THE OF THE NATION OF ISRAEL

Saul (ruled 12 tribes of Israel for 40 years. Died by uicide (1 Sam 31:4-5)(1 Chr 10:4-5)
Ishbosheth (Saul's son ruled 11 tribes for 2 years. Killed by Rechab and Baanah (2 Sam 4:5-7)
David (ruled Judah for 2 years and then after Ishbosheth's death he ruled 12 tribes for 40 years)
Solomon (ruled 12 tribes for 40 years)

After Solomon's reign ended and his son Rohoboah listened to the wrong counsel, the kingdom divided into what became known as the Southern Kingdom (Judah and Benjamin: but simply called Judah) and the Northern Kingdom (the remaining 10 tribes: called Israel). The number of years each king ruled is in parenthesis.

Kings Of Israel (Northern Kingdom) - All Evil	**Kings Of Judah** – 8 Good Kings *
1. Jeroboam 1 (22 yrs) "The Lord struck him and he died" (2 Chr 13:20)(1 Kin 14:20)	1. Rehoboam (17 yrs)
2. Nadab (2 yrs) Killed by Baasha (1 Kin 15:25-28)	2. Abijam (3 yrs)
3. Baasha (24 yrs)	3. Asa (41 yrs) *
4. Elah (2 yrs)Killed by his servant Zimri (1 Kings 16:9-10)	4. Jehoshaphat (25 yrs) *
5. Zimri (7 days)Suicide (1 Kin 16:17-18)	5. Jehoram (8 yrs)
6. Omri (12 yrs) ***	6. Ahaziah (1 yr)Killed by Jehu (2 Chr 22:9)(2 Kin 9:27)
7. Ahab (22 yrs)Killed in battle (1 Kin 22:34-37)(2 Chr 18:33-34)	7. Athaliah (Queen) (6 yrs)Killed by order of Jehoiada the priest (2 Kin 11:15-16)(2 Chr 23:14-15)
8. Ahaziah (2 yrs)Died from an injury (2 Kin 1:2,4,16-17)	8. Joash (40 yrs) * Killed by his servants: Jozachar and Jehozabad (2 Kin 12:20-21)(2 Chr 24:25-26)
9. Jehoram (Joram)(12 yrs) Killed by Jehu (2 Kin 9:24-25)	9. Amaziah (29 yrs) *Killed by enemies (2 Kin 14:19)(2 Chr 25:27)
10. Jehu (28 yrs)	10. Azariah (Uzziah)(52 yrs) * God struck him with leprosy (until the day he died) (2 Chr 26:20-21)(2 Kin 15:5)
11. Jehoahaz (17 yrs)	11. Jotham (16 yrs) *
12. Jehoash (16 yrs)	12. Ahaz (16 yrs)
13. Jeroboam 2 (41 yrs)	13. Hezekiah (29 yrs) *
14. Zachariah (6 mos)Killed by Shallum (2 Kin 15:10)	14. Manasseh (55 yrs)
15. Shallum (1 mo)	15. Amon (2 yrs) Killed by his servants (2 Kin 21:23)(2 Chr 33:24)
16. Menahem (10 yrs)	16. Josiah (31 yrs) *Killed in battle by Pharaoh Neco (2 Kin 23:29-30)(2 Chr 35:23-24)
17. Pekhiah (2 yrs) Killed by Pekah, one of his chief officers (2 Kin 15:25)	17. Jehoahaz (3 mos) Died as a prisoner of Pharaoh Neco (2 Kin 23:33-34)
18. Pekah (20 yrs)Killed by Hoshea (2 Kin 15:30)	18. Jehoiakim (11 yrs) Taken prisoner by King Nebuchadnezzar and likely died in Babylon (2 Chr 36:5-6)(2 Kin 24:6)
19. Hoshea (9 yrs)	19. Jehoiachin (3 mos) Taken prisoner by King Nebuchadnezzar (2 Kin 24:12,15)(2 Chr 36:10) Later released by King Evil-merodach (2 Kin 25:27-30)
	20. Zedekiah (11 yrs)Taken prisoner by King Nebuchadnezzar and likely died in Babylon (2 Kin 25:7)

*** Zimri killed King Elah, and became king (1 Kin 16:8-10). When the army of Israel found out what Zimri had done, "all Israel" made Omri who was commander of the army, the new king (1 Kin 16:16). The army attacked and overthrew the city of Tirzah where Zimri was; consequently Zimri killed himself (1 Kin 1:17-18). "Half of the people followed Tibni, and half followed Omri" (1 Kin 16:21). There was war between them for about 4 years until Tibni died. And then, Omri became the sole ruler.   http://jesusalive.cc/ques344.htm

PERSONIFIED WISDOM IS NOT CHRIST

"**Wisdom personified, and love incarnate.** Wisdom is one of the Divine attributes; and Christ 'is of God made unto us wisdom,' as well as 'righteousness, and sanctification, and redemption.' We may surely expect, then, that up to a certain point the utterances of Wisdom and of Christ would coincide; so that in these passages in the Book of Proverbs we should be able to find, as we find throughout the whole of the Old Testament, some portion of 'the testimony of Jesus.' But does it follow that because some, or even many, of Wisdom's utterances may be correctly spoken of as the words of Christ Himself, therefore all of them may be so regarded? To see how utterly foolish is this way of reasoning, we have only to remember how many of David's words not only coincide with those of Christ, but are actually quoted in the New Testament as if Christ Himself had uttered them; and yet no one is so foolish as to insist that all the words of David can be safely put into the mouth of Christ. As we said at the beginning, wisdom is one of the attributes of God; and therefore the words of Wisdom must be, up to a certain point, the expression of the Divine mind. We may say that Wisdom expresses the mind of God in creation, in providence, in the whole realm of law. And in this realm, as well as in the realm of grace, the Son of God has His place as the Revealer. We may regard Christ and Wisdom as identical throughout the realm of natural law; so that no error would result from the substitution of the one for the other within that range of truth; but when we leave the realm of law and enter that of grace, it is entirely different; then it may not only be injurious but fatal to take the utterances of mere wisdom and put them into the mouth of Christ. If Christ had been only wisdom, He could not have heard the sinner's prayer. But **He is also 'righteousness, and sanctification, and redemption'; and that makes all the difference, for now that He has made an atonement for our sins and opened up the way of life, He can speak, not only in the name of wisdom, but of pardoning mercy and redeeming grace; and, accordingly, far from laughing at calamity and scorning the penitent's prayer, which wisdom if it were alone might do, He can, and will, and does 'save them to the uttermost that come unto God by Him.'** Having thus considered the extent to which we may expect to find "the testimony of Jesus" in the words of Wisdom, let us now test the principle we have laid down by an examination of the passage. The paragraph begins with this bold and striking personification: 'Wisdom crieth without; she uttereth her voice in the streets: she crieth in the chief place of concourse, in the openings of the gates: in the city she uttereth her words, saying'--and then follows the passage with which we have mainly to do. Let us, then, listen to Wisdom's cry, and observe how truthfully and powerfully it is translated into the language of men. We shall see its truth to nature better if we first look back a little. She begins, not with a cry, but with tender words of counsel and of promise (verses 8, 9), 'My son, hear the instruction of thy father,' etc. These are the tender and kindly words of counsel in which she addresses the young man setting out in life. Following this are tender and yet solemn words of warning against the tempter whom every one must meet (verse 19): 'My, son, if sinners entice thee, consent thou not,' etc. But now time passes on, and Wisdom's *protegé* begins to go astray, to forget the instruction of the father and the loving law of the mother; and so now she lifts up her voice and cries, entreating the wanderer to turn before it is too late (verses 22, 23). Time passes on, and the warning cry has been as little heeded as had been the tender voice of Wisdom at the first. The son, instead of being prudent, has been rash; he has been, not economical, but extravagant; not temperate, but dissipated; and so he has gone on till his last opportunity has been thrown away, his patrimony squandered, his health gone, his last friend lost. Then once more his early monitor appears. The prodigal remembers the tender words of counsel and of promise. He remembers how, when he was just beginning to go astray, before he had become hopelessly entangled in evil, Wisdom lifted up her voice and cried. For a long time his old counsellor has not been present to his mind at all. He has been hurrying on in courses of evil, but now his very wretchedness forces him to stop and think. And, again, there stands Wisdom before him. How does she address him now? Does she speak to him in soothing tones? Does she promise to restore him his money, or his health, or his friends? Alas, no: she cannot. All she can say is, 'I told you it would be so. I warned you what would be the end; and now the end has come. You must eat the fruit of your own ways, and be filled with your own devices.' That is positively all that Wisdom can say; and there is no tenderness in her tone. She seems to mock him rather, she seems to laugh at his calamity. Such is the voice of Wisdom in the end to those who have despised her counsel in the beginning. And is not the whole representation true to nature? Yes, it is perfectly true that 'Wisdom crieth without, she uttereth her voice in the streets,' and says these things so loudly that no listening ear can fail to hear them. It is no matter of deep philosophy. It is no ecclesiastical or theological dogma. It belongs to the Proverbs, the proverbs of the streets. The merit of Solomon, in this chapter, is not in telling us something we should not otherwise have known; but in putting what everybody knows in a very striking form. I question whether in all literature there can be found any more vivid and alarming description of the terror and despair of a remorseful conscience, as it looks back and recalls, when too late, the neglected counsels alike of earthly and of heavenly wisdom. So far Wisdom; and **if it were only with her that sinners had to do, it would go hard, not only with the profligate and openly vicious, but with the most respectable. But He with whom we have to do is not known as wisdom. He is wise indeed; and all wisdom is from Him. But there is that in Him which is higher than wisdom. 'God is love.'** Wisdom is the expression of His will in the realm of law; but love is the expression of Himself. The love of God is not a lawless love. It is not at variance with wisdom. The law which ordains that the sinner must eat of the fruit of his own way and be filled with his own devices cannot be set aside by the mere emotion of compassion. Hence it was necessary, in order to redeem man from the condemnation of sin, that the Holy One of God should suffer. Hence, too, it is that, though by the suffering and death of Christ believers in Him are set free from the condemnation of sin, yet the natural consequences of the transgressions of wisdom's laws are not abolished. If health has been wasted, it will not be miraculously restored. If money has been squandered, there must be suffering from the want of it. If character has been forfeited by dishonesty and impurity, it may never be redeemed on this side the grave. The laws of wisdom are not repealed or set at naught; they remain in force. But such has been the ingenuity, so to speak, of the Divine love, that without infringing on the proper domain of wisdom expressing itself in law, the way has been opened up for the full pardon and ultimate restoration even of those who have wandered farthest and sinned most. And accordingly, a passage like this awful one in the first chapter of the Book of Proverbs, instead of obscuring the Divine love in the smallest degree, or interposing so much as a thread between the sinner and his Saviour, rather serves as a background on which to set forth the radiant form of the Saviour of mankind,

> 'Whose love appears more orient and more bright,
> Having a foil whereon to show its light.' (J. M. Gibson, D.D.)"

(From Joseph S. Exell, Editor, *The Biblical Illustrator,* 1887-1905, e-Sword 12.0.1.)

POETICAL DEVICES IN THE BOOK OF PROVERBS

Device	Definition	Samples from Proverbs
Synonymous Parallelism	The second line repeats the thought of the first line but in different words. The repetition intensifies the thoughts and feelings being expressed.	Pro 19:5 A false witness shall not be unpunished, and he that speaketh lies shall not escape. Pro 16:18 Pride goeth before destruction, and an haughty spirit before a fall. Pro 11:25 The liberal soul shall be made fat: and he that watereth shall be watered also himself.
Antithetic Parallelism	The second line is the opposite of the first. Usually the two ideas are connected with a conjunction which is translated 'but.'	Pro 19:16 He that keepeth the commandment keepeth his own soul; but he that despiseth his ways shall die. Pro 10:19 In the multitude of words there wanteth not sin: but he that refraineth his lips is wise.
Numerical Parallelism or Graded Numerical Sequence	The first line of the proverb states a number and the second gives examples in the quantity of one more than previously stated. By giving one number followed by another larger number, one gets the truthful impression that there are more of this type of insatiable things, but that only four are being listed in this verse.	Pro 6:16-19 These six things doth the LORD hate: yea, seven are an abomination unto him: A proud look, a lying tongue, and hands that shed innocent blood, An heart that deviseth wicked imaginations, feet that be swift in running to mischief, A false witness that speaketh lies, and he that soweth discord among brethren. Pro 30:18-19 There be three things which are too wonderful for me, yea, four which I know not: The way of an eagle in the air; the way of a serpent upon a rock; the way of a ship in the midst of the sea; and the way of a man with a maid. Pro 30:21-23 For three things the earth is disquieted, and for four which it cannot bear: For a servant when he reigneth; and a fool when he is filled with meat; For an odious woman when she is married; and an handmaid that is heir to her mistress.
Synthetic Parallelism	The second line advances the thought of the first. Each line is synonymous but each additional line adds to the thought of the first making it more specific.	Pro 19:11 The discretion of a man deferreth his anger; and it is his glory to pass over a transgression. Pro 18:8 The words of a talebearer are as wounds, and they go down into the innermost parts of the belly. Pro 10:1 The proverbs of Solomon. A wise son maketh a glad father: but a foolish son is the heaviness of his mother.
Simile	Comparison using the words "like" or "as"	Pro 12:18 There is that speaketh like the piercings of a sword: but the tongue of the wise is health. Pro 23:32 At the last it biteth like a serpent, and stingeth like an adder. Pro 25:11 A word fitly spoken is like apples of gold in pictures of silver.
Metaphor	Comparison made not using "like" or "as"	Pro 15:4 A wholesome tongue is a tree of life: but perverseness therein is a breach in the spirit. Pro 13:14 The law of the wise is a fountain of life, to depart from the snares of death.
Synecdoche	A part of something stands for the whole	Pro 30:17 The eye that mocketh at his father, and despiseth to obey his mother, the ravens of the valley shall pick it out, and the young eagles shall eat it.
Personification	Inanimate objects or ideals are given characteristics of living things: The most familiar of these sections is found in chapter eight where wisdom is personified.	Pro 8:1-3 Doth not wisdom cry? and understanding put forth her voice? She standeth in the top of high places, by the way in the places of the paths. She crieth at the gates, at the entry of the city, at the coming in at the doors.
Acrostic Poem	Uses the Hebrew alphabet as a device for structuring. It emphasizes completeness by describing something from beginning to end.	Pro 31:10-31 Gives the characteristics of the virtuous woman

Repetition	The repetition of phrases, sentences, and ideas is used for emphasis and memorization. Subjects encountered in Chapter 1 will be looked at from a different angle or using a different speaker in later chapters. Repetition of Entire Proverbs: (compare 6:10-11 with 24:33-34; 14:12 with 16:25; 18:8 with 26:22; 20:16 with 27:13; 21:19 with 25:24) Repetition with a Slight Variation: the same image is used to make a related point (as in 17:3; 27:21). Repetition with Word Substitution: to achieve greater clarity or a different emphasis (cf. 19:1; 28:6). In 26:4-5 the same line is repeated in a seemingly contradictory way to make two different points	Pro 30:11-14 **There is a generation** that curseth their father, and doth not bless their mother. **There is a generation** that are pure in their own eyes, and yet is not washed from their filthiness. **There is a generation**, O how lofty are their eyes! and their eyelids are lifted up. **There is a generation**, whose teeth are as swords, and their jaw teeth as knives, to devour the poor from off the earth, and the needy from among men.

A proverb is like a snapshot compared to a video i.e. it condenses experience and astute observations into a few memorable words.

Proverbs in Hebrew poetry were characterized by **brevity in line length, parallelism**, and **figurative language**. Hebrew poetry does not rhyme, but it uses parallel ideas. Chapters 1-9 and 30-31 are mostly discourses while Chapters 10-29 are mostly short sayings embodying a general truth or astute observation– such as "Pride goeth before destruction, and a haughty spirit before a fall." Two different words – "pride" and "haughty spirit" are presented in a parallel fashion. The reference chart gives a definition and example of the devices used in Proverbs. **Sometimes understanding the type of poetical device will give insight to the meaning.**

A proverb is concentrated and requires a great deal of thought, evaluation, study, comparing and prayer to reach an acceptable level of understanding. Chapter 2 makes it clear that God intended for the godly person to gain spiritual strength through the work involved in mining the truths embodied within the figurative language incorporated in Proverbs. Proverbs guides the Christian through this life while he walks with God and reveals the defeated life of the ungodly, those deficit of godly character and those lacking personal character.

Solomon's time and culture were very different from today's. His word pictures and symbols are based on matters foreign to the industrial age. "He speaks of mangers and oxen.. He describes commerce in terms of scales and weights. For him, the roofs of houses were flat and the highest human authority in the land was a king. The reader must be sensitive to these historical differences. He must always be careful to resist reading these terms and word pictures through the prism of his own experience. (Quoted from https://blog.tms.edu/how-to-interpret-proverbs-5-principles-to-guide-your-study.)

PROVERBS REFERRED TO IN NEW TESTAMENT

(Proverbs, as well as other Old Testament Scriptures, are sources of Divine authority often referred to in the New Testament.)

	Proverbs referred to in New Testament
Proverbs 1:16 For their feet run to evil, and make haste to shed blood.	Romans 3:15 Their feet are swift to shed blood:
Proverbs 3:7 Be not wise in thine own eyes: fear the LORD, and depart from evil.	Romans 12:16 Be of the same mind one toward another. Mind not high things, but condescend to men of low estate. Be not wise in your own conceits.
Proverbs 3:11-12 My son, despise not the chastening of the LORD; neither be weary of his correction: For whom the LORD loveth he correcteth; even as a father the son in whom he delighteth.	Hebrews 12:5 And ye have forgotten the exhortation which speaketh unto you as unto children, My son, despise not thou the chastening of the Lord, nor faint when thou art rebuked of him:
Proverbs 10:12 Hatred stirreth up strifes: but love covereth all sins.	1Peter 4:8 And above all things have fervent charity among yourselves: for charity shall cover the multitude of sins.
Proverbs 11:31 Behold, the righteous shall be recompensed in the earth: much more the wicked and the sinner.	1Peter 4:18 And if the righteous scarcely be saved, where shall the ungodly and the sinner appear?
Proverbs 20:9 Who can say, I have made my heart clean, I am pure from my sin?	1John 1:8...10 If we say that we have no sin, we deceive ourselves, and the truth is not in us... If we say that we have not sinned, we make him a liar, and his word is not in us.
Proverbs 20:20 Whoso curseth his father or his mother, his lamp shall be put out in obscure darkness.	Matthew 15:4 For God commanded, saying, Honour thy father and mother: and, He that curseth father or mother, let him die the death.
Proverbs 20:22 Say not thou, I will recompense evil; but wait on the LORD, and he shall save thee.	Romans 12:17 Recompense to no man evil for evil. Provide things honest in the sight of all men.
Proverbs 24:29 Say not, I will do so to him as he hath done to me: I will render to the man according to his work.	1Thessalonians 5:15 See that none render evil for evil unto any man; but ever follow that which is good, both among yourselves, and to all men.
Proverbs 25:6-7 Put not forth thyself in the presence of the king, and stand not in the place of great men: For better it is that it be said unto thee, Come up hither; than that thou shouldest be put lower in the presence of the prince whom thine eyes have seen.	Luke 14:7-9 And he put forth a parable to those which were bidden, when he marked how they chose out the chief rooms; saying unto them, When thou art bidden of any man to a wedding, sit not down in the highest room; lest a more honourable man than thou be bidden of him; And he that bade thee and him come and say to thee, Give this man place; and thou begin with shame to take the lowest room.
Proverbs 25:21-22 If thine enemy be hungry, give him bread to eat; and if he be thirsty, give him water to drink: For thou shalt heap coals of fire upon his head, and the LORD shall reward thee.	Romans 12:20 Therefore if thine enemy hunger, feed him; if he thirst, give him drink: for in so doing thou shalt heap coals of fire on his head.
Proverbs 26:11 As a dog returneth to his vomit, so a fool returneth to his folly.	2Peter 2:22 But it is happened unto them according to the true proverb, The dog is turned to his own vomit again; and the sow that was washed to her wallowing in the mire.
Proverbs 27:1 Boast not thyself of to morrow; for thou knowest not what a day may bring forth.	James 4:14 Whereas ye know not what shall be on the morrow. For what is your life? It is even a vapour, that appeareth for a little time, and then vanisheth away.

Time Line of King Solomon's Life

[There is much debate over Bible dates. These dates are approximate and are derived from a variety of sources.]

Solomon was born *about* 12 years after his father David became king of Israel. The Bible does not record, and so far no dates have been archaeologically uncovered to prove, his exact date of birth or the exact date he became king. The Time Line gives us the *approximate* dates of the events in Solomon's life in relation to his father David, his son Rehoboam and the dividing of the kingdom into Israel and Judah with Jeroboam becoming king of Israel and Rehoboam king of Judah.

Dates	Reference	Events
992 B.C.	2 Sam. 11:2-25	David sins with Bathsheba; she is with child. Using deceit David has her husband, Uriah the Hittite, killed in battle.
991 B.C.	2 Sam. 11:26-12:14 Psalm 32, 38, 51	After Uriah's death, David marries Bathsheba. Rebuked by the Prophet Nathan, David repents; but the child dies (2 Sam. 12:15-23) and the sword never departs from his house. Bathsheba conceives again. (Notice that the punishment of David also affects Solomon.)
991.B.C.	2 Sam. 12:24-25	**Solomon is born.** (David is approximately 40 years old.) Named Jedidiah by God through Nathan the Prophet.
990 B.C. - 985 B.C.	2 Sam. 13:1-22 2 Sam. 13:23-39 2 Sam. 14:	David's son, Amnon, rapes David's daughter Tamar. [Amnon was the eldest son of King David, his mother was Ahinoam, a Jezreelitess; 2 Sam 3:2] .Two years later Tamar's brother, Absalom, who is also David's son kills Absalom and flees to Geshur for 3 more years. David's general, Joab persuaded King David to allow Absalom to return to Jerusalem. Absalom lived 2 more years in Jerusalem, but did not see David's face. **Solomon is now approximately 5 years old.**
	2 Sam. 15 -17	Absalom rebels against David and begins to steal the heart of the people away from David. Absalom lies to David and goes to Hebron to sacrifice, there making himself king. David flees Jerusalem with all the royal court (2 Sam 15:13-37) leaving behind 10 concubines to watch the house. **Solomon and his mother Bathsheba flee with him.** Bathsheba's father, Ahithophel, becomes Absalom's counselor. David prays that Ahithophel's counsel will turn to foolishness. When his counsel is finally rejected, Ahithophel commits suicide.
972 B.C.	2 Sam. 16:15-17:23 2 Sam 17:24-19:8	David gains the upper hand over Absalom by means of intrigue and deception David's army defeats Absalom's army in battle and Absalom is killed by Joab. [David is around 63 years old; Absalom around 30. **Solomon is around 20.**] David mourns Absalom.
	2 Sam. 20:1-3; 14-22	Sheba conspires and rebels against King David and is slain. David consigns seven sons of Saul to the Gibeonites to be slain to atone for Saul's persecution of the Gibeonites. David's census brings on punishment from God. Battles with the Philistines.
	1 Chron. 22	**Solomon's preparations for building the temple are assisted by Solomon.**
	1 Chron. 28, 29 1 Kings 1-4 Psalm 72	**David's health fails.** Abishag is taken as David's concubine to give him heat. David writes Psalm 72 for Solomon. King David's fourth son, Adonijah son of Haggith, attempts to usurp the kingdom The Prophet Nathan has Bathsheba ask David to name Solomon king. **David gives the orders to crown Solomon king.**
970 B.C.	1 Kings 2:12 1 Chron. 29:28	**Solomon crowned king at about 20 years of age.** David delivers his charge to Solomon (1 Kings 2:1-11; 1 Chron. 22:6-19; 1 Chron 28-29) **Solomon is anointed king a second time in 1 Chron 29:22**
	1 Kings 2:10 1 Chron. 29:28 Acts 2:29-30	Death of David. [David was about 70 when he died; he reigned over Judah 7 years and 6 months, and over all Israel 33 years - 40 years total- 2 Sam 4:5; 1 Chron 29:7, 8 and 28; 1 Kings 2:11] **David and Solomon served as co-regents from the time of Adonijah's rebellion until David's death** (1Chr 29:1-25). Adonijah is killed when he sends Bathsheba to ask for Abishag for him.
967 B.C.	2 Chron. 1:7-12 1 Kings 3:5-14; 16-28	**God appears to Solomon in a dream.** At God's request, **Solomon asks for the gift of wisdom** which God grants in addition to wealth. **King Solomon judges a dispute by two harlots over a living baby, and through God's wisdom he determines which is the real mother.**
966 B.C. - 946 B.C.	1 Kings 5-6 2 Chron. 3-4	**When Solomon had reigned 4 years, he began construction of Temple** using materials David had collected and procuring other materials. **The construction of the Temple took approximately 20 years.**

946 B.C.	1 Kings 8 2 Chron. 5:1-7:11	**Solomon's prays to dedicate the temple** (2 Chron 6). **God's Glory fills the Temple** (2 Chron 7). **God renews His covenant with Solomon after the dedication of the Temple** (1 Kings 9:1-9; 2 Chron 7:12-22)
963 B.C. - 946 B.C.	1 Kings 7:1 2 Chron. 8:1	**Solomon began building his own Royal Palace** in the 7th year of his reign and completed it in the 20th year.
	1 Kings 3 2 Chron. 8:11 1 Kings 11:1-8 2 Kings 23:13	**Solomon's first foreign policy act was to yoke up with Pharaoh, King of Egypt, by marrying his daughter.** This practice of marrying "strange women" (foreign idol worshipers) would be continued. Solomon continued his practice of marrying "strange women" until he had a harem of 700 wives (princesses) and 300 concubines. **Solomon's wives turned him to worship their pagan gods to which he built temples and made sacrifices.**
	1 Kings 7:2-12 & 9:15; 17-19 Ecc. 2:4-11	**In addition to construction of the Temple, Solomon devoted his reign to great building projects** including: the walls of Jerusalem; the Millo (*an earthen fill made to enlarge Jerusalem -1 Kings 11:27*); the royal cities of Megiddo, Hazor, and Gezer; the store cities; the cities for his horsemen; and the cities for his chariots.
950 B.C.	Proverbs 1-31 Song of Songs 1-8	**Solomon started writing** and collecting Proverbs. The ***Book of Proverbs*** was not completed until the time of Hezekiah's reign. It was also during this period that he began writing ***Song of Songs.***
946 B.C.	1 Kings 10:1-13 2 Chron 9:1-12	**The Queen of Sheba** heard of the fame of King Solomon and visits him. I Kings 10:1 tells why she came: "And when the queen of Sheba heard of the fame of Solomon concerning the name of the LORD, she came to prove him with hard questions."
939 B.C.	1 Kings 11:9-14; 23-25	**Because of his idiolatry, God became angry with Solomon.** He promises to take the kingdom away from his son Rehoboam except for Judah, and give the rest of the kingdom to Jeroboam, the son of Solomon's servant. In addition God stirred up nations against Israel.
937 B.C.	Ecclesiastes 1-12	**King Solomon concludes the Book of Ecclesiastes** by saying "Fear God and keep His commandments for this is the whole duty of man. For God shall bring every work into judgment."
931 B.C.	1 Kings 11:42-43 2 Chron. 30-31	**King Solomon's 40 year reign ends with his death. He was about 58 years old.**

BIBLIOGRAPHY

BIBLIOGRAPHY

Barnes, Albert, *Notes on the Bible,* 1847-1885, e-Sword, 12.0.1.

Benner, Jeff A., Ancient Hebrew Research Center, *Ancient Hebrew Lexicon of the Bible,* 2006, e-Sword 12.0.1.

Benson, Joseph, *Commentary on the Old and New Testaments,* 1857, e-Sword 12.0.1.

Bridges, Charles, *Commentary on Proverbs,* 1906, e-Sword 12.0.1.

Brown, Francis, Driver, R., Briggs Charles, *Hebrew Definitions,* 1906, e-Sword 12.0.1.

Bullinger, E. W., *The Companion Bible,* 1909-1922, e-Sword 12.0.1.

Campbell, Morgan, G., *Exposition on the Whole Bible,* 2002 by Michael Andrews *[actually produced in 1959 after his death],* e-Sword 12.0.1.

Clarke, Adam, *Commentary on the Bible,* 1810-1826, e-Sword 12.0.1.

College Press Bible Textbook Series, David Hunt, "Pondering the Proverbs," 1983, e-Sword 12.0.1.

Easton, M. G., *Illustrated Bible Dictionary,* 1897, e-Sword 12.0.1.

Ellicott, Charles John, Editor, J. W. Nutt, "Proverbs," *A Bible Commentary for English Readers*, e-Sword, 12.0.1.

Exell, Joseph S., Editor, *The Biblical Illustrator,* 1887-1905, e-Sword 12.0.1.

Exell Joseph S., Editor, Harris W., "Proverbs", in *The Preachers Complete Homiletical Comm*entary, 1892, e-Sword 12.0.1.

Fausset, Andrew Robert, *Fausset's Bible Dictionary,* 1888, e-Sword 12.0.1.

Gaebelein, Arno Clement, *Annotated Bible*,1919, e-Sword 12.0.1.

George, Calvin, *KJV Marginal Notes, (In honor of the 400th Anniversary of the Authorized Version 1611-2011),* e-Sword 12.0.1.

Gill, John, *Exposition of the Bible*, 1746-1766, 1816, e-Sword 12.0.1.

Girdlestone, Robert Baker, *Synonyms of the Old Testament,* 1871, e-Sword 12.0.1.

Harris, W., *The Preacher's Complete Homiletic Commentary on the Book of Proverbs,* 1892,e-Sword 12.0.1

Hastings, James, Editor, *Great Texts of the Bible*, 1911-1916, e-Sword 12.0.1.

Hawker, Robert, *Poor Man's Commentary,* 1805, e-Sword 12.0.1.

Henry, Matthew, *Commentary on the Whole Bible*, 1708-1714, e-Sword 12.0.1.

Henry, Matthew, abridgment by George Burder and John Hughes, *Concise Commentary on the Whole Bible*, 1811, e-Sword 12.01.

Jamison, Robert, Fausset, A. R., Brown, David, *A Commentary, Critical and Explanatory, on the Old and New Testaments*, 1871, e-Sword,12.0.1.

Jamison, Robert, Fausset, A. R., Brown, David, *Unabridged Commentary*, 1878, e-Sword,12.2.0.

Hawker, Robert, *Poor Man's Commentary*, 1805, e-Sword 12.0.1.

Lange, John Peter, *Commentary on the Holy Scriptures: Critical, Doctrinal, and Homeletical*, 1900, e-sWord 12.0.1.

Kiel, Johann Carl Friedrich and Delitzsch, Franz, *Commentary on the Old Testament*, 1866-1891, e-Sword 12.0.1.

Lewis, C. S., *Mere Christianity* (New York: Simon & Schuster Touchstone edition, 1996), pp. 109, 111.

MacLaren, Alexander, *Expositions of Holy Scripture*, 1904-1910, e-sword 12.0.1

McClintock, John and Strong James, *Encyclopedia of Biblical, Theological and Ecclesiastical Literature*, 1895, e-Sword 12.0.1.

Morris, Henry M., *Defender's Study Bible*, 1955, e-Sword 13.0.0

Morrish, George, *A New and Concise Bible Dictionary*, London, 1897, e-Sword 12.2.2.

Morris, Henry G., *Defender's Study Bible*, 1995, 2004, e-Sword 12.0.1.

Nicoll, William Robertson and Horton, R.F., *Expositors Bible Commentary*, 1890-1891, e-Sword 12.0.1.

Nicoll, William Robertson, Editor, *Sermon Bible Commentary*, 1888-1893, e-Sword 12.0.1.S

Nesbit, James, Compiler and Editor, *The Church Pulpit Commentary, (12 Vol.)*, 1908, e-Sword 12.0.1.

Orr, James, *International Standard Bible Encyclopedia*, 1915, 1939, e-Sword 12.0.1.

Perowne, J.J.S., Editor, *The Cambridge Bible for Schools and Colleges*, 1882-1921, e-Sword, 12.0.1.

Pett, Peter, *Commentary Series on the Bible*, 2013, e-Sword 12.0.1.

Poole, Matthew, *Commentary*, 1853, e-Sword 12.0.1.

Jerome H. Smith, *The Ultimate Cross-Reference Treasury*, (Nashville: Thomas Nelson, Inc.), e-Sword, 12.0.1.

William Smith, *Smith's Bible Dictionary*, 1863, 12.0.1.

H. D. M. Spence and Joseph S. Exell, *The Pulpit Commentary*, 1897, e-Sword, 12.0.1.

Charles Haddon Spurgeon, *Treasury of David*, 1869-1885, (from Psalm 121:3), e-Sword 12.0.1.

James Strong, *Hebrew and Greek Dictionaries*, taken from *Strong's Exhaustive Concordance*, 1890, e-Sword 12.0.1.

Jeremy Taylor, *The rule and exercises of Holy Living*, Philadelphia: J.W. Bradley, 1860, p 100.

W. E. Vine, Merrill F. Unger, William White, Jr., *Vine's Complete Expository Dictionary of Old Testament Words*, Nashville: Thomas Nelson Publisher, 1968, 1908, 1985, 1986, e-Sword 12.0.1.

Walvoord, John F. and Zuck, Roy B., *The Bible Knowledge Commentary*, e-Sword, 12.0.1.

Ralph Wardlaw, *Lectures on the Book of Proverbs*, 3 Vols, edited by his son, J.S. Wardlaw, 1838-1844, e-Sword 12.0.1.

Merriam-Webster's Collegiate Dictionary, Version 3, Springfield, Massachusetts: 2003.

Webster, Noah, *Dictionary of American English (1828)*, e-Sword,12.0.1.

Whedon, Daniel D., Editor, Bur, J. K., Hunter, W., Hyde, A.B., "Job, Proverbs, Ecclesiastes, and Solomon's Song, *Whedon's Commentary on the Old and New Testaments*, 1874-1909, e-Sword 12.0.1.

Wight, Fred H, *Manners and Customs of Bible lands*, e-Sword 12.0.1.

Youngblood Ronald F., General Editor; General Editor of Original Edition: Herbert Lockyer, Sr., *Nelson's New Illustrated Bible Dictionary,* Thomas Nelson Publishers: 1986, 1995, e-Sword 12.0.1.

WEBSITES

Abbasi, Hamid. "Signs of a Dried Out Spinal Disc." <https://inspiredspine.com/signs-dried-spinal-disc/>.

Benner, Jeff, *Ancient Hebrew Word Meanings,* as quoted on <https://nuggets4u.files.wordpress.com/2013/04/ancient-hebrew-word-meanings.doc>.

Benner, Jeff A. (January 18, 2017), "Parent Roots of Hebrew Words," as published in <http://www.ancient-hebrew.org/vocabulary_parent.html>.

"Brain Fact: Moderate alcohol use doesn't kill brain cells, and while rampant alcohol use can damage the brain, it's not due to cell death." <https://www.brainhq.com/brain-resources/cool-brain-facts-myths/brain-mythology/brain-myth-alcohol-kills-brain-cells>.

Card, Michael. "Persecution of Christians on rise – in U.S." <https://www.wnd.com/2012/09/persecution-of-christians-on-rise-in-u-s/>.

Cloe, Adam. Updated March 13, 2018. <https://sciencing.com/what-functions-umbilical-cord-4672809.html>.

Cloud, David. "The Lion." Way of Life Literature. <https://www.wayoflife.org/reports/the-lion.php>.

<www.CompellingTruth.org>.

Dovey, Dana. "Alcohol And Your Eyes: 6 Ways Excessive Drinking Can Impair Your Vision." <https://www.medicaldaily.com/alcohol-and-your-eyes-6-ways-excessive-drinking-can-impair-your-vision-406993>.

"Envy." <https://www.vocabulary.com/dictionary/envy>.

"Facts + Statistics: Alcohol-impaired driving." <https://www.iii.org/fact-statistic/facts-statistics-alcohol-impaired-driving>.

"For what purpose did God create the world?" January 1, 2001. <https://bible.org/question/what-purpose-did-god-create-world>.

<"Fret." https://www.vocabulary.com/dictionary/fret>.

Gilcrest, Jim Gilcrest. "How much effort do you put into your work?" as quoted on <https://blog.bpir.com/human-resources/how-much-effort-do-you-put-into-your-work/>

"Gutenberg and the History of the Printed Bible." <https://museumofprinting.org/news-and-events/gutenberg-and-the-history-of-the-printed-bible/>

Henry, Phillip. "Be as much troubled by unjust praises, as by unjust slanders." "As quoted on: <https://gracequotes.org/author-quote/philip-henry/>.

"Honor for a Fool." <https://www.generations.org/devotionals/481>

"Marriage." <https://www.bible-history.com/biblestudy/marriage.html.>

Helmenstine, Anne Marie. "What Is Fermentation? Definition and Examples." ThoughtCo, Sep. 7, 2021, <thoughtco.com/what-is-fermentation-608199.

Institute Of Physics. "Spiders Make Best Ever Post-it Notes." ScienceDaily. ScienceDaily, 26 April 2004. <www.sciencedaily.com/releases/2004/04/040426054407.htm>.

"Linen." <https://www.biblegateway.com/resources/encyclopedia-of-the-bible/Linen.>

<Https://www.freethesaurus.com/virtuous>.

<https://www.apmex.com/what-is-fine-gold>.

<https://www.mayoclinic.org/healthy-lifestyle/stress-management/in-depth/stress-symptoms/art-20050987>.

https://www.medicalnewstoday.com/articles/285666.php.

"Perverse." Retrieved from <https://www.dictionary.com/browse/perverse>.

Rubin, David, 2018, January 22. " About Hebrew." Retrieved from <http://rubinspace.org/html/about_hebrew.html>.

Smith, Samuel. "100% of Christians Face Persecution in These 21 Countries." https://www.christianpost.com/news/100-percent-of-christians-face-persecution-in-21-countries-open-doors-world-watch-list-2017-172850/

Stefanov, Pavel. February, 2009. "The Lion and the Leopard in the Bible." <https://www.academia.edu/1189718>.

Thompson, Jeff. "Is body language really over 90% of how we communicate?." <https://www.psychologytoday.com/us/blog/beyond-words/201109/is-nonverbal-communication-numbers-game>.

"Virtuous." <https://www.thefreedictionary.com/virtuous>.

"What was the practice of casting lots?" https://www.gotquestions.org/casting-lots.html

INDEX

INDEX

-A-

a bear robbed of her whelps	297
a buckler to them that walk uprightly	24
a companion of fools	202
a deceitful witness speaketh lies	227
a divine sentence	271
a false witness shall not be unpunished	336
a father	63
a fire	575
a fool in his folly	297
a good man shall be satisfied from himself	218, 219
a good report	259
a just weight and balance are the LORD'S	271
a land	521
a man of understanding hath wisdom	131
a man shall eat good by the fruit of his mouth	186
a man's gift maketh room for him	324
a righteous man hateth lying	188
a roaring lion	544
a soft tongue	476
a true witness delivereth souls	227
a wicked mind	405
a wise man feareth, and departeth from evil	220
Abendnego	461
abhorred	423
Abigail	394, 488, 476
Abimelech	269, 383, 453, 488
abominable	365
abomination	45, 47, 77, 92, 96, 130, 137, 151, 181, 185, 201, 241, 242, 255, 263, 267, 272, 283, 299, 363, 376, 405, 453, 526, 546, 553, 563
abominations	526
Abraham	359, 360, 362, 555
Absalom	341, 327, 347, 358, 439, 341, 361, 362, 462, 625
abundant life	41, 132, 181, 182, 239
abusers of themselves with mankind	358
acceptable	136
accountable	544
accursed	399
accuse	573
Achan	399
acknowledge	34, 35
Adam and Eve	530
add	571
Adonijah	358, 439, 554
adulterer	81, 358
adulteress	1, 27, 28, 63, 66, 67, 68, 73, 78, 79, 80, 83, 85-87, 88, 89, 92, 94, 95, 105, 106, 109, 110, 112, 113, 164, 397, 499, 577, 594
adulterous	67, 576
adulterous woman	576
adultery	73, 78, 80, 358, 546
adversary	531
afflicted	246, 428, 437, 500, 585, 586
afraid	42, 44, 45, 519, 562, 580, 594
Agur	567, 570, 571, 576
Ahab	371, 408, 533
Ahasuerus	585
Ahaz	381
all have sinned	364
all liars	178
all the city	599
all the days of the afflicted are evil	246
all wisdom	311
am not I in sport	496
Amnon	341, 358, 439
Amram	377
an ungodly witness scorneth judgment	354
Ananias and Sapphira	377
ancient landmark	430
anger	81, 153, 173, 205, 230, 237, 248, 263, 274, 286, 297, 327, 347, 358, 393, 394, 418, 438, 459, 463, 485, 497, 505, 531, 551, 555, 560
angry	86, 186, 221, 237, 248, 274, 286, 298, 316, 324, 326, 335, 347, 358, 394, 399, 403, 415, 428, 429, 481, 485, 497, 506, 514, 560, 581
angry countenance	316, 373, 481, 497, 560
answereth a matter before he heareth it	320
ant	74
ants	578
anxiety	180
appearance of being ignorant	112
appeaseth strife	248
apple	84
apple of thine eye	83, 84
apples of gold	473
applications	8
apply thine heart to understanding	21
arise up	597
armed man	465
arrogance	92, 96, 157, 193, 195, 220, 292, 302, 320, 341, 385, 428, 489, 493, 517, 539, 558, 559, 560
arrogancy	9, 92, 95, 96, 276
arrogant	574
arrows	496
as a dog returneth to his vomit	493
as righteousness tendeth to life	128
ashamed	164
at the entry of the city	92
at the gates	92
at the right time, at the right place, and in the right spirit	473
Athaliah	408
attend	58, 64
attend to my words	94
attire of an harlot	85, 86
attitude	111, 250, 304, 367
aura	340
authority	544
avoid evil	79

avoiding wicked people 76
awesome respect for God 8, 9, 10, 21, 37, 39, 95, 111,
    197, 211, 228, 247, 268, 350, 414, 456, 587, 598
awesome respect. 95

-B-

Baalam 347, 408
babbling.. 446
backbiting 373, 481
backslider in heart shall be filled with his own ways. 218
bad relationships 31
Balak 408
barren womb 575
Bathsheba 584
be afraid... 363
be wise for thyself 112
bear rule... 179
bear 577
beauty is vain 589, 598
beauty of old men is the gray head 286
bed 494
before it be meddled with........................... 298
before the mountains 100
beg in harvest 360
beginning of strife.................................. 298
beginning of wisdom. 262
belly.. 315, 327, 372, 379
Belshazzar 585
Benaiah 358
beneficence.. 33
benevolence 46
Benhadad 585
besetting sins 441
betimes.. 205
better is a dinner of herbs........................... 248
better is little 247
better than 168
bewrayeth 513, 561, 562
bewrayeth... 562
bind 79, 84
bind them about thy neck 33, 214
bitterness 306
bitterness to her that bare him...................... 306
blaming 530
blessed 39, 42, 51, 69, 70, 71, 84, 91, 100, 102,
    105, 121, 131, 143, 147, 148, 154, 155, 171, 191, 194, 204, 220,
    224, 240, 263, 293, 306, 322, 342, 362, 374, 405, 408, 418, 434,
    450, 463, 473, 481, 535, 561, 583, 591, 597
blessed are the peacemakers........................ 177
blessed are they that keep my ways................. 102
blesseth 45, 48, 488, 513
blessing 31, 48, 131, 462, 536
blessing of the upright the city 143
blessings 120
blessings.. 535
blood 533
blot.. 110, 111
blueness 381
boast 503
boasteth 475
body 35
body language.. 64, 76, 88, 237, 360, 413, 433, 499, 512, 528, 580
bold 519, 520
boldness 454
born of a woman................................... 364
bosom of fools 174
bountiful eye................................ 418, 419, 541

bow down thine ear 64, 65, 426,
bow thine ear 64, 67
brawling 390, 482
bray 517
breach 46, 88, 189, 239
breach in the spirit 109, 175
bread 363, 596
bread eaten in secret........................ 112, 113
bread of deceit 370
bread of diligence............................... 597
bribery.. 563
bribes 256, 305, 544, 546
bringeth the wheel over them 363
broken 76, 13, 69, 147, 165, 175, 244, 304, 322, 323
broken spirit........................ 246, 247, 304, 322, 323
brother 316
brother is born for adversity 300
brother offended................................. 326
brought forth..................................... 100
brutish 122, 161, 240, 523, 543, 567, 568
buckler 5, 23
busybody 373
but transgressors shall be taken in their own naughtiness 139
butter 581
buyeth it... 591

-C-

Cain 327, 347, 407, 493, 509, 530, 563
Cain lied to God................................. 530
calamity 19, 76, 132, 460, 462, 514
calamity of his father 341
call her blessed.................................. 597
candle 459
candle goeth not out by night 592
candle of the LORD 379
carnal 39
casement 85
cast down many wounded 89
chaff 363, 378
chambers of death............................... 89
character 33, 34
chaseth away his mother 352
chasten 38, 346
chastened 381
chastening 38
chastisement................................. 19, 554
cheerful countenance 244, 259
child left to himself 553
child... 441
children 85, 89
children of Ammon.............................. 359
children of God................................. 177
choice.. 103
choice silver........................... 129, 130, 175
choose 246
choose the fear of the LORD..................... 130
chosen to be ignorant of wisdom 112
chosen to become wise 106
churning of milk................................. 581
cistern 69
city is blessed by the upright..................... 143
clamorous....................................... 112
clean... 9, 364
cleanse 364
closer than a brother 330
cloud of the latter rain........................... 274
coals of fire...................................... 480

come out of trouble	171
comely	579
command his children and his household after him	362
commandment	78, 79
commandment is a lamp	78, 79
commandments	31, 83, 84, 89
commit	265
commit wickedness	272
communicating with God	39
companion of fools1	70
conceit	528
concourse	17
condemn	162
condemnation	489
condemned	381
condemneth the just	299
condemns himself	112
conditional	32
confess	364, 530
confesseth	529, 530
confidence	42, 45, 228, 402, 478
confident	173
confidential	46
congregation	498
congregation of the dead	396
conies	578
conscience	14, 28, 36, 56, 79, 530, 531, 539
conscious thinking	31
consent	11
considereth	548
considereth a field	591
contempt	312, 373
contendeth	549, 550
contention	193, 315, 419
contentions	326, 341, 446
contentions of a wife	341
contentious	399, 497, 513, 514
contentious	560
continual dropping	341, 513, 514
continual feast	246
convenient	571, 572
Corban	374, 378, 539
cords	73
cords of his sins	71
corner of the housetop	390, 481
correct thy son	555
correcteth	38
correction 38, 128, 438	
cosigner	73, 146
cosigning	146, 301, 369, 429, 512
counsel	15, 19, 20, 47, 92, 96, 130, 132, 146, 360, 370, 371, 402, 427, 451, 452, 470, 487
counsel of the LORD	348
counsellors	146, 371
counsellors of peace	176
counselors	68
counselors of peace	176
counsels	65, 165
counsels of the wicked	165, 176
countenance	245
covenant	27
covereth	529, 530
covereth a transgression	295
coverings of tapestry	594
coveteth	404, 541
covetous	358, 533, 546
covetous person is driven to obtain unjust gain	256
covetousness	532, 533, 544
craveth	282
crown	164, 595
crown of glory	53, 55, 285
crown of the wise is their riches	226
crown of the wise	99
crown to her husband	164, 168, 169
cruel	148
cruel messenger	296
cry of the poor	392
curse	31, 45, 48, 364, 393, 462, 488, 513, 541, 573
curse causeless	467, 488
cursed	430
curseth	373
cursing	561, 562
cut off	29

-D-

dainties	433
dainty meats	435
damnation	363
dark sayings	3
darkness	58
darkness	26, 57
daughters	597
David	312, 321, 358, 359, 363, 371, 413, 461, 488, 512, 530, 550, 552, 556, 584
day of evil	266
day of vengeance	78, 81
days shall be multiplied	134
deal	178
deal falsely	368
deal truly	178
dealeth	198
death	28, 64, 66, 496
death and life are in the power of the tongue	328
deceit	165, 176, 178, 370, 374, 547, 552
deceitful	123, 149, 507, 508, 552
deceitful heart	176
deceitful witness	178
deceitful witness speaketh lies	175
deceitfulness	368
deceive	130, 364, 376, 464
deceived	66, 112, 357
deceiver is compelled to speak lies	174
deceiveth	496
deception	538
decline	54, 89
deep ditch	445
deep sleep	342
deep water	360
deep waters	313, 360
delight	102, 106, 137, 151, 178, 241, 242, 252, 258, 339, 381, 462, 541, 555
delight is not seemly for a fool	339
delighteth	38
Delilah	80
deliver	166, 346, 347
deliver him	347
deliver thyself	73
delivered	151
delivered out of trouble	141
depart	552
depart from evil	9, 36, 262
depths of hell	112

desire	194, 195, 404
desire accomplished	201
desire of a man is his kindness	349
desire of the righteous	152
desire to please God	255
desireth	187
desolation	19, 42, 132
desolation of the wicked	45
despise	8, 9
despised	167, 168
despised reproof	243
despised, and hath a servant	168
despiseth	144, 195, 208, 223, 576
despiseth the word	195
destitute of wisdom	250
destroy	138
destroyed	543
destroyed for want of judgment	204, 205
destroyer	374, 539
destroyeth his own soul	78
destroying himself	240
destruction	19, 88, 126, 131, 134, 138, 186, 243, 262, 276, 315, 318, 396, 449, 515, 585, 586
destruction of the poor is their poverty	126, 127
destructive	128
devices	348
devil	25, 531
devise	46
devise evil	224
devise good	224
deviseth	452
deviseth mischief continually	176
deviseth mischiefs	175
dew upon the grass	341, 358
did not hear	132
different types of bindings	73
diligence	59, 120
diligent	119, 180, 187, 368, 374, 387, 430
diligently	433
directeth his way	407
discernment	371
disciple	31
discipline	439
disciplined	554
discontented	87
discord	365
discreet	596
discretion	3, 6, 7, 26, 29, 42, 44, 51, 64, 65, 102, 152, 249, 340, 523, 534, 538, 560
dishonesty	374, 376
dishonour	78
dishonorable	359
disobedience	26, 284, 303
disposing	287
disquieted	577
disrespectful	292
dissatisfaction	575
dissembleth	498, 499
distaff	592, 593
distress	19
divers measures	364
divers weights	364, 376
divide the spoil	277
Divided Kingdom	521
do judgement	394, 395
doctrinal errors	527
doctrine	51, 52
doctrines	106
doing justice and judgement	386
doings	365
drieth the bones	304
drinketh damage	467, 490
dross	291, 471, 516
drowsiness	441, 442
drunk	448
drunkard	441, 442, 491
drunkards	358
drunkenness	358, 441, 586
dry morsel	289
due season	252
dumb	585, 586
durable riches	92, 98
dust of the world	101

-E-

eagle	576
eagle in the air	576
ear	526
ear of the wise seeketh knowledge	323
ear that heareth the reproof of life	260
earring	474
ears that can't hear	366
easy prey	88
eat the labour of thine hands	170
eaten the fruit of lies	329
eateth not the bread of idleness	596
Ebedmelech	550
effeminate	358
efficient	43
egotism	472
Elah	585
elder	595
Eli	346, 367, 554, 557
Elimelech	509
Elisha	488
emotion	35
emptied of self	567
emulations	358
encouraged himself in the LORD his God	323
enemy	284, 480, 481, 507, 508
Enoch	59
envious	449, 459
envy	45, 231
envyings	358
equitable	546
equity	3, 5, 24, 26, 284, 307, 376
err	224, 353
erreth	128
Esaias	367
Esau	394
establish	254
established	101, 163, 175, 176, 265, 272, 380, 553
established by counsel	371
establisheth the land	546
eternal life	32
eternity	40
Eve	353
even in laughter the heart is sorrowful	217
everlasting foundation	132, 163
everlasting life	361
every wise woman buildeth her house	207
evil	6, 7, 9, 11, 12, 13, 14, 24, 26, 27, 45,

57, 60, 61, 68, 88, 95, 102, 132, 150, 177, 363, 364, 365, 370, 381, 395, 459, 527, 529, 531, 532, 547, 551, 589
evil eye. 374, 419, 435, 533, 536
evil man 26
evil men 65, 449
evil pursueth sinners 203
evil shall not depart from his house 297
evil way 9, 92, 95, 96, 262
evil woman 78, 79
exaggeration 434
exalt 55
exalted 143
exalteth folly 230
excellent speech 293
excellent things 92, 94
excellest 597
excessive in praise 499
excuses 360
expectation 140, 152, 456
expectation of the wicked 134
external worship 38
extortioners 358
eyelids 78, 80
eyes of a fool are in the ends of the earth 306
eyes of man 515
eyes that can't see 366

-F-

facts 35
fair woman which is without discretion 152
faith 535, 536, 539, 540, 541, 563
faithful 31, 70, 210, 364, 484, 507, 535, 537, 552
faithful ambassador 199
faithful man 362, 374
faithful messenger 475
faithful spirit 145, 172, 179, 372
faithful witness 210
faithfully 553
faithfulness 515, 538
fall 276, 277, 458
false 210
false balance 137, 376
false gift 475
false lips 291
false prophets 353, 371
false witness 77, 174, 178, 210, 328, 365, 406, 477
false witnesses 175
false witness shall perish 175
false witness that speaketh lies 175
false witness will utter lies 175, 210
famish 118
fan is in his hand 363
far above rubies 587, 588
father of a fool hath no joy 250
father 14
father/son relationship 31
fatherless 437
favor 31, 34, 420
favour 33, 34, 162, 213, 214, 234, 341, 358, 363, 531, 598
favour both with the LORD, and also with men 34
favour is deceitful 598
favour of the LORD 183, 214
fear 19, 228, 350, 358, 489
fear of evil 20
fear of God 4, 439
fear of man 467, 562, 563
fear of the LORD 8, 9, 20-22, 32, 36, 37, 51, 95, 99, 110-112, 133, 228, 247, 261, 262, 286, 350, 444, 554, 592, 598
fear of the wicked 132
fear the king 460
Fear thou the LORD 460
feareth 531
feareth the commandment 195
feareth the LORD 208
fearful 9, 365
fears 132
feels 485
field 6, 465
fields 101
fig tree 515
figurative language 12
filled with his own ways 218
filled with the Spirit 358
final rewards 31
financial dealings 272
find good 338
find the knowledge of God 21
find them out 95
findeth 39
findeth wisdom 39
fine gold 40
fine linen 595
finer 471
fining pot 290, 291, 516
fire in his bosom 80
firebrands 496
first in his own cause 325
first line of defense 26
first step to receiving wisdom and prudence 213
firstfruit 38
firstfruits 37
fitly 473
five individuals "void of understanding" 170
flatter 538
flattereth 27, 83, 84, 473, 537, 547
flattering 27, 66, 85, 547
flattering mouth 500
flattery 78, 79, 516, 538, 563
flax 590
flesh 25, 59, 231, 435, 554
flourish 216
flourish as a branch 156, 157
flowing brook 360
follower 31
followeth 169, 170
followeth after righteousness 181
followeth after vain persons 170
followeth vain persons 169
folly 99, 280, 286, 320, 489, 493, 494, 517, 528
folly in taking care of business 164
folly is joy 250
folly of fools 176
folly of fools is deceit 212
food from afar 590
fool 14, 20, 35, 60, 68, 128, 129, 131, 157, 158, 164, 185, 198, 199, 213, 240, 250, 280, 295, 304, 311, 333, 452, 467, 487, 489, 491, 492, 493, 517, 523, 528, 540, 543, 551, 554, 577
fool despiseth his father's instruction 240
fool layeth open his folly 179, 198, 199
fool to the correction of the stocks 85, 89

fool uttereth all his mind	174
fool when he is filled with meat	577
fool's words	315
foolish	135, 212, 286, 400, 525, 531, 534, 545, 549, 550
foolish man	250
foolish son is a grief to his father	306
foolish son	117, 306, 341
foolish woman	112
foolishness	111, 178, 179, 213, 246, 280, 423, 453, 517, 554
foolishness of fools is folly	226
fools	8, 9, 19, 45, 49, 71, 92, 94, 13, 17, 130, 170, 489-491, 534, 551
fools despise wisdom	173
fool's lips	315
fools make a mock at sin	213
fool's mouth	315
fool's wrath is presently known	173
for a moment	175, 176
for conscience sake	363
for our good	112
for they shall be an ornament of grace unto thy head	79
forbear	454
forbearing	476
forget his poverty	586
forget the law	585
forgiveness	33, 530
fornication	67
fornicators	358
forsake	530
forsake the foolish	110
forsake the law	522
forsaketh	529, 530
forsaketh the way	243
foundation	132
foundations of the earth	101
fountain	70, 228
fountain of life	22, 196, 228
fountains	69, 70
fountains of the deep	101
fraud	370
free will to choose good or evil	267
free will	266, 267
fret	459
friend	330, 335, 420, 467, 507, 509, 514
friend loveth at all times	300
friends	330
from sin	180
froward	9, 26, 31, 45, 47, 49, 59, 60, 76, 92, 95, 123, 136, 151, 283, 284, 303, 365, 389, 415, 523, 524, 531, 534, 543
froward heart	151, 242, 303
froward mouth	96, 262
froward things	285
frowardness	76, 123, 132, 136, 176, 534
frowardness of the wicked	523
fruit	17, 20, 22, 32, 60, 71, 92, 98, 127, 128, 131, 158, 159, 162, 165, 170, 171, 172, 185, 308, 327, 328, 333, 345, 366, 399, 515, 543, 591, 592, 598, 610, 611
fruit of her hands	591, 592, 598
fruit of his doings	176
fruit of his mouth	172, 185, 186, 252, 327
fruit of the righteous	158
fruit of the righteous is a tree of life	127, 158
fruit of the Spirit	209
fruit of the wicked	127, 128, 183
fruit of their own way	20
full soul	508
furious	428, 560
furnace	290, 291, 516

-G-

gain of oppressions	363
Garden of Eden	7
garner	363
gate	452
gathereth in summer	120
generation	573
getteth	39
getteth understanding	39
gift	294, 305, 393, 475
gift of God is eternal life through Jesus Christ our Lord	183
gifts	256, 546
girdeth her loins with strength	591, 592
girdles	595
given to appetite	433
given to change	460, 461
gives place	485
glad	175, 444
gladness	134
glorious	364
glory	31, 45, 49, 340, 359, 364, 381, 470, 484, 517, 528, 529, 531, 534, 538, 541
glory of young men is their strength	286
glutton	441, 442
gluttony	441
go from the presence of a foolish man	212
go not in the way of evil men	285
goals	3
God is the Maker of every man, rich and poor	232
godliness	535
godly	361
God's chosen people	521
God's responses	31
goeth well with the righteous	142
Goliath	488
good	45, 46, 152, 153, 162, 185, 186, 203, 204, 363, 589
good man	129, 204
good man leaveth an inheritance to his children's children	204
good men	29
good name	411
good news	482
good report	259
good tidings	482
good understanding	34, 197
good word	175
good works	363
goodness	33
governs	42
grace	10, 11, 34, 41, 42, 43, 45, 46, 49, 50, 53, 55, 534, 541, 75, 78, 79, 131, 147, 152, 195, 197, 212, 304, 362, 411, 420, 474, 523, 527, 579, 592, 595, 610
gracious woman	147
graded numerical sequence	77, 575, 577, 579
gratitude	37
grave	575
great men	324
great revenues	525
great understanding	230
great waster	316

great wrath	346
greedily	404
greedy	256
greedy of gain	256
greyhound	579
grieveth	494
grievous words	237
guide	138
guide of her youth	27
guilt from sin	180
gullible	6

-H-

habitation	48
habitation the just	48
Haman	403, 347
hand	593
hand join in hand	177, 267
hand of the diligent	179
handmaid	577
handmaid that is heir to her mistress	577
hands	590
hands	593
hands that shed innocent blood	77
Hannah	245
Hanun	359
happiness	39, 223
happy	39, 41, 531, 541
hard	197
hardeneth his face	407
hardeneth his heart	531
hardeneth his neck	543
harvest	360
haste	375
hasteth with his feet	333
hastily	374
hasty	174, 371, 374, 387, 388, 551
hasty of spirit	230
hate	77, 125, 477, 480, 530, 550
hate and abhor lying	189
hated	223
hated instruction	243
hated knowledge	9, 130
hates the knowledge of God	213
hateth	161, 205, 498, 499, 554
hateth covetousness	257
hateth gifts	256
hateth lying	188
hateth reproof	243
hating covetousness	532
hating evil consists in a careful abstinence from all sin	96
hatred	128, 248
haughty	318, 403, 540
haughty spirit	561
haughty spirit before a fall	276, 277
have not sinned	364
have nothing	360
he goat	579, 580
he shall not be visited with evil	350
he that despiseth his neighbour sinneth	223
he that diligently seeketh good	155
he that exalteth his gate seeketh destruction	302
he that getteth wisdom loveth his own soul	338
he that hath mercy on the poor, happy is he	223
he that keepeth understanding shall find good	338
he that pursueth evil pursueth it to his own death	150
he that refraineth his lips is wise	129
he that refuseth instruction despiseth his own soul	260
he that seeketh mischief	155, 156
he that spareth his rod hateth his son	205
he that speaketh lies shall not escape	175, 336
he that troubleth his own house	157
he that watereth shall be watered also himself	154
he that winneth souls is wise	158
health	36, 37, 59, 175, 199
health to the bones	175, 281
hear	51, 55, 67, 94, 102, 122, 130, 360, 441, 524, 526
hear counsel	252
hear instruction	102, 214
hearing ear	366
hearing the law	526
hearken	102, 443, 526, 552
hearkeneth unto counsel	172
heart	31, 35, 59, 77, 78, 79, 83, 84, 231, 256, 323, 515
heart fretteth against the LORD	335
heart is deceitful	176
heart may discover itself	311
heart of fools	178, 179, 233
heart of her husband	588
heart of him that hath understanding	246
heart of men	361
heart of the foolish	241
heart of the prudent getteth knowledge	323
heart of the righteous	178, 257, 263
heart of the wicked	129, 175
heart of the wise teacheth his mouth	257
heart of them that imagine evil	176
heart sick	194
hearty counsel	467, 509, 510
heaviness	180, 217
heaviness in the heart of man maketh it stoop	175
heavy hearts	479, 585, 586
Hebron	362
hedge of thorns	249
hell	64, 66, 89, 243, 515
hell and destruction	243
help meet	589
her candle goeth not out by night	591
her children arise up	597
her own works praise her in the gates	598, 599
herds	517
heresies	358
Herod	403, 585
Herod Agrippa I	538
Hezekiah	469
hide	21
hide my commandments	21
hideth	513
hideth hatred with lying lips	172
high look	386
high places	92, 112, 113
high tower	318
high wall	317, 318
highway of the upright	275
him that followeth after righteousness	242
hinges	494
hoary head	285
holden	71
holdest thy tongue	363
holdeth his peace	144
holiness	376, 381
holy	92, 364, 378
holy temple	363

honey	456, 484, 517
honeycomb	65, 66, 456
honor	34, 38, 40
honor God	517
honorable	589
honorable person	176
honour	22, 32, 39, 67, 98, 261, 359, 401, 491, 528, 595
honoureth himself	168
hope	140
hope deferred	194
hope of the righteous	134
hornets	519
horns of the altar	358
horseleach	575
house	106, 207, 215, 254, 297, 449, 450
house and riches are the inheritance of fathers	342
house of the proud	254
house of the righteous	166, 167, 240
house of the wicked	31, 48, 215, 255, 391
human depravity	297
humble	137, 193, 278, 472, 560, 567, 561
humble spirit	277
humbly	517
humility	9, 22, 38, 96, 99 261, 318, 320, 414
hungry	480
hungry soul	508
husband is known in the gates	595
hyperbole	351, 494, 576, 577
hypocrisy	28, 130, 530 538
hypocrite	142, 438, 498, 499, 530

-I-

identities	64
identity	64
idiom or idiomatic expression	302, 592
idle soul shall suffer hunger	342
idle word	129
idleness	596
idolaters	358, 365
idolatry	358, 526
ignominy	312
ignorance	57
image of God	292
imagination of man's heart	364
imagine evil	176
impudent	85, 88
impurities	517
in all labour there is profit	226
in his own conceit	317, 489
in the beginning of his way	100
in the gates	598, 599
in the midst	99
in the mouth of the foolish is a rod of pride	208
in the multitude of words there wanteth not sin	179
in the way of righteousness is life	182
in vain	572
incline thine ear	21, 94
inclines	28
increaseth	153
indolent	360
industrious	180
infirmity	322
ingenuity	578
inherit the wind	157
inheritance	374, 430
iniquities	70, 71, 526, 544
iniquity	130, 134, 363, 395, 532

injustice	526
innocent	11, 12
instinct	578
instruction	3, 4, 8, 9, 10, 18, 53, 56, 59, 64, 68, 70, 92, 102, 106, 111, 128, 161, 185, 438, 443, 465, 543, 595
instruction of fools is folly	280
instruction of wisdom	261
instructions	58
integrity	60, 122, 138, 333, 362, 532, 535
intellect	32
intermeddle	214
intermeddleth	311
interpretation	8
inward peace and joy	245, 247
iron sharpeneth iron	514
irony	586
Isaac	377
Ishtob	359
issues of life	59
Ithiel	567, 570

-J-

Jacob	361, 394
Jacob's well	361
Jakeh	567
jealousy	78, 81
Jedidiah	584
Jehoshaphat	408, 495, 496
Jehu	362
Jereboam	290
Jeremiah	488, 550
Jericho	359
Jeroboam	362, 521
Jesus	364
jewel of gold	152
Jezebel	550, 533
Joab	358, 359
Jochebed	377
John the Baptist	585
Jonathan	550
Joseph	80, 375, 383, 431, 530
Joseph's brothers	530
Joshua	399, 488
Jotham	488
joy	176, 215, 250, 395, 396, 526
joy by the answer of his mouth	252
joy of the hypocrite but for a moment	176
joy of the LORD is your strength	247
Judas Iscariot	32
judge	381
judge righteously	585, 586
judgment	3, 5, 23, 24, 26, 132, 284, 358, 362, 376, 381, 388, 458, 523, 534, 541, 546, 462, 555
judgment cometh from the LORD	563
judgments	525, 544, 489
judgments are prepared for scorners	354
just	45, 57, 120, 129, 130, 142, 171, 204, 364 457, 488, 550, 563
just man	111, 362
just weight	137, 271, 272
justice	3, 5, 26, 284, 362, 363, 376, 440, 546
justice, judgment, and equity	5, 24-25
justified	129, 364

-K-

keep	7, 10, 21, 25 27, 28, 29, 31, 33, 36, 37, 39, 42, 43 44, 45, 50, 51, 53, 54, 58, 59, 60, 65, 73, 78, 79, 83, 84, 91, 100,

102, 112, 135, 157, 186, 189, 329, 343, 344, 346, 399, 415, 426, 511, 513, 522, 523, 556, 618	
keep my commandments and live	89
keep the law	522, 523
keep the way of the LORD	362
keep thy father's commandment	78
keeper at home	587
keepeth	128, 186, 189, 275, 343
keepeth company with harlots	545
keepeth his life	186
keepeth his mouth	186
keepeth his own soul	343
keepeth instruction	173
keepeth the law	525, 546, 556
kindness	589
kindness and peace	295
King Ahab	552
King Asa	557
King Cyrus	383
King Darius	320
King Hezekiah	381
King Lemuel	14, 583
King Maacah	359
King of kings	364
King Saul	312, 347
King Zedekiah	550
king, against whom there is no rising up	579, 580
king's honour	229
kingdom	529
kingdom of God	358, 524
kinswoman	85
kiss his lips	462
knowledge	3, 5, 6, 7-9,16, 17, 20, 21,22, 23 25, 42, 43, 51,54, 64, 65, 92, 122, 126,130, 142, 161,185, 198,211, 212, 241, 246, 323,371,391, 427, 438,449-451, 521, 522, 524, 526,534, 543,567,568,571
knowledge is easy unto him that understandeth	211
knowledge is power	451
knowledge of God	4, 5, 10, 17, 21, 22, 23, 25, 33, 39, 92, 211, 212, 213, 323, 334, 369, 421, 422, 427, 444, 450, 451, 568
knowledge of the holy	9, 110, 111, 134, 142
knowledge of wisdom	4, 456
Korah	461

-L-

Lot's daughters	358
Laban	394
labour	127, 226, 374,404
labour of the righteous tendeth to life	183
laboureth for himself	282
lacketh understanding	78, 80,109, 546
lacks discretion	112
Lamb of God	364
lamp	78, 79,192, 534, 554
lamp of the wicked	192, 193
lasciviousness	358
latter rain	363
laugh	549, 550
laughter	217
law	10,31,78, 84, 364
law is light	78, 79
law of the first fruits	38
law of the wise	196
law of thy mother	78
lay her hands	593
lay thine hand upon thy mouth	580

lay up	83
lay up wealth	400
layeth up	23
lazy	422
leadership	528, 580, 585, 595
lean	35
leave off contention	298
legal matters	585
Lemuel	583
length of days	32, 39, 40
lest	67
let not thy soul spare for his crying	346
liar	123, 150, 188, 189, 213, 290, 291, 292, 336, 339, 349, 350, 364, 388, 406, 475, 487, 496, 500, 552, 570, 571, 595
liars	9, 365
liberal soul	154
lie	368
lie in wait for blood	166
life	42, 59, 363, 401
life of evil	176
life of the flesh	231
life without righteousness	99
lifestyle	242
lifting up thyself	580
light	78,192, 534
light of Christ	58
light of the eyes rejoiceth the heart	259
light of the king's countenance	363,274
light of the righteous	192
lighteneth both their eyes	553
lion	422, 494, 579, 580
lip	361
lip of truth	175, 176, 178
lips	65,212, 498, 499
lips of knowledge	212, 369
lips of the righteous	130, 136, 241
lips of the wise	208, 209, 241
living water	361
loatheth	508
loathsome	188
locusts	578
loins	591
long life	31, 32
looketh well	596
LORD is far from the wicked	258
Lordship of Christ	213
lot	287, 326
lot is cast into the lap	287
loud	85, 87
love	33,173,248, 295,481, 535
love covereth all sins	173
love of money	131, 374, 537
loveth	161
loveth his own soul	338
loveth pleasure	397
loving favour	411
loving relationships	31
lovingkindness	381, 541
lowly	137
loyal wife and friend	27
lust	37,78, 516
lust not	79
lying	77, 128, 175,178, 188, 189, 365, 370,388, 530
lying lips	293, 294
lying lips are abomination to the LORD	176, 178
lying tongue	77, 175, 176, 178, 388,500

-M-

mad man	496
made fat	154, 187, 539, 540
maiden	596
maidens	590, 591
make it fit	463
make no friendship	560
maketh haste	535, 537
maketh himself rich	190
maketh himself poor	190
maketh the bones fat	259
man of understanding	7, 172, 173, 250, 361
man shall be satisfied with good	172
man with a maid	576
man's heart	270
Manasseh	381
manipulate	538
marriage vows	27
marrow	36, 37
masters	475
maul	477
mean	430
meat	590
meddle	359, 372, 460, 461
meddled	298
meddleth	495
meddling	359
medicine	37, 304
meditative thinking	387
meekness	535
memory of the just	121
Mephibosheth	321
merchandise	39, 40, 591
merchandise is good	592
merchant	595
merchants' ships	590
merciful	148
mercy	32, 33, 99, 223, 224, 225, 231, 380, 401, 496, 529, 530, 541
mercy and his truth	225
mercy and truth	22, 33, 34, 38, 50, 244, 244, 268, 380, 464,
mercy of the court	586
merry	246
merry heart	244, 245, 304
Meshach	461
messengers of death	358, 363
metaphor	71, 543
metonymy	577
Micaiah	371, 552
Michal	312, 498
mighty	326
mighty men	402
mind	551
mind of Christ	8, 23, 43 51, 92, 115, 130, 211
mind set	4
mingled	109
minister of God	363
mingled her wine	106
mirth	217
mischief	57, 76, 131, 132, 132, 177, 199, 283, 303, 449, 457, 487, 489, 499, 531, 543
mischievous	452
misery	19, 585, 586
mistreatment	374
Moab	488
mockery	550
mocketh	576
mocketh the poor	292
mocks God and the teachings of wisdom	110
moderation	476
mortar	517
Moses	377, 408, 555
motive	393
mourn	68
mouth	142-144, 402, 423
mouth calleth for strokes	315
mouth of a righteous man	171
mouth of fools	179, 246
mouth of the foolish	126
mouth of the just	136
mouth of the righteous	255
mouth of the upright	166
mouth of the wicked	172, 241, 257, 263
mouth of the wicked devoureth iniquity	354
mouth of the wicked poureth out evil things	257, 263
much better is it to get wisdom than gold	275
much food is in the tillage of the poor	204
multitude of counsellors	146, 173, 251
multitude of people	229
multitude of words	129
murderers	365
murders	358
must shew himself friendly	330
"My Heart Leaps Up" William Wordsworth	366
my peace I give unto you	231
my son	10, 21, 31, 38, 42, 43, 53, 55, 58, 73, 78, 89, 441, 445, 456, 460, 583

-N-

Nabal	394
Naboth	533
name	121
name of the LORD is a strong tower	317
name of the wicked	121
Nathan	417, 428, 583, 584
natural affection	33
naughtiness	140
naughty	60, 76
naughty tongue	291
navel	37
Nebuchadnezzar	403
needy	593
neglect	31
Nehemiah	403
neighbour	45, 46, 176, 181, 223, 464, 477
neighbour's wife	78, 80
net	13
nettles	6, 465
never satisfied	516, 575
no sorrow	131
new creature	515
no fear of God	213
no fountains	100
no good	303
no heart	299
no joy	554
no justification	47
no oxen are, the crib is clean	209
no peace	231, 557
no rest	549, 550

no rule over his own spirit	174
no sin	364
no sincerity	33
no uprightness	33
Noah	358, 419, 442, 555
nose	581
no conscience	33
no death	182
no delight in understanding	311
no depths	100
no evil happen to the just	177
non-verbal	176
not afraid of the snow	594
not be corrected by words	558
not good	307, 334, 376, 536
not hasty	591
not rendering evil for evil	177
notoriety	461
noun of direct address	64
nurture and admonition of the Lord	554

-O-

O ye children	64
Obadiah	550
obedience	34
obedient	474
obedient ear	369
obedient heart	31
obedient to His word	34, 197
obeyed	64
obeying	526
obscure darkness	373
obstinate	534
obtain favour of the LORD	102, 329
obtaining wisdom	4
odious	577
odious woman when she is married	577
of spirit	286
oil	400
old landmark	437
omnipresence	238
one that taketh a dog by the ears	495
open rebuke	507
open-minded	112
openeth her mouth with wisdom	596
opposed to God	128
opposition	26, 284, 303
oppress	526
oppresseth	231, 425, 522, 541
oppresseth the poor	231
oppression	370, 532
oppression of the poor	232
oppressor	45, 46, 47, 50, 147, 232, 522, 532, 544, 553
oppressors	526, 532
ornament of grace	10, 11, 53, 55, 595
out of control	560
out of the abundance of the heart the mouth speaketh	256, 258
out of the bosom	305
overthrow proper judgement	314
overthroweth	190, 391
overthrown	143, 144, 216, 421
ox goeth to the slaughter	85, 89

-P-

pacify	274
parable	465, 490, 491
parables	367
parental instruction	79
parenthetical instruction	110
partner with a thief	561, 562
partakers of the altar	38
pass over	340
pass over a transgression	249, 359
passengers	112
passeth by	495
path	12, 13, 24, 57, 60, 212
path of life	64, 67
paths	5, 27, 33, 34, 36, 39, 41, 44, 85
paths of judgment	92, 98, 99
paths of life	27
paths of the righteous	29
patience	535
Paul	550
peace	31, 32, 39, 41, 55, 231, 240, 268, 420, 427, 530, 532, 450
peaceful sleep	79
peace of God	540
peace of mind	59, 95, 98
peace offering	28, 88, 289
peace through truthfulness	176
penury	226
people	234
perceive	4
perceivest	212
perfect	29, 139, 140
perfect man	308
perfect peace	231
perish	544, 556
perisheth	140
permissive will of God	98
persecution	529
person of the wicked	314
personal diligence	518
personal oversight	517
personalities	14
personification	14, 93, 357, 442, 610, 612
personification of wisdom	14, 16
personified wisdom	1, 14, 15, 16, 17, 40, 41, 64, 93, 94, 95, 100, 102, 106, 108, 470, 543, 610
perverse	59, 60, 92, 167, 285, 303, 333, 467, 524, 531, 533, 534, 284
perverse in his ways	208
perverse tongue	303
perverseness	138, 175, 239
pervert	305
pervert justice	256
pervert the judgment	585, 586
pervert the ways of judgment	305
perverteth	122, 123, 335
pestle	517
Peter	550
pharaoh	384, 408
pharisees	530, 538, 539
physical discipline	205, 346
physical immoralities	527
pictures of silver	473
piece of bread	78, 80, 535, 536
piercings of a sword	175
pillars	106
pit	12, 423, 445, 527, 533
pity	344, 541
place of refuge	228

plain	249
plan	26, 65
plead the cause of the poor and needy	585, 586
pleasant	25, 113
pleasant words	175, 281
pleasantness	39, 41
pledge	369, 370, 512, 513
plenteousness	374, 387
plunder	588
ponder	60, 67, 70, 455
poor	119, 392, 397, 412, 541, 593
poor and needy	586
poor man	522
poor man is better than a liar	349
portion	590, 591
possessed	100
Potiphar	80
Potiphar's wife	413, 512
potsherd covered with silver dross	498
poverty	6, 74, 75, 119, 126, 127, 170, 223, 441, 465, 494, 526, 534, 536, 571, 572, 585, 586
power	450
power of the tongue	328
power of thine hand	45, 46
practical living	23
praise	362, 363, 503, 516, 522, 538, 598, 599
praised	589, 598
praiseth	597
prating	487
prating fool	121, 123
pray	489
prayer of the righteous	258
preaching	556
precious	39, 181, 182
precious life	78, 80
preparations of the heart	263
preservation	209
preserveth	24, 275
price in the hand	299
pride	9, 92, 95, 96, 137, 138, 193, 262, 277, 292, 302, 319, 359, 403, 517, 530, 538, 539, 560
pride goeth before destruction	276
prideful heart manifests itself with words	209
pride of parenthood	554
priest and prophet	585
priest's due from the people	38
priests "lived of the sacrifice"	38
prince	532
principle	210, 248, 279
principle of high moral character	138
principle of life	430
principles	11, 58, 143, 451
principles of leadership	577
principles of wisdom	73
priorities	463
privily	11
procureth favour	155
prodigal son	374, 545
profit	40, 226
prolong his days	257
prolongation of life	32
prolongs days	22, 133
promises	50
promotion of fools	49
proper preparations	594
prophecy	567, 568, 583
prosper	131
protection	450
protective watch	43
protector	24
proud	4, 36, 50, 77, 97, 138, 226, 254, 255, 267, 277, 278, 290, 329, 338, 359, 380, 386, 403, 419, 440, 453, 475, 487, 503, 538, 539, 540, 549, 552, 555, 560, 574, 580, 590
proud in heart	267
proud look	77
proud wrath	403
providence	376
provision	450
provisions of God	518
provoke not your children to wrath	554
prudence	6, 43, 95, 96, 102
prudent	4, 6, 7, 95, 128, 162, 173, 174, 178, 185, 198, 199, 212, 219, 221, 222, 235, 238, 239, 240, 279, 323, 342, 348, 413, 453, 487, 511, 312, 551, 596, 610
prudent man	173, 179
prudent man dealeth with knowledge	198
prudent man looketh well to his going	219
prudent wife is from the LORD	342
prudently	591
punish the just	307
punishment	346
pure	130, 364, 389, 570, 571
pure heart	242
pure in their own eyes	573, 574
pureness of heart	420
purer	363
purity	28
purple	594
purpose	441
put away	60
put out	192, 193
putting away lying	175

-Q-

quality of living	98
quit before a project is finished	181

-R-

rabbi	302
rage	549, 550
rain	475
ranging	531
ranging bear	531, 544
ransom	78, 191, 398, 399
ransom of a man's life	191
ravished	70
reacheth forth her hands	593
ready to perish	586
reasoning	35
reasons	450, 460
Rebekeh	377
rebellion	296, 526
rebels	461
rebuke	185, 191, 462, 536, 538, 554
rebuke a wise man	110
rebukes	507
rebuketh	537
receive instruction	252
recompence	375
recompence of a man's hands	172
recompensed	159
respect of persons	462, 535, 536
revenue	98

refreshing	475
refusal to hear	526
refuseth instruction	128, 200, 260
refuseth reproof	128, 173
regard	65
regardeth	168, 200
regardeth reproof	200, 240
Rehoboam	251, 290, 350, 521
rejoice	70, 102, 42, 250, 381, 443, 444, 467, 509, 514, 528, 531, 534, 542, 544, 548, 554, 556, 595, 596
rejoice in the LORD	247
rejoice the heart	180
rejoice to do evil	27, 523
rejoice to do wickedness	395
rejoiceth	192, 540, 542, 545
rejoicing always before him	102
remedy	543
render a reason	495
repeateth a matter	295
repeating a transgression	295
reproach	78, 80, 234, 352, 419
reproacheth his Maker	231, 292
reproof	9, 18-20, 38, 64, 68, 122, 128, 130, 132, 161, 185, 295, 296, 543
reproof of life	260
reproofs	78, 79
reproofs of instruction	78, 79, 261, 554
reproofs of instruction are the way of life	78
reprove	110, 570, 571, 572
reprove not a scorner	110
reproved	531, 543
reprover	369, 474
reproveth	244
required	571
resistance	31
respect	37, 573, 574
respect of persons	535
rest	555
resting place	457
restore sevenfold	80
retain riches	147
retaineth	39, 41
retaineth honour	147
revellings	358
revenger	363
revenues of the wicked	240
revilers	358
reward	49, 149, 393, 401, 456, 480, 481
rewardeth	492
rewards of listening and obeying	102
rhetorical questions	70, 569
rich	127, 131, 412, 434, 435, 524
rich man	318, 528
rich man's wealth	126, 127, 317, 318
riches	39, 92, 97, 191, 450, 517, 518, 572
riches and honour	40
right	165, 525
right hand of God	364
right in his own eyes	172
right paths	55
right things	92
right time, right place, right spirit	476
righteous	5, 7, 9, 23, 31, 45, 47, 94, 99, 118, 121, 124, 127, 130, 132, 134, 135, 138, 141, 151, 153, 156, 157, 159, 163, 171, 172, 175, 176, 181, 188, 190, 203, 206, 232, 233, 240, 242, 249, 283, 286, 317, 363, 364, 391, 398, 443, 444, 457, 458, 462, 467, 483, 519, 520, 524, 527, 528, 530, 541, 542, 544, 547, 548, 550-552, 555
righteous eateth to the satisfying of his soul	206
righteous hath hope in his death	233
righteous is delivered out of trouble	177
righteous is more excellent than his neighbour	181
righteous king	544
righteous lips	252, 363
righteous lips are the delight of kings	273
righteous man regardeth the life of his beast	168
righteousness of God	360
righteous way	243
righteous person is compelled to tell the truth	174
righteous person seeks God's help	249
righteous shall never be removed	135
righteousness	5, 24, 66, 79, 88, 92, 98, 111, 117, 118, 131, 139, 140, 149, 150, 189, 191, 216, 249, 269, 272, 283, 363, 374, 375, 381, 401, 451, 471, 525, 526, 535, 536, 538, 541, 542, 546, 548, 553, 555
righteousness delivereth from death	117, 183
righteousness exalteth a nation	234
righteousness of the perfect shall direct his way	139, 140
righteousness of the upright shall deliver them	139, 140
righteousness tendeth to life	150
riotous	80, 158, 441, 525, 545, 577
riotous eaters of flesh	398, 441
riotous living	80, 158, 290, 341, 442, 525, 534, 545
riotous men	525, 545
rivers of water	70, 383
roaring lion	531
roaring of a lion	340, 358
robbery by deceit	388
robbeth	539
rod	125, 126, 205, 346, 423, 438
rod and reproof	544, 553, 554
rod of correction	554
rod of pride	186
root	163
root of all evil	374
root of the righteous	163, 170
rooted out	29
rottenness in his bones	164, 231
rubies	39, 92, 369
ruin	460, 500
ruler	433, 544, 552
ruler's favour	563
rulers	363
ruleth his spirit	286

-S-

secret love	506
seed of the righteous shall be delivered	177
self-deception	216, 282
spirit is broken	244
spiritual darkness	57
strange woman	84
sacrifice	364, 386, 526
sacrifice of the wicked	241, 242, 405
sacrifices	242, 289, 364, 385
safe	533
safely	42, 44
safety	95, 146, 173, 408, 451, 563
saints	23, 24
salvation	37, 458
same mind	36
Samson	80
Samuel	34, 367, 554, 556

Sanballat and Tobiah	403, 408
sanctified	377
sanctify	364
sarcasm	351, 494, 534
satisfaction	532
satisfied	169, 170, 350
satisfied with bread	169, 170
Saul	413, 512, 530
scaleth	402
scarlet	594
scattereth	153, 363
scorner	110, 111, 185, 211, 240, 243, 244, 352, 365, 391, 403, 419, 421, 453, 489
scorner is an abomination to men	256
scorner seeketh wisdom, and findeth it not	211
scorners	17, 19, 31, 45, 49, 358
scorneth	49
scorneth judgment	354
scornful	396, 549
scorning	31
searchest for her as for hid treasures	21
searcheth	325
second death	365
secret	31, 45, 47
securely	46
security	541
seditions	358
seduceth	181
seductive or flattering words	27
seed	151
seeing eye	366
seek	524
seek me early	98
seekest her as silver	21
seemly	339
seest thou a man	493
self-conceit	37
self-centered	276, 318
self-promotion	472
Sennacherib	452
serpent	576
serpent upon a rock	576
servant	417, 558, 559, 573, 577
servant to have rule over princes	339
servant when he reigneth	577
set up	100
seven	457, 495
seven pillars	105
sexual wickedness	164
shabbath	587
shadow of thy wings	450
Shadrach	461
shall abide satisfied	350
shall die	344
shall not be visited with evil	350
shame	45, 49, 110, 120, 137, 173, 175, 188, 189, 200, 234, 320, 352, 472, 473, 539, 544, 553, 554
shameful situation	110
shapen in iniquity	364
sharp arrow	477
Shechem	488
sheol	243, 516
shield	570-572
Shimei	375, 488
shining light	57
ship	576
ship in the midst of the sea	576
shutteth his eyes from seeing evil	363
silk	594
silver	21, 275, 471
Simeon and Levi	347
simple	3, 6, 17, 19, 20, 86, 92, 94, 109, 112, 113, 391, 534
simple believeth every word	219
simple ones	85
simplicity	17
sin	127-129, 364
sinful	123
sing	548
single eye	60
sinner	159
sinners	11, 132, 440
sinneth against	103, 358
sinneth not	364
sins	526
sins are like cords that bind	73
sins of Jeroboam	362
sitteth among the elders	595
slack hand	119, 120, 180, 187, 368
slander	128, 487
sleep	42, 44, 57, 59, 74, 75, 367
sleepeth in harvest	120
slothful	6, 119, 188, 249, 316, 351, 404, 422, 465, 494
slothful man roasteth not that which he took in hunting	181
slothful shall be under tribute	179
slothfulness	342, 368, 590
slothfulness is also a spiritual issue	249
slow to anger	248, 286, 540
slow to speak	360
slow to wrath	230, 286, 360
sluggard	74, 75, 119, 133, 187, 360, 368, 404, 422, 494, 528
slumber	6, 465
smoke to the eyes	133
smoother than oil	64, 66
snare	85, 377, 428, 429, 467, 547, 549, 562
snare of his soul	315
snared	73, 74, 171
snares	228, 415
snares of death	196, 228
soft answer	237
soft tongue	476
solid foundation	598
Solomon	3, 363
son	559
son of my vows	584
son of my womb	584
son that causeth shame	290, 352
sons of man	94, 102
sorcerers	365
sorrow	446
sorrow of heart	244, 245
soul	35, 118, 185-188, 206, 402, 550
soul of the diligent	187, 188
soul of the sluggard	182, 187
soul of the transgressors	185, 186
soul of the wicked desireth evil	177
soul that sinneth, it shall die	112
sound	43
sound doctrine	527

sound heart	231
sound wisdom	14, 15, 23, 42, 43, 92, 96, 102, 470
soweth discord	76, 176
soweth righteousness	149
spareth his rod	554
spareth his words	308
speak	360
speaketh truth	174
speech reveals a person's heart	209
spendeth it up	400
spider	578
spinal fluid	305
spindle	592, 593
spirit	35
spirit of a man	322
spirit of excellence	590, 592, 594
spiritual adultery	69
spiritual darkness	57
spiritual death	28
spiritual fornication	80
spiritual hunger	283
spiritual living	23
spiritually minded	165
spoil	12, 588
spoken lie	176
sport	131
sport to a fool to do mischief	131
spreadeth a net for his feet	547
stability	546
stablished	164
stalled ox	248
state of thy flocks	517
stay	533
steal	368
stirreth up strife	248, 249
stolen waters	112, 370
stoop	175
stoppeth his ears	363, 392
straightened	55
strange	6, 21, 26, 389
strange woman	27, 24, 26, 27, 55, 63, 64, 65, 66, 67, 68, 70, 73, 78, 79, 83, 84, 85, 89, 95, 102, 189, 369, 370, 423, 444, 445, 512, 513, 583, 618
strange women	65, 102, 357, 423, 447
stranger	73, 214, 215, 369, 512, 553
strength	92, 96, 134, 375, 380, 381, 402, 451, 458, 470, 584, 587, 591, 592, 495
strength and honour are her clothing	595
strength of the ox	209
strengthened	101
strengthened the hands of the wicked	178
stretcheth out her hand	593
stricken thy hand	73
strife	47, 248, 283, 289, 302, 358, 359, 419, 495, 496 497, 539, 540, 560, 581
strifes	125
strike	307
strike hands	301, 369, 429, 513
strike princes for equity	307
stripes	375, 381
stripes for the back of fools	354
strive	472
strive not	45
strong	451
strong city	126, 127, 326
strong confidence	22
strong drink	446, 585, 586
strong men	147
stubborn	85, 87
stubbornness	489
student	31
studieth to answer	257, 263
subject unto the higher powers	363
substance	98, 181, 182 525, 545
substance of a diligent man is precious	181, 182
subtil of heart	85, 86
subtility	3, 6
sudden fear	42, 45
sufficient	476
surely	122
sureties	429
suretiship	369, 513
surety	73, 74, 146, 147, 301, 302, 330, 369, 370, 372, 429, 512, 513
sustain	322
sweet savour	364
sweet to the soul	281
sweetness of the lips	279
swift to hear	360
sword	363, 477
synecdoche	65, 576
Syrians	359

-T-

the bars of a castle	326
the poor	526
thine own understanding	34
thinking	35
to act	485
trial of your faith	291
triumphing of the wicked is short	176
tabernacle	38, 215
tabernacle of the upright	215
table of thine heart	33, 84
take	71, 80
taken	73, 74
talebearer	145, 283, 372, 496
talebearer revealeth secrets	172, 179
talk of the lips tendeth only to penury	226
teacheth	76
temple	38
tender mercies of the wicked	168, 169
tenderness	33
tendeth to life	22
tenth	378
the belly of the wicked shall want	206
the bread of idleness	596
the commandment	343
the cruel	67
the desire of a man is his kindness	349
the earth	101
the eyes of the LORD	420
the fear of the LORD	8, 95, 183
the guide of her youth	27
the law	585, 586
the law of kindness	596
the light of men	553
the LORD directeth his steps	270
the LORD trieth the hearts	290, 291
the mighty	286
the mind of Christ	51
the minister of God	363
the paths of life	28

the people	146, 546
the poor	60, 126, 127, 224, 329, 333, 337, 425, 428, 524-526, 528, 531, 534, 541, 544, 546, 548, 553, 573, 574
the poor is hated even of his own neighbour	223
the principal thing	54
the prudent are crowned with knowledge	221, 222
the rich	329
the rich hath many friends	223
the simple	352
the simple inherit folly	221
the state	521, 522
the way	189, 441
the way of good men	29
the way of life	396
the way of righteousness	396
the way of the righteous	396
the wicked	232, 390
the wicked shall not be unpunished	177
the words of a man's mouth	360
theft	370
they that hate me love death	102
thief	80
thieves	358
thine own understanding	35, 541
thinketh in his heart	435
thirsty earth	575
thorns	6, 249, 415, 465
thou excellest them all	597
thought	453
thought of foolishness is sin	256
thoughts	584
thoughts of the righteous	165, 176
thoughts of the wicked	255, 263
throne of judgement	363, 364
tilleth	534
tilleth his land	169, 170
time to come	595, 596
to react	485
tongue	402
tongue of the just	129, 130, 175
tongue of the wise	175
top of high places	92
tough love	416
tradition	378, 539
traditions	378
transgress	535
transgression	302, 340, 521, 539, 547, 555, 560
transgression of his lips	171
transgressor	398, 421
transgressors	29, 138, 185, 186, 197, 492, 445
treacherously	363
treasure	240, 247, 400
treasures	98, 99, 388
treasures of wickedness	117, 374, 388
tree of life	39, 41, 158, 194, 195, 239
tribulation	296
tribute	179
trouble	240, 247, 478
troubles	402
troubleth	256
troubleth his own flesh	148
troubleth his own house	256
true	9, 94
true witness	178
trust	34, 127, 134, 326, 454, 467, 539, 541, 562, 563, 570, 571, 588
trust in the LORD	250, 467, 562, 563
trusteth	156
trusteth in his own heart	540
trusteth in his riches	156
trusting	31
trustworthy	475
truth	33, 92, 111, 130, 176, 224, 364, 380, 443, 475, 527
truthful heart and mind	176
truthfulness	174
two edged sword	66

-U-

Ucal	567, 570
unbelieving	9, 365
uncleanness	358
under the influence of wrath	560
under the influence of drugs	560
under the influence of the Holy Spirit	560
understand	523, 524
understand his way	176
understandeth	211, 364
understanding	5, 7, 9, 23, 25, 26, 32, 34, 35, 39, 42, 43, 44, 51, 53, 64, 80, 81, 84-86, 92, 96, 99, 102, 110, 111, 122, 125, 128, 129-131, 134, 144, 169, 170, 212, 214, 250, 260, 262, 262, 275, 280, 286, 306, 352, 358, 369, 443, 445, 449, 450, 470, 489, 521, 522, 524, 525, 530, 534, 550, 551, 567, 568, 571
understanding heart	94, 395
unfaithful	478
ungodly	128, 396
ungodly witness	354
unhappy deceivers	176
unjust	140, 365, 563
unjust gain	525
unrighteous	358
unrighteousness	364, 536
unsearchable	470
unwillingness	489
unwise	31, 213, 228, 358
unwise decisions	73
upright	23, 29, 121, 135, 138, 151, 189, 215, 275, 407 526, 527, 550, 563
uprightly	5, 23, 122, 250, 467, 533, 534
uprightness	523, 524
Uriah	358
usury	525
utterance	583

-V-

vain	169, 170, 598
vain glory	530
vain persons	170, 534
vain words	130
vanity	388, 571, 572
variance	358
Vashti	585
vengeance	375, 480
vengeance is mine	375
victim mentality	74
vigilant	531
vile person	285
vinegar to the teeth	133
vineyard	6, 465, 533, 591
violence	57, 124, 185, 186, 285, 533
virtuous woman	164, 587, 591
vision	358, 556
void	169, 170

void of understanding 6, 85, 86, 89, 94, 125,
    126, 169,170, 301, 369, 465, 487, 489, 513
void of wisdom. 144
vomit 476
vow 378
vows. 88, 584

-W-

wages of sin is death wages of sin is death 183 183
waiteth on his master 515
walk 12,13, 42,208, 571, 572
walk in the law. 362
walk in the Spirit 270
walk with God 23, 396
walketh in his uprightness 208, 524
walketh uprightly 122
walketh with wise men 170, 202
walls 484
want of judgment 170
want of people is the destruction of the prince. 229
want of wisdom 130
wanteth understanding 109, 112, 113
wanton eyes 80
washing of water by the word 364
wasteth his father 352
watching daily at my gates 102
way 13, 24, 57,270
way of a fool. 172
way of a man with a maid 576
way of death 103
way of life 79, 103, 128, 173, 253
way of life is above to the wise 253
way of man 389
way of righteousness. 285
way of the LORD 134, 135
way of the slothful 249
way of the wicked. 181, 242
way of transgressors 197,214
way of understanding 110, 396
way of wisdom 55
way which seemeth right. 173, 181,282,216
ways 41,47 59, 60, 70
ways of death 173,216, 281
ways of her household. 596
wealth 67,526,552
wealth gotten by vanity. 194
wealth maketh many friends 335
wealth of the sinner 204
weary 38
weather 360
well advised. 193
well of life 124
wellspring of life 280
wellspring of wisdom 313
whatsoever a man soweth, that shall he also reap 128
whatsoever thy hand findeth to do, do it with thy might. 182
whatsoever ye do, do it heartily, as to the Lord, and not unto men
    180, 182
when a man's ways please the LORD 268
when to remain quiet 172
when to speak 172
where no counsel is 146,173
while there is hope 345
whirlwind. 132
whisperer 284
wholesome tongue 239
wholesome tongue is a tree of life 175
whore 445
whoremongers 365
whorish woman 78, 80
whoso findeth a wife findeth a good thing. 329
whoso findeth me findeth life 102, 183
whoso mocketh the poor reproacheth his Maker 232
whoso rewardeth evil for good 297
whosoever loveth and maketh a lie 178
why art thou cast down, O my soul 180
wicked 9, 13, 29, 45,48, 57, 71, 76, 99, 120,
    121,124, 127-129, 132, 134, 140, 149, 159, 163, 165, 166, 171,
    181, 186, 188, 189, 192, 206, 215, 232, 266, 283, 285, 305,363,
    365,369, 375, 391, 392, 395, 398, 457, 458,459,462, 467, 471,
    483,488, 519,522, 526, 528, 529, 531,536, 542-544, 548, 551,
    552, 555,563.
wicked desireth the net of evil men 170
wicked devices 162,221, 225, 285, 286,363
wicked doer 291
wicked heart 498
wicked imaginations 77
wicked man 128, 175,406
wicked messenger. 199
wicked people are known for their ungodly mouths 144
wicked shall be filled with mischief 177
wicked shall fall by his own wickedness 139
wicked shall not be unpunished 151
wicked shall not inhabit the earth 135
wicked speaking. 365
wicked thoughts 365
wickedness 57,58,92,131, 163,189, 363,370,
    71, 483,499 546, 553, 576
wickedness of the wicked shall be upon him 112
wickedness overthroweth the sinner 190
widow 254,398
wilful disregard 31
will. 35
windows of opportunity 119
wine 109,357, 446,447
winebibbers 398, 441, 442
winketh 76, 123
winnowing 363
wisdom 3, 4,5,8, 9, 14, 22, 23, 25, 32, 37, 39,
    42, 44, 51, 53, 58, 59, 64, 65, 83, 84, 85, 89,92, 93, 95, 96, 98,
    100, 101,102, 105, 106, 110, 111, 125, 130, 131, 136, 137, 167,
    193, 211, 250, 286, 299, 306, 360, 369, 371, 376, 381, 402, 427,
    435, 436, 443, 445, 449, 450, 451,456, 487, 489, 524, 526, 528,
    534, 539, 541, 545, 551, 553, 554, 571, 589, 592
wisdom is before him that hath understanding 306
wisdom of the prudent 176
wisdom of the prudent is to understand his way 212
wisdom resteth in the heart of him that hath understanding 233
wise 3, 7, 24, 31, 45, 47, 49, 65, 71,74, 110,
    121, 122, 126, 130, 167, 170,172, 179, 190,202,244,260,391,
    402,426,439,440, 444, 451, 489,499, 517, 518, 525,527 534,
    540, 541, 545, 546, 549-551
wise counsel. 251
wise counsels 3, 7, 122, 173
wise in heart. 279
wise in his own conceit . . 35, 74, 368, 404, 487, 489, 493, 494, 528
wise in thine own eyes 36
wise in your own conceits 36
wise king 363, 470
wise man 111, 173, 274, 295, 363
wise men lay up knowledge 126
wise of heart 157, 158
wise servant 234, 290

wise son	117, 185, 250
wise son maketh a glad father	250
wiser in his own conceit	173, 494, 495
witchcraft	358
with all his heart	362
with good advice make war	371
withholdeth corn	155
withholdeth more than is meet	153
within	498, 499
without	463
without counsel purposes are disappointed	251
without discretion	152
without instruction	71
without knowledge	333, 334
without remedy	543
without wisdom	71
witness	464, 174, 175
witty inventions	95
woe	358, 446
woman of Samaria	361
woman of strength	164
woman of valor	587
wonderful	576
wool	590
word	473
word fitly spoken	180
word of God	31
word spoken in due season	252
word play	534
words	84, 473
words of a talebearer are as wounds	315
words of knowledge	353
words of the pure are pleasant words	255
words of the wicked	166
words of the wise	3
words of thy mouth	73, 74
words of understanding	4
work	366
work of his hands	172
workers of iniquity	135, 395
worketh willingly	590
works	454-456, 598, 599
works of the flesh	358, 554
worldly wisdom	4
world's system	24, 25
wormwood	64, 66
wound	78
wounded spirit	322
wrath	152, 234, 249, 340, 346, 358, 360, 363, 393, 481, 531, 549, 581
wrath of a king is as messengers of death	274
wrathful man	248
wringing	581
wringing of the nose bringeth forth blood	581
wrongeth his own soul	103

-Y-

ye children	51, 102, 583
young man	3

-Z-

Ziba	321

www.ingramcontent.com/pod-product-compliance
Lightning Source LLC
Chambersburg PA
CBHW081141290426
44108CB00018B/2402